SEVENTH EDITION

Infants and Children
Prenatal Through Middle Childhood

Laura E. Berk
Illinois State University

Allyn & Bacon

Boston • Columbus • Indianapolis • New York • San Francisco • Upper Saddle River
Amsterdam • Cape Town • Dubai • London • Madrid • Milan • Munich • Paris • Montreal • Toronto
Delhi • Mexico City • Sao Paulo • Sydney • Hong Kong • Seoul • Singapore • Taipei • Tokyo

To Annie and Penny

Editor in Chief: Jessica Mosher
Managing Editor: Tom Pauken
Supplements Editor: Sara Harris
Media Editor: Beth Stoner
Development Editors: Judy Ashkenaz, Lisa McLellan
Editorial Assistants: Paige Clunie, Amelia Benner
Senior Marketing Manager: Wendy Albert
Senior Production Project Manager: Donna Simons
Manufacturing Buyer: Debbie Rossi

Cover Administrator and Designer: Joel Gendron
Electronic Composition: TexTech, Inc.
Interior Designer: Carol Somberg
Photo Researcher: Sarah Evertson—ImageQuest
Copyeditor: Margaret Pinette
References Editor: William Heckman
Proofreader: Beyond Words Proofreading
Supplements Project Management: LEAP Higher Education

Milestones of Development Table photo credits:

Page 286: column 1: © Blend Images/Alamy; column 2: © Laura Dwight Photography; column 3: © JGI/Getty Images/Blend Images

Page 287: column 1: © Ellen B. Senisi Photography; column 2: © Geri Engberg/The Image Works; column 3: © Myrleen Ferguson Cate/PhotoEdit

Page 408: column 1: © CLEO PHOTOGRAPHY/PhotoEdit; column 2: © John-Francis Bourke/zefa/Corbis; column 3: © Bill Aron/PhotoEdit

Page 409: column 1 top: © Ellen B. Senisi Photography; column 1 bottom: © Michael Newman/PhotoEdit; column 2: © Ellen B. Senisi

Photography; column 3 top: © Ellen B. Senisi/The Image Works; column 3 bottom: © Asia Images Group/photolibrary

Page 526: column 1 top: © i love images/Alamy; column 1 bottom: © blue jean images/Getty Images; column 2: © Catchlight Visual Services/Alamy; column 3: © Adams Picture Library t/a apl/Alamy

Page 527: column 1 top: © Michael Newman/PhotoEdit; column 1 bottom: © Annie Griffiths Belt/National Geographic Society/Corbis; column 2: © Fuse/Getty Images; column 3 top: © JLP/Jose L. Pelaez/Corbis; column 3 bottom: © ableimages/Alamy

Library of Congress Cataloging-in-Publication Data
Berk, Laura E.
    Infants and children : prenatal through middle childhood / Laura E. Berk. – 7th ed.
        p. cm.
    Includes bibliographical references and index.
    ISBN 978-0-205-83191-3 (alk. paper)
    1. Child development. I. Title.
    RJ131.B3863 2011
    618.92—dc22

                            2010047378

10   9   8   7   6   5   CKV   14   13   12

Allyn & Bacon
is an imprint of

www.pearsonhighered.com

ISBN-10: 0-205-83191-5
ISBN-13: 978-0-205-83191-3

Laura E. Berk is a distinguished professor of psychology at Illinois State University, where she has taught child and human development to both undergraduate and graduate students for more than three decades. She received her bachelor's degree in psychology from the University of California, Berkeley, and her master's and doctoral degrees in child development and educational psychology from the University of Chicago. She has been a visiting scholar at Cornell University, UCLA, Stanford University, and the University of South Australia.

Berk has published widely on the effects of school environments on children's development, the development of private speech, and, most recently, the role of make-believe play in development. Her research has been funded by the U.S. Office of Education and the National Institute of Child Health and Human Development. It has appeared in many prominent journals, including *Child Development, Developmental Psychology, Merrill-Palmer Quarterly, Journal of Abnormal Child Psychology, Development and Psychopathology,* and *Early Childhood Research Quarterly.* Her empirical studies have attracted the attention of the general public, leading to contributions to *Psychology Today* and *Scientific American.* She has also been featured on National Public Radio's *Morning Edition* and in *Parents Magazine, Wondertime,* and *Reader's Digest.*

Berk has served as research editor for *Young Children* and consulting editor for *Early Childhood Research Quarterly.* Currently, she is an associate editor for the *Journal of Cognitive Education and Psychology.* She is a frequent contributor to edited volumes on early childhood development, having recently authored chapters on the importance of parenting, on make-believe play and self-regulation, and on the kindergarten child. She has also written the chapter on development for *The Many Faces of Psychological Research in the Twenty-First Century* (Society for the Teaching of Psychology); the article on social development for *The Child: An Encyclopedic Companion;* the article on Vygotsky for the *Encyclopedia of Cognitive Science;* and the chapter on storytelling as a teaching strategy for *Voices of Experience: Memorable Talks from the National Institute on the Teaching of Psychology* (Association for Psychological Science).

Berk's books include *Private Speech: From Social Interaction to Self-Regulation; Scaffolding Children's Learning: Vygotsky and Early Childhood Education; Landscapes of Development: An Anthology of Readings;* and *A Mandate for Playful Learning in Preschool: Presenting the Evidence.* In addition to *Infants, Children, and Adolescents,* she is author of the best-selling texts *Child Development* and *Development Through the Lifespan,* published by Allyn and Bacon. Her book for parents and teachers is *Awakening Children's Minds: How Parents and Teachers Can Make a Difference.*

Berk is active in work for children's causes. In addition to service in her home community, she is a member of the national board of directors and chair of the Chicago advisory board of Jumpstart, a nonprofit organization that provides one-to-one literacy intervention to thousands of low-income preschoolers across the United States, using college and university students as interveners. Berk is a fellow of the American Psychological Association, Division 7: Developmental Psychology.

...OGY AND ENVIRONMENT

...silient Children 10

A Case of Epigenesis: Smoking During Pregnancy Alters Gene Expression 87

The Prenatal Environment and Health in Later Life 104

Prenatal Iron Deficiency and Memory Impairments in Infants of Diabetic Mothers 118

Parental Depression and Child Development 155

Brain Plasticity: Insights from Research on Brain-Damaged Children and Adults 170

"Tuning In" to Familiar Speech, Faces, and Music: A Sensitive Period for Culture-Specific Learning 191

Infantile Amnesia 221

Development of Shyness and Sociability 259

Low-Level Lead Exposure and Children's Development 296

"Mindblindness" and Autism 342

David: A Boy Who Was Reared as a Girl 392

Children with Attention-Deficit Hyperactivity Disorder 444

Bullies and Their Victims 502

CULTURAL INFLUENCES

Immigrant Youths: Adapting to a New Land 36

The African-American Extended Family 79

Cultural Variation in Infant Sleeping Arrangements 173

Social Origins of Make-Believe Play 226

The Powerful Role of Paternal Warmth in Development 276

Child Health Care in the United States and Other Western Nations 303

Children in Village and Tribal Cultures Observe and Participate in Adult Work 333

Cultural Variations in Personal Storytelling: Implications for Early Self-Concept 366

Ethnic Differences in the Consequences of Physical Punishment 383

Children's Understanding of God 495

Impact of Ethnic and Political Violence on Children 518

SOCIAL ISSUES: EDUCATION

Can Musical Experiences Enhance Intelligence? 44

Worldwide Education of Girls: Transforming Current and Future Generations 73

Development of Infants with Severe Visual Impairments 194

Baby Learning from TV and Video: The Video Deficit Effect 213

Parent–Child Interaction: Impact on Language and Cognitive Development of Deaf Children 243

Children's Questions: Catalyst for Cognitive Development 326

Children's Understanding of Health and Illness 426

School Recess—A Time to Play, a Time to Learn 433

Emotional Intelligence 457

Magnet Schools: Equal Access to High-Quality Education 471

SOCIAL ISSUES: HEALTH

The Pros and Cons of Reproductive Technologies 66

The Nurse–Family Partnership: Reducing Maternal Stress and Enhancing Child Development Through Social Support 116

A Cross-National Perspective on Health Care and Other Policies for Parents and Newborn Babies 140

The Mysterious Tragedy of Sudden Infant Death Syndrome 147

Does Child Care in Infancy Threaten Attachment Security and Later Adjustment? 273

Otitis Media and Development 304

The Obesity Epidemic: How Americans Became the Heaviest People in the World 420

Children's Eyewitness Testimony 521

APPLYING WHAT WE KNOW

Steps Prospective Parents Can Take Before Conception to Increase the Chances of a Healthy Baby 68

Do's and Don'ts for a Healthy Pregnancy 119

Soothing a Crying Baby 148

How Couples Can Ease the Transition to Parenthood 156

Reasons to Breastfeed 175

Play Materials That Support Infant and Toddler Cognitive Development 216

Features of a High-Quality Home Life for Infants and Toddlers: The HOME Infant–Toddler Subscales 229

Signs of Developmentally Appropriate Infant and Toddler Child Care 231

Supporting Early Language Learning 241

Encouraging Affectionate Ties Between Infants and Their Preschool Siblings 277

Helping Toddlers Develop Compliance and Self-Control 283

Encouraging Good Nutrition in Early Childhood 301

Reducing Unintentional Injuries in Early Childhood 307

Enhancing Make-Believe Play in Early Childhood 320

Supporting Emergent Literacy in Early Childhood 345

Features of a High-Quality Home Life for Preschoolers: The HOME Early Childhood Subscales 347

Signs of Developmentally Appropriate Early Childhood Programs 352

Helping Children Manage Common Fears of Early Childhood 370

Using Positive Discipline 384

Regulating TV and Computer Use 389

Strategies for Fostering Healthy Lifestyles in School-Age Children 427

Providing Developmentally Appropriate Organized Sports in Middle Childhood 432

Signs of High-Quality Education in Elementary School 467

Fostering a Mastery-Oriented Approach to Learning 489

Helping Children Adjust to Their Parents' Divorce 514

Resources That Foster Resilience in Middle Childhood 522

CONTENTS

A Personal Note to Students   xi
Preface for Instructors   xiii

PART I
THEORY AND RESEARCH IN CHILD DEVELOPMENT

CHAPTER 1
History, Theory, and Research Strategies   2

The Field of Child Development   4
Domains of Development   5
Periods of Development   6

Basic Issues   7
Continuous or Discontinuous Development?   7
One Course of Development or Many?   8
Relative Influence of Nature and Nurture?   9
A Balanced Point of View   9

BIOLOGY AND ENVIRONMENT *Resilient Children*   10

Historical Foundations   11
Medieval Times   11
The Reformation   12
Philosophies of the Enlightenment   12
Scientific Beginnings   13

Mid-Twentieth-Century Theories   14
The Psychoanalytic Perspective   15
Behaviorism and Social Learning Theory   17
Piaget's Cognitive-Developmental Theory   19

Recent Theoretical Perspectives   21
Information Processing   21
Ethology and Evolutionary Developmental Psychology   23
Vygotsky's Sociocultural Theory   24
Ecological Systems Theory   25
New Directions: Development as a Dynamic System   28

Comparing Child Development Theories   29

Studying the Child   30
Common Research Methods   31
General Research Designs   35

CULTURAL INFLUENCES *Immigrant Youths: Adapting to a New Land*   36
Designs for Studying Development   40
Ethics in Research on Children   43

SOCIAL ISSUES: EDUCATION *Can Musical Experiences Enhance Intelligence?*   44

Summary   47

Important Terms and Concepts   49

PART II
FOUNDATIONS OF DEVELOPMENT

CHAPTER 2
Genetic and Environmental Foundations   50

Genetic Foundations   52
The Genetic Code   52
The Sex Cells   53
Boy or Girl?   54
Multiple Births   55
Patterns of Genetic Inheritance   56
Chromosomal Abnormalities   60

Reproductive Choices   63
Genetic Counseling   63
Prenatal Diagnosis and Fetal Medicine   63
The Alternative of Adoption   65

SOCIAL ISSUES: HEALTH *The Pros and Cons of Reproductive Technologies*   66

Environmental Contexts for Development   69
The Family   69
Socioeconomic Status and Family Functioning   71
Affluence   72

SOCIAL ISSUES: EDUCATION *Worldwide Education of Girls: Transforming Current and Future Generations*   73
Poverty   74
Beyond the Family: Neighborhoods and Schools   75
The Cultural Context   77

CULTURAL INFLUENCES *The African-American Extended Family*   79

Understanding the Relationship Between Heredity and Environment   82
The Question, "How Much?"   82
The Question, "How?"   84

BIOLOGY AND ENVIRONMENT *A Case of Epigenesis: Smoking During Pregnancy Alters Gene Expression*   87

Summary   88

Important Terms and Concepts   89

CHAPTER 3
Prenatal Development   90

Motivations for Parenthood   92
Why Have Children?   92
How Large a Family?   93
Is There a Best Time During Adulthood to Have a Child?   94

Prenatal Development   95

Conception   96
Period of the Zygote   97
Period of the Embryo   99
Period of the Fetus   100

Prenatal Environmental Influences   102

Teratogens   102

BIOLOGY AND ENVIRONMENT *The Prenatal Environment and Health in Later Life   104*

Other Maternal Factors   112

SOCIAL ISSUES: HEALTH *The Nurse–Family Partnership: Reducing Maternal Stress and Enhancing Child Development Through Social Support   116*

The Importance of Prenatal Health Care   116

BIOLOGY AND ENVIRONMENT *Prenatal Iron Deficiency and Memory Impairments in Infants of Diabetic Mothers   118*

Preparing for Parenthood   120

Seeking Information   120
The Baby Becomes a Reality   120
Models of Effective Parenthood   121
The Parental Relationship   121

Summary   122

Important Terms and Concepts   123

CHAPTER 4
Birth and the Newborn Baby   124

The Stages of Childbirth   126

Stage 1: Dilation and Effacement of the Cervix   126
Stage 2: Delivery of the Baby   127
Stage 3: Birth of the Placenta   128
The Baby's Adaptation to Labor and Delivery   128
The Newborn Baby's Appearance   128
Assessing the Newborn's Physical Condition: The Apgar Scale   128

Approaches to Childbirth   129

Natural, or Prepared, Childbirth   130
Home Delivery   131

Medical Interventions   132

Fetal Monitoring   132
Labor and Delivery Medication   133
Instrument Delivery   133
Induced Labor   134
Cesarean Delivery   134

Birth Complications   135

Oxygen Deprivation   135
Preterm and Low-Birth-Weight Infants   136

SOCIAL ISSUES: HEALTH *A Cross-National Perspective on Health Care and Other Policies for Parents and Newborn Babies   140*

Birth Complications, Parenting, and Resilience   141

Precious Moments After Birth   142

The Newborn Baby's Capacities   143

Reflexes   143
States   145

SOCIAL ISSUES: HEALTH *The Mysterious Tragedy of Sudden Infant Death Syndrome   147*

Sensory Capacities   149
Neonatal Behavioral Assessment   152

The Transition to Parenthood   154

Changes in the Family System   154

BIOLOGY AND ENVIRONMENT *Parental Depression and Child Development   155*

Single-Mother Families   156
Parent Interventions   157

Summary   158

Important Terms and Concepts   159

PART III
INFANCY AND TODDLERHOOD: THE FIRST TWO YEARS

CHAPTER 5
Physical Development in Infancy and Toddlerhood   160

Body Growth   162

Changes in Body Size and Muscle-Fat Makeup   162
Changes in Body Proportions   162
Skeletal Growth   163

Brain Development   164

Development of Neurons   164
Neurophysiological Methods   166
Development of the Cerebral Cortex   167
Sensitive Periods in Brain Development   169

BIOLOGY AND ENVIRONMENT *Brain Plasticity: Insights from Research on Brain-Damaged Children and Adults   170*

Changing States of Arousal   172

CULTURAL INFLUENCES *Cultural Variation in Infant Sleeping Arrangements   173*

Influences on Early Physical Growth   174

Heredity   174
Nutrition   174
Malnutrition   176
Emotional Well-Being   178

Learning Capacities   178

Classical Conditioning   179
Operant Conditioning   180
Habituation   180
Imitation   181

Motor Development   183

The Sequence of Motor Development   183
Motor Skills as Dynamic Systems   184

Dynamic Motor Systems in Action   185
Cultural Variations in Motor Development   186
Fine-Motor Development: Reaching and Grasping   186
Bowel and Bladder Control   188

Perceptual Development   189

Hearing   189
Vision   190

BIOLOGY AND ENVIRONMENT *"Tuning In" to Familiar Speech, Faces, and Music: A Sensitive Period for Culture-Specific Learning   191*

SOCIAL ISSUES: EDUCATION *Development of Infants with Severe Visual Impairments   194*

Object Perception   196
Intermodal Perception   197
Understanding Perceptual Development   198

Summary   200

Important Terms and Concepts   201

CHAPTER 6

Cognitive Development in Infancy and Toddlerhood   202

Piaget's Cognitive-Developmental Theory   204

Piaget's Ideas About Cognitive Change   204
The Sensorimotor Stage   205
Follow-Up Research on Infant Cognitive Development   208
Evaluation of the Sensorimotor Stage   212

SOCIAL ISSUES: EDUCATION *Baby Learning from TV and Video: The Video Deficit Effect   213*

Information Processing   217

Structure of the Information-Processing System   217
Attention   218
Memory   219

BIOLOGY AND ENVIRONMENT *Infantile Amnesia   221*

Categorization   222
Evaluation of Information-Processing Findings   223

The Social Context of Early Cognitive Development   224

CULTURAL INFLUENCES *Social Origins of Make-Believe Play   226*

Individual Differences in Early Mental Development   227

Infant Intelligence Tests   227
Early Environment and Mental Development   228
Early Intervention for At-Risk Infants and Toddlers   231

Language Development   233

Three Theories of Language Development   233
Getting Ready to Talk   236
First Words   238
The Two-Word Utterance Phase   239
Comprehension versus Production   240
Individual and Cultural Differences   240
Supporting Early Language Development   241

SOCIAL ISSUES: EDUCATION *Parent–Child Interaction: Impact on Language and Cognitive Development of Deaf Children   243*

Summary   243

Important Terms and Concepts   245

CHAPTER 7

Emotional and Social Development in Infancy and Toddlerhood   246

Erikson's Theory of Infant and Toddler Personality   248

Basic Trust versus Mistrust   248
Autonomy versus Shame and Doubt   249

Emotional Development   249

Development of Basic Emotions   250
Understanding and Responding to the Emotions of Others   252
Emergence of Self-Conscious Emotions   253
Beginnings of Emotional Self-Regulation   254

Temperament and Development   256

The Structure of Temperament   256
Measuring Temperament   258
Stability of Temperament   258

BIOLOGY AND ENVIRONMENT *Development of Shyness and Sociability   259*

Genetic Influences   260
Environmental Influences   261
Temperament and Child Rearing: The Goodness-of-Fit Model   262

Development of Attachment   264

Bowlby's Ethological Theory   265
Measuring the Security of Attachment   266
Stability of Attachment   268
Cultural Variations   268
Factors That Affect Attachment Security   269

SOCIAL ISSUES: HEALTH *Does Child Care in Infancy Threaten Attachment Security and Later Adjustment?   273*

Multiple Attachments   274

CULTURAL INFLUENCES *The Powerful Role of Paternal Warmth in Development   276*

From Attachment to Peer Sociability   277
Attachment and Later Development   278

Self-Development   279

Self-Awareness   280
Categorizing the Self   282
Self-Control   282

Summary   284

Important Terms and Concepts   285

MILESTONES: Development in Infancy and Toddlerhood   286

PART IV
EARLY CHILDHOOD: TWO TO SIX YEARS

♦ CHAPTER **8**

Physical Development in Early Childhood   288

Body Growth   290
Skeletal Growth   290
Brain Development   291

Influences on Physical Growth and Health   295
BIOLOGY AND ENVIRONMENT *Low-Level Lead Exposure and Children's Development*   296
Heredity and Hormones   297
Emotional Well-Being   297
Sleep Habits and Problems   298
Nutrition   299
Infectious Disease   301
CULTURAL INFLUENCES *Child Health Care in the United States and Other Western Nations*   303
SOCIAL ISSUES: HEALTH *Otitis Media and Development*   304
Childhood Injuries   304

Motor Development   308
Gross-Motor Development   308
Fine-Motor Development   309
Individual Differences in Motor Skills   312
Enhancing Early Childhood Motor Development   313

Summary   314

Important Terms and Concepts   315

♦ CHAPTER **9**

Cognitive Development in Early Childhood   316

Piaget's Theory: The Preoperational Stage   318
Advances in Mental Representation   318
Make-Believe Play   318
Symbol–Real-World Relations   320
Limitations of Preoperational Thought   321
Follow-Up Research on Preoperational Thought   323
SOCIAL ISSUES: EDUCATION *Children's Questions: Catalyst for Cognitive Development*   326
Evaluation of the Preoperational Stage   327
Piaget and Education   328

Vygotsky's Sociocultural Theory   329
Private Speech   329
Social Origins of Early Childhood Cognition   330
Vygotsky and Early Childhood Education   332
Evaluation of Vygotsky's Theory   332
CULTURAL INFLUENCES *Children in Village and Tribal Cultures Observe and Participate in Adult Work*   333

Information Processing   334
Attention   334
Memory   335
Problem Solving   337
The Young Child's Theory of Mind   338
Early Literacy and Mathematical Development   341
BIOLOGY AND ENVIRONMENT *"Mindblindness" and Autism*   342

Individual Differences in Mental Development   346
Early Childhood Intelligence Tests   346
Home Environment and Mental Development   347
Preschool, Kindergarten, and Child Care   348
Educational Media   351

Language Development   354
Vocabulary   354
Grammar   356
Conversation   358
Supporting Language Learning in Early Childhood   359

Summary   360

Important Terms and Concepts   361

♦ CHAPTER **10**

Emotional and Social Development in Early Childhood   362

Erikson's Theory: Initiative versus Guilt   364

Self-Understanding   364
Foundations of Self-Concept   365
CULTURAL INFLUENCES *Cultural Variations in Personal Storytelling: Implications for Early Self-Concept*   366
Emergence of Self-Esteem   366

Emotional Development   367
Understanding Emotion   367
Emotional Self-Regulation   369
Self-Conscious Emotions   370
Empathy and Sympathy   371

Peer Relations   372
Advances in Peer Sociability   372
First Friendships   374
Peer Relations and School Readiness   375
Social Problem Solving   375
Parental Influences on Early Peer Relations   377

Foundations of Morality   378
The Psychoanalytic Perspective   378
Social Learning Theory   380
CULTURAL INFLUENCES *Ethnic Differences in the Consequences of Physical Punishment*   383
The Cognitive-Developmental Perspective   384
The Other Side of Morality: Development of Aggression   385

Gender Typing   390
Gender-Stereotyped Beliefs and Behaviors   390
Biological Influences on Gender Typing   391
BIOLOGY AND ENVIRONMENT *David: A Boy Who Was Reared as a Girl*   392

Environmental Influences on Gender Typing 393
Gender Identity 395
Reducing Gender Stereotyping in Young Children 397
Child Rearing and Emotional and Social Development 398
Styles of Child Rearing 398
What Makes Authoritative Child Rearing Effective? 400
Cultural Variations 400
Child Maltreatment 401
Summary 406
Important Terms and Concepts 407

MILESTONES: Development in Early Childhood 408

PART V

MIDDLE CHILDHOOD: SIX TO ELEVEN YEARS

CHAPTER 11

Physical Development in Middle Childhood 410

Body Growth 412
Worldwide Variations in Body Size 413
Secular Trends in Physical Growth 413
Skeletal Growth 414
Brain Development 414
Common Health Problems 415
Nutrition 416
Overweight and Obesity 416
SOCIAL ISSUES: HEALTH *The Obesity Epidemic: How Americans Became the Heaviest People in the World* 420
Vision and Hearing 422
Bedwetting 422
Illnesses 423
Unintentional Injuries 424
Health Education 425
SOCIAL ISSUES: EDUCATION *Children's Understanding of Health and Illness* 426
Motor Development and Play 427
Gross-Motor Development 427
Fine-Motor Development 429
Individual Differences in Motor Skills 430
Games with Rules 430
Adult-Organized Youth Sports 431
Shadows of Our Evolutionary Past 431
Physical Education 432
SOCIAL ISSUES: EDUCATION *School Recess-A Time to Play, a Time to Learn* 433
Summary 434
Important Terms and Concepts 435

CHAPTER 12

Cognitive Development in Middle Childhood 436

Piaget's Theory: The Concrete Operational Stage 437
Achievements of the Concrete Operational Stage 438
Limitations of Concrete Operational Thought 440
Follow-Up Research on Concrete Operational Thought 440
Evaluation of the Concrete Operational Stage 442
Information Processing 442
Attention 443
BIOLOGY AND ENVIRONMENT *Children with Attention-Deficit Hyperactivity Disorder* 444
Memory Strategies 446
The Knowledge Base and Memory Performance 446
Culture, Schooling, and Memory Strategies 447
The School-Age Child's Theory of Mind 447
Cognitive Self-Regulation 449
Applications of Information Processing to Academic Learning 450
Individual Differences in Mental Development 453
Defining and Measuring Intelligence 453
Recent Efforts to Define Intelligence 454
SOCIAL ISSUES: EDUCATION *Emotional Intelligence* 457
Explaining Individual and Group Differences in IQ 458
Reducing Cultural Bias in Testing 461
Language Development 462
Vocabulary 462
Grammar 463
Pragmatics 463
Learning Two Languages 464
Children's Learning in School 466
Class Size 466
Educational Philosophies 467
Teacher–Student Interaction 469
Grouping Practices 470
SOCIAL ISSUES: EDUCATION *Magnet Schools: Equal Access to High-Quality Education* 471
Computers and Academic Learning 472
Teaching Children with Special Needs 473
How Well-Educated Are U. S. Children? 476
Summary 478
Important Terms and Concepts 479

CHAPTER 13

Emotional and Social Development in Middle Childhood 480

Erikson's Theory: Industry versus Inferiority 482
Self-Understanding 482
Self-Concept 482
Cognitive, Social, and Cultural Influences on Self-Concept 483

Self-Esteem   484
Influences on Self-Esteem   485

Emotional Development   489
Self-Conscious Emotions   489
Emotional Understanding   490
Emotional Self-Regulation   490

Understanding Others: Perspective Taking   491

Moral Development   492
Moral and Social-Conventional Understanding   492
Understanding Individual Rights   493
Culture and Moral Understanding   494
Understanding Diversity and Inequality   494

CULTURAL INFLUENCES *Children's Understanding of God*   495

Peer Relations   497
Peer Groups   498
Friendships   499
Peer Acceptance   500

BIOLOGY AND ENVIRONMENT *Bullies and Their Victims*   502

Gender Typing   503
Gender-Stereotyped Beliefs   503
Gender Identity and Behavior   505

Family Influences   506
Parent–Child Relationships   506
Siblings   507
Only Children   508
Gay and Lesbian Families   508

Never-Married Single-Parent Families   509
Divorce   510
Blended Families   513
Maternal Employment and Dual-Earner Families   515

Some Common Problems of Development   517
Fears and Anxieties   517

CULTURAL INFLUENCES *Impact of Ethnic and Political Violence on Children*   518
Child Sexual Abuse   519
Fostering Resilience in Middle Childhood   520

SOCIAL ISSUES: HEALTH *Children's Eyewitness Testimony*   521

Summary   523

Important Terms and Concepts   525

MILESTONES: Development in Middle Childhood   526

Glossary   G-1
References   R-1
Name Index   NI-1
Subject Index   SI-1

My more than 30 years of teaching child development have brought me in contact with thousands of students like you-students with diverse college majors, future goals, interests, and needs. Some are affiliated with my own field of psychology, but many come from other related fields—education, sociology, anthropology, family studies, social service, nursing, and biology, to name just a few. Each semester, my students' aspirations have proved to be as varied as their fields of study. Many look toward careers in applied work—teaching, caregiving, nursing, counseling, social work, school psychology, and program administration. Some want to teach, and a few want to do research. Most hope someday to become parents, whereas others are already parents who come with a desire to better understand and rear their children. And almost all arrive with a deep curiosity about how they themselves developed from tiny infants into the complex human beings they are today.

My goal in preparing this seventh edition of *Infants and Children* is to provide a textbook that meets the instructional goals of your course as well as your personal interests and needs. To achieve these objectives, I have grounded this book in a carefully selected body of classic and current theory and research brought to life with stories and vignettes about children and families, most of whom I have known personally. In addition, the text highlights the joint contributions of biology and environment to the developing child, explains how the research process helps solve real-world problems, illustrates commonalities and differences among ethnic groups and cultures, and pays special attention to policy issues that are crucial for safeguarding children's well-being in today's world. Woven throughout the text is a unique pedagogical program that will assist you in mastering information, integrating the various aspects of development, critically examining controversial issues, applying what you have learned, and relating the information to real life.

I hope that learning about child development will be as rewarding for you as I have found it over the years. I would like to know what you think about both the field of child development and this book. I welcome your comments; please feel free to send them to me at Department of Psychology, Box 4620, Illinois State University, Normal, IL 61790, or in care of the publisher, who will forward them to me.

Laura E. Berk

My decision to write *Infants and Children* was inspired by a wealth of professional and personal experiences. First and foremost were the interests and concerns of hundreds of students of child development with whom I have worked in more than three decades of college teaching. I aimed for a text that is intellectually stimulating, provides depth as well as breadth of coverage, portrays the complexities of child development with clarity and excitement, and is relevant and useful in building a bridge from theory and research to children's everyday lives. Instructor and student enthusiasm for the book not only has been among my greatest sources of pride and satisfaction but also has inspired me to rethink and improve each edition.

The 18 years since *Infants and Children* first appeared have been a period of unprecedented expansion and change in theory and research. This seventh edition represents these rapidly transforming aspects of the field, with a wealth of new content and teaching tools:

■ *Diverse pathways of change are highlighted.* Investigators have reached broad consensus that variations in biological makeup, everyday tasks, and the people who support children in mastery of those tasks lead to wide individual differences in children's paths of change and resulting competencies. This edition pays more attention to variability in development and to recent theories—including ecological, sociocultural, and dynamic systems—that attempt to explain it. Multicultural and cross-cultural findings, including international comparisons, are enhanced throughout the text and in revised and expanded Cultural Influences boxes.

■ *The complex, bidirectional relationship between biology and environment is given greater attention.* Accumulating evidence on development of the brain, motor skills, cognitive competencies, temperament, and developmental problems underscores the way biological factors emerge in, are modified by, and share power with experience. The interconnection between biology and environment is revisited throughout the text narrative and in Biology and Environment boxes with new and updated topics.

■ *Inclusion of interdisciplinary research is expanded.* The move toward viewing thoughts, feelings, and behavior as an integrated whole, affected by a wide array of influences in biology, social context, and culture, has motivated developmental researchers to strengthen their ties with other areas of psychology and with other disciplines. Topics and findings included in this edition increasingly reflect the contributions of educational psychology, social psychology, health psychology, clinical psychology, neuropsychology, biology, pediatrics, sociology, anthropology, social service, and other fields.

■ *The links among theory, research, and applications—a theme of this book since its inception—are strengthened.* As researchers intensify their efforts to generate findings that can be applied to real-life situations, I have placed even greater weight on social policy issues and sound theory- and research-based practices. Further applications are provided in the Applying What We Know tables, which give students concrete ways of building bridges between their learning and the real world.

■ *The educational context of development becomes a stronger focus.* The home, school, and community are featured as vital educational contexts in which the child develops. Research on effective teaching practices appears in many chapters and in new and revised Social Issues: Education boxes.

■ *The role of active student learning is made more explicit.* The *Take a Moment...* feature, built into the chapter narrative, asks students to think deeply and critically as they read. Ask Yourself questions at the end of each major section have been revised and expanded to promote four approaches to engaging actively with the subject matter: *Review, Apply, Connect,* and *Reflect.* This feature assists students in reflecting on what they have read from multiple vantage points. And a new *Look and Listen* feature presents students with opportunities to observe what real children say and do and attend to influences on children in their everyday environments.

Text Philosophy

The basic approach of this book has been shaped by my own professional and personal history as a teacher, researcher, and parent. It consists of seven philosophical ingredients that I regard as essential for students to emerge from a course with a thorough understanding of child development:

1. An understanding of major theories and the strengths and shortcomings of each. The first chapter begins by emphasizing that only knowledge of multiple theories can do justice to the richness of child development. As I take up each age period and domain of development, I present a variety of theoretical perspectives, indicate how each highlights previously overlooked facets of development, and discuss research that evaluates it. Consideration of contrasting theories also serves as the context for an evenhanded analysis of many controversial issues.

2. An appreciation of research strategies for investigating child development. To evaluate theories, students must have a firm grounding in research methods and designs. In addition to a special section in Chapter 1 covering research strategies, throughout the book numerous studies are discussed in sufficient detail for students to use what they have learned to critically assess the findings, conclusions, and implications of research.

3. *Knowledge of both the sequence of child development and the processes that underlie it.* Students are provided with a description of the organized sequence of development along with processes of change. An understanding of process—how complex interactions of biological and environmental events produce development—has been the focus of most recent research. Accordingly, the text reflects this emphasis. But new information about the timetable of change has also emerged. In many ways, children have proved to be far more competent than they were believed to be in the past. Current evidence on the sequence and timing of development, along with its implications for process, is presented throughout the book.

4. *An appreciation of the impact of context and culture on child development.* A wealth of research indicates that children live in rich physical and social contexts that affect all domains of development. In each chapter, students travel to distant parts of the world as I review a growing body of cross-cultural evidence. The text narrative also discusses many findings on socioeconomically and ethnically diverse children within the United States and on children with varying abilities and disabilities. Besides highlighting the role of immediate settings, such as family, neighborhood, and school, I make a concerted effort to underscore the impact of larger social structures—societal values, laws, and government programs—on children's well-being.

5. *An understanding of the joint contributions of biology and environment to development.* The field recognizes more powerfully than ever before the joint roles of hereditary/constitutional and environmental factors—that these contributions to development combine in complex ways and cannot be separated in a simple manner. Numerous examples of how biological dispositions can be maintained as well as transformed by social contexts are presented throughout the book.

6. *A sense of the interdependency of all domains of development—physical, cognitive, emotional, and social.* Every chapter takes an integrated approach to understanding children. I show how physical, cognitive, emotional, and social development are interwoven. Within the text narrative and in a special series of Ask Yourself *Connect* questions at the end of major sections, students are referred to other sections of the book to deepen their grasp of relationships among various aspects of change.

7. *An appreciation of the interrelatedness of theory, research, and applications.* Throughout this book, I emphasize that theories of child development and the research stimulated by them provide the foundation for sound, effective practices with children. The links among theory, research, and applications are reinforced by an organizational format in which theory and research are presented first, followed by practical implications. In addition, a current focus in the field—harnessing child development knowledge to shape social policies that support children's needs—is reflected in every chapter. The text addresses the current condition of children in the United States and around the world and shows how theory and research have combined with public interest to spark successful interventions.

Text Organization

I have chosen a chronological organization for this text. The chronological approach assists students in thoroughly understanding each age period. It also eases the task of integrating the various domains of development because each is discussed in close proximity. At the same time, a chronologically organized book requires that theories covering several age periods be presented piecemeal. This creates a challenge for students, who must link the various parts together. To assist with this task, I frequently remind students of important earlier achievements before discussing new developments, referring back to related sections with page references. Also, chapters devoted to the same topic (for example, cognitive development) are similarly organized, making it easier for students to draw connections across age periods and construct an overall view of developmental change.

New Coverage in the Seventh Edition

Child development is a fascinating and ever-changing field, with constantly emerging new discoveries and refinements in existing knowledge. The seventh edition represents this burgeoning contemporary literature, with more than 1,500 new citations. Cutting-edge topics throughout the text underscore the book's major themes. Here is a sampling:

■ **CHAPTER 1** ■ Introduction to the concept of plasticity in development • Updated Biology and Environment box on resilience • New, applied examples of the contributions of behaviorism and social learning theory • Revised and updated section on developmental cognitive neuroscience as a new area of investigation • New examples of research using systematic observation, structured interviews, correlational design, and field experimentation • Updated Cultural Influences box on immigrant youths • Expanded discussion of ethics, including informed consent and the use of deception in research with children

■ **CHAPTER 2** ■ Updated Social Issues: Health box on the pros and cons of reproductive technologies • Updated section on development of adopted children • Enhanced attention to the impact of poverty on development • Expanded introduction to family influences on development, including the importance of coparenting • Updated research on neighborhood influences on children's physical and mental health • Updated section on public policies and child development, including current statistics on the condition of children and families in the United States compared with other Western nations • Expanded section and a new Biology and Environment box on epigenesis, including examples of environmental influences on gene expression

■ **CHAPTER 3** ■ New findings on family size and parenting quality • Updated research on fetal sensory and behavioral capacities • Updated Biology and Environment box on the prenatal environment and health in later life • Expanded and updated consideration of a wide range of teratogens • New evidence on the long-term consequences of emotional stress during pregnancy • New findings on older maternal age and prenatal and birth complications • New Biology and Environment box on prenatal iron deficiency, brain development, and memory impairments in infants of diabetic mothers • New Social Issues: Health box on the Nurse–Family Partnership—reducing maternal stress and enhancing child development through social support

■ **CHAPTER 4** ■ Role of placental *corticotrophin-releasing hormone (CRH)* in initiating labor • Updated evidence on the contributions of doula support during childbirth to the birth process and to newborn adjustment • Updated research on the impact of medical interventions on childbirth and on maternal and infant health and postbirth adjustment • New findings on preterm and low-birth-weight infants, including interventions that foster development • Expanded and updated Social Issues box on health care and other policies for parents and newborn babies • New findings on the roles of impaired brain functioning and of maternal smoking and drug abuse in sudden infant death syndrome (SIDS) • New research on the impact of "proximal care"—extensive holding of young babies—in reducing infant crying • Updated research on touch sensitivity in newborns, including techniques for reducing infant stress to painful medical procedures • New research on factors that affect adjustment to new parenthood, including marital quality and partner support • Updated Biology and Environment box on both maternal and paternal depression, including postpartum depression, on child development

■ **CHAPTER 5** ■ Expanded consideration of major methods of assessing brain functioning, including the EEG geodesic sensor net (GSN) and near-infrared spectroscopy (NIRS) • New research on children adopted from Romanian orphanages, including neurophysiological evidence, bearing on the question of whether infancy is a sensitive period of development • Updated Cultural Influences box on cultural variation in infant sleeping arrangements • Updated section on breastfeeding • New section on infants with faltering growth, highlighting the joint contributions of a disturbed parent–infant relationship and feeding difficulties • Expanded and updated section on newborn imitation, including evidence on mirror neurons • New dynamic systems research on development of walking and reaching • Up-

dated evidence on how environmental factors, including caregiving practices and the baby's physical surroundings, contribute to development of motor skills • Enhanced attention to cultural variations in motor development • New research on development of object perception, including the role of object manipulation • Expanded and updated section on intermodal perception, including its contributions to all aspects of psychological development

■ **CHAPTER 6** ■ New evidence on babies' gradual mastery of object permanence, as indicated by object-hiding tasks • Revised and updated section on infant and toddler imitation, revealing toddlers' ability to infer others' intentions • New section on symbolic understanding, including toddlers' developing grasp of words and pictures as symbolic tools • New Social Issues: Education box on baby learning from TV and video, including discussion of the video deficit effect • Updated Cultural Influences box on social origins of make-believe play • Expanded sections on development of attention memory • Revised and updated section on categorization, including various explanations of babies' remarkable categorization skills • Updated section on infant and toddler child care • New findings on the importance of caregiver responsiveness to infant babbling • New evidence on babies' joint attention and preverbal gestures • Updated research on babies' first words

■ **CHAPTER 7** ■ New findings on the early emergence of self-conscious emotions • Updated evidence on parental influences on early development of emotional self-regulation • New research on consequences of effortful control for development • New findings on emergence of an internal working model in the second year • Updated evidence on contextual factors that contribute to changes in attachment pattern over time • Revised and updated section on early caregiving for attachment security, processing of emotion, and adjustment, highlighting studies of children adopted from Eastern European orphanages • New findings on the joint contributions of infant temperament and parenting to disorganized/disoriented attachment • Updated research on extensive early exposure to child care and externalizing behavior problems • New evidence on contributions of fathers' play to attachment security and emotional and social development • Updated survey research on employed fathers' involvement in caregiving • Updated section on grandparents as primary caregivers • New research on contributions of parental sensitivity in toddlerhood to social competence in early childhood • New evidence on development of explicit body self-awareness, including scale errors • New research on cultural influences on early self-development • New findings on active resistance to parents in toddlerhood as a sign of healthy self-assertion and autonomy

■ **CHAPTER 8** ■ Updated consideration of advances in brain development in early childhood, with special attention to the prefrontal cortex and the amygdala • Updated evidence on the health of young U.S. children, including tooth decay, childhood immunizations, and overall health status • New research on development of handedness • Enhanced consideration of hormonal influences on physical growth, including insulin-like growth factor 1 (IGF-1) • New research on ethnic variations in early childhood sleep habits and problems • Expanded attention to the impact of adult mealtime practices on children's eating behavior • New findings on the contribution of child temperament, parenting practices, and societal conditions to unintentional injury in early childhood • Revised and updated Cultural Influences box on child health care in the United States compared with other Western nations, including implications of the U.S. Patient Protection and Affordable Care Act

■ **CHAPTER 9** ■ New evidence on preschoolers' magical beliefs • Updated evidence on preschoolers' grasp of the animate–inanimate distinction • New Social Issues: Education box on children's questions as a catalyst for cognitive development • Updated research on development of attention, highlighting gains in inhibition • New research on Tools of the Mind, a preschool program inspired by Vygotsky's theory • Enhanced discussion of development of autobiographical memory, including cultural variations • New evidence on cognitive attainments and social experiences that contribute to mastery of false belief • Updated Biology and Environment box on "mindblindness" and autism • Enhanced discussion of SES differences in emergent literacy and math knowledge, including interventions that reduce the SES gap in kindergarten readiness • Findings of the Head Start Impact Study, including follow-up at end of first grade • Updated discussion of educational media, including effects of television and computers on academic learning and social experiences • Expanded and updated research on the diverse strategies preschoolers use to figure out word meanings

■ **CHAPTER 10** ■ New evidence on preschoolers' emerging grasp of personality traits • New findings on the contribution of parent–child conversations about the past to early self-concept • New evidence on the contribution of attachment to parent–child narratives about emotions • Updated consideration of emotional self-regulation in early childhood, including the influence of temperament and parenting • Enhanced Cultural Influences box on ethnic differences in the consequences of physical punishment • New section on the role of positive peer relations in school readiness • New evidence on interventions for enhancing preschoolers' social problem solving • New longitudinal findings on the relationship of early corporal punishment to later behavior problems • Updated research on aggression, including proactive and reactive forms • New section on social information-processing deficits of aggressive children • New section on cultural variations in communication within gender-segregated peer groups • New findings on the harmful impact of parental psychological control on children's adjustment • Up-

dated consideration of consequences of child maltreatment, including new evidence on central nervous system damage

■ **CHAPTER 11** ■ Updated coverage of brain development in middle childhood and gains in efficient, flexible, and adaptive information processing • Revised and updated section on overweight and obesity, including contributing factors and consequences • Updated evidence on outcomes of participation in youth sports programs • Updated statistics on physical activity and fitness among U.S. school-age children

■ **CHAPTER 12** ■ Revised and updated Biology and Environment box on children with attention-deficit hyperactivity disorder • Enhanced discussion of school-age children's spatial reasoning, with special attention to map skills • New research on development of planning in middle childhood • Updated evidence on the school-age child's theory of mind • Expanded treatment of cultural influences on mathematical development • Updated Social Issues: Education box on emotional intelligence • Enhanced discussion of dynamic assessment, with implications for ethnic minority children's test performance • New evidence on how culturally acquired knowledge affects reasoning on mental test items • Attention to the educational impact of the U.S. No Child Left Behind Act • Updated research on academic achievement of children with limited English proficiency in U.S. schools • Expanded consideration of the effects of biased teacher judgments on ethnic minority children's academic achievement • New research on the educational consequences of SES and ethnic segregation in American schools • New Social Issues box on magnet schools as a means of attaining equal access to high-quality education • Expanded treatment of the impact of computer and Internet use on academic learning • Revised and updated section on U.S. academic achievement in international perspective

■ **CHAPTER 13** ■ Enhanced attention to cultural variations in school-age children's self-concepts • New research on the impact of gender-stereotyped expectations on self-esteem • Updated findings on parenting practices and children's achievement-related attributions • Updated research on cultural variations in children's moral judgments of truthfulness and lying • Updated evidence on school-age children's grasp of individual rights • Enhanced section on development of racial and ethnic prejudice and strategies for reducing children's prejudices • Updated findings on development of flexible gender attitudes in middle childhood • Consideration of the contemporary debate over how best to help children who feel gender atypical • Expanded attention to the role of fathers in children's development, with special attention to blended families and dual-career families • New evidence on the impact of self-care and after-school programs on school-age children's adjustment • New findings on children's eyewitness testimony, including factors that contribute to children's suggestibility

Pedagogical Features

Maintaining a highly accessible writing style—one that is lucid and engaging without being simplistic—continues to be one of my major goals. I frequently converse with students, encouraging them to relate what they read to their own lives. In doing so, I hope to make the study of child development involving and pleasurable.

CHAPTER INTRODUCTIONS AND VIGNETTES ABOUT CHILDREN To provide a helpful preview of chapter content, I include an outline and overview in each chapter introduction. To help students construct a clear image of development and to enliven the text narrative, each chronological age division is unified by case examples woven throughout that set of chapters. For example, within the infancy and toddlerhood section, we'll look in on three children, observe dramatic changes and striking individual differences, and address the impact of family background, child-rearing practices, and parents' and children's life experiences on development. Besides a set of main characters, many additional vignettes offer vivid examples of development among children and adolescents.

END-OF-CHAPTER SUMMARIES Comprehensive end-of-chapter summaries, organized according to the major divisions of each chapter and highlighting important terms, remind students of key points in the text discussion. Review questions are included in the summary to encourage active study.

TAKE A MOMENT... Built into the text narrative, this feature asks students to "take a moment" to think about an important point, integrate information on children's development, or engage in an exercise or an application to clarify a challenging concept. **TAKE A MOMENT...** highlights and reinforces the text's strength in conversing with and actively engaging students in learning and in inspiring critical thinking.

LOOK AND LISTEN This new active-learning feature presents students with opportunities to observe what real children say and do and attend to influences on children in their everyday environments. "Look and Listen" experiences are tied to relevant text sections, with the goal of making the study of development more authentic and meaningful.

ASK YOURSELF QUESTIONS Active engagement with the subject matter is also supported by revised and expanded study questions at the end of each major section. Four types of questions prompt students to think about child development in diverse ways: *Review* questions help students recall and comprehend information they have just read. *Apply* questions encourage the application of knowledge to controversial issues and problems faced by children, parents, and professionals who work with them. *Connect* questions help students build an image of the whole child by integrating what they have learned across age periods and domains of development. *Reflect* questions make the study of child development personally meaningful by asking students to reflect on their own development and life experiences. Each question is answered on the text's MyDevelopmentLab website.

THREE TYPES OF THEMATIC BOXES

Our thematic boxed features accentuate the philosophical themes of this book:

SOCIAL ISSUES boxes discuss the impact of social conditions on children and emphasize the need for sensitive social policies to ensure their well-being. They are divided into two types: **Social Issues: Education** boxes focus on home, school, and community influences on children's learning—for example, *Baby Learning from TV and Video: The Video Deficit Effect; Children's Questions: Catalyst for Cognitive Development; Magnet Schools: Equal Access to High-Quality Education;* and *Media Multitasking Disrupts Attention and Learning;* and **Social Issues: Health** boxes address values and practices relevant to children's physical and mental health. Examples include *The Nurse-Family Partnership: Reducing Maternal Stress and Enhancing Child Development Through Social Support;* and *A Cross-National Perspective on Health Care and Other Policies for Parents and Newborn Babies.*

BIOLOGY AND ENVIRONMENT boxes highlight the growing attention to the complex, bidirectional relationship between biology and environment. Examples include *A Case of Epigenesis: Smoking During Pregnancy Alters Gene Expression; Prenatal Iron Deficiency and Memory Impairments in Infants of Diabetic Mothers; Children with Attention-Deficit Hyperactivity Disorder; "Mindblindness" and Autism;* and *Bullies and Their Victims.*

CULTURAL INFLUENCES boxes deepen the attention to culture threaded throughout the text. They highlight both cross-cultural and multicultural variations in child development—for example, *Immigrant Youths: Adapting to a New Land; Cultural Variation in Infant Sleeping Arrangements; Child Health Care in the United States and Other Western Nations;* and *The Impact of Ethnic and Political Violence on Children.*

APPLYING WHAT WE KNOW TABLES   In this feature, I summarize research-based applications on many issues, speaking directly to students as parents or future parents and to those pursuing different careers or areas of study, such as teaching, health care, counseling, or social work. They include: *Do's and Don'ts for a Healthy Pregnancy; Keeping Infants and Toddlers Safe; Supporting Emergent Literacy in Early Childhood;* and *Regulating TV and Computer Use.*

MILESTONES TABLES A Milestones table appears at the end of each age division of the text. These tables summarize major physical, cognitive, language, emotional, and social attainments, providing a convenient aid for reviewing the chronology of child development.

ENHANCED ART AND PHOTO PROGRAM A revised art style presents concepts and research findings with clarity and attractiveness, thereby aiding student understanding and retention. Each photo has been carefully selected to complement the text discussion and to represent the diversity of children around the world.

IN-TEXT KEY TERMS WITH DEFINITIONS, END-OF-CHAPTER TERM LIST, AND END-OF-BOOK GLOSSARY Mastery of terms that make up the central vocabulary of the field is promoted through in-text highlighting of key terms and definitions, which encourages students to review the terminology of the field in greater depth by rereading related information. Key terms also appear in an end-of-chapter page-referenced term list and an end-of-book glossary.

Acknowledgments

The dedicated contributions of a great many individuals helped make this book a reality and contributed to refinements and improvements in this seventh edition. An impressive cast of reviewers provided many helpful suggestions and constructive criticisms, as well as encouragement and enthusiasm, for the organization and content of the text. I am grateful to each one of them.

Reviewers for the First Through Sixth Editions

Scott Adler, York University
Mark B. Alcorn, University of Northern Colorado
Joseph Allen, University of Virginia
William Aquilino, University of Wisconsin
Armin W. Arndt, Eastern Washington University
Lamia Barakat, Drexel University
Cecelia Benelli, Western Illinois University
Kathleen Bey, Palm Beach Community College
Heather Bouchey, University of Vermont
Donald Bowers, Community College of Philadelphia
Michele Y. Breault, Truman State University
Jerry Bruce, Sam Houston State College
Lanthan D. Camblin, University of Cincinnati
Joseph J. Campos, University of California, Berkeley
Linda A. Camras, DePaul University
Gustavo Carlo, University of Nebraska—Lincoln
Lynn Caruso, Seneca College
Nancy Taylor Coghill, University of Southwest Louisiana
Raymond Collings, SUNY Cortland
Diane Brothers Cook, Gainesville College
Jennifer Cook, Kent State University
Roswell Cox, Berea College
Ronald Craig, Edinboro University of Pennsylvania
Zoe Ann Davidson, Alabama A&M University
Sheridan DeWolf, Grossmont College
Matthew DiCintio, Delaware County Community College
Constance DiMaria-Kross, Union County College
Jacquelynne Eccles, University of Michigan
Bronwyn Fees, Kansas State University
F. Richard Ferraro, University of North Dakota
Kathleen Fite, Southwest Texas State University
Peter Flynn, Northern Essex Community College
Trisha Folds-Bennett, College of Charleston
Nancy Freeman, University of South Carolina
Jayne Gackenbach, MacEwan University
Eugene Geist, Ohio University
Sabine Gerhardt, University of Akron
Kristine Hansen, University of Winnipeg
Vivian Harper, San Joaquin Delta College
Algea Harrison, Oakland University
Janice Hartgrove-Freile, North Harris Community College
Vernon Haynes, Youngstown State University

Bert Hayslip, Jr., University of North Texas
Sandra Hellyer, Butler University
Joan Herwig, Iowa State University
Paula Hillmann, University of Wisconsin, Waukesha
Christie Honeycutt, Stanly Community College
Malia Huchendorf, Normandale Community College
Lisa Huffman, Ball State University
Clementine Hansley Hurt, Radford University
Scott Johnson, New York University
Joline Jones, Worcester State University
Kate Kenney, Howard Community College
Shirin Khosropour, Austin Community College
John S. Klein, Castleton State College
Claire Kopp, Claremont Graduate School
Eugene Krebs, California State University, Fresno
Carole Kremer, Hudson Valley Community College
Gary W. Ladd, University of Illinois, Urbana—Champaign
Deborah Laible, Southern Methodist University
Linda Lavine, State University of New York at Cortland
Sara Lawrence, California State University, Northridge
Gail Lee, Jersey City State College
Judith R. Levine, State University of New York at Farmingdale
David Lockwood, Humber College
Frank Manis, University of Southern California
Martin Marino, Atlantic Cape Community College
Mary Ann McLaughlin, Clarion University of Pennsylvania
Annie McManus, Parkland College
Cloe Merrill, Weber State University
Rich Metzger, University of Tennessee at Chattanooga
Karla Miley, Black Hawk College
Jennifer Trapp Myers, University of Michigan
Virginia Navarro, University of Missouri, St. Louis
Larry Nelson, Brigham Young University
Peggy Norwood, Red Rocks Community College
Peter V. Oliver, University of Hartford
Behnaz Pakizegi, William Patterson University
Virginia Parsons, Carroll College
Julie Poehlmann, University of Wisconsin—Madison
Kavita Prakash, Heritage College
Joe M. Price, San Diego State University
Cathy Proctor-Castillo, Long Beach Community College
Verna Raab, Mount Royal College
Raghu Rao, University of Minnesota
Mary Kay Reed, York College of Pennsylvania
Michael Rodman, Middlesex Community College
Alan Russell, Flinders University
Tizrah Schutzengel, Bergen Community College
Johnna Shapiro, Illinois Wesleyan University
Delores Smith, University of Tennessee
Gregory Smith, Dickinson College
Thomas Spencer, San Francisco State University
Carolyn Spies, Bloomfield College
Kathy Stansbury, University of New Mexico
Connie Steele, University of Tennessee, Knoxville
Janet Strayer, Simon Fraser University
Marcia Summers, Ball State University
Daniel Swingley, University of Pennsylvania

Christy Teranishi, Texas A&M International University
Dennis Thompson, Georgia State University
Tracy Thorndike-Christ, Western Washington University
Connie K. Varnhagen, University of Alberta
Athena Vouloumanos, McGill University
Judith Ward, Central Connecticut State University
Shawn Ward, Le Moyne College
Alida Westman, Eastern Michigan University
Colin William, Columbus State Community College
Belinda Wholeben, Rockford College
Sue Williams, Southwest Texas State University
Deborah Winters, New Mexico State University

Reviewers for the Seventh Edition

Martha Arterberry, Colby College
Kristy Burkholder, University of Wisconsin, Madison
Melissa Burnham, University of Nevada, Reno
Nicole Campione-Barr, University of Missouri, Columbia
Jeff Farrar, University of Florida
William Friedman, Oberlin College
Abi Gewirtz, University of Minnesota
Robert Hiltonsmith, Radford University
Shayla Holub, University of Texas, Dallas
Jennifer Jipson, California Polytechnic State University
Elisa Klein, University of Maryland
Debbie Laible, Lehigh University
Miriam Linver, Montclair State University
Trent Maurer, Georgia Southern University
Megan McLelland, Oregon State University
Daniel Messinger, University of Miami
Joyce Munsch, California State University, Northridge
Karen Peterson, University of Washington, Vancouver
Tom Power, Washington State University
Pamela Schulze, University of Akron
Elizabeth Short, Case Western Reserve University
Laura Sosinsky, Fordham University
Jayne White, Drury University
Ilona Yim, University of California, Irvine
Nicole Zarrett, University of South Carolina, Columbia

An outstanding editorial staff in my home community contributed immeasurably to the entire project. Sara Harris, Supplements Editor and visiting assistant professor of psychology, Bradley University, coordinated the preparation of the teaching ancillaries and wrote major sections of the Instructor's Resource Manual, bringing to these tasks great depth of knowledge, impressive writing skill, enthusiasm, and imagination. Amelia Benner, Editorial Assistant, spent countless hours searching, gathering, and organizing scholarly literature; writing portions of the Study Guide; designing highly creative MyDevelopmentLab simulations; contributing to the Explorations in Child Development video segments and video guide; and expertly handling many additional tasks as they arose.

I have been fortunate to work with a highly capable editorial team at Pearson Education. It has been a great pleasure to work once again with Tom Pauken, Managing Editor, who over-saw the preparation of the fourth edition of *Infants and Children* and who returned to edit this seventh edition. His careful review of manuscript, keen organizational skills, responsive day-to-day communication, insightful suggestions, astute problem solving, interest in the subject matter, and thoughtfulness have greatly enhanced the quality of the text and made its preparation especially enjoyable and rewarding. Judy Ashkenaz and Lisa McLellan, Development Editors, carefully reviewed and commented on each chapter, helping to ensure that every thought and concept would be clearly expressed and well-developed. My appreciation, also, to Jessica Mosher, Editor in Chief of Psychology, for reorganizing the management of my projects to enable the focused work that is vital for precise, inspired writing and timely manuscript preparation.

The supplements package benefited from the talents and diligence of several other individuals. Leah Shiro carefully revised the chapter summaries and outlines in the Instructor's Resource Manual. Kimberly Michaud prepared a superb Test Bank along with practice tests for the Study Guide, and Bill Tierney authored the excellent MyDevelopmentLab assessments. Diana Murphy designed and wrote a highly attractive PowerPoint presentation. Maria Henneberry and Phil Vandiver of Contemporary Visuals in Bloomington, IL, prepared an extraordinarily artistic and inspiring set of new video segments covering diverse topics in child development.

Donna Simons, Senior Production Project Manager, coordinated the complex production tasks that resulted in an exquisitely beautiful seventh edition. I am grateful for her keen aesthetic sense, attention to detail, flexibility, efficiency, and thoughtfulness. I thank Sarah Evertson for obtaining the exceptional photographs that so aptly illustrate the text narrative. I am also grateful for Judy Ashkenaz's fine contributions to the photo specifications and captions. Margaret Pinette, Bill Heckman, and Beyond Words Proofreading provided outstanding copyediting and proofreading.

Wendy Albert, Executive Marketing Manager, prepared the beautiful print ads and informative e-mails to the field about *Infants and Children,* Seventh Edition. She has also ensured that accurate and clear information reached Pearson Education's sales force and that the needs of prospective and current adopters were met.

A final word of gratitude goes to my family, whose love, patience, and understanding have enabled me to be wife, mother, teacher, researcher, and text author at the same time. My sons, David and Peter, grew up with my texts, passing from childhood to adolescence and then to adulthood as successive editions were written. David has a special connection with the books' subject matter as an elementary school teacher, and Peter is now an experienced attorney and married to his vivacious, talented, and caring Melissa. All three continue to enrich my understanding through reflections on events and progress in their own lives. My husband, Ken, willingly made room for yet another time-consuming endeavor in our life together and communicated his belief in its importance in a great many unspoken, caring ways.

Laura E. Berk

Supplementary Materials

Instructor Supplements

A variety of teaching tools are available for qualified instructors in organizing lectures, planning demonstrations and examinations, and ensuring student comprehension.

MyDevelopmentLab This interactive and instructive multimedia resource can be used as a supplement to a classroom course or to completely administer an online course. Prepared in collaboration with Laura Berk, MyDevelopmentLab includes a variety of assessments that enable continuous evaluation of students' learning. Extensive video footage, multimedia simulations, biographies of major figures in the field, and interactive activities that are unique to *Infants and Children* are also included. A new MyDevelopmentLab feature, "Careers in Human Development," explains how studying human development is essential for a wide range of career paths. The power of MyDevelopmentLab lies in its design as an all-inclusive teaching and learning tool. For a sampling of its rich content, contact your Pearson representative.

Instructor's Resource Manual (IRM) This thoroughly revised IRM can be used by first-time or experienced instructors to enrich classroom experiences. Each chapter includes a Chapter-at-a-Glance grid, Brief Chapter Summary, Learning Objectives, detailed Lecture Outlines, Lecture Enhancements, Learning Activities, Ask Yourself questions with answers, Suggested Student Readings, a PowerPoint Presentation, and a Media Materials list.

Test Bank The Test Bank contains over 2,000 multiple-choice questions, each of which is page-referenced to chapter content and classified by type (factual, applied, or conceptual). Each chapter also includes a selection of essay questions and sample answers.

Computerized Test Bank This computerized version of the Test Bank, in easy-to-use MyTest format, lets you prepare tests for printing as well as for network and online testing. It has full editing capability. Test items are also available in Course-Compass, Blackboard, and WebCT formats.

PowerPoint Presentation The PowerPoint presentation contains illustrations and outlines of key topics for each chapter from the text, presented in a clear and visually attractive format.

"Explorations in Child Development" DVD and Guide This new DVD is over four hours in length and contains 47 four- to ten-minute narrated segments, designed for effective classroom use, that illustrate the many theories, concepts, and milestones of child development. New additions include *Preterm Birth, Autism, First-Grade Science Education, Childhood Obesity, Civic Engagement in Adolescence,* and *Changing Parent–Adolescent Relationships.* "Explorations in Child Development" DVD and DVD Guide are available to instructors who adopt the text for in-class use and are also available as a student supplement for free when packaged with the text. The DVD Guide helps students use the DVD in conjunction with the textbook, deepening their understanding and applying what they have learned to everyday life.

Student Supplements

Beyond the study aids found in the textbook, Pearson offers a number of supplements for students:

MyDevelopmentLab This interactive and instructive multimedia resource is an all-inclusive learning tool. Prepared in collaboration with Laura Berk, MyDevelopmentLab engages students and reinforces learning through controlled assessments, extensive video footage, multimedia simulations, biographies of major figures in the field, and interactive activities that are unique to *Infants and Children.* In addition, "Careers in Human Development" explains how knowledge of human development is essential for a wide range of career paths. Easy to use, MyDevelopmentLab meets the individual learning needs of every student. For a sampling of its rich content, visit *www.mydevelopmentlab.com.*

Study Guide with Practice Tests This helpful study guide offers Chapter Summaries, Learning Objectives, Study Questions organized according to major headings in the text, Suggested Readings, Crossword Puzzles for mastering important terms, and two multiple-choice Practice Tests per chapter.

Milestones Study Cards Adapted from the popular Milestones tables featured in the text, these colorfully illustrated study cards outline key developmental attainments. Easy-to-use, they assist students in integrating the various domains of development and constructing a vision of the whole developing child.

About the Chapter Opening Art

I would like to extend grateful acknowledgments to the International Museum of Children's Art, Oslo, Norway; to the International Child Art Foundation, Washington, D.C.; to the World Awareness Children's Museum, Glens Falls, New York; and to the International Collection of Child Art, Milner Library, Illinois State University, for the exceptional cover image and chapter opening art, which depict the talents, concerns, and viewpoints of young artists from around the world. The awe-inspiring collection of children's art gracing this text expresses family, school, and community themes; good times and personal triumphs; profound appreciation for beauty; and great depth of emotion. I am pleased to share with readers this window into children's creativity, insightfulness, sensitivity, and compassion.

INFANTS and CHILDREN

"My Vision of the Future"
Bhea Vacio
11 years, Philippines

In this artist's vision of the future, people from around the globe join hands in peace and cooperation, with a rainbow of colors as a backdrop. Chapter 1 will introduce you to a rainbow of theories—a multiplicity of ways to think about and study children's development.

Reprinted with permission from the International Child Art Foundation, Washington, D.C.

History, Theory, and Research Strategies

$\mathcal{N}$ ot long ago, I left my Midwestern home to live for a year near the small city in northern California where I spent my childhood. One morning, I visited the neighborhood where I grew up—a place I had not seen since I was 12 years old.

I stood at the entrance to my old schoolyard. Buildings and grounds that had looked large to me as a child now seemed strangely small. I peered through the window of my first-grade classroom. The desks were no longer arranged in rows but grouped in intimate clusters. Computers rested against the far wall, near where I once sat. I walked my old route home from school, the distance shrunken by my longer stride. I stopped in front of my best friend Kathryn's house, where we once drew sidewalk pictures, crossed the street to play kickball, and produced plays in the garage. In place of the small shop where I had purchased penny candy stood a child-care center, filled with the voices and vigorous activity of toddlers and preschoolers.

As I walked, I reflected on early experiences that contributed to who and what I am today—weekends helping my father in his downtown clothing shop, the year my mother studied to become a high school teacher, moments of companionship and rivalry with my sister and brother, Sunday outings to museums and the seashore, and visits to my grandmother's house, where I became someone extra special.

As I passed the homes of my childhood friends, I thought of what I knew about their present lives. Kathryn, star student and president of our sixth-grade class— today a successful corporate lawyer and mother of two. Shy, withdrawn Phil, cruelly teased because of his cleft lip—now owner of a thriving chain of hardware stores and member of the city council. Julio, immigrant from Mexico who joined our class in third grade—today director of an elementary school bilingual education program and single parent of an adopted Mexican boy. And finally, my next-door neighbor Rick, who picked fights at recess, struggled with reading, repeated fourth grade, dropped out of high school, and (so I heard) moved from one job to another over the following 10 years.

The Field of Child Development
Domains of Development • Periods of Development

Basic Issues
Continuous or Discontinuous Development? • One Course of Development or Many? • Relative Influence of Nature and Nurture? • A Balanced Point of View

■ **BIOLOGY AND ENVIRONMENT**
Resilient Children

Historical Foundations
Medieval Times • The Reformation • Philosophies of the Enlightenment • Scientific Beginnings

Mid-Twentieth-Century Theories
The Psychoanalytic Perspective • Behaviorism and Social Learning Theory • Piaget's Cognitive-Developmental Theory

Recent Theoretical Perspectives
Information Processing • Ethology and Evolutionary Developmental Psychology • Vygotsky's Sociocultural Theory • Ecological Systems Theory • New Directions: Development as a Dynamic System

Comparing Child Development Theories

Studying the Child
Common Research Methods • General Research Designs • Designs for Studying Development • Ethics in Research on Children

■ **CULTURAL INFLUENCES**
Immigrant Youths: Adapting to a New Land

■ **SOCIAL ISSUES: EDUCATION**
Can Musical Experiences Enhance Intelligence?

As you begin this course in child development, perhaps you, too, wonder about some of the same questions that crossed my mind during that nostalgic neighborhood walk:

- In what ways are children's home, school, and neighborhood experiences the same today as they were in generations past, and in what ways are they different?
- How are the infant and young child's perceptions of the world the same as the adult's, and how are they different?
- What determines the features that humans have in common and those that make each of us unique—physically, mentally, and behaviorally?
- How did Julio, transplanted at age 8 to a new culture, master its language and customs and succeed in its society, yet remain strongly identified with his ethnic community?
- Why do some of us, like Kathryn and Rick, retain the same styles of responding that characterized us as children, whereas others, like Phil, change in essential ways?
- How do cultural changes—employed mothers, child care, divorce, smaller families, and new technologies—affect children's characteristics?

These are central questions addressed by **child development,** an area of study devoted to understanding constancy and change from conception through adolescence. Child development is part of a larger, interdisciplinary field known as **developmental science,** which includes all changes we experience throughout the lifespan (Lerner, 2006). Great diversity characterizes the interests and concerns of the thousands of investigators who study child development. But all have a common goal: to describe and identify those factors that influence the consistencies and changes in young people during the first two decades of life.

The Field of Child Development

The questions just listed are not just of scientific interest. Each has *applied,* or practical, importance as well. In fact, scientific curiosity is just one factor that led child development to become the exciting field of study it is today. Research about development has also been stimulated by social pressures to improve the lives of children. For example, the beginning of public education in the early twentieth century led to a demand for knowledge about what and how to teach children of different ages. Pediatricians' interest in improving children's health required an understanding of physical growth and nutrition. The social service profession's desire to treat children's anxieties and behavior problems required information about personality and social development. And parents have continually sought advice about child-rearing practices and experiences that would promote their children's development and well-being.

Our large storehouse of information about child development is *interdisciplinary.* It has grown through the combined efforts of people from many fields. Because of the need to solve everyday problems concerning children, researchers from psychology, sociology, anthropology, biology, and neuroscience have joined forces with professionals from education, family studies, medicine, public health, and social service—to name just a few. The field of child development, as it exists today, is a monument to the contributions of these many disciplines. Its body of knowledge is not just scientifically important but also relevant and useful.

© MICHAEL NEWMAN/PHOTOEDIT

- Theories have practical value in helping us improve the welfare and treatment of children. For example, theories have contributed to new approaches to education that emphasize exploration, discovery, and collaboration. ■

Domains of Development

To make the vast, interdisciplinary study of human constancy and change more orderly and convenient, development is often divided into three broad domains: *physical, cognitive,* and *emotional and social.* Refer to Figure 1.1 for a description and illustration of each. Within each period from infancy through adolescence, we will consider the three domains in the order just mentioned. Yet the domains are not really distinct. Rather, they combine in an integrated, holistic fashion to yield the living, growing child. Furthermore, each domain influences and is influenced by the others. For example, in Chapter 5 you will see that new motor capacities, such as reaching, sitting, crawling, and walking (physical), contribute greatly to infants' understanding of their surroundings (cognitive). When babies think and act more competently, adults stimulate them more with games, language, and expressions of delight at their new achievements (emotional and social). These enriched experiences, in turn, promote all aspects of development.

Although each chapter focuses on a particular domain, you will encounter instances of the interwoven nature of all domains on nearly every page of this book. In the margins of the text you will find occasional *Look and Listen* activities—opportunities for you to see every-day illustrations of development by observing what real children say and do or by attending to everyday influences on children. Through these experiences, I hope to make your study of development more authentic and meaningful.

Also, look for the *Ask Yourself* feature at the end of major sections, designed to deepen your understanding. Within it, I have included *Review* questions, which help you recall and think about information you have just read; *Apply* questions, which encourage you to apply your knowledge to controversial issues and problems faced by parents, teachers, and children; *Connect* questions, which help you form a coherent, unified picture of child development; and *Reflect* questions, which invite you to reflect on your own development and that of people you know well.

Physical Development

Changes in body size, proportions, appearance, functioning of body systems, perceptual and motor capacities, and physical health

Cognitive Development

Changes in intellectual abilities, including attention, memory, academic and everyday knowledge, problem solving, imagination, creativity, and language

Emotional and Social Development

Changes in emotional communication, self-understanding, knowledge about other people, interpersonal skills, friendships, intimate relationships, and moral reasoning and behavior

FIGURE 1.1

Major domains of development. The three domains are not really distinct. Rather, they overlap and interact.

Periods of Development

Besides distinguishing and integrating the three domains, another dilemma arises in discussing development: how to divide the flow of time into sensible, manageable parts. Researchers usually use the following age periods, according to which I have organized this book. Each brings new capacities and social expectations that serve as important transitions in major theories:

- *The prenatal period: from conception to birth*. In this nine-month period, the most rapid time of change, a one-celled organism is transformed into a human baby with remarkable capacities for adjusting to life in the surrounding world.
- *Infancy and toddlerhood: from birth to 2 years*. This period brings dramatic changes in the body and brain that support the emergence of a wide array of motor, perceptual, and intellectual capacities; the beginnings of language; and first intimate ties to others. Infancy spans the first year; toddlerhood spans the second, during which children take their first independent steps, marking a shift to greater autonomy.
- *Early childhood: from 2 to 6 years*. The body becomes longer and leaner, motor skills are refined, and children become more self-controlled and self-sufficient. Make-believe play blossoms, supporting every aspect of psychological development. Thought and language expand at an astounding pace, a sense of morality becomes evident, and children establish ties with peers.
- *Middle childhood: from 6 to 11 years*. Children learn about the wider world and master new responsibilities that increasingly resemble those they will perform as adults. Hallmarks of this period are improved athletic abilities; participation in organized games with rules; more logical thought processes; mastery of fundamental reading, writing, math, and other academic knowledge and skills; and advances in understanding the self, morality, and friendship.
- *Adolescence: from 11 to 18 years*. This period initiates the transition to adulthood. Puberty leads to an adult-sized body and sexual maturity. Thought becomes abstract and idealistic, and schooling is increasingly directed toward preparation for higher education and the world of work. Young people begin to establish autonomy from the family and to define personal values and goals.

For many contemporary youth in industrialized nations, the transition to adult roles has become increasingly prolonged—so much so that some researchers have posited a new period of development called *emerging adulthood*, which spans ages 18 to 25. Although emerging adults have moved beyond adolescence, they have not yet fully assumed adult roles. Rather, during higher education and sometimes beyond, these young people intensify their exploration of options in love, career, and personal values before making enduring commitments. Because emerging adulthood first became apparent during the past few decades, researchers have just begun to study it (Arnett, 2003, 2004; Arnett & Tanner, 2006). Perhaps it is *your* period of development.

With this introduction in mind, let's turn to some basic issues that have captivated, puzzled, and sparked debate among child development theorists. Then our discussion will trace the emergence of the field and survey major theories. We will return to each contemporary theory in greater detail in later chapters.

© UWE OMMER, 1,000 FAMILIES, TASCHEN

■ Child development is so dramatic that researchers divide it into periods. This large family of the Ivory Coast includes children in infancy, early childhood (boy in front row, girl seated in second row), middle childhood (girl in front row, girl standing in second row), and adolescence (girl standing in center). ■

Basic Issues

Research on child development did not begin until the late nineteenth and early twentieth centuries. But ideas about how children grow and change have a much longer history. As these speculations combined with research, they inspired the construction of *theories* of development. A **theory** is an orderly, integrated set of statements that describes, explains, and predicts behavior. For example, a good theory of infant–caregiver attachment would (1) *describe* the behaviors of babies around 6 to 8 months of age as they seek the affection and comfort of a familiar adult, (2) *explain* how and why infants develop this strong desire to bond with a caregiver, and (3) *predict* the consequences of this emotional bond for future relationships.

Theories are vital tools for two reasons. First, they provide organizing frameworks for our observations of children. In other words, they *guide and give meaning* to what we see. Second, theories that are verified by research often serve as a sound basis for practical action. Once a theory helps us *understand* development, we are in a much better position *to know how to improve* the welfare and treatment of children.

As we will see later, theories are influenced by the cultural values and belief systems of their times. But theories differ in one important way from mere opinion or belief: A theory's continued existence depends on *scientific verification*. This means that the theory must be tested using a fair set of research procedures agreed on by the scientific community, and its findings must endure, or be replicated over time.

Within the field of child development, many theories offer very different ideas about what children are like and how they change. The study of child development provides no ultimate truth because investigators do not always agree on the meaning of what they see. Also, children are complex beings; they change physically, cognitively, emotionally, and socially. No single theory has explained all these aspects. But the existence of many theories helps advance knowledge because researchers are continually trying to support, contradict, and integrate these different points of view.

Although there are many theories, we can easily organize them by looking at the stand they take on three basic issues: (1) Is the course of development continuous or discontinuous? (2) Does one course of development characterize all children, or are there many possible courses? (3) What are the roles of genetic and environmental factors—nature and nurture—in development? Let's look closely at each of these issues.

Continuous or Discontinuous Development?

Recently, the mother of 20-month-old Angelo reported to me with amazement that her young son had pushed a toy car across the living room floor while making a motorlike sound, "Brmmmm, brmmmm," for the first time. When he hit a nearby wall with a bang, Angelo let go of the car, exclaimed, "C'ash!" and laughed heartily.

"How come Angelo can pretend, but he couldn't a few months ago?" queried his mother. "And I wonder what 'Brmmmm, brmmmm' and 'Crash!' mean to Angelo. Does he understand motorlike sounds and collision the same way I do?"

Angelo's mother has raised a puzzling issue about development: How can we best describe the differences in capacities and behavior between small infants, young children, adolescents, and adults? As Figure 1.2 on page 8 illustrates, most major theories recognize two possibilities.

One view holds that infants and preschoolers respond to the world in much the same way as adults do. The difference between the immature and the mature being is simply one of *amount or complexity*. For example, little Angelo's thinking may be just as logical and well-organized as our own. Perhaps (as his mother reports) he can sort objects into simple categories, recognize whether he has more of one kind than of another, and remember where he left his favorite toy at child care the week before. Angelo's only limitation may be that he cannot perform these skills with as much information and precision as we can. If this is so, then Angelo's development is **continuous**—a process of gradually adding more of the same types of skills that were there to begin with.

FIGURE 1.2

Is development continuous or discontinuous? (a) Some theorists believe that development is a smooth, continuous process. Children gradually add more of the same types of skills. (b) Other theorists think that development takes place in discontinuous stages. Children change rapidly as they step up to a new level and then change very little for a while. With each step, the child interprets and responds to the world in a qualitatively different way.

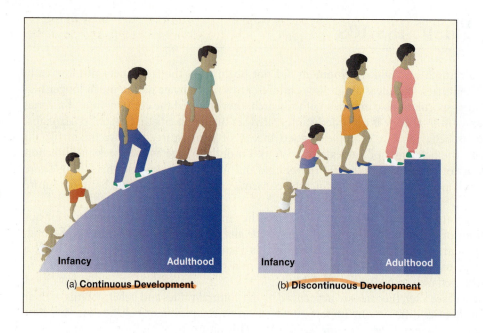

(a) **Continuous Development**　　(b) **Discontinuous Development**

According to a second view, Angelo's thoughts, emotions, and behavior differ considerably from those of adults. His development is **discontinuous**—a process in which new ways of understanding and responding to the world emerge at specific times. From this perspective, Angelo is not yet able to organize objects or remember and interpret experiences as we do. Instead, he will move through a series of developmental steps, each with unique features, until he reaches the highest level of functioning.

Theories that accept the discontinuous perspective regard development as taking place in **stages**—*qualitative* changes in thinking, feeling, and behaving that characterize specific periods of development. In stage theories, development is much like climbing a staircase, with each step corresponding to a more mature, reorganized way of functioning. The stage concept also assumes that children undergo periods of rapid transformation as they step up from one stage to the next, alternating with plateaus during which they stand solidly within a stage. In other words, change is fairly sudden rather than gradual and ongoing.

Does development actually occur in a neat, orderly sequence of stages? This ambitious assumption has faced significant challenges. Later in this chapter, we will review some influential stage theories.

One Course of Development or Many?

Stage theorists assume that people everywhere follow the same sequence of development. For example, in the domain of cognition, a stage theorist might try to identify the common influences that lead children to represent their world through language and make-believe play in early childhood, to think more logically and systematically in middle childhood, and to reason more systematically and abstractly in adolescence.

At the same time, the field of child development is becoming increasingly aware that children grow up in distinct **contexts**—unique combinations of personal and environmental circumstances that can result in different paths of change. For example, a shy child who fears social encounters develops in very different contexts from those of an outgoing agemate who readily seeks out other people (Kagan, 2003, 2008). Children in non-Western village societies have experiences in their families and communities that differ sharply from those of children in large Western cities. These different circumstances foster different cognitive capacities, social skills, and feelings about the self and others (Shweder et al., 2006).

As you will see, contemporary theorists regard the contexts that mold development as many-layered and complex. On the personal side, these include heredity and biological makeup. On the environmental side, they include both immediate settings—home, child-care center, school, and neighborhood—and circumstances that are more remote from children's everyday lives: community resources, societal values and priorities, and historical time period. Finally, researchers today are more conscious than ever before of cultural diversity in development.

Relative Influence of Nature and Nurture?

In addition to describing the course of child development, each theory takes a stand on a major question about its underlying causes: Are genetic or environmental factors more important in influencing development? This is the age-old **nature–nurture controversy.** By *nature,* we mean inborn biological givens—the hereditary information we receive from our parents at the moment of conception. By *nurture,* we mean the complex forces of the physical and social world that influence our biological makeup and psychological experiences before and after birth.

Although all theories grant roles to both nature and nurture, they vary in emphasis. Consider the following questions: Is the older child's ability to think in more complex ways largely the result of an inborn timetable of growth, or is it primarily influenced by stimulation from parents and teachers? Do children acquire language because they are genetically predisposed to do so or because parents intensively teach them from an early age? And what accounts for the vast individual differences among children—in height, weight, physical coordination, intelligence, personality, and social skills? Is nature or nurture more responsible?

A theory's position on the roles of nature and nurture affects how it explains individual differences. Some theorists emphasize *stability*—that children who are high or low in a characteristic (such as verbal ability, anxiety, or sociability) will remain so at later ages. These theorists typically stress the importance of *heredity*. If they do regard environment as important, they usually point to *early experiences* as establishing a lifelong pattern of behavior. Powerful negative events in the first few years, they argue, cannot be fully overcome by later, more positive ones (Bowlby, 1980; Johnson, 2000; Sroufe, 2005). Other theorists, taking a more optimistic view, see development as having substantial **plasticity** throughout life—as open to change in response to influential experiences (Baltes, Lindenberger, & Staudinger, 2006; Lerner & Overton, 2008; Lester, Masten, & McEwen, 2006).

Throughout this book, you will see that investigators disagree, often sharply, on the question of *stability versus plasticity.* Their answers have great applied significance. If you believe that development is largely due to nature, then providing experiences aimed at promoting change would seem to be of little value. If, on the other hand, you are convinced of the supreme importance of early experience, then you would intervene as soon as possible, offering high-quality stimulation and support to ensure that children develop at their best. Finally, if you think that environment is profoundly influential throughout development, you would provide assistance any time children or adolescents face difficulties, in the belief that, with the help of favorable life circumstances, they can recover from early negative events.

A Balanced Point of View

So far, we have discussed basic issues of child development in terms of extremes—solutions favoring one side or the other. But as we trace the unfolding of the field in the rest of this chapter, you will see that the positions of many theorists have softened. Today, some theorists believe that both continuous and discontinuous changes occur. Many acknowledge that development has both universal features and features unique to the individual and his or her contexts. And a growing number regard heredity and environment as inseparably interwoven, each affecting the potential of the other to modify the child's traits and capacities (Cole, 2006; Gottlieb, Wahlsten, & Lickliter, 2006; Lerner, 2006; Rutter, 2007b). We will discuss these new ideas about nature and nurture in Chapter 2.

Finally, as you will see later in this book, the relative impact of early and later experiences varies greatly from one domain of development to another and even—as the Biology and Environment box on pages 10–11 indicates—across individuals! Because of the complex network of factors contributing to human change and the challenges of isolating the effects of each, many theoretical points of view have gathered research support. Although debate continues, this circumstance has also sparked more balanced visions of child development.

BIOLOGY AND ENVIRONMENT

Resilient Children

*J*ohn and his best friend, Gary, grew up in a run-down, crime-ridden inner-city neighborhood. By age 10, each had experienced years of family conflict followed by parental divorce. Reared for the rest of childhood and adolescence in mother-headed households, John and Gary rarely saw their fathers. Both dropped out of high school and were in and out of trouble with the police.

Then their paths diverged. By age 30, John had fathered two children with women he never married, had spent time in prison, was unemployed, and drank alcohol heavily. In contrast, Gary had returned to finish high school, had studied auto mechanics at a community college, and became manager of a gas station and repair shop. Married with two children, he had saved his earnings and bought a home. He was happy, healthy, and well-adapted to life.

A wealth of evidence shows that environmental risks—poverty, negative family interactions and parental divorce, job loss, mental illness, and drug abuse—predispose children to future problems (Masten & Gewirtz, 2006; Sameroff, 2006; Wadsworth & Santiago, 2008). Why did Gary "beat the odds" and come through unscathed?

New evidence on **resilience**—the ability to adapt effectively in the face of threats to

development—is receiving increasing attention as investigators look for ways to protect young people from the damaging effects of stressful life conditions (Masten & Powell, 2003). This interest has been inspired by several long-term studies on the relationship of life stressors in childhood to competence and adjustment in adolescence and adulthood (Fergusson & Horwood, 2003; Masten et al., 1995; Werner & Smith, 2001). In each study, some individuals were shielded from negative outcomes, whereas others had lasting problems. Four broad factors seemed to offer protection from the damaging effects of stressful life events.

Personal Characteristics

A child's biologically endowed characteristics can reduce exposure to risk or lead to experiences that compensate for early stressful events. High intelligence and socially valued talents (in music or athletics, for example) increase the chances that a child will have

■ This boy's close, affectionate relationship with his father helps foster resilience. A strong bond with at least one parent who combines warmth with appropriate expectations for maturity can shield children from the damaging effects of stressful life conditions. ■

© ROBERT BRENNER/PHOTOEDIT

ASK YOURSELF

◆ **REVIEW** What is meant by a *stage* of development? Provide your own example of stagewise change. What stand do stage theorists take on the issue of continuous versus discontinuous development?

◆ **APPLY** Anna, a high school counselor, has devised a program that integrates classroom learning with vocational training to help adolescents at risk for school dropout stay in school and transition smoothly to work life. What is Anna's position on *stability versus plasticity* in development? Explain.

◆ **CONNECT** Provide an example of how one domain of development (physical, cognitive, or emotional/social) can affect development in another domain.

◆ **REFLECT** Cite an aspect of your development that differs from a parent's or a grandparent's when he or she was your age. How might *contexts* explain this difference?

rewarding experiences at school and in the community that offset the impact of a stressful home life. Temperament is particularly powerful. Children who have easygoing, sociable dispositions and who can readily inhibit negative emotions and impulses tend to have an optimistic outlook on life and a special capacity to adapt to change—qualities that elicit positive responses from others. In contrast, emotionally reactive and irritable children often tax the patience of people around them (Mathiesen & Prior, 2006; Vanderbilt-Adriance & Shaw, 2008; Wong et al., 2006). For example, both John and Gary moved several times during their childhoods. Each time, John became anxious and angry. Gary looked forward to making new friends and exploring new parts of the neighborhood.

A Warm Parental Relationship

A close relationship with at least one parent who provides warmth, appropriately high expectations, monitoring of the child's activities, and an organized home environment fosters resilience (Masten & Shaffer, 2006). But this factor (as well as the next one) is not independent of children's personal characteristics. Children who are relaxed, socially responsive, and able to deal with change are easier to rear and more likely to enjoy positive relationships with parents and other people. At the same time, some children may develop more attractive

dispositions as a result of parental warmth and attention (Conger & Conger, 2002; Gulotta, 2008).

Social Support Outside the Immediate Family

The most consistent asset of resilient children is a strong bond to a competent, caring adult. For children who do not have a close bond with either parent, a grandparent, aunt, uncle, or teacher who forms a special relationship with the child can promote resilience (Masten & Reed, 2002). Gary received support in adolescence from his grandfather, who listened to Gary's concerns and helped him solve problems. Gary's grandfather had a stable marriage and work life and handled stressors skillfully. Consequently, he served as a model of effective coping.

Associations with rule-abiding peers who value school achievement are also linked to resilience. But children who have positive relationships with adults are far more likely to establish these supportive peer ties.

Community Resources and Opportunities

Community supports—good schools, convenient and affordable health care and social services, libraries, and recreation centers—foster both parent's and children's well-being. In addition, opportunities to participate in community life

help older children and adolescents overcome adversity. Extracurricular activities at school, religious youth groups, scouting, and other organizations teach important social skills, such as cooperation, leadership, and contributing to others' welfare. As participants acquire these competencies, they gain in self-reliance, self-esteem, and community commitment (Benson et al., 2006). As a college student, Gary volunteered for Habitat for Humanity, joining a team building affordable housing in low-income neighborhoods. Community involvement offered Gary additional opportunities to form meaningful relationships, which further strengthened his resilience.

Research on resilience highlights the complex connections between heredity and environment. Armed with positive characteristics stemming from innate endowment, favorable rearing experiences, or both, children and adolescents can act to reduce stressful situations.

But when many risks pile up, they are increasingly difficult to overcome (Obradović et al., 2009). To inoculate children against the negative effects of risk, interventions must not only reduce risks but also enhance children's protective relationships at home, in school, and in the community. This means attending to both the person and the environment—strengthening children's capacities while also reducing hazardous experiences.

Historical Foundations

Contemporary theories of child development are the result of centuries of change in Western cultural values, philosophical thinking about children, and scientific progress. To understand the field as it exists today, we must return to its early beginnings—to ideas about children that long preceded scientific child study but that linger as important forces in current theory and research.

Medieval Times

Childhood was regarded as a separate period of life as early as medieval Europe—the sixth through the fifteenth centuries. Medieval painters often depicted children wearing loose, comfortable gowns, playing games, and looking up to adults. Written texts contained terms that distinguished children under age 7 or 8 from other people and that recognized even

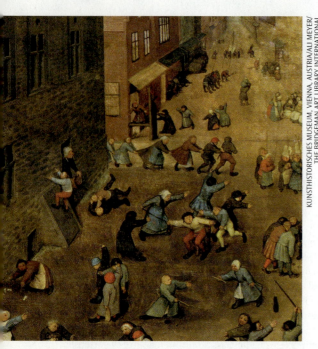

KUNSTHISTORISCHES MUSEUM, VIENNA, AUSTRIA/ALI MEYER/
THE BRIDGEMAN ART LIBRARY INTERNATIONAL

■ As early as medieval times, adults viewed childhood as a distinct developmental period. In this sixteenth-century painting, *Children's Games*, by Pieter Bruegel the Elder, boys and girls wearing loose, comfortable clothing play lively outdoor games. *[Children's games (Kinderspiele): Detail of top right hand corner, 1560 (oil on panel) (detail of 68945), Bruegel, Pieter the Elder (c.1525–69).]* ■

young teenagers as not fully mature. By the fourteenth century, manuals offering advice on many aspects of child care, including health, feeding, clothing, and games, were common (Alexandre-Bidon & Lett, 1997; Lett, 1997). Laws recognized that children needed protection from people who might mistreat them, and courts exercised leniency with lawbreaking youths because of their tender years (Hanawalt, 1993).

In sum, in medieval times, if not before, clear awareness existed of children as vulnerable beings and of childhood as a distinct developmental period. Religious writings, however, contained contradictory depictions of children's basic nature, sometimes portraying them as possessed by the devil and in need of purification, at other times as innocent and close to angels (Hanawalt, 2003). Both ideas foreshadowed later views of childhood.

The Reformation

In the sixteenth century, the Puritan belief in original sin gave rise to the view that children were born evil and stubborn and had to be civilized (Shahar, 1990). Harsh, restrictive child-rearing practices were recommended to tame the depraved child. Children were dressed in stiff, uncomfortable clothing that held them in adultlike postures, and disobedient students were routinely beaten by their schoolmasters. Nevertheless, love and affection for their children prevented most Puritan parents from using extremely repressive measures (Moran & Vinovskis, 1986).

As the Puritans emigrated from England to the American colonies, they brought the belief that child rearing was one of their most important obligations. Although they continued to regard the child's soul as tainted by original sin, they tried to teach their sons and daughters to use reason to tell right from wrong (Clarke-Stewart, 1998). As they trained their children in self-reliance and self-control, Puritan parents gradually adopted a moderate balance between severity and permissiveness.

Philosophies of the Enlightenment

The seventeenth-century Enlightenment brought new philosophies that emphasized ideals of human dignity and respect. Conceptions of childhood were more humane than those of the past.

JOHN LOCKE   The writings of British philosopher John Locke (1632–1704) served as the forerunner of a twentieth-century perspective that we will discuss shortly: behaviorism. Locke viewed the child as a *tabula rasa*—Latin for "blank slate." According to this idea, children begin as nothing at all; their characters are shaped entirely by experience. Locke (1690/1892) saw parents as rational tutors who can mold the child in any way they wish through careful instruction, effective example, and rewards for good behavior. He was ahead of his time in recommending child-rearing practices that present-day research supports—for example, the use of praise and approval as rewards, rather than money or sweets. He also opposed physical punishment: "The child repeatedly beaten in school cannot look upon books and teachers without experiencing fear and anger." Locke's philosophy led to a change from harshness toward children to kindness and compassion.

Look carefully at Locke's ideas, and you will see that he regarded development as *continuous*: Adultlike behaviors are gradually built up through the warm, consistent teachings of parents. His view of the child as a tabula rasa led him to champion *nurture*—the power of the environment to shape the child. And his faith in nurture suggests the possibility of *many courses of development* and of *high plasticity at later ages* due to new experiences. Finally, Locke's philosophy characterizes children as doing little to influence their own destiny, which is written on "blank slates" by others. This vision of a passive child has been discarded. All contemporary theories view children as active, purposeful beings who contribute substantially to their own development.

JEAN-JACQUES ROUSSEAU   In the eighteenth century, French philosopher Jean-Jacques Rousseau (1712–1778) introduced a new view of childhood. Children, Rousseau claimed, are not blank slates to be filled by adult instruction. Instead, they are *noble savages,* naturally endowed with a sense of right and wrong and an innate plan for orderly, healthy growth. Unlike Locke, Rousseau believed that children's built-in moral sense and unique ways of thinking and feeling would only be harmed by adult training. His was a child-centered philosophy in which the adult should be receptive to the child's needs at each of four stages: infancy, childhood, late childhood, and adolescence.

Rousseau's philosophy includes two influential concepts. The first is the concept of *stage,* which we discussed earlier. The second is the concept of **maturation,** which refers to a genetically determined, naturally unfolding course of growth. In contrast to Locke, Rousseau saw children as determining their own destinies. And he viewed development as a *discontinuous, stagewise* process that follows a *single, unified course* mapped out by *nature.*

Scientific Beginnings

The study of child development evolved quickly in the late nineteenth and early twentieth centuries. Early observations of children were soon followed by improved methods and theories. Each advance contributed to the firm foundation on which the field rests today.

DARWIN: FOREFATHER OF SCIENTIFIC CHILD STUDY   British naturalist Charles Darwin (1809–1882) joined an expedition to distant parts of the world, where he observed infinite variation among plant and animal species. He also saw that within a species, no two individuals are exactly alike. From these observations, he constructed his famous *theory of evolution.*

The theory emphasized two related principles: *natural selection* and *survival of the fittest.* Darwin explained that certain species survive in particular parts of the world because they have characteristics that fit with, or are adapted to, their surroundings. Other species die off because they are not as well-suited to their environments. Individuals within a species who best meet the environment's survival requirements live long enough to reproduce and pass their more beneficial characteristics to future generations. Darwin's emphasis on the adaptive value of physical characteristics and behavior eventually found its way into important developmental theories.

During his explorations, Darwin discovered that early prenatal growth is strikingly similar in many species. Other scientists concluded from Darwin's observation that the development of the human child followed the same general plan as the evolution of the human species. Although this belief eventually proved inaccurate, efforts to chart parallels between child growth and human evolution prompted researchers to make careful observations of all aspects of children's behavior. Out of these first attempts to document an idea about development, scientific child study was born.

THE NORMATIVE PERIOD   G. Stanley Hall (1844–1924), one of the most influential American psychologists of the early twentieth century, is generally regarded as the founder of the child-study movement (Cairns & Cairns, 2006). Inspired by Darwin's work, Hall and his well-known student Arnold Gesell (1880–1961) devised theories based on evolutionary ideas. These early leaders regarded development as a genetically determined process that unfolds automatically, much like a flower (Gesell, 1933; Hall, 1904).

Hall and Gesell are remembered less for their one-sided theories than for their intensive efforts to describe all aspects of child development. They launched the **normative approach,** in which measures of behavior are taken on large numbers of individuals and age-related averages are computed to represent typical development. Using this procedure, Hall constructed elaborate questionnaires asking children of different ages almost everything they could tell about themselves—interests, fears, imaginary playmates, dreams, friendships, everyday knowledge, and more. Similarly, through observations and parental interviews, Gesell collected detailed normative information on the motor achievements, social behaviors, and personality characteristics of infants and children.

LOOK AND LISTEN

Examine several recent parenting-advice books in your local bookstore or library, and identify the stance each book takes on the three basic issues about child development.

© LAURA DWIGHT PHOTOGRAPHY

■ Theories of child development have sparked an extensive parenting-advice literature. This expectant mother relies on an array of infant-care manuals to prepare for the challenges of caring for a new baby. ■

Gesell was also among the first to make knowledge about child development meaningful to parents. If, as he believed, the timetable of development is the product of millions of years of evolution, then children are naturally knowledgeable about their needs. His child-rearing advice, in the tradition of Rousseau, recommended sensitivity to children's cues (Thelen & Adolph, 1992). Along with Benjamin Spock's *Baby and Child Care,* Gesell's books became a central part of a rapidly expanding popular literature for parents.

THE MENTAL TESTING MOVEMENT   While Hall and Gesell were developing their theories and methods in the United States, French psychologist Alfred Binet (1857–1911) was also taking a normative approach to child development, but for a different reason. In the early 1900s, Binet and his colleague Theodore Simon were asked by Paris school officials to find a way to identify children with learning problems who needed to be placed in special classes. To address these practical educational concerns, Binet and Simon constructed the first successful intelligence test.

Binet began with a well-developed theory of intelligence. Capturing the complexity of children's thinking, he defined intelligence as good judgment, planning, and critical reflection (Sternberg & Jarvin, 2003). Then he created age-graded test items that directly measured these abilities.

In 1916, at Stanford University, Binet's test was adapted for use with English-speaking children. Since then, the English version has been known as the *Stanford-Binet Intelligence Scale.* Besides providing a score that could successfully predict school achievement, the Binet test sparked tremendous interest in individual differences in development. Comparisons of the scores of children who vary in gender, ethnicity, birth order, family background, and other characteristics became a major focus of research. And intelligence tests rose quickly to the forefront of the nature–nurture controversy.

ASK YOURSELF

◆ REVIEW Imagine a debate between John Locke and Jean-Jacques Rousseau on the nature–nurture controversy. Summarize the argument that each historical figure is likely to present.

◆ CONNECT What do the ideas of Rousseau, Darwin, and Hall have in common?

◆ REFLECT Find out whether your parents read any child-rearing advice books when you were growing up. What questions most concerned them? Do you think the concerns of today's parents differ from those of your parents' generation? Explain.

Mid-Twentieth-Century Theories

In the mid-twentieth century, the field of child development expanded. A variety of theories emerged, each of which continues to have followers today. In these theories, the European concern with the child's inner thoughts and feelings contrasts sharply with the North American academic focus on scientific precision and concrete, observable behavior.

The Psychoanalytic Perspective

By the 1930s and 1940s, parents were increasingly seeking professional help in dealing with children's emotional difficulties. The earlier normative movement had answered the question, What are children like? Now another question had to be addressed: How and why do children become the way they are? To treat psychological problems, psychiatrists and social workers turned to an emerging approach to personality development that emphasized the unique history of each child.

According to the **psychoanalytic perspective,** children move through a series of stages in which they confront conflicts between biological drives and social expectations. How these conflicts are resolved determines the person's ability to learn, to get along with others, and to cope with anxiety. Among the many individuals who contributed to the psychoanalytic perspective, two were especially influential: Sigmund Freud, founder of the psychoanalytic movement, and Erik Erikson.

FREUD'S THEORY   Freud (1856–1939), a Viennese physician, sought a cure for emotionally troubled adults by having them talk freely about painful events of their childhoods. Working with these recollections, Freud examined the unconscious motivations of his patients and constructed his **psychosexual theory,** which emphasizes that how parents manage their child's sexual and aggressive drives in the first few years is crucial for healthy personality development.

In Freud's theory, three parts of the personality—id, ego, and superego—become integrated during a sequence of five stages, summarized in Table 1.1 on page 16. The *id,* the largest portion of the mind, is the source of basic biological needs and desires. The *ego,* the conscious, rational part of personality, emerges in early infancy to redirect the id's impulses so that they are discharged in acceptable ways. Between 3 and 6 years of age, the *superego,* or conscience, develops through interactions with parents, who insist that children conform to the values of society. Now the ego faces the increasingly complex task of reconciling the demands of the id, the external world, and conscience (Freud, 1923/1974)—for example, the id impulse to grab an attractive toy from a playmate, versus the superego's awareness that such behavior is wrong. According to Freud, the relations established between id, ego, and superego during the preschool years determine the individual's basic personality.

Freud (1938/1973) believed that during childhood, sexual impulses shift their focus from the oral to the anal to the genital regions of the body. In each stage, parents walk a fine line between permitting too much or too little gratification of their child's basic needs. If parents strike an appropriate balance, then children grow into well-adjusted adults with the capacity for mature sexual behavior and investment in family life.

Freud's theory was the first to stress the influence of the early parent–child relationship on development—an emphasis that continues to play a role in many contemporary theories. But his perspective was eventually criticized. First, it overemphasized the influence of sexual feelings in development. Second, because it was based on the problems of sexually repressed, well-to-do adults in nineteenth-century Victorian society, it did not apply in other cultures. Finally, Freud had not studied children directly.

ERIKSON'S THEORY   Several of Freud's followers took what was useful from his theory and improved on his vision. The most important of these neo-Freudians is Erik Erikson (1902–1994), who expanded the picture of development at each stage. In his **psychosocial theory,** Erikson emphasized that in addition to mediating between id impulses and superego demands, the ego makes a positive contribution to development, acquiring attitudes and skills that make the individual an active, contributing member of society. A basic psychological conflict, which is resolved along a continuum from positive to negative, determines healthy or maladaptive outcomes at each stage. As Table 1.1 shows, Erikson's first five stages parallel Freud's stages, but Erikson added three adult stages. He was one of the first to recognize the lifespan nature of development.

Unlike Freud, Erikson pointed out that normal development must be understood in relation to each culture's life situation. For example, in the 1940s, he observed that Yurok Indians

| TABLE 1.1 | Freud's Psychosexual Stages and Erikson's Psychosocial Stages Compared |

APPROXIMATE AGE	FREUD'S PSYCHOSEXUAL STAGE	ERIKSON'S PSYCHOSOCIAL STAGE
Birth–1 year	*Oral:* If oral needs are not met through sucking from breast or bottle, the individual may develop such habits as thumb sucking, fingernail biting, overeating, or smoking.	*Basic trust versus mistrust:* From warm, responsive care, infants gain a sense of trust that the world is good. Mistrust occurs if infants are neglected or handled harshly.
1–3 years	*Anal:* Toddlers and preschoolers enjoy holding and releasing urine and feces. If parents toilet train before children are ready or make too few demands, conflicts about anal control may appear in the form of extreme orderliness or disorder.	*Autonomy versus shame and doubt:* Using new mental and motor skills, children want to decide for themselves. Autonomy is fostered when parents permit reasonable free choice and do not force or shame the child.
3–6 years	*Phallic:* As preschoolers take pleasure in genital stimulation, Freud's Oedipus conflict for boys and Electra conflict for girls arise: Children feel a sexual desire for the other-sex parent. To avoid punishment, they give up this desire and adopt the same-sex parent's values. As a result, the superego is formed, and children feel guilty when they violate its standards.	*Initiative versus guilt:* Through make-believe play, children gain insight into the person they can become. Initiative—a sense of ambition and responsibility—develops when parents support their child's sense of purpose. If parents demand too much self-control, children experience excessive guilt.
6–11 years	*Latency:* Sexual instincts die down, and the superego strengthens as the child acquires new social values from adults and same-sex peers.	*Industry versus inferiority:* At school, children learn to work and cooperate with others. Inferiority develops when negative experiences at home or school lead to feelings of incompetence.
Adolescence	*Genital:* With puberty, sexual impulses reappear. Successful development during earlier stages leads to marriage, mature sexuality, and child rearing.	*Identity versus role confusion* By exploring values and vocational goals, the young person forms a personal identity. The negative outcome is confusion about future adult roles.
Early adulthood		*Intimacy versus isolation:* Young adults establish intimate relationships. Because of earlier disappointments, some individuals cannot form close bonds and remain isolated.
Middle adulthood		*Generativity versus stagnation:* Generativity means giving to the next generation through child rearing, caring for others, or productive work. The person who fails in these ways feels an absence of meaningful accomplishment.
Old age		*Integrity versus despair:* Integrity results from feeling that life was worth living as it happened. Older people who are dissatisfied with their lives fear death.

Erik Erikson

© OLIVE PIERCE/BLACK STAR

of the U.S. northwest coast deprived babies of breastfeeding for the first 10 days after birth and instead fed them a thin soup. At age 6 months, infants were abruptly weaned—if necessary, by having the mother leave for a few days. From our cultural vantage point, these practices may seem cruel. But Erikson explained that because the Yurok depended on salmon, which fill the river just once a year, the development of considerable self-restraint was essential for survival. In this way, he showed that child rearing is responsive to the competencies valued and needed by the child's society.

CONTRIBUTIONS AND LIMITATIONS OF PSYCHOANALYTIC THEORY A special strength of the psychoanalytic perspective is its emphasis on the individual's unique life history as worthy of study and understanding. Consistent with this view, psychoanalytic theorists accept the *clinical,* or *case study, method,* which synthesizes information from a variety of sources into a detailed picture of the personality of a single child. (We will discuss this method further at the end of this chapter.) Psychoanalytic theory has also inspired a wealth of research on many aspects of emotional and social development, including infant–caregiver attachment, aggression, sibling relationships, child-rearing practices, morality, gender roles, and adolescent identity.

Despite its extensive contributions, the psychoanalytic perspective is no longer in the mainstream of child development research. Psychoanalytic theorists may have become isolated from the rest of the field because they were so strongly committed to the clinical approach that they failed to consider other methods. In addition, many psychoanalytic ideas, such as psychosexual stages and ego functioning, are too vague to be tested empirically (Crain, 2005; Thomas, 2005). Nevertheless, Erikson's broad outline of psychosocial change captures the essence of personality development during childhood and adolescence. Consequently, we will return to it in later chapters.

Behaviorism and Social Learning Theory

As the psychoanalytic perspective gained prominence, child study was also influenced by a very different perspective. According to **behaviorism,** directly observable events—stimuli and responses—are the appropriate focus of study. North American behaviorism began in the early twentieth century with the work of psychologist John Watson (1878–1958), who wanted to create an objective science of psychology.

■ Children of the Lacandon Mayan people of southern Mexico learn from their father how to make souvenir arrows similar to those of their hunter-gatherer ancestors. As Erikson recognized, these child-rearing practices can be understood only in relation to the Lacandon's distinct culture. ■

TRADITIONAL BEHAVIORISM Watson was inspired by Russian physiologist Ivan Pavlov's studies of animal learning. Pavlov knew that dogs release saliva as an innate reflex when they are given food. But he noticed that his dogs started salivating before they tasted any food—when they saw the trainer who usually fed them. The dogs, Pavlov reasoned, must have learned to associate a neutral stimulus (the trainer) with another stimulus (food) that produces a reflexive response (salivation). Because of this association, the neutral stimulus alone could bring about a response resembling the reflex. Eager to test this idea, Pavlov successfully taught dogs to salivate at the sound of a bell by pairing it with the presentation of food. He had discovered *classical conditioning*.

Watson wanted to find out if classical conditioning could be applied to children's behavior. In a historic experiment, he taught Albert, an 11-month-old infant, to fear a neutral stimulus—a soft white rat—by presenting it several times with a sharp, loud sound, which naturally scared the baby. Little Albert, who at first had reached out eagerly to touch the furry rat, began to cry and turn his head away at the sight of it (Watson & Raynor, 1920). In fact, Albert's fear was so intense that researchers eventually challenged the ethics of studies like this one. Consistent with Locke's tabula rasa, Watson concluded that environment is the supreme force in development and that adults can mold children's behavior by carefully controlling stimulus–response associations. He viewed development as continuous—a gradual increase with age in the number and strength of these associations.

Another form of behaviorism was B. F. Skinner's (1904–1990) *operant conditioning theory*. According to Skinner, the frequency of a behavior can be increased by following it with a wide variety of *reinforcers*—food, praise, a friendly smile, or a new toy—or decreased through *punishment*, such as disapproval or withdrawal of privileges. As a result of Skinner's work, operant conditioning became a broadly applied learning principle, which we will consider further when we explore the infant's learning capacities in Chapter 5.

SOCIAL LEARNING THEORY Psychologists wondered whether behaviorism might offer a more direct and effective explanation of the development of children's social behavior than the less precise concepts of psychoanalytic theory. This sparked approaches that built on the principles of conditioning, offering expanded views of how children and adults acquire new responses.

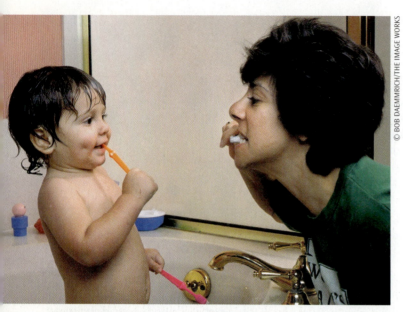

© BOB DAEMMRICH/THE IMAGE WORKS

 Social learning theory recognizes that children acquire many skills through modeling. By observing and imitating her mother's behavior, this 19-month-old learns an important skill. ∎

Several kinds of **social learning theory** emerged. The most influential, devised by Albert Bandura (1977), emphasizes *modeling,* also known as *imitation* or *observational learning,* as a powerful source of development. The baby who claps her hands after her mother does so, the child who angrily hits a playmate in the same way that he has been punished at home, and the teenager who wears the same clothes and hairstyle as her friends are all displaying observational learning.

Bandura's work continues to influence much research on children's social development. But today, like the field of child development as a whole, his theory stresses the importance of *cognition,* or thinking. Bandura has shown that children's ability to listen, remember, and abstract general rules from complex sets of observed behaviors affects their imitation and learning. In fact, the most recent revision of Bandura's (1992, 2001) theory places such strong emphasis on how children think about themselves and other people that he calls it a *social-cognitive* rather than a social learning approach.

In Bandura's revised view, children gradually become more selective in what they imitate. From watching others engage in self-praise and self-blame and through feedback about the worth of their own actions, children develop *personal standards* for behavior and a *sense of self-efficacy*—the belief that their own abilities and characteristics will help them succeed. These cognitions guide responses in particular situations (Bandura, 1999, 2001). For example, imagine a parent who often remarks, "I'm glad I kept working on that task, even though it was hard," and who encourages persistence by saying, "I know you can do a good job on that homework!" Soon the child starts to view herself as hardworking and high-achieving and selects people with these characteristics as models. In this way, as children acquire attitudes, values, and convictions about themselves, they control their own learning and behavior.

CONTRIBUTIONS AND LIMITATIONS OF BEHAVIORISM AND SOCIAL LEARNING THEORY Behaviorism and social learning theory have had a major impact on practices with children. **Behavior modification** consists of procedures that combine conditioning and modeling to eliminate undesirable behaviors and increase desirable responses. It has been used to relieve a wide range of serious developmental problems, such as persistent aggression, language delays, and extreme fears (Martin & Pear, 2007).

Behavior modification is also effective in dealing with common, everyday difficulties, including poor time management; unwanted habits such as nail biting and smoking; and anxiety over such recurrent events as test-taking, public speaking, and medical and dental treatments. In one study, researchers reduced 4- and 5-year-olds' unruliness in a preschool classroom by reinforcing them with tokens (which they could exchange for treats) when they behaved appropriately and punishing them by taking away tokens when they screamed, threw objects, attacked other children, or refused to comply with a teacher's request (Conyers et al., 2004). In another investigation, children with acute burn injuries played a virtual reality game while nurses engaged in the painful process of changing their bandages. Visual images and sound effects delivered though a headset made the children feel as if they were in a fantasy world. As the game reinforced children's concentration and pleasure, it distracted them from the medical procedure, causing their pain and anxiety to drop sharply compared with dressing changes in which the game was unavailable (Das et al., 2005).

Nevertheless, many theorists believe that behaviorism and social learning theory offer too narrow a view of important environmental influences. These extend beyond immediate reinforcements and modeled behaviors to children's rich physical and social worlds. Behaviorism and social learning theory have also been criticized for underestimating children's

LOOK AND LISTEN

◆ ◆

Describe an event you observed in which feedback from a parent or teacher likely strengthened a child's self-efficacy. How might the adult's message have influenced the child's self-perceptions and choice of models?

contributions to their own development. Bandura, with his emphasis on cognition, is unique among theorists whose work grew out of the behaviorist tradition in granting children an active role in their own learning.

Piaget's Cognitive-Developmental Theory

If one individual has influenced the contemporary field of child development more than any other, it is Swiss cognitive theorist Jean Piaget (1896–1980). North American investigators had been aware of Piaget's work since 1930. But they did not grant it much attention until the 1960s, mainly because Piaget's ideas were at odds with behaviorism, which dominated North American psychology in the mid-twentieth century (Cairns & Cairns, 2006). Piaget did not believe that children's learning depends on reinforcers, such as rewards from adults. According to his **cognitive-developmental theory**, children actively construct knowledge as they manipulate and explore their world.

PIAGET'S STAGES   Piaget's view of development was greatly influenced by his early training in biology. Central to his theory is the biological concept of *adaptation* (Piaget, 1971). Just as structures of the body are adapted to fit with the environment, so structures of the mind develop to better fit with, or represent, the external world. In infancy and early childhood, Piaget claimed, children's understanding is different from adults'. For example, he believed that young babies do not realize that an object hidden from view—a favorite toy or even the mother—continues to exist. He also concluded that preschoolers' thinking is full of faulty logic. For example, children younger than age 7 commonly say that the amount of a liquid changes when it is poured into a different-shaped container. According to Piaget, children eventually revise these incorrect ideas in their ongoing efforts to achieve an *equilibrium,* or balance, between internal structures and information they encounter in their everyday worlds.

In Piaget's theory, as the brain develops and children's experiences expand, they move through four broad stages, each characterized by qualitatively distinct ways of thinking. Table 1.2 provides a brief description of Piaget's stages. Cognitive development begins in the

■ In Piaget's sensorimotor stage, babies learn by acting on the world. As this 1-year-old bangs a mallet on a xylophone, he discovers that his movements have predictable effects on objects and that objects influence one another in regular ways. ■

TABLE 1.2   Piaget's Stages of Cognitive Development

STAGE	PERIOD OF DEVELOPMENT	DESCRIPTION
Sensorimotor	Birth–2 years	Infants "think" by acting on the world with their eyes, ears, hands, and mouth. As a result, they invent ways of solving sensorimotor problems, such as pulling a lever to hear the sound of a music box, finding hidden toys, and putting objects in and taking them out of containers.
Preoperational	2–7 years	Preschool children use symbols to represent their earlier sensorimotor discoveries. Development of language and make-believe play takes place. However, thinking lacks the logic of the two remaining stages.
Concrete operational	7–11 years	Children's reasoning becomes logical and better organized. School-age children understand that a certain amount of lemonade or play dough remains the same even after its appearance changes. They also organize objects into hierarchies of classes and subclasses. However, thinking falls short of adult intelligence. It is not yet abstract.
Formal operational	11 years on	The capacity for abstract, systematic thinking enables adolescents, when faced with a problem, to start with a hypothesis, deduce testable inferences, and isolate and combine variables to see which inferences are confirmed. Adolescents can also evaluate the logic of verbal statements without referring to real-world circumstances.

Jean Piaget

In Piaget's preoperational stage, preschoolers represent their earlier sensorimotor discoveries with symbols, and language and make-believe play develop rapidly. These 5-year-olds need only a few props to create an imaginary office scene. ■

sensorimotor stage with the baby's use of the senses and movements to explore the world. These action patterns evolve into the symbolic but illogical thinking of the preschooler in the *preoperational stage*. Then cognition is transformed into the more organized reasoning of the school-age child in the *concrete operational stage*. Finally, in the *formal operational stage,* thought becomes the abstract, systematic reasoning system of the adolescent and adult.

Piaget devised special methods for investigating how children think. Early in his career, he carefully observed his three infant children and also presented them with everyday problems, such as an attractive object that could be grasped, mouthed, kicked, or searched for. From their responses, Piaget derived his ideas about cognitive changes during the first two years. To study childhood and adolescent thought, Piaget adapted the clinical method of psychoanalysis, conducting open-ended *clinical interviews* in which a child's initial response to a task served as the basis for Piaget's next question. We will look more closely at this technique when we discuss research methods later in this chapter.

CONTRIBUTIONS AND LIMITATIONS OF PIAGET'S THEORY

Piaget convinced the field that children are active learners whose minds consist of rich structures of knowledge. Besides investigating children's understanding of the physical world, Piaget explored their reasoning about the social world. His stages have sparked a wealth of research on children's conceptions of themselves, other people, and human relationships. In practical terms, Piaget's theory encouraged the development of educational philosophies and programs that emphasize children's discovery learning and direct contact with the environment.

Despite Piaget's overwhelming contributions, his theory has been challenged. Research indicates that Piaget underestimated the competencies of infants and preschoolers. When young children are given tasks scaled down in difficulty and relevant to their everyday experiences, their understanding appears closer to that of the older child and adult than Piaget assumed. Also, adolescents generally reach their full intellectual potential only in areas of endeavor in which they have had extensive education and experience (Kuhn,

In Piaget's concrete operational stage, school-age children think in an organized, logical fashion about concrete objects. These 7-year-olds understand that the amount of milk remains the same after being poured into a differently shaped container, even though its appearance changes. ■

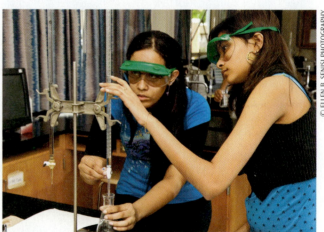

In Piaget's formal operational stage, adolescents think systematically and abstractly. They solve problems by generating hypotheses about procedures that might work, isolating and combining relevant variables, and conducting systematic tests to observe their real-world consequences. ■

2008). These discoveries have led many researchers to conclude that maturity of thinking depends heavily on the complexity of knowledge sampled and the individual's familiarity with the task. Furthermore, many studies show that children's performance on Piagetian problems can be improved with training—findings that call into question Piaget's assumption that discovery learning rather than adult teaching is the best way to foster development (Klahr & Nigam, 2004; Siegler & Sventina, 2006). Critics also point out that Piaget's stagewise account pays insufficient attention to social and cultural influences—and the resulting wide variation in thinking among children and adolescents of the same age.

Today, the field of child development is divided over its loyalty to Piaget's ideas (Desrochers, 2008). Those who continue to find merit in Piaget's stages often accept a modified view—one in which changes in children's thinking take place more gradually than Piaget believed (Case, 1998; Demetriou et al., 2002; Fischer & Bidell, 2006; Halford & Andrews, 2006). Among those who disagree with Piaget's stage sequence, some have embraced an approach that emphasizes continuous gains in children's cognition: information processing. And still others have been drawn to theories that highlight the role of children's social and cultural contexts. We take up these approaches in the next section.

ASK YOURSELF

◆ REVIEW What aspect of behaviorism made it attractive to critics of psychoanalytic theory? How did Piaget's theory respond to a major limitation of behaviorism?

◆ APPLY A 4-year-old becomes frightened of the dark and refuses to go to sleep at night. How would a psychoanalyst and a behaviorist differ in their views of how this problem developed?

◆ CONNECT Although social learning theory focuses on social development and Piaget's theory on cognitive development, each has enhanced our understanding of other domains. Mention an additional domain addressed by each theory.

Recent Theoretical Perspectives

New ways of understanding the child are constantly emerging—questioning, building on, and enhancing the discoveries of earlier theories. Today, a burst of fresh approaches and research emphases is broadening our understanding of children's development.

Information Processing

In the 1970s and 1980s, researchers turned to the field of cognitive psychology for ways to understand the development of children's thinking. The design of digital computers that use mathematically specified steps to solve problems suggested to psychologists that the human mind might also be viewed as a symbol-manipulating system through which information flows—a perspective called **information processing** (Klahr & MacWhinney, 1998; Munakata, 2006). From the time information is presented to the senses at *input* until it emerges as a behavioral response at *output,* information is actively coded, transformed, and organized.

CONCERN WITH RIGOR AND PRECISION Information-processing researchers often use flowcharts to map the precise steps individuals use to solve problems and complete tasks, much like the plans devised by programmers to get computers to perform a series of "mental operations" (Siegler & Alibali, 2005). To see the usefulness of this approach, let's look at an example.

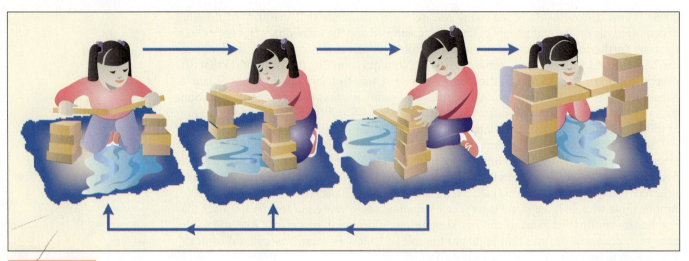

FIGURE 1.3

Information-processing flowchart showing the steps that a 5-year-old used to solve a bridge-building problem. Her task was to use blocks varying in size, shape, and weight, some of which were planklike, to construct a bridge across a "river" (painted on a floor mat) too wide for any single block to span. The child discovered how to counterweight and balance the bridge. The arrows reveal that even after building a successful counterweight, she returned to earlier, unsuccessful strategies, which seemed to help her understand why the counterweight approach worked. *(Adapted from Thornton, 1999.)*

In a study of problem solving, a researcher provided a pile of blocks varying in size, shape, and weight and asked school-age children to build a bridge across a "river" (painted on a floor mat) that was too wide for any single block to span (Thornton, 1999). Figure 1.3 shows one solution to the problem: Two planklike blocks span the water, each held in place by the counterweight of heavy blocks on the bridge's towers. Whereas older children easily built successful bridges, only one 5-year-old did. Careful tracking of her efforts revealed that she repeatedly tried unsuccessful strategies, such as pushing two planks together and pressing down on their ends to hold them in place. But eventually, her experimentation triggered the idea of using the blocks as counterweights. Her mistaken procedures helped her understand why the counterweight approach worked.

Many information-processing models exist. Some, like the one just considered, track children's mastery of one or a few tasks. Others describe the human cognitive system as a whole (Atkinson & Shiffrin, 1968; Lockhart & Craik, 1990). These general models are used as guides for asking questions about broad age changes in children's thinking: Does a child's ability to solve problems become more organized and "planful" with age? What strategies do younger and older children use to remember new information, and how do those strategies affect children's recall?

The information-processing approach is also being used to clarify the processing of social information. For example, flowcharts exist that track the steps children use to solve social problems (such as how to enter an ongoing play group) and acquire gender-linked preferences and behaviors (Crick & Dodge, 1994; Liben & Bigler, 2002). If we can identify how social problem solving and gender stereotyping arise in childhood, then we can design interventions that promote more favorable social development.

Like Piaget's theory, the information-processing approach regards children as active, sense-making beings who modify their own thinking in response to environmental demands (Halford, 2005; Munakata, 2006). But unlike Piaget's theory, it does not divide development into stages. Rather, the thought processes studied—perception, attention, memory, categorization of information, planning, problem solving, and comprehension of written and spoken prose—are regarded as similar at all ages but present to a lesser or greater extent. Therefore, the view of development is one of continuous change.

A great strength of the information-processing approach is its commitment to rigorous research methods. Because it has provided precise accounts of how children of different ages engage in many aspects of thinking, its findings have led to teaching methods that help children approach academic tasks in more advanced ways (Blumenfeld, Marx, & Harris, 2006). But information processing has fallen short in some respects. It has been better at analyzing thinking into its components than at putting them back together into a comprehensive theory. And it has had little to say about aspects of children's cognition that are not linear and logical, such as imagination and creativity (Birney et al., 2005).

DEVELOPMENTAL COGNITIVE NEUROSCIENCE   Over the past three decades, as information-processing research expanded, a new area of investigation arose, called **developmental cognitive neuroscience.** It brings together researchers from psychology, biology, neuroscience, and medicine to study the relationship between changes in the brain and the developing child's cognitive processing and behavior patterns.

Improved methods for analyzing brain activity while children perform various tasks have greatly enhanced knowledge of relationships between brain functioning and behavior (Johnson, 2005; Pennington, Snyder, & Roberts, 2007; Westermann et al., 2007). Armed with these brain-imaging techniques (which we will consider in Chapter 5), neuroscientists are tackling questions like these: How does genetic makeup combine with specific experiences at various ages to influence the growth and organization of the child's brain? How do changes in brain structures support rapid memory development in infancy and toddlerhood? What transformations in brain systems make it harder for adolescents and adults than for children to acquire a second language?

During infancy and early childhood, the brain is highly plastic—especially open to growth and reorganization as a result of experience. But a revolutionary finding of neuroscience research is that the brain retains considerable plasticity throughout life. Neuroscientists are making especially impressive progress in identifying the types of experiences that support or undermine brain development at diverse ages. They are also clarifying the brain bases of many learning and behavior disorders (Durston & Conrad, 2007; Schlaggar & McCandliss, 2007). And they are contributing to effective treatments for children with disabilities by examining the impact of various intervention techniques on both brain functioning and behavior (Luciana, 2007). Although much remains to be discovered, developmental cognitive neuroscience is already transforming our understanding of development and yielding major practical applications.

An advantage of having many theories is that they encourage researchers to attend to previously neglected dimensions of children's lives. The final four perspectives we will discuss focus on *contexts* for development. The first of these views emphasizes that the development of many capacities is influenced by our long evolutionary history.

Ethology and Evolutionary Developmental Psychology

Ethology is concerned with the adaptive, or survival, value of behavior and its evolutionary history. Its roots can be traced to the work of Darwin. Two European zoologists, Konrad Lorenz and Niko Tinbergen, laid its modern foundations. Watching diverse animal species in their natural habitats, Lorenz and Tinbergen observed behavior patterns that promote survival. The best known of these is *imprinting,* the early following behavior of certain baby birds, such as geese, which ensures that the young will stay close to the mother and be fed and protected from danger (Lorenz, 1952). Imprinting takes place during an early, restricted period of development. If the mother goose is absent during this time but an object resembling her in important features is present, young goslings may imprint on it instead.

Observations of imprinting led to a major concept in child development: the *critical period*. It is a limited time span during which the child is biologically prepared to acquire certain adaptive behaviors but needs the support of an appropriately stimulating environment. Many researchers have investigated whether complex cognitive and social behaviors must be learned during certain periods. For example, if children are deprived of adequate food or physical and social stimulation during their early years, will their intelligence be impaired? If language is not mastered in early childhood, is the child's capacity to acquire it reduced?

In later chapters, you will discover that the term *sensitive period* applies better to human development than the strict notion of a critical period (Bornstein, 1989). A **sensitive period** is

■ Ethology focuses on the adaptive, or survival, value of behavior and on similarities between human behavior and that of other species, especially our primate relatives. Observing this mother cuddling her 8-day-old infant helps us understand the human caregiver–infant relationship. ■

a time that is biologically optimal for certain capacities to emerge because the individual is especially responsive to environmental influences. However, its boundaries are less well-defined than are those of a critical period. Development can occur later, but it is harder to induce.

Inspired by observations of imprinting, British psychoanalyst John Bowlby (1969) applied ethological theory to understanding the human caregiver–infant relationship. He argued that infant smiling, babbling, grasping, and crying are built-in social signals that encourage the caregiver to approach, care for, and interact with the baby. By keeping the parent near, these behaviors help ensure that the baby will be fed, protected from danger, and provided with the stimulation and affection necessary for healthy growth. The development of attachment in human infants is a lengthy process involving changes in psychological structures that lead the baby to form a deep affectionate tie with the caregiver (Thompson, 2006). In Chapter 7, we will consider how infant, caregiver, and family context contribute to attachment and how attachment influences later development.

Observations by ethologists have shown that many aspects of children's social behavior, including emotional expressions, aggression, cooperation, and social play, resemble those of our primate relatives. Recently, researchers have extended this effort in a new area of research called **evolutionary developmental psychology.** It seeks to understand the adaptive value of species-wide cognitive, emotional, and social competencies as those competencies change with age (Geary, 2006b). Evolutionary developmental psychologists ask questions like these: What role does the newborn's visual preference for facelike stimuli play in survival? Does it support older infants' capacity to distinguish familiar caregivers from unfamiliar people? Why do children play in gender-segregated groups? What do they learn from such play that might lead to adult gender-typed behaviors, such as male dominance and female investment in caregiving?

As these examples suggest, evolutionary psychologists are not just concerned with the genetic and biological basis of development. They realize that humans' large brain and extended childhood resulted from the need to master an increasingly complex environment, so they are also interested in learning (Grotuss, Bjorklund, & Csinady, 2007). And they realize that today's lifestyles differ so radically from those of our evolutionary ancestors that certain evolved behaviors, such as life-threatening risk taking by adolescents and male-to-male violence, are no longer adaptive (Blasi & Bjorklund, 2003). By clarifying the origins and development of such behaviors, evolutionary developmental psychology may help spark more effective interventions.

In sum, evolutionary psychologists want to understand the entire *organism–environment system.* The next contextual perspective we will discuss, Vygotsky's sociocultural theory, serves as an excellent complement to the evolutionary viewpoint because it highlights the social and cultural dimensions of children's experiences.

Vygotsky's Sociocultural Theory

The field of child development has recently seen a dramatic increase in studies addressing the cultural context of children's lives. Investigations that make comparisons across cultures, and between ethnic groups within cultures, provide insight into whether developmental pathways apply to all children or are limited to particular environmental conditions (Goodnow, 2010).

Today, much research is examining the relationship of *culturally specific beliefs and practices* to development. The contributions of Russian psychologist Lev Vygotsky (1896–1934) have played a major role in this trend. Vygotsky's (1934/1987) perspective, known as **sociocultural theory,** focuses on how *culture*—the values, beliefs, customs, and skills of a social group—is transmitted to the next generation. According to Vygotsky, *social interaction*—in particular, cooperative dialogues with more knowledgeable members of society—is necessary for children to acquire the ways of thinking and behaving that make up a community's culture. Vygotsky believed that as adults and more expert peers help children master culturally meaningful activities, the communication between them becomes part of children's thinking. As children internalize features of these dialogues, they can use the language within them to guide their own thought and actions and to acquire new skills (Berk & Harris, 2003; Winsler, Fernyhough, & Montero, 2009). The young child instructing herself while working a puzzle or preparing a table for dinner has begun to produce the same kinds of guiding comments that an adult previously used to help her master important tasks.

Vygotsky's theory has been especially influential in the study of children's cognition. Vygotsky agreed with Piaget that children are active, constructive beings. But whereas Piaget emphasized children's independent efforts to make sense of their world, Vygotsky viewed cognitive development as a *socially mediated process,* in which children depend on assistance from adults and more expert peers as they tackle new challenges.

In Vygotsky's theory, children undergo certain stagewise changes. For example, when they acquire language, they gain in ability to participate in dialogues with others, and mastery of culturally valued competencies surges forward. When children enter school, they spend much time discussing language, literacy, and other academic concepts—experiences that encourage them to reflect on their own thinking (Bodrova & Leong, 2007; Kozulin, 2003). As a result, they gain dramatically in reasoning and problem solving.

At the same time, Vygotsky stressed that dialogues with experts lead to continuous changes in thinking that vary greatly from culture to culture. Consistent with this view, a major finding of cross-cultural research is that cultures select different tasks for children's learning (Rogoff, 2003). Social interaction surrounding those tasks leads to competencies essential for success in a particular culture. For example, in industrialized nations, teachers help people learn to read, drive a car, or use a computer. Among the Zinacanteco Indians of southern Mexico, adult experts guide young girls as they master complicated weaving techniques (Greenfield, 2004; Greenfield, Maynard, & Childs, 2000). In Brazil and other developing nations, child candy sellers with little or no schooling develop sophisticated mathematical abilities as the result of buying candy from wholesalers, pricing it in collaboration with adults and experienced peers, and bargaining with customers on city streets (Saxe, 1988).

Research stimulated by Vygotsky's theory reveals that children in every culture develop unique strengths. But Vygotsky's emphasis on culture and social experience led him to neglect the biological side of development. Although he recognized the importance of heredity and brain growth, he said little about their role in cognitive change. Furthermore, Vygotsky's focus on social transmission of knowledge meant that, compared with other theorists, he placed less emphasis on children's capacity to shape their own development. Followers of Vygotsky stress that children strive for social connection, actively participating in the conversations and social activities from which their development springs. From these joint experiences, they not only acquire culturally valued practices but also modify and transform those practices (Nelson, 2007; Rogoff, 2003). Contemporary sociocultural theorists grant the individual and society balanced, mutually influential roles.

Ecological Systems Theory

Urie Bronfenbrenner (1917–2005) is responsible for an approach to child development that has moved to the forefront of the field over the past two decades because it offers the most differentiated and complete account of contextual influences on children's development. **Ecological systems theory** views the child as developing within a complex *system* of relationships affected by multiple levels of

■ According to Lev Vygotsky, shown here with his daughter, many cognitive processes and skills are socially transferred from more knowledgeable members of society to children. Vygotsky's sociocultural theory helps explain the wide cultural variation in cognitive competencies. ■

■ With her mother's guidance, this Navajo child learns to use a vertical weaving loom. She acquires a culturally valued skill through interaction with an older, more experienced weaver. ■

the surrounding environment. Since the child's biologically influenced dispositions join with environmental forces to mold development, Bronfenbrenner characterized his perspective as a *bioecological model* (Bronfenbrenner, 2005; Bronfenbrenner & Morris, 2006).

Bronfenbrenner envisioned the environment as a series of interrelated, nested structures that form a complex functioning whole, or *system*. These include but also extend beyond the home, school, and neighborhood settings in which children spend their everyday lives (see Figure 1.4). Each layer joins with the others to powerfully affect development.

THE MICROSYSTEM   The innermost level of the environment, the **microsystem,** consists of activities and interaction patterns in the child's immediate surroundings. Bronfenbrenner emphasizes that to understand child development at this level, we must keep in mind that all relationships are *bidirectional:* Adults affect children's behavior, but children's biologically and socially influenced characteristics—their physical attributes, personalities, and capacities— also affect adults' behavior. A friendly, attentive child is likely to evoke positive, patient reactions from parents, whereas a distractible child is more likely to receive restriction and punishment. When these reciprocal interactions occur often over time, they have an enduring impact on development (Collins et al., 2000; Crockenberg & Leerkes, 2003b).

Third parties—other individuals in the microsystem—also affect the quality of any two-person relationship. If they are supportive, interaction is enhanced. For example, when parents encourage each other in their child-rearing roles, each engages in more effective parenting. In contrast, marital conflict is associated with inconsistent discipline and hostile reactions toward children. In response, children often react with fear and anxiety or with anger and aggression, and the well-being of both parent and child suffers (Caldera & Lindsey, 2006; Davies & Lindsay, 2004).

THE MESOSYSTEM   The second level of Bronfenbrenner's model, the **mesosystem,** encompasses connections between microsystems, such as home, school, neighborhood, and child-care center. For example, a child's academic progress depends not just on activities that take place in classrooms but also on parent involvement in school life and on the extent

FIGURE 1.4

Structure of the environment in ecological systems theory. The *microsystem* concerns relations between the child and the immediate environment; the *mesosystem,* connections among immediate settings; the *exosystem,* social settings that affect but do not contain the child; and the *macrosystem,* the values, laws, customs, and resources of the culture that affect activities and interactions at all inner layers. The *chronosystem* (not pictured) is not a specific context. Instead, it refers to the dynamic, ever-changing nature of the child's environment.

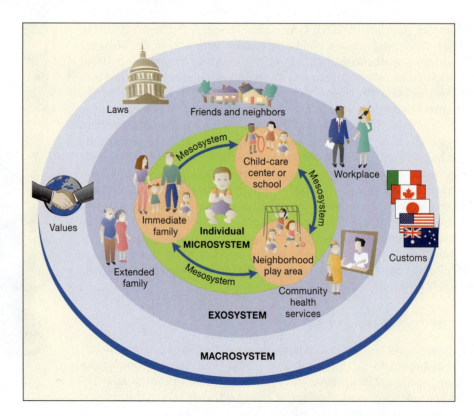

to which academic learning is carried over into the home (Gershoff & Aber, 2006). Similarly, parent–child interaction at home is likely to affect care-giver–child interaction in the child-care setting, and vice versa. Each relationship is more likely to support development when there are links between home and child care, in the form of visits and cooperative exchanges of information.

THE EXOSYSTEM The **exosystem** consists of social settings that do not contain children but that nevertheless affect children's experiences in immediate settings. These can be formal organizations, such as parents' workplaces, their religious institutions, and health and welfare services in the community. For example, parents' work settings can support child rearing and, indirectly, enhance development through flexible work schedules, paid maternity and paternity leave, and sick leave for parents whose children are ill. Exosystem supports also can be informal, such as parents' social networks—friends and extended-family members who provide advice, companionship, and even financial assistance. Research confirms the negative impact of a breakdown in exosystem activities. Families who are affected by unemployment or who are socially isolated, with few personal or community-based ties, show increased rates of conflict and child abuse (Coulton et al., 2007).

■ In ecological systems theory, development occurs within a complex system of relationships affected by multiple levels of the environment. This father says good-bye to his daughter at the start of the school day. The girl's experiences at school (microsystem) and the father's experiences at work (exosystem) affect the father-daughter relationship. ■

THE MACROSYSTEM The outermost level of Bronfenbrenner's model, the **macrosystem**, consists of cultural values, laws, customs, and resources. The priority that the macrosystem gives to children's needs affects the support they receive at inner levels of the environment. For example, in countries that require generous workplace benefits for employed parents and high-quality standards for child care, children are more likely to have favorable experiences in their immediate settings. As you will see in later chapters, such programs are far less available in the United States than in other industrialized nations (Children's Defense Fund, 2008).

AN EVER-CHANGING SYSTEM According to Bronfenbrenner, the environment is not a static force that affects children in a uniform way. Instead, it is ever-changing. Important life events, such as the birth of a sibling, the beginning of school, a move to a new neighborhood, or parents' divorce, modify existing relationships between children and their environments, producing new conditions that affect development. In addition, the timing of environmental change affects its impact. The arrival of a new sibling has very different consequences for a homebound toddler than for a school-age child with many relationships and activities beyond the family.

Bronfenbrenner called the temporal dimension of his model the **chronosystem** (the prefix *chrono-* means "time"). Life changes can be imposed on the child, as in the examples just given. Alternatively, they can arise from within the child, since as children get older they select, modify, and create many of their own settings and experiences. How they do so depends on their physical, intellectual, and personality characteristics and their environmental opportunities. Therefore, in ecological systems theory, development is neither entirely controlled by environmental circumstances nor driven solely by inner dispositions. Rather, children and their environments form a network of interdependent effects. Notice how our discussion of resilient children on pages 10–11 illustrates this idea. You will see many more examples in this book.

LOOK AND LISTEN

Ask a parent to explain his or her most worrisome child-rearing challenge. Describe one source of support at each level of Bronfenbrenner's model that could help ease the parent's stress and promote favorable child development.

© KABLONK/PHOTOLIBRARY

New Directions: Development as a Dynamic System

Today, researchers recognize both consistency and variability in children's development and want to do a better job of explaining variation. Consequently, a new wave of systems theorists focuses on how children alter their behavior to attain more advanced functioning. According to this **dynamic systems perspective,** the child's mind, body, and physical and social worlds form an *integrated system* that guides mastery of new skills. The system is *dynamic,* or constantly in motion. A change in any part of it—from brain growth to physical or social surroundings—disrupts the current organism–environment relationship. When this happens, the child actively reorganizes his or her behavior so the various components of the system work together again but in a more complex, effective way (Fischer & Bidell, 2006; Spencer & Schöner, 2003; Thelen & Smith, 2006).

Researchers adopting a dynamic systems perspective try to find out just how children attain new levels of organization by studying their behavior while they are in transition (Thelen & Corbetta, 2002). For example, when presented with an attractive toy, how does a 3-month-old baby who engages in many, varied movements discover how to reach for it? On hearing a new word, how does a 2-year-old figure out the category of objects or events to which it refers?

Dynamic systems theorists acknowledge that a common human genetic heritage and basic regularities in children's physical and social worlds yield certain universal, broad outlines of development. But biological makeup, everyday tasks, and the people who support children in mastery of those tasks vary greatly, leading to wide individual differences in specific skills. Even when children master the same skills, such as walking, talking, or adding and subtracting, they often do so in unique ways. And because children build competencies by engaging in real activities in real contexts, different skills vary in maturity within the same child. From this perspective, development cannot be characterized as a single line of change. As Figure 1.5 shows, it is more like a web of fibers branching out in many directions, each representing a different skill area that may undergo both continuous and stagewise transformations (Fischer & Bidell, 2006).

The dynamic systems view has been inspired by other scientific disciplines, especially biology and physics. It also draws on information-processing and contextual theories—evolutionary developmental psychology, sociocultural theory, and ecological systems theory. Dynamic systems research is still in its early stages. The perspective has been applied largely to children's motor and cognitive skills, but some investigators have drawn on it to explain emotional and social development as well (Campos, Frankel, &

■ The dynamic systems perspective views the child's mind, body, and physical and social worlds as a continuously reorganizing, integrated system. A change in any part of the system disrupts the current organism–environment relationship. As this girl experiences the physical, cognitive, and emotional changes of early adolescence, she and her father must devise new, more mature ways of relating to each other. ■

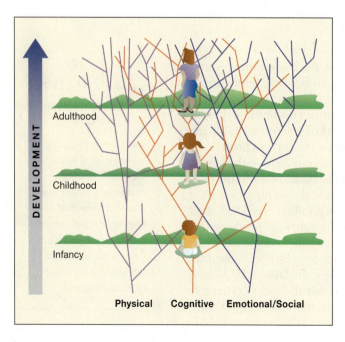

Physical   Cognitive   Emotional/Social

FIGURE 1.5

The dynamic systems view of development. Rather than envisioning a single line of stagewise or continuous change (refer to Figure 1.2 on page 8), dynamic systems theorists conceive of development as a web of fibers branching out in many directions. Each strand in the web represents a skill within the major domains of development—physical, cognitive, and emotional/social. The differing directions of the strands signify possible variations in paths and outcomes as the child masters skills necessary to participate in diverse contexts. The interconnections of the strands at each row of "hills" portray stagelike changes—periods of major transformation in which various skills work together as a functioning whole. As the web expands, skills become more numerous, complex, and effective. *(Adapted from Fischer & Bidell, 2006.)*

Camras, 2004; Fogel & Garvey, 2007; Lewis, 2000). Consider the young teenager, whose body and reasoning powers are changing massively and who also is confronting the challenges of secondary school. Researchers following parent–child interaction over time found that the transition to adolescence disrupted family communication. It became unstable and variable for several years—a mix of positive, neutral, and negative exchanges (Granic et al., 2003). Gradually, as parent and adolescent devised new, more mature ways of relating to one another, the system reorganized and stabilized. Once again, interaction became predictable and mostly positive.

As dynamic systems research illustrates, today investigators are tracking and analyzing development in all its complexity. In doing so, they hope to move closer to an all-encompassing approach to understanding change.

ASK YOURSELF

◆ **REVIEW** Explain how each recent theoretical perspective regards children as active contributors to their own development.

◆ **APPLY** Mario wants to find out precisely how children of different ages recall stories. Anna is interested in how adult–child communication in different cultures influences children's storytelling. Which theoretical perspective has Mario probably chosen? How about Anna? Explain.

◆ **CONNECT** Return to the Biology and Environment box on pages 10–11. How does the story of John and Gary illustrate bidirectional influences within the microsystem, as described in ecological systems theory?

◆ **REFLECT** To illustrate the chronosystem in ecological systems theory, select an important event from your childhood, such as a move to a new neighborhood or a class with an inspiring teacher. How did the event affect you? How might its impact have differed had you been five years younger? How about five years older?

Comparing Child Development Theories

In the preceding sections, we reviewed theoretical perspectives in child development research. They differ in many respects. First, they focus on different domains of development. Some, such as the psychoanalytic perspective and ethology, emphasize emotional and social development. Others, such as Piaget's cognitive-developmental theory, information processing, and Vygotsky's sociocultural theory, stress changes in thinking. The remaining approaches—behaviorism, social learning theory, evolutionary developmental psychology, ecological systems theory, and the dynamic systems perspective—discuss many aspects of children's functioning. Second, every theory contains a point of view about child development. **TAKE A MOMENT...** As we conclude our review of theoretical perspectives, identify the stand that each theory takes on the controversial issues presented at the beginning of this chapter. Then check your analysis of the theories against Table 1.3 on page 30.

Finally, we have seen that every theory has strengths and limitations. Perhaps you found that you are attracted to some theories, but you have doubts about others. As you read more about child development in later chapters, you may find it useful to keep a notebook in which you test your own theoretical likes and dislikes against the evidence. Don't be surprised if you revise your ideas many times, just as theorists have done throughout the past century. By the end of the course, you will have built your own personal perspective on child development. Very likely, it will be an *eclectic position,* or blend of several theories, since every viewpoint we have considered has contributed to what we know about children.

TABLE 1.3   Stances of Major Theories on Basic Issues in Child Development

THEORY	CONTINUOUS OR DISCONTINUOUS DEVELOPMENT?	ONE COURSE OF DEVELOPMENT OR MANY?	RELATIVE INFLUENCE OF NATURE AND NURTURE?
Psychoanalytic perspective	*Discontinuous:* Psychosexual and psychosocial development takes place in stages.	*One course:* Stages are assumed to be universal.	*Both nature and nurture:* Innate impulses are channeled and controlled through child-rearing experiences. *Early experiences* set the course of later development.
Behaviorism and social learning theory	*Continuous:* Development involves an increase in learned behaviors.	*Many possible courses:* Behaviors reinforced and modeled may vary from child to child.	*Emphasis on nurture:* Development results from conditioning and modeling. *Both early and later experiences* are important.
Piaget's cognitive-developmental theory	*Discontinuous:* Cognitive development takes place in stages.	*One course:* Stages are assumed to be universal.	*Both nature and nurture:* Development occurs as the brain grows and children exercise their innate drive to discover reality in a generally stimulating environment. *Both early and later experiences* are important.
Information processing	*Continuous:* Children gradually improve in perception, attention, memory, and problem-solving skills.	*One course:* Changes studied characterize most or all children.	*Both nature and nurture:* Children are active, sense-making beings who modify their thinking as the brain grows and they confront new environmental demands. *Both early and later experiences* are important.
Ethology and evolutionary developmental psychology	*Both continuous and discontinuous:* Children gradually develop a wider range of adaptive behaviors. Sensitive periods occur, in which qualitatively distinct capacities emerge fairly suddenly.	*One course:* Adaptive behaviors and sensitive periods apply to all members of a species.	*Both nature and nurture:* Evolution and heredity influence behavior, and learning lends greater flexibility and adaptiveness to it. In sensitive periods, *early experiences* set the course of later development.
Vygotsky's sociocultural theory	*Both continuous and discontinuous:* Language acquisition and schooling lead to stagewise changes. Dialogues with more expert members of society also lead to continuous changes that vary from culture to culture.	*Many possible courses:* Socially mediated changes in thought and behavior vary from culture to culture.	*Both nature and nurture:* Heredity, brain growth, and dialogues with more expert members of society jointly contribute to development. *Both early and later experiences* are important.
Ecological systems theory	*Not specified.*	*Many possible courses:* Children's characteristics join with environmental forces at multiple levels to mold development in unique ways.	*Both nature and nurture:* Children's characteristics and the reactions of others affect each other in a bidirectional fashion. Layers of the environment influence child-rearing experiences. *Both early and later experiences* are important.
Dynamic systems perspective	*Both continuous and discontinuous:* Change in the system is always ongoing. Stagelike transformations occur as children reorganize their behavior so components of the system work as a functioning whole.	*Many possible courses:* Biological makeup, everyday tasks, and social experiences vary, yielding wide individual differences in specific skills.	*Both nature and nurture:* The child's mind, body, and physical and social surroundings form an integrated system that guides mastery of new skills. *Both early and later experiences* are important.

Studying the Child

In every science, research usually begins with a *hypothesis*—a prediction drawn directly from a theory. Theories and hypotheses, however, merely initiate the many activities that result in sound evidence on child development. Conducting research according to scientifically accepted procedures involves many steps and choices. Investigators must decide which participants, and how many, to include. Then they must figure out what the participants will be asked to do and when, where, and how many times each will be seen. Finally, they must examine and draw conclusions from their data.

In the following sections, we look at research strategies commonly used to study children. We begin with common *research methods*—the specific activities of participants, such as taking tests, answering questionnaires, responding to interviews, or being observed. Then we turn to *research designs*—overall plans for research studies that permit the best possible test of the investigator's hypothesis. Finally, we discuss special ethical issues involved in doing research on children.

Why learn about research strategies? Why not leave these matters to research specialists and concentrate on what is already known about the child and how this knowledge can be applied? There are two reasons. First, each of us must be a wise and critical consumer of knowledge. Knowing the strengths and limitations of various research strategies is important in separating dependable information from misleading results. Second, individuals who work directly with children may be in a unique position to build bridges between research and practice by conducting studies, either on their own or in partnership with experienced investigators. Community agencies such as schools, mental health facilities, and parks and recreation programs sometimes collaborate with researchers in designing, implementing, and evaluating interventions aimed at enhancing children's development (Lerner & Overton, 2008). To broaden these efforts, a basic understanding of the research process is essential.

LOOK AND LISTEN

Ask a teacher, counselor, social worker, or nurse to describe a question about development he or she would like researchers to address, as a means of facilitating applied work with children. Recommend research strategies best suited to answering the question, citing their strengths and limitations.

Common Research Methods

How does a researcher choose a basic approach to gathering information about children? Common methods include systematic observation, self-reports (such as questionnaires and interviews), clinical or case studies of a single child, and ethnographies of the life circumstances of a specific group of children. Table 1.4 on page 32 summarizes the strengths and limitations of each of these methods.

SYSTEMATIC OBSERVATION Observations of the behavior of children, and of adults who are important in their lives, can be made in different ways. One approach is to go into the field, or natural environment, and observe the behavior of interest—a method called **naturalistic observation.**

A study of preschoolers' responses to their peers' distress provides a good example of this technique (Farver & Branstetter, 1994). Observing 3- and 4-year-olds in childcare centers, the researchers recorded each instance of a child crying and the reactions of nearby children—whether they ignored, watched curiously, commented on the child's unhappiness, scolded or teased, or shared, helped, or expressed sympathy. Caregiver behaviors—explaining why a child was crying, mediating conflict, or offering comfort—were noted to see if adult sensitivity was related to children's caring responses. A strong relationship emerged. The great strength of naturalistic observation is that investigators can see directly the everyday behaviors they hope to explain.

Naturalistic observation also has a major limitation: Not all individuals have the same opportunity to display a particular behavior in everyday life. In the study just mentioned, some children might have witnessed a child crying more often than others or been exposed to more cues for positive social responses from caregivers. For this reason, they might have displayed more compassion.

Researchers commonly deal with this difficulty by making **structured observations,** in which the investigator sets up a laboratory situation that evokes the behavior of interest

In naturalistic observation, the researcher goes into the field and records the behavior of interest. This researcher observes children at a summer camp. She may note their playmate choices, cooperation, helpfulness, or conflicts. ■

TABLE 1.4	Strengths and Limitations of Common Information-Gathering Methods

METHOD	DESCRIPTION	STRENGTHS	LIMITATIONS
Systematic Observation			
Naturalistic observation	Observation of behavior in natural contexts.	Reflects participants' everyday behaviors.	Cannot control conditions under which participants are observed.
Structured observation	Observation of behavior in a laboratory, where conditions are the same for all participants.	Grants each participant an equal opportunity to display the behavior of interest. Permits study of behaviors rarely seen in everyday life.	May not yield observations typical of participants' behavior in everyday life.
Self-Reports			
Clinical interview	Flexible interviewing procedure in which the investigator obtains a complete account of the participant's thoughts.	Comes as close as possible to the way participants think in everyday life. Great breadth and depth of information can be obtained in a short time.	May not result in accurate reporting of information. Flexible procedure makes comparing individuals' responses difficult.
Structured interview, questionnaires, and tests	Self-report instruments in which each participant is asked the same questions in the same way.	Permits comparisons of participants' responses and efficient data collection. Researchers can specify answer alternatives that participants might not think of in an open-ended interview.	Does not yield the same depth of information as a clinical interview. Responses are still subject to inaccurate reporting.
Clinical, or Case Study, Method	A full picture of one individual's psychological functioning, obtained by combining interviews, observations, and sometimes test scores.	Provides rich, descriptive insights into processes of development.	May be biased by researchers' theoretical preferences. Findings cannot be applied to individuals other than the participant.
Ethnography	Participant observation of a culture or distinct social group. By making extensive field notes, the researcher tries to capture the culture's unique values and social processes.	Provides a more complete and accurate description than can be derived from a single observational visit, interview, or questionnaire.	May be biased by researchers' values and theoretical preferences. Findings cannot be applied to individuals and settings other than the ones studied.

so that every participant has an equal opportunity to display the response. In one study, 2-year-olds' emotional reactions to harm that they thought they had caused were observed by asking them to take care of a rag doll that had been modified so its leg would fall off when the child picked it up. To make the child feel at fault, once the leg detached, an adult "talked for" the doll by saying, "Ow!" Researchers recorded children's facial expressions of sadness and concern for the injured doll, efforts to help the doll, and body tension—responses that indicated remorse and a desire to make amends. In addition, mothers were asked to engage in brief conversations about emotions with their children (Garner, 2003). Toddlers whose mothers more often explained the causes and consequences of emotion were more likely to express concern for the injured doll.

Structured observation permits greater control over the research situation than does naturalistic observation. In addition, the method is especially useful for studying behaviors—such as parent–child or friendship interactions—that investigators rarely have an opportunity to see in everyday life. When aggressive and nonaggressive 10-year-old boys were observed playing games with their best friend in a laboratory, the aggressive boys and their friends more often violated game rules, cheated, and encouraged each other to engage in these dishonest acts. In addition, observers rated these boys' interactions as angrier and less cooperative than the interactions of nonaggressive boys (Bagwell & Coie, 2004). The researchers concluded that aggressive boys' close peer ties provide a context in which they practice hostility and other negative behaviors, which may contribute to their antisocial behavior.

The procedures used to collect systematic observations vary, depending on the purpose of the research. Some investigators choose to describe the entire behavior stream—everything said and done over a certain time period. In one study, researchers wanted to find out whether maternal sensitivity in infancy and early childhood contributes to readiness for formal schooling at age 6 (Hirsh-Pasek & Burchinal, 2006). Between age 6 months and 4½ years, the investigators periodically videotaped 15-minute mother–child play sessions. Then they rated each session for maternal positive emotion, support, stimulating play, and respect for the child's autonomy—ingredients of sensitivity that did predict better language and academic progress when the children reached kindergarten.

Researchers have devised ingenious ways of observing difficult-to-capture behaviors. For example, to record instances of bullying, a group of investigators set up video cameras overlooking a classroom and a playground and had fourth to sixth graders wear small, remote microphones and pocket-sized transmitters (Craig, Pepler, & Atlas, 2000). Results revealed that bullying occurred often—at rates of 2.4 episodes per hour in the classroom and 4.5 episodes per hour on the playground. Yet only 15 to 18 percent of the time did teachers take steps to stop the harassment.

Systematic observation provides invaluable information on how children and adults behave, but it tells us little about the reasoning behind their responses. For this kind of information, researchers must turn to self-report techniques.

SELF-REPORTS   Self-reports ask research participants to provide information on their perceptions, thoughts, abilities, feelings, attitudes, beliefs, and past experiences. They range from relatively unstructured interviews to highly structured interviews, questionnaires, and tests.

In a **clinical interview,** a flexible, conversational style is used to probe for the participant's point of view. In the following example, Piaget questioned a 5-year-old child about his understanding of dreams:

> *Where does the dream come from?*—I think you sleep so well that you dream.—*Does it come from us or from outside?*—From outside.—*When you are in bed and you dream, where is the dream?*—In my bed, under the blanket. I don't really know. If it was in my stomach, the bones would be in the way and I shouldn't see it.—*Is the dream there when you sleep?*—Yes, it is in the bed beside me. (Piaget, 1926/1930, pp. 97–98)

The clinical interview has two major strengths. First, it permits people to display their thoughts in terms that are as close as possible to the way they think in everyday life. Second, the clinical interview can provide a large amount of information in a fairly brief period. For example, in an hour-long session, we can obtain a wide range of child-rearing information from a parent—much more than we could capture by observing for the same amount of time.

A major limitation of the clinical interview has to do with the accuracy with which people report their thoughts, feelings, and experiences. Some participants, desiring to please the interviewer, may make up answers. When asked about past events, some may have trouble recalling exactly what happened. And because the clinical interview depends on verbal ability and expressiveness, it may underestimate the capacities of individuals who have difficulty putting their thoughts into words.

The clinical interview has also been criticized because of its flexibility. When questions are phrased differently for each participant, variations in responses may reflect the manner of interviewing rather than real differences in the way people think about a topic. **Structured interviews** (including tests and questionnaires), in which each participant is asked the same questions in the same way, eliminate this problem. These instruments are also much more efficient. Answers are briefer, and researchers can obtain written responses from an entire group at the same time. Furthermore, by listing answer alternatives, researchers can indicate the specific activities and behaviors of interest—ones that participants might not think of in an open-ended clinical interview. For example, when parents were asked what they considered "the most important thing for children to prepare them for life," 62 percent checked "to think for themselves" when this alternative appeared on a list. Yet only 5 percent thought of it during a clinical interview (Schwarz, 1999).

Nevertheless, structured interviews do not yield the same depth of information as a clinical interview. And they can still be affected by inaccurate reporting.

Using the clinical, or case study, method, this researcher combines interviews with the mother and observations and testing of the child to construct an in-depth picture of one child's psychological functioning. ■

THE CLINICAL, OR CASE STUDY, METHOD An outgrowth of psychoanalytic theory, the **clinical,** or **case study, method** brings together a wide range of information on one child, including interviews, observations, and sometimes test scores. The aim is to obtain as complete a picture as possible of that child's psychological functioning and the experiences that led up to it.

The clinical method is well-suited to studying the development of certain types of individuals who are few in number but vary widely in characteristics. For example, the method has been used to find out what contributes to the accomplishments of *prodigies*—extremely gifted children who attain adult competence in a field before age 10 (Moran & Gardner, 2006). Consider Adam, a boy who read, wrote, and composed musical pieces before he was out of diapers. By age 4, Adam was deeply involved in mastering human symbol systems—French, German, Russian, Sanskrit, Greek, the computer programming language BASIC, ancient hieroglyphs, music, and mathematics. Adam's parents provided a home rich in stimulation and reared him with affection, firmness, and humor. They searched for schools in which he could both develop his abilities and form rewarding social relationships. He graduated from college at age 18 and continued to pursue musical composition. Would Adam have realized his potential without the chance combination of his special gift and nurturing, committed parents? Probably not, researchers concluded (Feldman, 2004).

The clinical method yields richly detailed case narratives that offer valuable insights into the multiplicity of factors affecting development. Nevertheless, like all other methods, it has drawbacks. Because information often is collected unsystematically and subjectively, researchers' theoretical preferences may bias their interpretations. In addition, investigators cannot assume that their conclusions apply, or generalize, to anyone other than the child studied (Stanovich, 2007). Even when patterns emerge across several cases, it is wise to confirm them with other research strategies.

METHODS FOR STUDYING CULTURE To study the impact of culture on child development, researchers adjust the methods just considered or tap procedures specially devised for cross-cultural and multicultural research (Triandis, 2007). Which approach investigators choose depends on their research goals.

Sometimes researchers are interested in characteristics that are believed to be universal but that vary in degree from one culture to the next: Are parents warmer or more directive in some cultures than in others? How strong are gender stereotypes in different nations? In each instance, several cultural groups will be compared, and all participants must be questioned or observed in the same way. Therefore, researchers draw on the observational and self-report procedures we have already considered, adapting them through translation so they can be understood in each cultural context. For example, to study cultural variation in parenting attitudes, the same questionnaire, asking for ratings on such items as "I often hug and kiss my child" or "I scold my child when his/her behavior does not meet my expectations," is given to all participants (Wu et al., 2002). Still, investigators must be mindful of cultural differences in familiarity with responding to self-report instruments that may bias their findings (Van de Vijver, Hofer, & Chasiotis, 2010).

At other times, researchers want to uncover the *cultural meanings* of children's and adults' behaviors by becoming as familiar as possible with their way of life. To achieve this goal, researchers rely on a method borrowed from the field of anthropology—**ethnography.** Like the clinical method, ethnographic research is a descriptive, qualitative technique. But instead of aiming to understand a single individual, it is directed toward understanding a culture or a distinct social group through *participant observation*. Typically, the researcher spends months and sometimes years in the cultural community, participating in its daily life. Extensive field notes are gathered, consisting of a mix of observations, self-reports from members of the culture, and careful interpretations by the investigator (Miller, Hengst, & Wang, 2003; Shweder et al., 2006). Later, these notes are put together into a description of the community that tries to capture its unique values and social processes.

The ethnographic method assumes that by entering into close contact with a social group, researchers can understand the beliefs and behaviors of its members in a way not possible with an observational visit, interview, or questionnaire. Some ethnographies take in many aspects of children's experience, as one researcher did in describing what it is like to grow up in a small American town. Others focus on one or a few settings, such as home, school, or neighborhood life (Higginbottom, 2006; Peshkin, 1997; Valdés, 1998). And still others are limited to a particular practice, such as uncovering cultural and religious influences on children's make-believe play. For example, ethnographic findings reveal that East Indian Hindu parents encourage preschoolers to communicate with "invisible" characters. They regard this activity as linked to *karma* (the cycle of birth and death) and believe that the child may be remembering a past life. In contrast, Christian fundamentalist parents often discourage children from pretending to be unreal characters, believing that such play promotes dangerous spiritual ideas and deceitful behavior (Taylor & Carlson, 2000). Researchers may supplement traditional self-report and observational methods with ethnography if they suspect that unique meanings underlie cultural differences, as the Cultural Influences box on page 36 reveals.

■ This Western ethnographer spent months living among the Efe people of the Republic of Congo. Here he observes young children sharing food. The Efe value and encourage cooperation and generosity at an early age. ■

Ethnographers strive to minimize their influence on the culture they are studying by becoming part of it. Nevertheless, as with clinical research, investigators' cultural values and theoretical commitments sometimes lead them to observe selectively or misinterpret what they see. Finally, the findings of ethnographic studies cannot be assumed to generalize beyond the people and settings in which the research was conducted.

ASK YOURSELF

◆ **REVIEW** Why might a researcher choose structured observation over naturalistic observation? How about the reverse? What might lead the researcher to opt for clinical interviewing over systematic observation?

◆ **APPLY** A researcher wants to study the thoughts and feelings of children who have a parent on active duty in the military. Which method should she use? Why?

◆ **CONNECT** What strengths and limitations do the clinical, or case study, method and ethnography have in common?

General Research Designs

In deciding on a research design, investigators choose a way of setting up a study that permits them to test their hypotheses with the greatest degree of certainty possible. Two main designs are used in all research on human behavior: *correlational* and *experimental*.

CULTURAL INFLUENCES

Immigrant Youths: Adapting to a New Land

During the past quarter century, a rising tide of immigrants has come to North America, fleeing war and persecution in their homelands or seeking better life chances. Today, nearly one-fourth of U.S. children and adolescents have foreign-born parents, making them the fastest growing sector of the U.S. youth population. About 20 percent of them are foreign-born themselves, mostly from Latin America, the Caribbean, and Asia (Hernandez, Denton, & Macartney, 2008; Suarez-Orozco, Todorova, & Qin, 2006).

How well are immigrant youths adapting to their new country? To find out, researchers use multiple research methods—academic testing, questionnaires assessing psychological adjustment, and in-depth ethnographies.

Academic Achievement and Adjustment

Although educators and laypeople often assume that the transition to a new country has a negative impact on psychological well-being, evidence reveals that many children of immigrant parents from diverse countries adapt amazingly well. Students who are first generation (foreign-born) or second generation (American-born, with immigrant parents) often achieve in school as well as or better than students of native-born parents, graduating from high school at similar or greater overall rates (Fuligni, 2004; Hernandez, Denton, & Macartney, 2008; Saucier et al., 2002). Findings on psychological adjustment are similar. Compared with their agemates, adolescents from immigrant families are less likely to commit delinquent and violent acts, to use drugs and alcohol, or to have early sex. They are also less likely to be obese or to have missed school because of illness. And they tend to report just as favorable, and at times higher, self-esteem as do young people with native-born parents (Fuligni, 1998; Saucier et al., 2002; Supple & Small, 2006).

These outcomes are strongest for Chinese, Filipino, Japanese, Korean, and East Indian youths (Fuligni, 2004; Louie, 2001; Portes & Rumbaut, 2005). Variation in adjustment is greater among Mexican, Central American, and Southeast Asian (Hmong, Cambodian, Laotian, Thai, and Vietnamese) young people, who show elevated rates of school failure and dropout, delinquency, teenage parenthood, and drug use. Disparities in parental economic resources, education, English-language proficiency, and sup-

port of children contribute to these trends (Supple & Small, 2006; Zhou & Xiong, 2005).

Still, many first- and second-generation youths whose parents face considerable financial hardship and who speak little English are successful (Fuligni & Yoshikawa, 2003; Hernandez, Denton, & Macartney, 2008). Factors other than income are responsible—notably, family values and strong ethnic-community ties.

Family and Ethnic-Community Influences

Ethnographies reveal that immigrant parents view education as the surest way to improve life chances (Goldenberg et al., 2001; Lee, 2001; Louie, 2001). Aware of the challenges their children face, they typically emphasize trying hard. They remind their children that, because educational opportunities were not available in their native countries, they themselves are often limited to menial jobs. And while preserving their culture's values, these parents also make certain adaptations—for example, supporting education for daughters even though their culture of origin endorses it only for sons.

Adolescents from these families internalize their parents' valuing of academic achievement, endorsing it more strongly than agemates with native-born parents (Asakawa, 2001; Fuligni, 2004). Because minority ethnicities usually stress allegiance to family and community over individual goals, first- and second-generation young people often feel a strong sense of obligation to their parents. They view school success as an important way of repaying their parents for the hardships they have endured (Bacallao & Smokowski, 2007; Fuligni, Yip, & Tseng, 2002). Both family relationships and school achievement protect these youths from risky behaviors (see the Biology and Environment box on pages 10–11).

Immigrant parents of successful youths typically develop close ties to an ethnic community, which exerts additional control through a high consensus on values and constant monitoring of young people's activities.

■ These Hmong boys perform in an ethnic festival in St. Paul, Minnesota, where many Hmong immigrants have settled. Cultural values that engender allegiance to family and community promote high achievement and protect many immigrant youths from involvement in risky behaviors. ■

The following comments capture the power of these family and community forces:

- *Elizabeth, age 16, from Vietnam, straight-A student, like her two older sisters:* My parents know pretty much all the kids in the neighborhood. Everybody here knows everybody else. It's hard to get away with much. (Zhou & Bankston, 1998, pp. 93, 130)
- *Juan, teenager from Mexico:* A really big part of the Hispanic population [is] being close to family, and the family being a priority all the time. I hate people who say, "Why do you want to go to a party where your family's at? Don't you want to get away from them?" You know, I don't really get tired of them. I've always been really close to them. That connection to my parents, that trust that you can talk to them, that makes me Mexican. (Bacallao & Smokowski, 2007, p. 62)

The experiences of well-adjusted immigrant youths are not problem-free. Chinese adolescents who had arrived in the United States within the previous year described their adjustment as very difficult because they were not proficient in English and, as a result, found many everyday tasks challenging and felt socially isolated (Yeh et al., 2008). Young immigrants also encounter racial and ethnic prejudices and experience tensions between family values and the new culture. In the long term, however, family and community cohesion, supervision, and high expectations promote favorable outcomes.

CORRELATIONAL DESIGN   In a **correlational design,** researchers gather information on individuals, generally in natural life circumstances, and make no effort to alter their experiences. Then they look at relationships between participants' characteristics and their behavior or development. Suppose we want to answer such questions as, Do parents' styles of interacting with their children have any bearing on children's intelligence? Does attending a child-care center promote children's friendliness with peers? How do child abuse and neglect affect children's feelings about themselves and their relationships with peers? In these and many other instances, the conditions of interest are difficult or impossible to arrange and control and must be studied as they currently exist.

Correlational studies have one major limitation: We cannot infer cause and effect. For example, if we find that parental interaction is related to children's intelligence, we would not know whether parents' behavior actually *causes* intellectual differences among children. In fact, the opposite is possible. The behaviors of highly intelligent children may be so attractive that they cause parents to interact more favorably. Or a third variable that we did not even consider, such as amount of noise and distraction in the home, may cause changes in both parental interaction and children's intelligence.

In correlational studies, and in other types of research designs, investigators often examine relationships by using a **correlation coefficient**—a number that describes how two measures, or variables, are associated with one another. We will encounter the correlation coefficient in discussing research findings throughout this book, so let's look at what it is and how it is interpreted. A correlation coefficient can range in value from +1.00 to –1.00. The *magnitude, or size, of the number* shows the *strength of the relationship.* A zero correlation indicates no relationship, but the closer the value is to either +1.00 or –1.00, the stronger the relationship (see Figure 1.6). For instance, a correlation of –.78 is high, –.52 is moderate, and –.18 is low. Note, however that correlations of +.52 and –.52 are equally strong. The *sign of the number* refers to the *direction of the relationship.* A positive sign (+) means that as one variable *increases,* the other also *increases.* A negative sign (–) indicates that as one variable *increases,* the other *decreases.*

Let's look at some examples of how a correlation coefficient works. One researcher reported a +.55 correlation between a measure of maternal language stimulation and the size of children's vocabularies at age 2 years (Hoff, 2003). This is a moderate correlation, which indicates that mothers who spoke more to their infants had children who were more advanced in language development. In two other studies, child-rearing practices were related to toddlers' compliance in consistent ways. First, maternal warmth and sensitivity during play correlated positively (+.34) with 2-year-olds' willingness to comply with their mother's directive to clean up toys (Feldman & Klein, 2003). Second, the extent to which mothers spoke harshly, interrupted, and controlled their 4-year-olds' play correlated negatively (–.31 for boys and –.42 for girls) with children's compliance (Smith et al., 2004).

All these investigations found a relationship between parenting and young children's behavior. **TAKE A MOMENT...** Are you tempted to conclude that parenting influenced children's responses? Although the researchers suspected this was so, they could not be sure of cause and effect. Can you think of other possible explanations? Finding a relationship in a correlational study suggests that tracking down its cause—using a more powerful experimental strategy, if possible—would be worthwhile.

EXPERIMENTAL DESIGN   An **experimental design** permits inferences about cause and effect because researchers use an evenhanded procedure to assign people to two or more treatment conditions. In an experiment, the events and behaviors of interest are divided into two types: independent and dependent variables. The **independent variable** is the one the investigator expects to cause changes in another variable. The **dependent variable** is the one the investigator expects to be influenced by the independent variable. Cause-and-effect relationships can be detected because the researcher directly *controls* or *manipulates* changes in the independent variable by exposing participants to the treatment

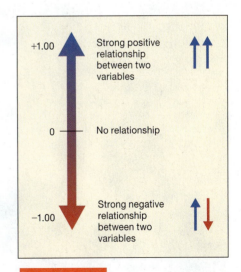

FIGURE 1.6

The meaning of correlation coefficients. The magnitude of the number indicates the *strength* of the relationship. The sign of the number (+ or –) indicates the *direction* of the relationship.

FIGURE 1.7

Does the way adults end their angry encounters affect children's emotional reactions?
A laboratory experiment showed that children who had previously witnessed adults resolving their disputes by apologizing and compromising were more likely to decline in distress when witnessing subsequent adult conflicts than were children who witnessed adults leaving their arguments unresolved. Notice in this graph that only 10 percent of children in the unresolved-anger treatment declined in distress (see bar on left), whereas 42 percent of children in the resolved-anger treatment did so (see bar on right). *(Adapted from El-Sheikh, Cummings, & Reiter, 1996.)*

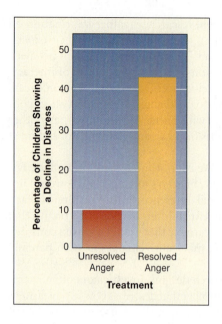

conditions. Then the researcher compares their performance on measures of the dependent variable.

In one *laboratory experiment,* researchers explored the impact of adults' angry interactions on children's adjustment (El-Sheikh, Cummings, & Reiter, 1996). They hypothesized that the way angry encounters end (independent variable) affects children's emotional reactions (dependent variable). Four- and 5-year-olds were brought one at a time to a laboratory, accompanied by their mothers. One group was exposed to an *unresolved-anger treatment,* in which two adult actors entered the room and argued but did not work out their disagreements. The other group witnessed a *resolved-anger treatment,* in which the adults ended their disputes by apologizing and compromising. As Figure 1.7 shows, when they witnessed a follow-up adult conflict, more children in the resolved-anger treatment showed a decline in distress, as measured by fewer anxious facial expressions, less freezing in place, and less seeking of closeness to their mothers. The experiment revealed that anger resolution can reduce the stressful impact of adult conflict on children.

In experimental studies, investigators must take special precautions to control for participants' characteristics that could reduce the accuracy of their findings. For example, in the study just described, if more children from homes high in parental conflict ended up in the unresolved-anger treatment, we could not tell what produced the results—the independent variable or the children's backgrounds. To protect against this problem, researchers engage in **random assignment** of participants to treatment conditions. By using an unbiased procedure, such as drawing numbers out of a hat or flipping a coin, investigators increase the chances that participants' characteristics will be equally distributed across treatment groups.

Sometimes researchers combine random assignment with another technique called *matching.* In this procedure, participants are measured before the experiment on the factor in question—in our example, exposure to parental conflict. Then children from homes high and low in parental conflict are assigned in equal numbers to each treatment condition. In this way, the experimental groups are deliberately matched, or made equivalent, on characteristics that are likely to distort the results.

MODIFIED EXPERIMENTAL DESIGNS: FIELD AND NATURAL EXPERIMENTS Most experiments are conducted in laboratories, where researchers can achieve the maximum possible control over treatment conditions. But as we have already indicated, findings obtained in laboratories may not apply to everyday situations. In *field experiments,* investigators capitalize on rare opportunities to assign participants randomly to treatment conditions in natural settings. In the experiment just described, we can conclude that the emotional climate established by adults affects children's behavior in the laboratory. But does it also do so in daily life?

Another study helps answer this question. Ethnically diverse, poverty-stricken families with a 2-year-old child were scheduled for a home visit, during which researchers assessed family functioning and child problem behaviors by asking parents to respond to questionnaires

When researchers cannot randomly assign children to conditions in the real world, they sometimes conduct natural experiments using treatments that already exist. For example, the learning environments of different child-care centers might be compared to explore the impact of storybook reading on preschoolers' language and literacy development. ■

and videotaping parent–child interaction. Then the families were randomly assigned to either an intervention condition, called the Family Check-Up, or a no-intervention control group. The intervention consisted of three home-based sessions in which a consultant gave parents feedback about their child-rearing practices and their child's adjustment, explored parents' willingness to improve, identified community services appropriate to each family's needs, and offered follow-up sessions on parenting practices and other concerns (Dishion et al., 2008). Findings showed that families assigned to the Family Check-Up (but not controls) gained in positive parenting, which predicted a reduction in child problem behaviors—outcomes still evident a year later, when participating children were reassessed at age 3.

Often researchers cannot randomly assign participants and manipulate conditions in the real world, as these investigators were able to do. Sometimes they can compromise by conducting *natural,* or *quasi-, experiments.* Treatments that already exist, such as different family environments, child-care centers, or schools, are compared. These studies differ from correlational research only in that groups of participants are carefully chosen to ensure that their characteristics are as much alike as possible. In this way, investigators do their best to rule out alternative explanations for their treatment effects. But despite these efforts, natural experiments cannot achieve the precision and rigor of true experimental research.

To help you compare correlational and experimental designs, Table 1.5 summarizes their strengths and limitations. It also includes an overview of designs for studying development, to which we turn next.

TABLE 1.5 Strengths and Limitations of Research Designs

DESIGN	DESCRIPTION	STRENGTHS	LIMITATIONS
GENERAL			
Correlational	The investigator obtains information on participants without altering their experiences.	Permits study of relationships between variables.	Does not permit inferences about cause-and-effect relationships.
Experimental	The investigator manipulates an independent variable and examines its effect on a dependent variable. Can be conducted in the laboratory or in the natural environment.	Permits inferences about cause-and-effect relationships.	When conducted in the laboratory, findings may not generalize to the real world. In *field experiments,* control over the treatment is usually weaker than in the laboratory. In *natural,* or *quasi-, experiments,* lack of random assignment substantially reduces the precision of research.
DEVELOPMENTAL			
Longitudinal	The investigator studies the same group of participants repeatedly at different ages.	Permits study of common patterns and individual differences in development and relationships between early and later events and behaviors.	Age-related changes may be distorted because of biased sampling, selective attrition, practice effects, and cohort effects.
Cross-sectional	The investigator studies groups of participants differing in age at the same point in time.	More efficient than the longitudinal design.	Does not permit study of individual developmental trends. Age differences may be distorted because of cohort effects.
Sequential	The investigator follows a sequence of samples (two or more age groups), collecting data on them at the same points in time.	Permits both longitudinal and cross-sectional comparisons. Reveals cohort effects. Permits tracking of age-related changes more efficiently than the longitudinal design.	May have the same problems as longitudinal and cross-sectional strategies, but the design itself helps identify difficulties.
Microgenetic	The investigator presents children with a novel task and follows their mastery over a series of closely spaced sessions.	Offers insights into the process of development.	Requires intensive study of participants' moment-by-moment behaviors. The time required for participants to change is difficult to anticipate. Practice effects may distort developmental trends.

Designs for Studying Development

Scientists interested in child development require information about the way research participants change over time. To answer questions about development, they must extend correlational and experimental approaches to include measurements at different ages. Longitudinal and cross-sectional designs are special *developmental research strategies.* In each, age comparisons form the basis of the research plan.

THE LONGITUDINAL DESIGN In a **longitudinal design,** participants are studied repeatedly, and changes are noted as they get older. The time spanned may be relatively short (a few months to several years) or very long (a decade or even a lifetime). The longitudinal approach has two major strengths. First, because it tracks the performance of each person over time, researchers can identify common patterns as well as individual differences in development. Second, longitudinal studies permit investigators to examine relationships between early and later events and behaviors. Let's illustrate these ideas.

A group of researchers wondered whether children who display extreme personality styles—either angry and explosive or shy and withdrawn—retain the same dispositions when they become adults. In addition, the researchers wanted to know what kinds of experiences promote stability or plasticity in personality and what consequences explosiveness and shyness have for long-term adjustment. To answer these questions, the researchers delved into the archives of the Guidance Study, a well-known longitudinal investigation that was initiated in 1928 at the University of California, Berkeley, and continued for several decades (Caspi, Elder, & Bem, 1987, 1988).

Results revealed that the two personality styles were moderately stable. Between ages 8 and 30, a good number of individuals remained the same, whereas others changed substantially. When stability did occur, it appeared to be due to a "snowballing effect," in which children evoked responses from adults and peers that acted to maintain their dispositions. Explosive youngsters were likely to be treated with anger, whereas shy children were apt to be ignored. As a result, the two types of children came to view their social worlds differently. Explosive children tended to view others as hostile; shy children regarded them as unfriendly (Caspi & Roberts, 2001). Together, these factors led explosive children to sustain or increase their unruliness and shy children to continue to withdraw.

Persistence of extreme personality styles affected many areas of adult adjustment. For men, the results of early explosiveness were most apparent in their work lives, in the form of conflicts with supervisors, frequent job changes, and unemployment. Since few women in this sample of an earlier generation worked after marriage, their family lives were most affected. Explosive girls grew up to be hotheaded wives and parents who were especially prone to divorce. Sex differences in the long-term consequences of shyness were even greater. Men who had been withdrawn in childhood were delayed in marrying, becoming fathers, and developing stable careers. However, because a withdrawn, unassertive style was socially acceptable for females in the mid-twentieth century, women who had shy personalities showed no special adjustment problems.

PROBLEMS IN CONDUCTING LONGITUDINAL RESEARCH Despite their strengths, longitudinal investigations pose a number of problems. For example, *biased sampling*—the failure to enlist participants who adequately represent the population of interest—is a common problem. People who willingly participate in research that requires them to be observed and tested over many years are likely to have distinctive characteristics—perhaps a special appreciation for the scientific value of research, or a unique need or desire for medical, mental health, or educational services provided by the investigators. Furthermore, longitudinal samples generally become more biased as the investigation proceeds because of *selective attrition.* Participants may move away or drop out of the study for other reasons, and the ones who remain are likely to differ in important ways from the ones who continue. Also, from repeated study, people may become "test-wise." Their performance may improve as a result of *practice effects*—better test-taking skills and increased familiarity with the test—not because of factors commonly associated with development.

The most widely discussed threat to the accuracy of longitudinal findings is cultural–historical change, commonly called **cohort effects.** Longitudinal studies examine the development of *cohorts*—children born at the same time, who are influenced by particular cultural and historical conditions. Results based on one cohort may not apply to children developing at other times. For example, look back at the findings on female shyness described in the previous section, which were gathered in the 1950s. Today's shy young women tend to be poorly adjusted—a difference that may be due to changes in gender roles in Western societies. Shy adults, whether male or female, feel more depressed, have fewer social supports, and may do less well in educational and career attainment than their agemates (Caspi, 2000; Caspi et al., 2003; Mounts et al., 2006). Similarly, a longitudinal study of social development would probably result in quite different findings if it were carried out in the second decade of the twenty-first century, around the time of World War II, or during the Great Depression of the 1930s.

Cohort effects don't just operate broadly on an entire generation. They also occur when specific experiences influence some children but not others in the same generation. For example, children who witnessed the terrorist attacks of September 11, 2001 (either because they were near Ground Zero or because they saw injury and death on TV), or who lost a parent in the disaster were far more likely than other children to display persistent emotional problems, including intense fear, anxiety, and depression (Mullett-Hume et al., 2008; Pfeffer et al., 2007). A study of one New York City sample suggested that as many as one-fourth of the city's children were affected (Hoven et al., 2005).

■ These children lost family members, friends, teachers, and other sources of support in the January 2010 earthquake in Haiti. They live and attend school in a refugee camp in Port-au-Prince, where rescue workers try to help them cope with the crisis. This powerfully destructive historical event is a cohort effect, with profound consequences for development. ■

THE CROSS-SECTIONAL DESIGN   The length of time it takes for many behaviors to change, even in limited longitudinal studies, has led researchers to turn to a more efficient strategy for studying development. In the **cross-sectional design,** groups of people differing in age are studied at the same point in time. Because participants are measured only once, researchers need not be concerned about such difficulties as participant dropout or practice effects.

An investigation in which students in grades 3, 6, 9, and 12 filled out a questionnaire about their sibling relationships provides a good illustration (Buhrmester & Furman, 1990). Findings revealed that sibling interaction was characterized by greater equality and less power assertion with age. Also, feelings of sibling companionship declined during adolescence. The researchers thought that several factors contributed to these age differences. As later-born children become more competent and independent, they no longer need, and are probably less willing to accept, direction from older siblings. And as adolescents move from psychological dependence on the family to greater involvement with peers, they may have less time and emotional need to invest in siblings. Subsequent research has confirmed these intriguing ideas about the development of sibling relationships.

PROBLEMS IN CONDUCTING CROSS-SECTIONAL RESEARCH   Despite its convenience, cross-sectional research does not provide evidence about change at the level at which it actually occurs: the individual. For example, in the cross-sectional study of sibling relationships just discussed, comparisons are limited to age-group averages. We cannot tell if important individual differences exist. Indeed, longitudinal findings reveal that adolescents vary considerably in the changing quality of their sibling relationships. Although many become more distant, others become more supportive and intimate, still others more rivalrous and antagonistic (Branje et al., 2004; Kim et al., 2006; Whiteman & Loken, 2006).

Cross-sectional studies—especially those that cover a wide age span—have another problem. Like longitudinal research, they can be threatened by cohort effects. For example, comparisons of 5-year-old cohorts and 15-year-old cohorts—groups born and reared in different years—may not really represent age-related changes. Instead, they may reflect unique experiences associated with the time period in which the age groups were growing up.

IMPROVING DEVELOPMENTAL DESIGNS   Researchers have devised ways of building on the strengths and minimizing the weaknesses of longitudinal and cross-sectional approaches. Several modified developmental designs have resulted.

Sequential Designs. To overcome some of the limitations of traditional developmental designs, investigators sometimes use **sequential designs,** in which they conduct several similar cross-sectional or longitudinal studies (called *sequences*) at varying times. As the illustration in Figure 1.8 reveals, some sequential designs combine longitudinal and cross-sectional strategies, an approach that has three advantages:

- We can find out whether cohort effects are operating by comparing participants of the same age who were born in different years. In Figure 1.8, for example, we can compare the longitudinal samples at seventh, eighth, and ninth grades. If they do not differ, we can rule out cohort effects.
- We can make both longitudinal and cross-sectional comparisons. If outcomes are similar, we can be especially confident about the findings.
- The design is efficient. In our example, we can find out about change over a five-year period by following each cohort for three years.

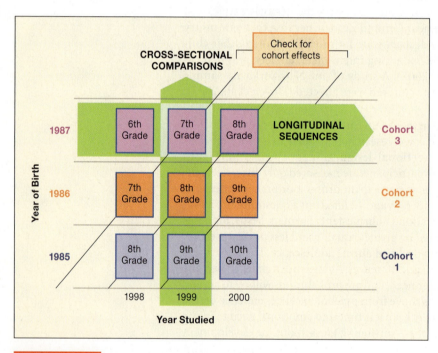

FIGURE 1.8

Example of a sequential design. Three cohorts, born in 1985 (blue), 1986 (orange), and 1987 (pink), respectively, are followed longitudinally for three years. Testing the cohorts in overlapping grades enables researchers to check for cohort effects by comparing participants born in different years when they reach the same grade (see diagonals). In a study using this design, same-grade adolescents who were members of different cohorts scored similarly on a questionnaire assessing family harmony, indicating no cohort effects. By following each cohort for just three years, the investigator could infer a developmental trend across five years, from sixth to tenth grade.

In a study that used the design in Figure 1.8, researchers wanted to find out if family harmony changed as young people experienced the dramatic physical and psychological changes of adolescence (Baer, 2002). A questionnaire assessing emotional bonding among family members was given to three adolescent cohorts, each born a year apart. In longitudinal follow-ups, each cohort again responded to the questionnaire during the following two years.

Findings for the three cohorts converged: All reported (1) a slight decline in family harmony with grade and (2) similar levels of family harmony as they reached the same grade, confirming that there were no cohort effects. Therefore, the researchers concluded that family closeness diminishes steadily from sixth to tenth grade, noting, however, that the change is mild—not enough to threaten supportive family ties. **TAKE A MOMENT...** Turn back to our discussion of parent–adolescent communication as a dynamic system on page 29 and our consideration of adolescent sibling relationships on page 41. How are those results helpful in interpreting the outcomes of the sequential study just described?

Examining Microcosms of Development. In the examples of developmental research we have discussed, observations of children are fairly widely spaced. When we observe once a year or every few years, we can describe development, but we cannot easily capture the processes that produce it. The **microgenetic design,** an adaptation of the longitudinal approach, presents children with a novel task and follows their mastery over a series of closely spaced sessions. Within this "microcosm" of development, researchers observe how change occurs (Flynn & Siegler, 2007; Kuhn, 1995; Siegler & Crowley, 1991). The microgenetic design is especially useful for studying cognitive development—for example, the strategies children use to acquire new knowledge in reading, mathematics, and science (Siegler, 2002, 2006). As you will see in Chapter 5, the microgenetic design has also been used to trace infants' mastery of motor skills.

Nevertheless, microgenetic studies are difficult to carry out. Researchers must pore over hours of recorded information, analyzing each participant's behavior many times. In addition, the time required for children to change is hard to anticipate. It depends on a careful match between the child's capabilities and the demands of the task. Finally, as in other longitudinal research, practice effects can distort microgenetic findings. But when researchers overcome these challenges, they reap the benefits of seeing development as it takes place.

■ How will these preschoolers become proficient at building a structure collaboratively? A microgenetic design, which permits researchers to follow children's mastery of a challenging task, is uniquely suited to answering this question. ■

Combining Experimental and Developmental Designs. Perhaps you noticed that all the examples of longitudinal and cross-sectional research we have considered permit only correlational, not causal, inferences. Yet causal information is also desirable, both for testing theories and for finding ways to enhance development. Sometimes researchers can explore the causal link between experiences and development by experimentally manipulating the experiences. If, as a result, development improves, then we have strong evidence for a causal association. Today, research that combines an experimental strategy with either a longitudinal or a cross-sectional approach, with the aim of augmenting development, is becoming increasingly common (Lerner & Overton, 2008). For an example, refer to the Social Issues: Education box on page 44.

Ethics in Research on Children

Research into human behavior creates ethical issues because, unfortunately, the quest for scientific knowledge can sometimes exploit people. When children take part in research, the ethical concerns are especially complex. Children are more vulnerable than adults to physical and psychological harm. In addition, immaturity makes it difficult or impossible for children to evaluate for themselves what participation in research will mean. For these reasons, special ethical guidelines for research on children have been developed by the federal government, by funding agencies, and by research-oriented associations such as the American Psychological Association (2002) and the Society for Research in Child Development (2007).

Table 1.6 on page 45 presents a summary of children's basic research rights. **TAKE A MOMENT…** After examining them, read about the following research situations, each of which poses a serious ethical dilemma. What precautions do you think should be taken in each instance? Is either so threatening to children's well-being that it should not be carried out?

■ In a study of moral development, a researcher wants to assess children's ability to resist temptation by videotaping their behavior without their knowledge. She promises 7-year-olds an attractive prize for solving difficult puzzles but tells them not to look at a classmate's correct solutions, which are deliberately placed at the back of the room. Telling

SOCIAL ISSUES: EDUCATION

Can Musical Experiences Enhance Intelligence?

In a 1993 experiment, researchers reported that college students who listened to a Mozart sonata for a few minutes just before taking a test of spatial reasoning abilities did better on the test than students who took the test after listening to relaxation instructions or sitting in silence (Rauscher, Shaw, & Ky, 1993). Strains of Mozart, the investigators concluded, seem to induce changes in the brain that "warm up" neural connections, thereby improving thinking. But the gain in performance, widely publicized as the "Mozart effect," lasted only 15 minutes and proved difficult to replicate. Rather than involving a real change in ability, Mozart seemed to improve arousal and mood, yielding better concentration on the test (Schellenberg et al., 2007).

Despite mounting evidence that the Mozart effect was uncertain at best, the media and politicians were enthralled with the idea that a brief exposure of the brain to classical music in infancy, when neural connections are forming rapidly, might yield lifelong intellectual

benefits. For a time, the states of Georgia, Tennessee, and South Dakota provided free classical music CDs for every newborn baby leaving the hospital. Yet no studies of the Mozart effect have ever been conducted on infants! And an experiment with school-age children failed to yield any intellectual gains as a result of simply listening to music (McKelvie & Low, 2002).

Research suggests that to produce lasting gains in mental test scores, interventions must be long-lasting and involve children's active participation. Consequently, Glenn Schellenberg (2004) wondered, Can music lessons enhance intelligence? Children who take music lessons must practice regularly, engage in extended focused attention, read music, memorize lengthy musical passages, understand diverse musical structures, and master technical skills. These experiences might foster cognitive processing, particularly during childhood, when regions of the brain are taking on specialized functions and are highly sensitive to environmental influences.

Schellenberg recruited 132 6-year-olds—children just old enough for formal lessons. First, the children took an intelligence test and were rated on social maturity, permitting the researchers to see whether music lessons would affect some aspects of development but not others. Next, the children were randomly assigned to one of four experimental conditions. Two were music groups; one received piano lessons and the other voice lessons. The third group took drama lessons—a condition that shed light on whether intellectual gains were unique to musical experiences. The fourth group—a no-lessons control—was offered music lessons the following year. All music and drama instruction took place at the prestigious Royal Conservatory of Music in Toronto, where experienced teachers taught the children in small groups. After 36 weeks of lessons, a longitudinal follow-up was conducted: The children's intelligence and social maturity were assessed again.

■ Children who take music lessons over many weeks gain in mental test performance compared to children who take drama lessons or who receive no lessons at all. To make music, children must engage in diverse intellectually challenging activities: reading musical notation, memorizing lengthy passages, analyzing musical structures, and mastering technical skills. ■

All four groups gained in mental test performance, probably because the participants had just entered grade school, which usually leads to an increase in intelligence test scores. But the two music groups consistently gained more than the drama and no-lesson control groups (see Figure 1.9). Their advantage, though just a few points, extended across many mental abilities, including verbal and spatial skills and speed of thinking. At the same time, only the drama group improved in social maturity.

In sum, active, sustained musical experiences can lead to small increases in intelligence among 6-year-olds that do not arise from comparable drama lessons. But other enrichment activities with similar properties, such as reading, science, math, and chess programs, may confer similar benefits. All demand that children invest far more time and effort than they would in listening to a Mozart sonata. Nevertheless—despite absence of evidence to support their claims—music companies persist in selling CDs entitled "Tune Your Brain with Mozart," "Music for Accelerating Learning," and "Mozart for Newborns: A Bright Beginning."

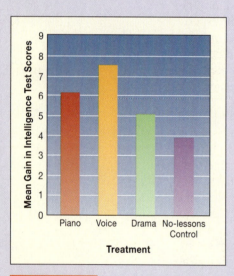

FIGURE 1.9

Music lessons promote gains in intelligence. In a study that combined experimental and longitudinal research strategies, children's mental test performance was tracked longitudinally, before and after they experienced one of four conditions: (1) piano lessons, (2) voice lessons, (3) drama lessons, or (4) no lessons. Children in the two groups receiving music lessons showed greater gains in test scores.

TABLE 1.6   Children's Research Rights

RESEARCH RIGHT	DESCRIPTION
Protection from harm	Children have the right to be protected from physical or psychological harm in research. If in doubt about the harmful effects of research, investigators should seek the opinion of others. When harm seems possible, investigators should find other means for obtaining the desired information or abandon the research.
Informed consent	All research participants, including children, have the right to have explained to them, in language appropriate to their level of understanding, all aspects of the research that may affect their willingness to participate. When children are participants, informed consent of parents as well as others who act on the child's behalf (such as school officials) should be obtained, preferably in writing. Children, and the adults responsible for them, have the right to discontinue participation in the research at any time.
Privacy	Children have the right to concealment of their identity on all information collected in the course of research. They also have this right with respect to written reports and any informal discussions about the research.
Knowledge of results	Children have the right to be informed of the results of research in language that is appropriate to their level of understanding.
Beneficial treatments	If experimental treatments believed to be beneficial are under investigation, children in control groups have the right to alternative beneficial treatments if they are available.

Sources: American Psychological Association, 2002; Society for Research in Child Development, 2007.

children ahead of time that cheating is being studied or that their behavior is being monitored will defeat the purpose of the study.

■ A researcher is interviewing fifth graders about their experiences with bullying. A girl describes frequent name-calling and derogatory comments by her older sister. Although the girl is unhappy, she wants to handle the problem on her own. If the researcher alerts the girl's parents to provide protection and help, he will violate his promise to keep participants' responses private.

Did you find it difficult to evaluate these examples? Virtually every organization that has devised ethical principles for research has concluded that conflicts arising in research situations do not have simple right or wrong answers. The ultimate responsibility for the ethical integrity of research lies with the investigator. But researchers are advised—and often required—to seek advice from others. Committees for this purpose exist in colleges, universities, and other institutions. These *institutional review boards (IRBs)* balance the costs of the research to participants in terms of time, stress, and inconvenience against the study's value for advancing knowledge and improving conditions of life. If any risks to the safety and welfare of participants outweigh the worth of the research, then preference is always given to the interests of the participants.

The ethical principle of *informed consent* requires special interpretation when participants cannot fully appreciate the research goals and activities. Parental consent is meant to protect the safety of children whose ability to decide is not yet mature. In addition, researchers should obtain the agreement of other individuals who act on children's behalf, such as institutional officials when research is conducted in schools, child-care centers, or hospitals. This is especially important when research includes special groups, such as abused children, whose parents may not always represent their best interests (Fisher, 1993; Thompson, 1990).

As soon as children are old enough to appreciate the purpose of the research, and certainly by 7 years of age, their own informed consent should be obtained in addition to parental consent. Around age 7, changes in children's thinking permit them to better understand basic scientific principles and the needs of others. Researchers should respect and enhance these capacities by giving school-age children a full explanation of research activities in language

© STOCKBYTE/GETTY IMAGES

■ Although this 10-year-old responds to the interviewer's questions, she may not know why she is being interviewed, or realize that she has the right to withdraw from the study without negative consequences. Because children have difficulty understanding the research process, extra steps must be taken to protect their research rights. ■

they can understand (Fisher, 1993). Extra care must be taken when telling children that the information they provide will be kept confidential and that they can end their participation at any time. Even adolescents may not understand, and sometimes do not believe, these promises (Bruzzese & Fisher, 2003; Ondrusek et al., 1998). And in certain ethnic minority communities, where deference to authority, maintaining pleasant relationships, and meeting the needs of a guest (the researcher) are highly valued, children and parents may be particularly likely to consent when they would rather not do so (Fisher et al., 2002).

Careful attention to informed consent helps resolve dilemmas about revealing children's responses to parents, teachers, or other authorities when those responses suggest that the child's welfare is in danger. Children can be told in advance that if they report that someone is harming them, the researcher will tell an appropriate adult to take action to ensure the child's safety (Mishna, Antle, & Regehr, 2004).

Finally, young children rely on a basic faith in adults to feel secure in unfamiliar situations. For this reason, they may find some types of research particularly disturbing. All ethical guidelines advise that special precautions be taken in the use of deception and concealment, as occurs when researchers observe children from behind one-way mirrors, give them false feedback about their performance, or do not tell them the truth regarding what the research is about. When these procedures are used with adults, *debriefing,* in which the researcher provides a full account and justification of the activities, occurs after the research session is over. Debriefing should also be done with children, and it sometimes works well. But young children often lack the cognitive skills to understand the reasons for deceptive procedures, and, despite explanations, they may leave the research situation questioning the honesty of adults. Ethical standards permit deception in research with children if investigators satisfy IRBs that such practices are necessary. Nevertheless, because deception may have serious emotional consequences for some youngsters, many child development specialists believe that researchers should use it only if the risk of harm is minimal.

ASK YOURSELF

◆ **REVIEW** Explain how cohort effects can distort the findings of both longitudinal and cross-sectional studies. How does the sequential design reveal cohort effects?

◆ **APPLY** A researcher compares children who went to summer leadership camps with children who attended athletic camps. She finds that those who attended leadership camps are friendlier. Should the investigator tell parents that sending children to leadership camps will cause them to be more sociable? Why or why not?

◆ **CONNECT** Review the experiment on music lessons and intelligence reported in the Social Issues: Education box on page 44. Why was it ethically important for the researchers to offer music lessons to the no-lessons control group during the year after completion of the study? (*Hint:* Refer to Table 1.6. onpage 45)

◆ **REFLECT** Suppose a researcher asks you to enroll your baby in a 10-year longitudinal study. What factors would lead you to agree and to stay involved? Do your answers shed light on why longitudinal studies often have biased samples? Explain.

Summary

The Field of Child Development

What is the field of child development, and what factors stimulated its expansion?

- **Child development** is an area of study devoted to understanding constancy and change from conception through adolescence. It is part of a larger interdisciplinary field known as **developmental science,** which includes all changes we experience throughout the lifespan. Research on child development has been stimulated both by scientific curiosity and by social pressures to better children's lives.

How can we divide child development into sensible, manageable periods and domains?

- Development is often divided into physical, cognitive, and emotional and social domains. These domains are not really distinct; rather, they combine in an integrated, holistic fashion.

- Researchers generally divide the flow of time into the following age periods: (1) the prenatal period (conception to birth), (2) infancy and toddlerhood (birth to 2 years), (3) early childhood (2 to 6 years), (4) middle childhood (6 to 11 years), and (5) adolescence (11 to 18 years). To describe the prolonged transition to adulthood typical of contemporary young people in industrialized nations, researchers have posited a new period of development, emerging adulthood, spanning ages 18 to 25.

Basic Issues

Identify three basic issues on which theories of child development take a stand.

- Each **theory** of child development takes a stand on three fundamental issues: (1) Is development a **continuous** process, or is it **discontinuous,** following a series of distinct **stages?** (2) Does one general course of development characterize all children, or are there many possible courses, influenced by the distinct **contexts** in which children grow up? (3) Are genetic or environmental factors more important in influencing development (the **nature–nurture controversy**), and are individual differences stable or characterized by substantial **plasticity?**

- Recent theories take a balanced stand on these issues. And contemporary researchers realize that answers may vary across domains of development and even, as research on **resilience** illustrates, across individuals.

Historical Foundations

Describe major historical influences on modern theories of child development.

- As early as medieval times, the sixth through the fifteenth centuries, childhood was regarded as a separate phase of life.

- In the sixteenth and seventeenth centuries, the Puritan conception of original sin led to a harsh philosophy of child rearing. The seventeenth-century Enlightenment brought a new emphasis on human dignity and respect that led to more humane views of childhood. Locke's notion of the child as a tabula rasa ("blank slate") provided the basis for twentieth-century behaviorism, while Rousseau's idea that children were noble savages foreshadowed the concepts of stage and **maturation.**

- Inspired by Darwin's theory of evolution, efforts to observe the child directly began in the late nineteenth and early twentieth centuries. Soon after, Hall and Gesell introduced the **normative approach,** which produced a large body of descriptive facts about children. Binet and Simon constructed the first successful intelligence test, which sparked interest in individual differences in development and led to a heated controversy over nature versus nurture.

Mid-Twentieth-Century Theories

What theories influenced child development research in the mid-twentieth century?

- In the 1930s and 1940s, psychiatrists and social workers turned to the **psychoanalytic perspective** for help in treating children's emotional problems. In Freud's **psychosexual theory,** children move through five stages, during which three portions of the personality—id, ego, and superego—become integrated.

- Erikson's **psychosocial theory** builds on Freud's theory, emphasizing the development of culturally relevant attitudes and skills and—with the addition of three adult stages—the lifespan nature of development. Despite its extensive contributions, the psychoanalytic perspective is no longer in the mainstream of child development research.

- As the psychoanalytic perspective gained in prominence, **behaviorism** emerged, focusing on directly observable events (stimuli and responses) in an effort to create an objective science of psychology. B. F. Skinner's operant conditioning theory emphasizes the role of reinforcement and punishment in increasing or decreasing the frequency of behaviors.

- A related approach, Albert Bandura's **social learning theory,** focuses on modeling as the major means through which children and adults acquire new responses. Its most recent revision stresses the role of cognition, or thinking, in children's imitation and learning and, therefore, is known as a social-cognitive approach.

- Behaviorism and social learning theory gave rise to techniques of **behavior modification** to eliminate undesirable behaviors and increase desirable responses.

■ Piaget's **cognitive-developmental theory** emphasizes that children actively construct knowledge as they move through four stages, beginning with the baby's sensorimotor action patterns and ending with the abstract, systematic reasoning system of the adolescent and adult. Piaget's work has stimulated a wealth of research on children's thinking and has encouraged educational programs that emphasize children's discovery learning.

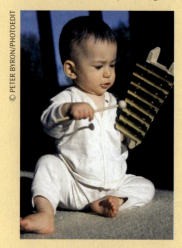

Recent Theoretical Perspectives

Describe recent theoretical perspectives on child development.

■ **Information processing** views the mind as a complex symbol-manipulating system, much like a computer. This approach helps investigators achieve a detailed understanding of what children of different ages do when faced with tasks and problems.

■ Over the past three decades, researchers in **developmental cognitive neuroscience** have begun to study the relationship between changes in the brain and the developing child's cognitive processing and behavior patterns. They have made progress in identifying the types of experiences to which the brain is sensitive at various ages and in clarifying the brain bases of many learning and behavior disorders.

■ Four contemporary perspectives emphasize contexts for development. **Ethology,** which stresses the adaptive value and evolutionary history of behavior, inspired the **sensitive period** concept. In a new area of research called **evolutionary developmental psychology,** researchers have extended this emphasis, seeking to understand the adaptiveness of species-wide competencies as they change over time.

■ Vygotsky's **sociocultural theory,** which focuses on how culture is transmitted from one generation to the net through social interaction, views cognitive development as a socially mediated process. Through cooperative dialogues with more expert members of society, children come to use language to guide their own thought and actions and acquire culturally relevant knowledge and skills..

■ **Ecological systems theory** views the child as developing within a complex system of relationships affected by multiple, nested layers of the surrounding environment—**microsystem, mesosystem, exosystem,** and **macrosystem.** Each of these levels is seen as a major influence on children's well-being. The **chronosystem** represents the dynamic, ever-changing nature of children and their experiences.

■ A new wave of theorists has adopted a **dynamic systems perspective** to better understand how children alter their behavior to attain more advanced functioning. According to this view, the mind, body, and physical and social worlds form an integrated system that guides mastery of new skills. A change in any part of the system prompts the child to reorganize her behavior so the various components work together again but in a more complex, effective way.

Comparing Child Development Theories

Identify the stand taken by each major theory on the basic issues of child development.

■ Theories that are major forces in child development research vary in their focus on different domains of development, in their view of how development occurs, and in their strengths and weaknesses. (For a full summary, see Table 1.3 on page 30.)

Studying the Child

Describe methods commonly used to gather information on children.

■ **Naturalistic observations,** which are gathered in everyday environments, permit researchers to see directly the everyday behaviors they hope to explain. In contrast, **structured observations** take place in laboratories, where every participant has an equal opportunity to display the behaviors of interest.

■ Self-report methods can be flexible and open-ended like the **clinical interview,** which permits participants to express their thoughts in ways similar to their thinking in everyday life. Alternatively, **structured interviews,** tests, and questionnaires are more efficient and permit researchers to specify activities and behaviors that participants might not think of in an open-ended interview.

■ Investigators use the **clinical,** or **case study, method** to obtain an in-depth understanding of a single child. It involves synthesizing a wide range of information, including interviews, observations, and sometimes test scores.

■ Researchers have adapted observational and self-report methods to permit direct comparisons of cultures. To uncover the cultural meanings of behavior, they rely on **ethnography,** engaging in participant observation.

Distinguish between correlational and experimental research designs, noting the strengths and limitations of each.

■ The **correlational design** examines relationships between variables, generally as they occur in natural life circumstances, without altering participants' experiences. The **correlation coefficient** describes how two measures, or variables, are associated with one another. Correlational studies do not permit inferences about cause and effect, but they can be helpful in identifying relationships that are worth exploring with a more powerful experimental strategy.

■ An **experimental design** permits inferences about cause and effect. Researchers manipulate an **independent variable** by exposing participants to two or more treatment conditions. Then they determine what effect this variable has on a **dependent variable. Random assignment** reduces the chances that characteristics of participants will affect the accuracy of experimental findings.

■ Field and natural, or quasi-, experiments compare treatments in natural environments. However, these approaches are less rigorous than laboratory experiments.

Describe designs for studying development, noting the strengths and limitations of each.

■ In a **longitudinal design,** participants are studied repeatedly at different ages, revealing common patterns as well as individual differences in development and the relationship between early and later events and behaviors. Longitudinal research poses several problems, including biased sampling, selective attrition, and **cohort effects**—difficulty generalizing to children developing at other historical times, or to children who did not experience a specific event.

■ The **cross-sectional design,** in which groups of children differing in age are studied at the same point in time, offers an efficient approach to investigating development. However, it is limited to comparisons of age-group averages. Cross-sectional studies, especially those that cover a wide age span, are also vulnerable to cohort effects.

■ By comparing participants of the same age who were born in different years, investigators use **sequential designs** to find out if cohort effects are operating. When sequential designs combine longitudinal and cross-sectional strategies, researchers can see if outcomes are similar, for added confidence in their findings.

■ In the **microgenetic design,** researchers track change as it occurs for unique insights into processes of development. However, the time required for children to change is hard to anticipate, and practice effects can bias findings.

■ When researchers combine experimental and developmental designs, they can examine causal influences on development. This combined strategy is increasingly common today.

What special ethical concerns arise in doing research on children?

■ Because of their immaturity, children are especially vulnerable to harm and often cannot evaluate the risks and benefits of research. Ethical guidelines and institutional review boards that weigh the risks and benefits of research help ensure that children's research rights are protected.

■ Besides obtaining consent from parents and others who act on children's behalf, researchers should seek the informed consent of children 7 years and older. The use of deception in research with children is especially risky because it may undermine their basic faith in the honesty of adults.

IMPORTANT TERMS AND CONCEPTS

behaviorism (p. 17)
behavior modification (p. 18)
child development (p. 4)
chronosystem (p. 27)
clinical interview (p. 33)
clinical, or case study, method (p. 34)
cognitive-developmental theory (p. 19)
cohort effects (p. 41)
contexts (p. 8)
continuous development (p. 7)
correlational design (p. 37)
correlation coefficient (p. 37)
cross-sectional design (p. 41)
dependent variable (p. 37)
developmental cognitive neuroscience (p. 23)
developmental science (p. 4)
discontinuous development (p. 8)

dynamic systems perspective (p. 28)
ecological systems theory (p. 25)
ethnography (p. 34)
ethology (p. 23)
evolutionary developmental psychology (p. 24)
exosystem (p. 27)
experimental design (p. 37)
independent variable (p. 37)
information processing (p. 21)
longitudinal design (p. 40)
macrosystem (p. 27)
maturation (p. 13)
mesosystem (p. 26)
microgenetic design (p. 43)
microsystem (p. 26)
naturalistic observation (p. 31)

nature–nurture controversy (p. 9)
normative approach (p. 13)
plasticity (p. 9)
psychoanalytic perspective (p. 15)
psychosexual theory (p. 15)
psychosocial theory (p. 15)
random assignment (p. 38)
resilience (p. 10)
sensitive period (p. 23)
sequential design (p. 42)
social learning theory (p. 18)
sociocultural theory (p. 24)
stage (p. 8)
structured interview (p. 33)
structured observation (p. 31)
theory (p. 7)

Untitled

Mohamed Salahedeen Abd Hamid

11 years, Egypt

A river flows past a city on one shore and a grassy bank on the other. Animals, birds, vehicles, and people are all part of the complexity of our world. Chapter 2 addresses a similarly complex blend of forces—genetic, family, neighborhood, school, and culture—that influence child development.

Reprinted with permission from the International Museum of Children's Art, Oslo, Norway

Genetic and Environmental Foundations

Genetic Foundations

The Genetic Code • The Sex Cells • Boy or Girl? • Multiple Births • Patterns of Genetic Inheritance • Chromosomal Abnormalities

Reproductive Choices

Genetic Counseling • Prenatal Diagnosis and Fetal Medicine • The Alternative of Adoption

■ **SOCIAL ISSUES: HEALTH**
The Pros and Cons of Reproductive Technologies

Environmental Contexts for Development

The Family • Socioeconomic Status and Family Functioning • Affluence • Poverty • Beyond the Family: Neighborhoods and Schools • The Cultural Context

■ **SOCIAL ISSUES: EDUCATION**
Worldwide Education of Girls: Transforming Current and Future Generations

■ **CULTURAL INFLUENCES**
The African-American Extended Family

Understanding the Relationship Between Heredity and Environment

The Question, "How Much?" • The Question, "How?"

■ **BIOLOGY AND ENVIRONMENT**
A Case of Epigenesis: Smoking During Pregnancy Alters Gene Expression

"*I*t's a girl!" announces the doctor, holding up the squalling newborn baby as her parents gaze with amazement at their miraculous creation.

"A girl! We've named her Sarah!" exclaims the proud father to eager relatives waiting for news of their new family member.

As we join these parents in thinking about how this wondrous being came into existence and imagining her future, we are struck by many questions. How could this baby, equipped with everything necessary for life outside the womb, have developed from the union of two tiny cells? What ensures that Sarah will, in due time, roll over, reach for objects, walk, talk, make friends, learn, imagine, and create—just like other typical children born before her? Why is she a girl and not a boy, dark-haired rather than blond, calm and cuddly instead of wiry and energetic? What difference will it make that Sarah is given a name and place in one family, community, nation, and culture rather than another?

To answer these questions, this chapter takes a close look at the foundations of development: heredity and environment. Because nature has prepared us for survival, all humans have features in common. Yet each of us is also unique. **TAKE A MOMENT...** Think about several children you know well, and jot down the most obvious physical and behavioral similarities between them and their parents. Did you find that one child shows combined features of both parents, another resembles just one parent, whereas a third is not like either parent? These directly observable characteristics are called **phenotypes.** They depend in part on the individual's **genotype**—the complex blend of genetic information that determines our species and influences all our unique characteristics. Yet phenotypes are also affected by each person's lifelong history of experiences.

We begin our discussion at the moment of conception, an event that establishes the hereditary makeup of the new individual. First we review basic genetic principles that help explain similarities and differences among children in appearance and behavior. Then we turn to aspects of the environment that play powerful roles in children's lives. As our discussion proceeds, some findings about the influence of nature and nurture may surprise you. For example, many people believe that when children inherit unfavorable characteristics, not much can be done to help them. Others are convinced that the damage done to a child by a harmful environment can easily be corrected. As we will see, neither of these assumptions is true. In the final section of this chapter, we consider how nature and nurture *work together* to shape the course of development.

Genetic Foundations

Each of us is made up of trillions of units called *cells*. Within every cell (except red blood cells) is a control center, or *nucleus*, that contains rodlike structures called **chromosomes, which store and transmit genetic information.** Human chromosomes come in 23 matching pairs (an exception is the XY pair in males, which we will discuss shortly). Each member of a pair corresponds to the other in size, shape, and genetic functions. One is inherited from the mother and one from the father (see Figure 2.1).

The Genetic Code

Chromosomes are made up of a chemical substance called **deoxyribonucleic acid** or **DNA.** As Figure 2.2 shows, DNA is a long, double-stranded molecule that looks like a twisted ladder. Each rung of the ladder consists of a pair of chemical substances called *bases*. Although the bases always pair up in the same way across the ladder rungs—A with T and C with G—they can occur in any order along its sides. It is this sequence of base pairs that provides genetic instructions. A **gene** is a segment of DNA along the length of the chromosome. Genes can be of different lengths—perhaps 100 to several thousand ladder rungs long. An estimated 20,000 to 25,000 genes lie along the human chromosomes (Human Genome Program, 2008).

We share some of our genetic makeup with even the simplest organisms, such as bacteria and molds, and most of it with other mammals, especially primates. Between 98 and 99 percent of chimpanzee and human DNA is identical. This means that only a small portion of our heredity is responsible for the traits that make us human, from our upright gait to our extraordinary language and cognitive capacities. And the genetic variation from one human to the next is even less! Individuals around the world are about 99.1 percent genetically identical

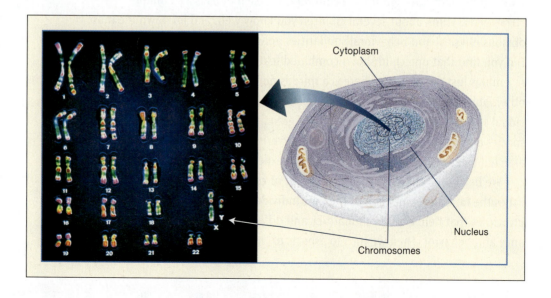

FIGURE 2.1

A karyotype, or photograph, of human chromosomes. The 46 chromosomes shown on the left were isolated from a human cell, stained, greatly magnified, and arranged in pairs according to decreasing size of the upper "arm" of each chromosome. The twenty-third pair, XY, reveals that the cell donor is a male. In a female, this pair would be XX. *(© CNRI/Science Photo Library/Photo Researchers, Inc.)*

Cytoplasm

Nucleus

Chromosomes

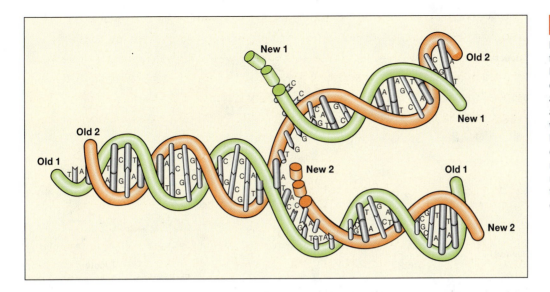

FIGURE 2.2

DNA's ladderlike structure. This figure shows that the pairings of bases across the rungs of the ladder are very specific: Adenine (A) always appears with thymine (T), and cytosine (C) always appears with guanine (G). Here, the DNA ladder duplicates by splitting down the middle of its ladder rungs. Each free base picks up a new complementary partner from the area surrounding the cell nucleus.

(Gibbons, 1998; Gibbons et al., 2004). But it takes a change in only a single base pair to influence human traits. And such tiny changes can combine in unique ways across multiple genes, thereby amplifying variability within the human species.

A unique feature of DNA is that it can duplicate itself through a process called **mitosis.** This special ability permits the one-celled fertilized ovum to develop into a complex human being composed of a great many cells. Refer again to Figure 2.2, and you will see that during mitosis, the chromosomes copy themselves. As a result, each new body cell contains the same number of chromosomes and the identical genetic information.

Genes accomplish their task by sending instructions for making a rich assortment of proteins to the *cytoplasm,* the area surrounding the cell nucleus. Proteins, which trigger chemical reactions throughout the body, are the biological foundation on which our characteristics are built. How do humans, with far fewer genes than scientists once thought (only twice as many as the worm or fly), manage to develop into such complex beings? The answer lies in the proteins our genes make, which break up and reassemble in staggering variety—about 10 to 20 million altogether. Simpler species have far fewer proteins. Furthermore, the communication system between the cell nucleus and cytoplasm, which fine-tunes gene activity, is more intricate in humans than in simpler organisms. Within the cell, a wide range of environmental factors modify gene expression (Lashley, 2007). So even at this microscopic level, biological events are the result of *both* genetic and nongenetic forces.

The Sex Cells

New individuals are created when two special cells called **gametes,** or sex cells—the sperm and ovum—combine. A gamete contains only 23 chromosomes, half as many as a regular body cell. Gametes are formed through a cell division process called **meiosis,** which halves the number of chromosomes normally present in body cells. When sperm and ovum unite at conception, the resulting cell, called a **zygote,** will again have 46 chromosomes. Meiosis ensures that a constant quantity of genetic material is transmitted from one generation to the next.

The steps involved in meiosis are shown in Figure 2.3 on page 54. First, the chromosomes pair up, and each one copies itself. Then a special event called **crossing over** occurs, in which chromosomes next to each other break at one or more points along their length and exchange segments, so that genes from one are replaced by genes from another. This shuffling of genes creates new hereditary combinations. Next, the chromosome pairs separate into different cells, but chance determines which member of each pair will gather with others and end up in the same gamete. Finally, each chromosome leaves its partner and becomes part of a gamete containing only 23 chromosomes instead of the usual 46.

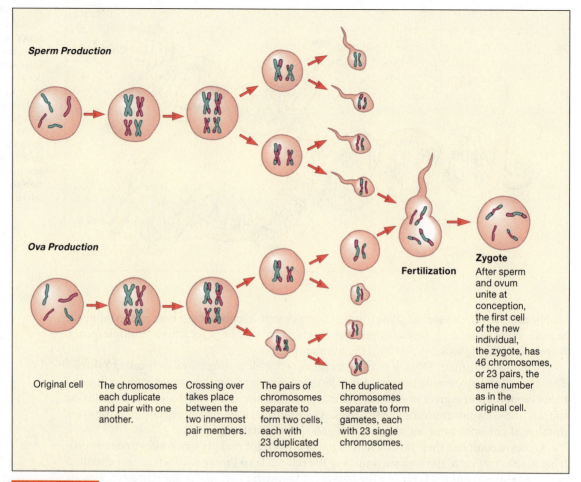

FIGURE 2.3

The cell division process of meiosis, leading to gamete formation. (Here, original cells are depicted with two rather than the full complement of 23 pairs.) Meiosis creates gametes with only half the usual number of chromosomes. When sperm and ovum unite at conception, the first cell of the new individual (the zygote) has the correct, full number of chromosomes.

These events make the likelihood extremely low—about 1 in 700 trillion—that nontwin siblings will be genetically identical (Gould & Keeton, 1996). The genetic variability produced by meiosis is adaptive: Because it generates offspring that vary in phenotype, it increases the chances that at least some members of a species will cope successfully with ever-changing environments and will survive.

In the male, four sperm are produced when meiosis is complete. Also, the cells from which sperm arise are produced continuously throughout life. For this reason, a healthy man can father a child at any age after sexual maturity. In the female, meiosis results in just one ovum; the remaining genetic material degenerates. In addition, the female is born with all her ova already present in her ovaries, and she can bear children for only three to four decades. Still, there are plenty of female sex cells. About 1 to 2 million are present at birth, 40,000 remain at adolescence, and approximately 350 to 450 will mature during a woman's childbearing years (Moore & Persaud, 2008).

Boy or Girl?

Return to Figure 2.1 on page 52, and note the 22 matching pairs of chromosomes, which geneticists number from longest (1) to shortest (22). These are called **autosomes** (meaning *not* sex chromosomes). The twenty-third pair consists of **sex chromosomes.** In females, this pair is called XX; in males, it is called XY. The X is a relatively large chromosome, whereas the Y is short and carries little genetic material. When gametes form in males, the X and Y chromosomes separate into different sperm cells. The gametes that form in females all carry an X chromosome. Therefore, the sex of the new organism is determined by whether an X-bearing or a Y-bearing sperm fertilizes the ovum. In fact, scientists have isolated a gene on the Y chromosome that initiates the formation of male sex organs during the prenatal period. But they also know that other genes, some yet to be discovered, are involved in the development of sexual characteristics (Bhagavath & Layman, 2007; Sekido & Lovell-Badge, 2009).

Multiple Births

Ruth and Peter, a couple I know well, tried for several years to have a child, without success. When Ruth reached age 33, her doctor prescribed a fertility drug, and Ruth gave birth to twins—Jeannie and Jason. Jeannie and Jason are **fraternal,** or **dizygotic, twins,** the most common type of multiple birth, resulting from the release and fertilization of two ova. Genetically, they are no more alike than ordinary siblings. Table 2.1 summarizes genetic and environmental factors that increase the chances of giving birth to fraternal twins. Older maternal age, fertility drugs, and in vitro fertilization (to be discussed shortly) are major causes of the dramatic rise in fraternal twinning and other multiple births in industrialized nations over the past several decades (Machin, 2005; Russell et al., 2003). Currently, fraternal twins account for 1 in about every 60 births in the United States (U.S. Department of Health and Human Services, 2010c).

Twins can be created in another way. Sometimes a zygote that has started to duplicate separates into two clusters of cells that develop into two individuals. These are called **identical,** or **monozygotic, twins** because they have the same genetic makeup. The frequency of identical twins is the same around the world—about 1 in every 330 births (Hall, 2003). Animal research has uncovered a variety of environmental influences that prompt this type of twinning, including temperature changes, variation in oxygen levels, and late fertilization of the ovum. In a minority of cases, the identical twinning runs in families, suggesting a genetic influence (Lashley, 2007).

During their early years, children of single births often are healthier and develop more rapidly than twins. Jeannie and Jason, like most twins, were born early—three weeks

© RACHEL EPSTEIN/PHOTOEDIT

■ These identical, or monozygotic, twins were created when a duplicating zygote separated into two clusters of cells and developed into two individuals with the same genetic makeup. Identical twins look alike, and as we will see later in this chapter, tend to resemble each other in a variety of psychological characteristics. ■

TABLE 2.1 Maternal Factors Linked to Fraternal Twinning

FACTOR	DESCRIPTION
Ethnicity	Occurs in 4 per 1,000 births among Asians, 8 per 1,000 births among whites, 12 to 16 per 1,000 births among blacks[a]
Family history of twinning	Occurs more often among women whose mothers and sisters gave birth to fraternal twins
Age	Rises with maternal age, peaking between 35 and 39 years, and then rapidly falls
Nutrition	Occurs less often among women with poor diets; occurs more often among women who are tall and overweight or of normal weight as opposed to slight body build
Number of births	Is more likely with each additional birth
Fertility drugs and in vitro fertilization	Is more likely with fertility hormones and in vitro fertilization (see pages 66–67), which also increase the chances of bearing triplets, quadruplets, or quintuplets

[a] Worldwide rates, not including multiple births resulting from use of fertility drugs.

Sources: Hall, 2003; Hoekstra et al., 2008; Lashley, 2007.

before Ruth's due date. And, like other premature infants, as you will see in Chapter 4, they required special care after birth. When the twins came home from the hospital, Ruth and Peter had to divide time between them. Perhaps because neither baby got quite as much attention as the average single infant, Jeannie and Jason walked and talked several months later than most other children their age, although both caught up in development by middle childhood (Lytton & Gallagher, 2002). Parental energies are further strained after the birth of triplets, whose early development is slower than that of twins (Feldman, Eidelman, & Rotenberg, 2004).

Patterns of Genetic Inheritance

Jeannie has her parents' dark, straight hair, whereas Jason is curly-haired and blond. Patterns of genetic inheritance—the way genes from each parent interact—explain these outcomes. Recall that except for the XY pair in males, all chromosomes come in corresponding pairs. Two forms of each gene occur at the same place on the chromosomes, one inherited from the mother and one from the father. Each form of a gene is called an **allele.** If the alleles from both parents are alike, the child is **homozygous** and will display the inherited trait. If the alleles are different, the child is **heterozygous,** and relationships between the alleles determine the phenotype.

DOMINANT–RECESSIVE INHERITANCE In many heterozygous pairings, **dominant–recessive inheritance** occurs: Only one allele affects the child's characteristics. It is called *dominant;* the second allele, which has no effect, is called *recessive.* Hair color is an example. The allele for dark hair is dominant (we can represent it with a capital *D*), whereas the one for blond hair is recessive (symbolized by a lowercase *b*). A child who inherits a homozygous pair of dominant alleles *(DD)* and a child who inherits a heterozygous pair *(Db)* will both be dark-haired, even though their genotypes differ. Blond hair (like Jason's) can result only from having two recessive alleles *(bb)*. Still, heterozygous individuals with just one recessive allele *(Db)* can pass that trait to their children. Therefore, they are called **carriers** of the trait.

Some human characteristics that follow the rules of dominant–recessive inheritance are listed in Table 2.2 and Table 2.3 on page 58. As you can see, many disabilities and diseases are the product of recessive alleles. One of the most frequently occurring recessive disorders is *phenylketonuria,* or *PKU*. It affects the way the body breaks down proteins contained in many foods. Infants born with two recessive alleles lack an enzyme that converts one of the basic amino acids that make up proteins (phenylalanine) into a byproduct essential for body functioning (tyrosine). Without this enzyme, phenylalanine quickly builds to toxic levels that damage the central nervous system. By 1 year, infants with PKU are permanently retarded.

Despite its potentially damaging effects, PKU provides an excellent illustration of the fact that inheriting unfavorable genes does not always lead to an untreatable condition. All U.S. states require that each newborn be given a blood test for PKU. If the disease is found, doctors place the baby on a diet low in phenylalanine. Children who receive this treatment nevertheless show mild deficits in certain cognitive skills, such as memory, planning, decision making, and problem solving, because even small amounts of phenylalanine interfere with brain functioning (Anderson et al., 2007; Christ et al., 2006; DeRoche & Welsh, 2008). But as long as dietary treatment begins early and continues, children with PKU usually attain an average level of intelligence and have a normal lifespan.

TABLE 2.2 Examples of Dominant and Recessive Characteristics

DOMINANT	RECESSIVE
Dark hair	Blond hair
Normal hair	Pattern baldness
Curly hair	Straight hair
Nonred hair	Red hair
Facial dimples	No dimples
Normal hearing	Some forms of deafness
Normal vision	Nearsightedness
Farsightedness	Normal vision
Normal vision	Congenital eye cataracts
Normally pigmented skin	Albinism
Double-jointedness	Normal joints
Type A blood	Type O blood
Type B blood	Type O blood
Rh-positive blood	Rh-negative blood

Note: Many normal characteristics that were previously thought to be due to dominant–recessive inheritance, such as eye color, are now regarded as due to multiple genes. For the characteristics listed here, there still seems to be general agreement that the simple dominant–recessive relationship holds.

Source: McKusick, 2007.

In dominant–recessive inheritance, if we know the genetic makeup of the parents, we can predict the percentage of children in a family who are likely to display or carry a trait. Figure 2.4 illustrates this for PKU. For a child to inherit the condition, each parent must have a recessive allele *(p)*. As the figure also illustrates, a single gene can affect more than one trait. Because of their inability to convert phenylalanine into tyrosine (which is responsible for pigmentation), children with PKU usually have light hair and blue eyes. Furthermore, children vary in the degree to which phenylalanine accumulates in their tissues and in the extent to which they respond to treatment. This is due to the action of **modifier genes,** which enhance or dilute the effects of other genes.

Only rarely are serious diseases due to dominant alleles. Think about why this is so. Children who inherit the dominant allele always develop the disorder. They seldom live long enough to reproduce, so the harmful dominant allele is eliminated from the family's heredity in a single generation. Some dominant disorders, however, do persist. One is *Huntington disease,* a condition in which the central nervous system degenerates. Why has this disorder endured? Its symptoms usually do not appear until age 35 or later, after the person has passed the dominant allele to his or her children.

INCOMPLETE DOMINANCE
In some heterozygous circumstances, the dominant–recessive relationship does not hold completely. Instead, we see **incomplete dominance,** a pattern of inheritance in which both alleles are expressed in the phenotype, resulting in a combined trait, or one that is intermediate between the two.

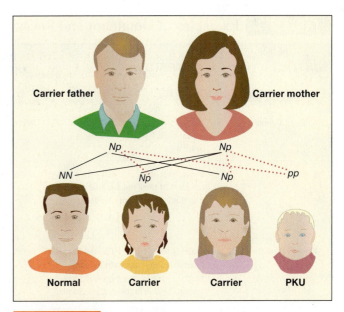

FIGURE 2.4

Dominant–recessive mode of inheritance, as illustrated by PKU. When both parents are heterozygous carriers of the recessive gene *(p)*, we can predict that 25 percent of their offspring are likely to be normal *(NN),* 50 percent are likely to be carriers *(Np),* and 25 percent are likely to inherit the disorder *(pp)*. Notice that the PKU-affected child, in contrast to his siblings, has light hair. The recessive gene for PKU affects more than one trait. It also leads to fair coloring.

The *sickle cell trait,* a heterozygous condition present in many black Africans, provides an example. *Sickle cell anemia* (see Table 2.3) occurs in full form when a child inherits two recessive alleles. They cause the usually round red blood cells to become sickle (crescent-moon) shaped, especially under low-oxygen conditions. The sickled cells clog the blood vessels and block the flow of blood, causing intense pain, swelling, and tissue damage. Despite medical advances that today allow 85 percent of affected children to survive to adulthood, North Americans with sickle cell anemia have a life expectancy of only 55 years (Driscoll, 2007). Heterozygous individuals are protected from the disease under most circumstances. However, when they experience oxygen deprivation—for example, at high altitudes or after intense physical exercise—the single recessive allele asserts itself, and a temporary, mild form of the illness occurs.

The sickle cell allele is common among black Africans for a special reason. Carriers of it are more resistant to malaria than are individuals with two alleles for normal red blood cells. In Africa, where malaria is common, these carriers have survived and reproduced more frequently than others, leading the gene to be maintained in the black population. But in regions of the world where the risk of malaria is low, the frequency of the gene is declining. For example, only 8 percent of African Americans are carriers, compared with 20 percent of black Africans (National Center for Biotechnology Information, 2007).

X-LINKED INHERITANCE
Males and females have an equal chance of inheriting recessive disorders carried on the autosomes, such as PKU and sickle cell anemia. But when a harmful allele is carried on the X chromosome, **X-linked inheritance** applies. Males are more likely to be affected because their sex chromosomes do not match. In females, any recessive allele on one X chromosome has a good chance of being suppressed by a dominant allele on the other X. But the Y chromosome is only about one-third as long and therefore lacks many corresponding alleles to override those on the X. A well-known example is *hemophilia,* a disorder in which the

TABLE 2.3 Examples of Dominant and Recessive Diseases

DISEASE	DESCRIPTION	MODE OF INHERITANCE	INCIDENCE	TREATMENT
AUTOSOMAL DISEASES				
Cooley's anemia	Pale appearance, retarded physical growth, and lethargic behavior begin in infancy.	Recessive	1 in 500 births to parents of Mediterranean descent	Frequent blood transfusions. Death from complications usually occurs by adolescence.
Cystic fibrosis	Lungs, liver, and pancreas secrete large amounts of thick mucus, leading to breathing and digestive difficulties.	Recessive	1 in 2,000 to 2,500 Caucasian births; 1 in 16,000 births to North Americans of African descent	Bronchial drainage, prompt treatment of respiratory infection, dietary management. Advances in medical care allow survival with good life quality into adulthood.
Phenylketonuria (PKU)	Inability to metabolize the amino acid phenylalanine, contained in many proteins, causes severe central nervous system damage in the first year of life.	Recessive	1 in 8,000 births	Placing the child on a special diet results in average intelligence and normal lifespan. Subtle difficulties in memory, planning, decision making, and problem solving are often present.
Sickle cell anemia	Abnormal sickling of red blood cells causes oxygen deprivation, pain, swelling, and tissue damage. Anemia and susceptibility to infections, especially pneumonia, occur.	Recessive	1 in 400 to 600 births to North Americans of African descent	Blood transfusions, painkillers, prompt treatment of infection. No known cure; 50 percent die by age 55.
Tay-Sachs disease	Central nervous system degeneration, with onset at about 6 months, leads to poor muscle tone, blindness, deafness, and convulsions.	Recessive	1 in 3,600 births to Jews of European descent and to French Canadians	None. Death occurs by 3 to 4 years of age.
Huntington disease	Central nervous system degeneration leads to muscular coordination difficulties, mental deterioration, and personality changes. Symptoms usually do not appear until age 35 or later.	Dominant	1 in 18,000 to 25,000 births to North Americans	None. Death occurs 10 to 20 years after symptom onset.
Marfan syndrome	Tall, slender build; thin, elongated arms and legs; and heart defects and eye abnormalities, especially of the lens. Excessive lengthening of the body results in a variety of skeletal defects.	Dominant	1 in 5,000 to 10,000 births	Correction of heart and eye defects sometimes possible. Death from heart failure in early adulthood is common.
X-LINKED DISEASES				
Duchenne muscular dystrophy	Degenerative muscle disease. Abnormal gait, loss of ability to walk between ages 7 and 13 years.	Recessive	1 in 3,000 to 5,000 male births	None. Death from respiratory infection or weakening of the heart muscle usually occurs in adolescence.
Hemophilia	Blood fails to clot normally; can lead to severe internal bleeding and tissue damage.	Recessive	1 in 4,000 to 7,000 male births	Blood transfusions. Safety precautions to prevent injury.
Diabetes insipidus	Insufficient production of the hormone vasopressin results in excessive thirst and urination. Dehydration can cause central nervous system damage.	Recessive	1 in 2,500 male births	Hormone replacement.

Note: For recessive disorders, carrier status can be detected in prospective parents through a blood test or genetic analyses. For all disorders listed, prenatal diagnosis is available (see page 63).

Sources: Kliegman et al., 2008; Lashley, 2007; McKusick, 2007.

blood fails to clot normally. Figure 2.5 shows its greater like-lihood of inheritance by male children whose mothers carry the abnormal allele.

Besides X-linked disorders, many sex differences reveal the male to be at a disadvantage. Rates of miscarriage, infant and childhood deaths, birth defects, learning disabilities, behavior disorders, and mental retardation all are higher for boys (Butler & Meaney, 2005). It is possible that these sex differences can be traced to the genetic code. The female, with two X chromosomes, benefits from a greater variety of genes. Nature, however, seems to have adjusted for the male's disadvantage. Worldwide, about 106 boys are born for every 100 girls, and judging from miscarriage and abor-tion statistics, an even greater number of boys are conceived (United Nations, 2006).

Nevertheless, in recent decades the proportion of male births has declined in many industrialized countries, includ-ing the United States, Canada, and European nations (Jongbloet et al., 2001). Some researchers attribute the trend to a rise in stressful living conditions, which heighten spon-taneous abortions, especially of male fetuses. In a test of this hypothesis, male-to-female birth ratios in East Germany were examined between 1946 and 1999. The ratio was low-est in 1991, the year that the country's economy collapsed (Catalano, 2003). Similarly, in a California study spanning the decade of the 1990s, the percentage of male fetal deaths increased in months in which unemployment (a major stressor) also rose above its typical level (Catalano et al., 2005, 2009).

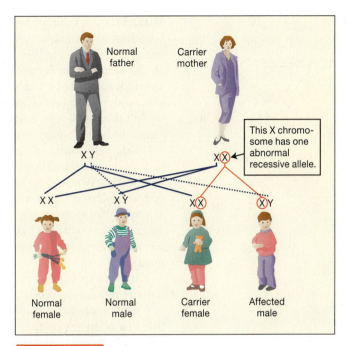

FIGURE 2.5

X-linked inheritance. In the example shown here, the allele on the father's X chromosome is normal. The mother has one normal and one abnormal recessive allele on her X chromosomes. By looking at the possible combinations of the parents' alleles, we can predict that 50 percent of these parents' male children are likely to have the disorder, and 50 percent of their female children are likely to be carriers of it.

GENOMIC IMPRINTING   More than 1,000 human characteristics follow the rules of dominant–recessive and incomplete-dominance inheritance (McKusick, 2007). In these cases, whichever parent contributes a gene to the new individual, the gene responds in the same way. Geneticists, however, have identified some exceptions. In **genomic imprinting,** alleles are *imprinted,* or chemically marked, in such a way that one pair member (either the mother's or the father's) is activated, regardless of its makeup. The imprint is often temporary; it may be erased in the next generation, and it may not occur in all individuals (Everman & Cassidy, 2000).

Imprinting helps us understand certain puzzling genetic patterns. For example, children are more likely to develop diabetes if their father, rather than their mother, suffers from it. And people with asthma or hay fever tend to have mothers, not fathers, with the illness. Imprinting is involved in several childhood cancers and in *Prader-Willi syndrome,* a disorder with symp-toms of mental retardation and severe obesity (Benarroch et al., 2007). It may also explain why Huntington disease, when inherited from the father, tends to emerge at an earlier age and to progress more rapidly (Navarrete, Martinez, & Salamanca, 1994).

Genomic imprinting can also operate on the sex chromosomes, as *fragile X syndrome*—the most common inherited cause of mental retardation—reveals. In this disorder, which affects about 1 in 4,000 males and 1 in 6,000 females, an abnormal repetition of a sequence of DNA bases occurs in a special spot on the X chromosome, damaging a particular gene. The defective gene at the fragile site is expressed only when it is passed from mother to child. Because the dis-order is X-linked, males are more severely affected (Hagerman et al., 2009). Females usually have a normally functioning gene on their other X chromosome (inherited from the father) that partially compensates for the abnormal gene. About 25 to 30 percent of individuals with fragile X syndrome also have symptoms of *autism,* a serious disorder usually diagnosed in early childhood that involves impaired social interaction, delayed or absent language and commu-nication, and repetitive motor behavior (Schwarte, 2008).

MUTATION   Although less than 3 percent of pregnancies result in the birth of a baby with a hereditary abnormality, these children account for about 20 percent of infant deaths and contribute substantially to lifelong impaired physical and mental functioning (U.S. Department of Health and Human Services, 2010c). How are harmful genes created in the first place? The answer is **mutation,** a sudden but permanent change in a segment of DNA. A mutation may affect only one or two genes, or it may involve many genes, as in the chromosomal disorders we will discuss shortly. Some mutations occur spontaneously, simply by chance. Others are caused by hazardous environmental agents.

Although nonionizing forms of radiation—electromagnetic waves and microwaves—have no demonstrated impact on DNA, ionizing (high-energy) radiation is an established cause of mutation. Women who receive repeated doses before conception are more likely to miscarry or give birth to children with hereditary defects. The incidence of genetic abnormalities, such as physical malformations and childhood cancer, is also higher in children whose fathers are exposed to radiation in their occupations. However, infrequent and mild exposure to radiation does not cause genetic damage (Jacquet, 2004). Rather, high doses over a long period impair DNA.

The examples just given illustrate *germline mutation,* which takes place in the cells that give rise to gametes. When the affected individual mates, the defective DNA is passed on to the next generation. In a second type, called *somatic mutation,* normal body cells mutate, an event that can occur at any time of life. The DNA defect appears in every cell derived from the affected body cell, eventually becoming widespread enough to cause disease (such as cancer) or disability.

It is easy to see how disorders that run in families can result from germline mutation. But somatic mutation may be involved in these disorders as well. Some people harbor a genetic susceptibility that causes certain body cells to mutate easily in the presence of triggering events (Weiss, 2005). This helps explain why some individuals develop serious illnesses (such as cancer) as a result of smoking, exposure to pollutants, or psychological stress, while others do not.

Although virtually all mutations that have been studied are harmful, some spontaneous ones (such as the sickle cell allele in malaria-ridden regions of the world) are necessary and desirable. By increasing genetic variation, they help individuals adapt to unexpected environmental challenges. Scientists, however, seldom go looking for mutations that underlie favorable traits, such as an exceptional talent or an especially sturdy immune system. They are far more concerned with identifying and eliminating unfavorable genes that threaten health and survival.

POLYGENIC INHERITANCE   So far, we have discussed patterns of inheritance in which people either display a particular trait or do not. These cut-and-dried individual differences are much easier to trace to their genetic origins than are characteristics that vary on a continuum among people, such as height, weight, intelligence, and personality. These traits are due to **polygenic inheritance,** in which many genes affect the characteristic in question. Polygenic inheritance is complex, and much about it is still unknown. In the final section of this chapter, we discuss how researchers infer the influence of heredity on human attributes when they do not know the precise patterns of inheritance.

Chromosomal Abnormalities

Besides harmful recessive alleles, abnormalities of the chromosomes are a major cause of serious developmental problems. Most chromosomal defects result from mistakes during meiosis, when the ovum and sperm are formed. A chromosome pair does not separate properly, or part of a chromosome breaks off. Because these errors involve far more DNA than problems due to single genes, they usually produce many physical and mental symptoms.

DOWN SYNDROME   The most common chromosomal disorder, occurring in 1 out of every 770 live births, is *Down syndrome.* In 95 percent of cases, it results from a failure of the twenty-first pair of chromosomes to separate during meiosis, so the new individual receives three of these chromosomes rather than the normal two. For this reason, Down syndrome is sometimes called *trisomy 21*. In other, less frequent forms, an extra broken piece of a twenty-first chromosome is attached to another chromosome (called *translocation* pattern). Or an error occurs during the early stages of mitosis, causing some but not all body cells to have the defective chromosomal makeup (called *mosaic* pattern) (U.S. Department of Health and Human Services, 2009d). Because the mosaic type involves less genetic material, symptoms may be less extreme.

The consequences of Down syndrome include mental retardation, memory and speech problems, limited vocabulary, and slow motor development. Affected individuals also have distinct physical features—a short, stocky build; a flattened face; a protruding tongue; almond-shaped eyes; and (in 50 percent of cases) an unusual crease running across the palm of the hand. In addition, infants with Down syndrome are often born with eye cataracts, hearing loss, and heart and intestinal defects (Sherman et al., 2007). Because of medical advances, fewer individuals with Down syndrome die early than was the case in the past. Many survive into their fifties and a few into their sixties to eighties. However, more than half of affected individuals who live past age 40 show symptoms of *Alzheimer's disease,* the most common form of dementia (Wiseman et al., 2009). Genes on chromosome 21 are linked to this disorder.

Infants with Down syndrome smile less readily, show poor eye-to-eye contact, have weak muscle tone, and explore objects less persistently (Slonims & McConachie, 2006). But when parents encourage them to engage with their surroundings, children with Down syndrome develop more favorably. They also benefit from infant and preschool intervention programs, although emotional, social, and motor skills improve more than intellectual performance (Carr, 2002). Clearly, environmental factors affect how well children with Down syndrome fare.

As Figure 2.6 shows, the risk of bearing a Down syndrome baby rises dramatically with maternal age (Schonberg & Tifft, 2007). But exactly why older mothers are more likely to release ova with meiotic errors is not yet known (Martin, 2008). In about 5 to 10 percent of cases, the extra genetic material originates with the father. Some studies suggest a role for advanced paternal age, while others show no age effects (De Souza, Alberman, & Morris, 2009; Dzurova & Pikhart, 2005; Sherman et al., 2005).

ABNORMALITIES OF THE SEX CHROMOSOMES Disorders of the autosomes other than Down syndrome usually disrupt development so severely that miscarriage occurs. When such babies are born, they rarely survive beyond early childhood. In contrast, abnormalities of the sex chromosomes usually lead to fewer problems. In fact, sex chromosome disorders often are not recognized until adolescence when, in

© LAUREN SHEAR/PHOTO RESEARCHERS, INC.

■ A 6-year-old boy with Down syndrome, at right, plays with a typically developing classmate. Despite impaired intellectual development, this boy benefits from exposure to stimulating environments and from opportunities to interact with peers. ■

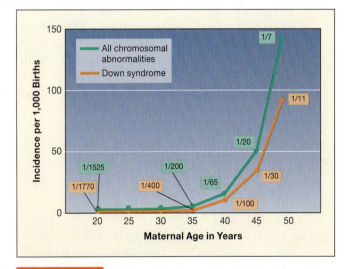

FIGURE 2.6

Risk of Down syndrome and all chromosomal abnormalities by maternal age. Risk rises sharply after age 35. *(Adapted from R. L. Schonberg & C. J. Tifft, 2007, "Birth Defects and Prenatal Diagnosis," from* Children with Disabilities, *6/e, M. L. Matshaw, L. Pellegrino, & N. J. Roizen, eds., p. 85. Baltimore: Paul H. Brookes Publishing Co., Inc. Reprinted by permission.)*

TABLE 2.4 Sex Chromosomal Disorders

DISORDER	DESCRIPTION	INCIDENCE	TREATMENT
XYY syndrome	Extra Y chromosome. Above-average height, large teeth, and sometimes severe acne. Intelligence, male sexual development, and fertility are normal.	1 in 1,000 male births	No special treatment necessary.
Triple X syndrome (XXX)	Extra X chromosome. Tallness and impaired verbal intelligence. Female sexual development and fertility are normal.	1 in 500 to 1,250 female births	Special education to treat verbal ability problems.
Klinefelter syndrome (XXY)	Extra X chromosome. Tallness, body fat distribution resembling females, incomplete development of sex characteristics at puberty, sterility, and impaired verbal intelligence.	1 in 900 male births	Hormone therapy at puberty to stimulate development of sex characteristics; special education to treat verbal ability problems.
Turner syndrome (XO)	Missing X chromosome. Short stature, webbed neck, incomplete development of sex characteristics at puberty, sterility, and impaired spatial intelligence.	1 in 2,500 to 8,000 female births	Hormone therapy in childhood to stimulate physical growth and at puberty to promote development of sex characteristics; special education to treat spatial ability problems.

Sources: Geerts, Steyaert, & Fryns, 2003; Kesler, 2007; Saitta & Zackai, 2005; Simpson et al., 2003.

some deviations, puberty is delayed. The most common problems involve the presence of an extra chromosome (either X or Y) or the absence of one X in females.

Research has discredited a variety of myths about individuals with sex chromosome disorders. For example, as Table 2.4 reveals, males with *XYY syndrome* are not necessarily more aggressive and antisocial than XY males. And most children with sex chromosome disorders do not suffer from mental retardation. Rather, their intellectual problems are usually very specific. Verbal difficulties—for example, with reading and vocabulary—are common among girls with *triple X syndrome* and boys with *Klinefelter syndrome,* both of whom inherit an extra X chromosome. In contrast, girls with *Turner syndrome,* who are missing an X, have trouble with spatial relationships—for example, drawing pictures, telling right from left, following travel directions, and noticing changes in facial expressions (Kesler, 2007; Lawrence et al., 2003; Simpson et al., 2003). Brain-imaging evidence confirms that adding to or subtracting from the usual number of X chromosomes alters the development of certain brain structures, yielding particular intellectual deficits (Cutter et al., 2006; Itti et al., 2006).

ASK YOURSELF

◆ **REVIEW** Cite evidence indicating that both heredity and environment contribute to the development of children with PKU and Down syndrome.

◆ **REVIEW** Using your knowledge of X-linked inheritance, explain why males are more vulnerable than females to miscarriage, infant death, genetic disorders, and other problems.

◆ **APPLY** Gilbert's genetic makeup is homozygous for dark hair. Jan's is homozygous for blond hair. What color is Gilbert's hair? How about Jan's? What proportion of their children are likely to be dark-haired? Explain.

◆ **CONNECT** Referring to ecological systems theory (Chapter 1, pages 25–27), explain why parents of children with genetic disorders often experience increased stress. What factors, within and beyond the family, can help these parents support their children's development?

Reproductive Choices

Two years after they married, Ted and Marianne gave birth to their first child. Kendra appeared to be a healthy infant, but by 4 months her growth had slowed, and she was diagnosed as having Tay-Sachs disease (see Table 2.3). When Kendra died at 2 years of age, Ted and Marianne were devastated. Although they did not want to bring another infant into the world who would endure such suffering, they badly wanted to have a child. They began to avoid family get-togethers, where little nieces and nephews were constant reminders of the void in their lives.

In the past, many couples with genetic disorders in their families chose not to bear a child at all rather than risk the birth of a baby with abnormalities. Today, genetic counseling and prenatal diagnosis help people make informed decisions about conceiving, carrying a pregnancy to term, or adopting a child.

Genetic Counseling

Genetic counseling is a communication process designed to help couples assess their chances of giving birth to a baby with a hereditary disorder and choose the best course of action in view of risks and family goals (Resta et al., 2006). Individuals likely to seek counseling are those who have had difficulties bearing children—for example, repeated miscarriages—or who know that genetic problems exist in their families. In addition, women who delay childbearing past age 35 are often candidates for genetic counseling. After this time, the overall rate of chromosomal abnormalities rises sharply (refer again to Figure 2.6) (Schonberg & Tifft, 2007). But because younger mothers give birth in far higher numbers than older mothers, they still bear the majority of babies with genetic defects. Therefore, some experts argue that maternal needs, not age, should determine referral for genetic counseling (Berkowitz, Roberts, & Minkoff, 2006).

If a family history of mental retardation, psychological disorders, physical defects, or inherited diseases exists, the genetic counselor interviews the couple and prepares a *pedigree*, a picture of the family tree in which affected relatives are identified. The pedigree is used to estimate the likelihood that parents will have an abnormal child, using the genetic principles discussed earlier in this chapter. For many disorders, blood tests or genetic analyses can reveal whether the parent is a carrier of the harmful gene. Carrier detection is possible for all the recessive diseases listed in Table 2.3, as well as others, and for fragile X syndrome.

When all the relevant information is in, the genetic counselor helps people consider appropriate options. These include taking a chance and conceiving, choosing from among a variety of reproductive technologies (see the Social Issues: Health box on pages 66–67), or adopting a child.

Prenatal Diagnosis and Fetal Medicine

If couples who might bear a child with abnormalities decide to conceive, several **prenatal diagnostic methods**—medical procedures that permit detection of developmental problems before birth—are available (see Table 2.5 on page 64). Women of advanced maternal age are prime candidates for *amniocentesis* or *chorionic villus sampling* (see Figure 2.7 on page 65). Except for *maternal blood analysis,* prenatal diagnosis should not be used routinely, since other methods have some chance of injuring the developing organism.

Prenatal diagnosis has led to advances in fetal medicine. For example, by inserting a needle into the uterus, doctors can administer drugs to the fetus. Surgery has been performed to repair such problems as heart, lung, and diaphragm malformations; urinary tract obstructions; and neural defects (Kunisaki & Jennings, 2008). Fetuses with blood disorders have been given blood transfusions. And those with immune deficiencies have received bone marrow transplants that succeeded in creating a normally functioning immune system (Williams, 2006).

TABLE 2.5 Prenatal Diagnostic Methods

METHOD	DESCRIPTION
Amniocentesis	The most widely used technique. A hollow needle is inserted through the abdominal wall to obtain a sample of fluid in the uterus. Cells are examined for genetic defects. Can be performed by the 14th week after conception; 1 to 2 more weeks are required for test results. Small risk of miscarriage.
Chorionic villus sampling	A procedure that can be used if results are desired or needed very early in pregnancy. A thin tube is inserted into the uterus through the vagina, or a hollow needle is inserted through the abdominal wall. A small plug of tissue is removed from the end of one or more chorionic villi, the hairlike projections on the membrane surrounding the developing organism. Cells are examined for genetic defects. Can be performed at 9 weeks after conception; results are available within 24 hours. Entails a slightly greater risk of miscarriage than does amniocentesis. Also associated with a small risk of limb deformities, which increases the earlier the procedure is performed.
Fetoscopy	A small tube with a light source at one end is inserted into the uterus to inspect the fetus for defects of the limbs and face. Also allows a sample of fetal blood to be obtained, permitting diagnosis of such disorders as hemophilia and sickle cell anemia as well as neural defects (see below). Usually performed between 15 and 18 weeks after conception but can be done as early as 5 weeks. Entails some risk of miscarriage.
Ultrasound	High-frequency sound waves are beamed at the uterus; their reflection is translated into a picture on a video screen that reveals the size, shape, and placement of the fetus. By itself, permits assessment of fetal age, detection of multiple pregnancies, and identification of gross physical defects. Also used to guide amniocentesis, chorionic villus sampling, and fetoscopy. When used five or more times, may increase the chances of low birth weight.
Maternal blood analysis	By the second month of pregnancy, some of the developing organism's cells enter the maternal bloodstream. An elevated level of alpha-fetoprotein may indicate kidney disease, abnormal closure of the esophagus, or neural tube defects, such as anencephaly (absence of most of the brain) and spina bifida (bulging of the spinal cord from the spinal column). Isolated cells can be examined for genetic defects.
Preimplantation genetic diagnosis	After in vitro fertilization and duplication of the zygote into a cluster of about 8 to 10 cells, 1 or 2 cells are removed and examined for hereditary defects. Only if that sample is free of detectable genetic disorders is the fertilized ovum implanted in the woman's uterus.

Sources: Hahn & Chitty, 2008; Kumar & O'Brien, 2004; Moore & Persaud, 2008; Sermon, Van Steirteghem, & Liebaers, 2004.

© JOEY McLEISTER/MCT/LANDOV

■ This mother sings while delivering medication through a nebulizer to her 2-year-old daughter, who has cystic fibrosis. The child also wears a vest for a twice-daily treatment that pounds her chest to clear her lungs of thick mucus. In the future, such children may benefit from gene-based treatments for hereditary disorders. ■

These techniques frequently result in complications, the most common being premature labor and miscarriage (Schonberg & Tifft, 2007). Yet parents may be willing to try almost any option, even one with only a slim chance of success. Currently, the medical profession is struggling with how to help parents make informed decisions about fetal surgery.

Advances in *genetic engineering* also offer new hope for correcting hereditary defects. As part of the Human Genome Project—an ambitious international research program aimed at deciphering the chemical makeup of human genetic material (genome)—researchers have mapped the sequence of all human DNA base pairs. Using this information, they are "annotating" the genome—identifying all its genes and their functions, including their protein products and what these products do. A major goal is to understand the estimated 4,000 human disorders, those due to single genes and those resulting from a complex interplay of multiple genes and environmental factors.

Already, thousands of genes have been identified, including those involved in hundreds of diseases, such as cystic fibrosis; Duchenne muscular dystrophy; Huntington disease; Marfan syndrome; heart, digestive, blood, eye, and nervous system abnormalities; and many forms of cancer (National Institutes of Health, 2008). As a result, new treatments are being explored, such as *gene therapy*—correcting genetic abnormalities by delivering DNA carrying a functional gene to the cells. In recent experiments, gene

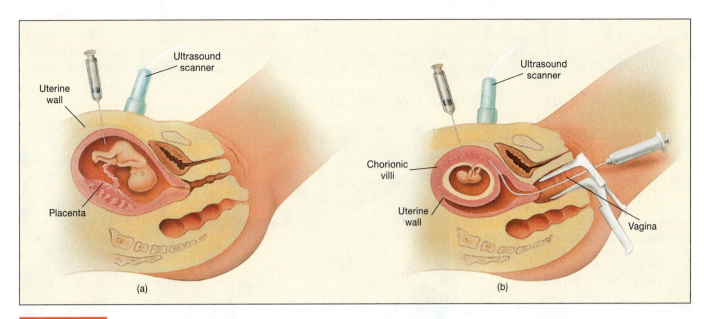

FIGURE 2.7

Amniocentesis and chorionic villus sampling. Today, hundreds of defects and diseases can be detected before birth using these two procedures. (a) In amniocentesis, a hollow needle is inserted through the abdominal wall into the uterus during the fourteenth week after conception or later. Fluid is withdrawn, and fetal cells are cultured, a process that takes one to two weeks. (b) Chorionic villus sampling can be performed much earlier in pregnancy, at nine weeks after conception, and results are available within 24 hours. Two approaches to obtaining a sample of chorionic villus are shown: inserting a thin tube through the vagina into the uterus and inserting a needle through the abdominal wall. In both amniocentesis and chorionic villus sampling, an ultrasound scanner is used for guidance. *(Adapted from* Before We Are Born, *7th ed. By K. L. Moore & T. V. N. Persaud, p. 69. Copyright © 2008, reprinted with permission from Elsevier, Inc.)*

therapy relieved symptoms in hemophilia patients and in patients with severe immune system dysfunction. A few, however, experienced serious side effects (Gillet et al., 2009). In another approach, called *proteomics*, scientists modify gene-specified proteins involved in disease (Van Eyk & Dunn, 2008).

Genetic treatments seem some distance in the future for most single-gene defects, however, and farther off for diseases involving multiple genes that combine in complex ways with each other and the environment. Applying What We Know on page 68 summarizes steps that prospective parents can take before conception to protect the genetic health of their child.

The Alternative of Adoption

Adults who are infertile, who are likely to pass along a genetic disorder, or who are older and single but want a family are turning to adoption in increasing numbers. Those who have children by birth, too, sometimes choose to expand their families through adoption. Adoption agencies try to ensure a good fit by seeking parents of the same ethnic and religious background as the child and, where possible, trying to choose parents who are the same age as typical biological parents. Because the availability of healthy babies has declined (fewer young unwed mothers give up their babies than in the past), more people in North America and Western Europe are adopting from other countries or accepting children who are past infancy or who have known developmental problems (Schweiger & O'Brien, 2005).

Adopted children and adolescents—whether or not they are born in their adoptive parents' country—tend to have more learning and emotional difficulties than other children, a difference that increases with the child's age at time of adoption (Nickman et al., 2005; van IJzendoorn, Juffer, & Poelhuis, 2005; Verhulst, 2008). There are many possible reasons for adoptees' more problematic childhoods. The biological mother may have been unable to care for the child because of problems believed to be partly genetic, such as alcoholism or severe depression, and may have passed this tendency to her offspring. Or perhaps she experienced stress, poor diet, or inadequate medical care during pregnancy—factors that can affect the

SOCIAL ISSUES: HEALTH

The Pros and Cons of Reproductive Technologies

Some couples decide not to risk pregnancy because of a history of genetic disease. Many others—in fact, one-sixth of all couples who try to conceive—discover that they are infertile. And some never-married adults and gay and lesbian partners want to bear children. Today, increasing numbers of individuals are turning to alternative methods of conception—technologies that, although they fulfill the wish for parenthood, have become the subject of heated debate.

Donor Insemination and In Vitro Fertilization

For several decades, *donor insemination*—injection of sperm from an anonymous man into a woman—has been used to overcome male reproductive difficulties. In recent years, it has also permitted women without a male partner to become pregnant. Donor insemination is 70 to 80 percent successful, resulting in about 40,000 deliveries and 52,000 newborn babies in the United States each year (Wright et al., 2008).

In *vitro fertilization* is another reproductive technology that has become increasingly common. Since the first "test tube" baby was born in England in 1978, 1 percent of all children in developed countries—about 40,000 babies in the United States—have been conceived through this technique annually (Jackson, Gibson, & Wu, 2004). With in vitro fertilization, a woman is given hormones that stimulate the ripening of several ova. These are removed surgically and placed in a dish of nutrients, to which sperm are added. Once an ovum is fertilized and begins to duplicate into several cells, it is injected into the mother's uterus.

By mixing and matching gametes, pregnancies can be brought about when either or both partners have a reproductive problem. Usually,

AP IMAGES/THE HOLLAND SENTINEL, DENNIS P. J. GEPPERT

Fertility drugs and in vitro fertilization often lead to multiple fetuses. Although these sextuplets are healthy, reproductive technologies can pose grave ethical dilemmas. When three or more fetuses fill the womb, pregnancy complications may be so severe that doctors recommend aborting one or more to save the others.

in vitro fertilization is used to treat women whose fallopian tubes are permanently damaged. But a recently developed technique permits a single sperm to be injected directly into an ovum, thereby overcoming most male fertility problems. And a "sex sorter" method helps ensure that couples who carry X-linked diseases (which usually affect males) have a daughter. Fertilized ova and sperm can even be frozen and stored in embryo banks for use at some future time, thereby guaranteeing healthy zygotes should age or illness lead to fertility problems.

The overall success rate of assisted reproductive techniques is about 35 percent. However,

success declines steadily with age, from 40 percent in women younger than age 35 to 8 percent in women age 43 and older (Pauli et al., 2009).

Children conceived through these methods may be genetically unrelated to one or both of their parents. In addition, most parents who have used in vitro fertilization do not tell their children about their origins. Does lack of genetic ties or secrecy surrounding these techniques interfere with parent–child relationships? Perhaps because of a strong desire for parenthood, caregiving is actually somewhat warmer for young children conceived through donor insemination or in vitro fertilization.

child (as we will see in Chapter 3). Furthermore, children adopted after infancy often have a preadoptive history of conflict-ridden family relationships, lack of parental affection, neglect and abuse, or deprived institutional rearing. Finally, adoptive parents and children, who are genetically unrelated, are less alike in intelligence and personality than are biological relatives—differences that may threaten family harmony.

Despite these risks, most adopted children fare well, and those with preexisting problems usually make rapid progress (Arcus & Chambers, 2008; Bimmel et al., 2003). In a study of internationally adopted children in the Netherlands, sensitive maternal care and secure attach-

Also, in vitro infants are as securely attached to their parents, and in vitro children and adolescents as well-adjusted, as their counterparts who were naturally conceived (Golombok et al., 2004; Punamaki, 2006; Wagenaar et al., 2008).

Although reproductive technologies have many benefits, serious questions have arisen about their use. In many countries, including the United States, doctors are not required to keep records of donor characteristics, though information about the child's genetic background might be critical in the case of serious disease (Adamson, 2005). Another concern is that the in vitro "sex sorter" method will lead to parental sex selection, thereby eroding the moral value that boys and girls are equally precious.

Furthermore, about 50 percent of in vitro procedures result in multiple births. Most are twins, but 9 percent are triplets and higher-order multiples. Consequently, among in vitro babies, the rate of low birth weight is nearly three times as high as in the general population (Wright et al., 2008). Risk of major birth defects also doubles because of many factors, including drugs used to induce ripening of ova and delays in fertilizing the ova outside the womb (Machin, 2005; Neri, Takeuchi, & Palermo, 2008). In sum, in vitro fertilization poses greater risks than natural conception to infant survival and healthy development.

Surrogate Motherhood

An even more controversial form of medically assisted conception is *surrogate motherhood*. In this procedure, in vitro fertilization may be used to impregnate a woman (called a surrogate) with a couple's fertilized ovum. Alternatively, sperm from a man whose partner is infertile may be used to inseminate the surrogate, who agrees to turn the baby over to the natural father. The child is then adopted by his partner. In both cases, the surrogate is paid a fee for her child-bearing services.

Although most of these arrangements proceed smoothly, those that end up in court highlight serious risks for all concerned. In one case, both parties rejected the infant with severe disabilities who resulted from the pregnancy. In several others, the surrogate mother wanted to keep the baby, or the couple changed their mind during the pregnancy. These children came into the world in the midst of conflict that threatened to last for years.

Because surrogacy usually involves the wealthy as contractors for infants and the less economically advantaged as surrogates, it may promote exploitation of financially needy women. In addition, most surrogates already have children of their own, who may be deeply affected by the pregnancy. Knowledge that their mother would give away a baby for profit may cause these children to worry about the security of their own family circumstances.

New Reproductive Frontiers

Reproductive technologies are evolving faster than societies can weigh the ethics of these procedures. Doctors have used donor ova from younger women in combination with in vitro fertilization to help postmenopausal women become pregnant. Most recipients are in their forties, but several women in their fifties and sixties have given birth. These cases raise questions about bringing children into the world whose parents may not live to see them reach adulthood. Based on U.S. life expectancy data, 1 in 3 mothers and 1 in 2 fathers having a baby at age 55 will die before their child enters college (U.S. Census Bureau, 2010b).

Currently, experts are debating other reproductive options. At donor banks, customers can select ova or sperm on the basis of physical characteristics and even IQ. And scientists are devising ways to alter the DNA of human ova, sperm, and embryos to protect against hereditary disorders—techniques that could be used to engineer other desired characteristics. Many worry that these practices are dangerous steps toward selective breeding through "designer babies"—controlling offspring traits by manipulating genetic makeup.

Although new reproductive technologies permit many barren couples to rear healthy newborn babies, laws are needed to regulate such practices. In Australia, New Zealand, Sweden, and Switzerland, individuals conceived with donated gametes have a right to information about their genetic origins (Frith, 2001). Pressure from those working in the field of assisted reproduction may soon lead to a similar policy in the United States. Australia, Canada, and the Netherlands prohibit any genetic alteration of human gametes, with other nations following suit (Isasi, Nguyen, & Knoppers, 2006). But some scientists argue that this total ban is too restrictive because it interferes with serving therapeutic needs.

In the case of surrogate motherhood, the ethical problems are so complex that 18 U.S. states have sharply restricted the practice. Australia, Canada, and many European nations have banned it, arguing that the status of a baby should not be a matter of commercial arrangement and that a part of the body should not be rented or sold (Chen, 2003; McGee, 1997). Denmark, France, and Great Britain have prohibited in vitro fertilization for women past menopause (Bioethics Consultative Committee, 2003). At present, nothing is known about the psychological consequences of being a product of these procedures. Research on how such children grow up, including later-appearing medical conditions and knowledge and feelings about their origins, is important for weighing the pros and cons of these techniques.

---

ment in infancy predicted cognitive and social competence at age 7 (Stams, Juffer, & van IJzendoorn, 2002).

Overall, international adoptees fare much better in development than birth siblings or institutionalized agemates who stay behind. By middle childhood, those who were adopted in infancy have mental test scores resembling those of their nonbiological siblings and school classmates, although they tend to achieve less well in school, to have more learning problems that require special treatment, and to be slightly delayed in language skills (van IJzendoorn, Juffer, & Poelhuis, 2005). Children adopted at older ages develop feelings of trust and affection

Applying What We Know

Steps Prospective Parents Can Take Before Conception to Increase the Chances of a Healthy Baby

RECOMMENDATION	EXPLANATION
Arrange for a physical exam.	A physical exam before conception permits detection of diseases and other medical problems that might reduce fertility, be difficult to treat during pregnancy, or affect the developing organism.
Consider your genetic makeup.	Find out if anyone in your family has had a child with a genetic disease or disability. If so, seek genetic counseling before conception.
Reduce or eliminate toxins under your control.	Because the developing organism is highly sensitive to damaging environmental agents during the early weeks of pregnancy (see Chapter 3), couples trying to conceive should avoid drugs, alcohol, cigarette smoke, radiation, pollution, chemical substances in the home and workplace, and infectious diseases. Furthermore, they should stay away from ionizing radiation and some industrial chemicals that are known to cause mutations.
Ensure proper nutrition.	A doctor-recommended vitamin–mineral supplement, begun before conception, helps prevent many prenatal problems. It should include folic acid, which reduces the chances of neural tube defects, prematurity, and low birth weight (see Chapter 3, page 114).
Consult a physician after 12 months of unsuccessful efforts at conception.	Long periods of infertility may be due to undiagnosed spontaneous abortions, which can be caused by genetic defects in either partner. If a physical exam reveals a healthy reproductive system, seek genetic counseling.

for their adoptive parents as they come to feel loved and supported in their new families (Verissimo & Salvaterra, 2006). As we will see in Chapter 5, however, later-adopted children—especially those with multiple early-life adversities—are more likely than their agemates to have persistent cognitive, emotional, and social problems.

By adolescence, adoptees' lives are often complicated by unresolved curiosity about their roots. Some have difficulty accepting the possibility that they may never know their birth parents. Others worry about what they would do if their birth parents suddenly reappeared. Nevertheless, the decision to search for birth parents is usually postponed until early adulthood, when marriage and childbirth may trigger it. Despite concerns about their origins, most adoptees appear well-adjusted as adults. And as long as their parents took steps to help them learn about their heritage in childhood, young people adopted into a different ethnic group or culture generally develop identities that are healthy blends of their birth and rearing backgrounds (Nickman et al., 2005; Thomas & Tessler, 2007).

As we conclude our discussion of reproductive choices, perhaps you are wondering how things turned out for Ted and Marianne. Through genetic counseling, Marianne discovered a history of Tay-Sachs disease on her mother's side of the family. Ted had a distant cousin who died of the disorder. The genetic counselor explained that the chances of giving birth to another affected baby were 1 in 4. Ted and Marianne took the risk. Their son Douglas is now 12 years old. Although Douglas is a carrier of the recessive allele, he is a normal, healthy boy. In a few years, Ted and Marianne will tell Douglas about his genetic history and explain the importance of genetic counseling and testing before he has children of his own.

© GOLDEN PIXELS LLC/ALAMY

■ Adoption is one option for adults who are infertile or have a family history of genetic disorders. This couple, who adopted their daughter from China, can promote her successful adjustment by helping her learn about her birth heritage. ■

◆ **REVIEW** Why is genetic counseling called a *communication process?* Who should seek it?

◆ **APPLY** Imagine that you must counsel a couple considering in vitro fertilization using the wife's ova and sperm from an anonymous man to overcome the husband's infertility. What medical and ethical risks would you raise?

◆ **CONNECT** How does research on adoption reveal resilience? Which factor related to resilience (see Chapter 1, pages 10–11) is central in positive outcomes for adoptees?

◆ **REFLECT** Imagine that you are a woman who is a carrier of fragile X syndrome but who wants to have children. Would you become pregnant, adopt, use a surrogate mother, or give up your desire for parenthood? If you became pregnant, would you opt for prenatal diagnosis? Explain your decisions.

Environmental Contexts for Development

Just as complex as the genetic inheritance is the surrounding environment—a many-layered set of influences that combine to help or hinder physical and psychological well-being. **TAKE A MOMENT...** Think back to your own childhood, and jot down a brief description of people and events that had a significant impact on your development. Do the items on your list resemble those of my students, who mostly mention experiences that involve their families? This emphasis is not surprising, since the family is the first and longest-lasting context for development. Other influences that make most students' top ten are friends, neighbors, school, and community and religious organizations.

Return to Bronfenbrenner's ecological systems theory, discussed in Chapter 1. It emphasizes that environments extending beyond the *microsystem*—the immediate settings just mentioned—powerfully affect development. Indeed, my students rarely mention one important context. Its impact is so pervasive that we seldom stop to think about it in our daily lives. This is the *macrosystem,* or broad social climate of society—its values and programs that support and protect children's development. All families need help in rearing their children—through affordable housing and health care, safe neighborhoods, good schools, well-equipped recreational facilities, and high-quality child care and other services that permit parents to meet both work and family responsibilities. And some families, because of poverty or special tragedies, need considerably more help than others.

In the following sections, we take up these contexts for development. Because they affect every age and aspect of change, we will return to them in later chapters. For now, our discussion emphasizes that environments, as well as heredity, can enhance or create risks for development.

The Family

In power and breadth of influence, no other microsystem context equals the family. The family introduces children to the physical world by providing opportunities for play and exploration of objects. It also creates unique bonds among people. Attachments to parents and siblings are usually lifelong and serve as models for relationships in the wider world. Within the family, children learn the language, skills, and social and moral values of their culture. And people of all ages turn to family members for information, assistance, and pleasurable interaction. Warm, gratifying family ties predict physical and psychological health throughout development. In contrast, isolation or alienation from the family is often associated with developmental problems (Deković & Buist, 2005; Parke & Buriel, 2006).

■ The family is a network of interdependent relationships, in which each person's behavior influences that of others. The positive mealtime atmosphere as these teenagers and their parents gather for breakfast is the result of many forces, including parents who respond to children with warmth and patience and children who, in turn, have developed cooperative dispositions. ■

Contemporary researchers view the family as a network of interdependent relationships (Bronfenbrenner & Morris, 2006; Lerner et al., 2002). Recall from ecological systems theory that *bidirectional influences* exist in which the behaviors of each family member affect those of others. Indeed, the very term *system* implies that the responses of all family members are related. These system influences operate both directly and indirectly.

DIRECT INFLUENCES Recently, as I passed through the checkout counter at the supermarket, I witnessed two episodes, each an example of how parents and children directly influence each other:

■ Four-year-old Danny looked longingly at the tempting rows of candy as his mother lifted groceries from her cart onto the counter. "Pleeeeease, can I have it, Mom?" Danny begged, holding up a large package of bubble gum. "Do you have a dollar? Just one?"

   "No, not today," his mother answered. "Remember, we picked out your special cereal. That's what I need the dollar for." Gently taking the bubble gum from his hand, Danny's mother handed him the box of cereal. "Here, let's pay," she said, lifting Danny so he could see the cash register.

■ Three-year-old Meg was sitting in the shopping cart while her mother transferred groceries to the counter. Suddenly Meg turned around, grabbed a bunch of bananas, and started pulling them apart.

   "Stop it, Meg!" shouted her mother, snatching the bananas from Meg's hand. But as she turned her attention to swiping her debit card, Meg reached for a chocolate bar from a nearby shelf. "Meg, how many times have I told you, don't touch!" Loosening the candy from Meg's tight little fist, Meg's mother slapped her hand. Meg's face turned red with anger as she began to wail.

These observations fit with a wealth of research on the family system. Studies of families of diverse ethnicities show that when parents are firm but warm, children tend to comply with their requests. And when children willingly cooperate, their parents are likely to be warm and gentle in the future. In contrast, children whose parents discipline harshly and impatiently are more likely to refuse and rebel. And because children's misbehavior is stressful, parents may increase their use of punishment, leading to more unruliness by the child (Stormshak et al., 2000; Whiteside-Mansell et al., 2003). In each case, the behavior of one family member helps sustain a form of interaction in the other that either promotes or undermines children's well-being.

INDIRECT INFLUENCES The impact of family relationships on child development becomes even more complicated when we consider that interaction between any two members is affected by others present in the setting. Bronfenbrenner calls these indirect influences the effect of *third parties* (see Chapter 1, page 26).

Third parties can serve as supports for or barriers to development. For example, when a marital relationship is warm and considerate, mothers and fathers are more likely to engage in effective **coparenting,** mutually supporting each other's parenting behaviors. Such parents are warmer, praise and stimulate children more, and nag and scold them less. In contrast, parents whose marriage is tense and hostile often interfere with one another's child-rearing efforts, are less responsive to children's needs, and are more likely to criticize, express anger, and punish (Caldera & Lindsey, 2006; McHale et al., 2002). Children who are chronically exposed to angry, unresolved parental conflict have serious emotional problems resulting from disrupted emotional security (Cummings & Merrilees, 2010; Schacht, Cummings, & Davies, 2009). These

LOOK AND LISTEN

❖❖

Observe several parent–young child pairs in a supermarket or department store, where parents are likely to place limits on children's behavior. How does the quality of parent communication seem to influence the child's response? How does the child's response affect the parent's subsequent interaction?

include both *internalizing difficulties* (especially among girls), such as feeling worried and fearful and trying to repair their parents' relationship, and *externalizing difficulties* (especially among boys), including anger and aggression (Cummings, Goeke-Morey, & Papp, 2004). These child problems can further disrupt parents' marital relationship.

Yet even when parental conflict strains children's adjustment, other family members may help restore effective interaction. Grandparents, for example, can promote children's development both directly, by responding warmly to the child, and indirectly, by providing parents with child-rearing advice, models of child-rearing skill, and even financial assistance. Of course, as with any indirect influence, grandparents can sometimes be harmful. When quarrelsome relations exist between parents and grandparents, parent–child communication may suffer.

ADAPTING TO CHANGE Think back to the *chronosystem* in Bronfenbrenner's theory (see page 27 in Chapter 1). The interplay of forces within the family is dynamic and ever-changing, as each member adapts to the development of other members.

For example, as children acquire new skills, parents adjust the way they treat their more competent youngsters. **TAKE A MOMENT...**The next time you have a chance, notice the way a parent relates to a tiny baby as compared with a walking, talking toddler. During the first few months, parents spend much time feeding, changing, bathing, and cuddling the infant. Within a year, things change dramatically. The 1-year-old points, shows, names objects, and makes his way through the household cupboards. In response, parents devote less time to physical care and more to talking, playing games, and disciplining. These new ways of interacting, in turn, encourage the child's expanding motor, cognitive, and social skills.

Parents' development affects children as well. In Chapter 14, we will see that the rise in parent–child conflict that often occurs in early adolescence is not solely due to teenagers' striving for independence. This is a time when most parents of adolescents have reached middle age and—conscious that their children will soon leave home and establish their own lives—are reconsidering their own commitments (Steinberg & Silk, 2002). Consequently, while the adolescent presses for greater autonomy, the parent presses for more togetherness. This imbalance promotes friction, which parent and teenager gradually resolve by accommodating to changes in each other. Indeed, no social unit other than the family is required to adjust to such vast changes in its members.

Historical time period also contributes to a dynamic family system. In recent decades, a declining birth rate, a high divorce rate, expansion of women's roles, increased acceptance of homosexuality, and postponement of parenthood have led to a smaller family size and a greater number of single parents, remarried parents, gay and lesbian parents, employed mothers, and dual-earner families. Clearly, families in industrialized nations have become more diverse than ever before. In later chapters we will take up these family forms, examining how each affects family relationships and, ultimately, children's development.

Nevertheless, some general patterns in family functioning do exist. In the United States and other industrialized nations, one important source of these consistencies is socioeconomic status.

Socioeconomic Status and Family Functioning

People in industrialized nations are stratified on the basis of what they do at work and how much they earn for doing it—factors that determine their social position and economic well-being. Researchers assess a family's standing on this continuum through an index called **socioeconomic status (SES),** which combines three related, but not completely overlapping, variables: (1) years of education and (2) the prestige of one's job and the skill it requires, both of which measure social status, and (3) income, which measures economic status. As SES rises and falls, parents and children face changing circumstances that profoundly affect family functioning.

SES is linked to timing of parenthood and to family size. People who work in skilled and semiskilled manual occupations (for example, construction workers, truck drivers, and custodians) tend to marry and have children earlier as well as give birth to more children than people in professional and technical occupations. The two groups also differ in child-rearing values and expectations. For example, when asked about personal qualities they desire for their children, lower-SES parents tend to emphasize external characteristics, such as obedience, politeness, neatness, and cleanliness. In contrast, higher-SES parents emphasize psychological traits, such as curiosity, happiness, self-direction, and cognitive and social maturity (Duncan & Magnuson, 2003; Hoff, Laursen, & Tardif, 2002; Tudge et al., 2000).

These differences are reflected in family interaction. Parents higher in SES talk to, read to, and otherwise stimulate their infants and preschoolers more and grant them greater freedom to explore. With older children and adolescents, higher-SES parents use more warmth, explanations, and verbal praise; set higher academic and other developmental goals; and allow their children to make more decisions. Commands ("You do that because I told you to"), criticism, and physical punishment all occur more often in low-SES households (Bush & Peterson, 2008; Mandara et al., 2009).

Education contributes substantially to these variations in child rearing. Higher-SES parents' interest in providing verbal stimulation, nurturing inner traits, and promoting academic achievement is supported by years of schooling, during which they learned to think about abstract, subjective ideas (Mistry et al., 2008; Vernon-Feagans et al., 2008). In diverse cultures around the world, as the Social Issues: Education box on the following page makes clear, education of women in particular fosters patterns of thinking and behaving that greatly improve quality of life, for both parents and children.

Because of limited education and low social status, many lower-SES parents feel a sense of powerlessness and lack of influence in their relationships beyond the home. At work, for example, they must obey rules made by others in positions of power and authority. When they get home, their parent–child interaction seems to duplicate these experiences—but now they are in authority. Higher levels of stress, along with a stronger belief in the value of physical punishment, contribute to low-SES parents' greater use of coercive discipline (Conger & Donnellan, 2007; Pinderhughes et al., 2000). Higher-SES parents, in contrast, typically have more control over their own lives. At work, they are used to making independent decisions and convincing others of their point of view. At home, they teach these skills to their children (Greenberger, O'Neil, & Nagel, 1994).

As early as the second year of life, higher SES is associated with enhanced cognitive and language development and with reduced incidence of emotional and behavior problems. And throughout childhood and adolescence, higher-SES children do better in school (Bradley & Corwyn, 2003; Melby et al., 2008). As a result, they attain higher levels of education, which greatly enhances their opportunities for a prosperous adult life. Researchers believe that differences in family functioning have much to do with these outcomes.

Affluence

Despite their advanced education and great material wealth, affluent parents—those in prestigious and high-paying occupations—too often fail to engage in family interaction and parenting that promote favorable development. In several studies, researchers tracked the adjustment of youths growing up in wealthy suburbs (Luthar & Latendresse, 2005a). By seventh grade, many showed serious problems that worsened in high school. Their school grades were poor, and they were more likely than low-SES youths to engage in alcohol and drug use and to report high levels of anxiety and depression (Luthar & Becker, 2002; Luthar & Goldstein, 2008). Furthermore, among affluent (but not low-SES) teenagers, substance use was correlated with anxiety and depression, suggesting that wealthy youths took drugs to self-medicate—a practice that predicts persistent abuse (Luthar & Sexton, 2004).

© INTI ST. CLAIR/GETTY IMAGES/PHOTODISC

■■ Advanced education and material wealth do not guarantee a healthy family life. When children in affluent families lack parental supervision and emotional closeness, they are at risk for academic and emotional difficulties, including poor grades, alcohol and drug use, and anxiety and depression. ■

SOCIAL ISSUES: EDUCATION

Worldwide Education of Girls: Transforming Current and Future Generations

When a new school opened in the Egyptian village of Beni Shara'an, Ahmen, an illiterate shopkeeper, immediately enrolled his 8-year-old daughter Rawia (Bellamy, 2004, p. 19). Until that day, Rawia had divided her days between back-breaking farming and confinement to her home.

Before long, Rawia's advancing language, literacy, and reasoning skills transformed her family's quality of life. "My store accounts were in a mess, but soon Rawia started straightening out the books," Ahmen recalled. She also began helping her older sister learn to read and write and explaining to her family the instructions on prescription medicines and the news on television. In addition, Rawia began to envision a better life for herself. "When I grow up," she told her father, "I want to be a doctor. Or maybe a teacher."

Over the past century, the percentage of children in the developing world who go to school has increased from a small minority of boys to a majority of all children in most regions. Still, some 73 million children, most of them poverty-stricken girls, do not start elementary school, and more than 200 million, again mostly girls, do not go to secondary school (UNICEF, 2009a).

Although schooling is vital for all children, educating girls has an especially powerful impact on the welfare of families, societies, and future generations. The diverse benefits of girls' schooling largely accrue in two ways: (1) through enhanced verbal skills—reading, writing, and oral communication; and (2) through empowerment—a growing desire to improve their life conditions (LeVine, LeVine, & Schnell, 2001).

Family Health

Education gives people the communicative skills and confidence to seek health services and to benefit from public health information. As a result, years of schooling strongly predicts women's preventive health behavior: prenatal visits, child immunizations, healthy diet, and sanitary practices (LeVine et al., 2004; Peña, Wall, & Person, 2000). In addition, because educated women have more life opportunities, they are more likely to take advantage of family planning services, delay marriage and child-bearing, and have more widely spaced and fewer children (Stromquist, 2007). All these practices are linked to increased maternal and child survival and family health.

Family Relationships and Parenting

In developed and developing nations alike, the empowerment that springs from education is associated with more equitable husband–wife relationships and a reduction in harsh disciplining of children (LeVine et al., 1991; LeVine, LeVine, & Schnell, 2001). Also, educated mothers engage in more verbal stimulation and teaching of literacy skills to their children, which fosters success in school, higher educational attainment, and economic gains in the next generation. Regions of the world that have invested more in girls' education, such as Southeast Asia and Latin America, tend to have higher levels of economic development (King & Mason, 2001).

According to a United Nations report, educating girls is the most effective means of combating the most profound, global threats to human development: poverty, maternal and child mortality, and disease (UNICEF, 2010). Rawia got the chance to go to school because of an Egyptian national initiative, which led to the establishment of several thousand one-classroom schools in rural areas with the poorest record in educating girls. Because of cultural beliefs about gender roles or reluctance to give up a daughter's work at home, parents sometimes resist. But the largest barrier is that many countries continue to charge parents a fee for each child enrolled in school, often amounting to nearly one-third of the income of poverty-stricken families. Under these conditions, parents—if they send any children—tend to send only sons.

In 2003, Kenya eliminated fees for primary school. Immediately, enrollments of both boys and girls surged—by more than 30 percent. Uganda followed suit, increasing its primary school enrollment by 70 percent (Alter, 2008; RESULTS, 2006). When governments abolish enrollment fees, provide information about the benefits of education for girls, and create employment possibilities for women, the overwhelming majority of parents—including the very poor—choose to send their daughters to school, and some make great sacrifices to do so.

© AP IMAGES/JOHN MCCONNICO

■ For these girls huddling in an open-air class in a village in Pakistan, attending school will dramatically improve their life opportunities and their nation's welfare. In both developed and developing nations, educating girls leads to gains in family income and relationships that carry over to improved health, education, and economic well-being in the next generation. ■

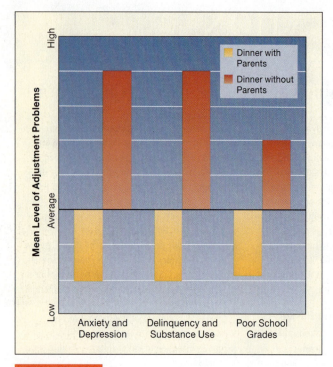

FIGURE 2.8

Relationship of regularly eating dinner with parents to affluent youths' adjustment problems. Compared with sixth graders who often ate dinner with their parents, those who rarely did so were far more likely to display anxiety and depression, delinquency and substance use, and poor school grades, even after many other aspects of parenting were controlled. In this study, frequent family mealtimes also protected low-SES youths from delinquency and substance use and from classroom learning problems. *(Adapted from Luthar & Latendresse, 2005b.)*

Why are so many affluent youths troubled? Compared to their better-adjusted counterparts, poorly adjusted affluent young people report less emotional closeness and supervision from their parents, who lead professionally and socially demanding lives. As a group, wealthy parents are nearly as physically and emotionally unavailable to their youngsters as parents coping with serious financial strain. At the same time, these parents often make excessive demands for achievement (Luthar & Becker, 2002). Adolescents whose parents value their accomplishments more than their character are more likely to have academic and emotional problems.

For both affluent and low-SES youths, a simple routine—eating dinner with parents—is associated with a reduction in adjustment difficulties, even after many other aspects of parenting are controlled (see Figure 2.8) (Luthar & Latendresse, 2005b). Interventions that make wealthy parents aware of the high costs of a competitive lifestyle and minimal family time are badly needed.

Poverty

When families slip into poverty, development is seriously threatened. Consider Zinnia Mae, who grew up in a close-knit black neighborhood located in a small southeastern American city (Heath, 1990). As unemployment struck the community and citizens moved away, 16-year-old Zinnia Mae caught a ride to Atlanta. Two years later, she was the mother of a daughter and twin boys, and she had moved into high-rise public housing.

Zinnia Mae worried constantly about scraping together enough money to put food on the table, finding babysitters so she could go to the laundry or grocery, freeing herself from a cycle of rising debt, and finding the twins' father, who had stopped sending money. Her most frequent words were, "I'm so tired." The children had only one set meal—breakfast; otherwise, they ate whenever they were hungry or bored. Their play space was limited to the living room sofa and a mattress on the floor. Toys consisted of scraps of a blanket, spoons and food cartons, a small rubber ball, a few plastic cars, and a roller skate abandoned in the building. At a researcher's request, Zinnia Mae agreed to tape record her interactions with her children. Cut off from family and community ties and overwhelmed by financial strains and feelings of helplessness, she found herself unable to join in activities with her children. In 500 hours of tape, she started a conversation with them only 18 times.

Although poverty rates in the United States declined slightly in the 1990s, in recent years they have risen. Today, about 13 percent—nearly 40 million Americans—are affected. Those hit hardest are parents under age 25 with young children and elderly people who live alone. Poverty is also magnified among ethnic minorities and women. For example, 19 percent of U.S. children are poor, rates that climb to 30 percent for Hispanic children, 32 percent for Native-American children, and 34 percent for African-American children. For single mothers with preschool children, the poverty rate is close to 50 percent (DeNavas-Walt, Proctor, & Smith, 2009).

Joblessness, a high divorce rate, a high rate of adolescent parenthood, and (as we will see later) inadequate government programs to meet family needs are responsible for these disheartening statistics. The poverty rate is higher among children than any other age group. And of all Western nations, the United States has the highest percentage of extremely poor children. Nearly 8 percent of U.S. children live in deep poverty (at less than half the poverty threshold, the income level judged necessary for a minimum living standard). In contrast, in Denmark, Finland, Norway, and Sweden, child poverty rates have remained at 5 percent or less for several decades, and deep child poverty is rare (UNICEF, 2007). The earlier poverty begins, the deeper it is, and the longer it lasts, the more devastating are its effects. Children of poverty are more likely than other children to suffer from lifelong poor physical health, persistent deficits in cognitive development and academic achievement, high school dropout, mental illness, and impulsivity, aggression, and antisocial behavior (Aber, Jones & Raver, 2007; Dearing, 2008; Morgan et al., 2009; Ryan, Fauth, & Brooks-Gunn, 2006).

The constant stressors that accompany poverty gradually weaken the family system. Poor families have many daily hassles—bills to pay, the car breaking down, loss of welfare and unemployment payments, something stolen from the house, to name just a few. When daily crises arise, family members become depressed, irritable, and distracted; hostile interactions increase; and children's development suffers (Conger & Donnellan, 2007; Evans, 2006). Negative outcomes are especially severe in single-parent families and families who must live in poor housing and dangerous neighborhoods—conditions that make everyday existence even more difficult, while reducing social supports that assist in coping with economic hardship (Hart, Atkins, & Matsuba, 2008; Leventhal & Brooks-Gunn, 2003).

■ Homelessness poses enormous challenges for maintaining positive family relationships. This family has spent the last three years living in Chicago-area shelters, a circumstance that can lead to feelings of helplessness and isolation and to weakening of the family system. ■

Besides poverty, another problem—one that has become more common in the past 30 years—has reduced the life chances of many children. On any given night, approximately 350,000 people in the United States have no place to live. An estimated 23 percent of the homeless are families with children (National Coalition for the Homeless, 2008). The rise in homelessness is mostly due to two factors: a decline in the availability of government-supported low-cost housing and the release of large numbers of mentally ill people from hospitals, without an increase in community treatment programs to help them adjust to ordinary life and get better.

Most homeless families consist of women with children under age 5. Besides health problems (which affect the majority of homeless people), many homeless children suffer from developmental delays and chronic emotional stress due to their harsh, insecure daily lives (Bratt, 2002). An estimated 25 to 30 percent of those who are old enough do not go to school. Those who do enroll achieve less well than other poverty-stricken children because of poor attendance and health and emotional difficulties (Obradović et al., 2009; Shinn et al., 2008).

Beyond the Family: Neighborhoods and Schools

As the concepts of *mesosystem* and *exosystem* in ecological systems theory make clear, connections between family and community are vital for children's well-being. From our discussion of poverty, perhaps you can see why: In poverty-stricken urban areas, community life is usually disrupted. Families move often, parks and playgrounds are in disarray, and community centers providing leisure-time activities do not exist. In such neighborhoods, family violence, child abuse and neglect, children's problem behavior, youth antisocial activity, and adult criminal behavior are especially high (Brody et al., 2003; Dunn, Schaefer-McDaniel, & Ramsay, 2010). In contrast, strong family ties to the community—as indicated by frequent contact with friends and relatives, organized youth activities, and regular church, synagogue, or mosque attendance—reduce family stress and adjustment problems (Boardman, 2004; Leventhal & Brooks-Gunn, 2003).

NEIGHBORHOODS   Let's look closely at the functions of communities in the lives of children by beginning with the neighborhood. **TAKE A MOMENT...** What were your childhood experiences like in the yards, streets, parks, and community centers surrounding your home?

© TONY AVELAR/AP IMAGES FOR SPRITE

■ These girls enjoy step-dancing lessons at a Boys and Girls Club in their California community. Neighborhood resources are especially important for economically disadvantaged children and families. ■

How did you spend your time, whom did you get to know, and how important were these moments to you?

Neighborhoods offer resources and social ties that play an important part in children's development. In several studies, low-SES families were randomly assigned vouchers to move out of public housing into neighborhoods varying widely in affluence. Compared with their peers who remained in poverty-stricken areas, children and youths who moved into low-poverty neighborhoods showed substantially better physical and mental health and school achievement (Goering, 2003; Leventhal & Brooks-Gunn, 2003).

Neighborhood resources have a greater impact on economically disadvantaged than on well-to-do young people. Higher-SES families are less dependent on their immediate surroundings for social support, education, and leisure pursuits. They can afford to transport their children to lessons and entertainment and, if necessary, to better-quality schools in distant parts of the community. In low-income neighborhoods, in-school and after-school programs that substitute for lack of other resources by providing art, music, sports, scouting, and other enrichment activities are associated with improved school performance and a reduction in emotional and behavior problems in middle childhood (Peters, Petrunka, & Arnold, 2003; Vandell & Posner, 1999; Vandell, Reisner, & Pierce, 2007). Neighborhood organizations, such as religious youth groups and special-interest clubs, contribute to favorable development in adolescence, including increased self-confidence, school achievement, and educational aspirations (Barnes et al., 2007; Gonzales et al., 1996).

Yet in dangerous, disorganized neighborhoods, high-quality activities for children and adolescents are usually scarce. Even when they are available, crime and social disorder limit young people's access, and attendance is low (Dynarski et al., 2004). Furthermore, home and neighborhood obstacles often combine to reduce involvement. Parents overwhelmed by financial and other stressors are less likely to provide the stimulation and encouragement that motivate their children to participate (Kohen et al., 2008). In an investigation of a large sample of elementary school students diverse in SES and neighborhood residence, those living in the least stimulating homes and the most chaotic neighborhoods were least likely to participate in after-school and community-center enrichment activities (Dearing et al., 2009). Thus, the neediest children were especially likely to miss out on these development-enhancing experiences.

Just how do family–neighborhood ties reduce parenting stress and promote child development? One answer lies in their provision of *social support,* which leads to the following benefits:

■ *Parental self-worth.* A neighbor or relative who listens and tries to relieve a parent's concern enhances her self-esteem. The parent, in turn, is likely to interact in a more sensitive and involved manner with her children.

■ *Parental access to valuable information and services.* A friend who suggests where a parent might find a job, housing, and affordable child care and youth activities helps make the multiple roles of spouse, parent, and provider easier to fulfill.

■ *Child-rearing controls and role models.* Friends, relatives, and other community members may encourage and demonstrate effective parenting practices and discourage ineffective practices.

■ *Direct assistance with child rearing.* As children and adolescents participate in their parents' social networks and in neighborhood settings, other adults can influence children through warmth, stimulation, and exposure to a wider array of competent models. In this way, family–neighborhood ties can reduce the impact of ineffective parenting (Silk et al., 2004). Nearby adults can also intervene when they see young people skipping school or behaving antisocially.

LOOK AND LISTEN

Ask several parents to list their school-age children's regular lessons and other enrichment activities. Then inquire about home and neighborhood factors that either encourage or impede their children's participation.

The Better Beginnings, Better Futures Project of Ontario, Canada, is a government-sponsored set of pilot programs aimed at preventing the dire consequences of home and neighborhood poverty, including child and adolescent externalizing difficulties, antisocial activity, school failure, and high school dropout (Gershoff & Aber, 2006). The most successful of these efforts, using a local elementary school as its base, provided children with in-class and summer enrichment activities. Project staff also visited each child's parents regularly, informed them about community resources, and encouraged their involvement in the child's school and neighborhood life (Peters, 2005; Peters, Petrunka, & Arnold, 2003). An evaluation after four years revealed wide-ranging benefits—gains in neighborhood satisfaction, family functioning, effective parenting, and children's reading skills, along with a reduction in emotional and behavior problems.

SCHOOLS   Unlike the informal worlds of family and neighborhood, school is a formal institution designed to transmit knowledge and skills that children need to become productive members of their society. Children in the developed world spend many hours in school— 6 hours a day, 5 days a week, 36 weeks a year—a total of about 14,000 hours, on average, by high school graduation. And today, because many children younger than age 5 attend "school-like" child-care centers or preschools, the impact of schooling begins even earlier and is more powerful than these figures suggest.

Schools are complex social systems that affect many aspects of development. Schools differ in their physical environments—student body size, number of children per class, and space available for work and play. They also vary in their educational philosophies— whether teachers regard children as passive learners to be molded by adult instruction; as active, curious beings who determine their own learning; or as collaborative partners assisted by adult experts, who guide their mastery of new skills. Finally, the social life of schools varies—for example, in the degree to which students cooperate or compete; in the extent to which students of different abilities, SES, and ethnic backgrounds learn together; and in whether classrooms, hallways, and play yards are safe, humane settings or are riddled with violence (Evans, 2006). We will discuss each of these aspects of schooling in later chapters.

■ Schools are complex social systems that powerfully affect development. By encouraging students' active participation, this fifth-grade teacher promotes mastery of new knowledge and skills along with enthusiastic attitudes toward learning. ■

Regular parent–school contact supports development at all ages. Students whose parents are involved in school activities and attend parent–teacher conferences show better academic achievement. Higher-SES parents, whose backgrounds and values are similar to those of teachers, are more likely to make phone calls and visits to school. In contrast, low-SES and ethnic minority parents often feel uncomfortable about coming to school, and daily stressors reduce the energy they have for school involvement (Grant & Ray, 2010; Jeynes, 2005; Reschly & Christenson, 2009). Parent–teacher contact is also more frequent in small towns, where most citizens know each other and schools serve as centers of community life (Peshkin, 1994). Teachers and administrators must take extra steps with low-SES and ethnic minority families and in urban areas to build supportive family–school ties.

When these efforts lead to cultures of good parenting and teaching, they deliver an extra boost to children's well-being. For example, students attending schools with many highly involved parents achieve especially well (Darling & Steinberg, 1997). And when excellent education becomes a team effort of teachers, administrators, and community members, its effects on learning are stronger and reach many more students (Hauser-Cram et al., 2006).

The Cultural Context

Our discussion in Chapter 1 emphasized that child development can be fully understood only when viewed in its larger cultural context. In the following sections, we expand on this important

LOOK AND LISTEN

Ask a teacher whose classroom has many students from low-SES families what percentage of parents attend parent–teacher conferences. What steps does the teacher take to promote parent–school involvement?

theme by taking up the role of the *macrosystem* in development. First, we discuss ways that cultural values and practices affect environmental contexts for development. Then we consider how healthy development depends on laws and government programs that shield children from harm and foster their well-being.

CULTURAL VALUES AND PRACTICES Cultures shape family interaction, school experiences, and community settings beyond the home—in short, all aspects of daily life. Many of us remain blind to aspects of our own cultural heritage until we see them in relation to the practices of others.

TAKE A MOMENT... Consider the question, Who should be responsible for rearing young children? How would you answer it? Here are some typical responses from my students: "If parents decide to have a baby, then they should be ready to care for it." "Most people are not happy about others intruding into family life." These statements reflect a widely held opinion in the United States—that the care and rearing of young children, and paying for that care, are the duty of parents, and only parents. This view has a long history—one in which independence, self-reliance, and the privacy of family life emerged as central American values (Halfon & McLearn, 2002). It is one reason, among others, that the public has been slow to endorse publicly supported benefits for all families, such as high-quality child care and paid employment leave for meeting family needs. And it has also contributed to the large number of U.S. children who remain poor, even though their parents are gainfully employed (Gruendel & Aber, 2007; Pohl, 2002; UNICEF, 2007).

Although the culture as a whole may value independence and privacy, not all citizens share the same values. Some belong to **subcultures**—groups of people with beliefs and customs that differ from those of the larger culture. Many ethnic minority groups in the United States have cooperative family structures, which help protect their members from the harmful effects of poverty. As the Cultural Influences box on the following page indicates, the African-American tradition of **extended-family households,** in which parent and child live with one or more adult relatives, is a vital feature of black family life that has enabled its members to survive, despite a long history of prejudice and economic deprivation. Within the extended family, grandparents play meaningful roles in guiding younger generations; adults who face employment, marital, or child-rearing difficulties receive assistance and emotional support; and caregiving is enhanced for children and the elderly. Active, involved extended families also characterize other minorities, such as Asian, Native-American, and Hispanic subcultures (Becker et al., 2003; Harwood et al., 2002).

Our discussion so far reflects a broad dimension on which cultures and subcultures differ: the extent to which *collectivism* versus *individualism* is emphasized. In **collectivist societies,** people define themselves as part of a group and stress group over individual goals. In **individualistic societies,** people think of themselves as separate entities and are largely concerned with their own personal needs (Triandis, 1995, 2005). As these definitions suggest, the two cultural patterns are associated with two distinct views of the self. Collectivist societies value an *interdependent self,* which stresses social harmony, obligations and responsibility to others, and collaborative endeavors. In contrast, individualistic societies value an *independent self,* which emphasizes personal exploration, discovery, and achievement and individual choice in relationships. Both interdependence and independence are part of the makeup of every person and occur in varying mixtures (Greenfield et al., 2003; Tamis-LeMonda et al., 2008). But societies vary greatly in the extent to which they emphasize each alternative and—as later chapters will reveal—instill it in their young.

Although individualism tends to increase as cultures become more complex, cross-national differences remain. The United States is strongly individualistic, whereas most Western European countries lean toward collectivism. As we will see next, collectivist versus individualistic values have a powerful impact on a nation's approach to protecting the well-being of its children and families.

PUBLIC POLICIES AND CHILD DEVELOPMENT When widespread social problems arise, such as poverty, homelessness, hunger, and disease, nations attempt to solve them by developing **public policies**—laws and government programs designed to improve current

CULTURAL INFLUENCES

The African-American Extended Family

The African-American extended family can be traced to the African heritage of most black Americans. In many African societies, newly married couples do not start their own households. Instead, they live with a large extended family, which assists its members with all aspects of daily life. This tradition of maintaining a broad network of kinship ties traveled to North America during the period of slavery. Since then, it has served as a protective shield against the destructive impact of poverty and racial prejudice on African-American family life. Today, more black than white adults have relatives other than their own children living in the same household. African-American parents also live closer to kin, often establish family-like relationships with friends and neighbors, see more relatives during the week, and perceive them as more important in their lives (Boyd-Franklin, 2006; Kane, 2000).

By providing emotional support and sharing income and essential resources, the African-American extended family helps reduce the stress of poverty and single parenthood. Extended-family members often help with child rearing, and adolescent mothers living in extended families are more likely to complete high school and get a job and less likely to be on welfare than mothers living on their own—factors that in turn benefit children's well-being (Gordon, Chase-Lansdale, & Brooks-Gunn, 2004; Trent & Harlan, 1994).

For single mothers who were very young at the time of their child's birth, extended-family living continues to be associated with more positive mother–child interaction during the preschool years. Otherwise, establishing an independent household with the help of nearby relatives is related to improved child rearing. Perhaps this arrangement permits the more mature teenage mother who has developed effective parenting skills to implement them (Chase-Lansdale, Brooks-Gunn, & Zamsky, 1994). In families rearing adolescents, kinship support increases the likelihood of effective parenting, which is related to adolescents' self-reliance, emotional well-being, and reduced antisocial behavior (Hamilton, 2005; Simons et al., 2006).

Finally, the extended family plays an important role in transmitting African-American culture. Compared with nuclear-family households (which include only parents and their children), extended-family arrangements place more emphasis on cooperation and on moral and religious values. And older black adults, such as grandparents and great-grandparents, regard educating children about their African heritage as especially important (Mosely-Howard & Evans, 2000; Taylor, 2000). Family reunions—sometimes held in grandparents' and great-grandparents' hometowns in the South—are especially common among African Americans, giving young people a strong sense of their roots (Boyd-Franklin, 2006). These influences strengthen family bonds, enhance children's development, and increase the chances that the extended-family lifestyle will carry over to the next generation.

■ A grandmother shares a photo album chronicling family history with her son and grandchildren. Strong bonds with extended-family members have helped protect many African-American children against the destructive effects of poverty and racial prejudice. ■

conditions. For example, when poverty increases and families become homeless, a country might decide to build more low-cost housing, provide economic aid to homeowners having difficulty making mortgage payments, and increase welfare benefits. When reports indicate that many children are not achieving well in school, federal and state governments might grant more tax money to school districts, strengthen teacher preparation, and make sure that help reaches children who need it most.

Nevertheless, U.S. public policies safeguarding children and youths have lagged behind policies in other developed nations. As Table 2.6 on page 80 reveals, the United States does not rank well on any key measure of children's health and well-being.

The problems of children and youths extend beyond the indicators in Table 2.6. Despite improved health-care provisions signed into law in 2010, the United States remains the only industrialized nation without a universal, publicly funded health-care system. Approximately 10 percent of U.S. children—most in low-income families—have no health insurance (Kenney, Lynch, & Cook, 2010). Furthermore, the United States has been slow to move toward national standards and funding for child care. Affordable care is in short supply, and much of it is substandard in quality (Lamb & Ahnert, 2006; Muenchow & Marsland, 2007). In families affected

TABLE 2.6   How Does the United States Compare to Other Nations on Indicators
of Children's Health and Well-Being?

INDICATOR	U.S. RANK[a]	SOME COUNTRIES THE UNITED STATES TRAILS
Childhood poverty (among 25 industrialized nations considered)	25th	Canada, Czech Republic, Germany, Norway, Sweden, Poland, Spain[b]
Infant deaths in the first year of life (worldwide)	28th	Canada, Hong Kong, Ireland, Singapore, Spain
Teenage pregnancy rate (among 28 industrialized nations considered)	28th	Australia, Canada, Czech Republic, Denmark, Hungary, Iceland, Poland, Slovak Republic
Public expenditure on education as a percentage of gross domestic product[c] (among 22 industrialized nations considered)	12th	Belgium, France, Iceland, New Zealand, Portugal, Spain, Sweden
Public expenditure on early childhood education and child care as a percentage of gross domestic product (among 14 industrialized nations considered)	9th	Austria, Germany, Italy, Netherlands, France, Sweden
Public expenditure on health as a percentage of total health expenditure, public plus private (among 29 industrialized nations considered)	29th	Austria, Australia, Canada, France, Hungary, Iceland, Switzerland, New Zealand

[a] 1 = highest, or best, rank.

[b] U.S. childhood poverty and, especially, deep poverty rates greatly exceed poverty in these nations. For example, the poverty rate is 9.5 percent in Canada, 6 percent in the Czech Republic, 4 percent in Norway, and 2.5 percent in Sweden. Deep poverty affects just 2.5 percent of children in Canada, and a fraction of 1 percent in the other countries just listed.

[c] Gross domestic product is the value of all goods and services produced by a nation during a specified time period. It provides an overall measure of a nation's wealth.

Sources: Canada Campaign 2000, 2009; OECD, 2006, 2008a, 2008b; UNICEF, 2007; U.S. Census Bureau, 2010b; U.S. Department of Education, 2010.

by divorce, weak enforcement of child support payments heightens poverty in mother-headed households. When they finish high school, many American non-college-bound young people lack the vocational preparation they need to contribute fully to society. And 8 percent of 16- to 24-year olds who dropped out of high school have not returned to earn a diploma (U.S. Department of Education, 2010).

Why have attempts to help children and youths been difficult to realize in the United States? A complex set of political and economic forces is involved. Cultural values of self-reliance and privacy have made government hesitant to become involved in family matters. Furthermore, good social programs are expensive, and they must compete for a fair share of a country's economic resources. Children can easily remain unrecognized in this process because they cannot vote or speak out to protect their own interests (Ripple & Zigler, 2003). Instead, they must rely on the goodwill of others to make them an important government priority.

Without vigilance from child advocates, policies directed at solving a particular social problem can work at cross-purposes with children's well-being, leaving them in dire straits or even worsening their condition. For example, U.S. welfare policy aimed at returning welfare recipients to the workforce—by reducing or terminating their welfare benefits after 24 continuous months—can either help or harm children, depending on whether it lifts a family out of poverty. When welfare-to-work reduces financial strain, it relieves maternal stress, improves quality of parenting, and is associated with cognitive gains and a reduction in child behavior problems (Dunifon, Kalil, & Danziger, 2003; Gennetian & Morris, 2003; Jackson, Bentler, & Franke, 2006). In contrast, former welfare recipients who must take very low-paying jobs that perpetuate poverty often engage in harsh, coercive parenting and have poorly adjusted children (Smith et al., 2001).

LOOKING TOWARD THE FUTURE   Public policies aimed at fostering children's development can be justified on two grounds. The first is that children are the future—the parents, workers, and citizens of tomorrow. Investing in children yields valuable returns to a nation's quality of life (Heckman & Masterov, 2004).

Second, child-oriented policies can be defended on humanitarian grounds—children's basic rights as human beings. In 1989, the U.N. General Assembly, with the assistance of experts from many child-related fields, drew up the *Convention on the Rights of the Child,* a legal agreement among nations that commits each cooperating country to work toward guaranteeing environments that foster children's development, protect them from harm, and enhance their community participation and self-determination. Examples of rights include the highest attainable standard of health; an adequate standard of living; free and compulsory education; a happy, understanding, and loving family life; protection from all forms of abuse and neglect; and freedom of thought, conscience, and religion, subject to appropriate parental guidance and national law.

Although the United States played a key role in drawing up the Convention, it is one of only two countries in the world whose legislature has not yet ratified it. (The other is war-torn Somalia, which currently does not have a recognized national government.) American individualism has stood in the way. Opponents maintain that the Convention's provisions would shift the burden of child rearing from the family to the state (Melton, 2005).

Although the worrisome state of many children and families persists, efforts are being made to improve their condition. Throughout this book, we will discuss many successful programs that could be expanded. Also, growing awareness of the gap between what we know and what we do to better children's lives has led experts in child development to join with concerned citizens as advocates for more effective policies. As a result, several influential interest groups devoted to the well-being of children have emerged.

In the United States, the most vigorous is the Children's Defense Fund—a private, nonprofit organization founded by Marian Wright Edelman in 1973—which engages in research, public education, legal action, drafting of legislation, congressional testimony, and community organizing. It also publishes many reports on U.S. children's condition, government-sponsored programs that serve children and families, and proposals for improving those programs. To learn more about the Children's Defense Fund, visit its website at *www.childrensdefense.org.*

Besides strong advocacy, public policies that enhance child development depend on policy-relevant research that documents needs and evaluates programs to spark improvements. Today, more researchers are collaborating with community and government agencies to enhance the social relevance of their investigations. They are also doing a better job of disseminating their findings to the public in easily understandable, compelling ways, through television documentaries, newspaper stories, magazine articles, websites, and direct reports to government officials. In these ways, they are helping to create the sense of immediacy about the condition of children and families that is necessary to spur a society into action.

■ Marian Wright Edelman, founder and president of the Children's Defense Fund, speaks in support of U.S. health-care reform legislation in Washington, DC. The bill, signed into law on March 23, 2010, immediately prevented children with pre-existing health conditions from being denied insurance coverage. ■

ASK YOURSELF

◆ **REVIEW** Links between family and community are essential for children's well-being. Provide examples and research findings from our discussion that support this idea.

◆ **APPLY** Check your local newspaper or one or two national news magazines or news websites to see how often articles on the condition of children and families appear. Why is it important for researchers to communicate with the general public about children's needs?

◆ **CONNECT** How does poverty affect the functioning of the family system, placing all aspects of development at risk?

◆ **REFLECT** Do you agree with the widespread American sentiment that government should not become involved in family life? Explain.

Understanding the Relationship Between Heredity and Environment

Throughout this chapter, we have discussed a wide variety of genetic and environmental influences, each of which has the power to alter the course of development. Yet children who are born into the same family (and who therefore share both genes and environments) are often quite different in characteristics. We also know that some children are affected more than others by their homes, neighborhoods, and communities. In some cases, a child who is given many advantages nevertheless does poorly, while another, though exposed to unfavorable rearing conditions, does well. How do scientists explain the impact of heredity and environment when they seem to work in so many different ways?

Behavioral genetics is a field devoted to uncovering the contributions of nature and nurture to this diversity in human traits and abilities. All contemporary researchers agree that both heredity and environment are involved in every aspect of development. But for polygenic traits (those due to many genes) such as intelligence and personality, scientists are a long way from knowing the precise hereditary influences involved. Although they are making progress in identifying the multiple variations in DNA sequences associated with complex traits, so far these genetic markers explain only a small amount of variation in human behavior, and a minority of cases of most psychological disorders (Plomin, 2005; Plomin & Davis, 2009). For the most part, scientists are still limited to investigating the impact of genes on complex characteristics indirectly.

Some believe that it is useful and possible to answer the question of *how much each factor contributes* to differences among children. A growing consensus, however, regards that question as unanswerable. These investigators believe that heredity and environment are inseparable (Gottlieb, Wahlsten, & Lickliter, 2006; Lerner & Overton, 2008). The important question, they maintain, is *how nature and nurture work together*. Let's consider each position in turn.

■ Children vary widely in mental abilities and personality traits. Most contemporary researchers seek to clarify how heredity and environment jointly contribute to individual differences in these complex characteristics. ■

The Question, "How Much?"

To infer the role of heredity in complex human characteristics, researchers use special methods, the most common being the *heritability estimate*. Let's look closely at the information this procedure yields, along with its limitations.

HERITABILITY **Heritability estimates** measure the extent to which individual differences in complex traits in a specific population are due to genetic factors. We will take a brief look at heritability findings on intelligence and personality here and will return to them in later chapters, when we consider these topics in greater detail. Heritability estimates are obtained from **kinship studies,** which compare the characteristics of family members. The most common type of kinship study compares identical twins, who share all their genes, with fraternal twins, who share only some. If people who are genetically more alike are also more similar in intelligence and personality, then the researcher assumes that heredity plays an important role.

Kinship studies of intelligence provide some of the most controversial findings in the field of child development. Some experts claim a strong genetic influence, whereas others believe that heredity is barely involved. Currently, most kinship findings support a moderate role for heredity. When many twin studies are examined, correlations between the scores of identical twins are consistently higher than those of fraternal twins. In a summary of more than 10,000 twin pairs, the average correlation was .86 for identical twins and .60 for fraternal twins (Plomin & Spinath, 2004).

Researchers use a complex statistical procedure to compare these correlations, arriving at a heritability estimate ranging from 0 to 1.00. The value for intelligence is about .50 for child and adolescent twin samples in Western industrialized nations. This suggests that differences in genetic makeup explain half the variation in intelligence. Adopted children's mental test scores are more strongly related to their biological parents' scores than to those of their adoptive parents, offering further support for the role of heredity (Petrill & Deater-Deckard, 2004).

Heritability research also reveals that genetic factors are important in personality. For frequently studied traits, such as sociability, anxiety, agreeableness, and activity level, heritability estimates obtained on child and adolescent and young adult twins are moderate, in the .40s and .50s (Caspi & Shiner, 2006; Rothbart & Bates, 2006; Wright et al., 2008).

Twin studies of schizophrenia—a psychological disorder involving delusions and hallucinations, difficulty distinguishing fantasy from reality, and irrational and inappropriate behaviors—consistently yield high heritabilities, around .80. The role of heredity in antisocial behavior and major depression, though still apparent, is less strong, with heritabilities in the .30s and .40s (Faraone, 2008). Again, adoption studies support these results. Biological relatives of schizophrenic and depressed adoptees are more likely than adoptive relatives to share the same disorder (Plomin et al., 2001; Ridenour, 2000; Tienari et al., 2003).

■ Adriana and Tamara, identical twins born in Mexico, were separated at birth and adopted into different homes in the New York City area. They were unaware of each other's existence until age 20, when they met through a mutual acquaintance. The twins found that they had many similarities—academic achievement, a love of dancing, even similar taste in clothing. The study of identical twins reared apart reveals that heredity contributes to many personality characteristics. But generalizing from twin evidence to the population is controversial. ■

LIMITATIONS OF HERITABILITY Serious questions have been raised about the accuracy of heritability estimates, which depends on the extent to which the twin pairs studied reflect genetic and environmental variation in the population. Within a population in which all people have very similar home, school, and community experiences, individual differences in intelligence and personality would be largely genetic, and heritability estimates would be close to 1.00. Conversely, the more environments vary, the more likely they are to account for individual differences, yielding lower heritability estimates. In twin studies, most twin pairs are reared together under highly similar conditions. Even when separated twins are available for study, social service agencies have often placed them in advantaged homes that are alike in many ways (Rutter et al., 2001). Because the environments of most twin pairs are less diverse than those of the general population, heritability estimates are likely to exaggerate the role of heredity.

Heritability estimates are controversial measures because they can easily be misapplied. For example, high heritabilities have been used to suggest that ethnic differences in intelligence, such as the poorer performance of black children compared to white children, have a genetic basis (Jensen, 1969, 1998, 2001; Rushton & Jensen, 2005, 2006). Yet this line of reasoning is widely regarded as incorrect. Heritabilities computed on mostly white twin samples do not tell us what causes test score differences between ethnic groups. We have already seen that large economic and cultural differences are involved. In Chapter 12, we will discuss research indicating that when black children are adopted into economically advantaged homes at an early age, their scores are well above average and substantially higher than those of children growing up in impoverished families.

Perhaps the most serious criticism of heritability estimates has to do with their limited usefulness. Though interesting, these estimates give us no precise information on how intelligence and personality develop or how children might respond to environments designed to help them develop as far as possible (Baltes, Lindenberger, & Staudinger, 2006; Rutter, 2002). Indeed, the heritability of children's intelligence increases as parental education and income increase—that is, as children grow up in conditions that allow them to make the most of their genetic endowment. In impoverished environments, children are prevented from realizing their potential. Consequently, enhancing experiences through interventions—such as parent education and high-quality preschool or child care—has a greater impact on the development of low-SES than higher-SES children (Bronfenbrenner & Morris, 2006; Turkheimer et al., 2003).

According to one group of experts, heritability estimates have too many problems to yield any firm conclusions about the relative strength of nature and nurture (Collins et al., 2000). Although these statistics confirm that heredity contributes to complex traits, they do not tell us how environment can modify genetic influences.

The Question, "How?"

Today, most researchers view development as the result of a dynamic interplay between heredity and environment. How do nature and nurture work together? Several concepts shed light on this question.

REACTION RANGE   The first of these ideas is **range of reaction**—each person's unique, genetically determined response to the environment (Gottesman, 1963). Let's explore this idea in Figure 2.9. Reaction range can apply to any characteristic; here it is illustrated for intelligence. Notice that when environments vary from extremely unstimulating to highly enriched, Ben's intelligence increases steadily, Linda's rises sharply and then falls off, and Ron's begins to increase only after the environment becomes modestly stimulating.

Reaction range highlights two important points. First, it shows that because each of us has a unique genetic makeup, we respond differently to the same environment. Note in Figure 2.9 how a poor environment results in similarly low scores for all three individuals. But when the environment provides an intermediate level of stimulation, Linda is by far the best-performing child. And in a highly enriched environment, Ben does best, followed by Ron, both of whom now outperform Linda.

Second, sometimes different genetic–environmental combinations can make two people look the same! For example, if Linda is reared in a minimally stimulating environment, her score will be about 100—average for children in general. Ben and Ron can also obtain this score, but to do so, they must grow up in a fairly enriched home. In sum, range of reaction reveals that unique blends of heredity and environment lead to both similarities and differences in behavior (Gottlieb, Wahlsten, & Lickliter, 2006).

CANALIZATION   Another way of understanding how heredity and environment combine comes from the concept of **canalization**—the tendency of heredity to restrict the development of some characteristics to just one or a few outcomes. A behavior that is strongly canalized develops similarly in a wide range of environments; only strong environmental forces can change it (Waddington, 1957). For example, infant perceptual and motor development seems to be strongly canalized because all normal human babies eventually roll over, reach for objects, sit up, crawl, and walk. It takes extreme conditions to modify these behaviors or cause them not to appear. In contrast, intelligence and personality are less strongly canalized; they vary much more with changes in the environment.

When we look at behaviors that are constrained by heredity, we can see that canalization is highly adaptive. Through it, nature ensures that children will develop certain species-typical skills under a wide range of rearing conditions, thereby promoting survival.

GENETIC–ENVIRONMENTAL CORRELATION   A major problem in trying to separate heredity and environment is that

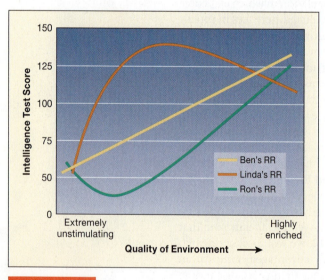

FIGURE 2.9

Intellectual ranges of reaction (RR) for three children in environments that vary from extremely unstimulating to highly enriched. Each child, because of his or her genetic makeup, responds differently to changes in quality of the environment. Ben's intelligence test score increases steadily, Linda's rises sharply and then falls off, and Ron's begins to increase only after the environment becomes modestly stimulating. *(Adapted from Wahlsten, 1994.)*

they are often correlated (Plomin, 2009; Scarr & McCartney, 1983). According to the concept of **genetic–environmental correlation,** our genes influence the environments to which we are exposed. The way this happens changes with age.

Passive and Evocative Correlation. At younger ages, two types of genetic–environmental correlation are common. The first is called *passive* correlation because the child has no control over it. Early on, parents provide environments influenced by their own heredity. For example, parents who are good athletes emphasize outdoor activities and enroll their children in swimming and gymnastics. Besides being exposed to an "athletic environment," the children may have inherited their parents' athletic ability. As a result, they are likely to become good athletes for both genetic and environmental reasons.

The second type of genetic–environmental correlation is *evocative.* The responses children evoke from others are influenced by the child's heredity, and these responses strengthen the child's original style. For example, an active, friendly baby is likely to receive more social stimulation than a passive, quiet infant. And a cooperative, attentive child probably receives more patient and sensitive interactions from parents than an inattentive, distractible child. In support of this idea, the less genetically alike siblings are, the more their parents treat them differently, in both warmth and negativity. Thus, parents' treatment of identical twins is highly similar, whereas their treatment of fraternal twins and nontwin biological siblings is only moderately so. And little resemblance exists in parents' warm and negative interactions with unrelated stepsiblings (see Figure 2.10) (Reiss, 2003).

Active Correlation. At older ages, *active* genetic–environmental correlation becomes common. As children extend their experiences beyond the immediate family and are given the freedom to make more choices, they actively seek environments that fit with their genetic tendencies. The well-coordinated, muscular child spends more time at after-school sports, the musically talented youngster joins the school orchestra and practices his violin, and the intellectually curious child is a familiar patron at her local library.

This tendency to actively choose environments that complement our heredity is called **niche-picking** (Scarr & McCartney, 1983). Infants and young children cannot do much niche-picking because adults select environments for them. In contrast, older children and adolescents are much more in charge of their environments.

The niche-picking idea explains why pairs of identical twins reared apart during childhood and later reunited may find, to their surprise, that they have similar hobbies, food preferences, and vocations—a trend that is especially marked when twins' environmental opportunities are similar (Plomin, 1994). Niche-picking also helps us understand why identical twins become somewhat more alike, and fraternal twins and adopted siblings less alike, in intelligence with age (Bouchard, 2004; Loehlin, Horn, & Willerman, 1997). And niche-picking sheds light on why adolescent identical twin pairs—far more often than same-sex fraternal pairs, ordinary siblings, and adopted siblings—report similar stressful life events influenced by personal decisions and actions, such as failing a course, quitting a job, or getting in trouble for drug-taking (Bemmels et al., 2008).

The influence of heredity and environment is not constant but changes over time. With age,

■ This mother shares her love of the piano with her daughter, who also may have inherited her mother's musical talent. When heredity and environment are correlated, they jointly foster the same capacities, and the influence of one cannot be separated from the influence of the other. ■

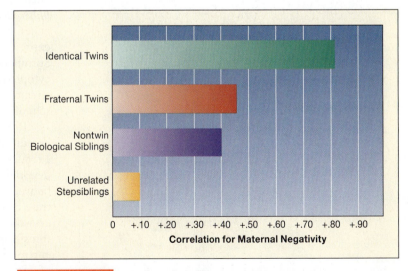

FIGURE 2.10

Similarity in mothers' interactions for pairs of siblings differing in genetic relatedness. The correlations shown are for maternal negativity. The pattern illustrates evocative genetic–environmental correlation. Identical twins evoke similar maternal treatment because of their identical heredity. As genetic resemblance between siblings declines, the strength of the correlation drops. Mothers vary their interactions as they respond to each child's unique genetic makeup. *(Adapted from Reiss, 2003.)*

genetic factors may become more important in influencing the environments we experience and choose for ourselves.

ENVIRONMENTAL INFLUENCES ON GENE EXPRESSION   Notice how, in the concepts just considered, heredity is granted priority. In range of reaction, it *determines* individual responsiveness to varying environments. In canalization, it *restricts* the development of certain behaviors. Similarly, genetic–environmental correlation is viewed as *driven* by genetics, in that children's genetic makeup causes them to receive, evoke, or seek experiences that actualize their inborn tendencies (Plomin, 2009; Rowe, 1994).

A growing number of researchers take issue with the supremacy of heredity, arguing that it does not dictate children's experiences or development in a rigid way. In one study, boys with a genetic tendency toward antisocial behavior (based on the presence of a gene on the X chromosome known to predispose both animals and humans to aggression) were no more aggressive than boys without this gene, *unless* they also had a history of severe child abuse (Caspi et al., 2002). Boys with and without the gene did not differ in their experience of abuse, indicating that the "aggressive genotype" did not increase exposure to abuse. And in a large Finnish adoption study, children whose biological mothers had schizophrenia but who were being reared by healthy adoptive parents showed little mental illness—no more than a control group with healthy biological and adoptive parents. In contrast, schizophrenia and other psychological impairments piled up in adoptees whose biological and adoptive parents were both disturbed (Tienari et al., 2003; Tienari, Wahlberg, & Wynne, 2006).

Furthermore, parents and other caring adults can *uncouple* unfavorable genetic–environmental correlations. They often provide children with positive experiences that modify the expression of heredity, yielding favorable outcomes. For example, in a study that tracked the development of 5-year-old identical twins, pair members tended to resemble each other in level of aggression. And the more aggression they displayed, the more maternal anger and criticism they received (a genetic–environmental correlation). Nevertheless, some mothers treated their twins differently. When followed up at age 7, twins who had been targets of more maternal negativity engaged in even more antisocial behavior. In contrast, their better-treated, genetically identical counterparts showed a reduction in disruptive acts (Caspi et al., 2004). Good parenting protected them from a spiraling, antisocial course of development.

Accumulating evidence reveals that the relationship between heredity and environment is not a one-way street, from genes to environment to behavior. Rather, like other system influences considered in this and the previous chapter, it is *bidirectional:* Genes affect children's behavior and experiences, but their experiences and behavior also affect gene expression (Diamond, 2009; Gottlieb, 2003; Rutter, 2007a). Stimulation—both *internal* to the child (activity within the cytoplasm of the cell, hormones released into the bloodstream) and *external* to the child (home, neighborhood, school, and society)—modifies gene activity.

Researchers call this view of the relationship between heredity and environment the *epigenetic framework* (Gottlieb, 1998, 2007). It is depicted in Figure 2.11. **Epigenesis** means development resulting from ongoing, bidirectional exchanges between heredity and all levels of the environment. To illustrate, providing a baby with a healthy diet promotes brain growth, leading to new connections among nerve cells, which transform gene expression. This opens the door to new gene–environment exchanges—for example, advanced exploration of objects and interaction with caregivers, which further enhance brain growth and gene expression. These ongoing bidirectional influences foster cognitive and social development. In contrast, harmful environments can interfere with gene expression (see the Biology and Environment box on the following page for an example). And at times, the impact

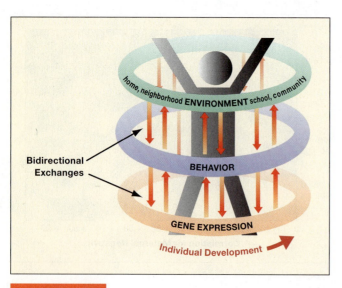

FIGURE 2.11

The epigenetic framework. Development takes place through ongoing, bidirectional exchanges between heredity and all levels of the environment. Genes affect behavior and experiences. Experiences and behavior also affect gene expression. *(Adapted from Gottlieb, 2007.)*

BIOLOGY AND ENVIRONMENT

A Case of Epigenesis: Smoking During Pregnancy Alters Gene Expression

A wealth of experimental research with animals confirms that environment can modify the genome in ways that have no impact on a gene's sequence of base pairs but nevertheless affect the operation of that gene (Zhang & Meaney, 2010). This epigenetic interplay, in which a gene's impact on the individual's phenotype depends on the gene's context, is now being vigorously investigated in humans.

Maternal smoking during pregnancy is among the risk factors for *attention-deficit hyperactivity disorder (ADHD)*—one of the most common disorders of childhood, which we will take up in greater detail in Chapter 12. ADHD symptoms—inattention, impulsivity, and overactivity—typically result in serious academic and social problems. Several studies report that individuals who are homozygous for a chromosome-12 gene (DD) containing a special repeat of base pairs are at increased risk for ADHD. Other research, however, has not confirmed any role for this gene (Fisher et al., 2002; Gill et al., 1997; Waldman et al., 1998).

Animal evidence suggests that one reason for this inconsistency is that environmental influences associated with ADHD—such as prenatal exposure to toxins—modify the gene's activity. To test this possibility, researchers recruited several hundred mothers and their 6-month-old babies, obtaining infant blood samples for genetic analysis and asking mothers whether they smoked regularly during pregnancy (Kahn et al., 2003). At a 5-year follow-up, parents responded to a widely used behavior rating scale that assesses children for ADHD symptoms.

Findings revealed that by itself, the DD genotype was unrelated to impulsivity, overactivity, or oppositional behavior. But children whose mothers had smoked during pregnancy scored higher in these behaviors than children of nonsmoking mothers. Furthermore, as Figure 2.12 illustrates, 5-year-olds with both prenatal nicotine exposure and the DD genetic makeup obtained substantially higher impulsivity, overactivity, and oppositional scores than all other groups—outcomes that persisted even after a variety of other factors (quality of the home environment and maternal ethnicity, marital status, and post-birth smoking) had been controlled.

Another investigation following participants into adolescence obtained similar findings, suggesting that the genotype–prenatal environment effect persists (Becker et al., 2008). What processes might account for it? In animal research, tobacco smoke stimulates the DD genotype to release chemicals in the brain that promote impulsivity and overactivity (Ernst, Moolchan, & Robinson, 2001). These behaviors, in turn, often evoke harsh, punitive parenting, which can trigger defiance in children.

The DD genotype is widespread, present in more than 50 percent of people. Thus, the majority of children prenatally exposed to nicotine are at high risk for learning and behavior problems. As we will see in Chapter 3, smoking during pregnancy has additional negative health consequences. And other genes, in epigenetic interplay with as yet unknown environmental factors, contribute to ADHD symptoms (Hudziak & Rettew, 2009).

© IMAGE SOURCE/GETTY IMAGES

■ Because his mother smoked during pregnancy, this baby may be at increased risk for developing attention-deficit hyperactivity disorder (ADHD). Prenatal exposure to nicotine seems to alter expression of a chromosome-12 gene in ways that greatly heighten impulsivity, overactivity, and oppositional behavior. ■

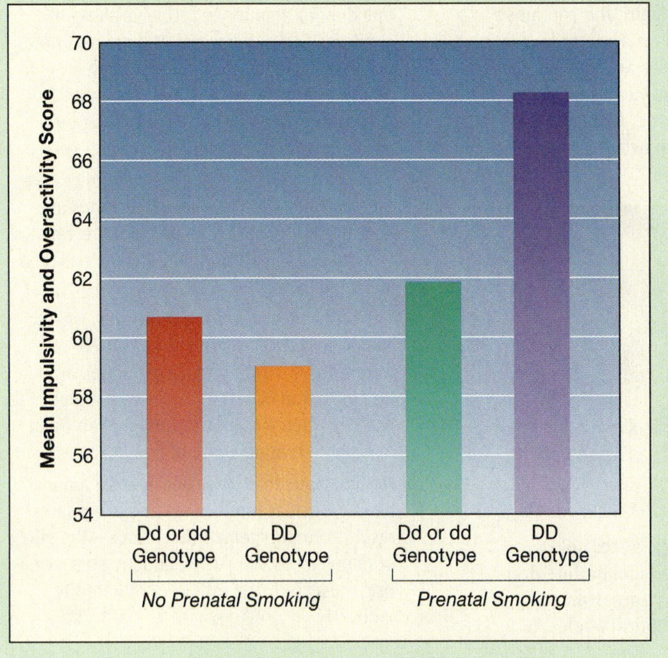

FIGURE 2.12

Combined influence of maternal prenatal smoking and genotype on impulsivity and overactivity at age 5. In the absence of prenatal smoking, 5-year-olds who were homozygous for a chromosome-12 gene (DD) showed no elevation in impulsivity and overactivity (orange bar) compared with children of other genotypes (Dd or dd) (red bar). Among children of all genotypes, prenatal smoking was associated with an increase in these behaviors (green and purple bars). And the combination of prenatal smoking and the DD genotype greatly magnified impulsivity and overactivity (purple bar). Children's oppositional behavior followed a similar epigenetic pattern. *(Adapted from Kahn et al., 2003.)*

is so profound that later experiences can do little to change characteristics (such as intelligence and personality) that originally were flexible.

A major reason that researchers are interested in the nature–nurture issue is that they want to improve environments so that children can develop as far as possible. The concept of epigenesis reminds us that development is best understood as a series of complex exchanges between nature and nurture. Although children cannot be changed in any way we might desire, environments can modify genetic influences. The success of any attempt to improve development depends on the characteristics we want to change, the genetic makeup of the child, and the type and timing of our intervention.

ASK YOURSELF

◆ **REVIEW** What is epigenesis, and how does it differ from range of reaction and genetic–environmental correlation? Provide an example of epigenesis.

◆ **APPLY** Bianca's parents are accomplished musicians. At age 4, Bianca began taking piano lessons. By age 10, she was accompanying the school choir. At age 14, she asked if she could attend a special music high school. Explain how genetic–environmental correlation promoted Bianca's talent.

◆ **CONNECT** Explain how each of the following concepts supports the conclusion that genetic influences on human characteristics are not constant but change over time: somatic mutation (page 60), niche-picking (page 85), and epigenesis (page 86).

◆ **REFLECT** What aspects of your own development— for example, interests, hobbies, college major, or vocational choice—are probably due to niche-picking? Explain.

Summary

Genetic Foundations

What are genes, and how are they transmitted from one generation to the next?

■ Each individual's **phenotype,** or directly observable characteristics, is a product of both **genotype** and environment. **Chromosomes,** rodlike structures within the cell nucleus, contain our hereditary endowment. Along their length are **genes,** segments of **deoxyribonucleic acid (DNA),** that send instructions for making a rich assortment of proteins to the cytoplasm of the cell—a process that makes us distinctly human and influences our development and characteristics.

■ **Gametes,** or sex cells, are produced through a cell division process called **meiosis. Crossing over** and chance assortment of chromosomes into gametes ensure that each receives a unique set of genes from each parent. Once sperm and ovum unite, the resulting **zygote** starts to develop into a complex human being through cell duplication, or **mitosis.**

■ If the fertilizing sperm carries an X chromosome, the child will be a girl; if it contains a Y chromosome, a boy. **Fraternal,** or **dizygotic, twins** result when two ova are released from the mother's ovaries and each is fertilized. **Identical,** or **monozygotic, twins** develop when a zygote divides in two during the early stages of cell duplication.

© RACHEL EPSTEIN/PHOTOEDIT

Describe various patterns of genetic inheritance.

■ Traits controlled by single genes follow **dominant–recessive** and **incomplete dominance** patterns of inheritance. **Homozygous** individuals have two identical **alleles,** or forms of a gene. **Heterozygous** individuals, with one dominant and one recessive allele, are **carriers** of the recessive trait. In **incomplete dominance,** both alleles are expressed in the phenotype, resulting in a trait that combines aspects of both. **Modifier genes** enhance or dilute the effects of other genes.

■ **X-linked inheritance** applies when recessive disorders are carried on the X chromosome and, therefore, are more likely to affect males. In **genomic imprinting,** one parent's allele is activated, regardless of its makeup.

■ Harmful genes arise from **mutation,** which can occur spontaneously or be caused by hazardous environmental agents. Germ-line mutation occurs in the cells that give rise to gametes; somatic mutation can occur in body cells at any time of life.

■ Human traits that vary continuously among people, such as intelligence and personality, result from **polygenic inheritance**—the effects of many genes. For such characteristics, scientists must study the influence of heredity indirectly.

Describe major chromosomal abnormalities, and explain how they occur.

- Most chromosomal abnormalities are due to errors in meiosis. The most common is Down syndrome, which results in physical defects and mental retardation. Disorders of the **sex chromosomes**—XYY, triple X, Klinefelter, and Turner syndromes—are milder than defects of the **autosomes.**

Reproductive Choices

What procedures can assist prospective parents in having healthy children?

- **Genetic counseling** helps couples at risk for giving birth to children with genetic abnormalities consider appropriate reproductive options. **Prenatal diagnostic methods** allow early detection of genetic problems.

- Reproductive technologies, such as donor insemination, in vitro fertilization, surrogate motherhood, and postmenopausal-assisted childbirth, permit many individuals to become parents who otherwise would not, but they raise serious legal and ethical concerns.
- Many parents who cannot conceive or who have a high likelihood of transmitting a genetic disorder decide to adopt. Although adopted children tend to have more learning and emotional problems than children in general, most fare well in the long run. Warm, sensitive parenting predicts favorable development.

Environmental Contexts for Development

Describe family functioning from the perspective of ecological systems theory, along with aspects of the environment that support family well-being and children's development.

- The first and foremost context for child development is the family, a dynamic system characterized by bidirectional influences, in which each family member's behaviors affect those of others. Both direct and indirect influences operate within the family system, which must continually adjust to new events and changes in its members.
- **Socioeconomic status (SES)** profoundly affects family functioning. Higher-SES families tend to be smaller, to emphasize psychological traits, and to engage in warm, verbally stimulating interaction with children. Lower-SES families often stress external characteristics and use more commands, criticism, and physical punishment. Many affluent families are physically and emotionally unavailable, thereby impairing their children's adjustment. Poverty and homelessness undermine effective parenting and pose serious threats to children's development.
- Children benefit from supportive ties between the family and the surrounding environment, including stable, socially cohesive neighborhoods that provide constructive leisure and enrichment activities and that offer parents access to social support. High-quality schools with frequent parent–teacher contact are also vital.
- The values and practices of cultures and **subcultures** affect all aspects of children's daily lives. **Extended-family households,** which are common among many ethnic minority groups, help protect children from negative effects of poverty and other stressful conditions.

- **Collectivist societies,** which emphasize group needs and goals, and **individualistic societies,** which emphasize individual well-being, take different approaches to developing **public policies** to address social problems, including those affecting children. Largely because of its strongly individualistic values, the United States lags behind other developed nations in policies safeguarding children and youths.

Understanding the Relationship Between Heredity and Environment

Explain the various ways heredity and environment may combine to influence complex traits.

- **Behavioral genetics** is a field that examines the contributions of nature and nurture to complex traits. Researchers use **kinship studies** to compute **heritability estimates,** which show that genetic factors influence such traits as intelligence and personality. However, the accuracy and usefulness of heritability estimates have been challenged.

- According to the concepts of **range of reaction** and **canalization,** heredity influences children's responsiveness to varying environments. **Genetic–environmental correlation** and **niche-picking** describe how children's genes affect the environments to which they are exposed. **Epigenesis** reminds us that development is best understood as a series of complex exchanges between nature and nurture.

IMPORTANT TERMS AND CONCEPTS

allele (p. 56)
autosomes (p. 54)
behavioral genetics (p. 82)
canalization (p. 84)
carrier (p. 56)
chromosomes (p. 52)
collectivist societies (p. 78)
coparenting (p. 70)
crossing over (p. 53)
deoxyribonucleic acid (DNA) (p. 52)
dominant–recessive inheritance (p. 56)
epigenesis (p. 86)
extended-family household (p. 78)
fraternal, or dizygotic, twins (p. 55)

gametes (p. 53)
gene (p. 52)
genetic counseling (p. 63)
genetic–environmental correlation (p. 85)
genomic imprinting (p. 59)
genotype (p. 51)
heritability estimate (p. 82)
heterozygous (p. 56)
homozygous (p. 56)
identical, or monozygotic, twins (p. 55)
incomplete dominance (p. 57)
individualistic societies (p. 78)
kinship studies (p. 82)
meiosis (p. 53)

mitosis (p. 53)
modifier genes (p. 57)
mutation (p. 60)
niche-picking (p. 85)
phenotype (p. 51)
polygenic inheritance (p. 60)
prenatal diagnostic methods (p. 63)
public policies (p. 78)
range of reaction (p. 84)
sex chromosomes (p. 54)
socioeconomic status (SES) (p. 71)
subculture (p. 78)
X-linked inheritance (p. 57)
zygote (p. 53)

chapter

3

"Pregnant Mummy"
Eliska Kocová
5 years, Czech Republic

In this painting, the rapidly growing fetus claims a central place in the parent's world. How is the one-celled organism transformed into a baby with the capacity to participate in family life? What factors support or undermine this earliest period of development? Chapter 3 provides answers to these questions.

Reprinted with permission from the International Museum of Children's Art, Oslo, Norway

Prenatal Development

When I met Yolanda and Jay one fall in my child development class, Yolanda was just two months pregnant. Approaching age 30, married for several years and their careers well under way, they had decided to have a baby. To prepare for the transition to parenthood, they enrolled in my evening section, arriving once a week after work full of questions: "How does the baby grow before birth?" "When is each organ formed?" "Has its heart begun to beat?" "Can it hear, feel, or sense our presence?"

Most of all, Yolanda and Jay wanted to do everything possible to make sure their baby would be born healthy. At first, they believed that the uterus completely shielded the developing organism from any dangers in the environment. All babies born with problems, they thought, had unfavorable genes. After browsing through several pregnancy books, Yolanda and Jay realized they were wrong. Yolanda wondered about her diet and whether she should keep up her daily aerobics routine. And she asked me whether an aspirin for a headache, a glass of wine at dinner, or a few cups of coffee during the workday might be harmful.

In this chapter, we answer Yolanda and Jay's questions, along with a great many more that scientists have asked about the events before birth. We begin our discussion during the time period before pregnancy with these puzzling questions: Why is it that generation after generation, most couples who fall in love and marry want to become parents? And how do they decide whether to have just one child or more than one?

Then we trace prenatal development, paying special attention to environmental supports for healthy growth, as well as damaging influences that threaten the child's health and survival. Finally, we look at how couples prepare psychologically for the arrival of the baby and start to forge a new sense of self as mother or father.

Motivations for Parenthood

Why Have Children? • How Large a Family? • Is There a Best Time During Adulthood to Have a Child?

Prenatal Development

Conception • Period of the Zygote • Period of the Embryo • Period of the Fetus

Prenatal Environmental Influences

Teratogens • Other Maternal Factors • The Importance of Prenatal Health Care

■ **BIOLOGY AND ENVIRONMENT**
The Prenatal Environment and Health in Later Life

■ **SOCIAL ISSUES: HEALTH**
The Nurse–Family Partnership: Reducing Maternal Stress and Enhancing Child Development Through Social Support

■ **BIOLOGY AND ENVIRONMENT**
Prenatal Iron Deficiency and Memory Impairments in Infants of Diabetic Mothers

Preparing for Parenthood

Seeking Information • The Baby Becomes a Reality • Models of Effective Parenthood • The Parental Relationship

Motivations for Parenthood

TAKE A MOMENT... What, in your view, are the benefits and drawbacks of having children? How large would your ideal family be, and why? As part of her semester project for my class, Yolanda interviewed her grandmother, asking why she had wanted children and how she had settled on a particular family size. Yolanda's grandmother, whose children were born in the 1950s, replied:

> We didn't think much about whether or not to have children in those days. We just had them—everybody did. It would have seemed odd not to! I was 22 years old when I had the first of my four children, and I had four because—well, I wouldn't have had just one because we all thought children needed brothers and sisters, and only children could end up spoiled and selfish. Life is more interesting with children, you know. And now that we're older, we've got family we can depend on and grandchildren to enjoy.

Why Have Children?

In some ways, the reasons Yolanda's grandmother wanted children are much like those of contemporary parents. In other ways, they are very different. In the past, the issue of whether to have children was, for many adults, a biological given or a compelling social expectation. Today, in Western industrialized nations, it is a matter of true individual choice. Effective birth control techniques enable adults to avoid having children in most instances. And changing cultural values allow people to remain childless with far less fear of social criticism and rejection than a generation or two ago (Scott, 2009). In 1950, 78 percent of U.S. married couples were parents. Today, 70 percent bear children—a choice affected by a complex array of factors including financial circumstances, career goals, personal and religious values, and health conditions (Theil, 2006).

When Americans are asked about their desire to have children, they mention a variety of advantages and disadvantages, which are listed in Table 3.1. Although some ethnic and regional differences exist, reasons for having children that are most important to all groups include the warm, affectionate relationship and the stimulation and fun that children provide. Also frequently mentioned are growth and learning experiences that children bring into the lives of adults, the desire to have someone carry on after one's own death, and feelings of accomplishment and creativity that come from helping children grow (Cowan & Cowan, 2000; Langdridge, Connolly, & Sheeran, 2000; O'Laughlin & Anderson, 2001).

Most adults are also aware that having children means years of extra burdens and responsibilities. Among disadvantages of parenthood, they cite "loss of freedom" most often, followed by "financial strain." According to a conservative estimate, new parents in the United States today will spend about $210,000 to rear a child from birth to age 18, and many will incur substantial additional expense for higher education and financial dependency during emerging adulthood—a reality that has contributed to the declining birthrate in industrialized nations (Lino & Carlson, 2009). Finally, many adults worry greatly about family–work conflict—not having enough time to meet both child-rearing and job responsibilities (Jacobs & Gerson, 2004).

Greater freedom to choose whether, when, and how to have children (see the discussion of reproductive choices in Chapter 2) makes contemporary family planning more challenging than it was in Yolanda's grandmother's day. As each partner expects to have equal say, childbearing often becomes a matter of delicate negotiation (Cowan & Cowan, 2000). Yet careful weighing of the pros and cons of having children means that many more couples are making informed and personally meaningful decisions—a trend that increases the chances that they will have children when ready and will find parenting an enriching experience.

LOOK AND LISTEN

Interview several parents of infants or preschoolers about the benefits and challenges of parenthood. Ask which issues they considered before starting a family. How deliberate about family planning were they?

■ Individuals from diverse cultures mention many of the same reasons for becoming parents. This young couple takes pleasure in the affectionate, playful relationship they have with their toddler son. ■

© MYRLEEN PEARSON/THE IMAGE WORKS

TABLE 3.1 Advantages and Disadvantages of Parenthood Mentioned by American Couples

ADVANTAGES	DISADVANTAGES
Giving and receiving warmth and affection	Loss of freedom, being tied down
Experiencing the stimulation and fun that children add to life	Financial strain
Being accepted as a responsible and mature member of the community	Family–work conflict—not enough time to meet both child-rearing and job responsibilities
Experiencing new growth and learning opportunities that add meaning to life	Interference with mother's employment opportunities and career progress
Having someone carry on after one's own death	Worries over children's health, safety, and well-being
Gaining a sense of accomplishment and creativity from helping children grow	Risks of bringing up children in a world plagued by crime, war, and pollution
Having someone to provide care in old age	Reduced time to spend with partner
Learning to become less selfish and to sacrifice	Loss of privacy
Having offspring who help with parents' work or add their own income to the family's resources	Fear that children will turn out badly, through no fault of one's own

Sources: Cowan & Cowan, 2000; O'Laughlin & Anderson, 2001.

How Large a Family?

In contrast to her grandmother, Yolanda plans to have no more than two children. And she and Jay are talking about whether to limit their family to a single child. In 1960, the average number of children per North American couple was 3.1. Currently, it is 2.1 in the United States; 1.9 in the United Kingdom; 1.8 in Australia; 1.7 in Sweden; 1.6 in Canada; 1.4 in Germany; and 1.3 in Italy and Japan (U.S. Census Bureau, 2010a; 2010b). In addition to more effective birth control, a major reason for this decline is that a family size of one or two children is more compatible with a woman's decision to divide her energies between family and career. Marital instability has also contributed to smaller families: More couples today get divorced before their childbearing plans are complete.

Popular advice to prospective parents often recommends limiting family size in the interests of "child quality"—more parental affection, attention, and material resources per child, which enhance children's intellectual development. Do large families make less intelligent children, as prevailing attitudes suggest? Or do less intelligent parents—as a result of heredity, environment, or both—tend to have larger families? To find out researchers turned to a large, two-generation longitudinal study.

Starting in 1972, the U.S. National Longitudinal Survey of Youth (NLSY) followed a nationally representative sample of several thousand U.S. 14- to 22-year-olds; in 1986 the children of the original participants were added to the investigation. Because both cohorts took intelligence tests, the researchers could (1) examine the relationship of sibling birth order within families to mental test scores, to find out whether having more children depresses children's intellectual functioning; and (2) correlate maternal scores with family size, for insight into whether mothers who score poorly are prone to have larger families.

As the horizontal lines in Figure 3.1 reveal, children's mental test performance did not decline with later birth

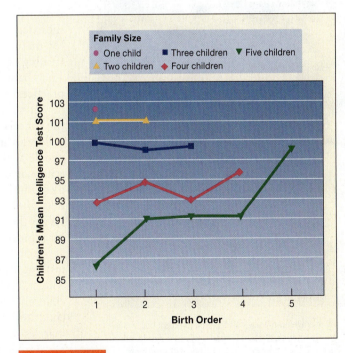

FIGURE 3.1

Relationship of birth order and family size to intelligence. In the U.S. National Longitudinal Survey of Youth, children's intelligence test scores did not decline with later birth order, as would be predicted if large families diluted the quality of children's experiences. To the contrary, in the largest families, the youngest children tended to score higher than their siblings. But note the differences among the lines, which indicate that the larger the family, the lower the scores of all siblings. *(From J. L. Rodgers, H. H. Cleveland, E. van den Oord, & D. C. Rowe, 2000, "Resolving the Debate Over Birth Order, Family Size, and Intelligence,"* American Psychologist, *55, p. 607. © 2000 by the American Psychological Association. Reprinted with permission.)*

TABLE 3.2	Advantages and Disadvantages of a One-Child Family		
ADVANTAGES		**DISADVANTAGES**	
Mentioned by Parents	*Mentioned by Children*	*Mentioned by Parents*	*Mentioned by Children*
Having time to pursue one's own interests and career	Having no sibling rivalry	Walking a "tightrope" between healthy attention and overindulgence	Not getting to experience the closeness of a sibling relationship
Less financial pressure	Having more privacy	Having only one chance to "make good" as a parent	Feeling too much pressure from parents to succeed
Not having to worry about "playing favorites" among children	Enjoying greater affluence	Being left childless in case of the child's death	Having no one to help care for parents when they get old
	Having a closer parent–child relationship		

Source: Hawke & Knox, 1978.

order—a finding that contradicts the belief that having more children depresses children's intellectual ability. At the same time, the differences among the lines show that the larger the family, the lower the scores of all siblings. The researchers found that the link between family size and children's scores can be explained by the strong trend for mothers who are low in intelligence to give birth to more children (Rodgers et al., 2000). In other NLSY research, among children of bright, economically advantaged mothers, the family size–intelligence correlation disappeared (Guo & VanWey, 1999).

Other evidence confirms that rather than parenting quality declining as new children are born, parents reallocate their energies. In a longitudinal study of Canadian two-parent families, new births led to a decrease in maternal affection toward older siblings, though most mothers probably remained generally warm. At the same time, the consistency of parenting—the extent to which mothers insisted older children meet their expectations for mature behavior, such as completing chores, doing homework, and treating others respectfully—rose over time (Strohschein et al., 2008). After a new baby joined the family, mothers seemed to reorganize their parenting practices to best meet all their children's needs.

In sum, although many good reasons exist for limiting family size, the concern that additional births will reduce parenting quality and, thus, children's intelligence and life chances is not warranted. Rather, young people with lower mental test scores—many of whom dropped out of school, live in poverty, lack hope for their future, and fail to engage in family planning—are most likely to have large families (Amato et al., 2008). Return to the Social Issues: Education box on page 73 in Chapter 2 to review the close link between education and family planning. Both are vital for improving children's quality of life.

Is Yolanda's grandmother right when she says that parents who have just one child are likely to end up with a spoiled, selfish youngster? As we will see in Chapter 13, research also challenges this widely held belief. Only children are just as well-adjusted as children with siblings. Still, the one-child family, like all family lifestyles, has both pros and cons. Table 3.2 summarizes results of a survey in which only children and their parents were asked what they liked and disliked about living in a single-child family. The list is useful for parents to consider when deciding how many children would best fit their life plans.

■ Average family size has declined in recent decades in North America, Western Europe, and other developed nations. But, contrary to popular belief, having more children does not reduce the intelligence or life chances of later-born children. ■

© PHOTODISC/GETTY IMAGES

Is There a Best Time During Adulthood to Have a Child?

Yolanda's grandmother had her first child in her early twenties. Yolanda, at age 29, is pregnant for the first time. Many people believe that women should, ideally, give birth in their twenties, not only because the risk of having a baby with a chromosomal disorder increases with age (see Chapter 2) but also because younger parents have more energy to keep up with active children.

However, as Figure 3.2 reveals, first births to women in their thirties have increased greatly over the past several decades. Many people are delaying childbearing until their education is complete, their careers are established, and they know they can support a child. Older parents may be somewhat less energetic than they once were, but they are financially better off and emotionally more mature. For these reasons, they may be better able to invest in parenting.

Nevertheless, reproductive capacity does decline with age. Fertility problems among women increase from age 15 to 50, with a sharp rise in the mid-thirties. Between ages 25 and 34, nearly 20 percent of women are affected, a figure that climbs to 34 percent for 35- to 39-year-olds and to 43 percent for 40- to 44-year-olds. Age also affects male reproductive capacity. Amount of semen and concentration of sperm in each ejaculation decline gradually after age 35. Consequently, compared to a 25-year-old man, a 45-year-old is 12 times as likely to take more than two years to achieve a conception (Lambert, Masson, & Fisch, 2006; U.S. Department of Health and Human Services, 2009e). Women with demanding careers are especially likely to delay parenthood (Tough et al., 2007). Many believe, incorrectly, that if they have difficulty conceiving, they can rely on reproductive technologies. But recall from Chapter 2 that the success of these procedures drops steadily with age. Although no one time during adulthood is best to begin parenthood, individuals who decide to put off childbirth until well into their thirties or early forties risk having fewer children than they desire or none at all.

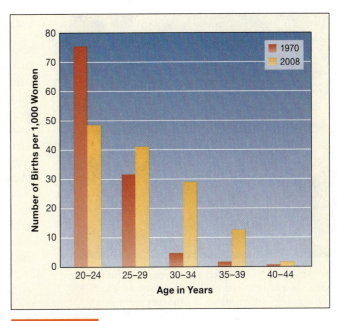

FIGURE 3.2

First births to American women of different ages in 1970 and 2008. The birthrate decreased during this period for women 20 to 24 years of age, whereas it increased for women 25 years of age and older. For women in their thirties, the birthrate more than doubled. Similar trends have occurred in other industrialized nations. *(Adapted from U.S. Census Bureau, 2010b.)*

ASK YOURSELF

◆ **REVIEW** Using research findings, explain why the common assumption that larger families make less intelligent children is incorrect.

◆ **APPLY** Rhonda and Mark are career-oriented, 35-year-old parents of an only child. They are thinking about having a second baby. What factors should they keep in mind as they decide whether to add to their family at this time in their lives?

◆ **CONNECT** Why is it incorrect for couples who postpone childbearing until age 35 or later to conclude that medical advances can overcome fertility problems? (See Chapter 2, pages 66–67.)

◆ **REFLECT** Ask one of your parents or grandparents to list his or her motivations for having children. How do those motivations compare with your own? What factors—for example, education or cultural changes—might account for any differences?

Prenatal Development

The sperm and ovum that unite to form the new individual are uniquely suited for the task of reproduction. The ovum is a tiny sphere, measuring $1/175$ inch in diameter, that is barely visible to the naked eye as a dot the size of the period at the end of this sentence. But in its microscopic world, it is a giant—the largest cell in the human body. The ovum's size makes it a perfect target for the much smaller sperm, which measure only $1/500$ inch.

In this photo taken with the aid of a powerful microscope, sperm penetrate the surface of the enormous-looking ovum, the largest cell in the human body. When one sperm successfully fertilizes the ovum, the resulting zygote begins to duplicate. ■

Conception

About once every 28 days, in the middle of a woman's menstrual cycle, an ovum bursts from one of her *ovaries*, two walnut-sized organs located deep inside her abdomen, and is drawn into one of two *fallopian tubes*—long, thin structures that lead to the hollow, soft-lined uterus (see Figure 3.3). While the ovum is traveling, the spot on the ovary from which it was released, now called the *corpus luteum*, secretes hormones that prepare the lining of the uterus to receive a fertilized ovum. If pregnancy does not occur, the corpus luteum shrinks, and the lining of the uterus is discarded two weeks later with menstruation.

The male produces sperm in vast numbers—an average of 300 million a day—in the *testes*, two glands located in the *scrotum*, sacs that lie just behind the penis. In the final process of maturation, each sperm develops a tail that permits it to swim long distances upstream in the female reproductive tract, through the *cervix* (opening of the uterus), and into the fallopian tube, where fertilization usually takes place. The journey is difficult, and many sperm die. Only 300 to 500 reach the ovum, if one happens to be present. Sperm live for up to six days and can lie in wait for the ovum, which survives for only one day after being released into the fallopian tube. However, most conceptions result from intercourse during a three-day period—on the day of ovulation or during the two days preceding it (Wilcox, Weinberg, & Baird, 1995).

With conception, the story of prenatal development begins to unfold. The vast changes that take place during the 38 weeks of pregnancy are usually divided into three phases: (1) the period of the zygote, (2) the period of the embryo, and (3) the period of the fetus. As we look at what happens in each, you may find it useful to refer to Table 3.3, which summarizes milestones of prenatal development.

Female reproductive organs, showing fertilization, early cell duplication, and implantation. *(From* Before We Are Born, *6th ed., by K. L. Moore and T. V. N. Persaud, p. 87. Copyright © 2003, reprinted with permission from Elsevier, Inc.)*

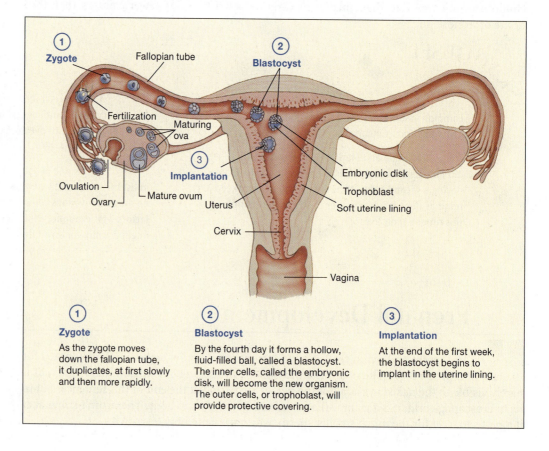

1 Zygote

As the zygote moves down the fallopian tube, it duplicates, at first slowly and then more rapidly.

2 Blastocyst

By the fourth day it forms a hollow, fluid-filled ball, called a blastocyst. The inner cells, called the embryonic disk, will become the new organism. The outer cells, or trophoblast, will provide protective covering.

3 Implantation

At the end of the first week, the blastocyst begins to implant in the uterine lining.

TABLE 3.3 Milestones of Prenatal Development

TRIMESTER	PERIOD	WEEKS	LENGTH AND WEIGHT	MAJOR EVENTS
First	Zygote	1		The one-celled zygote multiplies and forms a blastocyst.
		2		The blastocyst burrows into the uterine lining. Structures that feed and protect the developing organism begin to form—*amnion, chorion, yolk sac, placenta,* and *umbilical cord.*
	Embryo	3–4	¼ inch (6 mm)	A primitive brain and spinal cord appear. Heart, muscles, ribs, backbone, and digestive tract begin to develop.
		5–8	1 inch (2.5 cm); ⅟₇ ounce (4 g)	Many external body structures (face, arms, legs, toes, fingers) and internal organs form. The sense of touch begins to develop, and the embryo can move.
	Fetus	9–12	3 inches (7.6 cm); less than 1 ounce (28 g)	Rapid increase in size begins. Nervous system, organs, and muscles become organized and connected, and new behavioral capacities (kicking, thumb sucking, mouth opening, and rehearsal of breathing) appear. External genitals are well-formed, and the fetus's sex is evident.
Second		13–24	12 inches (30 cm); 1.8 pounds (820 g)	The fetus continues to enlarge rapidly. In the middle of this period, fetal movements can be felt by the mother. Vernix and lanugo keep the fetus's skin from chapping in the amniotic fluid. Most of the brain's neurons are present by 24 weeks. Eyes are sensitive to light, and the fetus reacts to sound.
Third		25–38	20 inches (50 cm); 7.5 pounds (3,400 g)	The fetus has a good chance of survival if born during this time. Size increases. Lungs mature. Rapid brain development causes sensory and behavioral capacities to expand. In the middle of this period, a layer of fat is added under the skin. Antibodies are transmitted from mother to fetus to protect against disease. Most fetuses rotate into an upside-down position in preparation for birth.

Source: Moore & Persaud, 2008.

Photos (from top to bottom): © Claude Cortier/Photo Researchers, Inc.; © G. Moscoso/Photo Researchers, Inc.; © John Watney/Photo Researchers, Inc.; © James Stevenson/Photo Researchers, Inc.; © Lennart Nilsson, *A Child Is Born*/Scanpix.

Period of the Zygote

The period of the zygote lasts about two weeks, from fertilization until the tiny mass of cells drifts down and out of the fallopian tube and attaches itself to the wall of the uterus. The zygote's first cell duplication is long and drawn out; it is not complete until about 30 hours after conception. Gradually, new cells are added at a faster rate. By the fourth day, 60 to 70 cells exist that form a hollow, fluid-filled ball called a **blastocyst** (refer again to Figure 3.3). The cells on the inside of the blastocyst, called the **embryonic disk,** will become the new organism; the thin outer ring of cells, termed the **trophoblast,** will become the structures that provide protective covering and nourishment.

IMPLANTATION   Between the seventh and ninth days, **implantation** occurs: The blastocyst burrows deep into the uterine lining. Surrounded by the woman's nourishing blood, it starts to grow in earnest. At first, the trophoblast (protective outer layer) multiplies fastest. It forms a membrane, called the **amnion,** that encloses the developing organism in **amniotic fluid,** which helps keep the temperature of the prenatal world constant and provides a cushion against any jolts caused by the woman's movement. A *yolk sac* emerges that produces blood cells until the developing liver, spleen, and bone marrow are mature enough to take over this function (Moore & Persaud, 2008).

The events of these first two weeks are delicate and uncertain. As many as 30 percent of zygotes do not survive this period. In some, the sperm and ovum did not join properly. In others, for some unknown reason, cell duplication never begins. By preventing implantation in these cases, nature eliminates most prenatal abnormalities (Sadler, 2009).

THE PLACENTA AND UMBILICAL CORD   By the end of the second week, cells of the trophoblast form another protective membrane—the **chorion,** which surrounds the amnion. From the chorion, tiny fingerlike *villi,* or blood vessels, emerge.[1] As these villi burrow into the uterine wall, the placenta starts to develop. By bringing the mother's and the embryo's blood close together, the **placenta** permits food and oxygen to reach the developing organism and waste products to be carried away. A membrane forms that allows these substances to be exchanged but prevents the mother's and the embryo's blood from mixing directly (see Figure 3.4).

The placenta is connected to the developing organism by the **umbilical cord,** which first appears as a primitive body stalk and, during the course of pregnancy, grows to a

■ **Period of the zygote: seventh to ninth day.** The fertilized ovum duplicates at an increasingly rapid rate, forming a hollow ball of cells, or blastocyst, by the fourth day after fertilization. Here the blastocyst, magnified thousands of times, burrows into the uterine lining between the seventh and ninth day. ■

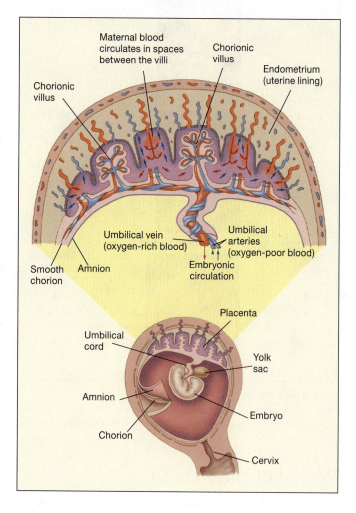

FIGURE 3.4

Cross-section of the uterus, showing detail of the placenta. The embryo's blood flows from the umbilical cord arteries into the chorionic villi and returns via the umbilical cord vein. The mother's blood circulates in spaces surrounding the chorionic villi. A membrane between the two blood supplies permits food and oxygen to be delivered and waste products to be carried away. The two blood supplies do not mix directly. The umbilical arteries carry oxygen-poor blood (shown in blue) to the placenta, and the umbilical vein carries oxygen-rich blood (shown in red) to the fetus. *(From Before We Are Born, 6th ed., by K. L. Moore and T. V. N. Persaud, p. 95. Copyright © 2003, reprinted with permission from Elsevier, Inc.)*

---

[1]Recall from Chapter 2 that *chorionic villus sampling* is the prenatal diagnostic method that can be performed earliest, at nine weeks after conception. In this procedure, tissues from the ends of the villi are removed and examined for genetic abnormalities.

length of 1 to 3 feet. The umbilical cord contains one large vein that delivers blood loaded with nutrients and two arteries that remove waste products. The force of blood flowing through the cord keeps it firm, much like a garden hose, so it seldom tangles while the embryo, like a space-walking astronaut, floats freely in its fluid-filled chamber (Moore & Persaud, 2008).

By the end of the period of the zygote, the developing organism has found food and shelter. Already, it is a very complex being. These dramatic beginnings take place before most mothers know they are pregnant.

Period of the Embryo

The period of the **embryo** lasts from implantation through the eighth week of pregnancy. During these brief six weeks, the most rapid prenatal changes take place, as the groundwork is laid for all body structures and internal organs. Because all parts of the body are forming, the embryo is especially vulnerable to interference with healthy development. But the short time span of embryonic growth helps limit opportunities for serious harm.

LAST HALF OF THE FIRST MONTH   In the first week of this period, the embryonic disk forms three layers of cells: (1) the *ectoderm*, which will become the nervous system and skin; (2) the *mesoderm*, from which will develop the muscles, skeleton, circulatory system, and other internal organs; and (3) the *endoderm*, which will become the digestive system, lungs, urinary tract, and glands. These three layers give rise to all parts of the body.

At first, the nervous system develops fastest. The ectoderm folds over to form the **neural tube,** or spinal cord. At $3\frac{1}{2}$ weeks, the top swells to form the brain. Production of *neurons* (nerve cells that store and transmit information) begins deep inside the neural tube at the astounding pace of more than 250,000 per minute. Once formed, neurons travel along tiny threads to their permanent locations, where they will form the major parts of the brain (Nelson, Thomas, & de Haan, 2006).

While the nervous system is developing, the heart begins to pump blood, and muscles, backbone, ribs, and digestive tract start to appear. At the end of the first month, the curled embryo—only $\frac{1}{4}$ inch long—consists of millions of organized groups of cells with specific functions.

THE SECOND MONTH   In the second month, growth continues rapidly. The eyes, ears, nose, jaw, and neck form. Tiny buds become arms, legs, fingers, and toes. Internal organs are more distinct: The intestines grow, the heart develops separate chambers, and the liver and spleen take over production of blood cells so that the yolk sac is no longer needed. Changing body proportions cause the embryo's posture to become more upright. Now 1 inch long and $\frac{1}{7}$ ounce in weight, the embryo can sense its world. It responds to touch, particularly in the mouth area and on the soles of the feet. And it can move, although its tiny flutters are still too light to be felt by the mother (Moore & Persaud, 2008).

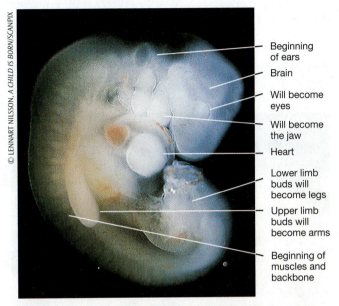

© LENNART NILSSON, *A CHILD IS BORN*/SCANPIX

Beginning of ears
Brain
Will become eyes
Will become the jaw
Heart
Lower limb buds will become legs
Upper limb buds will become arms
Beginning of muscles and backbone

■ **Period of the embryo: fourth week.** This 4-week-old embryo is only ¼ inch long, but many body structures have begun to form. ■

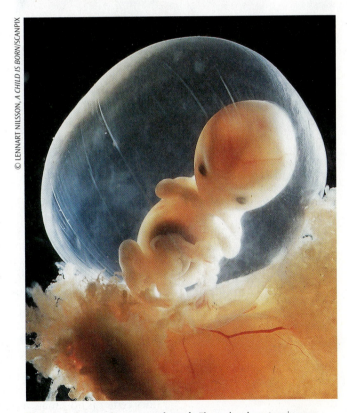

© LENNART NILSSON, *A CHILD IS BORN*/SCANPIX

■ **Period of the embryo: seventh week.** The embryo's posture is more upright. Body structures—eyes, nose, arms, legs, and internal organs—are more distinct. The embryo now responds to touch. It also can move, although at less than one inch long and an ounce in weight, it is still too tiny to be felt by the mother. ■

Period of the Fetus

The period of the **fetus,** from the ninth week to the end of pregnancy, is the longest prenatal period. During this "growth and finishing" phase, the developing organism increases rapidly in size, especially from the ninth to the twentieth week.

THE THIRD MONTH   In the third month, the organs, muscles, and nervous system start to become organized and connected. When the brain signals, the fetus kicks, bends its arms, forms a fist, curls its toes, turns its head, opens its mouth, and even sucks its thumb, stretches, and yawns. Body position changes are frequent, occurring as often as 25 times per hour (Einspieler, Marschik, & Prechtl, 2008). The tiny lungs begin to expand and contract in an early rehearsal of breathing movements. By the twelfth week, the external genitals are well-formed, and the sex of the fetus can be detected with ultrasound (Sadler, 2009). Other finishing touches appear, such as fingernails, toenails, tooth buds, and eyelids that open and close. The heartbeat can now be heard through a stethoscope.

Prenatal development is sometimes divided into **trimesters,** or three equal time periods. At the end of the third month, the *first trimester* is complete.

THE SECOND TRIMESTER   By the middle of the second trimester, between 17 and 20 weeks, the new being has grown large enough that the mother can feel its movements. A white, cheeselike substance called **vernix** protects its skin from chapping during the long months spent bathing in the amniotic fluid. White, downy hair called **lanugo** also appears over the entire body, helping the vernix stick to the skin.

At the end of the second trimester, many organs are well-developed. And most of the brain's billions of neurons are in place; few will be produced after this time. However, *glial cells,* which support and feed the neurons, continue to increase at a rapid rate throughout the remaining months of pregnancy, as well as after birth. Consequently, brain weight increases tenfold from the twentieth week until birth (Roelfsema et al., 2004).

Brain growth means new behavioral capacities. The 20-week-old fetus can be stimulated as well as irritated by sounds. Slow eye movements appear, with rapid eye movements following at 22 weeks. And if a doctor looks inside the uterus using fetoscopy (see Chapter 2, page 64), fetuses try to shield their eyes from the light with their hands, indicating that sight has begun to emerge (Moore & Persaud, 2008). Still, a fetus born at this time cannot survive. Its lungs are immature, and the brain cannot yet control breathing movements or body temperature.

THE THIRD TRIMESTER   During the final trimester, a fetus born early has a chance for survival. The point at which the baby can first survive, called the **age of viability,** occurs sometime between 22 and 26 weeks (Moore & Persaud, 2008). A baby born between the seventh and eighth month, however, usually needs oxygen assistance to breathe. Although the brain's respiratory center is now mature, tiny air sacs in the lungs are not yet ready to inflate and exchange carbon dioxide for oxygen.

The brain continues to make great strides. The *cerebral cortex,* the seat of human intelligence, enlarges. Convolutions and grooves in its surface appear, permitting a dramatic increase

© LENNART NILSSON, *A CHILD IS BORN*/SCANPIX

■ **Period of the fetus: eleventh week.** The organism grows rapidly, and body structures are completed. At 11 weeks, the brain and muscles are better connected. The fetus can kick, bend its arms, open and close its hands and mouth, and suck its thumb. Notice the yolk sac, which shrinks as pregnancy advances. The internal organs have taken over its function of producing blood cells. ■

in surface area that allows for maximum prenatal brain growth without the full-term baby's head becoming too large to pass through the birth canal. As neurological organization improves, the fetus spends more time awake. At 20 weeks, fetal heart rate reveals no periods of alertness. But by 28 weeks, fetuses are awake about 11 percent of the time, a figure that rises to 16 percent just before birth (DiPietro et al., 1996). Between 30 and 34 weeks, fetuses show rhythmic alternations between sleep and wakefulness that gradually increase in organization (Rivkees, 2003). Around this time, synchrony between fetal heart rate and motor activity peaks: A rise in heart rate is usually followed within five seconds by a burst of motor activity (DiPietro et al., 2006). These are clear signs that coordinated neural networks are beginning to form in the brain.

By the end of pregnancy, the fetus also takes on the beginnings of a personality. Higher fetal activity in the last weeks of pregnancy predicts a more active infant in the first month of life—a relationship that, for boys, persists into early childhood (Groome et al., 1999). Fetal activity is linked in other ways to infant temperament. In one study, more active fetuses during the third trimester became 1-year-olds who could better handle frustration and 2-year-olds who were less fearful, in that they more readily interacted with toys and with an unfamiliar adult in a laboratory (DiPietro et al., 2002). Perhaps fetal activity level is an indicator of healthy neurological development, which fosters adaptability in childhood. The relationships just described, however, are only modest. As we will see in Chapter 7, sensitive caregiving can modify the temperaments of children who have difficulty adapting to new experiences.

■ **Period of the fetus: twenty-second week.** This fetus is almost a foot long and weighs slightly more than one pound. Its movements can be felt easily by the mother and by other family members who place a hand on her abdomen. The fetus has reached the age of viability; if born, it has a slim chance of surviving. ■

The third trimester also brings greater responsiveness to external stimulation. As we will see later when we discuss newborn capacities, fetuses acquire taste and odor preferences from bathing in and swallowing amniotic fluid (its makeup is influenced by the mother's diet). Between 23 and 30 weeks, connections form between the cerebral cortex and brain regions involved in pain sensitivity. By this time, painkillers should be used in any surgical procedures performed on a fetus (Lee et al., 2005). Around 28 weeks, fetuses blink their eyes in reaction to nearby sounds (Kisilevsky & Low, 1998; Saffran, Werker, & Werner, 2006). And at 30 weeks, fetuses presented with a repeated auditory stimulus against the mother's abdomen initially react with a rise in heart rate and body movements. But over the next 5 to 6 minutes, responsiveness gradually declines, indicating habituation (adaptation) to the sound. If the stimulus is reintroduced after a 10-minute delay, heart rate falls off far more quickly (Dirix et al., 2009). This suggests that fetuses can remember for at least a brief period.

Within the next six weeks, fetuses distinguish the tone and rhythm of different voices and sounds. They show systematic heart rate changes in response to a male versus a female speaker, to the mother's voice versus a stranger's, to a stranger speaking their native language (English) versus a foreign language (Mandarin Chinese), and to a simple familiar melody (descending tones) versus an unfamiliar melody (ascending tones) (Granier-Deferre et al., 2003; Huotilainen et al., 2005; Kisilevsky et al., 2003, 2009; Lecanuet et al., 1993). And in one clever study, mothers read aloud Dr. Seuss's lively book *The Cat in the Hat* each day during the last six weeks of pregnancy. After birth, their infants learned to turn on recordings of the mother's voice by sucking on nipples. They sucked hardest to hear *The Cat in the Hat*—the sound they had come to know while still in the womb (DeCasper & Spence, 1986).

TAKE A MOMENT... On the basis of these findings, would you recommend that expectant mothers provide fetuses with stimulation specially designed to enhance later mental

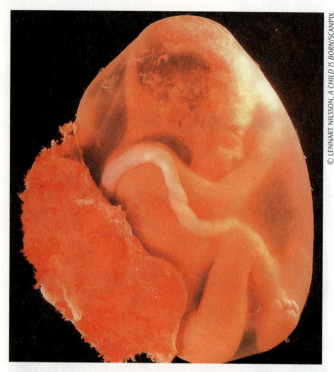

(Photo credit, vertical:) © LENNART NILSSON, *A CHILD IS BORN*/SCANPIX

■ **Period of the fetus: thirty-sixth week.** This fetus fills the uterus. To support its need for nourishment, the umbilical cord and placenta have grown large. The vernix (cheeselike substance) on the skin protects it from chapping. The fetus has accumulated a layer of fat to assist with temperature regulation after birth. In two more weeks, it will be full-term. ■

development? Notice how risky it is to draw such conclusions. First, specific forms of fetal stimulation, such as reading aloud or playing classical music, are unlikely to have a long-lasting impact on cognitive development because of the developing child's constantly changing capacities and experiences, which can override the impact of fetal stimulation (Lecanuet, Granier-Deferre, & DeCasper, 2005). Second, although ordinary stimulation contributes to the functioning of sensory systems, excessive input can be dangerous. For example, animal studies indicate that a sensitive period (see pages 23–24 in Chapter 1) exists in which the fetal ear is highly susceptible to injury. During that time, prolonged exposure to sounds that are harmless to the mature ear can permanently damage fetal inner-ear structures (Pierson, 1996).

In the final three months, the fetus gains more than 5 pounds and grows 7 inches. As it fills the uterus, it gradually moves less often. In addition, brain development, which enables the organism to inhibit behavior, contributes to a decline in physical activity (DiPietro et al., 1996). In the eighth month, a layer of fat is added to assist with temperature regulation. The fetus also receives antibodies from the mother's blood to protect against illnesses, since the newborn's own immune system will not work well until several months after birth. In the last weeks, most fetuses assume an upside-down position, partly because of the shape of the uterus and partly because the head is heavier than the feet. Growth slows, and birth is about to take place.

ASK YOURSELF

◆ **REVIEW** Why is the period of the embryo regarded as the most dramatic prenatal phase? Why is the period of the fetus called the "growth and finishing" phase?

◆ **APPLY** Amy, two months pregnant, wonders how the embryo is being fed and what parts of the body have formed. "I don't look pregnant yet, so does that mean not much development has taken place?" she asks. How would you respond to Amy?

◆ **CONNECT** How is brain development related to fetal capacities and behavior? What implications do individual differences in fetal behavior have for infant temperament after birth?

Prenatal Environmental Influences

Although the prenatal environment is far more constant than the world outside the womb, a great many factors can affect the embryo and fetus. Yolanda and Jay learned that parents—and society as a whole—can do a great deal to create a safe environment for development before birth.

Teratogens

The term **teratogen** refers to any environmental agent that causes damage during the prenatal period. Scientists chose this label (from the Greek word *teras,* meaning "malformation" or "monstrosity") because they first learned about harmful prenatal influences from cases in which babies had been profoundly damaged. But the harm done by teratogens is not always simple and straightforward. It depends on the following factors:

■ *Dose.* As we discuss particular teratogens, you will see that larger doses over longer time periods usually have more negative effects.

■ *Heredity.* The genetic makeup of the mother and the developing organism plays an important role. Some individuals are better able than others to withstand harmful environments.

■ *Other negative influences.* The presence of several negative factors at once, such as additional teratogens, poor nutrition, and lack of medical care, can worsen the impact of a single harmful agent.

■ *Age.* The effects of teratogens vary with the age of the organism at time of exposure. To understand this last idea, think of the *sensitive period* concept. Recall that a sensitive period is a limited time span in which a part of the body or a behavior is biologically prepared to develop rapidly. During that time, it is especially sensitive to its surroundings. If the environment is harmful, then damage occurs, and recovery is difficult and sometimes impossible.

Figure 3.5 summarizes prenatal sensitive periods. Look at it carefully, and you will see that some parts of the body, such as the brain and eye, have long sensitive periods that extend throughout prenatal development. Other sensitive periods, such as those for the limbs and palate, are much shorter. Figure 3.5 also indicates that we can make some general statements

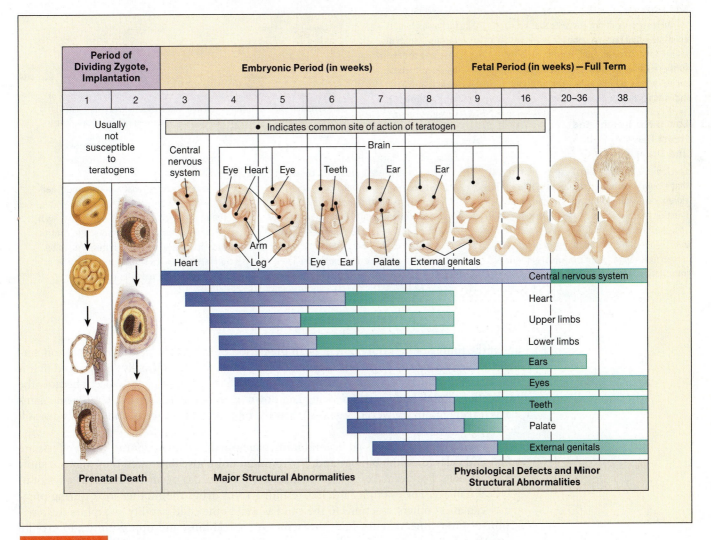

FIGURE 3.5

Sensitive periods in prenatal development. Each organ or structure has a sensitive period, during which its development may be disturbed. Blue horizontal bars indicate highly sensitive periods. Green horizontal bars indicate periods that are somewhat less sensitive to teratogens, although damage can occur. *(Adapted from* Before We Are Born, *7th ed., by K. L. Moore and T. V. N. Persaud, p. 313. Copyright © 2008, reprinted by permission from Elsevier, Inc.)*

BIOLOGY AND ENVIRONMENT

The Prenatal Environment and Health in Later Life

When Michael entered the world 55 years ago, 6 weeks premature and weighing only 4 pounds, the doctor delivering him wasn't sure he would make it. Michael not only survived but enjoyed good health until his mid-forties, when, during a routine medical checkup, he was diagnosed with high blood pressure and type 2 diabetes. Michael had no apparent risk factors for these conditions: He wasn't overweight, didn't smoke, and didn't eat high-fat foods. Nor did the illnesses run in his family. Could the roots of Michael's health problems date back to his prenatal development?

Increasing evidence suggests that prenatal environmental factors—ones that are not toxic (as are tobacco or alcohol) but rather fairly subtle, such as the flow of nutrients and hormones across the placenta—can affect an individual's health decades later.

Low Birth Weight and Heart Disease, Stroke, and Diabetes

Carefully controlled animal experiments reveal that a poorly nourished, underweight fetus experiences changes in body structure and function that greatly increase the risk of cardiovascular disease in adulthood (Franco et al., 2002). To explore this relationship in humans, researchers tapped public records, gathering information on the birth weights of 15,000 British men and women and the occurrence of disease in middle adulthood. Those weighing less than 5 pounds at birth had a 50 percent greater chance of dying of heart disease and stroke, even after SES and a variety of other health risks were controlled. The connection between birth weight and cardiovascular disease was strongest for people whose weight-to-length ratio at birth was very low—a sign of prenatal growth stunting (Godfrey & Barker, 2000; Martyn, Barker, & Osmond, 1996).

In other large-scale studies, a consistent link between low birth weight and high blood pressure, heart disease, stroke, and diabetes in middle adulthood emerged—for both sexes and in diverse countries (Barker, 2008; Kaijser et al., 2009; Whincup et al., 2008). Smallness itself does not cause later health problems; rather, researchers believe,

© ELLEN B. SENISI PHOTOGRAPHY

■ Prenatal environmental factors—even subtle ones, such as the flow of nutrients across the placenta—can affect an individual's health in later life. This baby's high birth weight places her at increased risk for breast cancer in adulthood. ■

complex factors associated with it are involved.

Some speculate that a poorly nourished fetus diverts large amounts of blood to the brain, causing organs in the abdomen, such as the liver and kidneys (involved in controlling cholesterol and blood pressure), to be undersized (Hales & Ozanne, 2003). The result is heightened later risk of heart

---

about the timing of harmful influences. In the period of the zygote, before implantation, teratogens rarely have any impact. If they do, the tiny mass of cells is usually so damaged that it dies. The *embryonic period* is the time when serious defects are most likely to occur because the foundations for all body parts are being laid down. During the *fetal period,* teratogenic damage is usually minor. However, organs such as the brain, ears, eyes, teeth, and genitals can still be strongly affected.

The effects of teratogens go beyond immediate physical damage. Some health effects are subtle and delayed. As the Biology and Environment box above illustrates, they may not show up for decades. Furthermore, psychological consequences may occur indirectly, as a result of physical damage. For example, a defect resulting from drugs the mother took during pregnancy can affect others' reactions to the child as well as the child's ability to explore the environment. Over time, parent–child interaction, peer relations, and opportunities to explore may suffer. Furthermore, prenatally exposed children may be less resilient in the face of environmental risks, such as single parenthood, parental emotional disturbance, or maladaptive parenting (Yumoto, Jacobson, & Jacobson, 2008). As a result, their long-term adjustment may be compromised.

disease and stroke. In the case of diabetes, inadequate prenatal nutrition may permanently impair functioning of the pancreas, leading glucose intolerance to rise as the person ages (Wu et al., 2004). Yet another hypothesis, supported by both animal and human research, is that the malfunctioning placentas of some expectant mothers permit high levels of stress hormones to reach the fetus, which retards fetal growth, increases fetal blood pressure, and promotes excess blood glucose, predisposing the developing person to later disease (Stocker, Arch, & Cawthorne, 2005).

Finally, prenatally growth-stunted babies often gain excessive weight in childhood, once they have access to plentiful food. This excess weight usually persists, greatly increasing the risk of diabetes (Hyppönen, Power, & Smith, 2003).

High Birth Weight and Breast Cancer

The other prenatal growth extreme—high birth weight—is linked to breast cancer, the most common malignancy in adult women (Ahlgren et al., 2004). In one study of more than 2,000 British women, high birth weight—especially weight above 8.8 pounds—was associated with a greatly increased incidence of breast cancer, even after other cancer risks were controlled (see Figure 3.6) (dos Santos Silva et al., 2004). Researchers suspect that the culprit is excessive maternal estrogen in the overweight expectant mother, which promotes large fetal size and alters the makeup of beginning breast tissue so

that it may respond to estrogen in adulthood by becoming malignant (Barker et al., 2008).

High birth weight is also associated with increases in prostate cancer in men and digestive, blood, and lymphatic cancers in both genders (Caughey & Michels, 2009; Cnattingius et al., 2009; McCormack et al., 2005). As yet, the reasons are unclear.

Prevention

The relationships between prenatal development and later-life illnesses emerging in research do not mean that the illnesses are inevitable. Rather, prenatal environmental conditions *influence* adult health, and the steps we take to protect our health can prevent prenatal risks from becoming reality. Researchers advise individuals who were low-weight or high-weight at birth to get regular medical checkups and screening tests that increase the odds of early disease

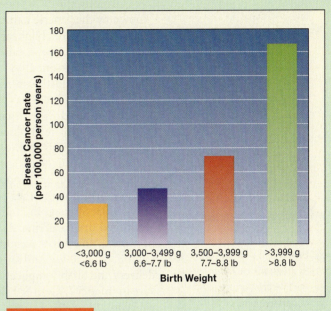

FIGURE 3.6

Relationship of birth weight to breast cancer risk in adulthood. In a study of more than 2,000 British births with follow-ups in adulthood, birth weight predicted breast cancer incidence after many other prenatal and postnatal health risks were controlled. The breast cancer risk was especially high for women whose birth weights were greater than 3,999 grams, or 8.8 pounds. *(Adapted from dos Santos Silva et al., 2004.)*

detection. They also recommend consistent attention to diet, weight, fitness, and stress—controllable factors that contribute to cardiovascular disease, adult-onset diabetes, and cancer.

Notice how an important idea about development that we discussed in earlier chapters is at work here: *bidirectional influences* between child and environment. Now let's look at what scientists have discovered about a variety of teratogens.

PRESCRIPTION AND NONPRESCRIPTION DRUGS In the early 1960s, the world learned a tragic lesson about drugs and prenatal development. At that time, a sedative called *thalidomide* was widely available in Canada, Europe, and South America. When taken by mothers four to six weeks after conception, thalidomide produced gross deformities of the embryo's developing arms and legs and, less frequently, damage to the ears, heart, kidneys, and genitals. About 7,000 infants worldwide were affected (Moore & Persaud, 2008). As children exposed to thalidomide grew older, many scored below average in intelligence. Perhaps the drug damaged the central nervous system directly. Or the child-rearing conditions of these severely deformed youngsters may have impaired their intellectual development.

Another medication, a synthetic hormone called *diethylstilbestrol (DES),* was widely prescribed between 1945 and 1970 to prevent miscarriages. As daughters of these mothers reached adolescence and young adulthood, they showed unusually high rates of cancer of the vagina, malformations of the uterus, and infertility. When they tried to have children, their pregnancies more often resulted in prematurity, low birth weight, and miscarriage than those of non-DES-exposed women. Young men showed an increased risk of genital abnormalities and cancer of the testes (Hammes & Laitman, 2003; Palmer et al., 2001).

Currently, the most widely used potent teratogen is a vitamin A derivative called *Accutane* (known by the generic name *isotretinoin),* prescribed to treat severe acne. Hundreds of thousands of women of childbearing age in industrialized nations take it. Exposure during the first trimester results in eye, ear, skull, brain, heart, and immune system abnormalities (Honein, Paulozzi, & Erickson, 2001). Accutane's packaging warns users to avoid pregnancy by using two methods of birth control, but many women do not heed this advice (Garcia-Bournissen et al., 2008).

Indeed, any drug with a molecule small enough to penetrate the placental barrier can enter the embryonic or fetal bloodstream. Yet many pregnant women continue to take over-the-counter medications without consulting their doctors. Aspirin is one of the most common. Several studies suggest that regular aspirin use is linked to low birth weight, infant death around the time of birth, poorer motor development, and lower intelligence test scores in early childhood, although other research fails to confirm these findings (Barr et al., 1990; Kozer et al., 2003; Streissguth et al., 1987). Coffee, tea, cola, and cocoa contain another frequently consumed drug, caffeine. As amounts exceed 100 milligrams per day (equivalent to one cup of coffee), low birth weight and miscarriage increase (CARE Study Group, 2008; Weng, Odouli, & Li, 2008). And antidepressant medications are linked to increased risk of premature delivery and birth complications, including respiratory distress and persistent high blood pressure in infancy (Alwan & Friedman, 2009; Lund, Pedersen, & Henriksen, 2009; Oberlander et al., 2006).

Because children's lives are involved, we must take findings like these seriously. At the same time, we cannot be sure that these frequently used drugs actually cause the problems just mentioned. Often mothers take more than one drug. If the embryo or fetus is injured, it is hard to tell which drug might be responsible or whether other factors correlated with drug taking are really at fault. Until we have more information, the safest course is the one Yolanda took: Avoid these drugs entirely. Unfortunately, many women do not know that they are pregnant during the early weeks of the embryonic period, when exposure to medications (and other teratogens) can be of greatest threat.

ILLEGAL DRUGS   The use of highly addictive mood-altering drugs, such as cocaine and heroin, has become more widespread, especially in poverty-stricken inner-city areas, where these drugs provide a temporary escape from a daily life of hopelessness. Nearly 4 percent of U.S. pregnant women take these substances (U.S. Department of Health and Human Services, 2007a).

Babies born to users of cocaine, heroin, or methadone (a less addictive drug used to wean people away from heroin) are at risk for a wide variety of problems, including prematurity, low birth weight, physical defects, breathing difficulties, and death around the time of birth (Behnke et al., 2001; Howell, Coles, & Kable, 2008; Schuetze & Eiden, 2006). In addition, these infants are born drug-addicted. They are often feverish and irritable and have trouble sleeping, and their cries are abnormally shrill and piercing—a common symptom among stressed newborns (Bauer et al., 2005). When mothers with many problems of their own must care for these babies, who are difficult to calm, cuddle, and feed, behavior problems are likely to persist.

Throughout the first year, heroin- and methadone-exposed infants are less attentive to the environment than nonexposed babies, and their motor development is slow. After infancy, some children get better, while others remain jittery and inattentive (Cosden, Peerson, & Elliott, 1997). The kind of parenting they receive may explain why problems persist for some but not for others (Hans & Jeremy, 2001).

Evidence on cocaine suggests that some prenatally exposed babies develop lasting difficulties. Cocaine constricts the blood vessels, causing oxygen delivered to the developing organism to fall for 15 minutes following a high dose. It also can alter the production and functioning of neurons and the chemical balance in the fetus's brain. These effects may contribute to an array of cocaine-associated physical defects, including eye, bone, genital, urinary tract, kidney, and

LOOK AND LISTEN

On a trip to your grocery or drugstore, examine the fine print on nonprescription medication labels, such as pain relievers, and on energy drinks containing high levels of caffeine. Are the prenatal risks of these products clearly conveyed?

heart deformities; brain hemorrhages and seizures; and severe growth retardation (Covington et al., 2002; Feng, 2005; Mayes, 1999). Some studies report perceptual, motor, attention, memory, language, and impulse-control problems that persist into the preschool years (Dennis et al., 2006; Lester et al., 2003; Linares et al., 2006; Noland et al., 2005; Singer et al., 2004).

But other investigations reveal no major negative effects of prenatal cocaine exposure (Behnke et al., 2006; Frank et al., 2005; Hurt et al., 2005). These contradictory findings indicate how difficult it is to isolate the precise damage caused by illegal drugs. Cocaine users vary greatly in the amount, potency, and purity of the cocaine they ingest. Also, they often take several drugs, display other high-risk behaviors, suffer from poverty and other stresses, and engage in insensitive caregiving—factors that worsen outcomes for children (Jones, 2006). But researchers have yet to determine exactly what accounts for findings of cocaine-related damage in some studies but not in others.

Another illegal drug, marijuana, is used more widely than heroin and cocaine. Studies examining its relationship to low birth weight and prematurity reveal mixed findings (Fried, 1993). Several researchers have linked prenatal marijuana exposure to smaller head size (a measure of brain growth); to sleep, attention, memory, and academic achievement difficulties and to depression in childhood; and to poorer problem-solving performance in adolescence (Dahl et al., 1995; Goldschmidt et al., 2004; Gray et al., 2005; Huizink & Mulder, 2006). As with cocaine, however, lasting consequences are not well-established. Overall, the effects of illegal drugs are far less consistent than the impact of two legal substances to which we now turn: tobacco and alcohol.

■ This 3-day-old infant, who was born many weeks before his due date, breathes with the aid of a respirator. Prematurity and low birth weight can result from a variety of environmental influences during pregnancy, including maternal drug use and cigarette smoking. ■

TOBACCO Although smoking has declined in Western nations, an estimated 14 percent of U.S. women smoke during their pregnancies (Tong et al., 2009). The best-known effect of smoking during the prenatal period is low birth weight. But the likelihood of other serious consequences, such as miscarriage, prematurity, impaired heart rate and breathing during sleep, infant death, and asthma and cancer later in childhood, is also increased (Howell, Coles, & Kable, 2008; Jaakkola & Gissler, 2004). The more cigarettes a mother smokes, the greater the chances that her baby will be affected. If a pregnant woman decides to stop smoking at any time, even during the last trimester, she reduces the likelihood that her infant will be born underweight and suffer from future problems (Klesges et al., 2001).

Even when a baby of a smoking mother appears to be born in good physical condition, slight behavioral abnormalities may threaten the child's development. Newborns of smoking mothers are less attentive to sounds, display more muscle tension, are more excitable when touched and visually stimulated, and more often have colic (persistent crying). These findings suggest subtle negative effects on brain development (Law et al., 2003; Sondergaard et al., 2002). Consistent with this view, prenatally exposed children and adolescents tend to have shorter attention spans, difficulties with impulsivity and overactivity, poorer memories, lower mental test scores, and more externalizing behavior problems (Fryer, Crocker, & Mattson, 2008; Huizink & Mulder, 2006; Nigg & Breslau, 2007; Rogers, 2009).

Exactly how can smoking harm the fetus? Nicotine, the addictive substance in tobacco, constricts blood vessels, lessens blood flow to the uterus, and causes the placenta to grow abnormally. This reduces the transfer of nutrients, so the fetus gains weight poorly. Also, nicotine raises the concentration of carbon monoxide in the bloodstreams of both mother and fetus. Carbon monoxide displaces oxygen from red blood cells, damaging the central nervous system and slowing body growth in the fetuses of laboratory animals. Similar effects may occur in humans. Also, recall from Chapter 2 that nicotine-exposed fetuses with a certain genotype are at high risk for becoming impulsive, overactive, and oppositional children and adolescents (see page 87).

From one-third to one-half of nonsmoking pregnant women are "passive smokers" because their husbands, relatives, or co-workers use cigarettes. Passive smoking is also related to low birth weight, infant death, childhood respiratory illnesses, and possible long-term attention, learning, and behavior problems (Hanke, Sobala, & Kalinka, 2004; Makin, Fried, & Watkinson, 1991; Pattenden et al., 2006). Clearly, expectant mothers should avoid smoke-filled environments.

ALCOHOL   In his moving book *The Broken Cord,* Michael Dorris (1989), a Dartmouth College anthropology professor, described what it was like to raise his adopted son Abel (called Adam in the book), whose biological mother drank heavily throughout pregnancy and died of alcohol poisoning shortly after his birth. A Sioux Indian, Abel was born with **fetal alcohol spectrum disorder (FASD),** a term that encompasses a range of physical, mental, and behavioral outcomes caused by prenatal alcohol exposure. As Table 3.4 shows, children with FASD are given one of three diagnoses, which vary in severity:

1. **Fetal alcohol syndrome (FAS),** distinguished by (a) slow physical growth, (b) a pattern of three facial abnormalities (short eyelid openings; a thin upper lip; a smooth or flattened philtrum, or indentation running from the bottom of the nose to the center of the upper lip), and (c) brain injury, evident in a small head and impairment in at least three areas of functioning—for example, memory, language and communication, attention span and activity level (overactivity), planning and reasoning, motor coordination, or social skills. Other defects—of the eyes, ears, nose, throat, heart, genitals, urinary tract, or immune system—may also be present. Abel was diagnosed as having FAS. As is typical for this disorder, his mother drank heavily throughout pregnancy.
2. **Partial fetal alcohol syndrome (p-FAS),** characterized by (a) two of the three facial abnormalities just mentioned and (b) brain injury, again evident in at least three areas of impaired functioning. Mothers of children with p-FAS generally drank alcohol in smaller quantities, and children's defects vary with the timing and length of alcohol exposure. Furthermore, recent evidence suggests that paternal alcohol use around the time of conception can alter gene expression (see page 86 in Chapter 2), thereby contributing to symptoms (Ouko et al., 2009).

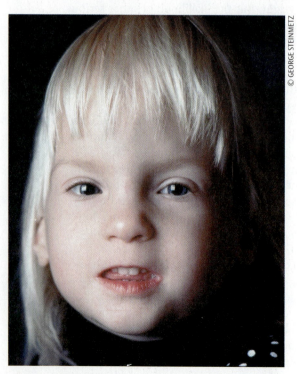

■ This toddler's mother drank heavily during pregnancy. Her widely spaced eyes, thin upper lip, and short eyelid openings are typical of fetal alcohol syndrome (FAS). ■

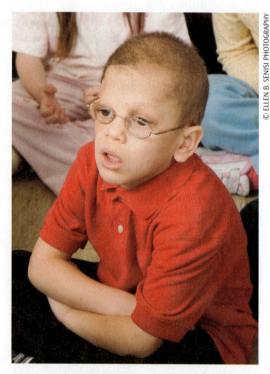

■ This 6-year-old has the distinctive facial abnormalities of FAS. He is also small for his age, due to the slow physical growth that accompanies the disorder. ■

TABLE 3.4 Fetal Alcohol Spectrum Disorder: Criteria for Diagnosis

Criteria	DIAGNOSTIC CATEGORY		
	FAS	**p-FAS**	**ARND**
Slow physical growth	Yes	No	No
Facial abnormalities: • Short eyelid openings • Thin upper lip • Smooth or flattened philtrum	All three are present	Two of the three are present	None are present
Brain injury	Impairment in a minimum of three areas of functioning	Impairment in a minimum of three areas of functioning	Impairment in a minimum of three areas of functioning

Source: Loock et al., 2005.

3. **Alcohol-related neurodevelopmental disorder (ARND),** in which at least three areas of mental functioning are impaired, despite typical physical growth and absence of facial abnormalities. Again, prenatal alcohol exposure, though confirmed, is less pervasive than in FAS (Chudley et al., 2005; Loock et al., 2005).

Even when provided with enriched diets, FAS babies fail to catch up in physical size during infancy or childhood. Mental impairment associated with all three FASD diagnoses is also permanent: In his teens and twenties, Abel Dorris had trouble concentrating and keeping a routine job, and he suffered from poor judgment. For example, he would buy something and not wait for change or would wander off in the middle of a task. He died in 1991, at age 23, after being hit by a car.

The more alcohol a woman consumes during pregnancy, the poorer the child's motor coordination, speed of information processing, reasoning, and intelligence and achievement test scores during the preschool and school years (Burden, Jacobson, & Jacobson, 2005; Korkman, Kettunen, & Autti-Raemoe, 2003; Mattson, Calarco, & Lang, 2006). In adolescence and early adulthood, FASD is associated with persisting attention and motor-coordination deficits, poor school performance, trouble with the law, inappropriate sexual behavior, alcohol and drug abuse, and lasting mental health problems (Barr et al., 2006; Fryer, Crocker, & Mattson, 2008; Howell et al., 2006; Streissguth et al., 2004).

How does alcohol produce its devastating effects? First, it interferes with production and migration of neurons in the primitive neural tube. Brain-imaging research reveals reduced brain size, damage to many brain structures, and abnormalities in brain functioning, including the electrical and chemical activity involved in transferring messages from one part of the brain to another (Riley, McGee, & Sowell, 2004; Spadoni et al., 2007). Second, the body uses large quantities of oxygen to metabolize alcohol. A pregnant woman's heavy drinking draws away oxygen that the developing organism needs for cell growth.

About 25 percent of U.S. mothers reported drinking at some time during their pregnancies. As with heroin and cocaine, alcohol abuse is higher in poverty-stricken women. On some Native-American reservations, the incidence of FAS is as high as 10 to 20 percent (Szlemko, Wood, & Thurman, 2006; U.S. Department of Health and Human Services, 2007a). Unfortunately, when affected girls later become pregnant, the poor judgment caused by the syndrome often prevents them from understanding why they themselves should avoid alcohol. Thus, the tragic cycle is likely to be repeated in the next generation.

How much alcohol is safe during pregnancy? Even mild drinking, less than one drink per day, is associated with reduced head size and body growth among children followed into adolescence (Jacobson et al., 2004; Martinez-Frias et al., 2004). Recall that other factors—both genetic and environmental—can make some fetuses more vulnerable to teratogens. Therefore, no amount of alcohol is safe. Couples planning a pregnancy and expectant mothers should avoid alcohol entirely.

© CAROLINE PENN/CORBIS

■ This child's deformities are linked to radiation exposure during the Chernobyl nuclear power plant disaster of 1986. Her mother was just a few weeks pregnant at the time. Prenatal radiation exposure also increased the risk of low intelligence and language and emotional disorders. ■

RADIATION In Chapter 2, we saw that ionizing radiation can cause mutation, damaging DNA in ova and sperm. When mothers are exposed to radiation during pregnancy, the embryo or fetus can suffer additional harm. Defects due to radiation were tragically apparent in children born to pregnant women who survived the bombing of Hiroshima and Nagasaki during World War II. Similar abnormalities surfaced in the nine months following the 1986 Chernobyl, Ukraine, nuclear power plant accident. After each disaster, the incidence of miscarriage and babies born with underdeveloped brains, physical deformities, and slow physical growth rose dramatically (Hoffmann, 2001; Schull, 2003).

Even when a radiation-exposed baby seems normal, problems may appear later. For example, even low-level radiation, as the result of industrial leakage or medical X-rays, can increase the risk of childhood cancer (Fattibene et al., 1999). In middle childhood, prenatally exposed Chernobyl children had abnormal brain-wave activity, lower intelligence test scores, and rates of language and emotional disorders two to three times greater than those of nonexposed Russian children. Furthermore, the more tension parents reported, due to forced evacuation from their homes and worries about living in irradiated areas, the poorer their children's emotional functioning (Loganovskaja & Loganovsky, 1999; Loganovsky et al., 2008). Stressful rearing conditions seemed to combine with the damaging effects of prenatal radiation to impair children's development.

Women should do their best to avoid medical X-rays during pregnancy. If dental, thyroid, chest, or other X-rays are necessary, insisting on the use of an abdominal X-ray shield is a key protective measure.

ENVIRONMENTAL POLLUTION In industrialized nations, an astounding number of potentially dangerous chemicals are released into the environment. More than 75,000 are in common use in the United States, and many new pollutants are introduced each year. When 10 newborns were randomly selected from U.S. hospitals for analysis of umbilical cord blood, researchers uncovered a startling array of industrial contaminants—287 in all! They concluded that many babies are "born polluted" by chemicals that not only impair prenatal development but also increase the chances of life-threatening diseases and health problems later on (Houlihan et al., 2005).

In the 1950s, an industrial plant released waste containing high levels of *mercury* into a bay providing seafood and water for the town of Minamata, Japan. Many children born at the time displayed physical deformities, mental retardation, abnormal speech, difficulty in chewing and swallowing, and uncoordinated movements. High levels of prenatal mercury exposure disrupt production and migration of neurons, causing widespread brain damage (Clarkson, Magos, & Myers, 2003; Hubbs-Tait et al., 2005). Pregnant women are wise to avoid eating long-lived predatory fish, such as swordfish, albacore tuna, and shark, which are heavily contaminated with mercury.

For many years, *polychlorinated biphenyls (PCBs)* were used to insulate electrical equipment, until research showed that, like mercury, they found their way into waterways and entered the food supply. In Taiwan, prenatal exposure to very high levels of PCBs in rice oil resulted in low birth weight, discolored skin, deformities of the gums and nails, brain-wave abnormalities, and delayed cognitive development (Chen & Hsu, 1994; Chen et al., 1994). Steady, low-level PCB exposure is also harmful. Women who frequently ate PCB-contaminated fish, compared with those who ate little or no fish, had infants with lower birth weights, smaller heads, persisting attention and memory difficulties, and lower intelligence test scores in childhood (Boucher, Muckle, & Bastien, 2009; Jacobson & Jacobson, 2003; Stewart et al., 2008).

Another teratogen, *lead,* is present in paint flaking off the walls of old buildings and in certain materials used in industrial occupations. High levels of prenatal lead exposure are consistently related to prematurity, low birth weight, brain damage, and a wide variety of physical defects. Even low levels may be dangerous. In some studies, affected babies showed slightly poorer mental and motor development (Bellinger, 2005). In one investigation, unfavorable effects—in the form of increased delinquent and antisocial behaviors—were evident in adolescence (Dietrich et al., 2001).

Finally, prenatal exposure to *dioxins*—toxic compounds resulting from incineration—is linked to brain, immune system, and thyroid damage in babies and to an increased incidence of breast and uterine cancers in women, perhaps through altering hormone levels (ten Tusscher & Koppe, 2004). Furthermore, even tiny amounts of dioxin in the paternal bloodstream cause a dramatic change in sex ratio of offspring: Affected men father nearly twice as many girls as boys (Ishihara et al., 2007; Mocarell et al., 2000). Dioxin seems to impair the fertility of Y-bearing sperm prior to conception.

INFECTIOUS DISEASE During her first prenatal visit, Yolanda's doctor asked her if she and Jay had already had measles, mumps, chickenpox, and several other illnesses. In addition, Yolanda was checked for the presence of several infections—and for good reason. As you can see in Table 3.5, certain diseases are major causes of miscarriage and birth defects.

Viruses. In the mid-1960s, a worldwide epidemic of *rubella* (three-day, or German, measles) led to the birth of more than 20,000 American babies with serious defects and to 13,000 fetal and newborn deaths. Consistent with the sensitive-period concept, the greatest damage occurs when rubella strikes during the embryonic period. More than 50 percent of infants whose mothers become ill during that time show deafness; eye deformities, including cataracts; heart, genital, urinary, intestinal, bone, and dental defects; and mental retardation. Infection during the fetal period is less harmful, but low birth weight, hearing loss, and bone defects may still

TABLE 3.5 Effects of Some Infectious Diseases During Pregnancy

DISEASE	MISCARRIAGE	PHYSICAL MALFORMATIONS	MENTAL RETARDATION	LOW BIRTH WEIGHT AND PREMATURITY
VIRAL				
Acquired immune deficiency syndrome (AIDS)	0	?	+	?
Chickenpox	0	+	+	+
Cytomegalovirus	+	+	+	+
Herpes simplex 2 (genital herpes)	+	+	+	+
Mumps	+	?	0	0
Rubella (German measles)	+	+	+	+
BACTERIAL				
Chlamydia	+	?	0	+
Syphilis	+	+	+	?
Tuberculosis	+	?	+	+
PARASITIC				
Malaria	+	0	0	+
Toxoplasmosis	+	+	+	+

+ = established finding; 0 = no present evidence; ? = possible effect that is not clearly established.

Sources: Jones, Lopez, & Wilson, 2003; Kliegman et al., 2008; Mardh, 2002; O'Rahilly & Müller, 2001.

© UNICEF/NYHQ2009-0697/CHRISTINE NESBITT

■ In Zambia, Africa, a mother who is HIV-positive learns that her 11-week-old infant tested negative for the virus. The baby benefited from prenatal and post-birth antiviral drug treatment, provided by a UNICEF-sponsored clinic that focuses on preventing HIV transmission from mother to child. ■

occur. The organ damage inflicted by prenatal rubella often leads to lifelong health problems, including severe mental illness, diabetes, cardiovascular disease, and thyroid and immune-system dysfunction in adulthood (Brown, 2006; Duszak, 2009). Routine vaccination in infancy and childhood has made new rubella outbreaks unlikely in industrialized nations. But an estimated 100,000 cases of prenatal infection continue to occur each year, primarily in developing countries in Africa and Asia with weak or absent immunization programs (Robinson et al., 2006).

The *human immunodeficiency virus (HIV)*, which can lead to *acquired immune deficiency syndrome (AIDS)*, a disease that destroys the immune system, has infected increasing numbers of women over the past two decades. Currently, women account for one-fourth of cases in North America, Western Europe, and East Asia. Although the incidence of AIDS has declined in industrialized nations, the disease is rampant in developing countries, where 95 percent of new infections occur, more than half of which affect women. In South Africa, for example, nearly 30 percent of all pregnant women are HIV-positive (Quinn & Overbaugh, 2005; South African Department of Health, 2009). HIV-infected expectant mothers pass the deadly virus to the fetus 20 to 30 percent of the time.

AIDS progresses rapidly in infants. By 6 months, weight loss, diarrhea, and repeated respiratory illnesses are common. The virus also causes brain damage, as indicated by seizures, gradual loss in brain weight, and delayed mental and motor development. Nearly half of prenatal AIDS babies die by 1 year of age and 90 percent by age 3 (Devi et al., 2009). The antiviral drug zidovudine (ZDV) reduces prenatal AIDS transmission by as much as 95 percent, with no harmful consequences of drug treatment for children (Culnane et al., 1999). ZDV has led to a dramatic decline in prenatally acquired AIDS in Western nations. Although distribution is increasing, the drug is still not widely available in impoverished regions of the world (UNICEF, 2009b).

As Table 3.5 reveals, the developing organism is especially sensitive to the family of herpes viruses, for which no vaccine or treatment exists. Among these, *cytomegalovirus* (the most frequent prenatal infection, transmitted through respiratory or sexual contact, often without symptoms) and *herpes simplex 2* (which is sexually transmitted) are especially dangerous. In both, the virus invades the mother's genital tract, infecting babies either during pregnancy or at birth. Both diseases often have no symptoms, very mild symptoms, or symptoms with which people are unfamiliar, thereby increasing the likelihood of contagion. Pregnant women who are not in a mutually monogamous relationship are at greatest risk.

Bacterial and Parasitic Diseases. Table 3.5 also includes several bacterial and parasitic diseases. Among the most common is *toxoplasmosis*, an infection caused by a parasite found in many animals. Pregnant women may become infected from eating raw or undercooked meat or from contact with the feces of infected cats. About 40 percent of women who have the disease transmit it to the developing organism. If it strikes during the first trimester, it is likely to cause eye and brain damage. Infection during the second and third trimesters is linked to mild visual and cognitive impairments. And about 80 percent of affected newborns with no obvious signs of damage develop learning or visual disabilities in later life (Jones, Lopez, & Wilson, 2003). Expectant mothers can avoid toxoplasmosis by making sure that the meat they eat is well-cooked, having pet cats checked for the disease, and turning over the care of litter boxes to other family members.

Other Maternal Factors

Besides avoiding teratogens, expectant parents can support the embryo and fetus in other ways. Regular exercise, good nutrition, and emotional well-being of the mother are essential. Problems that may result from maternal and fetal blood type differences can be prevented.

Finally, many prospective parents wonder how a mother's age affects the course of pregnancy. We examine each of these factors in the following sections.

EXERCISE   Yolanda continued her half-hour of aerobics three times a week into the third trimester, although her doctor cautioned against bouncing, jolting, and jogging movements that might subject the fetus to too many shocks and startles. In healthy, physically fit women, regular moderate exercise, such as walking, swimming, biking, or an aerobic workout, is related to increased birth weight and a reduction in risk for certain complications, such as pregnancy-induced maternal diabetes and high blood pressure (Leiferman & Evenson, 2003; Olson et al., 2009). However, frequent, vigorous, extended exercise—working up a sweat for more than 30 minutes, four or five days a week, especially late in pregnancy—results in lower birth weight than in healthy, nonexercising controls (Clapp et al., 2002; Leet & Flick, 2003). Hospital-sponsored childbirth education programs frequently offer exercise classes and suggest appropriate routines that help prepare for labor and delivery.

During the last trimester, when the abdomen grows very large, mothers have difficulty moving freely and often must cut back on exercise. Most women, however, do not engage in sufficient moderate exercise during pregnancy to promote their own and their baby's health (Hausenblas & Downs, 2005). An expectant mother who remains fit experiences fewer physical discomforts, such as back pain, upward pressure on the chest, or difficulty breathing in the final weeks.

Pregnant women with health problems, such as circulatory difficulties or a history of miscarriages, should consult their doctor about a physical fitness routine. For these mothers, exercise (especially the wrong kind) can endanger the pregnancy.

NUTRITION   During the prenatal period, when children are growing more rapidly than at any other time, they depend totally on the mother for nutrients. A healthy diet, consisting of a gradual increase in calories—an extra 100 calories a day in the first trimester, 265 in the second, and 430 in the third—resulting in a weight gain of 25 to 30 pounds (10 to 13.5 kilograms), helps ensure the health of mother and baby.

Consequences of Prenatal Malnutrition. During World War II, a severe famine occurred in the Netherlands, giving scientists a rare opportunity to study the impact of nutrition on prenatal development. Findings revealed that the sensitive-period concept operates with nutrition, just as it does with teratogens. Women affected by the famine during the first trimester were more likely to have miscarriages or give birth to babies with physical defects. When women were past the first trimester, fetuses usually survived, but many were born underweight and had small heads (Stein et al., 1975).

Prenatal malnutrition can cause serious damage to the central nervous system. The poorer the mother's diet, the greater the loss in brain weight, especially if malnutrition occurred during the third trimester. During that time, the brain is increasing rapidly in size, and for it to reach its full potential, the mother must have a diet high in all the basic nutrients (Morgane et al., 1993). An inadequate diet during pregnancy can also distort the structure of other organs, including the liver, kidney, and pancreas, resulting in lifelong health problems (refer again to the Biology and Environment box on pages 104–105).

Because poor nutrition suppresses development of the immune system, prenatally malnourished babies frequently catch respiratory illnesses (Chandra, 1991). In addition, they often are irritable and unresponsive to stimulation. Like drug-addicted newborns, they have a high-pitched cry that is particularly distressing to their caregivers. In poverty-stricken families, these effects quickly combine with a stressful home life. With age, low intelligence test scores and serious learning problems become more apparent (Pollitt, 1996).

Prevention and Treatment. Many studies show that providing pregnant women with adequate food has a substantial impact on the health of their

■ These pregnant women of Sierra Leone share a healthy meal they prepared together. They are members of a support group that seeks to improve maternal and infant health by preventing prenatal malnutrition. ■

newborn babies. Yet the growth demands of the prenatal period require more than just increased quantity of food. Vitamin–mineral enrichment is also crucial. For example, taking a folic acid supplement around the time of conception reduces by more than 70 percent abnormalities of the neural tube, such as *anencephaly* and *spina bifida* (see Table 2.5 on page 64). Folic acid supplementation early in pregnancy also reduces the risk of other physical defects, including cleft lip and palate, urinary tract abnormalities, and limb deformities. Furthermore, adequate folic acid intake during the last 10 weeks of pregnancy cuts in half the risk of premature delivery and low birth weight (Goh & Koren, 2008; MCR Vitamin Study Research Group, 1991; Scholl, Hediger, & Belsky, 1996).

Because of these findings, U.S. government guidelines recommend that all women of childbearing age consume 0.4 milligrams of folic acid per day. For women who have previously had a pregnancy affected by neural tube defect, the recommended amount is 4 or 5 milligrams (dosage must be carefully monitored, as excessive intake can be harmful) (American Academy of Pediatrics, 2006). About half of U.S. pregnancies are unplanned, so government regulations mandate that bread, flour, rice, pasta, and other grain products be fortified with folic acid.

Other vitamins and minerals also have established benefits. Enriching women's diets with calcium helps prevent maternal high blood pressure and premature births. Adequate magnesium and zinc reduce the risk of many prenatal and birth complications (Durlach, 2004; Kontic-Vucinic, Sulovic, & Radunovic, 2006). Fortifying table salt with iodine virtually eradicates *cretinism*—a condition of stunted growth and cognitive impairment, caused by prenatal iodine deficiency, that is a common cause of mental retardation in many parts of the world (Williams, 2008). And sufficient vitamin C and iron beginning early in pregnancy promote growth of the placenta and healthy birth weight (Mathews, Yudkin, & Neil, 1999). Nevertheless, a supplement program should complement, not replace, efforts to improve maternal diets during pregnancy. For women who do not get enough food or an adequate variety of foods, multivitamin tablets are a necessary, but not a sufficient, intervention.

When poor nutrition continues throughout pregnancy, infants usually require more than dietary improvement. In response to their tired, restless behavior, parents tend to be less sensitive and stimulating. The babies, in turn, become even more passive and withdrawn. Successful interventions must break this cycle of apathetic caregiver–baby interaction. Some do so by teaching parents how to interact effectively with their infants; others focus on stimulating infants to promote active engagement with their physical and social surroundings (Grantham-McGregor et al., 1994; Grantham-McGregor, Schofield, & Powell, 1987).

Although prenatal malnutrition is highest in poverty-stricken regions of the world, it is not limited to developing countries. The U.S. Special Supplemental Food Program for Women, Infants, and Children (WIC), which provides food packages and nutrition education to low-income pregnant women, reaches about 90 percent of those who qualify because of their extremely low incomes (U.S. Department of Agriculture, 2009). But many U.S. women who need nutrition intervention are not eligible for WIC.

EMOTIONAL STRESS   When women experience severe emotional stress during pregnancy, their babies are at risk for a wide variety of difficulties. Intense anxiety—especially during the first two trimesters—is associated with higher rates of miscarriage, prematurity, low birth weight, infant respiratory and digestive illnesses, colic (persistent infant crying), sleep disturbances, and irritability during the child's first three years (Field et al., 2007; Huizink, Mulder, & Buitelaar, 2004; Lazinski, Shea, & Steiner, 2008; van der Wal, van Eijsden, & Bonsel, 2007). Prenatal stress is also related to several commonly occurring physical defects, such as cleft lip and palate, heart deformities, and pyloric stenosis (tightening of the infant's stomach outlet, which often must be treated surgically) (Carmichael & Shaw, 2000).

How can maternal stress affect the developing organism? **TAKE A MOMENT...** To understand this process, list the changes you sensed in your own body the last time you were under stress. When we experience fear and anxiety, stimulant hormones released into our bloodstream cause us to be "poised for action." Large amounts of blood are sent to parts of the body involved in the defensive response—the brain, the heart, and muscles in the arms, legs, and trunk. Blood flow to other organs, including the uterus, is reduced. As a result, the fetus is deprived of a full supply of oxygen and nutrients.

Maternal stress hormones also cross the placenta, causing a dramatic rise in fetal stress hormones (evident in the amniotic fluid) and in fetal heart rate, blood pressure, and activity level (Monk et al., 2000, 2004; Weinstock, 2008). Excessive fetal stress may permanently alter neurological functioning, thereby heightening stress reactivity in later life. In one study, researchers identified mothers who had been directly exposed to the September 11, 2001, World Trade Center collapse during their pregnancies. At age 9 months, their babies were tested for saliva concentrations of *cortisol,* a hormone involved in regulating the stress response. Infants whose mothers had reacted to the disaster with severe anxiety had cortisol levels that were abnormally low—a symptom of reduced physiological capacity to manage stress. Consistent with this finding, these 9-month-olds showed greater distress when confronted with novel stimuli than did other infants (Brand et al., 2006; Yehuda et al., 2005). Maternal emotional stress during pregnancy also predicts anxiety, short attention span, anger, aggression, overactivity, and lower mental test scores among preschool and school-age children, above and beyond the impact of other risks, such as maternal smoking during pregnancy, low birth weight, postnatal maternal anxiety, and low SES (de Weerth & Buitelaar, 2005; Gutteling et al., 2006; Lazinski, Shea, & Steiner, 2008; Van den Bergh, 2004).

But stress-related prenatal complications are greatly reduced when mothers have partners, other family members, and friends who offer social support (Glover, Bergman, & O'Connor, 2008). The relationship of social support to positive pregnancy outcomes and subsequent child development is particularly strong for low-income women, who often lead highly stressful lives (see the Social Issues: Health box on page 116) (Olds et al., 2002, 2004).

BLOOD INCOMPATIBILITY   When the inherited blood types of mother and fetus differ, serious problems sometimes result. The most common cause of these difficulties is **Rh factor incompatibility.** When the mother is Rh-negative (lacks the Rh blood protein) and the father is Rh-positive (has the protein), the baby may inherit the father's Rh-positive blood type. (Recall from Table 2.2 on page 57 that Rh-positive blood is dominant and Rh-negative blood is recessive, so the chances are good that a baby will be Rh-positive.) If even a little of a fetus's Rh-positive blood crosses the placenta into the Rh-negative mother's bloodstream, she begins to form antibodies to the foreign Rh protein. If these enter the fetus's system, they destroy red blood cells, reducing the oxygen supply to organs and tissues. Mental retardation, miscarriage, heart damage, and infant death can occur.

It takes time for the mother to produce Rh antibodies, so firstborn children are rarely affected. The danger increases with each additional pregnancy. Fortunately, Rh incompatibility can be prevented in most cases. After the birth of each Rh-positive baby, Rh-negative mothers are routinely given a vaccine to prevent the buildup of antibodies. In emergency cases, blood transfusions can be performed immediately after delivery or, if necessary, even before birth.

MATERNAL AGE AND PREVIOUS BIRTHS   In Chapter 2, we noted that women who delay childbearing until their thirties or forties face increased risk of infertility, miscarriage, and babies born with chromosomal defects. Are other pregnancy complications also more common for older mothers? Research consistently indicates that healthy women in their thirties have about the same rates as those in their twenties (Bianco et al., 1996; Dildy et al., 1996; Prysak, Lorenz, & Kisly, 1995). Thereafter, as Figure 3.7 reveals, complication rates increase, with a sharp rise among women age 50 to 55—an age at which, because of menopause (end of menstruation) and aging reproductive organs, few women can conceive naturally (Salihu et al., 2003; Usta & Nassar, 2008).

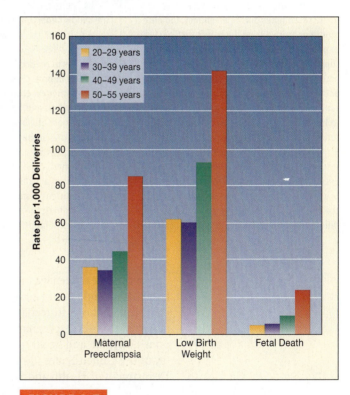

FIGURE 3.7

Relationship of maternal age to prenatal and birth complications. Complications increase after age 40, with a sharp rise between 50 and 55 years. See page 117 for a description of preeclampsia. *(Adapted from Salihu et al., 2003.)*

SOCIAL ISSUES: HEALTH

The Nurse–Family Partnership: Reducing Maternal Stress and Enhancing Child Development Through Social Support

At age 17, Denise—an unemployed high-school dropout living with her disapproving parents—gave birth to Tara. Having no one to turn to for help during pregnancy and beyond, Denise felt overwhelmed and anxious much of the time. Tara was premature and cried uncontrollably, slept erratically, and suffered from frequent minor illnesses throughout her first year. When she reached school age, she had trouble keeping up academically, and her teachers described her as distractible, unable to sit still, angry, and uncooperative.

The Nurse–Family Partnership, currently implemented in hundreds of counties across 29 U.S. states, is a voluntary home visiting program for first-time, low-income expectant mothers like Denise. Its goals are to reduce pregnancy and birth complications, promote competent early caregiving, and improve family conditions, thereby protecting children from lasting adjustment difficulties. A registered nurse visits the home seven times during pregnancy and once a month or more during the baby's first two years to provide the mother with intensive social support—a sympathetic ear; assistance in accessing health and other community services and the help of family members (especially fathers and grandmothers); and encouragement to finish high school, find work, and engage in future family planning.

To evaluate the program's effectiveness, researchers randomly assigned over 1,000 mothers at risk for high prenatal stress (due to teenage pregnancy, poverty, and other negative life conditions) to nurse-visiting or comparison conditions (just prenatal care, or prenatal care plus infant referral for developmental problems). Families were followed through their child's first three years of elementary school (Olds et al., 2004, 2007).

As kindergartners, Nurse–Family Partnership children obtained higher language and intelligence test scores. And at both ages 6 and 9, children of home-visited mothers in the poorest mental health during pregnancy exceeded comparison children in academic achievement and displayed fewer behavior problems. Furthermore, from their baby's birth on, home-visited mothers were on a more favorable life course: They had fewer subsequent births, longer intervals between their first and second births, more frequent contact with the child's father, more stable intimate partnerships, less welfare dependence, and a greater sense of control over their lives—key factors in reducing subsequent prenatal stress and in protecting children's development.

In another experiment involving over 700 at-risk mothers and babies, professional nurses were far more effective than trained paraprofessionals in preventing outcomes associated with prenatal stress, including high infant fearfulness to novel stimuli and delayed mental development (Olds et al., 2002). Nurses were probably more proficient in individualizing program guidelines to fit the strengths and challenges faced by each family. They also might have

■ Through the Nurse–Family Partnership, this 15-year-old first-time mother-to-be receives regular home visits from a registered nurse, which will continue after her baby is born. In follow-up research, the children of home-visited mothers developed more favorably—cognitively, emotionally, and socially—than did comparison children whose mothers did not receive this individualized intervention. ■

had unique legitimacy as experts in the eyes of stressed mothers, more easily convincing them to take steps to reduce pregnancy complications that can trigger persisting developmental problems—such as those Tara displayed.

The Nurse–Family Partnership is highly cost-effective. For $1 spent, it saves more than $5 in public spending on pregnancy complications, preterm births, and child and youth learning and behavior problems (Dawley, Loch, & Bindrich, 2007). To find out more about the Nurse–Family Partnership, visit *www.nursefamilypartnership.org*.

In the case of teenage mothers, does physical immaturity cause prenatal problems? Nature tries to ensure that once a girl can conceive, she is physically ready to carry and give birth to a baby. Infants born to teenagers have a higher rate of problems, but not directly because of maternal age. Most pregnant teenagers come from low-income backgrounds, where stress, poor nutrition, and health problems are common. Also, many are afraid to seek medical care or, in the United States, do not have access to care because they lack health insurance (U.S. Department of Health and Human Services, 2009b).

The Importance of Prenatal Health Care

Yolanda had her first prenatal appointment three weeks after missing her menstrual period. After that, she visited the doctor's office once a month until she was seven months pregnant, then twice during the eighth month. As birth grew near, Yolanda's appointments increased to once a week. The doctor kept track of her general health, her weight gain, and the capacity of her uterus and cervix to support the fetus. The fetus's growth was also carefully monitored.

Yolanda's pregnancy, like most others, was free of complications. But unexpected difficulties can arise, especially if mothers have health problems. For example, women with diabetes need careful monitoring. Extra sugar in the diabetic mother's bloodstream increases the risk of pregnancy and birth problems, as well as brain damage and later learning difficulties (see the Biology and Environment box on page 118). Another complication, experienced by 5 to 10 percent of pregnant women, is *preeclampsia* (sometimes called *toxemia*), in which blood pressure increases sharply and the face, hands, and feet swell in the second half of pregnancy. If untreated, preeclampsia can cause convulsions in the mother and fetal death. Usually, hospitalization, bed rest, and drugs can lower blood pressure to a safe level (Vidaeff, Carroll, & Ramin, 2005). If not, the baby must be delivered at once.

Unfortunately, 8 percent of pregnant women in the United States wait until after the first trimester to seek prenatal care or receive none at all. As Figure 3.8 shows, inadequate care is far more common among adolescent and low-income, ethnic minority mothers. Their infants are three times as likely to be born underweight and five times as likely to die as are babies of mothers who receive early medical attention (Child Trends, 2007). Why do these mothers delay going to the doctor? One reason is that they lack health insurance. Although the very poorest of them are eligible for government-sponsored health services, many low-income women do not qualify. As we will see when we take up birth complications in Chapter 4, in nations where affordable medical care is universally available, such as Australia, Canada, Japan, and European countries, late-care pregnancies and maternal and infant health problems are greatly reduced.

Besides financial hardship, some mothers have other reasons for not seeking early prenatal care. These include both *situational barriers* (difficulty finding a doctor, getting an appointment, and arranging transportation, and insensitive or unsatisfying experiences with clinic staff) and *personal barriers* (psychological stress, the demands of taking care of other young children, family crises, lack of knowledge about signs of pregnancy and benefits of prenatal care, and ambivalence about the pregnancy). Many also engage in high-risk behaviors, such as smoking and drug abuse, which they do not want to reveal to health professionals (Maupin et al., 2004). These women, who receive little or no prenatal care, are among those who need it most!

Clearly, public education about the importance of early and sustained prenatal care for all pregnant women is badly needed. For women who are young, less-educated, low-income, or under stress and therefore at risk for inadequate prenatal care, assistance in making appointments, drop-in child-care centers, and convenient, free, or low-cost transportation are vital.

Culturally sensitive health-care practices are also helpful. Low-SES minority women often report depersonalizing experiences during prenatal appointments, including condescending interactions with medical staff and hurried

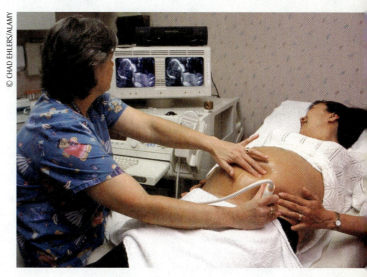

During a routine prenatal visit, a doctor uses ultrasound to evaluate the development of this expectant mother's 5-month-old fetus. All pregnant women should receive regular prenatal care to protect their own health as well as the health of their babies. ■

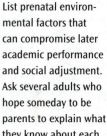

LOOK AND LISTEN

List prenatal environmental factors that can compromise later academic performance and social adjustment. Ask several adults who hope someday to be parents to explain what they know about each factor. How great is their need for prenatal education?

FIGURE 3.8

Expectant mothers in the United States with late (after the first trimester) or no prenatal care. More than 10 percent of low-income minority mothers, and nearly 30 percent of adolescent mothers, receive inadequate prenatal care. *(From Hueston, Geesey, & Diaz, 2008; U.S. Department of Health and Human Services, 2009b.)*

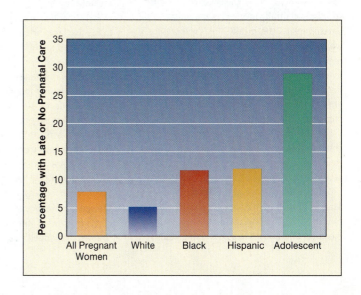

BIOLOGY AND ENVIRONMENT

Prenatal Iron Deficiency and Memory Impairments in Infants of Diabetic Mothers

Diabetes affects nearly 11 percent of Americans age 20 and older—a rate that has risen sharply over the past quarter century as a result of widespread overweight and obesity. Although it is increasingly prevalent among all sectors of the population, diabetes is at least twice as likely to affect low-income ethnic minority as white adults. Today, about 5 percent of pregnant mothers are diabetic—a 50 percent increase over the past decade. Most had the disease before becoming pregnant; others developed it during pregnancy (American Diabetes Association, 2010). In either case, their newborn babies are at risk for long-term developmental problems.

In the early weeks of pregnancy, when organs are forming, a diabetic mother's out-of-control blood glucose increases the risk of birth defects. Later in pregnancy, excess blood glucose causes the fetus to be "overfed" and to grow unusually large, often causing birth complications. Furthermore, to metabolize this flood of maternal glucose, the fetus secretes abnormally high levels of insulin—a circumstance that greatly increases demand for oxygen. To extract extra oxygen from the mother's system, the fetus increases production of oxygen-carrying red blood cells. This expanding red blood-cell mass requires extra iron, which the fetus can obtain only by taxing its own iron stores in the liver, muscles, heart, and brain.

In animal research on maternal diabetes, by late pregnancy iron stores decline sharply in the brain's temporal lobes (located on each side of the brain, just above the ears), which house structures centrally involved in memory development—specifically, the *hippocampus,* which plays a crucial role in the formation of new memories. Prenatal iron depletion interferes with growth of brain cells and their connections, permanently reducing the size and altering the structure of the hippocampus in laboratory rats (deUngria et al., 2000).

In human research, diabetic mothers bear children who, at school age, tend to score lower than their agemates on intelligence tests (Rizzo et al., 1997). Is prenatal iron deficiency and resulting early damage to the brain's memory areas responsible? In a series of studies, Charles Nelson (2007a) and his collaborators recorded electrical brain waves to assess young infants'

memory performance, focusing on a particular slow brain wave in the temporal lobes believed to reflect memory processing.

Typically developing newborns come to recognize their mother's voice through repeated exposure during pregnancy; they suck more on a nipple to hear a recording of it than the voice of an unfamiliar woman (DeCasper & Spence, 1988). In a comparison of newborns of diabetic mothers likely to have a brain iron deficiency (based on a measure of body iron stores) with normal-iron controls, brain waves were recorded as the babies listened to sound clips of their mother's or a stranger's voice (Sidappa et al., 2004). The controls showed a distinctive slow wave to each stimulus, indicating recognition of the mother's voice. The brain iron–deficient babies showed no difference in brain waves to the two stimuli, suggesting memory impairment of prenatal origin.

Do these memory deficits persist beyond the newborn period—evidence that diabetes-linked prenatal brain damage has lasting consequences? At 6 months, the researchers recorded brain waves while infants alternately viewed a videotaped image of their mother's face and that of an unfamiliar woman. Consistent with the newborn findings, control infants responded with distinct slow waves in the temporal lobes to the two faces, while infants of diabetic mothers displayed no difference. Even after months of experience, they could not recognize their mother's facial image (Nelson et al., 2000).

At an 8-month follow-up, babies were given a more challenging memory task. After feeling a novel object (an unusually shaped wooden block) held beneath an apron so they could not see it, the infants were tested visually: They viewed photos of the novel object interspersed with photos of familiar objects (Nelson et al., 2003). Again, infants of diabetic mothers showed no evidence of distinguishing the novel object from other stimuli. The control babies, in contrast, responded to the novel object with a

COURTESY OF DR. CHARLES NELSON

■ Prenatal iron supplementation is especially important for pregnant mothers with diabetes, which increases the fetus's risk of iron depletion and resulting memory impairments. To study the impact of prenatal diabetes on early memory development, researchers recorded this 8-month-old's electrical brain waves during a challenging memory task. ■

stronger temporal-lobe slow wave, suggesting an ability to recognize the novel stimulus, even when presented in a different sensory modality.

Nelson and his colleagues have followed their research participants through the preschool years, amassing additional evidence for poorer memory (especially more rapid forgetting) in children born to diabetic mothers than in controls (deRegnier et al., 2007). The findings highlight a previously hidden pregnancy complication: As a result of iron depletion in critical brain areas, a diabetic pregnancy places the fetus at risk for lasting memory deficits and thus for long-term learning and academic problems. The researchers believe that damage to the hippocampus, located deep inside the temporal lobes, is responsible.

Nelson's research underscores the need to find more effective ways of intervening with iron supplementation in diabetic pregnancies, as well as the importance of sufficient dietary iron for every expectant mother and her developing fetus. Diabetes prevention is also vital, through weight control, increased exercise, and improved diet beginning in childhood.

Applying What We Know

Do's and Don'ts for a Healthy Pregnancy

DO	DON'T
Do make sure that you have been vaccinated against infectious diseases dangerous to the embryo and fetus, such as rubella, before you get pregnant. Most vaccinations are not safe during pregnancy.	Don't take any drugs without consulting your doctor.
Do see a doctor as soon as you suspect that you are pregnant, and continue to get regular medical checkups throughout pregnancy.	Don't smoke. If you have already smoked during part of your pregnancy, cut down or, better yet, quit. If other members of your family smoke, ask them to quit or to smoke outside.
Do eat a well-balanced diet and take vitamin–mineral supplements, as prescribed by your doctor, both prior to and during pregnancy. On average, a woman should increase her intake by 100 calories a day in the first trimester, 265 in the second, and 430 in the third. Gain 25 to 30 pounds gradually.	Don't drink alcohol from the time you decide to get pregnant.
	Don't engage in activities that might expose your embryo or fetus to environmental hazards, such as radiation or chemical pollutants. If you work in an occupation that involves these agents, ask for a safer assignment or a leave of absence.
Do obtain literature from your doctor, local library, and bookstore about prenatal development and care, and ask questions about anything that concerns you.	Don't engage in activities that might expose your embryo or fetus to harmful infectious diseases, such as toxoplasmosis.
Do keep physically fit through moderate exercise. If possible, join a special exercise class for expectant mothers.	Don't choose pregnancy as a time to go on a diet.
Do avoid emotional stress. If you are a single expectant mother, find a relative or friend on whom you can count for emotional support.	Don't gain too much weight during pregnancy. A very large weight gain is associated with complications.
Do get plenty of rest. An overtired mother is at risk for pregnancy complications.	
Do enroll in a prenatal and childbirth education class with your partner or other companion. When you know what to expect, the nine months before birth can be one of the most joyful times of life.	

checkups with no opportunity to ask questions. These behaviors are especially disturbing to women whose cultures emphasize warm, personalized interaction styles and a relaxed sense of time—causing many to avoid returning (Daniels, Noe, & Mayberry, 2006; Downe et al., 2009). In a strategy called *group prenatal care,* after each medical checkup, trained leaders provide minority expectant mothers with a group discussion session after each medical checkup, which is conducted in their native language and encourages them to talk about important health issues (Massey, Rising, & Ickovics, 2006). Compared to mothers receiving traditional brief appointments, participants engaged in more health-promoting behaviors and also gave birth to babies with a reduced incidence of prematurity and low birth weight—major predictors of newborn survival and healthy development. Applying What We Know above lists "do's and don'ts" for a healthy pregnancy, based on our discussion of the prenatal environment.

ASK YOURSELF

◆ **REVIEW** Why is it difficult to determine the prenatal effects of many environmental agents, such as drugs and pollution?

◆ **APPLY** Nora, pregnant for the first time, believes that a few cigarettes and a glass of wine a day won't be harmful. Provide Nora with research-based reasons for not smoking or drinking.

◆ **CONNECT** How do teratogens illustrate the notion of epigenesis, presented in Chapter 2, that environments can affect gene expression? (See page 86 to review.)

◆ **REFLECT** If you had to choose five environmental influences to publicize in a campaign aimed at promoting healthy prenatal development, which ones would you choose, and why?

Preparing for Parenthood

Although we have discussed many ways that development can be thrown off course during the prenatal period, more than 90 percent of pregnancies in industrialized nations result in healthy newborn babies. For most expectant parents, the prenatal period is not a time of medical hazard. Rather, it is a period of major life change accompanied by excitement, anticipation, and looking inward. The nine months before birth not only permit the fetus to grow but also give men and women time to develop a new sense of themselves as mothers and fathers.

This period of psychological preparation is vital. In one study, more than 100 first-time expectant married couples, varying widely in age and SES, were interviewed about their pregnancy experiences. Participants reported a wide range of reactions to learning they were expecting. Nearly two-thirds were positive, about one-third mixed or neutral, and only a handful negative (Feeney et al., 2001). An unplanned pregnancy was especially likely to spark negative or ambivalent feelings. But as the pregnancy moved along, these reactions subsided. By the third trimester, no participants felt negatively, and only about 10 percent remained mixed or neutral. Couples' increasingly upbeat attitudes reflected acceptance of parenthood—a coming to terms with this imminent, radical change in their lives.

How effectively individuals construct a parental identity during pregnancy has important consequences for the parent–child relationship. A great many factors contribute to the personal adjustments that take place.

Seeking Information

We know most about how mothers adapt to the psychological challenges of pregnancy, although some evidence suggests that fathers use many of the same techniques. One common strategy is to seek information, as Yolanda and Jay did when they read books on pregnancy and childbirth and enrolled in my class. In fact, expectant mothers regard books as an extremely valuable source of information, rating them as second in importance only to their doctors. And the more a pregnant woman seeks information—by reading, accessing relevant websites, asking friends, consulting her own mother, or attending a prenatal class—the more confident she tends to feel about her own ability to be a good mother (Cowan & Cowan, 2000; Deutsch et al., 1988).

■ These parents express affection toward their preschooler while preparing him for the birth of a sibling. In this way, they expand their identity as a family to include the new baby while fostering the older child's sense of security. ■

© MYRLEEN FERGUSON CATE/PHOTOEDIT

The Baby Becomes a Reality

At the beginning of pregnancy, the baby seems far in the future. But gradually, the woman's abdomen enlarges, and the baby starts to become a reality. A major turning point occurs when expectant parents have concrete proof that a fetus is, indeed, developing inside the uterus. For Yolanda and Jay, this happened 13 weeks into the pregnancy, when their doctor showed them an ultrasound image. As Jay described the experience, "We saw it, these little hands and feet waving and kicking. It's really a baby in there!" Sensing the fetus's movements for the first time can be just as thrilling. Of course, the mother feels these "kicks" first, but soon after, the partner (and siblings) can participate by touching her abdomen.

Parents get to know the fetus as an individual through these signs of life. And both are likely to form an emotional attachment to the new being, especially when their relationship is positive, extended family members are supportive, and the mother reports favorable psychological well-being (Alhusen, 2008). In a Swedish study, the stronger mothers' and fathers' attachment to their fetus, the more positively they related to each other and to their baby after birth, and the more upbeat the baby's mood at age 8 months (White et al., 1999).

Models of Effective Parenthood

As pregnancy proceeds, expectant parents think about important models of parenthood in their own lives. When men and women have had good relationships with their own parents, they are more likely to develop positive images of themselves as parents during pregnancy (Deutsch et al., 1988). These images, in turn, predict harmonious marital communication and effective parenting during infancy and early childhood (Curran et al., 2005; Klitzing et al., 1999; McHale et al., 2004).

If their own parental relationships are mixed or negative, expectant mothers and fathers may have trouble building a healthy picture of themselves as parents. Some adults handle this challenge by seeking other examples of effective parenthood. One expectant father named Roger shared these thoughts with his wife and several couples, who met regularly with a counselor to talk about their concerns during pregnancy:

> I rethink past experiences with my father and my family and am aware of how I was raised. I just think I don't want to do that again. . . . I wish there had been more connection and closeness and a lot more respect for who I was. For me, my father-in-law . . . is a mix of empathy and warmth plus stepping back and being objective that I want to be as a father. (Colman & Colman, 1991, p. 148)

Like Roger, many people come to terms with negative experiences in their own childhood, recognize that other options are available to them, and build healthier and happier relationships with their children (Thompson, 2006). Roger achieved this understanding after participating in a special intervention program for expectant mothers and fathers. Couples who take part in such programs feel better about themselves and their marital relationships, communicate more effectively, feel more competent as parents after the baby arrives, and adapt more easily when family problems arise (Glade, Bean, & Vira, 2005; Petch & Halford, 2008).

The Parental Relationship

The most important preparation for parenthood takes place in the context of the parents' relationship. Expectant couples who are unhappy in their marriages and who have difficulty working out their differences continue to be distant, dissatisfied, and poor problem solvers after childbirth (Cowan & Cowan, 2000; Curran et al., 2005). Deciding to have a baby in hopes of improving a troubled relationship is a serious mistake. In a distressed marriage, pregnancy adds to rather than lessens family conflict (Perren et al., 2005).

When a couple's relationship is faring well and both partners want and plan for the baby, the excitement of a first pregnancy may bring husband and wife closer (Feeney et al., 2001). Parents who have forged a solid foundation of love and respect are well-equipped for the challenges of pregnancy. They are also prepared to handle the much more demanding changes that will take place as soon as their baby is born.

■ Couples who have a warm, respectful relationship and who look forward to parenthood often find that pregnancy brings them closer. As a result, they are well-equipped to handle the changes that will come after the baby arrives. ■

ASK YOURSELF

◆ REVIEW List psychological factors during pregnancy that predict parenting effectiveness after childbirth.

◆ APPLY Muriel, who is expecting her first child, recalls her own mother as cold and distant. Suggest steps she can take to form a confident, positive picture of herself as a new parent.

◆ REFLECT Ask your parents and/or your grandparents to describe attitudes and experiences that fostered or interfered with their capacity to build a positive parental identity when they were expecting their first child. Do you think building a healthy picture of oneself as a parent is more challenging today than it was in your parents' or grandparents' generation?

Summary

Motivations for Parenthood

How has decision making about childbearing changed over the past half-century, and what are the consequences for child rearing and child development?

■ Today, adults in Western industrialized nations have greater freedom to choose whether, when, and how to have children. In industrialized nations, family size has declined over the past half-century. But no link has been found between later birth order and lower mental test performance. Rather, less intelligent parents—as a result of heredity, environment, or both—tend to have larger families.

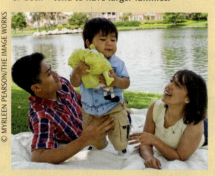

© MYRLEEN PEARSON/THE IMAGE WORKS

■ Although reproductive capacity declines with age, adults who delay childbearing until their education is complete, their careers are established, and they are emotionally more mature may be better able to invest in parenting.

Prenatal Development

List the three phases of prenatal development, and describe the major milestones of each.

■ The first prenatal phase, the period of the zygote, lasts about two weeks, from fertilization through **implantation** of the **blastocyst** in the uterine lining. During this time, structures that will support prenatal growth begin to form, including the **placenta** and the **umbilical cord.**

■ During the period of the **embryo,** from weeks 2 to 8, the foundations for all body structures are laid down. The nervous system develops fastest, starting with the formation of the **neural tube,** the top of which swells to form the brain. Other organs follow and grow rapidly. At the end of this phase, the embryo responds to touch and can move.

■ The period of the **fetus,** lasting until the end of pregnancy, involves a dramatic increase in body size and completion of physical structures. At the end of the second trimester, most of the brain's neurons are in place. At the beginning of the third trimester, between 22 and 26 weeks, the fetus reaches the **age of viability.** The brain continues to develop rapidly, and new sensory and behavioral capacities emerge. Gradually the lungs mature, the fetus fills the uterus, and birth is near.

Prenatal Environmental Influences

What are teratogens, and what factors influence their impact?

■ **Teratogens** are environmental agents that cause damage during the prenatal period. Their impact varies with the amount and length of exposure, the genetic makeup of mother and fetus, the presence or absence of other harmful agents, and the age of the organism at time of exposure. The developing organism is especially vulnerable during the embryonic period. In addition to immediate physical damage, some health outcomes may appear later in development, and physical defects may lead to psychological consequences as well.

List agents known to be or suspected of being teratogens, and discuss evidence supporting their harmful impact.

■ Drugs, cigarettes, alcohol, radiation, environmental pollution, and infectious diseases are teratogens that can endanger the developing organism. Currently, the most widely used potent teratogen is Accutane, a drug used to treat severe acne. The prenatal impact of many other commonly used medications, such as aspirin and caffeine, is hard to separate from other factors correlated with drug taking. Babies born to users of heroin, methadone, or cocaine are at risk for a wide variety of problems, including prematurity, low birth weight, physical defects, and breathing difficulties around the time of birth.

- Infants whose parents use tobacco are often born underweight and have attention, learning, and behavior problems in early childhood. Maternal alcohol consumption can lead to **fetal alcohol spectrum disorder (FASD). Fetal alcohol syndrome (FAS)** involves slow physical growth, facial abnormalities, and impairment in mental functioning. Milder forms—**partial fetal alcohol syndrome (p-FAS)** or **alcohol-related neurodevelopmental disorder (ARND)**—affect children whose mothers consumed smaller quantities of alcohol.

- Prenatal exposure to high levels of radiation, mercury, lead, dioxins, and PCBs leads to physical malformations and severe brain damage. Low-level exposure to these teratogens has also been linked to diverse impairments, including cognitive deficits and emotional and behavior disorders.

- Among infectious diseases, rubella causes a wide variety of abnormalities. Babies with prenatally transmitted HIV rapidly develop AIDS, leading to brain damage and early death. Cytomegalovirus, herpes simplex 2, and toxoplasmosis can also be devastating to the embryo and fetus.

Describe the impact of other maternal factors on prenatal development.

- Regular moderate exercise during pregnancy contributes to general health and readiness for childbirth and is related to higher birth weight. However, very vigorous exercise results in lower birth weight.

- When the mother's diet is inadequate, low birth weight and damage to the brain and other organs are major concerns. Vitamin–mineral supplementation, including folic acid, before conception and continuing during pregnancy can prevent prenatal and birth complications.

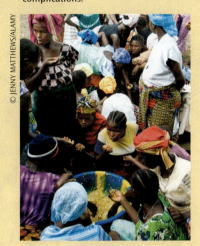

- Severe emotional stress is linked to many pregnancy complications and may permanently alter fetal neurological functioning, resulting in anxiety, short attention span, behavior problems, and lower mental tests scores in childhood The negative impact of prenatal stress can be reduced by providing the mother with emotional support.

- **Rh factor incompatibility**—an Rh-positive fetus developing within an Rh-negative mother—can lead to oxygen deprivation, brain and heart damage, and infant death.

- Aside from the risk of chromosomal abnormalities in older women, maternal age through the early forties is not a major cause of prenatal problems. Poor health and environmental risks associated with poverty are the strongest predictors of pregnancy complications in both teenagers and older women.

Why is early and regular health care vital during the prenatal period?

- Unexpected difficulties, such as preeclampsia, can arise, especially when pregnant women have health problems to begin with. Prenatal care is especially crucial for those women least likely to seek it—in particular, those who are young or poverty-stricken. Among low-SES ethnic minority mothers, culturally sensitive health-care practices—such as group prenatal care—can lead to more health-promoting behaviors.

Preparing for Parenthood

What factors contribute to preparation for parenthood during the prenatal period?

- Over the course of pregnancy, reactions to expectant parenthood become increasingly positive. Mothers and fathers prepare for their new role by seeking information from books and other sources. Ultrasound images and fetal movements make the baby a reality, and parents may form an emotional attachment to the new being. They also rely on effective models of parenthood to build positive images of themselves as mothers and fathers.

- The most important preparation for parenthood takes place in the context of the couple's relationship. During pregnancy, parents adjust their roles and their expectations of each other as they prepare to welcome the baby into the family.

IMPORTANT TERMS AND CONCEPTS

age of viability (p. 100)
alcohol-related neurodevelopmental disorder (ARND) (p. 109)
amnion (p. 98)
amniotic fluid (p. 98)
blastocyst (p. 98)
chorion (p. 98)
embryo (p. 99)

embryonic disk (p. 98)
fetal alcohol spectrum disorder (FASD) (p. 108)
fetal alcohol syndrome (FAS) (p. 108)
fetus (p. 100)
implantation (p. 98)
lanugo (p. 100)
neural tube (p. 99)
partial fetal alcohol syndrome (p-FAS) (p. 108)

placenta (p. 98)
Rh factor incompatibility (p. 115)
teratogen (p. 102)
trimesters (p. 100)
trophoblast (p. 98)
umbilical cord (p. 98)
vernix (p. 100)

chapter

4

"I'll Love Becoming a Mother"
Tina Crnjak
12 years, Slovenia

Safely held and nurtured by his mother and older sister, this baby thrives both physically and emotionally. In Chapter 4, we explore the birth process, the marvelous competencies of the newborn, and the challenges of new parenthood.

Birth and the Newborn Baby

The Stages of Childbirth

Stage 1: Dilation and Effacement of the Cervix • Stage 2: Delivery of the Baby • Stage 3: Birth of the Placenta • The Baby's Adaptation to Labor and Delivery • The Newborn Baby's Appearance • Assessing the Newborn's Physical Condition: The Apgar Scale

Approaches to Childbirth

Natural, or Prepared, Childbirth • Home Delivery

Medical Interventions

Fetal Monitoring • Labor and Delivery Medication • Instrument Delivery • Induced Labor • Cesarean Delivery

Birth Complications

Oxygen Deprivation • Preterm and Low-Birth-Weight Infants • Birth Complications, Parenting, and Resilience

■ **SOCIAL ISSUES: HEALTH**
A Cross-National Perspective on Health Care and Other Policies for Parents and Newborn Babies

Precious Moments After Birth

The Newborn Baby's Capacities

Reflexes • States • Sensory Capacities • Neonatal Behavioral Assessment

■ **SOCIAL ISSUES: HEALTH**
The Mysterious Tragedy of Sudden Infant Death Syndrome

The Transition to Parenthood

Changes in the Family System • Single-Mother Families • Parent Interventions

■ **BIOLOGY AND ENVIRONMENT**
Parental Depression and Child Development

Although Yolanda and Jay completed my course three months before their baby was born, both agreed to return the following spring to share with my next class their reactions to birth and new parenthood. Two-week-old Joshua came along as well. Yolanda and Jay's story revealed that the birth of a baby is one of the most dramatic and emotional events in human experience. Jay was present throughout Yolanda's labor and delivery. Yolanda explained:

> By morning, we knew I was in labor. It was Thursday, so we went in for my usual weekly appointment. The doctor said, yes, the baby was on the way, but it would be a while. He told us to go home and relax, and come to the hospital in 3 or 4 hours. We checked in at 3 in the afternoon; Joshua arrived at 2 o'clock the next morning. When, finally, I was ready to deliver, it went quickly; a half hour or so and some good hard pushes, and there he was! His face was red and puffy, and his head was misshapen, but I thought, "Our son! I can't believe he's really here."

Jay was also elated by Joshua's birth. "I wanted to support Yolanda and to experience as much as I could. It was awesome, indescribable," he said, holding little Joshua over his shoulder and patting and kissing him gently.

In this chapter, we explore the experience of childbirth, from both the parents' and the baby's point of view. As recently as 40 years ago, the birth process was treated more like an illness than a natural part of life. Today, women in industrialized nations have many choices about where and how they give birth, and hospitals go to great lengths to make the arrival of a new baby a rewarding, family-centered event.

Joshua reaped the benefits of Yolanda and Jay's careful attention to his needs during pregnancy. He was strong, alert, and healthy at birth. Nevertheless, the birth process does not always go smoothly. We will consider the pros and cons of medical interventions, such as pain-relieving drugs and surgical deliveries, designed to ease a difficult birth and protect the health of mother and baby. Our discussion also addresses the problems of infants born underweight or too early.

Finally, Yolanda and Jay spoke candidly about how their lives had changed since Joshua's arrival. "It's exciting and wonderful," reflected Yolanda, "but the adjustments are enormous. I wasn't quite prepared for the intensity of Joshua's 24-hour-a-day demands." In the concluding sections of this chapter, we look closely at the remarkable capacities of newborns to adapt to the external world and to communicate their needs. We also consider how parents adjust to the realities of everyday life with a new baby.

The Stages of Childbirth

It is not surprising that childbirth is often referred to as labor. It is the hardest physical work a woman may ever do. A complex series of hormonal changes initiates the process. As pregnancy advances, the placenta releases increasing amounts of *corticotropin-releasing hormone (CRH)*, a hormone involved in the stress response. High levels of CRH trigger additional placental hormone adjustments that induce uterine contractions. And as CRH rises in the fetal bloodstream in the final prenatal weeks, it stimulates fetal production of the stress hormone cortisol, which promotes development of the lungs in preparation for breathing (Norwitz, 2009; Smith, 2007). An abnormal increase in maternal CRH in the third trimester of pregnancy is currently being evaluated as an early predictor of premature birth (Smith et al., 2009).

Several signs indicate that labor is near:

- Yolanda occasionally felt the upper part of her uterus contract. These contractions are often called *false labor* or *prelabor* because they remain brief and unpredictable for several weeks.
- About two weeks before birth, an event called *lightening* occurred; Joshua's head dropped low into the uterus. Placental hormone changes had caused Yolanda's cervix to soften, and it no longer supported Joshua's weight so easily.
- A sure sign that labor is only hours or days away is the *bloody show*. As the cervix begins to open, the plug of mucus that sealed it during pregnancy is released, producing a reddish discharge. Soon after, uterine contractions become more frequent, and mother and baby have entered the first of three stages of labor (see Figure 4.1).

Stage 1: Dilation and Effacement of the Cervix

Stage 1 is the longest, lasting an average of 12 to 14 hours with a first birth and 4 to 6 hours with later births. **Dilation and effacement of the cervix** take place—that is, as uterine contractions gradually become more frequent and powerful, they cause the cervix to open (dilate) and thin (efface), forming a clear channel from the uterus into the birth canal, or vagina. The uterine contractions that open the cervix are forceful and regular, starting out 10 to 20 minutes apart and lasting about 15 to 20 seconds. Gradually, they get closer together, occurring every 2 to 3 minutes, and become stronger, persisting for as long as 60 seconds.

During this stage, Yolanda could do nothing to speed up the process. Jay held her hand, provided sips of juice and water, and helped her get comfortable. Throughout the first few hours, Yolanda walked, stood, or sat upright. As the contractions became more intense, she leaned against pillows or lay on her side.

The climax of Stage 1 is a brief phase called **transition,** in which the frequency and strength of contractions are at their peak and the cervix opens completely. Although transition

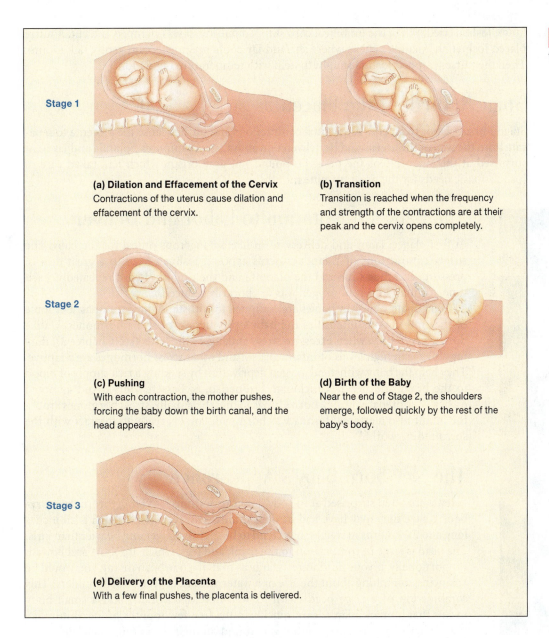

FIGURE 4.1

The three stages of labor.

Stage 1

(a) Dilation and Effacement of the Cervix
Contractions of the uterus cause dilation and effacement of the cervix.

(b) Transition
Transition is reached when the frequency and strength of the contractions are at their peak and the cervix opens completely.

Stage 2

(c) Pushing
With each contraction, the mother pushes, forcing the baby down the birth canal, and the head appears.

(d) Birth of the Baby
Near the end of Stage 2, the shoulders emerge, followed quickly by the rest of the baby's body.

Stage 3

(e) Delivery of the Placenta
With a few final pushes, the placenta is delivered.

is the most uncomfortable part of childbirth, it is especially important that the mother relax. If she tenses or bears down with her muscles before the cervix is completely dilated and effaced, she may bruise the cervix and slow the progress of labor.

Stage 2: Delivery of the Baby

In Stage 2, which lasts about 50 minutes for a first baby and 20 minutes in later births, the infant is born. Strong contractions of the uterus continue, but the mother also feels a natural urge to squeeze and push with her abdominal muscles. As she does so with each contraction, she forces the baby down and out.

Between contractions, Yolanda dozed lightly. When the doctor announced that the baby's head was *crowning*—the vaginal opening had stretched around the entire head—Yolanda felt renewed energy; she knew that soon the baby would arrive. Quickly, with several more pushes, Joshua's forehead, nose, and chin emerged, then his upper body and trunk. The doctor held him up, wet with amniotic fluid and still attached to the umbilical cord. As air rushed into his lungs, Joshua cried. When the umbilical cord stopped pulsing, it was clamped and cut. A nurse placed Joshua on Yolanda's chest, where she and Jay could see, touch, and gently talk to him. Then the nurse wrapped Joshua snugly, to help with temperature regulation.

Stage 3: Birth of the Placenta

Stage 3 brings labor to an end. A few final contractions and pushes cause the placenta to separate from the wall of the uterus and be delivered in about 5 to 10 minutes. Yolanda and Jay were surprised at the large size of the thick 1½-pound red-gray organ, which had taken care of Joshua's basic needs for the previous nine months.

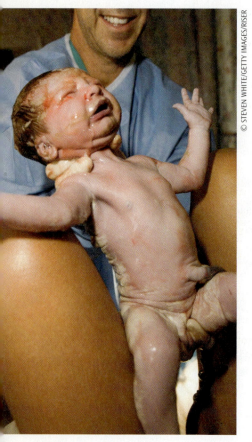

■ To accommodate the well-developed brain, a newborn's head is large in relation to the trunk and legs. This newborn's body readily turns pink as he takes his first few breaths. ■

The Baby's Adaptation to Labor and Delivery

At first glance, labor and delivery seem like a dangerous ordeal for the baby. The strong contractions of Yolanda's uterus exposed Joshua's head to a great deal of pressure, and they squeezed the placenta and the umbilical cord repeatedly. Each time, Joshua's supply of oxygen was temporarily reduced.

Fortunately, healthy babies are equipped to withstand these traumas. The force of the contractions intensifies the baby's production of stress hormones. Unlike during pregnancy, when excessive stress endangers the fetus (see Chapter 3), during childbirth high levels of infant cortisol and other stress hormones are adaptive. They help the baby withstand oxygen deprivation by sending a rich supply of blood to the brain and heart (Gluckman, Sizonenko, & Bassett, 1999). And as noted earlier, they prepare the newborn's lungs to breathe. Finally, stress hormones arouse the infant into alertness. Joshua was born wide-awake, ready to interact with the surrounding world.

The Newborn Baby's Appearance

Parents are often surprised at the odd-looking newborn—a far cry from the storybook image they may have had in their minds. The average newborn is 20 inches long and 7½ pounds in weight; boys tend to be slightly longer and heavier than girls. The head is large in comparison to the trunk and legs, which are short and bowed. Proportionally, if your head were as large as that of a newborn infant, you would be balancing something about the size of a watermelon between your shoulders! This combination of a large head (with its well-developed brain) and a small body means that human infants learn quickly in the first few months of life. But unlike most other mammals, they cannot get around on their own until much later.

Even though newborn babies may not match parents' idealized image, some features do make them attractive. Their round faces, chubby cheeks, large foreheads, and big eyes make adults feel like picking them up and cuddling them (Berman, 1980).

Assessing the Newborn's Physical Condition: The Apgar Scale

Infants who have difficulty making the transition to life outside the uterus must be given special help at once. To assess the newborn's physical condition quickly, doctors and nurses use the **Apgar Scale.** As Table 4.1 shows, a rating of 0, 1, or 2 on each of five characteristics is made at 1 minute and again at 5 minutes after birth. A combined Apgar score of 7 or better indicates that the infant is in good physical condition. If the score is between 4 and 6, the baby requires assistance in establishing breathing and other vital signs. If the score is 3 or below, the infant is in serious danger and requires emergency medical attention. Two Apgar ratings are given because some babies have trouble adjusting at first but do quite well after a few minutes (Apgar, 1953).

TABLE 4.1 The Apgar Scale

	SCORE		
Sign[a]	*0*	*1*	*2*
Heart rate	No heartbeat	Under 100 beats per minute	100 to 140 beats per minute
Respiratory effort	No breathing for 60 seconds	Irregular, shallow breathing	Strong breathing and crying
Reflex irritability (sneezing, coughing, and grimacing)	No response	Weak reflexive response	Strong reflexive response
Muscle tone	Completely limp	Weak movements of arms and legs	Strong movements of arms and legs
Color[b]	Blue body, arms, and legs	Body pink with blue arms and legs	Body, arms, and legs completely pink

[a]To remember these signs, you may find it helpful to use a technique in which the original labels are reordered and renamed as follows: color = **A**ppearance; heart rate = **P**ulse; reflex irritability = **G**rimace; muscle tone = **A**ctivity; and respiratory effort = **R**espiration. Together, the first letters of the new labels spell **Apgar.**

[b]The skin tone of nonwhite babies makes it difficult to apply the "pink" color criterion. However, newborns of all races can be rated for pinkish glow resulting from the flow of oxygen through body tissues.

Source: Apgar, 1953.

ASK YOURSELF

◆ REVIEW Name and briefly describe the three stages of labor.

◆ APPLY On seeing her newborn baby for the first time, Caroline exclaimed, "Why is she so out of proportion?" What observations prompted Caroline to ask this question? Explain why her baby's appearance is adaptive.

◆ CONNECT Contrast the positive impact of the baby's production of stress hormones during childbirth with the negative impact of maternal stress on the fetus, discussed on pages 114–115 in Chapter 3.

Approaches to Childbirth

Childbirth practices, like other aspects of family life, are molded by the society of which mother and baby are a part. In many village and tribal cultures, expectant mothers are well-acquainted with the childbirth process. For example, the Jarara of South America and the Pukapukans of the Pacific Islands treat birth as a vital part of daily life. The Jarara mother gives birth in full view of the entire community, including small children. The Pukapukan girl is so familiar with the events of labor and delivery that she can frequently be seen playing at it. Using a coconut to represent the baby, she stuffs it inside her dress, imitates the mother's pushing, and lets the nut fall at the proper moment. In most nonindustrialized cultures, women are assisted—though often not by medical personnel—during labor and delivery. Among the Mayans of the Yucatán, the mother leans against the body of a woman called the "head helper," who supports her weight and breathes with her during each contraction. And in Bolivia, a Siriono mother delivers her own baby in a hammock with a crowd of women close by, who keep her company. The father cuts the umbilical cord and joins the mother in tending to the newborn for the first few days (Jordan, 1993; Mead & Newton, 1967; Reed, 2005).

In Western nations, childbirth has changed dramatically over the centuries. Before the late 1800s, birth usually took place at home and was a family-centered event. The industrial revolution brought greater crowding to cities, along with new health problems. As a result, childbirth moved from home to hospital, where the health of mothers and babies could be protected.

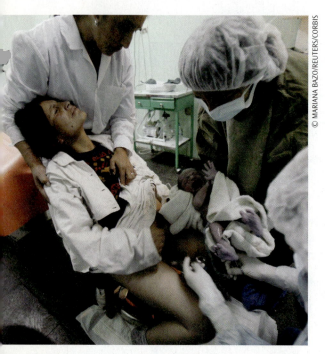

© MARIANA BAZO/REUTERS/CORBIS

■ In this Peruvian health clinic, families are encouraged to incorporate practices of their village culture into the birth experience. Here, a familiar attendant supports and soothes a new mother as her baby is delivered. ■

Once doctors assumed responsibility for childbirth, women's knowledge of it declined, and relatives and friends no longer participated (Borst, 1995).

By the 1950s and 1960s, women had begun to question the medical procedures that had come to be used routinely during labor and delivery. Many felt that routine use of strong drugs and delivery instruments had robbed them of a precious experience and was often neither necessary nor safe for the baby. Gradually, a natural childbirth movement arose in Europe and spread to North America. Its purpose was to make hospital birth as comfortable and rewarding for mothers as possible. Today, most hospitals offer birth centers that are family-centered and homelike. *Freestanding birth centers,* which permit greater maternal control over labor and delivery, including choice of delivery positions, presence of family members and friends, and early contact between parents and baby, also exist. And a small number of North American women reject institutional birth entirely and choose to have their babies at home.

Natural, or Prepared, Childbirth

Yolanda and Jay chose **natural,** or **prepared, childbirth**—a group of techniques aimed at reducing pain and medical intervention and making childbirth as rewarding an experience as possible. Most natural childbirth programs draw on methods developed by Grantly Dick-Read (1959) in England and Fernand Lamaze (1958) in France. These physicians recognized that cultural attitudes had taught women to fear the birth experience. An anxious, frightened woman in labor tenses her muscles, heightening the pain that usually accompanies strong contractions.

In a typical natural childbirth program, the expectant mother and a companion (a partner, relative, or friend) participate in three activities:

■ *Classes.* Yolanda and Jay attended a series of classes in which they learned about the anatomy and physiology of labor and delivery. Knowledge about the birth process reduces a mother's fear.
■ *Relaxation and breathing techniques.* During each class, Yolanda was taught relaxation and breathing exercises aimed at counteracting the pain of uterine contractions.
■ *Labor coach.* Jay learned how to help Yolanda during childbirth by reminding her to relax and breathe, massaging her back, supporting her body, and offering encouragement and affection.

Studies reveal many benefits for mothers who experience natural childbirth compared with those who do not. Because mothers feel more in control of labor and delivery, their attitudes toward the childbirth experience are more positive. They also feel less pain. As a result, they require less pain-relieving medication—very little or none at all (Taylor, 2002; Waldenström, 1999).

SOCIAL SUPPORT AND NATURAL CHILDBIRTH Social support is important to the success of natural childbirth techniques. In Guatemalan and American hospitals that routinely isolated patients during childbirth, some mothers were randomly assigned a *doula*—a Greek word referring to a trained lay attendant—who stayed with them throughout labor and delivery, talking to them, holding their hands, and rubbing their backs to promote relaxation. These mothers had fewer birth complications, and their labors were several hours shorter than those of women who did not have supportive companionship. Guatemalan mothers who received doula support also interacted more positively with their babies after delivery, talking, smiling, and gently stroking (Kennell et al., 1991; Sosa et al., 1980).

LOOK AND LISTEN

Talk to several mothers about social supports available to them during labor and delivery. From the mothers' perspectives, how did those supports (or lack of support) affect the birth experience?

Other studies indicate that mothers who are supported during labor—either by a lay birth attendant or a relative or friend with doula training—less often have instrument-assisted or cesarean (surgical) deliveries or need medication to control pain. Also, their babies' Apgar scores are higher, and they are more likely to be breastfeeding at a two-month follow-up (Campbell et al., 2006, 2007; Hodnet et al., 2003; McGrath & Kennell, 2008).

The continuous rather than intermittent support of a doula during labor and delivery strengthens these outcomes. It is particularly helpful during a first childbirth, when mothers are more anxious (DiMatteo & Kahn, 1997; Scott, Berkowitz, & Klaus, 1999). And this aspect of natural childbirth makes Western hospital-birth customs more acceptable to women from parts of the world where assistance from family and community members is the norm (Dundek, 2006).

POSITIONS FOR DELIVERY   When natural childbirth is combined with delivery in a birth center or at home, mothers often give birth in an upright, sitting position rather than lying flat on their backs with their feet in stirrups (the traditional hospital delivery room practice). Use of special seats to enable an upright birth has become more common. One type of birthing seat permits the partner to sit behind the mother, providing physical support (see Figure 4.2).

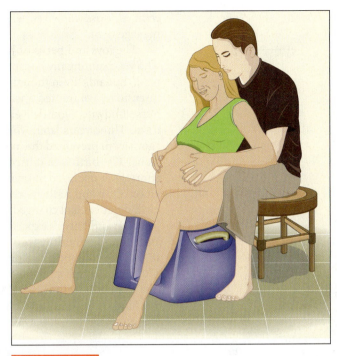

A birthing seat. The mother gives birth in an upright posture. Her partner can sit behind, supporting her body.

Research findings favor the sitting position. When mothers are upright, labor is shortened because pushing is easier and more effective. The baby benefits from a richer supply of oxygen because blood flow to the placenta is increased. Because the mother can see the delivery, she can track the effectiveness of each contraction in pushing the baby out of the birth canal. This helps her work with the doctor or midwife to ensure that the baby's head and shoulders emerge slowly, which reduces the chances of tearing the mother's tissues and, thus, the need for an *episiotomy* (incision that increases the size of the vaginal opening). Compared with those who give birth lying on their backs, women who choose an upright position are less likely to use pain-relieving medication (Eberhard, Stein, & Geissbuehler, 2005; Romano & Lothian, 2008).

In another increasingly popular method, water birth, the mother sits in a warm tub of water, which supports her weight, relaxes her, and provides her with the freedom to move into any position she finds most comfortable. Recent evidence indicates that water birth is associated with reduced maternal stress, shorter labor, lower episiotomy rate, and a greater likelihood of medication-free delivery than both back-lying and birthing-stool approaches (Cluett & Burns, 2009; Eberhard, Stein, & Geissbuehler, 2005; Ohlsson et al., 2001). As long as water birth is carefully managed by health professionals, it poses no additional risk of infection or safety to mothers or babies (Zanetti-Daellenbach et al., 2007).

Home Delivery

Home birth has always been popular in certain industrialized nations, such as England, the Netherlands, and Sweden. The number of American women choosing to have their babies at home rose during the 1970s and 1980s but remains small, at less than 1 percent (U.S. Department of Health and Human Services, 2009b). Although some home births are attended by doctors, many more are handled by

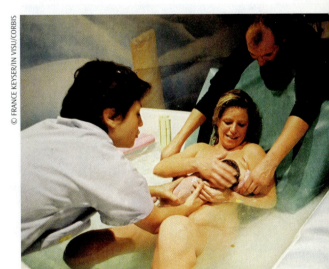

■ This woman has chosen a water birth, an increasingly popular childbirth option. Sitting in a warm tub of water relaxes the mother, supports her weight, and gives her the freedom to move into a comfortable position. ■

certified nurse-midwives, who have degrees in nursing and additional training in childbirth management.

The joys and perils of home delivery are well illustrated by the story I heard from Don, who was painting my house as I worked on this book. "Our first child was delivered in the hospital," he said. "Even though I was present, Kathy and I found the atmosphere to be rigid and insensitive. We wanted a warmer, more personal birth environment." With the coaching of a nurse-midwife, Don delivered their second child, Cindy, at their farmhouse, 3 miles out of town. Three years later, when Kathy went into labor with Marnie, their third child, a heavy snowstorm prevented the midwife from reaching the house on time, so Don delivered the baby alone. The birth was difficult, and Marnie failed to breathe for several minutes. With great effort, Don managed to revive her. The frightening memory of Marnie's limp, blue body convinced Don and Kathy to return to the hospital to have their last child. By then, the hospital's birth practices had changed, and the event was a rewarding one for both parents.

Don and Kathy's experience raises the question: Is it just as safe to give birth at home as in a hospital? For healthy women who are assisted by a well-trained doctor or midwife, it seems so because complications rarely occur (Fullerton, Navarro, & Young, 2007; Johnson & Daviss, 2005). However, if attendants are not carefully trained and prepared to handle emergencies, the rate of infant death is high (Mehlmadrona & Madrona, 1997). When mothers are at risk for any kind of complication, the appropriate place for labor and delivery is the hospital, where life-saving treatment is available.

Medical Interventions

Medical interventions during childbirth occur in both industrialized and non-industrialized cultures. For example, some tribal and village societies have discovered labor-inducing drugs and devised surgical techniques to deliver babies (Jordan, 1993). Yet childbirth in North America, more so than elsewhere in the world, is a medically monitored and controlled event. Use of some medical procedures has reached epic proportions—in part because of rising rates of multiple births and other high-risk deliveries, which are associated with increased maternal age and use of fertility treatments. But births unaffected by these factors are also highly medicalized.

What medical techniques are doctors likely to use during labor and delivery? When are they justified, and what dangers do they pose to mothers and babies?

Fetal Monitoring

Fetal monitors are electronic instruments that track the baby's heart rate during labor. An abnormal heartbeat pattern may indicate that the baby is in distress due to lack of oxygen and needs to be delivered immediately. Continuous fetal monitoring, which is required in most U.S. hospitals, is used in over 80 percent of U.S. births (Natale & Dodman, 2003). The most popular type of monitor is strapped across the mother's abdomen throughout labor. A second, more accurate method involves threading a recording device through the cervix and placing it directly under the baby's scalp.

Fetal monitoring is a safe medical procedure that has saved the lives of many babies in high-risk situations. But in healthy pregnancies, it does not reduce the already low rates of infant brain damage and death (Haws et al., 2009). Furthermore, most infants have some heartbeat irregularities during labor, and critics worry that fetal monitors identify many babies as in danger who, in fact, are not. Monitoring is linked to an increase in the number of instrument and cesarean

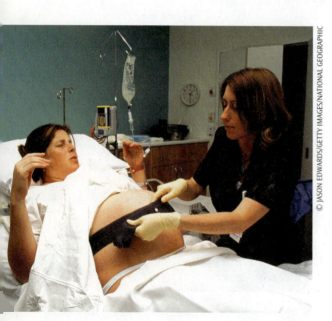

© JASON EDWARDS/GETTY IMAGES/NATIONAL GEOGRAPHIC

■ The fetal monitor strapped across this mother's abdomen uses ultrasound to record fetal heart rate throughout labor. In high-risk situations, fetal monitoring saves many lives. But it also may encourage unnecessary instrument and cesarean deliveries. ■

(surgical) deliveries, practices we will discuss shortly (Thacker & Stroup, 2003). In addition, some women complain that the devices are uncomfortable and interfere with the normal course of labor.

Still, fetal monitors will probably continue to be used routinely in the United States, even though they are not necessary in most cases. Doctors fear that they will be sued for malpractice if an infant dies or is born with problems and they cannot show that they did everything possible to protect the baby.

Labor and Delivery Medication

Some form of medication is used in more than 80 percent of U.S. births (Althaus & Wax, 2005). *Analgesics,* drugs used to relieve pain, may be given in mild doses during labor to help a mother relax. *Anesthetics* are a stronger type of painkiller that blocks sensation. Currently, the most common approach to controlling pain during labor is *epidural analgesia,* in which a regional pain-relieving drug is delivered continuously through a catheter into a small space in the lower spine. Unlike older spinal block procedures, which numb the entire lower half of the body, epidural analgesia limits pain reduction to the pelvic region. Because the mother retains the capacity to feel the pressure of the contractions and to move her trunk and legs, she is able to push during the second stage of labor.

Although pain-relieving drugs help women cope with childbirth and enable doctors to perform essential medical interventions, they also can cause problems. Epidural analgesia, for example, weakens uterine contractions. As a result, labor is prolonged, and the chances of cesarean (surgical) delivery increase (Klein, 2006). And because drugs rapidly cross the placenta, exposed newborns tend to have lower Apgar scores, to be sleepy and withdrawn, to suck poorly during feedings, and to be irritable when awake (Caton et al., 2002; Eltzschig, Lieberman, & Camann, 2003; Emory, Schlackman, & Fiano, 1996).

Do heavy doses of childbirth medication have a lasting impact on physical and mental development? Some researchers have claimed so (Brackbill, McManus, & Woodward, 1985), but their findings have been challenged (Riordan et al., 2000). Use of medication may be related to other risk factors that could account for the long-term consequences in some studies. Nevertheless, the negative impact of these drugs on the newborn's adjustment supports the current trend to limit their use.

Instrument Delivery

Forceps, metal clamps placed around the baby's head to pull the infant from the birth canal, have been used since the sixteenth century to speed up delivery (see Figure 4.3). A more recent instrument, the *vacuum extractor,* consists of a plastic cup (placed on the baby's head) attached to a suction tube. Instrument delivery is appropriate if the mother's pushing during the second stage of labor does not move the baby through the birth canal in a reasonable period of time.

Instrument use has declined considerably over the past two decades, partly because doctors more often deliver babies surgically when labor problems arise. Nevertheless, forceps and vacuum extractors continue to be used in about 5 percent of American births (U.S. Department of Health and Human Services, 2009b). These figures suggest that instruments are applied too freely in U.S. hospitals.

Using forceps to pull the baby through most or all of the birth canal greatly increases the risk of brain damage. As a result, forceps are seldom used this way today. Low-forceps delivery (carried out when the baby is most of the way through the vagina) is associated with risk of injury to the baby's head and the mother's tissues. Vacuum extractors, rapidly replacing forceps as the dominant instrument, are less likely to tear the mother's tissues. Cup suction does cause bleeding beneath the baby's skin and on the outside of the skull in about 15 percent of cases and more serious complications, including bleeding within the eye and beneath the skull (which can damage the brain), in 5 percent of cases (Ali &

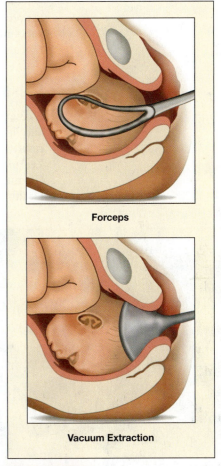

Forceps

Vacuum Extraction

FIGURE 4.3

Instrument delivery. The pressure that must be applied to pull the infant from the birth canal with forceps can injure the baby's head. An alternative method, the vacuum extractor, is less likely than forceps to injure the mother's tissues. Nevertheless, risk of infant scalp injuries and internal bleeding in the eyes and skull remains.

Norwitz, 2009). Consequently, neither method should be used when mothers can be encouraged to deliver normally and there is no special reason to hurry the birth.

Induced Labor

An **induced labor** is one that is started artificially, usually by breaking the amnion, or bag of waters (an event that typically occurs naturally in the first stage of labor), and giving the mother synthetic oxytocin, a hormone that stimulates contractions. About 22 percent of American labors are induced—a figure that has more than doubled over the past two decades (U.S. Department of Health and Human Services, 2009b).

Induced labors are justified when continuing the pregnancy threatens the well-being of mother or baby. Often, though, they are performed for the doctor's or the patient's convenience—a major reason they have increased. An induced labor often proceeds differently from a naturally occurring one. Contractions are longer, harder, and closer together, increasing the possibility of inadequate oxygen supply to the baby. In addition, mothers often find it more difficult to stay in control of an induced labor, even when they have been coached in natural childbirth techniques. As a result, labor and delivery medication is likely to be used in larger amounts, and the chances of instrument delivery are slightly greater (Cammu et al., 2002; Hoffman et al., 2006).

Occasionally, induction is performed before the mother is physically ready to give birth, and the procedure fails. When this happens, a cesarean delivery is necessary. The rate of cesareans is substantially higher in induced than spontaneous labors. Ripening of the cervix—initial dilation and effacement—is the best predictor of the success of labor induction (Clark et al., 2009).

Cesarean Delivery

A **cesarean delivery** is a surgical birth; the doctor makes an incision in the mother's abdomen and lifts the baby out of the uterus. Forty years ago, cesarean delivery was rare. Since then, cesarean rates have climbed internationally, reaching 16 percent in Finland, 20 percent in New Zealand, 22 percent in Australia, 26 percent in Canada, and 31 percent in the United States (Betrán et al., 2007; Society of Obstetricians and Gynaecologists, 2008; U.S. Department of Health and Human Services, 2009b).

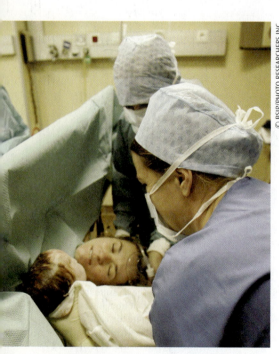

© BSIP/PHOTO RESEARCHERS, INC.

Cesareans have always been warranted by medical emergencies, such as Rh incompatibility, premature separation of the placenta from the uterus, or serious maternal illness or infection (for example, the herpes simplex 2 virus, which can infect the baby during a vaginal delivery). Cesareans are also justified when babies are in **breech position,** turned so that the buttocks or feet would be delivered first (about 1 in every 25 births). The breech position increases the chances of squeezing of the umbilical cord as the large head moves through the birth canal, thereby depriving the infant of oxygen. Head injuries are also more likely (Golfier et al., 2001). But the infant's exact position makes a difference. Certain breech babies fare just as well with a normal delivery as with a cesarean (Giuliani et al., 2002). Sometimes the doctor can gently turn the baby into a head-down position during the early part of labor.

Until recently, many women who have had a cesarean have been offered the option of a vaginal birth in subsequent pregnancies. But growing evidence indicates that compared with repeated cesareans, a natural labor after a cesarean is associated with slightly increased rates of rupture of the uterus and infant death (Cahill & Macones, 2007). As a result, the rule "Once a cesarean, always a cesarean" has made a comeback.

Repeated cesareans, however, do not explain the worldwide rise in cesarean deliveries. Instead, medical control over childbirth is largely responsible. Because many needless cesareans are performed, pregnant women should ask questions about the procedure when choosing a doctor. Although the operation itself is safe, mother and baby require more time for recovery. Anesthetic may have crossed the placenta, making cesarean newborns sleepy and unresponsive and putting them at increased risk for breathing difficulties (McDonagh, Osterweil, & Guise, 2005).

■ A nurse shows a mother her newborn following a cesarean delivery. Cesareans have become increasingly common over the past forty years, largely because of medical control over childbirth. ■

◆ REVIEW Describe the features and benefits of natural childbirth. What aspect contributes greatly to favorable outcomes, and why?

◆ APPLY Sharon, a heavy smoker, has just arrived at the hospital in labor. Which one of the medical interventions discussed in the preceding sections is her doctor justified in using? (For help in answering this question, review the prenatal effects of tobacco on page 107 in Chapter 3.)

◆ CONNECT How might use of epidural analgesia negatively affect the parent–newborn relationship? Explain how your answer illustrates bidirectional influences between parent and child, emphasized in ecological systems theory.

◆ REFLECT If you were an expectant parent, would you choose home birth? Why or why not?

Birth Complications

We have seen that some babies—in particular, those whose mothers are in poor health, do not receive good medical care, or have a history of pregnancy problems—are especially likely to experience birth complications. Inadequate oxygen, a pregnancy that ends too early, and a baby who is born underweight are serious risks to development that we have touched on many times. A baby remaining in the uterus too long is yet another risk. Let's look at the impact of each complication on later development.

Oxygen Deprivation

Some years ago, I got to know 4-year-old Melinda and her mother, Judy, both of whom participated in a special program for children with disabilities at our laboratory school. Melinda has *cerebral palsy*, a general term for a variety of impairments in muscle coordination caused by brain damage before, during, or just after birth. The disorder can range from very mild tremors to severe crippling and mental retardation. One out of every 500 American children has cerebral palsy. About 10 percent experienced **anoxia**, or inadequate oxygen supply, along with a buildup of harmful acids and deficiency of vital blood substrates, as a result of decreased maternal blood supply during labor and delivery (Bracci, Perrone, & Buonocore, 2006; Clark, Ghulmiyyah, & Hankins, 2008).

Melinda walks with a halting, lumbering gait and has difficulty keeping her balance. "Some mothers don't know how the palsy happened," confided Judy, "but I do. I got pregnant accidentally, and my boyfriend didn't want to have anything to do with it. I was frightened and alone most of the time. I arrived at the hospital at the last minute. Melinda was breech, and the cord was wrapped around her neck."

Squeezing of the umbilical cord, as in Melinda's case, is one cause of anoxia. Another cause is *placenta abruptio*, or premature separation of the placenta, a life-threatening event with a high rate of infant death. Factors related to it include multiple fetuses and teratogens that cause constriction of blood vessels and abnormal development of the placenta, such as tobacco and cocaine (Ovelese & Ananth, 2006). Just as serious is *placenta previa*, a condition caused by implantation of the blastocyst so low in the uterus that the placenta covers the cervical opening. As the cervix dilates and effaces in the third trimester, part of the placenta may detach. Women who have had previous cesareans or who are carrying multiple fetuses are at increased risk (Ovelese & Smulian, 2006). Although placenta abruptio and placenta previa occur in only 1 to 2 percent of births, they can cause severe hemorrhaging, which requires that an emergency cesarean be performed.

In still other instances, the birth seems to go along all right, but the baby fails to start breathing within a few minutes. Healthy newborns can survive periods of little or no oxygen longer than adults can; they reduce their metabolic rate, thereby conserving the limited oxygen available. Nevertheless, brain damage is likely if a baby is suffering from infection and therefore cannot initiate these protective reactions or if regular breathing is delayed more than 10 minutes (Kendall & Peebles, 2005). **TAKE A MOMENT...** Can you think of other possible causes of oxygen deprivation that you learned about as you studied prenatal development and birth?

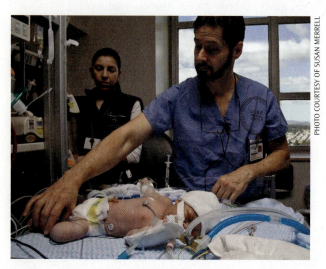

PHOTO COURTESY OF SUSAN MERRELL

■ Treatment for this newborn, who experienced oxygen deprivation, combines a cooling head cap with a cooling water blanket to lower the baby's body temperature, which helps prevent brain damage. ■

After initial brain injury from anoxia, another phase of cell death can occur several hours later. Currently, researchers are experimenting with ways to prevent this secondary damage. Compared with routine hospital care, placing anoxic newborns in a head-cooling device shortly after birth for 72 hours substantially reduces brain injury (detected through brain scans) and increases scores on a newborn behavioral assessment (Hoehn et al., 2008; Lin et al., 2006). Another alternative—whole-body cooling by having anoxic newborns lie on a precooled water blanket—leads to an impressive reduction in death and disability rates during the first two years (Shankaran et al., 2005).

How do children who experience anoxia during labor and delivery fare as they get older? Research suggests that the greater the oxygen deprivation, the poorer children's cognitive and language skills in early and middle childhood (Hopkins-Golightly, Raz, & Sander, 2003). Although effects of even mild to moderate anoxia often persist, many children improve over time (Bass et al., 2004; Raz, Shah, & Sander, 1996). In Melinda's case, her physical disability was permanent, but with warm, stimulating intervention services, she was just slightly behind in mental development as a preschooler.

When development is severely impaired, the anoxia was probably extreme. Perhaps it was caused by prenatal insult to the baby's respiratory system, or it may have happened because the infant's lungs were not yet mature enough to breathe. For example, infants born more than six weeks early commonly have *respiratory distress syndrome* (otherwise known as *hyaline membrane disease*). Their tiny lungs are so poorly developed that the air sacs collapse, causing serious breathing difficulties. Today, mechanical respirators keep many such infants alive. In spite of these measures, some babies suffer permanent brain damage from lack of oxygen, and in other cases their delicate lungs are harmed by the treatment itself. Respiratory distress syndrome is only one of many risks for babies born too soon, as we will see in the following section.

Preterm and Low-Birth-Weight Infants

Janet, almost six months pregnant, and her husband, Rick, boarded a flight in Hartford, Connecticut, on their way to a vacation in Hawaii. During a stopover in San Francisco, Janet told Rick she was bleeding. Rushed to a hospital, she gave birth to Keith, who weighed less than 1½ pounds. Delivered 23 weeks after conception, he had barely reached the age of viability (see Chapter 3, page 100).

During Keith's first month, he experienced one crisis after another. Three days after birth, an ultrasound scan suggested that fragile blood vessels feeding Keith's brain had hemorrhaged, a complication that can cause brain damage. Within three weeks, Keith had surgery to close a heart valve that seals automatically in full-term babies. Keith's immature immune system made infections difficult to contain. Repeated illnesses and the drugs used to treat them caused permanent hearing loss. Keith also had respiratory distress syndrome and breathed with the help of a respirator. Soon there was evidence of lung damage. More than three months of hospitalization passed before Keith's rough course of complications and treatment eased.

Babies born three weeks or more before the end of a full 38-week pregnancy or who weigh less than 5½ pounds (2,500 grams) have for many years been referred to as "premature." A wealth of research indicates that premature babies are at risk for many problems. Birth weight is the best available predictor of infant survival and healthy development. Many newborns who weigh less than 3⅓ pounds (1,500 grams) experience difficulties that are not overcome, an effect that becomes stronger as length of pregnancy and birth weight decrease (see Figure 4.4) (Bolisetty et al., 2006; Dombrowski, Noonan, & Martin, 2007). Brain structural abnormalities, frequent illness, inattention, overactivity, sensory impairments, poor motor coordination, language delays, low intelligence test scores, deficits in school learning, and emotional and behavior problems are some of the difficulties that persist through childhood and adolescence and into adulthood (Aarnoudse-Moens, Weisglas-Kuperus, & van Goudoever, 2009; Bayless & Stevenson, 2007; Clark et al., 2008; Delobel-Ayoub et al., 2009).

About 1 in 13 American infants is born underweight. The problem can strike unexpectedly, as it did for Janet and Rick. But it is highest among poverty-stricken women (U.S. Department of Health and Human Services, 2009b). These mothers, as indicated in Chapter 3, are more likely to be undernourished, under stress, and exposed to other harmful environmental influences—factors strongly linked to low birth weight. In addition, they often do not receive the prenatal care necessary to protect their vulnerable babies.

Recall from Chapter 2 that prematurity is also common in multiple births. About 60 percent of twins and more than 90 percent of triplets are born early and low birth weight (U.S. Department of Health and Human Services, 2009b). Because space inside the uterus is restricted, multiples gain less weight than singletons in the second half of pregnancy.

PRETERM VERSUS SMALL-FOR-DATE INFANTS Although low-birth-weight infants face many obstacles to healthy development, most go on to lead normal lives; about half of those born at 23 to 24 weeks gestation and weighing only a couple of pounds at birth have no disability (refer again to Figure 4.4). To better understand why some babies do better than others, researchers divide them into two groups. **Preterm infants** are born several weeks or more before their due date. Although they are small, their weight may still be appropriate, based on time spent in the uterus. **Small-for-date infants** are below their expected weight considering length of the pregnancy. Some small-for-date infants are actually full-term. Others are preterm babies who are especially underweight.

Of the two types of babies, small-for-date infants usually have more serious problems. During the first year, they are more likely to die, catch infections, and show evidence of brain damage. By middle childhood, they are smaller in stature, have lower intelligence test scores, are less attentive, achieve more poorly in school, and are socially immature (Hediger et al., 2002; O'Keefe et al., 2003; Sullivan et al., 2008). Small-for-date infants probably experienced inadequate nutrition before birth. Perhaps their mothers did not eat properly, the placenta did not function normally, or the babies themselves had defects that prevented them from growing as they should. In some of these babies, an abnormally functioning placenta permitted ready transfer of stress hormones from mother to fetus. Consequently, small-for-date infants are especially likely to suffer from prenatal neurological impairments that permanently weaken their capacity to manage stress (Wust et al., 2005).

Even among preterm newborns whose weight is appropriate for length of pregnancy, just seven more days—from 34 to 35 weeks—greatly reduces rates of illness, costly medical procedures, and lengthy hospital stays (although they need greater medical intervention than full-term babies) (Gladstone & Katz, 2004). And despite being relatively low-risk for disabilities, a substantial number of 34-week preterms are below average in physical growth and mildly to moderately delayed in cognitive development in early and middle childhood (Morse et al., 2009; Pietz et al., 2004; Stephens & Vohr, 2009). Yet doctors often induce births several weeks preterm, under the misconception that these babies are developmentally "mature."

CONSEQUENCES FOR CAREGIVING Imagine a scrawny, thin-skinned infant whose body is only a little larger than the size of your hand. You try to play with the baby by stroking and

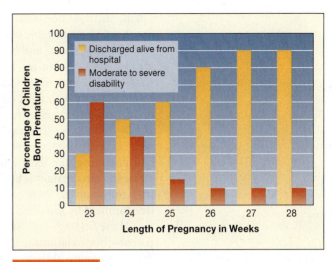

FIGURE 4.4

Rates of infant survival and child disabilities by length of pregnancy. In a follow-up of more than 2,300 babies born between 23 and 28 weeks gestation, the percentage of infants who survived decreased and the percentage who displayed moderate to severe disabilities (assessed during the preschool years) increased with reduced length of pregnancy. Severe disabilities included cerebral palsy (unlikely to ever walk), severely delayed mental development, deafness, and blindness. Moderate disabilities included cerebral palsy (able to walk with assistance), moderately delayed mental development, and hearing impairments partially correctable with a hearing aid. *(Adapted from Bolisetty et al., 2006.)*

talking softly, but he is sleepy and unresponsive. When you feed him, he sucks poorly. During the short, unpredictable periods in which he is awake, he is usually irritable.

The appearance and behavior of preterm babies can lead parents to be less sensitive and responsive in caring for them. Compared to full-term infants, preterm babies—especially those who are very ill at birth—are less often held close, touched, and talked to gently. At times, mothers of these infants resort to interfering pokes and verbal commands, in an effort to obtain a higher level of response from the baby (Barratt, Roach, & Leavitt, 1996; Feldman, 2007b). This may explain why preterm babies as a group are at risk for child abuse. When they are born to isolated, poverty-stricken mothers who cannot provide good nutrition, health care, and parenting, the likelihood of unfavorable outcomes increases. In contrast, parents with stable life circumstances and social supports usually can overcome the stresses of caring for a preterm infant. In these cases, even sick preterm babies have a good chance of catching up in development by middle childhood (Ment et al., 2003).

These findings suggest that how well preterm babies develop has a great deal to do with the parent–child relationship. Consequently, interventions directed at supporting both sides of this tie are more likely to help these infants recover.

■ *Top photo:* New mothers in a hospital ward in the Philippines practice skin-to-skin "kangaroo care," widely used in developing countries to promote the survival and recovery of preterm babies. *Bottom photo:* In Western nations, kangaroo care may be used to supplement hospital intensive care. Here, a U.S. mother engages in the technique with her fragile newborn. ■

INTERVENTIONS FOR PRETERM INFANTS   A preterm baby is cared for in a special Plexiglas-enclosed bed called an *isolette.* Temperature is carefully controlled because these infants cannot yet regulate their own body temperature effectively. To help protect the baby from infection, air is filtered before it enters the isolette. When a preterm infant is fed through a stomach tube, breathes with the aid of a respirator, and receives medication through an intravenous needle, the isolette can be very isolating indeed! Physical needs that otherwise would lead to close contact and other human stimulation are met mechanically.

Special Infant Stimulation.   At one time doctors believed that stimulating such fragile babies could be harmful. Now we know that in proper doses, certain kinds of stimulation can help preterm infants develop. In some intensive care nurseries, preterm babies can be seen rocking in suspended hammocks or lying on waterbeds designed to replace the gentle motion they would have received while still in the mother's uterus. Other forms of stimulation have also been used—an attractive mobile or a tape recording of a heartbeat, soft music, or the mother's voice. These experiences promote faster weight gain, more predictable sleep patterns, and greater alertness (Arnon et al., 2006; Marshall-Baker, Lickliter, & Cooper, 1998; Standley, 1998).

Touch is an especially important form of stimulation. In baby animals, touching the skin releases certain brain chemicals that support physical growth—effects believed to occur in humans as well. When preterm infants were gently massaged several times each day in the hospital, they gained weight faster and, at the end of the first year, were more advanced in mental and motor development than preterm babies not given this stimulation (Field, 2001; Field, Hernandez-Reif, & Freedman, 2004).

In developing countries where hospitalization is not always possible, skin-to-skin "kangaroo care" is the most readily available intervention for promoting the survival and recovery of preterm babies. It involves placing the infant in a vertical position between the mother's breasts or next to the father's chest (under the parent's clothing) so the parent's body functions as a human incubator. Kangaroo care offers fathers a unique opportunity to increase their involvement in caring for the preterm newborn. Because of its many physical and psychological benefits, the technique is used often in Western nations as a supplement to hospital intensive care.

Kangaroo skin-to-skin contact fosters improved oxygenation of the baby's body, temperature regulation, sleep, breastfeeding, alertness, and infant survival (Feldman, 2007a; Feldman & Eidelman, 2003). In addition, the kangaroo position provides the baby with gentle stimulation of all sensory modalities: hearing (through the parent's voice), smell (through proximity to the parent's body), touch (through skin-to-skin contact), and visual (through the upright position). Mothers and fathers practicing kangaroo care feel more confident about caring for their fragile babies, interact more sensitively and affectionately, and feel more attached to them (Dodd, 2005; Feldman et al., 2002, 2003).

Together, these factors may explain why preterm babies given many hours of kangaroo care in their early weeks, compared to those given little or no such care, are less likely to react negatively to and more likely to explore novel toys and score higher on measures of mental and motor development during the first year (Charpak, Ruiz-Peláez, & Figueroa, 2005; Feldman, 2007a; Tessier et al., 2003). Because of its diverse benefits, more than 80 percent of U.S. hospital nurseries now offer kangaroo care to preterm newborns (Field et al., 2006).

Training Parents in Infant Caregiving Skills. Interventions that support parents of preterm infants generally teach them about the infant's characteristics and promote caregiving skills. For parents with the economic and personal resources to care for a preterm infant, just a few sessions of coaching in recognizing and responding to the baby's needs are linked to enhanced parent–infant interaction, reduced infant crying and improved sleep, more rapid language development in the second year, and steady gains in mental test performance that equal those of full-term children by middle childhood (Achenbach, Howell, & Aoki, 1993; Newnham, Milgrom, & Skouteris, 2009).

When preterm infants live in stressed, low-income households, long-term intensive intervention is necessary. In the Infant Health and Development Project, preterm babies born into poverty received a comprehensive intervention that combined medical follow-up, weekly parent training sessions, and cognitively stimulating child care from 1 to 3 years of age. More than four times as many intervention children as no-intervention controls (39 versus 9 percent) were within normal range at age 3 in intelligence, psychological adjustment, and physical growth (Bradley et al., 1994). In addition, mothers in the intervention group were more affectionate and more often encouraged play and cognitive mastery in their children—one reason their 3-year-olds may have been developing so favorably (McCarton, 1998).

At ages 5 and 8, children who had attended the child-care program regularly—for more than 350 days over the three-year period—continued to show better intellectual functioning. The more they attended, the higher they scored, with greater gains among those whose birth weights were higher—between 4½ and 5½ pounds (2,001 to 2,500 grams) (see Figure 4.5). In contrast, children who attended only sporadically gained little or even lost ground (Hill, Brooks-Gunn, & Waldfogel, 2003). A follow-up at age 18 revealed persisting benefits for the higher-birth-weight participants: They remained advantaged over controls in academic achievement, and they also engaged in fewer risky behaviors (such as unprotected sexual activity and alcohol and drug use) (McCormick et al., 2006).

These findings confirm that babies who are both preterm and economically disadvantaged require *intensive* intervention. And special strategies, such as extra adult–child interaction, may be necessary to achieve lasting changes in children with the lowest birth weights.

VERY LOW BIRTH WEIGHT, ENVIRONMENTAL ADVANTAGES, AND LONG-TERM OUTCOMES
Although very-low-birth-weight individuals often have lasting problems, in a Canadian study, young adults who weighed between 1 and 2.2 pounds (500 to 1,000 grams) at birth were doing well in overall quality of life (Saigal et al., 2006). At 22 to 25 years of age, they resembled normal-birth-weight individuals

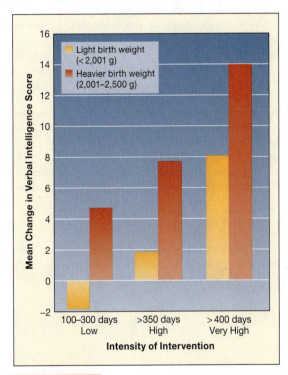

FIGURE 4.5

Influence of intensity of early intervention for low-income, preterm babies on intellectual functioning at age 8. Infants born preterm received cognitively stimulating child care from 1 through 3 years of age. Those who attended the program sporadically gained little in intellectual functioning (heavier-weight babies) or lost ground (lighter-weight babies). The more often children attended, the greater their intellectual gains. Heavier babies consistently gained more than light babies. But boosting the intensity of intervention above 400 days led to a dramatic increase in the performance of the light-weight group. *(Adapted from Hill, Brooks-Gunn, & Waldfogel, 2003.)*

SOCIAL ISSUES: HEALTH

A Cross-National Perspective on Health Care and Other Policies for Parents and Newborn Babies

*I*nfant mortality—the number of deaths in the first year of life per 1,000 live births—is an index used around the world to assess the overall health of a nation's children. The United States has the most up-to-date health-care technology in the world, including a newborn intensive care capacity per number of births far exceeding that of other industrialized nations (Thompson, Goodman, & Little, 2002). Nevertheless, it has made less progress in reducing infant deaths than many other countries. Over the past three decades, it has slipped in the international rankings, from seventh in the 1950s to twenty-eighth in 2009. Members of America's poor ethnic minorities are at greatest risk. African-American and Native-American babies are twice as likely as white infants to die in the first year of life (U.S. Census Bureau, 2010a, 2010b).

Neonatal mortality, the rate of death within the first month of life, accounts for 67 percent of the infant death rate in the United States. Two factors are largely responsible for neonatal mortality. The first is serious physical defects, most of which cannot be prevented. The percentage of babies born with physical defects is about the same in all ethnic and income groups. The second leading cause of neonatal mortality

is low birth weight, which is largely preventable. African-American and Native-American babies are more than twice as likely as white infants to be born early and underweight (U.S. Census Bureau, 2010b).

Widespread poverty and weak health-care programs for mothers and young children are largely responsible for these trends. Each country listed in Figure 4.6 that outranks the United States in infant survival provides all its citizens with government-sponsored health-care benefits. And each takes extra steps to make sure that pregnant mothers and

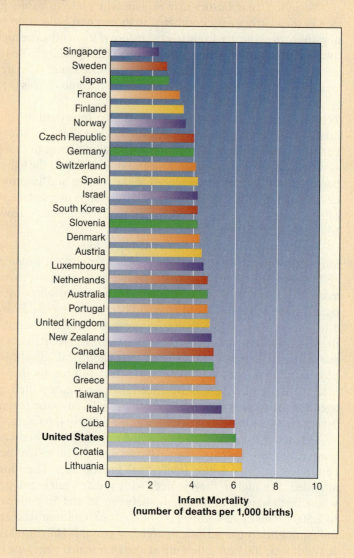

FIGURE 4.6

Infant mortality in 30 nations. Despite its advanced health-care technology, the United States ranks poorly. It is twenty-eighth in the world, with a death rate of 6.1 infants per 1,000 births. *(Adapted from U.S. Census Bureau, 2010a.)*

in educational attainment, rates of marriage and parenthood, and (for those who had no neurological or sensory impairments) employment status. What explains these excellent outcomes? Researchers believe that home, school, and societal advantages are largely responsible (Hack & Klein, 2006). Most participants in this study were reared in two-parent middle-SES homes, attended good schools where they received special services, and benefited from Canada's universal health care system.

Nevertheless, even the best environments cannot "fix" the enormous biological risks associated with very low birth weight. Think back to Keith, the very sick baby you met at the beginning of this section. Despite advanced medical technology and new ways of helping parents, most infants born as early and with as low a birth weight as Keith either die or end up with serious disabilities (Larroque et al., 2008; Mathews & MacDorman, 2006). Six months after he was born, Keith died without ever having left the hospital.

babies have access to good nutrition, high-quality medical care, and social and economic supports that promote effective parenting.

For example, all Western European nations guarantee women a certain number of prenatal visits at very low or no cost. After a baby is born, a health professional routinely visits the home to provide counseling about infant care and to arrange continuing medical services. Home assistance is especially extensive in the Netherlands. For a token fee, each mother is granted a specially trained maternity helper, who assists with infant care, shopping, house-keeping, meal preparation, and the care of other children during the days after delivery (Bradley & Bray, 1996; Zwart, 2007).

Paid, job-protected employment leave is another vital societal intervention for new parents. Canadian mothers are eligible for 15 weeks' maternity leave at 55 percent of prior earnings (up to a maximum of $413 per week), and Canadian mothers or fathers can take an additional 35 weeks of parental leave at the same rate. Paid leave is widely available in other industrialized nations as well. Sweden has the most generous parental leave program in the world. Mothers can begin maternity leave 60 days prior to expected delivery, extending it to six weeks after birth; fathers are granted two weeks of birth leave. In addition, either parent can take full leave for 16 months at 80 percent of prior earnings, followed by an additional three months at a modest flat rate. Each parent is also entitled to another 18 months of unpaid leave. Even less-developed nations provide parental leave benefits. For example, in the People's Republic of China, a new mother is granted three months' leave at regular pay. Furthermore, many countries supplement basic paid leave. In Germany, for example, after a fully paid three-month leave, a parent may take one more year at a flat rate and three additional years at no pay (OECD, 2006; Waldfogel, 2001).

Yet in the United States, the federal government mandates *only 12 weeks of unpaid leave* for employees in companies with at least 50 workers. Most women, however, work in smaller businesses, and even those who work in large enough companies may be unable to afford to take unpaid leave (Hewlett, 2003). And because of financial pressures, many new mothers who are eligible for unpaid work leave take far less than 12 weeks. Similarly, though paternal leave predicts fathers' increased involvement in infant care at the end of first year, many take little or none at all (Nepomnyaschy & Waldfogel, 2007; OECD, 2006). In 2002, California became the first state to guarantee a mother or father paid leave—up to six weeks at half salary, regardless of the size of the company.

Nevertheless, six weeks of childbirth leave (the norm in the United States) is not enough. When a family is stressed by a baby's arrival, leaves of six weeks or less are linked to increased maternal anxiety, depression, marital dissatisfaction, sense of role overload (conflict between work and family responsibilities), and negative interactions with the baby. A longer leave (12 weeks or more) predicts favorable maternal mental health, supportive marital interaction, and sensitive, responsive caregiving (Feldman, Sussman, & Zigler, 2004; Hyde et al., 2001). Single women and their babies are most

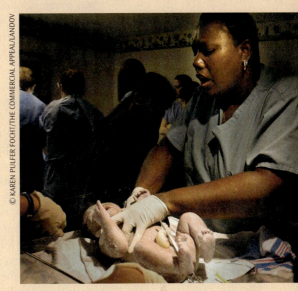

■ This doctor works with high-risk pregnancies, delivering babies whose poverty-stricken mothers have had little or no prenatal care. Nations that provide government-sponsored health-care benefits for all citizens outrank the United States in infant survival. ■

hurt by the absence of a generous national paid-leave policy. These mothers, who are usually the sole source of support for their families, can least afford to take time from their jobs.

In countries with low infant mortality rates, expectant mothers need not wonder how they will get health care and other resources to support their baby's development. The powerful impact of universal, high-quality health care; generous parental leave; and other social services on maternal and infant well-being provides strong justification for these policies.

Keith's premature birth was unavoidable, but the high rate of underweight babies in the United States—one of the worst in the industrialized world—could be greatly reduced by improving the health and social conditions described in the Social Issues: Health box above. Fortunately, today we can save many preterm babies, but an even better course of action would be to prevent this serious threat to infant survival and development before it happens.

Birth Complications, Parenting, and Resilience

In the preceding sections, we considered a variety of birth complications. Now let's try to put the evidence together. Can any general principles help us understand how infants who survive a traumatic birth are likely to develop? A landmark study carried out in Hawaii provides answers to this question.

In 1955, Emmy Werner began to follow the development of nearly 700 infants on the island of Kauai who experienced either mild, moderate, or severe birth complications. Each was matched, on the basis of SES and ethnicity, with a healthy newborn (Werner & Smith, 1982). Findings showed that the likelihood of long-term difficulties increased if birth trauma was severe. But among mildly to moderately stressed children, those growing up in stable families did almost as well on measures of intelligence and psychological adjustment as those with no birth problems. Those exposed to poverty, family disorganization, and mentally ill parents often developed serious learning difficulties, behavior problems, and emotional disturbance.

The Kauai study tells us that as long as birth injuries are not overwhelming, a supportive home can restore children's growth. But the most intriguing cases in this study were the handful of exceptions. A few children with serious birth complications and troubled family environments grew into competent adults who fared as well as controls in career attainment and psychological adjustment. Werner found that these children relied on factors outside the family and within themselves to overcome stress. Some had attractive personalities that drew positive responses from relatives, neighbors, and peers. In other instances, a grandparent, aunt, uncle, or babysitter provided the needed emotional support (Werner, 1989, 2001; Werner & Smith, 1992).

Do these outcomes remind you of the characteristics of resilient children, discussed in Chapter 1? The Kauai study and other similar investigations reveal that the impact of early biological risks often wanes as children's personal characteristics and social experiences contribute increasingly to their functioning (Laucht, Esser, & Schmidt, 1997; Resnick et al., 1999). In sum, when the overall balance of life events tips toward the favorable side, children with serious birth problems can develop successfully. And when negative factors outweigh positive ones, even a sturdy newborn can become a lifelong casualty.

ASK YOURSELF

◆ **REVIEW** Sensitive care can help preterm infants recover, but they are less likely than full-term newborns to receive such care. Explain why.

◆ **APPLY** Cecilia and Adena each gave birth to a 3-pound baby seven weeks preterm. Cecilia is single and on welfare. Adena and her husband are happily married and earn a good income. Plan an intervention appropriate for helping each baby develop.

◆ **CONNECT** List factors discussed in this chapter and in Chapter 3 that increase the chances that an infant will be born underweight. How many of these factors could be prevented by better health care for expectant mothers?

◆ **REFLECT** Many people object to the use of extra-ordinary medical measures to save extremely low-birth-weight babies because of their high risk for persistent, serious developmental problems. Do you agree or disagree? Explain.

Precious Moments After Birth

Yolanda and Jay's account of Joshua's birth revealed that the time spent holding and touching him right after delivery was filled with intense emotion. A mother given her infant at this time will usually stroke the baby gently, look into the infant's eyes, and talk softly (Klaus & Kennell, 1982). Fathers respond similarly. Most are overjoyed at their baby's birth; characterize the experience as "awesome," "indescribable," or "unforgettable"; and display intense interest in their newborn child (Bader, 1995; Rose, 2000). Regardless of SES or participation in childbirth classes, fathers touch, look at, talk to, and kiss their newborn infants just as much as mothers do. When they hold the baby, they sometimes exceed mothers in stimulation and affection (Parke & Tinsley, 1981).

Certain parental hormonal changes in the presence of the newborn help foster parents' involvement and sensitivity. Toward the end of pregnancy, mothers begin producing higher levels of the hormone *oxytocin,* which causes the breasts to "let down" milk and heightens responsiveness to the baby (Russell, Douglas, & Ingram, 2001). And in several studies, fathers showed hormonal changes when holding their newborn babies that were compatible with those of mothers—specifically, slight increases in *prolactin* (a hormone that stimulates milk production in females) and *estrogens* (sex hormones produced in larger quantities in females) and a drop in *androgens* (sex hormones produced in larger quantities in males). In animal and human research, these changes are associated with positive emotional reactions to infants and with paternal caregiving (Delahunty et al., 2007; Storey et al., 2000; Wynne-Edwards, 2001).

But do human parents require close physical contact in the hours after birth for **bonding, or feelings of affection and concern for the infant,** to develop—as many animal species do? Current evidence shows that the human parent–infant relationship does not depend on a precise, early period of togetherness. Some parents report sudden, deep feelings of affection on first holding their babies. For others, these emotions emerge gradually (Lamb, 1994). And as successful adoption reveals (see pages 65–68 in Chapter 2), humans can parent effectively without experiencing birth-related hormonal changes. Human bonding is a complex process that depends on many factors, not just on what happens during a short sensitive period.

Still, contact with the baby after birth may be one of several factors that help build a good parent–infant relationship. Research shows that mothers learn to discriminate their newborn baby from other infants on the basis of touch, smell, and sight (a photograph) after as little as one hour of contact (Kaitz et al., 1987, 1988, 1993a). Fathers, as well, can recognize their baby by touch and sight after brief exposure (Bader & Phillips, 2002; Kaitz et al., 1993b). This early recognition probably facilitates responsiveness to the infant.

Clearly, early contact supports parental engagement with the newborn, although it is neither necessary nor a guarantee of it. Realizing this, today hospitals offer **rooming in,** in which the infant stays in the mother's hospital room all or most of the time. If parents do not choose this option or cannot do so for medical reasons, there is no evidence that their competence as caregivers will be compromised or that the baby will suffer emotionally.

■ This father displays great affection for and involvement with his newborn baby. Like mothers, fathers typically express their elation by touching, looking at, talking to, and kissing the infant. ■

The Newborn Baby's Capacities

Newborn infants have a remarkable set of capacities that are crucial for survival and for evoking adult attention and care. In relating to the physical and social world, babies are active from the very start.

Reflexes

A **reflex** is an inborn, automatic response to a particular form of stimulation. Reflexes are the newborn baby's most obvious organized patterns of behavior. As Jay placed Joshua on a table in my classroom, we saw several. When Jay bumped the side of the table, Joshua reacted by flinging his arms wide and bringing them back toward his body. As Yolanda stroked Joshua's cheek, he turned his head in her direction. When she put her finger in Joshua's palm, he grabbed on tightly. **TAKE A MOMENT...** Look at Table 4.2 on page 144 and see if you can name the newborn reflexes that Joshua displayed. Then let's consider the meaning and purpose of these curious behaviors.

ADAPTIVE VALUE OF REFLEXES   Some reflexes have survival value. The rooting reflex helps a breastfed baby find the mother's nipple. Babies display it only when hungry and touched by another person, not when they touch themselves (Rochat & Hespos, 1997). And if sucking were not automatic, our species would be unlikely to survive for a single generation! At birth, babies adjust their sucking pressure to how easily milk flows from the nipple (Craig & Lee, 1999). The swimming reflex helps a baby who is accidentally dropped into a body of water stay afloat, increasing the chances of retrieval by the caregiver.

TABLE 4.2 Some Newborn Reflexes

REFLEX	STIMULATION	RESPONSE	AGE OF DISAPPEARANCE	FUNCTION
Eye blink	Shine bright light at eyes or clap hand near head	Infant quickly closes eyelids	Permanent	Protects infant from strong stimulation
Rooting	Stroke cheek near corner of mouth	Head turns toward source of stimulation	3 weeks (becomes voluntary head turning at this time)	Helps infant find the nipple
Sucking	Place finger in infant's mouth	Infant sucks finger rhythmically	Replaced by voluntary sucking after 4 months	Permits feeding
Swimming	Place infant face down in pool of water	Baby paddles and kicks in swimming motion	4–6 months	Helps infant survive if dropped into water
Moro	Hold infant horizontally on back and let head drop slightly, or produce a sudden loud sound against surface supporting infant	Infant makes an "embracing" motion by arching back, extending legs, throwing arms outward, and then bringing arms in toward the body	6 months	In human evolutionary past, may have helped infant cling to mother
Palmar grasp	Place finger in infant's hand and press against palm	Spontaneous grasp of finger	3–4 months	Prepares infant for voluntary grasping
Tonic neck	Turn baby's head to one side while infant is lying awake on back	Infant lies in a "fencing position." One arm is extended in front of eyes on side to which head is turned, other arm is flexed	4 months	May prepare infant for voluntary reaching
Stepping	Hold infant under arms and permit bare feet to touch a flat surface	Infant lifts one foot after another in stepping response	2 months in infants who gain weight quickly; sustained in lighter infants	Prepares infant for voluntary walking
Babinski	Stroke sole of foot from toe toward heel	Toes fan out and curl as foot twists in	8–12 months	Unknown

Sources: Knobloch & Pasamanick, 1974; Prechtl & Beintema, 1965; Thelen, Fisher, & Ridley-Johnson, 1984.

© LAURA DWIGHT PHOTOGRAPHY

■ The palmar grasp reflex is so strong during the first week after birth that many infants can use it to support their entire weight. ■

Other reflexes probably helped babies survive during our evolutionary past. For example, the Moro, or "embracing," reflex is believed to have helped infants cling to their mothers when they were carried about all day. If the baby happened to lose support, the reflex caused the infant to embrace and, along with the palmar grasp reflex (so strong during the first week that it can support the baby's entire weight), regain its hold on the mother's body (Kessen, 1967; Prechtl, 1958).

Several reflexes help parents and infants establish gratifying interaction. A baby who searches for and successfully finds the nipple, sucks easily during feedings, and grasps when her hand is touched encourages parents to respond lovingly and feel competent as caregivers. Reflexes can also help parents comfort the baby because they permit infants to control distress and amount of stimulation. For example, on short trips with Joshua to the grocery store, Yolanda brought along a pacifier. If he became fussy, sucking helped quiet him until she could feed, change, or hold and rock him.

REFLEXES AND THE DEVELOPMENT OF MOTOR SKILLS   A few reflexes form the basis for complex motor skills that will develop later. For example, the tonic neck reflex may prepare the baby for voluntary reaching. When infants lie on their backs in this "fencing position," they naturally gaze at the hand in front of their eyes. The reflex may encourage them to combine vision with arm movements and, eventually, reach for objects (Knobloch & Pasamanick, 1974).

Certain reflexes—such as the palmar grasp, swimming, and stepping—drop out early, but the motor functions involved are renewed later. The stepping reflex, for example, looks like a primitive walking response. Unlike other reflexes, it appears in a wide range of situations—

with the newborn's body in a sideways or upside-down position, with feet touching walls or ceilings, and even with legs dangling in the air (Adolph & Berger, 2006). One reason that babies frequently engage in the alternating leg movements of stepping is their ease compared with other movement patterns; repetitive movement of one leg or of both legs at once requires more effort.

In infants who gain weight quickly in the weeks after birth, stepping drops out because thigh and calf muscles are not strong enough to lift the baby's chubby legs. But if the lower part of the infant's body is dipped in water, the reflex reappears because the buoyancy of the water lightens the load on the baby's muscles (Thelen, Fisher, & Ridley-Johnson, 1984). When stepping is exercised regularly, babies display more spontaneous stepping movements and gain muscle strength. Consequently, they tend to walk several weeks earlier than if stepping is not practiced (Zelazo et al., 1993). However, there is no special need for infants to practice the stepping reflex—all normal babies walk in due time.

In the case of the swimming reflex, trying to build on it is risky. Although young babies placed in a swimming pool will paddle and kick, they swallow large amounts of water. This lowers the concentration of salt in the baby's blood, which can cause brain swelling and seizures. Despite this remarkable reflex, swimming lessons are best postponed until at least 3 years of age.

THE IMPORTANCE OF ASSESSING NEWBORN REFLEXES

Look at Table 4.2 again, and you will see that most newborn reflexes disappear during the first six months. Researchers believe that this is due to a gradual increase in voluntary control over behavior as the cerebral cortex develops. Pediatricians test reflexes carefully, especially if a newborn has experienced birth trauma, because reflexes can reveal the health of the baby's nervous system. Weak or absent reflexes, overly rigid or exaggerated reflexes, and reflexes that persist beyond the point in development when they should normally disappear can signal brain damage (Schott & Rossor, 2003; Zafeiriou, 2000). However, individual differences in reflexive responses exist that are not cause for concern. An observer must assess newborn reflexes along with other characteristics to accurately distinguish normal from abnormal central nervous system functioning.

States

Throughout the day and night, newborn infants move in and out of the five **states of arousal,** or degrees of sleep and wakefulness, described in Table 4.3 on page 146. During the first month, these states alternate frequently. The most fleeting is quiet alertness, which usually moves quickly toward fussing and crying. Much to the relief of their fatigued parents, newborns spend the greatest amount of time asleep—about 16 to 18 hours a day. Because the fetus tends to synchronize periods of rest and activity with those of the mother, newborns—even those who are 4 to 6 weeks preterm—sleep more at night than during the day (Heraghty et al., 2008; Rivkees, 2003). Nevertheless, young babies' sleep–wake cycles are affected more by fullness–hunger than by darkness–light (Davis, Parker, & Montgomery, 2004; Goodlin-Jones, Burnham, & Anders, 2000).

However, striking individual differences in daily rhythms exist that affect parents' attitudes toward and interactions with the baby. A few newborns sleep for long periods, increasing the energy their well-rested parents have for sensitive, responsive care. Other babies cry a great deal, and their parents must exert great effort to soothe them. If these parents do not succeed, they may feel less competent and less positive toward their infant. Babies who spend more time alert probably receive more social stimulation and

■ In the Moro reflex, loss of support or a sudden loud sound causes the baby to arch her back, extend her arms outward, and then bring them in toward her body. ■

■ This baby shows the Babinski reflex. When an adult strokes the sole of the foot, the toes fan out. Then they curl as the foot twists in. ■

■ When held upright under the arms, newborn babies show reflexive stepping movements. ■

TABLE 4.3	Infant States of Arousal	

STATE	DESCRIPTION	DAILY DURATION IN NEWBORN
Regular, or NREM, sleep	The infant is at full rest and shows little or no body activity. The eyelids are closed, no eye movements occur, the face is relaxed, and breathing is slow and regular.	8–9 hours
Irregular, or REM, sleep	Gentle limb movements, occasional stirring, and facial grimacing occur. Although the eyelids are closed, occasional rapid eye movements can be seen beneath them. Breathing is irregular.	8–9 hours
Drowsiness	The infant is either falling asleep or waking up. Body is less active than in irregular sleep but more active than in regular sleep. The eyes open and close; when open, they have a glazed look. Breathing is even but somewhat faster than in regular sleep.	Varies
Quiet alertness	The infant's body is relatively inactive, with eyes open and attentive. Breathing is even.	2–3 hours
Waking activity and crying	The infant shows frequent bursts of uncoordinated body activity. Breathing is very irregular. Face may be relaxed or tense and wrinkled. Crying may occur.	1–4 hours

Source: Wolff, 1966.

opportunities to explore and, therefore, may have a slight advantage in mental development (Sadeh et al., 2007; Smart & Hiscock, 2007).

Of the states listed in Table 4.3 the two extremes—sleep and crying—have been of greatest interest to researchers. Each tells us something about normal and abnormal early development.

SLEEP Observing Joshua as he slept, Yolanda and Jay wondered why his eyelids and body twitched and his rate of breathing varied. Sleep is made up of at least two states. During irregular, or **rapid-eye-movement (REM), sleep,** brain-wave activity is remarkably similar to that of the waking state. The eyes dart beneath the lids; heart rate, blood pressure, and breathing are uneven; and slight body movements occur. The expression "sleeping like a baby" was probably not meant to describe this state! In contrast, during regular, or **non-rapid-eye-movement (NREM), sleep,** the body is almost motionless, and heart rate, breathing, and brain-wave activity are slow and even.

Like children and adults, newborns alternate between REM and NREM sleep. However, they spend far more time in the REM state than they ever will again. REM sleep accounts for 50 percent of the newborn baby's sleep time. By 3 to 5 years, it has declined to an adultlike level of 20 percent (Louis et al., 1997).

Why do young infants spend so much time in REM sleep? In older children and adults, the REM state is associated with dreaming. Babies probably do not dream, at least not in the same way we do. But researchers believe that the stimulation of REM sleep is vital for growth of the central nervous system. Young infants seem to have a special need for this stimulation because they spend so little time in an alert state, when they can get input from the environment. In support of this idea, the percentage of REM sleep is especially great in the fetus and in preterm babies, who are even less able than full-term newborns to take advantage of external stimulation (de Weerd & van den Bossche, 2003; Peirano, Algarin, & Uauy, 2003).

Whereas the brain-wave activity of REM sleep safeguards the central nervous system, the rapid eye movements protect the health of the eye. Eye movements cause the vitreous (gelatin-like substance within the eye) to circulate, thereby delivering oxygen to parts of the eye that do not have their own blood supply. During sleep, when the eyes and the vitreous are still, visual structures are at risk for anoxia. As the brain cycles through REM-sleep periods, rapid eye movements stir up the vitreous, ensuring that the eye is fully oxygenated (Blumberg & Lucas, 1996).

Because the normal sleep behavior of the newborn baby is organized and patterned, observations of sleep states can help identify central nervous system abnormalities. In infants who are brain-damaged or who have experienced serious birth trauma, disturbed REM–NREM sleep cycles are often present. Babies with poor sleep organization are likely to be behaviorally disorganized and, therefore, to have difficulty learning and eliciting caregiver interactions that enhance their development. In follow-ups during the preschool years, they show delayed

SOCIAL ISSUES: HEALTH

The Mysterious Tragedy of Sudden Infant Death Syndrome

Millie awoke with a start one morning and looked at the clock. It was 7:30, and Sasha had missed both her night waking and her early morning feeding. Wondering if she was all right, Millie and her husband, Stuart, tiptoed into the room. Sasha lay still, curled up under her blanket. She had died silently during her sleep.

Sasha was a victim of **sudden infant death syndrome (SIDS),** the unexpected death, usually during the night, of an infant younger than 1 year of age that remains unexplained after thorough investigation. In industrialized nations, SIDS is the leading cause of infant mortality between 1 week and 12 months, accounting for about 20 percent of these deaths in the United States (Mathews & MacDorman, 2008).

SIDS victims usually show physical problems from the beginning. Early medical records of SIDS babies reveal higher rates of prematurity and low birth weight, poor Apgar scores, and limp muscle tone. Abnormal heart rate and respiration and disturbances in sleep–wake cycles are also involved (Cornwell & Feigenbaum, 2006; Kato et al., 2003). At the time of death, many SIDS babies have a mild respiratory infection (Samuels, 2003). This seems to increase the chances of respiratory failure in an already vulnerable baby.

Mounting evidence suggests that impaired brain functioning is a major contributor to SIDS. Between 2 and 4 months, when SIDS is most likely to occur, reflexes decline and are replaced by voluntary, learned responses. Neurological weaknesses may prevent SIDS babies from acquiring behaviors that replace defensive reflexes (Lipsitt, 2003). As a result, when breathing difficulties occur during sleep, these infants do not wake up, shift their position, or cry out for help. Instead, they simply give in to oxygen deprivation and death. In support of this

interpretation, autopsies reveal that the brains of SIDS babies contain unusually low levels of serotonin (a brain chemical that assists with arousal when survival is threatened) as well as other abnormalities in centers controlling breathing and arousal (Duncan et al., 2010; Paterson et al., 2006).

Several environmental factors are linked to SIDS. Maternal cigarette smoking, both during and after pregnancy, as well as smoking by other caregivers, doubles risk of the disorder. Babies exposed to cigarette smoke arouse less easily from sleep and have more respiratory infections (Anderson, Johnson, & Batal, 2005; Shah, Sullivan, & Carter, 2006). Prenatal abuse of drugs that depress central nervous system functioning (alcohol, opiates, and barbiturates) increases the risk of SIDS as much as fifteenfold (Hunt & Hauck, 2006). Babies of drug-abusing mothers are especially likely to display SIDS-related brain abnormalities (Kinney, 2009).

SIDS babies are also more likely to sleep on their stomachs than on their backs and often are wrapped very warmly in clothing and blankets. Infants who sleep on their stomachs less often wake when their breathing is disturbed (Richardson, Walker, & Horne, 2008). In other cases, healthy babies sleeping face down in soft bedding may die from continually breathing their own exhaled breath.

Quitting smoking and drug taking, changing an infant's sleeping position, and removing a few bedclothes can reduce the incidence of SIDS. For example, if women refrained from smoking while pregnant, an estimated 30 percent of SIDS cases would be prevented. Public education campaigns that encourage parents to put their infants down on their backs have cut the incidence of SIDS by more than half in many Western nations (Moon, Horne, & Hauck, 2007). Another protective measure is pacifier use: Sleeping babies who suck arouse more

easily in response to breathing and heart-rate irregularities (Li et al., 2006). Nevertheless, compared with white infants, SIDS rates are two to six times higher in poverty-stricken minority groups, where parental stress, substance abuse, reduced access to health care, and lack of knowledge about safe sleep practices are widespread (Pickett, Luo, & Lauderdale, 2005).

When SIDS does occur, surviving family members require a great deal of help to overcome a sudden and unexpected death. As Millie commented six months after Sasha's death, "It's the worst crisis we've ever been through. What's helped us most are the comforting words of others who've experienced the same tragedy."

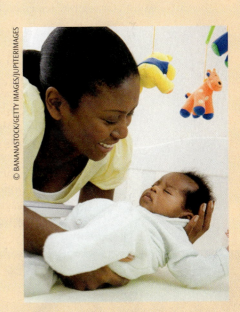

© BANANASTOCK/GETTY IMAGES/JUPITERIMAGES

■ Public education campaigns encouraging parents to put their infants down on their backs to sleep have helped to reduce the incidence of SIDS, which has dropped by more than half in many Western nations. ■

motor, cognitive, and language development (de Weerd & van den Bossche, 2003; Feldman, 2006; Holditch-Davis, Belyea, & Edwards, 2005). And the brain-functioning problems that underlie newborn sleep irregularities may culminate in sudden infant death syndrome, a major cause of infant mortality (see the Social Issues: Health box above).

CRYING Crying is the first way that babies communicate, letting parents know that they need food, comfort, and stimulation. During the weeks after birth, all babies seem to have some fussy periods when they are difficult to console. But most of the time, the nature of the cry,

Applying What We Know

Soothing a Crying Baby

TECHNIQUE	EXPLANATION
Lift the baby to the shoulder and rock or walk.	This combination of physical contact, upright posture, and motion is an effective soothing technique, causing young infants to become quietly alert.
Swaddle the baby.	Restricting movement and increasing warmth often soothe a young infant.
Offer a pacifier.	Sucking helps babies control their own level of arousal.
Talk softly or play rhythmic sounds.	Continuous, monotonous, rhythmic sounds (such as a clock ticking, a fan whirring, or peaceful music) are more effective than intermittent sounds.
Take the baby for a short car ride or a walk in a baby carriage; swing the baby in a cradle.	Gentle, rhythmic motion of any kind helps lull the baby to sleep.
Massage the baby's body.	Stroking the baby's torso and limbs with continuous, gentle motions relaxes the baby's muscles.
Combine several of the methods just listed.	Stimulating several of the baby's senses at once is often more effective than stimulating only one.
If these methods do not work, let the baby cry for a short period.	Occasionally, a baby responds well to just being put down and will, after a few minutes, fall asleep.

Sources: Evanoo, 2007; Campos, 1989; Lester, 1985; Reisman, 1987.

combined with the experiences that led up to it, helps guide parents toward its cause. The baby's cry is a complex stimulus that varies in intensity, from a whimper to a message of all-out distress (Gustafson, Wood, & Green, 2000). As early as the first few weeks, infants can be identified by the unique vocal "signature" of their cries, which helps parents locate their baby from a distance (Gustafson, Green, & Cleland, 1994).

Young infants usually cry because of physical needs. Hunger is the most common cause, but babies may also cry in response to temperature change when undressed, a sudden noise, or a painful stimulus. Newborns (as well as older babies) often cry at the sound of another crying baby (Dondi, Simion, & Caltran, 1999). Some researchers believe that this response reflects an inborn capacity to react to the suffering of others. Furthermore, crying typically increases during the early weeks, peaks at about 6 weeks, and then declines. Because this trend appears in many cultures with vastly different infant care practices, researchers believe that normal readjustments of the central nervous system underlie it (Barr, 2001).

TAKE A MOMENT... The next time you hear a baby cry, notice your own reaction. The sound stimulates strong feelings of arousal and discomfort in men and women, parents and nonparents alike (Murray, 1985). This powerful response is probably innately programmed to help ensure that babies receive the care and protection they need to survive.

Soothing Crying Infants. Although parents do not always interpret their baby's cry correctly, their accuracy improves with experience. Fortunately, there are many ways to soothe a crying baby when feeding and diaper changing do not work (see Applying What We Know above). The technique that Western parents usually try first, lifting the baby to the shoulder and rocking or walking, is most effective. Another common soothing method is swaddling—wrapping the baby snugly in a blanket. The Quechua, who live in the cold, high-altitude desert regions of Peru, dress young babies in several layers of clothing and blankets that cover the head and body, a technique that reduces crying and promotes sleep (Tronick, Thomas, & Daltabuit, 1994). It also enables the baby to conserve energy for early growth in the harsh Peruvian highlands.

In many tribal and village societies and in non-Western developed nations, infants spend most of the day and night in close physical contact

© KEVIN DODGE/CORBIS

■ To soothe his crying infant, this father holds the baby upright against his gently moving body. The combination of physical contact, upright posture, and motion causes infants to stop crying and become quietly alert. ■

with their caregivers. Among the !Kung of the desert regions of Botswana, Africa, mothers carry their young babies in grass-lined, animal-skin slings hung on their hips, so the infants can see their surroundings and can nurse at will. Japanese mothers also spend much time holding their babies (Small, 1998). Infants in these cultures show shorter bouts of crying than their American counterparts (Barr, 2001). When Western parents choose to practice "proximal care" by holding their babies extensively, amount of crying in the early months is reduced by about one-third (St James-Roberts et al., 2006).

Abnormal Crying. Like reflexes and sleep patterns, the infant's cry offers a clue to central nervous system distress. The cries of brain-damaged babies and those who have experienced prenatal and birth complications are often shrill, piercing, and shorter in duration than the cries of healthy infants (Boukydis & Lester, 1998; Green, Irwin, & Gustafson, 2000). Even newborns with a fairly common problem—*colic,* or persistent crying—tend to have high-pitched, harsh-sounding cries (Zeskind & Barr, 1997). Although the cause of colic is unknown, certain newborns, who react especially strongly to unpleasant stimuli, are susceptible. Because their crying is intense, they find it harder to calm down than other babies. Colic generally subsides between 3 and 6 months (Barr et al., 2005; St James-Roberts, 2007).

In an intervention aimed at reducing colic, nurses made periodic home visits, providing parents with help in identifying their baby's early warning signs of becoming overly aroused, in using effective soothing techniques, and in modifying light, noise, and activity in the home to promote predictable sleep–wake cycles (Keefe et al., 2005). Colicky infants who received the intervention spent far less time crying than no-intervention controls—1.3 versus 3 hours per day.

Most parents try to respond to a crying baby's call for help with extra care and attention, but sometimes the cry is so unpleasant and the infant so difficult to soothe that parents become frustrated, resentful, and angry. Preterm and ill babies are more likely to be abused by highly stressed parents, who sometimes mention a high-pitched, grating cry as one factor that caused them to lose control and harm the baby (St. James-Roberts, 2007; Zeskind & Lester, 2001). We will discuss a host of additional influences on child abuse in Chapter 10.

■ These Quechua women, who live in the cold, high-altitude desert regions of Peru, dress their young babies in layers of clothing and blankets that cover the head and body. In addition to reducing crying and promoting sleep, swaddling helps babies conserve energy for early growth in the harsh Peruvian highlands. ■

Sensory Capacities

On his visit to my class, Joshua looked wide-eyed at my bright pink blouse and turned to the sound of his mother's voice. During feedings, he lets Yolanda know by the way he sucks that he prefers the taste of breast milk to a bottle of plain water. Clearly, Joshua has some well-developed sensory capacities. In the following sections, we explore the newborn baby's responsiveness to touch, taste, smell, sound, and visual stimulation.

TOUCH   In our discussion of preterm infants, we saw that touch helps stimulate early physical growth. And as we will see in Chapter 7, it is vital for emotional development as well. Therefore, it is not surprising that sensitivity to touch is well-developed at birth.

The reflexes listed in Table 4.2 on page 144 reveal that the newborn baby responds to touch, especially around the mouth, on the palms, and on the soles of the feet. During the prenatal period, these areas, along with the genitals, are the first to become sensitive to touch (Humphrey, 1978; Streri, 2005). Using their palms, newborns can even distinguish the shapes (prism versus cylinder) and textures (smooth versus rough) of small objects, as indicated by their tendency to hold on longer to an object with an unfamiliar shape or texture than to a familiar object (Sann & Streri, 2008; Streri, Lhote, & Dutilleul, 2000).

At birth, infants are quite sensitive to pain. If male newborns are circumcised, anesthetic is sometimes not used because of the risk of giving drugs to a very young infant. Babies often respond with a high-pitched, stressful cry and a dramatic rise in heart rate, blood pressure,

LOOK AND LISTEN

In a public setting, watch several parents soothe their crying babies. What techniques did the parents use, and how successful were they?

palm sweating, pupil dilation, and muscle tension (Lehr et al., 2007; Warnock & Sandrin, 2004). Brain-imaging research suggests that because of central nervous system immaturity, preterm and male babies feel the pain of a medical injection especially intensely (Bartocci et al., 2006).

Recent research establishing the safety of certain local anesthetics for newborns promises to ease the pain of these procedures. Offering a nipple that delivers a sugar solution is also helpful; it quickly reduces crying and discomfort in young babies, preterm and full-term alike. Breast milk may be especially effective: Even the smell of the milk of the baby's mother reduces infant stress to a routine blood-test heelstick more effectively than the odor of another mother's milk or of formula (Nishitani et al., 2009). And combining sweet liquid with gentle holding by the parent lessens pain even more. Research on infant mammals indicates that physical touch releases *endorphins*—painkilling chemicals in the brain (Axelin, Salantera, & Lehtonen, 2006; Gormally et al., 2001).

Allowing a baby to endure severe pain overwhelms the nervous system with stress hormones, which can disrupt the child's developing capacity to handle common, everyday stressors. The result is heightened pain sensitivity, sleep disturbances, feeding problems, and difficulty calming down when upset (Mitchell & Boss, 2002).

TASTE AND SMELL Facial expressions reveal that newborns can distinguish several basic tastes. Like adults, they relax their facial muscles in response to sweetness, purse their lips when the taste is sour, and show a distinct archlike mouth opening when it is bitter (Steiner, 1979; Steiner et al., 2001). These reactions are important for survival: The food that best supports the infant's early growth is the sweet-tasting milk of the mother's breast. Not until 4 months do babies prefer a salty taste to plain water, a change that may prepare them to accept solid foods (Mennella & Beauchamp, 1998).

Nevertheless, newborns can readily learn to like a taste that at first evoked either a neutral or a negative response. For example, babies allergic to cow's milk formula who are given a soy or other vegetable-based substitute (typically very strong and bitter-tasting) soon prefer it to regular formula. A taste previously disliked can come to be preferred when it is paired with relief of hunger (Harris, 1997).

As with taste, certain odor preferences are present at birth. For example, the smell of bananas or chocolate causes a relaxed, pleasant facial expression, whereas the odor of rotten eggs makes the infant frown (Steiner, 1979). During pregnancy, the amniotic fluid is rich in tastes and smells that vary with the mother's diet—early experiences that influence newborns' preferences. In a study carried out in the Alsatian region of France, where anise is frequently used to flavor foods, researchers tested newborns for their reaction to the anise odor (Schaal, Marlier, & Soussignan, 2000). The mothers of some babies had regularly consumed anise during the last two weeks of pregnancy; the other mothers had never consumed it. When presented with the anise odor on the day of birth, the babies of non-anise-consuming mothers were far more likely to turn away with a negative facial expression (see Figure 4.7). These different reactions were still apparent four days later, even though all mothers had refrained from consuming anise during this time.

In many mammals, the sense of smell plays an important role in feeding and in protecting the young from predators by helping mothers and babies identify each other. Although smell is less well-developed in humans, traces of its survival value remain.

Immediately after birth, infants placed face-down between their mother's breasts latch on to a nipple and begin

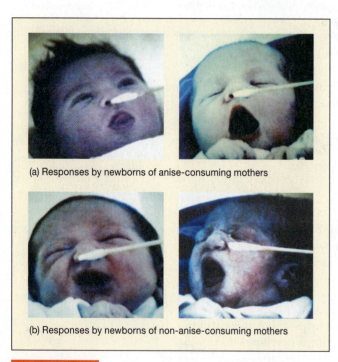

(a) Responses by newborns of anise-consuming mothers

(b) Responses by newborns of non-anise-consuming mothers

FIGURE 4.7

Examples of facial expressions of newborns exposed to the odor of anise whose mothers' diets differed in anise-flavored foods during late pregnancy. (a) Babies of anise-consuming mothers spent more time turning toward the odor and sucking, licking, and chewing. (b) Babies of non-anise-consuming mothers more often turned away with a negative facial expression. *(From B. Schaal, L. Marlier, & R. Soussignan, 2000, "Human Foetuses Learn Odours from Their Pregnant Mother's Diet," Chemical Senses, 25, p. 731. Reprinted by permission of Benoist Schaal.)*

sucking within an hour. If one breast is washed to remove its natural scent, most newborns move toward the unwashed breast, indicating that they are guided by smell (Varendi & Porter, 2001). At 4 days of age, breastfed babies prefer the smell of their own mother's breast to that of an unfamiliar lactating woman (Cernoch & Porter, 1985). And both breast- and bottle-fed 3- to 4-day-olds orient more and display more mouthing to the smell of unfamiliar human milk than to formula milk, indicating that (even without postnatal exposure) the odor of human milk is more attractive to newborns (Marlier & Schaal, 2005). Newborns' dual attraction to the odors of their mother and of breast milk helps them locate an appropriate food source and, in the process, distinguish their caregiver from other people.

HEARING Although conduction of sound through the structures of the ear and transmission of auditory information to the brain are inefficient at birth, newborn infants can hear a wide variety of sounds—sensitivity that improves greatly over the first few months (Saffran, Werker, & Werner, 2006; Tharpe & Ashmead, 2001). At birth, infants prefer complex sounds, such as noises and voices, to pure tones. And babies only a few days old can tell the difference between a variety of sound patterns: a series of tones arranged in ascending versus descending order; tone sequences with a rhythmic downbeat (as in music) versus those without; utterances with two versus three syllables; the stress patterns of words, such as "*ma*-ma" versus "ma-*ma*"; happy-sounding speech as opposed to speech with negative or neutral emotional qualities; and even two languages spoken by the same bilingual speaker, as long as those languages differ in their rhythmic features—for example, French from Russian (Mastropieri & Turkewitz, 1999; Ramus, 2002; Sansavini, Bertoncini, & Giovanelli, 1997; Trehub, 2001; Winkler et al., 2009).

Young infants listen longer to human speech than to structurally similar nonspeech sounds (Vouloumanos & Werker, 2004). And they can detect the sounds of any human language. Newborns make fine-grained distinctions among many speech sounds. For example, when given a nipple that turns on a recording of the "*ba*" sound, babies suck vigorously for a while and then slow down as the novelty wears off. When the sound switches to "*ga*," sucking picks up, indicating that infants detect this subtle difference. Using this method, researchers have found only a few speech sounds that newborns cannot discriminate. Their ability to perceive sounds not found in their own language is more precise than an adult's (Aldridge, Stillman, & Bower, 2001; Jusczyk & Luce, 2002). These capacities reveal that the baby is marvelously prepared for the awesome task of acquiring language.

Responsiveness to sound also supports the newborn baby's exploration of the environment. Infants as young as 3 days turn their eyes and head in the general direction of a sound. The ability to identify the precise location of a sound improves greatly over the first six months and shows further gains through the preschool years (Litovsky & Ashmead, 1997).

TAKE A MOMENT... Listen carefully to yourself the next time you talk to a young baby. You will probably speak in ways that highlight important parts of the speech stream—use a high-pitched, expressive voice with a rising tone at the ends of phrases and sentences and a pause before continuing. Adults probably communicate this way with infants because they notice that babies are more attentive when they do so. Indeed, newborns prefer speech with these characteristics (Saffran, Werker, & Werner, 2006). They will also suck more on a nipple to hear a recording of their own mother's voice than that of an unfamiliar woman and to hear their native language as opposed to a foreign language (Moon, Cooper, & Fifer, 1993; Spence & DeCasper, 1987). These preferences may have developed from hearing the muffled sounds of the mother's voice before birth.

VISION Vision is the least developed of the newborn baby's senses. Visual structures in both the eye and the brain are not yet fully formed at birth. For example, cells in the *retina*, the membrane lining the inside of the eye that captures light and transforms it into messages that are sent to the brain, are not as mature or densely packed as they will be in several months. The optic nerve that relays these messages, and visual centers in the brain that receive them, will not be adultlike for several years. And muscles of the *lens*, which permit us to adjust our visual focus to varying distances, are weak (Kellman & Arterberry, 2006).

As a result, newborn babies cannot focus their eyes well, and their **visual acuity,** or fineness of discrimination, is limited. At birth, infants perceive objects at a distance of 20 feet about

FIGURE 4.8

View of the human face by the newborn and the adult. The newborn baby's limited focusing ability and poor visual acuity lead the mother's face, even when viewed from close up, to look much like the fuzzy image in (a) rather than the clear image in (b). Also, newborn infants have some color vision, although they have difficulty discriminating colors. Researchers speculate that colors probably appear similar, but less intense, to newborns than to older infants and adults. *(From Kellman & Arterberry 2006; Slater, 2001.)*

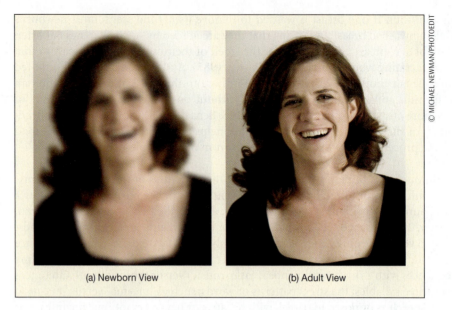

(a) Newborn View   (b) Adult View

as clearly as adults do at 600 feet (Slater, 2001). In addition, unlike adults (who see nearby objects most clearly), newborn babies see unclearly across a wide range of distances (Banks, 1980; Hainline, 1998). As a result, images such as the parent's face, even from close up, look like the blurry image in Figure 4.8. Nevertheless, as we will see in Chapter 5, newborns can detect human faces. And as with their preference for their mother's smell and voice, from repeated exposures they quickly learn to prefer her face to that of an unfamiliar woman, although they are more sensitive to its broad outlines than its fine-grained, internal features (Bartrip, Morton, & de Schonen, 2001; Walton, Armstrong, & Bower, 1998).

Although they cannot yet see well, newborns actively explore their environment by scanning it for interesting sights and tracking moving objects. However, their eye movements are slow and inaccurate (von Hofsten & Rosander, 1998). Joshua's captivation with my pink blouse reveals that he is attracted to bright objects. Nevertheless, once newborns focus on an object, they tend to look only at a single feature—for example, the corner of a triangle instead of the entire shape. And despite their preference for colored over gray stimuli, newborn babies are not yet good at discriminating colors. It will take about four months for color vision to become adultlike (Adams & Courage, 1998; Kellman & Arterberry, 2006).

Neonatal Behavioral Assessment

A variety of instruments permit doctors, nurses, and researchers to assess the behavior of newborn babies. The most widely used of these tests, T. Berry Brazelton's **Neonatal Behavioral Assessment Scale (NBAS),** evaluates the baby's reflexes, muscle tone, state changes, responsiveness to physical and social stimuli, and other reactions (Brazelton & Nugent, 1995). A recently developed instrument consisting of similar items, called the *Neonatal Intensive Care Unit Network Neurobehavioral Scale (NNNS),* is specially designed for use with newborns at risk for developmental problems—because of low birth weight, preterm delivery, prenatal substance exposure, or other conditions (Lester & Tronick, 2004). Scores are used to recommend appropriate interventions and to guide parents in meeting their baby's unique needs.

The NBAS has been given to many infants around the world. As a result, researchers have learned about individual and cultural differences in newborn behavior and how child-rearing practices can maintain or change a baby's reactions. For example, NBAS scores of Asian and Native-American babies reveal that they are less irritable than Caucasian infants. Mothers in these cultures often encourage their babies' calm dispositions through holding and nursing at the first signs of discomfort (Muret-Wagstaff & Moore, 1989; Small, 1998). In contrast, maternal care quickly changes the poor NBAS scores of undernourished infants in Zambia, Africa. The Zambian mother carries her baby about on her hip all day, providing a rich variety of sensory stimulation. As a result, a once unresponsive newborn becomes an alert, contented 1-week-old (Brazelton, Koslowski, & Tronick, 1976).

■ This mother of the El Molo people of northern Kenya carries her baby about all day, providing close physical contact, a rich variety of stimulation, and ready feeding. Many Western parents find similar benefits in using a sling to keep their babies physically close. ■

TAKE A MOMENT... Using these examples, can you explain why a single neonatal assessment score is not a good predictor of later development? Because newborn behavior and parenting styles combine to shape development, *changes in scores* over the first week or two of life (rather than a single score) provide the best estimate of the baby's ability to recover from the stress of birth. NBAS "recovery curves" predict intelligence and absence of emotional and behavior problems with moderate success well into the preschool years (Brazelton, Nugent, & Lester, 1987; Ohgi et al., 2003a, 2003b).

In some hospitals, health professionals use the NBAS or the NNNS to help parents get to know their newborns through discussion or demonstration of the capacities these instruments assess. Parents of both preterm and full-term newborns who participate in these programs interact more effectively with their babies (Browne & Talmi, 2005; Bruschweiler-Stern, 2004). Although lasting effects on development have not been demonstrated, neonatal behavioral assessment interventions are useful in helping the parent–infant relationship get off to a good start.

ASK YOURSELF

◆ **REVIEW** What functions does REM sleep serve in young infants? Can sleep tell us anything about the health of the newborn's central nervous system? Explain.

◆ **APPLY** After a difficult delivery, Jackie observes her 2-day-old daughter, Kelly, being given the NBAS. Kelly scores poorly on many items. Seeing this, Jackie wonders if Kelly will develop normally. How would you respond to Jackie's concern?

◆ **CONNECT** How do the diverse capacities of newborn babies contribute to their first social relationships? Provide as many examples as you can.

◆ **REFLECT** Are newborns more competent than you thought they were before you read this chapter? Which of their capacities most surprised you?

The Transition to Parenthood

The early weeks after a new baby enters the family are full of profound changes. The mother needs to recover from childbirth and adjust to massive hormone shifts in her body. If she is breastfeeding, energies must be devoted to working out this intimate relationship. The father must become a part of this new threesome while supporting the mother in her recovery. At times, he may feel ambivalent about the baby, who constantly demands and gets the mother's attention.

While all this is going on, the tiny infant is assertive about his urgent physical needs, demanding to be fed, changed, and comforted at odd times of the day and night. The family schedule becomes irregular and uncertain. Yolanda spoke candidly about the changes she and Jay experienced:

> When we brought Joshua home, he seemed so small and helpless, and we worried about whether we would be able to take proper care of him. It took us 20 minutes to change the first diaper. I rarely feel rested because I'm up two to four times every night, and I spend a good part of my waking hours trying to anticipate Joshua's rhythms and needs. If Jay weren't so willing to help by holding and walking Joshua, I think I'd find it much harder.

Changes in the Family System

The demands of new parenthood—constant caregiving, added financial responsibilities, and less time for couples to devote to one another—usually cause the gender roles of husband and wife to become more traditional (Cowan & Cowan, 2000; Salmela-Aro et al., 2000). This is true even for couples like Yolanda and Jay, who are strongly committed to gender equality and are used to sharing household tasks. Yolanda took a leave of absence from work, whereas Jay's career continued as it had before. As a result, Yolanda spent more time at home with the baby, while Jay focused more on his provider role.

For most new parents, however, the arrival of a baby—though often associated with mild declines in relationship satisfaction and communication quality—does not cause significant marital strain. Marriages that are gratifying and supportive tend to remain so (Doss et al., 2009; Feeney et al., 2001; Miller, 2000). But troubled marriages usually become more distressed after a baby is born. In a study of newlyweds who were interviewed annually for six years, the husband's affection, expression of "we-ness" (values and goals similar to his wife's), and awareness of his wife's daily life predicted mothers' stable or increasing marital satisfaction after childbirth. In contrast, the husband's negativity and the couple's out-of-control conflict predicted a drop in mothers' satisfaction (Shapiro, Gottman, & Carrere, 2000). When expectant couples anticipate lack of partner support in parenting, their prediction generally becomes reality, yielding an especially difficult post-birth adjustment (McHale & Rotman, 2007). For some new parents, problems are severe (see the Biology and Environment box on the following page).

Violated expectations about division of labor in the home powerfully affect family well-being. In dual-earner marriages, the larger the difference between men's and women's caregiving responsibilities, the greater the decline in marital satisfaction after childbirth, especially for women—with negative consequences for parent–infant interaction. In contrast, sharing caregiving predicts greater parental happiness and sensitivity to the baby (McHale et al., 2004; Moller, Hwang, & Wickberg, 2008). An exception exists, however, for employed lower-SES women who endorse traditional gender roles. When their husbands help extensively with child care, these mothers tend to report more distress, perhaps because they feel disappointed at being unable to fulfill their desire to do most of the caregiving (Goldberg & Perry-Jenkins, 2003).

Postponing parenthood until the late twenties or thirties, as more couples do today, eases the transition to parenthood. Waiting permits couples to pursue occupational goals and gain life experience. Under these circumstances, men are more enthusiastic about becoming fathers and therefore more willing to participate. And women whose careers are well under way and whose marriages are happy are more likely to encourage their husbands to share housework and child care, which fosters fathers' involvement (Lee & Doherty, 2007; Schoppe-Sullivan et al., 2008).

BIOLOGY AND ENVIRONMENT

Parental Depression and Child Development

About 8 to 10 percent of women experience chronic depression—mild to severe feelings of sadness and withdrawal that continue for months or years. Often, the beginnings of this emotional state cannot be pinpointed. In other instances, depression emerges or strengthens after childbirth but fails to subside as the new mother adjusts to hormonal changes in her body and gains confidence in caring for her baby. This is called *postpartum depression*.

Although it is less recognized and studied, fathers, too, experience chronic depression. About 3 to 5 percent of fathers report symptoms after the birth of a child (Madsen & Juhl, 2007; Spector, 2006). Parental depression can interfere with effective parenting and seriously impair children's development. Genetic makeup increases the risk of depressive illness, but social and cultural factors are also involved.

Maternal Depression

During Julia's pregnancy, her husband, Kyle, showed so little interest in the baby that Julia worried that having a child might be a mistake. Then, shortly after Lucy was born, Julia's mood plunged. She felt anxious and weepy, overwhelmed by Lucy's needs, and angry at loss of control over her own schedule. When Julia approached Kyle about her own fatigue and his unwillingness to help with the baby, he snapped that she was overreacting. Julia's childless friends stopped by just once to see Lucy but did not call again.

Julia's depressed mood quickly affected her baby. In the weeks after birth, infants of depressed mothers sleep poorly, are less attentive to their surroundings, and have elevated levels of the stress hormone cortisol (Field, 1998). The more extreme the depression and the greater the number of stressors in a mother's life (such as marital discord, little or no social support, and poverty), the more the parent–child relationship suffers (Simpson et al., 2003). Julia rarely smiled at, comforted, or talked to Lucy, who responded to her mother's sad, vacant gaze by turning away, crying, and often looking sad or angry herself (Herrera, Reissland, & Shepherd, 2004; Stanley, Murray, & Stein, 2004). Julia, in turn, felt guilty and inadequate, and her depression deepened. By age 6 months, Lucy showed mental and emotional symptoms common in babies of depressed mothers—delays in development, an irritable mood, and attachment difficulties (Cornish et al., 2005; McMahon et al., 2006).

When maternal depression persists, the parent–child relationship worsens. Depressed parents view their infants more negatively than independent observers do (Forman et al., 2007). And they use inconsistent discipline—sometimes lax, at other times too forceful. As we will see in later chapters, children who experience these maladaptive parenting practices often have serious adjustment problems. Some withdraw into a depressive mood themselves; others become impulsive and aggressive. In one study, infants born to mothers who were depressed during pregnancy were four times as likely as babies of nondepressed mothers to have engaged in violent antisocial behavior (such as fighting, bullying, assault with a weapon, and extreme bodily harm) by age 16, after other stressors in the mother's life that could contribute to youth antisocial conduct had been controlled (Hay et al., 2010).

Paternal Depression

Paternal depression is also linked to dissatisfaction with marriage and family life after childbirth and to other life stressors, including job loss and divorce (Bielawska-Batorowicz & Kossakowska-Petrycka, 2006). In a study of a large representative sample of British parents and babies, researchers assessed depressive symptoms of fathers shortly after birth and again the following year. Then they tracked the children's development into the preschool years. Persistent paternal depression was, like maternal depression, a strong predictor of child behavior problems—especially overactivity, defiance, and aggression in boys (Ramchandani et al., 2008).

Paternal depression is linked to frequent father–child conflict as children grow older (Kane & Garber, 2004). Over time, children subjected to parental negativity develop a pessimistic worldview—one in which they lack self-confidence and perceive their parents and other people as threatening. Children who constantly feel in danger are especially likely to become overly aroused in stressful situations, easily losing control in the face of cognitive and social challenges (Sturge-Apple et al., 2008). Although children of depressed parents may inherit a tendency toward emotional and behavior problems, quality of parenting is a major factor in their adjustment.

Interventions

Early treatment is vital to prevent parental depression from interfering with the parent–child relationship. Julia's doctor referred her to a therapist, who helped Julia and Kyle with their marital problems. At times, antidepressant medication is prescribed.

In addition to alleviating parental depression, therapy that encourages depressed mothers to revise their negative views of their babies and to engage in emotionally positive, responsive caregiving is vital for reducing young children's attachment and other developmental problems (Forman et al., 2007). When a depressed parent does not respond easily to treatment, a warm relationship with the other parent or another caregiver can safeguard children's development (Mezulis, Hyde, & Clark, 2004).

© RICHARD NEWTON/ALAMY

■ This depressed mother appears completely uninterested in her infant. If her disengagement continues, the baby is likely to become negative and irritable, eventually withdraw, and develop serious emotional and behavior problems. ■

Applying What We Know

How Couples Can Ease the Transition to Parenthood

STRATEGY	DESCRIPTION
Devise a plan for sharing household tasks.	As soon as possible, discuss division of household responsibilities. Decide who does a particular chore based on who has the needed skill and time, not gender. Schedule regular times to reevaluate your plan to fit changing family circumstances.
Begin sharing child care right after the baby's arrival.	For fathers, strive to spend equal time with the baby early. For mothers, refrain from imposing your standards on your partner. Instead, share the role of "child-rearing expert" by discussing parenting values and concerns often. Attend a new-parenthood course together.
Talk over conflicts about decision making and responsibilities.	Face conflict through communication. Clarify your feelings and needs, and express them to your partner. Listen and try to understand your partner's point of view. Then be willing to negotiate and compromise.
Establish a balance between work and parenting.	Critically evaluate the time you devote to work in view of new parenthood. If it is too much, try to cut back.
Press for workplace and public policies that assist parents in rearing children.	Difficulties faced by new parents may be partly due to lack of workplace and societal supports. Encourage your employer to provide benefits that help combine work and family roles, such as paid employment leave, flexible work hours, and on-site high-quality, affordable child care. Communicate with lawmakers and other citizens about improving policies for children and families, including paid, job-protected leave to support the transition to parenthood.

In a study of well-educated mothers, those who had recently given birth to their second child reported just as much stress as first-time mothers (Krieg, 2007). A second birth typically requires that fathers take an even more active role in parenting—by caring for the firstborn while the mother is recuperating and by sharing in the high demands of tending to both a baby and a young child. Consequently, well-functioning families with a newborn second child typically pull back from the traditional division of responsibilities that occurred after the first birth. In a study that tracked parents from the end of pregnancy through the first year after their second child's birth, fathers' willingness to place greater emphasis on the parenting role was strongly linked to mothers' adjustment after the arrival of a second baby (Stewart, 1990). And the support and encouragement of family, friends, and partner are crucial for fathers' well-being.

Finally, both parents must help their firstborn child adjust. Preschool-age siblings understandably may feel displaced and react with jealousy and anger—a topic we will take up in Chapter 7. For strategies couples can use to ease the transition to parenthood, refer to Applying What We Know above.

Single-Mother Families

Nearly 39 percent of babies in the United States are born to single mothers, one-third of whom are teenagers (U.S. Department of Health and Human Services, 2009b). Because of poverty, poor health care, stressful life conditions, high rates of drug and alcohol abuse, and weak parenting skills, adolescent mothers and their newborns are at high risk for developmental problems.

At the other extreme, planned births and adoptions by single 30- to 45-year-old women are increasing. These mothers are generally financially secure, have readily available social support from family members and friends, and adapt to parenthood with relative ease. In fact, older single mothers in well-paid occupations who plan carefully for a new baby may encounter fewer parenting difficulties than married couples, largely because their family structure is simpler: They do not have to coordinate parenting roles with a partner, and they have no unfulfilled expectations for shared caregiving (Ambert, 2006). And because of their psychological maturity, these mothers are likely to cope effectively with parenting challenges.

The majority of nonmarital births are unplanned and to women in their twenties. Most of these single mothers have incomes below the poverty level and experience a stressful transition

LOOK AND LISTEN

Ask a couple or a single mother to describe the challenges of new parenthood, along with factors that aided or impeded this transition.

to parenthood. Although many live with the baby's father or another partner, cohabiting relationships in the United States are less socially acceptable than those in Western Europe, involve less commitment and cooperation, and are far more likely to break up—especially after an unplanned baby arrives (Fussell & Gauthier, 2005). Furthermore, these single mothers often lack emotional and parenting support—strong predictors of psychological distress and infant caregiving difficulties (Keating-Lefler et al., 2004).

Parent Interventions

Special interventions are available to help parents adjust to life with a new baby. For those who are not at high risk for problems, counselor-led groups focusing on couple and adjustment and parenting skills are highly effective (Glade, Bean, & Vira, 2005; Petch & Halford, 2008). In one program, first-time expectant couples gathered once a week for six months to discuss their dreams for the family and the changes in relationships sparked by the baby's arrival. Eighteen months after the program ended, participating fathers described themselves as more involved with their child than did fathers in a no-intervention condition. Perhaps because of fathers' caregiving assistance, participating mothers maintained their prebirth satisfaction with family and work roles. Three years after the birth, the marriages of all participating couples were still intact and just as happy as they had been before parenthood. In contrast, 15 percent of couples receiving no intervention had divorced (Cowan & Cowan, 1997; Schulz, Cowan, & Cowan, 2006).

■ A growing number of single women in their thirties and early forties are choosing to give birth or adopt a child. With social support from family and friends, this mother is likely to have a relatively smooth transition to parenthood. ■

High-risk parents struggling with poverty or the birth of a child with disabilities need more intensive interventions. Programs in which a professional intervener visits the home and focuses on enhancing social support and parenting have resulted in improved parent–infant interaction and benefits for children's cognitive and social development into middle childhood (review one example on page 116 in Chapter 3) (Petch & Halford, 2008). Many low-income single parents also require tangible support—money, food, transportation, and affordable child care—to ease stress and allow them to engage in effective caregiving.

When marital relationships are positive, social support is available, and families have sufficient income, the stress caused by the birth of a baby remains manageable. Nevertheless, as one pair of counselors who have worked with many new parents point out, "As long as children are dependent on their parents, those parents find themselves preoccupied with thoughts of their children. This does not keep them from enjoying other aspects of their lives, but it does mean that they never return to being quite the same people they were before they became parents" (Colman & Colman, 1991, p. 198).

ASK YOURSELF

◆ **REVIEW** Explain how persisting postpartum depression seriously impairs children's development.

◆ **APPLY** Derek, father of a 3-year-old and a newborn, reported that he had a harder time adjusting to the birth of his second child than to that of his first child. Explain why this might be so.

◆ **CONNECT** Louise has just given birth to her first child. Because her husband works long hours and is seldom available to help, she feels overwhelmed by the pressures of caring for a new baby. Why does Louise's four-week maternity leave pose a risk to her mental health? (*Hint:* Consult the Social Issues: Health box on page 141.)

◆ **REFLECT** If you are a parent, what was the transition to parenthood like for you? What factors helped you adjust to this major life change? What factors made it more difficult? If you are not a parent, pose these questions to someone you know who recently became a parent.

Summary

The Stages of Childbirth

Describe the three stages of childbirth, the baby's adaptation to labor and delivery, and the newborn baby's appearance.

■ In the first stage of childbirth, **dilation and effacement of the cervix** occur as uterine contractions increase in strength and frequency. This stage culminates in **transition,** a brief period in which contractions are at their peak and the cervix opens completely. In the second stage, the mother feels an urge to bear down with her abdominal muscles, and the baby is born. In the final stage, the placenta is delivered.

■ During labor, the force of the contractions causes infants to produce high levels of stress hormones, which help them withstand oxygen deprivation, clear the lungs for breathing, and arouse them into alertness at birth.

■ Newborn infants have large heads and small bodies. The **Apgar Scale** is used to assess the baby's physical condition at birth.

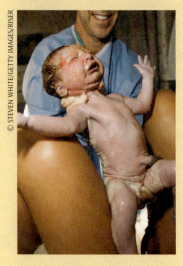

© STEVEN WHITE/GETTY IMAGES/RISER

Approaches to Childbirth

Describe natural childbirth and home delivery, noting benefits and concerns associated with each.

■ In **natural,** or **prepared, childbirth,** the expectant mother and a companion typically attend classes where they learn about labor and delivery, master relaxation and breathing techniques to counteract pain, and prepare for coaching during childbirth. The method reduces pain and use of medication and fosters more positive maternal attitudes toward the birth experience. Social support, from a partner, relative, or doula, reduces the length of labor and the incidence of birth complications.

■ Home birth is relatively rare in the United States but is common in some other industrialized nations. It is safe for healthy mothers who are assisted by a well-trained doctor or midwife, but mothers at risk for any kind of complication are safer giving birth in a hospital.

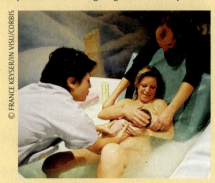

© FRANCE KEYSER/IN VISU/CORBIS

Medical Interventions

List common medical interventions during childbirth, circumstances that justify their use, and any dangers associated with each.

■ **Fetal monitors** help save the lives of many babies whose mothers have a history of pregnancy and birth complications. But they also may identify infants as in danger who, in fact, are not, and are linked to an increase in cesarean deliveries.

■ Use of analgesics and anesthetics to control pain during childbirth can prolong labor and cause newborns to be withdrawn and irritable. Instrument delivery using *forceps* or a *vacuum extractor* may be appropriate if the mother's pushing does not move the infant through the birth canal in a reasonable period of time. However, because they can cause serious complications, they should be avoided if possible.

■ **Induced labor** is more difficult than naturally occurring labor and is more likely to be associated with the use of labor and delivery medication and instrument delivery. Inductions should be scheduled only when continuing the pregnancy threatens the well-being of mother or baby.

■ **Cesarean deliveries** are justified in cases of medical emergency or serious maternal illness and when the baby is in **breech position.** A dramatic worldwide rise has occurred in cesarean deliveries, many of which are unnecessary.

Birth Complications

What are the risks of oxygen deprivation, preterm birth, and low birth weight, and what factors can help infants who survive a traumatic birth?

■ Squeezing of the umbilical cord during childbirth, placenta abruptio, and placenta previa can cause **anoxia** (oxygen deprivation), with risk of brain damage and infant death. Effects of even mild to moderate anoxia on cognitive and language development are still evident in middle childhood, though many children improve over time. Infants born more than six weeks early commonly have respiratory distress syndrome, which can cause brain damage due to immaturity of the lungs and associated anoxia.

■ Low birth weight, a major cause of **neonatal** and **infant mortality** and wide-ranging developmental problems, is most common in infants born to poverty-stricken women. Compared with **preterm** babies, whose weight is appropriate for time spent in the uterus, **small-for-date** infants usually have longer-lasting difficulties.

■ Some interventions provide special infant stimulation in the intensive care nursery. Others teach parents how to care for and interact with their babies. Preterm infants in stressed, low-income households need long-term, intensive intervention.

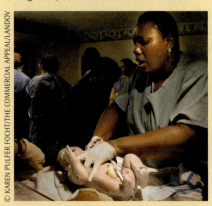

© KAREN PULFER FOCHT/THE COMMERCIAL APPEAL/LANDOV

■ When babies experience birth trauma, a supportive family environment or relationships with other caring adults can help restore their growth. Even infants with fairly serious birth complications can recover with the help of positive life events.

Precious Moments After Birth

Is close parent–infant contact shortly after birth necessary for bonding?

■ Human parents do not require close physical contact with the baby immediately after birth for **bonding** and effective parenting to occur. Nevertheless, early contact supports parents' feelings of caring and affection. Hospital practices that promote parent–infant closeness, such as **rooming in,** may help parents build a good relationship with their newborn.

The Newborn Baby's Capacities

Describe the newborn baby's reflexes and states of arousal, including sleep characteristics and ways to soothe a crying baby.

■ **Reflexes** are the newborn baby's most obvious organized patterns of behavior. Some have survival value, others help parents and infants establish gratifying interaction, and still others provide the foundation for voluntary motor skills.

■ Although newborns move in and out of five **states of arousal,** they spend most of their time asleep. Sleep includes at least two states: **rapid-eye-movement (REM) sleep** and **non-rapid-eye-movement (NREM) sleep.** Newborns spend about 50 percent of their sleep time in REM sleep, far more than they ever will again. REM sleep provides young infants with stimulation essential for central nervous system development. Disturbed REM–NREM cycles are a sign of central nervous system abnormalities, which may lead to **sudden infant death syndrome (SIDS),** a major cause of infant mortality.

■ A crying baby stimulates strong feelings of discomfort in nearby adults. The intensity of the cry and the experiences that led up to it help parents identify what is wrong. Once feeding and diaper changing have been tried, lifting the baby to the shoulder and rocking or walking is the most effective soothing technique. Other helpful soothing methods include swaddling, offering a pacifier, and talking softly.

Describe the newborn baby's sensory capacities.

■ The senses of touch, taste, smell, and sound are well-developed at birth. Newborns can use their palms to distinguish the shapes of small objects. They are also sensitive to pain, prefer sweet tastes and smells, and orient toward the odor of their own mother's lactating breast and toward human milk rather than formula milk.

■ Newborns can distinguish a few sound patterns, as well as nearly all speech sounds. They are especially responsive to human speech, high-pitched expressive voices, their own mother's voice, and speech in their native language.

■ Vision is the least developed of the newborn's senses. At birth, focusing ability and **visual acuity** are limited. Nevertheless, newborns can detect human faces and prefer their mother's familiar face to the face of a stranger. In exploring the visual field, they are attracted to bright objects but limit their looking to single features. Newborn babies have difficulty discriminating colors.

Why is neonatal behavioral assessment useful?

■ The most widely used instrument for assessing the behavior of the newborn infant, Brazelton's **Neonatal Behavioral Assessment Scale (NBAS),** has helped researchers understand individual and cultural differences in newborn behavior. Sometimes it is used to teach parents about their baby's capacities.

The Transition to Parenthood

Describe typical changes in the family after the birth of a new baby, along with interventions that foster the transition to parenthood.

■ In response to the demands of new parenthood, the gender roles of husband and wife usually become more traditional. Parents in gratifying marriages who continue to support each other's needs generally adapt well. But a large difference between a husband's and wife's caregiving responsibilities can strain the marriage and negatively affect parent–infant interaction. Favorable adjustment to a second birth typically requires that fathers take an even more active role in parenting.

■ Most nonmarital births are unplanned and to young mothers who have incomes below the poverty level and experience a stressful transition to parenthood. Planned births and adoptions by financially secure single women in their thirties and forties are increasing. These mothers adapt to new parenthood as well as, and sometimes more favorably than, married couples.

■ When parents are at low risk for problems, counselor-led parenting groups involving discussion of changing family relationships can ease the transition to parenthood. High-risk parents struggling with poverty or the birth of a baby with disabilities are more likely to benefit from intensive home interventions focusing on enhancing social support and parenting.

IMPORTANT TERMS AND CONCEPTS

anoxia (p. 135)
Apgar Scale (p. 128)
bonding (p. 143)
breech position (p. 134)
cesarean delivery (p. 134)
dilation and effacement of the cervix (p. 126)
fetal monitors (p. 132)
induced labor (p. 134)

infant mortality (p. 140)
natural, or prepared, childbirth (p. 130)
Neonatal Behavioral Assessment Scale (NBAS) (p. 152)
neonatal mortality (p. 140)
non-rapid-eye-movement (NREM) sleep (p. 146)
preterm infants (p. 137)

rapid-eye-movement (REM) sleep (p. 146)
reflex (p. 143)
rooming in (p. 143)
small-for-date infants (p. 137)
states of arousal (p. 145)
sudden infant death syndrome (SIDS) (p. 147)
transition (p. 126)
visual acuity (p. 151)

"We Are Playing in the House Garden"
Uttharaa Ranaweera
10 years, Sri Lanka

Encouraged by her older brothers and sisters, a baby explores a garden and experiences the physical potential of her growing body. During the first year, infants grow rapidly, move on their own, increasingly investigate their surroundings, and make sense of complex sights and sounds.

Reprinted with permission from the International Museum of Children's Art, Oslo, Norway

Physical Development in Infancy and Toddlerhood

On a brilliant June morning, 16-month-old Caitlin emerged from her front door, ready for the short drive to the child-care home where she spent her weekdays while her mother, Carolyn, and her father, David, worked. Clutching a teddy bear in one hand and her mother's arm with the other, Caitlin descended the steps. "One! Two! Threeeee!" Carolyn counted as she helped Caitlin down. "How much she's changed!" Carolyn thought to herself, looking at the child who, not long ago, had been a newborn. With her first steps, Caitlin had passed from *infancy* to *toddlerhood*—a period spanning the second year of life. At first, Caitlin did, indeed, "toddle" with an awkward gait, tipping over frequently. But her face reflected the thrill of conquering a new skill.

As they walked toward the car, Carolyn and Caitlin spotted 3-year-old Eli and his father, Kevin, in the neighboring yard. Eli dashed toward them, waving a bright yellow envelope. Carolyn bent down to open the envelope and took out a card. It read, "Announcing the arrival of Grace Ann. Born: Cambodia. Age: 16 months." Carolyn turned toward Kevin and Eli. "That's wonderful news! When can we see her?"

"Let's wait a few days," Kevin suggested. "Monica's taken Grace to the doctor this morning. She's underweight and malnourished." Kevin described Monica's first night with Grace in a hotel room in Phnom Penh. Grace lay on the bed, withdrawn and fearful. Eventually she fell asleep, gripping crackers in both hands.

Carolyn felt Caitlin's impatient tug at her sleeve. Off they drove to child care, where Vanessa had just dropped off her 18-month-old son, Timmy. Within moments, Caitlin and Timmy were in the sandbox, shoveling sand into plastic cups and buckets with the help of their caregiver, Ginette.

A few weeks later, Grace joined Caitlin and Timmy at Ginette's child-care home. Although still tiny and unable to crawl or walk, she had grown taller and heavier, and her sad, vacant gaze had given way to an alert expression, a ready smile, and an enthusiastic desire to imitate and explore. When Caitlin headed for the sandbox,

Body Growth

Changes in Body Size and Muscle–Fat Makeup • Changes in Body Proportions • Skeletal Growth

Brain Development

Development of Neurons • Neurophysiological Methods • Development of the Cerebral Cortex • Sensitive Periods in Brain Development • Changing States of Arousal

■ **BIOLOGY AND ENVIRONMENT**
Brain Plasticity: Insights from Research on Brain-Damaged Children and Adults

■ **CULTURAL INFLUENCES**
Cultural Variation in Infant Sleeping Arrangements

Influences on Early Physical Growth

Heredity • Nutrition • Malnutrition • Emotional Well-Being

Learning Capacities

Classical Conditioning • Operant Conditioning • Habituation • Imitation

Motor Development

The Sequence of Motor Development • Motor Skills as Dynamic Systems • Dynamic Motor Systems in Action • Cultural Variations in Motor Development • Fine-Motor Development: Reaching and Grasping • Bowel and Bladder Control

Perceptual Development

Hearing • Vision • Object Perception • Intermodal Perception • Understanding Perceptual Development

■ **BIOLOGY AND ENVIRONMENT**
"Tuning in" to Familiar Speech, Faces, and Music: A Sensitive Period for Culture-Specific Learning

■ **SOCIAL ISSUES: EDUCATION**
Development of Infants with Severe Visual Impairments

Grace stretched out her arms, asking Ginette to carry her there, too. Soon Grace was pulling herself up at every opportunity. Finally, at age 18 months, she walked!

This chapter traces physical growth during the first two years—one of the most remarkable and busiest times of development. We will see how rapid changes in the infant's body and brain support learning, motor skills, and perceptual capacities. Caitlin, Grace, and Timmy will join us along the way to illustrate individual differences and environmental influences on physical development.

Body Growth

TAKE A MOMENT... The next time you're walking in your neighborhood park or at the mall, note the contrast between infants' and toddlers' physical capabilities. One reason for the vast changes in what children can do over the first two years is that their bodies change enormously—faster than at any other time after birth.

Changes in Body Size and Muscle–Fat Makeup

By the end of the first year a typical infant's height is about 32 inches—more than 50 percent greater than at birth. By 2 years, it is 75 percent greater (36 inches). Similarly, by 5 months of age, birth weight has doubled, to about 15 pounds. At 1 year it has tripled, to 22 pounds, and at 2 years it has quadrupled, to about 30 pounds.

Figure 5.1 illustrates this dramatic increase in body size. But rather than making steady gains, infants and toddlers grow in little spurts. In one study, children who were followed over the first 21 months of life went for periods of 7 to 63 days with no growth, then added as much as half an inch in a 24-hour period! Almost always, parents described their babies as irritable and very hungry on the day before the spurt (Lampl, 1993; Lampl, Veldhuis, & Johnson, 1992).

One of the most obvious changes in infants' appearance is their transformation into round, plump babies by the middle of the first year. This early rise in "baby fat," which peaks at about 9 months, helps the infant maintain a constant body temperature. In the second year, most toddlers slim down, a trend that continues into middle childhood (Fomon & Nelson, 2002). In contrast, muscle tissue increases very slowly during infancy and will not reach a peak until adolescence. Babies are not very muscular; their strength and physical coordination are limited.

In infancy, girls are slightly shorter and lighter than boys, with a higher ratio of fat to muscle. These small sex differences persist throughout early and middle childhood and are greatly magnified at adolescence. Ethnic differences in body size are apparent as well. Grace was below the *growth norms* (height and weight averages for children her age). Early malnutrition played a part, but even after substantial catch-up, Grace—as is typical for Asian children—remained below North American norms. In contrast, Timmy is slightly above average in size, as African-American children tend to be (Bogin, 2001).

Changes in Body Proportions

As the child's overall size increases, parts of the body grow at different rates. Two growth patterns describe these changes. The first is the **cephalocaudal trend**—from the Latin for "head to tail." During the prenatal period, the head develops more rapidly than the lower part of the body. At birth, the head takes up one-fourth of total body length, the legs only one-third. Notice how, in Figure 5.1, the lower portion of the body catches up. By age 2, the head accounts for only one-fifth and the legs for nearly one-half of total body length.

In the second pattern, the **proximodistal trend,** growth proceeds, literally, from "near to far"—from the center of the body outward. In the prenatal period, the head, chest, and trunk grow first, then the arms and legs, and finally the hands and feet. During infancy and childhood, the arms and legs continue to grow somewhat ahead of the hands and feet.

Andy at 1 month

Andy at 4 months

Amy at birth

Amy at 5 months

Andy at 18 months

Andy at 28 months

Amy at 16 months

Amy at 26 months

FIGURE 5.1

Body growth during the first two years. Andy and Amy are brother and sister, born two years apart. These photos, taken by their parents, depict the dramatic changes in body size and proportions during infancy and toddlerhood. In the first year, the head is quite large in proportion to the rest of the body, and height and weight gain are especially rapid. During the second year, the lower portion of the body catches up. Notice, also, how Andy and Amy added "baby fat" in the early months of life and then slimmed down, a trend that continues into middle childhood. From birth on, Andy was slightly taller and heavier than Amy—a typical sex difference. We will revisit Andy's and Amy's growth in Chapters 8, 11, and 14.

Skeletal Growth

Children of the same age differ in *rate* of physical growth; some make faster progress toward a mature body size than others. But current body size is not enough to tell us how quickly a child's physical growth is moving along. Although Timmy is larger and heavier than Caitlin and Grace, he is not physically more mature. In a moment, you will see why.

GENERAL SKELETAL GROWTH   The best estimate of a child's physical maturity is **skeletal age,** a measure of development of the bones of the body. The embryonic skeleton is first formed out of soft, pliable tissue called *cartilage.* In the sixth week of pregnancy, cartilage cells begin to harden into bone, a gradual process that continues throughout childhood and adolescence (Moore & Persaud, 2008).

Just before birth, special growth centers, called **epiphyses,** appear at the two extreme ends of each of the long bones of the body (see Figure 5.2). Cartilage cells continue to be produced at the growth plates of these epiphyses, which increase in number

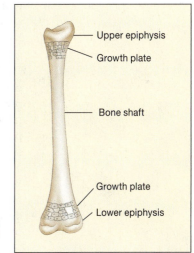

Upper epiphysis

Growth plate

Bone shaft

Growth plate

Lower epiphysis

FIGURE 5.2

Diagram of a long bone showing upper and lower epiphyses. Cartilage cells are produced at the growth plates of the epiphyses and gradually harden into bone. *(Adapted and reprinted by permission of the publisher from* Fetus into Man: Physical Growth from Conception to Maturity *by J. M. Tanner, pp. 16, 32. Cambridge, Mass.: Harvard University Press and Castlemead Publications. Copyright © 1978, 1989 by J. M. Tanner.)*

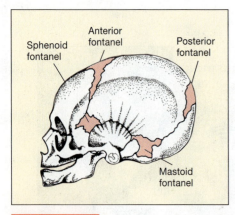

The skull at birth, showing the fontanels and sutures. The fontanels gradually close during the first two years, forming sutures that permit the skull to expand easily as the brain grows.

throughout childhood and then, as growth continues, get thinner and disappear. After that, no further growth in bone length is possible. Skeletal age can be estimated by X-raying the bones and seeing the number of epiphyses and the extent to which they are fused.

African-American children tend to be slightly ahead of Caucasian-American children in skeletal age. And girls are considerably ahead of boys—the reason Timmy's skeletal age lags behind that of Caitlin and Grace. At birth, the sexes differ by about 4 to 6 weeks, a gap that widens over infancy and childhood (Tanner, Healy, & Cameron, 2001). Girls are advanced in development of other organs as well. This greater physical maturity may contribute to girls' greater resistance to harmful environmental influences. As noted in Chapter 2, girls experience fewer developmental problems than boys and have lower infant and childhood mortality rates.

GROWTH OF THE SKULL   Pediatricians routinely measure children's head size between birth and age 2 years, when skull growth is especially rapid because of large increases in brain size. At birth, the bones of the skull are separated by six gaps, or "soft spots," called **fontanels** (see Figure 5.3). The gaps permit the bones to overlap as the large head of the baby passes through the mother's narrow birth canal. You can easily feel the largest gap, the anterior fontanel, which measures slightly more than an inch across at the top of a baby's skull. It gradually shrinks and is filled in during the second year. The other fontanels are smaller and close more quickly. As the skull bones come in contact with one another, they form *sutures,* or seams. These permit the skull to expand easily as the brain grows. The sutures disappear completely in adolescence, when skull growth is complete.

Brain Development

At birth, the brain is nearer to its adult size than any other physical structure, and it continues to develop at an astounding pace throughout infancy and toddlerhood. We can best understand brain growth by looking at it from two vantage points: (1) the microscopic level of individual brain cells and (2) the larger level of the cerebral cortex, the most complex brain structure and the one responsible for the highly developed intelligence of our species.

Development of Neurons

The human brain has 100 to 200 billion **neurons,** or nerve cells, that store and transmit information, many of which have thousands of direct connections with other neurons. Unlike other body cells, neurons are not tightly packed together. Between them are tiny gaps, or **synapses,** where fibers from different neurons come close together but do not touch (see Figure 5.4). Neurons send messages to one another by releasing chemicals called **neurotransmitters,** which cross the synapse.

The basic story of brain growth concerns how neurons develop and form this elaborate communication system. Figure 5.5 summarizes major milestones of brain development. In the prenatal period, neurons are produced in the embryo's primitive neural tube. From there, they migrate to form the major parts of the brain (see Chapter 3, page 99). Once neurons are in place, they differentiate, establishing their unique functions by extending their fibers to form synaptic connections with neighboring cells. During infancy and toddlerhood, neural fibers and synapses increase at an astounding pace (Huttenlocher, 2002; Moore & Persaud, 2008). Because developing neurons require space for these connective structures, a surprising aspect of brain growth is that as synapses form, many surrounding neurons die—20 to 80 percent, depending on the brain region (de Haan & Johnson, 2003; Stiles, 2008). Fortunately, during the prenatal period, the neural tube produces far more neurons than the brain will ever need.

As neurons form connections, *stimulation* becomes vital to their survival. Neurons that are stimulated by input from the surrounding environment continue to establish new synapses, forming increasingly elaborate systems of communication that support more complex abilities. At first, stimulation results in a massive overabundance of synapses, many of which serve identical functions, thereby ensuring that the child will acquire the motor, cognitive, and social skills that our species needs to survive. Neurons that are seldom stimulated soon lose their synapses, in a process called **synaptic pruning** that returns neurons not needed at the moment to an uncommitted state so they can support future development. In all, about 40 percent of synapses are pruned during childhood and adolescence (Webb, Monk, & Nelson, 2001). For this process to go forward, appropriate stimulation of the child's brain is vital during periods in which the formation of synapses is at its peak (Nelson, Thomas, & de Haan, 2006).

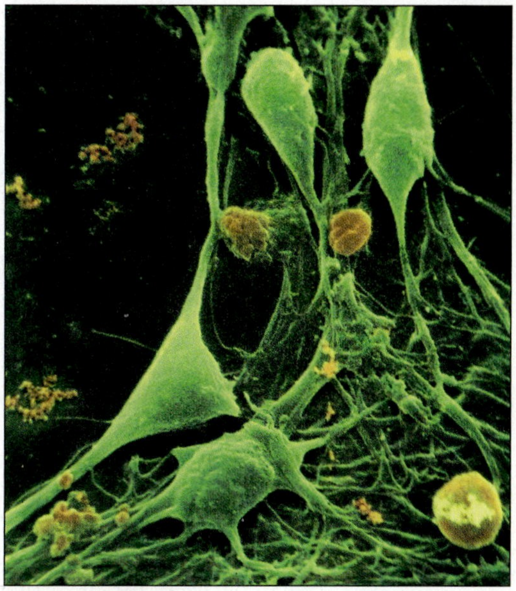

If few neurons are produced after the prenatal period, what causes the dramatic increase in brain size during the first two years? About half the brain's volume is made up of **glial cells,** which are responsible for **myelination,** the coating of neural fibers with an insulating fatty sheath (called *myelin*) that improves the efficiency of message transfer. Certain types of glial cells also participate directly in neural communication, by picking up and passing on neuronal signals and releasing neurotransmitters (LoTurco, 2000). Glial cells multiply rapidly from the end of pregnancy through the second year of life—a process that continues at a slower pace through middle childhood and accelerates again in adolescence. Gains in neural fibers and myelination are responsible for the extraordinary gain in overall size of the brain—from nearly 30 percent of its adult weight at birth to 70 percent by age 2 (Johnson, 2005; Knickmeyer et al., 2008).

Brain development can be compared to molding a "living sculpture." After neurons and synapses are overproduced, cell death and synaptic pruning sculpt away excess building material

FIGURE 5.4

Neurons and their connective fibers. This photograph of several neurons, taken with the aid of a powerful microscope, shows the elaborate synaptic connections that form with neighboring cells.

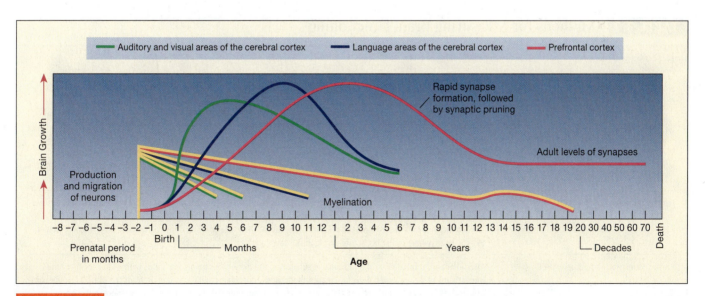

FIGURE 5.5

Major milestones of brain development. Formation of synapses is rapid during the first two years, especially in the auditory, visual, and language areas of the cerebral cortex. The prefrontal cortex undergoes more extended synaptic growth. In each area, overproduction of synapses is followed by synaptic pruning. The prefrontal cortex is among the last regions to attain an adult level of synaptic connections—in mid- to late adolescence. Myelination occurs at a dramatic pace during the first two years and then at a slower pace through childhood, followed by an acceleration at adolescence. The multiple yellow lines indicate that the timing of myelination varies among different brain areas. For example, neural fibers myelinate over a longer period in the language areas, and especially in the prefrontal cortex, than in the visual and auditory areas. *(Adapted from Thompson & Nelson, 2001.)*

to form the mature brain—a process jointly influenced by genetically programmed events and the child's experiences. The resulting sculpture is a set of interconnected regions, each with specific functions—much like countries on a globe that communicate with one another (Johnston et al., 2001). This "geography" of the brain permits researchers to study its organization and the activity of its regions using *neurophysiological* techniques.

Neurophysiological Methods

Table 5.1 describes major measures of brain functioning. The first two methods detect changes in *electrical activity* in the cerebral cortex. Researchers can examine *EEG brain-wave patterns* for stability and organization—signs of mature cortical functioning (see Figure 5.6). And as a child processes a particular stimulus, *ERPs* detect the general location of brain-wave activity— a method often used to study preverbal infants' responsiveness to various stimuli, the impact of experience on specialization of specific brain regions, and atypical brain functioning in children at risk for learning and emotional problems (DeBoer, Scott, & Nelson, 2007; deRegnier, 2005).

Neuroimaging techniques, which yield detailed, three-dimensional computerized pictures of the entire brain and its active areas, provide the most precise information about which brain regions are specialized for certain capacities. In *PET,* the child must lie quietly on a scanner bed, and in fMRI, inside a tunnel-like apparatus. But unlike PET, fMRI does not depend on X-ray photography, which requires injection of a radioactive substance. Rather, when a child is exposed to a stimulus, fMRI detects changes in blood flow and oxygen metabolism magnetically; a computer combines frequently recorded images into a colorful, moving picture of parts of the brain used to perform a given activity (see Figure 5.7a and b).

Because PET and fMRI require that the participant to lie as motionless as possible for an extended time, they are not suitable for infants and young children (Nelson, Thomas, & de Haan, 2006). A neuroimaging technique that works well in infancy and early childhood is *near infrared spectroscopy (NIRS),* in which infrared (invisible) light is beamed at regions of the cerebral cortex to measure blood flow and oxygen metabolism while the child attends to a stimulus (refer again to Table 5.1). Because the apparatus consists only of thin, flexible optical

---

TABLE 5.1 Methods for Measuring Brain Functioning

METHOD	DESCRIPTION
Electroencephalogram (EEG)	Electrodes embedded in a head cap record electrical brain-wave activity in the brain's outer layers—the cerebral cortex. Researchers use an advanced tool called a geodesic sensor net (GSN) to hold interconnected electrodes (up to 128 for infants and 256 for children and adults) in place through a cap that adjusts to each person's head shape, yielding improved brain-wave detection.
Event-related potentials (ERPs)	Using the EEG, the frequency and amplitude of brain waves in response to particular stimuli (such as a picture, music, or speech) are recorded in the cerebral cortex. Enables identification of general regions of stimulus-induced activity.
Functional magnetic resonance imaging (fMRI)	While the person lies inside a tunnel-shaped apparatus that creates a magnetic field, a scanner magnetically detects increased blood flow and oxygen metabolism in areas of the brain as the individual processes particular stimuli. The scanner typically records images every 1 to 4 seconds; these are combined into a computerized moving picture of activity anywhere in the brain (not just its outer layers).
Positron emission tomography (PET)	After injection or inhalation of a radioactive substance, the person lies on an apparatus with a scanner that emits fine streams of X-rays, which detect increased blood flow and oxygen metabolism in areas of the brain as the person processes particular stimuli. As with fMRI, the result is a computerized image of activity anywhere in the brain.
Near-infrared spectroscopy (NIRS)	Using thin, flexible optical fibers attached to the scalp through a head cap, infrared (invisible) light is beamed at the brain; its absorption by areas of the cerebral cortex varies with changes in blood flow and oxygen metabolism as the individual processes particular stimuli. The result is a computerized moving picture of active areas in the cerebral cortex. Unlike fMRI and PET, NIRS is appropriate for infants and young children, who can move within limited range during testing.

fibers attached to the scalp using a head cap, a baby can sit on the parent's lap and move during testing—as Figure 5.7c illustrates (Hespos et al., 2010; Meek, 2002). But unlike PET and fMRI, which map activity changes throughout the brain, NIRS is limited to examining the functioning of the cerebral cortex.

Neurophysiological methods are powerful tools for uncovering relationships between the brain and psychological development. But like all research methods, they have limitations. Even though a stimulus produces a consistent pattern of brain activity, investigators cannot be certain that an individual has processed it in a certain way. And a researcher who takes a change in brain activity as an indicator of information processing must make sure that the change was not due instead to hunger, boredom, fatigue, or body movements. Consequently, other methods must be combined with brain-wave and -imaging findings to clarify their meaning (Nicholson, 2006). Now let's turn to the developing organization of the cerebral cortex.

Development of the Cerebral Cortex

The **cerebral cortex** surrounds the rest of the brain, resembling half of a shelled walnut. It is the largest brain structure—accounting for 85 percent of the brain's weight and containing the greatest number of neurons and synapses. Because the cerebral cortex is the last part of the brain to stop growing, it is sensitive to environmental influences for a much longer period than any other part of the brain.

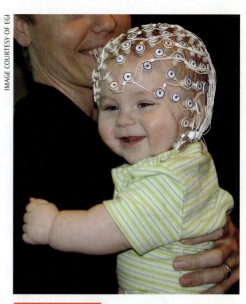

FIGURE 5.6

Electroencephalogram (EEG) using the geodesic sensor net (GSN). Interconnected electrodes embedded in the head cap record electrical brain-wave activity in the cerebral cortex.

REGIONS OF THE CORTEX Figure 5.8 on page 168 shows specific functions of regions of the cerebral cortex, such as receiving information from the senses, instructing the body to move, and thinking. The order in which cortical regions develop corresponds to the order in which various capacities emerge in the infant and growing child. For example, a burst of synaptic growth occurs in the auditory and visual cortexes and in areas responsible for body movement over the first year—a period of dramatic gains in auditory and visual perception and mastery of motor skills (Johnson, 2005). Language areas are especially active from late infancy through the preschool years, when language development flourishes (Pujol et al., 2006; Thompson et al., 2000).

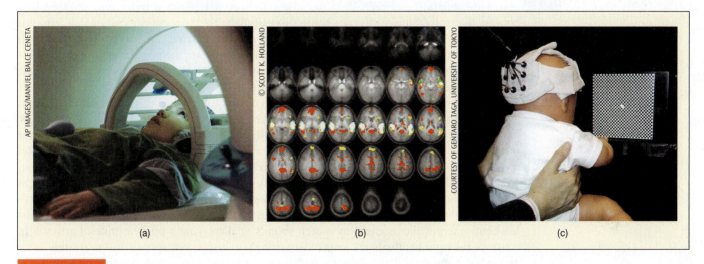

(a)   (b)   (c)

FIGURE 5.7

Functional magnetic resonance imaging (fMRI) and near infrared spectroscopy (NIRS). (a) This 6-year-old is part of a study that uses fMRI to find out how his brain processes light and motion. (b) The fMRI image shows which areas of the boy's brain are active while he views changing visual stimuli. (c) Here, NIRS is used to investigate a 2-month-old's response to a visual stimulus. During testing, the baby can move freely within a limited range. *(Photo (c) From G. Taga, K. Asakawa, A. Maki, Y. Konishi, & H. Koisumi, 2003, "Brain Imaging in Awake Infants by Near-Infrared Optical Topography," Proceedings of the National Academy of Sciences, 100, p. 10723. Reprinted by permission.)*

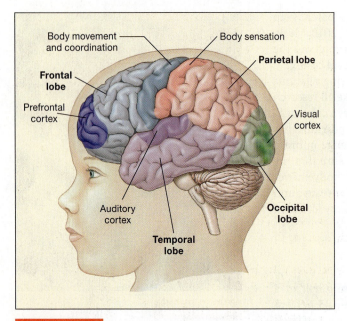

FIGURE 5.8

The left side of the human brain, showing the cerebral cortex. The cortex is divided into different lobes, each of which contains a variety of regions with specific functions. Some major regions are labeled here.

The cortical regions with the most extended period of development are the *frontal lobes.* The **prefrontal cortex,** lying in front of areas controlling body movement, is responsible for thought—in particular, for consciousness, inhibition of impulses, integration of information, and use of memory, reasoning, planning, and problem-solving strategies. From age 2 months on, the prefrontal cortex functions more effectively. But it undergoes especially rapid myelination and formation and pruning of synapses during the preschool and school years, followed by another period of accelerated growth in adolescence, yielding an adult level of synaptic connections around mid- to late adolescence (Nelson, 2002; Nelson, Thomas, & de Haan, 2006; Sowell et al., 2002).

LATERALIZATION AND PLASTICITY OF THE CERE-BRAL CORTEX The cerebral cortex has two *hemispheres,* or sides, that differ in their functions. Some tasks are done mostly by the left hemisphere, others by the right. For example, each hemisphere receives sensory information from the side of the body opposite to it and controls only that side.[1] For most of us, the left hemisphere is largely responsible for verbal abilities (such as spoken and written language) and positive emotion (for example, joy). The right hemisphere handles spatial abilities (judging distances, reading maps, and recognizing geometric shapes) and negative emotion (such as distress) (Banish & Heller, 1998; Nelson & Bosquet, 2000). In left-handed people, this pattern may be reversed or, more commonly, the cerebral cortex may be less clearly specialized than in right-handers.

Why does this specialization of the two hemispheres, called **lateralization,** occur? Studies using fMRI reveal that the left hemisphere is better at processing information in a sequential, analytic (piece-by-piece) way, a good approach for dealing with communicative information—both verbal (language) and emotional (a joyful smile). In contrast, the right hemisphere is specialized for processing information in a holistic, integrative manner, ideal for making sense of spatial information and regulating negative emotion. A lateralized brain may have evolved because it enabled humans to cope more successfully with changing environmental demands (Falk, 2005). It permits a wider array of functions to be carried out effectively than if both sides processed information in exactly the same way. However, the popular notion of a "right-brained" or "left-brained" person is an oversimplification. The two hemispheres communicate and work together, doing so more rapidly and effectively with age.

Researchers study when brain lateralization occurs to learn more about **brain plasticity.** A highly *plastic* cerebral cortex, in which many areas are not yet committed to specific functions, has a high capacity for learning. And if a part of the cortex is damaged, other parts can take over the tasks it would have handled. But once the hemispheres lateralize, damage to a specific region means that the abilities it controls cannot be recovered to the same extent or as easily as earlier.

At birth, the hemispheres have already begun to specialize. Most newborns favor the right side of the body in their head position and reflexive reactions (Grattan et al., 1992; Rönnqvist & Hopkins, 1998). Most also show greater activation (detected either with ERP or NIRS) in the left hemisphere while listening to speech sounds or displaying a positive state of arousal. In contrast, the right hemisphere reacts more strongly to nonspeech sounds and to stimuli (such as a sour-tasting fluid) that evoke a negative reaction (Davidson, 1994; Fox & Davidson, 1986; Hespos et al., 2010).

---

[1]The eyes are an exception. Messages from the right half of each retina go to the right hemisphere; messages from the left half of each retina go to the left hemisphere. Thus, visual information from *both* eyes is received by *both* hemispheres.

Nevertheless, research on brain-damaged children and adults offers dramatic evidence for substantial plasticity in the young brain, summarized in the Biology and Environment box on page 170. Furthermore, early experience greatly influences the organization of the cerebral cortex. For example, deaf adults who, as infants and children, learned sign language (a spatial skill) depend more than hearing individuals on the right hemisphere for language processing (Neville & Bavelier, 2002). And toddlers who are advanced in language development show greater left-hemispheric specialization for language than their more slowly developing age-mates (Casey et al., 2002; Luna et al., 2001; Mills et al., 2005). Apparently, the very process of acquiring language and other skills promotes lateralization.

In sum, the brain is more plastic during the first few years than it will ever be again. An overabundance of synaptic connections supports brain plasticity and, therefore, young children's ability to learn, which is fundamental to their survival. And although the cortex is genetically programmed for hemispheric specialization, experience greatly influences the rate and success of its advancing organization.

Sensitive Periods in Brain Development

Animal studies confirm that early, extreme sensory deprivation results in permanent brain damage and loss of functions—findings that verify the existence of sensitive periods in brain development. For example, early, varied visual experiences must occur for the brain's visual centers to develop normally. If a 1-month-old kitten is deprived of light for just three or four days, these areas of the brain degenerate. If the kitten is kept in the dark during the fourth week of life and beyond, the damage is severe and permanent (Crair, Gillespie, & Stryker, 1998). And the general quality of the early environment affects overall brain growth. When animals reared from birth in physically and socially stimulating surroundings are compared with those reared in isolation, the brains of the stimulated animals show much denser synaptic connections (Greenough & Black, 1992).

**HUMAN EVIDENCE: VICTIMS OF DEPRIVED EARLY ENVIRON-
MENTS** For ethical reasons, we cannot deliberately deprive some infants of normal rearing experiences and observe the impact on their brains and competencies. Instead, we must turn to natural experiments, in which children were victims of deprived early environments that were later rectified. Such studies have revealed some parallels with the animal evidence just described.

For example, when babies are born with cataracts in both eyes (clouded lenses, preventing clear visual images), those who have corrective surgery within four to six months show rapid improvement in vision, except for subtle aspects of face perception, which require early visual input to the right hemisphere to develop (Le Grand et al., 2001, 2003). But the longer cataract surgery is postponed beyond infancy, the less complete the recovery in visual skills. And if surgery is delayed until adulthood, vision is severely and permanently impaired (Lewis & Maurer, 2005; Maurer et al., 1999).

Studies of infants placed in orphanages who were later exposed to ordinary family rearing confirm the importance of a generally stimulating environment for psychological development. In one investigation, researchers followed the progress of a large sample of children transferred between birth and 3½ years from extremely deprived Romanian orphanages to adoptive families in Great Britain (Beckett et al., 2006; O'Connor et al., 2000; Rutter et al., 1998, 2004, 2010). On arrival, most were impaired in all domains of development. Cognitive catch-up was impressive for children adopted before 6 months, who consistently attained average mental test scores in childhood and adolescence, performing as well as a comparison group of early-adopted British-born children.

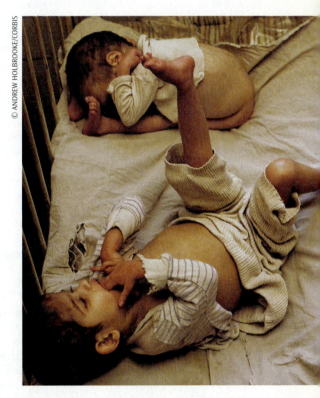

■ These children in an orphanage in Romania receive very little adult contact or stimulation. The longer they remain in this barren environment, the more they will withdraw and wither, displaying profound impairments in all domains of development. ■

BIOLOGY AND ENVIRONMENT

Brain Plasticity: Insights from Research on Brain-Damaged Children and Adults

*I*n the first few years of life, the brain is highly plastic. It can reorganize areas committed to specific functions in a way that the mature brain cannot. Consistently, adults who suffered brain injuries in infancy and early childhood show fewer cognitive impairments than adults with later-occurring injuries (Holland, 2004; Huttenlocher, 2002). Nevertheless, the young brain is not totally plastic. When it is injured, its functioning is compromised. The extent of plasticity depends on several factors, including age at time of injury, site of damage, and skill area.

Brain Plasticity in Infancy and Early Childhood

In a large study of children with injuries to the cerebral cortex that occurred before birth or in the first six months of life, language and spatial skills were assessed repeatedly into adolescence (Akshoomoff et al., 2002; Stiles, 2001a; Stiles et al., 2005, 2008). All the children had experienced early brain seizures or hemorrhages. Brain-imaging techniques (fMRI and PET) revealed the precise site of damage.

Regardless of whether injury occurred in the left or right cerebral hemisphere, the children showed delays in language development that persisted until about 3½ years of age. That damage to either hemisphere affected early language competence indicates that at first, language functioning is broadly distributed in the brain. But by age 5, the children caught up in vocabulary and grammatical skills. Undamaged areas—in either the left or the right hemisphere—had taken over these language functions.

Compared with language, spatial skills were more impaired after early brain injury. When preschool through adolescent-age youngsters were asked to copy designs, those with early right-hemispheric damage had trouble with holistic processing—accurately representing the overall shape. In contrast, children with left-hemispheric damage captured the basic shape but omitted fine-grained details. Nevertheless, the children showed improvements in their drawings with age—gains that did not occur in brain-injured adults (Akshoomoff et al., 2002; Stiles et al., 2003, 2008).

Clearly, recovery after early brain injury is greater for language than for spatial skills. Why is this so? Researchers speculate that spatial processing is the older of the two capacities in our evolutionary history and, therefore, more lateralized at birth (Stiles, 2001b; Stiles et al., 2002, 2008). But early brain injury has far less impact than later injury on both language and spatial skills. In sum, the young brain is remarkably plastic.

The Price of High Plasticity in the Young Brain

Despite impressive recovery of language and (to a lesser extent) spatial skills, children with early brain injuries show deficits in a wide variety of complex mental abilities during the school years. For example, their reading and math progress is slow. And in telling stories, they produce simpler narratives than agemates without early brain injuries (although many catch up in narrative skills by early adolescence) (Reilly, Bates, & Marchman, 1998; Reilly et al., 2004). Furthermore, the more brain tissue destroyed in infancy or early childhood, the poorer children score on intelligence tests (Anderson et al., 2006).

High brain plasticity, researchers explain, comes at a price. When healthy brain regions take over the functions of damaged areas, a "crowding effect" occurs: Multiple tasks must be done by a smaller-than-usual volume of brain tissue. Consequently, the brain processes information less quickly and accurately than it would if it were intact. Complex mental abilities of all kinds suffer into middle childhood, and often longer, because performing them well requires considerable space in the cerebral cortex (Huttenlocher, 2002).

Later Plasticity

Brain plasticity is not restricted to early childhood. Although far more limited, reorganization in the brain can occur later, even in adulthood. For example, adult stroke victims often display considerable recovery, especially in response to stimulation of language and motor skills. Brain-imaging techniques reveal that structures adjacent to the permanently damaged area or in the opposite cerebral hemisphere reorganize to support the impaired ability (Kalra & Ratan, 2007; Murphy & Corbett, 2009).

In infancy and childhood, the goal of brain growth is to form neural connections that ensure mastery of essential skills. Animal research reveals that plasticity is greatest while the brain is forming many new synapses; it declines during synaptic pruning (Murphy & Corbett, 2009). At older ages, specialized brain structures are in place, but after injury they can still reorganize to some degree. The adult brain can produce a small number of new neurons. And when an individual practices relevant tasks, the brain strengthens existing synapses and generates new ones (Nelson, Thomas, & de Haan, 2006). Plasticity seems to be a basic property of the nervous system. Researchers hope to discover how experience and brain plasticity work together throughout life, so they can help people of all ages—with and without brain injuries—develop at their best.

■ This preschooler, who experienced brain damage in infancy, has been spared massive impairments because of high plasticity of the brain. Here, a teacher guides his hand in drawing shapes to strengthen spatial skills, which remain more impaired than language after early brain injury. ■

© JIM WEST/THE IMAGE WORKS

But Romanian children who had been institutionalized for more than the first six months showed serious intellectual deficits (see Figure 5.9). Although they improved in test scores during middle childhood and adolescence, they remained substantially below average. And most displayed at least three serious mental health problems, such as inattention, overactivity, unruly behavior, and autistic-like symptoms (social disinterest, stereotyped behavior) (Kreppner et al., 2007, 2010). A major correlate of both time spent in the institution and poor cognitive and emotional functioning was below-average head size, suggesting that early lack of stimulation permanently damaged the brain (Sonuga-Barke, Schlotz, & Kreppner, 2010).

Neurophysiological findings indicate that early, prolonged institutionalization leads to a generalized reduction in brain-wave and metabolic activity in the cerebral cortex—especially the prefrontal cortex, which governs complex cognition and impulse control. Neural fibers connecting the prefrontal cortex with other brain structures involved in control of emotion are also reduced (Eluvathingal et al., 2006; Nelson, 2007b).

Additional evidence shows that the chronic stress of early, deprived orphanage rearing disrupts the brain's capacity to manage stress. In another investigation, researchers followed the development of children who had spent their first eight months or more in Romanian institutions and were then adopted into Canadian homes (Gunnar et al., 2001; Gunnar & Cheatham, 2003). Compared with agemates adopted shortly after birth, these children showed extreme stress reactivity, as indicated by high concentrations of the stress hormone

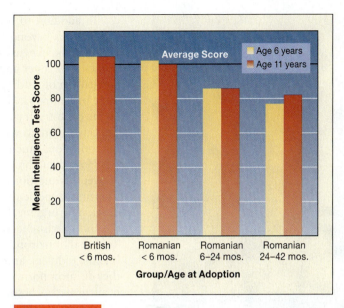

FIGURE 5.9

Relationship of age at adoption to mental test scores at ages 6 and 11 among British and Romanian adoptees. Children transferred from Romanian orphanages to British adoptive homes in the first six months of life attained average scores and fared as well as British early-adopted children, suggesting that they had fully recovered from extreme early deprivation. Romanian children adopted after 6 months of age performed well below average. And although those adopted after age 2 improved between ages 6 and 11, they continued to show serious intellectual deficits. *(Adapted from Beckett et al., 2006.)*

cortisol in their saliva—a physiological response linked to illness, retarded physical growth, and learning and behavior problems, including deficits in attention and control of anger and other impulses. The longer the children spent in orphanage care, the higher their cortisol levels—even 6½ years after adoption. In other research, orphanage children displayed abnormally low cortisol—a blunted physiological stress response that may be the central nervous system's adaptation to earlier, frequent cortisol elevations (Carlson & Earls, 1997; Gunnar & Vasquez, 2001).

Finally, early deprived rearing may also disrupt the brain's typical response to pleasurable social experiences. After sitting on their mother's lap and playing an enjoyable game, preschoolers adopted, on average, at age 1½ years from Romanian orphanages had abnormally low urine levels of *oxytocin*—a hormone released by the brain that evokes calmness and contentment in the presence of familiar, trusted people (Fries et al., 2005). As we will see in Chapter 7, children who spend their infancy in neglectful institutions often display attachment difficulties that even a caring adoptive family cannot completely overcome.

APPROPRIATE STIMULATION   Unlike the orphanage children just described, Grace, whom Monica and Kevin had adopted in Cambodia at 16 months of age, showed favorable progress. Two years earlier, they had adopted Grace's older brother, Eli. When Eli was 2 years old, Monica and Kevin sent a letter and a photo of Eli to his biological mother, describing a bright, happy child. The next day, the Cambodian mother tearfully asked an adoption agency to send her baby daughter to join Eli and his American family.

Although Grace's early environment was very depleted, her biological mother's loving care—holding gently, speaking softly, and breastfeeding—may have prevented irreversible damage to her brain. Besides offering gentle, appropriate stimulation, sensitive adult care helps normalize cortisol production in both typically developing and emotionally traumatized infants and young children (Gunnar & Quevedo, 2007; Tarullo & Gunnar, 2006). Good parenting seems to protect the young brain from the potentially damaging effects of both excessive and inadequate stress-hormone exposure.

 Experience-expectant brain growth takes place naturally, through ordinary, stimulating experiences. This toddler shoveling pebbles into her bucket engages in the type of activity that best promotes brain development in the early years. ■

In addition to impoverished environments, ones that overwhelm children with expectations beyond their current capacities interfere with the brain's potential. In recent years, expensive early learning centers have sprung up, in which infants are trained with letter and number flash cards and slightly older toddlers are given a full curriculum of reading, math, science, art, gym, and more. There is no evidence that these programs yield smarter, better "superbabies" (Hirsh-Pasek & Golinkoff, 2003). To the contrary, trying to prime infants with stimulation for which they are not ready can cause them to withdraw, thereby threatening their interest in learning and creating conditions much like stimulus deprivation!

How, then, can we characterize appropriate stimulation during the early years? To answer this question, researchers distinguish between two types of brain development. The first, **experience-expectant brain growth,** refers to the young brain's rapidly developing organization, which depends on ordinary experiences—opportunities to see and touch objects, to hear language and other sounds, and to move about and explore the environment. As a result of millions of years of evolution, the brains of all infants, toddlers, and young children expect to encounter these experiences and, if they do, grow normally. The second type of brain development—**experience-dependent brain growth**—occurs throughout our lives. It consists of additional growth and the refinement of established brain structures as a result of specific learning experiences that vary widely across individuals and cultures (Greenough & Black, 1992). Reading and writing, playing computer games, weaving an intricate rug, and practicing the violin are examples. The brain of a violinist differs in certain ways from the brain of a poet because each has exercised different brain regions for a long time.

Experience-expectant brain development occurs early and naturally, as caregivers offer babies and preschoolers age-appropriate play materials and engage them in enjoyable daily routines—a shared meal, a game of peekaboo, a bath before bed, a picture book to talk about, or a song to sing. The resulting growth provides the foundation for later-occurring, experience-dependent development (Huttenlocher, 2002; Shonkoff & Phillips, 2001). No evidence exists for a sensitive period in the first few years of life for mastering skills that depend on extensive training, such as reading, musical performance, or gymnastics (Bruer, 1999). To the contrary, rushing early learning also harms the brain by overwhelming its neural circuits, thereby reducing the brain's sensitivity to the everyday experiences it needs for a healthy start in life.

Changing States of Arousal

Rapid brain growth means that the organization of sleep and wakefulness changes substantially between birth and 2 years, and fussiness and crying also decline. The newborn baby takes round-the-clock naps that total about 16 to 18 hours (Davis, Parker, & Montgomery, 2004). Total sleep time declines slowly; the average 2-year-old still needs 12 to 13 hours. But periods of sleep and wakefulness become fewer and longer, and the sleep–wake pattern increasingly conforms to a night–day schedule. Most 6- to 9-month-olds take two daytime naps; by about 18 months, children generally need only one nap. Finally, between ages 3 and 5, napping subsides (Iglowstein et al., 2003).

These changing arousal patterns are due to brain development, but they are also affected by the social environment. In Western nations, many parents try to get their babies to sleep through the night around 4 months of age by feeding them solid foods before bedtime, then putting them down in a separate, quiet room—practices that may be at odds with young infants' neurological development. Not until the middle of the first year is the secretion of *melatonin*, a hormone within the brain that promotes drowsiness, much greater at night than during the day (Sadeh, 1997). Babies of this age, whose caregivers take them out on regular early-afternoon outings and expose them to more bright sunlight, sleep better at night (Harrison, 2004).

As the Cultural Influences box on the following page reveals, isolating infants to promote sleep is rare elsewhere in the world. When babies sleep with their parents, their average sleep period remains constant at three hours from 1 to 8 months of age. Only at the end of the first year, as REM sleep (the state that usually prompts waking) declines, do infants move in the direction of an adultlike sleep–wake schedule (Ficca et al., 1999).

LOOK AND LISTEN

Interview a parent of a baby about sleep challenges. What strategies has the parent tried to ease these difficulties? Are the techniques likely to be effective, in view of evidence on infant sleep development?

CULTURAL INFLUENCES

Cultural Variation in Infant Sleeping Arrangements

While awaiting the birth of a new baby, North American parents typically furnish a room as the infant's sleeping quarters. For decades, child-rearing advice from experts strongly encouraged the nighttime separation of baby from parent. For example, the most recent edition of Benjamin Spock's *Baby and Child Care* recommends that babies sleep in their own room by 3 months of age, explaining, "By 6 months, a child who regularly sleeps in her parents' room may become dependent on this arrangement" (Spock & Needlman, 2004, p. 60). And the American Academy of Pediatrics (2005) has issued a controversial warning that parent–infant bedsharing may increase the risk of sudden infant death syndrome (SIDS).

Yet parent–infant "cosleeping" is the norm for approximately 90 percent of the world's population, in cultures as diverse as the Japanese, the rural Guatemalan Maya, the Inuit of northwestern Canada, and the !Kung of Botswana. Japanese and Korean children usually lie next to their mothers throughout infancy and early childhood, and many continue to sleep with a parent or other family member until adolescence (Takahashi, 1990; Yang & Hahn, 2002). Among the Maya, mother–infant cosleeping is interrupted only by the birth of a new baby, at which time the older child is moved next to the father or to another bed in the same room (Morelli et al., 1992). Cosleeping is also common in U.S. ethnic minority families (McKenna & Volpe, 2007). African-American children, for example, frequently fall asleep with their parents and remain with them for part or all of the night (Buswell & Spatz, 2007).

Cultural values—specifically, collectivism versus individualism (see Chapter 2, page 78)—strongly influence infant sleeping arrangements. In one study, researchers interviewed Guatemalan Mayan mothers and American middle-SES mothers about their sleeping practices. Mayan mothers stressed a collectivist perspective, explaining that cosleeping builds a close parent–child bond, which is necessary for children to learn the ways of people around them. In contrast, American mothers conveyed an individualistic perspective, mentioning the importance of instilling early independence, preventing bad habits, and protecting their own privacy (Morelli et al., 1992).

Over the past two decades, cosleeping has increased in Western nations. In the United States, an estimated 13 percent of infants routinely bedshare, and an additional 30 to 35 percent sometimes do so (Buswell & Spatz, 2007; Willinger et al., 2003). Proponents of the practice say that it helps infants sleep, makes breastfeeding more convenient, and provides valuable bonding time—especially for employed parents who have limited contact with their baby during the day (McKenna & Volpe, 2007).

During the night, cosleeping babies breastfeed three times longer than infants who sleep alone. Because infants arouse to nurse more often when sleeping next to their mothers, some researchers believe that cosleeping may actually help safeguard babies at risk for SIDS. Consistent with this view, SIDS is rare in Asian cultures where cosleeping is widespread, including Cambodia, China, Japan, Korea, Thailand, and Vietnam (McKenna, 2002; McKenna & McDade, 2005). And contrary to popular belief, cosleeping does not reduce mothers' total sleep time, although they experience more brief awakenings, which permit them to check on their baby (Mao et al., 2004).

Infant sleeping practices affect other aspects of family life. For example, Mayan babies doze off in the midst of ongoing family activities and are carried to bed by their mothers. In contrast, for many North American parents, bedtime often requires a lengthy, elaborate ritual. Perhaps bedtime struggles, so common in Western homes but rare elsewhere in the world, are related to the stress young children feel when they must fall asleep without assistance (Latz, Wolf, & Lozoff, 1999).

Critics of bedsharing warn that cosleeping children will develop emotional problems, especially excessive dependency. Yet a longitudinal study following children from the end of pregnancy through age 18 showed that young people who had bedshared in the early years were no different from others in any aspect of adjustment (Okami, Weisner, & Olmstead, 2002). Another concern is that infants might become trapped under the parent's body or in soft covers, mattresses, or sofas and suffocate. Parents who are obese or who use alcohol, tobacco, or illegal drugs do pose a serious risk to their sleeping babies, as does the use of quilts and comforters or an overly soft mattress (Willinger et al., 2003).

But with appropriate precautions, parents and infants can cosleep safely (McKenna & Volpe, 2007). In cultures where cosleeping is widespread, parents and infants usually sleep with light covering on hard surfaces, such as firm mattresses, floor mats, and wooden planks, or infants sleep in a cradle or hammock next to the parents' bed (McKenna, 2001, 2002). And when sharing the same bed, infants typically lie on their back or side facing the mother—positions that promote frequent, easy communication between parent and baby and arousal if breathing is threatened.

Finally, breastfeeding mothers usually assume a distinctive sleeping posture. They face the infant, with knees drawn up under the baby's feet and arm above the baby's head. Besides facilitating feeding, the position prevents the infant from sliding down under covers or up under pillows (Ball, 2006). Because this posture is also seen in female great apes while sharing sleeping nests with their infants, researchers believe it may have evolved to enhance infant safety.

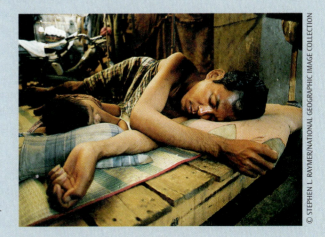

■ This Cambodian father and child sleep together, a practice common in their culture and around the globe. The family sleeps on hard wooden surfaces, which protect cosleeping children from entrapment in soft bedding. ■

© STEPHEN L. RAYMER/NATIONAL GEOGRAPHIC IMAGE COLLECTION

Even after infants sleep through the night, they continue to wake occasionally. When babies begin to crawl and walk, they often show temporary periods of disrupted sleep (Scher, Epstein, & Tirosh, 2004). And studies carried out in Australia, Great Britain, and Israel revealed that night wakings increased between 1½ and 2 years, then declined (Scher, Epstein, & Tirosh, 2004; Scher et al., 1995). As we will see in Chapter 7, the challenges of the second year—ability to range farther from the familiar caregiver and awareness of the self as separate from others— often prompt anxiety in toddlers, evident in disturbed sleep and clinginess. When parents offer comfort, these behaviors subside.

ASK YOURSELF

◆ **REVIEW** How do overproduction of synapses and synaptic pruning support infants' and children's ability to learn?

◆ **APPLY** Which infant enrichment program would you choose: one that emphasizes gentle talking and touching and social games, or one that includes reading and number drills and classical music lessons? Explain.

◆ **CONNECT** Explain how inappropriate stimulation— either too little or too much—can impair cognitive and emotional development in the early years.

◆ **REFLECT** What is your attitude toward parent–infant cosleeping? Is it influenced by your cultural background? Explain.

Influences on Early Physical Growth

Physical growth, like other aspects of development, results from the continuous and complex interplay between genetic and environmental factors. Heredity, nutrition, relative freedom from disease, and emotional well-being all affect early physical growth.

Heredity

Because identical twins are much more alike in body size than fraternal twins, we know that heredity is important in physical growth (Estourgie-van Burk et al., 2006). When diet and health are adequate, height and rate of physical growth are largely determined by heredity. In fact, as long as negative environmental influences such as poor nutrition or illness are not severe, children and adolescents typically show *catch-up growth*—a return to a genetically determined growth path—once conditions improve. After her adoption, Grace grew rapidly until, at age 2, she was nearly average in size by Cambodian standards. Still, the health of many organs may be permanently compromised by inadequate early nutrition.

Twin studies reveal that genetic makeup also contributes considerably to body weight (Kinnunen, Pietilainen, & Rissanen, 2006). At the same time, environment—in particular, nutrition and eating habits—plays a powerful role.

Nutrition

Nutrition is especially crucial for development in the first two years because the baby's brain and body are growing so rapidly. Pound for pound, an infant's energy needs are at least twice those of an adult. Twenty-five percent of infants' total caloric intake is devoted to growth, and babies need extra calories to keep rapidly developing organs functioning properly (Meyer, 2009).

BREASTFEEDING VERSUS BOTTLE-FEEDING   Babies not only need enough food; they also need the right kind of food. In early infancy, breast milk is ideally suited to their needs, and bottled formulas try to imitate it. Applying What We Know on the following page summarizes major nutritional and health advantages of breastfeeding.

Applying What We Know

Reasons to Breastfeed

NUTRITIONAL AND HEALTH ADVANTAGES	EXPLANATION
Provides the correct balance of fat and protein	Compared with the milk of other mammals, human milk is higher in fat and lower in protein. This balance, as well as the unique proteins and fats contained in human milk, is ideal for a rapidly myelinating nervous system.
Ensures nutritional completeness	A mother who breastfeeds need not add other foods to her infant's diet until the baby is 6 months old. The milks of all mammals are low in iron, but the iron contained in breast milk is much more easily absorbed by the baby's system. Consequently, bottle-fed infants need iron-fortified formula.
Helps ensure healthy physical growth	One-year-old breastfed babies are leaner (have a higher percentage of muscle to fat), a growth pattern that persists through the preschool years and that may help prevent later overweight and obesity.
Protects against many diseases	Breastfeeding transfers antibodies and other infection-fighting agents from mother to baby and enhances functioning of the immune system. Compared with bottle-fed infants, breastfed babies have far fewer allergic reactions and respiratory and intestinal illnesses. Breast milk also has anti-inflammatory effects, which reduce the severity of illness symptoms. Breastfeeding in the first four months (especially when exclusive) is linked to lower blood cholesterol levels in adulthood and, thereby, may help prevent cardiovascular disease.
Protects against faulty jaw development and tooth decay	Sucking the mother's nipple instead of an artificial nipple helps avoid malocclusion, a condition in which the upper and lower jaws do not meet properly. It also protects against tooth decay due to sweet liquid remaining in the mouths of infants who fall asleep while sucking on a bottle.
Ensures digestibility	Because breastfed babies have a different kind of bacteria growing in their intestines than do bottle-fed infants, they rarely suffer from constipation or other gastrointestinal problems.
Smooths the transition to solid foods	Breastfed infants accept new solid foods more easily than do bottle-fed infants, perhaps because of their greater experience with a variety of flavors, which pass from the maternal diet into the mother's milk.

Sources: American Academy of Pediatrics, 2005a; Buescher, 2001; Michels et al., 2007; Owen et al., 2008; Rosetta & Baldi, 2008; Weyermann, Rothenbacher, & Brenner, 2006.

Because of these benefits, breastfed babies in poverty-stricken regions of the world are much less likely to be malnourished and 6 to 14 times more likely to survive the first year of life. The World Health Organization recommends breastfeeding until age 2 years, with solid foods added at 6 months. These practices, if widely followed, would save the lives of more than a million infants annually (World Health Organization, 2010b). Even breastfeeding for just a few weeks offers some protection against respiratory and intestinal infections, which are devastating to young children in developing countries. Also, because a nursing mother is less likely to get pregnant, breastfeeding helps increase spacing among siblings, a major factor in reducing infant and childhood deaths in nations with widespread poverty. (Note, however, that breastfeeding is not a reliable method of birth control.)

Yet many mothers in the developing world do not know about these benefits. In Africa, the Middle East, and Latin America, most babies get some breastfeeding, but fewer than 40 percent are exclusively breastfed for the first six months, and one-third are fully weaned from the breast before 1 year (Lauer et al., 2004). In place of breast milk, mothers give their babies commercial formula or low-grade nutrients, such as rice water or highly diluted cow or goat milk. Contamination of these foods as a result of poor sanitation is common and often leads to illness and infant death. The United Nations has encouraged all hospitals and maternity units in developing countries to promote breastfeeding as long as mothers do not have viral or bacterial infections (such as HIV or tuberculosis) that can be transmitted to the baby. Today, most developing countries have banned the practice of giving free or subsidized formula to new mothers.

Partly as a result of the natural childbirth movement, breastfeeding has become more common in industrialized nations, especially among well-educated women. Today, 74 percent of American mothers breastfeed, but half of them stop after a few months (U.S. Centers for Disease Control, 2009). And despite the health benefits of breast milk, only 50 percent of

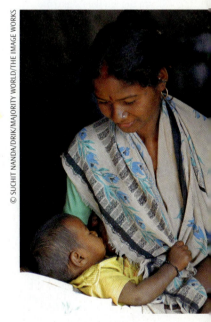

■ Breastfeeding is especially important in developing countries. This breastfed baby from a village in India is likely to grow normally during the first year. ■

By providing nutritious meals and snacks, this mother supports her toddler's desire to feed herself while also promoting healthy eating habits that protect against overweight and obesity. ■

preterm infants are breastfed at hospital discharge. Breastfeeding a preterm baby presents special challenges, including maintaining a sufficient milk supply with artificial pumping until the baby is mature enough to suck at the breast and providing the infant with enough sucking experience to learn to feed successfully (Callen & Pinelli, 2005). Kangaroo care (see pages 138–139 in Chapter 4) and the support of health professionals are helpful.

Breast milk is so easily digestible that a breastfed infant becomes hungry quite often—every 1½ to 2 hours, compared to every 3 or 4 hours for a bottle-fed baby. This makes breastfeeding inconvenient for many employed women. Not surprisingly, mothers who return to work sooner wean their babies from the breast earlier (Kimbro, 2006). But mothers who cannot be with their babies all the time can still combine breast- and bottle-feeding. The U.S. Department of Health and Human Services (2009a) advises exclusive breastfeeding for the first 6 months and inclusion of breast milk in the baby's diet until at least 1 year.

Women who do not breastfeed sometimes worry that they are depriving their baby of an experience essential for healthy psychological development. Yet breastfed and bottle-fed infants in industrialized nations do not differ in quality of the mother–infant relationship or in later emotional adjustment (Fergusson & Woodward, 1999; Jansen, de Weerth, & Riksen-Walraven, 2008). Some studies report a slight advantage in intelligence test performance for children and adolescents who were breastfed, after controlling for many factors. Most, however, find no cognitive benefits (Der, Batty, & Deary, 2006).

ARE CHUBBY BABIES AT RISK FOR LATER OVERWEIGHT AND OBESITY? From early infancy, Timmy was an enthusiastic eater who nursed vigorously and gained weight quickly. By 5 months, he began reaching for food on his parents' plates. Vanessa wondered: Was she overfeeding Timmy and increasing his chances of being permanently overweight?

Most chubby babies thin out during toddlerhood and the preschool years, as weight gain slows and they become more active. Infants and toddlers can eat nutritious foods freely without risk of becoming overweight. But recent evidence does indicate a strengthening relationship between rapid weight gain in infancy and later obesity (Botton et al., 2008; Chomtho et al., 2008). The trend may be due to the rise in overweight and obesity among adults, who promote unhealthy eating habits in their young children. Interviews with more than 3,000 U.S. parents of 4- to 24-month-olds revealed that many routinely served them french fries, pizza, candy, sugary fruit drinks, and soda. For example, 60 percent of 12-month-olds ate candy at least once a day! On average, infants consumed 20 percent and toddlers 30 percent more calories than they needed. At the same time, one-third ate no fruits or vegetables (Briefel et al., 2004).

How can concerned parents prevent their infants from becoming overweight children and adults? One way is to breastfeed for the first six months, which is associated with slower weight gain over the first year and leaner body build through early childhood (Gunnarsdottir et al., 2010; Sloan et al., 2008). Another is to avoid giving them foods loaded with sugar, salt, and saturated fats. Once toddlers learn to walk, climb, and run, parents can also provide plenty of opportunities for energetic play. Finally, because research shows a correlation between excessive television viewing and overweight in older children, parents should limit the time very young children spend in front of the TV.

Malnutrition

Osita is an Ethiopian 2-year-old whose mother has never had to worry about his gaining too much weight. When she weaned him at 1 year, he had little to eat besides starchy rice flour cakes. Soon his belly enlarged, his feet swelled, his hair fell out, and a rash appeared on his skin. His bright-eyed curiosity vanished, and he became irritable and listless.

In developing countries and war-torn areas where food resources are limited, malnutrition is widespread. Recent evidence indicates that about 27 percent of the world's children suffer

LOOK AND LISTEN

Ask several parents of 1- to 2-year-olds to keep a diary of all the foods and drinks they offer their toddler over a weekend. How healthy are the toddlers' diets? Did any of the parents report heightened awareness of family nutrition as a result of the diary exercise?

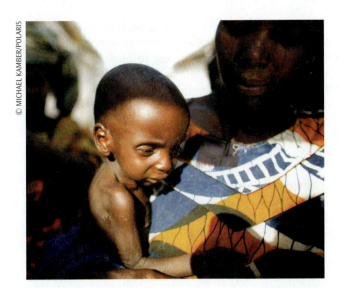

■ The baby on the left, of Niger, Africa, has marasmus, a wasted condition caused by a diet low in all essential nutrients. The swollen abdomen of the toddler on the right, also from Niger, is a symptom of kwashiorkor, which results from a diet very low in protein. If these children survive, they are likely to be growth stunted and to suffer from lasting organ damage as well as serious cognitive and emotional impairments. ■

from malnutrition before age 5 (World Health Organization, 2009b). The 10 percent who are severely affected suffer from two dietary diseases.

Marasmus is a wasted condition of the body caused by a diet low in all essential nutrients. It usually appears in the first year of life when a baby's mother is too malnourished to produce enough breast milk and bottle-feeding is also inadequate. Her starving baby becomes painfully thin and is in danger of dying.

Osita has **kwashiorkor,** caused by an unbalanced diet very low in protein. The disease usually strikes after weaning, between 1 and 3 years of age. It is common in regions where children get just enough calories from starchy foods but little protein. The child's body responds by breaking down its own protein reserves, which causes the swelling and other symptoms that Osita experienced.

Children who survive these extreme forms of malnutrition often grow to be smaller in all body dimensions and suffer from lasting damage to the brain, heart, liver, or other organs (Müller & Krawinkel, 2005). When their diets do improve, they tend to gain excessive weight (Uauy et al., 2008). A malnourished body protects itself by establishing a low basal metabolism rate, which may endure after nutrition improves. Also, malnutrition may disrupt appetite control centers in the brain, causing the child to overeat when food becomes plentiful.

Learning and behavior are also seriously affected. In one long-term study of marasmic children, an improved diet led to some catch-up growth in height, but not in head size (Stoch et al., 1982). The malnutrition probably interfered with growth of neural fibers and myelination, causing a permanent loss in brain weight. And animal evidence reveals that a deficient diet alters the production of neurotransmitters in the brain—an effect that can disrupt all aspects of development (Haller, 2005). These children score low on intelligence tests, show poor fine-motor coordination, and have difficulty paying attention (Galler et al., 1990; Liu et al., 2003). They also display a more intense stress response to fear-arousing situations, perhaps caused by the constant, gnawing pain of hunger (Fernald & Grantham-McGregor, 1998).

Recall from our discussion of prenatal malnutrition in Chapter 3 that the passivity and irritability of malnourished children worsen the impact of poor diet. These behaviors may appear even when protein-calorie deprivation is only mild to moderate. They also accompany *iron-deficiency anemia,* a condition common among poverty-stricken infants and children that interferes with many central nervous system processes. Withdrawal and listlessness reduce the nutritionally deprived child's ability to pay attention, explore, and evoke sensitive caregiving from parents, whose lives are already disrupted by poverty and stressful living conditions (Corapci, Radan, & Lozoff, 2006; Grantham-McGregor & Ani, 2001). For this reason, interventions for malnourished children must improve the family situation as well as the child's nutrition.

Inadequate nutrition is not confined to developing countries. Because government-supported supplementary food programs do not reach all families in need, an estimated 22 percent of U.S. children suffer from *food insecurity*—uncertain access to enough food for a healthy, active life. Food insecurity is especially high among single-parent families (35 percent) and low-income ethnic minority families—for example, Hispanics and African Americans (26 and 27 percent, respectively) (Nord, Andrews, & Carlson, 2009). Although few of these children have marasmus or kwashiorkor, their physical growth and ability to learn are still affected.

Emotional Well-Being

We may not think of affection as necessary for healthy physical growth, but it is as vital as food. **Growth faltering** is a term applied to infants whose weight, height, and head circumference are substantially below age-related growth norms and who are withdrawn and apathetic (Black, 2005). In as many as half such cases, a disturbed parent–infant relationship contributes to this failure to grow normally.

Lana, an observant nurse at a public health clinic, became concerned about 8-month-old Melanie, who was 3 pounds lighter than she had been at her last checkup. Lana noted that Melanie kept her eyes on nearby adults, anxiously watching their every move, and rarely smiled at her mother. During feeding and diaper changing, Melanie's mother sometimes appeared depressed and distant, at other times impatient and hostile. Melanie tried to protect herself by tracking her mother's whereabouts and, when she approached, avoiding her gaze.

Often an unhappy marriage and parental psychological disturbance contribute to these serious caregiving problems. And most of the time, the baby is irritable and displays abnormal feeding behaviors, such as poor sucking or vomiting, that both disrupt growth and lead parents to feel anxious and helpless, which stress the parent–infant relationship further (Batchelor, 2008; Linscheid, Budd, & Rasnake, 2005).

In Melanie's case, her alcoholic father was out of work, and her parents argued constantly. Melanie's mother had little energy to meet Melanie's psychological needs. When treated early, by intervening in infant feeding problems, helping parents with their own life challenges, and encouraging sensitive caregiving, babies show quick catch-up growth. But if the disorder is not corrected in infancy, most of these children remain small and show lasting cognitive and emotional difficulties (Black et al., 2007; Drewett, Corbett, & Wright, 2006).

ASK YOURSELF

◆ **REVIEW** Explain why breastfeeding can have lifelong consequences for the development of babies born in poverty-stricken regions of the world.

◆ **APPLY** Eight-month-old Shaun is well below average in height and painfully thin. He cries during feedings and is listless and irritable. Shaun's single mother feels overwhelmed and discouraged. Why do Shaun and his mother need intervention quickly? What should health professionals do?

◆ **CONNECT** How are bidirectional influences between parent and child involved in the impact of malnutrition on psychological development? After her adoption, how did those influences change for Grace?

◆ **REFLECT** Imagine that you are the parent of a newborn baby. Describe feeding practices you would use, and ones you would avoid, to prevent overweight and obesity.

Learning Capacities

Learning refers to changes in behavior as the result of experience. Babies come into the world with built-in learning capacities that permit them to profit from experience immediately. Infants are capable of two basic forms of learning, which were introduced in Chapter 1: classical and operant conditioning. They also learn through their natural preference for novel stimulation. Finally, shortly after birth, babies learn by observing others; they can imitate the facial expressions and gestures of adults.

Classical Conditioning

Newborn reflexes, discussed in Chapter 4, make **classical conditioning** possible in the young infant. In this form of learning, a neutral stimulus is paired with a stimulus that leads to a reflexive response. Once the baby's nervous system makes the connection between the two stimuli, the neutral stimulus produces the behavior by itself. Classical conditioning helps infants recognize which events usually occur together in the everyday world, so they can anticipate what is about to happen next. As a result, the environment becomes more orderly and predictable. Let's take a closer look at the steps of classical conditioning.

As Carolyn settled down in the rocking chair to nurse Caitlin, she often stroked Caitlin's forehead. Soon Carolyn noticed that each time she did this, Caitlin made active sucking movements. Caitlin had been classically conditioned. Here is how it happened (see Figure 5.10):

1. Before learning takes place, an **unconditioned stimulus (UCS)** must consistently produce a reflexive, or **unconditioned, response (UCR).** In Caitlin's case, sweet breast milk (UCS) resulted in sucking (UCR).
2. To produce learning, a *neutral stimulus* that does not lead to the reflex is presented just before, or at about the same time as, the UCS. Carolyn stroked Caitlin's forehead as each nursing period began. The stroking (neutral stimulus) was paired with the taste of milk (UCS).
3. If learning has occurred, the neutral stimulus alone produces a response similar to the reflexive response. The neutral stimulus is then called a **conditioned stimulus (CS),** and the response it elicits is called a **conditioned response (CR).** We know that Caitlin has been classically conditioned because stroking her forehead outside the feeding situation (CS) results in sucking (CR).

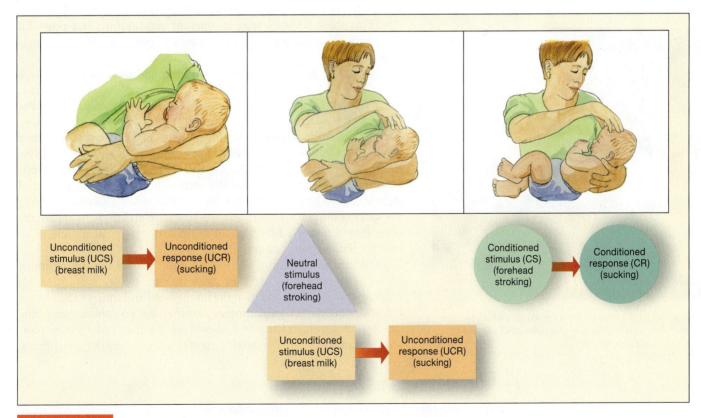

FIGURE 5.10

The steps of classical conditioning. This example shows how Caitlin's mother classically conditioned her to make sucking movements by stroking her forehead at the beginning of feedings.

If the CS is presented alone enough times, without being paired with the UCS, the CR will no longer occur, an outcome called *extinction*. In other words, if Carolyn repeatedly strokes Caitlin's forehead without feeding her, Caitlin will gradually stop sucking in response to stroking.

Young infants can be classically conditioned most easily when the association between two stimuli has survival value. Learning which stimuli regularly accompany feeding improves the infant's ability to get food and survive (Blass, Ganchrow, & Steiner, 1984). In contrast, some responses, such as fear, are very difficult to classically condition in young babies. Until infants have the motor skills to escape unpleasant events, they have no biological need to form these associations. After age 6 months, however, fear is easy to condition. **TAKE A MOMENT...** Return to Chapter 1, page 17, to review John Watson's well-known experiment in which he conditioned Little Albert to withdraw and cry at the sight of a furry white rat. Then test your knowledge of classical conditioning by identifying the UCS, UCR, CS, and CR in Watson's study.

Operant Conditioning

In classical conditioning, babies build expectations about stimulus events in the environment, but they do not influence the stimuli that occur. In **operant conditioning,** infants act, or *operate,* on the environment, and stimuli that follow their behavior change the probability that the behavior will occur again. A stimulus that increases the occurrence of a response is called a **reinforcer.** For example, sweet liquid *reinforces* the sucking response in newborns. Removing a desirable stimulus or presenting an unpleasant one to decrease the occurrence of a response is called **punishment.** A sour-tasting fluid *punishes* newborn babies' sucking response. It causes them to purse their lips and stop sucking entirely.

Many stimuli besides food can serve as reinforcers of infant behavior. For example, newborns will suck faster on a nipple that produces interesting sights and sounds, including visual designs, music, or human voices (Floccia, Christophe, & Bertoncini, 1997). Even preterm babies will seek reinforcing stimulation. In one study, they increased their contact with a soft teddy bear that "breathed" at a rate reflecting the infant's respiration, whereas they decreased their contact with a nonbreathing bear (Thoman & Ingersoll, 1993). As these findings suggest, operant conditioning is a powerful tool for finding out what stimuli babies can perceive and which ones they prefer.

As infants get older, operant conditioning expands to include a wider range of responses and stimuli. For example, researchers have hung special mobiles over the cribs of 2- to 6-month-olds. When the baby's foot is attached to the mobile with a long cord, the infant can, by kicking, make the mobile turn. Under these conditions, it takes only a few minutes for infants to start kicking vigorously (Rovee-Collier, 1999; Rovee-Collier & Barr, 2001). As you will see in Chapter 6, operant conditioning with mobiles is frequently used to study infants' memory and their ability to group similar stimuli into categories. Once babies learn the kicking response, researchers see how long and under what conditions they retain it when exposed again to the original mobile or to mobiles with varying features.

Operant conditioning also plays a vital role in the formation of social relationships. As the baby gazes into the adult's eyes, the adult looks and smiles back, and then the infant looks and smiles again. As the behavior of each partner reinforces the other, both continue their pleasurable interaction. In Chapter 7, we will see that this contingent responsiveness contributes to the development of infant–caregiver attachment.

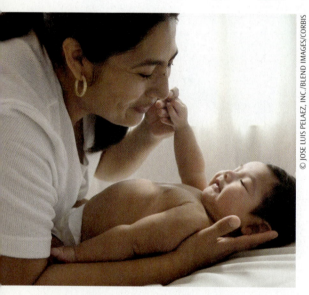

© JOSE LUIS PELAEZ, INC./BLEND IMAGES/CORBIS

■ As this baby and his mother gaze into each other's eyes and smile, the behavior of each reinforces the other, sustaining their pleasurable interaction. ■

Habituation

At birth, the human brain is set up to be attracted to novelty. Infants tend to respond more strongly to a new element that has entered their environment, an inclination that ensures that they will continually add to their knowledge base. **Habituation** refers to a gradual reduction in the strength of a response due to repetitive stimulation. Looking, heart rate, and respiration rate may all decline, indicating a loss of interest. Once this has occurred, a new stimulus—a change in the environment—causes responsiveness to return to a high level, an increase called **recovery.** For example, when you walk through a familiar space, you notice things that are new and different—a recently hung picture on the wall or a piece of furniture that has been moved. Habituation and recovery promote learning by focusing our attention on those aspects of the environment we know least about.

Researchers studying infants' understanding of the world rely on habituation and recovery more than any other learning capacity. For example, a baby who first *habituates* to a visual pattern (a photo of a baby) and then *recovers* to a new one (a photo of a bald man) appears to remember the first stimulus and perceive the second one as new and different from it. This method of studying infant perception and cognition, illustrated in Figure 5.11, can be used with newborns, including preterm infants. It has even been used to study the fetus's sensitivity to external stimuli—for example, by measuring changes in fetal heart rate when various repeated sounds are presented (Dirix et al., 2009; Doherty & Hepper, 2000). Habituation to an auditory stimulus is evident in the third trimester of pregnancy.

Recovery to a new stimulus, or *novelty preference*, assesses infants' *recent memory*. **TAKE A MOMENT...** Think about what happens when you return to a place you have not seen for a long time. Instead of attending to novelty, you are likely to focus on aspects that are familiar: "I recognize that—I've been here before!" Like adults, infants shift from a novelty preference to a familiarity preference as more time intervenes between habituation and test phases in research. That is, babies recover to the familiar stimulus rather than to a novel stimulus (see Figure 5.11) (Bahrick, Hernandez-Reif, & Pickens, 1997; Bahrick & Pickens, 1995; Courage & Howe, 1998; Richmond, Colombo, & Hayne, 2007). By focusing on that shift, researchers can also use habituation to assess *remote memory*, or memory for stimuli to which infants were exposed weeks or months earlier.

With age, babies habituate and recover to stimuli more quickly, indicating that they process information more efficiently. Habituation and recovery have been used to assess a wide range of infant perceptual and cognitive capacities—speech perception, musical and visual pattern perception, object perception, categorization, and knowledge of the social world. But despite the strengths of habituation research, its findings are not clear-cut. When looking, sucking, or heart rate declines and recovers, what babies actually know about the stimuli to which they responded is sometimes uncertain. We will return to this difficulty in Chapter 6.

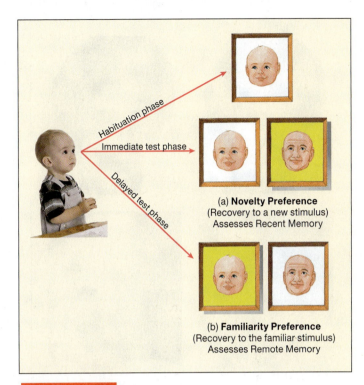

(a) **Novelty Preference**
(Recovery to a new stimulus)
Assesses Recent Memory

(b) **Familiarity Preference**
(Recovery to the familiar stimulus)
Assesses Remote Memory

FIGURE 5.11

Using habituation to study infant perception and cognition. In the habituation phase, infants view a photo of a baby until their looking declines. In the test phase, infants are again shown the baby photo, but this time it appears alongside a photo of a bald-headed man. (a) When the test phase occurs soon after the habituation phase (within minutes, hours, or days, depending on the age of the infants), participants who remember the baby face and distinguish it from the man's face show a *novelty preference;* they recover to (spend more time looking at) the new stimulus. (b) When the test phase is delayed for weeks or months, infants who continue to remember the baby face shift to a *familiarity preference;* they recover to the familiar baby face rather than to the novel man's face.

Imitation

Babies come into the world with a primitive ability to learn through **imitation**—by copying the behavior of another person. For example, Figure 5.12 on page 182 shows a human newborn imitating two adult facial expressions (Meltzoff & Moore, 1977). The newborn's capacity to imitate extends to certain gestures, such as head and index-finger movements, and has been demonstrated in many ethnic groups and cultures (Meltzoff & Kuhl, 1994; Nagy et al., 2005). As the figure reveals, even newborn chimpanzees, our closest evolutionary ancestors, imitate some behaviors (Myowa-Yamakoshi et al., 2004).

Imitation by human and chimpanzee newborns. The human infants in the middle row imitating (left) tongue protrusion and (right) mouth opening are 2 to 3 weeks old. The chimpanzee imitating both facial expressions is 2 weeks old. *(From A. N. Meltzoff & M. K. Moore, 1977, "Imitation of Facial and Manual Gestures by Human Neonates," Science, 198, p. 75; and M. Myowa-Yamakoshi et al., 2004, "Imitation in Neonatal Chimpanzees [Pan Troglodytes]." Developmental Science, 7, p. 440. Copyright © 1977 by AAAS, copyright 2004 by Blackwell Publishing. Reprinted by permission.)*

Although newborns' capacity to imitate is widely accepted, a few studies have failed to reproduce the human findings (see, for example, Anisfeld et al., 2001). And because newborn mouth and tongue movements occur with increased frequency to almost any arousing change in stimulation (such as lively music or flashing lights), some researchers argue that certain newborn "imitative" responses are actually mouthing—a common early exploratory response to interesting stimuli (Jones, 2006). Furthermore, imitation is harder to induce in babies 2 to 3 months old than just after birth. Therefore, skeptics believe that the newborn imitative response is little more than an automatic response that declines with age, much like a reflex (Heyes, 2005).

Others claim that newborns imitate a variety of facial expressions and head movements with effort and determination, even after short delays—when the adult is no longer demonstrating the behavior (Hayne, 2002; Meltzoff & Moore, 1999). Furthermore, these investigators argue that imitation—unlike reflexes—does not decline. Human babies several months old often do not imitate an adult's behavior right away because they first try to play familiar social games—mutual gazing, cooing, smiling, and waving their arms. But when an adult models a gesture repeatedly, older human infants soon get down to business and imitate (Meltzoff & Moore, 1994). Similarly, imitation declines in baby chimps around 9 weeks of age, when mother–baby mutual gazing and other face-to-face exchanges increase.

According to Andrew Meltzoff, newborns imitate much as older children and adults do—by actively trying to match body movements they *see* with ones they *feel* themselves make (Meltzoff, 2007). Later we will encounter evidence that young babies are remarkably adept at coordinating information across sensory systems.

Indeed, scientists have identified specialized cells in many areas of the cerebral cortex of primates—called **mirror neurons**—that underlie these capacities. Mirror neurons fire identically when a primate hears or sees an action and when it carries out that action on its own (Rizzolatti & Craighero, 2004). Humans have especially elaborate systems of mirror neurons, which enable us to observe another person's behavior (such as smiling or throwing a ball) while simulating the behavior in our own brain. Mirror neurons are believed to be the biological basis of a variety of interrelated, complex social abilities, including imitation, empathic sharing of emotions, and understanding others' intentions (Iocaboni et al., 2005; Schulte-Ruther et al., 2007).

Brain-imaging findings support a functioning mirror-neuron system as early as 6 months of age. Using NIRS, researchers found that the same motor areas of the cerebral cortex were activated in 6-month-olds and in adults when they observed a model engage in a behavior that could be imitated (tapping a box to make a toy pop out) as when they themselves engaged in the motor action (Shimada & Hiraki, 2006). In contrast, when infants and adults observed an object that appeared to move on its own, without human intervention (a ball hanging from the ceiling on a string, swinging like a pendulum), motor areas were not activated.

Still, Meltzoff's view of newborn imitation as a flexible, voluntary capacity remains controversial. Mirror neurons, though possibly functional at birth, undergo an extended period of development (Bertenthal & Longo, 2007; Lepage & Théoret, 2007). Similarly, as we will see in Chapter 6, the capacity to imitate expands greatly over the first two years. But however limited it is at birth, imitation is a powerful means of learning. Using imitation, young infants explore their social world, getting to know people by matching their behavioral states. As babies notice similarities between their own actions and those of others, they learn about themselves. By tapping into infants' ability to imitate, adults can get infants to exhibit desirable behaviors. Finally, caregivers take great pleasure in a baby who imitates their facial gestures and actions, which helps get the infant's relationship with parents off to a good start.

ASK YOURSELF

◆ **REVIEW** Provide an example of classical conditioning, of operant conditioning, and of habituation/recovery in young infants.

◆ **APPLY** Nine-month-old Byron has a toy with large, colored push buttons on it. Each time he pushes a button, he hears a nursery tune. Which learning capacity is the manufacturer of this toy taking advantage of? What can Byron's play with the toy reveal about his perception of sound patterns?

◆ **CONNECT** Which learning capacities contribute to an infant's first social relationships? Explain, providing examples.

Motor Development

Carolyn, Monica, and Vanessa each kept a baby book, filled with proud notations about when their children held up their heads, reached for objects, sat by themselves, and walked alone. Parents are understandably excited about these new motor skills, which allow babies to master their bodies and the environment in new ways. For example, sitting upright gives infants a new perspective on the world. Reaching permits babies to find out about objects by acting on them. And when infants can move on their own, their opportunities for exploration multiply.

Babies' motor achievements have a powerful effect on their social relationships. When Caitlin crawled at 7½ months, Carolyn and David began to restrict her movements by saying no and expressing mild impatience. When she walked three days after her first birthday, the first "testing of wills" occurred (Biringen et al., 1995). Despite her mother's warnings, she sometimes pulled items from shelves that were off limits. "I said, 'Don't do that!'" Carolyn would repeat firmly, taking Caitlin's hand and redirecting her attention.

At the same time, newly walking babies more actively attend to and initiate social interaction (Clearfield, Osborne, & Mullen, 2008). Caitlin frequently toddled over to her parents to express a greeting, give a hug, or initiate a gleeful game of hide-and-seek. Soon after, she held out a book and then turned its pages as she and her parents named each picture. Carolyn and David, in turn, increased their expressions of affection and playful activities. Caitlin's delight as she worked on new motor skills triggered pleasurable reactions in others, which encouraged her efforts further (Mayes & Zigler, 1992). Motor, social, cognitive, and language competencies developed together and supported one another.

The Sequence of Motor Development

Gross-motor development refers to control over actions that help infants get around in the environment, such as crawling, standing, and walking. *Fine-motor development* has to do with smaller movements, such as reaching and grasping. Table 5.2 on page 184 shows the average ages at which U.S. infants and toddlers achieve a variety of gross- and fine-motor skills. It also presents the age range during which most babies accomplish each skill, indicating large

TABLE 5.2 Gross- and Fine-Motor Development in the First Two Years

MOTOR SKILL	AVERAGE AGE ACHIEVED	AGE RANGE IN WHICH 90 PERCENT OF INFANTS ACHIEVE THE SKILL
When held upright, holds head erect and steady	6 weeks	3 weeks–4 months
When prone, lifts self by arms	2 months	3 weeks–4 months
Rolls from side to back	2 months	3 weeks–5 months
Grasps cube	3 months, 3 weeks	2–7 months
Rolls from back to side	4½ months	2–7 months
Sits alone	7 months	5–9 months
Crawls	7 months	5–11 months
Pulls to stand	8 months	5–12 months
Plays pat-a-cake	9 months, 3 weeks	7–15 months
Stands alone	11 months	9–16 months
Walks alone	11 months, 3 weeks	9–17 months
Builds tower of two cubes	11 months, 3 weeks	10–19 months
Scribbles vigorously	14 months	10–21 months
Walks up stairs with help	16 months	12–23 months
Jumps in place	23 months, 2 weeks	17–30 months
Walks on tiptoe	25 months	16–30 months

© JIM CRAIGMYLE/CORBIS
© LAURA DWIGHT/CORBIS
© ELIZABETH CREWS/THE IMAGE WORKS

Sources: Bayley, 1969, 1993, 2005.

individual differences in *rate* of motor progress. Also, a baby who is a late reacher will not necessarily be a late crawler or walker. We would be concerned about a child's development only if many motor skills were seriously delayed.

Historically, researchers assumed that the motor milestones listed in Table 5.2 are separate, innate abilities that emerge in a fixed sequence governed by a built-in maturational timetable. This view has long been discredited. Rather, motor skills are interrelated: Each is a product of earlier motor attainments and a contributor to new ones. And children acquire motor skills in highly individual ways. For example, before her adoption, Grace spent most of her days lying in a hammock. Because she was rarely placed on her tummy and on firm surfaces that enabled her to move on her own, she did not try to crawl. As a result, she pulled to a stand and walked before she crawled! Even Western babies display such skills as rolling, sitting, crawling, and walking in diverse orders rather than in the sequence implied by motor norms (Adolph, Karasik, & Tamis-LeMonda, 2010).

Many influences—both internal and external to the child—join together to support the vast transformations in motor competencies of the first two years. The *dynamic systems perspective,* introduced in Chapter 1 (see pages 28–29), helps us understand how motor development takes place.

Motor Skills as Dynamic Systems

According to the **dynamic systems theory of motor development,** mastery of motor skills involves acquiring increasingly complex *systems of action*. When motor skills work as a *system,* separate abilities blend together, each cooperating with others to produce more effective ways of exploring and controlling the environment. For example, control of the head and upper chest combine into sitting with support. Kicking, rocking on all fours, and reaching combine to become crawling. Then crawling, standing, and stepping are united into walking (Adolph & Berger, 2006; Thelen, 1989).

Each new skill is a joint product of the following factors: (1) central nervous system development, (2) the body's movement capacities, (3) the goals the child has in mind, and (4) environmental supports for the skill. Change in any element makes the system less stable, and the child starts to explore and select new, more effective motor patterns. The factors that induce change vary with age. In the early weeks of life, brain and body growth are especially important as infants achieve control over the head, shoulders, and upper torso. Later, the baby's goals (getting a toy or crossing the room) and environmental supports (parental encouragement, objects in the infants' everyday setting) play a greater role.

The broader physical environment also profoundly influences motor skills. Infants with stairs in their home learn to crawl up stairs at an earlier age and also more readily master a back-descent strategy—the safest but also the most challenging position because the baby must turn around at the top, give up visual guidance of her goal, and crawl backward (Berger, Theuring, & Adolph, 2007). And if children were reared on the moon with its reduced gravity, they would prefer jumping to walking or running!

When a skill is first acquired, infants must refine it. For example, in trying to crawl, Caitlin often collapsed on her tummy and moved backward. Soon she figured out how to propel herself forward by alternately pulling with her arms and pushing with her feet, "belly-crawling" in various ways for several weeks (Vereijkin & Adolph, 1999). As they attempt a new skill, most babies move back and forth between its presence and absence: An infant might roll over, sit, crawl, or take a few steps on Monday but not do so again until Friday, and then not again until the following week. And related, previously mastered skills often become less secure. As the novice walker experiments with balancing the body vertically over two small moving feet, balance during sitting may become temporarily less stable (Adolph & Berger, 2006; Chen et al., 2007). This variability is evidence of loss of stability in the system—in dynamic systems theory, a necessary transition between a less mature and a more mature stable state.

Furthermore, motor mastery involves intense practice. In learning to walk, for example, toddlers practice six or more hours a day, traveling the length of 29 football fields! Gradually their small, unsteady steps change to a longer stride, their feet move closer together, their toes point to the front, and their legs become symmetrically coordinated (Adolph, Vereijken, & Shrout, 2003). As movements are repeated thousands of times, they promote new synaptic connections in the brain that govern motor patterns.

Dynamic systems theory shows us why motor development cannot be genetically determined. Because it is motivated by exploration and the desire to master new tasks, heredity can map it out only at a general level. Rather than being *hardwired* into the nervous system, behaviors are *softly assembled*, allowing for different paths to the same motor skill (Adolph, 2008; Thelen & Smith, 2006).

Dynamic Motor Systems in Action

To find out how infants acquire motor capacities, researchers conduct microgenetic studies (see Chapter 1, page 43), following babies from their first attempts at a skill until it becomes smooth and effortless. Using this strategy, James Galloway and Esther Thelen (2004) held sounding toys alternately in front of infants' hands and feet, from the time they first showed interest until they engaged in well-coordinated reaching and grasping. As Figure 5.13 illustrates, the infants violated the normative sequence of arm and hand control preceding leg and foot control, shown in Table 5.2. They

LOOK AND LISTEN

Spend an hour observing a newly crawling or walking baby. Note the goals that motivate the baby to move, along with the baby's effort and motor experimentation. Describe parenting behaviors and features of the environment that promote mastery of the skill.

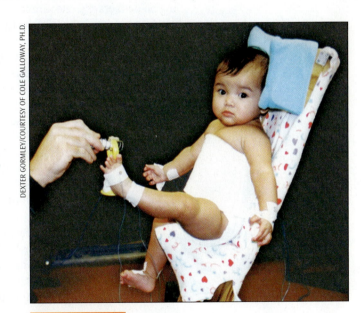

DEXTER GORMLEY/COURTESY OF COLE GALLOWAY, PH.D.

FIGURE 5.13

Reaching "feet first." When sounding toys were held in front of babies' hands and feet, they reached with their feet as early as 8 weeks of age, a month or more before they reached with their hands—a clear violation of the cephalocaudal pattern. Reduced freedom of movement in the hip joint makes leg movements easier to control than arm movements. This 2½-month-old skillfully explores an object with her foot.

The West Indians of Jamaica believe that exercise helps infants grow up strong and physically attractive. This mother "walks" her baby up her body—an activity that contributes to earlier mastery of walking. ■

first explored the toys with their feet—as early as 8 weeks of age, at least a month before reaching with their hands!

Why did babies reach "feet first"? Because the hip joint constrains the legs to move less freely than the shoulder joint constrains the arms, infants could more easily control their leg movements. Consequently, foot reaching required far less practice than hand reaching. As these findings confirm, rather than following a strict, predetermined cephalocaudal pattern, the order in which motor skills develop depends on the anatomy of the body part being used, the surrounding environment, and the baby's efforts.

Cultural Variations in Motor Development

Cross-cultural research further illustrates how early movement opportunities and a stimulating environment contribute to motor development. Half a century ago, Wayne Dennis (1960) observed infants in Iranian orphanages who were deprived of the tantalizing surroundings that induce infants to acquire motor skills. These babies spent their days lying on their backs in cribs, without toys to play with—conditions far worse than Grace experienced lying in a hammock in her Cambodian home. As a result, most did not move on their own until after 2 years of age. When they finally did move, the constant experience of lying on their backs led them to scoot in a sitting position rather than crawl on their hands and knees. Because babies who scoot come up against furniture with their feet, not their hands, they are far less likely to pull themselves to a standing position in preparation for walking. Indeed, by 3 to 4 years of age, only 15 percent of the Iranian orphans were walking alone.

Cultural variations in infant-rearing practices also affect motor development. **TAKE A MOMENT...** Take a quick survey of several parents you know: Should sitting, crawling, and walking be deliberately encouraged? Answers vary widely from culture to culture. Japanese mothers, for example, believe such efforts are unnecessary (Seymour, 1999). Among the Zinacanteco Indians of southern Mexico and the Gusii of Kenya, rapid motor progress is actively discouraged. Babies who walk before they know enough to keep away from cooking fires and weaving looms are viewed as dangerous to themselves and disruptive to others (Greenfield, 1992).

In contrast, among the Kipsigis of Kenya and the West Indians of Jamaica, babies hold their heads up, sit alone, and walk considerably earlier than North American infants. Kipsigis parents deliberately teach these motor skills. In the first few months, babies are seated in holes dug in the ground, with rolled blankets to keep them upright. Walking is promoted by frequently standing babies in adults' laps and bouncing them on their feet. Infants respond with stepping movements, often "walking" up the adult's body (Hopkins & Westra, 1988; Super, 1981). And as parents in these cultures support babies in upright postures and rarely put them down on the floor, their infants usually skip crawling—a motor skill regarded as crucial in Western nations!

Finally, because it decreases exposure to "tummy time," the current Western practice of having babies sleep on their backs to protect them from SIDS (see page 147 in Chapter 4) delays gross-motor milestones of rolling, sitting, and crawling (Majnemer & Barr, 2005; Scrutton, 2005). To prevent these delays, caregivers can regularly expose babies to the tummy-lying position during waking hours.

Fine-Motor Development: Reaching and Grasping

Of all motor skills, reaching may play the greatest role in infant cognitive development. By grasping things, turning them over, and seeing what happens when they are released, infants learn a great deal about the sights, sounds, and feel of objects.

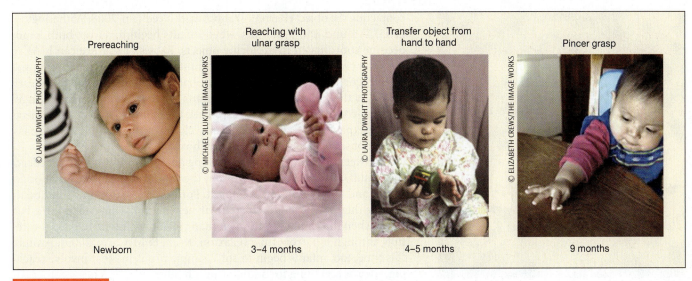

FIGURE 5.14

Some milestones of reaching. The average age at which each skill is attained is given. (Ages from Bayley, 1969; Rochat, 1989.)

Reaching and grasping, like many other motor skills, start out as gross, diffuse activity and move toward mastery of fine movements. Figure 5.14 illustrates some milestones of voluntary reaching over the first nine months. Newborns will actively work to bring their hands into their field of vision: In a dimly lit room, they keep their hand within a narrow beam of light, moving the hand when the light beam moves (van der Meer, 1997). Newborns also make poorly coordinated swipes, called **prereaching**, toward an object in front of them, but because of poor arm and hand control they rarely contact the object. Like newborn reflexes, prereaching drops out around 7 weeks of age, when babies improve in eye movements involved in tracking and fixating on objects, which are essential for accurate reaching. Yet these early behaviors suggest that babies are biologically prepared to coordinate hand with eye in the act of exploring (Rosander & von Hofsten, 2002; von Hofsten, 2004).

DEVELOPMENT OF REACHING AND GRASPING   At about 3 to 4 months, as infants develop the necessary eye, head, and shoulder control, reaching appears as purposeful, forward arm movements in the presence of a nearby toy and gradually improves in accuracy (Bhat, Heathcock, & Galloway, 2005; Spencer et al., 2000). By 5 to 6 months, infants reach for an object in a room that has been darkened during the reach by switching off the lights—a skill that improves over the next few months (Clifton et al., 1994; McCarty & Ashmead, 1999). This indicates that the baby does not need to use vision to guide the arms and hands in reaching. Rather, reaching is largely controlled by *proprioception*—our sense of movement and location in space, arising from stimuli within the body. When vision is freed from the basic act of reaching, it can focus on more complex adjustments, such as fine-tuning actions to fit the distance and shape of objects.

Reaching improves as depth perception advances and as infants gain greater control of body posture and arm and hand movements. Four-month-olds aim their reaches ahead of a moving object so they can catch it (von Hofsten, 1993). Around 5 months, babies reduce their efforts when an object is moved beyond their reach (Robin, Berthier, & Clifton, 1996). By 7 months, the arms become more independent: Infants reach for an object by extending one arm rather than both (Fagard & Pezé, 1997). During the next few months, infants become more efficient at reaching for moving objects—ones that spin, change direction, and move sideways, closer, or farther away (Fagard, Spelke, & von Hofsten, 2009; Wentworth, Benson, & Haith, 2000).

Once infants can reach, they modify their grasp. The newborn's grasp reflex is replaced by the **ulnar grasp,** a clumsy motion in which the young infant's fingers close against the palm. Still, even 4-month-olds adjust their grasp to the size and shape of an object—a capacity that improves over the first year as infants orient the hand more precisely and do so in advance of

■ The capacity to sit unsupported contributes to independent movement of the two arms, enabling this 7-month-old to reach for a tantalizing toy with one hand rather than both. ■

contacting the object (Barrett, Traupman, & Needham, 2008; Witherington, 2005). Around 4 to 5 months, when infants begin to sit up, both hands become coordinated in exploring objects. Babies of this age can hold an object in one hand while the other scans it with the tips of the fingers, and they frequently transfer objects from hand to hand (Rochat & Goubet, 1995). By the end of the first year, infants use the thumb and index finger in a well-coordinated **pincer grasp.** Then the ability to manipulate objects greatly expands. The 1-year-old can pick up raisins and blades of grass, turn knobs, and open and close small boxes.

Between 8 and 11 months, reaching and grasping are well-practiced. As a result, attention is released from the motor skill to events that occur before and after obtaining the object. For example, 10-month-olds easily modify their reach to anticipate their next action. They reach for a ball faster when they intend to throw it than when they intend to drop it carefully through a narrow tube (Claxton, Keen, & McCarty, 2003). Around this time, too, infants begin to solve simple problems that involve reaching, such as searching for and finding a hidden toy.

Finally, the capacity to reach for and manipulate an object increases infants' attention to the way an adult reaches for and plays with that same object (Hauf, Aschersleben, & Prinz, 2007). As babies watch what others do, they broaden their understanding of others' behaviors and of the range of actions that can be performed on various objects, gradually incorporating those possibilities into their own object-related behaviors.

EARLY EXPERIENCE AND REACHING   Like other motor milestones, reaching is affected by early experience. In cultures where mothers carry their infants on their hips or in slings for most of the day, babies have rich opportunities to explore with their hands. Among the !Kung of Botswana, infants grasp their mothers' colorful, beaded necklaces to steady themselves while breastfeeding as the mother moves. While riding along, they also frequently swipe at and manipulate their mother's jewelry and other dangling objects (Konner, 1977). As a result, !Kung infants are advanced in development of reaching and grasping. And because babies of Mali and Uganda spend half or more of their day held in sitting or standing positions, which facilitate reaching, they, too, develop manual skills earlier than Western infants, who spend much of their day lying down (Adolph, Karasik, & Tamis-LeMonda, 2010).

Babies' visual surroundings are also influential. In a well-known study, institutionalized infants given a moderate amount of visual stimulation—at first, simple designs and, later, a mobile hung over their crib—reached for objects six weeks earlier than infants given nothing to look at. A third group given massive stimulation—patterned crib bumpers and mobiles at an early age—also reached sooner than unstimulated babies. But this heavy enrichment took its toll. These infants looked away and cried a great deal, and they were less advanced in reaching than the moderately stimulated group (White & Held, 1966). Recall from our discussion of brain development that more stimulation is not necessarily better. Trying to push infants beyond their readiness to handle stimulation can undermine the development of important motor skills.

Bowel and Bladder Control

More than any other aspect of early muscular development, parents wonder about bowel and bladder control. Two or three generations ago, many mothers tried to toilet train infants, but they only caught the baby's reflexive release of urine or a bowel movement at a convenient moment.

Toilet training is best delayed until the months following the second birthday, when children can consistently identify the signals from a full bladder or rectum and wait for the right place to open these muscles—physiological developments essential for the child to cooperate with training. A toddler who stays dry for several hours at a time, stops playing during urination or a bowel movement, and is bothered by a wet or full diaper shows signs of readiness. Children whose parents postpone intensive training until the beginning or middle of the third year are generally fully trained within four months. Starting before 27 months simply prolongs the process (Choby & George, 2008; Brazelton & Sparrow, 2004).

Effective training techniques include establishing regular toileting routines (for example, after getting up, after eating, before going to bed), using gentle encouragement, and praising children for their efforts (Christophersen & Mortweet, 2003). As we will see in Chapter 7, pressuring too much in this area, as in others, can negatively affect the toddler's emotional well-being.

ASK YOURSELF

◆ REVIEW Cite evidence that motor development is a joint product of biological, psychological, and environmental factors.

◆ APPLY List everyday experiences that support mastery of reaching, grasping, sitting, and crawling. Why should caregivers place young infants in a variety of waking-time body positions?

◆ CONNECT Provide several examples of how motor development influences infants' and toddlers' social experiences. How do social experiences, in turn, influence motor development?

◆ REFLECT Do you favor early, systematic training of infants in motor skills such as crawling, walking, running, hopping, and stair climbing? Why or why not?

Perceptual Development

In Chapter 4, you learned that the senses of touch, taste, smell, and hearing—but not vision—are remarkably well-developed at birth. Now let's turn to a related question: How does perception change over the first year? Our discussion will address hearing and vision, the focus of almost all research. Unfortunately, little evidence exists on how touch, taste, and smell develop after birth. Also, in Chapter 4 we used the word *sensation* to talk about these capacities. It suggests a fairly passive process—what the baby's receptors detect when exposed to stimulation. Now we use the word *perception,* which is active: When we perceive, we organize and interpret what we see.

As we review the perceptual achievements of infancy, you may find it hard to tell where perception leaves off and thinking begins. The research we are about to discuss provides an excellent bridge to the topic of Chapter 6—cognitive development during the first two years.

Hearing

On Timmy's first birthday, Vanessa bought several CDs of nursery songs, and she turned one on each afternoon at naptime. Soon Timmy let her know his favorite tune. If she put on "Twinkle, Twinkle," he stood up in his crib and whimpered until she replaced it with "Jack and Jill." Timmy's behavior illustrates the greatest change in hearing over the first year of life: Babies start to organize sounds into complex patterns.

Between 4 and 7 months, infants display a sense of musical phrasing. They prefer Mozart minuets with pauses between phrases to those with awkward breaks (Krumhansl & Jusczyk, 1990). Around 6 to 7 months, they can distinguish musical tunes on the basis of variations in rhythmic patterns, including beat structure (duple or triple) and accent structure (emphasis on the first note of every beat unit or at other positions) (Hannon & Johnson, 2004). And by the end of the first year, infants recognize the same melody when it is played in different keys (Trehub, 2001). As we will see next, 6- to 12-month-olds make comparable discriminations in human speech: They readily detect sound regularities that will facilitate later language learning.

SPEECH PERCEPTION   Recall from Chapter 4 that newborns can distinguish nearly all sounds in human languages and that they prefer listening to speech over nonspeech sounds and to their native tongue rather than a rhythmically distinct foreign language. As infants listen to people talking, they learn to focus on meaningful sound variations. ERP brain-wave recordings reveal that around 5 months, infants become sensitive to syllable stress patterns in their own language (Weber et al., 2004). Between 6 and 8 months, they start to "screen out" sounds not

■ This baby already responds to sound regularities in his mother's speech. As he listens, he becomes sensitive to syllable stress patterns and will eventually screen out sounds not used in his own language. ■

used in their own language (Anderson, Morgan, & White, 2003; Polka & Werker, 1994). As the Biology and Environment box on the following page explains, this increased responsiveness to native-language sounds is part of a general "tuning" process in the second half of the first year—a possible sensitive period in which babies acquire a range of perceptual skills for picking up socially important information.

Soon after, infants focus on larger speech units that are critical to figuring out meaning. They recognize familiar words in spoken passages and listen longer to speech with clear clause and phrase boundaries (Johnson & Seidl, 2008; Jusczyk & Hohne, 1997; Soderstrom et al., 2003). Around 7 to 9 months, infants extend this sensitivity to speech structure to individual words: They begin to divide the speech stream into wordlike units (Jusczyk, 2002; Saffran, Werker, & Werner, 2006).

ANALYZING THE SPEECH STREAM   How do infants make such rapid progress in perceiving the structure of speech? Research reveals that they have an impressive **statistical learning capacity.** By analyzing the speech stream for patterns—repeatedly occurring sequences of sounds—they acquire a stock of speech structures for which they will later learn meanings, long before they start to talk around age 12 months.

For example, when presented with controlled sequences of nonsense syllables, babies listened for statistical regularities: They locate words by discriminating syllables that often occur together (indicating that they belong to the same word) from syllables that seldom occur together (indicating a word boundary). Consider the English word sequence *pretty#baby.* After listening to the speech stream for just one minute (about 60 words), babies can distinguish a word-internal syllable pair *(pretty)* from a word-external syllable pair *(ty#ba).* They prefer to listen to new speech that preserves the word-internal pattern (Saffran, Aslin, & Newport, 1996; Saffran & Thiessen, 2003).

Once infants locate words, they focus on the words and, around 7 to 8 months, detect regular syllable-stress patterns—for example, in English and Dutch, that the onset of a strong syllable (*hap*-py, *rab*-bit) often signals a new word (Swingley, 2005; Thiessen & Saffran, 2007). By 10 months, infants can detect words that start with weak syllables, such as "sur*prise,*" by listening for sound regularities before and after the words (Jusczyk, 2001; Kooijman, Hagoort, & Cutler, 2009).

Infants also attend to regularities in word sequences. In a study using nonsense words, 7-month-olds distinguished the ABA structure of "ga ti ga" and "li na li" from the ABB structure of "wo fe fe" and "ta la la" (Marcus et al., 1999). They seemed to detect simple word-order rules—a capacity that may eventually help them figure out basic grammar. After extracting these rules, babies generalize them to nonspeech sounds. Seven-month-olds who were exposed to regularities in sequences of nonsense words could identify similar patterns in strings of musical tones and animal sounds. But when presented alone, these stimuli yielded no rule learning (Marcus, Fernandes, & Johnson, 2007). Analyzing speech seems to help babies structure other aspects of their auditory world.

Clearly, babies have a powerful ability to extract patterns from complex, continuous speech. As a result, they acquire a great deal of language-specific knowledge—including a stock of words and other speech structures for which they will later learn meanings—before they start to talk around 12 months of age. As we will see in Chapter 6, adults' style of communicating with infants greatly facilitates analysis of the structure of speech.

Vision

For exploring the environment, humans depend on vision more than any other sense. Although at first a baby's visual world is fragmented, it undergoes extraordinary changes during the first 7 to 8 months of life.

Visual development is supported by rapid maturation of the eye and visual centers in the cerebral cortex. Recall from Chapter 4 that the newborn baby focuses and perceives color poorly. Around 2 months, infants can focus on objects about as well as adults, and their color vision is adultlike by 4 months (Kellman & Arterberry, 2006). Visual acuity (fineness of discrimination) increases steadily throughout the first year, reaching a near-adult level of about

BIOLOGY AND ENVIRONMENT

"Tuning in" to Familiar Speech, Faces, and Music: A Sensitive Period for Culture-Specific Learning

To share experiences with members of their family and community, babies must become skilled at making perceptual discriminations that are meaningful in their culture. As we have seen, at first babies are sensitive to virtually all speech sounds but, around 6 months, they narrow their focus, limiting the distinctions they make to the language they hear and will soon learn.

The ability to perceive faces shows a similar path of development. After habituating to one member of each pair of faces in Figure 5.15, 6-month-olds were shown the familiar and novel faces side by side. For both pairs, they recovered to (looked longer at) the novel face,

indicating that they could discriminate the individual faces of both humans and monkeys equally well (Pascalis, de Haan, & Nelson, 2002). But at 9 months, infants no longer showed a novelty preference when viewing the monkey pair. Like adults, they could distinguish only the human faces.

This developmental trend appears again in musical rhythm perception. Western adults are accustomed to the even-beat pattern of Western music—repetition of the same rhythmic structure in every measure of a tune—and easily notice rhythmic changes that disrupt this familiar beat. But present them with music that does not follow this typical Western rhythmic form—Baltic folk tunes, for example—and they fail to pick up on rhythmic-pattern deviations. Six-month-olds, however, can detect such disruptions in both Western and non-Western melodies. But by 12 months, after added exposure to Western music, babies

are no longer aware of deviations in foreign musical rhythms, although their sensitivity to Western rhythmic structure remains unchanged (Hannon & Trehub, 2005b).

Several weeks of regular interaction with a foreign-language speaker and of daily opportunities to listen to non-Western music fully restore 12-month-olds' sensitivity to wide-ranging speech sounds and music rhythms (Hannon & Trehub, 2005a; Kuhl, Tsao, & Liu, 2003). Adults given similar extensive experiences, by contrast, show little improvement in perceptual sensitivity.

Taken together, these findings suggest a heightened capacity—or sensitive period—in the second half of the first year, when babies are biologically prepared to "zero in" on socially meaningful perceptual distinctions. Notice how, between 6 and 12 months, learning is especially rapid across several domains (speech, faces, and music) and is easily modified by experience. This suggests a broad neurological change—perhaps a special time of experience-expectant brain growth (see page 172) in which babies analyze everyday stimulation of all kinds similarly, in ways that prepare them to participate in their cultural community.

FIGURE 5.15

Discrimination of human and monkey faces. Which of these pairs is easiest for you to tell apart? After habituating to one of the photos in each pair, infants were shown the familiar and the novel face side-by-side. For both pairs, 6-month-olds recovered to (looked longer at) the novel face, indicating that they could discriminate human and monkey faces equally well. By 12 months, babies lost their ability to distinguish the monkey faces. Like adults, they showed a novelty preference only to human stimuli. *(From O. Pascalis et al., 2002, "Is Face Processing Species-Specific During the First Year of Life?" Science, 296, p. 1322. Reprinted with permission from AAAS.)*

20/20 by 6 months (Slater, 2001). Scanning the environment and tracking moving objects also improve over the first half-year as infants see more clearly and better control their eye movements. In addition, as young infants build an organized perceptual world, they scan more thoroughly and systematically, strategically picking up important information (Johnson, Slemmer, & Amso, 2004; von Hofsten & Rosander, 1998). Consequently, scanning enhances perception, and—in bidirectional fashion—perception also enhances scanning.

As babies explore their visual field, they figure out the characteristics of objects and how they are arranged in space. To understand how they do so, let's examine the development of three aspects of vision: depth, pattern, and object perception.

© MARK RICHARDS/PHOTOEDIT

FIGURE 5.16

The visual cliff. Plexiglas covers the deep and shallow sides. By refusing to cross the deep side and showing a preference for the shallow side, this infant demonstrates the ability to perceive depth.

DEPTH PERCEPTION   *Depth perception* is the ability to judge the distance of objects from one another and from ourselves. It is important for understanding the layout of the environment and for guiding motor activity.

Figure 5.16 shows the well-known *visual cliff,* designed by Eleanor Gibson and Richard Walk (1960) and used in the earliest studies of depth perception. It consists of a Plexiglas-covered table with a platform at the center, a "shallow" side with a checkerboard pattern just under the glass, and a "deep" side with a checkerboard several feet below the glass. The researchers found that crawling babies readily crossed the shallow side, but most avoided the deep side. They concluded that around the time infants crawl, most distinguish deep from shallow surfaces and avoid drop-offs.

The visual cliff shows that crawling and avoidance of drop-offs are linked, but not how they are related or when depth perception first appears. Recent research has looked at babies' ability to detect specific depth cues, using methods that do not require that they crawl.

Emergence of Depth Perception. How do we know when an object is near rather than far away? **TAKE A MOMENT...** Try these exercises to find out. Pick up a small object (such as your cup) and move it toward and away from your face. Did its image grow larger as it approached and smaller as it receded? Next time you take a bike or car ride, notice that nearby objects move past your field of vision more quickly than those far away.

Motion is the first depth cue to which infants are sensitive. Babies 3 to 4 weeks old blink their eyes defensively when an object moves toward their face as though it is going to hit (Nánez & Yonas, 1994). As they are carried about and people and things turn and move before their eyes, infants learn more about depth. By the time they are 3 months old, motion has helped them figure out that objects are not flat but three-dimensional (Arterberry, Craton, & Yonas, 1993).

Binocular depth cues arise because our two eyes have slightly different views of the visual field. The brain blends these two images, resulting in perception of depth. Research in which two overlapping images are projected before the baby, who wears special goggles to ensure that each eye receives only one image, reveals that sensitivity to binocular cues emerges between 2 and 3 months and improves rapidly over the first year (Birch, 1993; Brown & Miracle, 2003). Infants soon make use of binocular cues in their reaching, adjusting arm and hand movements to match the distance of objects from the eyes.

Finally, between 5 and 7 months, infants display sensitivity to *pictorial depth cues*—the ones artists often use to make a painting look three-dimensional. Examples include receding lines that create the illusion of perspective, changes in texture (nearby textures are more detailed than faraway ones), overlapping objects (an object partially hidden by another object is perceived to be more distant), height-in-the-picture-plane (objects closer to the horizon appear farther away), and shadows cast on surfaces (indicating a separation in space between the object and the surface) (Arterberry, 2008; Sen, Yonas, & Knill, 2001; Yonas, Elieff, & Arterberry, 2002; Yonas & Granrud, 2006).

Why does perception of depth cues emerge in the order just described? Researchers speculate that motor development is involved. For example, control of the head during the early weeks of life may help babies notice motion and binocular cues. Around 5 to 6 months, the ability to turn, poke, and feel the surface of objects may promote perception of pictorial cues (Bushnell & Boudreau, 1993). And as we will see next, one aspect of motor progress—independent movement—plays a vital role in refinement of depth perception.

Independent Movement and Depth Perception. At 6 months, Timmy started crawling. "He's fearless!" exclaimed Vanessa. "If I put him down in the middle of the bed, he crawls right over the edge. The same thing happens by the stairs." Will Timmy become wary of the side of the bed and the staircase as he becomes a more experienced crawler? Research suggests that he will. Infants with more crawling experience (regardless of when they started to crawl) are far more likely to refuse to cross the deep side of the visual cliff (Campos et al., 2000).

© ELLEN B. SENISI PHOTOGRAPHY

■ Increased experience at crawling will help this 7-month-old gain in three-dimensional understanding, including how to avoid falling and where objects are in relation to herself and to other objects. ■

From extensive everyday experience, babies gradually figure out how to use depth cues to detect the danger of falling. But because the loss of body control that leads to falling differs greatly for each body position, babies must undergo this learning separately for each posture. In one study, 9-month-olds, who were experienced sitters but novice crawlers, were placed on the edge of a shallow drop-off that could be widened (Adolph, 2002, 2008). While in the familiar sitting position, infants avoided leaning out for an attractive toy at distances likely to result in falling. But in the unfamiliar crawling position, they headed over the edge, even when the distance was extremely wide! And newly walking babies, while avoiding sharp drop-offs, careen down slopes and over uneven surfaces without making the necessary postural adjustments, even when their mothers discourage them from proceeding! Thus, they fall frequently (Adolph et al., 2008; Joh & Adolph, 2006). As infants discover how to avoid falling in different postures and situations, their understanding of depth expands.

Crawling experience promotes other aspects of three-dimensional understanding. For example, seasoned crawlers are better than their inexperienced agemates at remembering object locations and finding hidden objects (Bai & Bertenthal, 1992; Campos et al., 2000). Why does crawling make such a difference? **TAKE A MOMENT...** Compare your own experience of the environment when you are driven from one place to another with what you experience when you walk or drive yourself. When you move on your own, you are much more aware of landmarks and routes of travel, and you take more careful note of what things look like from different points of view. The same is true for infants. In fact, crawling promotes a new level of brain organization, as indicated by more organized EEG brain-wave activity in the cerebral cortex (Bell & Fox, 1996). Perhaps crawling strengthens certain neural connections, especially those involved in vision and understanding of space. As the Social Issues: Education box on page 194 reveals, the link between independent movement and spatial knowledge is also evident in a population with very different perceptual experience: infants with severe visual impairments.

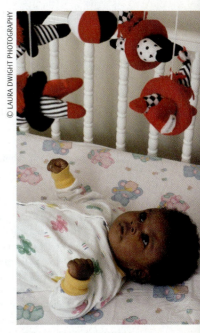

■ This 2-month-old's visual acuity has improved greatly since birth. She detects the contrast in complex patterns and spends more time looking at them. ■

PATTERN PERCEPTION Even newborns prefer to look at patterned rather than plain stimuli—for example, a drawing of the human face or one with scrambled facial features rather than a black-and-white oval (Fantz, 1961). As they get older, infants prefer more complex patterns. For example, 3-week-olds look longest at black-and-white checkerboards with a few large squares, whereas 8- and 14-week-olds prefer those with many squares (Brennan, Ames, & Moore, 1966).

A general principle, called **contrast sensitivity,** explains early pattern preferences (Banks & Ginsburg, 1985). *Contrast* refers to the difference in the amount of light between adjacent regions in a pattern. If babies are *sensitive to* (can detect) the contrast in two or more patterns, they prefer the one with more contrast. To understand this idea, look at the checkerboards in the top row of Figure 5.17. To us, the one with many small squares has more contrasting elements. Now look at the bottom row, which shows how these checkerboards appear to infants in the first few weeks of life. Because of their poor vision, very young babies cannot resolve the small features in more complex patterns, so they prefer to look at the large, bold checkerboard. Around 2 months, when detection of fine-grained detail has improved, infants become sensitive to the contrast in complex patterns and spend more time looking at them (Gwiazda & Birch, 2001).

Bold checkerboard   Complex checkerboard

Appearance of checkerboards to very young infants

FIGURE 5.17

The way two checkerboards differing in complexity look to infants in the first few weeks of life. Because of their poor vision, very young infants cannot resolve the fine detail in the *complex checkerboard.* It appears blurred, like a gray field. The large, *bold checkerboard* appears to have more contrast, so babies prefer to look at it. *(Adapted from M. S. Banks & P. Salapatek, 1983, "Infant Visual Perception," in M. M. Haith & J. J. Campos (Eds.),* Handbook of Child Psychology: Vol. 2. Infancy and Developmental Psychobiology *[4th ed.], New York: John Wiley & Sons, p. 504. Reprinted with permission from John Wiley & Sons, Inc.)*

SOCIAL ISSUES: EDUCATION

Development of Infants with Severe Visual Impairments

Research on infants who can see little or nothing at all dramatically illustrates the interdependence of vision, motor exploration, social interaction, and understanding of the world. In a longitudinal study, infants with a visual acuity of 20/800 or worse—that is, they had only dim light perception or were blind—were followed through the preschool years. Compared to agemates with less severe visual impairments, they showed serious delays in all aspects of development. Motor and cognitive functioning suffered the most. With age, performance in both domains became increasingly distant from that of other children (Hatton et al., 1997).

What explains these profound developmental delays? Minimal or absent vision can alter the child's experiences in at least two crucial, interrelated ways.

Impact on Motor Exploration and Spatial Understanding

Infants with severe visual impairments attain gross- and fine-motor milestones many months later than their sighted counterparts (Levtzion-Korach et al., 2000). For example, on average, blind infants do not reach for and manipulate objects until 12 months, crawl until 13 months, or walk until 19 months (compare these averages to the norms in Table 5.2 on page 184). Why is this so?

Infants with severe visual impairments must rely on sound to identify the whereabouts of objects. But sound does not function as a precise clue to object location until much later than vision—around the middle of the first year (Litovsky & Ashmead, 1997). And because infants who cannot see have difficulty engaging their caregivers, adults may not provide them with rich, early exposure to sounding objects. As a result, the baby comes to understand relatively late that there is a world of interesting objects to explore.

Until "reaching on sound" is achieved, infants with severe visual impairments are not motivated to move independently. Because of their own uncertainty and their parents' protectiveness and restraint to prevent injury, blind infants are typically tentative in their movements. These factors delay motor development further.

Motor and cognitive development are closely linked, especially for infants with little or no vision. These babies build an understanding of the location and arrangement of objects in space only after reaching and crawling (Bigelow, 1992). Inability to imitate the motor actions of others presents additional challenges as these children get older, contributing to declines in motor and cognitive progress relative to peers with better vision (Hatton et al., 1997).

Impact on the Caregiver–Infant Relationship

Infants who see poorly have great difficulty evoking stimulating caregiver interaction. They cannot make eye contact, imitate, or pick up nonverbal social cues. Their emotional expressions are muted; for example, their smile is fleeting and unpredictable. And because they cannot gaze in the same direction as a partner, they are greatly delayed in establishing a shared focus of attention on objects as the basis for play (Bigelow, 2003). Consequently, these infants may receive little adult attention and other stimulation vital for all aspects of development.

When a visually impaired child does not learn how to participate in social interaction during infancy, communication is compromised in early childhood. In an observational study of blind children enrolled in preschools with sighted agemates, the blind children seldom initiated contact with peers and teachers. When they did interact, they had trouble interpreting the meaning of others' reactions and responding appropriately (Preisler, 1991, 1993).

Interventions

Parents, teachers, and caregivers can help infants with minimal vision overcome early

COURTESY OF PERKINS SCHOOL FOR THE BLIND, WATERTOWN, MA

■ This child has no light perception as a result of an optic nerve disorder. His caregiver encourages manipulative play with objects, which enhances awareness of his physical and social surroundings and promotes both motor and cognitive development. ■

developmental delays through stimulating, responsive interaction. Until a close emotional bond with an adult is forged, babies with visual impairments cannot establish vital links with their environments.

Techniques that help infants become aware of their physical and social surroundings include heightened sensory input through combining sound and touch (holding, touching, or bringing the baby's hands to the adult's face while talking or singing), engaging in many repetitions, and consistently reinforcing the infant's efforts to make contact. Manipulative play with objects that make sounds is also vital.

Finally, rich language stimulation can compensate for visual loss (Conti-Ramsden & Pérez-Pereira, 1999). It gives young children a ready means of finding out about objects, events, and behaviors they cannot see. Once language emerges, many children with limited or no vision show impressive rebounds. Some acquire a unique capacity for abstract thinking, and most master social and practical skills that enable them to lead productive, independent lives (Warren, 1994).

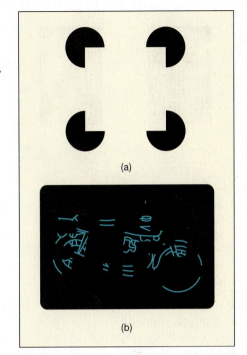

FIGURE 5.18

Subjective boundaries in visual patterns. (a) Do you perceive a square in the middle of the figure? By 4 months of age, infants do, too. (b) What does the image, missing two-thirds of its outline, look like to you? By 12 months, infants detect a motorcycle. After habituating to the incomplete motorcycle image, they were shown an intact motorcycle figure paired with a novel form. Twelve-month-olds recovered to (looked longer at) the novel figure, indicating that they recognized the motorcycle pattern on the basis of very little visual information. *(Adapted from Ghim, 1990; Rose, Jankowski, & Senior, 1997.)*

Combining Pattern Elements. In the early weeks of life, infants respond to the separate parts of a pattern. They stare at single high-contrast features, generally on the edges, and have difficulty shifting their gaze away toward other interesting stimuli (Hunnius & Geuze, 2004a, 2004b). At 2 to 3 months, when scanning ability and contrast sensitivity improve, infants thoroughly explore a pattern's internal features, pausing briefly to look at each part (Bronson, 1994).

Once babies can take in all aspects of a pattern, they integrate the parts into a unified whole. Around 4 months, babies are so good at detecting pattern organization that they perceive subjective boundaries that are not really present. For example, they perceive a square in the center of Figure 5.18a, just as you do (Ghim, 1990). And like adults, 3- to 4-month-olds engage in *boundary extension:* When re-exposed to a photo of a natural scene, they remember it as extending beyond its original boundaries. The visual system seems to interpret the photographed scene like a view through a window, which is understood to extend beyond the edges of the window (Quinn & Intraub, 2007).

Older infants carry this sensitivity to subjective form further. For example, 9-month-olds look much longer at an organized series of moving lights that resembles a human being walking than at an upside-down or scrambled version. Three- to 5-month-olds, though able to discriminate the three patterns, do not prefer the walking-human display (Proffitt & Bertenthal, 1990). At 12 months, infants can detect familiar objects represented by incomplete drawings, even when as much as two-thirds of the drawing is missing (see Figure 5.18b) (Rose, Jankowski, & Senior, 1997). As these findings reveal, infants' increasing knowledge of objects and actions supports pattern perception.

Face Perception. Infants' tendency to search for structure in a patterned stimulus applies to face perception. Newborns prefer to look at photos and simplified drawings of faces with features arranged naturally (upright) rather than unnaturally (upside down or sideways) (see Figure 5.19a and b on page 196) (Cassia, Turati, & Simion, 2004; Mondloch et al., 1999). They also track a facelike pattern moving across their visual field farther than they track other stimuli (Johnson, 1999). And although they rely more on outer features (hairline and chin) than inner features to distinguish real faces, newborns prefer photos of faces with eyes open and a direct gaze (Farroni et al., 2002; Turati et al., 2006). Yet another amazing capacity is their tendency to look longer at faces judged by adults as attractive—a preference that may be the origin of the widespread social bias favoring physically attractive people (Slater et al., 2000).

Some researchers claim that these behaviors reflect a built-in capacity to orient toward members of one's own species, just as many newborn animals do (Johnson, 2001a; Slater & Quinn, 2001). In support of this view, the upright face preference occurs only when newborns view stimuli in the periphery of their visual field—an area of the retina governed by primitive brain centers (Cassia, Simion, & Umiltá, 2001). Others assert that newborns simply prefer any stimulus in which the most salient elements are arranged horizontally in the upper part of a pattern—like the "eyes" in Figure 5.19b. Indeed, newborns do prefer patterns with these characteristics over other arrangements (Cassia, Turati, & Simion, 2004; Simion et al., 2001). But a bias favoring the facial pattern possibly promotes such preferences. Still other researchers argue that newborns are exposed to faces more often than to other stimuli—early experiences that could quickly "wire" the brain to detect faces and prefer attractive ones (Nelson, 2001).

Although newborns respond to facelike structures, they cannot discriminate a complex facial pattern from other, equally complex patterns (see Figure 5.19c). But from repeated exposures to their mother's face, they quickly learn to prefer her face to that of an unfamiliar woman, although they mostly attend to its broad outlines.

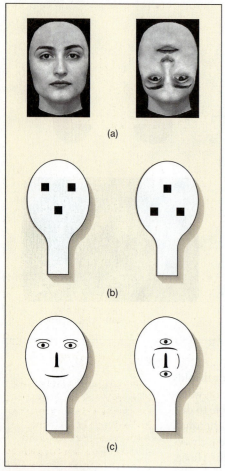

FIGURE 5.19

Early face perception.
Newborns prefer to look at the photo of a face (a) and the simple pattern resembling a face (b) over the upside-down versions. (c) When the complex drawing of a face on the left and the equally complex, scrambled version on the right are moved across newborns' visual field, they follow the face longer. But if the two stimuli are stationary, infants show no preference for the face until around 2 months of age. *(From Cassia, Turati, & Simion, 2004; Johnson, 1999; Mondloch et al., 1999.)*

Around 2 months, when they can combine pattern elements into an organized whole, babies prefer a complex drawing of the human face to other equally complex stimulus arrangements (Dannemiller & Stephens, 1988). And they clearly prefer their mother's detailed facial features to those of another woman (Bartrip, Morton, & de Schonen, 2001).

Around 3 months, infants readily make fine distinctions among the features of different faces—for example, between photographs of two strangers, even when the faces are moderately similar (Farroni et al., 2007). At 5 months—and strengthening over the second half-year—infants perceive emotional expressions as meaningful wholes. They treat positive faces (happy and surprised) as different from negative ones (sad and fearful) (Bornstein & Arterberry, 2003; Ludemann, 1991).

Experience influences face processing, leading babies to form group biases at a tender age. As early as 3 months, infants prefer and more easily discriminate among female faces than among male faces, probably because they typically spend much more time with female adults (Quinn et al., 2002). Furthermore, 3- to 6-month-olds exposed mostly to members of their own race prefer to look at the faces of members of that race and more easily detect differences among those faces—perceptual narrowing that increases in the next few months (Bar-Haim et al., 2006; Kelly et al., 2007a, 2007b). This own-race preference is absent in babies who have frequent contact with members of other races, and it can be reversed through exposure to racial diversity (Sangrigoli et al., 2005).

Clearly, extensive face-to-face interaction with caregivers contributes to infants' refinement of face perception. And as babies recognize and respond to the expressive behavior of others, face perception supports their earliest social relationships.

Object Perception

Research on pattern perception involves only two-dimensional stimuli, but our environment is made up of stable, three-dimensional objects. Do young infants perceive a world of independently existing objects—knowledge essential for distinguishing among the self, other people, and things?

SIZE AND SHAPE CONSTANCY

As we move around the environment, the images that objects cast on our retina constantly change in size and shape. To perceive objects as stable and unchanging, we must translate these varying retinal images into a single representation.

Size constancy—perception of an object's size as the same, despite changes in the size of its retinal image—is evident in the first week of life. To test for it, researchers habituated infants to a small cube at varying distances from the eye, in an effort to desensitize them to changes in the cube's retinal image size and direct their attention to the object's actual size. When the small cube was presented together with a new, large cube—but at different distances so that they cast retinal images of the same size—all babies recovered to (looked longer at) the novel large cube, indicating that they distinguished objects on the basis of actual size, not retinal image size (Slater, 2001).

Perception of an object's shape as stable, despite changes in the shape projected on the retina, is called **shape constancy.** Habituation research reveals that it, too, is present within the first week of life, long before babies can actively rotate objects with their hands and view them from different angles (Slater & Johnson, 1999).

In sum, both size and shape constancy seem to be built-in capacities that assist babies in detecting a coherent world of objects. Yet they provide only a partial picture of young infants' object perception.

PERCEPTION OF OBJECT IDENTITY

At first, babies rely heavily on motion and spatial arrangement to identify objects (Jusczyk et al., 1999; Spelke & Hermer, 1996). When two objects are touching and either move in unison or stand still, babies younger than 4 months cannot distinguish them. Infants, of course, are fascinated by moving objects. As they observe objects' motions, they pick up additional information about objects' boundaries, such as shape, color, and texture.

For example, as Figure 5.20 reveals, around 2 months, babies realize that a moving rod whose center is hidden behind a box is a complete rod rather than two rod pieces. Motion, a patterned background, alignment of the top and bottom of the rod, and a small box (so most of the rod is visible) are necessary for young infants to infer object unity. Because their ability to scan for relevant information is still immature, infants need all these cues to heighten the distinction between the objects in the display (Amso & Johnson, 2006; Johnson, 2009).

As infants become familiar with many types of objects, they rely more on object features, such as shape and surface pattern, and less on motion (Cohen & Cashon, 2001). Babies as young as 4½ months can distinguish two touching objects on the basis of these features in very simple, easy-to-process situations. And prior visual exposure to one of the objects enhances the ability of 4½-month-olds to discern the boundary between two touching objects—a finding that highlights the role of experience (Dueker, Modi, & Needham, 2003; Needham, 2001).

In everyday life, objects frequently move in and out of sight, so infants must keep track of their disappearance and reappearance to perceive their identity. Habituation research, in which a ball moves back and forth behind a screen, reveals that at age 4 months, infants first perceive the ball's path as continuous (Johnson et al., 2003). Between 4 and 5 months, infants can monitor more intricate paths of objects. As indicated by their future-oriented eye movements (looking ahead to where they expect an object to reappear from behind a barrier), 5-month-olds even keep track of an object that travels on a curvilinear course at varying speeds (Rosander & von Hofsten, 2004). From 4 to 11 months, infants increasingly rely on featural information to detect the identity of an object traveling behind a screen—at first, form (size and shape) and later in the first year, surface features (pattern and then color) (Wilcox & Woods, 2009). Again, experience—in particular, physically manipulating the object—enhances older infants' attention to its surface features.

In sum, perception of object identity is mastered gradually over the first year. We will consider a related attainment—infants' understanding of object permanence, awareness that an object still exists when hidden—in Chapter 6.

Intermodal Perception

Our world provides rich, continuous *intermodal stimulation*—simultaneous input from more than one *modality,* or sensory system. In **intermodal perception,** we make sense of these running streams of light, sound, tactile, odor, and taste information, perceiving them as integrated wholes. We know, for example, that an object's shape is the same whether we see it or touch it, that lip movements are closely coordinated with the sound of a voice, and that dropping a rigid object on a hard surface will cause a sharp, banging sound.

Recall that newborns turn in the general direction of a sound and reach for objects in a primitive way. These behaviors suggest that infants expect sight, sound, and touch to go together. Research reveals that babies perceive input from different sensory systems in a unified way by detecting **amodal sensory properties,** information that is not specific to a single modality but that overlaps two or more sensory systems, such as rate, rhythm, duration, intensity, temporal synchrony (for vision and hearing), and texture and shape (for vision and touch). Consider the sight and sound of a bouncing ball or the face and voice of a speaking person. In each event, visual and auditory information are conveyed simultaneously and with the same rate, rhythm, duration, and intensity.

Even newborns are impressive perceivers of amodal properties. After touching an object (such as a cylinder) placed in their palms, they recognize it visually, distinguishing it from a

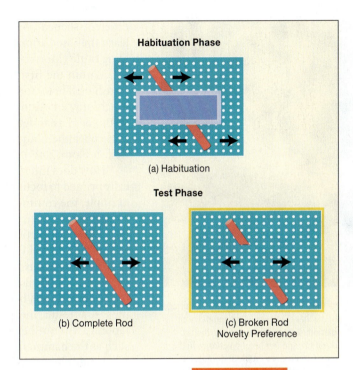

Habituation Phase

(a) Habituation

Test Phase

(b) Complete Rod

(c) Broken Rod
Novelty Preference

FIGURE 5.20

Testing infants' ability to perceive object unity. (a) Infants were habituated to a rod moving back and forth behind a box against a textured background. Next, they were shown two test displays in alternation: (b) a complete rod and (c) a broken rod with a gap corresponding to the location of the box. Each stimulus was moved back and forth against the textured background, in the same way as the habituation stimulus. Infants 2 months of age and older recovered to (looked longer at) the broken rod than the complete rod. Their novelty preference suggests that they perceive the rod behind the box in the first display as a single unit. *(Adapted from Johnson, 1997.)*

■ This 10-month-old exploring the surface of a guitar readily picks up amodal information, such as common rate, rhythm, duration, and temporal synchrony, in the visual appearance and sounds of its moving strings. Detection of amodal properties seems to provide the basis for more specific intermodal matches—for example, between the shape of a guitar and its verbal label. ■

LOOK AND LISTEN

While watching a parent and infant playing, list instances of parental intermodal stimulation and communication. What is the baby likely learning about people, objects, or language from each intermodal experience?

different-shaped object (Sann & Streri, 2007). And they require just one exposure to learn the association between the sight and sound of a toy, such as a rhythmically jangling rattle (Morrongiello, Fenwick, & Chance, 1998).

Within the first half-year, infants master a remarkable range of intermodal relationships. Three- to 4-month-olds can match faces with voices on the basis of lip–voice synchrony, emotional expression, and even age and gender of the speaker (Bahrick, Netto, & Hernandez-Reif, 1998). Between 4 and 6 months, infants can perceive and remember the unique face–voice pairings of unfamiliar adults (Bahrick, Hernandez-Reif, & Flom, 2005).

How does intermodal perception develop so quickly? Young infants seem biologically primed to focus on amodal information. Their detection of amodal relations—for example, the common tempo and rhythm in sights and sounds—precedes and seems to provide the basis for detecting more specific intermodal matches, such as the relation between a particular person's face and the sound of her voice or between an object and its verbal label (Bahrick, Hernandez-Reif, & Flom, 2005).

Intermodal sensitivity is crucial for perceptual development. In the first few months, when much stimulation is unfamiliar and confusing, it enables babies to notice meaningful correlations between sensory inputs and rapidly make sense of their surroundings. As a result, inexperienced perceivers notice a unitary event, such as a hammer's tapping, without being distracted by momentarily irrelevant aspects of the situation, such as the hammer's color or orientation (Bahrick, Lickliter, & Flom, 2004).

In addition to easing perception of the physical world, intermodal perception facilitates processing of the social world. For example, as 3- to 4-month-olds gaze at an adult's face, they initially require both vocal and visual input to distinguish positive from negative emotional expressions (Walker-Andrews, 1997). Only later do infants discriminate positive from negative emotion in each sensory modality—first in voices (around 4 to 5 months), later (from 5 months on) in faces (Bahrick, Hernandez-Reif, & Flom, 2005).

Finally, because communication is often intermodal (simultaneously verbal, visual, and tactile), infants receive much support from other senses in detecting units of speech. When parents speak to infants, they often provide temporal synchrony between words, object motions, and touch—for example, saying "doll" while moving a doll and occasionally having the doll touch the infant. In doing so, caregivers greatly increase the chances that babies will remember the association between the word and the object (Gogate & Bahrick, 1998, 2001).

In sum, intermodal stimulation fosters all aspects of psychological development. When caregivers provide many concurrent sights, sounds, and touches, babies process more information and learn faster (Lickliter & Bahrick, 2000). Intermodal perception is yet another fundamental capacity that assists infants in their active efforts to build an orderly, predictable world.

Understanding Perceptual Development

Now that we have reviewed the development of infant perceptual capacities, how can we put together this diverse array of amazing achievements? Widely accepted answers come from the work of Eleanor and James Gibson. According to the Gibsons' **differentiation theory,** infants actively search for *invariant features* of the environment—those that remain stable—in a constantly changing perceptual world. In pattern perception, for example, young babies search for features that stand out and orient toward faces. Soon they explore internal features, noticing *stable relationships* among them. As a result, they detect patterns, such as complex designs and individual faces. Similarly, infants analyze the speech stream for regularities, detecting words, word-order sequences, and—within words—syllable-stress patterns. The development of intermodal perception also reflects this principle. Babies seek out invariant relationships—first, amodal properties, such as common rate and rhythm, in a voice and face, later more detailed associations, such as unique voice–face matches.

The Gibsons described their theory as *differentiation* (where *differentiate* means "analyze" or "break down") because over time the baby detects finer and finer invariant features among stimuli. In addition to pattern perception and intermodal perception, differentiation applies to depth and object perception: Recall how in each, sensitivity to motion precedes detection of fine-grained features. So one way of understanding perceptual development is to think of it as a built-in tendency to seek order and consistency—a capacity that becomes increasingly fine-tuned with age (Gibson, 1970; Gibson, 1979).

Acting on the environment is vital in perceptual differentiation. According to the Gibsons, perception is guided by the discovery of **affordances**—the action possibilities that a situation offers an organism with certain motor capabilities (Gibson, 2000, 2003). By moving about and exploring the environment, babies figure out which objects can be grasped, squeezed, bounced, or stroked and whether a surface is safe to

FIGURE 5.21

Acting on the environment plays a major role in perceptual differentiation. Crawling and walking change the way babies perceive a sloping surface. The newly crawling infant on the left plunges headlong down the slope. He has not yet learned that it affords the possibility of falling. The toddler on the right, who has been walking for more than a month, approaches the slope cautiously. Experience in trying to remain upright but frequently tumbling over has made him more aware of the consequences of his movements. He perceives the incline differently than he did at a younger age. *(Courtesy of Karen Adolph, New York University.)*

cross or presents the possibility of falling. Sensitivity to these affordances means that we spend far less time correcting ineffective actions than we would otherwise: It makes our actions future-oriented and largely successful rather than reactive and blundering.

To illustrate, recall how infants' changing capabilities for independent movement affect their perception. When babies crawl, and again when they walk, they gradually realize that a sloping surface *affords the possibility* of falling (see Figure 5.21). With added weeks of practicing each skill, they hesitate to crawl or walk down a risky incline. Experience in trying to keep their balance on various surfaces makes crawlers and walkers more aware of the consequences of their movements. Crawlers come to detect when surface slant places so much body weight on their arms that they will fall forward, and walkers come to sense when an incline shifts body weight so their legs and feet can no longer hold them upright. Learning is gradual and effortful because newly crawling and walking babies traverse many types of surfaces in their homes each day (Adolph, 2008; Adolph & Joh, 2009). As they experiment with balance and postural adjustments to accommodate each, they perceive surfaces in new ways that guide their movements. As a result, they act more competently.

As we conclude this chapter, it is only fair to note that some researchers believe that babies do more than make sense of experience by searching for invariant features and discovering affordances: They also *impose meaning on* what they perceive, constructing categories of objects and events in the surrounding environment. We have seen the glimmerings of this cognitive point of view in this chapter. For example, older babies *interpret* a familiar face as a source of pleasure and affection and a pattern of blinking lights as a moving human being. This cognitive perspective also offers insight into the achievements of infancy. In fact, many researchers combine these two positions, regarding infant development as proceeding from a perceptual to a cognitive emphasis over the first year of life.

ASK YOURSELF

◆ **REVIEW** Using examples, explain why intermodal stimulation is vital for infants' developing understanding of their physical and social worlds.

◆ **APPLY** After several weeks of crawling, Ben learned to avoid going headfirst down a steep incline. Now he has started to walk. Can his mother trust him not to try walking down a steep surface? Explain, using the concept of affordances.

◆ **CONNECT** According to differentiation theory, perceptual development reflects infants' active search for invariant features. Provide examples from research on hearing, pattern perception, and intermodal perception.

◆ **REFLECT** Are young infants more competent than you thought they were before you read this chapter? List the capacities that most surprised you.

Summary

Body Growth

Describe major changes in body size, proportions, muscle–fat makeup, and skeletal growth over the first two years.

- Height and weight gains are greater during the first two years than at any other time after birth. Body fat is laid down quickly during the first nine months, whereas muscle development is slow and gradual. Parts of the body grow at different rates, following the **cephalocaudal** and **proximodistal trends,** resulting in changing body proportions.

- **Skeletal age,** a measure based on the number of **epiphyses** and the extent to which they are fused, is the best way to estimate the child's overall physical maturity. At birth, the bones of an infant's skull are separated by six gaps, or **fontanels,** which permit the skull to expand as the brain grows.

Brain Development

Describe brain development during infancy and toddlerhood, current methods of measuring brain functioning, and appropriate stimulation to support the brain's potential.

- Early in development, the brain grows faster than any other organ of the body. Once **neurons** are in place, they rapidly form **synapses** and release **neurotransmitters,** which cross synapses to send messages to other neurons. During the peak period of synaptic growth in any brain area, many surrounding neurons die. Neurons that are seldom stimulated lose their synapses in a process called **synaptic pruning. Glial cells,** responsible for **myelination,** multiply rapidly through the second year, contributing to large gains in brain weight.

- Neurophysiological methods for measuring brain functioning include those that detect changes in electrical activity in the cerebral cortex (EEG, ERPs), neuroimaging techniques (PET, fMRI), and NIRS, which uses infrared light and is suitable for infants and young children.

- The **cerebral cortex** is the largest, most complex brain structure and the last to stop growing. Its regions develop in the general order in which various capacities emerge in the growing child, with the frontal lobes (which contain the **prefrontal cortex**) having the most extended period of development. The hemispheres of the cerebral cortex specialize, a process called **lateralization.** In the first few years of life, there is high **brain plasticity,** with many areas not yet committed to specific functions.

- Both heredity and early experience contribute to brain organization. Stimulation of the brain is essential during sensitive periods—periods in which the brain is developing most rapidly. Prolonged early deprivation, as in some babies reared in orphanages, can disrupt brain growth and interfere with the brain's capacity to manage stress, with long-term physical and psychological consequences.

- Appropriate early stimulation promotes **experience-expectant brain growth,** which depends on ordinary experiences. No evidence exists for a sensitive period in the first few years for **experience-dependent brain growth,** which relies on specific learning experiences. In fact, environments that overwhelm children with inappropriately advanced expectations can undermine the brain's potential.

How does the organization of sleep and wakefulness change over the first two years?

- Infants' changing arousal patterns are primarily affected by brain growth, but the social environment also plays a role. Periods of sleep and wakefulness become fewer but longer over the first two years, conforming to a night–day schedule. Parents in Western nations try to get their babies to sleep through the night much earlier than parents throughout most of the world, who are more likely to sleep with their babies.

© STEPHEN L. RAYMER/NATIONAL GEOGRAPHIC IMAGE COLLECTION

Influences on Early Physical Growth

Cite evidence indicating that heredity, nutrition, and parental affection and stimulation contribute to early physical growth.

- Twin and adoption studies reveal that heredity contributes to body size and rate of physical growth.

- Breast milk is ideally suited to infants' growth needs. Breastfeeding protects against disease and prevents malnutrition and infant death in poverty-stricken areas of the world.

- Most infants and toddlers can eat nutritious foods freely without risk of becoming overweight. However, the relationship between rapid weight gain in infancy and obesity at older ages is strengthening, perhaps because of a rise in unhealthy early feeding practices, in which babies are given high-fat foods and sugary drinks.

© KEITH BROFSKY/BLEND IMAGES/CORBIS

- **Marasmus** and **kwashiorkor** are dietary diseases caused by malnutrition that affect many children in developing countries and, if prolonged, can permanently stunt body growth and brain development. **Growth faltering** illustrates the importance of parental affection for normal physical growth.

Learning Capacities

Describe infant learning capacities, the conditions under which they occur, and the unique value of each.

- **Classical conditioning** is based on the infant's ability to associate events that usually occur together in the everyday world. Infants can be classically conditioned most easily when the pairing of an **unconditioned stimulus (UCS)** and a **conditioned stimulus (CS)** has survival value—for example, learning which stimuli regularly accompany feeding.

- In **operant conditioning,** infants act on their environment and their behavior is followed by either **reinforcers,** which increase the occurrence of a preceding behavior, or **punishment,** which either removes a desirable stimulus or presents an unpleasant one to decrease the occurrence of a response. In young infants, interesting sights and sounds and pleasurable caregiver interaction serve as effective reinforcers.

- **Habituation** and **recovery** reveal that at birth, babies are attracted to novelty. Novelty preference (recovery to a novel stimulus) assesses recent memory, whereas familiarity preference (recovery to the familiar stimulus) assesses remote memory.

- Newborns also have a primitive ability to imitate adults' facial expressions and gestures. **Imitation** is a powerful means of learning, which contributes to the parent–infant bond. Scientists have identified specialized cells called **mirror neurons** that underlie these capacities. However, whether newborn imitation is a voluntary capacity remains controversial.

Motor Development

Describe the general course of motor development during the first two years, along with factors that influence it.

- According to the **dynamic systems theory of motor development,** children acquire new motor skills by combining existing skills into increasingly complex systems of action. Each new skill is a joint product of central nervous system development, the body's movement possibilities, the child's goals, and environmental supports for the skill.

- Movement opportunities and a stimulating environment profoundly affect motor development, as shown by research on infants reared in deprived institutions. Cultural values and child-rearing customs contribute to the emergence and refinement of early motor skills.

- During the first year, infants perfect their reaching and grasping. The poorly coordinated **prereaching** of the newborn period drops out. Gradually, reaching becomes more flexible and accurate, and the clumsy **ulnar grasp** is transformed into a refined **pincer grasp** by the end of the first year.

- Young children are not physically and psychologically ready for toilet training until the months following their second birthday. Effective training techniques include regular toileting routines, gentle encouragement, and praise.

Perceptual Development

What changes in hearing and in depth, pattern, object, and intermodal perception take place during infancy?

- Infants organize sounds into increasingly complex patterns and, in the middle of the first year, become more sensitive to the sounds of their own language. They have an impressive **statistical learning capacity,** which enables them to detect speech regularities for which they will later learn meanings.

© REGINE MAHAUX/GETTY IMAGES/DIGITAL VISION

- Rapid maturation of the eye and visual centers in the cerebral cortex supports the development of focusing, color discrimination, and visual acuity during the first few months. The ability to scan the environment and track moving objects also improves.

- Research on depth perception reveals that responsiveness to motion develops first, followed by sensitivity to binocular and then to pictorial depth cues. Experience in crawling enhances depth perception and other aspects of three-dimensional understanding, but babies must learn to avoid drop-offs for each body position.

- **Contrast sensitivity** accounts for infants' early pattern preferences. At first, babies stare at single, high-contrast features. At 2 to 3 months, they thoroughly explore internal features of a pattern and start to detect pattern organization. Over time, they discriminate increasingly complex and meaningful patterns.

- Newborns prefer to look at photos and simplified drawings of faces, but whether they have a built-in tendency to orient toward human faces is a matter of dispute. Around 2 months, they recognize and prefer their mother's facial features, and at 3 months, they distinguish the features of different faces. From 5 months on, they perceive emotional expressions as meaningful wholes.

- At birth, **size** and **shape constancy** help babies build a coherent world of objects. At first, infants depend on motion and spatial arrangement to identify objects. After 4 months of age, they rely increasingly on object features, such as distinct shape and surface pattern. Around this time, they first perceive the path of a ball moving back and forth behind a screen as continuous. Soon they can monitor increasingly intricate paths of objects, and they look for featural information to detect the identity of a moving object.

- From the start, infants are capable of **intermodal perception**—combining information across sensory modalities. Detection of **amodal sensory properties,** such as common rate, rhythm, or intensity, may provide the basis for detecting many intermodal matches.

Explain the Gibsons' differentiation theory of perceptual development.

- According to **differentiation theory,** perceptual development is a matter of detecting increasingly fine-grained invariant features in a constantly changing perceptual world. Perceptual differentiation is guided by discovery of **affordances**—the action possibilities that a situation offers the individual.

IMPORTANT TERMS AND CONCEPTS

affordances (p. 199)
amodal sensory properties (p. 197)
brain plasticity (p. 168)
cephalocaudal trend (p. 162)
cerebral cortex (p. 167)
classical conditioning (p. 179)
conditioned response (CR) (p. 179)
conditioned stimulus (CS) (p. 179)
contrast sensitivity (p. 193)
differentiation theory (p. 198)
dynamic systems theory of motor development (p. 184)
epiphyses (p. 163)
experience-dependent brain growth (p. 172)
experience-expectant brain growth (p. 172)

fontanels (p. 164)
glial cells (p. 165)
growth faltering (p. 178)
habituation (p. 180)
imitation (p. 181)
intermodal perception (p. 197)
kwashiorkor (p. 177)
lateralization (p. 168)
marasmus (p. 177)
mirror neurons (p. 182)
myelination (p. 165)
neurons (p. 164)
neurotransmitters (p. 164)
operant conditioning (p. 180)
pincer grasp (p. 188)

prefrontal cortex (p. 168)
prereaching (p. 187)
proximodistal trend (p. 162)
punishment (p. 180)
recovery (p. 181)
reinforcer (p. 180)
shape constancy (p. 196)
size constancy (p. 196)
skeletal age (p. 163)
statistical learning capacity (p. 190)
synapses (p. 164)
synaptic pruning (p. 165)
ulnar grasp (p. 187)
unconditioned response (UCR) (p. 179)
unconditioned stimulus (UCS) (p. 179)

"My Family"
Aldo Pablo Fernandez
5 years, Mexico

With a glorious wash of earth and sky as a backdrop, a family accompanies a toddler on an expedition of discovery. In Chapter 6, you will see that a stimulating environment combined with the guidance of more mature members of their culture ensures that young children's cognition will develop at its best.

Reprinted with permission from the International Museum of Children's Art, Oslo, Norway

Cognitive Development in Infancy and Toddlerhood

Piaget's Cognitive-Developmental Theory

Piaget's Ideas About Cognitive Change • The Sensorimotor Stage • Follow-Up Research on Infant Cognitive Development • Evaluation of the Sensorimotor Stage

■ **SOCIAL ISSUES: EDUCATION**
Baby Learning from TV and Video: The Video Deficit Effect

Information Processing

Structure of the Information-Processing System • Attention • Memory • Categorization • Evaluation of Information-Processing Findings

■ **BIOLOGY AND ENVIRONMENT**
Infantile Amnesia

The Social Context of Early Cognitive Development

■ **CULTURAL INFLUENCES**
Social Origins of Make-Believe Play

Individual Differences in Early Mental Development

Infant Intelligence Tests • Early Environment and Mental Development • Early Intervention for At-Risk Infants and Toddlers

Language Development

Three Theories of Language Development • Getting Ready to Talk • First Words • The Two-Word Utterance Phase • Comprehension versus Production • Individual and Cultural Differences • Supporting Early Language Development

■ **SOCIAL ISSUES: EDUCATION**
Parent–Child Interaction: Impact on Language and Cognitive Development of Deaf Children

W hen Caitlin, Grace, and Timmy gathered at Ginette's child-care home, the playroom was alive with activity. The three spirited explorers, each nearly 18 months old, were bent on discovery. Grace dropped shapes through holes in a plastic box that Ginette held and adjusted so the harder ones would fall smoothly into place. Once a few shapes were inside, Grace grabbed the box and shook it, squealing with delight as the lid fell open and the shapes scattered around her. The clatter attracted Timmy, who picked up a shape, carried it to the railing at the top of the basement steps, and dropped it overboard, then followed with a teddy bear, a ball, his shoe, and a spoon. Meanwhile, Caitlin pulled open a drawer, unloaded a set of wooden bowls, stacked them in a pile, knocked it over, and then banged two bowls together. With each action, the children seemed to be asking, "How do things work? What makes interesting events happen? Which ones can I control?"

As the toddlers experimented, I could see the beginnings of spoken language—a whole new way of influencing the world. "All gone baw!" Caitlin exclaimed as Timmy tossed the bright red ball down the basement steps. "Bye-bye," Grace chimed in, waving as the ball disappeared from sight. Later that day, Grace revealed the beginnings of make-believe. "Night-night," she said, putting her head down and closing her eyes, ever so pleased that she could decide for herself when and where to go to bed.

Over the first two years, the small, reflexive newborn baby becomes a self-assertive, purposeful being who solves simple problems and starts to master the most amazing human ability: language. Parents wonder, how does all this happen so quickly? This question has also captivated researchers, yielding a wealth of findings along with vigorous debate over how to explain the astonishing pace of infant and toddler cognition.

In this chapter we take up three perspectives on early cognitive development: Piaget's *cognitive-developmental theory, information processing,* and Vygotsky's *sociocultural theory*. We also consider the usefulness of tests that measure infants' and toddlers' intellectual progress. Finally, we look at the beginnings of language. We will see how toddlers' first words build on early cognitive achievements and how, very soon, new words and expressions greatly increase the speed and flexibility of their thinking. Throughout development, cognition and language mutually support each other.

Piaget's Cognitive-Developmental Theory

Swiss theorist Jean Piaget inspired a vision of children as busy, motivated explorers whose thinking develops as they act directly on the environment. Influenced by his background in biology, Piaget believed that the child's mind forms and modifies psychological structures so they achieve a better fit with external reality. Recall from Chapter 1 that in Piaget's theory, children move through four stages between infancy and adolescence. During these stages, Piaget claimed, all aspects of cognition develop in an integrated fashion, changing in a similar way at about the same time.

Piaget's first stage, the **sensorimotor stage,** spans the first two years of life. Piaget believed that infants and toddlers "think" with their eyes, ears, hands, and other sensorimotor equipment. They cannot yet carry out many activities inside their heads. But by the end of toddlerhood, children can solve everyday practical problems and represent their experiences in speech, gesture, and play. To appreciate Piaget's view of how these vast changes take place, let's consider some important concepts.

Piaget's Ideas About Cognitive Change

According to Piaget, specific psychological structures—organized ways of making sense of experience called **schemes**—change with age. At first, schemes are sensorimotor action patterns. For example, at 6 months, Timmy dropped objects in a fairly rigid way, simply by letting go of a rattle or teething ring and watching with interest. By 18 months, his "dropping scheme" had become deliberate and creative. In tossing objects down the basement stairs, he threw some in the air, bounced others off walls, released some gently and others forcefully. Soon, instead of just acting on objects, he will show evidence of thinking before he acts. For Piaget, this change marks the transition from sensorimotor to preoperational thought.

In Piaget's theory, two processes, *adaptation* and *organization,* account for changes in schemes.

ADAPTATION   **TAKE A MOMENT...** The next time you have a chance, notice how infants and toddlers tirelessly repeat actions that lead to interesting effects. **Adaptation** involves building schemes through direct interaction with the environment. It consists of two complementary activities: *assimilation* and *accommodation*. During **assimilation,** we use our current schemes to interpret the external world. For example, when Timmy dropped objects, he was assimilating them all into his sensorimotor "dropping scheme." In **accommodation,** we create new schemes or adjust old ones after noticing that our current ways of thinking do not capture the environment completely. When Timmy dropped objects in different ways, he modified his dropping scheme to take account of the varied properties of objects.

According to Piaget, the balance between assimilation and accommodation varies over time. When children are not changing much, they assimilate

© LAURA DWIGHT PHOTOGRAPHY

■ In Piaget's theory, first schemes are sensorimotor action patterns. As this 11-month-old experiments with her dropping scheme, her dropping behavior becomes more deliberate and varied. ■

more than they accommodate. Piaget called this a state of cognitive *equilibrium,* implying a steady, comfortable condition. During rapid cognitive change, however, children are in a state of *disequilibrium,* or cognitive discomfort. Realizing that new information does not match their current schemes, they shift away from assimilation toward accommodation. After modifying their schemes, they move back toward assimilation, exercising their newly changed structures until they are ready to be modified again.

Each time this back-and-forth movement between equilibrium and disequilibrium occurs, more effective schemes are produced. Because the times of greatest accommodation are the earliest ones, the sensorimotor stage is Piaget's most complex period of development.

ORGANIZATION Schemes also change through **organization,** a process that takes place internally, apart from direct contact with the environment. Once children form new schemes, they rearrange them, linking them with other schemes to create a strongly interconnected cognitive system. For example, eventually Timmy will relate "dropping" to "throwing" and to his developing understanding of "nearness" and "farness." According to Piaget, schemes reach a true state of equilibrium when they become part of a broad network of structures that can be jointly applied to the surrounding world (Piaget, 1936/1952).

In the following sections, we will first describe infant development as Piaget saw it, noting research that supports his observations. Then we will consider evidence demonstrating that in some ways, babies' cognitive competence is more advanced than Piaget believed.

The Sensorimotor Stage

The difference between the newborn baby and the 2-year-old child is so vast that Piaget divided the sensorimotor stage into six substages, summarized in Table 6.1. Piaget based this sequence on observations of his own three children—a very small sample. But he watched his son and two daughters carefully and also presented them with everyday problems (such as hidden objects) that helped reveal their understanding of the world.

According to Piaget, at birth infants know so little about their world that they cannot purposefully explore it. The **circular reaction** provides a special means of adapting their first schemes. It involves stumbling onto a new experience caused by the baby's own motor activity. The reaction is "circular" because, as the infant tries to repeat the event again and again, a sensorimotor response that originally occurred by chance becomes strengthened into a new scheme.

TABLE 6.1 Summary of Piaget's Sensorimotor Stage

SENSORIMOTOR SUBSTAGE	TYPICAL ADAPTIVE BEHAVIORS
1. Reflexive schemes (birth–1 month)	Newborn reflexes (see Chapter 4, page 143)
2. Primary circular reactions (1–4 months)	Simple motor habits centered around the infant's own body; limited anticipation of events
3. Secondary circular reactions (4–8 months)	Actions aimed at repeating interesting effects in the surrounding world; imitation of familiar behaviors
4. Coordination of secondary circular reactions (8–12 months)	Intentional, or goal-directed, behavior; ability to find a hidden object in the first location in which it is hidden (object permanence); improved anticipation of events; imitation of behaviors slightly different from those the infant usually performs
5. Tertiary circular reactions (12–18 months)	Exploration of the properties of objects by acting on them in novel ways; imitation of novel behaviors; ability to search in several locations for a hidden object (accurate A–B search)
6. Mental representation (18 months–2 years)	Internal depictions of objects and events, as indicated by sudden solutions to problems; ability to find an object that has been moved while out of sight (invisible displacement); deferred imitation; and make-believe play

■ This 3-month-old sees his hands touch, open, and close. He tries to repeat these movements, in a primary circular reaction that helps him gain voluntary control over his behavior. ■

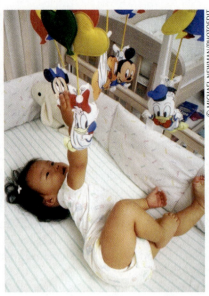

■ When this 4-month-old accidentally hits a toy hung in front of her, her action causes it to swing. Using the secondary circular reaction, she tries to recapture this interesting effect. In the process, she forms a new "hitting scheme." ■

Consider Caitlin, who at age 2 months accidentally made a smacking sound after a feeding. Finding this new sound intriguing, she tried to repeat it until, after a few days, she became quite expert at smacking her lips.

The circular reaction initially centers on the infant's own body but later turns outward, toward manipulation of objects. In the second year, it becomes experimental and creative, aimed at producing novel outcomes. Infants' difficulty inhibiting new and interesting behaviors may underlie the circular reaction. This immaturity in inhibition seems to be adaptive, helping to ensure that new skills will not be interrupted before they strengthen (Carey & Markman, 1999). Piaget considered revisions in the circular reaction so important that, as Table 6.1 shows, he named the sensorimotor substages after them.

REPEATING CHANCE BEHAVIORS
Piaget saw newborn reflexes as the building blocks of sensorimotor intelligence. In Substage 1, babies suck, grasp, and look in much the same way, no matter what experiences they encounter. In one amusing example, Carolyn described how 2-week-old Caitlin lay on the bed next to her sleeping father. Suddenly, he awoke with a start. Caitlin had latched on and begun to suck on his back!

Around 1 month, as babies enter Substage 2, they start to gain voluntary control over their actions through the *primary circular reaction,* by repeating chance behaviors largely motivated by basic needs. This leads to some simple motor habits, such as sucking their fists or thumbs. Babies of this substage also begin to vary their behavior in response to environmental demands. For example, they open their mouths differently for a nipple than for a spoon. And they start to anticipate events. At age 3 months, when Timmy awoke from his nap, he cried out with hunger. But as soon as Vanessa entered the room, his crying stopped. He knew that feeding time was near.

During Substage 3, from 4 to 8 months, infants sit up and become skilled at reaching for and manipulating objects. These motor achievements strengthen the *secondary circular reaction,* through which babies try to repeat interesting events in the surrounding environment that are caused by their own actions. For example, 4-month-old Caitlin accidentally knocked a toy hung in front of her, producing a fascinating swinging motion. Over the next three days, Caitlin tried to repeat this effect, gradually forming a new "hitting" scheme. Improved control over their own behavior permits infants to imitate others' behavior more effectively. However, 4- to 8-month-olds cannot adapt flexibly and quickly enough to imitate novel behaviors (Kaye & Marcus, 1981). Therefore, although they enjoy watching an adult demonstrate a game of pat-a-cake, they are not yet able to participate.

INTENTIONAL BEHAVIOR
In Substage 4, 8- to 12-month-olds combine schemes into new, more complex action sequences. As a result, actions that lead to new schemes no longer have a random, hit-or-miss quality—*accidentally* bringing the thumb to the mouth or *happening* to hit the toy. Instead, 8- to 12-month-olds can engage in **intentional,** or **goal-directed, behavior,** coordinating schemes deliberately to solve simple problems. The clearest example is provided

■ The capacity to find a hidden object, a major advance in cognitive development, emerges between 8 and 12 months. To find the toy under the cloth, this 10-month-old engages in intentional, goal-directed behavior—the basis for all problem solving. ■

by Piaget's famous object-hiding task, in which he shows the baby an attractive toy and then hides it behind his hand or under a cover. Infants of this substage can find the object by coordinating two schemes—"pushing" aside the obstacle and "grasping" the toy. Piaget regarded these *means–end action sequences* as the foundation for all problem solving.

Retrieving hidden objects reveals that infants have begun to master **object permanence,** the understanding that objects continue to exist when they are out of sight. But awareness of object permanence is not yet complete. Babies still make the **A-not-B search error:** If they reach several times for an object at a first hiding place (A), then see it moved to a second (B), they still search for it in the first hiding place (A). Consequently, Piaget concluded that they do not have a clear image of the object as persisting when hidden from view.

Infants of Substage 4, who can better anticipate events, sometimes use their capacity for intentional behavior to try to change those events. At 10 months, Timmy crawled after Vanessa when she put on her coat, whimpering to keep her from leaving. Also, babies can now imitate behaviors slightly different from those they usually perform. After watching someone else, they try to stir with a spoon, push a toy car, or drop raisins into a cup. Again, they draw on intentional behavior, purposefully modifying schemes to fit an observed action (Piaget, 1945/1951).

In Substage 5, from 12 to 18 months, the *tertiary circular reaction,* in which toddlers repeat behaviors with variation, emerges. Recall how Timmy dropped objects over the basement steps, trying this action, then that, then another. Because they approach the world in this deliberately exploratory way, 12- to 18-month-olds become better problem solvers. For example, Grace figured out how to fit a shape through a hole in a container by turning and twisting it until it fell through, and she discovered how to use a stick to get toys that were out of reach. According to Piaget, this capacity to experiment leads to a more advanced understanding of object permanence. Toddlers look for a hidden toy in several locations, displaying an accurate A–B search. Their more flexible action patterns also permit them to imitate many more behaviors, such as stacking blocks, scribbling on paper, and making funny faces.

MENTAL REPRESENTATION   Substage 6 brings the ability to create **mental representations**—internal depictions of information that the mind can manipulate. Our most powerful mental representations are of two kinds: (1) *images,* or mental pictures of objects, people, and spaces; and (2) *concepts,* or categories in which similar objects or events are grouped together. We can use a mental image to retrace our steps when we've misplaced something or to imitate someone's behavior long after we've observed it. And by thinking in concepts and labeling them (for example, "ball" for all rounded, movable objects used in play), we become more efficient thinkers, organizing our diverse experiences into meaningful, manageable, and memorable units.

Piaget noted that 18- to 24-month-olds arrive at solutions suddenly rather than through trial-and-error behavior. In doing so, they seem to experiment with actions inside their heads—evidence that they can mentally represent their experiences. For example, at 19 months, Grace—after bumping her new push toy against a wall—paused for a moment as if to "think," and then immediately turned the toy in a new direction.

Representation enables older toddlers to solve advanced object permanence problems involving *invisible displacement*—finding a toy moved while out of sight, such as into a small box while under a cover. It also permits **deferred imitation**—the ability to remember and copy the behavior of models who are not present. And it makes possible **make-believe play,** in which children act out everyday and imaginary activities. Grace's pretending to go to sleep, in the opening to this chapter, illustrates the very simple make-believe of toddlers. Make-believe expands greatly in early childhood, and it is so important for psychological development that we will return to it again. In sum, as the sensorimotor stage draws to a close, mental symbols have become major instruments of thinking.

■ Using a tertiary circular reaction, this baby twists, turns, and pushes until a block fits through its matching hole in her shape sorter. Between 12 and 18 months, toddlers take a deliberately experimental approach to problem solving, repeating behaviors with variation. ■

■ The capacity for mental representation enables this 2-year-old to engage in make-believe play. With the expansion of make-believe in early childhood, mental symbols become major instruments of thinking. ■

Follow-Up Research on Infant Cognitive Development

Many studies suggest that infants display a wide array of understandings earlier than Piaget believed. Recall the operant conditioning research reviewed in Chapter 5, in which newborns sucked vigorously on a nipple to gain access to interesting sights and sounds. This behavior, which closely resembles Piaget's secondary circular reaction, shows that babies try to explore and control the external world long before 4 to 8 months. In fact, they do so as soon as they are born.

To discover what infants know about hidden objects and other aspects of physical reality, researchers often use the **violation-of-expectation method.** They may *habituate* babies to a physical event (expose them to the event until their looking declines) to familiarize them with a situation in which their knowledge will be tested. Or they may simply show babies an *expected event* (one that is consistent with reality) or an *unexpected event* (a variation of the first event that violates reality). Heightened attention to the unexpected event suggests that the infant is "surprised" by a deviation from physical reality and, therefore, is aware of that aspect of the physical world.

The violation-of-expectation method is controversial. Some critics believe that it indicates limited awareness of physical events, not the full-blown, conscious understanding that was Piaget's focus in requiring infants to act on their surroundings, as in searching for hidden objects (Munakata, 2001; Thelen & Smith, 1994). Others maintain that the method reveals only babies' perceptual preference for novelty, not their understanding of experience (Bremner & Mareschal, 2004; Hood, 2004; Kagan, 2008). Let's examine this debate in light of recent evidence.

OBJECT PERMANENCE   In a series of studies using the violation-of-expectation method, Renée Baillargeon and her collaborators claimed to have found evidence for object permanence in the first few months of life. One of Baillargeon's studies is illustrated in Figure 6.1 (Aguiar & Baillargeon, 2002; Baillargeon & DeVos, 1991). After habituating to a short and a tall carrot moving behind a screen, infants were given two test events: (1) an *expected event,* in which the short carrot moved behind a screen, could not be seen in its window, and reappeared on the other side, and (2) an *unexpected event,* in which the tall carrot moved behind a screen, could not be seen in its window (although it was taller than the window's lower edge), and reappeared. Infants as young as 2½ to 3½ months looked longer at the unexpected event, suggesting that they had some awareness that an object moved behind a screen would continue to exist.

Additional violation-of-expectation studies yielded similar results (Baillargeon, 2004; Wang, Baillargeon, & Paterson, 2005). But several researchers using similar procedures failed to confirm some of Baillargeon's findings (Bogartz, Shinskey, & Shilling, 2000; Cashon & Cohen, 2000; Cohen & Marks, 2002; Rivera, Wakeley, & Langer, 1999). Baillargeon and others maintain that these opposing investigations did not include crucial controls. And they emphasize that infants look longer at a wide variety of unexpected events involving hidden objects (Newcombe, Sluzenski, & Huttenlocher, 2005; Wang, Baillargeon, & Paterson, 2005). Still, critics question what babies' looking preferences tell us about what they actually know.

But another type of looking behavior suggests that young infants are aware that objects persist when out of view. Four- and 5-month-olds will track a ball's path of movement as it disappears and

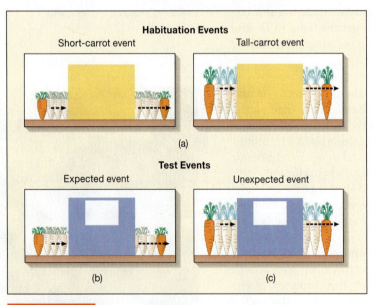

FIGURE 6.1

Testing young infants for understanding of object permanence using the violation-of-expectation method. (a) First, infants were habituated to two events: a short carrot and a tall carrot moving behind a yellow screen, on alternate trials. Next, the researchers presented two test events. The color of the screen was changed to help infants notice its window. (b) In the *expected event,* the carrot shorter than the window's lower edge moved behind the blue screen and reappeared on the other side. (c) In the *unexpected event,* the carrot taller than the window's lower edge moved behind the screen and did not appear in the window, but then emerged intact on the other side. Infants as young as 2½ to 3½ months recovered to (looked longer at) the *unexpected event,* suggesting that they had some understanding of object permanence. *(Adapted from R. Baillargeon & J. DeVos, 1991, "Object Permanence in Young Infants: Further Evidence,"* Child Development, 62, *p. 1230. © The Society for Research in Child Development. Adapted with permission.)*

reappears from behind a barrier, even gazing ahead to where they expect it to emerge (Bertenthal, Longo, & Kenny, 2007; Rosander & von Hofsten, 2004). With age, babies are more likely to fixate on the predicted place of the ball's reappearance and wait for it—evidence of an increasingly secure grasp of object permanence.

In related research, investigators recorded 6-month-olds' ERP brain-wave activity as the babies watched two events on a computer screen. In one event, a black square moved until it covered an object, then moved away to reveal the object (object permanence). In the other event, as a black square started to move across an object, the object disintegrated (object disappearance) (Kaufman, Csibra, & Johnson, 2005). Only while watching the first event did the infants show a particular brain-wave pattern in the right temporal lobe—the same pattern adults exhibit when told to sustain a mental image of an object.

If young infants do have some notion of object permanence, how do we explain Piaget's finding that even infants capable of reaching do not try to search for hidden objects before 8 months of age? Violation-of-expectation tasks require only that the baby react (through looking) to whether a post-object-hiding scene accords with ordinary experience. Searching for a hidden object is far more cognitively demanding: The baby must *predict* where the hidden object is. Consistent with this idea, infants solve some object-hiding tasks before others: Eight- to 10-month-olds remove the cover from a partially hidden object before they are able to do so from a fully covered object (Moore & Meltzoff, 2008). And 10-month-olds search for an object placed on a table and covered by a cloth before they search for an object that a hand deposits under a cloth (Moore & Meltzoff, 1999). In the second, more difficult task, infants seem to expect the object to reappear in the hand because that is where the object initially disappeared. When the hand emerges without the object, they conclude that there is no other place the object could be. Not until 14 months can most babies infer that the hand deposited the object under the cloth.

Around this age, toddlers demonstrate a thorough understanding of hidden objects. Fourteen-month-olds know that objects continue to exist in their hidden locations even after the infants have left the location. After seeing an object hidden in a cupboard, when the toddlers returned the next day, they correctly searched for the specific object in its original location. When exposed to a similar cupboard in a new room, the infants behaved just as adults do: They saw no reason to search (Moore & Meltzoff, 2004).

SEARCHING FOR OBJECTS HIDDEN IN MORE THAN ONE LOCATION

Once 8- to 12-month-olds search for hidden objects, they make the A-not-B search error. Some research suggests that they search at A (where they found the object on previous reaches) instead of B (its most recent location) because they have trouble inhibiting a previously rewarded motor response (Diamond, Cruttenden, & Neiderman, 1994). In support of this view, the more prior reaches to A, the greater the likelihood that the infant will reach again toward A when the object is hidden at B. Another possibility is that after finding the object several times at A, babies do not attend closely when it is hidden at B (Ruffman & Langman, 2002). A more comprehensive explanation is that a complex, dynamic system of factors—having built a habit of reaching toward A, continuing to look at A, having the hiding place at B appear similar to the one at A, and maintaining a constant body posture—increases the chances that the baby will make the A-not-B search error. Research shows that disrupting any one of these factors increases 10-month-olds' accurate searching at B (Thelen et al., 2001).

In sum, mastery of object permanence is a gradual achievement. Babies' understanding becomes increasingly complex with age: They must perceive an object's identity by integrating feature and movement information (see Chapter 5, page 197), distinguish the object from the barrier concealing it and the surface on which it rests, keep track of the object's whereabouts, and use this knowledge to obtain the object (Cohen & Cashon, 2006; Moore & Meltzoff, 2008; Munakata & Stedron, 2002). Success at object search tasks coincides with rapid development of the frontal lobes of the cerebral cortex (Bell, 1998). Also crucial are a wide variety of experiences perceiving, acting on, and remembering objects.

MENTAL REPRESENTATION

In Piaget's theory, infants lead purely sensorimotor lives. They cannot represent experience until about 18 months of age. Yet 8- to 10-month-olds' ability to recall the location of hidden objects after delays of more than a minute, and 14-month-olds' recall after delays of a day or more, clearly indicate that babies construct mental

LOOK AND LISTEN

Using an attractive toy and cloth, try several object-hiding tasks with 8- to 14-month-olds. Is their searching behavior consistent with research findings?

representations of objects and their whereabouts (McDonough, 1999; Moore & Meltzoff, 2004). In studies of deferred imitation and problem solving, representational thought is evident even earlier. And toddlers make impressive strides in symbolic understanding, as their grasp of words and photos reveals.

Deferred and Inferred Imitation. Piaget studied imitation by noting when his three children demonstrated it in their everyday behavior. Under these conditions, a great deal must be known about the infant's daily life to be sure that deferred imitation—which requires infants to represent another's past behavior—has occurred.

Laboratory research reveals that deferred imitation is present at 6 weeks of age! Infants who watched an unfamiliar adult's facial expression imitated it when exposed to the same adult the next day (Meltzoff & Moore, 1994). As motor capacities improve, infants copy actions with objects. In one study, adults showed 6- and 9-month-olds a novel series of actions with a puppet: taking its glove off, shaking the glove to ring a bell inside, and replacing the glove. When tested a day later, infants who had seen the novel actions were far more likely to imitate them (see Figure 6.2). And when researchers paired a second, motionless puppet with the first puppet a day before the demonstration, 6-month-olds generalized the actions to this new, very different-looking puppet (Barr, Marrott, & Rovee-Collier, 2003). Even more impressive, after having seen Puppet A paired with B and Puppet B paired with C on successive days, infants transferred modeled actions from A to C and from C to A, though they had not directly observed this pair together (Townsend & Rovee-Collier, 2007). Already, infants can form flexible mental representations that include chains of relevant associations.

Gains in recall, expressed through deferred imitation, are accompanied by changes in brain-wave activity during memory tasks, as measured by ERPs. This suggests that improvements in memory storage in the cerebral cortex contribute to these advances (Bauer et al., 2006). Between 12 and 18 months, toddlers use deferred imitation skillfully to enrich their range of schemes. They retain modeled behaviors for at least several months, copy the actions of peers as well as adults, and imitate across a change in context—for example, enact at home a behavior seen at child care (Klein & Meltzoff, 1999).

Toddlers even imitate rationally, by *inferring* others' intentions! They are more likely to imitate purposeful than accidental behaviors (Carpenter, Akhtar, & Tomasello, 1998). And they adapt their imitative acts to a model's goals. If 12-month-olds see an adult perform an unusual

(a)   (b)

FIGURE 6.2

Testing infants for deferred imitation. After researchers performed a novel series of actions with a puppet, this 6-month-old imitated the actions a day later—(a) removing the glove; (b) shaking the glove to ring a bell inside. With age, gains in recall are evident in deferred imitation of others' behaviors over longer delays.

action for fun (make a toy dog enter a miniature house by jumping through the chimney, even though its door is wide open), they copy the behavior. But if the adult engages in the odd behavior because she *must* (she makes the dog go through the chimney only after first trying to use the door and finding it locked), 12-month-olds typically imitate the more efficient action (putting the dog through the door) (Schwier et al., 2006).

Between 14 and 18 months, toddlers become increasingly adept at imitating actions an adult *tries* to produce, even if these are not fully realized (Bellagamba, Camaioni, & Colonnesi, 2006; Meltzoff, 1995; Olineck & Poulin-Dubois, 2007). On one occasion, Ginette attempted to pour some raisins into a small bag but missed, spilling them onto the counter. A moment later, Grace began dropping the raisins into the bag, indicating that she had inferred Ginette's goal.

Though advanced in terms of Piaget's predictions, toddlers' ability to represent others' intentions—a cornerstone of social understanding and communication—seems to have roots in earlier sensorimotor activity. In several studies, infants' skill at engaging in goal-directed actions—reaching for objects at 3 to 4 months, pointing to objects at 9 months—predicted their awareness of an adult's similar behavior as goal-directed in a violation-of-expectation task (Gerson & Woodward, 2010; Woodward, 2009). And the better 10-month-olds are at detecting the goals of others' gazes and reaches, the more successful they are four months later at inferring an adult's intention from her incomplete actions in an imitation task (Olineck & Poulin-Dubois, 2009).

Problem Solving. As Piaget indicated, around 7 to 8 months, infants develop intentional means–end action sequences, which they use to solve simple problems, such as pulling on a cloth to obtain a toy resting on its far end (Willatts, 1999). Soon after, infants' representational skills permit more effective problem solving than Piaget's theory suggests.

By 10 to 12 months, infants can *solve problems by analogy*—apply a solution strategy from one problem to other relevant problems. In one study, babies of this age were given three similar problems, each requiring them to overcome a barrier, grasp a string, and pull it to get an attractive toy. The problems differed in many aspects of their superficial features—texture and color of the string, barrier, and floor mat and type of toy (horse, doll, or car). For the first problem, the parent demonstrated the solution and encouraged the infant to imitate. Babies obtained the toy more readily on each additional problem (Chen, Sanchez, & Campbell, 1997). Similarly, 12-month-olds who were repeatedly presented with a spoon in the same orientation (handle to one side) readily adapted their motor actions when the spoon was presented in the opposite orientation (handle to the other side), successfully transporting food to their mouths most of the time (McCarty & Keen, 2005).

These findings suggest that at the end of the first year, infants form flexible mental representations of how to use tools to get objects. They have some ability to move beyond trial-and-error experimentation, represent a solution mentally, and use it in new contexts.

Symbolic Understanding. One of the most momentous advances in early development is the realization that words can be used to cue mental images of things not physically present—a symbolic capacity called **displaced reference** that emerges around the first birthday. It greatly expands toddlers' capacity to learn about the world through communicating with others. Observations of 12-month-olds reveal that they respond to the label of an absent toy by looking at and gesturing toward the spot where it usually rests (Saylor, 2004). And on hearing the name of a parent or sibling who has just left the room, most 13-month-olds turn toward the door (DeLoache & Ganea, 2009). The more experience toddlers have with an object and its verbal label, the more likely they are to call up a mental representation when they hear the object's name. As memory and vocabulary improve, skill at displaced reference expands.

But at first, toddlers have difficulty using language to acquire new information about an absent object—an ability that is essential to learn from symbols. In one study, an adult taught 19- and 22-month-olds a name for a stuffed animal—"Lucy" for a frog. Then, with the frog out of sight, the toddler was told that some water had spilled, so "Lucy's all wet!" Finally, the adult showed the toddler three stuffed animals—a wet frog, a dry frog, and a pig—and said, "Get Lucy!" (Ganea et al., 2007). Although all the children remembered that Lucy was a frog, only the 22-month-olds identified the wet frog as Lucy. Nevertheless, older toddlers' reliance on verbal information is fragile. When a verbal message about a toy's new location conflicts with a previously observed location, most 23-month-olds simply go to the initial location. At

© ELLEN B. SENISI PHOTOGRAPHY

■ A 17-month-old points to a picture in a book, revealing her beginning awareness of the symbolic function of pictures. But pictures must be highly realistic for toddlers to treat them symbolically. ■

30 months, children succeed at finding the toy (Ganea & Harris, 2010). The capacity to use language as a flexible symbolic tool—to modify an existing mental representation—improves from the end of the second into the third year.

Awareness of the symbolic function of pictures also emerges in the second year. Even newborns perceive a relation between a picture and its referent, as indicated by their preference for looking at a photo of their mother's face (see page 195 in Chapter 5). At the same time, infants do not treat pictures as symbols. Rather, they touch, rub, and pat a color photo of an object or pick it up and manipulate it—behaviors that reveal confusion about the picture's true nature. This manual exploration increases from 4 to 9 months and then declines, becoming rare around 18 months (DeLoache et al., 1988; DeLoache & Ganea, 2009).

As long as pictures strongly resemble real objects, by the middle of the second year toddlers treat them symbolically. After hearing a novel label ("blicket") applied to a color photo of an unfamiliar object, most 15- to 24-month-olds—when presented with both the real object and its picture and asked to indicate the "blicket"—gave a symbolic response. They selected either the real object or both the object and its picture, not the picture alone, a tendency that strengthened with age (Ganea et al., 2009). Around this time, toddlers increasingly use pictures as vehicles for communicating with others and acquiring new knowledge. They point to, name, and talk about pictures, and they can apply something learned from a book with realistic-looking pictures to real objects, and vice versa (Ganea, Pickard, & DeLoache, 2008).

But even after coming to appreciate the symbolic nature of pictures, young children continue to have difficulty grasping the distinction between some pictures (such as line drawings) and their referents, as we will see in Chapter 8. How do infants and toddlers interpret another ever-present, pictorial medium—video? Turn to the Social Issues: Education box on the following page to find out.

Evaluation of the Sensorimotor Stage

Table 6.2 summarizes the remarkable cognitive attainments we have just considered. **TAKE A MOMENT...** Compare this table with the description of Piaget's sensorimotor substages in Table 6.1 on page 205. You will see that infants anticipate events, actively search for hidden objects, master the A–B object search, flexibly vary their sensorimotor schemes, engage in make-believe play, and treat pictures and video images symbolically within Piaget's time frame. Yet

TABLE 6.2 Some Cognitive Attainments of Infancy and Toddlerhood

AGE	COGNITIVE ATTAINMENTS
Birth–1 month	Secondary circular reactions using limited motor skills, such as sucking a nipple to gain access to interesting sights and sounds
1–4 months	Awareness of object permanence, object solidity, and gravity, as suggested by violation-of-expectation findings; deferred imitation of an adult's facial expression over a short delay (one day)
4–8 months	Improved knowledge of object properties and basic numerical knowledge, as suggested by violation-of-expectation findings; deferred imitation of an adult's novel actions on objects over a short delay (one to three days)
8–12 months	Ability to search for a hidden object when covered by a cloth; ability to solve simple problems by analogy to a previous problem
12–18 months	Ability to search in several locations for a hidden object when a hand deposits it under a cloth and when it is moved from one location to another (accurate A–B search); deferred imitation of an adult's novel actions on an object over a long delay (at least several months) and across a change in situation (from child care to home); rational imitation, inferring the model's intentions; displaced reference of words
18 months–2 years	Deferred imitation of actions an adult tries to produce, even if these are not fully realized, again indicating a capacity to infer others' intentions; imitation of everyday behaviors in make-believe play; beginning awareness of pictures and video as symbols of reality

TAKE A MOMENT... Which of the capacities listed in this table indicate that mental representation emerges earlier than Piaget believed?

SOCIAL ISSUES: EDUCATION

Baby Learning from TV and Video: The Video Deficit Effect

Children first become TV and video viewers in early infancy, as they are exposed to programs watched by parents and older siblings. Many parents also turn on TV shows or videos aimed at viewers not yet out of diapers, such as the Baby Einstein products. About 40 percent of U.S. 3-month-olds watch regularly, a figure that rises to 90 percent at age 2, a period during which average viewing time increases from just under an hour to 1½ hours a day (Zimmerman, Christakis, & Meltzoff, 2007). Although parents assume that babies learn from TV and videos, research indicates that they cannot take full advantage of them.

Initially, infants respond to videos of people as if viewing people directly—smiling, moving their arms and legs, and (by 6 months) imitating actions of a televised adult. But they confuse the images with the real thing (Barr, Muentener, & Garcia, 2007; Marian, Neisser, & Rochat, 1996). When 9- to 19-month-olds were shown videos of attractive toys, the 9-month-olds manually explored the screen, as they do with pictures. By 19 months, touching and grabbing had declined in favor of pointing at the images (Pierroutsakos & Troseth, 2003). Nevertheless, toddlers continue to have difficulty applying what they see on video to real situations.

In a series of studies, some 2-year-olds watched through a window while a live adult hid an object in an adjoining room, while others watched the same event on a video screen. Children in the direct viewing condition retrieved the toy easily; those in the video condition had difficulty (Troseth, 2003; Troseth & DeLoache, 1998). This **video deficit effect**—poorer performance after a video than a live demonstration—has also been found for 2-year-olds' deferred imitation, word learning, and means–end problem solving (Deocampo, 2003; Hayne, Herbert, & Simcock, 2003; Krcmar, Grela, & Linn, 2007).

One explanation for the video deficit effect is that 2-year-olds typically do not view a video character as offering socially relevant information.

After an adult on video announced where she hid a toy, few 2-year-olds searched (Schmidt, Crawley-Davis, & Anderson, 2007). In contrast, when the adult stood in front of the child and uttered the same words, 2-year-olds promptly retrieved the object.

Toddlers seem to discount information on video as relevant to their everyday experiences because people do not look at and converse with them directly or establish a shared focus on objects, as their caregivers do. In one study, researchers gave some 2-year-olds an interactive video experience (using a two-way, closed-circuit video system). An adult on video interacted with the child for five minutes—calling the child by name, talking about the child's siblings and pets, waiting for the child to respond, and playing interactive games (Troseth, Saylor, & Archer, 2006). Compared with 2-year-olds who viewed the same adult in a noninteractive video, those in the interactive condition were far more successful in using a verbal cue from a person on video to retrieve a toy.

Around age 2½, the video deficit effect declines. Before this age, the American Academy of Pediatrics (2001) recommends against mass

media exposure, emphasizing that babies require rich responsive exchanges with caregivers and exploration of their physical surroundings for optimal brain growth and psychological development (see Chapter 5, page 169). In support of this advice, amount of TV viewing is negatively related to 8- to 18-month-olds' language progress (Tanimura et al., 2004; Zimmerman, Christakis, & Meltzoff, 2007). And heavy 1- to 3-year-old viewers tend to have attention, memory, and reading difficulties in the early school years (Christakis et al., 2004; Zimmerman & Christakis, 2005).

Toddlers face a complex task in making sense of video. Although they no longer confuse it with reality, they do not know how to mentally represent the relationship between video images and real objects and people. Video for 2-year-olds is likely to work best as a teaching tool when it is rich in social cues—close-ups of characters who look directly at the camera, address questions to viewers, and pause to invite their response. Repetition of video programs also helps children over age 2 make sense of video content (Anderson, 2004).

© NIAMH BALDOCK/ALAMY

■ This baby reaches for the TV screen because she thinks the child she sees there is real. Not until about age 2½ will she understand how onscreen images relate to real people and objects. ■

other capacities—including secondary circular reactions, understanding of object properties, first signs of object permanence, deferred imitation, problem solving by analogy, and displaced reference of words—emerge earlier than Piaget expected. These findings show that the cognitive attainments of infancy and toddlerhood do not develop together in the neat, stepwise fashion Piaget predicted.

Recent research raises questions about Piaget's view of how infant development takes place. Consistent with Piaget's ideas, sensorimotor action helps infants construct some forms of knowledge. For example, in Chapter 5 we saw that crawling enhances depth perception and ability to find hidden objects and that handling objects fosters awareness of object properties. Yet we have also seen evidence that infants comprehend a great deal before they are capable of the motor behaviors that Piaget assumed led to those understandings. How can we account for babies' amazing cognitive accomplishments?

ALTERNATIVE EXPLANATIONS   Unlike Piaget, who thought young babies constructed all mental representations out of sensorimotor activity, most researchers now believe that young babies have some built-in cognitive equipment for making sense of experience. But intense disagreement exists over the extent of this initial understanding. As we have seen, much evidence on young infants' cognition rests on the violation-of-expectation method. Researchers who lack confidence in this method argue that babies' cognitive starting point is limited (Campos et al., 2008; Cohen & Cashon, 2006; Kagan, 2008). For example, some believe that newborns begin life with a set of biases for attending to certain information and with general-purpose learning procedures—such as powerful techniques for analyzing complex perceptual information. Together, these capacities enable infants to construct a wide variety of schemes (Bahrick, Lickliter, & Flom, 2004; Huttenlocher, 2002; Mandler, 2004; Quinn, 2008).

Others, convinced by violation-of-expectation findings, believe that infants start out with impressive understandings. According to this **core knowledge perspective,** babies are born with a set of innate knowledge systems, or *core domains of thought.* Each of these "prewired" understandings permits a ready grasp of new, related information and therefore supports early, rapid development (Carey & Markman, 1999; Leslie, 2004; Spelke, 2004; Spelke & Kinzler, 2007). Core knowledge theorists argue that infants could not make sense of the complex stimulation around them without having been genetically "set up" in the course of evolution to comprehend its crucial aspects.

Researchers have conducted many studies of infants' *physical knowledge,* including object permanence, object solidity (that one object cannot move through another), and gravity (that an object will fall without support). Violation-of-expectation findings suggest that in the first few months, infants have some awareness of all these basic object properties and quickly build on this knowledge (Baillargeon, 2004; Hespos & Baillargeon, 2001; Luo & Baillargeon, 2005; Spelke, 2000). Core knowledge theorists also assume that an inherited foundation of *linguistic knowledge* enables swift language acquisition in early childhood—a possibility we will consider later in this chapter. Further, these theorists argue, infants' early orientation toward people initiates swift development of *psychological knowledge*—in particular, understanding of mental states, such as intentions, emotions, desires, and beliefs, which we will address further in Chapter 7.

Researchers have even examined infants' *numerical knowledge!* In the best-known study, 5-month-olds saw a screen raised to hide a single toy animal and then watched a hand place a second toy behind a screen. Finally, the screen was removed to reveal either one or two toys. If infants kept track of the two objects (requiring them to add one object to another), then they should look longer at the unexpected, one-toy display—which is what they did (see Figure 6.3) (Wynn, Bloom, & Chiang, 2002). These findings and others suggest that babies can discriminate quantities up to three and use that knowledge to perform simple arithmetic—both addition and subtraction (in which two objects are covered and one is removed) (Kobayashi et al., 2004; Kobayashi, Hiraki, & Hasegawa, 2005; Wynn, Bloom, & Chiang, 2002). As further support, ERP brain-wave recordings taken while babies view correct and incorrect simple arithmetic solutions reveal a response pattern identical to the pattern adults show when detecting errors (Berger, Tzur, & Posner, 2006).

Further evidence suggests that infants can distinguish among large sets of items, as long as the difference between those sets is great enough. For example,

© STEPHEN MALLABY/ALAMY

■ Did this 3-year-old acquire the physical knowledge necessary to create this structure through repeatedly acting on objects, as Piaget assumed? Or did he begin life with innate knowledge that helps him understand objects and their relationships quickly, with little hands-on exploration? ■

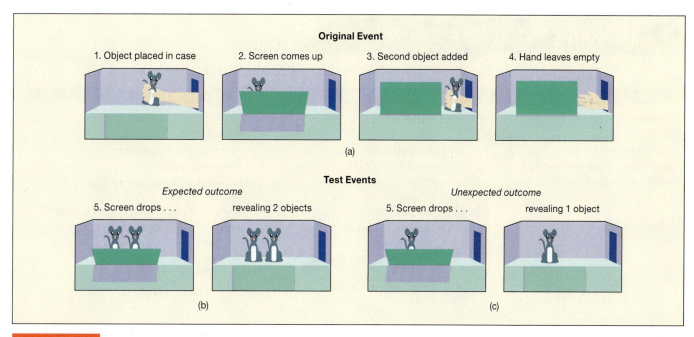

FIGURE 6.3

Testing infants for basic number concepts. (a) First, infants saw a screen raised in front of a toy animal. Then an identical toy was added behind the screen. Next, the researchers presented two outcomes. (b) In the *expected outcome,* the screen dropped to reveal two toy animals. (c) In the *unexpected outcome,* the screen dropped to reveal one toy animal. Five-month-olds shown the unexpected outcome looked longer than 5-month-olds shown the expected outcome. The researchers concluded that infants can discriminate the quantities "one" and "two" and use that knowledge to perform simple addition: 1 + 1 = 2. A variation of this procedure suggested that 5-month-olds could also do simple subtraction: 2 − 1 = 1. *(From K. Wynn, 1992, "Addition and Subtraction by Human Infants,"* Nature, 358, p. 749. © 1992 by Nature Publishing Group. Reprinted by permission of Nature Publishing Group. Adapted by permission of Macmillan Publishers, Ltd.)

6-month-olds can tell the difference between 8 versus 16 dots but not 8 versus 12, and 9-month-olds can discriminate 8 versus 12 but not 8 versus 10 (Lipton & Spelke, 2003; Xu, Spelke, & Goddard, 2005). As a result, some researchers believe that infants can represent approximate large-number values, in addition to the small-number discriminations evident in Figure 6.3.

These findings—like other violation-of-expectation results—are controversial. In other experiments similar to those just described, looking preferences were inconsistent (Langer, Gillette, & Arriaga, 2003; Wakeley, Rivera, & Langer, 2000). These researchers point out that claims for infants' knowledge of number concepts are surprising, given other research indicating that before 14 to 16 months, toddlers have difficulty with less-than and greater-than relationships between small sets. And, as we will see in Chapter 9, not until the preschool years do children add and subtract small sets correctly.

Even when violation-of-expectation results are consistent, critics take issue with the assumption that infants are endowed with *knowledge*. They argue that young infants' looking behaviors may indicate only a perceptual preference, not the existence of concepts and reasoning (Cohen, 2009; Cohen & Cashon, 2006). Similarly, investigators of brain development add that little evidence exists for prewiring of complex cognitive functions in the brain (Johnson, 2001b; Nelson, Thomas, & de Haan, 2006). Instead, they say, the cerebral cortex is initially highly plastic and gradually specializes, largely as the result of children's experiences (see Chapter 5, pages 167–169).

Finally, although the core knowledge perspective emphasizes native endowment, it acknowledges that experience is essential for children to extend this initial knowledge. But so far, it has said little about which experiences are most important in each core domain of thought and how those experiences advance children's thinking. Despite ongoing challenges from critics, core knowledge research has sharpened the field's focus on clarifying the starting point for human cognition and on carefully tracking the changes that build on it.

Applying What We Know

Play Materials That Support Infant and Toddler Cognitive Development

FROM 2 MONTHS	FROM 6 MONTHS	FROM 1 YEAR
Crib mobile	Squeeze toys	Large dolls, toy dishes, toy telephone
Rattles and other handheld sound-making toys, such as a bell on a handle	Nesting cups	Cars and trucks
	Clutch and texture balls	Large blocks, cardboard boxes
Adult-operated music boxes and music recordings with gentle, regular rhythms, songs, and lullabies	Stuffed animals and soft-bodied dolls	Hammer-and-peg toy
	Filling and emptying toys	Pull and push toys, riding toys that can be pushed with feet
	Large and small blocks	Rhythm instruments for shaking and banging, such as bells, cymbals, and drums
	Pots, pans, and spoons from the kitchen	Simple puzzles
	Simple, floating objects for the bath	Sandbox, shovel, and pail
	Picture books with realistic color images	Shallow wading pool and water toys
		Balls of various sizes

PIAGET'S LEGACY   Follow-up research on Piaget's sensorimotor stage yields broad agreement on two issues. First, many cognitive changes of infancy are gradual and continuous rather than abrupt and stagelike, as Piaget thought (Bjorklund, 2004; Courage & Howe, 2002). Second, rather than developing together, various aspects of infant cognition change unevenly because of the challenges posed by different types of tasks and infants' varying experiences with them. These ideas serve as the basis for another major approach to cognitive development—*information processing*—which we take up next.

Before we turn to this alternative point of view, let's recognize Piaget's enormous contributions. Piaget's work inspired a wealth of research on infant cognition, including studies that challenged his theory. Today, researchers are far from consensus on how to modify or replace his account of infant cognitive development, and some believe that his general approach continues to make sense and fits most of the evidence (Cohen, 2010). Piaget's observations also have been of great practical value. Teachers and caregivers continue to look to the sensorimotor stage for guidelines on how to create developmentally appropriate environments for infants and toddlers.

TAKE A MOMENT...   Now that you are familiar with some milestones of the first two years, what play materials do you think would support the development of sensorimotor and early representational schemes? Prepare a list, justifying it by referring to the cognitive attainments described in the previous sections. Then compare your suggestions to the ones given in Applying What We Know above.

Ask Yourself

◆ **REVIEW** Using the text discussion on pages 204–212, construct your own table providing an overview of infant and toddler cognitive development. Which entries in your table are consistent with Piaget's sensorimotor stage? Which ones develop earlier than Piaget anticipated?

◆ **APPLY** Several times, after her father hid a teething biscuit under a red cup, 12-month-old Mimi retrieved it easily. Then Mimi's father hid the biscuit under a nearby yellow cup. Why did Mimi persist in searching for it under the red cup?

◆ **CONNECT** Recall from Chapter 5 (page 197) that around the middle of the first year, infants identify objects by their features and by their paths of movement, even when they cannot observe the entire path. How might these attainments contribute to infants' understanding of object permanence?

◆ **REFLECT** Which explanation of infants' cognitive competencies do you prefer, and why?

Information Processing

Information-processing researchers agree with Piaget that children are active, inquiring beings. But instead of providing a single, unified theory of cognitive development, they focus on many aspects of thinking, from attention, memory, and categorization skills to complex problem solving.

Recall from Chapter 1 that the information-processing approach frequently relies on computer-like flowcharts to describe the human cognitive system. Information-processing researchers are not satisfied with general concepts, such as assimilation and accommodation, to describe how children think. Instead, they want to know exactly what individuals of different ages do when faced with a task or problem (Halford, 2002; Miller, 2009). The computer model of human thinking is attractive because it is explicit and precise.

Structure of the Information-Processing System

Most information-processing researchers assume that we hold information in three parts of the mental system for processing: the *sensory register; working,* or *short-term, memory;* and *long-term memory* (see Figure 6.4). As information flows through each, we can use **mental strategies** to operate on and transform it, increasing the chances that we will retain information, use it efficiently, and think flexibly, adapting the information to changing circumstances. To understand this more clearly, let's look at each aspect of the mental system.

First, information enters the **sensory register,** where sights and sounds are represented directly and stored briefly. **TAKE A MOMENT...** Look around you, and then close your eyes. An image of what you saw persists for a few seconds, but then it decays, or disappears, unless you use mental strategies to preserve it. For example, by *attending to* some information more carefully than to other information, you increase the chances that it will transfer to the next step of the information-processing system.

In the second part of the mind, **working,** or **short-term, memory,** we actively apply mental strategies as we "work" on a limited amount of information. For example, if you are studying this book effectively, you are taking notes, repeating information to yourself, or grouping

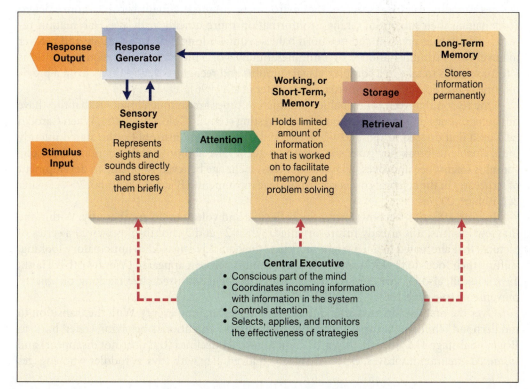

FIGURE 6.4

Model of the human information-processing system. Information flows through three parts of the mental system: the *sensory register; working,* or *short-term, memory;* and *long-term memory.* In each, mental strategies can be used to manipulate information, increasing the efficiency and flexibility of thinking and the chances that information will be retained. The *central executive* is the conscious, reflective part of working memory. It coordinates incoming information already in the system, decides what to attend to, and oversees the use of strategies.

pieces of information together. Why do you apply these strategies? The sensory register, though limited, can take in a wide panorama of information. The capacity of working memory is more restricted. By meaningfully connecting pieces of information into a single representation, we reduce the number of pieces we must attend to, thereby making room in working memory for more. Also, the more thoroughly we learn information, the more *automatically* we use it. Automatic cognitive processing expands working memory by permitting us to focus on other information simultaneously.

To manage its complex activities, a special part of working memory—called the **central executive**—directs the flow of information. It decides what to attend to, coordinates incoming information with information already in the system, and selects, applies, and monitors strategies (Baddeley, 2000; Pressley & Hilden, 2006). The central executive is the conscious, reflective part of our mental system. It works closely with working memory to direct such activities as comprehension, reasoning, and problem solving.

The longer we hold information in working memory, the more likely it will transfer to the third and largest storage area—**long-term memory,** our permanent knowledge base, which is unlimited. In fact, we store so much in long-term memory that *retrieval*—getting information back from the system—can be problematic. To aid retrieval, we apply strategies, just as we do in working memory. Information in long-term memory is *categorized* according to a master plan based on content, much like a library shelving system that allows us to retrieve items by following the same network of associations used to store them in the first place.

Information-processing researchers believe that the basic structure of the human mental system remains similar throughout life. But the *capacity* of the system—the amount of information that can be retained and processed at once—and the speed with which it can be processed increases, making more complex forms of thinking possible with age (Case, 1998; Kail, 2003). Gains in information-processing capacity are due in part to brain development and in part to improvements in strategies—such as attending to information and categorizing it effectively—that are already under way in the first two years of life.

Attention

How does attention develop in early infancy? Recall from our discussion of perceptual development in Chapter 5 that between 1 and 2 months of age, infants shift from focusing on single, high-contrast features of their visual world to exploring objects and patterns more thoroughly. Besides attending to more aspects of the environment, infants gradually become more efficient at managing their attention, taking in information more quickly with age. Habituation research reveals that preterm and newborn babies require a long time to habituate and recover to novel visual stimuli—about 3 or 4 minutes. But by 4 or 5 months, infants require as little as 5 to 10 seconds to take in a complex visual stimulus and recognize that it differs from a previous one (Rose, Feldman, & Janowski, 2001; Slater et al., 1996).

One reason that very young babies' habituation times are so much longer is that they have difficulty disengaging their attention from interesting stimuli (Colombo, 2002). When Carolyn held up a doll dressed in red-and-white checked overalls, 2-month-old Caitlin stared intently until, unable to break her gaze, she burst into tears. The ability to shift attention from one stimulus to another improves by 3 to 4 months—a change believed to be due to development of structures in the cerebral cortex controlling eye movements (Blaga & Colombo, 2006; Posner & Rothbart, 2007a).

Infants' attention becomes increasingly flexible and voluntary in another way: Within the first few months, it is already future-oriented. When 2- and 3-month-olds viewed a series of pictures that alternated in a left–right sequence, they quickly engaged in anticipatory looking, shifting their focus to the location of the next stimulus before it appeared (Wentworth & Haith, 1998). Recall, also, 4- and 5-month-olds' ability to engage in predictive tracking of objects' movements (see page 208).

Over the first year, infants attend to novel and eye-catching events. With the transition to toddlerhood, children become increasingly capable of intentional behavior (refer back to Piaget's Substage 4). Consequently, attraction to novelty declines (but does not disappear) and *sustained attention* improves, especially when children play with toys. A toddler who engages even in simple goal-directed behavior, such as stacking blocks or putting them in a container, must sustain attention to reach the goal (Ruff & Capozzoli, 2003). As plans and activities gradually become more complex, so does the duration of attention.

Adults can foster sustained attention by taking note of an infant or toddler's current interest, encouraging it ("Oh, you like that bell!"), and prompting the child to stay focused ("See, it makes a noise!"). Consistently helping babies focus attention at 10 months predicts higher mental test scores at 18 months (Bono & Stifter, 2003). Also, infants and toddlers gradually become more interested in what others are attending to. Later we will see that this joint attention between caregiver and child is important for language development.

Memory

Operant conditioning and habituation provide windows into early memory. Both methods show that retention of visual events increases dramatically over infancy and toddlerhood.

OPERANT CONDITIONING RESEARCH Using operant conditioning, researchers study infant memory by teaching 2- to 6-month-olds to move a mobile by kicking a foot tied to it with a long cord. Two-month-olds remember how to activate the mobile for 1 to 2 days after training, and 3-month-olds for one week. By 6 months, memory increases to two weeks (Rovee-Collier, 1999; Rovee-Collier & Bhatt, 1993). Around the middle of the first year, babies can manipulate switches or buttons to control stimulation. When 6- to 18-month-olds pressed a lever to make a toy train move around a track, duration of memory continued to increase with age; 13 weeks after training, 18-month-olds still remembered how to press the lever (Hartshorn et al., 1998b). Figure 6.5 on page 220 shows this dramatic rise in retention of operant responses over the first year and a half.

Even after 2- to 6-month-olds forget an operant response, they need only a brief prompt—an adult who shakes the mobile—to reinstate the memory (Hildreth & Rovee-Collier, 2002). And when 6-month-olds are given a chance to reactivate the response themselves for just a couple of minutes—jiggling the mobile by kicking or moving the train by lever-pressing—their memory not only returns but also extends dramatically, to about 17 weeks (Hildreth, Sweeney, & Rovee-Collier, 2003). Furthermore, with just five widely spaced adult-provided reminders of the train task extending over 1½ years, babies trained at age 6 months still remembered the response after reaching their second birthday (Hartshorn, 2003).

At first, infants' memory for operant responses is highly *context-dependent*. If 2- to 6-month-olds are not tested in the same situation in which they were trained—with the same mobile and crib bumper and in the same room—they remember poorly (Hayne, 2004; Hayne & Rovee-Collier, 1995). After 9 months, the importance of context declines. Older infants and toddlers remember how to make the toy train move even when its features are altered and testing takes place in a different room (Hartshorn et al., 1998a; Hayne, Boniface, & Barr, 2000). As babies move on their own and experience frequent changes in context, they apply learned responses more flexibly, generalizing them to relevant new situations.

HABITUATION RESEARCH Habituation studies show that infants learn and retain a wide variety of information just by watching objects and events, without being physically active. Sometimes, they do so for much longer time spans than in operant conditioning studies. Babies

■ As toddlers become increasingly capable of goal-directed play, sustained attention improves. Adults can promote the development of sustained attention by encouraging the child's current interest and prompting the child to stay focused. ■

■ Memory for operant responses improves dramatically over the first 18 months. Here, a 12-month-old has learned to press a lever to make a toy train move around a track—a response she is likely to remember when re-exposed to the task after an interval as long as six weeks (see Figure 6.5 on page 220). ■

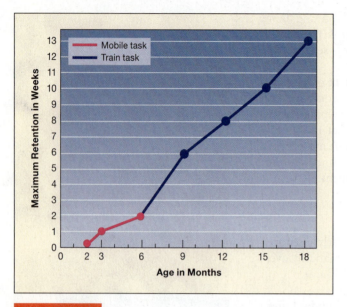

FIGURE 6.5

Increase in retention in two operant conditioning tasks from 2 to 18 months. Two- to 6-month-olds were trained to make a kicking response that turned a mobile. Six- to 18-month-olds were trained to press a lever that made a toy train move around a track. Six-month-olds learned both responses and retained them for an identical length of time, indicating that the tasks are comparable. Consequently, researchers could plot a single line tracking gains in retention of operant responses from 2 to 18 months of age. The line shows that memory improves dramatically. *(From C. Rovee-Collier & R. Barr, 2001, "Infant Learning and Memory," in G. Bremner & A. Fogel, eds., Blackwell Handbook of Infant Development, Oxford, U.K.: Blackwell, p. 150. Reprinted by permission of Blackwell Publishing Ltd.)*

are especially attentive to the movements of objects and people. In one investigation, 5½-month-olds remembered a woman's captivating action (such as blowing bubbles or brushing hair) seven weeks later, as indicated by a *familiarity preference* (see page 181 in Chapter 5) (Bahrick, Gogate, & Ruiz, 2002). The babies were so attentive to the woman's action that they did not remember her face, even when tested one minute later for a *novelty preference.*

In Chapter 4, we saw that 3- to 5-month-olds are excellent at discriminating faces. But their memory for the faces of unfamiliar people and for other visual patterns is short-lived—at 3 months, only about 24 hours; at the end of the first year, several days to a few weeks (Fagan, 1973; Pascalis, de Haan, & Nelson, 1998). By contrast, 3-month-olds' memory for the unusual movements of objects (such as a metal nut swinging on the end of a string) persists for at least three months (Bahrick, Hernandez-Reif, & Pickens, 1997).

By 10 months, infants remember both novel actions and features of objects involved in those actions equally well (Horst, Oakes, & Madole, 2005). Thus, over the second half-year, sensitivity to object appearance increases. This change, as noted earlier, is fostered by infants' increasing ability to manipulate objects, which helps them learn about objects' observable properties.

Habituation research confirms that infants need not be physically active to acquire new information. Nevertheless, as illustrated by research presented in Chapter 5 on the facilitating role of crawling in finding hidden objects (see page 193), motor activity does promote certain aspects of learning and memory.

RECALL MEMORY   So far, we have discussed only **recognition**—noticing when a stimulus is identical or similar to one previously experienced. It is the easiest form of memory: All babies have to do is indicate (by kicking, pressing a lever, or looking) whether a new experience is identical or similar to a previous one. **Recall** is more challenging because it involves remembering something without perceptual support. To recall, you must generate a mental image of the past experience. Can infants engage in recall? By the middle of the first year, they can, as indicated by their ability to imitate actions hours or days after observing the behavior.

Recall memory improves steadily with age. In several studies, 1-year-olds who briefly observed an adult's actions on a novel toy imitated those behaviors one month later. Among 2-year-olds, retention persisted for at least three months (Herbert & Hayne, 2000; Klein & Meltzoff, 1999). Other evidence suggests that toddlers' recall endures even longer—three months for short sequences of adult-modeled actions at 1 year and up to 12 months for sequences observed at 1½ years. The ability to recall modeled behaviors in the order in which the actions occurred—evident as early as 6 months—strengthens over the second year (Rovee-Collier & Cuevas, 2009). And when toddlers imitate in correct sequence, processing not just separate actions but relations between actions, they remember more (Knopf, Kraus, & Kressley-Mba, 2006).

Long-term recall depends on connections among multiple regions of the cerebral cortex, especially with the prefrontal cortex. During infancy and toddlerhood, these neural circuits develop rapidly (Nelson, Thomas, & de Haan, 2006). The evidence as a whole indicates that infants' memory processing is remarkably similar to that of older children and adults: Babies acquire information quickly, retain it over time, and apply it flexibly—doing so more effectively with age (Bauer, 2009; Rovee-Collier & Cuevas, 2009). Yet a puzzling finding is that older children and adults no longer recall their earliest experiences! See the Biology and Environment box on the following page for a discussion of *infantile amnesia.*

BIOLOGY AND ENVIRONMENT

Infantile Amnesia

*I*f infants and toddlers recall many aspects of their everyday lives, how do we explain **infantile amnesia**—that most of us cannot retrieve events that happened to us before age 3? The reason cannot be merely the passage of time because we can recall many personally meaningful one-time events from both the recent and the distant past: the day a sibling was born or a move to a new house—recollections known as **autobiographical memory.**

Several explanations of infantile amnesia exist. One theory credits brain development, suggesting that vital changes in the frontal lobes of the cerebral cortex pave the way for an *explicit* memory system—one in which children remember deliberately rather than *implicitly*, without conscious awareness (Boyer & Diamond, 1992). But as we have seen, mounting evidence indicates that even young infants engage in conscious recall (Rovee-Collier & Cuevas, 2009).

Another conjecture is that older children and adults often use verbal means for storing information, whereas infants' and toddlers' memory processing is largely nonverbal—an incompatibility that may prevent long-term retention of early experiences. To test this idea, researchers sent two adults to the homes of 2- to 4-year-olds with an unusual toy that the children were likely to remember: The Magic

Shrinking Machine, shown in Figure 6.6. One adult showed the child how, after inserting an object in an opening on top of the machine and turning a crank that activated flashing lights and musical sounds, the child could retrieve a smaller, identical object (discreetly dropped down a chute by the second adult) from behind a door on the front of the machine.

A day later, the researchers tested the children to see how well they recalled the event. Their nonverbal memory—based on acting out the "shrinking" event and recognizing the "shrunken" objects in photos—was excellent. But even when they had the vocabulary, children younger than age 3 had trouble describing features of the "shrinking" experience. Verbal recall increased sharply between ages 3 and 4—the period during which children "scramble over the amnesia barrier" (Simcock & Hayne, 2003, p. 813). In a second study, preschoolers could not translate their nonverbal memory for the game into language six months to one year later, when their language had improved dramatically. Their verbal reports were "frozen in time," reflecting their limited language skill at the age they played the game (Simcock & Hayne, 2002).

These findings help us reconcile infants' and toddlers' remarkable memory skills with infantile amnesia. During the first few years, children

rely heavily on nonverbal memory techniques, such as visual images and motor actions. But as language develops, their ability to use it to refer to preverbal memories requires strong contextual cues, such as direct exposure to the physical setting of the to-be-recalled experience (Morris & Baker-Ward, 2007). Only after age 3 do children often represent events verbally. As children encode autobiographical events in verbal form, they can use language-based cues to retrieve them, increasing the accessibility of those memories at later ages (Hayne, 2004).

Other findings suggest that the advent of a clear self-image contributes to the end of infantile amnesia. Toddlers who were advanced in development of a sense of self demonstrated better verbal memories a year later while conversing about past events with their mothers (Harley & Reese, 1999). Very likely, both biology and social experience contribute to the decline of infantile amnesia. Brain development and adult–child interaction may jointly foster self-awareness, language, and improved memory, which enable children to talk with adults about significant past experiences (Bauer, 2007; Nelson & Fivush, 2004). As a result, preschoolers begin to construct a long-lasting autobiographical narrative of their lives and enter into the history of their family and community.

(a)

(b)

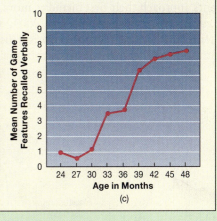
(c)

FIGURE 6.6

The Magic Shrinking Machine, used to test young children's verbal and nonverbal memory of an unusual event. After being shown how the machine worked, the child participated in selecting objects from a polka-dot bag, dropping them into the top of the machine (a), and turning a crank, which produced a "shrunken" object (b). When tested the next day, 2- to 4-year-olds' nonverbal memory for the event was excellent. But below 36 months, verbal recall was poor, based on the number of features recalled about the game during an open-ended interview (c). Recall improved between 36 and 48 months, the period during which infantile amnesia subsides. *(From G. Simcock & H. Hayne, 2003, "Age-Related Changes in Verbal and Nonverbal Memory During Early Childhood," Developmental Psychology, 39, pp. 807, 809. Copyright © 2003 by the American Psychological Association. Reprinted with permission of the American Psychological Association.) Photos: Ross Coombes/Courtesy of Harlene Hayne.*

Categorization

Even young infants can categorize, grouping similar objects and events into a single representation. Categorization helps infants make sense of experience—reduce the enormous amount of new information they encounter every day so they can learn and remember (Cohen, 2003; Oakes & Madole, 2003).

Some creative variations of operant conditioning research with mobiles have been used to find out about infant categorization. One such study, of 3-month-olds, is described and illustrated in Figure 6.7. Similar investigations reveal that in the first few months, babies categorize stimuli on the basis of shape, size, and other physical properties (Wasserman & Rovee-Collier, 2001). By 6 months of age, they can categorize on the basis of two correlated features—for example, the shape and color of an alphabet letter (Bhatt et al., 2004). This ability to categorize using clusters of features prepares babies for acquiring many complex everyday categories.

Habituation has also been used to study infant categorization. Researchers show babies a series of pictures belonging to one category and then see whether they recover to (look longer at) a picture that is not a member of the category (see Figure 6.8). Findings reveal that in the second half of the first year, as long as they have sufficient familiarity with category members, infants group objects into an impressive array of categories—food items, furniture, birds, land animals, air animals, sea animals, plants, vehicles, kitchen utensils, and spatial location ("above" and "below," "on" and "in") (Bornstein, Arterberry, & Mash, 2010; Casasola, Cohen, & Chiarello, 2003; Mandler & McDonough, 1998; Oakes, Coppage, & Dingel, 1997). Besides organizing the physical world, infants of this age categorize their emotional and social worlds. Their looking responses reveal that they sort people and their voices by gender and age, have begun to distinguish emotional expressions, can separate people's natural actions (walking) from other motions, and expect people (but not inanimate objects) to move spontaneously (Spelke, Phillips, & Woodward, 1995; see also Chapter 5, pages 180–181).

Babies' earliest categories are based on similar overall appearance or prominent object parts: legs for animals, wheels for vehicles. But as infants approach their first birthday, more categories appear to be based on subtle sets of features (Cohen, 2003; Mandler, 2004; Quinn, 2008). Older infants can even make categorical distinctions when the perceptual contrast between two categories is minimal (birds versus airplanes).

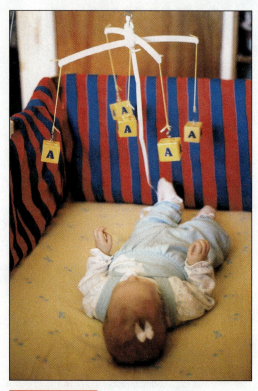

FIGURE 6.7

Investigating infant categorization using operant conditioning. Three-month-olds were taught to kick to move a mobile that was made of small blocks, all with the letter *A* on them. After a delay, kicking returned to a high level only if the babies were shown a mobile whose blocks were labeled with the same form (the letter *A*). If the form was changed (from *A*s to *2*s), infants no longer kicked vigorously. While making the mobile move, the babies had grouped together its features. They associated the kicking response with the category *A* and, at later testing, distinguished it from the category *2 (Bhatt, Rovee-Collier, & Weiner, 1994; Hayne, Rovee-Collier, & Perris, 1987)*.

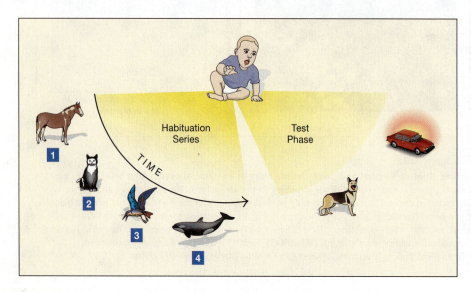

Habituation Series

Test Phase

TIME

FIGURE 6.8

Using habituation to study infant categorization. After habituating to a series of items belonging to one category (in this example, animals), infants are shown two novel items, one that is a member of the category (dog) and one that is not (car). If infants recover to (look longer at or spend more time manipulating) the out-of-category item (car), this indicates that they distinguish it from the set of within-category items (animals). Habituating another group of infants to a series of vehicles and seeing if, when presented with the two test items above, they recover to the dog confirms that babies can distinguish animals from vehicles. This pattern of responding has been found in many infant categorization studies.

As they gain experience in comparing to-be-categorized items in varied ways and their store of verbal labels expands, toddlers start to categorize flexibly: When 14-month-olds are given four balls and four blocks, some made of soft rubber and some of rigid plastic, their sequence of object touching reveals that after classifying by shape, they can switch to classifying by material (soft versus hard) if an adult calls their attention to the new basis for grouping (Ellis & Oakes, 2006).

In addition to touching and sorting, toddlers' categorization skills are evident in their play behaviors. After watching an adult give a toy dog a drink from a cup, most 14-month-olds shown a rabbit and a motorcycle offered the drink only to the rabbit (Mandler & McDonough, 1998). They clearly understood that certain actions are appropriate for some categories of items (animals) but not for others (vehicles).

By the end of the second year, toddlers' grasp of the animate–inanimate distinction expands. Nonlinear motions are typical of animates (a person or a dog jumping), linear motions of inanimates (a car or a table pushed along a surface). At 18 months, toddlers more often imitate a nonlinear motion with a toy that has animate-like parts (legs), even if it represents an inanimate (a bed). At 22 months, displaying a much fuller understanding, they imitate a nonlinear motion only with toys in the animate category (a cat but not a bed) (Rakison, 2005). They seem to realize that whereas animates are self-propelled and therefore have varied paths of movement, inanimates move only when acted on, in highly restricted ways (Rakison, 2006).

Researchers disagree on how babies arrive at these impressive attainments. One view holds that older infants and toddlers categorize more effectively because they become increasingly sensitive to fine-grained perceptual features and to stable relations among those features—for example, objects with flapping wings and feathers belong to one category; objects with rigid wings, windows, and a smooth surface belong to another category (Cohen & Cashon, 2006; Oakes et al., 2009; Rakison & Lupyan, 2008). An alternative view is that before the end of the first year, babies undergo a fundamental shift from a perceptual to a conceptual basis for constructing categories, increasingly grouping objects by their common function or behavior (birds versus airplanes, cars versus motorcycles, dogs versus cats) (Mandler, 2004). And yet a third view, stemming from the core knowledge perspective, assumes an inherited foundation of conceptual knowledge, which is enlarged and refined with experience (Gelman & Kalish, 2006).

All researchers acknowledge that infants' and toddlers' exploration of objects and expanding knowledge of the world contribute to advances in categorization, eventually enriching conceptual understanding. In addition, adult labeling of a set of objects with a consistently applied word ("Look at the car!" "Do you see the car?") calls babies' attention to commonalities among objects, fostering categorization as early as 3 to 4 months of age. Words are uniquely facilitating, as pairing the same tone with each object is ineffective (Ferry, Hespos, & Waxman, 2010). Toddlers' vocabulary growth, in turn, fosters categorization (Cohen & Brunt, 2009; Waxman, 2003).

Variations among languages lead to cultural differences in development of categories. Korean toddlers, who learn a language in which object names are often omitted from sentences, develop object-sorting skills later than their English-speaking counterparts (Gopnik & Choi, 1990). At the same time, Korean contains a common word, *kkita*, with no English equivalent, referring to a tight fit between objects in contact (a ring on a finger, a cap on a pen), and Korean toddlers are advanced in forming the spatial category "tight-fit" (Choi et al., 1999). After English-speaking 18-month-olds heard the word *tight* while observing several instances of objects fitting together tightly, they readily acquired the tight-fit category (Casasola, Bhagwat, & Burke, 2009). Those who viewed the events without the label did not form this challenging category.

LOOK AND LISTEN

Observe a toddler playing with a variety of small toys—some representing animals and some representing household objects. What play behaviors reveal the child's ability to categorize?

Evaluation of Information-Processing Findings

The information-processing perspective underscores the continuity of human thinking from infancy into adult life. In attending to the environment, remembering everyday events, and categorizing objects, Caitlin, Grace, and Timmy think in ways that are remarkably similar to our own, though their mental processing is far from proficient. Findings on memory and categorization join with other research in challenging Piaget's view of early cognitive development. Infants' capacity to recall events and to categorize stimuli attests, once again, to their ability to mentally represent their experiences.

Information-processing research has contributed greatly to our view of infants and toddlers as sophisticated cognitive beings. But its central strength—analyzing cognition into its components, such as perception, attention, memory, and categorization—is also its greatest drawback: Information processing has had difficulty putting these components back together into a broad, comprehensive theory.

One approach to overcoming this weakness has been to combine Piaget's theory with the information-processing approach, an effort we will take up in Chapter 12. A more recent trend has been the application of a *dynamic systems view* (see Chapter 1, page 28) to early cognition. In this approach, researchers analyze each cognitive attainment to see how it results from a complex system of prior accomplishments and the child's current goals (Courage & Howe, 2002; Spencer & Perone, 2008; Thelen & Smith, 2006). Once these ideas are fully tested, they may move the field closer to a more powerful view of how the minds of infants and children develop.

The Social Context of Early Cognitive Development

Recall the description at the beginning of this chapter of Grace dropping shapes into a container. Notice that she learns about the toy with Ginette's help. With adult support, Grace will gradually become better at matching shapes to openings and dropping them into the container. Then she will be able to perform the activity (and others like it) on her own.

Vygotsky's sociocultural theory emphasizes that children live in rich social and cultural contexts that affect the way their cognitive world is structured (Bodrova & Leong, 2007; Rogoff, 2003). Vygotsky believed that complex mental activities, such as voluntary attention, deliberate memory, categorization, and problem solving, have their origins in social interaction. Through joint activities with more mature members of their society, children master activities and think in ways that have meaning in their culture.

A special Vygotskian concept explains how this happens. The **zone of proximal** (or potential) **development** refers to a range of tasks that the child cannot yet handle alone but can do with the help of more skilled partners. To understand this idea, think about how a sensitive adult (such as Ginette) introduces a child to a new activity. The adult picks a task that the child can master but that is challenging enough that the child cannot do it by herself. Or the adult capitalizes on an activity that the child has chosen. The adult guides and supports, adjusting the level of support offered to fit the child's current level of performance. As the child joins in the interaction and picks up mental strategies, her competence increases, and the adult steps back, permitting the child to take more responsibility for the task. This form of teaching—known as *scaffolding*—promotes learning at all ages, and we will consider it further in Chapter 9.

Vygotsky's ideas have been applied mostly to preschool and school-age children, who are more skilled in language and social communication. Recently, however, his theory has been extended to infancy and toddlerhood. Recall that babies are equipped with capabilities that ensure that caregivers will interact with them. Then adults adjust the environment and their communication in ways that promote learning adapted to their cultural circumstances.

A study by Barbara Rogoff and her collaborators (1984) illustrates this process. Placing a jack-in-the-box nearby, the researchers watched how several adults played with Rogoff's son and daughter over the first two years. In the early months, adults tried to focus the baby's attention by working the toy and, as the bunny popped out, saying something like "My, what happened?" By the end of the first year, when the baby's cognitive and motor skills had improved, interaction centered on how to use the toy: The adults guided the baby's hand in turning the crank and putting the bunny back in the box. During the second year, adults helped from a distance, using gestures and verbal prompts, such as making a turning motion with the hand near the crank. Research indicates that this fine-tuned support is related to advanced play, language, and problem solving during the second year (Bornstein et al., 1992; Charman et al., 2001; Tamis-LeMonda & Bornstein, 1989).

As early as the first year, cultural variations in social experiences affect mental strategies. In the jack-in-the-box example, adults and children focused their attention on a single activity. This strategy, common in Western families, is well-suited to lessons in which children master skills apart from the everyday situations in which they will later use those skills. In contrast, Guatemalan Mayan adults and babies often attend to several events at once. For example, one 12-month-old skillfully put objects in a jar while watching a passing truck and blowing into a toy whistle his mother had slipped in his mouth (Chavajay & Rogoff, 1999). Processing several competing events simultaneously may be vital in cultures where

■ With gentle physical support and simple words, this father helps his young son put together a puzzle. By bringing the task within the child's zone of proximal development and adjusting his communication to suit the child's needs, the father transfers mental strategies to the child, promoting his cognitive development. ■

children largely learn not through lessons but through keen observation of others' ongoing activities at home, at work, and in public life. Children of Guatemalan Mayan, Mexican, and Native-American parents without extensive education continue to display this style of attention well into middle childhood (Chavajay & Rogoff, 2002; Correa-Chavez, Rogoff, & Arauz, 2005; Philips, 1983).

Earlier we saw how infants and toddlers create new schemes by acting on the physical world (Piaget) and how certain skills become better-developed as children represent their experiences more efficiently and meaningfully (information processing). Vygotsky adds a third dimension to our understanding by emphasizing that many aspects of cognitive development are socially prompted and encouraged. The Cultural Influences box on page 226 presents additional evidence for this idea. And we see even more evidence in the next section, where we look at individual differences in mental development during the first two years.

ASK YOURSELF

◆ **REVIEW** What impact does toddlers' more advanced play with toys have on the development of attention?

◆ **APPLY** When Timmy was 18 months old, his mother stood behind him, helping him throw a large ball into a box. As his skill improved, she stepped back, letting him try on his own. Using Vygotsky's ideas, explain how Timmy's mother is supporting his cognitive development.

◆ **CONNECT** Review the research on page 211, indicating that by age 10 to 12 months, infants can solve problems by analogy. How might this attainment be related to the development of categorization (less emphasis on similar appearance, more on common function and behavior) over the second half-year?

◆ **REFLECT** Describe your earliest autobiographical memory. How old were you when the event occurred? Do your responses fit with research on infantile amnesia?

CULTURAL INFLUENCES

Social Origins of Make-Believe Play

One of the activities my husband, Ken, used to do with our two sons when they were young was to bake pineapple upside-down cake, a favorite treat. One Sunday afternoon when a cake was in the making, 21-month-old Peter stood on a chair at the kitchen sink, busily pouring water from one cup to another.

"He's in the way, Dad!" complained 4-year-old David, trying to pull Peter away from the sink.

"Maybe if we let him help, he'll give us some room," Ken suggested. As David stirred the batter, Ken poured some into a small bowl for Peter, moved his chair to the side of the sink, and handed him a spoon.

"Here's how you do it, Petey," instructed David, with an air of superiority. Peter watched as David stirred, then tried to copy his motion. When it was time to pour the batter, Ken helped Peter hold and tip the small bowl.

"Time to bake it," said Ken.

"Bake it, bake it," repeated Peter, watching Ken slip the pan into the oven.

Several hours later, we observed one of Peter's earliest instances of make-believe play. He got his pail from the sandbox and, after filling it with a handful of sand, carried it into the kitchen and put it down on the floor in front of the oven. "Bake it, bake it," Peter called to Ken. Together, father and son placed the pretend cake in the oven.

Piaget and his followers concluded that toddlers discover make-believe independently, once they are capable of representational schemes. Vygotsky's theory has challenged this view. He believed that society provides children with opportunities to represent culturally meaningful activities in play. Make-believe, like other complex mental activities, is first learned under the guidance of experts (Berk, Mann, & Ogan, 2006). In the example just described, Peter extended his capacity to represent daily events when Ken drew him into the baking task and helped him act it out in play.

Current evidence supports the idea that early make-believe is the combined result of children's readiness to engage in it and social experiences that promote it. In one observational study of U.S. middle-SES toddlers, 75 to 80 percent of make-believe involved mother–child interaction (Haight & Miller, 1993). At 12 months, make-believe was fairly one-sided: Almost all play episodes were initiated by mothers. But by the end of the second year, half of pretend episodes were initiated by each.

During make-believe, mothers offer toddlers a rich array of cues that they are pretending—looking and smiling at the child more, making more exaggerated movements, and using more "we" talk (acknowledging that pretending is a joint endeavor) than they do during the same real-life event (Lillard et al., 2007). These maternal cues encourage toddlers to join in and probably facilitate their ability to distinguish pretend from real acts, which strengthens over the second and third years (Lillard & Witherington, 2004; Ma & Lillard, 2006).

Also, when adults participate, toddlers' make-believe is more elaborate (Keren et al., 2005). They are more likely to combine schemes into complex sequences, as Peter did when he put the sand in the bucket ("making the batter"), carried it into the kitchen, and, with Ken's help, put it in the oven ("baking the cake"). The more parents pretend with their toddlers, the more time their children devote to make-believe. In certain collectivist societies, such as Argentina and Japan, mother–toddler other-directed pretending, as in feeding or putting a doll to sleep, is particularly rich in maternal expressions of affection and praise (Bornstein et al., 1999a).

In some cultures, such as those of Indonesia and Mexico, where extended-family households and sibling caregiving are common, make-believe is more frequent and more complex with older siblings than with mothers. As early as age 3 to 4, children provide rich, challenging stimulation to their younger brothers and sisters, take these teaching responsibilities seriously, and, with age, become better at them (Zukow-Goldring, 2002). In a study of Zinacanteco Indian children of southern Mexico, by age 8, sibling teachers were highly skilled at showing 2-year-olds how to play at everyday tasks, such as washing and cooking. They often guided toddlers verbally and physically through the task and provided feedback (Maynard, 2002).

In Western middle-SES families, older siblings less often teach deliberately but still serve as influential models of playful behavior. In a study of New Zealand families of Western European descent, when both a parent and an older sibling were available, toddlers more often imitated the actions of the sibling, especially when siblings engaged in make-believe (Barr & Hayne, 2003).

As Chapters 9 and 10 will reveal, make-believe is a major means through which children extend their cognitive and social skills and learn about important activities in their culture. Vygotsky's theory, and the findings that support it, tell us that providing a stimulating environment is not enough to promote early cognitive development. In addition, toddlers must be invited and encouraged by more skilled members of their culture to participate in the social world around them. Parents and teachers can enhance early make-believe by playing often with toddlers, guiding and elaborating their make-believe themes.

© CAROLINE PENN/PANOS PICTURES

■ In cultures where sibling caregiving is common, make-believe play is more frequent and complex with older siblings than with mothers. These Kenyan brothers pretend with sand and rocks—"toys" that are plentiful in their surroundings. The older boy easily engages his toddler sibling, teaching him how to play. ■

Individual Differences in Early Mental Development

Because of Grace's deprived early environment, Kevin and Monica had a child psychologist give her one of many tests available for assessing mental development in infants and toddlers. Worried about Timmy's progress, Vanessa also arranged for him to be tested. At age 22 months, he had only a handful of words in his vocabulary, played in a less mature way than Caitlin and Grace, and seemed restless and overactive.

The cognitive theories we have just discussed try to explain the *process* of development—how children's thinking changes. Mental tests, in contrast, focus on cognitive *products*. Their goal is to measure behaviors that reflect development and to arrive at scores that *predict* future performance, such as later intelligence, school achievement, and adult vocational success. This concern with prediction arose nearly a century ago, when French psychologist Alfred Binet designed the first successful intelligence test, which predicted school achievement (see Chapter 1). It inspired the design of many new tests, including ones that measure intelligence at very early ages.

Infant Intelligence Tests

Accurately measuring infants' intelligence is a challenge because young babies cannot answer questions or follow directions. All we can do is present them with stimuli, coax them to respond, and observe their behavior. As a result, most infant tests emphasize perceptual and motor responses. But increasingly, new tests are being developed that tap early language, cognition, and social behavior, especially with older infants and toddlers.

One commonly used test, the *Bayley Scales of Infant Development,* is suitable for children between 1 month and 3½ years. The most recent edition, the Bayley-III, has three main subtests: (1) the Cognitive Scale, which includes such items as attention to familiar and unfamiliar objects, looking for a fallen object, and pretend play; (2) the Language Scale, which taps understanding and expressions of language—for example, recognition of objects and people, following simple directions, and naming objects and pictures; and (3) the Motor Scale, which includes gross- and fine-motor skills, such as grasping, sitting, stacking blocks, and climbing stairs (Bayley, 2005).

Two additional Bayley-III scales depend on parental report: (4) the Social-Emotional Scale, which asks caregivers about such behaviors as ease of calming, social responsiveness, and imitation in play; and (5) the Adaptive Behavior Scale, which asks about adaptation to the demands of daily life, including communication, self-control, following rules, and getting along with others.

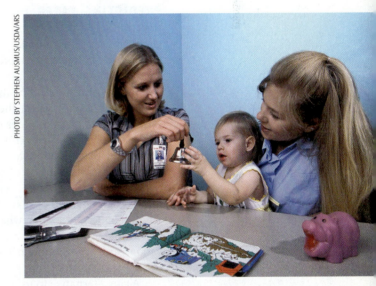

■ A trained examiner administers a test based on the Bayley Scales of Infant Development to a 1-year-old sitting in her mother's lap. Compared with earlier editions, the Bayley-III Cognitive and Language Scales better predict preschool mental test performance. ■

PHOTO BY STEPHEN AUSMUS/USDA/ARS

COMPUTING INTELLIGENCE TEST SCORES Intelligence tests for infants, children, and adults are scored in much the same way—by computing an **intelligence quotient (IQ),** which indicates the extent to which the raw score (number of items passed) deviates from the typical performance of same-age individuals. To make this comparison possible, test designers engage in **standardization**—giving the test to a large, representative sample and using the results as the *standard* for interpreting scores. The standardization sample for the Bayley-III included 1,700 infants, toddlers, and young preschoolers, reflecting the U.S. population in SES and ethnic diversity.

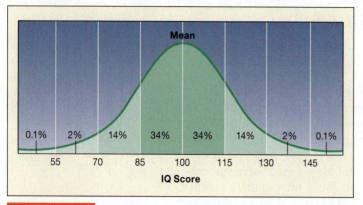

FIGURE 6.9

Normal distribution of intelligence test scores. To determine what percentage of same-age individuals in the population a person with a certain IQ outperformed, add the figures to the left of that IQ score. For example, an 8-year-old child with an IQ of 115 scored better than 84 percent of the population of 8-year-olds.

Within the standardization sample, performances at each age level form a **normal distribution,** in which most scores cluster around the mean, or average, with progressively fewer falling toward the extremes (see Figure 6.9). This *bell-shaped distribution* results whenever researchers measure individual differences in large samples. When intelligence tests are standardized, the mean IQ is set at 100. An individual's IQ is higher or lower than 100 by an amount that reflects how much his or her test performance deviates from the standardization-sample mean.

The IQ offers a way of finding out whether an individual is ahead, behind, or on time (average) in mental development compared with others of the same age. For example, if Timmy's score is 100, then he did better than 50 percent of his agemates, and his score will be 100. A child with an IQ of 85 did better than only 16 percent, whereas a child with an IQ of 130 outperformed 98 percent. The IQs of 96 percent of individuals fall between 70 and 130; only a few achieve higher or lower scores.

PREDICTING LATER PERFORMANCE FROM INFANT TESTS   Despite careful construction, most infant tests—including previous editions of the Bayley—predict later intelligence poorly. Longitudinal research reveals that the majority of children show substantial fluctuations in IQ between toddlerhood and adolescence—typically 10 to 20 points, and sometimes much more (McCall, 1993; Weinert & Hany, 2003).

Infants and toddlers easily become distracted, fatigued, or bored during testing, so their scores often do not reflect their true abilities. And infant perceptual and motor items differ from the tasks given to older children, which increasingly emphasize verbal, conceptual, and problem-solving skills. In contrast, the Bayley-III Cognitive and Language Scales, which better dovetail with childhood tests, are good predictors of preschool mental test performance (Albers & Grieve, 2007). But because most infant test scores do not tap the same dimensions of intelligence measured at older ages, they are conservatively labeled **developmental quotients (DQs)** rather than IQs.

Infant tests are somewhat better at making long-term predictions for extremely low-scoring babies. Today, they are largely used for *screening*—helping to identify for further observation and intervention babies whose very low scores mean that they are likely to have developmental problems.

As an alternative to infant tests, some researchers have turned to information-processing measures, such as habituation, to assess early mental progress. Their findings show that speed of habituation and recovery to novel visual stimuli are among the best available infant predictors of IQ from early childhood to early adulthood, with correlations ranging from the .30s to the .60s (Fagan, Holland, & Wheeler, 2007; Kavsek, 2004; McCall & Carriger, 1993).

Habituation and recovery seem to be especially effective early indexes of intelligence because they assess memory as well as quickness and flexibility of thinking, which underlie intelligent behavior at all ages (Colombo, 1995; Rose & Feldman, 1997). Piagetian object-permanence tasks are also relatively good predictors of later IQ, perhaps because they, too, reflect a basic intellectual process—problem solving (Rose, Feldman, & Wallace, 1992). The consistency of these findings has prompted designers of the Bayley-III to include items that tap such cognitive skills as habituation, object permanence, and categorization.

Early Environment and Mental Development

In Chapter 2, we indicated that intelligence is a complex blend of hereditary and environmental influences. Many studies have examined the relationship of environmental factors to infant and toddler mental test scores. As we consider this evidence, you will encounter findings that highlight the role of heredity as well.

Applying What We Know

Features of a High-Quality Home Life for Infants and Toddlers: The HOME Infant–Toddler Subscales

HOME SUBSCALE	SAMPLE ITEM
Emotional and verbal responsiveness of the parent	Parent caresses or kisses child at least once during observer's visit.
	Parent spontaneously speaks to child twice or more (excluding scolding) during observer's visit.
Parental acceptance of the child	Parent does not interfere with child's actions or restrict child's movements more than three times during observer's visit.
Organization of the physical environment	Child's play environment appears safe and free of hazards.
Provision of appropriate play materials	Parent provides toys or interesting activities for child during observer's visit.
Parental involvement with the child	Parent tends to keep child within view and to look at child often during observer's visit.
Opportunities for variety in daily stimulation	Child eats at least one meal per day with mother and/or father, according to parental report.
	Child frequently has a chance to get out of house (for example, accompanies parent on trips to grocery store).

Source: Bradley, 1994; Bradley et al., 2001.

HOME ENVIRONMENT The **Home Observation for Measurement of the Environment (HOME)** is a checklist for gathering information about the quality of children's home lives through observation and parental interview (Caldwell & Bradley, 1994). Applying What We Know above lists the factors measured by HOME during the first three years. Each is positively related to toddlers' mental test performance. Regardless of SES and ethnicity, an organized, stimulating physical setting and parental affection, involvement, and encouragement of new skills repeatedly predict better language and IQ scores in toddlerhood and early childhood (Fuligni, Han, & Brooks-Gunn, 2004; Linver, Martin, & Brooks-Gunn, 2004; Tamis-LeMonda et al., 2004; Tong et al., 2007). The extent to which parents talk to infants and toddlers is particularly important. It contributes strongly to early language progress, which, in turn, predicts intelligence and academic achievement in elementary school (Hart & Risley, 1995).

Yet we must interpret these correlational findings cautiously. In all the studies, children were reared by their biological parents, with whom they share not just a common environment but also a common heredity. Parents who are genetically more intelligent may provide better experiences while also giving birth to genetically brighter children, who evoke more stimulation from their parents. Research supports this hypothesis, which refers to *genetic–environmental correlation* (see Chapter 2, pages 84–85) (Saudino & Plomin, 1997). Still, heredity does not account for the entire association between home environment and mental test scores. Family living conditions—both HOME scores and affluence of the surrounding neighborhood—continue to predict children's IQ beyond the contribution of parental IQ and education (Chase-Lansdale et al., 1997; Klebanov et al., 1998). In one study, infants and children growing up in less crowded homes had parents who were far more verbally responsive to them—a major contributor to language, intellectual, and academic progress (Evans, Maxwell, & Hart, 1999).

How can the research summarized so far help us understand Vanessa's concern about Timmy's development? Ben, the psychologist who tested Timmy, found that he scored only slightly below average. Ben talked with Vanessa about her child-rearing practices and watched her play with Timmy. A single parent who worked long hours, Vanessa had little energy for Timmy at the end of the day. Ben also noticed that Vanessa, anxious about Timmy's progress, tended to pressure him, dampening his active behavior and bombarding him with directions: "That's enough ball play. Stack these blocks."

Ben explained that when parents are intrusive in these ways, infants and toddlers are likely to be distractible, play immaturely, and do poorly on mental tests (Bono & Stifter, 2003;

■ High-quality child care centers, with small group sizes and well-trained caregivers who provide developmentally appropriate stimulation, can be especially beneficial for children from low-SES homes. ■

Ask several employed parents of infants or toddlers to describe what they sought in a child-care setting, along with challenges they faced in finding child care. Are the parents knowledgeable about the ingredients of high-quality care?

Stilson & Harding, 1997). He coached Vanessa in how to interact sensitively with Timmy, while also assuring her that Timmy's current performance need not forecast his future development. Warm, responsive parenting that builds on toddlers' current capacities is a much better indicator than an early mental test score of how children will do later.

INFANT AND TODDLER CHILD CARE Today, more than 60 percent of U.S. mothers with a child under age 2 are employed (U.S. Census Bureau, 2010b). Child care for infants and toddlers has become common, and its quality—though not as influential as parenting—affects mental development. Research consistently shows that young children exposed to long hours of mediocre to poor-quality child care—whether they come from middle-class or from low-SES homes—score lower on measures of cognitive, language, and social skills during the preschool and elementary school years (Belsky et al., 2007; Hausfather et al., 1997; NICHD Early Child Care Research Network, 2000b, 2001, 2003b, 2006).

In contrast, good child care can reduce the negative impact of a stressed, poverty-stricken home life, and it sustains the benefits of growing up in an economically advantaged family (Lamb & Ahnert, 2006; McCartney et al., 2007; NICHD Early Child Care Research Network, 2003b). In Swedish longitudinal research, entering high-quality child care in infancy and toddlerhood was associated with cognitive, emotional, and social competence in middle childhood and adolescence (Andersson, 1989, 1992; Broberg et al., 1997).

In contrast to most European countries and to Australia and New Zealand, where child care is nationally regulated and funded to ensure its quality, reports on U.S. child care raise serious concerns. Standards are set by the individual states and vary widely. In studies of quality, only 20 to 25 percent of child-care centers and family child-care settings provided infants and toddlers with sufficiently positive, stimulating experiences to promote healthy psychological development. Most settings offered substandard care (NICHD Early Child Care Research Network, 2000a, 2004).

Unfortunately, many U.S. children from low-income families experience inadequate child care (Brooks-Gunn, 2004). But U.S. settings providing the very worst care tend to serve middle-SES families. These parents are especially likely to place their children in for-profit centers, where quality tends to be lowest. Low-SES children more often attend publicly subsidized, nonprofit centers, which have smaller group sizes and better teacher–child ratios (Lamb & Ahnert, 2006), Still, child-care quality for low-SES children varies widely. And probably because of greater access to adult stimulation, infants and toddlers in high-quality family child care score higher than those in center care in cognitive and language development (NICHD Early Child Care Research Network, 2000b).

See Applying What We Know on the following page for signs of high-quality child care for infants and toddlers, based on standards for **developmentally appropriate practice.** These standards, devised by the U.S. National Association for the Education of Young Children, specify program characteristics that serve young children's developmental and individual needs, based on both current research and consensus among experts. Caitlin, Grace, and Timmy are fortunate to be in family child care that meets these standards.

Child care in the United States is affected by a macrosystem of individualistic values and weak government regulation and funding. Furthermore, many parents think that their children's child-care experiences are better than they really are. Unable to identify good care, they do not demand it (Helburn, 1995). In recent years, recognizing that child care is in a state of crisis, the U.S. federal government and some states have allocated additional funds to subsidize its cost, especially for low-income families. Though far from meeting the need, this increase in resources has had a positive impact on child-care quality and accessibility (Children's Defense Fund, 2009).

Good child care is a cost-effective means of protecting children's well-being. And much like the programs we are about to consider, it can serve as effective early intervention for children whose development is at risk.

Applying What We Know

Signs of Developmentally Appropriate Infant and Toddler Child Care

PROGRAM CHARACTERISTIC	SIGNS OF QUALITY
Physical setting	Indoor environment is clean, in good repair, well-lighted, and well-ventilated. Fenced outdoor play space is available. Setting does not appear overcrowded when children are present.
Toys and equipment	Play materials are appropriate for infants and toddlers and are stored on low shelves within easy reach. Cribs, highchairs, infant seats, and child-sized tables and chairs are available. Outdoor equipment includes small riding toys, swings, slide, and sandbox.
Caregiver–child ratio	In child-care centers, caregiver–child ratio is no greater than one to three for infants and one to six for toddlers. Group size (number of children in one room) is no greater than six infants with two caregivers and 12 toddlers with two caregivers. In family child care, caregiver is responsible for no more than six children; within this group, no more than two are infants or toddlers. Staffing is consistent, so infants and toddlers can form relationships with particular caregivers.
Daily activities	Daily schedule includes times for active play, quiet play, naps, snacks, and meals. It is flexible rather than rigid, to meet the needs of individual children. Atmosphere is warm and supportive, and children are never left unsupervised.
Interactions among adults and children	Caregivers respond promptly to infants' and toddlers' distress; hold, talk to, sing, and read to them; and interact with them in a manner that respects the individual child's interests and tolerance for stimulation.
Caregiver qualifications	Caregiver has some training in child development, first aid, and safety.
Relationships with parents	Parents are welcome anytime. Caregivers talk frequently with parents about children's behavior and development.
Licensing and accreditation	Child-care setting, whether a center or a home, is licensed by the state or province. Voluntary accreditation by the National Academy of Early Childhood Programs *(www.naeyc.org/accreditation)* or the National Association for Family Child Care *(www.nafcc.org)* is evidence of an especially high-quality program.

Source: Copple & Bredekamp, 2009.

Early Intervention for At-Risk Infants and Toddlers

Children living in poverty are likely to show gradual declines in intelligence test scores and to achieve poorly when they reach school age (Bradley et al., 2001; Gutman, Sameroff, & Cole, 2003). These problems are largely due to stressful home environments that undermine children's ability to learn and increase the likelihood that they will remain poor as adults (McLoyd, Aikens, & Burton, 2006). A variety of intervention programs have been developed to break this tragic cycle of poverty. Although most begin during the preschool years (we will discuss these in Chapter 9), a few start during infancy and continue through early childhood.

In center-based interventions, children attend an organized child-care or preschool program where they receive educational, nutritional, and health services and their parents receive child-rearing and other social service supports. In home-based interventions, a skilled adult visits the home and works with parents, providing social support and teaching them how to stimulate a very young child's development. In most programs of either type, participating children score higher than untreated controls on mental tests by age 2. The earlier intervention begins, the longer it lasts, and the greater its scope and intensity (for example, year-round high-quality child care plus generous support services for parents), the better participants' cognitive and academic performance is throughout childhood and adolescence (Brooks-Gunn, 2004; Ramey, Ramey, & Lanzi, 2006; Sweet & Appelbaum, 2004).

The Carolina Abecedarian Project illustrates these positive outcomes. In the 1970s, more than 100 infants from poverty-stricken families, ranging in age from 3 weeks to 3 months, were randomly assigned to either a treatment group or a control group. Treatment infants were enrolled in full-time, year-round child care through the preschool years. There they received

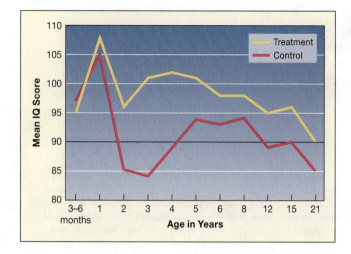

FIGURE 6.10

IQ scores of treatment and control children from infancy to 21 years in the Carolina Abecedarian Project. At 1 year, treatment children outperformed controls, an advantage consistently maintained through age 21. The IQ scores of both groups declined gradually during childhood and adolescence—a trend probably due to the damaging impact of poverty on mental development. *(Adapted from Campbell et al., 2001.)*

stimulation aimed at promoting motor, cognitive, language, and social skills and, after age 3, literacy and math concepts. Special emphasis was placed on rich, responsive adult–child verbal communication. All children received nutrition and health services; the primary difference between treatment and controls was the intensive child-care experience.

As Figure 6.10 shows, by 12 months of age, the IQs of the two groups diverged. Treatment children sustained their advantage until last tested—at age 21. In addition, throughout their years of schooling, treatment youths achieved considerably higher scores in reading and math. These gains translated into more years of schooling completed, higher rates of college enrollment and employment in skilled jobs, and lower rates of drug use and adolescent parenthood (Campbell et al., 2001, 2002; Ramey & Ramey, 1999).

Without early intervention, many children born into economically disadvantaged families will not reach their potential. Recognition of this reality led the U.S. Congress to provide limited funding for intervention services directed at infants and toddlers who already have serious developmental problems or who are at risk for problems because of poverty. Early Head Start, begun in 1995, currently has 700 sites serving 65,000 low-income families. It offers an array of coordinated services—child care, educational experiences for infants and toddlers, parenting education, family social support, and health care—delivered through a center-based, home-based, or mixed approach, depending on community needs. A recent evaluation, conducted when children reached age 3, showed that intervention led to warmer, more stimulating parenting, a reduction in harsh discipline, gains in cognitive and language development, and lessening of child aggression. The strongest effects occurred at sites offering a mix of center- and home-based services (Love et al., 2005; Love, Chazan-Cohen, & Raikes, 2007). Though not yet plentiful enough to meet the need, such programs are a promising beginning.

■ Interventions like Early Head Start show parents how to create a stimulating home environment for their young children. Here, mothers and toddlers gather for a session devoted to picture-book reading, an activity that promotes cognitive and language development. ■

ASK YOURSELF

◆ **REVIEW** What probably accounts for the finding that speed of habituation and recovery to visual stimuli predicts later IQ better than an infant mental test score?

◆ **APPLY** Fifteen-month-old Joey's developmental quotient (DQ) is 115. His mother wants to know exactly what this means and what she should do to support his mental development. How would you respond?

◆ **CONNECT** Using what you learned about brain development in Chapter 5, explain why it is best to initiate intervention for poverty-stricken children in the first two years rather than later.

◆ **REFLECT** Suppose you were seeking a child-care setting for your baby. What would you want it to be like, and why?

Language Development

Improvements in perception and cognition during infancy pave the way for an extraordinary human achievement—language. In Chapter 5, we saw that by the second half of the first year, infants make dramatic progress in distinguishing the basic sounds of their language and in segmenting the flow of speech into word and phrase units. They also start to comprehend some word meanings and, around 12 months of age, say their first word. Sometime between 1½ and 2 years, toddlers combine two words (Gleason, 2009). By age 6, children have a vocabulary of about 10,000 words, speak in elaborate sentences, and are skilled conversationalists.

To appreciate this awesome task, think about the many abilities involved in your own flexible use of language. When you speak, you must select words that match the underlying concepts you want to convey. To be understood, you must pronounce words correctly. Then you must combine them into phrases and sentences using a complex set of grammatical rules. Finally, you must follow the rules of everyday conversation—taking turns, making comments relevant to what your partner just said, and using an appropriate tone of voice.

How do infants and toddlers make such remarkable progress in launching these skills? To address this question, let's examine several prominent theories of language development.

■ Infants communicate from the very beginning of life, as seen in this interchange between a father and his baby. How will this child become a fluent speaker of his native language within just a few years? Theorists disagree sharply. ■

Three Theories of Language Development

In the 1950s, researchers did not take seriously the idea that very young children might be able to figure out important properties of language. As a result, the first two theories of how children acquire language were extreme views. One, *behaviorism,* regards language development as entirely due to environmental influences. The second, *nativism,* assumes that children are "prewired" to master the intricate rules of their language.

THE BEHAVIORIST PERSPECTIVE   Behaviorist B. F. Skinner (1957) proposed that language, like any other behavior, is acquired through *operant conditioning.* As the baby makes sounds, parents reinforce those that are most like words with smiles, hugs, and speech in return. For example, at 12 months, my older son, David, often babbled something like "book-a-book-a-dook-a-dook-a-book-a-nook-a-book-aaa." One day as he babbled away, I held up his picture book and said, "Book!" Soon David was saying "book-aaa" in the presence of books.

Some behaviorists believe that children rely on *imitation* to rapidly acquire complex utterances, such as whole phrases and sentences (Moerk, 2000). Imitation can combine with reinforcement to promote language, as when a parent coaxes, "Say 'I want a cookie,'" and delivers praise and a treat after the toddler responds, "Wanna cookie!"

Although reinforcement and imitation contribute to early language development, they are best viewed as supporting rather than fully explaining it. "It's amazing how creative Caitlin is with language," Carolyn remarked one day. "She combines words in ways she's never heard before, like 'needle it' when she wants me to sew up her teddy bear and 'allgone outside' when she has to come in."

Carolyn's observations are accurate: Young children create many novel utterances that are not reinforced by or copied from others. And when they do imitate others' language, they do so selectively, focusing mainly on building their vocabularies and on refining aspects of language that they are working on at the moment (Owens, 2008).

THE NATIVIST PERSPECTIVE   Linguist Noam Chomsky (1957) proposed a *nativist* account that regards the young child's amazing language skill as a uniquely human accomplishment, etched into the structure of the brain. Focusing on grammar, Chomsky reasoned that the rules for sentence organization are much too complex to be directly taught to or discovered by even a cognitively adept young child. Rather, he argued, all children have a **language acquisition device (LAD),** an innate system that contains a *universal grammar,* or set of rules common to all languages. It enables children, no matter which language they hear, to understand and speak in a rule-oriented fashion as soon as they pick up enough words. In sharp contrast to the behaviorist view, nativists regard deliberate training by parents as unnecessary (Pinker, 1999).

Are children biologically primed to acquire language? Recall from Chapter 4 that newborn babies are remarkably sensitive to speech sounds. And children everywhere reach major language milestones in a similar sequence (Gleitman & Newport, 1996). Also, the ability to master a grammatically complex language system seems to be unique to humans, as efforts to teach language to nonhuman primates—using either specially devised artificial symbol systems or American Sign Language (ASL), a gestural language used by the deaf—have met with limited success. Even after extensive training, chimpanzees (who are closest to humans in terms of evolution) master only a basic vocabulary and short word combinations, and they produce these far less consistently than human preschoolers (Tomasello, Call, & Hare, 2003).

Evidence for specialized language areas in the brain and a sensitive period for language development have also been interpreted as supporting Chomsky's theory. Let's take a closer look at these findings.

Language Areas in the Brain. Recall from Chapter 5 that for most individuals, language is housed in the left hemisphere of the cerebral cortex. Within it are two important language-related structures (see Figure 6.11). To clarify their functions, researchers have, for several decades, studied adults who experienced damage to these structures and display *aphasias,* or communication disorders. *Broca's area,* located in the left frontal lobe, supports grammatical processing and language production. *Wernicke's area,* located in the left temporal lobe, plays a role in comprehending word meaning.

But recent brain-imaging research suggests more complicated relationships between language functions and brain structures. The impaired pronunciation and grammar of patients with Broca's aphasia and the meaningless speech streams of patients with Wernicke's aphasia involve the spread of injury to nearby cortical areas and widespread abnormal activity in the left cerebral hemisphere, triggered by the brain damage (Bates et al., 2003; Keller et al., 2009).

Contrary to long-held belief, then, Broca's and Wernicke's areas are not solely or even mainly responsible for specific language functions. Nevertheless, depending on the site of injury to the adult left hemisphere, language deficits do vary predictably. Damage to frontal-lobe areas usually yields language production problems, whereas damage to areas in the other lobes yields comprehension problems (Dick et al., 2004).

The broad association of language functions with left-hemispheric regions is consistent with Chomsky's notion of a brain prepared to process language. But critics point out that at birth, the brain is not fully lateralized; it is highly plastic. Language areas in the cerebral cortex *develop* as children acquire language (Mills & Conboy, 2005). Although the left hemisphere is biased for language processing, if it is injured in the first few years, other regions take over language functions, and most such children eventually attain normal language competence. Thus, left-hemispheric localization, though typical, is not necessary for effective language processing. Additional research reveals that many regions of the cerebral cortex participate in language activities to different degrees, depending on the language skill and the individual's mastery of that skill (Shafer & Garrido-Nag, 2007).

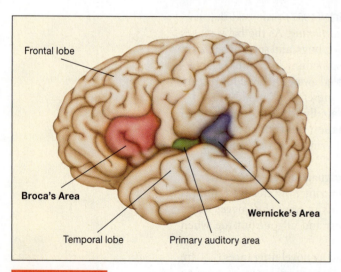

FIGURE 6.11

Broca's and Wernicke's areas, in the left hemisphere of the cerebral cortex. Broca's area, located in the frontal lobe, supports grammatical processing and language production. Wernicke's area, located in the temporal lobe, is involved in comprehending word meaning. Contrary to what was once believed, however, neither area is solely or even mainly responsible for these functions.

Nevertheless, when the young brain allocates language to the right hemisphere—as a result of left-hemispheric damage or learning of sign language (see page 169 in Chapter 5)—it localizes it in roughly the same regions that typically support language in the left hemisphere (Newman et al., 2002; Rosenberger et al., 2009). This suggests that those brain structures are uniquely disposed for language processing.

A Sensitive Period for Language Development. Must language be acquired early in life, during an age span in which the brain is particularly responsive to language stimulation? Evidence for a sensitive period that coincides with brain lateralization would support the view that language development has unique biological properties.

To test this idea, researchers have examined the language competence of deaf adults who acquired their first language—American Sign Language (ASL)—at different ages. The later learners, whose parents chose to educate them through the oral method, which relies on speech and lip-reading, did not acquire spoken language because of their profound deafness. And consistent with the sensitive-period notion, those who learned ASL in adolescence or adulthood never became as proficient as those who learned in childhood (Mayberry, 1994; Newport, 1991; Singleton & Newport, 2004). However, a precise age cutoff for a decline in first-language competence has not been established.

Is acquiring a second language also harder after a sensitive period has passed? In one study, researchers examined U.S. census data, selecting immigrants from non-English-speaking countries who had resided in the United States for at least ten years. The census form had asked the immigrants to rate how competently they spoke English, from "not at all" to "very well"—self-reports that correlate strongly with objective language measures. As age of immigration increased from infancy and early childhood into adulthood, English proficiency declined (Hakuta, Bialystok, & Wiley, 2003). Furthermore, ERP and fMRI measures of brain activity indicate that second-language processing is less lateralized in older than in younger learners (Neville & Bruer, 2001). But second-language competence does not drop sharply at a certain age. Rather, a continuous, age-related decrease occurs.

In sum, research on both first- and second-language learning reveals a biologically based timeframe for optimum language development. However, the boundaries of this sensitive period remain unclear.

■ Immigrant mothers read English with their children as part of a literacy program at a library in Queens, New York. Although the capacity to learn a second language does not drop sharply at a certain age, childhood seems to be a sensitive period for optimum language development. As a result, these mothers may never become as proficient in English as their children. ■

LIMITATIONS OF THE NATIVIST PERSPECTIVE Chomsky's theory has had a major impact on current views of language development. It is now widely accepted that humans have a unique, biologically based capacity to acquire language. Still, Chomsky's account of development has been challenged on several grounds.

First, researchers have had great difficulty specifying Chomsky's universal grammar. A major problem is the absence of a complete description of these abstract grammatical structures or even an agreed-on list of how many exist or the best examples of them. Chomsky's critics doubt that one set of rules can account for the extraordinary variation in grammatical forms among the world's languages (Christiansen & Chater, 2008; Tomasello, 2003, 2005). How children manage to link such rules with the strings of words they hear is also unclear.

Second, Chomsky's assumption that grammatical knowledge is innately determined does not fit with certain observations of language development. Once children begin to use an innate grammatical structure, we would expect them to apply it to all relevant instances in their language. But children refine and generalize many grammatical forms gradually, engaging in much piecemeal learning and making errors along the way. For example, one 3-year-old, in grappling with prepositions, initially added *with* to the verb *open* ("You open with scissors") but not to the word *hit* ("He hit me stick") (Tomasello, 2000, 2003, 2006). As we will see in Chapter 12, complete mastery of some grammatical forms, such as the passive voice, is not achieved until well into middle childhood (Tager-Flusberg & Zukowski, 2009). This suggests that more experimentation and learning are involved than Chomsky assumed.

THE INTERACTIONIST PERSPECTIVE   Recent ideas about language development emphasize *interactions* between inner capacities and environmental influences. One type of interactionist theory applies the information-processing perspective to language development. A second type emphasizes social interaction.

Some information-processing theorists assume that children make sense of their complex language environments by applying powerful cognitive capacities of a general kind (Bates, 2004; Elman, 2001; Munakata, 2006; Saffran, 2009). These theorists note that regions of the brain housing language also govern similar perceptual, motor, and cognitive abilities. For example, damage to parts of the left hemisphere, including Wernicke's area, results in difficulty comprehending both language and other patterned stimuli, such as music and a series of moving lights that depict familiar shapes (Koelsch et al., 2002; Saygin et al., 2004).

Other theorists blend this information-processing view with Chomsky's nativist perspective. They agree that infants are amazing statistical analyzers of speech and other information (see Chapter 5). But, they argue, these capacities probably are not sufficient to account for mastery of higher-level aspects of language, such as intricate grammatical structures (Aslin & Newport, 2009; Newport & Aslin, 2000). They also point out that grammatical competence may depend more on specific brain structures than other components of language. When 2- to 2½-year-olds and adults listened to short sentences—some grammatically correct, others with phrase-structure violations—both groups showed similarly distinct ERP brain-wave patterns for each sentence type in the left frontal and temporal lobes of the cerebral cortex (Oberecker & Friederici, 2006; Oberecker, Friedrich, & Friederici, 2005). This suggests that 2-year-olds process sentence structures using the same neural system as adults do. Furthermore, in studies of older children and adults with left-hemispheric brain damage, grammar is more impaired than other language functions (Baynes & Gazzaniga, 1988; Stromswold, 2000).

Still other interactionists emphasize that children's social skills and language experiences are centrally involved in language development. In this social-interactionist view, an active child, well-endowed for making sense of language, strives to communicate. In doing so, she cues her caregivers to provide appropriate language experiences, which help her relate content and structure of language to its social meanings (Bohannon & Bonvillian, 2009; Chapman, 2000, 2006).

Among social interactionists, disagreement continues over whether or not children are equipped with specialized language structures (Lidz, 2007; Shatz, 2007; Tomasello, 2003, 2006). Nevertheless, as we chart the course of language development, we will encounter much support for their central premise—that children's social competencies and language experiences greatly affect their language progress. In reality, native endowment, cognitive-processing strategies, and social experience probably operate in different balances with respect to each aspect of language: pronunciation, vocabulary, grammar, and communication skills. Table 6.3 provides an overview of early language milestones that we will examine in the next few sections.

Getting Ready to Talk

Before babies say their first word, they make impressive progress toward understanding and speaking their native tongue. They listen attentively to human speech, and they make speech-like sounds. As adults, we can hardly help but respond.

COOING AND BABBLING   Around 2 months, babies begin to make vowel-like noises, called **cooing** because of their pleasant "oo" quality. Gradually, consonants are added, and around 6 months **babbling** appears, in which infants repeat consonant–vowel combinations, often in long strings, such as "babababab" or "nanananana."

Babies everywhere (even those who are deaf) start babbling at about the same age and produce a similar range of early sounds. But for babbling to develop further, infants must be able to hear human speech. In hearing-impaired babies, these speechlike sounds are greatly delayed. And a deaf infant not exposed to sign language will stop babbling entirely (Oller, 2000).

TABLE 6.3	Milestones of Language Development During the First Two Years

APPROXIMATE AGE	MILESTONE
2 months	Infants coo, making pleasant vowel sounds.
4 months on	Infants observe with interest as the caregiver plays turn-taking games, such as pat-a-cake and peekaboo.
6 months on	Infants babble, adding consonants to their cooing sounds and repeating syllables. By 7 months, babbling starts to include many sounds of spoken languages. Infants comprehend commonly heard words.
8–12 months	Infants become more accurate at establishing joint attention with the caregiver, who often verbally labels what the baby is looking at. Infants actively participate in turn-taking games, trading roles with the caregiver. Infants use preverbal gestures, such as showing and pointing, to influence others' goals and behavior and to convey information.
12 months	Babbling includes sound and intonation patterns of the child's language community. Speed and accuracy of word comprehension increase rapidly. Toddlers say their first recognizable word.
18–24 months	Spoken vocabulary expands from about 50 to 200 words. Toddlers combine two words.

In one case, a deaf-born 5-month-old received a *cochlear implant*—an electronic device surgically inserted into the ear that converts external sounds into a signal to stimulate the auditory nerve. She showed typical babbling in infancy and resembled her hearing agemates in language development at 3 to 4 years (Schauwers et al., 2004). But if auditory input is not restored until after age 2 (the usual time for cochlear implant surgery), children remain behind in language development. And if implantation occurs after age 4, language delays are severe and persistent (Govaerts et al., 2002; Svirsky, Teoh, & Neuburger, 2004). These outcomes suggest an early sensitive period for the brain to develop the necessary organization for normal speech processing.

TAKE A MOMENT... When a baby coos or babbles and gazes at you, how do you respond? One day, as I stood in line at the post office behind a mother and her 7-month-old, the baby babbled, and three adults—myself and two people standing beside me—started to talk to the infant. We cooed and babbled in return, and we also said things like "Oooo, really?" "My, you're a big girl! Out to help Mommy mail letters today?" The baby smiled and babbled all the more. As infants listen to spoken language, babbling increases. Around 7 months, it starts to include many sounds of spoken languages. And as caregivers respond contingently to infant babbles, older infants modify their babbling to include sound patterns like those in the adult's speech (Goldstein & Schwade, 2008). By 8 to 10 months, babbling reflects the sound and intonation patterns of children's language community, some of which are transferred to their first words (Boysson-Bardies & Vihman, 1991).

Deaf infants exposed to sign language from birth babble with their hands much as hearing infants do through speech (Petitto & Marentette, 1991). Furthermore, hearing babies of deaf, signing parents produce babblelike hand motions with the rhythmic patterns of natural sign languages (Petitto et al., 2001, 2004). This sensitivity to language rhythm, evident not just in perception of speech but also in babbling, whether spoken or signed, supports both discovery and production of meaningful language units.

BECOMING A COMMUNICATOR At birth, infants are prepared for some aspects of conversational behavior. For example, they initiate interaction through eye contact and terminate it by looking away. By 3 to 4 months, infants start to gaze in the same general direction adults are looking—a skill that becomes more accurate at 10 to 11 months, as babies realize that others' focus offers information about their communicative intentions (to talk about an object) or other goals (to obtain an object) (Brooks & Meltzoff, 2005; Senju, Csibra, & Johnson, 2008).

 This baby uses a preverbal gesture to draw his father's attention to the birdhouse. His father's verbal response promotes the baby's transition to spoken language. ■

Indeed, 12-month-olds look where an adult is looking only when the adult's eyes are open. And 12- to 14-month olds are more likely to engage in gaze following when no obstacles block an adult's line of sight to an object (Brooks & Meltzoff, 2002; Dunphy-Lelii & Wellman, 2004). Around their first birthday, infants realize that a person's visual gaze signals a vital connection between the viewer and his or her surroundings, and they want to participate.

This **joint attention,** in which the child attends to the same object or event as the caregiver, who often labels it, contributes greatly to early language development. Infants and toddlers who often engage in it sustain attention longer, comprehend more language, produce meaningful gestures and words earlier, and show faster vocabulary development through 2 years of age (Brooks & Meltzoff, 2008; Carpenter, Nagel, & Tomasello, 1998; Flom & Pick, 2003; Silvén, 2001). Gains in joint attention at the end of the first year enable babies to establish a "common ground" with the adult, through which they can figure out the meaning of the adult's verbal labels (Tomasello, 2003).

Between 4 and 6 months, interactions between caregivers and babies begin to include *give-and-take,* as in pat-a-cake and peekaboo games. At first, the parent starts the game and the baby is an amused observer. But even 4-month-olds are sensitive to the structure and timing of these interactions, smiling more to an organized than to a disorganized peekaboo exchange (Rochat, Querido, & Striano, 1999). By 12 months, babies participate actively, trading roles with the caregiver. As they do so, they practice the turn-taking pattern of human conversation, a vital context for acquiring language and communication skills. Infants' play maturity and vocalizations during games predict advanced language progress in the second year (Rome-Flanders & Cronk, 1995).

At the end of the first year, infants use *preverbal gestures* to direct adults' attention, to influence their behavior, and to convey helpful information (Tomasello, Carpenter, & Liszkowski, 2007). For example, Caitlin held up a toy to show it, pointed to the cupboard when she wanted a cookie, and pointed at her mother's car keys lying on the floor. Carolyn responded to these gestures and also labeled them ("That's your bear!" "You want a cookie!" "Oh, there are my keys!"). In this way, toddlers learn that using language leads to desired results. Like gaze following, infant pointing predicts faster vocabulary development over the second year (Brooks & Meltzoff, 2008).

Besides using preverbal gestures to serve their own goals, 12-month-olds adapt these gestures to the needs of others. In one study, they pointed more often to an object whose location a searching adult did not know than to an object whose location the adult did know (Liszkowski, Carpenter, & Tomasello, 2008). Already, the cooperative processes essential for effective communication—modifying messages to suit others' intentions and knowledge—are under way. Soon toddlers integrate words with gestures, using the gesture to expand their verbal message, as in pointing to a toy while saying "give" (Capirci et al., 2005). Gradually, gestures recede, and words become dominant. But the earlier toddlers form word–gesture combinations, the sooner they produce two-word utterances at the end of the second year (Goldin-Meadow & Butcher, 2003).

LOOK AND LISTEN

Observe a toddler for 30 to 60 minutes at home or child care. Jot down preverbal gestures, words, and word–gesture combinations that the baby produces. Do the toddler's language skills fit with research findings?

First Words

In the second half of the first year, infants begin to understand word meanings. When 6-month-olds listened to the words "Mommy" or "Daddy" while looking at side-by-side videos of their parents, they looked longer at the video of the named parent (Tincoff & Jusczyk, 1999). At 9 months, after hearing a word paired with an object, babies looked longer at other objects in the same category than at those in a different category (Balaban & Waxman, 1997).

First spoken words, around 1 year, build on the sensorimotor foundations Piaget described and on categories infants have formed. In a study tracking the first 10 words used by several hundred U.S. and Chinese (both Mandarin- and Cantonese-speaking) babies, common objects ("ball," "bread"), important people ("Mama," "Dada"), and sound effects ("woof-woof," "vroom") were mentioned most often. Action words ("hit," "grab," "hug") and social routines ("hi," "bye"), though also appearing in all three groups, were more often produced by

Chinese than U.S. babies—differences we will consider shortly (Tardif et al., 2008). Other investigations concur that earliest words usually include people, objects that move, foods, animals (in families with pets), familiar actions, outcomes of such actions ("hot," "wet"), and social terms (Hart, 2004; Nelson, 1973). In their first 50 words, toddlers rarely name things that just *sit there*, like "table" or "vase."

When young children first learn words, they sometimes apply them too narrowly, an error called **underextension.** At 16 months, Caitlin used "bear" only to refer to the worn and tattered teddy bear she carried nearly constantly. As vocabulary expands, a more common error is **overextension**—applying a word to a wider collection of objects and events than is appropriate. For example, Grace used "car" for buses, trains, trucks, and fire engines. Toddlers' overextensions reflect their sensitivity to categories (MacWhinney, 2005). They apply a new word to a group of similar experiences: "car" to wheeled objects, "open" to opening a door, peeling fruit, and untying shoelaces. This suggests that children often overextend deliberately because they have difficulty recalling or have not acquired a suitable word. And when a word is hard to pronounce, toddlers are likely to substitute a related one they can say (Bloom, 2000). As vocabulary and pronunciation improve, overextensions disappear.

The Two-Word Utterance Phase

Young toddlers add to their spoken vocabularies at a rate of one to three words a week. Because gains in word production between 18 and 24 months are so impressive (one or two words per day), many researchers concluded that toddlers undergo a *spurt in vocabulary*—a transition from a slower to a faster learning phase. But recent evidence indicates that most children show a steady, continuous increase in rate of word learning that extends through the preschool years (Ganger & Brent, 2004).

How do toddlers build their vocabularies so quickly? Over the second year, they improve in ability to categorize experience, recall words, and grasp others' social cues to meaning, such as eye gaze, pointing, and handling objects (Dapretto & Bjork, 2000; Golinkoff & Hirsh-Pasek, 2006; Liszkowski, Carpenter, & Tomasello, 2007). Furthermore, as toddlers' experiences broaden, they have a wider range of interesting objects and events to label. For example, children approaching age 2 more often mention places to go ("park," "store"). And as they construct a clearer self-image, they add more words that refer to themselves ("me," "mine," "Katy") and to their own and others' bodies and clothing ("eyes," "mouth," "jacket" (Hart, 2004). In Chapter 9, we will consider young children's specific strategies for word learning.

■ Toddlers typically utter their first word around 1 year. As their experiences broaden, they label more objects and events, first with single words and then with two-word utterances known as telegraphic speech. ■

Once toddlers produce about 200 words, they start to combine two words: "Mommy shoe," "go car," "more cookie." These two-word utterances are called **telegraphic speech** because, like a telegram, they focus on high-content words, omitting smaller, less important ones ("can," "the," "to"). Children the world over use them to express an impressive variety of meanings.

Two-word speech consists largely of simple formulas ("more + X," "eat + X"), with different words inserted in the "X" position. Toddlers rarely make gross grammatical errors, such as saying "chair my" instead of "my chair." But their word-order regularities are usually copies of adult word pairings, as when Carolyn remarked to Caitlin, "How about *more sandwich?*" or "Let's see if you can *eat the berries?*" (Tomasello, 2003; Tomasello & Brandt, 2009). When 18- to 23-month-olds were taught noun and verb nonsense words (for example, "meek" for a doll and "gop" for a snapping action), they easily combined the new nouns with words they knew well ("more meek"). But they seldom formed word combinations with the new verbs (Tomasello, 2000; Tomasello et al., 1997). This suggests that they did not yet grasp subject–verb and verb–object relations, which are the foundation of grammar.

In sum, toddlers are absorbed in figuring out word meanings and using their limited vocabularies in whatever way possible to get their thoughts across. They first acquire "concrete pieces of language," gradually generalizing from those pieces to construct the word-order and other grammatical rules of their native tongue (Tomasello, 2006). As we will see in Chapter 7, they make steady progress over the preschool years.

Comprehension versus Production

So far, we have focused on language **production**—the words and word combinations children use. What about **comprehension**—the language they understand? At all ages, comprehension develops ahead of production. A five-month lag exists between the time toddlers comprehend 50 words (around 13 months) and the time they produce that many (around 18 months) (Menyuk, Liebergott, & Schultz, 1995).

Think back to the distinction made earlier in this chapter between two types of memory—recognition and recall. Comprehension requires only that children *recognize* the meaning of a word. But for production, children must *recall*, or actively retrieve from their memories, not only the word but also the concept for which it stands. Still, the two capacities are related. The speed and accuracy of toddlers' comprehension of spoken language increase dramatically over the second year. And toddlers who are faster and more accurate in comprehension tend to show more rapid growth in words understood and produced as they approach age 2 (Fernald, Perfors, & Marchman, 2006). Quick comprehension frees space in working memory for picking up new words and for the more demanding task of using them to communicate.

Individual and Cultural Differences

Although, on average, children produce their first word around their first birthday, the range is large, from 8 to 18 months—variation due to a complex blend of genetic and environmental influences. Earlier we saw that Timmy's spoken language was delayed, in part because of Vanessa's tense, directive communication with him. But Timmy is also a boy, and many studies show that girls are slightly ahead of boys in early vocabulary growth (Fenson et al., 1994). The most common explanation is girls' faster rate of physical maturation, which is believed to promote earlier development of the left cerebral hemisphere.

Temperament matters, too. Shy toddlers often wait until they understand a great deal before trying to speak. Once they do speak, their vocabularies increase rapidly, although they remain slightly behind their agemates (Spere et al., 2004). Temperamentally negative toddlers also acquire language more slowly because their high emotional reactivity diverts them from processing linguistic information (Salley & Dixon, 2007).

The surrounding environment also plays a role: The more words caregivers use, the more children learn (Weizman & Snow, 2001). Mothers talk much more to toddler-age girls than to boys, and parents converse less often with shy than with sociable children (Leaper, Anderson, & Sanders, 1998; Patterson & Fisher, 2002). Low-SES children, who receive less verbal stimulation in their homes than higher-SES children, usually have smaller vocabularies (Hoff, 2006). Limited parent–child book reading is a major factor. On average, a middle-SES child is read to for 1,000 hours between 1 and 5 years, a low-SES child for only 25 hours (Neuman, 2003). As a result, low-SES kindergartners have vocabularies only one-fourth as large as those of their higher-SES agemates (Lee & Burkam, 2002).

Young children have distinct styles of early language learning. Caitlin and Grace, like most toddlers, used a **referential style;** their vocabularies consisted mainly of words that referred to objects. A smaller number of toddlers use an **expressive style;** compared to referential children, they produce many more social formulas and pronouns ("thank you," "done," "I want it") uttered as compressed phrases that sound like single words ("Iwannit"). These styles reflect early ideas about the functions of language. Grace, for example, thought words were for naming things. In the week after her adoption, she uttered only a single word in Khmer, her native language. But after two months of listening to English conversation, Grace added words quickly: "Eli," then "doggie," "kitty," "Mama," "Dada," "book," "ball," "car," "cup," "clock," and "chicken"—all within one week. In contrast, expressive-style children believe words are for talking about people's feelings and needs. The vocabularies of referential-style toddlers grow faster because all languages contain many more object labels than social terms (Bates et al., 1994).

© TINA MANLEY/ASIA/ALAMY

■ This Chinese mother's communication with her toddler probably includes many words for actions and social routines. Her child—like other Chinese children—is likely to display an expressive style, focused on strengthening social relationships. ■

What accounts for a toddler's language style? Rapidly developing referential-style children often have an especially active interest in exploring objects. They also eagerly imitate their parents' frequent naming of objects, and their parents imitate back—a strategy that supports swift vocabulary growth by helping children remember new labels (Masur & Rodemaker, 1999). Expressive-style children tend to be highly sociable, and their parents more often use verbal routines ("How are you?" "It's no trouble") that support social relationships (Goldfield, 1987).

The two language styles are also linked to culture. Object words (nouns) are particularly common in the vocabularies of English-speaking toddlers, but Chinese, Japanese, and Korean toddlers have more words for actions (verbs) and social routines. When mothers' speech is examined in each culture, it reflects this difference (Choi & Gopnik, 1995; Fernald & Morikawa, 1993; Tardif, Gelman, & Xu, 1999). American mothers frequently label objects when interacting with their babies. Asian mothers, perhaps because of a cultural emphasis on the importance of group membership, emphasize actions and social routines as soon as their babies begin to speak.

At what point should parents become concerned if their child talks very little or not at all? If a toddler's development is greatly delayed when compared with the norms in Table 6.3, then parents should consult the child's doctor or a speech and language therapist. Late babbling may be a sign of slow language development that can be prevented with early intervention (Fasolo, Majorano, & D'Odorico, 2008). Some toddlers who do not follow simple directions or who, after age 2, have difficulty putting their thoughts into words may suffer from a hearing impairment or a language disorder that requires immediate treatment.

Supporting Early Language Development

Consistent with the interactionist view, a rich social environment builds on young children's natural readiness to speak their native tongue. For a summary of how caregivers can consciously support early language learning, see Applying What We Know below. Caregivers also do so unconsciously—through a special style of speech.

Adults in many countries speak to young children in **child-directed speech (CDS),** a form of communication made up of short sentences with high-pitched, exaggerated expression, clear pronunciation, distinct pauses between speech segments, clear gestures to support verbal meaning, and repetition of new words in a variety of contexts ("See the ball." "The ball bounced!") (Fernald et al., 1989; O'Neill et al., 2005). Deaf parents use a similar style of communication when signing to their deaf babies (Masataka, 1996). From birth on, infants prefer CDS over other kinds of adult talk, and by 5 months they are more emotionally responsive to it (Aslin, Jusczyk, & Pisoni, 1998).

■ This mother speaks to her baby in short, clearly pronounced sentences with high-pitched, exaggerated intonation. This form of communication, called child-directed speech, eases language learning for infants and toddlers. ■

© STOCK CONNECTION DISTRIBUTION/ALAMY

 ## Applying What We Know

Supporting Early Language Learning

STRATEGY	CONSEQUENCE
Respond to coos and babbles with speech sounds and words.	Encourages experimentation with sounds that can later be blended into first words
	Provides experience with the turn-taking pattern of human conversation
Establish joint attention and comment on what child sees.	Predicts earlier onset of language and faster vocabulary development
Play social games, such as pat-a-cake and peekaboo.	Provides experience with the turn-taking pattern of human conversation
Engage toddlers in joint make-believe play.	Promotes all aspects of conversational dialogue
Engage toddlers in frequent conversations.	Predicts faster early language development and academic success during the school years
Read to toddlers often, engaging them in dialogues about picture books.	Provides exposure to many aspects of language, including vocabulary, grammar, communication skills, and information about written symbols and story structures

CDS builds on several communicative strategies we have already considered: joint attention, turn-taking, and caregivers' sensitivity to toddlers' preverbal gestures. Here is an example of Carolyn using CDS with 18-month-old Caitlin as she picks her up from child care:

Caitlin:	"Go car."
Carolyn:	"Yes, time to go in the car. Where's your jacket?"
Caitlin:	[*Looks around; walks to the closet.*] "Dacket!" [*Points to her jacket.*]
Carolyn:	"There's that jacket! [*She helps Caitlin into the jacket.*] On it goes! Let's zip up. [*Zips up the jacket.*] Now, say bye-bye to Grace and Timmy."
Caitlin:	"Bye-bye, G-ace. Bye-bye, Te-te."
Carolyn:	"Where's your bear?"
Caitlin:	[*Looks around.*]
Carolyn:	[*Pointing*] "See? By the sofa." [*Caitlin gets the bear.*]

LOOK AND LISTEN

While observing a parent and toddler playing, describe how the parent adapts his or her language to the child's needs. Did the parent use child-directed speech?

Notice how Carolyn kept her utterance length just ahead of Caitlin's, creating a sensitive match between language stimulation and Caitlin's current capacities. Parents constantly fine-tune the length and content of their utterances in CDS to fit children's needs—adjustments that enable toddlers to join in and that foster both language comprehension and production (Cameron-Faulkner, Lieven, & Tomasello, 2003; Rowe, 2008). As the Social Issues: Education box on the following page makes clear, when a child's disability makes it difficult for parents to engage in the sensitive communication of CDS, language and cognitive development are drastically delayed.

As we saw earlier, parent–toddler conversation strongly predicts language development and later academic success. It provides many examples of speech just ahead of the child's current level and a sympathetic environment in which children can try out new skills. Dialogues about picture books are particularly effective. They expose children to great breadth of language and literacy knowledge, from vocabulary, grammar, and communication skills to information about written symbols and story structures. From the end of the first year through early childhood, children who experience regular adult–child book reading are substantially ahead of their agemates in language skills (Karrass & Braungart-Rieker, 2005; Whitehurst & Lonigan, 1998).

Do social experiences that promote language development remind you of those that strengthen cognitive development in general? CDS and parent–child conversation create a *zone of proximal development* in which children's language expands. In contrast, impatience with and rejection of children's efforts to talk lead them to stop trying and result in immature language skills (Baumwell, Tamis-LeMonda, & Bornstein, 1997; Cabrera, Shannon, & Tamis-LeMonda, 2007). In the next chapter, we will see that sensitivity to children's needs and capacities supports their emotional and social development as well.

ASK YOURSELF

◆ **REVIEW** Why is the social-interactionist perspective attractive to many investigators of language development? Cite evidence that supports it.

◆ **APPLY** Fran frequently corrects her 17-month-old son Jeremy's attempts to talk and—fearing that he won't use words—refuses to respond to his gestures. How might Fran be contributing to Jeremy's slow language progress?

◆ **CONNECT** Cognition and language are interrelated. List examples of how cognition fosters language development. Next, list examples of how language fosters cognitive development.

◆ **REFLECT** Find an opportunity to speak to an infant or toddler. How did your manner of speaking differ from the way you typically speak to an adult? What features of your speech are likely to promote early language development, and why?

SOCIAL ISSUES: EDUCATION

Parent–Child Interaction: Impact on Language and Cognitive Development of Deaf Children

About 2 to 3 out of every 1,000 American infants is born profoundly or fully deaf (Deafness Research Foundation, 2010). When a deaf child cannot participate fully in communication with caregivers, development is severely compromised. Yet the consequences of deafness for children's language and cognition vary with social context, as comparisons of deaf children of hearing parents with deaf children of deaf parents reveal.

Over 90 percent of deaf children have hearing parents who are not fluent in sign language. In toddlerhood and early childhood, these children often are delayed in development of language and make-believe play. In middle childhood, many achieve poorly in school, are deficient in social skills, and display impulse-control problems (Arnold, 1999; Edmondson, 2006). Yet deaf children of deaf parents escape these difficulties! Their language (use of sign) and play maturity are on a par with hearing children's. After school entry, deaf children of deaf parents learn easily and get along well with adults and peers (Bornstein et al., 1999b; Spencer & Lederberg, 1997).

These differences can be traced to early parent–child communication. Beginning in infancy, hearing parents of deaf children are less positive, less responsive to their child's efforts to communicate, less effective at achieving joint attention and turn-taking, less involved in play, and more directive and intrusive (Spencer, 2000;

Spencer & Meadow-Orlans, 1996). In contrast, the quality of interaction between deaf children and deaf parents resembles that of hearing children and hearing parents.

Hearing parents are not to blame for their deaf child's problems. Rather, they lack experience with visual communication, which enables deaf parents to respond readily to a deaf child's needs. Deaf parents know they must wait for the child to turn toward them before interacting (Loots & Devise, 2003). Hearing parents tend to speak or gesture while the child's attention is directed elsewhere—a strategy that works with a hearing but not with a deaf partner. When the child is confused or unresponsive, hearing parents often feel overwhelmed and become overly controlling (Jamieson, 1995).

The impact of deafness on language and cognitive development can best be understood by considering how it affects parents and other significant people in the child's life. Deaf children need access to language models—deaf adults and peers—to experience natural language learning. And their hearing parents benefit from social support along with training in how to interact sensitively with a nonhearing partner.

Screening techniques can identify deaf babies at birth. Many U.S. states and an increasing number of Western nations require that every newborn be tested, enabling immediate enrollment in programs aimed at fostering

effective parent–child interaction. When children with profound hearing loss start to receive intervention within the first year of life, they show much better language, cognitive, and social development (Vohr et al., 2008; Yoshinaga-Itano, 2003).

As this mother signs words to her toddler, who is deaf, the child responds with babblelike hand motions, similar to the vocal babbling of hearing infants. Babbling, whether spoken or signed, supports production of meaningful language. ■

Summary

Piaget's Cognitive-Developmental Theory

According to Piaget, how do schemes change over the course of development?

■ By acting directly on the environment, children move through four stages in which psychological structures, or **schemes,** achieve a better fit with external reality.

■ Schemes change in two ways: through **adaptation,** which is made up of two complementary activities—**assimilation** and **accommodation;** and through **organization,** the internal rearrangement of schemes into a strongly interconnected cognitive system.

Describe the major cognitive achievements of the sensorimotor stage.

■ In the **sensorimotor stage,** the **circular reaction** provides a means of adapting first schemes, and the newborn baby's reflexes gradually transform into the more flexible action patterns of the older infant. Around 8 months, infants develop **intentional,** or **goal-directed, behavior** and begin to understand **object permanence.**

■ Twelve- to 18-month-olds engage in more deliberate, varied exploration and no longer make the **A-not-B search error.** Between 18 and 24 months, **mental representation** is evident in sudden solutions to sensorimotor problems, mastery of object-permanence problems involving invisible displacement, **deferred imitation,** and **make-believe play.**

What does follow-up research say about the accuracy of Piaget's sensorimotor stage?

■ Many studies suggest that infants display a variety of understandings earlier than Piaget believed. Some awareness of object permanence, as revealed by the **violation-of-expectation method** and object-tracking research, may be evident in the first few months, although searching for hidden objects is a true cognitive advance, as Piaget suggested.

■ Furthermore, young infants display deferred imitation, and by 10 to 12 months, they engage in analogical problem solving— attainments that that require mental representation. Toddlers even imitate rationally, by inferring others' intentions.

■ A major advance in symbolic understanding, occurring around the first birthday, is **displaced reference**—the realization that words can be used to cue mental images of things not physically present. The capacity to use language to modify mental representations improves from the end of the second into the third year. By the middle of the second year, toddlers treat realistic-looking pictures symbolically. At about 2½ years, children grasp the symbolic meaning of video.

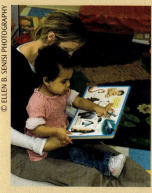

© ELLEN B. SENISI PHOTOGRAPHY

■ Today, researchers believe that newborns have more built-in equipment for making sense of their world than Piaget assumed, although they disagree on how much initial understanding infants have. According to the **core knowledge perspective,** infants are born with core domains of thought that support rapid cognitive development.

■ Although findings on early, ready-made knowledge are mixed, broad agreement exists on two issues. First, many cognitive changes of infancy are continuous rather than stagelike. Second, various aspects of cognition develop unevenly, rather than in an integrated fashion.

Information Processing

Describe the information-processing view of cognitive development and the general structure of the information- processing system.

■ Information-processing researchers want to know precisely what individuals of different ages do when faced with a task or problem. Most assume that we hold information in three parts of the mental system: the **sensory register; working,** or **short-term, memory;** and **long-term memory.** As information flows through the system, **mental strategies** operate on it so that it can be retained and used efficiently. To manage the complex activities of working memory, the **central executive** directs the flow of information.

What changes in attention, memory, and categorization take place over the first two years?

■ With age, infants attend to more aspects of the environment, take information in more quickly, anticipate future events, and flexibly shift their attention from one stimulus to another. In the second year, attention to novelty declines and sustained attention improves, especially during play with toys.

■ Young infants are capable of **recognition** memory. By the middle of the first year, they also engage in **recall** and can even retain modeled behaviors in the order in which they occurred. Both recognition and recall improve steadily with age.

■ Infants group stimuli into increasingly complex categories, shifting from categorical distinctions based on similar overall appearance to ones based on subtle sets of features. In the second year, toddlers begin to categorize flexibly, switching their basis of object sorting, and their grasp of the animate–inanimate distinction expands. Babies' exploration of objects, expanding knowledge of the world, and advancing language skills foster categorization.

Describe the contributions and limitations of the information-processing approach to our understanding of early cognitive development.

■ Information-processing findings challenge Piaget's view of infants as purely sensorimotor beings who cannot mentally represent experiences. But information processing has not yet provided a broad, comprehensive theory of children's thinking.

The Social Context of Early Cognitive Development

How does Vygotsky's concept of the zone of proximal development expand our understanding of early cognitive development?

■ Vygotsky believed that children master tasks within the **zone of proximal development**— ones just ahead of their current capacities— through the support and guidance of more skilled partners. As early as the first year, cultural variations in social experiences affect mental strategies.

© JAMES SHAFFER/PHOTOEDIT

Individual Differences in Early Mental Development

Describe the mental testing approach, the meaning of intelligence test scores, and the extent to which infant tests predict later performance.

■ The mental testing approach measures intellectual development in an effort to predict future performance. Scores are arrived at by computing an **intelligence quotient,** or **IQ,** which compares an individual's performance with that of a **standardization** sample of same-age individuals, whose performances form a **normal distribution.**

■ Infant tests, which consist largely of perceptual and motor responses, predict later intelligence poorly. As a result, scores on infant tests are called **developmental quotients,** or **DQs,** rather than IQs. Speed of habituation and recovery to visual stimuli and object permanence are better predictors of future performance.

Discuss environmental influences on early mental development, including home, child care, and early intervention for at-risk infants and toddlers.

■ Research with the **Home Observation for Measurement of the Environment (HOME)** shows that an organized, stimulating home environment and parental affection, involvement, and encouragement of new skills repeatedly predict higher mental test scores. Although the HOME–IQ relationship is partly due to heredity, family living conditions also affect mental development.

- Quality of infant and toddler child care influences cognitive, language, and social skills. Standards for **developmentally appropriate practice** specify program characteristics that meet young children's developmental needs.

- Intensive early intervention beginning in infancy and extending through early childhood can prevent the gradual declines in intelligence and the poor academic performance evident in many poverty-stricken children.

Language Development

Describe three theories of language development, and indicate the emphasis each places on innate abilities and environmental influences.

- According to the *behaviorist* perspective, parents train children in language skills through operant conditioning and imitation. Behaviorism has difficulty accounting for children's novel utterances.

- In contrast, Chomsky's *nativist* theory regards children as naturally endowed with a **language acquisition device (LAD).** Consistent with this perspective, a complex language system is unique to humans.

- Although language-related structures—Broca's and Wernicke's areas—exist in the left hemisphere of the cerebral cortex, their roles are more complex than previously assumed. But the broad association of language functions with left-hemispheric regions is consistent with Chomsky's notion of a brain prepared to process language. Evidence for a sensitive period for language development also supports this view.

- Difficulty specifying the universal grammar that underlies the vast diversity among languages challenges the nativist perspective. Children's gradual, piecemeal learning of many constructions is also inconsistent with Chomsky's theory.

- Recent theories suggest that language development results from *interactions* between inner capacities and environmental influences. Some interactionists apply the information-processing perspective to language development. Others emphasize the importance of children's social skills and language experiences.

Describe major milestones of language development in the first two years, individual differences, and ways adults can support infants' and toddlers' emerging capacities.

- Infants begin **cooing** at 2 months and **babbling** around 6 months. At 10 to 11 months, babies' skill at establishing **joint attention** improves, and by 12 months they actively engage in turn-taking games and use preverbal gestures. Adults can encourage language progress by responding to infants' coos and babbles, playing turn-taking games, establishing joint attention and labeling what babies see, and responding verbally to their preverbal gestures.

- Around 12 months, toddlers say their first word. Young children often make errors of **underextension** and **overextension.** Rate of word learning increases steadily, and once vocabulary reaches about 200 words, two-word utterances called **telegraphic speech** appear. At all ages, language **comprehension** develops ahead of **production.**

- Individual differences in early language development exist. Girls show faster progress than boys, and reserved, cautious toddlers may wait before trying to speak. Low-SES children, who receive less verbal stimulation than higher- SES children, usually have smaller vocabularies.

- Most toddlers use a **referential style** of language learning, in which early words consist largely of names for objects. A few use an **expressive style,** in which social formulas and pronouns are common and vocabulary grows more slowly.

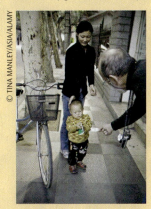

- Adults in many cultures speak to young children in **child-directed speech (CDS),** a simplified form of language that is well-suited to their learning needs. Parent–toddler conversation is one of the best predictors of early language development and academic competence during the school years.

IMPORTANT TERMS AND CONCEPTS

accommodation (p. 204)
adaptation (p. 204)
A-not-B search error (p. 207)
assimilation (p. 204)
autobiographical memory (p. 221)
babbling (p. 236)
central executive (p. 218)
child-directed speech (CDS) (p. 241)
circular reaction (p. 205)
comprehension (p. 240)
cooing (p. 236)
core knowledge perspective (p. 214)
deferred imitation (p. 207)
developmentally appropriate practice (p. 230)
developmental quotient (DQ) (p. 228)

displaced reference (p. 211)
expressive style (p. 240)
Home Observation for Measurement of the Environment (HOME) (p. 229)
infantile amnesia (p. 221)
intelligence quotient (IQ) (p. 227)
intentional, or goal-directed, behavior (p. 206)
joint attention (p. 238)
language acquisition device (LAD) (p. 234)
long-term memory (p. 218)
make-believe play (p. 207)
mental representation (p. 207)
mental strategies (p. 217)
normal distribution (p. 228)
object permanence (p. 207)

organization (p. 205)
overextension (p. 239)
production (p. 240)
recall (p. 220)
recognition (p. 220)
referential style (p. 240)
scheme (p. 204)
sensorimotor stage (p. 204)
sensory register (p. 217)
standardization (p. 227)
telegraphic speech (p. 239)
underextension (p. 239)
video deficit effect (p. 213)
violation-of-expectation method (p. 208)
working, or short-term, memory (p. 217)
zone of proximal development (p. 224)

"Our Baby Sister"
Marna
Age 13, Kentucky

A mother provides a soft, intimate shelter, protecting the baby from danger while supporting her mastery of the environment. Chapter 7 considers the importance of parental love and sensitivity for infants' and toddlers' feelings of security and competence.

Emotional and Social Development in Infancy and Toddlerhood

A s Caitlin reached 8 months of age, her parents noticed that she had become more fearful. One evening, when Carolyn and David left her with a babysitter, she wailed as they headed for the door—an experience she had accepted easily a few weeks earlier. Caitlin and Timmy's caregiver Ginette also observed an increasing wariness of strangers. When she turned to go to another room, both babies dropped their play to crawl after her. At the mail carrier's knock at the door, they clung to Ginette's legs, reaching out to be picked up.

At the same time, each baby seemed more willful. Removing an object from the hand produced little response at 5 months. But at 8 months, when Timmy's mother, Vanessa, took away a table knife he had managed to reach, Timmy burst into angry screams and could not be consoled or distracted.

All Monica and Kevin knew about Grace's first year was that she had been deeply loved by her destitute, homeless mother. Separation from her, followed by a long journey to an unfamiliar home, had left Grace in shock. At first she was extremely sad, turning away when Monica or Kevin picked her up. She did not smile for over a week. But as Grace's new parents held her close, spoke gently, and satisfied her craving for food, Grace returned their affection. Two weeks after her arrival, her despondency gave way to a sunny, easygoing disposition. She burst into a wide grin, reached out at the sight of Monica and Kevin, and laughed at her brother Eli's funny faces. Among her first words were the names of family members—"Eli," "Mama," and "Dada." As her second birthday approached, she pointed to herself, exclaiming "Gwace!" and laid claim to treasured possessions. "Gwace's chicken!" she would announce at mealtimes, sucking the marrow from the drumstick, a practice she had brought with her from Cambodia.

Taken together, the children's reactions reflect two related aspects of personality that develop during the first two years: close ties to others and a sense of self.

Erikson's Theory of Infant and Toddler Personality

Basic Trust versus Mistrust • Autonomy versus Shame and Doubt

Emotional Development

Development of Basic Emotions • Understanding and Responding to the Emotions of Others • Emergence of Self-Conscious Emotions • Beginnings of Emotional Self-Regulation

Temperament and Development

The Structure of Temperament • Measuring Temperament • Stability of Temperament • Genetic Influences • Environmental Influences • Temperament and Child Rearing: The Goodness-of-Fit Model

■ **BIOLOGY AND ENVIRONMENT**
Development of Shyness and Sociability

Development of Attachment

Bowlby's Ethological Theory • Measuring the Security of Attachment • Stability of Attachment • Cultural Variations • Factors That Affect Attachment Security • Multiple Attachments • From Attachment to Peer Sociability • Attachment and Later Development

■ **SOCIAL ISSUES: HEALTH**
Does Child Care in Infancy Threaten Attachment Security and Later Adjustment?

■ **CULTURAL INFLUENCES**
The Powerful Role of Paternal Warmth in Development

Self-Development

Self-Awareness • Categorizing the Self • Self-Control

We begin with Erikson's psychosocial theory, which provides an overview of personality development during infancy and toddlerhood. Then, as we chart the course of emotional development, we will discover why fear and anger became more apparent in Caitlin's and Timmy's range of emotions by the end of the first year. Our attention then turns to individual differences in temperament. We will examine biological and environmental contributions to these differences and their consequences for future development.

Next, we take up attachment to the caregiver, the child's first affectionate tie. We will see how the feelings of security that grow out of this important bond support the child's exploration, sense of independence, and expanding social relationships.

Finally, we focus on early self-development. By the end of toddlerhood, Grace recognized herself in mirrors and photographs, labeled herself as a girl, and showed the beginnings of self-control. "Don't touch!" she instructed herself one day as she resisted the desire to pull a lamp cord out of its socket. Cognitive advances combine with social experiences to produce these changes during the second year.

Erikson's Theory of Infant and Toddler Personality

Our discussion of major theories in Chapter 1 revealed that psychoanalytic theory is no longer in the mainstream of child development research. But one of its lasting contributions is its ability to capture the essence of personality development during each period of development. Recall that Sigmund Freud, founder of the psychoanalytic movement, believed that psychological health and maladjustment could be traced to the early years—in particular, to the child's relationships with parents. Although Freud's preoccupation with the channeling of biological drives and his neglect of important experiences beyond infancy and early childhood came to be heavily criticized, the basic outlines of his theory were accepted and elaborated in several subsequent theories. The most influential is Erik Erikson's *psychosocial theory*, also introduced in Chapter 1.

Basic Trust versus Mistrust

Erikson accepted Freud's emphasis on the importance of the parent–infant relationship during feeding, but he expanded and enriched Freud's view. A healthy outcome during infancy, Erikson believed, does not depend on the *amount* of food or oral stimulation offered but rather on the *quality* of caregiving: relieving discomfort promptly and sensitively, holding the infant gently, waiting patiently until the baby has had enough milk, and weaning when the infant shows less interest in breast or bottle.

Erikson recognized that no parent can be perfectly in tune with the baby's needs. Many factors affect parental responsiveness—feelings of personal happiness, current life conditions (for example, additional young children in the family), and culturally valued child-rearing practices. But when the *balance of care* is sympathetic and loving, the psychological conflict of the first year—**basic trust versus mistrust**—is resolved on the positive side. The trusting infant expects the world to be good and gratifying. As a result, he feels confident about venturing out and exploring it, and he emerges from this stage well-prepared for the challenges of toddlerhood. The mistrustful baby cannot count on the kindness and compassion of others, so she protects herself by withdrawing from people and things around her.

Autonomy versus Shame and Doubt

With the transition to toddlerhood, Freud viewed the parent's manner of toilet training as decisive for psychological health. In Erikson's view, toilet training is only one of many influential experiences. The familiar refrains of newly walking, talking toddlers—"No!" "Do it myself!"—reveal that they have entered a new period of budding selfhood. They want to decide for themselves, not just in toileting but also in other situations. The conflict of toddlerhood, **autonomy versus shame and doubt,** is resolved favorably when parents provide young children with suitable guidance and reasonable choices. A self-confident, secure 2-year-old has parents who do not criticize or attack him when he fails at new skills—using the toilet, eating with a spoon, or putting away toys. And they meet his assertions of independence with tolerance and understanding—for example, by giving him an extra five minutes to finish his play before leaving for the grocery store. In contrast, when parents are over- or undercontrolling, the outcome is a child who feels forced and shamed and who doubts his ability to control his impulses and act competently on his own.

In sum, basic trust and autonomy grow out of warm, sensitive parenting and reasonable expectations for impulse control starting in the second year. If children emerge from the first few years without sufficient trust in caregivers and without a healthy sense of individuality, the seeds are sown for adjustment problems. Adults who have difficulty establishing intimate ties, who are overly dependent on a loved one, or who continually doubt their own ability to meet new challenges may not have fully mastered the tasks of trust and autonomy during infancy and toddlerhood.

■ Toddlers who are given appropriate opportunities to try new skills without criticism develop a sense of autonomy—a feeling of being able to act competently on their own. ■

ASK YOURSELF

◆ **APPLY** Derek's mother fed him in a warm and loving manner during the first year. But when he became a toddler, she kept him in a playpen for many hours because he got into too much mischief while exploring freely. Use Erikson's theory to evaluate Derek's early experiences.

◆ **CONNECT** Do Erikson's recommendations for fostering autonomy in toddlerhood fit with Vygotsky's concept of the zone of proximal development, described on page 224 in Chapter 6? Explain.

■■ Emotional Development

■■ **TAKE A MOMENT...** Observe several infants and toddlers, noting the emotions each displays, the cues you rely on to interpret the baby's emotional state, and how caregivers respond. Researchers have conducted many such observations to find out how babies convey their emotions and interpret those of others. They have discovered that emotions play powerful roles in organizing the attainments that Erikson regarded as so important: social relationships, exploration of the environment, and discovery of the self (Halle, 2003; Saarni et al., 2006).

Think back to the *dynamic systems perspective* introduced in Chapters 1 and 5. As you read about early emotional development in the sections that follow, notice how emotions are an integral part of young children's dynamic systems of action. Emotions energize development. At the same time, they are an aspect of the system that develops, becoming more varied and complex as children reorganize their behavior to attain new goals (Campos, Frankel, & Camras, 2004; Witherington, Campos, & Hertenstein, 2001).

Because infants cannot describe their feelings, determining exactly which emotions they are experiencing is a challenge. Although vocalizations and body movements provide some information, facial expressions offer the most reliable cues. Cross-cultural evidence reveals that people around the world associate photographs of different facial expressions with emotions in the same way (Ekman, 2003; Ekman & Friesen, 1972). These findings inspired researchers to analyze infants' facial patterns to determine the range of emotions they display at different ages.

Nevertheless, assuming a close correspondence between a pattern of behavior and an underlying emotional state can lead to error. Infants, children, and adults use diverse responses to express a particular emotion. For example, babies on the visual cliff (see page 192 in Chapter 5) generally do not display a fearful facial expression, though they do show other signs of fear—drawing back and refusing to crawl over the deep side. Recall, also, from Chapter 5 that the emotional expressions of blind babies, who cannot make eye contact, are muted, prompting parents to withdraw (see page 194). When therapists show parents how blind infants express emotions through finger movements, parents become more interactive (Saarni et al., 2006; Fraiberg, 1971). Furthermore, the same general response can express several emotions. Depending on the situation, a smile might convey joy, embarrassment, contempt, or a social greeting.

In line with the dynamic systems view, emotional expressions vary with the person's developing capacities, goals, and context. To infer babies' emotions more accurately, researchers must attend to multiple interacting expressive cues—vocal, facial, and gestural—and see how they vary across situations believed to elicit different emotions (Lewis, 2000, 2008). With these ideas in mind, let's chart the course of early emotional development.

Development of Basic Emotions

Basic emotions—happiness, interest, surprise, fear, anger, sadness, and disgust—are universal in humans and other primates and have a long evolutionary history of promoting survival. Do infants come into the world with the ability to express basic emotions? Although signs of some emotions are present, babies' earliest emotional life consists of little more than two global arousal states: attraction to pleasant stimulation and withdrawal from unpleasant stimulation. Only gradually do emotions become clear, well-organized signals (Camras et al., 2003; Fox, 1991).

The dynamic systems perspective helps us understand how this happens: Children coordinate separate skills into more effective, emotionally expressive systems as the central nervous system develops and the child's goals and experiences change. Videotaping the facial expressions of her daughter from 6 to 14 weeks, Linda Camras (1992) found that in the early weeks, the baby displayed a fleeting angry face as she was about to cry and a sad face as her crying waned. These expressions first appeared on the way to or away from full-blown distress and were not clearly linked to the baby's experiences and desires. With age, she was better able to sustain an angry signal when she encountered a blocked goal and a sad signal when she could not overcome an obstacle.

According to one view, sensitive, contingent caregiver communication, in which parents selectively mirror aspects of the baby's diffuse emotional behavior, helps infants construct emotional expressions that more closely resemble those of adults (Gergely & Watson, 1999). Around 6 months, face, gaze, voice, and posture form organized patterns that vary meaningfully with environmental events. For example, Caitlin typically responded to her parents' playful interaction with a joyful face, pleasant babbling, and a relaxed posture, as if to say, "This is fun!" In contrast, an unresponsive parent often evokes a sad face, fussy sounds, and a drooping body (sending the message, "I'm despondent") or an angry face, crying, and "pick-me-up" gestures (as if to say, "Change this unpleasant event!") (Weinberg & Tronick, 1994; Yale et al., 1999). By the middle of the first year, emotional expressions are well-organized and specific—and therefore able to tell us a great deal about the infant's internal state.

We will begin by looking at four basic emotions—happiness, anger, sadness, and fear—that have received the most research attention. Later in the chapter, we will examine other emotions that develop in the first two years.

HAPPINESS Happiness—expressed first in blissful smiles, later through exuberant laughter—contributes to many aspects of development. When infants achieve new skills, they smile and laugh, displaying delight in motor and cognitive mastery. As the smile encourages caregivers to be affectionate and stimulating, the baby smiles even more (Aksan & Kochanska, 2004). Happiness binds parent and baby into a warm, supportive relationship that fosters the infant's developing competencies.

During the early weeks, newborn babies smile when full, during REM sleep, and in response to gentle touches and sounds, such as stroking of the skin, rocking, and the mother's soft, high-pitched voice. By the end of the first month, infants smile at dynamic, eye-catching sights, such as a bright object jumping suddenly across their field of vision. And as infants attend to the parent's face, and the parent talks and smiles, babies knit their brows, open their mouths to coo, and move their arms and legs excitedly, gradually becoming more emotionally positive until, between 6 and 10 weeks, the parent's communication evokes a broad grin called the **social smile** (Lavelli & Fogel, 2005; Sroufe & Waters, 1976). These changes parallel the development of infant perceptual capacities—in particular, sensitivity to visual patterns, including the human face (see Chapter 5). And social smiling becomes better-organized and stable as babies learn to use it to evoke and sustain pleasurable face-to-face interaction with the parent.

Laughter, which appears around 3 to 4 months, reflects faster processing of information than smiling. But, as with smiling, the first laughs occur in response to very active stimuli, such as the parent saying playfully, "I'm gonna get you!" and kissing the baby's tummy. As infants understand more about their world, they laugh at events with subtler elements of surprise, such as a silent game of peekaboo (Sroufe & Wunsch, 1972).

■ This baby's laughter encourages his mother to respond in kind, binding them together in a warm, affectionate relationship that promotes all aspects of development. ■

Around the middle of the first year, babies smile and laugh more often when interacting with familiar people, a preference that strengthens the parent–child bond. Between 8 and 10 months, infants more often interrupt their play with an interesting toy to relay their delight to an attentive adult (Venezia et al., 2004). And like adults, 10- to 12-month-olds have several smiles, which vary with context—a broad, "cheek-raised" smile in response to a parent's greeting; a reserved, muted smile for a friendly stranger; and a "mouth-open" smile during stimulating play (Bolzani et al., 2002; Dickson, Fogel, & Messinger, 1998). By the end of the first year, the smile has become a deliberate social signal.

ANGER AND SADNESS   Newborn babies respond with generalized distress to a variety of unpleasant experiences, including hunger, painful medical procedures, changes in body temperature, and too much or too little stimulation (see Chapter 4). From 4 to 6 months into the second year, angry expressions increase in frequency and intensity. Older infants react with anger in a wider range of situations—when an object is taken away, an expected pleasant event does not occur, their arms are restrained, the caregiver leaves for a brief time, or they are put down for a nap (Camras et al., 1992; Stenberg & Campos, 1990; Sullivan & Lewis, 2003).

Why do angry reactions increase with age? As infants become capable of intentional behavior (see Chapter 6), they want to control their own actions and the effects they produce. They are also more persistent about obtaining desired objects (Mascolo & Fischer, 2007). Furthermore, older infants are better at identifying who caused them pain or removed a toy. Their anger is particularly intense when a caregiver from whom they have come to expect warm behavior causes discomfort. The rise in anger is also adaptive. New motor capacities enable an angry infant to defend herself or overcome an obstacle (Izard & Ackerman, 2000). Finally, anger motivates caregivers to relieve the infant's distress and, in the case of separation, may discourage them from leaving again soon.

Although expressions of sadness also occur in response to pain, removal of an object, and brief separations, they are less common than anger. In contrast, sadness occurs often when infants are deprived of a familiar, loving caregiver (as illustrated by Grace's despondency in the weeks after her adoption) and when parent–infant interaction is seriously disrupted. In several studies, researchers had parents assume either a still-faced, unreactive pose or a depressed emotional state. Their 2- to 7-month-olds tried facial expressions, vocalizations, and body

When an unfamiliar adult attempts to hold her, this 8-month-old makes it clear that she prefers her mother! Fear rises during the second half of the first year. Its most frequent expression is stranger anxiety. ■

movements to get their mother or father to respond again. When these efforts failed, they turned away, frowned, and cried (Moore, Cohn, & Campbell, 2001; Papoušek, 2007). The still-face reaction is identical among American, Canadian, and Chinese babies, suggesting that it is a built-in withdrawal response to caregivers' lack of communication (Kisilevsky et al., 1998). Return to Chapter 4, page 155, and note that infants of depressed parents respond this way. When allowed to persist, a sad, vacant outlook disrupts all aspects of early development.

FEAR   Like anger, fear rises during the second half of the first year. Older infants hesitate before playing with a new toy, and newly crawling infants soon back away from heights (see Chapter 5). But the most frequent expression of fear is to unfamiliar adults, a response called **stranger anxiety.** Many infants and toddlers are quite wary of strangers, although the reaction does not always occur. It depends on several factors: temperament (some babies are generally more fearful), past experiences with strangers, and the current situation. When an unfamiliar adult picks up the infant in a new situation, stranger anxiety is likely. But if the adult sits still while the baby moves around and a parent is nearby, infants often show positive and curious behavior (Horner, 1980). The stranger's style of interaction—expressing warmth, holding out an attractive toy, playing a familiar game, and approaching slowly rather than abruptly—reduces the baby's fear.

Cross-cultural research reveals that infant-rearing practices can modify stranger anxiety. Among the Efe hunters and gatherers of the Republic of Congo, where the maternal death rate is high, infant survival is safeguarded by a collective caregiving system in which, starting at birth, Efe babies are passed from one adult to another. Consequently, Efe infants show little stranger anxiety (Tronick, Morelli, & Ivey, 1992). In contrast, among infants in Israeli kibbutzim (cooperative agricultural settlements), who live in isolated communities vulnerable to terrorist attacks, wariness of strangers is widespread. By the end of the first year, when infants look to others for cues about how to respond emotionally, kibbutz babies display far greater stranger anxiety than their city-reared counterparts (Saarni et al., 2006).

The rise in fear after 6 months of age keeps newly mobile babies' enthusiasm for exploration in check. Once wariness develops, infants use the familiar caregiver as a **secure base,** or point from which to explore, venturing into the environment and then returning for emotional support. As part of this adaptive system, encounters with strangers lead to two conflicting tendencies: approach (indicated by interest and friendliness) and avoidance (indicated by fear). The infant's behavior is a balance between the two.

As cognitive development permits toddlers to discriminate more effectively between threatening and nonthreatening people and situations, stranger anxiety and other fears of the first two years decline. Fear also wanes as children acquire a wider array of strategies for coping with it, as you will see when we discuss emotional self-regulation.

LOOK AND LISTEN

While observing an 8- to 18-month-old with his or her parent, gently approach the baby, offering a toy. Does the baby respond with stranger anxiety? To better understand the baby's behavior, ask the parent to describe his or her temperament and past experiences with strangers.

Understanding and Responding to the Emotions of Others

Infants' emotional expressions are closely tied to their ability to interpret the emotional cues of others. We have seen that in the first few months, babies match the feeling tone of the caregiver in face-to-face communication. Some researchers claim that young babies respond in kind to others' emotions through a built-in, automatic process of *emotional contagion* (Stern, 1985). Others, however, believe that infants acquire these emotional contingencies through operant conditioning—for example, learning that a smile generally triggers caregiver responsiveness and that distress prompts a comforting response (Saarni et al., 2006).

Around 3 to 4 months, infants become sensitive to the structure and timing of face-to-face interactions (see Chapter 6, page 238). When they gaze, smile, or vocalize, they now expect their social partner to respond in kind, and they reply with positive vocal and emotional reactions (Markova & Legerstee, 2006; Rochat, Striano, & Blatt, 2002). Within these exchanges, babies become increasingly aware of the range of emotional expressions (Montague & Walker-Andrews, 2001). According to some researchers, out of this early imitative communication, infants start to view others as "like me"—an awareness believed to lay the foundation for understanding others' thoughts and feelings (Gergeley & Watson, 1996; Meltzoff, 2007).

By 4 to 5 months, infants distinguish positive from negative emotion in voices, and soon after, they do so in facial expressions (see Chapter 5). Gradually, they become better at matching specific facial and vocal displays of emotion. By 7 months, they look longer at an appropriate face–voice pairing (such as a happy face with a happy voice) than at an inappropriate one (a happy face with an angry voice) (de Haan & Matheson, 2009). Responding to emotional expressions as organized wholes suggests that these signals are becoming meaningful to babies. Between 7 and 12 months, ERPs recorded while babies attend to facial expressions reveal reorganized brain-wave patterns resembling those of adults, suggesting enhanced processing of emotional cues (Grossmann, Striano, & Friederici, 2007). As skill at establishing joint attention improves (see Chapter 6), infants realize that an emotional expression not only has meaning but is also a meaningful reaction to a specific object or event (Moses et al., 2001; Tomasello, 1999).

Once these understandings are in place, infants engage in **social referencing**—actively seeking emotional information from a trusted person in an uncertain situation (Mumme et al., 2007). Many studies show that a caregiver's emotional expression (happy, angry, or fearful) influences whether a 1-year-old will be wary of strangers, play with an unfamiliar toy, or cross the deep side of the visual cliff (Repacholi, 1998; Stenberg, 2003; Striano & Rochat, 2000). The adult's voice—either alone or combined with a facial expression—is more effective than a facial expression alone (Vaish & Striano, 2004). The voice conveys both emotional and verbal information, and the baby need not turn toward the adult but, instead, can focus on evaluating the novel event.

As recall memory and language skills improve, and as parents' warnings to their newly walking youngsters become more frequent and intense, babies retain these emotional messages over longer time intervals. At 11 months, they respond appropriately after a delay of a few minutes, at 14 months after a delay of an hour or more (Hertenstein & Campos, 2004). By the middle of the second year, social referencing expands to include indirect emotional signals. After observing an adult react angrily to a second adult's play with a toy, 18-month-olds increased their monitoring of the angry adult's facial expression and reduced their touching of the object (Repacholi & Meltzoff, 2007).

As toddlers begin to appreciate that others' emotional reactions may differ from their own, social referencing allows them to compare their own and others' assessments of events. In one study, an adult showed 14- and 18-month-olds broccoli and crackers. In one condition, she acted delighted with the taste of broccoli but disgusted with the taste of crackers. In the other condition, she showed the reverse preference. When asked to share the food, 14-month-olds offered only the type of food they themselves preferred—usually crackers. In contrast, 18-month-olds gave the adult whichever food she appeared to like, regardless of their own preferences (Repacholi & Gopnik, 1997).

In sum, in social referencing, toddlers move beyond simply reacting to others' emotional messages. They use those signals to evaluate the safety and security of their surroundings, to guide their own actions, and to gather information about others' intentions and preferences. These experiences, along with cognitive and language development, probably help toddlers refine the meanings of emotions of the same valence—for example, happiness versus surprise, anger versus fear—during the second year (Gendler, Witherington, & Edwards, 2008; Saarni et al., 2006).

Emergence of Self-Conscious Emotions

Besides basic emotions, humans are capable of a second, higher-order set of feelings, including guilt, shame, embarrassment, envy, and pride. These are called **self-conscious emotions** because each involves injury to or enhancement of our sense of self. We feel guilt when we

> ### LOOK AND LISTEN
>
> ❖
>
> Observe a toddler and parent at a playground, park, or shopping mall, noting circumstances that trigger social referencing. How does the parent convey emotional information? How does the toddler respond?

■ This 2-year-old proudly displays his artistic accomplishment. Pride and other self-conscious emotions appear in the middle of the second year as children become firmly aware of the self as a separate, unique individual. ■

know that we have harmed someone and want to correct the wrongdoing. When we are ashamed or embarrassed, we have negative feelings about our behavior, and we want to retreat so others will no longer notice our failings. In contrast, pride reflects delight in the self's achievements, and we are inclined to tell others what we have accomplished and to take on further challenges (Saarni et al., 2006).

Self-conscious emotions appear in the middle of the second year, as 18- to 24-month-olds become firmly aware of the self as a separate, unique individual. Toddlers show shame and embarrassment by lowering their eyes, hanging their heads, and hiding their faces with their hands. They show guilt-like reactions, too. After noticing Grace's unhappiness, 22-month-old Caitlin returned a toy she had grabbed and patted her upset playmate. Pride also emerges around this time, and envy by age 3 (Barrett, 2005; Garner, 2003; Lewis et al., 1989).

Besides self-awareness, self-conscious emotions require an additional ingredient: adult instruction in *when* to feel proud, ashamed, or guilty. Parents begin this tutoring early when they say, "Look how far you can throw that ball!" or "You should feel ashamed for grabbing that toy!" Self-conscious emotions play important roles in children's achievement-related and moral behaviors. The situations in which adults encourage these feelings vary from culture to culture. In Western individualistic nations, most children are taught to feel pride over personal achievement—throwing a ball the farthest, winning a game, and (later on) getting good grades. In collectivist cultures such as China and Japan, calling attention to individual success evokes embarrassment and self-effacement. And violating cultural standards by failing to show concern for others—a parent, a teacher, or an employer—sparks intense shame (Akimoto & Sanbinmatsu, 1999; Lewis, 1992).

Beginnings of Emotional Self-Regulation

Besides expressing a wider range of emotions, infants and toddlers begin to manage their emotional experiences. **Emotional self-regulation** refers to the strategies we use to adjust our emotional state to a comfortable level of intensity so we can accomplish our goals (Eisenberg & Spinrad, 2004; Thompson & Goodvin, 2007). When you remind yourself that an anxiety-provoking event will be over soon, suppress your anger at a friend's behavior, or decide not to see a scary horror film, you are engaging in emotional self-regulation.

Emotional self-regulation requires voluntary, effortful management of emotions. This capacity for *effortful control* improves gradually, as the result of development of the prefrontal cortex and the assistance of caregivers, who help children manage intense emotion and teach them strategies for doing so (Fox & Calkins, 2003; Rothbart, Posner, & Kieras, 2006). Individual differences in control of emotion are evident in infancy and, by early childhood, play such a vital role in children's adjustment that—as we will see later—effortful control is regarded as a major dimension of temperament. A good start in regulating emotion during the first two years contributes greatly to autonomy and mastery of cognitive and social skills. Poorly regulated toddlers, by contrast, are likely to be delayed in mental development and to have behavior problems in the preschool years and are at risk for long-lasting problems (Eisenberg et al., 2004b; Lawson & Ruff, 2004).

In the early months, infants have only a limited capacity to regulate their emotional states. When their feelings get too intense, they are easily overwhelmed. They depend on the soothing interventions of caregivers for distraction and reorienting of attention—being lifted to the shoulder, rocked, gently stroked, and talked to softly.

More effective functioning of the prefrontal cortex increases the baby's tolerance for stimulation. Between 2 and 4 months, caregivers build on this capacity by initiating face-to-face play and attention to objects. In these interactions, parents arouse pleasure in the baby while adjusting the pace of their own behavior so the infant does not become overwhelmed and distressed. As a result, the baby's tolerance for stimulation increases further (Kopp & Neufeld, 2003).

By 4 to 6 months, the ability to shift attention and to engage in self-soothing helps infants control emotion. Babies who more readily turn away from unpleasant events or engage in self-soothing are less prone to distress (Crockenberg & Leerkes, 2003a). At the end of the first year, crawling and walking enable infants to regulate emotion more effectively by approaching or retreating from various situations. And further gains in attention permit toddlers to sustain interest in their surroundings and in play activities for a longer time (Rothbart & Bates, 2006).

As caregivers help infants regulate their emotional states, they contribute to the child's style of emotional self-regulation. Infants whose parents "read" and respond contingently and sympathetically to their emotional cues tend to be less fussy, to express more pleasurable emotion, to be more interested in exploration, and to be easier to soothe (Crockenberg & Leerkes, 2004; Volling et al., 2002). In contrast, parents who respond impatiently or angrily or who wait to intervene until the infant has become extremely agitated reinforce the baby's rapid rise to intense distress. This makes it harder for parents to soothe the baby in the future—and for the baby to learn to calm herself. When caregivers fail to regulate stressful experiences for infants who cannot yet regulate them for themselves,

■ Chinese and Japanese adults discourage the expression of strong emotion in infants. This baby's calm demeanor is typical of Chinese infants, who tend to smile and cry less than American babies. ■

brain structures that buffer stress may fail to develop properly, resulting in an anxious, reactive child who has a reduced capacity for regulating emotion problems (Crockenberg & Leerkes, 2000; Feldman, 2007b; Little & Carter, 2005).

Caregivers also provide lessons in socially approved ways of expressing feelings. Beginning in the first few months, parents encourage infants to suppress negative emotion by imitating their expressions of interest, happiness, and surprise more often than their expressions of anger and sadness. Boys get more of this training than infant girls, in part because boys have a harder time regulating negative emotion (Else-Quest et al., 2006; Malatesta et al., 1986). As a result, the well-known sex difference—females as emotionally expressive and males as emotionally controlled—is promoted at a tender age. Collectivist cultures place particular emphasis on socially appropriate emotional behavior. Compared with North Americans, Japanese and Chinese adults discourage the expression of strong emotion in babies (Fogel, 1993; Kuchner, 1989). By the end of the first year, Chinese and Japanese infants smile and cry less than American babies (Camras et al., 1998).

In the second year, growth in representation and language leads to new ways of regulating emotions. A vocabulary for talking about feelings—"happy," "love," "surprised," "scary," "yucky," "mad"—develops rapidly after 18 months, but toddlers are not yet good at using language to manage their emotions. Temper tantrums tend to occur because toddlers cannot control the intense anger that often arises when an adult rejects their demands, particularly when they are fatigued or hungry (Mascolo & Fischer, 2007). Toddlers whose parents are emotionally sympathetic but set limits (by not giving in to tantrums), who distract the child by offering acceptable alternatives, and who later suggest better ways to handle adult refusals display more effective anger-regulation strategies and social skills during the preschool years (Lecuyer & Houck, 2006).

Patient, sensitive parents also encourage toddlers to describe their internal states. Then, when 2-year-olds feel distressed, they can guide caregivers in helping them (Cole, Armstrong, & Pemberton, 2010). For example, while listening to a story about monsters, Grace whimpered, "Mommy, scary." Monica put the book down and gave Grace a comforting hug.

Older toddlers' use of words to label emotions shows that they have a remarkable understanding of themselves and others as emotional beings. The more parents label and talk about mental states in the second year, the greater their 2-year-olds' emotion vocabulary and ability to identify how others feel from situational cues—for example, a cartoon of a child being chased by a lion (Taumoepeau & Ruffman, 2006). As we will see in later chapters, with the ability to think about feelings, emotional self-regulation improves greatly in early and middle childhood.

ASK YOURSELF

◆ **REVIEW** Why do many infants show stranger anxiety in the second half of the first year? What factors can increase or decrease wariness of strangers?

◆ **APPLY** At 14 months, Reggie built a block tower and gleefully knocked it down. But at age 2, he called to his mother and pointed proudly at his tall block tower. What explains this change in Reggie's emotional behavior?

◆ **CONNECT** Why do children of depressed parents have difficulty regulating emotion (see page 155 in Chapter 4)? What implications do their weak self-regulatory skills have for their response to cognitive and social challenges?

◆ **REFLECT** How do you typically manage negative emotion? Describe several recent examples. How might your early experiences, gender, and cultural background have influenced your style of emotional self-regulation?

Temperament and Development

From early infancy, Caitlin's sociability was unmistakable. She smiled and laughed while interacting with adults and, in her second year, readily approached other children. Meanwhile, Monica marveled at Grace's calm, relaxed disposition. At 19 months, she sat contentedly in a highchair through a two-hour family celebration at a restaurant. In contrast, Timmy was active and distractible. Vanessa found herself chasing him as he dropped one toy, moved on to the next, and climbed on chairs and tables.

When we describe one person as cheerful and "upbeat," another as active and energetic, and still others as calm, cautious, or prone to angry outbursts, we are referring to **temperament**—early-appearing, stable individual differences in reactivity and self-regulation. *Reactivity* refers to quickness and intensity of emotional arousal, attention, and motor activity. *Self-regulation*, as we have seen, refers to strategies that modify that reactivity (Rothbart & Bates, 2006). The psychological traits that make up temperament are believed to form the cornerstone of the adult personality.

In 1956, Alexander Thomas and Stella Chess initiated the New York Longitudinal Study, a groundbreaking investigation of the development of temperament that followed 141 children from early infancy well into adulthood. Results showed that temperament can increase a child's chances of experiencing psychological problems or, alternatively, protect a child from the negative effects of a highly stressful home life. At the same time, Thomas and Chess (1977) discovered that parenting practices can modify children's emotional styles considerably.

These findings stimulated a growing body of research on temperament, including its stability, biological roots, and interaction with child-rearing experiences. Let's begin to explore these issues by looking at the structure, or makeup, of temperament and how it is measured.

The Structure of Temperament

Thomas and Chess's model of temperament inspired all others that followed. When detailed descriptions of infants' and children's behavior obtained from parental interviews were rated on nine dimensions of temperament, certain characteristics clustered together, yielding three types of children:

- The **easy child** (40 percent of the sample) quickly establishes regular routines in infancy, is generally cheerful, and adapts easily to new experiences.
- The **difficult child** (10 percent of the sample) is irregular in daily routines, is slow to accept new experiences, and tends to react negatively and intensely.

- The **slow-to-warm-up child** (15 percent of the sample) is inactive, shows mild, low-key reactions to environmental stimuli, is negative in mood, and adjusts slowly to new experiences.

Note that 35 percent of the children did not fit any of these categories. Instead, they showed unique blends of temperamental characteristics.

The "difficult" pattern has sparked the most interest because it places children at high risk for adjustment problems—both anxious withdrawal and aggressive behavior in early and middle childhood (Bates, Wachs, & Emde, 1994; Ramos et al., 2005; Thomas, Chess, & Birch, 1968). Compared with difficult children, slow-to-warm-up children present fewer problems in the early years. However, they tend to show excessive fearfulness and slow, constricted behavior in the late preschool and school years, when they are expected to respond actively and quickly in classrooms and peer groups (Chess & Thomas, 1984; Schmitz et al., 1999).

Today, the most influential model of temperament is Mary Rothbart's, described in Table 7.1. It combines related traits proposed by Thomas and Chess and other researchers, yielding a concise list of just six dimensions. For example, distractibility and persistence are considered opposite ends of the

- Despite his older brother's comforting offer of a stuffed animal, this toddler reacts with distress to a new situation. Patient, supportive parenting can help him modify his biologically based temperament and better manage his reactivity. ■

same dimension, which is labeled "attention span/persistence." A unique feature of Rothbart's model is inclusion of both "fearful distress" and "irritable distress," which distinguish between reactivity triggered by fear and reactivity due to frustration. And the model deletes overly broad dimensions such as regularity of body functions and intensity of reaction (Rothbart, Ahadi, & Evans, 2000; Rothbart & Mauro, 1990). A child who is regular in sleeping is not necessarily regular in eating or bowel habits. And a child who smiles and laughs intensely is not necessarily intense in fear, irritability, or motor activity.

Rothbart's dimensions represent the three underlying components included in the definition of temperament: (1) emotion ("fearful distress," "irritable distress," "positive affect," and "soothability"), (2) attention ("attention span/persistence"), and (3) action ("activity level"). According to Rothbart, individuals differ not just in their reactivity on each dimension but also in the self-regulatory dimension of temperament, **effortful control**—the capacity to

TABLE 7.1 Rothbart's Model of Temperament

DIMENSION	DESCRIPTION
REACTIVITY	
Activity level	Level of gross-motor activity
Attention span/persistence	Duration of orienting or interest
Fearful distress	Wariness and distress in response to intense or novel stimuli, including time to adjust to new situations
Irritable distress	Extent of fussing, crying, and distress when desires are frustrated
Positive affect	Frequency of expression of happiness and pleasure
SELF-REGULATION	
Effortful control	Capacity to voluntarily suppress a dominant, reactive response in order to plan and execute a more adaptive response

voluntarily suppress a dominant response in order to plan and execute a more adaptive response (Rothbart, 2003; Rothbart & Bates, 2006). Variations in effortful control are evident in how effectively a child can focus and shift attention, inhibit impulses, and manage negative emotion. Beginning in early childhood, capacity for effortful control predicts favorable development and adjustment in cultures as diverse as China and the United States (Zhou, Lengua, & Wang, 2009). Positive outcomes include persistence, task mastery, academic achievement, cooperation, moral maturity (such as concern about wrongdoing and willingness to apologize), and positive social behaviors of sharing and helpfulness (Eisenberg, 2010; Harris et al., 2007; Kochanska & Aksan, 2006; Posner & Rothbart, 2007b).

Measuring Temperament

Temperament is often assessed through interviews or questionnaires given to parents. Behavior ratings by pediatricians, teachers, and others familiar with the child and laboratory observations by researchers have also been used. Parental reports are convenient and take advantage of parents' depth of knowledge about their child across many situations (Gartstein & Rothbart, 2003). Although information from parents has been criticized as being biased, parental reports are moderately related to researchers' observations of children's behavior (Majdandžić & van den Boom, 2007; Mangelsdorf, Schoppe, & Buur, 2000). And parent perceptions are vital for understanding how parents view and respond to their child.

Observations by researchers in the home or laboratory avoid the subjectivity of parent reports but can lead to other inaccuracies. In homes, observers find it hard to capture all relevant information, especially events that are rare but important, such as infants' response to frustration. And in the unfamiliar lab setting, fearful children who calmly avoid certain experiences at home may become too upset to complete the session (Wachs & Bates, 2001). Still, researchers can better control children's experiences in the lab. And they can conveniently combine observations of behavior with physiological measures to gain insight into the biological basis of temperament.

Most neurophysiological research has focused on children who fall at opposite extremes of the positive-affect and fearful-distress dimensions of temperament: **inhibited, or shy, children,** who react negatively to and withdraw from novel stimuli, and **uninhibited, or sociable, children,** who display positive emotion and approach novel stimuli. As the Biology and Environment box on the following page reveals, biologically based reactivity—evident in heart rate, hormone levels, and EEG brain waves in the frontal region of the cerebral cortex— differentiates children with inhibited and uninhibited temperaments.

Stability of Temperament

Young children who score low or high on attention span, irritability, sociability, shyness, or effortful control tend to respond similarly when assessed again several months to a few years later and, occasionally, even into the adult years (Caspi et al., 2003; Kochanska & Knaack, 2003; Komsi et al., 2006; Majdandžić & van den Boom, 2007; Rothbart, Ahadi, & Evans, 2000; Ruff & Rothbart, 1996). However, the overall stability of temperament is low in infancy and toddlerhood and only moderate from the preschool years on (Putnam, Samson, & Rothbart, 2000). Some children remain the same, but many others change.

Why isn't temperament more stable? A major reason is that temperament itself develops with age. To illustrate, let's look at irritability and activity level. Recall from Chapter 4 that the early months are a period of fussing and crying for most babies. As infants better regulate their attention and emotions, many who initially seemed irritable become calm and content. In the case of activity level, the meaning of the behavior changes. At first, an active, wriggling infant tends to be highly aroused and uncomfortable, whereas an inactive baby is often alert and attentive. Once infants move on their own, the reverse is so! An active crawler is usually alert and interested in exploration, whereas an inactive baby may be fearful and withdrawn.

These discrepancies help us understand why long-term prediction from early temperament is best achieved after age 3, when children's styles of responding are better established (Roberts & DelVecchio, 2000). In line with this idea, between 2½ and 3, children improve substantially and also perform more consistently across a wide range of tasks requiring effortful

BIOLOGY AND ENVIRONMENT

Development of Shyness and Sociability

Two 4-month-old babies, Larry and Mitch, visited the laboratory of Jerome Kagan, who observed their reactions to a variety of unfamiliar experiences. When exposed to new sights and sounds, such as a moving mobile decorated with colorful toys, Larry tensed his muscles, moved his arms and legs with agitation, and began to cry. In contrast, Mitch remained relaxed and quiet, smiling and cooing at the excitement around him.

As toddlers, Larry and Mitch returned to the laboratory, where they experienced a variety of procedures designed to induce uncertainty. Electrodes were placed on their bodies and blood pressure cuffs on their arms to measure heart rate; toy robots, animals, and puppets moved before their eyes; and unfamiliar people entered and behaved in unexpected ways or wore novel costumes. While Larry whimpered and quickly withdrew, Mitch watched with interest, laughed at the strange sights, and approached the toys and strangers.

On a third visit, at age 4½, Larry barely talked or smiled during an interview with an unfamiliar adult. In contrast, Mitch asked questions and communicated his pleasure at each new activity. In a playroom with two unfamiliar peers, Larry pulled back and watched, while Mitch made friends quickly.

In longitudinal research on several hundred Caucasian infants followed into adolescence, Kagan found that about 20 percent of 4-month-olds were, like Larry, easily upset by novelty; another 40 percent, like Mitch, were comfortable, even delighted, with new experiences. About 20 to 30 percent of these extreme groups retained their temperamental styles as they grew older (Kagan, 2003; Kagan & Saudino, 2001; Kagan et al., 2007). But most children's dispositions became less extreme over time. Genetic makeup and child-rearing experiences jointly influenced stability and change in temperament.

Neurophysiological Correlates of Shyness and Sociability

Individual differences in arousal of the *amygdala,* an inner brain structure that controls avoidance reactions, contribute to these contrasting temperaments. In shy, inhibited children, novel stimuli easily excite the amygdala and its connections to the cerebral cortex and sympathetic nervous system, which prepares the body to act in the face of threat. In sociable, uninhibited children, the same level of stimulation evokes minimal neural excitation (Kagan & Fox, 2006). In support of this theory, while viewing photos of unfamiliar faces, adults who had been classified as inhibited in the second year of life showed greater fMRI activity in the amygdala than adults who had been uninhibited as toddlers (Schwartz et al., 2003). And additional neurophysiological responses known to be mediated by the amygdala distinguish these two emotional styles:

- *Heart rate.* From the first few weeks of life, the heart rates of shy children are consistently higher than those of sociable children, and they speed up further in response to unfamiliar events (Schmidt et al., 2007; Snidman et al., 1995).
- *Cortisol.* Saliva concentrations of the stress hormone cortisol tend to be higher, and to rise more in response to a stressful event, in shy than in sociable children (Schmidt et al., 1997, 1999; Zimmermann & Stansbury, 2004).
- *Pupil dilation, blood pressure, and skin surface temperature.* Compared with sociable children, shy children show greater pupil dilation, rise in blood pressure, and cooling of the fingertips when faced with novelty (Kagan et al., 1999, 2007).

Another physiological correlate of approach–withdrawal to people and objects is the pattern of brain waves in the frontal lobes of the cerebral cortex. Shy infants and preschoolers show greater EEG activity in the right frontal lobe, which is associated with negative emotional reactivity; sociable children show the opposite pattern (Kagan & Snidman, 2004; Kagan et al., 2007). Neural activity in the amygdala, which is transmitted to the frontal lobes, probably contributes to these differences. Inhibited children also show greater generalized activation of the cerebral cortex, an indicator of high emotional arousal and monitoring of new situations for potential threats (Henderson et al., 2004).

Child-Rearing Practices

According to Kagan, extremely shy or sociable children inherit a physiology that biases them toward a particular temperamental style. Yet heritability research indicates that genes contribute only modestly to shyness and sociability

■ A strong physiological response to uncertain situations prompts this child to cling to her mother. With patient, insistent encouragement, her parents can help her overcome the urge to retreat from unfamiliar events. ■

(Kagan & Fox, 2006). Experience has a profound impact.

Child-rearing practices affect the chances that an emotionally reactive baby will become a fearful child. Warm, supportive parenting reduces shy infants' and preschoolers' intense physiological reaction to novelty, whereas cold, intrusive parenting heightens anxiety (Hane et al., 2008; Rubin, Burgess, & Hastings, 2002). And if parents overprotect infants and young children who dislike novelty, they make it harder for the child to overcome an urge to retreat. Parents who make appropriate demands for their child to approach new experiences help shy youngsters overcome fear (Rubin & Burgess, 2002).

When inhibition persists, it leads to excessive cautiousness, low self-esteem, and loneliness (Fordham & Stevenson-Hinde, 1999; Rubin, Stewart, & Coplan, 1995). In adolescence, persistent shyness increases the risk of severe anxiety, especially social phobia—intense fear of being humiliated in social situations (Kagan & Fox, 2006). For inhibited children to acquire effective social skills, parenting must be tailored to their temperaments—a theme we will encounter again in this and later chapters.

© FIRST LIGHT/ALAMY

control, such as waiting for a reward, lowering their voice to a whisper, succeeding at games like "Simon Says," and selectively attending to one stimulus while ignoring competing stimuli (Kochanska, Murray, & Harlan, 2000; Li-Grining, 2007). Researchers believe that around this time, areas in the prefrontal cortex involved in suppressing impulses develop rapidly (Gerardi-Caulton, 2000; Rothbart & Bates, 2006).

Nevertheless, the ease with which children manage their reactivity in early childhood depends on the type and strength of the reactive emotion involved. Preschoolers who were highly fearful as toddlers score slightly better than their agemates in effortful control. In contrast, angry, irritable toddlers tend to be less effective at effortful control at later ages (Bridgett et al., 2009; Kochanska & Knaack, 2003; Kochanska, Murray, & Harlan, 2000). Other evidence confirms that child rearing plays an important role in modifying biologically based temperamental traits. Toddlers and young preschoolers who have fearful or negative, irritable temperaments but experience patient, supportive parenting are better at managing their reactivity and are especially likely to decline in difficultness (Warren & Simmens, 2005).

In sum, many factors affect the extent to which a child's temperament remains stable, including development of the biological systems on which temperament is based, the child's capacity for effortful control, and the success of her efforts, which depend on the quality and intensity of her emotional reactivity. When we consider the evidence as a whole, the low to moderate stability of temperament makes sense. It also confirms that experience can modify biologically based temperamental traits considerably, although children rarely change from one extreme to the other—that is, a shy toddler practically never becomes highly sociable, and irritable toddlers seldom become easy-going. With these ideas in mind, let's turn to genetic and environmental contributions to temperament and personality.

Genetic Influences

The word *temperament* implies a genetic foundation for individual differences in personality. Research indicates that identical twins are more similar than fraternal twins across a wide range of temperamental traits (activity level, attention span, shyness/sociability, irritability, and effortful control) and personality measures (introversion/extroversion, anxiety, agreeableness, curiosity and imaginativeness, and impulsivity) (Bouchard, 2004; Bouchard & Loehlin, 2001; Caspi & Shiner, 2006; Roisman & Fraley, 2006; Saudino & Cherny, 2001). In Chapter 2, we noted that heritability estimates derived from twin studies suggest a moderate role for genetic factors in temperament and personality: About half of individual differences have been attributed to differences in genetic makeup.

Consistent ethnic and sex differences in early temperament exist, again implying a role for heredity. Compared with Caucasian-American infants, Chinese and Japanese babies tend to be less active, irritable, and vocal, more easily soothed when upset, and better at quieting them-

■ Sex differences in temperament are evident in children's play styles. Boys tend to engage in more active, high-intensity play. And girls' large advantage in effortful control helps explain their greater cooperativeness. ■

selves (Kagan et al., 1994; Lewis, Ramsay, & Kawakami, 1993). Grace's capacity to remain contentedly seated in her high chair through a long family dinner certainly fits with this evidence.

Timmy's high rate of activity illustrates a typical sex difference (Gartstein & Rothbart, 2003). From an early age, boys are more active and daring, more irritable when frustrated, more likely to express high-intensity pleasure in play, and slightly more impulsive than girls—factors that contribute to boys' higher injury rates throughout childhood and adolescence. Girls, in contrast, tend to be more anxious and timid. And girls' large advantage in effortful control undoubtedly contributes to their greater cooperativeness, better school performance, and lower incidence of behavior problems (Eisenberg et al., 2004a; Else-Quest et al., 2006).

Nevertheless, genetic influences vary with the temperamental trait and with the age of individuals being studied. For example, heritability estimates are higher for expressions of negative emotion than for positive emotion. And the role of heredity is considerably smaller in infancy than in childhood and later years, when temperament becomes more stable (Wachs & Bates, 2001).

Environmental Influences

Environment also has a powerful influence on temperament. For example, persistent nutritional and emotional deprivation profoundly alters temperament, resulting in maladaptive emotional reactivity. Recall from Chapter 5 that children exposed to severe malnutrition in infancy remain more distractible and fearful than their agemates, even after dietary improvement. And infants reared in deprived orphanages are easily overwhelmed by stressful events. Their poor regulation of emotion results in inattention and weak impulse control, including frequent expressions of anger (see pages 171 and 177).

GENETIC–ENVIRONMENTAL CORRELATION   Other evidence confirms that heredity and environment often jointly contribute to temperament, since a child's approach to the world affects the experiences to which she is exposed—an instance of genetic–environmental correlation (see page 85 in Chapter 2). To illustrate how this works, let's take a second look at ethnic and sex differences in temperament.

Japanese mothers usually say that babies come into the world as independent beings who must learn to rely on their parents through close physical contact. American mothers typically believe just the opposite—that they must wean babies away from dependency toward autonomy. And while Asian cultures tend to view calmness as an ideal emotional state, Americans highly value the arousal and excitement generated by new places and activities (Kagan, 2010). Consistent with these beliefs, Asian mothers interact gently, soothingly, and gesturally with their babies, whereas Caucasian mothers use a more active, stimulating, verbal approach (Rothbaum et al., 2000a). Also, recall from our discussion of emotional self-regulation that Chinese and Japanese adults discourage babies from expressing strong emotion, which contributes further to their infants' tranquility.

A similar process seems to contribute to sex differences in temperament. Within 24 hours after birth (before they have had much experience with the baby), parents already perceive male and female newborns differently. Sons are rated as larger, better coordinated, more alert, and stronger; daughters as softer, weaker, and more delicate and awkward (Stern & Karraker, 1989; Vogel et al., 1991). In line with these gender-stereotyped beliefs, parents more often encourage their young sons to be physically active and assertive and their daughters to seek help and physical closeness—through the toys they provide (trucks and footballs for boys, dolls and tea sets for girls) and through more positive reactions when their child exhibits temperamental traits consistent with gender stereotypes (Bryan & Dix, 2009; Ruble, Martin, & Berenbaum, 2006).

CHILDREN'S UNIQUE EXPERIENCES   In families with several children, an additional influence on temperament is at work. Parents often look for differences between siblings: "She's a lot more active." "He's more sociable." "She's far more persistent." As a result, parents often regard siblings as more distinct than other observers do. In a large study of 1- to 3-year-old twin pairs, parents rated identical twins as resembling each other less in temperament than researchers' ratings indicated. And whereas researchers rated fraternal twins as moderately

LOOK AND LISTEN

Ask several parents of siblings to describe their children's personalities, along with child-rearing practices they use with each. Do the parents tend to emphasize differences? Are their child-rearing practices responsive to their views of each child's unique qualities?

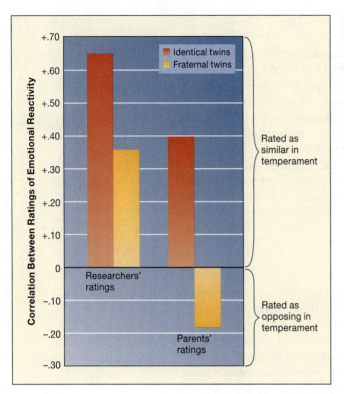

FIGURE 7.1

Temperament correlations for identical and fraternal twin pairs, as rated by researchers and parents. Parents rated 1- to 3-year-old identical twins as resembling each other less in temperament than researchers did. And whereas researchers rated fraternal twins as moderately similar, parents rated them as somewhat opposing in temperament. The correlations depicted here are for emotional reactivity. Activity level, shyness, and attention span/persistence yielded similar findings. *(Adapted from Saudino, 2003.)*

similar, parents viewed them as somewhat opposite in temperamental style (see Figure 7.1) (Saudino, 2003).

Parents' tendency to emphasize each child's unique qualities affects their child-rearing practices. In an investigation of identical-twin toddlers, mothers' differential treatment predicted differences in psychological adjustment. The twin who received more warmth and less harshness was more positive in mood and social behavior (Deater-Deckard et al., 2001). Each child, in turn, evokes responses from caregivers that are consistent with parental beliefs and the child's developing temperament.

Besides different experiences within the family, siblings have distinct experiences with teachers, peers, and others in their community that affect development. And in middle childhood and adolescence, they often seek ways to differ from one another. For all these reasons, both identical and fraternal twins tend to become increasingly dissimilar in personality with age (Loehlin & Martin, 2001; McCartney, Harris, & Bernieri, 1990). In sum, temperament and personality can be understood only in terms of complex interdependencies between genetic and environmental factors.

Temperament and Child Rearing: The Goodness-of-Fit Model

If a child's disposition interferes with learning or getting along with others, adults must gently but consistently counteract the child's maladaptive style. Thomas and Chess (1977) proposed a **goodness-of-fit model** to explain how temperament and environment can together produce favorable outcomes. Goodness of fit involves creating child-rearing environments that recognize each child's temperament while simultaneously encouraging more adaptive functioning.

Goodness of fit helps explain why difficult children (who withdraw from new experiences and react negatively and intensely) frequently experience parenting that fits poorly with their dispositions, putting them at high risk for later adjustment problems. As infants, they are less likely to receive sensitive caregiving (van den Boom & Hoeksma, 1994). By the second year, their parents tend to resort to angry, punitive discipline, which undermines the development of effortful control. As the child reacts with defiance and disobedience, parents become increasingly stressed (Bridgett et al., 2009; Paulussen-Hoogeboom et al., 2007). As a result, they continue their coercive tactics and also discipline inconsistently, sometimes rewarding the child's noncompliance by giving in to it. These practices sustain and even increase the child's irritable, conflict-ridden style (van Aken et al., 2007; Pesonen et al., 2008). In contrast, when parents are positive and sensitive, which helps infants and toddlers regulate emotion, difficultness declines by age 2 or 3 (Feldman, Greenbaum, & Yirmiya, 1999; Raikes et al., 2007).

Effective parenting, however, also depends on life conditions—good parental mental health, marital happiness, and favorable economic conditions (Schoppe-Sullivan et al., 2007). In a comparison of the temperaments of Russian and U.S. babies, Russian infants were more emotionally negative, fearful, and upset when frustrated (Gartstein, Slobodskaya, & Kinsht, 2003). At the time of the study, Russian parents faced a severely depressed national economy. Because of financial worries and longer work hours, Russian parents may have lacked time and energy for the patient parenting that protects against difficultness.

Cultural values also affect the fit between parenting and child temperament, as research in China illustrates. In the past, collectivist values, which discourage self-assertion, led Chinese adults to evaluate shy children positively. Several studies showed that shy Chinese children of a decade or two ago appeared well-adjusted, both academically and socially (Chen, Rubin, & Li, 1995; Chen et al., 1998). But rapid expansion of a market economy in China, which requires assertiveness and sociability for success, may be responsible for a recent change in Chinese parents' and teachers' attitudes toward childhood shyness (Chen, Wang, & DeSouza, 2006; Yu, 2002). Among Shanghai fourth graders, the association between shyness and adjustment also changed over time. Whereas shyness was positively correlated with teacher-rated competence, peer acceptance, leadership, and academic achievement in 1990, these relationships weakened in 1998 and reversed in 2002, when they mirrored findings of Western research (see Figure 7.2) (Chen et al., 2005). Cultural context makes a difference in whether shy children receive support or disapproval and whether they adjust well or poorly.

■ "Goodness of fit" describes the interaction between a child's temperament and the child-rearing environment. This mother's calm, soothing manner will help her child learn to regulate intense emotional reactions. ■

An effective match between rearing conditions and child temperament is best accomplished early, before unfavorable temperament–environment relationships produce maladjustment. Both difficult and shy children benefit from warm, accepting parenting that makes firm but reasonable demands for mastering new experiences. With reserved, inactive toddlers, highly stimulating parental behavior—encouraging, questioning, and pointing out objects—fosters exploration. Yet for highly active babies, this approach is too directive, dampening their play and curiosity (Miceli et al., 1998). Recall from Chapter 6 that Vanessa often behaved in a harsh, directive way with Timmy. A poor fit between her parenting and Timmy's active temperament may have contributed to his tendency to move from one activity to the next with little involvement.

The goodness-of-fit model reminds us that babies have unique dispositions that adults must accept. Parents can neither take full credit for their children's virtues nor be blamed for all their faults. But parents can turn an environment that exaggerates a child's problems into one that builds on the child's strengths. As we will see, goodness of fit is also at the heart of infant–caregiver attachment. This first intimate relationship grows out of interaction between parent and baby, to which the emotional styles of both partners contribute.

FIGURE 7.2

Changes over time in correlations between shyness and adjustment among Chinese fourth graders. In 1990, shy Chinese children appeared well-adjusted. But as China's market economy expanded and valuing of self-assertion and sociability increased, the direction of the correlations shifted. In 2002, shyness was negatively associated with adjustment. These findings are for teacher-rated competence and peer acceptance. Those for leadership (holding offices in student organizations) and academic achievement changed similarly. (*Adapted from Chen et al., 2005.*)

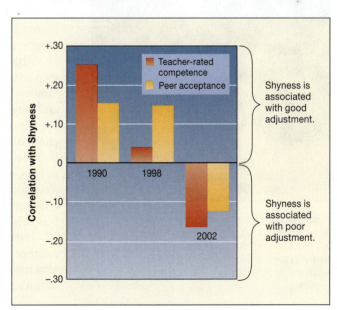

Development of Attachment

Attachment is the strong affectionate tie we have for special people in our lives that leads us to experience pleasure and joy when we interact with them and to be comforted by their nearness in times of stress. By the second half of the first year, infants have become attached to familiar people who have responded to their needs. **TAKE A MOMENT...** Watch how babies of this age single out their parents for special attention: When the parent enters the room, the baby breaks into a broad, friendly smile. When she picks him up, he pats her face, explores her hair, and snuggles against her. When he feels anxious or afraid, he crawls into her lap and clings closely.

Freud first suggested that the infant's emotional tie to the mother is the foundation for all later relationships. Contemporary research indicates that—although the infant–parent bond is vitally important—later development is influenced not just by early attachment experiences but also by the continuing quality of the parent–child relationship.

Attachment has also been the subject of intense theoretical debate. Recall that the *psychoanalytic perspective* regards feeding as the central context in which caregivers and babies build this close emotional bond. *Behaviorism,* too, emphasizes the importance of feeding, but for different reasons. According to a well-known behaviorist account, infants learn to prefer the mother's soft caresses, warm smiles, and tender words because these events are paired with tension relief as she satisfies the baby's hunger.

Although feeding is an important context for building a close relationship, attachment does not depend on hunger satisfaction. In the 1950s, a famous experiment showed that rhesus monkeys reared with terry-cloth and wire-mesh "surrogate mothers" clung to the soft terry-cloth substitute, even though the wire-mesh "mother" held the bottle and infants had to climb onto it to be fed (Harlow & Zimmerman, 1959). Human infants, too, become attached to family members who seldom feed them, including fathers, siblings, and grandparents. And toddlers in Western cultures who sleep alone and experience frequent daytime separations from their parents sometimes develop strong emotional ties to cuddly objects, such as blankets and teddy bears, that play no role in infant feeding!

Both psychoanalytic and behaviorist accounts of attachment have another problem: They emphasize the caregiver's contribution to the attachment relationship but pay little attention to the importance of the infant's characteristics.

■ Baby monkeys reared with "surrogate mothers" preferred to cling to a soft terry-cloth "mother" instead of a wire-mesh "mother" that held a bottle. These findings contradict the drive-reduction explanation of attachment, which assumes that the parent–infant relationship is based on feeding. ■

Bowlby's Ethological Theory

Today, **ethological theory of attachment,** which recognizes the infant's emotional tie to the caregiver as an evolved response that promotes survival, is the most widely accepted view. John Bowlby (1969), who first applied this idea to the infant–caregiver bond, retained the psychoanalytic idea that quality of attachment to the caregiver has profound implications for the child's feelings of security and capacity to form trusting relationships.

At the same time, Bowlby was inspired by Konrad Lorenz's studies of imprinting in baby geese (see Chapter 1). Bowlby believed that the human infant, like the young of other animal species, is endowed with a set of built-in behaviors that keep the parent nearby to protect the infant from danger and to provide support for exploring and mastering the environment (Waters & Cummings, 2000). Contact with the parent also ensures that the baby will be fed, but Bowlby was careful to point out that feeding is not the basis for attachment. Rather, attachment can best be understood in an evolutionary context in which survival of the species—through ensuring both safety and competence—is of utmost importance.

■ Clear-cut attachment to the familiar caregiver is evident in separation anxiety, which increases between 6 and 15 months. This 9-month-old actively protests his mother's departure. ■

According to Bowlby, the infant's relationship with the parent begins as a set of innate signals that call the adult to the baby's side. Over time, a true affectionate bond forms, supported by new cognitive and emotional capacities as well as by a history of warm, sensitive care. Attachment develops in four phases:

1. *Preattachment phase* (birth to 6 weeks). Built-in signals—grasping, smiling, crying, and gazing into the adult's eyes—help bring newborn babies into close contact with other humans, who comfort them. Babies of this age recognize their own mother's smell, voice, and face (see Chapter 4). But they are not yet attached to her, since they do not mind being left with an unfamiliar adult.
2. *"Attachment in the making" phase* (6 weeks to 6 to 8 months). During this phase, infants respond differently to a familiar caregiver than to a stranger. For example, at 4 months, Timmy smiled, laughed, and babbled more freely when interacting with his mother and quieted more quickly when she picked him up. As infants learn that their own actions affect the behavior of those around them, they begin to develop a *sense of trust*—the expectation that the caregiver will respond when signaled—but they still do not protest when separated from her.
3. *"Clear-cut" attachment phase* (6 to 8 months to 18 months to 2 years). Now attachment to the familiar caregiver is evident. Babies display **separation anxiety,** becoming upset when their trusted caregiver leaves. Like stranger anxiety (see page 252), separation anxiety does not always occur; it depends on infant temperament and the current situation. But in many cultures, separation anxiety increases between 6 and 15 months, suggesting that infants have developed a clear understanding that the caregiver continues to exist when not in view. Besides protesting the parent's departure, older infants and toddlers try hard to maintain her presence. They approach, follow, and climb on her in preference to others. And they use the familiar caregiver as a secure base from which to explore.
4. *Formation of a reciprocal relationship* (18 months to 2 years and on). By the end of the second year, rapid growth in representation and language enables toddlers to understand some of the factors that influence the parent's coming and going and to predict her return. As a result, separation protest declines. Now children negotiate with the caregiver, using requests and persuasion to alter her goals. For example, at age 2, Caitlin asked Carolyn and David to read her a story before leaving her with a babysitter. The extra time with her parents, along with a better understanding of where they were going ("to have dinner with Uncle Sean") and when they would be back ("right after you go to sleep"), helped Caitlin withstand her parents' absence.

LOOK AND LISTEN

Watch an 8- to 18-month-old at play for 20 to 30 minutes. Describe the baby's use of the parent or other familiar caregiver as a secure base from which to explore.

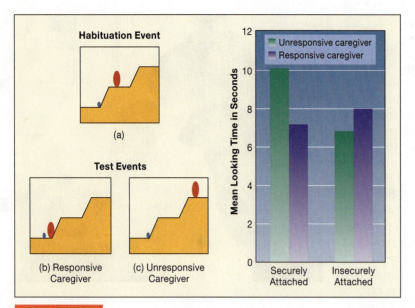

Habituation Event

(a)

Test Events

(b) Responsive Caregiver

(c) Unresponsive Caregiver

■ Unresponsive caregiver
■ Responsive caregiver

Mean Looking Time in Seconds

Securely Attached   Insecurely Attached

FIGURE 7.3

Testing toddlers for internal working models of attachment. (a) First, 12- to 16-month-olds were habituated to a video of two animated shapes, one large (the "caregiver") and one small (the "child"). The caregiver traveled halfway up an incline to a plateau, and the child began to "cry," depicted by pulsing and bouncing accompanied by an infant cry. Next the researchers presented two test events: (b) In the *responsive caregiver outcome,* the caregiver returned to the child. (c) In the *unresponsive caregiver outcome,* the caregiver continued up the slope away from the child. Securely attached toddlers looked longer at the unresponsive outcome, depicting caregiver behavior inconsistent with their expectations. Insecurely attached toddlers did not differentiate between the two test events. *(Adapted from Johnson, Dweck, & Chen, 2007.)*

According to Bowlby (1980), out of their experiences during these four phases, children construct an enduring affectionate tie to the caregiver that they can use as a secure base in the parent's absence. This image serves as an **internal working model,** or set of expectations about the availability of attachment figures, their likelihood of providing support during times of stress, and the self's interaction with those figures. The internal working model becomes a vital part of personality, serving as a guide for all future close relationships (Bretherton & Munholland, 1999).

Consistent with these ideas, as early as the second year, toddlers form attachment-related expectations about parental comfort and support. In one study, securely attached 12- to 16-month-olds looked longer at a video of an unresponsive caregiver (inconsistent with their expectations) than a video of a responsive caregiver. Insecurely attached toddlers, in contrast, did not distinguish between the two (see Figure 7.3) (Johnson, Dweck, & Chen, 2007).

With cognitive development and continuing experiences in close relationships, this budding internal working model expands into a broader, more complex representation. Children continue to revise it as they interact with parents and form other bonds with adults, siblings, and friends.

Measuring the Security of Attachment

Although all family-reared babies become attached to a familiar caregiver by the second year, the quality of this relationship differs from child to child. Some infants appear relaxed and secure in the presence of the caregiver; they know they can count on her for protection and support. Others seem anxious and uncertain.

A widely used laboratory technique for assessing the quality of attachment between 1 and 2 years of age is the **Strange Situation.** In designing it, Mary Ainsworth and her colleagues reasoned that securely attached infants and toddlers should use the parent as a secure base from which to explore in an unfamiliar playroom. In addition, when the parent leaves, an unfamiliar adult should be less comforting than the parent. The Strange Situation takes the baby through eight short episodes in which brief separations from and reunions with the parent occur (see Table 7.2).

Observing infants' responses to these episodes, researchers identified a secure attachment pattern and three patterns of insecurity; a few babies cannot be classified (Ainsworth et al., 1978; Barnett & Vondra, 1999; Main & Solomon, 1990; Thompson, 2006). Although separation anxiety varies among the groups, the baby's reunion responses largely define attachment quality. **TAKE A MOMENT...** From the description at the beginning of this chapter, which pattern do you think Grace displayed after adjusting to her adoptive family?

■ **Secure attachment.** These infants use the parent as a secure base. When separated, they may or may not cry, but if they do, it is because the parent is absent and they prefer her to the stranger. When the parent returns, they actively seek contact, and their crying is reduced immediately. About 60 percent of North American infants in middle-SES families show this pattern. (In low-SES families, a smaller proportion of babies show the secure pattern, with higher proportions falling into the insecure patterns.)

| TABLE 7.2 | Episodes in the Strange Situation |

EPISODE	EVENTS	ATTACHMENT BEHAVIOR OBSERVED
1	Researcher introduces parent and baby to playroom and then leaves.	
2	Parent is seated while baby plays with toys.	Parent as a secure base
3	Stranger enters, is seated, and talks to parent.	Reaction to unfamiliar adult
4	Parent leaves room. Stranger responds to baby and offers comfort if baby is upset.	Separation anxiety
5	Parent returns, greets baby, and offers comfort if necessary. Stranger leaves room.	Reaction to reunion
6	Parent leaves room.	Separation anxiety
7	Stranger enters room and offers comfort.	Ability to be soothed by stranger
8	Parent returns, greets baby, offers comfort if necessary, and tries to reinterest baby in toys.	Reaction to reunion

Note: Episode 1 lasts about 30 seconds; each of the remaining episodes lasts about 3 minutes. Separation episodes are cut short if the baby becomes very upset. Reunion episodes are extended if the baby needs more time to calm down and return to play.

Source: Ainsworth et al., 1978.

■ **Avoidant attachment.** These infants seem unresponsive to the parent when she is present. When she leaves, they usually are not distressed, and they react to the stranger in much the same way as to the parent. During reunion, they avoid or are slow to greet the parent, and when picked up, they often fail to cling. About 15 percent of North American infants in middle-SES families show this pattern.

■ **Resistant attachment.** Before separation, these infants seek closeness to the parent and often fail to explore. When the parent leaves, they are usually distressed, and on her return they combine clinginess with angry, resistive behavior, struggling when held and sometimes hitting and pushing. Many continue to cry after being picked up and cannot be comforted easily. About 10 percent of North American infants in middle-SES families show this pattern.

■ **Disorganized/disoriented attachment.** This pattern reflects the greatest insecurity. At reunion, these infants show confused, contradictory behaviors—for example, looking away while the parent is holding them or approaching the parent with flat, depressed emotion. Most display a dazed facial expression, and a few cry out unexpectedly after having calmed down or display odd, frozen postures. About 15 percent of North American infants in middle-SES families show this pattern.

An alternative method, the **Attachment Q-Sort,** suitable for children between 1 and 4 years, depends on home observations (Waters et al., 1995). Either the parent or a highly trained observer sorts 90 behaviors—such as "Child greets mother with a big smile when she enters the room," "If mother moves very far, child follows along," and "Child uses mother's facial expressions as a good source of information when something looks risky or threatening"—into nine categories ranging from "highly descriptive" to "not at all descriptive" of the child. Then a score, ranging from high to low in security, is computed.

Because the Q-Sort taps a wider array of attachment-related behaviors than the Strange Situation, it may better reflect the parent–infant relationship in everyday life. However, the Q-sort method is time-consuming, requiring a nonparent informant to spend several hours observing the child before sorting the descriptors, and it does not differentiate between types of insecurity. The Q-Sort responses of expert observers correspond well with babies' secure-base behavior in the Strange Situation, but parents' Q-Sorts do not (van IJzendoorn et al., 2004). Parents of insecure children, especially, may have difficulty accurately reporting their child's attachment behaviors.

Stability of Attachment

Research on the stability of attachment patterns between 1 and 2 years of age yields a wide range of findings. In some studies, as many as 70 to 90 percent of children remain the same in their reactions to parents; in others, only 30 to 40 percent do (Thompson, 2000, 2006). A close look at which babies stay the same and which ones change yields a more consistent picture. Quality of attachment is usually secure and stable for middle-SES babies experiencing favorable life conditions. And infants who move from insecurity to security typically have well-adjusted mothers with positive family and friendship ties. Perhaps many became parents before they were psychologically ready but, with social support, grew into the role.

In contrast, in low-SES families with many daily stresses and little social support, attachment generally moves away from security or changes from one insecure pattern to another (Belsky et al., 1996; Fish, 2004; Vondra, Hommerding, & Shaw, 1999; Vondra et al., 2001). In one long-term follow-up of a poverty-stricken sample, many securely attached infants ended up insecure when reassessed in early adulthood. Child maltreatment, maternal depression, and poor family functioning in adolescence distinguished these young people from the few who stayed securely attached (Weinfield, Sroufe, & Egeland, 2000; Weinfield, Whaley, & Egeland, 2004).

These findings indicate that securely attached babies more often maintain their attachment status than insecure babies, whose relationship with the caregiver is, by definition, fragile and uncertain. The exception is disorganized/disoriented attachment—an insecure pattern that is as stable as attachment security: Nearly 70 percent retain this classification over time (Hesse & Main, 2000; Weinfield, Whaley, & Egeland, 2004). As you will soon see, many disorganized/disoriented infants experience extremely negative caregiving, which may disrupt emotional self-regulation so severely that confused, ambivalent feelings toward parents persist.

Cultural Variations

Cross-cultural evidence indicates that attachment patterns may have to be interpreted differently in certain cultures. For example, as Figure 7.4 reveals, German infants show considerably more avoidant attachment than American babies do. But German parents value independence and encourage their infants to be nonclingy, so the baby's behavior may be an intended outcome of cultural beliefs and practices (Grossmann et al., 1985). In contrast, a study of infants of the Dogon people of Mali, Africa, revealed that none showed avoidant attachment to their mothers (True, Pisani, & Oumar, 2001). Even when grandmothers are primary caregivers (as they are with firstborn sons), Dogon mothers remain available to their babies, holding them close and nursing them promptly in response to hunger and distress.

Japanese infants, as well, rarely show avoidant attachment (refer again to Figure 7.4). Rather, many are resistantly attached, but this reaction may not represent true insecurity. Japanese mothers rarely leave their babies in others' care, so the Strange Situation probably induces greater stress in them than in infants who frequently experience maternal separations (Takahashi, 1990). Also, many Japanese mothers expect their babies to be quite upset during reunion in the Strange Situation. They view the

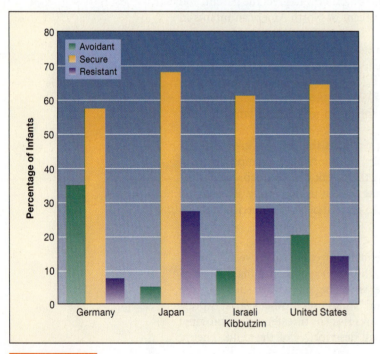

FIGURE 7.4

A cross-cultural comparison of infants' reactions in the Strange Situation. A high percentage of German babies seem avoidantly attached, whereas a substantial number of Japanese and Israeli kibbutz infants appear resistantly attached. Note that these responses may not reflect true insecurity. Instead, they are probably due to cultural differences in child-rearing practices. *(Adapted from Sagi et al., 1995; van IJzendoorn & Kroonenberg, 1988.)*

attention-seeking that is part of resistant attachment as a normal indicator of infants' efforts to satisfy dependency and security needs (Rothbaum et al., 2000b, 2007). Likewise, infants in Israeli kibbutzim frequently show resistant attachment. For these babies, who can sense the fear of unfamiliar people that is pervasive in their communities (see page 252), the Strange Situation probably induces unusual distress (van IJzendoorn & Sagi, 1999). Despite these and other cultural variations, the secure pattern is still the most common attachment quality in all societies studied to date.

Factors That Affect Attachment Security

What factors might influence attachment security? Researchers have looked closely at four important influences: (1) early availability of a consistent caregiver, (2) quality of caregiving, (3) the baby's characteristics, and (4) family context, including parents' internal working models.

EARLY AVAILABILITY OF A CONSISTENT CAREGIVER What happens when a baby does not have the opportunity to establish a close tie to a caregiver? In a series of studies, René Spitz (1946) observed institutionalized infants whose mothers had given them up between 3 and 12 months of age. After being placed in a large ward where each shared a nurse with at least seven others, the babies lost weight, wept, withdrew from their surroundings, and had difficulty sleeping. If a consistent caregiver did not replace the mother, the depression deepened rapidly. These institutionalized babies had emotional problems because they were prevented from forming a bond with one or a few adults (Rutter, 1996).

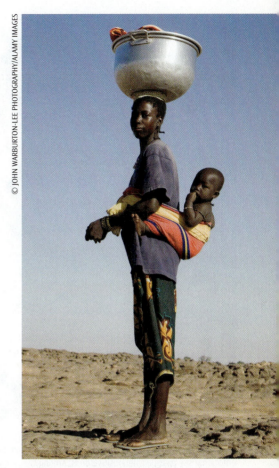

■ Dogon mothers of Mali, West Africa, stay close to their babies and respond promptly and gently to infant distress. Unlike German infants, whose mothers discourage clinginess, no Dogon babies show avoidant attachment. ■

Another study supports this conclusion. Researchers followed the development of infants in an institution with a good caregiver–child ratio and a rich selection of books and toys. However, staff turnover was so rapid that the average child had 50 caregivers by age 4½. Many of these children became "late adoptees" who were placed in homes after age 4. Most developed deep ties with their adoptive parents, indicating that a first attachment can develop as late as 4 to 6 years of age (Hodges & Tizard, 1989; Tizard & Rees, 1975). But these children were more likely to display attachment difficulties, including an excessive desire for adult attention, "overfriendliness" to unfamiliar adults and peers, failure to check back with the parent in anxiety-arousing situations, and few friendships.

Adopted children who spent their first year or more in deprived Eastern European orphanages—though also able to bond with their adoptive parents—show elevated rates of attachment insecurity (van den Dries et al., 2009). And they, too, are at high risk for emotional and social difficulties. Whereas many are indiscriminately friendly, others are sad, anxious, and withdrawn (Chisholm, 1998; Fisher et al., 1997; O'Connor et al., 2003). These symptoms typically persist and are associated with wide-ranging mental health problems in middle childhood and adolescence, including cognitive impairments, inattention and hyperactivity, depression, and either social avoidance or aggressive behavior (O'Connor et al., 2003; Rutter et al., 2007, 2010; Zeanah, 2000).

Furthermore, as early as 7 months, Eastern European orphanage children show reduced ERP brain waves in response to facial expressions of emotion and have trouble discriminating such expressions—outcomes that suggest disrupted formation of neural structures involved in "reading" emotions (Parker et al., 2005). These problems are still evident in preschoolers adopted during the second year, who find it hard to match appropriate facial expressions with situations in stories (Fries & Pollak, 2004). The longer the institutional stay, the worse adopted children perform on these emotion-processing tasks—deficits believed to contribute to their social-relationship and adjustment problems. Taken together, the evidence indicates that fully normal emotional development depends on establishing a close tie with a caregiver early in life.

© GERI ENGBERG/THE IMAGE WORKS

■ This father and baby engage in a sensitively tuned form of communication called interactional synchrony, in which they match emotional states, especially positive ones. Among Western babies, interactional synchrony supports secure attachment. But it does not characterize parent–infant attachment in all cultures. ■

QUALITY OF CAREGIVING Dozens of studies report that **sensitive caregiving**—responding promptly, consistently, and appropriately to infants and holding them tenderly and carefully—is moderately related to attachment security in both biological and adoptive mother–infant pairs and in diverse cultures and SES groups (De Wolff & van IJzendoorn, 1997; Posada et al., 2002, 2004; van IJzendoorn et al., 2004). In contrast, insecurely attached infants tend to have mothers who engage in less physical contact, handle them awkwardly or in a "routine" manner, and are sometimes resentful and rejecting, particularly in response to infant distress (Ainsworth et al., 1978; Isabella, 1993; McElwain & Booth-LaForce, 2006; Pederson & Moran, 1996).

Also, in studies of Western babies, a special form of communication called **interactional synchrony** separated the experiences of secure from insecure babies. It is best described as a sensitively tuned "emotional dance," in which the caregiver responds to infant signals in a well-timed, rhythmic, appropriate fashion. In addition, both partners match emotional states, especially the positive ones (Bigelow et al., 2010; Isabella & Belsky, 1991; Nievar & Becker, 2008). For example, when Caitlin excitedly shook a rattle, Carolyn responded with a broad smile and an enthusiastic "That-a-girl!" In return, Caitlin smiled and cooed. And when Caitlin fussed and cried, Carolyn soothed with gentle touches and soft, sympathetic words.

Earlier we saw that sensitive face-to-face play, in which interactional synchrony occurs, increases babies' sensitivity to others' emotional messages and helps them regulate emotion. But moderate adult–infant coordination is a better predictor of attachment security than "tight" coordination, in which the adult responds to most infant cues (Jaffee et al., 2001). Perhaps warm, sensitive caregivers use a relaxed, flexible style of communication in which they comfortably accept and repair emotional mismatches, returning to a synchronous state.

Cultures vary in their view of sensitivity toward infants. Among the Gusii people of Kenya, mothers rarely cuddle, hug, or interact playfully with their babies, although they are very responsive to their babies' needs. Yet most Gusii infants appear securely attached (LeVine et al., 1994). This suggests that security depends on attentive caregiving, not necessarily on moment-by-moment contingent interaction. Puerto Rican mothers, who highly value obedience and socially appropriate behavior, often physically direct and limit their babies' actions—a caregiving style linked to attachment security in Puerto Rican culture (Carlson & Harwood, 2003). Yet in many Western cultures, such physical control predicts insecurity.

Compared with securely attached infants, avoidant babies tend to receive overstimulating, intrusive care. Their mothers might, for example, talk energetically to them while they are looking away or falling asleep. By avoiding the mother, these infants appear to be escaping from overwhelming interaction. Resistant infants often experience inconsistent care. Their mothers are unresponsive to infant signals. Yet when the baby begins to explore, these mothers interfere, shifting the infant's attention back to themselves. As a result, the baby is overly dependent as well as angry at the mother's lack of involvement (Cassidy & Berlin, 1994; Isabella & Belsky, 1991).

Highly inadequate caregiving is a powerful predictor of disruptions in attachment. Child abuse and neglect (topics we will consider in Chapter 10) are associated with all three forms of attachment insecurity. Among maltreated infants, disorganized/disoriented attachment is especially high (van IJzendoorn, Schuengel, & Bakermans-Kranenburg, 1999). Persistently depressed mothers, mothers with very low marital satisfaction, and parents suffering from a traumatic event, such as serious illness or loss of a loved one, also tend to promote the uncertain behaviors of this pattern (Campbell et al., 2004; Moss et al., 2005; van IJzendoorn, 1995).

And some mothers of disorganized/disoriented infants engage in frightening, contradictory, and unpleasant behaviors, such as looking scared, teasing the baby, holding the baby stiffly at a distance, roughly pulling the baby by the arm, or seeking reassurance from the upset child (Lyons-Ruth, Bronfman, & Parsons, 1999; Madigan, Moran, & Pederson, 2006; Moran et al., 2008). Perhaps the baby's disorganized behavior reflects a conflicted reaction to the parent, who sometimes comforts but at other times arouses fear.

INFANT CHARACTERISTICS   Because attachment is the result of a *relationship* between two partners, infant characteristics should affect how easily it is established. In Chapters 3 and 4 we saw that prematurity, birth complications, and newborn illness make caregiving more taxing. In families under stress, these difficulties are linked to attachment insecurity. In one study, the *combination* of preterm birth and maternal depression—but not preterm birth alone—increased the likelihood of insecure attachment at 12 months (Poehlmann & Fiese, 2001). Infants with special needs probably require greater parental sensitivity, which stressed parents often cannot provide. But at-risk newborns whose parents have adequate time and patience to care for them fare quite well in attachment security (Cox, Hopkins, & Hans, 2000).

The role of infant temperament in attachment security has been intensely debated. Some researchers believe that infants who are irritable and fearful may simply react to brief separations with intense anxiety, regardless of the parent's sensitivity to the baby (Kagan, 1998; Kagan & Fox, 2006). Consistent with this view, emotionally reactive, difficult babies are more likely to develop later insecure attachments (van IJzendoorn et al., 2004; Vaughn & Bost, 1999). And disorganized newborn behavior, evident in scores on the Neonatal Behavioral Assessment Scale (NBAS, see Chapter 4), increases the risk of disorganized/disoriented attachment at the end of the first year (Spangler, Fremmer-Bomik, & Grossmann, 1996).

Again, however, other evidence suggests that parental mental health and caregiving are involved. In a study extending from birth to age 2, difficult infants more often had highly anxious mothers—a combination that, by the second year, frequently resulted in a "disharmonious relationship" characterized by both maternal insensitivity and attachment insecurity (Symons, 2001). Infant difficultness and maternal anxiety seemed to perpetuate each other, impairing caregiving and the security of the parent–infant bond. Similarly, in another study, mothers' experience of traumatic events was associated with disorganized/disoriented attachment only in infants with a chromosome-11 gene having a certain repetition of DNA base pairs (called DRD4 7-repeat), which is linked to deficient self-regulation (van IJzendoorn & Bakermans-Kranenburg, 2006). Babies with this genetic marker, who face special challenges in managing intense emotion, were more susceptible to the negative impact of maternal adjustment problems.

If children's temperaments alone determined attachment quality, we would expect attachment, like temperament, to be at least moderately heritable. Yet the heritability of attachment is virtually nil (O'Connor & Croft, 2001). In fact, about two-thirds of siblings establish similar attachment patterns with their parents, although the siblings often differ in temperament (Cole, 2006; Dozier et al., 2001). This suggests that most parents try to adjust their caregiving to each child's individual needs.

Why don't infant characteristics show strong relationships with attachment quality? Their influence probably depends on goodness of fit. From this perspective, *many* child attributes can lead to secure attachment as long as caregivers sensitively adjust their behavior to fit the baby's needs (Seifer & Schiller, 1995).

Interventions that teach parents to interact sensitively with difficult-to-care-for infants and toddlers are highly successful in enhancing both sensitive care and attachment security (Velderman et al., 2006). One program that focused on both maternal sensitivity and effective discipline was particularly effective in reducing stress reactivity (as indicated by lower cortisol levels) and disruptive behavior among toddlers with the DRD4 7-repeat gene, who are at risk for later attention-deficit hyperactivity disorder and externalizing behavior problems (Bakermans-Kranenburg et al., 2008a, 2008b). But when parents' capacity for sensitivity is strained—by their own personalities or by stressful living conditions—then infants with illnesses, disabilities, and difficult temperaments are at risk for attachment problems.

■ Family circumstances are linked to attachment quality. Observing her parents' heated quarrels may undermine this child's sense of emotional security. ■

FAMILY CIRCUMSTANCES   Shortly after Timmy's birth, his parents divorced, and his father moved to a distant city. Anxious and distracted, Vanessa placed 1-month-old Timmy in Ginette's child-care home and began working 50-hour weeks to make ends meet. On days Vanessa stayed late at the office, a babysitter picked Timmy up, gave him dinner, and put him to bed. Once or twice a week, Vanessa went to get Timmy from child care. As he neared his first birthday, Vanessa noticed that, unlike the other children, who reached out, crawled, or ran to their parents, Timmy ignored her.

Timmy's behavior reflects a repeated finding: Job loss, a failing marriage, and financial difficulties can undermine attachment indirectly by interfering with parental sensitivity. These stressors can also affect babies' sense of security directly by altering the emotional climate of the family (for example, exposing them to angry adult interactions) or by disrupting familiar daily routines (Finger et al., 2009; Raikes & Thompson, 2005). Parents who manage to sustain a favorable relationship with their baby despite environmental stressors protect the child's development. Social support fosters attachment security by reducing parental stress and improving the quality of parent–child communication (Belsky & Fearon, 2002b; Moss et al., 2005). Ginette's sensitivity toward Timmy was helpful, as was the parenting advice Vanessa received from Ben, a psychologist. As Timmy turned 2, his relationship with his mother seemed warmer.

PARENTS' INTERNAL WORKING MODELS   Parents bring to the family context their own history of attachment experiences, from which they construct internal working models that they apply to the bonds they establish with their babies. Monica, who recalled her mother as tense and preoccupied, expressed regret that they had not had a closer relationship. Is her image of parenthood likely to affect Grace's attachment security?

To assess parents' internal working models, researchers have asked them to evaluate childhood memories of attachment experiences (Main & Goldwyn, 1998). Parents who discuss their childhoods with objectivity and balance, regardless of whether their experiences were positive or negative, tend to have securely attached infants and to behave sensitively toward them. In contrast, parents who dismiss the importance of early relationships or describe them in angry, confused ways usually have insecurely attached babies and engage in less sensitive caregiving (Slade et al., 1999; van IJzendoorn, 1995).

But we must not assume any direct transfer of parents' childhood experiences to quality of attachment with their own children. Internal working models are *reconstructed memories* affected by many factors, including relationship experiences over the life course, personality, and current life satisfaction. Longitudinal research reveals that negative life events can weaken the link between an individual's own attachment security in infancy and a secure internal working model in adulthood. And insecurely attached babies who become adults with insecure internal working models often have lives that, based on self-reports in adulthood, are filled with family crises (Waters et al., 2000; Weinfield, Sroufe, & Egeland, 2000).

In sum, our early rearing experiences do not destine us to become either sensitive or insensitive parents. Rather, the way we *view* our childhoods—our ability to come to terms with negative events, to integrate new information into our working models, and to look back on our own parents in an understanding, forgiving way—appears to be much more influential in how we rear our children than the actual history of care we received (Main, 2000).

ATTACHMENT IN CONTEXT   Carolyn and Vanessa returned to work when their babies were 2 to 3 months old. Monica did the same a few weeks after Grace's adoption. When parents divide their time between work and parenting and place their infants and toddlers in child care, is quality of attachment and child adjustment affected? See the Social Issues: Health box on the following page for research that addresses this issue.

SOCIAL ISSUES: HEALTH

Does Child Care in Infancy Threaten Attachment Security and Later Adjustment?

Research suggests that infants placed in full-time child care before 12 months of age are more likely than infants who remain at home to display insecure attachment—especially avoidance—in the Strange Situation (Belsky, 2001, 2005). Does this mean that infants who experience daily separations from their employed parents and early placement in child care are at risk for developmental problems? Let's look closely at the evidence.

Attachment Quality

In U.S. studies reporting an association between child care and attachment quality, the rate of insecurity among child-care infants is somewhat higher than among non-child-care infants—about 36 versus 29 percent (Lamb, Sternberg, & Prodromidis, 1992). But not all investigations report that babies in child care differ in attachment quality from those cared for solely by parents (NICHD Early Child Care Research Network, 1997; Roggman et al., 1994). Rather, the relationship between child care and emotional well-being depends on both family and child-care experiences.

Family Circumstances

We have seen that family conditions affect attachment security. For employed parents, balancing work and child care can be stressful. Mothers who are fatigued and anxious because they feel overloaded by work and family pressures may respond less sensitively to their babies, thereby risking the infant's security. And as paternal involvement in caregiving has risen (see page 274), many more U.S. fathers in dual-earner families also report work–family life conflict (Galinsky, Aumann, & Bond, 2009). Other employed parents may value and encourage their infant's independence. Or their babies may be unfazed by the Strange Situation because they are used to separating from their parents. In these cases, avoidance in the Strange Situation may represent healthy autonomy, not insecurity (Clarke-Stewart, Allhusen, & Goosens, 2001).

Quality and Extent of Child Care

Long periods spent in poor-quality child care may contribute to a higher rate of insecure attachment. In the U.S. National Institute of Child Health and Development (NICHD) Study of Early Child Care—the largest longitudinal study to date, including more than 1,300 infants and their families—child care alone did not contribute to attachment inse-

curity. But when babies were exposed to combined home and child-care risk factors—insensitive caregiving at home along with insensitive caregiving in child care, long hours in child care, or more than one child-care arrangement—the rate of insecurity increased. Overall, mother–child interaction was more favorable when children attended higher-quality child care and also spent fewer hours in child care (NICHD Early Child Care Research Network, 1997, 1999).

Furthermore, when these children reached age 3, a history of higher-quality child care predicted better social skills (NICHD Early Child Care Research Network, 2002b). However, at age 4½ to 5, children averaging more than 30 child-care hours per week displayed more behavior problems, especially defiance, disobedience, and aggression, an outcome that—for those who had been in child-care centers as opposed to family child-care homes—persisted through elementary school (Belsky et al., 2007; NICHD Early Child Care Research Network, 2003a, 2006). And in kindergarten, children with limited child-care experience but who had many classmates with extensive child-care exposure were rated by their teachers as slightly more aggressive and disobedient (Dmitrieva, Steinberg, & Belsky, 2007). This suggests that externalizing difficulties can spread to peers who interact regularly with child-care exposed children.

These findings do not necessarily mean that child care causes behavior problems. Rather, heavy exposure to substandard care, which is widespread in the United States, may promote these difficulties. In Australia, infants enrolled full-time in government-funded, high-quality child-care centers have a higher rate of secure attachment than infants informally cared for by relatives, friends, or babysitters. And amount of time spent in child care is unrelated to Australian children's behavior problems (Love et al., 2003).

Still, some children may be particularly stressed by long child-care hours. Many infants, toddlers, and preschoolers attending child-care centers for full days show a mild increase in saliva concentrations of the stress hormone cortisol across the day—a pattern that does not occur on days they spend at home. In one study, children rated as highly fearful by their caregivers experienced an especially sharp increase in cortisol levels (Watamura et al., 2003). Inhibited children may find the constant company of large numbers of peers particularly stressful.

Conclusions

Taken together, research suggests that some infants may be at risk for attachment insecurity and adjustment problems due to inadequate child care, long hours in child care, and the joint pressures their parents experience from full-time employment and parenthood. But it is inappropriate to use these findings to justify a reduction in infant child-care services. Instead, it makes sense to increase the availability of high-quality child care, to provide paid employment leave so parents can limit the hours their children spend in child care (see page 141 in Chapter 4), and to educate parents about the vital role of sensitive caregiving and child-care quality in early emotional development.

For child care to foster attachment security, the professional caregiver's relationship with the baby is vital. When caregiver–child ratios are generous, group sizes are small, and caregivers are educated about child development and child rearing, caregivers' interactions are more positive and children develop more favorably (McCartney et al., 2007; NICHD Early Child Care Research Network, 2000b, 2002a, 2006). Child care with these characteristics can become part of an ecological system that relieves rather than intensifies parental and child stress, thereby promoting healthy attachment and development.

© ELLEN B. SENISI PHOTOGRAPHY

■ At the end of his day in child care, this 10-month-old is happy to see his mother. High-quality child care and fewer hours in child care are associated with favorable mother–child interaction, which contributes to attachment security. ■

After reading the box, consider each factor that influences the development of attachment—infant and parent characteristics, the parents' relationship with each other, outside-the-family stressors, the availability of social supports, parents' views of their attachment history, and child-care arrangements. Although attachment builds within the warmth and intimacy of caregiver–infant interaction, it can be fully understood only from an ecological systems perspective (Bornstein, 2002). Return to Chapter 1, pages 25–27, to review Bronfenbrenner's ecological systems theory. Notice how research confirms the importance of each level of the environment for attachment security.

Multiple Attachments

As we have indicated, babies develop attachments to a variety of familiar people—not just mothers, but also fathers, grandparents, siblings, and professional caregivers. Although Bowlby (1969) believed that infants are predisposed to direct their attachment behaviors to a single special person, especially when they are distressed, his theory allowed for these multiple attachments.

FATHERS   An anxious, unhappy 1-year-old who is permitted to choose between the mother and the father as a source of comfort and security will usually choose the mother. But this preference typically declines over the second year. And when babies are not distressed, they approach, vocalize to, and smile equally often at both parents, who in turn are equally responsive to their infant's social bids (Bornstein, 2006; Parke, 2002).

Fathers' sensitive caregiving and interactional synchrony with infants, like mothers', predict attachment security (Lundy, 2003; van IJzendoorn et al., 2004). And fathers of 1- to 5-year-olds enrolled in full-time child care report feeling just as much anxiety as mothers about separating from their child and just as much concern about the impact of these daily separations on the child's well-being (Deater-Deckard et al., 1994). But as infancy progresses, mothers and fathers in many cultures, including Australia, Canada, Germany, India, Israel, Italy, Japan, and the United States, tend to interact differently with their babies: Mothers devote more time to physical care and expressing affection, fathers to playful interaction (Freeman & Newland, 2010; Roopnarine et al., 1990).

Mothers and fathers also play differently. Mothers more often provide toys, talk to infants, and gently play conventional games like pat-a-cake and peekaboo. In contrast, fathers—especially with their infant sons—tend to engage in highly stimulating physical play with bursts of excitement and surprise that increase as play progresses (Feldman, 2003). As long as fathers are also sensitive, this stimulating, startling play style helps babies regulate emotion in intensely arousing situations and may prepare them to venture confidently into active, unpredictable contexts, including novel physical environments and play with peers (Cabrera et al., 2007; Hazen et al., 2010; Paquette, 2004). In a German study, fathers' sensitive, challenging play with preschoolers predicted favorable emotional and social adjustment from kindergarten to early adulthood (Grossman et al, 2008).

Play is a vital context in which fathers build secure attachments (Newland, Coyl, & Freeman, 2008). It may be especially influential in cultures where long work hours prevent most fathers from sharing in infant caregiving, such as Japan (Hewlett, 2004; Shwalb et al., 2004). In many Western nations, however, a strict division of parental roles—mother as caregiver, father as playmate—has changed over the past several decades in response to women's workforce participation and to cultural valuing of gender equality.

A recent U.S. national survey of several thousand employed workers indicated that U.S. fathers under age 29 devote about 85 percent as much time as mothers do to children—on average, just over 4 hours per workday, nearly double the hours young fathers reported three decades ago. Although fathers age 29 to 42 spend somewhat less time with children, their involvement has also increased substantially (see Figure 7.5). Today, nearly one-third of U.S. employed women say that their spouse or partner shares equally in or takes most responsibility for child-care tasks (Galinsky, Aumann, & Bond, 2009). Paternal availability to children is fairly similar across SES and ethnic groups, with one exception: Hispanic fathers spend more time engaged, probably because of the particularly high value that Hispanic cultures place on family involvement (Cabrera & García Coll, 2004; Parke et al., 2004).

LOOK AND LISTEN

Observe parents at play with infants at home or a family gathering, describing both similarities and differences in mothers' and fathers' behaviors. Are your observations consistent with research findings?

Mothers in dual-earner families tend to engage in more playful stimulation of their babies than mothers who are at home full-time (Cox et al., 1992). But fathers who are primary caregivers retain their arousing play style (Lamb & Oppenheim, 1989). These highly involved fathers are less gender-stereotyped in their beliefs, have sympathetic, friendly personalities, often had fathers who were more involved in rearing them, and regard parenthood as an especially enriching experience (Cabrera et al., 2000; Levy-Shiff & Israelashvili, 1988).

Fathers' involvement with babies occurs within a complex system of family attitudes and relationships. When both mothers and fathers believe that men are capable of nurturing infants, fathers devote more time to caregiving (Beitel & Parke, 1998). A warm marital bond and supportive coparenting (see page 70 in Chapter 2) promote both parents' sensitivity and involvement and children's attachment security, but it is especially important for fathers (Brown et al., 2010; Lamb & Lewis, 2004; Laurent, Kim, & Capaldi, 2008). See the Cultural Influences box on page 276 for cross-cultural evidence documenting this conclusion—and also highlighting the powerful role of paternal warmth in children's development.

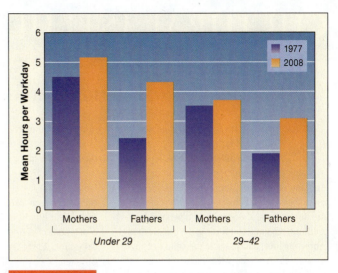

FIGURE 7.5

Average amount of time per workday U.S. employed mothers and fathers reported spending with their children (age 12 and younger) in 1977 and 2008. In national surveys of several thousand employed parents, mothers' time with children remained fairly stable from 1977 to 2008; fathers' time increased substantially. *(Adapted from Galinsky, Aumann, & Bond, 2009.)*

GRANDPARENT PRIMARY CAREGIVERS   Nearly 2.4 million U.S. children—4 to 5 percent of the child population—live with their grandparents but apart from parents, in so-called *skipped-generation families* (U.S. Census Bureau, 2010b). The number of grandparents rearing grandchildren has increased over the past two decades. The arrangement occurs in all ethnic groups, though more often in African-American, Hispanic, and Native-American families than in Caucasian families. Although grandparent caregivers are more likely to be women than men, many grandfathers participate. Grandparents generally step in when parents' troubled lives—as a result of substance abuse, child abuse and neglect, mental illness, or adolescent parenthood—threaten children's well-being (Fuller-Thomson & Minkler, 2005, 2007; Minkler & Fuller-Thomson, 2005). Often these families take in two or more children.

As a result, grandparents tend to assume the parenting role under highly stressful life circumstances. Unfavorable child-rearing experiences have left their mark on children, who show high rates of learning difficulties, depression, and antisocial behavior. Absent parents' adjustment difficulties strain family relationships. Parents may interfere by violating the grandparents' behavioral limits, taking grandchildren away without permission, or making promises to children that they do not keep. These youngsters also introduce financial burdens into households that often are already low-income (Mills, Gomez-Smith, & De Leon, 2005; Williamson, Softas-Nall, & Miller, 2003). And grandparent caregivers, at a time when they anticipated having more time for spouses, friends, and leisure, instead have less. Many report feeling emotionally drained, depressed, and worried about what will happen to the children if their own health fails (Hayslip et al., 2002; Kolomer & McCallion, 2005).

Nevertheless, because they provide physical and emotional care for an extended time and are invested in the child's well-being, grandparent caregivers forge significant attachment relationships with their grandchildren (Poehlmann, 2003). Warm grandparent–grandchild bonds help protect children from worsening adjustment problems,

■ This woman's daughter, a drug addict, dropped each of her sons on her mother's doorstep shortly after they were born. Though she undertook the parenting role under highly stressful conditions, this grandmother has forged deep attachments with her grandsons. ■

CULTURAL INFLUENCES

The Powerful Role of Paternal Warmth in Development

Research in diverse cultures demonstrates that fathers' warmth contributes greatly to children's long-term favorable development. In studies of many societies and ethnic groups around the world, researchers coded paternal expressions of love and nurturance—evident in such behaviors as cuddling, hugging, comforting, playing, verbally expressing love, and praising the child's behavior. Fathers' sustained affectionate involvement predicted later cognitive, emotional, and social competence as strongly as did mothers' warmth—and occasionally more strongly (Rohner & Veneziano, 2001; Veneziano, 2003). And in Western cultures, paternal warmth and secure attachment is associated with children's mature social behavior and protects them against a wide range of difficulties, including childhood emotional and behavior problems and adolescent substance abuse and delinquency (Grant et al., 2000; Michiels et al., 2010; Nelson & Coyne, 2009; Tacon & Caldera, 2001).

Fathers who devote little time to physical caregiving express warmth through play. In a German study, fathers' play sensitivity—accepting toddlers' play initiatives, adapting play behaviors to toddlers' capacities, and responding appropriately to toddlers' expressions of emotion—predicted children's secure internal working models of attachment during middle childhood and adolescence (Grossmann et al., 2002). Through play, fathers seemed to transfer to young children a sense of confidence about parental support, which may strengthen their capacity to master many later challenges.

What factors promote paternal warmth? Cross-cultural research reveals a consistent association between the amount of time fathers spend near infants and toddlers and their expressions of caring and affection (Rohner & Veneziano, 2001). Consider the Aka hunters and gatherers of Central Africa, where fathers spend more time in physical proximity to their babies than in any other known society. Observations reveal that Aka fathers are within arm's reach of infants more than half the day. They pick up, cuddle, and play with their babies at least five times as often as fathers in other hunting-and-gathering societies. Why are Aka fathers so involved? The bond between Aka husband and wife is unusually cooperative and intimate. Throughout the day, couples share hunting, food preparation, and social and leisure activities. The more Aka parents are together, the greater the father's loving interaction with his baby (Hewlett, 1992).

In Western cultures as well, fathers in gratifying marriages feel more confident about their parenting skills and spend more time with and interact more effectively with their infants. In contrast, marital dissatisfaction is associated with insensitive paternal care (Grych & Clark, 1999; Lundy, 2002; Sevigny & Loutzenhiser, 2010). Clearly, mothers' and fathers' warm

In both Western and non-Western nations, paternal warmth predicts long-term favorable cognitive, emotional, and social development. ■

interactions with each other and with their babies are closely linked. But paternal warmth promotes long-term favorable development, beyond the influence of maternal warmth (Rohner & Veneziano, 2001). Evidence for the power of fathers' affection, reported in virtually every culture and ethnic group studied, is reason to encourage more men to engage in nurturing care of young children.

even under conditions of great hardship (Hicks & Goedereis, 2009). Still, grandparent caregivers have a tremendous need for social and financial support and intervention services for their at-risk grandchildren.

SIBLINGS   Despite declines in family size, 80 percent of North American and European children grow up with at least one sibling (Dunn, 2004). The arrival of a new baby is a difficult experience for most preschoolers, who—realizing that they must now share their parents' attention and affection—often become demanding, clingy, and deliberately naughty for a time. Attachment security also typically declines, especially for children over age 2 (old enough to feel threatened and displaced) and for those with mothers under stress (Baydar, Greek, & Brooks-Gunn, 1997; Teti et al., 1995).

Yet resentment is only one feature of the rich emotional relationship that starts to build between siblings after a baby's birth. Older children also show affection and concern—kissing and patting the baby and calling out, "Mom, he needs you," when the infant cries. By the end of the first year, babies typically spend much time with older siblings and are comforted by the presence of a preschool-age brother or sister during short parental absences. Throughout

Applying What We Know

Encouraging Affectionate Ties Between Infants and Their Preschool Siblings

SUGGESTION	DESCRIPTION
Spend extra time with the older child.	To minimize the older child's feelings of being deprived of affection and attention, set aside time to spend with her. Fathers can be especially helpful, planning special outings with the preschooler and taking over care of the baby so the mother can be with the older child.
Handle sibling misbehavior with patience.	Respond patiently to the older sibling's misbehavior and demands for attention, recognizing that these reactions are temporary. Give the preschooler opportunities to feel proud of being more grown-up than the baby. For example, encourage the older child to assist with feeding, bathing, dressing, and offering toys, and show appreciation for these efforts.
Discuss the baby's wants and needs.	By helping the older sibling understand the baby's point of view, parents can promote friendly, considerate behavior. Say, for example, "He's so little that he just can't wait to be fed" or "He's trying to reach his rattle, and he can't."
Express positive emotion toward your partner and engage in joint problem solving.	When parents model effective problem solving, their good communication helps the older sibling cope adaptively with jealousy and conflict. Also, when family life is happy, children have less reason to feel jealous.

childhood, children continue to treat older siblings as attachment figures, turning to them for comfort in stressful situations when parents are unavailable (Seibert & Kerns, 2009). And in the second year, as toddlers imitate and join in play with their brothers and sisters, siblings start to become gratifying sources of companionship (Barr & Hayne, 2003).

Nevertheless, individual differences in sibling relationships emerge soon after the new baby's arrival. Temperament plays an important role. For example, conflict is greater when one sibling is emotionally intense or highly active (Brody, Stoneman, & McCoy, 1994; Dunn, 1994). And maternal warmth toward both children is related to positive sibling interaction and to preschoolers' support of a distressed younger sibling (Volling, 2001; Volling & Belsky, 1992). Mothers who frequently play with their children and explain the toddler's wants and needs to the preschool sibling foster sibling cooperation. In contrast, maternal harshness and lack of involvement are linked to antagonistic sibling relationships (Howe, Aquan-Assee, & Bukowski, 2001). Finally, a good marriage is correlated with older preschool siblings' capacity to cope adaptively with jealousy and conflict (Volling, McElwain, & Miller, 2002). Perhaps good communication between parents serves as a model of effective problem solving. It may also foster a generally happy family environment, giving children less reason to feel jealous.

Refer to Applying What We Know above for ways to promote positive relationships between babies and their preschool siblings. Siblings offer a rich social context in which children learn and practice a wide range of skills, including affectionate caring, conflict resolution, and control of hostile and envious feelings.

From Attachment to Peer Sociability

In cultures where agemates have regular contact during the first year of life, peer sociability begins early. By age 6 months, Caitlin and Timmy occasionally looked, reached, smiled, and babbled when they saw each other. These isolated social acts increased until, by the end of the first year, an occasional reciprocal exchange occurred in which the children grinned, gestured, or otherwise imitated a playmate's behavior (Vandell & Mueller, 1995).

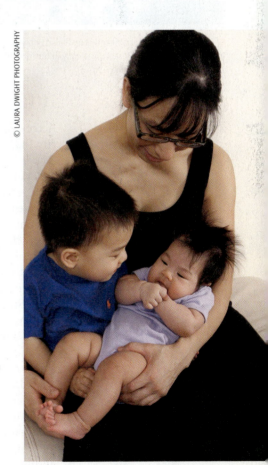

© LAURA DWIGHT PHOTOGRAPHY

■ The arrival of a baby brother or sister is a difficult experience for most preschoolers. Maternal warmth toward both children assures the older sibling of continuing parental love, models affectionate caring, and is related to positive sibling interaction. ■

Advances in peer sociability during the second year are evident in toddlers' coordinated interaction, mostly in the form of mutual imitation. ■

Between 1 and 2 years, as toddlers appreciate that others have intentions, desires, and emotions distinct from their own, they increasingly view one another as playmates (Brownell & Kopp, 2007). As a result, coordinated interaction occurs more often, largely in the form of mutual imitation involving jumping, chasing, or banging a toy. These imitative, turn-taking games create joint understandings that aid verbal communication. Around age 2, toddlers use words to talk about and influence a peer's behavior, as when Caitlin said to Grace, "Let's play chase," and after the game got going, "Hey, good running!" (Eckerman & Peterman, 2001; Eckerman & Whitehead, 1999). Reciprocal play and positive emotion are especially frequent in toddlers' interactions with familiar agemates, suggesting that they are building true peer relationships (Ross et al., 1992).

Though quite limited, peer sociability is present in the first two years and is promoted by the early caregiver–child bond. From interacting with sensitive adults, babies learn how to send and interpret emotional signals in their first peer associations (Trevarthen, 2003). Toddlers who have a warm parental relationship or who attend high-quality child care with a small group size and a generous caregiver–child ratio—features that promote warm, stimulating caregiving and secure attachment to professional caregivers—engage in more positive and extended peer exchanges. These children, in turn, display more socially competent behavior as preschoolers (Deynoot-Schaub & Riksen-Walraven, 2006a, 2006b; Howes & Matheson, 1992).

Attachment and Later Development

According to psychoanalytic and ethological theories, the inner feelings of affection and security that result from a healthy attachment relationship support all aspects of psychological development. Consistent with this view, an extensive longitudinal study by Alan Sroufe and his collaborators found that preschoolers who had been securely attached as babies were rated by their teachers as higher in self-esteem, social skills, and empathy than were their insecurely attached counterparts, who displayed more behavior problems. When studied again at age 11 in summer camp, children who had been secure infants had more favorable relationships with peers, closer friendships, and better social skills, as judged by camp counselors. And as these well-functioning school-age children became adolescents and young adults, they continued to benefit from more supportive social networks, formed more stable and gratifying romantic relationships, and attained higher levels of education (Elicker, Englund, & Sroufe, 1992; Sroufe, 2002; Sroufe et al., 2005).

For some researchers, these findings seem to indicate that secure attachment in infancy causes improved cognitive, emotional, and social competence in later years. Yet contrary evidence exists. In other longitudinal studies, secure infants generally fared better than insecure infants, but not always (Fearon et al., 2010; McCartney et al., 2004; Schneider, Atkinson, & Tardif, 2001; Stams, Juffer, & van IJzendoorn, 2002). Disorganized/disoriented attachment, however, is an exception: It is consistently related to internalizing problems (fear and anxiety) and externalizing problems (anger and aggression) during the preschool and school years. Disorganized children also show inappropriate role reversals: In an apparent effort to compensate for their parent's confused communication, they use either exaggerated comforting or hostility to try to control the parent's behavior (Lyons-Ruth, 1996; Lyons-Ruth, Easterbrooks, & Cibelli, 1997; Moss et al., 2004, 2006; Moss, Cyr, & Dubois-Comtois, 2004).

What accounts for unevenness in research findings on the consequences of early attachment quality? Mounting evidence indicates that *continuity of caregiving* determines whether attachment security is linked to later development (Lamb et al., 1985; Thompson, 2006).

Children whose parents respond sensitively not just in infancy but also in later years are likely to develop favorably. In contrast, children whose parents react insensitively or who, over a long period, are exposed to a negative family climate tend to establish lasting patterns of avoidant, resistant, or disorganized behavior and are at greater risk for developmental difficulties.

A close look at the relationship between parenting and children's adjustment in the first few years supports this emphasis on continuity of caregiving. Recall that parents of disorganized/disoriented infants tend to have serious psychological problems or engage in highly maladaptive caregiving—conditions that usually persist and that are strongly linked to poor adjustment in children (Lyons-Ruth, Bronfman, & Parsons, 1999). And when more than 1,000 children were tracked from age 1 to 3 years, those with histories of secure attachment followed by sensitive parenting scored highest in cognitive, emotional, and social outcomes. Those with histories of insecure attachment followed by insensitive parenting scored lowest, while those with mixed histories of attachment and maternal sensitivity scored in between (Belsky & Fearon, 2002a). Specifically, insecurely attached infants whose mothers became more positive and supportive in early childhood showed signs of developmental recovery.

Does this trend remind you of our discussion of *resilience* in Chapter 1? A child whose parental caregiving improves or who has other compensating affectionate ties can bounce back from adversity. In contrast, a child who experiences tender care in infancy but lacks sympathetic ties later on is at risk for problems.

Although a secure attachment in infancy does not guarantee continued good parenting, it does launch the parent–child relationship on a positive path that is likely to continue. Much research shows that an early warm, positive parent–child tie, sustained over time, promotes many aspects of children's development: a more confident and complex self-concept, more advanced emotional understanding, more favorable relationships with teachers and peers, more effective social skills, a stronger sense of moral responsibility, and higher motivation to achieve in school (Thompson, 2006; Thompson, Easterbrooks, & Padilla-Walker, 2003). But the effects of early attachment security are *conditional*—dependent on the quality of the baby's future relationships. Finally, as you will see again in future chapters, attachment is just one of the complex influences on children's psychological development.

ASK YOURSELF

◆ **REVIEW** What factors explain stability in attachment pattern for some children and change for others? Are these factors also involved in the link between attachment in infancy and later development? Explain.

◆ **APPLY** What attachment pattern did Timmy display when Vanessa arrived home from work, and what factors probably contributed to it?

◆ **CONNECT** Review research on emotional self-regulation on pages 254–255. How do the caregiving experiences of securely attached infants promote the development of emotional self-regulation?

◆ **REFLECT** How would you characterize your internal working model? What factors, in addition to your early relationship with your parents, might have influenced it?

Self-Development

Infancy is a rich formative period for the development of physical and social understanding. In Chapter 6, you learned that infants develop an appreciation of the permanence of objects. And in this chapter, we have seen that over the first year, infants recognize and respond appropriately to others' emotions and distinguish familiar from unfamiliar people. That both objects and people achieve an independent, stable existence for the infant implies that knowledge of the self as a separate, permanent entity is also emerging.

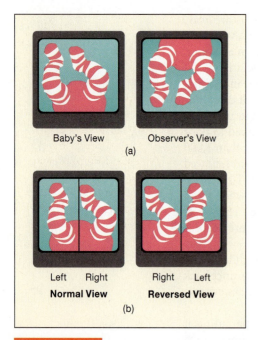

Baby's View   Observer's View
(a)

Left   Right   Right   Left
Normal View   **Reversed View**
(b)

Three-month-olds' emerging self-awareness, as indicated by reactions to video images.
(a) When shown two side-by-side views of their kicking legs, babies looked longer at the novel, observer's view than at their own view. (b) When shown a normal view of their leg positions alongside a reversed view, infants looked longer at the novel, reversed view. *(Adapted from Rochat, 1998.)*

■ This 18-month-old's response to her reflection indicates that she recognizes her unique physical features and is aware of herself as a separate being, distinct from other people and objects. ■

Self-Awareness

After Caitlin's bath, Carolyn often held her in front of the bathroom mirror. As early as the first few months, Caitlin smiled and returned friendly behaviors to her image. At what age did she realize that the charming baby gazing and grinning back was herself?

BEGINNINGS OF SELF-AWARENESS   At birth, infants sense that they are physically distinct from their surroundings. For example, newborns display a stronger rooting reflex in response to external stimulation (an adult's finger touching their cheek) than to self-stimulation (their own hand contacting their cheek) (Rochat & Hespos, 1997). Newborns' remarkable capacity for intermodal perception (see pages 197–198 in Chapter 5) supports the beginnings of self-awareness (Rochat, 2003). As they feel their own touch, feel and watch their limbs move, and feel and hear themselves cry, babies experience intermodal matches that differentiate their own body from surrounding bodies and objects.

Over the first few months, infants distinguish their own visual image from other stimuli, but their self-awareness is limited—expressed only in perception and action. When shown two side-by-side video images of their kicking legs, one from their own perspective (camera behind the baby) and one from an observer's perspective (camera in front of the baby), 3-month-olds looked longer at the observer's view (see Figure 7.6a). In another video-image comparison, they looked longer at a reversal of their leg positions than at a normal view (see Figure 7.6b) (Rochat, 1998). This suggests that young babies have a sense of their own body as a distinct entity, since they have habituated to it, as indicated by their interest in novel views of the body. By 4 months, infants look and smile more at video images of others than video images of themselves, indicating that they distinguish between the two and treat another person (as opposed to the self) as a potential social partner (Rochat & Striano, 2002).

This discrimination of one's own limb and facial movements from those of others in real-time video presentations reflects an *implicit sense of self–world differentiation*. It serves as the foundation for the development of *explicit self-awareness:* an objective understanding that the self is a unique object in a world of objects, which includes representations of one's own physical features and body dimensions.

EXPLICIT SELF-AWARENESS   During the second year, toddlers become consciously aware of the self's physical features. In several studies, 9- to 28-month-olds were placed in front of a mirror. Then, under the pretext of wiping the baby's face, each mother rubbed red dye on her child's nose or forehead. Younger babies touched the mirror as if the red mark had nothing to do with them. But those older than 20 months touched or rubbed their strange-looking noses or foreheads, a response indicating clear awareness of their unique facial appearance (Bard et al., 2006; Lewis & Brooks-Gunn, 1979). And some toddlers act silly or coy in front of the mirror, playfully experimenting with the way the self looks (Bullock & Lutkenhaus, 1990).

Around age 2, *self-recognition*—identification of the self as a physically unique being—is well under way. Children point to themselves in photos and refer to themselves by name or with a personal pronoun ("I" or "me") (Lewis & Ramsay, 2004). And soon they will identify themselves in images with less detail and fidelity than mirrors. Around age 2½, most reach for a sticker surreptitiously placed on top of their heads when shown themselves in a live video, and around age 3 most recognize their own shadow (Cameron & Gallup, 1988; Suddendorf, Simcock, & Nielsen, 2007).

As self-recognition takes shape, older toddlers also construct an explicit *body self-awareness*. At the end of the second year, they realize that their own body can serve as an obstacle. When asked to push a shopping cart while standing on a mat attached to its rear axle, most 18- to 21-month-olds (but not younger children) figured out how to remove themselves from the mat so the cart would move—an ability that improved with age (Moore et al., 2007).

Nevertheless, toddlers lack an objective understanding of their own body dimensions. They make **scale errors,** attempting to do things that their body size makes impossible. For example, they will try to put on dolls' clothes, fit themselves into a doll-sized chair, or walk through a doorway too narrow for them to pass through (Brownell, Zerwas, & Ramani, 2007; DeLoache, Uttal, & Rosengren, 2004). They are amazingly persistent, even seeking an adult's help after they repeatedly do not succeed! Scale errors decline around age 2, but many 2½-year-olds still make them. Young preschoolers are still learning to process physical information about their own bodies in the same way they do for other objects.

INFLUENCES ON SELF-AWARENESS   What experiences contribute to gains in self-awareness? During the first year, as infants act on the environment, they probably notice effects that help them sort out self, other people, and objects (Nadel, Prepin, & Okanda, 2005; Rochat, 2001). For example, batting a mobile and seeing it swing in a pattern different from the infant's own actions gives the baby information about the relation between self and physical world. Smiling and vocalizing at a caregiver who smiles and vocalizes back helps specify the relation between self and social world. And watching the movements of one's own hands and feet provides still another kind of feedback—one under much more direct control than the movements of other people or objects. The contrast between these experiences helps infants sense that they are separate from external reality.

Researchers do not yet know exactly how toddlers acquire the various aspects of explicit self-awareness. But sensitive caregiving seems to play a role. Compared to their insecurely attached agemates, securely attached toddlers display more complex self-related actions during play, such as making a doll labeled as the self take a drink or kiss a teddy bear. They also show greater knowledge of their own physical features—for example, in labeling body parts (Pipp, Easterbrooks, & Brown, 1993; Pipp, Easterbrooks, & Harmon, 1992). And 18-month-olds who often establish joint attention with their caregivers are advanced in mirror self-recognition (Nichols, Fox, & Mundy, 2005). Joint attention offers toddlers many opportunities to engage in social referencing—to compare their own and others' reactions to objects and events—which may enhance toddlers' awareness of their own physical uniqueness.

Cultural variations exist in early self-development. Urban German and Greek toddlers attain mirror self-recognition earlier than toddlers of the Nso people of Cameroon, a collectivist rural farming society that highly values social harmony and responsibility to others (Keller et al., 2004, 2005). Compared to their German and Greek counterparts, Nso mothers engage in less face-to-face communication and object stimulation and more body contact and physical stimulation of their babies. German and Greek practices reflect a distal parenting style common in cultures that emphasize *independence,* the Nso practice a proximal parenting style typical in cultures that promote *interdependence.* In line with these differences, Nso proximal parenting is associated with later attainment of self-recognition but earlier emergence of toddlers' compliance with adult requests (see Figure 7.7).

LOOK AND LISTEN

Ask several parents of 1½- to 2-year-olds if they have observed any instances of scale errors. Have the parent hand the toddler doll-sized clothing (hat, jacket, or shoe) or furniture (table, slide, or car) and watch for scale errors.

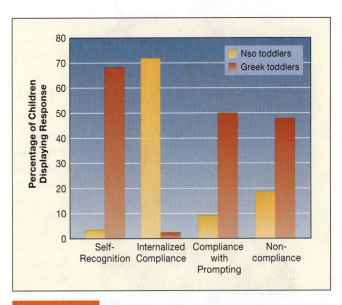

FIGURE 7.7

Self-recognition and compliance among Nso and Greek toddlers. At 10 and 20 months, toddlers were tested for mirror self-recognition and for compliance (they were told not to open a transparent container with an attractive food). Among Greek toddlers, whose culture values independence, many more had attained self-recognition. But Nso toddlers, reared in an interdependent culture, were greatly advanced in compliance (following directions without prompting), whereas Greek toddlers either needed reminders or did not comply. *(Adapted from Keller et al., 2004.)*

SELF-AWARENESS AND EARLY EMOTIONAL AND SOCIAL DEVELOPMENT Self-awareness quickly becomes a central part of children's emotional and social lives. Recall that self-conscious emotions depend on a strengthening sense of self. Self-awareness also leads to first efforts to understand another's perspective. We have seen that toddlers increasingly appreciate others' intentions, feelings, and desires. Older toddlers who have experienced sensitive caregiving and emotionally available parents draw on their advancing cognitive, language, and social skills to express first signs of **empathy**—the ability to understand another's emotional state and *feel with* that person, or respond emotionally in a similar way. For example, they communicate concern when others are distressed and may offer what they themselves find comforting—a hug, a reassuring comment, or a favorite doll or blanket (Hoffman, 2000; Moreno, Klute, & Robinson, 2008).

At the same time, toddlers demonstrate clearer awareness of how to upset others. One 18-month-old heard her mother talking to another adult about an older sibling: "Anny is really frightened of spiders. In fact, there's a particular toy spider that we've got that she just hates" (Dunn, 1989, p. 107). The innocent-looking toddler ran to the bedroom, returned with the toy spider, and pushed it in front of Anny's face!

Categorizing the Self

By the end of the second year, language becomes a powerful tool in self-development. Between 18 and 30 months, children can categorize themselves and others on the basis of age ("baby," "boy," or "man"), sex ("boy" or "girl"), physical characteristics ("big," "strong"), and even goodness and badness ("I good girl." "Tommy mean!"). They also start to refer to the self's competencies ("Did it!" "I can't") (Stipek, Gralinski, & Kopp, 1990).

Toddlers use their limited understanding of these social categories to organize their own behavior. As early as 17 months, children select and play in a more involved way with toys that are stereotyped for their own gender—dolls and tea sets for girls, trucks and cars for boys. Their ability to label their own gender predicts a sharp rise in these play preferences over the next few months (Zosuls et al., 2009). Then parents encourage gender-typed behavior by responding more positively when toddlers display it (Ruble, Martin, & Berenbaum, 2006). As we will see in Chapter 10, gender-typing increases dramatically during early childhood.

Self-Control

Self-awareness also contributes to *effortful control,* the extent to which children can inhibit impulses, manage negative emotion, and behave in socially acceptable ways. Indeed, a firmer sense of self may underlie the increasing stability and organization of effortful control in the third year (see pages 258 and 260). To behave in a self-controlled fashion, children must think of themselves as separate, autonomous beings who can direct their own actions. And they must have the representational and memory capacities to recall a caregiver's directive ("Caitlin, don't touch that light socket!") and apply it to their own behavior.

As these capacities emerge between 12 and 18 months, toddlers first become capable of **compliance:** They show clear awareness of caregivers' wishes and expectations and can obey simple requests and commands. And, as every parent knows, they can also decide to do just the opposite! Although defiance in preschoolers is associated with negative parent–child relationships and poor adjustment, toddlers who sometimes strongly resist parental demands tend to have sensitive, supportive parents with whom they interact positively. These parents recognize the young child's need for self-assertion and autonomy (Dix et al., 2007). Indeed, active resistance in toddlerhood does not predict later, persisting defiance. Rather, for most toddlers, assertiveness and opposition occur alongside compliance with an eager, willing spirit, which suggests that the child is beginning to adopt the adult's directives as his own (Kochanska, Murray, & Harlan, 2000). Compliance quickly

© SW PRODUCTIONS/GETTY IMAGES/PHOTODISC GREEN

■ This father encourages compliance and the beginnings of self-control. The toddler joins in the task with an eager, willing spirit, which suggests he is adopting the adult's directive as his own. ■

Applying What We Know

Helping Toddlers Develop Compliance and Self-Control

SUGGESTION	RATIONALE
Respond to the toddler with sensitivity and encouragement.	Toddlers whose parents are sensitive and supportive at times actively resist, but they are also are more compliant and self-controlled.
Provide advance notice when the toddler must stop an enjoyable activity.	Toddlers find it more difficult to stop a pleasant activity that is already under way than to wait before engaging in a desired action.
Offer many prompts and reminders.	Toddlers' ability to remember and comply with rules is limited; they need continuous adult oversight and patient assistance.
Respond to self-controlled behavior with verbal and physical approval.	Praise and hugs reinforce appropriate behavior, increasing the likelihood that it will occur again.
Encourage selective and sustained attention (see Chapter 6, pages 218–219).	Development of attention is related to self-control. Children who can shift attention from a captivating stimulus and focus on a less attractive alternative are better at controlling their impulses.
Support language development (see Chapter 6, pages 241–242).	Early language development is related to self-control. In the second year, children begin to use language to remind themselves of adult expectations and to delay gratification.
Gradually increase rules in a manner consistent with the toddler's developing capacities.	As cognition and language improve, toddlers can follow more rules related to safety, respect for people and property, family routines, manners, and simple chores.

leads to toddlers' first consciencelike verbalizations—for example, correcting the self by saying "No, can't" before reaching for a treat or jumping on the sofa.

Researchers often study the early emergence of self-control by giving children tasks that, like the situations just mentioned, require **delay of gratification**—waiting for an appropriate time and place to engage in a tempting act. Between ages 1½ and 3, children show an increasing capacity to wait before eating a treat, opening a present, or playing with a toy (Vaughn, Kopp, & Krakow, 1984). Children who are advanced in development of attention and language tend to be better at delaying gratification—findings that help explain why girls are typically more self-controlled than boys (Else-Quest et al., 2006). Some toddlers already use verbal and other attention-diverting techniques—talking to themselves, singing, or looking away—to keep from engaging in prohibited acts.

Like effortful control in general, young children's capacity to delay gratification is influenced by both temperament and quality of caregiving (Kochanska & Aksan, 2006; Kochanska & Knaack, 2003). Inhibited children find it easier to wait than angry, irritable children do. But toddlers who experience parental warmth and gentle encouragement are more likely to be cooperative and to resist temptation. Such parenting—which encourages and models patient, nonimpulsive behavior—is particularly important for temperamentally reactive babies. In one study, anger-prone 7-month-olds with gentle, responsive mothers became eagerly compliant 15-month-olds. Angry infants with insensitive mothers, by contrast, developed into strikingly uncooperative toddlers (Kochanska, Aksan, & Carlson, 2005). **TAKE A MOMENT...** Turn back to page 262, and note how these findings provide yet another example of the importance of goodness of fit between temperament and child rearing.

As self-control improves, parents gradually expand the rules they expect toddlers to follow, from safety and respect for property and people to family routines, manners, and simple chores (Gralinski & Kopp, 1993). Still, toddlers' control over their own actions depends on constant parental oversight and reminders. Several prompts ("Remember, we're going to go in just a minute") and gentle insistence were usually necessary to get Caitlin to stop playing so that she and her parents could go on an errand. Applying What We Know above summarizes ways to help toddlers develop compliance and self-control.

As the second year of life drew to a close, Carolyn, Monica, and Vanessa were delighted at their children's readiness to learn the rules of social life. As we will see in Chapter 10, advances in cognition and language, along with parental warmth and reasonable demands for maturity, lead preschoolers to make tremendous strides in this area.

ASK YOURSELF

◆ **REVIEW** Why is insisting that infants comply with parental directives inappropriate? What competencies are necessary for the emergence of compliance and self-control?

◆ **APPLY** Len, a caregiver of 1- and 2-year-olds, wonders whether toddlers recognize themselves. List signs of self-recognition in the second year that Len can observe. What behaviors reveal that toddlers are still forming objective representations of their own physical features?

◆ **CONNECT** What type of early parenting fosters the development of emotional self-regulation, secure attachment, and self-control? Why, in each instance, is it effective?

◆ **REFLECT** In view of research on toddlers' compliance, active resistance, and budding capacity to delay gratification, do you think that "the terrible twos," a commonly used expression to characterize typical toddler behavior, is an apt description? Explain.

Summary

Erikson's Theory of Infant and Toddler Personality

What personality changes take place during Erikson's stages of basic trust versus mistrust and autonomy versus shame and doubt?

■ Warm, responsive caregiving leads infants to resolve Erikson's psychological conflict of **basic trust versus mistrust** on the positive side. During toddlerhood, **autonomy versus shame and doubt** is resolved favorably when parents provide appropriate guidance and reasonable choices. If children emerge from the first few years without sufficient trust and autonomy, the seeds are sown for adjustment problems.

Emotional Development

Describe the development of basic emotions over the first year, noting the adaptive function of each.

■ During the first half-year, **basic emotions** gradually become clear, well-organized signals. The **social smile** appears between 6 and 10 weeks, laughter around 3 to 4 months. Happiness strengthens the parent–child bond and reflects as well as supports physical and cognitive mastery.

■ Anger and fear, especially in the form of **stranger anxiety,** increase in the second half of the first year as infants' cognitive and motor capacities improve. Newly mobile babies use the familiar caregiver as a **secure base** from which to explore.

Summarize changes that occur during the first two years in understanding others' emotions, expression of self-conscious emotions, and emotional self-regulation.

■ The ability to understand others' feelings expands over the first year. From 5 months on, babies perceive facial expressions as organized patterns. Between 8 and 10 months, infants engage in **social referencing,** actively seeking emotional information from caregivers in uncertain situations. By the middle of the second year, infants become aware that others' emotional reactions may differ from their own.

■ During toddlerhood, self-awareness and adult instruction provide the foundation for **self-conscious emotions:** shame, embarrassment, guilt, envy, and pride. **Emotional self-regulation** emerges as the prefrontal cortex functions more effectively and as caregivers sensitively assist infants in adjusting their emotional reactions. In the second year, growth in representation and language leads to more effective ways of regulating emotion.

© ABLEIMAGES/ALAMY IMAGES

Temperament and Development

What is temperament, and how is it measured?

■ Children differ greatly in **temperament**—early appearing, stable individual differences in reactivity and self-regulation. The New York Longitudinal Study identified three patterns: the **easy child,** the **difficult child,** and the **slow-to-warm-up child.** The most influential model of temperament, devised by Mary Rothbart, includes dimensions representing emotion, attention, and action, along with **effortful control,** the ability to regulate one's reactivity.

■ Temperament is assessed through parental reports, behavior ratings by others familiar with the child, and laboratory observations. Most neurophysiological research has focused on distinguishing **inhibited,** or **shy, children** from **uninhibited,** or **sociable, children.**

Discuss the roles of heredity and environment in the stability of temperament, including the goodness-of-fit model.

■ Temperament has low to moderate stability: It develops with age and can be modified by experience. Long-term prediction from early temperament is best achieved after age 3.

■ Temperament has a genetic foundation, but child rearing and cultural beliefs and practices have much to do with maintaining or changing it.

■ The **goodness-of-fit model** describes how temperament and environment work together to affect later development. Parenting practices that fit well with the child's temperament help children achieve more adaptive functioning.

Development of Attachment

What are the unique features of ethological theory of attachment?

- The most widely accepted perspective on development of **attachment**—our strong, affectionate tie with special people in our lives—is **ethological theory,** which recognizes the infant's emotional tie to the caregiver as an evolved response that promotes survival. In early infancy, a set of built-in behaviors encourages the parent to remain close to the baby.

- Around 6 to 8 months, **separation anxiety** and use of the parent as a secure base indicate the existence of a true attachment bond. Separation anxiety declines as representation and language develop, letting toddlers understand the parent's coming and going. From early caregiving experiences, children construct an **internal working model** that guides all future close relationships.

© LAURA DWIGHT PHOTOGRAPHY

Cite the four attachment patterns assessed by the Strange Situation and the Attachment Q-Sort, and discuss factors that affect attachment security.

- Using the **Strange Situation,** a common technique for measuring the quality of attachment between 1 and 2 years of age, researchers have identified four attachment patterns: **secure, avoidant, resistant,** and **disorganized/ disoriented attachment.** The **Attachment Q-Sort,** based on home observations of children between ages 1 and 5, yields a score ranging from low to high security.

- Securely attached babies in middle-SES families under favorable life conditions more often maintain their attachment pattern than insecure babies. However, the disorganized/ disoriented pattern is highly stable. Cultural conditions must be considered in interpreting the meaning of attachment patterns.

- Attachment security is influenced by early availability of a consistent caregiver, quality of caregiving, the fit between the baby's temperament and parenting practices, and family circumstances. **Sensitive caregiving** is moderately related to secure attachment.

- In some cultures, **interactional synchrony** characterizes the experiences of securely attached babies. Parents' internal working models are good predictors of infant attachment patterns, but parents' childhood experiences do not transfer directly to quality of attachment with their own children.

Discuss infants' formation of multiple attachments, and indicate how attachment paves the way for early peer sociability.

- Infants develop strong affectionate ties to fathers, who tend to engage in more exciting, physical play with babies than do mothers. Especially in cultures where fathers devote little time to infant care, play is a vital context in which fathers and babies build secure attachments, predicting favorable emotional and social adjustment.

- Grandparents who serve as primary caregivers for grandchildren in skipped-generation families forge significant attachment ties that help protect children with troubled family lives from adjustment problems.

© ELLEN B. SENISI PHOTOGRAPHY

- Early in the first year, infants start to form rich emotional relationships with siblings that combine rivalry and resentment with affection and sympathetic concern. Individual differences in these relationships are influenced by temperament, parenting practices, and marital quality.

- Peer sociability begins in infancy with isolated social acts, followed by reciprocal exchanges (largely in the form of mutual imitation) in the second year of life. A warm caregiver–child bond promotes peer sociability.

Describe and interpret the relationship between secure attachment in infancy and psychological development in childhood.

- A secure attachment in infancy launches the parent–child relationship on a positive path. But continuity of caregiving determines whether attachment security is linked to later development. If caregiving improves, children can recover from an insecure attachment history.

Self-Development

Describe the development of self-awareness in infancy and toddlerhood, along with the emotional and social capacities it supports.

- Self-awareness begins at birth, when infants implicitly sense that they are physically distinct from their surroundings, and expands over the early months. At the end of the second year, self-recognition emerges as toddlers become explicitly aware of the self's physical features. However, toddlers lack an objective understanding of their own body size, as indicated by their **scale errors.**

- Self-awareness sets the stage for social referencing and, in the second year, self-conscious emotions. It also leads to toddlers' first efforts to appreciate others' perspectives, including early signs of **empathy.** Between 18 and 30 months, as language develops, children categorize themselves and others on the basis of age, sex, physical characteristics, and competencies.

- Self-awareness also contributes to effortful control and, between 12 and 18 months, to the emergence of **compliance.** Between ages 1½ and 3, **delay of gratification** strengthens. Toddlers who experience parental warmth and gentle encouragement are likely to be advanced in self-control.

IMPORTANT TERMS AND CONCEPTS

attachment (p. 264)
Attachment Q-Sort (p. 267)
autonomy versus shame and doubt (p. 249)
avoidant attachment (p. 267)
basic emotions (p. 250)
basic trust versus mistrust (p. 248)
compliance (p. 282)
delay of gratification (p. 283)
difficult child (p. 256)
disorganized/disoriented attachment (p. 267)
easy child (p. 256)

effortful control (p. 257)
emotional self-regulation (p. 254)
empathy (p. 282)
ethological theory of attachment (p. 265)
goodness-of-fit model (p. 262)
inhibited, or shy, child (p. 258)
interactional synchrony (p. 270)
internal working model (p. 266)
resistant attachment (p. 267)
scale errors (p. 281)
secure attachment (p. 266)

secure base (p. 252)
self-conscious emotions (p. 253)
sensitive caregiving (p. 270)
separation anxiety (p. 265)
slow-to-warm-up child (p. 257)
social referencing (p. 253)
social smile (p. 251)
stranger anxiety (p. 252)
Strange Situation (p. 266)
temperament (p. 256)
uninhibited, or sociable, child (p. 258)

Milestones

Development in Infancy and Toddlerhood

Birth–6 months

PHYSICAL

- Height and weight increase rapidly. (162)
- Newborn reflexes decline. (145)
- Sleep is increasingly organized into a night–day schedule. (172)
- Responses can be classically and operantly conditioned. (179–180)
- Habituates to unchanging stimuli; recovers to novel stimuli. (181)
- Holds head up, rolls over, and grasps objects. (184)
- Shows sensitivity to motion, then binocular, and finally pictorial depth cues. (191–193)
- Recognizes and prefers human facial pattern; recognizes features of mother's face. (195–196)
- Perceives auditory and visual stimuli as organized patterns. (198)
- By end of this period, moves from relying on motion and spatial arrangement to using shape, color, and texture to visually identify objects. (197)
- Masters a wide range of intermodal (visual, auditory, and tactile) relationships. (197–198)

COGNITIVE

- Engages in immediate and deferred imitation of adults' facial expressions. (210–211)
- Repeats chance behaviors that lead to pleasurable and interesting results. (206)
- Has some awareness of many physical properties (including object permanence) and basic numerical knowledge. (208)

- Attention becomes more efficient and flexible. (218)
- Recognition memory for visual events improves. (219)
- Forms categories based on objects' similar physical properties. (222)

LANGUAGE

- Engages in cooing and, by the end of this period, babbling. (236)
- Begins to establish joint attention with caregiver, who labels objects and events. (238)

EMOTIONAL/SOCIAL

- Social smile and laughter emerge. (251)

- Matches feeling tone of caregiver in face-to-face communication; later, expects matched responses. (252)
- Emotional expressions become well organized and meaningfully related to environmental events. (253)
- Distinguishes positive from negative emotion in voices and facial expressions. (253)
- Regulates emotion by shifting attention and self-soothing. (255)
- Smiles, laughs, and babbles more to caregiver than to a stranger. (265)
- Awareness of self as physically distinct from surroundings increases. (280)

7–12 months

PHYSICAL

- Approaches adultlike sleep–wake schedule. (172)
- Sits alone, crawls, and walks. (184)

- Reaching and grasping improve in flexibility and accuracy; shows refined pincer grasp. (187–188)
- "Screens out" sounds not used in own language; perceives meaningful speech. (189–190)
- Relies on shape, color, and texture to distinguish objects from their surroundings. (197)
- Intermodal perception continues to improve. (198)

COGNITIVE

- Engages in intentional, or goal-directed, behavior. (206–207)
- Finds an object hidden in an initial location. (207)
- Recall memory improves, as indicated by gains in deferred imitation of adults' actions with objects. (210)
- Solves simple problems by analogy to a previous problem. (211)
- Categorizes objects by similar function and behavior. (222)
- Uses words to call up mental images of objects not physically present. (211)

NOTE: Numbers in parentheses indicate the page or pages on which each milestone is discussed.

LANGUAGE

- Babbling expands to include sounds of spoken languages and patterns of the child's language community. (237)
- Skill in joint attention with caregiver improves. (238)

- Takes turns in games, such as pat-a-cake and peekaboo. (238)
- Uses preverbal gestures (showing, pointing) to influence others' goals and behavior and to convey information. (238)
- Comprehends some word meanings. (238)
- Around 1 year, says first words. (238)

EMOTIONAL/SOCIAL

- Smiling and laughter increase in frequency and expressiveness. (251)
- Anger and fear increase in frequency and intensity. (251–252)
- Stranger anxiety and separation anxiety appear. (252, 265–266)
- Uses caregiver as a secure base for exploration. (252)
- Shows "clear-cut" attachment to a familiar caregiver. (265)
- Increasingly detects the meaning of others' emotional expressions and engages in social referencing. (253)
- Regulates emotion by approaching and retreating from stimulation. (254–255)

13–18 months

PHYSICAL

- Height and weight gain are rapid, but not as great as in first year; toddlers slim down. (162–163)
- Walking is better coordinated. (184)

- Manipulates small objects with improved coordination. (188, 206)

COGNITIVE

- Takes a deliberately experimental approach to problem solving, repeating behaviors with variation. (206)
- Searches in several locations for a hidden object. (209)
- Engages in deferred imitation of adults' actions with objects over longer delays and across a change in context—for example, from child care to home. (210)
- Sustained attention improves. (218)
- Recall memory for people, places, objects, and actions improves. (220)
- Sorts objects into categories. (222)
- Becomes aware that pictures can symbolize real objects. (212)

LANGUAGE

- Steadily adds to vocabulary. (239)
- Comprehends 50 words at 13 months; produces 50 words at 18 months. (240)

EMOTIONAL/SOCIAL

- Joins in play with familiar adults, siblings, and peers. (277–278)

- Realizes that others' emotional reactions may differ from one's own. (253)
- Uses social referencing to better evaluate events and understand emotions of the same valence. (253)
- Shows signs of empathy. (282)
- Complies with simple directives. (282)

19–24 months

PHYSICAL

- Jumps, walks on tiptoe, runs, and climbs. (184)
- Manipulates small objects with good coordination. (188, 206)

COGNITIVE

- Solves simple problems suddenly, through representation. (207)
- Finds a hidden object that has been moved while out of sight. (207)
- Engages in make-believe play, using simple actions experienced in everyday life. (207)

- Engages in deferred imitation of actions an adult tries to produce, even if not fully realized. (211)
- Sorts objects into categories more effectively. (223)
- Begins to use language as a flexible symbolic tool, to modify existing mental representations. (212)

LANGUAGE

- Produces about 200 words. (239)
- Combines two words. (239)

EMOTIONAL/SOCIAL

- Self-conscious emotions (shame, embarrassment, guilt, envy, and pride) emerge. (253–254)
- Acquires a vocabulary for talking about feelings. (255)
- Begins to use language to assist with emotional self-regulation. (255)
- Begins to tolerate caregiver's absences more easily; separation anxiety declines. (265)
- Recognizes image of self and by end of this period, uses own name or personal pronoun to refer to self. (280)
- Constructs explicit body self-awareness, and scale errors decline. (281)
- Categorizes self and others on the basis of age, sex, physical characteristics, goodness and badness, and competencies. (282)
- Shows gender-stereotyped toy preferences. (282)
- Self-control, as indicated by delay of gratification, emerges. (283)
- Starts to use words to influence a playmate's behavior. (278)

"On the Slope"
Natasha
6 years, Russia

These young skiers express pride in mastery of new motor skills. Chapter 8 highlights the close link between physical growth and other aspects of development in early childhood.

Reprinted with permission from the International Collection of Child Art, Milner Library, Illinois State University, Normal, Illinois

Physical Development in Early Childhood

Body Growth
Skeletal Growth • Brain Development

Influences on Physical Growth and Health
Heredity and Hormones • Emotional Well-Being • Sleep Habits and Problems • Nutrition • Infectious Disease • Childhood Injuries

■ **BIOLOGY AND ENVIRONMENT**
Low-Level Lead Exposure and Children's Development

■ **CULTURAL INFLUENCES**
Child Health Care in the United States and Other Western Nations

■ **SOCIAL ISSUES: HEALTH**
Otitis Media and Development

Motor Development
Gross-Motor Development • Fine-Motor Development • Individual Differences in Motor Skills • Enhancing Early Childhood Motor Development

For more than a decade, my fourth-floor office window over-looked the preschool and kindergarten play yard of our university laboratory school. On mild fall and spring mornings, the doors of classrooms swung open, and sand table, easels, and large blocks spilled out into a small courtyard. Alongside the building was a grassy area with jungle gyms, swings, a playhouse, and a flower garden planted by the children; beyond it, a circular path lined with tricycles and wagons. Each day, the setting was alive with activity.

Even from my distant vantage point, the physical changes of early childhood were evident. Children's bodies were longer and leaner than they had been a year or two earlier. The awkward gait of toddlerhood had disappeared in favor of more refined movements that included running, climbing, jumping, galloping, and skipping. Children scaled the jungle gym, raced across the lawn, turned somersaults, and vigorously pedaled tricycles. Just as impressive as these gross-motor achievements were gains in fine-motor skills. At the sand table, children built hills, valleys, caves, and roads and prepared trays of pretend cookies and cupcakes. And as they grew older, their paintings at the outdoor easels took on greater structure and detail as family members, houses, trees, birds, sky, monsters, and letterlike forms appeared in the colorful creations.

The years from 2 to 6 are often called "the play years"—aptly so, since play blossoms during this time and supports every aspect of development. Our discussion of early childhood opens with the physical achievements of this period—growth in body size, improvements in motor coordination, and refinements in perception. We pay special attention to genetic and environmental factors that support these changes, as well as to their intimate connection with other domains of development. The children I came to know well, first by watching from my office window and later by observing at close range in their classrooms, will provide many examples of developmental trends and individual differences.

Body Growth

In early childhood, the rapid increase in body size of the first two years tapers off into a slower growth pattern. On average, children add 2 to 3 inches in height and about 5 pounds in weight each year. Boys continue to be slightly larger than girls. As the "baby fat" that began to decline in toddlerhood drops off further, children gradually become thinner, although girls retain somewhat more body fat than boys, who are slightly more muscular. As the torso lengthens and widens, internal organs tuck neatly inside, and the spine straightens. As Figure 8.1 shows, by age 5 the top-heavy, bowlegged, potbellied toddler has become a more streamlined, flat-tummied, longer-legged child with body proportions similar to those of adults. Consequently, posture and balance improve—changes that foster gains in motor coordination.

Individual differences in body size are even more apparent during early childhood than in infancy and toddlerhood. Speeding around the bike path in the play yard, 5-year-old Darryl—at 48 inches tall and 55 pounds—towered over his kindergarten classmates. (The average North American 5-year-old boy is 43 inches tall and weighs 42 pounds.) Priti, an Asian-Indian child, was unusually small because of genetic factors linked to her cultural ancestry. And Lynette and Hal, two Caucasian children with impoverished home lives, were well below average for reasons we will discuss shortly.

The existence of these variations in body size reminds us that growth norms for one population are not good standards for children elsewhere in the world. Consider the Efe of the Republic of Congo, whose typical adult height is less than 5 feet. For genetic reasons, the impact of hormones controlling body size is reduced in Efe children (Bailey, 1991). By age 5, the average Efe child is shorter than more than 97 percent of North American 5-year-olds. The Efe's small size probably evolved because it reduces their caloric requirements in the face of food scarcity in the rain forests of Central Africa and enables them to move easily through the dense forest underbrush (Perry & Dominy, 2009). Efe children's short stature does not indicate growth or health problems. But for other children, such as Lynette and Hal, extremely slow growth is cause for concern.

Skeletal Growth

The skeletal changes of infancy continue throughout early childhood. Between ages 2 and 6, approximately 45 new *epiphyses,* or growth centers in which cartilage hardens into bone, emerge in various parts of the skeleton. Other epiphyses will appear in middle childhood. X-rays of these growth centers enable doctors to estimate children's *skeletal age,* or progress toward physical maturity (see page 163 in Chapter 5)—information helpful in diagnosing growth disorders.

By the end of the preschool years, children start to lose their primary, or "baby," teeth. The age at which they do so is heavily influenced by genetic factors. For example, girls, who are ahead of boys in physical development, lose their primary teeth sooner. Cultural ancestry also makes a difference. North American children typically get their first secondary (permanent) tooth at 6½ years, children in Ghana at just over 5 years, and children in Hong Kong around the sixth birthday (Burns, 2000). But nutritional factors also influence dental development. Prolonged malnutrition delays the appearance of permanent teeth, whereas overweight and obesity accelerate it (Hilgers et al., 2006).

Diseased baby teeth can affect the health of permanent teeth, so preventing decay in primary teeth is essential—by brushing consistently, avoiding sugary foods, drinking fluoridated water, and getting topical fluoride treatments and sealants (plastic coatings that protect tooth surfaces). Another factor is exposure to tobacco smoke, which suppresses children's immune system, including the ability to fight bacteria responsible for tooth decay. The risk associated with this suppression is greatest in infancy and early childhood, when the immune system is not yet fully

© BLEND IMAGES/ALAMY

■ During early childhood, body fat declines, the torso enlarges to better accommodate the internal organs, and the spine straightens. Compared to her younger brother, this 5-year-old is more streamlined. ■

PHOTOS COURTESY OF PAT SELFE

Andy at 3 years

Andy at 4 years

Andy at 5 years

Andy at 5¾ years

Amy at 3 years

Amy at 3½ years

Amy at 4½ years

Amy at 5½ years

Body growth during early childhood. Andy and Amy grew more slowly during the preschool years than in infancy and toddlerhood (see Chapter 5, page 163). By age 5, their bodies became flat-tummied and longer-legged. Boys continue to be slightly taller and heavier and more muscular than girls. But generally, the two sexes are similar in body proportions and physical capacities.

mature (Aligne et al., 2003). Young children in homes with regular smokers are three times as likely as their agemates to have decayed teeth, even after other factors influencing dental health have been controlled (Shenkin et al., 2004).

Unfortunately, an estimated 30 percent of U.S. preschoolers have tooth decay, a figure that rises to 60 percent by age 18. Causes include poor diet and inadequate health care—factors that are more likely to affect low-SES children. About 12 percent of U.S. children living in poverty have untreated tooth decay (U.S. Department of Health and Human Services, 2007c).

Brain Development

Between ages 2 and 6, the brain increases from 70 percent of its adult weight to 90 percent. At the same time, preschoolers improve in a wide variety of skills—physical coordination, perception, attention, memory, language, logical thinking, and imagination.

■ Regular dental checkups are important for preschoolers. Diseased baby teeth can affect the long-term health of permanent teeth, which start to appear at the end of the preschool years. ■

In addition to increasing in weight, the brain undergoes much reshaping and refining. By age 4, many parts of the cerebral cortex have overproduced synapses. In some regions, such as the prefrontal cortex, the number of synapses is nearly double the adult value. Together, synaptic growth and myelination of neural fibers result in a high energy need. In fact, fMRI evidence reveals that energy metabolism in the cerebral cortex reaches a peak around this age (Huttenlocher, 2002; Nelson, Thomas, & de Haan, 2006).

Recall from Chapter 5 that overabundance of synaptic connections supports *plasticity* of the young brain, helping to ensure that the child will acquire certain abilities even if some areas are damaged. *Synaptic pruning* follows: Neurons that are seldom stimulated lose their connective fibers, and the number of synapses is reduced (see page 165). As the structures of stimulated neurons become more elaborate and require more space, surrounding neurons die, and brain plasticity declines. By age 8 to 10, energy consumption of most cortical regions diminishes to near-adult levels (Nelson, 2002). In addition, cognitive functions are no longer as widely distributed in the cerebral cortex. Rather, they increasingly localize in distinct neural systems, reflecting a developmental shift toward a more fine-tuned, efficient neural organization (Durston & Casey, 2006; Tsujimoto, 2008).

EEG, NIRS, and fMRI measures of neural activity reveal especially rapid growth from early to middle childhood in prefrontal-cortical areas devoted to inhibition of impulses, attention, working memory (temporary storage, manipulation, and selection of information), and planning and organizing behavior (Bunge & Wright, 2007; Durston & Casey, 2006). Furthermore, for most children, the left cerebral hemisphere is especially active between 3 and 6 years and then levels off. In contrast, activity in the right hemisphere increases steadily throughout early and middle childhood, with a slight spurt between ages 8 and 10 (Thatcher, Walker, & Giudice, 1987; Thompson et al., 2000).

Studies of the brains of children who have died confirm these trends. For example, Figure 8.2 shows age-related trends in density of synapses in three left-hemispheric cortical areas involved in language processing: the primary auditory area, Broca's area, and Wernicke's area. (To review the location of these structures, refer to page 234.) Notice how synaptic density rises during the first three years and then, as a result of synaptic pruning, falls to an adult level around age 10.

The findings just summarized fit nicely with what we know about several aspects of cognitive development. Early childhood is a time of marked gains on tasks that depend on the prefrontal cortex—ones that require suppression of impulses in favor of thoughtful responses

FIGURE 8.2

Age-related changes in synaptic density of three areas of the cerebral cortex involved in language processing. Density of synapses in all three areas rises sharply during the first three years—the same period in which children rapidly develop language skills. As a result of pruning, density of synapses falls during the late preschool and school years. During this time, plasticity of the cerebral cortex is reduced. *(Adapted from P. Huttenlocher, 1999, "Synaptogenesis in Human Cerebral Cortex and the Concept of Critical Periods," in N. A. Fox, L. A. Leavitt, & J. G. Warhol, Eds., The Role of Early Experience in Development, pp. 15–28. Calverton, NY: Johnson & Johnson Pediatric Institute, L.L.C. Reprinted with permission.)*

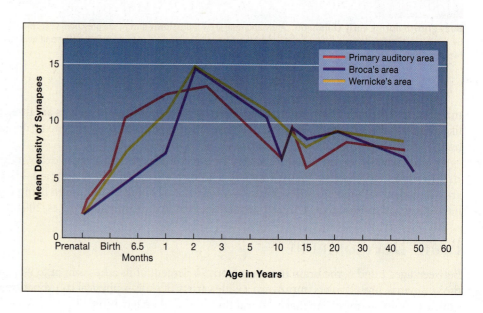

(Rothbart & Bates, 2006). Further, language skills (typically housed in the left hemisphere) increase at an astonishing pace in early childhood, and they support children's increasing control over behavior, also mediated by the prefrontal cortex. In contrast, spatial skills (usually located in the right hemisphere), such as giving directions, drawing pictures, and recognizing geometric shapes, develop gradually over childhood and adolescence.

Differences in rate of development between the two hemispheres suggest that they are continuing to *lateralize* (specialize in functions). Let's take a closer look at brain lateralization during early childhood by focusing on handedness.

HANDEDNESS   On a visit to the preschool, I watched 3-year-old Moira as she drew pictures, worked puzzles, ate a snack, and played outside. Unlike most of her classmates, Moira does most things—drawing, eating, and zipping her jacket—with her left hand. But she uses her right hand for a few activities, such as throwing a ball. Research on handedness, along with other evidence covered in Chapter 5, supports the joint contribution of nature and nurture to brain lateralization.

As early as the tenth prenatal week, most fetuses show a right-hand preference during thumb-sucking (Hepper, McCartney, & Shannon, 1998). And by age 6 months, infants typically display a smoother, more efficient movement when reaching with their right than their left arm. These early tendencies may contribute to the right-handed bias of most children by the end of the first year (Hinojosa, Sheu, & Michael, 2003; Ronnqvist & Domellof, 2006). During toddlerhood and early childhood, handedness gradually extends to a wider range of skills.

Handedness reflects the greater capacity of one side of the brain—the individual's **dominant cerebral hemisphere**—to carry out skilled motor action. Other important abilities are generally located on the dominant side as well. For right-handed people—in Western nations, 90 percent of the population—language is housed in the left hemisphere with hand control. For the left-handed 10 percent, language is occasionally located in the right hemisphere or, more often, shared between the hemispheres (Perelle & Ehrman, 2009). This indicates that the brains of left-handers tend to be less strongly lateralized than those of right-handers. Consistent with this idea, many left-handed individuals (like Moira) are also *ambidextrous*. Although they prefer their left hand, they sometimes use their right hand skillfully as well (McManus et al., 1988).

Left-handed parents show only a weak tendency to have left-handed children (Vuoksimaa et al., 2009). One genetic theory proposes that most children inherit a gene that *biases* them for right-handedness and a left-dominant cerebral hemisphere. But that bias is not strong enough to overcome experiences that might sway children toward a left-hand preference (Annett, 2002). Even prenatal events may profoundly affect handedness. Both identical and fraternal twins are more likely than ordinary siblings to differ in hand preference, probably because twins usually lie in opposite orientations in the uterus (Derom et al., 1996). The orientation of most singleton fetuses—facing toward the left—is believed to promote greater control over movements on the body's right side (Previc, 1991).

Handedness also involves practice. Newborns' bias in head position causes them to spend more time looking at and using one hand, which contributes to greater skillfulness of that hand (Hinojosa, Sheu, & Michael, 2003). Handedness is strongest for complex skills requiring extensive training, such as eating with utensils, writing, and engaging in athletic activities. Also, wide cultural differences exist in rates of left-handedness. In Tanzania, Africa, where children are physically restrained and punished for favoring the left hand, less than 1 percent of adults are left-handed (Provins, 1997).

Although left-handedness occurs more often in people with mental retardation and mental illness than in the general population, atypical brain lateralization

■ Twins are more likely than ordinary siblings to differ in hand preference, perhaps because twins usually lie in opposite orientations in the uterus. ■

is probably not responsible for these individuals' problems. Rather, early damage to the left hemisphere may have caused their disabilities while also leading to a shift in handedness. In support of this idea, left-handedness is associated with prenatal and birth difficulties that can result in brain damage, including maternal stress, prolonged labor, prematurity, Rh incompatibility, and breech delivery (O'Callaghan et al., 1993; Powls et al., 1996; Rodriguez & Waldenström, 2008).

Most left-handers, however, have no developmental problems—in fact, unusual lateralization may have certain advantages. Left- and mixed-handed young people are slightly advantaged in speed and flexibility of thinking, and they are more likely than their right-handed agemates to develop outstanding verbal and mathematical talents (Flannery & Liederman, 1995; Gunstad et al., 2007). More even distribution of cognitive functions across both hemispheres may be responsible.

OTHER ADVANCES IN BRAIN DEVELOPMENT   Besides the cerebral cortex, several other areas of the brain make strides during early childhood (see Figure 8.3). All of these changes involve establishing links between parts of the brain, increasing the coordinated functioning of the central nervous system.

At the rear and base of the brain is the **cerebellum,** a structure that aids in balance and control of body movement. Fibers linking the cerebellum to the cerebral cortex grow and myelinate from birth through the preschool years. This change contributes to dramatic gains in motor coordination: By the end of the preschool years, children can play hopscotch, throw a ball with well-coordinated movements, and print letters of the alphabet. Connections between the cerebellum and the cerebral cortex also support thinking (Diamond, 2000). Children with damage to the cerebellum usually display both motor and cognitive deficits, including problems with memory, planning, and language (Noterdaeme et al., 2002; Riva & Giorgi, 2000).

The **reticular formation,** a structure in the brain stem that maintains alertness and consciousness, generates synapses and myelinates throughout early childhood and into adolescence. Neurons in the reticular formation send out fibers to other areas of the brain. Many go to the prefrontal cortex, contributing to improvements in sustained, controlled attention.

An inner-brain structure called the **hippocampus,** which plays a vital role in memory and in images of space that help us find our way, undergoes rapid synapse formation and myelination in the second half of the first year, when recall memory and independent movement emerge. Over the preschool and elementary school years, the hippocampus and surrounding areas of the cerebral cortex continue to develop swiftly, establishing connections with one another and with the prefrontal cortex (Nelson, Thomas, & de Haan, 2006). These changes make possible the dramatic gains in memory and spatial understanding of early and middle childhood—ability to use strategies to store and retrieve information, expansion of autobio-

FIGURE 8.3

Cross-section of the human brain, showing the location of the cerebellum, the reticular formation, the hippocampus, the amygdala, and the corpus callosum.   These structures undergo considerable development during early childhood. Also shown is the pituitary gland, which secretes hormones that control body growth (see page 297).

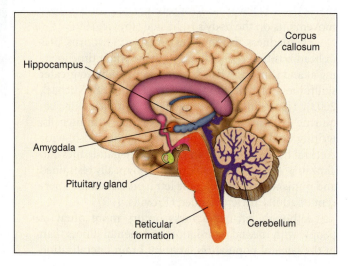

graphical memory (which brings an end to infantile amnesia), and drawing and reading of maps (which we will take up in Chapter 9).

Also located in the inner brain, adjacent to the hippocampus, is the **amygdala,** a structure that plays a central role in processing emotional information. The amygdala is sensitive to facial emotional expressions, especially fear (Whalen et al., 2009). It also enhances memory for emotionally salient events, thereby ensuring that information relevant for survival—stimuli that evoke fear or signify safety—will be retrieved on future occasions. This capacity for emotional learning seems to emerge in early childhood: Damage to the amygdala in the first few years leads to loss of ability to learn about fear and safety signals and typically results in wide-ranging socially inappropriate behaviors (Shaw, Brierley, & David, 2005). Throughout childhood and adolescence, connections between the amygdala and the prefrontal cortex, which governs regulation of emotion, form and myelinate (Tottenham, Hare, & Casey, 2009). Recall from Chapter 7 that in socially anxious children, the amygdala is overly reactive to threatening situations (see page 259).

The **corpus callosum** is a large bundle of fibers connecting the two cerebral hemispheres. Production of synapses and myelination of the corpus callosum increase at 1 year, peak between 3 and 6 years, then continue at a slower pace through middle childhood and adolescence (Thompson et al., 2000). The corpus callosum supports smooth coordination of movements on both sides of the body and integration of many aspects of thinking, including perception, attention, memory, language, and problem solving. The more complex the task, the more essential is communication between the hemispheres.

© ELLEN B. SENISI PHOTOGRAPHY

■ In early childhood, the hippocampus develops rapidly, forming connections with surrounding areas of the cerebral cortex and with the prefrontal cortex—changes that contribute to these preschoolers' spatial understanding. ■

ASK YOURSELF

◆ **REVIEW** What aspects of brain development support the tremendous gains in language, thinking, and motor control of early childhood?

◆ **APPLY** Dental checkups revealed a high incidence of untreated tooth decay in a U.S. preschool program serving low-income children. Using findings presented in this and previous chapters, list possible contributing factors.

◆ **CONNECT** What stand on the nature–nurture issue do findings on development of handedness support? Explain, using research findings.

◆ **REFLECT** How early, and to what extent, did you experience tooth decay in childhood? What factors might have been responsible?

Influences on Physical Growth and Health

As we consider factors affecting growth and health in early childhood, you will encounter some familiar themes. Heredity remains important, but environmental factors—including emotional well-being, good nutrition, relative freedom from disease, and physical safety—are also essential. And as the Biology and Environment box on page 296 illustrates, environmental pollutants can threaten children's healthy development. The extent to which low-level lead—one of the most common—undermines children's mental and emotional functioning is the focus of intensive research.

BIOLOGY AND ENVIRONMENT

Low-Level Lead Exposure and Children's Development

Lead is a highly toxic element that, at blood levels exceeding 60 μg/dL (micrograms per deciliter), causes brain swelling and hemorrhaging. Risk of death rises as blood-lead level exceeds 100 μg/dL. Before 1980, lead exposure resulted from use of lead-based paints in residences (infants and young children often ate paint flakes) and from use of leaded gasoline (car exhaust resulted in a highly breathable form of lead). Laws limiting the lead content of paint and mandating lead-free gasoline led to a sharp decline in children's lead levels, from an average of 15 μg/dL in 1980 to 1.8 μg/dL today (Jones et al., 2009; Meyer et al., 2003).

But in neighborhoods near industries that use lead production processes, or where lead-based paint remains in older homes, children's blood levels are still markedly elevated. About 15 percent of low-income children living in large central cities, and 19 percent of African-American children, have blood-lead levels exceeding 10 μg/dL (the official "level of concern"), warranting immediate efforts to reduce exposure (Jones et al., 2009).

How much lead exposure is too much? Does lead contamination impair children's mental functioning even in small quantities? Until recently, answers were unclear. Studies reporting a negative relationship between children's current lead levels and cognitive performance had serious limitations. Researchers knew nothing about children's history of lead exposure and

often failed to control for factors associated with both blood-lead levels and mental test scores (such as SES, home environmental quality, and nutrition) that might account for the findings.

Over the past two decades, seven longitudinal studies of the developmental consequences of lead have been conducted—three in the United States, two in Australia, one in Mexico City, and one in Yugoslavia. Some focused on inner-city, low-SES minority children, others on middle- and upper-middle SES suburban children, and one on children living close to a lead smelter. Each tracked children's lead exposure over an extended time and included relevant controls.

Five sites reported negative relationships between lead exposure and children's IQs (Hubbs-Tait et al., 2005). Higher blood levels were also associated with deficits in verbal and visual-motor skills and with distractibility, overactivity, poor organization, and behavior problems. And an array of findings suggested that persistent childhood lead exposure contributes to antisocial behavior in adolescence (Dietrich et al., 2001; Needleman et al., 2002; Nevin, 2000; Stretesky & Lynch, 2001).

The investigations did not agree on an age period of greatest vulnerability. In some, relationships were strongest in toddlerhood and early childhood; in others, at the most recently studied age—suggesting cumulative effects over time. Still other studies reported similar lead-related cognitive deficits from infancy through adolescence. Overall, poorer mental test scores associated with lead exposure persisted over time and seemed to be permanent. Children given drugs to induce excretion of lead (chelation) did not improve in

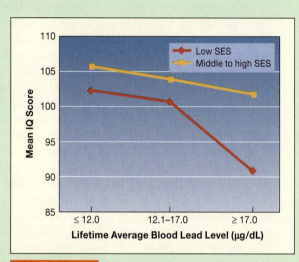

FIGURE 8.4

Relationship of lifetime average lead exposure to 11-to-13-year-old IQ by SES. In this study, conducted in the lead-smelting city of Port Pirie, Australia, blood-lead levels of 375 children were measured repeatedly from birth to age 11 to 13. The lead-exposure-related drop in IQ was much greater for low-SES than higher-SES children. *(Adapted from Tong, McMichael, & Baghurst, 2000.)*

long-term outcomes (Dietrich et al., 2004; Rogan et al., 2001). And negative cognitive consequences were evident at all levels of lead exposure—even below 10 μg/dL (Lamphear et al., 2005).

Although the overall impact of low-level lead exposure on all outcomes is modest, in three longitudinal investigations, cognitive consequences were much greater for low-SES than higher-SES children (see, for example, Figure 8.4) (Bellinger, Leviton, & Sloman, 1990; Ris et al., 2004; Tong, McMichael, & Baghurst, 2000). A stressed, disorganized home life seems to heighten lead-induced damage. Dietary factors can also magnify lead's toxic effects. Iron and zinc deficiencies, especially common in low-SES children, increase lead concentration in the blood (Noonan et al., 2003; Wolf, Jimenez, & Lozoff, 2003; Wright et al., 2003).

In sum, lead impairs learning and contributes to behavior problems. Low-SES children are more likely both to live in lead-contaminated areas and to experience additional risks that magnify lead-induced damage. Because lead is a stable element, its release into the air and soil is difficult to reverse. Therefore, in addition to laws that control lead pollution, interventions that reduce the negative impact of lead—through involved parenting, better schools, and dietary enrichment—are vital.

■ Children play near a factory in Cairo, Egypt, one of the world's most polluted cities in levels of lead and other toxins. Studies consistently show lasting negative effects of lead exposure, including learning and behavior problems. ■

AP IMAGES/MOHAMED EL-DAKHAKHNY

Heredity and Hormones

The impact of heredity on physical growth is evident throughout childhood. Children's physical size and rate of growth are related to those of their parents (Bogin, 2001). Genes influence growth by controlling the body's production of hormones. Figure 8.3 on page 294 shows the **pituitary gland,** located at the base of the brain, which plays a critical role by releasing two hormones that induce growth.

The first, **growth hormone (GH),** is necessary from birth on for development of almost all body tissues. GH acts directly but also accomplishes its task with the help of an intermediary. It stimulates the liver and epiphyses of the skeleton to release another hormone called *insulin-like growth factor 1 (IGF-1),* which triggers cell duplication throughout the body, especially the skeleton, muscles, nerves, bone marrow (origin of blood cells), liver, kidney, skin, and lungs.

About 2 percent of children suffer from inherited conditions that cause either GH deficiency or IGF-1 deficiency (in which GH fails to stimulate IGF-1). Without medical intervention, such children reach an average mature height of only 4 to 4½ feet. When treated early with injections of GH or IGF-1 (depending on the disorder), such children show catch-up growth and then grow at a normal rate, becoming much taller than they would have without treatment (Bright, Mendoza, & Rosenfeld, 2009; Saenger, 2003).

The availability of synthetic GH has also made it possible to treat short, normal-GH children with hormone injections, in hopes of increasing their final height. Thousands of parents, concerned that their children will suffer social stigma because of their shortness, have sought this GH therapy. But most normal-GH children given GH treatment grow only slightly taller than their previously predicted mature height (Rosenbloom, 2009). And contrary to popular belief, normal-GH short children are not deficient in self-esteem or other aspects of psychological adjustment (Sandberg & Voss, 2002). So despite the existence of "heightism" in Western cultures, little justification exists for medically intervening in short stature that is merely the result of biologically normal human diversity.

A second pituitary hormone, **thyroid-stimulating hormone (TSH),** prompts the thyroid gland in the neck to release *thyroxine,* which is necessary for brain development and for GH to have its full impact on body size. Infants born with a deficiency of thyroxine must receive it at once, or they will be mentally retarded. Once the most rapid period of brain development is complete, children with too little thyroxine grow at a below-average rate, but the central nervous system is no longer affected. With prompt treatment, such children catch up in body growth and eventually reach normal size (Salerno et al., 2001).

■ When a child is extremely short because of growth hormone (GH) deficiency, early treatment with injections of GH leads to substantial gains in height. But little justification exists for medical intervention with normal-GH children whose short stature simply reflects human diversity. ■

Emotional Well-Being

In childhood as in infancy, emotional well-being can profoundly affect growth and health. Preschoolers with very stressful home lives (due to divorce, financial difficulties, or parental job loss) suffer more respiratory and intestinal illnesses and more unintentional injuries than others (Cohen & Herbert, 1996; Kemeny, 2003).

In addition, high stress suppresses the release of GH (Deltondo et al., 2008). Consequently, extreme emotional deprivation can lead to **psychosocial dwarfism,** a growth disorder that appears between ages 2 and 15. Typical characteristics include decreased GH secretion, very short stature, immature skeletal age, and serious adjustment problems, which help distinguish psychosocial dwarfism from normal shortness (Tarren-Sweeney, 2006). Lynette, the 4-year-old mentioned earlier in this chapter, was diagnosed with this condition. She was placed in foster care after child welfare authorities discovered that she spent most of the day at home alone, unsupervised, and also might have been physically abused. When children like Lynette are removed from their emotionally inadequate environments, their GH levels quickly return to normal, and they grow rapidly. But if treatment is delayed, the dwarfism can be permanent.

© BLEND IMAGES/ALAMY

■ Compared with their Caucasian peers, African-American preschoolers are more likely to share a bedroom with siblings or cosleep with parents. As a result, they less often depend on a security object to reduce the discomfort of being left alone in a darkened room. ■

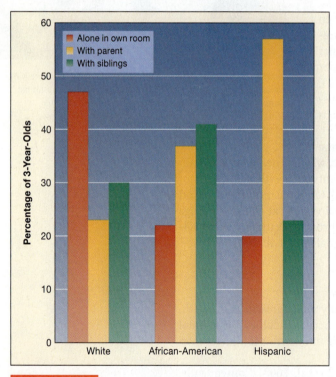

FIGURE 8.5

Sleeping arrangements of U.S. 3-year-olds by ethnicity. A survey of several thousand mothers who were asked about their 3-year-old's typical sleep location revealed that white preschoolers were far more likely to sleep alone in their own bedroom than African-American and Hispanic preschoolers. Among minority children, more Hispanic preschoolers slept with a parent, more African-American preschoolers with siblings. *(Adapted from Milan, Snow, & Belay, 2007.)*

Sleep Habits and Problems

Sleep contributes to body growth, since GH is released during the child's sleeping hours. A well-rested child is better able to play, learn, and contribute positively to family functioning. Many studies confirm that sleep difficulties are associated with impaired cognitive performance, including decreased attention, speed of thinking, working memory, and intelligence and achievement test scores. The impact of disrupted sleep on cognitive functioning is more pronounced for low-SES children. Perhaps insufficient sleep heightens the impact of other environmental stressors prevalent in their daily lives (Buckhalt et al., 2009; Sadeh, 2007). Also, children who sleep poorly disturb their parents' sleep, which can generate significant family stress—a major reason that sleep difficulties are among the most frequent concerns parents raise with their preschooler's doctor (Mindell, 2005).

Total sleep declines in early childhood; on average, 2- and 3-year-olds sleep 11 to 12 hours, 4- to 6-year-olds 10 to 11 hours. But substantial variability exists, with lesser- or greater-than-average sleep remaining fairly stable over time (Jenni et al., 2007). Younger preschoolers typically take a 1- to 2-hour nap in the early afternoon, although daytime sleep need also varies widely. Some continue to take two naps, as they did in toddlerhood; others give up napping entirely. Most Caucasian-American children stop napping between ages 3 and 4, although a quiet play period or rest after lunch helps them rejuvenate for the rest of the day (Howard & Wong, 2001). Perhaps because of greater cultural acceptance, napping remains common among African-American and Hispanic children throughout the preschool years, balanced by a tendency to sleep less at night (Crosby, LeBourgeois, & Harsh, 2005; Lavigne et al., 1999).

The majority of Western parents engage in bedtime routines with their preschoolers, though in the United States this is slightly more common among white than African-American and Hispanic parents. As Figure 8.5 shows, Caucasian preschoolers are less likely to cosleep with their parents or to share a room with siblings than their African-American agemates. White children more often go to bed with a security object, which may help them adjust to feelings of uneasiness at being left by themselves in a darkened room (Milan, Snow, & Belay, 2007). In most cases, cosleeping is not associated with problems during the preschool years, other than more frequent night wakings by parents due to children's movements during sleep (Gaylor et al., 2005; Thiedke, 2001). Western cosleeping children generally ask to sleep in their own bed by age 6 or 7.

Difficulty falling asleep—calling to the parent or asking for another drink of water—is common in early childhood, occurring in about one-third of preschoolers. But Caucasian parents more often express concern about their child falling asleep at a regular time than do African-American parents (Milan, Snow, & Belay, 2007). Perhaps Caucasian parents more highly value a scheduled bedtime and tend to view falling asleep without protest as a sign of maturity—expectations likely to be unmet at least occasionally.

Sometimes, sleep problems stem from a mismatch between parental demands and children's biology. The parent may step up pressure on the child, who vigorously resists because of a lower-than-average need for sleep. Consequently, sleep interventions should include parent education about individual differences in young children's sleep requirements (Jenni & O'Connor, 2005). Intense bedtime struggles sometimes result from family turmoil, as children worry about how their parents may get along when they are asleep and not available to distract them. In these cases, addressing family stress and conflict is the key to improving children's sleep.

Finally, most children waken during the night from time to time, and those who cannot return to sleep on their own may suffer from a sleep disorder. Because young children have vivid imaginations and difficulty separating fantasy from reality, *nightmares* are common; half of 3- to 6-year-olds experience them from time to time. And about 4 percent of children are frequent *sleepwalkers,* who are unaware of their wanderings during the night. Gently awakening and returning the child to bed helps avoid self-injury. *Sleep terrors,* which affect 3 percent of young children, are perhaps the most upsetting sleep problem to parents. In these panic-stricken arousals from deep sleep, the child may scream, thrash, speak incoherently, show a sharp rise in heart rate and breathing, and initially be unresponsive to parents' attempts to comfort. Sleepwalking and sleep terrors tend to run in families, suggesting a genetic influence (Guilleminault et al., 2003; Thorpy & Yager, 2001). But they can also be triggered by stress or extreme fatigue.

Fortunately, sleep disorders of early childhood usually subside without treatment. In the few cases that persist, children require a medical and psychological evaluation (Gregory et al., 2004). Their disturbed sleep may be a sign of neurological or emotional difficulties.

Nutrition

With the transition to early childhood, many children become unpredictable, picky eaters. One father I know wistfully recalled how his son, as a toddler, eagerly sampled Chinese food: "He ate rice, chicken chow mein, egg rolls—and now, at age 3, the only thing he'll try is the ice cream!"

Preschoolers' appetites decline because their growth has slowed. Their wariness of new foods is also adaptive: If they stick to familiar foods, they are less likely to swallow dangerous substances when adults are not around to protect them (Birch & Fisher, 1995). Parents need not worry about variations in amount eaten from meal to meal. Over the course of a day, preschoolers compensate for eating little at one meal by eating more at a later one (Hursti, 1999).

Though they eat less, preschoolers need a high-quality diet, including the same foods adults need, but in smaller amounts. Milk and milk products, meat or meat alternatives (such as eggs, dried peas or beans, and peanut butter), vegetables and fruits, and breads and cereals should be included. Fats, oils, and salt should be

© GETTY IMAGES/RED CHOPSTICKS

■ As this child's grandmother shows him how to eat with chopsticks, he also acquires a taste for foods commonly served in his culture. ■

kept to a minimum because of their link to high blood pressure and heart disease in adulthood. And foods high in sugar should be eaten only in small amounts to prevent tooth decay and protect against overweight and obesity—a topic we will take up in Chapter 11.

The social environment powerfully influences young children's food preferences. Children tend to imitate the food choices and eating practices of people they admire, both adults and peers. For example, mothers who drink milk or soft drinks tend to have 5-year-old daughters with a similar beverage preference (Fisher et al., 2001). In Mexico, where children see family members delighting in the taste of peppery foods, preschoolers enthusiastically eat chili peppers, whereas most American children reject them (Birch, Zimmerman, & Hind, 1980).

Repeated, unpressured exposure to a new food also increases acceptance (Fuller et al., 2005). In one study, preschoolers were given one of three versions of a food they had never eaten before (sweet, salty, or plain tofu). After 8 to 15 exposures, they readily ate the food. But they preferred the version they had already tasted. For example, children in the "sweet" condition liked sweet tofu best, and those in the "plain" condition liked plain tofu best (Sullivan & Birch, 1990). These findings reveal that adding sugar or salt in hopes of increasing a young child's willingness to eat healthy foods simply strengthens the child's desire for a sugary or salty taste. Similarly, offering children sweet fruit or soft drinks promotes "milk avoidance." Compared to their milk-drinking agemates, milk-avoiders are shorter in stature and have a lower bone density—a condition that leads to a lifelong reduction in strength and to increased risk of bone fractures (Black et al., 2002).

The emotional climate at mealtimes has a powerful impact on children's eating habits. When parents are worried about how well their preschoolers are eating, meals can become unpleasant and stressful. Offering bribes ("Finish your vegetables, and you can have an extra cookie"), as some parents do, causes children to like the healthy food less and the treat more (Birch, Fisher, & Davison, 2003).

Similarly, restricting access to tasty foods focuses children's attention on those foods and increases their desire to eat them. After caregivers in a child-care center prevented 3- to 6-year-olds from selecting apple-bar cookies at snack time by enclosing them in a transparent jar but gave them free access to peach-bar cookies (which they liked just as well), the children more often talked about and requested the apple-bar cookies and otherwise attempted to obtain them (see Figure 8.6) (Fisher & Birch, 1999). And when given access, they ate more apple-bar cookies than they had during previous, unrestricted snack times.

Children's healthy eating depends on a healthy food environment, but too much adult control limits their opportunities to develop self-control, thereby promoting overeating. For ways to encourage healthy, varied eating in young children, refer to Applying What We Know on the following page.

Finally, as indicated in earlier chapters, many children in North America and in developing countries lack access to sufficient high-quality food to support healthy growth. Five-year-old Hal rode a bus from a poor neighborhood to our laboratory preschool. His mother's paycheck barely covered her rent, let alone food. Hal's diet was deficient in protein and in essential vitamins and minerals—iron (to prevent anemia), calcium (to support development of bones and teeth), zinc (to support immune system functioning, neural communication, and cell duplication), vitamin A (to help maintain eyes, skin, and a variety of internal organs), and vitamin C (to facilitate iron absorption and wound healing). These are the most common dietary deficiencies of the preschool years (Ganji, Hampl, & Betts, 2003).

Hal was small for his age, pale, inattentive, and unruly at preschool. By the school years, low-SES U.S. children are, on average, about ½ to 1 inch shorter than their economically advantaged counterparts (Cecil et al., 2005; Yip, Scanlon, & Trowbridge, 1993). And throughout childhood and adolescence, a nutritionally deficient diet is associated with

LOOK AND LISTEN

Arrange to join a family with at least one preschooler for a meal, and closely observe parental mealtime practices. Are they likely to promote healthy eating habits? Explain.

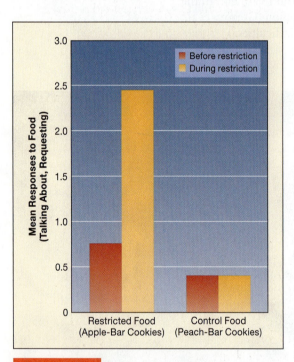

FIGURE 8.6

Children's spontaneous behavioral responses to a tasty food before and during restriction at snack times. Three- to 6-year-olds talked about, requested, and otherwise attempted to obtain a tasty food (apple-bar cookies) three times more often after they were restricted from eating it. They rarely responded this way to an equally tasty control food (peach-bar cookies) that remained unrestricted throughout the study. *(Adapted from Fisher & Birch, 1999.)*

Applying What We Know

Encouraging Good Nutrition in Early Childhood

SUGGESTION	DESCRIPTION
Offer a varied, healthy diet.	Provide a well-balanced variety of nutritious foods that are colorful and attractively served. Avoid including sweets and "junk" foods in the child's regular food environment.
Offer predictable meals as well as several snacks each day.	Preschoolers' stomachs are small, and they may not be able to eat enough in three meals to satisfy their energy requirements. They benefit from extra opportunities to eat.
Offer small portions, and permit the child to serve him- or herself and to ask for seconds.	When too much food is put on the plate, preschoolers (like adults) often overeat, increasing the risk of obesity. On average, preschoolers consume 25 percent less at a meal when permitted to serve themselves.
Offer healthy new foods early in a meal and repeatedly at subsequent meals, and respond with patience if the child rejects the food.	Introduce healthy new foods before the child's appetite is satisfied. Let children see you eat and enjoy the new food. If the child rejects it, accept the refusal and serve it again at another meal. As foods become more familiar, they are more readily accepted.
Keep mealtimes pleasant, and include the child in mealtime conversations.	A pleasant, relaxed eating environment helps children develop positive attitudes about food. Refrain from constantly offering food and prompting eating; these practices are associated with excessively fast eating and overeating. Avoid confrontations over disliked foods and table manners, which may lead to refusal to eat.
Avoid using food as a reward and forbidding access to certain foods.	Saying "No dessert until you clean your plate" tells children that they must eat even if they are not hungry and that dessert is the best part of the meal. Restricting access to a food increases children's valuing of that food and efforts to obtain it.

Sources: Birch, 1999; Fisher, Rolls, & Birch, 2003; Spruijt-Metz et al., 2002.

attention and memory difficulties, poorer intelligence and achievement test scores, and behavior problems—especially hyperactivity and aggression—even after family factors that might account for these relationships (such as stressors, parental psychological health, education, warmth, and stimulation of the child) are controlled (Liu et al., 2004; Pollitt, 2001; Slack & Yoo, 2005).

Infectious Disease

One day, I noticed that Hal had been absent from the play yard for several weeks, so I asked Leslie, his preschool teacher, what was wrong. "Hal's been hospitalized with the measles," she explained. "He's had difficulty recovering—lost weight when there wasn't much to lose in the first place." In well-nourished children, ordinary childhood illnesses have no effect on physical growth. But when children are undernourished, disease interacts with malnutrition in a vicious spiral, with potentially severe consequences.

INFECTIOUS DISEASE AND MALNUTRITION Hal's reaction to the measles is commonplace in developing nations, where a large proportion of the population lives in poverty and children do not receive routine immunizations. Illnesses such as measles and chicken pox, which typically do not appear until after age 3 in industrialized nations, occur much earlier. Poor diet depresses the body's immune system, making children far more susceptible to disease. Of the 10 million annual deaths of children under age 5 worldwide, 98 percent are in developing countries, and 70 percent are due to infectious diseases (World Health Organization, 2008a).

Disease, in turn, is a major contributor to malnutrition, hindering both physical growth and cognitive development. Illness reduces appetite and limits the body's ability to absorb foods, especially in children with intestinal infections. In developing countries, widespread diarrhea,

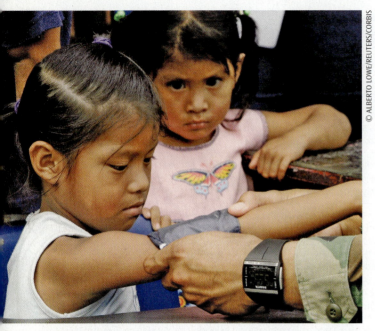

■ A health care worker examines a child of the Ngobe people of Panama. The Ngobes are subsistence farmers whose homes lack basic amenities, including clean water. As a result, diarrhea is widespread, placing Ngobe children at risk for growth stunting and impaired mental development. ■

resulting from unsafe water and contaminated foods, leads to growth stunting and nearly two million childhood deaths each year (World Health Organization, 2008a). Studies carried out in the slums and shantytowns of Brazil and Peru reveal that the more persistent diarrhea is in early childhood, the shorter children are in height and the lower they score on mental tests during the school years (Checkley et al., 2003; Niehaus et al., 2002).

Most developmental impairments and deaths due to diarrhea can be prevented with nearly cost-free *oral rehydration therapy (ORT),* in which sick children are given a glucose, salt, and water solution that quickly replaces fluids the body loses. Since 1990, public health workers have taught nearly half the families in the developing world how to administer ORT. Also, supplements of zinc (essential for immune system functioning), which cost only 30 cents for a month's supply, substantially reduce the incidence of severe and prolonged diarrhea (Aggarwal, Sentz, & Miller, 2007). Through these interventions, the lives of millions of children are saved each year.

IMMUNIZATION In industrialized nations, childhood diseases have declined dramatically during the past half-century, largely as a result of widespread immunization of infants and young children. Hal got the measles because, unlike his classmates from more advantaged homes, he did not receive a full program of immunizations.

About 20 percent of U.S. infants and toddlers are not fully immunized. Of the 80 percent who receive a complete schedule of vaccinations in the first two years, some do not receive the immunizations they need later, in early childhood. Overall, 24 percent of U.S. preschoolers lack essential immunizations. The rate rises to 28 percent for poverty-stricken children, many of whom do not receive full protection until age 5 or 6, when it is required for school entry (U.S. Department of Health and Human Services, 2008b). In contrast, fewer than 10 percent of preschoolers lack immunizations in Denmark and Norway, and fewer than 7 percent in Great Britain, Canada, the Netherlands, and Sweden (United Nations, 2002; UNICEF, 2008).

Why does the United States lag behind these other countries in immunization? As noted in earlier chapters, many U.S. children do not have access to the health care they need. The Cultural Influences box on the following page compares child health care in the United States with that in other Western nations.

In 1994, all medically uninsured children in the United States were guaranteed free immunizations, a program that has led to gains in immunization rates. Still, the cost of the doctor's visit to obtain the immunization may not be covered. Inability to pay for vaccines is only one cause of inadequate immunization. Parents with stressful daily lives often fail to schedule vaccination appointments, and those without a primary care physician do not want to endure long waits in crowded U.S. public health clinics. Some parents have been influenced by media reports suggesting a link between a mercury-based preservative used for decades in vaccines and a rise in the number of children diagnosed with autism. But large-scale studies show no association with autism and no consistent effects on cognitive performance (Dales, Hammer, & Smith, 2001; Richler et al., 2006; Stehr-Green et al., 2003; Thompson et al., 2007). Still, as a precautionary measure, mercury-free versions of childhood vaccinations are now available. In areas where many parents refuse to immunize their children, disease outbreaks of whooping cough and rubella have occurred, with life-threatening consequences (Kennedy & Gust, 2008; Tuyen & Bisgard, 2003). Public education programs directed at increasing parental knowledge about the importance of timely immunizations are badly needed.

A final point regarding communicable disease in early childhood deserves mention. Childhood illness rises with child-care attendance. On average, an infant or toddler in child

CULTURAL INFLUENCES

Child Health Care in the United States and Other Western Nations

The U.S. Patient Protection and Affordable Care Act, signed into law in March 2010, will expand health-insurance coverage to millions of Americans who are currently uninsured, requiring every citizen to purchase health insurance by 2014 while improving its affordability through industry regulation and subsidies for low-income families. The law's greatest immediate benefits for children include a prohibition on denial of coverage by insurance companies because of preexisting conditions and expansion of Medicaid—government-sponsored health insurance for very-low-income families.

Still, health insurance in the United States will remain an optional employment-related fringe benefit. Larger companies will suffer penalties for not providing affordable coverage to full-time workers and their families, but many parents who work part-time or for small businesses may face continued challenges in obtaining high-quality, reasonably priced insurance.

At the time of the Affordable Care Act's passage, about 7.3 million children (10 percent of the child population), many with working parents, were uninsured (U.S. Census Bureau, 2010b). In the United States, uninsured children are three times as likely as insured children to go without needed doctor visits (Newachek et al., 2002). Partly because of weak health-care services, an estimated one-fifth of U.S. children younger than age 5 who come from economically disadvantaged families are in less than very good health. And 12 percent of children living in poverty have activity limitations due to chronic illnesses—a rate nearly double the national average (U.S. Department of Health and Human Services, 2009f).

U.S. child health-care policies contrast with services provided in Australia, Canada, New Zealand, Western Europe, and other industrialized nations, where government-sponsored health insurance is regarded as a fundamental human right and is made available to all citizens at low or no cost. Let's look at two examples.

In the Netherlands, every child receives free medical examinations from birth through adolescence. Children's health care also includes parental counseling in nutrition, disease prevention, and child development (de Winter, Balledux, & de Mare, 1997). The Netherlands

achieves its extraordinarily high childhood immunization rate by giving parents of every newborn baby a written schedule that shows exactly when and where the child should be immunized. If a parent does not bring the child at the specified time, a public health nurse calls the family. When appointments are missed repeatedly, the nurse goes to the home to ensure that the child receives the recommended immunizations (de Pree-Geerlings, de Pree, & Bulk-Bunschoten, 2001).

In Norway, federal law requires that all communities establish well-baby and child clinics and that health checkups occur three times in the first year, then at ages 2 and 4. On other occasions, children are seen by specialized nurses who monitor their development, provide immunizations, and counsel parents on physical and mental health (AWC Oslo, 2005). Although citizens pay a small fee for routine medical visits, hospital services are free.

Currently, many government officials, organizations, and concerned citizens are working to guarantee every American child basic health care. Under the Children's Health Insurance Program (CHIP), launched in 1997, the states receive federal matching funds for upgrading children's health insurance. State control over program implementation enables each state to adapt insurance coverage to meet its unique needs. In 2009, CHIP federal funding was greatly expanded. By 2013, it is expected to provide coverage to 4 million additional children whose families are low-income but not eligible for Medicaid (Kaiser Commission on Medicaid and the Uninsured, 2009).

But even many insured U.S. children do not see a doctor regularly. Parents with no health benefits of their own are less inclined to make appointments for their children—circumstances likely to improve with activation of

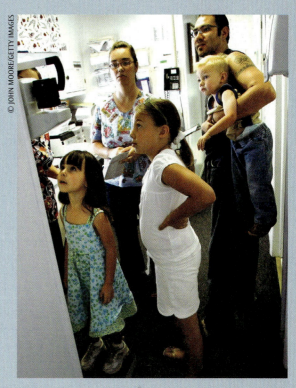

■ Parents bring their three children to a rural Colorado public clinic offering low-cost medical checkups. Although the father works full-time, his job offers no health insurance. Recent expansion of the Children's Health Insurance Program (CHIP) and provisions of the U.S. Patient Protection and Affordable Care Act of 2010 aim to guarantee affordable health care to families like this one. ■

the Affordable Care law's provisions. Still, because of low insurance-reimbursement rates, many doctors refuse to take public-aid patients. As a result, children with public insurance frequently do not have a primary care physician. Instead, they endure long waits in crowded public health clinics, and their parents often say they cannot gain access to needed services (Dombrowski, Lantz, & Freed, 2004; Hughes & Ng, 2003).

Finally, millions of eligible children are not enrolled in CHIP because their parents either do not understand the eligibility requirements or find the application process confusing. The 2009 CHIP reauthorization simplified enrollment procedures, further augmenting gains in the health-care arena for American children. Still, the United States has some distance to go before all its children have access to excellent health care.

SOCIAL ISSUES: HEALTH

Otitis Media and Development

During his first year in child care, 2-year-old Alex caught five colds, had the flu on two occasions, and experienced repeated *otitis media* (middle ear infection). Alex is not unusual. By age 3, 75 percent of U.S. children have had respiratory illnesses that resulted in at least one bout of otitis media; nearly half of these have had three or more bouts (Aronson & Henderson, 2006). Although antibiotics eliminate the bacteria responsible for otitis media, they do not reduce fluid buildup in the middle ear, which causes mild to moderate hearing loss that can last for weeks or months.

The incidence of otitis media is greatest between 6 months and 3 years, when children are first acquiring language. Frequent infections predict delayed language progress in early childhood and poorer academic performance after school entry that, in one study, was still evident in adolescence (Bennett et al., 2001; Casby, 2001; Miccio et al., 2002).

How might otitis media disrupt language and academic progress? Difficulties in perceiving and processing speech sounds, particularly in noisy settings, may be responsible (Polka & Rvachew, 2005). Children with many bouts are less attentive to others' speech and less persistent at tasks (Asbjornsen et al., 2005; Petinou et al., 2001). Their distractibility may result from an inability to make out what people around them are saying—which, in turn, may reduce the quality of others' interactions with them.

Because otitis media is so widespread, current evidence argues strongly in favor of early prevention. Crowded living conditions and exposure to cigarette smoke and other pollutants are linked to the disease, probably accounting for its high incidence among low-SES children. And rates of otitis media are greatly elevated in children who attend child-care centers, where severe, antibacterial-resistant strains of respiratory infections can easily develop and spread (Greenberg et al., 2008).

Early otitis media can be prevented in the following ways:

- *Frequent screening for the disease, followed by prompt medical intervention.* Plastic tubes that drain the narrow Eustachian tubes of the middle ear often are used to treat chronic otitis media in children, although their effectiveness has been disputed.
- *Child-care settings that control infection.* Because infants and young children often put toys in their mouths, these objects should be rinsed frequently with a disinfectant. Pacifier use has also been linked to a greater risk of otitis media (Rovers et al., 2008). Spacious, well-ventilated rooms and small group sizes help limit spread of the disease.
- *Verbally stimulating adult–child interaction.* Developmental problems associated with otitis media are reduced or eliminated in high-quality child-care centers. When caregivers are verbally stimulating and keep noise to a minimum, children have more opportunities to hear, and benefit from, spoken language (Roberts et al., 1998; Vernon-Feagans, Hurley, & Yont, 2002).
- *Vaccines.* Researchers have developed several vaccines that seem to prevent otitis media. But more evidence is needed before they can be made widely available (O'Brien et al., 2009).

■ Otitis media is widespread among children who attend child-care centers, where close contact leads to rapid spread of respiratory infection. ■

care becomes sick 9 to 10 times a year, a preschooler 6 to 7 times. The diseases that spread most rapidly are those most frequently suffered by young children—diarrhea and respiratory infections. The risk that a respiratory infection will result in *otitis media,* or middle ear infection, is almost double that for children remaining at home (Nafstad et al., 1999). To learn about the consequences of otitis media and how to prevent it, consult the Social Issues: Health box above.

Childhood Injuries

More than any other child in the preschool classroom, 3-year-old Tommy had trouble sitting still and paying attention. Instead, he darted from one place and activity to another. One day, he narrowly escaped serious injury when he put his mother's car in gear while she was outside scraping ice from its windows. The vehicle rolled through a guardrail and over the side of a 10-foot concrete underpass, where it hung until rescue workers arrived. Police charged Tommy's mother with failing to use a restraint seat for a child younger than age 8.

International death rates due to unintentional injury among 1- to 14-year-olds. Compared with other industrialized nations, the United States has a high injury death rate, largely because of widespread childhood poverty and shortages of high-quality child care. Injury death rates are many times higher in developing nations, where poverty, rapid population growth, overcrowding in cities, and inadequate safety measures endanger children's lives. *(Adapted from World Health Organization, 2008b.)*

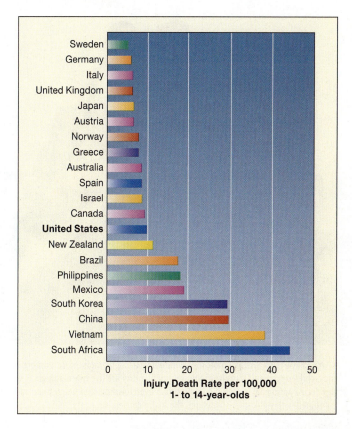

Injury Death Rate per 100,000
1- to 14-year-olds

Unintentional injuries are the leading cause of childhood mortality in industrialized nations. Although U.S. childhood injury fatalities have declined steadily over the past 35 years due to state laws and community policies aimed at improving child safety, as Figure 8.7 reveals, the United States continues to rank poorly in these largely preventable events. Nearly 35 percent of childhood deaths and 50 percent of adolescent deaths are due to injury (Children's Defense Fund, 2008; Safe Kids USA, 2008). And among injured children and youths who survive, thousands suffer pain, brain damage, and permanent physical disabilities.

Auto and traffic accidents, drownings, and burns are the most common childhood injuries (Safe Kids USA, 2008). Motor vehicle collisions are by far the most frequent source of injury across all ages, ranking as the leading cause of death among children more than 1 year old.

FACTORS RELATED TO CHILDHOOD INJURIES The common view of childhood injuries as "accidental" suggests that they are due to chance and cannot be prevented (Sleet & Mercy, 2003). In fact, these injuries occur within a complex *ecological system* of individual, family, community, and societal influences—and we can do something about them.

As Tommy's case suggests, individual differences exist in the safety of children's behaviors. Because of their higher activity level and greater impulsivity and risk taking, boys are 1.5 times more likely to be injured than girls, and their injuries are more severe (Safe Kids USA, 2009). Parents realize that they need to take more steps to protect their young sons than daughters from injury, and most do so. Still, mothers judge the chances of preventing injury in sons to be lower—a belief that may keep them from exercising sufficient oversight and control over the most injury-prone boys (Morrongiello & Kiriakou, 2004; Morrongiello, Ondejko, & Littlejohn, 2004).

Children with certain temperamental characteristics—inattentiveness, overactivity, irritability, defiance, and aggression—are also at greater risk for injury (Ordonana, Caspi, & Moffitt, 2008; Schwebel & Gaines, 2007). As we saw in Chapter 7, these children present child-rearing challenges. They are likely to protest when placed in auto seat restraints, to refuse to take a companion's hand when crossing the street, and to disobey after repeated instruction and discipline.

Poverty, single parenthood, and low parental education are also strongly associated with injury (Schwebel & Brezausek, 2007; World Health Organization, 2008b). Parents who must cope with many daily stresses often have little time or energy to monitor the safety of their children. And their homes and neighborhoods are likely to be noisy, crowded, and run-down, posing further risks (Dal Santo et al., 2004).

Broad societal conditions also affect childhood injury. In developing countries, the rate of death from injury before age 15 is five times as high as

© GARY S. CHAPMAN/GETTY IMAGES

■ Boys' higher activity level and greater impulsivity and risk taking explain why they are more likely to be injured and to suffer severe injuries than girls. ■

■ A family in India rides a motorbike without wearing helmets. In developing countries, childhood death rates from unintentional injury are five times as high as in developed nations. Population growth, urban overcrowding, and heavy road traffic, combined with weak safety measures, are major causes. ■

in developed nations and soon may exceed disease as the leading cause of childhood mortality (World Health Organization, 2008b). Rapid population growth, overcrowding in cities, and heavy road traffic combined with weak safety measures are major causes. Safety devices, such as car safety seats and bicycle helmets, are neither readily available nor affordable.

Childhood injury rates are high in the United States because of extensive poverty, shortages of high-quality child care (to supervise children in their parents' absence), and a high rate of births to teenagers, who are neither psychologically nor financially ready for parenthood (Ekeus, Christensson, & Hjern, 2003; Safe Kids USA, 2008). But U.S. children from advantaged families are also at considerably greater risk for injury than children in Western Europe (World Health Organization, 2008b). This indicates that besides reducing poverty and teenage pregnancy and upgrading the status of child care, additional steps are needed to ensure children's safety.

PREVENTING CHILDHOOD INJURIES   Childhood injuries have many causes, so a variety of approaches are needed to control them. Laws prevent many injuries by requiring car safety seats, child-resistant caps on medicine bottles, flameproof clothing, and fencing around backyard swimming pools (the site of 50 percent of early childhood drownings) (Brenner & Committee on Injury, Violence, and Poison Prevention, 2003). Communities can help by modifying their physical environments. Providing inexpensive and widely available public transportation can reduce the amount of time that children spend in cars. Playgrounds, a common site of injury, can be covered with protective surfaces (Safe Kids USA, 2009). Free, easily installed window guards can be given to families in high-rise apartment buildings to prevent falls. And media campaigns can inform parents and children about safety issues.

But even though they know better, many parents and children behave in ways that compromise safety. During the past three decades, parents have changed very little in the amount they do to protect their children, citing such reasons as "the chances of serious injury are slim," taking necessary steps "is a hassle," and (among low-income families) safety devices (such as home fire extinguishers and bicycle helmets) "cost too much" (Safe Kids USA, 2008). For example, 27 percent of U.S. parents (like Tommy's mother) fail to place their children in car safety seats, and 84 percent of infant seats and 41 percent of child booster seats are improperly used. Yet research confirms that young children properly restrained in car safety seats have an 80 percent reduced risk of fatal injury (Safe Kids USA, 2007). American parents, especially, seem willing to ignore familiar safety practices, perhaps because of the high value they place on individual rights and personal freedom (Damashek & Peterson, 2002).

Furthermore, many parents begin relying on children's knowledge of safety rules, rather than monitoring and controlling access to hazards, as early as 2 or 3 years of age—a premature transition associated with a rise in home injuries (Morrongiello, Ondejko, & Littlejohn, 2004). But even older preschoolers spontaneously recall only about half the safety rules their parents teach them. And even with well-learned rules, they need supervision to ensure that they comply (Morrongiello, Midgett, & Shields, 2001).

Parent interventions that highlight risk factors and that model and reinforce safety practices are effective in reducing home hazards and childhood injuries (Kendrick et al., 2008). But attention must also be paid to family conditions that can prevent childhood injury: relieving crowd-

Applying What We Know

Reducing Unintentional Injuries in Early Childhood

SUGGESTION	DESCRIPTION
Provide age-appropriate supervision and safety instruction.	Despite increasing understanding and self-control, preschoolers need nearly constant supervision. Establish and enforce safety rules, explain the reasons behind them, and praise children for following them, thereby encouraging the child to remember and obey.
Know the child's temperament.	Children who are unusually active, distractible, negative, or curious have more than their share of injuries and need extra monitoring.
Eliminate the most serious dangers from the home.	Examine all spaces for safety. For example, in the kitchen, store dangerous products in high cabinets out of sight, and keep sharp implements in a latched drawer. Remove guns; if that is impossible, store them unloaded in a locked cabinet. Always accompany young preschoolers to the bathroom, and keep all medicines in containers with safety caps.
During automobile travel, always restrain the child properly in the back seat of the car.	Use an age-appropriate, properly installed car safety seat or booster seat up to age 8 or until the child is 4 feet 9 inches tall, and strap the child in correctly every time. Children should always ride in the back seat; passenger-side air bags in the front seat deploy so forcefully that they can cause injury or death to a child. Never leave a child alone in a car, even on a cool, sunny day; a child's core body temperature increases 3 to 5 times faster than an adult's, with risk of permanent injury or death.
Select safe playground equipment and sites.	Make sure sand, wood chips, or rubberized matting has been placed under swings, see-saws, and jungle gyms. Check yards for dangerous plants. Always supervise outdoor play.
Be extra cautious around water.	Constantly observe children during water play; even shallow, inflatable pools are frequent sites of drownings. While they are swimming, young children's heads should not be immersed in water; they may swallow so much that they develop water intoxication, which can lead to convulsions and death.
Practice safety around animals.	Wait to get a pet until the child is mature enough to handle and care for it—usually around age 5 or 6. Never leave a young child alone with an animal; bites often occur during playful roughhousing. Model and teach humane pet treatment.

Source: Damashek & Peterson, 2002; Safe Kids USA, 2008.

ing in the home, providing social supports to ease parental stress, and teaching parents to use effective discipline—a topic we will take up in Chapter 10. Positive parenting—an affectionate, supportive relationship with the child; consistent, reasonable expectations for maturity; and oversight—substantially reduces injury rates, especially in overactive and temperamentally difficult children (Schwebel et al., 2004). But to implement these strategies, parents must have ample time and emotional resources as well as relevant knowledge and skills. Refer to Applying What We Know above for ways to minimize unintentional injuries in early childhood.

Ask Yourself

◆ **REVIEW** Describe ethnic variations in sleep problems during the preschool years. What factors likely contribute to those differences?

◆ **APPLY** One day, Leslie prepared a new snack to serve at preschool: celery stuffed with ricotta cheese and pineapple. The first time she served it, few children touched it. How can Leslie encourage her students to accept the snack? What tactics should she avoid?

◆ **CONNECT** Using research on malnutrition or on unintentional injuries, show how physical growth and health in early childhood result from a continuous, complex interplay between heredity and environment.

◆ **REFLECT** Ask a parent or other family member whether, as a preschooler, you were a picky eater, suffered from many infectious diseases, or sustained any serious injuries. In each instance, what factors might have been responsible?

Motor Development

TAKE A MOMENT... Observe several 2- to 6-year-olds at play in a neighborhood park, preschool, or child-care center. You will see that an explosion of new motor skills occurs in early childhood, each of which builds on the simpler movement patterns of toddlerhood.

During the preschool years, children continue to integrate previously acquired skills into more complex, *dynamic systems*. Then they revise each new skill as their bodies grow larger and stronger, their central nervous systems develop, their environments present new challenges, and they set new goals, aided by gains in perceptual and cognitive capacities.

Gross-Motor Development

As children's bodies become more streamlined and less top-heavy, their center of gravity shifts downward, toward the trunk. As a result, balance improves greatly, paving the way for new motor skills involving large muscles of the body. By age 2, preschoolers' gaits become smooth and rhythmic—secure enough that soon they leave the ground, at first by running and later by jumping, hopping, galloping, and skipping.

As children become steadier on their feet, their arms and torsos are freed to experiment with new skills—throwing and catching balls, steering tricycles, and swinging on horizontal bars and rings. Then upper- and lower-body skills combine into more refined actions. Five- and 6-year-olds simultaneously steer and pedal a tricycle and flexibly move their whole body when throwing, catching, hopping, and jumping. By the end of the preschool years, all skills are performed with greater speed and endurance. Table 8.1 provides a closer look at gross-motor development in early childhood.

Changes in ball skills provide an excellent illustration of preschoolers' gross-motor progress. Young preschoolers stand still, facing the target, throwing with their arm thrust forward. Catching is equally awkward. Two-year-olds extend their arms and hands rigidly, using them as a single unit to trap the ball. By age 3, children flex their elbows enough to trap the ball against the chest. But if the ball arrives too quickly, they cannot adapt, and it may bounce off the body (Haywood & Getchell, 2005).

Gradually, children call on the shoulders, torso, trunk, and legs to support throwing and catching. By age 4, the body rotates as the child throws, and at 5 years, preschoolers shift their weight forward, stepping as they release the ball. As a result, the ball travels faster and farther. When the ball is returned, older preschoolers predict its place of landing by moving forward, backward, or sideways (see Figure 8.8). Soon, they will catch it with their hands and fingers, "giving" with arms and body to absorb the force of the ball.

LOOK AND LISTEN

Play a game of catch with a 2- to 3-year-old, then with a 4- to 6-year-old. What differences in movement and coordination are evident?

FIGURE 8.8

Changes in catching during early childhood. At age 2, children extend their arms rigidly, and the ball tends to bounce off the body. At age 3, they flex their elbows in preparation for catching, trapping the ball against the chest. By ages 5 and 6, children involve the entire body. Instead of pressing the ball against the chest, they catch it with only the hands and fingers.

Age 2   Age 3   Age 5–6

TABLE 8.1	Changes in Gross- and Fine-Motor Skills During Early Childhood	
AGE	**GROSS-MOTOR SKILLS**	**FINE-MOTOR SKILLS**
2–3 years	Walks more rhythmically; hurried walk changes to run Jumps, hops, throws, and catches with rigid upper body Pushes riding toy with feet; little steering	Puts on and removes simple items of clothing Zips and unzips large zippers Uses spoon effectively

3–4 years	Walks up stairs, alternating feet, and down stairs,
	    leading with one foot
	Jumps and hops, flexing upper body
	Throws and catches with slight involvement of upper body; still
	    catches by trapping ball against chest
	Pedals and steers tricycle
		Fastens and unfastens large buttons
		Serves self food without assistance
		Uses scissors
		Copies vertical line and circle
		Draws first picture of person, using tadpole image

4–5 years	Walks down stairs, alternating feet Runs more smoothly Gallops and skips with one foot Throws ball with increased body rotation and transfer of weight on feet; catches ball with hands Rides tricycle rapidly, steers smoothly	Uses fork effectively Cuts with scissors following line Copies triangle, cross, and some letters
5–6 years	Increases running speed Gallops more smoothly; engages in true skipping Displays mature throwing and catching pattern Rides bicycle with training wheels	Uses knife to cut soft food Ties shoes Draws person with six parts Copies some numbers and simple words

Sources: Cratty, 1986; Haywood & Getchell, 2005; Malina & Bouchard, 1991.

Fine-Motor Development

Like gross-motor development, fine-motor skills take a giant leap forward in the preschool years. As control of the hands and fingers improves, young children put puzzles together, build with small blocks, cut and paste, and string beads. To parents, fine-motor progress is most apparent in two areas: (1) children's care of their own bodies, and (2) the drawings and paintings that fill the walls at home, child care, and preschool.

SELF-HELP SKILLS As Table 8.1 shows, young children gradually become self-sufficient at dressing and feeding. Two-year-olds put on and take off simple items of clothing. By age 3, children can dress and undress well enough to take care of toileting needs by themselves. Between ages 4 and 5, children can dress and undress without supervision. At mealtimes, young preschoolers use a spoon well, and they can serve themselves. By age 4 they are adept with a fork, and around 5 to 6 years they can use a knife to cut soft foods. Roomy clothing with large buttons and zippers and child-sized eating utensils help children master these skills.

Preschoolers get great satisfaction from managing their own bodies. They are proud of their independence, and their new skills also make life easier for adults. But parents must be patient about these abilities: When tired and in a hurry, young children often revert to eating with their fingers. And the 3-year-old who dresses himself in the morning sometimes ends up with his shirt on inside out, his pants on backward, and his left snow boot on his right foot! Perhaps the most complex self-help skill of early childhood is shoe tying, mastered around age 6. Success requires a longer attention span, memory for an intricate series of hand movements, and the dexterity to perform them. Shoe tying illustrates the close connection between motor and cognitive development, as do two other skills: drawing and writing.

DRAWING When given crayon and paper, even toddlers scribble in imitation of others. As the young child's ability to mentally represent the world expands, marks on the page take on meaning. A variety of factors combine with fine-motor control in

© LAURA DWIGHT PHOTOGRAPHY

■ Preschoolers take great satisfaction in their growing independence. For this child, using a knife to spread cream cheese on a bagel is a challenging but rewarding task. ■

the development of children's artful representations (Golomb, 2004). These include the realization that pictures can serve as symbols, improved planning and spatial understanding, and the emphasis that the child's culture places on artistic expression.

Typically, drawing progresses through the following sequence:

1. *Scribbles.* Western children begin to draw during the second year. At first, the intended representation is contained in gestures rather than in the resulting marks on the page. For example, one 18-month-old made her crayon hop and, as it produced a series of dots, explained, "Rabbit goes hop-hop" (Winner, 1986).

   Recall from Chapter 6 that 2-year-olds treat realistic-looking pictures symbolically, but they have difficulty interpreting line drawings. When an adult held up a drawing indicating which of two objects preschoolers should drop down a chute, 3-year-olds used the drawing as a symbol to guide their behavior but 2-year-olds did not (Callaghan, 1999).

2. *First representational forms.* Around age 3, children's scribbles start to become pictures. Often children make a gesture with the crayon, notice that they have drawn a recognizable shape, and then label it. In one case, a 2-year-old made some random marks on a page and then, realizing the resemblance between his scribbles and noodles, named the creation "chicken pie and noodles" (Winner, 1986).

   Few 3-year-olds spontaneously draw so others can tell what their picture represents. However, after an adult demonstrated how drawings can be used to stand for objects in a game, more 3-year-olds drew recognizable forms (Callaghan & Rankin, 2002). Western parents and teachers spend much time promoting 2- and 3-year-olds' language and make-believe play but relatively little time showing them how they can use drawings to represent their world. When adults draw with children and point out resemblances between drawings and objects, preschoolers' pictures become more comprehensible and detailed (Braswell & Callanan, 2003).

   A major milestone in drawing occurs when children use lines to represent the boundaries of objects. This enables 3- and 4-year-olds to draw their first picture of a person. Fine-motor and cognitive limitations lead the preschooler to reduce the figure to the simplest form that still looks human—the universal "tadpole" image, a circular shape with lines attached, shown on the left in Figure 8.9. Four-year-olds add features, such as eyes, nose, mouth, hair, fingers, and feet, as the tadpole drawings illustrate.

3. *More realistic drawings.* Five- and 6-year-olds create more complex drawings, like the one on the right in Figure 8.9, containing more conventional human and animal figures, with the head and body differentiated. Older preschoolers' drawings still contain perceptual distortions because they have just begun to represent depth (Cox & Littlejohn, 1995). Use of depth cues, such as overlapping objects, smaller size for distant than for near objects, diagonal placement, and converging lines, increases during middle childhood (Nicholls & Kennedy, 1992).

LOOK AND LISTEN

Visit a preschool or child-care center where artwork by 3- to 5-year-olds is plentiful. Note age differences in rendering of human and animal figures and in the complexity of children's drawings.

FIGURE 8.9

Examples of young children's drawings. The universal tadpole-like shape that children use to draw their first picture of a person is shown on the left. The tadpole soon becomes an anchor for greater detail as arms, fingers, toes, and facial features sprout from the basic shape. By the end of the preschool years, children produce more complex, differentiated pictures like the one on the right, drawn by a 6-year-old child. *(Left: From H. Gardner, 1980,* Artful Scribbles: The Significance of Children's Drawings, *New York: Basic Books, p. 64. Reprinted by permission of Basic Books, a member of Perseus Books Group. Right: From E. Winner, August 1986, "Where Pelicans Kiss Seals,"* Psychology Today, *20[8], p. 35. Reprinted by permission from the collection of Ellen Winner.)*

Drawing Category and Approximate Age Range	Cube	Cylinder
Single Units (3 to 7 years)		
Object Parts (4 to 13 years)		
Integrated Whole (8 years and older)		

FIGURE 8.10

Development of children's drawings of geometric objects—a cube and a cylinder. As these examples show, drawings change from single units to representation of object parts. Then the parts are integrated into a realistic whole. *(Adapted from Toomela, 1999.)*

■ As cognitive and fine-motor skills advance, children's drawings increase in detail and realism. This 5-year-old depicts a house with door and windows, a flower with petals, and people with an array of distinctive features—eyes, nose, mouth, hair, and hands. ■

Realism in drawings appears gradually, as perception, language (ability to describe visual details), memory, and fine-motor capacities improve (Toomela, 2002). Drawing of geometric objects follows the steps illustrated in Figure 8.10. (1) Three- to 7-year olds draw a single unit to stand for an object. To represent a cube, they draw a square; to represent a cylinder, they draw a circle, an oval, or a rectangle. (2) During the late preschool and school years, children represent salient object parts. They draw several squares to stand for a cube's sides and draw two circles and some lines to represent a cylinder. However, the parts are not joined properly. (3) Older school-age children and adolescents integrate object parts into a realistic whole (Toomela, 1999).

Preschoolers' free depiction of reality makes their artwork look fanciful and inventive. Accomplished artists often must work hard to achieve what they did effortlessly as 5- and 6-year-olds.

CULTURAL VARIATIONS IN DEVELOPMENT OF DRAW-ING In cultures with rich artistic traditions, children create elaborate drawings that reflect the conventions of their culture. Adults encourage young children by offering suggestions, modeling ways to draw, and asking children to label their pictures. Peers, as well, discuss one another's drawings and copy from one another's work (Boyatzis, 2000; Braswell, 2006). All of these practices enhance young children's drawing progress.

But in cultures with little interest in art, even older children and adolescents produce simple forms. In the Jimi Valley, a remote region of Papua New Guinea with no indigenous pictorial art, many children do not go to school and therefore have little opportunity to develop drawing skills. When a Western researcher asked nonschooled Jimi 10- to 15-year-olds to draw a human figure for the first time, most produced nonrepresentational scribbles and shapes or simple "stick" or "contour" images (see Figure 8.11) (Martlew & Connolly, 1996). These forms, which resemble those of preschoolers, seem to be a universal beginning in drawing. Once children realize that lines must evoke human features, they find solutions to figure drawing that vary somewhat from culture to culture but, overall, follow the sequence described earlier.

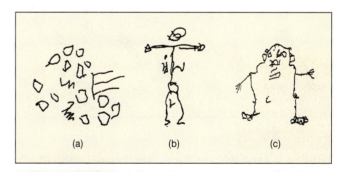

(a) (b) (c)

FIGURE 8.11

Drawings produced by nonschooled 10- to 15-year-old children of the Jimi Valley of Papua New Guinea when asked to draw a human figure for the first time. Many produced nonrepresentational scribbles and shapes (a), "stick" figures (b), or "contour" figures (c). Compared with the Western tadpole form, the Jimi "stick" and "contour" figures emphasize the hands and feet. Otherwise, the drawings of these older children resemble those of young preschoolers. *(From M. Martlew & K. J. Connolly, 1996, "Human Figure Drawings by Schooled and Unschooled Children in Papua New Guinea," Child Development, 67, pp. 2750–2751. © The Society for Research in Child Development. Adapted by permission.)*

© LAURA DWIGHT PHOTOGRAPHY

■ Gains in fine-motor control and perception, along with experience with written materials, contribute to this 5-year-old's skill at printing. ■

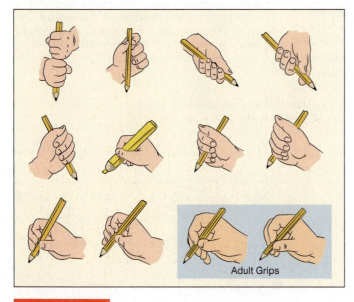

Adult Grips

FIGURE 8.12

Variations in 3-year-olds' pencil grip. Through experimenting with different grips, preschoolers gradually discover an adult grip with one or two fingers on top of the pencil, which maximizes writing stability and efficiency. *(Adapted from Greer & Lockman, 1998.)*

EARLY PRINTING   When preschoolers first try to write, they scribble, making no distinction between writing and drawing. As they experiment with lines and shapes, notice print in storybooks, and observe people writing, they attempt to print letters and, later, words. Around age 4, children's writing shows some distinctive features of print, such as separate forms arranged in a line on the page. But children often include picturelike devices. For example, they might use a circular shape to write "sun." Or they might call a large scribble the word *lion,* a small scribble the word *caterpillar,* and a red scribble the word *apple* (Ehri & Roberts, 2006; Levin & Bus, 2003). Applying their understanding of the symbolic function of drawings, 4-year-olds asked to write typically make a "drawing of print." Only gradually, as they learn to name the letters of the alphabet and to link them with language sounds, do preschoolers realize that writing stands for language.

Preschoolers' first attempts to print often involve their name, generally using a single letter. "How do you make a *D?*" my older son, David, asked at age 3½. When I printed a large uppercase *D,* he tried to copy. "*D* for David," he proclaimed, quite satisfied with his backward, imperfect creation. A year later, David added several letters, and around age 5, he printed his name clearly enough that others could read it.

Between ages 3 and 5, children acquire skill in gripping a pencil. As Figure 8.12 shows, 3-year-olds display diverse grip patterns and pencil angles, varying their grip depending on the direction and location of the marks they want to make. By trying out different forms of pencil-holding, they discover the grip and angle that maximize stability and writing efficiency. By age 5, most children use an adult grip pattern and a fairly constant pencil angle across a range of drawing and writing conditions (Greer & Lockman, 1998).

In addition to gains in fine-motor control, advances in perception contribute to the ability to print. Like many children, David continued to reverse letters until well into second grade. Once preschoolers distinguish writing from nonwriting around age 4, they make progress in identifying individual letters. Many preschoolers confuse letter pairs that are alike in shape with subtle distinctive features, such as *C* and *G, E* and *F,* and *M* and *W* (Bornstein & Arterberry, 1999). Mirror-image letter pairs (*b* and *d, p* and *q*) are especially hard to discriminate. Until children start to read, they do not find it especially useful to notice the difference between these forms.

The ability to tune in to mirror images and to scan a printed line from left to right improves as children gain experience with written materials (Casey, 1986). The more parents and teachers assist preschoolers in their efforts to print, the more advanced children are in writing and other aspects of literacy development (Aram & Levin, 2001, 2002). We will consider early childhood literacy in greater detail in Chapter 9.

Individual Differences in Motor Skills

Wide individual differences exist in the ages at which children reach motor milestones. A child with a tall, muscular body tends to move more quickly and to acquire certain skills earlier than a short, stocky youngster. And as in other domains, parents and teachers probably provide more encouragement to children with biologically based motor-skill advantages.

Sex differences in motor skills are evident in early childhood. Boys are ahead of girls in skills that emphasize force and power. By age 5, they can jump slightly farther, run slightly faster, and throw a ball about 5 feet farther. Girls have an edge in fine-motor skills and in certain gross-motor skills that require a combination of good balance and foot movement, such as hopping and skipping (Fischman, Moore, & Steele, 1992; Haywood & Getchell, 2005). Boys' greater muscle mass and, in the case of throwing, slightly longer forearms contribute to their skill advantages. And girls' greater overall physical maturity may be partly responsible for their better balance and precision of movement.

From an early age, boys and girls are usually channeled into different physical activities. For example, fathers are more likely to play catch with their sons than with their daughters. Baseballs and footballs are purchased for boys, jump ropes and sewing materials for girls. Sex differences in motor skills increase with age, but they remain small throughout childhood. This suggests that social pressures for boys to be active and physically skilled and for girls to play quietly at fine-motor activities exaggerate small genetically based sex differences (Greendorfer, Lewko, & Rosengren, 1996). In support of this view, boys can throw a ball much farther than girls only when using their dominant hand. When they use their nondominant hand, the sex difference is minimal (Williams, Haywood, & Painter, 1996). Boys' superior throwing largely results from practice.

■ Sex differences in motor development are already apparent in early childhood. Girls have an edge in skills that require balance and precision of movement. But in throwing, catching, and running, boys benefit from greater encouragement to improve their skill level. ■

Enhancing Early Childhood Motor Development

Many Western parents provide preschoolers with early training in gymnastics, tumbling, and other physical activities. These experiences offer excellent opportunities for exercise and social interaction. But aside from throwing (where direct instruction is helpful), formal lessons during the preschool years have little impact on motor development. Rather, children master the motor skills of early childhood naturally, as part of their everyday play.

Nevertheless, the physical environment in which informal play takes place can affect mastery of complex motor skills. The National Association for Sport and Physical Education (2009) recommends that preschoolers engage in at least 60 minutes, and up to several hours, of unstructured physical activity every day. When children have play spaces and equipment appropriate for running, climbing, jumping, and throwing and are encouraged to use them, they respond eagerly to these challenges. But if balls are too large and heavy to be properly grasped and thrown, or jungle gyms, ladders, and horizontal bars are suitable for only the largest and strongest children, then preschoolers cannot easily acquire new motor skills. Playgrounds must offer a range of equipment to meet the diverse needs of individual children.

■ When play spaces are properly designed and equipped, young children respond eagerly to motor challenges and develop new skills through informal play. ■

Simil[...]ent of fine-motor skills can be supported through daily routines, such as dressing and pouring juice, and through play that involves puzzles, construction sets, drawing, painting, sculpting, cutting, and pasting. Exposure to artwork of their own and others' cultures enhances children's awareness of the creative possibilities of artistic media. And opportunities to represent their own ideas and feelings, rather than coloring in predrawn forms, foster artistic development.

Finally, the social climate created by adults can enhance or dampen preschoolers' motor development. When parents and teachers criticize a child's performance, push specific motor skills, or promote a competitive attitude, they risk undermining children's self-confidence and, in turn, their motor progress (Berk, 2006). Adult involvement in young children's motor activities should focus on fun rather than on winning or perfecting the "correct" technique.

ASK YOURSELF

◆ **REVIEW** Describe typical changes in children's drawings in early childhood, along with factors that contribute to those changes.

◆ **APPLY** Mabel and Chad want to do everything they can to support their 3-year-old daughter's athletic development. What advice would you give them?

◆ **CONNECT** How are experiences that best support preschoolers' motor development consistent with experience-expectant brain growth of the early years? (Return to page 172 in Chapter 5 to review.)

Summary

Body Growth

Describe changes in body size, proportions, and skeletal maturity during early childhood.

■ Gains in body size taper off in early childhood as children become longer and leaner, and individual differences in body size and rate of growth are more apparent. In various parts of the skeleton, new epiphyses emerge, where cartilage hardens into bone.

■ By the end of the preschool years, children start to lose their primary teeth. Care of primary teeth is essential because diseased baby teeth can affect the health of permanent teeth. Childhood tooth decay remains common, especially among low-SES children.

Describe brain development in early childhood.

■ Neural fibers in the brain continue to form synapses and myelinate. By this time, many parts of the cerebral cortex have overproduced synapses, and *synaptic pruning* occurs. To make room for the connective structures of active neurons, many surrounding neurons die, leading to reduced brain plasticity.

■ Prefrontal-cortical areas devoted to inhibition, attention, working memory, and planning show rapid growth from early to middle childhood. In addition, for most children, the left cerebral hemisphere develops ahead of the right, supporting rapidly expanding language skills.

© LAURA DWIGHT PHOTOGRAPHY

■ Hand preference, which reflects an individual's **dominant cerebral hemisphere,** strengthens during early childhood. Research on handedness supports the joint contribution of nature and nurture to brain lateralization.

■ During early childhood, connections are established between brain structures. Fibers linking the **cerebellum** to the cerebral cortex grow and myelinate, enhancing motor coordination. The **reticular formation,** responsible for alertness and consciousness; the **hippocampus,** which plays a vital role in memory; the **amygdala,** which plays a central role in processing emotional information; and the **corpus callosum,** which connects the two cortical hemispheres, also form synapses and myelinate.

Influences on Physical Growth and Health

Explain how heredity influences physical growth.

■ Heredity influences physical growth by controlling production and release of two vital hormones from the **pituitary gland: growth hormone (GH),** which affects the development of almost all body tissues, and **thyroid-stimulating hormone (TSH),** which affects brain growth and body size.

Describe the effects of emotional well-being, restful sleep, nutrition, and infectious disease on physical growth and health in early childhood.

■ Emotional well-being continues to influence body growth and health. Extreme emotional deprivation can lead to **psychosocial dwarfism.**

■ Restful sleep contributes to body growth, since GH is released during the child's sleeping hours. Sleep difficulties impair cognitive functioning, especially for low-SES children. Although total sleep need declines, substantial variability exists.

■ Sleep problems sometimes stem from a mismatch between parental demands and children's sleep needs. Many preschoolers have difficulty falling asleep, and most awaken occasionally at night. A few children suffer from sleep disorders, such as sleepwalking or sleep terrors, which run in families, suggesting a genetic influence. These problems can also be triggered by stress or extreme fatigue.

■ As growth rate slows, preschoolers' appetites decline, and they often become wary of new foods. Young children's social environments powerfully influence their food preferences. Modeling by others, repeated exposure to new foods, and a positive emotional climate at mealtimes can promote healthy, varied eating in young children.

■ Dietary deficiencies—most commonly in protein, vitamins, and minerals—are associated with attention and memory difficulties, academic and behavior problems, and greater susceptibility to infectious diseases. Disease also contributes to malnutrition, especially when intestinal infections cause persistent diarrhea. In developing countries, inexpensive oral rehydration therapy (ORT) and supplements of zinc can prevent most developmental impairments and deaths due to diarrhea.

■ Immunization rates are lower in the United States than in other industrialized nations because many economically disadvantaged children lack access to necessary health care. Parental stress and misconceptions about vaccine safety also contribute.

What factors increase the risk of unintentional injuries, and how can childhood injuries be prevented?

■ Unintentional injuries are the leading cause of childhood mortality in industrialized nations. Injury victims are more likely to be boys; to be temperamentally irritable, inattentive, overactive, and defiant; and to live in stressed, poverty-stricken, crowded family environments.

■ Effective injury prevention includes passing laws that promote child safety; creating safer home, travel, and play environments; relieving sources of family stress; improving public education; and changing parent and child behaviors.

Motor Development

Cite major milestones of gross- and fine-motor development in early childhood.

■ As the child's center of gravity shifts toward the trunk, balance improves, paving the way for new gross-motor achievements. Preschoolers' gaits become smooth and rhythmic; they run, jump, hop, gallop; eventually skip, throw, and catch; and generally become better coordinated.

■ Increasing control of the hands and fingers leads to dramatic improvements in fine-motor skills. Preschoolers gradually dress themselves and use a fork and knife.

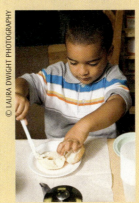

■ By age 3, children's scribbles become pictures. As perceptual, cognitive, and fine-motor capacities improve, children's drawings increase in complexity and realism. Children's drawings are also influenced by their culture's artistic traditions.

■ Between 3 and 5 years, children experiment with pencil grip; by age 5, most use an adult-like grip that maximizes stability and writing efficiency.

■ Advances in perception and exposure to written materials contribute to progress in discriminating and accurately printing individual letters. When parents and teachers support children's efforts to print, preschoolers are more advanced in writing and other aspects of literacy development.

Describe individual differences in preschoolers' motor skills and ways to enhance motor development in early childhood.

■ Body build and opportunity for physical play affect early childhood motor development. Sex differences that favor boys in skills requiring force and power and girls in skills requiring good balance and fine movements are partly genetic, but social pressures exaggerate them.

■ Children master the motor skills of early childhood through informal play experiences, with little benefit from exposure to formal training. Richly equipped play environments that accommodate a wide range of physical abilities are important. Emphasizing pleasure in motor activities is the best way to foster motor development during the preschool years.

IMPORTANT TERMS AND CONCEPTS

amygdala (p. 295)
cerebellum (p. 294)
corpus callosum (p. 295)
dominant cerebral hemisphere (p. 293)

growth hormone (GH) (p. 297)
hippocampus (p. 294)
pituitary gland (p. 297)

psychosocial dwarfism (p. 297)
reticular formation (p. 294)
thyroid-stimulating hormone (TSH) (p. 297)

"My Weekend"
Jingyi Liu
6 years, China

This avid painter's creations reflect her rapidly expanding knowledge of the wider world. Mental representation blossoms in early childhood, contributing greatly to cognitive and language development.

Reprinted with permission from the International Museum of Children's Art, Oslo, Norway

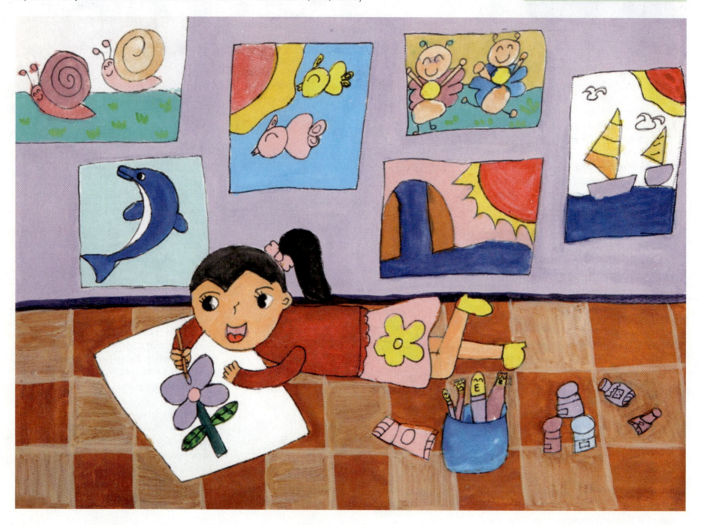

Cognitive Development in Early Childhood

One rainy morning, as I observed in our laboratory preschool, Leslie, the children's teacher, joined me at the back of the room for a moment. "Preschoolers' minds are such a curious blend of logic, fantasy, and faulty reasoning," Leslie reflected. "Every day, I'm startled by the maturity and originality of what they say and do. Yet at other times, their thinking seems limited and inflexible."

Leslie's comments sum up the puzzling contradictions of early childhood cognition. That day, for example, 3-year-old Sammy looked up, startled, after a loud crash of thunder outside. "A magic man turned on the thunder!" he pronounced. Even when Leslie patiently explained that thunder is caused by lightning, not by a person turning it on or off, Sammy persisted: "Then a magic lady did it."

In other respects, Sammy's thinking was surprisingly advanced. At snack time, he accurately counted, "One, two, three, four!" and then got four cartons of milk, one for each child at his table. Sammy's keen memory and ability to categorize were also evident. He could recite by heart *The Very Hungry Caterpillar*, a story he had heard many times. And he could name and classify dozens of animals.

But when his snack group included more than four children, Sammy's counting broke down. And some of his notions about quantity seemed as fantastic as his understanding of thunder. After Priti dumped out her raisins, scattering them in front of her, Sammy asked, "How come you got lots, and I only got this little bit?" He didn't realize that he had just as many raisins; his were simply all bunched up in a tiny red box. While Priti was washing her hands after snack, Sammy put her remaining raisins in her cubby. When Priti returned and looked for her raisins, Sammy pronounced, "You know where they are!" He failed to grasp that Priti, who hadn't seen him move the raisins, would expect them to be where she had left them.

In this chapter, we explore early childhood cognition, drawing on three theories with which you are already familiar. To understand Sammy's reasoning, we turn first to Piaget's and Vygotsky's theories along with evidence highlighting the

Piaget's Theory: The Preoperational Stage

Advances in Mental Representation • Make-Believe Play • Symbol–Real-World Relations • Limitations of Preoperational Thought • Follow-Up Research on Preoperational Thought • Evaluation of the Preoperational Stage • Piaget and Education

■ SOCIAL ISSUES: EDUCATION
Children's Questions: Catalyst for Cognitive Development

Vygotsky's Sociocultural Theory

Private Speech • Social Origins of Early Childhood Cognition • Vygotsky and Early Childhood Education • Evaluation of Vygotsky's Theory

■ CULTURAL INFLUENCES
Children in Village and Tribal Cultures Observe and Participate in Adult Work

Information Processing

Attention • Memory • Problem Solving • The Young Child's Theory of Mind • Early Literacy and Mathematical Development

■ BIOLOGY AND ENVIRONMENT
"Mindblindness" and Autism

Individual Differences in Mental Development

Early Childhood Intelligence Tests • Home Environment and Mental Development • Preschool, Kindergarten, and Child Care • Educational Media

Language Development

Vocabulary • Grammar • Conversation • Supporting Language Learning in Early Childhood

strengths and limitations of each. Then we examine additional research on young children's cognition inspired by the information-processing perspective. Next, we address factors that contribute to individual differences in mental development—the home environment, the quality of preschool and child care, and the many hours young children spend watching television and using computers. Our chapter concludes with the dramatic expansion of language in early childhood.

Piaget's Theory: The Preoperational Stage

As children move from the sensorimotor to the **preoperational stage,** which spans the years 2 to 7, the most obvious change is an extraordinary increase in representational, or symbolic, activity. Recall that infants and toddlers have considerable ability to mentally represent their world. In early childhood, this capacity blossoms.

Advances in Mental Representation

Piaget acknowledged that language is our most flexible means of mental representation. By detaching thought from action, it permits far more efficient thinking than was possible earlier. When we think in words, we overcome the limits of our momentary experiences. We can deal with past, present, and future at once and combine concepts in unique ways, as when we imagine a hungry caterpillar eating bananas or monsters flying through the forest at night.

But Piaget did not regard language as a primary ingredient in childhood cognitive change. Instead, he believed that sensorimotor activity leads to internal images of experience, which children then label with words (Piaget, 1936/1952). In support of Piaget's view, recall from Chapter 6 that children's first words have a strong sensorimotor basis. And toddlers acquire an impressive range of categories long before they use words to label them (see pages 222–223). But as we will see, other theorists regard Piaget's account of the link between language and thought as incomplete.

Make-Believe Play

Make-believe play is another excellent example of the development of representation in early childhood. Piaget believed that through pretending, young children practice and strengthen newly acquired representational schemes. Drawing on his ideas, several investigators have traced changes in make-believe play during the preschool years.

DEVELOPMENT OF MAKE-BELIEVE   One day, Sammy's 20-month-old brother, Dwayne, visited the classroom. Dwayne wandered around, picked up a toy telephone receiver, eyed his mother, said, "Hi, Mommy," and then dropped it. Next, he found an empty cup, pretended to drink, and then toddled off again. Meanwhile, Sammy joined Vance and Lynette in the block area for a space shuttle launch.

"That can be our control tower," Sammy suggested, pointing to a corner by a bookshelf. "Countdown!" he announced, speaking into his "walkie-talkie"—a small wooden block. "Five, six, two, four, one, blastoff!" Lynette made a doll push a pretend button, and the rocket was off!

© LAURA DWIGHT PHOTOGRAPHY

■ Make-believe play increases in sophistication during the preschool years. Children increasingly coordinate make-believe roles and pretend with less realistic toys, so a toy truck can stand for an electric hair clipper. ■

Comparing Dwayne's pretend play with Sammy's, we see three important changes that reflect the preschool child's growing symbolic mastery:

■ *Play detaches from the real-life conditions associated with it.* In early pretending, toddlers use only realistic objects—a toy telephone to talk into or a cup to drink from. Their earliest pretend acts usually imitate adults' actions and are not yet flexible. Children younger than age 2, for example, will pretend to drink from a cup but refuse to pretend a cup is a hat (Rakoczy, Tomasello, & Striano, 2005). They have trouble using an object (cup) that already has an obvious use as a symbol of another object (hat).

   After age 2, children pretend with less realistic toys—for example, a block for a telephone receiver. Gradually, they can flexibly imagine objects and events without support from the real world, as Sammy's imaginary control tower illustrates (O'Reilly, 1995; Striano, Tomasello, & Rochat, 2001).

■ *Play becomes less self-centered.* At first, make-believe is directed toward the self. For example, Dwayne pretends to feed only himself. Soon, children begin to direct pretend actions toward objects, as when a child feeds a doll. Early in the third year, they become detached participants, making a doll feed itself or pushing a button to launch a rocket. Make-believe becomes less self-centered as children realize that agents and recipients of pretend actions can be independent of themselves (McCune, 1993).

■ *Play includes more complex combinations of schemes.* Dwayne can pretend to drink from a cup, but he does not yet combine drinking with pouring. Later, children combine schemes with those of peers in **sociodramatic play,** the make-believe with others that is under way by the end of the second year and that increases rapidly in complexity during early childhood (Kavanaugh, 2006a). Already, Sammy and his classmates can create and coordinate several roles in an elaborate plot. By the end of the preschool years, children have a sophisticated understanding of role relationships and story lines.

Children as young as age 2 display awareness that make-believe is a representational activity. They distinguish make-believe from real experiences and grasp that pretending is a deliberate effort to act out imaginary ideas—an understanding that strengthens over early childhood (Lillard, 2003; Rakoczy, Tomasello, & Striano, 2004; Sobel, 2006). **TAKE A MOMENT...** Listen closely to preschoolers as they assign roles and negotiate plans in sociodramatic play: "*You pretend to be* the astronaut, *I'll act like* I'm operating the control tower!" "Wait, *I gotta set up* the spaceship." In communicating about pretend, children think about their own and others' fanciful representations—evidence that they have begun to reason about people's mental activities, a topic we will return to later in this chapter.

BENEFITS OF MAKE-BELIEVE   Today, Piaget's view of make-believe as mere practice of representational schemes is regarded as too limited. Play not only reflects but also contributes to children's cognitive and social skills. Sociodramatic play has been studied most thoroughly. Compared with social nonpretend activities (such as drawing or putting puzzles together), during sociodramatic play preschoolers' interactions last longer, show more involvement, draw more children into the activity, and are more cooperative (Creasey, Jarvis, & Berk, 1998).

It is not surprising, then, that preschoolers who spend more time in sociodramatic play are seen as more socially competent by their teachers (Connolly & Doyle, 1984). And many studies reveal that make-believe strengthens a wide variety of mental abilities, including sustained attention, memory, logical reasoning, language and literacy, imagination, creativity, and the ability to reflect on one's own thinking, regulate one's own emotions and behavior, and take another's perspective (Bergen & Mauer, 2000; Berk, Mann, & Ogan, 2006; Elias & Berk, 2002; Hirsh-Pasek et al., 2009; Lindsey & Colwell, 2003; Ogan & Berk, 2009; Ruff & Capozzoli, 2003).

Between 25 and 45 percent of preschoolers and young school-age children spend much time in solitary make-believe, creating *imaginary companions*—special fantasized friends endowed with humanlike qualities. For example, one preschooler created Nutsy and Nutsy, a pair of boisterous birds who lived outside her bedroom window and often went along on family outings (Gleason, Sebanc, & Hartup, 2000; Taylor et al., 2004). Imaginary companions were once viewed as a sign of maladjustment, but research challenges this assumption. Children with an

LOOK AND LISTEN

Observe the make-believe play of several 2- to 4-year-olds at home or in a preschool or child-care center. Describe pretend acts that exemplify important developmental changes.

Applying What We Know

Enhancing Make-Believe Play in Early Childhood

STRATEGY	DESCRIPTION
Provide sufficient space and play materials.	Generous space and materials allow for many play options and reduce conflict.
Encourage children's play without controlling it.	Model, guide, and build on young preschoolers' play themes. Provide open-ended suggestions (for example, "Would the animals like a train ride?"), and talk with the child about the thoughts, motivations, and emotions of play characters. These forms of adult support lead to more elaborate pretending. Refrain from directing the child's play; excessive adult control destroys the creativity and pleasure of make-believe.
Offer a variety of both realistic materials and materials without clear functions.	Children use realistic materials, such as trucks, dolls, tea sets, dress-up clothes, and toy scenes (house, farm, garage, airport) to act out everyday roles in their culture. Materials without clear functions (such as blocks, cardboard cylinders, paper bags, and sand) inspire fantastic role play, such as "pirate" and "creature from outer space."
Ensure that children have many rich, real-world experiences to inspire positive fantasy play.	Opportunities to participate in real-world activities with adults and to observe adult roles in the community provide children with rich social knowledge to integrate into make-believe. Restricting television viewing, especially programs with violent content, limits the degree to which violent themes and aggressive behavior become part of children's play. (See Chapter 10, pages 387–389.)
Help children solve social conflicts constructively.	Cooperation is essential for sociodramatic play. Guide children toward positive relationships with agemates by helping them resolve disagreements constructively. For example, ask, "What could you do if you want a turn?" If the child cannot think of possibilities, suggest options, and assist the child in implementing them.

Sources: Berk, Mann, & Ogan, 2006; Nielsen & Christie, 2008; Ogan & Berk, 2009.

invisible playmate typically treat it with care and affection and say it offers caring, comfort, and good company, just as their real friendships do (Gleason & Hohmann, 2006; Hoff, 2005). Such children also display more complex and imaginative pretend play, are advanced in understanding others' viewpoints and emotions, and are more sociable with peers (Bouldin, 2006; Gleason, 2002; Taylor & Carlson, 1997).

Applying What We Know above lists ways to enhance preschoolers' make-believe. Later we will return to the origins and consequences of make-believe from an alternative perspective—that of Vygotsky.

■ Children who experience a variety of symbols come to understand dual representation—for example, that this dollhouse is both an object in its own right and can stand for another, a full-sized house that people live in. ■

© ELLEN B. SENISI PHOTOGRAPHY

Symbol–Real-World Relations

In a corner of the classroom, Leslie set up a dollhouse, replete with tiny furnishings. Sammy liked to arrange the furniture to match his real-world living room, kitchen, and bedroom. Representations of reality, like Sammy's, are powerful cognitive tools. When we understand that a picture, model, or map corresponds to something specific in everyday life, we can use these tools to find out about objects and places we have not experienced.

In Chapter 6, we saw that by the middle of the second year, children grasp the symbolic function of realistic-looking pictures (such as photos). When do children comprehend scale models as symbols for real-world spaces? In one study, 2½- and 3-year-olds watched an adult hide a small toy (Little Snoopy) in a scale model of a room and then were asked to retrieve it. Next, they had to find a larger toy (Big Snoopy) hidden in the room that the model represented. Not until age 3 could most children use the model as a guide to finding Big Snoopy in the real room (DeLoache, 1987). The 2½-year-olds did not realize that the model could be both *a toy room* and *a symbol of another room.* They had trouble with **dual representation**—viewing a symbolic object as both an object in its own right and a symbol. In support of this interpretation, when researchers made the model room less prominent as an object, by placing it behind a window and preventing children from touching it, more 2½-year-olds succeeded at the search task (DeLoache, 2000, 2002).

Recall that in make-believe play, 1½- to 2-year-olds cannot use an object that has an obvious use (cup) to stand for another object (hat). Likewise, 2-year-olds do not yet grasp that a line drawing—an object in its own right—also represents real-world objects (see page 310 in Chapter 8). Difficulty with dual representation may contribute to 2-year-olds' scale errors—for example, attempts to put on dolls' clothes or sit in a doll-sized chair (see page 281 in Chapter 7).

How do children grasp the dual representation of symbolic objects? When adults point out similarities between models and real-world spaces, 2½-year-olds perform better on the find-Snoopy task (Peralta de Mendoza & Salsa, 2003). Also, insight into one type of symbol–real-world relation helps preschoolers master others. For example, children regard realistic-looking pictures as symbols early, around 1½ to 2 years, because a picture's primary purpose is to stand for something; it is not an interesting object in its own right (Preissler & Carey, 2004; Simcock & DeLoache, 2006). And 3-year-olds who can use a model of a room to locate Big Snoopy readily transfer their understanding to a simple map (Marzolf & DeLoache, 1994).

In sum, exposing young children to diverse symbols—picture books, photographs, drawings, make-believe, and maps—helps them appreciate that one object can stand for another. With age, children come to understand a wide range of symbols that have little physical similarity to what they represent (Liben, 2009). As a result, doors open to vast realms of knowledge.

Limitations of Preoperational Thought

Aside from gains in representation, Piaget described preschoolers in terms of what they *cannot* understand (Beilin, 1992). As the term *preoperational* suggests, he compared them to older, more competent children who have reached the concrete operational stage. According to Piaget, young children are not capable of *operations*—mental actions that obey logical rules. Rather, their thinking is rigid, limited to one aspect of a situation at a time, and strongly influenced by the way things appear at the moment.

EGOCENTRISM   For Piaget, the most fundamental deficiency of preoperational thinking is **egocentrism**—failure to distinguish the symbolic viewpoints of others from one's own. He believed that when children first mentally represent the world, they tend to focus on their own viewpoint and assume that others perceive, think, and feel the same way they do.

Piaget's most convincing demonstration of egocentrism involves his *three-mountains problem,* described in Figure 9.1. He also regarded egocentrism as responsible for preoperational children's **animistic thinking**—the belief that inanimate objects have lifelike qualities, such as thoughts, wishes, feelings, and intentions (Piaget, 1926/1930). Recall Sammy's insistence that someone must have turned on the thunder. According to Piaget, because young children egocentrically assign human purposes to physical events, magical thinking is common during the preschool years.

Piaget argued that preschoolers' egocentric bias prevents them from *accommodating,* or reflecting on and revising their faulty reasoning in response to their physical and social worlds. To understand this shortcoming, let's consider some additional tasks that Piaget gave to children.

INABILITY TO CONSERVE   Piaget's famous conservation tasks reveal several deficiencies of preoperational thinking. **Conservation** refers to the idea that certain physical characteristics of objects remain the same, even when their outward appearance changes. At snack time, Sammy and Priti had identical boxes of raisins, but when Priti spread her raisins out on the table, Sammy was convinced that she had more.

FIGURE 9.1

Piaget's three-mountains problem. Each mountain is distinguished by its color and by its summit. One has a red cross, another a small house, and the third a snow-capped peak. Children at the preoperational stage respond egocentrically. They cannot select a picture that shows the mountains from the doll's perspective. Instead, they simply choose the photo that reflects their own vantage point.

FIGURE 9.2

Some Piagetian conservation tasks. Children at the preoperational stage cannot yet conserve. These tasks are mastered gradually over the concrete operational stage. Children in Western nations typically acquire conservation of number, mass, and liquid sometime between 6 and 7 years and of weight between 8 and 10 years.

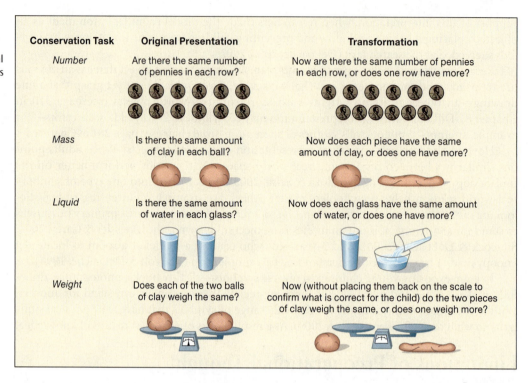

Conservation Task	Original Presentation	Transformation
Number	Are there the same number of pennies in each row?	Now are there the same number of pennies in each row, or does one row have more?
Mass	Is there the same amount of clay in each ball?	Now does each piece have the same amount of clay, or does one have more?
Liquid	Is there the same amount of water in each glass?	Now does each glass have the same amount of water, or does one have more?
Weight	Does each of the two balls of clay weigh the same?	Now (without placing them back on the scale to confirm what is correct for the child) do the two pieces of clay weigh the same, or does one weigh more?

In another conservation task involving liquid, the child is shown two identical tall glasses of water and asked if they contain equal amounts. Once the child agrees, the water in one glass is poured into a short, wide container, changing its appearance but not its amount. Then the child is asked whether the amount of water is the same or has changed. Preoperational children think the quantity has changed. They explain, "There is less now because the water is way down here" (that is, its level is so low) or, "There is more now because it is all spread out." Figure 9.2 illustrates other conservation tasks that you can try with children.

The inability to conserve highlights several related aspects of preoperational children's thinking. First, their understanding is *centered,* or characterized by **centration.** They focus on one aspect of a situation, neglecting other important features. In conservation of liquid, the child *centers* on the height of the water, failing to realize that changes in width compensate for the changes in height. Second, children are easily distracted by the *perceptual appearance* of objects. Third, children treat the initial and final *states* of the water as unrelated events, ignoring the *dynamic transformation* (pouring of water) between them.

The most important illogical feature of preoperational thought is its **irreversibility**—an inability to mentally go through a series of steps in a problem and then reverse direction, returning to the starting point. *Reversibility* is part of every logical operation. After Priti spills her raisins, Sammy cannot reverse by thinking, "I know Priti doesn't have more raisins than I do. If we put them back in that little box, her raisins and mine would look just the same."

LACK OF HIERARCHICAL CLASSIFICATION Preoperational children have difficulty with **hierarchical classification**—the organization of objects into classes and subclasses on the basis of similarities and differences. Piaget's famous *class inclusion problem,* illustrated in Figure 9.3, demonstrates this limitation. Preoperational children *center* on the overriding feature, red. They do not think reversibly, moving from the whole class (flowers) to the parts (red and blue) and back again.

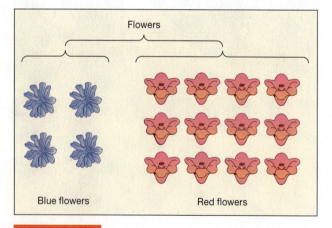

Flowers

Blue flowers

Red flowers

FIGURE 9.3

A Piagetian class inclusion problem. Children are shown 16 flowers, 4 of which are blue and 12 of which are red. Asked, "Are there more red flowers or flowers?" the preoperational child responds, "More red flowers," failing to realize that both red and blue flowers are included in the category "flowers."

Follow-Up Research on Preoperational Thought

Over the past three decades, researchers have challenged Piaget's view of preschoolers as cognitively deficient. Because many Piagetian problems contain unfamiliar elements or too many pieces of information for young children to handle at once, preschoolers' responses often do not reflect their true abilities. Piaget also missed many naturally occurring instances of effective reasoning by preschoolers. Let's look at some examples.

EGOCENTRIC, ANIMISTIC, AND MAGICAL THINKING   Do young children really believe that a person standing elsewhere in a room sees exactly what they see? When researchers change the nature of Piaget's three-mountains problem to include familiar objects and use methods other than picture selection (which is difficult even for 10-year-olds), 4-year-olds show clear awareness of others' vantage points (Borke, 1975; Newcombe & Huttenlocher, 1992). Even 2-year-olds realize that what they see sometimes differs from what another person sees. When asked to help an adult look for a lost object, 24-month-olds—but not 18-month-olds—handed her a toy resting behind a bucket that was within their line of sight but not the adult's (Moll & Tomasello, 2006).

Nonegocentric responses also appear in young children's conversations. For example, preschoolers adapt their speech to fit the needs of their listeners. Four-year-olds use shorter, simpler expressions when talking to 2-year-olds than to agemates or adults (Gelman & Shatz, 1978). And in describing objects, children do not use such words as "big" and "little" in a rigid, egocentric fashion. Instead, they *adjust* their descriptions to allow for context. By age 3, children judge a 2-inch shoe as small when seen by itself (because it is much smaller than most shoes) but as big for a tiny 5-inch-tall doll (Ebeling & Gelman, 1994).

In previous chapters, we saw that toddlers have already begun to infer others' intentions and perspectives. And in his later writings, Piaget (1945/1951) did describe preschoolers' egocentrism as a tendency rather than an inability. As we revisit the topic of perspective taking, we will see that it develops gradually throughout childhood and adolescence.

Piaget also overestimated preschoolers' animistic beliefs. Even infants have begun to distinguish animate from inanimate, as indicated by their remarkable categorical distinctions among living and nonliving things (see Chapter 6, pages 222–223). By age 2½, children give psychological explanations ("he likes to" or "she wants to") for people and other animals but rarely for objects (Hickling & Wellman, 2001). And 3- to 5-year-olds asked whether a variety of animals and objects can eat, grow, talk, think, remember, see, or feel mostly attribute these capacities to animals, not objects. In addition, they rarely attribute biological properties (like eating and growing) to robots, indicting that they are well aware that even a self-moving object with lifelike features is not alive. But unlike adults, preschoolers often say that robots have perceptual and psychological capacities—for example, seeing, thinking, and remembering (Jipson & Gelman, 2007; Subrahmanyam, Gelman, & Lafosse, 2002). These responses result from incomplete knowledge about certain objects, and they decline with age.

Similarly, preschoolers think that magic accounts for events they otherwise cannot explain, as in Sammy's magical explanation of thunder in the opening to this chapter. Consequently, most 3- and 4-year-olds believe in the supernatural powers of fairies, goblins, and other enchanted creatures (Rosengren & Hickling, 2000). But their notions of magic are flexible and appropriate. For example, older

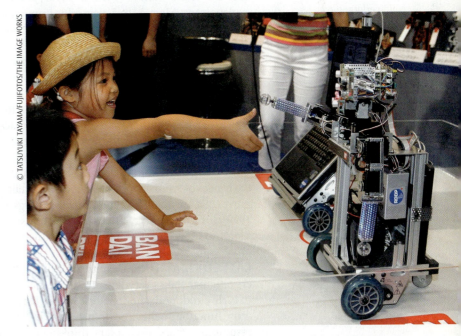

© TATSUYUKI TAYAMA/FUJIFOTOS/THE IMAGE WORKS

■ Most 3- to 5-year-olds have a well-developed understanding of the distinction between animate and inanimate. For example, they realize that a robot with lifelike features is really not alive and cannot eat or grow. But because of incomplete knowledge, they often claim that robots have perceptual and psychological capacities, such as seeing, thinking, and remembering. ■

3-year-olds and 4-year-olds think that violations of physical laws (walking through a wall) require magic more than violations of social conventions (taking a bath with shoes on) (Browne & Woolley, 2004). And they are more likely to say that a magical process—wishing—caused an event (an object to appear in a box) when a person made the wish before the event occurred, the event was consistent with the wish (the wished-for object rather than another object appeared in the box), and no alternative causes were apparent (Woolley, Browne, & Boerger, 2006). These features of causality are the same ones preschoolers rely on in ordinary situations.

Between ages 4 and 8, as children gain familiarity with physical events and principles, their magical beliefs decline. They figure out who is really behind Santa Claus and the Tooth Fairy, and they realize that the antics of magicians are due to trickery (Subbotsky, 2004). And increasingly, they say that events in fantastical stories couldn't really happen and that characters in such stories aren't real (Wooley & Cox, 2007). Still, because children entertain the possibility that something they imagine might materialize, they may react with anxiety to scary stories, TV shows, and nightmares. In one study, researchers had 4- to 6-year-olds imagine that a monster was inside one empty box and a puppy inside another. Almost all the children approached the "puppy" box, but many avoided putting their finger in the "monster" box, even though they knew that imagination cannot create reality (Harris et al., 1991).

Religion and culture play a role in how quickly children give up certain fantastic ideas. For example, Jewish children are more likely than their Christian agemates to express disbelief in Santa Claus and the Tooth Fairy. Having heard at home that Santa is imaginary, they seem to generalize this attitude to other magical figures (Woolley, 1997). And cultural myths about wishing—for example, the custom of making a wish before blowing out birthday candles—probably underlie the conviction of most 3- to 6-year-olds that by wishing, you can sometimes make your desires come true (Woolley, 2000).

LOGICAL THOUGHT Many studies show that when preschoolers are given tasks that are simplified and made relevant to their everyday lives, they do not display the illogical characteristics that Piaget saw in the preoperational stage. For example, when a conservation-of-number task is scaled down to include only three items instead of six or seven, 3-year-olds perform well (Gelman, 1972). And when preschoolers are asked carefully worded questions about what happens to substances (such as sugar) after they are dissolved in water, they give accurate explanations. Most 3- to 5-year-olds know that the substance is conserved—that it continues to exist, can be tasted, and makes the liquid heavier, even though it is invisible in the water (Au, Sidle, & Rollins, 1993; Rosen & Rozin, 1993).

Preschoolers' ability to reason about transformations is evident on other problems. They can engage in impressive *reasoning by analogy* about physical changes. When presented with the picture-matching problem "Play dough is to cut-up play dough as apple is to . . . ?," even 3-year-olds choose the correct answer (a cut-up apple) from a set of alternatives, several of which (a bitten apple, a cut-up loaf of bread) share physical features with the right choice (Goswami, 1996). These findings indicate that in familiar contexts, preschoolers can overcome appearances and think logically about cause and effect.

Finally, even without detailed biological or mechanical knowledge, preschoolers realize that the insides of animals are responsible for certain cause–effect sequences (such as willing oneself to move) that are impossible for nonliving things, such as machines (Gelman, 2003; Keil & Lockhart, 1999). Preschoolers seem to use illogical reasoning only when they must grapple with unfamiliar topics, too much information, or contradictory facts that they cannot reconcile (Ruffman, 1999).

CATEGORIZATION Despite their difficulty with Piagetian class inclusion tasks, preschoolers organize their everyday knowledge into nested categories at an early age. By the beginning of early childhood, children's categories include objects that go together because of their common function, behavior, or natural kind (animate versus inanimate), challenging Piaget's assumption that preschoolers' thinking is wholly governed by appearances.

Indeed, 2- to 5-year-olds readily draw appropriate inferences about nonobservable characteristics shared by category members. For example, after being told that a bird has warm blood and that a stegosaurus (dinosaur) has cold blood, preschoolers infer that a pterodactyl (labeled a dinosaur) has cold blood, even though it closely resembles a bird (Gopnik & Nazzi, 2003).

LOOK AND LISTEN

Try the conservation of number and mass tasks in Figure 9.2 with a 3- or 4-year-old. Next, simplify conservation of number by reducing the number of pennies, and relate conservation of mass to the child's experience by pretending the clay is baking dough and transforming it into cupcakes. Did the child perform more competently?

And when shown a set of three characters—two of whom look different but share an inner trait ("outgoing") and two of whom look similar but have different inner traits (one "shy," one "outgoing")—preschoolers rely on the trait category, not physical appearance, to predict similar preferred activities (Heyman & Gelman, 2000).

During the second and third years, and perhaps earlier, children's categories differentiate. They form many *basic-level categories*—ones at an intermediate level of generality, such as "chairs," "tables," and "beds." By the third year, children easily move back and forth between basic-level categories and *general categories,* such as "furniture." And they break down the basic-level categories into *subcategories,* such as "rocking chairs" and "desk chairs." In fact, a case study of a highly verbal toddler with a strong interest in birds revealed that by age 2, he had constructed a hierarchical understanding of the bird domain that included such basic-level categories and sub-categories as "waterbirds" ("ducks" and "swans"),

■ Preschoolers form many categories based on nonobservable characteristics. These 4-year-olds clearly understand which of a wide array of animals are prone to fight. ■

"landbirds" ("roosters" and "turkeys"), and "other birds" ("bluebirds," "cardinals," and "seagulls") (Mervis, Pani, & Pani, 2003). The boy's category structure was not quite the same as that of many adults, but it was, indeed, hierarchical. And he used that knowledge to make many correct inferences about category membership—for example, that baby birds and their parents must be members of the same species (both "robins") even though they look strikingly different.

Preschoolers' rapidly expanding vocabularies and general knowledge support their impressive skill at categorizing (Gelman & Koenig, 2003). As they learn more about their world, they devise theories about underlying characteristics that category members share, which help them identify new instances (Gelman & Kalish, 2006; Gelman & Koenig, 2003). For example, they realize that animals have an inborn potential for certain physical characteristics and behaviors that determine their identity. In categorizing, they look for causal links among these features. In one study, researchers invented two categories of animals—one with horns, armor, and a spiky tail; the other with wings, large ears, long toes, and a monkeylike tail (see Figure 9.4). Four-year-olds who were given a theory that identified an inner cause for the coexistence of the animals' features—animals in the first category "like to fight"; those in the second category "like to hide in trees"—easily classified new examples of animals. But 4-year-olds for whom animal features were merely pointed out or who were given a separate function for each feature could not remember the categories (Krascum & Andrews, 1998).

Finally, adult–child conversations are major sources of categorical learning. Adults frequently label and explain categories to young children. When they use the word *bird* for hummingbirds, turkeys, and swans, they signal to children that something other than physical

FIGURE 9.4

Categories of imaginary animals shown to preschoolers. When an adult provided a theory about the coexistence of animals' features—"likes to fight" and "likes to hide in trees"—4-year-olds easily classified new examples of animals with only one or two features. Without the theory, preschoolers could not remember the categories. Theories about underlying characteristics support the formation of many categories in early childhood. *(From R. M. Krascum & S. Andrews, 1998, "The Effects of Theories on Children's Acquisition of Family-Resemblance Categories," Child Development, 69, p. 336. © The Society for Research in Child Development, Inc. Reprinted by permission.)*

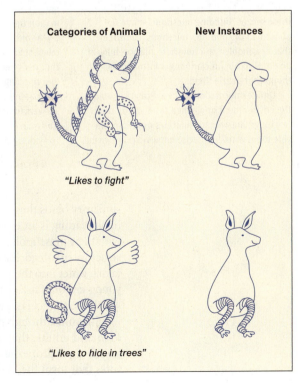

Categories of Animals   New Instances

"Likes to fight"

"Likes to hide in trees"

SOCIAL ISSUES: EDUCATION

Children's Questions: Catalyst for Cognitive Development

"Dad, what's that?" asked 4-year-old Emily as her father chopped vegetables for dinner.

"It's an onion," her father said.

"Is an onion a fruit?" Emily asked.

"It's a vegetable," her father replied. "A root vegetable because it grows underground."

Emily wrinkled her nose. "Why does it smell yucky?"

"I don't know," her father admitted. "But after dinner we can look it up online and find out."

When young children converse with adults, they ask, on average, more than one question per minute! Do inquisitive children like Emily really want answers to their many questions? Or are they—as their parents sometimes conclude—merely clamoring for attention?

An analysis of diaries that parents diverse in SES and ethnicity kept of their children's questions and of audio recordings of parent–child interactions revealed that at every age between 1 and 5 years, 70 to 90 percent of children's questions were information-seeking ("What's that [pointing to a crawfish]?") as opposed to non-information-seeking ("Can I have a cookie?") (Chouinard, 2007). And from age 2 on, children increasingly built on their fact-oriented questions with follow-up questions that asked for causes and explanations ("What do crawfish eat?" "Why does it have claws?"). By age 3½, these sets of "building questions" made up about half of children's questions, confirming that preschoolers ask questions purposefully, in an effort to obtain clarifying information about things that puzzle them.

Unlike information gathered casually from the environment or gleaned from adults' direct teachings, answers to children's questions provide them with the precise knowledge they need

at the precise moment they need it. Even before children can talk, they ask questions by gesturing at objects in their environment. A pointing gesture, for example, might lead a parent to say, "That's a ball. See, it bounces!" And the content of children's questions is related to their cognitive development. At a time when vocabulary is advancing rapidly, about 60 percent of 1½- to 2-year-olds' questions ask for names of objects. With age, preschoolers increasingly ask about function ("What's it do?"), activity ("What's he doing?"), state ("Is she hungry?"), and theory of mind ("How does the pilot *know* where to fly?").

Context also makes a difference. Compared with everyday situations, a visit to a zoo elicits many more questions about biological information from 2- to 4-year-olds: "Why is the lion sleeping?" "Is he dead?" "What do bats eat?" "Will the baby lion grow bigger?" Biological questions calling for explanations increased with age as 3- and 4-year-olds tried to make sense of such processes as growth, life, illness, and death—concepts they are currently grappling with and that will soon advance (see page 426 in Chapter 11).

The usefulness of children's questions depends on adults' answers. Most of the time, parents respond informatively. If they do not, preschoolers are amazingly persistent: They ask again until they get the information they wanted. Especially for 1- and 2-year-olds, parents often include additional relevant knowledge aimed at enhancing children's understanding and guiding further thinking. An earlier study also revealed that parents adjust the complexity of their answers to fit their children's maturity (Callanan & Oakes, 1992). To a question like "Why does the light come on?" 3-year-olds

typically get simpler, "prior cause" explanations ("I turned on the switch"). Slightly older children frequently get "mechanism" explanations ("The switch allows electricity to reach the light bulb").

Clearly, asking questions is a major means through which children expand their knowledge and reorganize their conceptual structures as they strive to attain adultlike understandings. Children's questions offer parents and teachers a fascinating window into their factual and conceptual knowledge, along with a wealth of opportunities to help them learn.

© BOB DAEMMRICH/PHOTOEDIT

■ A high percentage of preschoolers' questions are purposeful efforts to understand things that puzzle them. Adults' answers provide the precise knowledge children need at the precise moment they need it, making question-asking a powerful source of cognitive development. ■

---

similarity binds these instances together (Gelman, 2003, 2006; Gelman & Kalish, 2006). Picturebook reading is an especially rich context for understanding categories. While looking at books with their preschoolers, parents provide information that guides children's inferences about the structure of categories: "Penguins live at the South Pole, swim, and catch fish" or "Fish breathe by taking water into their mouths." Furthermore, as the Social Issues: Education box above indicates, young children ask many questions about their world and generally get informative answers, which are particularly well-suited to advancing their conceptual understanding.

In sum, although preschoolers' category systems are less complex than those of older children and adults, they already have the capacity to classify hierarchically and on the basis of nonobvious properties. And they use logical, causal reasoning to identify the interrelated features that form the basis of a category and to classify new members.

APPEARANCE VERSUS REALITY As we have seen, when presented with familiar situations and simplified problems, preschoolers show remarkably advanced reasoning—including the capacity to overcome perceptual appearances. But what happens when preschoolers encounter objects that have two identities—an apparent one and a real one? Can they distinguish appearance from reality? In a series of studies, John Flavell and his colleagues presented children with objects that were disguised in various ways and asked what each "looks like" and what each "is really and truly." Preschoolers had difficulty. For example, when asked whether a candle that looks like a crayon "is really and truly" a crayon or whether a stone painted to look like an egg "is really and truly" an egg, they often responded, "Yes!" Not until age 6 or 7 did children do well on these tasks (Flavell, Green, & Flavell, 1987).

Younger children's poor performance, however, is not due to a general difficulty in distinguishing appearance from reality, as Piaget suggested. Rather, they have trouble with the language of these tasks (Deák, Ray, & Brenneman, 2003). When permitted to solve appearance–reality problems nonverbally, by selecting from an array of objects the one that "really" has a particular identity, most 3-year-olds perform well (Sapp, Lee, & Muir, 2000).

These findings suggest that preschoolers begin to grasp the appearance–reality distinction sometime during the third year. Note how it involves an attainment we discussed earlier: *dual representation*—the realization that an object can be one thing (a candle) while symbolizing another (a crayon). At first, however, children's understanding is fragile. After putting on a Halloween mask, young preschoolers may be frightened when they see themselves in a mirror. Performing well on verbal appearance–reality tasks signifies a more secure understanding and is related to further progress in representational ability (Bialystok & Senman, 2004).

■ This 3-year-old has begun to grasp the distinction between appearance and reality—that this object, which looks like a pig, is really and truly a bank. Around age 6 to 7, his knowledge will be solid and secure. ■

Evaluation of the Preoperational Stage

Table 9.1 on page 328 provides an overview of the cognitive attainments of early childhood just considered. **TAKE A MOMENT...** Compare them with Piaget's description of the preoperational child on pages 321–322. The evidence as a whole indicates that Piaget was partly wrong and partly right about young children's cognitive capacities. When given simplified tasks based on familiar experiences, preschoolers show the beginnings of logical thinking. How can we make sense of the contradictions between Piaget's conclusions and the findings of recent research?

That preschoolers have some logical understandings that strengthen with age indicates that they attain logical operations gradually. Over time, children rely on increasingly effective mental (as opposed to perceptual) approaches to solving problems. For example, children who cannot use counting to compare two sets of items do not conserve number. Rather, they rely on perceptual cues to compare the amounts in two sets of items (Rouselle, Palmers, & Noël, 2004; Sophian, 1995). Once preschoolers can count, they apply this skill to conservation-of-number tasks involving just a few items. As counting improves, they extend the strategy to problems with more items. By age 6, they understand that number remains the same after a transformation in the length and spacing of a set of items as long as nothing is added or taken away (Halford & Andrews, 2006). Consequently, they no longer need to count to verify their answer.

Evidence that preschool children can be trained to perform well on Piagetian problems also supports the idea that operational thought is not absent at one point in time and present at another (Ping & Goldin-Meadow, 2008; Siegler & Svetina, 2006). Children who possess some understanding would naturally benefit from training, unlike those with no understanding at all. The gradual development of logical operations poses a serious challenge to Piaget's assumption of abrupt change toward logical reasoning around age 6 or 7. Does a preoperational stage really exist? Some no longer think so. Recall from Chapter 6 that according to the

TABLE 9.1	Some Cognitive Attainments of Early Childhood

APPROXIMATE AGE	COGNITIVE ATTAINMENTS
2–4 years © ELLEN B. SENISJ/THE IMAGE WORKS	Shows a dramatic increase in representational activity, as reflected in the development of language, make-believe play, understanding of dual representation, and categorization
	Takes the perspective of others in simplified, familiar situations and in everyday, face-to-face communication
	Distinguishes animate beings from inanimate objects; denies that magic can alter everyday experiences
	Grasps conservation, notices transformations, reverses thinking, and understands many cause-and-effect relationships in familiar contexts
	Categorizes objects on the basis of common function, behavior, and natural kind. Devises ideas about underlying characteristics that category members share and uses inner causal features to categorize objects varying widely in external appearance.
	Sorts familiar objects into hierarchically organized categories
	Distinguishes appearance from reality
4–7 years © STEVE STARR/CORBIS	Becomes increasingly aware that make-believe (and other thought processes) are representational activities
	Replaces magical beliefs about fairies, goblins, and events that violate expectations with plausible explanations
	Solves verbal appearance–reality problems, signifying a more secure understanding

information-processing perspective, children work out their understanding of each type of task separately, and their thought processes are basically the same at all ages—just present to a greater or lesser extent.

Other experts think that the stage concept is still valid, with modifications. For example, some *neo-Piagetian theorists* combine Piaget's stage approach with the information-processing emphasis on task-specific change (Case, 1998; Halford & Andrews, 2006). They believe that Piaget's strict stage definition must be transformed into a less tightly knit concept, one in which a related set of competencies develops over an extended period, depending on brain development and specific experiences. These investigators point to findings indicating that as long as the complexity of tasks and children's exposure to them are carefully controlled, children approach those tasks in similar, stage-consistent ways (Andrews & Halford, 2002; Case & Okamoto, 1996). For example, in drawing pictures, preschoolers depict objects separately, ignoring their spatial arrangement (return to the drawing on page 310 in Chapter 8 for an example). In understanding stories, they grasp a single story line but have trouble with a main plot plus one or more subplots.

This flexible stage notion recognizes the unique qualities of early childhood thinking. At the same time, it provides a better account of why, as Leslie put it, "Preschoolers' minds are such a blend of logic, fantasy, and faulty reasoning."

Piaget and Education

Three educational principles derived from Piaget's theory continue to influence teacher training and classroom practices, especially during early childhood:

- *Discovery learning.* In a Piagetian classroom, children are encouraged to discover for themselves through spontaneous interaction with the environment. Instead of presenting ready-made knowledge verbally, teachers provide a rich variety of activities designed to promote exploration and discovery, including art, puzzles, table games, dress-up clothing, building blocks, books, measuring tools, and musical instruments.

■ *Sensitivity to children's readiness to learn.* In a Piagetian classroom, teachers introduce activities that build on children's current thinking, challenging their incorrect ways of viewing the world. But they do not try to speed up development by imposing new skills before children indicate they are interested and ready.

■ *Acceptance of individual differences.* Piaget's theory assumes that all children go through the same sequence of development, but at different rates. Therefore, teachers must plan activities for individual children and small groups, not just for the whole class. In addition, teachers evaluate each child's educational progress in relation to the child's previous development, rather than on the basis of normative standards, or average performance of same-age peers.

Like his stages, educational applications of Piaget's theory have met with criticism. Perhaps the greatest challenge has to do with his insistence that young children learn primarily through acting on the environment (Brainerd, 2003). As we have already seen, children also use language-based routes to knowledge—a point emphasized by Vygotsky's sociocultural theory, to which we now turn. Nevertheless, Piaget's influence on education has been powerful. He gave teachers new ways to observe, understand, and enhance young children's development and offered strong theoretical justification for child-oriented approaches to classroom teaching and learning.

ASK YOURSELF

◆ **REVIEW** Select two of the following features of preoperational thought: egocentrism, a focus on perceptual appearances, difficulty reasoning about transformations, and lack of hierarchical classification. Present evidence indicating that preschoolers are more capable thinkers than Piaget assumed.

◆ **APPLY** Three-year-old Will understands that his tricycle isn't alive and can't feel or move on its own. But at the beach, while watching the sun dip below the horizon, Will exclaimed, "The sun is tired. It's going to sleep!" What explains this apparent contradiction in Will's reasoning?

◆ **CONNECT** Make-believe play promotes both cognitive and social development (see page 319). Explain why this is so.

◆ **REFLECT** Did you have an imaginary companion as a young child? If so, what was your companion like, and why did you create it? Were your parents aware of your companion? What was their attitude toward it?

Vygotsky's Sociocultural Theory

Piaget's deemphasis on language as a source of cognitive development brought on yet another challenge, this time from Vygotsky's sociocultural theory, which stresses the social context of cognitive development. In Vygotsky's view, the child and the social environment collaborate to mold cognition in culturally adaptive ways. During early childhood, rapid growth of language broadens preschoolers' participation in social dialogues with more knowledgeable individuals, who encourage them to master culturally important tasks. Soon children start to communicate with themselves in much the same way they converse with others. This greatly enhances the complexity of their thinking and their ability to control their own behavior. Let's see how this happens.

Private Speech

TAKE A MOMENT... Watch preschoolers as they play and explore the environment, and you will see that they frequently talk out loud to themselves. For example, as Sammy worked a puzzle, he said, "Where's the red piece? I need the red one. Now, a blue one. No, it doesn't fit. Try it here."

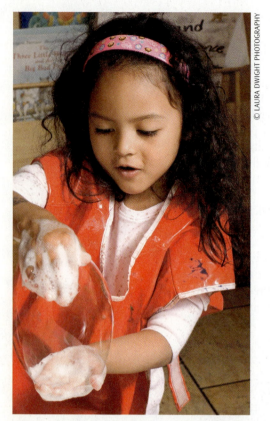

© LAURA DWIGHT PHOTOGRAPHY

■ A preschooler explores the possibilities in a handful of soap bubbles with the aid of private speech. Research supports Vygotsky's theory that children use private speech to guide their own thinking and behavior. ■

Piaget (1923/1926) called these utterances *egocentric speech*, reflecting his belief that young children have difficulty taking the perspectives of others. Their talk, he said, is often "talk for self" in which they express thoughts in whatever form they happen to occur, regardless of whether a listener can understand. Piaget believed that cognitive development and certain social experiences eventually bring an end to egocentric speech. Specifically, through disagreements with peers, children see that others hold viewpoints different from their own. As a result, egocentric speech declines in favor of social speech, in which children adapt what they say to their listeners.

Vygotsky (1934/1987) disagreed strongly with Piaget's conclusions. Because language helps children think about their mental activities and behavior and select courses of action, Vygotsky viewed it as the foundation for all higher cognitive processes, including controlled attention, deliberate memorization and recall, categorization, planning, problem solving, and self-reflection. In Vygotsky's view, children speak to themselves for self-guidance. As they get older and find tasks easier, their self-directed speech is internalized as silent, *inner speech*—the internal verbal dialogues we carry on while thinking and acting in everyday situations.

Over the past three decades, almost all studies have supported Vygotsky's perspective (Berk & Harris, 2003; Winsler, 2009). As a result, children's self-directed speech is now called **private speech** instead of egocentric speech. Research shows that children use more of it when tasks are appropriately challenging—neither too easy nor too hard but within their *zone of proximal development*, or range of mastery (see page 224 in Chapter 6). For example, Figure 9.5 shows how 5- and 6-year-olds' private speech increased as researchers made a problem-solving task moderately difficult, then decreased as the task became very difficult (Fernyhough & Fradley, 2005).

With age, as Vygotsky predicted, private speech goes underground, changing into whispers and silent lip movements. Furthermore, children who freely use private speech during a challenging activity are more attentive and involved and show better task performance than their less talkative agemates (Al-Namlah, Fernyhough, & Meins, 2006; Fernyhough & Fradley, 2005; Winsler, Naglieri, & Manfra, 2006).

Finally, compared with their agemates, children with learning and behavior problems engage in private speech over a longer period of development (Berk, 2001b; Ostad & Sorensen, 2007; Paladino, 2006; Winsler et al., 2007). They seem to use private speech to help compensate for impairments in attention and cognitive processing that make many tasks more difficult for them.

Social Origins of Early Childhood Cognition

Where does private speech come from? Recall from Chapter 6 that Vygotsky believed children's learning takes place within the *zone of proximal development*—a range of tasks too difficult for the child to do alone but possible with the help of others. Consider the joint activity of Sammy and his mother, who helps him put together a difficult puzzle:

Sammy: I can't get this one in. [*Tries to insert a piece in the wrong place.*]

Mother: Which piece might go down here? [*Points to the bottom of the puzzle.*]

Sammy: His shoes. [*Looks for a piece resembling the clown's shoes but tries the wrong one.*]

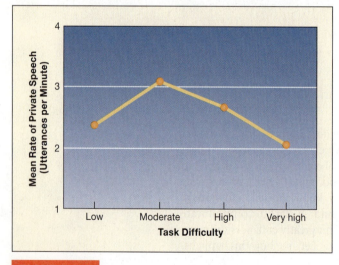

FIGURE 9.5

Relationship of private speech to task difficulty among 5- and 6-year-olds. Researchers increased the difficulty of a problem-solving task. Private speech rose as the task became moderately difficult, then declined as it became highly difficult. Children are more likely to use private speech for self-guidance when tasks are within their zone of proximal development, or range of mastery. *(Adapted from Fernyhough & Fradley, 2005.)*

Mother: Well, what piece looks like this shape? [*Pointing again to the bottom of the puzzle.*]

Sammy: The brown one. [*Tries it, and it fits; then attempts another piece and looks at his mother.*]

Mother: Try turning it just a little. [*Gestures to show him.*]

Sammy: There! [*Puts in several more pieces while his mother watches.*]

Sammy's mother keeps the puzzle within his zone of proximal development, at a manageable level of difficulty, by questioning, prompting, and suggesting strategies.

EFFECTIVE SOCIAL INTERACTION To promote cognitive development, social interaction must have two vital features. The first is **intersubjectivity,** the process by which two participants who begin a task with different understandings arrive at a shared understanding (Newson & Newson, 1975). Intersubjectivity creates a common ground for communication, as each partner adjusts to the other's perspective. Adults try to promote it when they translate their own insights in ways that are within the child's grasp. As the child stretches to understand the adult, she is drawn into a more mature approach to the situation (Rogoff, 1998).

The capacity for intersubjectivity is present early, in parent–infant mutual gaze, exchange of emotional signals, and imitation. Later, language facilitates it. As conversational skills improve, preschoolers increasingly seek others' help and direct that assistance to ensure that it is beneficial (Whitington & Ward, 1999). Between ages 3 and 5, children strive for intersubjectivity in dialogues with peers, as when they affirm a playmate's message, add new ideas, and make contributions to ongoing play to sustain it. They can also be heard saying, "I think [this way]. What do you think?"—evidence of a willingness to share viewpoints (Berk, 2001b). In these ways, children create zones of proximal development for one another.

A second important feature of social experience is **scaffolding**—adjusting the support offered during a teaching session to fit the child's current level of performance. When the child has little notion of how to proceed, the adult uses direct instruction, breaking the task into manageable units, suggesting strategies, and offering rationales for using them. As the child's competence increases, effective scaffolders—like Sammy's mother— gradually and sensitively withdraw support, turning over responsibility to the child. Then children take the language of these dialogues, make it part of their private speech, and use this speech to organize their independent efforts.

■ A grandfather engages in scaffolding by breaking a challenging construction task into manageable units, suggesting strategies, and gradually turning over responsibility to his 3-year-old grandchild. ■

Scaffolding captures the form of teaching interaction that occurs as children work on school or school-like tasks, such as puzzles, model building, picture matching, and (later) academic assignments. It may not apply to other contexts that are equally vital for cognitive development—for example, play or everyday activities, during which adults usually support children's efforts without deliberately teaching. To encompass children's diverse opportunities to learn through involvement with others, Barbara Rogoff (1998, 2003) suggests the term **guided participation,** a broader concept than scaffolding. It refers to shared endeavors between more expert and less expert participants, without specifying the precise features of communication. Consequently, it allows for variations across situations and cultures.

RESEARCH ON SOCIAL INTERACTION AND COGNITIVE DEVELOPMENT What evidence supports Vygotsky's ideas on the social origins of cognitive development? In previous chapters, we reviewed evidence indicating that when adults establish intersubjectivity by being stimulating, responsive, and supportive, they foster many competencies—attention, language, complex play, and understanding of others' perspectives. In several studies, children whose parents

LOOK AND LISTEN

Ask a preschooler to join you in working a difficult puzzle or other challenging task. How did you scaffold the child's progress? Did the child display any self-guiding private speech?

were effective scaffolders used more private speech, were more successful when attempting difficult tasks on their own, and were advanced in overall cognitive development (Berk & Spuhl, 1995; Conner & Cross, 2003; Mulvaney et al., 2006). Adult cognitive support—teaching in small steps and offering strategies—predicts children's mature thinking. And adult emotional support—offering encouragement and transferring responsibility to the child—predicts children's effort (Neitzel & Stright, 2003). The result is a winning combination for school success.

Other research shows that although young children benefit from working on tasks with same-age peers, their planning and problem solving improve more when their partner is either an "expert" peer (especially capable at the task) or an adult (Radziszewska & Rogoff, 1988). And peer disagreement (emphasized by Piaget) seems to be less important for cognitive development than the extent to which children achieve intersubjectivity—resolve differences of opinion and cooperate (Kobayashi, 1994; Tudge, 1992).

Vygotsky and Early Childhood Education

Both Piagetian and Vygotskian classrooms emphasize active participation and acceptance of individual differences. But a Vygotskian classroom goes beyond independent discovery to promote *assisted discovery*. Teachers guide children's learning with explanations, demonstrations, and verbal prompts, tailoring their interventions to each child's zone of proximal development. Assisted discovery is aided by *peer collaboration*, as children with varying abilities work in groups, teaching and helping one another.

Vygotsky (1935/1978) saw make-believe play as the ideal social context for fostering cognitive development in early childhood. As children create imaginary situations, they learn to follow internal ideas and social rules rather than their immediate impulses. For example, a child pretending to go to sleep follows the rules of bedtime behavior. A child imagining himself as a father and a doll as a child conforms to the rules of parental behavior. According to Vygotsky, make-believe play is a unique, broadly influential zone of proximal development in which children try out a wide variety of challenging activities and acquire many new competencies.

© ELLEN B. SENISI PHOTOGRAPHY

■ In this Vygotksy-inspired classroom, 4- and 5-year-olds benefit from peer collaboration. As they jointly make music, their conductor ensures that each player stays on beat. ■

Turn back to page 319 to review findings that make-believe play enhances a diverse array of cognitive and social skills. Pretending is also rich in private speech—a finding that supports its role in helping children bring action under the control of thought (Krafft & Berk, 1998). And preschoolers who spend more time engaged in sociodramatic play are better at taking personal responsibility for following classroom rules and at regulating emotion (Berk, Mann, & Ogan, 2006; Lemche et al., 2003). These findings support the role of make-believe in children's increasing self-control.

Evaluation of Vygotsky's Theory

In granting social experience a fundamental role in cognitive development, Vygotsky's theory underscores the vital role of teaching and helps us understand the wide cultural variation in children's cognitive skills. Nevertheless, it has not gone unchallenged. Verbal communication may not be the only means through which children's thinking develops—or even, in some cultures, the most important means. When Western parents scaffold their young children's mastery of challenging tasks, they assume much responsibility for children's motivation by frequently

CULTURAL INFLUENCES

Children in Village and Tribal Cultures Observe and Participate in Adult Work

*I*n Western societies, children are largely excluded from participating in adult work, which generally takes place outside the home. The role of equipping children with the skills they need to become competent workers is assigned to school. In early childhood, middle-SES parents' interactions with children dwell on preparing children to succeed in school through child-focused activities—especially adult–child conversations and play that enhance language, literacy, and other school-related knowledge. In village and tribal cultures, children receive little or no schooling, spend their days in contact with or participating in adult work, and start to assume mature responsibilities in early childhood (Rogoff et al., 2003). Consequently, parents have little need to rely on conversation and play to teach children.

A study comparing 2- and 3-year-olds' daily lives in four cultures—two U.S. middle-SES suburbs, the Efe hunters and gatherers of the Republic of Congo, and a Mayan agricultural town in Guatemala—documented these differences (Morelli, Rogoff, & Angelillo, 2003). In the U.S. communities, young children had little access to adult work and spent much time conversing and playing with adults. In contrast, the Efe and Mayan children rarely engaged in these child-focused activities. Instead, they spent their days close to—and frequently observing—adult work, which often took place in or near the Efe campsite or the Mayan family home.

An ethnography of a remote Mayan village in Yucatán, Mexico, shows that when young children are legitimate onlookers and participants in a daily life structured around adult work, their competencies differ from those of Western preschoolers (Gaskins, 1999; Gaskins, Haight, & Lancy, 2007). Yucatec Mayan adults are subsis-

tence farmers. Men tend cornfields, aided by sons age 8 and older. Women oversee the household and yard; they prepare meals, wash clothes, and care for the livestock and garden, assisted by daughters and by sons not yet old enough to work in the fields. Children join in these activities from the second year on. When not participating, they are expected to be self-sufficient. Young children make many nonwork decisions for themselves—how much to sleep and eat, what to wear, when to take their daily bath, and even when to start school. As a result, Yucatec Mayan preschoolers are highly competent at self-care. In contrast, their make-believe play is limited; when it occurs, they usually imitate adult work. Otherwise, they watch others—for hours each day.

Yucatec Mayan parents rarely converse or play with preschoolers or scaffold their learning. Rather, when children imitate adult tasks, parents conclude that they are ready for more responsibility. Then they assign chores, selecting tasks the child can do with little help so that adult work is not disturbed. If a child cannot do a task, the adult takes over and the child observes, reengaging when able to contribute.

Expected to be autonomous and helpful, Yucatec Mayan children seldom display attention-getting behaviors or ask others for something interesting to do. From an early age, they can sit quietly for long periods—through a long

religious service or a three-hour truck ride. And when an adult interrupts their activity and directs them to do a chore, they respond eagerly to a command that Western children frequently avoid or resent. By age 5, Yucatec Mayan children spontaneously take responsibility for tasks beyond those assigned.

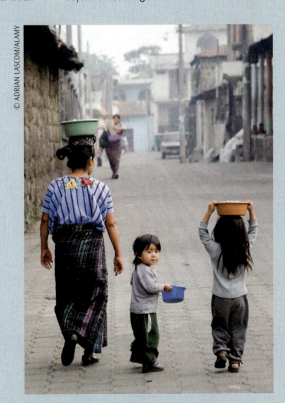

■ A Mayan 3-year-old imitates her mother in balancing a basin of water on her head, while her younger sibling prepares to attempt the skill. From an early age, children in Yucatec Mayan culture spend many hours observing adults and join in the work of their community. ■

instructing and conversing with the child. Their communication resembles the teaching that takes place in school, where their children will spend years preparing for adult life. But in cultures that place less emphasis on schooling and literacy, parents often expect children to take greater responsibility for acquiring new skills through keen observation and participation in community activities (Paradise & Rogoff, 2009; Rogoff, 2003). See the Cultural Influences box above for research illustrating this difference.

Vygotsky's theory has also been criticized for saying little about how basic motor, perceptual, attention, memory, and problem-solving skills, discussed in Chapters 5 and 6, contribute to socially transmitted higher cognitive processes. For example, his theory does not address how these elementary capacities spark changes in children's social experiences, from which more advanced cognition springs (Miller, 2009; Moll, 1994). Piaget paid far more attention than Vygotsky to the development of basic cognitive processes. It is intriguing to speculate about the broader theory that might exist today had Piaget and Vygotsky—the two twentieth-century giants of cognitive development—had a chance to meet and weave together their extraordinary accomplishments.

ASK YOURSELF

◆ **REVIEW** Describe features of social interaction that support children's cognitive development. How does such interaction create a zone of proximal development?

◆ **APPLY** Tanisha sees her 5-year-old son Toby talking aloud to himself as he plays. She wonders whether she should discourage this behavior. Use Vygotsky's theory to explain why Toby talks to himself. How would you advise Tanisha?

◆ **CONNECT** Explain how Piaget's and Vygotsky's theories complement each other. How would classroom practices inspired by these theories be similar? How would they differ?

◆ **REFLECT** When do you use private speech? Does it serve a self-guiding function for you, as it does for children? Explain.

Information Processing

Return to the model of information processing discussed on pages 217–218 in Chapter 6. Recall that information processing focuses on *mental strategies* that children use to transform stimuli flowing into their mental systems. During early childhood, advances in representation and in children's ability to guide their own behavior lead to more efficient and flexible ways of attending, manipulating information, and solving problems. Preschoolers also become more aware of their own mental life and begin to acquire academically relevant knowledge important for school success.

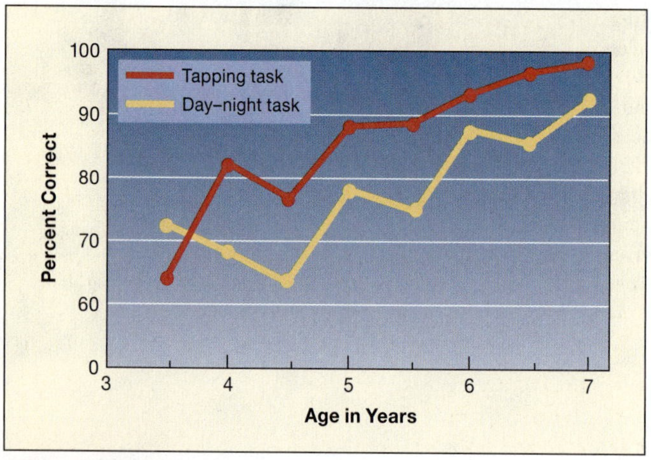

Attention

As parents and teachers know, preschoolers—compared with school-age children—spend shorter times involved in tasks and are more easily distracted. But recall from Chapter 5 that sustained attention improves in toddlerhood, a trend that continues during early childhood.

INHIBITION A major reason is a steady gain in children's ability to inhibit impulses and keep their mind on a competing goal. Consider a task in which the child must tap once when the adult taps twice and tap twice when the adult taps once, or must say "night" to a picture of the sun and "day" to a picture of the moon with stars. As Figure 9.6 shows, 3- and 4-year-olds make many errors. But by age 6 to 7, children find such tasks easy (Johnson, Im-Bolter, & Pascual-Leone, 2003; Kirkham, Cruess, & Diamond, 2003; Zelazo et al., 2003). They can resist the "pull" of their attention toward a dominant stimulus—a skill that, as early as age 3 to 5, predicts social maturity as well as subsequent reading and math achievement from kindergarten through high school (Blair & Razza, 2007; Duncan et al., 2007; Rhoades, Greenberg, & Domitrovich,

FIGURE 9.6

Gains between ages 3 and 7 in performance on tasks requiring children to inhibit an impulse and focus on a competing goal. In the tapping task, children had to tap once when the adult tapped twice and tap twice when the adult tapped once. In the day–night task, children had to say "night" to a picture of the sun and "day" to a picture of the moon with stars. *(From A. Diamond, 2004, "Normal Development of Prefrontal Cortex from Birth to Young Adulthood: Cognitive Functions, Anatomy, and Biochemistry," as appeared in D. T. Stuss & R. T. Knight, (Eds.),* Principles of Frontal Lobe Function, *New York: Oxford University Press, p. 474. Reprinted by permission of Adele Diamond.)*

2009). Simultaneously, ERP and fMRI measures reveal a steady age-related increase in activation of the prefrontal cortex while children engage in activities requiring suppression of inappropriate responses (Bartgis, Lilly, & Thomas, 2003; Luna et al., 2001).

The capacity to generate increasingly complex play goals (requiring concentration) and adult scaffolding of attention also contribute to development of attention (Ruff & Cappozoli, 2003). Preschoolers whose parents help them maintain a focus, by offering suggestions, questions, and comments about the child's current interest, are more mature, cognitively and socially, when reassessed a year or two later (Bono & Stifter, 2003; Landry et al., 2000).

High-quality preschool education also makes a difference. In *Tools of the Mind*—a preschool curriculum inspired by Vygotsky's theory—scaffolding of attention skills is woven into virtually all classroom activities. For example, teachers provide external aids to support attention: A child might hold a drawing of an ear as a reminder to listen and

■ In Tools of the Mind preschool classrooms, scaffolding of attention skills is woven into virtually all activities. Here, during "buddy reading," one child holds a drawing of an ear as a reminder to listen and not interrupt her classmate's storytelling. ■

refrain from interrupting a classmate who is telling a story. Teachers also lead games requiring frequent inhibition and memory for instructions. And they encourage make-believe play, which helps children follow rules and use thought to guide behavior (Bodrova & Leong, 2007).

When preschoolers from low-income families were randomly assigned to either Tools of the Mind or comparison classrooms, Tools children performed substantially better on end-of-year tasks assessing inhibition and other attentional capacities (Diamond et al., 2007). Nurturing attention through the Tools curriculum may prove powerful in early prevention of academic, emotional, and behavior problems. Many capacities, including language, exploration, problem solving, social interaction, and cooperation, benefit from an improved ability to concentrate.

PLANNING   During early childhood, children also become better at **planning**—thinking out a sequence of acts ahead of time and allocating attention accordingly to reach a goal. As long as tasks are familiar and not too complex, preschoolers can generate and follow a plan. For example, 4-year-olds can search for a lost object in a play area systematically if possible locations are few (McColgan & McCormack, 2008). But when asked to compare detailed pictures, preschoolers fail to search thoroughly. And on tasks with several steps, they often fail to decide what to do first and what to do next in an orderly fashion (Baughman & Cooper, 2006; Friedman & Scholnick, 1997; Kaller et al., 2008). They seem to have difficulty postponing action in favor of mapping out a sequence of moves and evaluating the consequences of each— procedures that require inhibition and increased working-memory capacity in addition to planning skill.

Children learn much from cultural tools that support planning—directions for playing games, patterns for construction, recipes for cooking—especially when they collaborate with more expert planners. When 4- to 7-year-olds were observed jointly constructing a toy with their mothers, the mothers provided basic information about the usefulness of plans and how to implement specific steps: "Do you want to look at the picture and see what goes where? What piece do you need first?" After working with their mothers, younger children more often referred to the plan when building on their own (Gauvain, 2004; Gauvain, de la Ossa, & Hurtado-Ortiz, 2001). When parents encourage planning in everyday activities, from loading the dishwasher to packing for a vacation, they help children plan more effectively.

Memory

Unlike infants and toddlers, preschoolers have the language skills to describe what they remember, and they can follow directions on simple memory tasks. As a result, memory becomes easier to study in early childhood.

RECOGNITION AND RECALL **TAKE A MOMENT...** Show a young child a set of 10 pictures or toys. Then mix them up with some unfamiliar items, and ask the child to point to the ones in the original set. You will find that preschoolers' *recognition* memory—ability to tell whether a stimulus is the same as or similar to one they have seen before—is remarkably good. It becomes even more accurate by the end of early childhood. In fact, 4- and 5-year-olds perform nearly perfectly.

Now keep the items out of view, and ask the child to name the ones she saw. This more demanding task requires *recall*—generating a mental image of an absent stimulus. Young children's recall is much poorer than their recognition. At age 2, they can recall no more than one or two items, at age 4 only about three or four (Perlmutter, 1984).

Of course, recognition is much easier than recall for adults as well, but in comparison to adults, children's recall is quite deficient. Better recall in early childhood is strongly associated with language development, which greatly enhances long-lasting representations of past experiences (Simcock & Hayne, 2003). But even preschoolers with good language skills recall poorly because they are not skilled at using **memory strategies,** deliberate mental activities that improve our chances of remembering. For example, to retain information, you may *rehearse,* repeating the items over and over, or *organize,* intentionally grouping items that are alike so that you can easily retrieve them by thinking of their similar characteristics.

Preschoolers do show the beginnings of memory strategies. When circumstances permit, they arrange items in space to aid their memories. In one study, an adult placed either an M&M or a wooden peg in each of 12 identical containers and handed them one by one to preschoolers, asking them to remember where the candy was hidden. By age 4, children put the candy containers in one place and the peg containers in another, a strategy that almost always led to perfect recall (DeLoache & Todd, 1988). But preschoolers do not yet rehearse or organize items (for example, all the vehicles together, all the animals together) to aid recall, even when they are trained to do so (Gathercole, Adams, & Hitch, 1994).

Why do young children seldom use memory strategies? One reason is that strategies tax their limited working memories. *Digit span* tasks, in which children try to repeat an adult-provided string of numbers, assess the capacity of working memory, which improves slowly, from an average of two digits at age 2½ to five digits at age 7 (Kail, 2003). With such limits, preschoolers have difficulty holding on to pieces of information while simultaneously applying a strategy.

MEMORY FOR EVERYDAY EXPERIENCES Think about the difference between your recall of listlike information and your memory for everyday experiences—what researchers call **episodic memory.** In remembering lists, you recall isolated bits, reproducing them exactly as you originally learned them. In remembering everyday experiences, you recall complex, meaningful information. Between 3 and 6 years, children improve sharply in memory for relations among stimuli. For example, in a set of photos, they remember not just the animals they saw but the contexts in which they saw them—a bear emerging from a tunnel, a zebra tied to a tree on a city street (Sluzenski, Newcombe, & Kovacs, 2006). The capacity to *bind together stimuli* when encoding and retrieving them supports the development of an increasingly rich event memory during early childhood.

Memory for Familiar Events. Like adults, preschoolers remember familiar, repeated events—what you do when you go to child care or have dinner—in terms of **scripts,** general descriptions of what occurs and when it occurs in a particular situation. Young children's scripts begin as a structure of main acts. For example, when asked to tell what happens at a restaurant, a 3-year-old might say, "You go in, get the food, eat, and then pay." Although children's first scripts contain only a few acts, as long as events in a situation take place in logical order, they are almost always recalled in correct sequence (Bauer, 2002, 2006). With age, scripts become more spontaneous and elaborate, as in this 5-year-old's account of going to a restaurant: "You go in. You can sit in a booth or at a table. Then you tell the waitress what you want. You eat. If you want dessert, you can have some. Then you pay and go home" (Hudson, Fivush, & Kuebli, 1992).

Scripts help children organize, interpret, and predict everyday experiences. Once formed, they can be used to predict what will happen on similar

■ Like adults, preschoolers remember everyday experiences, like brushing teeth, in terms of scripts—general descriptions of what occurs and when it occurs. Over time, children construct more elaborate scripts: "You squeeze out the toothpaste and brush your teeth. You rinse your mouth and then your toothbrush." ■

© ANDY SACKS/GETTY IMAGES/RISER

occasions in the future. Children rely on scripts to assist recall when listening to and telling stories. They also act out scripts in make-believe play as they pretend to put the baby to bed, go on a trip, or play school. And scripts support children's earliest efforts at planning by helping them represent sequences of actions that lead to desired goals (Hudson, Sosa, & Shapiro, 1997).

Memory for One-Time Events.   In Chapter 6, we considered a second type of episodic memory—*autobiographical memory,* or representations of personally meaningful, one-time events. As 3- to 6-year-olds' cognitive and conversational skills improve, their descriptions of special events become better organized in time, more detailed, enriched with a personal perspective, and related to the larger context of their lives (Fivush, 2001). A young preschooler simply reports, "I went camping." Older preschoolers include specifics: where and when the event happened and who was present. And with age, preschoolers increasingly include subjective information—why, for example, an event was exciting, funny, sad, or made them feel proud or embarrassed ("I loved sleeping all night in the tent!")—that explains the event's personal significance (Fivush, 2001).

Adults use two styles to elicit children's autobiographical narratives. In the *elaborative style,* they follow the child's lead, ask varied questions, add information to the child's statements, and volunteer their own recollections and evaluations of events. For example, after a field trip to the zoo, Leslie asked, "What was the first thing we did? Why weren't the parrots in their cages? I thought the roaring lion was scary. What did you think?" In this way, she helped the children reestablish and reorganize their memory of the field trip. In contrast, adults who use the *repetitive style* provide little information and keep repeating the same questions, regardless of the child's interest: "Do you remember the zoo? What did we do at the zoo? Which animals did you see at the zoo?"

Preschoolers who experience the elaborative style recall more information about past events and also produce more organized and detailed personal stories when followed up one to two years later (Cleveland & Reese, 2005; Farrant & Reese, 2000). Parents can be trained to use an elaborative style, which also enhances the richness of preschoolers' event memories (Reese & Newcombe, 2007).

As children converse with adults about the past, they not only improve their autobiographical memory but also create a shared history that strengthens close relationships and self-understanding. Parents and preschoolers with secure attachment bonds engage in more elaborate reminiscing (Bost et al., 2006; Reese, Newcombe, & Bird, 2006). And 5- and 6-year-olds of elaborative-style parents describe themselves in clearer, more consistent ways (Bird & Reese, 2006).

■ As she converses with her father about past experiences, this young child in Shanghai builds an autobiographical memory. Perhaps because Asian parents tend to discourage children from talking about themselves, Asian adults' autobiographical memories focus less on their own roles than on those of others. ■

Girls produce more organized and detailed narratives about past events than boys. And Western children typically include more comments about their own thoughts, emotions, and preferences than do Asian children. These differences fit with variations in parent–child conversations. Parents reminisce in more detail with daughters (Bruce, Dolan, & Phillips-Grant, 2000). And collectivist cultural values lead many Asian parents to discourage children from talking about themselves. Chinese parents, for example, engage in less detailed and evaluative past-event dialogues with their preschoolers (Fivush & Wang, 2005; Wang, 2006a). Consistent with these early experiences, women report an earlier age of first memory and more vivid early memories than men. And Western adults' autobiographical memories include earlier, more detailed events that focus more on their own roles than do the memories of Asians, who tend to highlight the roles of others (Wang, 2006b).

Problem Solving

How do preschoolers use their cognitive competencies to discover new problem-solving strategies? To find out, let's look in on 5-year-old Darryl as he adds marbles tucked into pairs of small bags that Leslie set out on a table.

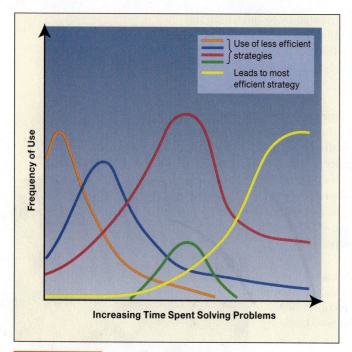

Overlapping-waves pattern of strategy use in problem solving. When given challenging problems, a child generates a variety of strategies, each represented by a wave. The waves overlap because the child tries several different strategies at the same time. Use of each strategy, depicted by the height of the wave, is constantly changing. As the child observes which strategies work best, which work less well, and which are ineffective, the one that results in the most rapid, accurate solutions wins out. *(From R. S. Siegler,* Emerging Minds: The Process of Change in Children's Thinking. *Copyright © 1996 by Oxford University Press, Inc. Used by permission of Oxford University Press, Inc.)*

As Darryl deals with adding each pair, his strategies vary. Sometimes he guesses, without applying any strategy. At other times, he counts from one on his fingers. For example, for bags containing 2 + 4 marbles, his fingers pop up one by one as he exclaims, "One, two, three, four, five, six!" On still other occasions, he starts with the lower digit, 2, and "counts on" ("two, three, four, five, six"). Or he begins with the higher digit, 4, and "counts on" ("four, five, six")—a strategy called *min* because it minimizes the work. Sometimes, he simply retrieves the answer from memory.

To study children's problem solving, Robert Siegler (1996, 2006) used the microgenetic research design (see Chapter 1, page 43), presenting children with many problems over an extended time. He found that children experiment with diverse strategies on many types of problems—basic math facts, numerical estimation, conservation, memory for lists of items, reading first words, spelling, even tic-tac-toe. And their strategy use follows the overlapping-waves pattern shown in Figure 9.7. According to **overlapping-waves theory,** when given challenging problems, children try out various strategies and observe which work best, which work less well, and which are ineffective. Gradually, they select strategies on the basis of two criteria: *accuracy* and *speed*—for basic addition, the *min* strategy. As children home in on effective strategies for solving the problems at hand, correct solutions become more strongly associated with problems, and children display the most efficient strategy—automatic retrieval of the answer.

How do children move from less to more efficient strategies? Often they discover a faster procedure by using a more time-consuming technique. For example, by repeatedly counting on fingers, Darryl began to recognize the number of fingers he held up (Siegler & Jenkins, 1989). Also, certain problems dramatize the need for a better strategy. When Darryl opened a pair of bags, one containing ten marbles and the other with only two, he realized that *min* would be best. Teaching children to reason logically with concepts relevant to the problems is also helpful (Alibali, Phillips, & Fischer, 2009; Siegler & Svetina, 2006). Once Darryl understood that he got the same result regardless of the order in which he combined two sets (3 + 6 = 9 and 6 + 3 = 9), he more often used *min* and arrived at correct answers. Finally, a large improvement in the accuracy of a newly discovered strategy over previous strategies generally leads to rapid adoption of the new approach (Siegler, 2006; Siegler & Booth, 2004).

Many factors, including practice, reasoning, tasks with new challenges, and adult assistance, contribute to improved problem solving. And experimenting with less mature strategies lets children see the limitations of those techniques. In sum, overlapping-waves theory emphasizes that trying many strategies is vital for developing new, more effective solution techniques. Even 2-year-olds use an overlapping-waves pattern to solve problems, such as how to use a tool to obtain an out-of-reach toy (Chen & Siegler, 2000). The pattern characterizes problem solving across a wide range of ages. And in the tradition of the information-processing approach, the theory views development as occurring gradually, rather than in discontinuous stages.

The Young Child's Theory of Mind

As representation of the world, memory, and problem solving improve, children start to reflect on their own thought processes. They begin to construct a *theory of mind,* or coherent set of ideas about mental activities. This understanding is also called **metacognition,** or "thinking about thought" (the prefix *meta-* means "beyond" or "higher"). As adults, we have a complex appreciation of our inner mental worlds, which we use to interpret our own and others' behavior and to improve our performance on various tasks. How early are children aware of their mental lives, and how complete and accurate is their knowledge?

AWARENESS OF MENTAL LIFE   At the end of the first year, babies view people as intentional beings who can share and influence one another's mental states, a milestone that opens the door to new forms of communication—joint attention, social referencing, preverbal gestures, and spoken language. These early milestones serve as the foundation for later mental understandings. In longitudinal research, 10-month-olds' ability to discern others' intentions predicted theory-of-mind competence at age 4 (Wellman et al., 2008).

As they approach age 2, children display a clearer grasp of others' emotions and desires, evident in their realization that people often differ from one another and from themselves in likes, dislikes, wants, needs, and wishes ("Mommy like broccoli. Daddy like carrots. I no like carrots."). As 2-year-olds' vocabularies expand, their first verbs include such words as *think, remember,* and *pretend* (Wellman, 2002).

By age 3, children realize that thinking takes place inside their heads and that a person can think about something without seeing, touching, or talking about it (Flavell, Green, & Flavell, 1995). But 2- to 3-year-olds' verbal responses indicate that they think people always behave in ways consistent with their *desires* and that they do not understand less obvious, more interpretive mental states, such as *beliefs,* also affect behavior.

Between ages 3 and 4, children use *think* and *know* to refer to their own and others' thoughts and beliefs (Wellman, 2002). And from age 4 on, they realize that both *beliefs* and *desires* determine behavior. Dramatic evidence for this advance comes from games that test whether preschoolers realize that *false beliefs*—ones that do not represent reality accurately—can guide people's behavior. **TAKE A MOMENT...** For example, show a child two small closed boxes—a familiar Band-Aid box and a plain, unmarked box (see Figure 9.8). Then say, "Pick the box you think has the Band-Aids in it." Children usually pick the marked container. Next, open the boxes and show the child that, contrary to her own belief, the marked one is empty, and the unmarked one contains the Band-Aids. Finally, introduce the child to a hand puppet and explain, "Here's Pam. She has a cut, see? Where do you think she'll look for Band-Aids? Why would she look in there? Before you looked inside, did you think that the plain box contained the Band-Aids? Why?" (Bartsch & Wellman, 1995). Only a handful of 3-year-olds can explain Pam's—and their own—false beliefs, but many 4-year-olds can.

Some researchers claim that the procedures just described, which require verbal responses, grossly underestimate younger children's ability to attribute false beliefs to others. Relying on the violation-of-expectation method (which depends on looking behavior), these investigators assert that children comprehend others' false beliefs by age 15 months (Baillargeon, Scott, & He, 2010). But like other violation-of-expectation evidence, this conclusion is controversial (see page 208 in Chapter 6) (Ruffman & Perner, 2005; Sirios & Jackson, 2007). In another study using an active behavioral measure (helping), most 18-month-olds—after witnessing an object moved from one box to another while an adult was not looking—helped the adult, when he tried to open the original box, locate the object in the new box (Buttelmann, Carpenter, & Tomasello, 2009). Still, much more evidence is needed to confirm that toddlers implicitly grasp mental states as complex as false belief (Poulin-Dubois, Brooker, & Chow, 2009).

FIGURE 9.8

Example of a false-belief task. (a) An adult shows a child the contents of a Band-Aid box and of an unmarked box. The Band-Aids are in the unmarked container. (b) The adult introduces the child to a hand puppet named Pam and asks the child to predict where Pam would look for the Band-Aids and to explain Pam's behavior. The task reveals whether children understand that without having seen that the Band-Aids are in the unmarked container, Pam will hold a false belief.

(a)   (b)

Among children of diverse cultural and SES backgrounds, false-belief understanding assessed in verbal tasks strengthens after age 3½, becoming more secure between ages 4 and 6 (Amsterlaw & Wellman, 2006; Callaghan et al., 2005; Flynn, 2006). During that time, it becomes a powerful tool for reflecting on the thoughts and emotions of oneself and others and a good predictor of social skills (Harwood & Farrar, 2006; Watson et al., 1999). Understanding of false belief also is also associated with early reading ability, probably because it helps children comprehend story narratives (Astington & Pelletier, 2005). To follow a story line, children generally must link plot actions with characters' motives and beliefs.

FACTORS CONTRIBUTING TO PRESCHOOLERS' THEORY OF MIND How do children develop a theory of mind at such a young age? Language, cognitive abilities, make-believe play, and social interaction all contribute.

Language and Verbal Reasoning. The prefrontal cortex seems to play a crucial role in theory-of-mind development. ERP brain-wave recordings obtained while 4- to 6-year-olds reasoned about others' beliefs revealed that children who pass false-belief tasks (as opposed to those who fail) display a pattern of activity in the left prefrontal cortex similar to that of adults engaged in the same tasks (Liu et al., 2009). This left-prefrontal ERP pattern typically appears when adults reason verbally about mental concepts.

Indeed, understanding the mind requires the ability to reflect on thoughts, which is greatly aided by language. Many studies indicate that language ability strongly predicts preschoolers' grasp of false belief (Milligan, Astington, & Dack, 2007). Children who spontaneously use, or who are trained to use, complex sentences with mental-state words are especially likely to pass false-belief tasks (de Villiers & de Villiers, 2000; Hale & Tager-Flusberg, 2003). The Quechua people of the Peruvian highlands refer to mental states such as "think" and "believe" indirectly, because their language lacks mental-state terms. Quechua children have difficulty with false-belief tasks for years after children in industrialized nations have mastered them (Vinden, 1996). In contrast, Chinese languages have verb markers that can label the word *believe* as decidedly false. When adults use those markers in false-belief tasks, Chinese preschoolers perform better (Tardif, Wellman, & Cheung, 2004).

Cognitive Abilities. The ability to inhibit inappropriate responses, think flexibly, and plan fosters mastery of false belief (Hughes, 1998; Sabbagh et al., 2006). Gains in inhibition are strongly related to mastery of false belief, perhaps because to do well on false-belief tasks, children must suppress an irrelevant response—the tendency to assume that others' knowledge and beliefs are the same as their own (Birch & Bloom, 2003; Carlson, Moses, & Claxton, 2004).

Make-Believe Play. Make-believe offers a rich context for thinking about the mind. As children act out roles, they often express the thoughts and emotions of the characters they portray and then reason about their implications (Kavanaugh, 2006b). These experiences may increase children's awareness that belief influences behavior. In support of this idea, preschoolers who engage in extensive fantasy play or who have imaginary companions—and, thus, are deeply absorbed in creating make-believe characters—are advanced in understanding false belief and other aspects of the mind (Astington & Jenkins, 1995; Lalonde & Chandler, 1995). And the better 3- and 4-year-olds can reason about situations that contradict a real-world state of affairs, the more likely they are to pass false-belief tasks (Riggs & Peterson, 2000).

Social Interaction. Social experience also promotes understanding of the mind. In longitudinal research, mothers of securely attached babies were more likely to comment appropriately on their infants' mental states: "Do you *remember* Grandma?" "You really *like* that swing!" These mothers continued to describe their children, when they reached preschool age, in terms of mental characteristics: "She's got *a mind of her own!*" This maternal "mind-mindedness" was positively associated with later performance on false-belief and other theory-of-mind tasks (Meins et al., 1998, 2003; Ruffman et al., 2006). As we saw earlier, secure attachment is related to more elaborative parent–child narratives, which often include discussions of mental states—conversations that expose preschoolers to concepts and language that help them think about their own and others' mental lives (Ontai & Thompson, 2008; Taumoepeau & Ruffman, 2006).

Also, preschoolers with siblings who are children (but not infants)—especially older siblings or two or more siblings—tend to be more aware of false belief because they experience more family talk about others' perspectives (Jenkins et al., 2003; McAlister & Peterson, 2006, 2007). Similarly, preschool friends who often engage in mental-state talk are ahead in false-belief understanding (de Rosnay & Hughes, 2006). Interacting with more mature members of society contributes, too. In a study of Greek preschoolers, daily contact with many adults and older children predicted mastery of false belief (Lewis et al., 1996). All these encounters offer extra opportunities to observe different viewpoints and talk about inner states.

Core knowledge theorists (see Chapter 6, page 214) believe that to profit from the social experiences just described, children must be biologically prepared to develop a theory of mind. They claim that children with *autism,* for whom mastery of false belief is either greatly delayed or absent, are deficient in the brain mechanism that enables humans to detect mental states. See the Biology and Environment box on page 342 to find out more about the biological basis of reasoning about the mind.

■ Interaction with siblings, especially older siblings, contributes to preschoolers' awareness of others' perspectives and, therefore, promotes understanding of false belief. ■

LIMITATIONS OF THE YOUNG CHILD'S THEORY OF MIND   Though surprisingly advanced, preschoolers' awareness of mental activities is far from complete. For example, 3- and 4-year-olds are unaware that people continue to think while they wait, look at pictures, listen to stories, or read books—that is, when there are no obvious cues that they are thinking. Preschoolers also do not realize that when two people view the same object, their trains of thought will differ because of variations in their knowledge and other characteristics (Eisbach, 2004; Flavell, Green, & Flavell, 1993, 1995; Flavell et al., 1997).

A major reason for these findings is that children younger than age 5 pay little attention to the *process* of thinking. When asked about subtle distinctions between mental states, such as *know* and *forget,* they express confusion (Lyon & Flavell, 1994). And they often say they have always known information they just learned (Taylor, Esbenson, & Bennett, 1994). Finally, they believe that all events must be directly observed to be known. They do not understand that *mental inferences* can be a source of knowledge (Miller, Hardin, & Montgomery, 2003).

These findings suggest that preschoolers view the mind as a passive container of information. Consequently, they greatly underestimate the amount of mental activity that people engage in and are poor at inferring what people know or are thinking about (Flavell, 2000; Wellman, 2002). In contrast, older children view the mind as an active, constructive agent that selects and interprets information—a change we will consider in Chapter 12.

Early Literacy and Mathematical Development

Researchers have begun to study how children's information-processing capacities affect the development of basic reading, writing, and mathematical skills that prepare them for school. The study of how preschoolers start to master these complex activities gives us additional information about their cognitive strengths and limitations—knowledge we can use to foster early literacy and mathematical development.

LITERACY   One week, Leslie's students created a make-believe grocery store. They brought empty food boxes from home, placed them on shelves in the classroom, labeled items with prices, made shopping lists, and wrote checks at the cash register. A sign at the entrance announced the daily specials: "APLS BNS 5¢" ("apples bananas 5¢").

As such play reveals, preschoolers understand a great deal about written language long before they learn to read or write in conventional ways. This is not surprising: Children in industrialized nations live in a world filled with written symbols. Each day, they observe

BIOLOGY AND ENVIRONMENT

"Mindblindness" and Autism

Michael stood at the water table in Leslie's classroom, repeatedly filling a plastic cup and dumping out its contents—dip-splash, dip-splash—until Leslie came over and redirected his actions. Without looking at Leslie's face, Michael moved to a new repetitive pursuit: pouring water from one cup into another and back again. As other children entered the play space and conversed, Michael hardly noticed. He rarely spoke, and when he did, he usually used words to get things he wanted, not to exchange ideas.

Michael has *autism* (a term that means "absorbed in the self"), the most severe behavior disorder of childhood. Like other children with autism, by age 3 he displayed deficits in three core areas of functioning. First, he had only limited ability to engage in nonverbal behaviors required for successful social interaction, such as eye gaze, facial expressions, gestures, imitation, and give-and-take. Second, his language was delayed and stereotyped. He used words to echo what others said and to get things he wanted, not to exchange ideas. Third, he engaged in much less make-believe play than other children (Frith, 2003; Walenski, Tager-Flusberg, & Ullman, 2006). And Michael showed another typical feature of autism: His interests were narrow and overly intense. For example, one day he sat for more than an hour spinning a toy Ferris wheel.

Researchers agree that autism stems from abnormal brain functioning, usually due to genetic or prenatal environmental causes. Beginning in the first year, children with the disorder have larger-than-average brains, perhaps due to massive overgrowth of synapses and lack of synaptic pruning, which accompanies normal development of cognitive, language, and communication skills (Courchesne, Carper, & Akshoomoff, 2003).

The amygdala, especially, grows abnormally large in childhood, followed by a greater than average reduction in size in adolescence and adulthood. This deviant growth pattern is believed to contribute to deficits in emotion processing and social interaction involved in the disorder (Schumann et al., 2009; Schumann & Amaral, 2010). The larger the amygdala compared with typically developing preschoolers, the more severe the child's social and communication impairments. Furthermore, fMRI studies reveal that autism is associated with reduced activity in areas of the cerebral cortex involved in emotional and social responsiveness and

with weaker connections between the amygdala and the temporal lobes (important for processing facial expressions) (Monk et al., 2010; Théoret et al., 2005).

Growing evidence reveals that children with autism have a deficient theory of mind. Long after they reach the intellectual level of an average 4-year-old, they have great difficulty with false belief. Most find it hard to attribute mental states to themselves or others (Steele, Joseph, & Tager-Flusberg, 2003). They rarely use mental-state words such as *believe, think, know, feel,* and *pretend*.

As early as the second year, children with autism show deficits in emotional and social capacities believed to contribute to an understanding of mental life. Compared with other children, they less often establish eye contact and joint attention, have difficulty distinguishing facial expressions, and seldom engage in social referencing or imitate an adult's novel behaviors (Chawarska & Shic, 2009; Mundy & Stella, 2000; Vivanti et al., 2008). And because children with autism are relatively insensitive to eye gaze as a cue to what a speaker is talking about, they often assume that another person's language refers to what they themselves are looking at—a possible reason for their frequent nonsensical expressions (Baron-Cohen, Baldwin, & Crowson, 1997).

Do these findings indicate that autism is due to impairment in an innate, core brain function, which leaves the child "mindblind" and therefore deficient in human sociability? Some researchers think so (Baron-Cohen & Belmonte, 2005; Scholl & Leslie, 2000). But others point out that individuals with mental retardation but not autism also do poorly on tasks assessing mental understanding (Yirmiya et al., 1998). This suggests that some kind of general intellectual impairment may be involved.

One conjecture is that children with autism are impaired in *executive processing* (refer to the *central executive* in the information-processing

■ This child, who has autism, is barely aware of his teacher and classmates. Researchers disagree on whether the "mindblindness" accompanying autism results from a specific deficit in social understanding, a general impairment in executive processing, or a style of information processing that focuses on parts rather than patterns and coherent wholes. ■

model on page 217 in Chapter 6). This leaves them deficient in skills involved in flexible, goal-oriented thinking, including shifting attention to address relevant aspects of a situation, inhibiting irrelevant responses, applying strategies to hold information in working memory, and generating plans (Joseph & Tager-Flusberg, 2004; Robinson et al., 2009).

Another possibility is that children with autism display a peculiar style of information processing, preferring to process the parts of stimuli over patterns and coherent wholes (Happé & Frith, 2006). Deficits in thinking flexibly and in holistic processing of stimuli would each interfere with understanding the social world because social interaction requires quick integration of information from various sources and evaluation of alternative possibilities.

It is not clear which of these hypotheses is correct. Some research suggests that impairments in social awareness, flexible thinking, processing coherent wholes, and verbal ability contribute independently to autism (Morgan, Maybery, & Durkin, 2003; Pellicano et al., 2006). Perhaps several biologically based cognitive deficits underlie the tragic social isolation of children like Michael.

and participate in activities involving storybooks, calendars, lists, and signs. Children's active efforts to construct literacy knowledge through informal experiences are called **emergent literacy.**

Young preschoolers search for units of written language as they "read" memorized versions of stories and recognize familiar signs ("PIZZA"). But they do not yet understand the symbolic function of the elements of print (Bialystok & Martin, 2003). Many preschoolers think that a single letter stands for a whole word or that each letter in a person's signature represents a separate name. Initially, as we noted in Chapter 8, preschoolers do not distinguish between drawing and writing but often believe that letters (like pictures) resemble the meanings they represent. For example, one child explained that the word *sun* begins with the letter *O* because that letter is shaped like the sun; to demonstrate, he drew an *O* surrounded with rays to produce a picture of the sun.

Children revise these ideas as their perceptual and cognitive capacities improve, as they encounter writing in many contexts, and as adults help them with written communication. Gradually preschoolers notice more features of written language and depict writing that varies in function, as in the "story" and "grocery list" in Figure 9.9.

Eventually children figure out that letters are parts of words and are linked to sounds in systematic ways, as seen in the invented spellings that are typical between ages 5 and 7. At first, children rely on sounds in the names of letters: "ADE LAFWTS KRMD NTU A LAVATR" ("eighty elephants crammed into a[n] elevator"). Soon they grasp sound–letter correspondences and learn that some letters have more than one common sound and that context affects their use ("*a*" is pronounced differently in "cat" than in "table") (McGee & Richgels, 2008).

Literacy development builds on a broad foundation of spoken language and knowledge about the world. Over time, children's language and literacy progress facilitate each other. **Phonological awareness**—the ability to reflect on and manipulate the sound structure of spoken language, as indicated by sensitivity to changes in sounds within words, to rhyming, and to incorrect pronunciation—is a strong predictor of emergent literacy and later reading and spelling achievement (Dickinson et al., 2003; Paris & Paris, 2006). When combined with sound–letter knowledge, it enables children to isolate speech segments and link them with their written symbols. Vocabulary and grammatical knowledge are also influential. And adult–child narrative conversations enhance diverse language skills essential for literacy progress.

The more informal literacy experiences young children have, the better their language and emergent literacy development and their later reading skills (Dickinson & McCabe, 2001; Speece et al., 2004). Pointing out letter–sound correspondences and playing language-sound games enhance children's awareness of the sound structure of language and how it is represented in print (Ehri & Roberts, 2006; Foy & Mann, 2003). *Interactive* reading, in which adults discuss storybook content with preschoolers, promotes many aspects of language and literacy development. And adult-supported writing activities that focus on narrative, such as preparing a letter or a story, also have wide-ranging benefits (Purcell-Gates, 1996; Wasik & Bond, 2001). In longitudinal research, each of these literacy experiences is linked to improved reading achievement in middle childhood (Hood, Conlon, & Andrews, 2008; Senechal & LeFevre, 2002; Storch & Whitehurst, 2001).

Preschoolers from low-SES families have fewer home and preschool language and literacy learning opportunities—a major reason that they are behind in emergent literacy skills and in reading achievement throughout the school years (Foster et al., 2005; Foster & Miller, 2007; Turnbull et al., 2009). Age-appropriate books, for example, are scarce in their environments. In one survey of four middle- and

■ Preschoolers acquire literacy knowledge informally by participating in everyday activities involving written symbols. This young chef "jots down" a phone order for a take-out meal. ■

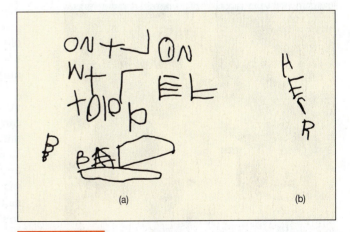

(a)   (b)

FIGURE 9.9

A story (a) and a grocery list (b) written by a 4-year-old child. This child's writing has many features of real print. It also reveals an awareness of different kinds of written expression. *(From McGee & Richgels,* Literacy's Beginnings, *Figure 3.10 "A Story and a Grocery List" p. 76. © 2004. Reproduced by permission of Pearson Education.)*

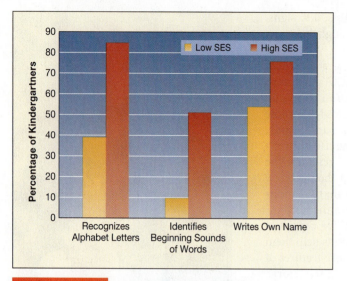

FIGURE 9.10

Some reading readiness skills at kindergarten entry by SES. The SES gap in emergent literacy development is large. *(Adapted from Lee & Burkham, 2002.)*

low-income communities, the middle-income neighborhoods averaged 13 books per child, the low-income neighborhoods just 1 book for every 300 children (Neuman & Celano, 2001).

On average, a low SES child is read to for a total of 25 hours during the preschool years, a higher-SES child for 1,000 hours. The SES gap in early literacy experiences translates into large differences in knowledge and skills vital for reading readiness at kindergarten entry (see Figure 9.10). Kindergartners who are behind in emergent literacy development tend to remain behind, performing poorly in reading in the early grades (National Early Literacy Panel, 2008). Over time, skilled readers acquire wide-ranging knowledge more efficiently, progressing more rapidly than poor readers in all achievement areas (Neuman, 2006). In this way, literacy deficiencies at the start of school contribute to widening achievement disparities between economically advantaged and disadvantaged children that often persist into high school.

High-quality intervention can reduce the SES gap in early literacy development substantially. Providing low-SES parents with children's books, along with guidance in how to stimulate emergent literacy, greatly enhances literacy activities in the home (High et al., 2000). And in a program that "flooded" child-care centers with children's books and provided caregivers with training on how to get 3- and 4-year-olds to spend time with books, low-SES children showed far greater gains in emergent literacy than a no-intervention control group (Neuman, 1999). Teachers who were given a tuition-free college course on effective early childhood literacy instruction readily applied what they learned, offering many more literacy activities in their classrooms (Dickinson & Sprague, 2001). For ways to support early childhood literacy development, refer to Applying What We Know on the following page.

MATHEMATICAL REASONING Mathematical reasoning, like literacy, builds on informal knowledge. Between 14 and 16 months, toddlers display a beginning grasp of **ordinality,** or order relationships between quantities—for example, that 3 is more than 2, and 2 is more than 1. In the early preschool years, children attach verbal labels *(lots, little, big, small)* to amounts and sizes. Sometime in the third year, they begin to count. By the time children turn 3, most can count rows of about five objects, although they do not yet know what the words mean. For example, when asked for *one,* they give one item, but when asked for *two, three, four,* or *five,* they usually give a larger, but incorrect, amount. Nevertheless, 2½- to 3½-year-olds realize that a number word refers to a unique quantity—that when a number label changes (for example, from *five* to *six*), the number of items should also change (Sarnecka & Gelman, 2004).

By age 3½ to 4, most children have mastered the meaning of numbers up to ten, count correctly, and grasp the vital principle of **cardinality**—that the last number in a counting sequence indicates the quantity of items in the set (Geary, 2006a). In the preschool scene described in the opening of this chapter, Sammy showed an understanding of cardinality when he counted four children at his snack table and then retrieved four milk cartons. Mastery of cardinality increases the efficiency of counting. By age 4, children use counting to solve simple arithmetic problems. At first, their strategies are tied to the order of numbers presented; when given 2 + 4, they count on from 2 (Bryant & Nunes, 2002). But soon they experiment with other strategies and master the *min* strategy, a more efficient approach (see page 338). Around this time, children realize that subtraction cancels out addition. Knowing, for example, that 4 + 3 = 7, they infer without counting that 7 − 3 = 4

■ Preschoolers understand basic arithmetic sooner when they have many opportunities to count, compare quantities, and talk about number concepts. ■

Applying What We Know

Supporting Emergent Literacy in Early Childhood

STRATEGY	EXPLANATION
Provide literacy-rich home and preschool environments.	Homes and preschools with abundant reading and writing materials—including a wide variety of children's storybooks, some relevant to children's ethnic backgrounds—open the door to a wealth of language and literacy experiences. Make-believe play, in which children have many opportunities to use newly acquired literacy skills in meaningful ways, spurs literacy development.
Engage in interactive book reading.	When adults discuss story content, ask open-ended questions about story events, explain the meaning of words, and point out features of print, they promote language development, comprehension of story content, knowledge of story structure, and awareness of units of written language.
Provide outings to libraries, museums, parks, zoos, and other community settings.	Visits to child-oriented community settings enhance children's general knowledge and offer many opportunities to see how written language is used in everyday life. They also provide personally meaningful topics for narrative conversation, which promote many language skills essential for literacy development.
Point out letter–sound correspondences, play rhyming and other language-sound games, and read rhyming poems and stories.	Experiences that help children isolate the sounds in words foster *phonological awareness*—a powerful predictor of early childhood literacy knowledge and later reading and spelling achievement.
Support children's efforts at writing, especially narrative products.	Assisting children in their efforts to write—especially letters, stories, and other narratives—fosters many language and literacy skills.
Model literacy activities.	When children see adults engaged in reading and writing activities, they better understand the diverse everyday functions of literacy skills and the knowledge and pleasure that literacy brings. As a result, children's motivation to become literate is strengthened.

Sources: McGee & Richgels, 2008; Neuman, 2006.

(Rasmussen, Ho, & Bisanz, 2003). Grasping basic arithmetic rules greatly facilitates rapid, accurate computation.

Understanding of basic arithmetic makes possible beginning *estimation*—the ability to generate approximate answers, which are useful for evaluating the accuracy of exact answers. After watching several doughnuts being added to or removed from a plate of four to ten doughnuts, 3- and 4-year-olds make sensible predictions about how many are on the plate (Zur & Gelman, 2004). Still, children can estimate only just beyond their calculation competence (Dowker, 2003). For example, preschoolers who can solve addition problems with sums up to 10 can estimate answers with sums up to about 20. And as with arithmetic operations, children try out diverse estimation strategies, gradually moving to more efficient, accurate techniques.

The arithmetic knowledge just described emerges universally around the world. But when adults provide many occasions for counting, comparing quantities, and talking about number concepts, children acquire these understandings sooner (Ginsburg, Lee, & Boyd, 2008; Klibanoff et al., 2006). Math proficiency at kindergarten entry strongly predicts math achievement years later, in elementary and secondary school (Duncan et al., 2007; Geary, 2006a).

As with emergent literacy, children from low-SES families begin kindergarten with considerably less math knowledge than their higher-SES agemates—a gap due to differences in environmental supports. Just a few sessions devoted to playing a number board game with an adult (see Figure 9.11) led to a dramatic improvement in low-SES 4-year-olds' number concepts and proficiency at counting from 1 to 10 (Siegler,

FIGURE 9.11

A number board game. An adult and child took turns using a spinner with a "1" section and a "2" section, which indicated how far to move a token on each turn. Children were asked to say the number spun and the numbers on the spaces as they moved. For example, a child on 5 who spun 2 would say "6, 7." Compared with agemates who played a color version of the game (it had only colored spaces on the board and a spinner with matching color sections), low-SES 4-year-olds who played the number board game showed large gains in number concepts and counting proficiency from 1 to 10. *(From R. S. Siegler, 2009, "Improving Preschoolers' Number Sense Using Information-Processing Theory," in O. A. Barbarin & B. H. Wasik, eds.,* Handbook of Child Development and Early Education. *New York: Guilford, p. 438. Reprinted by permission of Guilford Publications, Inc.)*

2009). And in an early childhood math curriculum called *Building Blocks,* materials that promote math concepts and skills through three types of media—computers, manipulatives, and print—enable teachers to weave math into many preschool daily activities, from building blocks to art and stories (Clements & Sarama, 2008). Compared with agemates randomly assigned to other preschool programs, low-SES preschoolers experiencing Building Blocks showed substantially greater year-end gains in math concepts and skills, including counting, sequencing, arithmetic computation, and geometric shapes.

ASK YOURSELF

◆ **REVIEW** Describe a typical 4-year-old's understanding of mental activities, noting both strengths and limitations.

◆ **APPLY** Lena, mother of 4-year-old Gregor, wonders why his preschool teacher provides extensive playtime in learning centers instead of formal lessons in literacy and math skills. Explain to Lena why adult-supported play is the best way for preschoolers to develop academically.

◆ **CONNECT** Cite evidence on the development of preschoolers' memory, theory of mind, and literacy and mathematical understanding that is consistent with Vygotsky's sociocultural theory.

◆ **REFLECT** Describe informal experiences important for literacy and math development that you experienced while growing up. How do you think those experiences contributed to your academic progress in school?

Individual Differences in Mental Development

Psychologists and educators typically measure how well preschoolers are developing mentally by giving them intelligence tests. Scores are computed in the same way as they are for infants and toddlers (return to Chapter 6, pages 227–228, to review). But instead of emphasizing perceptual and motor responses, tests for preschoolers sample a wide range of mental abilities. Understanding the link between early childhood experiences and mental test performance highlights ways to intervene in support of children's cognitive development.

Early Childhood Intelligence Tests

Five-year-old Hal sat in a small, unfamiliar testing room while Sarah gave him an intelligence test. Some of Sarah's questions were *verbal.* For example, she showed Hal a picture of a shovel and said, "Tell me what this is"—an item measuring vocabulary. She tested Hal's memory by asking him to repeat sentences and lists of numbers back to her. She probed his quantitative knowledge and problem solving by seeing if he could count and solve simple addition and subtraction problems. Finally, to assess Hal's spatial reasoning, Sarah used *nonverbal* tasks: Hal copied designs with special blocks, figured out the pattern in a series of shapes, and indicated what a piece of paper folded and cut would look like when unfolded (Roid, 2003; Wechsler, 2002).

Sarah knew that Hal came from an economically disadvantaged family. When low-SES and certain ethnic minority preschoolers are bombarded with questions by an unfamiliar adult, they sometimes react with anxiety. Also, such children may not define the testing situation in achievement terms. Instead, they may look for attention and approval from the adult and may settle for lower performance than their abilities allow. Sarah spent time playing with Hal before she began testing and encouraged him while the test was in progress. Under these conditions, low-SES preschoolers improve in performance (Bracken, 2000).

The questions Sarah asked Hal tap knowledge and skills that not all children have had an equal opportunity to learn. In Chapter 12, we will take up the hotly debated issue of *cultural bias* in mental testing. For now, keep in mind that intelligence tests do not sample all human abilities, and performance is affected by cultural and situational factors (Sternberg, 2005). Nevertheless, test scores remain important: By age 6 to 7, they are good predictors of later IQ and academic achievement, which are related to vocational success in industrialized societies. Let's see how the environments in which children spend their days—home, preschool, and child care—affect mental test performance.

Home Environment and Mental Development

A special version of the *Home Observation for Measurement of the Environment (HOME)*, covered in Chapter 6, assesses aspects of 3- to 6-year-olds' home lives that foster intellectual growth (see Applying What We Know below). Preschoolers who develop well intellectually have homes rich in educational toys and books. Their parents are warm and affectionate, stimulate language and academic knowledge, and arrange interesting outings. They also make reasonable demands for socially mature behavior—for example, that the child perform simple chores and behave courteously toward others. And these parents resolve conflicts with reason instead of physical force and punishment (Bradley & Caldwell, 1982; Espy, Molfese, & DiLalla, 2001; Roberts, Burchinal, & Durham, 1999).

As we saw in Chapter 2, these characteristics are less often seen in low-SES families. When parents manage, despite low education and income, to obtain high HOME scores, their preschoolers do substantially better on intelligence tests and measures of language and emergent literacy skills (Berger, Paxson, & Waldfogel, 2009; Foster et al., 2005; Mistry et al., 2008). And in a study of African-American 3- and 4-year-olds in low-income families, HOME cognitive stimulation and emotional support subscales predicted reading achievement four years later (Zaslow et al., 2006). These findings (along with others we will discuss in Chapter 12) indicate that the home plays a major role in the generally poorer intellectual performance of low-SES children compared to their higher-SES peers.

Applying What We Know

Features of a High-Quality Home Life for Preschoolers: The HOME Early Childhood Subscales

HOME SUBSCALE	SAMPLE ITEMS
Cognitive stimulation through toys, games, and reading material	Home includes toys to learn colors, sizes, and shapes.
Language stimulation	Parent teaches child about animals through books, games, and puzzles.
	Parent converses with child at least twice during observer's visit.
Organization of the physical environment	All visible rooms are reasonably clean and minimally cluttered.
Emotional support	Parent spontaneously praises child's qualities or behavior twice during observer's visit.
	Parent caresses, kisses, or hugs child at least once during observer's visit.
Stimulation of academic behavior	Child is encouraged to learn colors.
Modeling and encouragement of social maturity	Parent introduces interviewer to child.
Opportunities for variety in daily stimulation	Family member takes child on one outing at least every other week (picnic, shopping).
Avoidance of physical punishment	Parent neither slaps nor spanks child during observer's visit.

Sources: Bradley, 1994; Bradley et al., 2001.

Preschool, Kindergarten, and Child Care

Children between ages 2 and 6 spend even more time away from their homes and parents than infants and toddlers do. Largely because of the rise in maternal employment, over the past several decades the number of young children enrolled in preschool or child care has steadily increased to more than 60 percent in the United States (U.S. Census Bureau, 2010b).

A *preschool* is a program with planned educational experiences aimed at enhancing the development of 2- to 5-year-olds. In contrast, *child care* includes a variety of arrangements for supervising children of employed parents, ranging from care in the caregiver's or the child's home to some type of center-based program. The line between preschool and child care is fuzzy. Parents often select a preschool as a child-care option. And in response to the needs of employed parents, many U.S. preschools, as well as most public school kindergartens, have increased their hours from half to full days (U.S. Department of Education, 2010).

With age, preschoolers tend to shift from home-based to center programs. But many children experience several types of arrangements at once. In the United States, children of higher-income parents and children of very low-income parents are especially likely to be in preschools or child-care centers (Federal Interagency Forum on Child and Family Statistics, 2009). Many low-income working parents rely on care by relatives because they are not eligible for public preschool or government-subsidized center child care.

Good child care means more than simply keeping children safe and adequately fed. It should provide the same high-quality educational experiences that an effective preschool does, the only difference being that children attend for an extended day.

TYPES OF PRESCHOOL AND KINDERGARTEN   Preschool and kindergarten programs range along a continuum from child-centered to teacher-directed. In **child-centered programs,** teachers provide activities from which children select, and much learning takes place through play. In contrast, in **academic programs,** teachers structure children's learning, teaching letters, numbers, colors, shapes, and other academic skills through formal lessons, often using repetition and drill.

Despite evidence that formal academic training undermines young children's motivation and emotional well-being, early childhood teachers have felt increased pressure to take this approach. Preschoolers and kindergartners who spend much time passively sitting and completing worksheets, as opposed to being actively engaged in learning centers, display more stress behaviors (such as wiggling and rocking), have less confidence in their abilities, prefer less challenging tasks, and are less advanced in motor, academic, language, and social skills at the end of the school year (Marcon, 1999a; Stipek et al., 1995). Follow-ups reveal lasting effects through elementary school in poorer study habits and lower achievement test scores (Burts et al., 1992; Hart et al., 1998, 2003). These outcomes are strongest for low-SES children, with whom teachers more often use an academic approach—a disturbing trend in view of its negative impact on motivation and learning (Stipek, 2004; Stipek & Byler, 1997). Yet another concern is that public preschool programs serving low-SES children are more likely to be staffed by teachers who lack a bachelor's degree and who therefore tend to communicate in less stimulating and encouraging ways (Clifford et al., 2005; Pianta et al., 2005).

A special type of child-centered approach is *Montessori education,* devised more than a century ago by Italian physician and child development researcher Maria Montessori, who originally applied her method to poverty-stricken children. Features of Montessori schooling include multiage classrooms, teaching materials specially designed to promote exploration and discovery, long time periods for individual and small-group learning in child-chosen activities, and equal emphasis on academic and social development (Lillard, 2007). In an evaluation of Montessori public preschools serving mostly urban minority children in Milwaukee, researchers compared students randomly assigned to either Montessori or other classrooms (Lillard & Else-Quest, 2006). Five-year-olds who had completed two years of Montessori education outperformed controls in literacy and math skills, cognitive flexibility, false-belief understanding, concern with fairness in solving conflicts with peers, and cooperative play with agemates.

EARLY INTERVENTION FOR AT-RISK PRESCHOOLERS   In the 1960s, as part of the "War on Poverty" in the United States, many intervention programs for low-SES preschoolers were initiated in an effort to address learning problems before formal schooling begins. The most extensive of these federal programs, **Project Head Start,** began in 1965. A typical Head Start center provides children with a year or two of preschool, along with nutritional and health services. Parent involvement is central to the Head Start philosophy. Parents serve on policy councils, contribute to program planning, work directly with children in classrooms, attend special programs on parenting and child development, and receive services directed at their own emotional, social, and vocational needs. Currently, more than 18,000 U.S. Head Start centers serve about 908,000 children (Head Start Bureau, 2008).

Benefits of Preschool Intervention.   More than two decades of research have established the long-term benefits of preschool intervention. The most extensive of these studies combined data from seven interventions implemented by universities or research foundations. Results showed that poverty-stricken children who attended programs scored higher in IQ and achievement than controls during the first two to three years of elementary school. After that, differences declined (Lazar & Darlington, 1982). But on real-life measures of school adjustment, children and adolescents who had received intervention remained ahead. They were less likely to be placed in special education or retained in grade, and a greater number graduated from high school.

A separate report on one program—the High/Scope Perry Preschool Project—revealed benefits lasting well into adulthood. Two years' exposure to cognitively enriching preschool was associated with increased employment and reduced pregnancy and delinquency rates in adolescence. At age 27, those who had attended preschool were more likely than no-preschool counterparts to have graduated from high school and college, have higher earnings, be married, and own their own home—and less likely to have been involved with the criminal justice system (see Figure 9.12) (Weikart, 1998). In the most recent follow-up, at age 40, the intervention group sustained its advantage on all measures of life success, including education, income, family life, and law-abiding behavior (Schweinhart et al., 2005).

Do the effects on school adjustment of these well-designed and well-delivered programs generalize to Head Start and other community-based preschool interventions? Gains are similar, though not as strong. Head Start preschoolers, who are more economically disadvantaged than children in university-based programs, have more severe learning and behavior problems. And quality of services is more variable across community programs (Barnett, 2004; U.S. Department of Health and Human Services, 2010b). But interventions of documented high quality are associated with diverse, long-lasting favorable outcomes, including higher rates of high school graduation and college enrollment and lower rates of adolescent drug use and delinquency (Garces, Thomas, & Currie, 2002; Love et al., 2006; Mashburn, 2008).

A consistent finding is that gains in IQ and achievement test scores from attending Head Start and other interventions quickly dissolve. In the Head Start Impact Study, a nationally representative sample of 5,000 Head Start–eligible 3- and 4-year-olds was randomly assigned to one year of Head Start or to a control group that could attend other types of preschool programs (U.S. Department of Health and Human Services, 2010b). By year's end, Head Start 3-year-olds had gained relative to controls in vocabulary, emergent

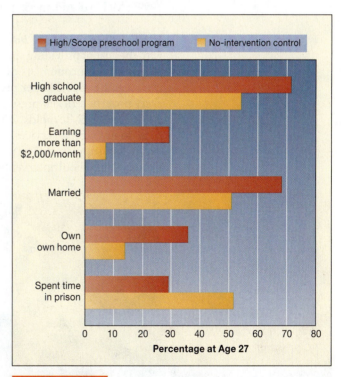

FIGURE 9.12

Some outcomes of the High/Scope Perry Preschool Project on follow-up at age 27. Although two years of a cognitively enriching preschool program did not eradicate the effects of growing up in poverty, children who received intervention were advantaged over no-intervention controls on all measures of life success when they reached adulthood. *(Adapted from Schweinhart et al., 2005.)*

■ Project Head Start provides children from poverty-stricken families with preschool education and nutritional and health services. High-quality early educational intervention has benefits lasting into adulthood. ■

literacy, and math skills; 4-year-olds in vocabulary, emergent literacy, and color identification. Head Start 3-year-olds also benefitted socially, displaying declines in overactivity and withdrawn behavior. But except for language skills, academic advantages were no longer evident by the end of first grade.

What explains these disappointing outcomes? Head Start children typically enter inferior public schools in poverty-stricken neighborhoods, which undermine the benefits of preschool education (Brooks-Gunn, 2003; Ramey, Ramey, & Lanzi, 2006). Among children who attended the Chicago Child–Parent Centers, a program emphasizing literacy intervention and parent involvement that began at age 3 and continued through third grade, gains in academic achievement were still evident in junior high school (Reynolds & Temple, 1998). And recall from Chapter 6 that when intensive intervention persists from infancy through early childhood and children enter good-quality schools, IQ gains endure into adulthood (see page 232).

Still, the improved school adjustment that results from attending a one- or two-year Head Start program is impressive. Program effects on parents may contribute: The more involved parents are in Head Start, the better their child-rearing practices and the more stimulating their home learning environments—factors positively related to preschoolers' independence, task persistence in the classroom, and year-end academic, language, and social skills (Marcon, 1999b; McLoyd, Aidens, & Burton, 2006; Parker et al., 1999).

Strengthening Preschool Intervention. Head Start is highly cost-effective when compared with the cost of providing special education, treating criminal behavior, and supporting unemployed adults. Economists estimate a lifetime return to society of more than $250,000 on an investment of $15,000 per preschool child—a potential savings of many billions of dollars if every poverty-stricken preschooler in the United States were enrolled (Heckman & Masterov, 2004; Temple & Reynolds, 2006). Because of funding shortages, however, many eligible children do not receive services.

A few supplementary programs have responded to this shortage—and to the need to intensify preschool intervention to strengthen its impact—by delivering extra educational enrichment to children in Head Start and other preschool classrooms serving low-income children. The largest of these programs is Jumpstart for Young Children. Two or three times a week, Jumpstart corps members (college students and older adults) go to an early childhood center, where they read to and converse with 1 to 3 designated 3-to-5-year-olds, engage in additional individualized learning activities, and play collaborative games in small groups.

■ A Jumpstart corps member reads to and converses with a 4-year-old in a Head Start classroom. By delivering extra educational enrichment, this supplementary intervention program yields gains in language, literacy, task persistence, and social skills for participating children. ■

Currently, Jumpstart reaches more than 13,000 children in over 60 communities. Evaluations indicate that preschoolers who experience Jumpstart show greater end-of-year gains in language, literacy, task persistence, and social skills than non-Jumpstart comparison children in the same Head Start or other centers (Harris & Berk, 2011; Jumpstart Evaluation Team, 2008).

CHILD CARE We have seen that high-quality early intervention can enhance the development of economically disadvantaged children. As noted in Chapter 6, however, much U.S. child care lacks quality. Preschoolers exposed to substandard child care, particularly for long hours, score lower in cognitive and social skills and display more behavior problems (Belsky, 2006; Lamb & Ahnert, 2006; NICHD Early Child Care Research Network, 2003b, 2006). Externalizing difficulties are especially likely to endure into the school years after extensive exposure to mediocre center-based (as opposed to home-based) care (Belsky et al., 2007). Psychological well-being also declines when children experience the instability of several child-care settings. The emotional problems of temperamentally difficult preschoolers worsen considerably (De Schipper, van IJzendoorn, & Tavecchio, 2004; De Schipper et al., 2004).

In contrast, good child care enhances cognitive, language, and social development, especially for low-SES children—effects that persist into elementary school (Belsky et al., 2007; Lamb & Ahnert, 2006; NICHD Early Child Care Research Network, 2006). In a study that followed 400 very-low-income children over the preschool years, center-based care was more strongly associated with cognitive gains than were other child-care arrangements, probably because good-quality child-care centers are more likely than family child-care homes to provide a systematic educational program (Loeb et al., 2004).

■ Ingredients of high-quality child care include small group size, generous caregiver–child ratios, richly equipped activity areas, and well-educated caregivers. Child care that meets these criteria enhances development, especially for low-SES preschoolers. ■

What are the ingredients of high-quality child care for preschoolers? Large-scale studies identify several important factors: group size (number of children in a single space), caregiver–child ratio, caregivers' educational preparation, and caregivers' personal commitment to learning about and caring for children. When these characteristics are favorable, adults are more verbally stimulating and sensitive to children's needs (Lamb & Ahnert, 2006). Applying What We Know on page 352 summarizes characteristics of high-quality early childhood programs, based on standards for developmentally appropriate practice devised by the U.S. National Association for the Education of Young Children. These standards offer a set of worthy goals as the United States strives to upgrade child-care and educational services for young children.

Educational Media

Besides home and preschool, young children spend much time in another learning environment: electronic media, including both television and computers. In the United States and other industrialized nations, nearly all homes have at least one television set, and most have two or more. About 85 percent of U.S. children live in homes with one or more computers, two-thirds of which have an Internet connection (Roberts, Foehr, & Rideout, 2005; U.S. Census Bureau, 2010b).

EDUCATIONAL TELEVISION Sammy's favorite TV program, *Sesame Street,* uses lively visual and sound effects to stress basic literacy and number concepts and presents engaging puppet and human characters to teach general knowledge, emotional and social understanding, and social skills. Today, *Sesame Street* is broadcast in more than 120 countries, making it the most widely viewed children's program in the world (Sesame Workshop, 2008).

Time devoted to watching children's educational programs is associated with gains in early literacy and math skills and academic progress in elementary school (Ennemoser & Schneider, 2007; Linebarger et al., 2004; Wright et al., 2001). Consistent with these findings, one study reported a link between preschool viewing of *Sesame Street* and other similar educational programs and getting higher grades, reading more books, and placing more value on achievement

LOOK AND LISTEN

◆◆

Arrange to observe at a child-care center and to talk to its director. Jot down signs of quality, referring to Applying What We Know on page 352. How would you rate the center's overall quality?

Applying What We Know

Signs of Developmentally Appropriate Early Childhood Programs

PROGRAM CHARACTERISTIC	SIGNS OF QUALITY
Physical setting	Indoor environment is clean, in good repair, and well-ventilated. Classroom space is divided into richly equipped activity areas, including make-believe play, blocks, science, math, games and puzzles, books, art, and music. Fenced outdoor play space is equipped with swings, climbing equipment, tricycles, and sandbox.
Group size	In preschools and child-care centers, group size is no greater than 18 to 20 children with two teachers.
Caregiver–child ratio	In preschools and child-care centers, teacher is responsible for no more than 8 to 10 children. In family child-care homes, caregiver is responsible for no more than 6 children.
Daily activities	Children mainly work individually or in small groups, selecting many of their own activities and learning through experiences relevant to their own lives. Teachers facilitate children's involvement, accept individual differences, and adjust expectations to children's developing capacities.
Interactions between adults and children	Teachers move among groups and individuals, asking questions, offering suggestions, and adding more complex ideas. Teachers use positive guidance techniques, such as modeling and encouraging expected behavior and redirecting children to more acceptable activities.
Teacher qualifications	Teachers have college-level specialized preparation in early childhood development, early childhood education, or a related field.
Relationships with parents	Parents are encouraged to observe and participate. Teachers talk frequently with parents about children's behavior and development.
Licensing and accreditation	Child-care setting, whether a center or a home, is licensed by the state. Voluntary accreditation by the National Academy of Early Childhood Programs *(www.naeyc.org/accreditation)* or the National Association for Family Child Care *(www.nafcc.org)* is evidence of an especially high-quality program.

Sources: Copple & Bredekamp, 2009.

in high school (Anderson et al., 2001). In recent years, *Sesame Street* has modified its rapid-paced format in favor of more leisurely episodes with a clear story line. Watching children's programs with slow-paced action and easy-to-follow narratives, such as *Barney and Friends,* leads to more elaborate make-believe play than viewing programs that present quick, disconnected bits of information (Singer & Singer, 2005).

Despite the spread of computers, television remains the dominant form of youth media, with children first becoming viewers in early infancy. About 40 percent of U.S. 3-month-olds regularly watch either TV or videos, a figure that rises to 90 percent by age 2 (Zimmerman, Christakis, & Meltzoff, 2007). The average U.S. 2- to 6-year-old watches TV programs and videos from 1½ to 2½ hours a day. In middle childhood, viewing time increases to an average of 3½ hours a day, then declines slightly in adolescence (Rideout & Hamel, 2006; Scharrer & Comstock, 2003).

Low-SES children are more frequent TV viewers, perhaps because few alternative forms of entertainment are available in their neighborhoods or affordable for their parents. On the positive side, preschoolers in low-SES families watch as much educational television as their economically advantaged agemates (Vandewater & Bickham, 2004). But parents with limited education are more likely to engage in practices that heighten TV viewing of all kinds, including eating family meals in front of the set and failing to limit children's TV access (Hesketh et al., 2007). About one-third of U.S. preschoolers and two-thirds of school-age children and adolescents have a TV set in their bedroom. These children spend from 40 to 90 minutes more per day watching TV, usually without any parental restrictions on what they view (Rideout & Hamel, 2006).

Does extensive TV viewing take children away from worthwhile activities? The more preschool and school-age children watch prime-time television and cartoons, the less time they spend reading and interacting with others and the poorer their academic skills (Ennemoser & Schneider, 2007; Huston et al., 1999; Wright et al., 2001). Educational programs, as noted above, are beneficial, but watching entertainment TV—especially heavy viewing—detracts from children's school success and social experiences. More than one-third of U.S. children live in homes where the TV is on constantly, or nearly so. Kindergartners and first graders in such families, regardless of SES, are far less likely than their agemates to have acquired beginning reading skills (Vandewater et al., 2005).

LEARNING WITH COMPUTERS According to a survey of 1,000 U.S. parents, 70 percent of 4- to 6-year-olds have used a computer at one time or another, and more than one-fourth use one regularly, spending on average just over an hour a day at the keyboard. Preschoolers of higher-SES parents have greater computer access (Calvert et al., 2005; Rideout, Vandewater, & Wartella, 2003). Children as young as age 3 can type simple keyboard commands, use a mouse to point and click, and load a CD or DVD on their own.

Because computers can have rich educational benefits, many early childhood classrooms include computer-learning centers. Computer storybooks and other literacy programs expand children's general knowledge and encourage diverse language and emergent literacy skills (Hutinger et al., 1998). When adults turn over control of the mouse to preschoolers, allowing them to interact directly with computer stories, children's sustained attention and interest increase (Calvert, Strong, & Gallagher, 2005). Kindergartners who use computers to draw or write produce more elaborate pictures and text, make fewer writing errors, and edit their work much as older children do. And combining everyday and computer experiences with math manipulatives is especially effective in promoting math concepts and skills (Clements & Sarama, 2003).

Simplified computer languages that children can use to make designs or build structures introduce them to programming skills. As long as adults support children's efforts, computer programming promotes improved problem solving and metacognition (awareness of thought processes) because children must plan and reflect on their thinking to get their programs to work. Furthermore, while programming, children are especially likely to help one another and to persist in the face of challenge (Nastasi & Clements, 1994; Resnick & Silverman, 2005). Small groups often gather around classroom computers, and children more often collaborate than in other pursuits (Svensson, 2000).

As with television, children spend much time using computers for entertainment, especially game playing. Although parental reports suggest that only 3 percent of preschoolers play video games on a daily basis, that figure rises to 35 percent in middle childhood and adolescence, when—as we will see in Chapter 12—a large sex difference favoring boys emerges. Nevertheless, game consoles are among the bedroom furnishings of 10 percent of children age 6 and younger (Rideout, Vandewater, & Wartella, 2003; Roberts, Foehr, & Rideout, 2005).

Video games designed for young children generally have specific educational goals, including literacy, math, science, colors, and other concepts (Garrison & Christakis, 2005). But on the whole, TV and computer-game media are rife with gender stereotypes and violence. We will consider the impact of media on emotional and social development in the next chapter.

ASK YOURSELF

◆ **REVIEW** What findings indicate that child-centered rather than academic preschools and kindergartens are better suited to fostering academic development?

◆ **APPLY** Your senator has heard that IQ gains resulting from Head Start do not last, so he plans to vote against additional funding. Write a letter explaining why he should support Head Start.

◆ **CONNECT** Compare outcomes resulting from preschool intervention programs with those from interventions beginning in infancy (see pages 231–232 in Chapter 6). Which are more likely to lead to lasting cognitive gains? Explain.

◆ **REFLECT** How much and what kinds of TV viewing and computer use did you engage in as a child? How do you think your home media environment influenced your development?

Language Development

Language is intimately related to virtually all the cognitive changes discussed in this chapter. Between ages 2 and 6, children make momentous advances in language. Their remarkable achievements, as well as their mistakes along the way, reveal their active, rule-oriented approach to mastering their native tongue.

Vocabulary

At age 2, Sammy had a spoken vocabulary of 200 words. By age 6, he will have acquired around 10,000 words (Bloom, 1998). To accomplish this feat, Sammy will learn about five new words each day. How do children build their vocabularies so quickly? Research shows that they can connect new words with their underlying concepts after only a brief encounter, a process called **fast mapping.** Even toddlers comprehend new labels remarkably quickly, but they need more repetitions of the word's use across several situations than preschoolers, who process speech-based information faster and are better able to categorize and recall it (Akhtar & Montague, 1999; Fernald, Perfors, & Marchman, 2006). During the preschool years, children become increasingly adept at fast-mapping two or more new words encountered in the same situation (Wilkinson, Ross, & Diamond, 2003).

TYPES OF WORDS One day, Leslie announced to the children that they would soon take a field trip. That night, Sammy excitedly told his mother, "We're going on a field trip!" When she asked where the class would go, Sammy responded matter-of-factly, "To a field!" Sammy's error suggests that young children fast-map some words more easily than others.

Children in many Western and non-Western language communities fast-map labels for objects especially rapidly because these refer to concepts that are easy to perceive (Gentner & Namy, 2004; Kern, 2007). When adults point to, label, and talk about an object, they help the child figure out the word's meaning (Gershoff-Stowe & Hahn, 2007). Soon children add verbs (*go, run, broke*), which require understandings of relationships between objects and actions. Because learning verbs is more cognitively challenging, preschoolers speaking quite different languages take longer to extend a new verb ("*push* the bike") to other instances of the same action ("*push* the box") than they do to extend a novel noun to other objects in the same category (Imai et al., 2008). In mastering verb meanings, they benefit from many examples of the same verb used in different contexts.

Nevertheless, young children learning Chinese, Japanese, and Korean—languages in which nouns are often omitted from adults' sentences, while verbs are stressed—acquire verbs more readily than their English-speaking agemates (Kim, McGregor, & Thompson, 2000; Tardif, 2006). Besides increased exposure to verbs, Chinese-speaking children hear a greater variety of verbs denoting physical actions, which are easiest to master—for example, several verbs for *carry*, each referring to a different way of carrying, such as on one's back, in one's arms, or with one's hands (Ma et al., 2009).

Gradually, preschoolers add modifiers (*red, round, sad*). First they make general distinctions (*big–small*), then more specific ones (*tall–short, high–low, wide–narrow*) (Stevenson & Pollitt, 1987).

STRATEGIES FOR WORD LEARNING Children figure out the meanings of words by contrasting them with words they already know and assigning the new label to a gap in their vocabulary (Clark, 1990). On hearing a new word in conversation, 2-year-olds repeat the word or acknowledge it with "yeah" or "uh-huh" in their next verbalization 60 percent of the time (Clark, 2007). This suggests that they assign the word a preliminary meaning and start to use it right away. Over time, they refine its meaning, striving to match its conventional use in their language community.

© ELLEN B. SENISI PHOTOGRAPHY

■ To engage in effective verbal communication, preschoolers must master and combine principles of word meaning, grammar, and everyday conversation. How they accomplish this feat so rapidly is the focus of intensive research and debate. ■

When learning a new noun, toddlers and preschoolers acquiring diverse languages tend to assume it refers to an object category at the basic level—an intermediate level of generality (see page 325). This preference helps young children narrow the range of possible meanings. Once they acquire a basic-level name *(dog)*, they add names at other hierarchical levels, both more general *(animal)* and more specific *(beagle, greyhound)* (Imai & Haryu, 2004; Waxman & Lidz, 2006).

How do children discover which concept each word picks out? This process is not yet fully understood. One speculation is that early in vocabulary growth, children adopt a **mutual exclusivity bias**—the assumption that words refer to entirely separate (nonoverlapping) categories (Markman, 1992). Two-year-olds seem to rely on mutual exclusivity when the objects named are perceptually distinct—for example, differ clearly in shape. After hearing the labels for two distinct novel objects (for example, *clip* and *horn*), they assign each word correctly, to the whole object, not just a part of it (Waxman & Senghas, 1992).

Indeed, children's first several hundred nouns refer mostly to objects well-organized by shape. In a study in which toddlers repeatedly played with and heard names for novel objects of different shapes ("That's a *wif*") over a nine-week period, they soon formed the generalization that only similar-shaped objects have the same name (Smith et al., 2002; Yoshida & Smith, 2003). Toddlers with this training added more than three times as many object names to their vocabularies outside the laboratory as did untrained controls. Because shape is a perceptual property relevant to most object categories for which they have already learned names, this *shape bias* helps preschoolers master additional names of objects, and vocabulary accelerates.

Once the name of a whole object is familiar, on hearing a new name for the object, 2- and 3-year-olds set aside the mutual exclusivity assumption. For example, if the object *(bottle)* has a part that stands out *(spout)*, children readily apply the new label to it (Hansen & Markman, 2009). In these instances, mutual exclusivity helps limit the possibilities the child must consider. Still, mutual exclusivity and object shape cannot account for preschoolers' remarkably flexible responses when objects have more than one name.

By age 3, preschoolers' memory, categorization, and language skills have expanded, and they assign multiple labels to many objects (Deák, Yen, & Pettit, 2001). For example, they refer to a sticker of a gray goose as "sticker," "goose," and "gray." In these instances, children often call on other aspects of language. According to one proposal, preschoolers discover many word meanings by observing how words are used in *syntax,* or the structure of sentences—a hypothesis called **syntactic bootstrapping** (Gleitman et al., 2005; Naigles & Swenson, 2007). Consider an adult who says, "This is a *citron* one," while showing the child a yellow car. Two- and 3-year-olds conclude that a new word used as an adjective for a familiar object (car) refers to a property of that object (Hall & Graham, 1999; Imai & Haryu, 2004). As preschoolers hear the word in various sentence structures ("That lemon is bright *citron*"), they use syntactic information to refine the word's meaning and generalize it to other categories.

Young children also take advantage of the rich social information that adults frequently provide when they introduce new words. In one study, an adult performed an action on an object and then used a new label while looking back and forth between the child and the object, as if inviting the child to play. Two-year-olds concluded that the label referred to the action, not the object (Tomasello & Akhtar, 1995). And when an adult first designates the whole object ("The bird has something . . .") and then points to a part of it ("in its beak"), 3-year-olds realize that *beak* is a certain part, not the whole bird (Saylor, Sabbagh, & Baldwin, 2002).

Adults also inform children directly about word meanings. Parents commonly highlight the meaning of adjectives by using the new label with several objects (a "red car," a "red truck")—information that helps children infer that the word refers to an object property (Hall, Burns, & Pawluski, 2003). And adults often explain which of two or more words to use, by saying, for example, "You can call it a sea creature, but it's better to say *dolphin*" (Callanan & Sabbagh, 2004). In these situations, preschoolers often call on their expanding theory of mind to facilitate word learning. For example, by age 3 they can use a speaker's recently expressed desire ("I really want to play with the *riff*") to figure out the label belonging to one of two novel

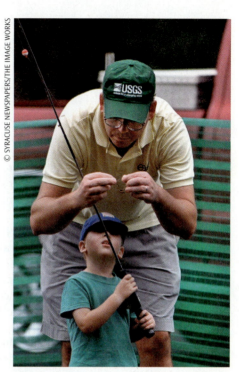

■ Young children rely on any useful information available to add to their vocabulary. This 3-year-old attends to a variety of perceptual, social, and linguistic cues to grasp the meanings of unfamiliar fishing words, such as *bait, line, bobber,* and *sinker.* ■

objects (Saylor & Troseth, 2006). And when an adult expresses certainty about a word's meaning, 3- and 4-year-olds are far more likely to accept her referent than when she expresses uncertainty ("I'm not sure that's a *beluga*") (Sabbagh & Baldwin, 2001).

Furthermore, to fill in for words they have not yet learned, children as young as age 3 coin new words using ones they already know—for example, "plant-man" for a gardener or "crayoner" for a child using crayons. Preschoolers also extend language meanings through metaphor—like the 3-year-old who described a stomachache as a "fire engine in my tummy" (Winner, 1988). Young preschoolers' metaphors involve concrete sensory comparisons: "Clouds are pillows," "Leaves are dancers." As their vocabulary and general knowledge expand, they appreciate nonsensory comparisons: "Friends are like magnets," "Time flies by" (Keil, 1986; Ozçaliskan & Goldin-Meadow, 2005). Metaphors permit young children to communicate in amazingly vivid and memorable ways.

EXPLAINING VOCABULARY DEVELOPMENT   Children acquire vocabulary so efficiently and accurately that some theorists believe that they are innately biased to induce word meanings using certain principles, such as mutual exclusivity and syntactic bootstrapping (Lidz, Gleitman, & Gleitman, 2004; Woodward & Markman, 1998). But critics observe that a small set of built-in, fixed principles cannot account for the varied, flexible manner in which children master vocabulary (Deák, 2000). And many word-learning strategies cannot be innate because children acquiring different languages use different approaches to mastering the same meanings.

An alternative view is that vocabulary growth is governed by the same cognitive strategies that children apply to nonlinguistic information. According to one account, children draw on a *coalition* of cues—perceptual, social, and linguistic—which shift in importance with age (Golinkoff & Hirsh-Pasek, 2006, 2008). Infants rely solely on perceptual features. Toddlers and young preschoolers, while still sensitive to perceptual features (such as object shape and physical action), increasingly attend to social cues—the speaker's direction of gaze, gestures, expressions of intention and desire, and soon the speaker's knowledge (Hollich, Hirsh-Pasek, & Golinkoff, 2000; Pruden et al., 2006). And as language develops further, linguistic cues—sentence structure and intonation (stress, pitch, and loudness)—play larger roles.

Preschoolers are most successful at figuring out new word meanings when several kinds of information are available (Saylor, Baldwin, & Sabbagh, 2005). Researchers have just begun to study the multiple cues that children use for different kinds of words and how their combined strategies change with development.

Grammar

Grammar refers to the way we combine words into meaningful phrases and sentences. Between ages 2 and 3, English-speaking children use simple sentences that follow a subject–verb–object word order. Children learning other languages adopt the word orders of the adult speech to which they are exposed.

BASIC RULES   Studies of children acquiring diverse languages indicate that their first use of grammatical rules is piecemeal—limited to just a few verbs. As children listen for familiar verbs in adults' speech, they expand their own utterances containing those verbs, relying on adult speech as their model (Gathercole, Sebastián, & Soto, 1999; Lieven, Pine, & Baldwin, 1997). Sammy, for example, added the preposition *with* to the verb *open* ("You open with scissors") but not to the word *hit* ("He hit me stick").

To test preschoolers' ability to generate novel sentences that conform to basic English grammar, researchers had them use a new verb in the subject–verb–object form after hearing it in a different construction, such as passive: "Ernie is getting *gorped* by the dog." When children were asked what the dog was doing, the percentage who could respond, "He's *gorping* Ernie," rose steadily with age. But as Figure 9.13 shows, not until age 3½ to 4 could the majority of children apply the fundamental subject–verb–object structure broadly, to newly acquired verbs (Tomasello, 2000, 2003, 2006).

As these examples suggest, once children form three-word sentences, they also make small additions and changes in words that enable speakers to express meanings flexibly and efficiently. For example, they add -*s* for plural *(cats),* use prepositions (*in* and *on*), and form various tenses of the verb *to be* (*is, are, were, has been, will*). All English-speaking children master these grammatical markers in a regular sequence, starting with those that involve the simplest meanings and structures (Brown, 1973; de Villiers & de Villiers, 1973). For example, children master the plural form *-s* before they learn tenses of the verb *to be*.

Once children acquire these markers, they sometimes overextend the rules to words that are exceptions, a type of error called **overregularization.** "We each got two *foots*" and "My toy car *breaked*" are expressions that appear between ages 2 and 3 and persist into middle childhood (Maratsos, 2000; Marcus, 1995). Children less often make this error on frequently used irregular verbs, such as the past tense of *go (went)* and *say (said)*, which they hear often enough to learn by rote. For rarely used verbs such as *grow* and *sing*, children alternate for months—or even several years—between overregularized forms (*growed, singed*) and correct forms, until the irregular form eventually wins out. Since children do not hear mature speakers use these forms, overregularization provides evidence that children apply grammatical rules creatively.

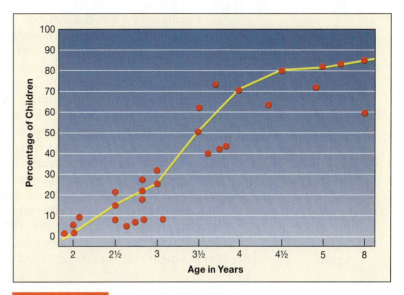

FIGURE 9.13

Percentage of children in different studies who could use a new verb in the subject–verb–object form after hearing it in another construction. Each dot in the graph represents the findings of one study. The ability to use the new verb—an indicator of the child's capacity to apply the subject–verb–object structure broadly—rose steadily with age. Children mastered this fundamental grammatical construction gradually. *(From M. Tomasello, 2000, "Do Young Children Have Adult Syntactic Competence?" Cognition, 74, p. 223. Reprinted with permission from Elsevier.)*

COMPLEX STRUCTURES Gradually, preschoolers master more complex grammatical structures, although they make errors along the way. In first creating questions, 2- and 3-year-olds use many formulas: "Where's *X*?" "Can I *X*?" (Dabrowska, 2000; Tomasello, 1992, 2003). Question asking remains variable for the next couple of years. An analysis of one child's questions revealed that he inverted the subject and verb when asking certain questions but not others ("What she will do?" "Why he can go?"). The correct expressions were the ones he heard most often in his mother's speech (Rowland & Pine, 2000). And sometimes children produce errors in subject–verb agreement ("Where does the dogs play?") and subject case ("Where can me sit?") (Rowland, 2007).

Similarly, children have trouble with some passive sentences. When told, "The car was pushed by the truck," young preschoolers often make a toy car push a truck. By age 5, they understand such expressions, but full mastery of the passive form is not complete until the end of middle childhood (Horgan, 1978; Lempert, 1990).

Nevertheless, preschoolers' grasp of grammar is remarkable. By age 4 to 5, they form embedded sentences ("I think *he will come*"), tag questions ("Dad's going to be home soon, *isn't he?*"), and indirect objects ("He showed *his friend* the present"). As the preschool years draw to a close, children use most of the grammatical constructions of their language competently (Tager-Flusberg & Zukowski, 2009).

EXPLAINING GRAMMATICAL DEVELOPMENT Evidence that grammatical development is an extended process has raised questions about Chomsky's *language acquisition device (LAD),* which assumes that children have innate knowledge of grammatical rules (see Chapter 6, page 234). Some experts believe that grammar is a product of general cognitive development—children's tendency to search the environment for consistencies and patterns of all sorts (Bloom, 1999; Chang, Dell, & Bock, 2006; Tomasello, 2003). Yet among these theorists, debate continues over just how children master grammar.

According to one view, young children rely on *semantics,* or word meanings, to figure out grammatical rules—an approach called **semantic bootstrapping.** For example, children might begin by grouping together words with "agent qualities" (things that cause actions) as *subjects* and words with "action qualities" as *verbs.* Then they merge these categories with observations of how words are used in sentences (Bates & MacWhinney, 1987; Braine, 1994).

Others believe that children master grammar through direct observation of the structure of language: They notice which words appear in the same positions in sentences and are combined in the same way with other words. Over time, they group words into grammatical categories and use them appropriately in sentences (Bloom, 1999; Chang, Dell, & Bock, 2006; Tomasello, 2003).

Still other theorists agree with the essence of Chomsky's theory. One idea accepts semantic bootstrapping but proposes that the grammatical categories into which children group word meanings are innate—present at the outset (Pinker, 1989, 1999). Critics, however, point out that toddlers' two-word utterances do not show a grasp of grammar (return to Chapter 6, page 239, to review). Another theory holds that children do not start with innate knowledge but, rather, have a *special language-making capacity*—a set of procedures for analyzing the language they hear, which supports the discovery of grammatical regularities. Research on children learning more than 40 different languages reveals common patterns, consistent with a basic set of strategies (Slobin, 1985, 1997). Yet controversy persists over whether a universal, built-in language-processing device exists or whether children who hear different languages devise unique strategies (Lidz, 2007; Marchman & Thal, 2005).

Conversation

Besides acquiring vocabulary and grammar, children must learn to engage in effective and appropriate communication—by taking turns, staying on the same topic, stating their messages clearly, and conforming to cultural rules for social interaction. This practical, social side of language is called **pragmatics,** and preschoolers make considerable headway in mastering it.

As early as age 2, children are skilled conversationalists. In face-to-face interaction, they take turns and respond appropriately to their partner's remarks (Pan & Snow, 1999). With age, the number of turns over which children can sustain interaction and their ability to maintain a topic over time increase, but even 2-year-olds converse effectively (Snow et al., 1996). These surprisingly advanced abilities probably grow out of early interactive experiences (see Chapter 6).

Indeed, the presence of a sibling seems to be especially conducive to acquiring the pragmatics of language. Preschoolers closely monitor conversations between their twin or older siblings and parents, and they often try to join in. When they do, these verbal exchanges last longer, with each participant taking more turns (Barton & Strosberg, 1997; Barton & Tomasello, 1991). As they listen to these conversations, young language learners pick up important skills, such as use of personal pronouns (*I* versus *you*), which are more common in the early vocabularies of later-born than of firstborn siblings (Pine, 1995). Furthermore, older siblings' remarks to a younger brother or sister often focus on regulating interaction: "Do you like Kermit?" "OK, your turn" (Oshima-Takane & Robbins, 2003). This emphasis probably contributes to younger siblings' conversational skills.

By age 4, children adapt their language to social expectations. For example, in acting out roles with hand puppets, they show that they understand the stereotypic features of different social positions. They use more commands when playing socially dominant and male roles (teacher, doctor, father) but speak more politely and use more indirect requests when playing less dominant and female roles (student, patient, mother) (Andersen, 2000).

Preschoolers' conversational skills occasionally do break down—for example, when talking on the phone. Here is an excerpt from one 4-year-old's phone conversation with his grandfather:

Grandfather: "How old will you be?"

John: "Dis many." [*Holding up four fingers*]

Grandfather: "Huh?"

John: "Dis many." [*Again holding up four fingers*] (Warren & Tate, 1992, pp. 259–260)

Young children's conversations appear less mature in highly demanding situations in which they cannot see their listeners' reactions or rely on typical conversational aids, such as gestures and objects to talk about. But when asked to tell a listener how to solve a simple puzzle, 3- to 6-year-olds give more specific directions over the phone than in person, indicating that they realize that more verbal description is necessary on the phone (Cameron & Lee, 1997).

Between ages 4 and 8, both conversing and giving directions over the phone improve greatly. Telephone talk provides yet another example of how preschoolers' competencies depend on the demands of the situation.

Supporting Language Learning in Early Childhood

How can adults foster preschoolers' language development? As in toddlerhood, interaction with more skilled speakers remains vital in early childhood. Conversational give-and-take with adults, either at home or in preschool, is consistently related to language progress (Hart & Risley, 1995; NICHD Early Child Care Research Network, 2000b). Furthermore, recall that language learning and literacy development are closely linked. Return to Applying What We Know on page 345, and notice how each strategy for supporting emergent literacy also fosters language progress.

■ Adults can support preschoolers' grammatical learning through indirect feedback, including recasts and expansions. However, exposure to a rich language environment may be more important than these strategies, which are not used in all cultures. ■

Sensitive, caring adults use additional techniques that promote language skills. When children use words incorrectly or communicate unclearly, they give helpful, explicit feedback: "I can't tell which ball you want. Do you mean a large or small one or a red or green one?" But they do not overcorrect, especially when children make grammatical mistakes. Criticism discourages children from freely using language in ways that lead to new skills.

Instead, adults often provide indirect feedback about grammar by using two strategies, often in combination: **recasts**—restructuring inaccurate speech into correct form, and **expansions**—elaborating on children's speech, increasing its complexity (Bohannon & Stanowicz, 1988; Chouinard & Clark, 2003). For example, if a child says, "I gotted new red shoes," the parent might respond, "Yes, you got a pair of new red shoes." In one study, after such corrective input, 2- to 4-year-olds often shifted to correct forms—improvements still evident several months later (Saxton, Backley, & Galloway, 2005). However, the impact of such feedback has been challenged. The techniques are not used in all cultures and, in a few investigations, had no impact on children's grammar (Strapp & Federico, 2000; Valian, 1999). Rather than eliminating errors, perhaps expansions and recasts model grammatical alternatives and encourage children to experiment with them.

Do the findings just described remind you once again of Vygotsky's theory? In language, as in other aspects of intellectual growth, parents and teachers gently prompt young children to take the next developmental step forward. Children strive to master language because they want to connect with other people. Adults, in turn, respond to children's desire to become competent speakers by listening attentively, elaborating on what children say, modeling correct usage, and stimulating children to talk further. In the next chapter, we will see that this combination of warmth and encouragement of mature behavior is at the heart of early childhood emotional and social development as well.

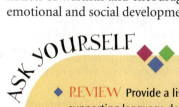

◆ **REVIEW** Provide a list of recommendations for supporting language development in early childhood, noting research that supports each.

◆ **APPLY** Sammy's mother explained to him that the family would take a vacation in Miami. The next morning, Sammy announced, "I gotted my bags packed. When are we going to Your-ami?" What explains Sammy's errors?

◆ **CONNECT** Explain how children's strategies for word learning support the interactionist perspective on language development, described on page 236 in Chapter 6.

Summary

Piaget's Theory: The Preoperational Stage

Describe advances in mental representation, and limitations of thinking, during the preoperational stage.

- Rapid advances in mental representation, notably language and make-believe play, mark the beginning of Piaget's **preoperational stage.** With age, make-believe becomes increasingly complex, evident in **sociodramatic play** with peers. Make-believe supports many aspects of cognitive and social development. **Dual representation** improves rapidly over the third year of life as children realize that models, drawings, and simple maps correspond to circumstances in the real world.

- Aside from representation, Piaget described preschoolers in terms of deficits rather than strengths. Because **egocentrism** prevents them from reflecting on their own thinking and accommodating, it contributes to **animistic thinking, centration,** and **irreversibility.** These difficulties cause preschoolers to fail **conservation** and **hierarchical classification** tasks.

What does follow-up research imply about the accuracy of Piaget's preoperational stage?

- When young children are given familiar and simplified problems, their performance appears more mature than Piaget assumed. Preschoolers recognize differing perspectives, distinguish animate from inanimate objects, have flexible and appropriate notions of magic, and notice and reason about transformations and cause-and-effect relations. They also show impressive skill at categorizing on the basis of nonobservable characteristics and notice distinctions between appearance and reality, revealing that their thinking is not dominated by perceptual appearances.
- These findings challenge Piaget's concept of stage. Rather than being absent in the preschool years, operational thinking develops gradually.

What educational principles can be derived from Piaget's theory?

- A Piagetian classroom promotes discovery learning, sensitivity to children's readiness to learn, and acceptance of individual differences.

Vygotsky's Sociocultural Theory

Describe Vygotsky's perspective on the social origins and significance of children's private speech.

- In contrast to Piaget, Vygotsky regarded language as the foundation for all higher cognitive processes. According to Vygotsky, **private speech,** or language used for self-guidance, emerges out of social communication as adults and more skilled peers help children master challenging tasks within the zone of proximal development. Eventually, private speech is internalized as inner, verbal thought.
- **Intersubjectivity** and **scaffolding** are two features of social interaction that promote transfer of cognitive processes to children. **Guided participation** recognizes situational and cultural variations in adult support of children's efforts.

Describe applications of Vygotsky's theory to education, and evaluate his major ideas.

- A Vygotskian classroom emphasizes assisted discovery, in which both teacher guidance and peer collaboration are vitally important. Make-believe play is a unique, broadly influential zone of proximal development in early childhood.
- Vygotsky's theory helps us understand the wide cultural variation in cognitive skills. In some cultures, verbal communication is not the only means—or even the most important means— through which children learn. Vygotsky said little about how basic cognitive and motor capacities, which develop in infancy, contribute to socially transmitted higher cognitive processes.

Information Processing

How do attention, memory, and problem solving change during early childhood?

- Sustained attention increases sharply between ages 2½ and 3, due to increased activation of the prefrontal cortex, the capacity to generate complex play goals, adult scaffolding, and high-quality preschool education. **Planning** also improves, though on tasks with several steps, they are often unsystematic.
- Young children's recognition memory is remarkably accurate. But their recall of listlike information is poor because they use **memory strategies** less effectively than older children.

- **Episodic memory,** or memory for everyday experiences, improves greatly in early childhood. Like adults, preschoolers remember recurring events as **scripts,** which become more elaborate with age.
- As cognitive and conversational skills improve, children's autobiographical memories become better organized, detailed, and related to the larger context of their lives, especially when adults use an elaborative style to talk about the past.
- According to **overlapping-waves theory,** children try out various strategies to solve challenging problems, gradually selecting those that result in rapid, accurate solutions. Practice with strategies, reasoning, tasks with new challenges, and adult assistance contribute to improved problem solving.

Describe the young child's theory of mind.

- Preschoolers begin to construct a theory of mind, indicating that they are capable of **metacognition,** or thinking about thought. From age 4 on, they realize that both beliefs and desires can influence behavior, in that they pass verbal false-belief tasks.
- Language and cognitive skills, make-believe play, and mental-state talk with older siblings, friends, and adults all contribute to young children's awareness of false belief.

- Preschoolers regard the mind as a passive container of information. As a result, they have difficulty inferring what people know or are thinking about.

Summarize children's literacy and mathematical knowledge during early childhood.

- Young children's **emergent literacy** reveals that they understand a great deal about written language before they read and write in conventional ways. Preschoolers gradually revise incorrect ideas about the meaning of written symbols as their perceptual and cognitive capacities improve, as they encounter writing in many contexts, and as adults help them make sense of written information.

- Literacy development builds on a foundation of spoken language and knowledge about the world. **Phonological awareness** strongly predicts emergent literacy and later reading and spelling achievement. Adult–child narrative conversations and informal literacy experiences, such as interactive storybook reading, foster literacy development.

- Mathematical reasoning also builds on informal knowledge. Toddlers' beginning grasp of **ordinality** serves as the basis for more complex understandings. By age 3½ to 4, they grasp the principle of **cardinality,** which increases the efficiency of counting. Soon children experiment with diverse strategies to solve simple arithmetic problems. When adults provide many occasions for counting and comparing quantities, children construct basic numerical concepts sooner.

Individual Differences in Mental Development

Describe the content of early childhood intelligence tests and the impact of home, preschool and kindergarten programs, child care, and educational media on mental development.

- Intelligence tests in early childhood sample a range of verbal and nonverbal skills, including vocabulary, memory, quantitative knowledge, problem solving, and spatial reasoning. By age 6 to 7, scores are good predictors of later IQ and academic achievement.

- Children growing up in warm, stimulating homes with parents who make reasonable demands for mature behavior score higher on mental tests. Home environment plays a major role in the poorer intellectual performance of low-SES children in comparison to their higher-SES peers.

- Preschools and kindergartens range along a continuum from **child-centered programs,** in which much learning occurs through play, to **academic programs,** in which teachers structure children's learning, often using repetition and drill. Emphasizing formal academic training undermines children's motivation and negatively influences later achievement.

- **Project Head Start** is the most extensive federally funded preschool program for low-income children in the United States. High-quality preschool intervention results in immediate IQ and achievement gains and long-term improvements in school adjustment, educational attainment, and life success. The more parents are involved in Head Start, the higher their children's year-end academic, language, and social skills.

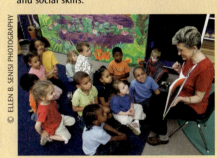

© ELLEN B. SENISI PHOTOGRAPHY

- Poor-quality child care undermines preschoolers' cognitive and social skills. In contrast, good child care enhances cognitive, language, and social development, especially for low-SES children.

- Children pick up academic knowledge from educational television and computer software. TV shows with slow-paced action and easy-to-follow story lines help preschoolers comprehend program content. Heavy exposure to entertainment TV, cartoons, and inappropriate computer games reduces time spent reading and interacting with others and is associated with poorer academic skills.

Language Development

Trace the development of vocabulary, grammar, and conversational skills in early childhood.

- Supported by **fast mapping,** preschoolers' vocabularies increase dramatically. According to one view, children are innately biased to induce word meanings using a **mutual exclusivity bias** and **syntactic bootstrapping.** An alternative perspective is that children use the same cognitive strategies they apply to nonlinguistic information. According to one account, preschoolers figure out word meanings from a coalition of cues—perceptual, social, and linguistic—which shift in importance with age.

- Between ages 2 and 3, children adopt the word order of their language. As they master grammatical constructions, they occasionally **overregularize,** applying the rules to words that are exceptions. By the end of the preschool years, children have acquired a wide variety of complex grammatical forms.

- Some experts believe that grammar is a product of general cognitive development. According to one view, children engage in **semantic bootstrapping,** relying on word meanings to figure out grammatical rules. Others agree with the essence of Chomsky's theory that children's brains are innately tuned for acquiring grammar.

- **Pragmatics** refers to the practical, social side of language. In face-to-face interaction with peers, young preschoolers are already skilled conversationalists. By age 4, they adapt their language to social expectations.

Cite factors that support language learning in early childhood.

- Conversational give-and-take with more skilled speakers fosters preschoolers' language skills. Adults provide both explicit feedback on the clarity of children's utterances and indirect feedback about grammar through **recasts** and **expansions.** However, these strategies, which are not used in all cultures, may be less important than mere exposure to a rich language environment.

IMPORTANT TERMS AND CONCEPTS

academic programs (p. 348)
animistic thinking (p. 321)
cardinality (p. 344)
centration (p. 322)
child-centered programs (p. 348)
conservation (p. 321)
dual representation (p. 320)
egocentrism (p. 321)
emergent literacy (p. 343)
episodic memory (p. 336)
expansions (p. 359)
fast mapping (p. 354)

guided participation (p. 331)
hierarchical classification (p. 322)
intersubjectivity (p. 331)
irreversibility (p. 322)
memory strategies (p. 336)
metacognition (p. 338)
mutual exclusivity bias (p. 355)
ordinality (p. 344)
overlapping-waves theory (p. 338)
overregularization (p. 357)
phonological awareness (p. 343)

planning (p. 335)
pragmatics (p. 358)
preoperational stage (p. 318)
private speech (p. 330)
Project Head Start (p. 349)
recasts (p. 359)
scaffolding (p. 331)
scripts (p. 336)
semantic bootstrapping (p. 357)
sociodramatic play (p. 319)
syntactic bootstrapping (p. 355)

"I Am Walking with Mama"
Tanya
4 years, Russia

A young child accompanies her mother on a winter walk. Warm, suppportive parenting provides a firm foundation for many facets of emotional and social development in early childhood, including self-concept and self-esteem, emotional understanding, peer relations, and morality.

Reprinted with permission from the International Collection of Child Art, Milner Library, Illinois State University, Normal, Illinois

Emotional and Social Development in Early Childhood

As the children in Leslie's classroom moved through the preschool years, their personalities took on clearer definition. By age 3, they voiced firm likes and dislikes as well as new ideas about themselves. "Stop bothering me," Sammy said to Mark, who was reaching for Sammy's beanbag as Sammy aimed it toward the mouth of a large clown face. "See, I'm great at this game," Sammy announced with confidence, an attitude that kept him trying, even though he missed most of the throws.

The children's conversations also revealed their first notions about morality. Often they combined statements about right and wrong with forceful attempts to defend their own desires. "You're 'posed to share," stated Mark, grabbing the beanbag out of Sammy's hand.

"I was here first! Gimme it back," demanded Sammy, pushing Mark. The two boys struggled for the beanbag until Leslie intervened, provided an extra set of beanbags, and showed them how they could both play.

As the interaction between Sammy and Mark reveals, preschoolers have become complex social beings. Young children argue, grab, and push, but cooperative exchanges are far more frequent. Between ages 2 and 6, first friendships form, in which children converse, act out complementary roles, and learn that their own desires for companionship and toys are best met when they consider others' needs and interests.

The children's developing understanding of their social world was especially apparent in their growing attention to the dividing line between male and female. While Lynette and Karen cared for a sick baby doll in the housekeeping area, Sammy, Vance, and Mark transformed the block corner into a busy intersection. "Green light, go!" shouted police officer Sammy as Vance and Mark pushed large wooden cars and trucks across the floor. Already, the children preferred same-sex peers, and their play themes mirrored their culture's gender stereotypes.

This chapter is devoted to the many facets of early childhood emotional and social development. We begin with Erik Erikson's theory, which provides an

Erikson's Theory: Initiative versus Guilt

Self-Understanding
Foundations of Self-Concept • Emergence of Self-Esteem

■ **CULTURAL INFLUENCES**
Cultural Variations in Personal Storytelling: Implications for Early Self-Concept

Emotional Development
Understanding Emotion • Emotional Self-Regulation • Self-Conscious Emotions • Empathy and Sympathy •

Peer Relations
Advances in Peer Sociability • First Friendships • Peer Relations and School Readiness • Social Problem Solving • Parental Influences on Early Peer Relations

Foundations of Morality
The Psychoanalytic Perspective • Social Learning Theory • The Cognitive-Developmental Perspective • The Other Side of Morality: Development of Aggression

■ **CULTURAL INFLUENCES**
Ethnic Differences in the Consequences of Physical Punishment

Gender Typing
Gender-Stereotyped Beliefs and Behaviors • Biological Influences on Gender Typing • Environmental Influences on Gender Typing • Gender Identity • Reducing Gender Stereotyping in Young Children

■ **BIOLOGY AND ENVIRONMENT**
David: A Boy Who Was Reared as a Girl

Child Rearing and Emotional and Social Development
Styles of Child Rearing • What Makes Authoritative Child Rearing Effective? • Cultural Variations • Child Maltreatment

overview of personality change in the preschool years. Then we consider children's concepts of themselves, their insights into their social and moral worlds, their gender typing, and their increasing ability to manage their emotional and social behaviors. Finally, we ask, What is effective child rearing? And we consider the complex conditions that support good parenting or lead it to break down, including the serious and widespread problems of child abuse and neglect.

Erikson's Theory: Initiative versus Guilt

Erikson (1950) described early childhood as a period of "vigorous unfolding." Once children have a sense of autonomy, they become less contrary than they were as toddlers. Their energies are freed for tackling the psychological conflict of the preschool years: **initiative versus guilt.** As the word *initiative* suggests, young children have a new sense of purposefulness. They are eager to tackle new tasks, join in activities with peers, and discover what they can do with the help of adults. They also make strides in conscience development.

Erikson regarded play as a means through which young children learn about themselves and their social world. Play permits preschoolers to try new skills with little risk of criticism and failure. It also creates a small social organization of children who must cooperate to achieve common goals. Around the world, children act out family scenes and highly visible occupations—police officer, doctor, and nurse in Western societies, rabbit hunter and potter among the Hopi Indians, hut builder and spear maker among the Baka of West Africa (Göncü, Patt, & Kouba, 2004).

Recall that Erikson's theory builds on Freud's psychosexual stages (see Chapter 1, page 16). In Freud's Oedipus and Electra conflicts, to avoid punishment and maintain the affection of parents, children form a *superego,* or conscience, by *identifying* with the same-sex parent. As a result, they adopt the moral and gender-role standards of their society. For Erikson, the negative outcome of early childhood is an overly strict superego that causes children to feel too much guilt because they have been threatened, criticized, and punished excessively by adults. When this happens, preschoolers' exuberant play and bold efforts to master new tasks break down.

Although Freud's ideas are no longer accepted as satisfactory explanations of conscience development, Erikson's image of initiative captures the diverse changes in young children's emotional and social lives. Early childhood is, indeed, a time when children develop a confident self-image, more effective control over their emotions, new social skills, the foundations of morality, and a clear sense of themselves as boy or girl. Now let's look closely at each of these aspects of development.

© DORANNE JACOBSON

■ This 3-year-old in India pretends to do laundry on the washing stone outside her family's home. Young children around the world act out family scenes and adult occupations, developing a sense of initiative as they gain insight into what they can do. ■

Self-Understanding

The development of language enables children to talk about their own subjective experience of being. In Chapter 9, we noted that preschoolers acquire a vocabulary for talking about their inner mental lives and refine their understanding of mental states. As self-awareness strengthens, children focus more intently on qualities that make the self unique. They begin to develop a **self-concept,** the set of attributes, abilities, attitudes, and values that an individual believes defines who he or she is. This mental representation of the self has profound implications for children's emotional and social lives, influencing their preferences for activities and social partners and their vulnerability to stress.

Foundations of Self-Concept

Ask a 3- to 5-year-old to tell you about him- or herself, and you are likely to hear something like this: "I'm Tommy. See, I got this new red T-shirt. I'm 4 years old. I can brush my teeth, and I can wash my hair all by myself. I have a new Tinkertoy set, and I made this big, big tower." Preschoolers' self-concepts largely consist of observable characteristics, such as their name, physical appearance, possessions, and everyday behaviors (Harter, 2006; Watson, 1990).

By age 3½, children also describe themselves in terms of typical emotions and attitudes ("I'm happy when I play with my friends"; "I don't like scary TV programs"; "I usually do what Mommy says"), suggesting a beginning understanding of their unique psychological characteristics (Eder & Mangelsdorf, 1997). And by age 5, children's degree of agreement with a battery of such statements coincides with maternal reports of their personality traits, indicating that older preschoolers have a sense of their own timidity, agreeableness, and positive or negative affect (Brown et al., 2008). As further support for this emerging grasp of personality, when given a trait label ("shy," "mean"), 4-year-olds infer appropriate motives and feelings. For example, they know that a shy person doesn't like to be with unfamiliar people (Heyman & Gelman, 1999). But preschoolers do not yet say "I'm helpful" or "I'm shy." Direct references to personality traits must wait for greater cognitive maturity.

A warm, sensitive parent–child relationship seems to foster a more positive, coherent early self-concept. In one study, 4-year-olds with a secure attachment to their mothers were more likely than their insecurely attached agemates to describe themselves in favorable terms at age 5—with statements that reflect agreeableness and positive affect (Goodvin et al., 2008). Also, recall from Chapter 9 that securely attached preschoolers participate in more elaborative parent–child conversations about personally experienced events, which help them understand themselves. Elaborative reminiscing is associated with a more organized, detailed autobiographical memory and with greater consistency in 5- and 6-year-olds' reports of their personal characteristics (see page 337). When, in past-event conversations, a child discovers that she finds swimming, getting together with friends, and going to the zoo fun, she can begin to connect these specific experiences into a general understanding of "what I enjoy," yielding a clearer image of herself (Farrant & Reese, 2000).

As early as age 2, parents use narratives of past events to impart rules, standards for behavior, and evaluative information about the child: "You added the milk when we made the mashed potatoes. That's a very important job!" (Nelson, 2003). As the Cultural Influences box on page 366 reveals, these self-evaluative narratives are a major means through which caregivers imbue the young child's self-concept with cultural values.

As they talk about personally significant events and as their cognitive skills advance, preschoolers gradually come to view themselves as persisting over time. Around age 4, children first become certain that a video image of themselves replayed shortly after it was filmed is still "me" (Povinelli, 2001). Similarly, when researchers asked 3- to 5-year-olds to imagine a future event (walking next to a waterfall) and to envision a future personal state by choosing from three items (a raincoat, money, a blanket) the one they would need to bring with them, performance—along with future-state justifications ("I'm gonna get wet")—increased sharply from age 3 to 4 (Atance & Meltzoff, 2005).

■ When asked to tell about themselves, preschoolers typically mention observable characteristics—physical appearance, possessions, and everyday behaviors and skills, such as "I can tie my own shoes." They also have an emerging grasp of their unique psychological characteristics—for this 5-year-old, persistence and determination! ■

CULTURAL INFLUENCES

Cultural Variations in Personal Storytelling: Implications for Early Self-Concept

Preschoolers of many cultural backgrounds participate in personal storytelling with their parents. Striking cultural differences exist in parents' selection and interpretation of events in these narratives, affecting the way children view themselves.

In one study, researchers spent hundreds of hours over a two-year period studying the storytelling practices of six middle-SES Irish-American families in Chicago and six middle-SES Chinese families in Taiwan. From extensive videotapes of adults' conversations with 2½-year-olds, the investigators identified personal stories and coded them for content, quality of their endings, and evaluation of the child (Miller, Fung, & Mintz, 1996; Miller et al., 1997).

Parents in both cultures discussed pleasurable holidays and family excursions in similar ways and with similar frequency. But Chinese parents more often told long stories about the child's misdeeds—using impolite language, writing on the wall, or playing in an overly rowdy way. These narratives were conveyed with warmth and caring, stressed the impact of misbehavior on others ("You made Mama lose face"), and often ended with direct teaching of proper behavior ("Saying dirty words is not good"). By contrast, in the few instances in which Irish-American stories referred to transgressions, parents downplayed their seriousness, attributing them to the child's spunk and assertiveness.

Early narratives about the child seem to launch preschoolers' self-concepts on culturally distinct paths (Miller, Fung, & Koven, 2007). Influenced by Confucian traditions of strict discipline and social obligations, Chinese parents integrated these values into their stories, affirming the importance of not disgracing the family and explicitly conveying expectations in the story's conclusion. Although Irish-American parents disciplined their children, they rarely dwelt on misdeeds in storytelling. Rather, they cast the child's shortcomings in a positive light, perhaps to promote self-esteem.

Whereas most Americans believe that favorable self-esteem is crucial for healthy development, Chinese adults generally see it as unimportant or even negative—as impeding the child's willingness to listen and to be corrected (Miller et al., 2002). Consistent with this view, the Chinese parents did little to cultivate their child's individuality. Instead, they used storytelling to guide the child toward socially responsible behavior. Hence, by the end of the preschool years, the Chinese child's self-image emphasizes membership in the collective and obligations to others ("I belong to the Lee family"; "I like to help my mom wash dishes"), whereas the American child's is more autonomous, consisting largely of personal descriptions ("I do lots of puzzles"; "I like hockey") (Wang, 2004).

A Chinese mother speaks gently to her children about proper behavior. Chinese parents often point out how their child's misdeeds affect others. The Chinese child's self-concept, in turn, emphasizes social obligations. ■

Emergence of Self-Esteem

Another aspect of self-concept emerges in early childhood: **self-esteem,** the judgments we make about our own worth and the feelings associated with those judgments. **TAKE A MOMENT...** Make a list of your own self-judgments. Notice that, besides a global appraisal of your worth as a person, you have a variety of separate self-evaluations concerning different activities. These evaluations are among the most important aspects of self-development because they affect our emotional experiences, future behavior, and long-term psychological adjustment.

By age 4, preschoolers have several self-judgments—for example, about learning things well in school, making friends, getting along with parents, and treating others kindly (Marsh, Ellis, & Craven, 2002). But because they have difficulty distinguishing between their desired and their actual competence, they usually rate their own ability as extremely high and often underestimate task difficulty, as Sammy did when he asserted, despite his many misses, that he was great at beanbag throwing (Harter, 2003, 2006).

High self-esteem contributes greatly to preschoolers' initiative during a period in which they must master many new skills. By age 3, children whose parents patiently encourage while offering information about how to succeed are enthusiastic and highly motivated. In contrast, children with a history of parental criticism of their worth and performance give up easily when faced with a challenge and express shame and despondency after failing (Kelley, Brownell, & Campbell, 2000). When preschool nonpersisters use dolls to act out an adult's reaction to failure, they anticipate disapproval—saying, for example, "He's punished because he can't do the puzzle" (Burhans & Dweck, 1995). They are also likely to report that their parents berate them for making small mistakes (Heyman, Dweck, & Cain, 1992). Adults can avoid promoting these self-defeating reactions by adjusting their expectations to children's capacities, scaffolding children's attempts at difficult tasks (see Chapter 9, page 331), and pointing out effort and improvement in children's work or behavior.

■ This 4-year-old probably overestimates how adept she is at playing catch with her older sister. But her high self-esteem contributes to her enthusiasm and motivation to master new skills. ■

ASK YOURSELF

◆ **REVIEW** Why is self-esteem typically extremely high in early childhood?

◆ **APPLY** Reread the description of Sammy and Mark's argument at the beginning of this chapter. On the basis of what you know about self-development, why was it a good idea for Leslie to resolve the dispute by providing an extra set of beanbags?

◆ **REFLECT** When you were a child, did your parents actively promote your self-esteem? How did their efforts reflect your family's cultural background? Explain.

Emotional Development

Gains in representation, language, and self-concept support emotional development in early childhood. Between ages 2 and 6, children make strides in the emotional abilities that, collectively, researchers refer to as *emotional competence* (Halberstadt, Denham, & Dunsmore, 2001; Saarni et al., 2006). First, preschoolers gain in emotional understanding, becoming better able to talk about feelings and to respond appropriately to others' emotional signals. Second, they become better at emotional self-regulation—in particular, at coping with intense negative emotion. Finally, preschoolers more often experience *self-conscious emotions* and *empathy,* which contribute to their developing sense of morality.

Parenting strongly influences preschoolers' emotional competence. Emotional competence, in turn, is vital for successful peer relationships and overall emotional health.

Understanding Emotion

Preschoolers' vocabulary for talking about emotion expands rapidly, and they use it skillfully to reflect on their own and others' behavior. Here are some excerpts from conversations in which 2-year-olds and 6-year-olds commented on emotionally charged experiences:

Two-year-old: [*After father shouted at child, she became angry, shouting back*] "I'm mad at you, Daddy. I'm going away. Good-bye."

Two-year-old: [*Commenting on another child who refused to nap and cried*] "Mom, Annie cry. Annie sad."

Six-year-old: [*In response to mother's comment, "It's hard to hear the baby crying"*] "Well, it's not as hard for me as it is for you." [*When mother asked why*] "Well, you like Johnny better than I do! I like him a little, and you like him a lot, so I think it's harder for you to hear him cry."

Six-year-old: [*Trying to comfort a small boy in church whose mother had gone up to communion*] "Aw, that's all right. She'll be right back. Don't be afraid. I'm here." (Bretherton et al., 1986, pp. 536, 540, 541)

COGNITIVE DEVELOPMENT AND EMOTIONAL UNDERSTANDING   As these examples show, early in the preschool years, children refer to causes, consequences, and behavioral signs of emotion, and over time their understanding becomes more accurate and complex (Stein & Levine, 1999). By age 4 to 5, they correctly judge the causes of many basic emotions ("He's happy because he's swinging very high"; "He's sad because he misses his mother"). Preschoolers' explanations tend to emphasize external factors over internal states, a balance that changes with age (Levine, 1995). In Chapter 9, we saw that after age 4, children appreciate that both desires and beliefs motivate behavior. Once these understandings are secure, children's grasp of how internal factors can trigger emotion expands.

Preschoolers can also predict what a playmate expressing a certain emotion might do next. Four-year-olds know that an angry child might hit someone and that a happy child is more likely to share (Russell, 1990). And they realize that thinking and feeling are interconnected—that a person reminded of a previous sad experience is likely to feel sad (Lagattuta, Wellman, & Flavell, 1997). Furthermore, they come up with effective ways to relieve others' negative feelings, such as hugging to reduce sadness (Fabes et al., 1988). Overall, preschoolers have an impressive ability to interpret, predict, and change others' feelings.

At the same time, preschoolers have difficulty interpreting situations that offer conflicting cues about how a person is feeling. When shown a picture of a happy-faced child with a broken bicycle, 4- and 5-year-olds tended to rely only on the emotional expression: "He's happy because he likes to ride his bike." Older children more often reconciled the two cues: "He's happy because his father promised to help fix his broken bike" (Gnepp, 1983; Hoffner & Badzinski, 1989). As in their approach to Piagetian tasks, young children focus on the most obvious aspect of a complex emotional situation to the neglect of other relevant information.

SOCIAL EXPERIENCE AND EMOTIONAL UNDERSTANDING   The more mothers label emotions, explain them, and express warmth and enthusiasm when conversing with preschoolers, the more "emotion words" children use and the better developed their emotional understanding (Fivush & Haden, 2005; Laible & Song, 2006). Maternal prompting of emotional thoughts ("What makes him afraid?") is a good predictor of 2-year-olds' emotion language. For older preschoolers, explanations ("He's sad because his dog ran away") are more important (Cervantes & Callanan, 1998). Does this remind you of the concept of *scaffolding*—that to be effective, adult teaching must adjust to children's increasing competence?

Preschoolers whose parents frequently acknowledge their children's emotional reactions and talk about diverse emotions are better able to judge others' emotions when tested at later ages (Denham & Kochanoff, 2002). Discussions in which family members disagree are particularly helpful. In one study, when mothers explained feelings and negotiated and compromised during conflicts with their 2½-year-olds, their children, at age 3, were advanced in emotional understanding and used similar strategies to resolve disagreements (Laible & Thompson, 2002). Such dialogues seem to help children reflect on the causes and consequences of emotion while also modeling mature communication skills. Furthermore, preschoolers who are securely attached to their mothers better understand emotion. Attachment security, as we have seen, is related to more elaborative parent–child narratives, including discussions of feelings that highlight the emotional significance of past events (Laible, 2004; Laible & Song, 2006; Raikes & Thompson, 2006).

As preschoolers learn more about emotion from interacting with adults, they engage in more emotion talk with siblings and friends, especially during make-believe play (Brown,

Donelan-McCall, & Dunn, 1996; Hughes & Dunn, 1998). Make-believe, in turn, contributes to emotional understanding, especially when children play with siblings (Youngblade & Dunn, 1995). The intense nature of the sibling relationship, combined with frequent acting out of feelings, makes pretending an excellent context for early learning about emotions. And when parents intervene in sibling disputes by reasoning and negotiating, preschoolers gain in sensitivity to their siblings' feelings (Perlman & Ross, 1997). They more often refer to their sibling's emotional perspective ("You get mad when I don't share") and engage in less fighting.

Knowledge about emotions helps children greatly in their efforts to get along with others. As early as 3 to 5 years of age, it is related to friendly, considerate behavior, willingness to make amends after harming another, and constructive responses to disputes with agemates (Brown & Dunn, 1996; Dunn, Brown, & Maguire, 1995; Garner & Estep, 2001). Also, the more preschoolers refer to feelings when interacting with playmates, the better liked they are by their peers (Fabes et al., 2001). Children seem to recognize that acknowledging others' emotions and explaining their own enhance the quality of relationships.

■ During the preschool years, children's understanding of the causes, consequences, and behavioral signs of emotion expands rapidly. Children whose mothers label and explain emotions use more "emotion words" and have better developed emotional understanding. ■

Emotional Self-Regulation

Language also contributes to preschoolers' improved *emotional self-regulation,* or ability to control the expression of emotion. By age 3 to 4, children verbalize a variety of strategies for adjusting their emotional arousal to a more comfortable level. For example, they know they can blunt emotions by restricting sensory input (covering their eyes or ears to block out a scary sight or sound), talking to themselves ("Mommy said she'll be back soon"), or changing their goals (deciding that they don't want to play anyway after being excluded from a game) (Thompson & Goodvin, 2007).

As children use these strategies, emotional outbursts decline. *Effortful control*—in particular, inhibiting impulses and shifting attention—also continues to be vital in managing emotion in early childhood. Three-year-olds who can distract themselves when frustrated tend to become cooperative school-age children with few problem behaviors (Gilliom et al., 2002). By age 3, effortful control predicts children's skill at portraying an emotion they do not feel—for example, reacting cheerfully after receiving an undesirable gift (Kieras et al., 2005). These emotional "masks" are largely limited to the positive feelings of happiness and surprise. Children of all ages (and adults as well) find it harder to act sad, angry, or disgusted than pleased (Denham, 1998). To promote good social relations, most cultures teach children to communicate positive feelings and inhibit unpleasant ones.

Temperament affects the development of emotional self-regulation. Children who experience negative emotion intensely find it harder to inhibit feelings and shift attention away from disturbing events. They are more likely to be anxious and fearful, respond with irritation to others' distress, react angrily or aggressively when frustrated, and get along poorly with teachers and peers (Chang et al., 2003; Eisenberg et al., 2005; Raikes et al., 2007).

To avoid social difficulties, emotionally reactive children must develop effective emotion-regulation strategies (Rothbart & Bates, 2006). By watching parents manage their feelings, children learn strategies for regulating their own. Warm, sensitive parents who use verbal guidance, including suggesting and explaining emotion-regulation strategies, strengthen children's capacity to handle stress (Colman et al., 2006). In contrast, when parents rarely express positive emotion, dismiss children's feelings as unimportant, and have difficulty controlling their own anger, children have continuing problems in managing emotion that seriously interfere with psychological adjustment (Hill et al., 2006; Katz & Windecker-Nelson, 2004; Thompson & Meyer, 2007). And because emotionally reactive children become increasingly difficult to rear, they are often targets of ineffective parenting, which compounds their poor self-regulation.

Applying What We Know

Helping Children Manage Common Fears of Early Childhood

FEAR	SUGGESTION
Monsters, ghosts, and darkness	Reduce exposure to frightening stories in books and on TV until the child is better able to distinguish between appearance and reality. Make a thorough "search" of the child's room for monsters, showing him that none are there. Leave a night-light burning, sit by the child's bed until he falls asleep, and tuck in a favorite toy for protection.
Preschool or child care	If the child resists going to preschool but seems content once there, the fear is probably separation. Provide a sense of warmth and caring while gently encouraging independence. If the child fears being at preschool, try to find out what is frightening—the teacher, the children, or a crowded, noisy environment. Provide extra support by accompanying the child and gradually lessening the amount of time you are present.
Animals	Do not force the child to approach a dog, cat, or other animal that arouses fear. Let the child move at her own pace. Demonstrate how to hold and pet the animal, showing the child that when treated gently, the animal is friendly. If the child is larger than the animal, emphasize this: "You're so big. That kitty is probably afraid of *you*!"
Intense fears	If a child's fear is intense, persists for a long time, interferes with daily activities, and cannot be reduced in any of the ways just suggested, it has reached the level of a *phobia*. Sometimes phobias are linked to family problems, and counseling is needed to reduce them. At other times, phobias diminish without treatment as the child's capacity for emotional self-regulation improves.

Adults' conversations with children also foster emotional self-regulation (Thompson, 2006). Parents who prepare children for difficult experiences by describing what to expect and ways to handle anxiety offer coping strategies that children can apply. Preschoolers' vivid imaginations and incomplete grasp of the distinction between appearance and reality make fears common in early childhood. Consult Applying What We Know above for ways adults can help young children manage fears.

Self-Conscious Emotions

One morning in Leslie's classroom, a group of children crowded around for a bread-baking activity. Leslie asked them to wait patiently while she got a baking pan. But Sammy reached over to feel the dough, and the bowl tumbled off the table. When Leslie returned, Sammy looked at her, then covered his eyes with his hands, and said, "I did something bad." He felt ashamed and guilty.

As their self-concepts develop, preschoolers become increasingly sensitive to praise and blame or (as Sammy did) to the possibility of such feedback. As a result, they more often experience *self-conscious emotions*—feelings that involve injury to or enhancement of their sense of self (see Chapter 7). By age 3, self-conscious emotions are clearly linked to self-evaluation (Lewis, 1995). But because preschoolers are still developing standards of excellence and conduct, they depend on the messages of parents, teachers, and others who matter to them to know *when* to feel proud, ashamed, or guilty, often viewing adult expectations as obligatory rules ("Dad said you're 'posed to take turns") (Thompson, Meyer, & McGinley, 2006).

When parents repeatedly comment on the worth of the child and her performance ("That's a bad job! I thought you were a good girl"), children experience self-conscious emotions intensely—more shame after failure, more pride after success. In contrast, when parents focus on how to improve performance ("You did it this way; now try doing it that way"), they induce moderate, more adaptive levels of shame and pride and greater persistence on difficult tasks (Kelley, Brownell, & Campbell, 2000; Lewis, 1998).

Beginning in early childhood, intense shame is associated with feelings of personal inadequacy ("I'm stupid"; "I'm a terrible person") and with maladjustment—withdrawal and depression as well as intense anger and aggression toward those who participated in the shame-evoking situation (Lindsay-Hartz, de Rivera, & Mascolo, 1995; Mills, 2005). In contrast, guilt—when it occurs in appropriate circumstances and is neither excessive nor accompanied by shame—is related to good adjustment. Guilt helps children resist harmful impulses, and it motivates a misbehaving child to repair the damage and behave more considerately (Mascolo

& Fischer, 2007; Tangney, Stuewig, & Mashek, 2007). But overwhelming guilt—involving such high emotional distress that the child cannot make amends—is linked to depressive symptoms as early as age 3 (Luby et al., 2009).

Finally, the consequences of shame for children's adjustment may vary across cultures. As illustrated in the Cultural Influences box on page 366, people in Asian collectivist societies, who define themselves in relation to their social group, view shame as an adaptive reminder of an interdependent self and of the importance of others' judgments (Bedford, 2004).

Empathy and Sympathy

Another emotional capacity that becomes more common in early childhood is *empathy,* which serves as an important motivator of **prosocial,** or **altruistic, behavior**—actions that benefit another person without any expected reward for the self (Eisenberg, Fabes, & Spinrad, 2006). Compared with toddlers, preschoolers rely more on words to communicate empathic feelings, a change that indicates a more reflective level of empathy. When a 4-year-old received a Christmas gift that she hadn't included on her list for Santa, she assumed it belonged to another little girl and pleaded with her parents, "We've got to give it back—Santa's made a big mistake. I think the girl's crying 'cause she didn't get her present!" As the ability to take the per-spective of others improves, empathic responding increases.

Yet empathy—*feeling with* another person and respond-ing emotionally in a similar way—does not always yield acts of kindness and helpfulness. For some children, empathiz-ing with an upset adult or peer escalates into *personal dis-tress.* In trying to reduce these feelings, the child focuses on his own anxiety rather than on the person in need. As a result, empathy does not lead to **sympathy**—feelings of con-cern or sorrow for another's plight.

Temperament plays a role in whether empathy prompts sympathetic, prosocial behavior or a personally distressed, self-focused response. Children who are sociable, assertive, and good at regulating emotion are more likely to help, share, and comfort others in distress. But poor emotion reg-ulators less often display sympathetic concern and prosocial behavior (Bengtson, 2005; Eisenberg et al., 1998; Valiente et al., 2004). When faced with someone in need, they react with facial and physiological distress—frowning, lip biting, a rise in heart rate, and a sharp increase in EEG brain-wave activity in the right cerebral hemisphere, which houses neg-ative emotion—indications that they are overwhelmed by their feelings (Jones, Field, & Davalos, 2000; Pickens, Field, & Nawrocki, 2001).

© ELLEN B. SENISI PHOTOGRAPHY

■ As children's language skills and ability to take the perspective of others improve, empathy also increases, motivating prosocial, or altruistic, behavior. ■

As with other aspects of emotional development, par-enting affects empathy and sympathy. When parents are warm, encourage emotional expressiveness, and show sensitive, empathic concern for their preschoolers' feelings, their children are likely to react in a concerned way to the distress of others—relationships that persist into adolescence and young adulthood (Koestner, Franz, & Weinberger, 1990; Michalik et al., 2007; Strayer & Roberts, 2004). Besides modeling sympathy, parents can teach children the importance of kindness and can intervene when they display inappropriate emotion—strategies that predict high levels of sympathetic responding (Eisen-berg, 2003).

In contrast, angry, punitive parenting disrupts the development of empathy at an early age—particularly among children who are poor emotion regulators and who therefore respond to parental hostility with especially high personal distress (Valiente et al., 2004). In one study, physically abused preschoolers at a child-care center rarely expressed concern at a peer's unhappiness but, rather, reacted with fear, anger, and physical attacks (Klimes-Dougan & Kistner, 1990). The children's behavior resembled their parents' insensitive responses to the suffering of others.

◆ **REVIEW** What do preschoolers understand about emotion, and how do cognition and social experience contribute to their understanding?

◆ **APPLY** Four-year-old Tia had her face painted at a carnival. As she walked around with her mother, the heat of the afternoon caused her balloon to pop. When Tia started to cry, her mother said, "Oh, Tia, balloons aren't such a good idea when it's hot outside. We'll get another on a cooler day. If you cry, you'll mess up your

beautiful face painting." What aspect of emotional development is Tia's mother trying to promote, and why is her intervention likely to help Tia?

◆ **CONNECT** Cite ways that parenting contributes to preschoolers' self-concept, self-esteem, emotional understanding, emotional self-regulation, self-conscious emotions, and empathy and sympathy. Do you see any patterns? Explain.

Peer Relations

As children become increasingly self-aware and better at communicating and understanding the thoughts and feelings of others, their skill at interacting with peers improves rapidly. Peers provide young children with learning experiences they can get in no other way. Because peers interact on an equal footing, they must keep a conversation going, cooperate, and set goals in play. With peers, children form friendships—special relationships marked by attachment and common interests. Let's look at how peer interaction changes over the preschool years.

Advances in Peer Sociability

Mildred Parten (1932), one of the first to study peer sociability among 2- to 5-year-olds, noticed a dramatic rise with age in joint, interactive play. She concluded that social development proceeds in a three-step sequence. It begins with **nonsocial activity**—unoccupied, onlooker behavior and solitary play. Then it shifts to **parallel play,** a limited form of social participation in which a child plays near other children with similar materials but does not try to influence their behavior. At the highest level are two forms of true social interaction. In **associative play,** children engage in separate activities but exchange toys and comment on one another's behavior. Finally, in **cooperative play,** a more advanced type of interaction, children orient toward a common goal, such as acting out a make-believe theme.

■ These 4-year-olds *(left)* engage in parallel play. Cooperative play *(right)* develops later than parallel play, but preschool children continue to move back and forth between the two types of sociability, often using parallel play as a respite from the complex demands of cooperation. ■

FOLLOW-UP RESEARCH ON PEER SOCIABILITY   Longitudinal evidence indicates that these play forms emerge in the order Parten suggested but that later-appearing ones do not replace earlier ones in a developmental sequence (Rubin, Bukowski, & Parker, 2006). Rather, all types coexist during early childhood.

TAKE A MOMENT... Watch preschool children move from one type of play to another in a play group or classroom, and you will see that they often transition from onlooker to parallel to cooperative play and back again (Robinson et al., 2003). Preschoolers seem to use parallel play as a way station. To successfully join the ongoing play of peers, they often first engage in parallel play nearby, easing into the group's activities—a strategy that increases the likelihood of being accepted. Later, they may return to parallel play as a respite from the high demands of complex social interaction and as a crossroad to new activities. And although nonsocial activity declines with age, it is still the most frequent form among 3- to 4-year-olds. Even among kindergartners it continues to occupy about one-third of children's free-play time. Both solitary and parallel play remain fairly stable from 3 to 6 years, accounting for as much of the young child's play as highly social, cooperative interaction (Rubin, Fein, & Vandenberg, 1983).

We now understand that it is the *type,* not the amount, of solitary and parallel play that changes during early childhood. In studies of preschoolers' play in Taiwan and the United States, researchers rated the *cognitive maturity* of nonsocial, parallel, and cooperative play by applying the categories shown in Table 10.1. Within each play type, older children displayed more cognitively mature behavior than younger children (Pan, 1994; Rubin, Watson, & Jambor, 1978).

Often parents wonder whether a preschooler who spends large amounts of time playing alone is developing normally. But only *certain types* of nonsocial activity—aimless wandering, hovering near peers, and functional play involving immature, repetitive motor action—are cause for concern. Children who behave reticently, by watching peers without playing, are usually temperamentally inhibited—high in social fearfulness. Their parents frequently overprotect them, criticize their social awkwardness, and unnecessarily control their play activities instead of patiently encouraging them to approach other children and helping them form at least one rewarding friendship, which protects against persisting adjustment problems (Coplan et al., 2004; Rubin, Bukowski, & Parker, 2006; Rubin, Burgess, & Hastings, 2002). And preschoolers who engage in solitary, repetitive behavior (banging blocks, making a doll jump up and down) tend to be immature, impulsive children who find it difficult to regulate anger and aggression (Coplan et al., 2001). In the classroom, both reticent and impulsive children experience peer ostracism, with boys at greater risk for rejection than girls (Coplan & Arbeau, 2008).

But other preschoolers with low rates of peer interaction are not socially anxious or impulsive. They simply prefer to play alone, and their solitary activities are positive and constructive. Teachers encourage such play by setting out art materials, books, puzzles, and building toys. Children who spend much time at these activities are usually well-adjusted youngsters who, when they do play with peers, show socially skilled behavior (Coplan & Armer, 2007). Still, a few preschoolers who engage in such age-appropriate solitary play—again, more often boys— are rebuffed by peers. Perhaps because quiet play is inconsistent with the "masculine" gender role, boys who engage in it are at risk for negative reactions from both parents and peers and, eventually, for adjustment problems (Coplan et al., 2001, 2004).

LOOK AND LISTEN

Observe several 3- to 5-year-olds during a free-play period in a preschool or child-care program. How much time does each child devote to nonsocial activity, parallel play, and socially interactive play? Do children seem to use parallel play as a way station between activities?

TABLE 10.1   Developmental Sequence of Cognitive Play Categories

PLAY CATEGORY	DESCRIPTION	EXAMPLES
Functional play	Simple, repetitive motor movements with or without objects, especially common during the first two years	Running around a room, rolling a car back and forth, kneading clay with no intent to make something
Constructive play	Creating or constructing something, especially common between 3 and 6 years	Making a house out of toy blocks, drawing a picture, putting together a puzzle
Make-believe play	Acting out everyday and imaginary roles, especially common between 2 and 6 years	Playing house, school, or police officer; acting out storybook or television characters

Source: Rubin, Fein, & Vandenberg, 1983.

■ These village children in India play a "circle tapping" game requiring high levels of cooperation. The child in the center recites a poem, the alphabet, or numbers, then walks around the circle saying, "Whomever I tap, it will be their turn." The tapped child moves to the center to recite. ■

As noted in Chapter 9, *sociodramatic play*—an advanced form of cooperative play—becomes especially common over the preschool years and supports cognitive, emotional, and social development (Göncü, Patt, & Kouba, 2004). In joint make-believe, preschoolers act out and respond to one another's pretend feelings. They also explore and gain control of fear-arousing experiences when they play doctor or pretend to search for monsters in a magical forest. As a result, they can better understand others' feelings and regulate their own (Smith, 2003). Finally, preschoolers spend much time negotiating roles and rules in play. To create and manage complex plots, they must resolve their disputes through negotiation and compromise. With age, preschoolers' conflicts center less on toys and other resources and more on differences of opinion—an indication of their expanding capacity to consider others' attitudes and ideas (Chen, Fein, & Tam, 2001; Hay, Payne, & Chadwick, 2004).

CULTURAL VARIATIONS   Peer sociability in collectivist societies, which stress group harmony, takes different forms than in individualistic cultures (Chen & French, 2008). For example, children in India generally play in large groups. Much of their behavior is imitative, occurs in unison, and involves close physical contact—a play style requiring high levels of cooperation. In a game called Bhatto Bhatto, children act out a script about a trip to the market, touching one another's elbows and hands as they pretend to cut and share a tasty vegetable (Roopnarine et al., 1994).

As another example, Chinese preschoolers—unlike North American preschoolers, who tend to reject reticent classmates—are typically willing to include a quiet, reserved child in play (Chen et al., 2006). In Chapter 7, we saw that until recently collectivist values, which discourage self-assertion, led to positive evaluations of shyness in China (see page 263). Apparently, this benevolent attitude is still evident in the play behaviors of young Chinese children.

Cultural beliefs about the importance of play also affect early peer associations. Caregivers who view play as mere entertainment are less likely to provide props or to encourage pretend than those who value its cognitive and social benefits (Farver & Wimbarti, 1995). Preschool children of Korean-American parents, who emphasize task persistence as vital for learning, spend less time than Caucasian-American children in joint make-believe and more time unoccupied and in parallel play (Farver, Kim, & Lee, 1995).

Recall the description of children's daily lives in village and tribal cultures, described on page 333 in Chapter 9. Mayan parents, for example, do not promote children's play—yet Mayan children are socially competent (Gaskins, 2000). Perhaps Western-style sociodramatic play, with its elaborate materials and wide-ranging themes, is particularly important for social development in societies where the worlds of adults and children are distinct. It may be less crucial in village cultures where children participate in adult activities from an early age.

First Friendships

As preschoolers interact, first friendships form that serve as important contexts for emotional and social development. **TAKE A MOMENT...** Jot down a description of what *friendship* means to you. You probably pictured a mutual relationship involving companionship, sharing, understanding of thoughts and feelings, and caring for and comforting one another in times of need. In addition, mature friendships endure over time and survive occasional conflicts.

Preschoolers understand something about the uniqueness of friendship. They say that a friend is someone "who likes you" and with whom you spend a lot of time playing. Yet their ideas about friendship are far from mature. Four- to 7-year-olds regard friendship as pleasurable play and sharing of toys. But friendship does not yet have a long-term, enduring quality based on mutual trust (Damon, 1988; Hartup, 2006). "Mark's my best friend," Sammy would declare on days when the boys got along well. But when a dispute arose, he would reverse himself: "Mark, you're not my friend!"

Nevertheless, interactions between young friends are unique. Preschoolers give twice as much reinforcement—greetings, praise, and compliance—to children they identify as friends, and they also receive more from them. Friends play together in more complex ways and are more cooperative and emotionally expressive—talking, laughing, and looking at each other more often than nonfriends do (Hartup, 2006; Vaughn et al., 2001). And early childhood friendships offer social support: Children who begin kindergarten with friends in their class or readily make new friends adjust to school more favorably (Ladd, Birch, & Buhs, 1999; Ladd & Price, 1987). Perhaps the company of friends serves as a secure base from which to develop new relationships, enhancing children's feelings of comfort in the new classroom.

Peer Relations and School Readiness

The ease with which kindergartners make new friends and are accepted by their classmates predicts cooperative participation in classroom activities and self-directed completion of learning tasks. These behaviors, in turn, are related to gains in achievement over the kindergarten year (Ladd, Birch, & Buhs, 1999; Ladd, Buhs, & Seid, 2000). Of course, kindergartners with friendly, prosocial behavioral styles make new friends easily, whereas those with weak emotional self-regulation skills and argumentative, aggressive, or peer-avoidant styles establish poor-quality relationships and make few friends. These negative social outcomes impair children's liking for school, classroom participation, and academic learning (Birch & Ladd, 1998).

■ In evaluating readiness for school, children's capacity for friendly, cooperative interaction is just as important as their academic skills. ■

The capacity to form mutually rewarding friendships, cooperate with peers, and build positive relationships with teachers enables kindergartners to integrate themselves into classroom environments in ways that foster both academic and social competence. In a longitudinal follow-up of more than 900 4-year-olds, children of average intelligence but with above-average social skills fared better in academic achievement in first grade than children of equal mental ability who were socially below average (Konold & Pianta, 2005). Because social maturity in early childhood contributes to later academic performance, a growing number of experts propose that readiness for kindergarten be assessed in terms of not just academic skills but also social skills, including capacity to form supportive bonds with teachers and peers, to participate actively and positively in interactions with classmates, and to behave prosocially (Ladd, Herald, & Kochel, 2006; Thompson & Raikes, 2007).

Preschool programs, too, should attend to these vital social prerequisites. Warm, responsive teacher–child interaction is vital, especially for temperamentally shy, impulsive, and emotionally negative children, who are at high risk for social difficulties (McClelland et al., 2007). In studies involving several thousand 4-year-olds in public preschools in six states, teacher sensitivity and emotional support were especially potent predictors of children's social competence during preschool and in a follow-up after kindergarten entry (Curby et al., 2009; Mashburn et al., 2008). Along with excellent teacher preparation, other indicators of program quality—small group sizes, generous teacher–child ratios, and developmentally appropriate daily activities (see page 352)—create classroom conditions that make positive teacher–child relationships more likely.

Social Problem Solving

As noted earlier, children, even those who are best friends, come into conflict—events that provide invaluable learning experiences in resolving disputes constructively. Preschoolers' disagreements only rarely result in hostile encounters. Although friends argue more than other peers do, they are also more likely to work out their differences through negotiation and to continue interacting (Hartup, 1999).

TAKE A MOMENT... At your next opportunity, observe preschoolers' play, noting disputes over objects ("That's mine!" "I had it first!"), entry into and control over play activities ("I'm on your team, Jerry." "No, you're not!"), and disagreements over facts, ideas, and beliefs ("I'm taller than he is." "No, you aren't!"). Children take these matters quite seriously. In Chapter 9, we noted that resolution of conflict, rather than conflict per se, promotes development. Social conflicts provide repeated occasions for **social problem solving**—generating and applying strategies that prevent or resolve disagreements, resulting in outcomes that are both acceptable to others and beneficial to the self. To engage in social problem solving, children must bring together diverse social understandings.

FIGURE 10.1

An information-processing model of social problem solving. The model is circular because children often engage in several information-processing activities at once—for example, interpreting information as they notice it and continuing to consider the meaning of another's behavior while they generate and evaluate problem-solving strategies. The model also takes into account the impact of mental state on social information processing—in particular, children's knowledge of social rules, their representations of past social experiences, and their expectations for future experiences. Peer evaluations and responses to enacted strategies are also important factors in social problem solving. *(Adapted from N. R. Crick & K. A. Dodge, 1994, "A Review and Reformulation of Social Information-Processing Mechanisms in Children's Social Adjustment," Psychological Bulletin, 115, 74–101, Figure 2 [adapted], p. 76. Copyright © 1994 by the American Psychological Association. Reprinted with permission of the American Psychological Association and Nicki Crick.)*

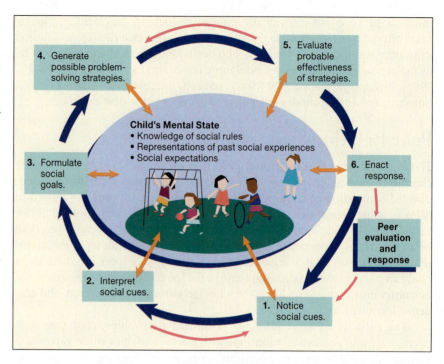

THE SOCIAL PROBLEM-SOLVING PROCESS   Nicki Crick and Kenneth Dodge (1994) organize the steps of social problem solving into the circular model shown in Figure 10.1. Notice how this flowchart takes an *information-processing approach,* clarifying exactly what a child must do to grapple with and solve a social problem. It enables identification of processing deficits, so intervention can be tailored to meet individual needs.

Social problem solving profoundly affects peer relations. Children who get along well with agemates interpret social cues accurately, formulate goals (being helpful to peers) that enhance relationships, and have a repertoire of effective problem-solving strategies—for example, politely asking to play, requesting an explanation when they do not understand a peer's behavior, and working out a compromise when faced with peer disagreement. In contrast, children with peer difficulties often hold biased social expectations. Consequently, they attend selectively to social cues (such as hostile acts) and misinterpret others' behavior (view an unintentional jostle as hostile). Their social goals (satisfying an impulse, getting even with or avoiding a peer) often lead to strategies that damage relationships (Dodge, Coie, & Lynam, 2006; Youngstrom et al., 2000). They might barge into a play group without asking, use threats and physical force, or fearfully hover around peers' activities.

Children improve greatly in social problem solving over the preschool and early school years. Instead of grabbing, hitting, or insisting that another child obey, 5- to 7-year-olds tend to rely on friendly persuasion and compromise, to think of alternative strategies when an initial one does not work, and to resolve disagreements without adult intervention (Chen et al., 2001; Mayeiux & Cillessen, 2003). Sometimes they suggest creating new, mutual goals, reflecting awareness that how they solve current problems will influence the future of the relationship (Yeates, Schultz, & Selman, 1991). By kindergarten, the accuracy and effectiveness of each component of social problem solving are related to socially competent behavior (Dodge et al., 1986).

ENHANCING SOCIAL PROBLEM SOLVING   Intervening with children who have weak social problem-solving skills can foster development in several ways. Besides improving peer relations, effective social problem solving offers children a sense of mastery in the face of stressful life events. It reduces the risk of adjustment difficulties in children from low-SES and troubled families (Goodman, Gravitt, & Kaslow, 1995).

In one intervention—the Promoting Alternative Thinking Strategies (PATHS) curriculum for preschool children—teachers provide children with weekly lessons in the ingredients of social problem solving. Using stories, puppet characters, discussion, and role-play demonstra-

LOOK AND LISTEN

At a playground, beach, or other public setting, watch for an hour or so as young children play, noting how they resolve conflicts. Do nearby adults guide them in social problem solving? How effective are adult interventions?

tions, they teach such skills as detecting others' feelings, planning sequences of action, generating effective strategies, and anticipating probable outcomes. In evaluations of PATHS, preschoolers who had completed 30 lessons in their Head Start classrooms scored higher than no-intervention controls in accurately "reading" others' emotions, inferring how others are likely to feel based on situational cues, selecting competent solutions to social conflicts, and teacher-rated peer cooperation and verbal communication (Bierman et al., 2008; Domitrovich, Cortes, & Greenberg, 2007).

Often preschoolers know how to solve a social problem effectively but do not apply their knowledge (Rudolph & Heller, 1997). And children who have repeatedly enacted maladaptive responses may need to rehearse alternatives to overcome their habitual behaviors and to spark more adaptive social information processing. A unique feature of PATHS is the inclusion of "extension activities" following each lesson—cooperative projects and games through which children practice targeted skills with teacher support. In addition, PATHS provides teachers with mentoring in effective classroom management and use of inductive discipline. These program elements likely strengthened its power to foster children's social competence.

Parental Influences on Early Peer Relations

Children first acquire skills for interacting with peers within the family. Parents influence children's peer sociability both *directly,* through attempts to influence children's peer relations, and *indirectly,* through their child-rearing practices and play behaviors (Ladd & Pettit, 2002; Rubin et al., 2005).

DIRECT PARENTAL INFLUENCES   Outside preschool, child care, and kindergarten, young children depend on parents to help them establish rewarding peer associations. Preschoolers whose parents frequently arrange informal peer play activities tend to have larger peer networks and to be more socially skilled (Ladd, LeSieur, & Profilet, 1993). In providing play opportunities, parents show children how to initiate peer contacts and encourage them to be good "hosts" who consider their playmates' needs.

Parents also influence their children's peer interaction skills by offering guidance on how to act toward others. Their skillful suggestions for managing conflict, discouraging teasing, and entering a play group are associated with preschoolers' social competence and peer acceptance (Laird et al., 1994; Mize & Pettit, 1997; Parke et al., 2004).

INDIRECT PARENTAL INFLUENCES   Many parenting behaviors not directly aimed at promoting peer sociability nevertheless influence it. For example, secure attachments to parents are linked to more responsive, harmonious peer interactions; larger peer networks; and warmer, more supportive friendships throughout childhood and adolescence (Laible, 2007; Lucas-Thompson & Clarke-Stewart, 2007; Wood, Emmerson, & Cowan, 2004). The sensitive, emotionally expressive communication that contributes to attachment security may be responsible. In several studies, highly involved, emotionally positive parent–child conversations and play predicted prosocial behavior and positive peer relations in preschool children (Clark & Ladd, 2000; Lindsey & Mize, 2000).

Parent–child play seems particularly effective for promoting peer interaction skills. During play, parents interact with their child on a "level playing field," much as peers do. And perhaps because parents play more with children of their own sex, mothers' play is more strongly linked to daughters' competence, fathers' play to sons' competence (Lindsey & Mize, 2000; Pettit et al., 1998).

As we have seen, some preschoolers already have great difficulty with peer relations. In Leslie's classroom, Robbie was one of them. Wherever he happened to be, comments like "Robbie ruined our block tower" and "Robbie hit me for no reason" could be heard. As we take up moral development in the next section, you will learn more about how parenting contributed to Robbie's peer problems.

© CULTURA/CORBIS

■ Parents' play with young children, especially same-sex children, is linked to social competence. By playing with his father as he would with a peer, this child acquires social skills that facilitate peer interaction. ■

ASK YOURSELF

◆ REVIEW Among children who spend much time playing alone, what factors distinguish those who are likely to have adjustment difficulties from those who are well-adjusted and socially skilled?

◆ APPLY Three-year-old Ben lives in the country, with no other preschoolers nearby. His parents wonder whether it is worth driving Ben into town once a week to participate in a peer play group. What advice would you give Ben's parents, and why?

◆ CONNECT Illustrate the influence of temperament on social problem solving by explaining how an impulsive child and a shy child might respond at each social problem-solving step in Figure 10.1 on page 376.

◆ REFLECT Think back to your first friendship. How old were you? Describe the quality of your relationship. What did your parents do, directly and indirectly, that might have influenced your earliest peer associations?

Foundations of Morality

Young children's behavior provides many examples of their budding moral sense. In Chapter 4, we noted that newborn (and older) infants often cry in response to the cries of other babies, a possible precursor of empathy. And after watching scenes in which one puppet helps a climber up a hill while a second pushes a climber down a hill, babies as young as 6 months overwhelming reached for the helpful character over a hinderer (Hamlin, Wynn, & Bloom, 2007). They seem implicitly drawn to the "nice" guy and repelled by the "mean" guy.

By age 2, children use words to evaluate their own and others' actions: "I naughty. I wrote on the wall" or (after being hit by another child) "Connie not nice." They also react with distress to aggressive or potentially harmful behaviors (Kochanska, Casey, & Fukumoto, 1995). And we have seen that children of this age share toys, help others, and cooperate in games—early indicators of considerate, responsible, prosocial attitudes.

Adults everywhere take note of this developing capacity to distinguish right from wrong and to accommodate the needs of others. Some cultures have special terms for it. The Utku Indians of Hudson Bay say the child develops *ihuma* (reason). The Fijians believe that *vakayalo* (sense) appears. In response, parents hold children more responsible for their behavior (Dunn, 2005). By the end of early childhood, children can state many moral rules: "Don't take someone's things without asking." "Tell the truth!" In addition, they argue over matters of justice: "You sat there last time, so it's my turn." "It's not fair. He got more!"

All theories of moral development recognize that conscience begins to take shape in early childhood. And most agree that at first, the child's morality is *externally controlled* by adults. Gradually, it becomes regulated by *inner standards.* Truly moral individuals do not do the right thing just to conform to others' expectations. Rather, they have developed compassionate concerns and principles of good conduct, which they follow in many situations.

Each major theory of development emphasizes a different aspect of morality. Psychoanalytic theory stresses the *emotional side* of conscience development—in particular, identification and guilt as motivators of good conduct. Social learning theory focuses on how *moral behavior* is learned through reinforcement and modeling. Finally, the cognitive-developmental perspective emphasizes *thinking*—children's ability to reason about justice and fairness.

The Psychoanalytic Perspective

Recall that according to Freud, young children form a *superego,* or conscience, by *identifying* with the same-sex parent, whose moral standards they adopt. Children obey the superego to avoid *guilt,* a painful emotion that arises each time they are tempted to misbehave. Moral development, Freud believed, is largely complete by 5 to 6 years of age.

Today, most researchers disagree with Freud's view of conscience development. In his theory (see page 16 in Chapter 1), fear of punishment and loss of parental love motivate conscience formation and moral behavior (Tellings, 1999). Yet children whose parents frequently use threats, commands, or physical force tend to violate standards often and feel little guilt, whereas parental warmth and responsiveness predict greater guilt following transgressions (Kochanska et al., 2002, 2005, 2008). And if a parent withdraws love after misbehavior—for example, refuses to speak to or states a dislike for the child—children often respond with high levels of self-blame, thinking, "I'm no good," or "Nobody loves me." Eventually, to protect themselves from overwhelming guilt, these children may deny the emotion and, as a result, also develop a weak conscience (Kochanska, 1991; Zahn-Waxler et al., 1990).

INDUCTIVE DISCIPLINE   In contrast, conscience formation is promoted by a type of discipline called **induction,** in which an adult helps make the child aware of feelings by pointing out the effects of the child's misbehavior on others, especially noting their distress and making clear that the child caused it. For example, a parent might say, "If you keep pushing him, he'll fall down and cry" or "She's crying because you won't give back her doll" (Hoffman, 2000). When generally warm parents provide explanations that match the child's capacity to understand, while firmly insisting that the child listen and comply, induction is effective as early as age 2. Preschoolers whose parents use it are more likely to refrain from wrongdoing, confess and repair damages after misdeeds, and display prosocial behavior (Kerr et al., 2004; Volling, Mahoney, & Rauer, 2009; Zahn-Waxler, Radke-Yarrow, & King, 1979).

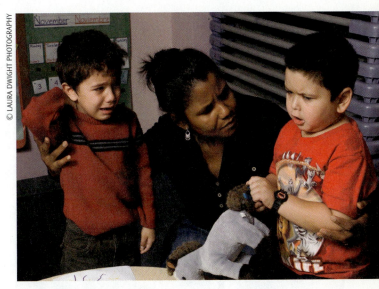

■ This teacher uses inductive discipline to explain to a child how his misbehavior affects others. She indicates how the child should behave, encouraging empathy and sympathetic concern. ■

The success of induction may lie in its power to motivate children's active commitment to moral standards, in the following ways:

- Induction gives children information about how to behave that they can use in future situations.
- By emphasizing the impact of the child's actions on others, induction encourages empathy and sympathetic concern, which motivate prosocial behavior (Krevans & Gibbs, 1996).
- Giving children reasons for changing their behavior encourages them to adopt moral standards because those standards make sense.
- Children who consistently experience induction may form a *script* for the negative emotional consequences of harming others: Child causes harm, inductive message points out harm, child feels empathy for victim, child makes amends (Hoffman, 2000). The script deters future transgressions.

In contrast, discipline that relies too heavily on threats of punishment or withdrawal of love makes children so anxious and frightened that they cannot think clearly enough to figure out what they should do. As a result, these practices do not get children to internalize moral rules and—as noted earlier—also interfere with empathy and prosocial responding (Eisenberg, Fabes, & Spinrad, 2006). Nevertheless, warnings, disapproval, and commands are sometimes necessary to get an unruly child to listen to an inductive message (Grusec, 2006).

THE CHILD'S CONTRIBUTION   Although good discipline is crucial, children's characteristics also affect the success of parenting techniques. Twin studies suggest a modest genetic contribution to empathy and prosocial behavior (Knafo & Plomin, 2006; Zahn-Waxler et al., 2001). More empathic children require less power assertion and are more responsive to induction.

Temperament is also influential. Mild, patient tactics—requests, suggestions, and explanations—are sufficient to prompt guilt reactions and conscience development in anxious, fearful preschoolers (Kochanska et al., 2002). But with fearless, impulsive children, gentle discipline has little impact. Power assertion also works poorly. It undermines the child's capacity for effortful control, which strongly predicts good conduct, empathy, sympathy, and prosocial

© JACK HOLLINGSWORTH/GETTY IMAGES/DIGITAL VISION

■ When children are impulsive and low in anxiety, a secure attachment relationship motivates conscience development. This preschooler wants to follow parental rules to preserve an affectionate, supportive relationship with his father. ■

behavior (Kochanska & Aksan, 2006; Kochanska & Knaack, 2003). Parents of impulsive children can foster conscience development by ensuring a secure attachment relationship and combining firm correction of misbehavior with induction (Kochanska, Aksan, & Joy, 2007). When children are so low in anxiety that parental disapproval causes them little discomfort, a close parent–child bond provides an alternative foundation for morality. It motivates children to listen to parents as a means of preserving an affectionate, supportive relationship.

In sum, to foster early moral development, parents must tailor their disciplinary strategies to their child's personality. Does this remind you of *goodness of fit,* discussed in Chapter 7? Return to page 262 to review this idea.

THE ROLE OF GUILT Although little support exists for Freudian ideas about conscience development, Freud was correct that guilt is an important motivator of moral action. By the end of toddlerhood, guilt reactions are evident, and preschoolers' assertions reveal that they have internalized the parent's moral voice: "Didn't you hear my mommy? We'd better not play with these toys" (Thompson, 2009).

Inducing *empathy-based* guilt (expressions of personal responsibility and regret, such as "I'm sorry I hurt him") by explaining that the child is causing someone distress and has disappointed the parent is a means of influencing children without using coercion. Empathy-based guilt reactions are associated with stopping harmful actions, repairing damage caused by misdeeds, and engaging in future prosocial behavior (Baumeister, 1998). At the same time, parents must help children deal with guilt feelings constructively—by guiding them to make up for immoral behavior rather than minimizing or excusing it (Bybee, Merisca, & Velasco, 1998).

But contrary to what Freud believed, guilt is not the only force that compels us to act morally. Nor is moral development complete by the end of early childhood. Rather, it is a gradual process, extending into adulthood.

Social Learning Theory

According to social learning theory, morality does not have a unique course of development. Rather, moral behavior is acquired just like any other set of responses: through reinforcement and modeling.

IMPORTANCE OF MODELING *Operant conditioning*—reinforcement for good behavior, in the form of approval, affection, and other rewards—is not enough for children to acquire moral responses. For a behavior to be reinforced, it must first occur spontaneously. Yet many prosocial acts—sharing, helping, comforting an unhappy playmate—occur so rarely at first that reinforcement cannot explain their rapid development in early childhood. Rather, social learning theorists believe that children learn to behave morally largely through *modeling*—by observing and imitating people who demonstrate appropriate behavior (Bandura, 1977; Grusec, 1988). Once children acquire a moral response, such as sharing or telling the truth, reinforcement in the form of praise for the act ("That was a very nice thing to do") and for the child's character ("You're a very kind and considerate boy") increases its frequency (Mills & Grusec, 1989).

Many studies show that having helpful or generous models increases young children's prosocial responses. And certain characteristics of the model affect children's willingness to imitate:

■ *Warmth and responsiveness.* Preschoolers are more likely to copy the prosocial actions of an adult who is warm and responsive than those of a cold, distant adult (Yarrow, Scott, & Waxler, 1973). Warmth seems to make children more attentive and receptive to the model and is itself an example of a prosocial response.

■ *Competence and power.* Children admire and therefore tend to imitate competent, powerful models—especially older peers and adults (Bandura, 1977).

■ *Consistency between assertions and behavior.* When models say one thing and do another—for example, announce that "it's important to help others" but rarely engage in helpful acts—children generally choose the most lenient standard of behavior that adults demonstrate (Mischel & Liebert, 1966).

Models are most influential in the early years. In one study, toddlers' eager, willing imitation of their mothers' behavior predicted moral conduct (not cheating in a game) and guilt following transgressions at age 3 (Forman, Aksan, & Kochanska, 2004). At the end of the preschool years, children who have had consistent exposure to caring adults tend to behave prosocially whether or not a model is present: They have internalized prosocial rules from repeated observations and encouragement by others (Mussen & Eisenberg-Berg, 1977).

EFFECTS OF PUNISHMENT   Many parents are aware that angrily yelling at, slapping, and spanking children are ineffective disciplinary tactics. A sharp reprimand or physical force to restrain or move a child is justified when immediate obedience is necessary—for example, when a 3-year-old is about to run into the street. In fact, parents are most likely to use forceful methods under these conditions. But to foster long-term goals, such as acting kindly toward others, they tend to rely on warmth and reasoning (Kuczynski, 1984). And in response to serious transgressions, such as lying or stealing, they often combine power assertion with reasoning (Grusec, 2006; Grusec & Goodnow, 1994).

Frequent punishment, however, promotes only immediate compliance, not lasting changes in behavior. For example, Robbie's parents often punished by hitting, shouting, and criticizing. But as soon as they were out of sight, Robbie usually engaged in the unacceptable behavior again. The more harsh threats, angry physical control, and physical punishment children experience, the more likely they are to develop serious, lasting mental health problems. These include weak internalization of moral rules; depression, aggression, antisocial behavior, and poor academic performance in childhood and adolescence; and depression, alcohol abuse, criminality, and partner and child abuse in adulthood (Afifi et al., 2006; Bender et al., 2007; Gershoff, 2002; Kochanska, Aksan, & Nichols, 2003; Lynch et al., 2006).

Harsh punishment has several undesirable side effects:

■ Parents often spank in response to children's aggression (Holden, Coleman, & Schmidt, 1995). Yet the punishment itself models aggression!

■ Harshly treated children react with anger, resentment, and a chronic sense of being personally threatened, which prompts a focus on the self's distress rather than a sympathetic orientation to others' needs.

■ Children who are frequently punished develop a more conflict-ridden and less supportive parent–child relationship and also learn to avoid the punitive parent (McLoyd & Smith, 2002; Shaw, Lacourse, & Nagin, 2005). Consequently, the parent's effectiveness at teaching desirable behaviors is substantially reduced.

■ By stopping children's misbehavior temporarily, harsh punishment gives adults immediate relief, reinforcing them for using coercive discipline. For this reason, a punitive adult is likely to punish with greater frequency over time, a course of action that can spiral into serious abuse.

■ Children, adolescents, and adults whose parents used *corporal punishment*—the use of physical force to inflict pain but not injury—are more accepting of such discipline (Bower-Russa, Knutson, & Winebarger, 2001; Deater-Deckard et al., 2003). In this way, use of physical punishment may transfer to the next generation.

Although corporal punishment spans the SES spectrum, its frequency and harshness are elevated among less educated, economically disadvantaged parents (Giles-Sims, Strauss, & Sugarman, 1995; Lansford et al., 2004b, 2009). And consistently, parents with conflict-ridden marriages and with mental health problems (who are emotionally reactive, depressed, or aggressive) are more likely to be punitive and also to have hard-to-manage children, whose disobedience evokes more parental harshness (Berlin et al., 2009; Erath et al., 2006; Knafo &

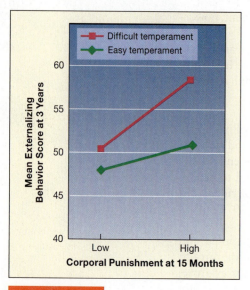

FIGURE 10.2

Relationship of parental corporal punishment at age 15 months to externalizing behavior, by child temperament. Corporal punishment was associated with increased externalizing behavior (anger and aggression) for both easy and difficult children, even after controlling for family and parenting characteristics. The rise in externalizing behavior was greater for difficulty children—a difference also evident in a follow-up during first grade. *(From M. K. Mulvaney & C. J. Mebert, 2007, "Parental Corporal Punishment Predicts Behavior Problems in Early Childhood,"* Journal of Family Psychology, 21, *p. 394. Copyright © 2007 by the American Psychological Association. Reprinted with permission of the American Psychological Association.)*

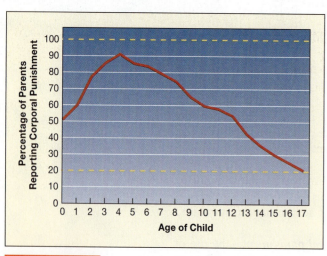

FIGURE 10.3

Prevalence of corporal punishment by child's age. Estimates are based on the percentage of parents in a nationally representative U.S. sample of nearly 1,000 reporting one or more instances of spanking, slapping, pinching, shaking, or hitting with a hard object in the past year. Physical punishment increases sharply during early childhood and then declines, but it is high at all ages. *(From M. A. Straus & J. H. Stewart, 1999, "Corporal Punishment by American Parents: National Data on Prevalence, Chronicity, Severity, and Duration in Relation to Child and Family Characteristics,"* Clinical Child and Family Psychology Review, 2, *p. 59. Adapted with kind permission from Springer Science and Business Media and the author.)*

Plomin, 2006; Taylor et al., 2010). These parent–child similarities suggest that heredity contributes to the link between punitive discipline and children's adjustment difficulties. But heredity is not a complete explanation. **TAKE A MOMENT...** Return to page 86 in Chapter 2 to review findings indicating that good parenting can shield children genetically at risk for aggression and antisocial activity from developing those behaviors.

Furthermore, in a longitudinal study extending from 15 months to 3 years, early corporal punishment predicted externalizing behavior problems in preschoolers of diverse temperaments (see Figure 10.2) (Mulvaney & Mebert, 2007). Negative outcomes were simply more pronounced among temperamentally difficult children. Other longitudinal findings reveal a similar link between physical punishment and later child and adolescent aggression, even after child, parenting, and family characteristics that might otherwise account for the relationship were controlled (Berlin et al., 2009; Lansford et al., 2009; Taylor et al., 2010).

In view of these outcomes, the widespread use of corporal punishment by American parents is cause for concern. A survey of a nationally representative sample of U.S. households revealed that although corporal punishment increases from infancy to age 5 and then declines, it is high at all ages (see Figure 10.3) (Straus & Stewart, 1999). Repeated use of physical punishment is more common with toddlers and preschoolers. And more than one-fourth of physically punishing U.S. parents report having used a hard object, such as a brush or a belt (Gershoff, 2002).

A prevailing American belief is that corporal punishment, if implemented by caring parents, is harmless, perhaps even beneficial. In a recent U.S. opinion poll, 72 percent of adults agreed that it is "OK to spank a child" (Survey USA, 2005). But as the Cultural Influences box on the following page reveals, this assumption is valid only under conditions of limited use in certain social contexts.

ALTERNATIVES TO HARSH PUNISHMENT Alternatives to criticism, slaps, and spankings can reduce the side effects of punishment. A technique called **time out** involves removing children from the immediate setting—for example, by sending them to their rooms—until they are ready to act appropriately. When a child is out of control, a few minutes in time out can be enough to change behavior while also giving angry parents a cooling-off period. Another approach is *withdrawal of privileges,* such as playing outside or watching a favorite TV program. Like time out, removing privileges allows parents to avoid using harsh techniques that can easily intensify into violence.

When parents do decide to use punishment, they can increase its effectiveness in three ways:

- *Consistency.* Permitting children to act inappropriately on some occasions but scolding them on others confuses children, and the unacceptable act persists (Acker & O'Leary, 1996).
- *A warm parent–child relationship.* Children of involved, caring parents find the interruption in parental affection that accompanies punishment especially unpleasant. They want to regain parental warmth and approval as quickly as possible.
- *Explanations.* Providing reasons for mild punishment helps children relate the misdeed to expectations for future behavior. This approach leads to far greater reduction in misbehavior than using punishment alone (Larzelere et al., 1996).

CULTURAL INFLUENCES

Ethnic Differences in the Consequences of Physical Punishment

In an African-American community, six elders, all of whom had volunteered to serve as mentors for parents facing child-rearing challenges, met to discuss parenting issues at a social service agency. Their attitudes toward discipline were strikingly different from those of the white social workers who had brought them together. Each elder argued that successful child rearing required the use of appropriate physical tactics. At the same time, they voiced strong disapproval of screaming or cursing at children, calling such out-of-control parental behavior "abusive." Ruth, the oldest and most respected member of the group, characterized good parenting as a complex combination of warmth, teaching, talking nicely, and disciplining physically. She related how an older neighbor advised her to handle her own children when she was a young parent:

> She said to me says, don't scream . . . you talk to them real nice and sweet and when they do something ugly . . . she say you get a nice little switch and you won't have any trouble with them and from that day that's the way I raised 'em. (Mosby et al., 1999, pp. 511–512)

Use of physical punishment is highest among low-SES ethnic minority parents, who are more likely than middle-SES white parents to advocate slaps and spankings (Pinderhughes et al., 2000; Straus & Stewart, 1999; Taylor et al., 2010). And although corporal punishment is linked to a wide array of negative child outcomes, exceptions do exist.

In one longitudinal study, researchers followed several hundred families for 12 years, collecting information from mothers on disciplinary strategies in early and middle childhood and from both mothers and their children on youth problem behaviors in adolescence. Even after many child and family characteristics were controlled, the findings were striking: In Caucasian-American families, physical punishment was positively associated with adolescent aggression and antisocial behavior. In African-American families, by contrast, the more mothers had disciplined physically in childhood, the less their teenagers displayed angry, acting-out behavior and got in trouble at school and with the police (Lansford et al., 2004a).

African-American and Caucasian-American parents seem to mete out physical punishment differently. In black families, such discipline is culturally approved, generally mild, delivered in a context of parental warmth, and aimed at helping children become responsible adults. White parents, in contrast, typically consider physical punishment to be wrong, so when they resort to it, they are often highly agitated and rejecting of the child (Dodge, McLoyd, & Lansford, 2006). As a result, most black children may view spanking as a practice carried out with their best interests in mind, whereas white children may regard it as an "act of personal aggression" (Gunnoe & Mariner, 1997, p. 768).

In support of this view, when several thousand ethnically diverse children were followed from the preschool through the early school years, spanking was associated with a rise in behavior problems if parents were cold and rejecting but not if they were warm and supportive (McLoyd & Smith, 2002). In another study, spanking predicted depressive symptoms only among a minority of African-American children whose mothers disapproved of the practice and, as a result, tended to use it when they were highly angry and frustrated (McLoyd et al., 2007).

These findings are not an endorsement of physical punishment. Other forms of discipline, including time out, withdrawal of privileges, and the positive strategies listed on page 384, are far more effective. But it is noteworthy that the meaning and impact of physical discipline vary sharply with cultural context.

■ In African-American families, physical discipline is often culturally approved, generally mild, and delivered in a context of parental warmth. As a result, most African-American children may view spanking as a practice carried out with their best interests in mind, not as an act of aggression. ■

POSITIVE RELATIONSHIPS, POSITIVE DISCIPLINE The most effective forms of discipline encourage good conduct—by building a mutually respectful bond with the child, letting the child know ahead of time how to act, and praising mature behavior (Zahn-Waxler & Robinson, 1995). When sensitivity, cooperation, and shared positive emotion are evident in joint activities between parents and preschoolers, children show firmer conscience development—expressing empathy after transgressions, behaving responsibly, playing fairly in games, and considering others' welfare (Kochanska et al., 2005, 2008). Parent–child closeness leads children to heed parental demands because children feel a sense of commitment to the relationship.

Consult Applying What We Know on page 384 for ways to discipline positively. Parents who use these strategies focus on long-term social and life skills—cooperation, problem solving, and consideration for others. As a result, they greatly reduce the need for punishment.

Applying What We Know

Using Positive Discipline

STRATEGY	EXPLANATION
Use transgressions as opportunities to teach.	When a child engages in harmful or unsafe behavior, intervene firmly, and then use induction, which motivates children to make amends and behave prosocially.
Reduce opportunities for misbehavior.	On long car trips, bring back-seat activities that relieve children's restlessness. At the supermarket, converse with children, and let them help with shopping. As a result, children learn to occupy themselves constructively when options are limited.
Provide reasons for rules.	When children appreciate that rules are fair to all concerned, not arbitrary, they strive to follow the rules because they are reasonable and rational.
Arrange for children to participate in family routines and duties.	By joining with adults in preparing a meal, washing dishes, or raking leaves, children develop a sense of responsible participation in family and community life and acquire many practical skills.
When children are obstinate, try compromising and problem solving.	When a child refuses to obey, express understanding of the child's feelings ("I know it's not fun to clean up"), suggest a compromise ("You put those away, I'll take care of these"), and help the child think of ways to avoid the problem in the future. Responding firmly but kindly and respectfully increases the likelihood of willing cooperation.
Encourage mature behavior.	Express confidence in children's capacity to learn and appreciation for effort and cooperation, as in "You gave that your best!" "Thanks for helping!" Adult encouragement fosters pride and satisfaction in succeeding, thereby inspiring children to improve further.
Be sensitive to children's physical and emotional resources.	When children are tired, ill, or bored, they are likely to engage in attention-getting, disorganized, or otherwise improper behavior as a reaction to discomfort. In these instances, meeting the child's needs makes more sense than disciplining.

Sources: Berk, 2001a; Grusec, 2006; Nelson, 1996.

© BLEND IMAGES/ALAMY

■ This 3-year-old understands that the style and color of her new shoes are matters of personal choice, distinct from moral imperatives and social conventions. ■

The Cognitive-Developmental Perspective

The psychoanalytic and behaviorist approaches to morality focus on how children acquire ready-made standards of good conduct from adults. In contrast, the cognitive-developmental perspective regards children as *active thinkers* about social rules. As early as the preschool years, children make moral judgments, deciding what is right or wrong on the basis of concepts they construct about justice and fairness (Gibbs, 2010; Turiel, 2006).

PRESCHOOLERS' MORAL UNDERSTANDING   Young children have some well-developed ideas about morality. As long as researchers emphasize people's intentions, 3-year-olds say that a person with bad intentions—someone who deliberately frightens, embarrasses, or otherwise hurts another—is more deserving of punishment than a well-intentioned person (Helwig, Zelazo, & Wilson, 2001; Jones & Thompson, 2001). Around age 4, children know that a person who expresses an insincere intention—says, "I'll come over and help you rake leaves" but doesn't intend to do so—is lying. And 4-year-olds approve of telling the truth and disapprove of lying, even when a lie remains undetected (Bussey, 1992).

Furthermore, preschoolers in diverse cultures distinguish **moral imperatives,** which protect people's rights and welfare, from two other types of rules and expectations: **social conventions,** customs determined solely by consensus, such as table manners and politeness rituals (saying "please" and "thank you"); and **matters of personal choice,** such as choice of friends, hairstyle, and leisure activities, which do not violate rights and are up to the individual (Killen, Margie, & Sinno, 2006; Nucci, 1996; Smetana, 2006). Interviews with 3- and 4-year-olds reveal that they consider moral violations (unprovoked hitting, stealing an apple) as more wrong than violations of social conventions (eating ice cream with your fingers). They also say that moral violations would still be wrong even if an adult did not see them and no rules existed to prohibit them because they harm others. And preschoolers' concern with personal choice, conveyed through statements like "I'm gonna wear *this* shirt," serves as the springboard for moral concepts of individual rights, which will expand greatly in middle childhood and adolescence (Nucci, 2005).

Within the moral domain, however, preschool and young school-age children tend to reason *rigidly*, making judgments based on salient features and consequences while neglecting other important information. For example, they are more likely than older children to claim that stealing and lying are always wrong, even when a person has a morally sound reason for engaging in these acts (Lourenco, 2003). They view inflicting physical damage (breaking a peer's toy) as a more serious transgression than treating others unfairly (not sharing) (Nucci, 2002). And their focus on outcomes means that they fail to realize that a promise is still a promise, even if it is unfulfilled (Maas, 2008; Maas & Abbeduto, 2001).

Still, preschoolers' ability to distinguish moral imperatives from social conventions is impressive. How do they do so? According to cognitive-developmental theorists, they *actively make sense* of their experiences (Turiel, 2006). They observe that after a moral offense, peers respond with strong negative emotion, describe their own injury or loss, tell another child to stop, or retaliate. And an adult who intervenes is likely to call attention to the rights and feelings of the victim. In contrast, violations of social convention elicit less intense peer reactions. And in these situations, adults usually demand obedience without explanation or point to the importance of keeping order.

SOCIAL EXPERIENCE AND MORAL UNDERSTANDING   Cognition and language support preschoolers' moral understanding, but social experiences are vital. Disputes with siblings and peers over rights, possessions, and property allow preschoolers to negotiate, compromise, and work out their first ideas about justice and fairness. Children also learn from warm, sensitive parental communication and from observing the way adults handle rule violations to care about the welfare of others (Turiel & Killen, 2010). And they benefit greatly from adult–child discussions of moral issues. Children who are advanced in moral thinking tend to have parents who adapt their communications about fighting, honesty, and ownership to what their children can understand, tell stories with moral implications, encourage prosocial behavior, and gently stimulate the child to think further, without being hostile or critical (Janssens & Deković, 1997; Walker & Taylor, 1991).

Preschoolers who verbally and physically assault others, often with little or no provocation, are already delayed in moral reasoning (Helwig & Turiel, 2004; Sanderson & Siegal, 1988). Without special help, such children show long-term disruptions in moral development, deficits in self-control, and ultimately an antisocial lifestyle.

The Other Side of Morality: Development of Aggression

Beginning in late infancy, all children display aggression from time to time, and as opportunities to interact with siblings and peers increase, aggressive outbursts occur more often (Tremblay, 2004). By the second year, aggressive acts with two distinct purposes emerge. Initially, the most common is **proactive** (or *instrumental*) **aggression,** in which children act to fulfill a need or desire—to obtain an object, privilege, space, or social reward, such as adult or peer attention—and unemotionally attack a person to achieve their goal. The other type, **reactive** (or *hostile*) **aggression,** is an angry, defensive response to provocation or a blocked goal and is meant to hurt another person (Dodge, Cole, & Lynam, 2006; Little et al., 2005).

Proactive and reactive aggression come in three varieties, which are the focus of most research:

■ **Physical aggression** harms others through physical injury—pushing, hitting, kicking, or punching others, or destroying another's property.
■ **Verbal aggression** harms others through threats of physical aggression, name-calling, or hostile teasing.

■ These preschoolers display proactive aggression, pushing and grabbing as they argue over a game. Proactive aggression declines with age as children learn to compromise and share, and as their capacity to delay gratification improves. ■

■ **Relational aggression** damages another's peer relationships through social exclusion, malicious gossip, or friendship manipulation.

Although verbal aggression is always direct, physical and relational aggression can be either *direct* or *indirect*. For example, hitting injures a person directly, whereas destroying property indirectly inflicts physical harm. Similarly, saying, "Do what I say, or I won't be your friend," conveys relational aggression directly, while spreading rumors, refusing to talk to a peer, or manipulating friendship by saying behind someone's back, "Don't play with her; she's a nerd," does so indirectly.

In early childhood, verbal aggression gradually replaces physical aggression as language develops and adults and peers react negatively and strongly to physical attacks (Alink et al., 2006; Tremblay et al., 1999). And proactive aggression declines as preschoolers' improved capacity to delay gratification enables them to resist grabbing others' possessions. But reactive aggression in verbal and relational forms tends to rise over early and middle childhood (Côté et al., 2007; Tremblay, 2000). Older children are better able to recognize malicious intentions and, as a result, more often retaliate in hostile ways.

By age 17 months, boys are more physically aggressive than girls—a difference found throughout childhood in many cultures (Baillargeon et al., 2007; Card et al., 2008). The sex difference is due in part to biology—in particular, to male sex hormones (androgens) and temperamental traits (activity level, irritability, impulsivity) on which boys score higher. Gender-role conformity is also important. As soon as preschoolers are aware of gender stereotypes—that males and females are expected to behave differently—physical aggression drops off more sharply for girls than for boys (Fagot & Leinbach, 1989). Parents also respond far more negatively to physical fighting in girls (Arnold, McWilliams, & Harvey-Arnold, 1998).

Although girls have a reputation for being both verbally and relationally more aggressive than boys, the sex difference is small (Crick et al., 2004, 2006; Crick, Ostrov, & Werner, 2006). Beginning in the preschool years, girls concentrate most of their aggressive acts in the relational category. Boys inflict harm in more variable ways. Physically and verbally aggressive boys also tend to be relationally aggressive (Card et al., 2008). Therefore, boys display overall rates of aggression that are much higher than girls'.

At the same time, girls more often use indirect relational tactics that—in disrupting intimate bonds especially important to girls—can be particularly mean. Whereas physical attacks are usually brief, acts of indirect relational aggression may extend for hours, weeks, or even months (Nelson, Robinson, & Hart, 2005; Underwood, 2003). In one instance, a 6-year-old girl formed a "pretty-girls club" and—for nearly an entire school year—convinced its members to exclude several classmates by saying they were "dirty and smelly."

An occasional aggressive exchange between preschoolers is normal. Children sometimes assert their sense of self through these encounters, which become important learning experiences as adults intervene and teach social problem solving (Vaughn et al., 2003). But some children—especially those who are emotionally negative, impulsive, and disobedient—are prone to early, high rates of physical or relational aggression (or both) that often persist. These aggressive children are at risk for later internalizing and externalizing difficulties and social skills deficits, including loneliness, anxiety, depression, poor-quality friendships, and antisocial activity in middle childhood and adolescence (Campbell et al., 2006; Côté et al., 2007; Crick, Ostrov, & Werner, 2006).

THE FAMILY AS TRAINING GROUND FOR AGGRESSIVE BEHAVIOR   "I can't control him; he's impossible," Robbie's mother, Nadine, complained to Leslie one day. When Leslie asked if Robbie might be troubled by something happening at home, she discovered that his parents fought constantly and resorted to harsh, inconsistent discipline. The same child-rearing practices that undermine moral internalization—love withdrawal, power assertion, physical punishment, negative comments and emotions, and inconsistency—are linked to aggression from early childhood through adolescence in children of both sexes and in many cultures, with most of these practices predicting both physical and relational forms (Bradford et al., 2003; Côté et al., 2007; Nelson et al., 2006; Rubin et al., 2003; Yang et al., 2003).

In families like Robbie's, anger and punitiveness quickly create a conflict-ridden family atmosphere and an "out-of-control" child. The pattern begins with forceful discipline, which occurs more often with stressful life experiences (such as economic hardship or an unhappy marriage), a parent with an unstable personality, or a temperamentally difficult child (Dodge, Coie, & Lynam, 2006). Typically, the parent threatens, criticizes, and punishes, and the child whines, yells, and refuses until the parent "gives in." At the end of each exchange, both parent and child get relief from stopping the unpleasant behavior of the other, so the behaviors repeat and escalate.

As these cycles become more frequent, they generate anxiety and irritability among other family members, who soon join in the hostile interactions. Compared with siblings in typical families, preschool siblings who have critical, punitive parents are more aggressive toward one another. Physically, verbally, and relationally destructive sibling conflict, in turn, quickly spreads to peer relationships, contributing to poor impulse control and antisocial behavior by the early school years (Garcia et al., 2000; Ostrov, Crick, & Stauffacher, 2006).

Boys are more likely than girls to be targets of harsh, inconsistent discipline because they are more active and impulsive and therefore harder to control. When children who are extreme in these characteristics are exposed to emotionally negative, inept parenting, their capacity for emotional self-regulation, empathic responding, and guilt after transgressions is severely disrupted (Eisenberg, Eggum, & Edwards, 2010). Consequently, they lash out when disappointed, frustrated, or faced with a sad or fearful victim.

SOCIAL INFORMATION-PROCESSING DEFICITS   Children who are products of these family processes soon acquire a distorted view of the social world. Those who are high in reactive aggression often see hostile intent where it does not exist—in situations where peers' intentions are unclear, where harm is accidental, and even where peers are trying to be helpful (Lochman & Dodge, 1998; Orobio de Castro et al., 2002). When such children feel threatened (for example, a researcher tells them that a peer partner is in a bad mood and might pick a fight), they are especially likely to interpret accidental mishaps as hostile (Williams et al., 2003). As a result, they make many unprovoked attacks, which trigger aggressive retaliations.

Children high in proactive aggression have different deficits in social information processing. Compared with their agemates, they believe there are more benefits and fewer costs for engaging in destructive acts (Arsenio, 2010; Dodge et al., 1997). And they are more likely to think that aggression "works," producing material rewards and reducing others' unpleasant behaviors (Arsenio & Lemerise, 2001; Goldstein & Tisak, 2004). Thus, they callously use aggression to advance their own goals and are relatively unconcerned about causing suffering in others—an aggressive style associated with later, more severe conduct problems, violent behavior, and delinquency (Marsee & Frick, 2010).

TAKE A MOMENT... Return to the information-processing model of social problem solving on page 376. Notice how reactive aggression is linked to deficiencies in noticing and interpreting social cues. In contrast, proactive aggression is associated with deficiencies in formulating social goals (caring more about satisfying one's own needs than getting along with others) and generating and evaluating strategies (engaging in aggression and evaluating it favorably) (Arsenio, 2010). A substantial number of aggressive children engage in both reactive and proactive acts, while others largely display one type (Fite et al., 2008; Little et al., 2003; Polman et al., 2007).

Highly aggressive children tend to be rejected by peers, to fail in school, and (by adolescence) to seek out deviant peers. Together, these factors contribute to the long-term stability of aggression.

VIOLENT MEDIA AND AGGRESSION   In the United States, 57 percent of American TV programs between 6 A.M. and 11 P.M. contain violent scenes, often portraying repeated aggressive acts that go unpunished. TV victims of violence are rarely shown experiencing serious harm, and few programs condemn violence or depict other ways of solving problems. Violent

■ TV violence increases the likelihood of hostile thoughts and emotions and tolerance of real-world aggression. Playing violent video and computer games has similar effects. ■

content is 9 percent above average in children's programming, and cartoons are the most violent (Center for Communication and Social Policy, 1998).

Reviewers of thousands of studies—using a wide variety of research designs, methods, and participants from diverse cultures—have concluded that TV violence increases the likelihood of hostile thoughts and emotions and of verbally, physically, and relationally aggressive behavior (Comstock & Scharrer, 2006; Ostrov, Gentile, & Crick, 2006). And a growing number of studies show that playing violent video and computer games has similar effects (Anderson, 2004; Anderson et al., 2008). Although young people of all ages are susceptible, preschool and young school-age children are especially likely to imitate TV violence because they believe that much TV fiction is real and accept what they see uncritically.

Violent programming not only creates short-term difficulties in parent and peer relations but also has lasting negative consequences. In several longitudinal studies, time spent watching TV in childhood and adolescence predicted aggressive behavior in early adulthood, after other factors linked to TV viewing (such as prior child and parent aggression, IQ, parent education, family income, and neighborhood crime) were controlled (see Figure 10.4) (Graber et al., 2006; Huesmann, 1986; Huesmann et al., 2003; Johnson et al., 2002). Aggressive children and adolescents have a greater appetite for violent TV and computer games. And boys devote more time to violent media than girls, in part because of male-oriented themes of conquest and adventure and use of males as lead characters. But even in nonaggressive children, violent TV sparks hostile thoughts and behavior; its impact is simply less intense (Bushman & Huesmann, 2001).

Furthermore, media violence "hardens" children to aggression, making them more willing to tolerate it in others. Viewers quickly habituate, responding with reduced arousal to real-world instances and tolerating more aggression in others (Anderson et al., 2003). Heavy viewers believe that there is much more violence in society than there actually is—an effect that is especially strong for children who perceive media violence to be relevant to their own lives (Donnerstein, Slaby, & Eron, 1994). As these responses indicate, exposure to violent media images modifies children's attitudes toward social reality so they increasingly match media images.

The ease with which television and computer games can manipulate children's beliefs and behavior has led to strong public pressure to improve its content. In the United States, the First Amendment right to free speech has hampered efforts to regulate TV broadcasting. Instead, all programs must be rated for violent and sexual content, and all new TV sets are required to contain the V-chip, which allows parents to block undesired material. In contrast, Canada's nationwide broadcasting code bans from children's shows realistic scenes of violence that minimize consequences and cartoons with violence as the central theme. Further, violent programming intended for adults cannot be shown on Canadian channels before 9 P.M. (Canadian children, however, have access to violent TV fare on U.S. channels.)

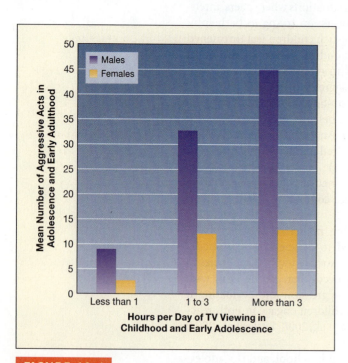

FIGURE 10.4

Relationship of television viewing in childhood and early adolescence to aggressive acts in adolescence and early adulthood.
Interviews with more than 700 parents and youths revealed that the more TV watched in childhood and early adolescence, the greater the annual number of aggressive acts committed by the young person, as reported in follow-up interviews at ages 16 and 22. *(Adapted from Johnson et al., 2002.)*

Applying What We Know

Regulating TV and Computer Use

STRATEGY	EXPLANATION
Limit TV viewing and computer use.	Provide clear rules limiting what children can view on TV and do on the computer, and stick to them. Avoid using the TV or the computer as a babysitter. Do not place a TV or a computer in a child's bedroom; doing so substantially increases use and makes the child's activity hard to monitor.
Avoid using TV or computer time as a reward.	When TV or computer access is used as a reward or withheld as punishment, children become increasingly attracted to it.
When possible, watch TV with children, helping them understand what they see.	When adults raise questions about realism in TV depictions, express disapproval of on-screen behavior, and encourage discussion, they help children understand and critically evaluate TV content.
Link TV content to everyday learning experiences.	Parents can extend TV learning in ways that encourage children to engage actively with their surroundings. For example, a program on animals might spark a trip to the zoo, a visit to the library for books about animals, or new ways of observing and caring for the family pet.
Model good TV and computer practices.	Parents' media behavior influences children's behavior. Avoid excessive TV and computer use, and limit your own exposure to violent media content.
Use a warm, rational approach to child rearing.	Children of warm parents who make reasonable demands for mature behavior prefer TV and computer experiences with educational and prosocial content and are less attracted to violent media fare.

At present, parents bear most responsibility for regulating their children's exposure to media violence and other inappropriate content. Besides TV and computer games, the Internet poses risks. As with the V-chip for TV, parents can control children's Internet access by using filters or programs that monitor website visits. Yet surveys of U.S. parents indicate that 20 to 30 percent of preschoolers and 40 percent of school-age children experience no limits on TV or computer use at home. Some children begin visiting websites without parental supervision as early as age 4 (Rideout & Hamel, 2006; Roberts, Foehr, & Rideout, 2005; Varnhagen, 2007). Applying What We Know above lists strategies parents can use to protect children from undesirable TV and computer fare.

HELPING CHILDREN AND PARENTS CONTROL AGGRESSION Treatment for aggressive children must begin early, before their antisocial behavior becomes well-practiced and difficult to change. Breaking the cycle of hostilities between family members and promoting effective ways of relating to others is crucial. The coercive cycles of punitive parents and aggressive children are so persistent that these children often are punished when they do behave appropriately!

Leslie suggested that Robbie's parents see a family therapist, who observed their inept practices and coached them in alternatives. They learned not to give in to Robbie, to pair commands with reasons, and to replace verbal insults and spankings with more effective punishments, such as time out and withdrawal of privileges. After several weeks of such training, children's aggression declines, and parents view their children more positively—benefits still evident one to four years later (Kazdin, 2003; Patterson & Fisher, 2002). The therapist also encouraged Robbie's parents to be warmer and to give him attention and approval for prosocial acts. Finally, she helped them with their marital problems. This, in addition to their improved ability to manage Robbie's behavior, greatly reduced tension and conflict in the household.

At the same time, Leslie began teaching Robbie more successful ways of relating to peers, had him practice these skills, and praised him whenever she noticed him using them. And as opportunities arose, she encouraged Robbie to talk about a playmate's feelings and to express his own. As Robbie practiced taking the perspective of others, empathizing, and feeling sympathetic concern, his lashing out at peers declined (Izard et al., 2004). Robbie participated in a social problem-solving intervention as well (return to pages 376–377 to review).

LOOK AND LISTEN

Watch a half-hour of Saturday morning cartoons and a prime-time movie on TV, and tally the number of violent acts, including those that go unpunished. How often did violence occur in each type of program? What do young viewers learn about the consequences of violence?

Finally, relieving stressors that stem from poverty and neighborhood disorganization and providing families with social supports help prevent childhood aggression (Boyle & Lipman, 2002). When parents better cope with difficulties in their own lives, interventions aimed at reducing children's aggression are even more effective (Kazdin & Whitley, 2003).

ASK YOURSELF

◆ **REVIEW** What experiences help preschoolers differentiate moral imperatives, social conventions, and matters of personal choice?

◆ **APPLY** Alice and Wayne want their two young children to become morally mature, caring individuals. List some parenting practices they should use and some they should avoid.

◆ **CONNECT** What must parents do to foster conscience development in fearless, impulsive children? How does this illustrate goodness of fit (see page 262 in Chapter 7)? Explain.

◆ **REFLECT** Which types of punishment for a misbehaving preschooler do you endorse, and which types do you reject? Why?

Gender Typing

Gender typing refers to any association of objects, activities, roles, or traits with one sex or the other in ways that conform to cultural stereotypes (Liben & Bigler, 2002). In Leslie's classroom, girls spent more time in the housekeeping, art, and reading corners, while boys gathered more often in spaces devoted to blocks, woodworking, and active play. Already, the children had acquired many gender-linked beliefs and preferences and tended to play with peers of their own sex.

The same theories that provide accounts of morality have been used to explain children's gender typing: *social learning theory,* with its emphasis on modeling and reinforcement, and *cognitive-developmental theory,* with its focus on children as active thinkers about their social world. As we will see, neither is adequate by itself. *Gender schema theory,* a third perspective that combines elements of both, has gained favor. In the following sections, we consider the early development of gender typing.

Gender-Stereotyped Beliefs and Behaviors

Even before children can label their own sex consistently, they have begun to acquire subtle associations with gender that most of us hold—men as rough and sharp, women as soft and round. In one study, 18-month-olds linked such items as fir trees and hammers with males, although they had not yet learned comparable feminine associations (Eichstedt et al., 2002). Recall from Chapter 7 that around age 2, children use such words as "boy," "girl," "lady," and "man" appropriately. As soon as gender categories are established, children sort out what they mean in terms of activities and behaviors.

Preschoolers associate toys, articles of clothing, tools, household items, games, occupations, colors (pink and blue), and behaviors (physical and relational aggression) with one sex or the other (Giles & Heyman, 2005; Poulin-Dubois et al., 2002; Ruble, Martin, & Berenbaum, 2006). And their actions reflect their beliefs, not only in play preferences but in personality traits as well. As we have seen, boys tend to be more active, impulsive, assertive, and physically aggressive. Girls tend to be more fearful, dependent, emotionally sensitive, compliant, advanced in effortful control, and skilled at understanding self-conscious emotions and at inflicting indirect relational aggression (Bosacki & Moore, 2004; Else-Quest et al., 2006; Underwood, 2003).

During early childhood, children's gender-stereotyped beliefs strengthen—so much so that many children apply them as blanket rules than as flexible guidelines. When children were asked whether gender stereotypes could be violated, half or more of 3- and 4-year-olds answered "no" to clothing, hairstyle, certain play styles (girls playing roughly), and play with certain toys (Barbie dolls and GI Joes) (Blakemore, 2003). Furthermore, most 3- to 6-year-olds are firm about not wanting to be friends with a child who violates a gender stereotype (a boy who wears nail polish, a girl who plays with trucks) or to attend a school where such violations are allowed (Ruble et al., 2007).

The rigidity of preschoolers' gender stereotypes helps us understand some commonly observed everyday behaviors. When Leslie showed her class a picture of a Scottish bagpiper wearing a kilt, the children insisted, "Men don't wear skirts!" During free play, they often exclaimed that girls can't be police officers and boys don't take care of babies. These one-sided judgments are a joint product of gender stereotyping in the environment and young children's cognitive limitations—in particular, their difficulty coordinating conflicting sources of information (Trautner et al., 2005). Most preschoolers do not yet realize that characteristics *associated with* one's sex—activities, toys, occupations, hairstyle, and clothing—do not *determine* whether a person is male or female. They have trouble understanding that males and females can be different in terms of their bodies but similar in many other ways.

■ Gender typing is well under way in the preschool years. Girls tend to play with girls and are drawn to toys and activities that emphasize nurturance, cooperation, and physical attractiveness. ■

Biological Influences on Gender Typing

The sex differences in play and personality traits just described appear in many cultures around the world (Munroe & Romney, 2006; Whiting & Edwards, 1988). Certain ones—male activity level and physical aggression, female emotional sensitivity, and a preference for same-sex playmates—are widespread among mammalian species (de Waal, 1993, 2001). According to an evolutionary perspective, the adult life of our male ancestors was oriented toward competing for mates, that of our female ancestors toward rearing children. Therefore, males became genetically primed for dominance and females for intimacy, responsiveness, and cooperativeness. Evolutionary theorists claim that family and cultural forces can influence the intensity of genetically based sex differences, leading some individuals to be more gender-typed than others. But experience cannot eradicate those aspects of gender typing that served adaptive functions in human history (Geary, 1999; Maccoby, 2002).

Experiments with animals reveal that prenatally administered androgens increase active play and suppress maternal caregiving in both male and female mammals (Sato et al., 2004). Eleanor Maccoby (1998) argues that sex hormones also affect human play styles, leading to rough, noisy movements among boys and calm, gentle actions among girls. Then, as children interact with peers, they choose partners whose interests and behaviors are compatible with their own. Preschool girls increasingly seek out other girls and like to play in pairs because they share a preference for quieter activities involving cooperative roles. Boys come to prefer larger-group play with other boys, who share a desire to run, climb, play-fight, compete, and build up and knock down (Fabes, Martin, & Hanish, 2003). At age 4, children spend three times as much time with same-sex as with other-sex playmates. By age 6, this ratio has climbed to 11 to 1 (Martin & Fabes, 2001).

Even stronger support for the role of biology in human gender typing comes from research on girls exposed prenatally to high levels of androgens due either to normal variation in hormone levels or to a genetic defect. In both instances, these girls showed more "masculine"

BIOLOGY AND ENVIRONMENT

David: A Boy Who Was Reared as a Girl

As a married man and father in his mid-thirties, David Reimer talked freely about his everyday life—his problems at work and the challenges of child rearing. But when asked about his first 15 years, he distanced himself, speaking as if the child of his early life were another person. In essence, she was.

David—named Bruce at birth—underwent the first infant sex reassignment ever reported on a genetically and hormonally normal child. To find out about David's development, researchers interviewed him intensively and studied his medical and psychotherapy records (Colapinto, 2001; Diamond & Sigmundson, 1999).

When Bruce was 8 months old, his penis was accidentally severed during circumcision. Soon afterward, his desperate parents heard about psychologist John Money's success in assigning a sex to children born with ambiguous genitals. They traveled from their home in Canada to Johns Hopkins University in Baltimore, where, under Money's oversight, 22-month-old Bruce had surgery to remove his testicles and sculpt his genitals to look like those of a girl. The operation complete, Bruce's parents named their daughter Brenda.

Brenda's upbringing was tragic. From the outset, she resisted her parents' efforts to steer her in a "feminine" direction. A dominant, rough-and-tumble child, Brenda picked fights with other children and usually won. Brian (Brenda's identical twin brother) recalled that Brenda looked like a delicate, pretty girl—until she moved or spoke. "She walked like a guy. She talked about guy things. . . . She played with my toys: Tinkertoys, dump trucks" (Colapinto, 2001, p. 57).

At school, Brenda's boyish behavior led classmates to taunt and tease her. When she played with girls, she tried organizing large-group, active games, but they weren't interested. Friendless and uncomfortable as a girl, Brenda increasingly displayed behavior problems. During periodic medical follow-ups, she drew pictures of herself as a boy and refused additional surgery to create a vagina.

As adolescence approached, Brenda's parents moved her from school to school and therapist to therapist in an effort to help her fit in socially and accept a female identity—pressures that increased Brenda's anxiety and conflict with her parents. At puberty, when Brenda's shoulders broadened and her body added muscle, her parents insisted that she begin estrogen therapy to feminize her appearance. Soon she grew breasts and added fat around her waist and hips. Repelled by her feminizing shape, Brenda began overeating to hide it. Her classmates reacted to her confused appearance with stepped-up brutality.

At last, Brenda was transferred to a therapist who recognized her despair and encouraged her parents to tell her about her infancy. When Brenda was 14, her father explained the circumcision accident. David recalled reacting with relief. Deciding to return to his biological sex immediately, he chose for himself the name David, after the biblical lad who slew a giant and overcame adversity. David soon started injections of the androgen hormone testosterone to masculinize his body, and he underwent surgery to remove his breasts and to construct a penis. Although his adolescence continued to be troubled, in his twenties he fell in love with Jane, a single mother of three children, and married her.

David's case confirms the impact of genetic sex and prenatal hormones on a person's sense of self as male or female. His gender reassignment failed because his male biology overwhelmingly

■ Because of a medical accident when he was a baby, David Reimer underwent the first sex reassignment on a genetically and hormonally normal child: He was reared as a girl. David's story shows the overwhelming impact of biology on gender identity. At age 36, as shown here, he was a married man and father. But two years later, the troubled life that sprang from David's childhood ended tragically, in suicide. ■

demanded a consistent sexual identity. At the same time, his childhood highlights the importance of experience. David expressed outrage at adult encouragement of dependency in girls—after all, he had experienced it firsthand.

Although David tried to surmount his tragic childhood, the troubled life that sprang from it persisted. When David was in his mid-thirties, his twin brother, Brian, committed suicide. Then, after David had lost his job and had been swindled out of his life savings in a shady investment deal, his wife left him, taking the children with her. Grief-stricken, David sank into a deep depression. On May 4, 2004, at age 38, he shot himself.

behaviors—a preference for trucks and blocks over dolls, for active over quiet play, and for boys as playmates—even when their parents encouraged them to engage in gender-typical play (Cohen-Bendahan, van de Beek, & Berenbaum, 2005; Pasterski et al., 2005). Similarly, boys with reduced prenatal androgen exposure due to hereditary defects tended to engage in "feminine" behaviors, including toy choices, play behaviors, and preference for girl playmates (Jürgensen et al., 2007).

Additional evidence comes from a case study of a boy who experienced serious sexual-identity and adjustment problems because his biological makeup and sex of rearing were at odds. Refer to the Biology and Environment box above to find out about David's development.

Environmental Influences on Gender Typing

In a study following almost 14,000 British children from ages 2½ to 8, gender-typed behavior rose steadily over early childhood, with the most gender-typed young preschoolers showing the sharpest increase (Golombok et al., 2008). A wealth of evidence reveals that environmental forces—at home, at school, and in the community—build on genetic influences to promote vigorous gender typing in early childhood.

THE FAMILY   Beginning at birth, parents have different expectations of sons than of daughters (see Chapter 7). Many parents prefer that their children play with "gender-appropriate" toys. And they tend to describe achievement, competition, and control of emotion as important for sons and warmth, "ladylike" behavior, and closely supervised activities as important for daughters (Brody, 1999; Turner & Gervai, 1995).

Actual parenting practices reflect these beliefs. Parents give their sons toys that stress action and competition (guns, cars, tools, and footballs) and their daughters toys that emphasize nurturance, cooperation, and physical attractiveness (dolls, tea sets, and jewelry) (Leaper, 1994; Leaper & Friedman, 2007). Parents also actively reinforce independence in boys and closeness and dependency in girls. For example, parents react more positively when a son plays with cars and trucks, demands attention, runs and climbs, or tries to take toys from others. When interacting with daughters, they more often direct play activities, provide help, encourage participation in household tasks, make supportive statements (approval, praise, and agreement), and refer to emotions (Clearfield & Nelson, 2006; Fagot & Hagan, 1991; Kuebli, Butler, & Fivush, 1995; Leaper et al., 1995). Gender-typed play contexts amplify these communication differences. For example, when playing housekeeping, mothers engage in high rates of supportive emotion talk with girls (Leaper, 2000).

Furthermore, parents provide children with indirect cues about gender categories and stereotypes through the language they use. In one study, researchers observed mothers talking about picture books with their 2- to 6-year-olds (Gelman, Taylor, & Nguyen, 2004). Mothers often labeled gender, even when they did not have to do so ("That's a boy." "Is that a she?"). And they frequently expressed *generic utterances,* which referred to many, or nearly all, males and females as alike, ignoring exceptions: "Boys can be sailors." "Most girls don't like trucks." As Figure 10.5 shows, with age, both mothers and children produced more of these generic statements, which—even when they denied a stereotype ("Boys can be ballet dancers, too")—viewed individuals of the same gender as alike and ignored exceptions. At age 2, mothers introduced these sweeping generalizations nearly three times as often as children. By age 6, children were producing generics more often than mothers, suggesting that children picked up many of these expressions from parental speech. And 4- to 6-year-olds frequently made stereotyped generic statements, which their mothers often affirmed (*Child:* "Only boys can drive trucks." *Mother:* "OK.").

Of the two sexes, boys are more gender-typed. Fathers, especially, are more insistent that boys conform to gender roles. They place more pressure to achieve on sons than on daughters and are less tolerant of "cross-gender" behavior in sons—more concerned when a boy acts like a "sissy" than when a girl acts like a "tomboy" (Sandnabba & Ahlberg, 1999; Wood, Desmarais, & Gugula, 2002). Parents who hold nonstereotyped values and consciously avoid behaving in these ways have children who are less gender-typed (Tenenbaum & Leaper, 2002; Weisner & Wilson-Mitchell, 1990). Other family members may also reduce gender typing. For example, children with older, other-sex siblings have many more opportunities to imitate and participate

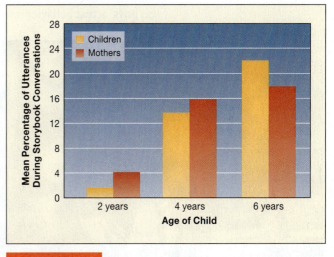

FIGURE 10.5

Mothers' and children's use of generic references to gender during storybook conversations. Generic utterances were broad in scope, in that they referred to many, or nearly all, males and females. Mothers' and children's use of generics increased dramatically between ages 2 and 6. At age 2, mothers produced more generics than children. By age 6, children produced more generics than mothers. *(From S. A. Gelman, M. G. Taylor, & S. P. Nguyen, "Mother–Child Conversations About Gender," Monographs of the Society for Research in Child Development, 69[1, Serial No. 275], p. 46. Reprinted by permission of Wiley-Blackwell Publishers.)*

LOOK AND LISTEN

Observe a parent discussing a picture book with a 3- to 6-year-old. How many times did the parent make generic statements about gender? How about the child? Did the parent accept or correct the child's generic utterances?

in "cross-gender" activities and, as a result, are less gender-typed in play preferences, attitudes, and personality traits (McHale et al., 2001; Rust et al., 2000).

TEACHERS   Teachers often act in ways that extend gender-role learning. Several times, Leslie caught herself emphasizing gender distinctions when she called out, "Will the girls line up on one side and the boys on the other?" or pleaded "Boys, I wish you'd quiet down like the girls!"

Like parents, preschool teachers give girls more encouragement to participate in adult-structured activities. Girls frequently cluster around the teacher, following directions, while boys are attracted to play areas where adults are minimally involved (Campbell, Shirley, & Candy, 2004; Powlishta, Serbin, & Moller, 1993). As a result, boys and girls engage in different social behaviors. Compliance and bids for help occur more often in adult-structured contexts; assertiveness, leadership, and creative use of materials in unstructured pursuits.

Teachers also use more disapproval and controlling discipline with boys. When girls misbehave, teachers tend to negotiate, coming up with a joint plan to improve behavior (Erden & Wolfgang, 2004). Teachers seem to expect boys to misbehave more often—a belief based partly on boys' actual behavior and partly on gender stereotypes.

PEERS   Children's same-sex peer associations make the peer context an especially potent source of gender-role learning. The more preschoolers play with same-sex partners, the more their behavior becomes gender-typed—in toy choices, activity level, aggression, and adult involvement (Martin & Fabes, 2001).

Gender-Role Learning in Gender-Segregated Peer Groups.   By age 3, same-sex peers positively reinforce one another for gender-typed play by praising, imitating, or joining in. In contrast, when preschoolers engage in "cross-gender" activities— for example, when boys play with dolls or girls with cars and trucks—peers criticize them. Boys are especially intolerant of cross-gender play in other boys (Fagot, 1984). A boy who frequently crosses gender lines is likely to be ignored by other boys, even when he does engage in "masculine" activities!

Children also develop different styles of social influence in gender-segregated peer groups. To get their way in large-group play, boys often rely on commands, threats, and physical force. Girls' preference for playing in pairs leads to greater concern with a partner's needs, evident in girls' use of polite requests, persuasion, and acceptance. Girls soon find that these gentle tactics succeed with other girls but not with boys, who ignore their courteous overtures (Leaper, 1994; Leaper, Tenenbaum, & Shaffer, 1999). Boys' unresponsiveness gives girls another reason to stop interacting with them.

Over time, children come to believe in the "correctness" of gender-segregated play, which further strengthens gender segregation and gender-stereotyped activities (Martin et al., 1999). As boys and girls separate, *in-group favoritism*—more positive evaluations of members of one's own gender—becomes another factor that sustains the separate social worlds of boys and girls, resulting in "two distinct subcultures" of shared knowledge, beliefs, interests, and behaviors (Maccoby, 2002; Ruble, Martin, & Berenbaum, 2006).

Cultural Variations.   Although gender segregation is pervasive, cultures and subcultures differ in the extent of gender-typed communication within those groups. African-American and Hispanic lower-SES girls, for example, are generally more assertive and independent in their interactions with one another and with boys than are Caucasian-American girls (Goodwin, 1998). A comparison of Chinese and U.S. preschoolers' play revealed similar differences.

© CINDY CHARLES/PHOTOEDIT

■ These boys positively reinforce one another's gender-typed behavior. Preschoolers, especially boys, tend to be critical of peers who play with "cross-gender" toys or enjoy activities associated with the other sex. ■

LOOK AND LISTEN

While observing 3- to 5-year-olds during a free-play period in a preschool or child-care program, note the extent of gender segregation and gender-typed play. Did styles of social influence differ in boys' and girls' gender-segregated groups? Jot down examples.

Chinese 5-year-old girls used more direct commands, complaints, and critical statements when interacting with both same- and other-sex peers than their American counterparts. And Chinese boys frequently combined commands with warning, appeasing, and justifying statements, which reduced expressions of dominance in boys' playgroups: "Better not open that. You'll spill it." "I'll do it! I'm here to help you" (Kyratis & Guo, 2001).

In collectivist societies where group cohesion is highly valued, children may not feel a need to work as hard at maintaining same-sex peer relations through traditional interaction patterns. In addition to their other benefits, ethnically diverse classrooms might reduce gender-typed peer communication as the "cross-gender" influence attempts of some children rub off on others.

THE BROADER SOCIAL ENVIRONMENT   Although children's everyday environments have changed to some degree, they continue to present many examples of gender typing—in occupations, leisure activities, media portrayals, and achievements of men and women. For example, although today's TV programs include more career-oriented women than in the past, female characters continue to be young, attractive, caring, emotional, and victimized and to be seen in romantic and family contexts. In contrast, male characters are usually dominant and powerful (Signorielli, 2001). Gender stereotypes even pervade preschool educational software, which emphasize male characters exhibiting "masculine" traits (Sheldon, 2004). And stereotypes are especially prevalent in cartoons, computer games, and other entertainment media for children and youths.

As we will see next, children do more than imitate the many gender-linked responses they observe. They soon come to view themselves and their social surroundings through a "gender-biased lens"—a perspective that can seriously restrict their interests and learning opportunities.

Gender Identity

As adults, each of us has a **gender identity**—an image of oneself as relatively masculine or feminine in characteristics. By middle childhood, researchers can measure gender identity by asking children to rate themselves on personality traits. A child or adult with a "masculine" identity scores high on traditionally masculine items (such as *ambitious, competitive,* and *self-sufficient*) and low on traditionally feminine items (such as *affectionate, cheerful,* and *soft-spoken*). Someone with a "feminine" identity does the reverse. And a substantial minority (especially females) have a gender identity called **androgyny,** scoring high on *both* masculine and feminine personality characteristics.

Gender identity is a good predictor of psychological adjustment. "Masculine" and androgynous children and adults have higher self-esteem than "feminine" individuals, perhaps because many typically feminine traits are not highly valued by society (Boldizar, 1991; Bronstein, 2006; Harter, 2006). Also, androgynous individuals are more adaptable—able to show masculine independence or feminine sensitivity, depending on the situation (Huyck, 1996; Taylor & Hall, 1982). The existence of an androgynous identity demonstrates that children can acquire a mixture of positive qualities traditionally associated with each gender—an orientation that may best help them realize their potential.

EMERGENCE OF GENDER IDENTITY   How do children develop a gender identity? According to *social learning theory,* behavior comes before self-perceptions. Preschoolers first acquire gender-typed responses through modeling and reinforcement and only later organize these behaviors into gender-linked ideas about themselves. In contrast, *cognitive-developmental theory* maintains that self-perceptions come before behavior. Over the preschool years, children acquire a cognitive appreciation of the permanence of their sex, or **gender constancy**—a full understanding of the biologically based permanence of their gender, including the realization that sex remains the same over time, even if clothing, hairstyle, and play activities change. Then children use this knowledge to guide their behavior (Kohlberg, 1966).

When 3- to 5-year-olds are asked such questions as "When you (a girl) grow up, could you ever be a daddy?" or "Could you be a boy if you wanted to?" they freely answer yes. And children younger than age 6 who watch an adult dressing a doll in "other-gender" clothing typically insist that the doll's sex has also changed (Chauhan, Shastri, & Mohite, 2005; Fagot, 1985). Mastery of gender constancy occurs in a three-step sequence: *gender labeling* (correct naming of one's own and others' sex), *gender stability* (understanding that gender remains the same over time), and *gender consistency* (realization that gender is not altered by superficial changes in clothing or activities). Full attainment of gender constancy is strongly related to ability to pass Piagetian conservation and verbal appearance–reality tasks (see page 327 in Chapter 9) (De Lisi & Gallagher, 1991; Trautner, Gervai, & Nemeth, 2003). Indeed, gender constancy tasks can be considered a type of appearance–reality problem, in that children must distinguish what a person looks like from who he or she really is.

In many cultures, young children do not have access to basic biological knowledge about gender because they rarely see members of the other sex naked. But giving preschoolers information about genital differences does not result in gender constancy. Preschoolers who have such knowledge usually say that changing a doll's clothing will not change its sex, but when asked to justify their response, they do not refer to sex as an innate, unchanging quality of people (Szkrybalo & Ruble, 1999). This suggests that cognitive immaturity, not social experience, is responsible for preschoolers' difficulty grasping the permanence of sex.

Is cognitive-developmental theory correct that gender constancy is responsible for children's gender-typed behavior? Evidence for this assumption is weak. "Gender-appropriate" behavior appears so early in the preschool years that its initial appearance must result from modeling and reinforcement, as social learning theory suggests. Although outcomes are not entirely consistent, some evidence suggests that gender constancy actually contributes to the emergence of more flexible gender-role attitudes during the school years (Ruble et al., 2007). But overall, the impact of gender constancy on gender typing is not great. As research in the following section reveals, gender-role adoption is more powerfully affected by children's beliefs about how close the connection must be between their own gender and their behavior.

GENDER SCHEMA THEORY **Gender schema theory** is an information-processing approach to gender typing that combines social learning and cognitive-developmental features. It explains how environmental pressures and children's cognitions work together to shape gender-role development (Martin & Halverson, 1987; Martin, Ruble, & Szkrybalo, 2002). At an early age, children pick up gender-stereotyped preferences and behaviors from others. At the same time, they organize their experiences into *gender schemas,* or masculine and feminine categories, that they use to interpret their world. As soon as preschoolers can label their own gender, they select gender schemas consistent with it ("Only boys can be doctors" or "Cooking is a girl's job") and apply those categories to themselves. Their self-perceptions then become gender-typed and serve as additional schemas that children use to process information and guide their own behavior.

We have seen that individual differences exist in the extent to which children endorse gender-typed views. Figure 10.6 shows different cognitive pathways for children who often apply gender schemas to their experiences and those who rarely do (Liben & Bigler, 2002). Consider Billy, who encounters a doll. If Billy is a *gender-schematic child,* his *gender-salience filter* immediately makes gender highly relevant. Drawing on his prior learning, he asks himself, "Should boys play with dolls?" If he answers "yes" and the toy interests him, he will approach it, explore it, and learn more about it. If he answers "no," he will respond by avoiding the "gender-inappropriate" toy. But if Billy is a *gender-aschematic child*—one who seldom views the world in gender-linked terms—he simply asks himself, "Do I like this toy?" and responds on the basis of his interests.

To examine the consequences of gender-schematic processing, researchers showed 4- and 5-year-olds toys that were gender-neutral and that varied in attractiveness. An adult labeled some as boys' toys and others as girls' toys, leaving a third group unlabeled. Most children engaged in gender-schematic reasoning, preferring toys labeled for their gender and predicting that same-sex peers would also like those toys (Martin, Eisenbud, & Rose, 1995). Highly attractive toys, especially, lost their appeal when they were labeled as for the other gender. And because gender-schematic preschoolers typically conclude, "What I like, children of my own sex will also like," they often use their own preferences to add to their gender biases! For example, a girl who dislikes oysters may declare, "Only boys like oysters!" even though she has never actually been given information supporting such a stereotype (Liben & Bigler, 2002).

Gender-schematic thinking is so powerful that when children see others behaving in "gender-inconsistent" ways, they often cannot remember the behavior or they distort their memory to

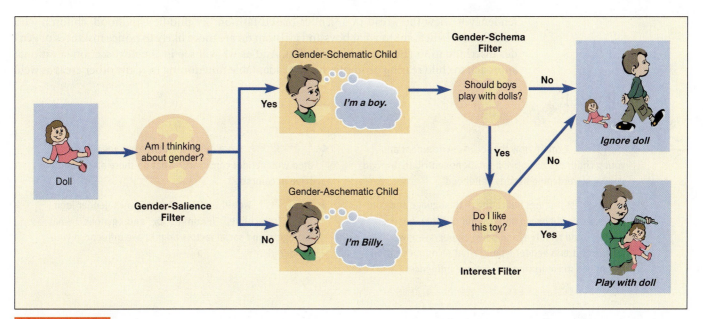

FIGURE 10.6

Cognitive pathways for gender-schematic and gender-aschematic children. In *gender-schematic children,* the gender-salience filter immediately makes gender highly relevant: Billy sees a doll and thinks, "I'm a boy. Should boys play with dolls?" Drawing on his experiences, he answers "yes" or "no." If he answers "yes" and the doll interests him, he plays with the doll. If he answers "no," he avoids the "gender-inappropriate" toy. *Gender-aschematic children* rarely view the world in gender-linked terms. Billy simply asks, "Do I like this toy?" and responds on the basis of his interests. *(Reprinted by permission of Rebecca Bigler, University of Texas, Austin.)*

make it "gender-consistent"—for example, when shown a picture of a male nurse, remembering him as a doctor (Liben & Signorella, 1993; Marin & Ruble, 2004). Over time, children learn much more about people, objects, and events that fit with their gender schemas than they do about "cross-gender" activities and behaviors. Of course, gender-schematic processing could not operate if society did not teach a wide variety of gender-linked associations.

Reducing Gender Stereotyping in Young Children

How can we help young children avoid rigid gender schemas that restrict their behavior and learning opportunities? No easy recipe exists. Biology clearly affects children's gender typing, channeling boys, on average, toward active, competitive play and girls toward quieter, more intimate interaction. But most aspects of gender typing are not built into human nature (Ruble, Martin, & Berenbaum, 2006).

Because young children's cognitive limitations lead them to assume that cultural practices determine gender, parents and teachers are wise to try to delay preschoolers' exposure to gender-stereotyped messages. Adults can begin by limiting traditional gender roles in their own behavior and by providing children with nontraditional alternatives. For example, parents can take turns making dinner, bathing children, and driving the family car, and they can give their sons and daughters both trucks and dolls and both pink and blue clothing. Teachers can make sure that all children spend time in mixed-gender play activities and in both adult-structured and unstructured pursuits. Finally, adults can avoid language that conveys gender stereotypes and can shield children from media presentations that do the same.

Once children notice the vast array of gender stereotypes in their society, parents and teachers can point out exceptions. For example, they can arrange for children to see men and women pursuing nontraditional careers and can explain that interests and skills, not sex, should determine a person's occupation. Research shows that such reasoning is highly effective in reducing children's

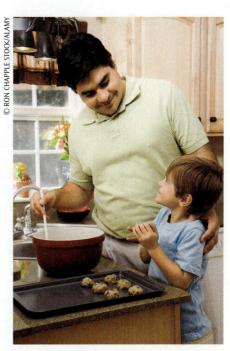

© RON CHAPPLE STOCK/ALAMY

■ Parents and teachers can reduce preschoolers' gender stereotyping by modeling nonstereotyped behaviors and providing nontraditional alternatives. For this boy, making cookies is not "for girls." It's an activity he and his father enjoy together. ■

tendency to view the world in a gender-biased fashion. By middle childhood, children who hold flexible beliefs about what boys and girls can do are more likely to notice instances of gender discrimination (Brown & Bigler, 2004). And as we will see in the next section, a rational approach to child rearing promotes healthy, adaptable functioning in many other areas as well.

Child Rearing and Emotional and Social Development

In this and previous chapters, we have seen how parents can foster children's competence—by building a parent–child relationship based on affection and cooperation, by serving as models and reinforcers of mature behavior, by using reasoning and inductive discipline, and by guiding and encouraging mastery of new skills. Now let's put these practices together into an overall view of effective parenting.

Styles of Child Rearing

Child-rearing styles are combinations of parenting behaviors that occur over a wide range of situations, creating an enduring child-rearing climate. In a landmark series of studies, Diana Baumrind gathered information on child rearing by watching parents interact with their preschoolers (Baumrind, 1971). Her findings, and those of others who have extended her work, reveal three features that consistently differentiate an effective style from less effective ones: (1) acceptance and involvement, (2) control, and (3) autonomy granting (Gray & Steinberg, 1999; Hart, Newell, & Olsen, 2003). Table 10.2 shows how child-rearing styles differ in these features. Let's discuss each style in turn.

AUTHORITATIVE CHILD REARING The **authoritative child-rearing style**—the most successful approach—involves high acceptance and involvement, adaptive control techniques, and appropriate autonomy granting. Authoritative parents are warm, attentive, and sensitive to their child's needs. They establish an enjoyable, emotionally fulfilling parent–child relationship that draws the child into close connection. At the same time, authoritative parents exercise firm, reasonable control: They insist on mature behavior, give reasons for their expectations, and use disciplinary encounters as "teaching moments" to promote the child's self-regulation. Finally, authoritative parents engage in gradual, appropriate autonomy granting, allowing the child to make decisions in areas where he is ready to do so (Kuczynski & Lollis, 2002; Russell, Mize, & Bissaker, 2004).

Throughout childhood and adolescence, authoritative parenting is linked to many aspects of competence—an upbeat mood, self-control, task persistence, cooperativeness, high self-esteem, social and moral maturity, and favorable school performance (Amato & Fowler, 2002; Aunola, Stattin, & Nurmi, 2000; Gonzalez & Wolters, 2006; Mackey, Arnold, & Pratt, 2001; Milevsky et al., 2007; Steinberg, Darling, & Fletcher, 1995).

TABLE 10.2 Features of Child-Rearing Styles

CHILD-REARING STYLE	ACCEPTANCE AND INVOLVEMENT	CONTROL	AUTONOMY GRANTING
Authoritative	Is warm, responsive, attentive, and sensitive to the child's needs	Makes reasonable demands for maturity and consistently enforces and explains them	Permits the child to make decisions in accord with readiness Encourages the child to express thoughts, feelings, and desires When parent and child disagree, engages in joint decision making when possible
Authoritarian	Is cold and rejecting and frequently degrades the child	Makes many demands coercively, using force and punishment; often uses psychological control, withdrawing love and intruding on the child's individuality	Makes decisions for the child Rarely listens to the child's point of view
Permissive	Is warm but overindulgent or inattentive	Makes few or no demands	Permits the child to make many decisions before the child is ready
Uninvolved	Is emotionally detached and withdrawn	Makes few or no demands	Is indifferent to the child's decision making and point of view

AUTHORITARIAN CHILD REARING The **authoritarian child-rearing style** is low in acceptance and involvement, high in coercive control, and low in autonomy granting. Authoritarian parents appear cold and rejecting. To exert control, they yell, command, criticize, and threaten. "Do it because I said so!" is their attitude. They make decisions for their child and expect their child to accept their word unquestioningly. If the child resists, authoritarian parents resort to force and punishment.

Children of authoritarian parents are anxious, unhappy, and low in self-esteem and self-reliance. When frustrated, they tend to react with hostility and, like their parents, resort to force when they do not get their way. Boys, especially, show high rates of defiance and aggression. Although girls also engage in acting-out behavior, they are more likely to be dependent, lacking interest in exploration, and overwhelmed by challenging tasks (Hart, Newell, & Olsen, 2003; Nix et al., 1999; Thompson, Hollis, & Richards, 2003). Children and adolescents exposed to the authoritarian style typically do poorly in school. However, because of their parents' concern with control, they tend to achieve better and to commit fewer antisocial acts than peers with undemanding parents—that is, whose parents use one of the parenting styles we will consider next (Steinberg, Blatt-Eisengart, & Cauffman, 2006).

In addition to unwarranted direct control, authoritarian parents engage in a more subtle type called **psychological control,** in which they intrude on and manipulate children's verbal expression, individuality, and attachments to parents. In an attempt to decide virtually everything for the child, these parents frequently interrupt or put down the child's ideas, decisions, and choice of friends. When they are dissatisfied, they withdraw love, making their affection contingent on the child's compliance. They also hold excessively high expectations that do not fit the child's developing capacities. Children subjected to psychological control exhibit adjustment problems involving both anxious, withdrawn behavior and defiance and aggression—especially the relational form, which (like parental psychological control) damages relationships through manipulation and exclusion (Barber et al., 2005; Kuppens et al., 2009; Nelson et al., 2006; Silk et al., 2003).

PERMISSIVE CHILD REARING The **permissive child-rearing style** is warm and accepting but uninvolved. Permissive parents are either overindulgent or inattentive and, thus, engage in little control. Instead of gradually granting autonomy, they allow children to make many of their own decisions at an age when they are not yet capable of doing so. Their children can eat meals and go to bed when they feel like it and watch as much television as they want. They do not have to learn good manners or do household chores. Although some permissive parents truly believe in this approach, many others simply lack confidence in their ability to influence their child's behavior (Oyserman et al., 2005).

Children of permissive parents are impulsive, disobedient, and rebellious. Compared with children whose parents exert more control, they are also overly demanding and dependent on adults, and they show less persistence on tasks, poorer school achievement, and more antisocial behavior. The link between permissive parenting and dependent, nonachieving, rebellious behavior is especially strong for boys (Barber & Olsen, 1997; Baumrind, 1971; Steinberg, Blatt-Eisengart, & Cauffman, 2006).

UNINVOLVED CHILD REARING The **uninvolved child-rearing style** combines low acceptance and involvement with little control and general indifference to issues of autonomy. Often these parents are emotionally detached and depressed and so overwhelmed by life stress that they have little time and energy for children. At its extreme, uninvolved parenting is a form of child maltreatment called *neglect.* Especially when it begins early, it disrupts virtually all aspects of development (see Chapter 4, page 155). Even with less extreme parental disengagement, children and adolescents display many problems—poor emotional self-regulation, school achievement difficulties, and antisocial behavior (Aunola, Stattin, & Nurmi, 2000; Kurdek & Fine, 1994).

What Makes Authoritative Child Rearing Effective?

Like other correlational findings, relationships between parenting styles and children's competence are open to interpretation. Perhaps parents of well-adjusted children are authoritative because their youngsters have especially cooperative dispositions. Children's characteristics do contribute to the ease with which parents can apply the authoritative style. An impulsive, noncompliant child makes it hard for parents to be warm, firm, and rational. But longitudinal research reveals that authoritative child rearing promotes maturity in children of diverse temperaments (Hart, Newell, & Olson, 2003; Olson et al., 2000; Rubin, Burgess, & Coplan, 2002). It seems to create a positive emotional context for parental influence in the following ways:

- Warm, involved parents who are secure in the standards they hold for their children provide models of caring concern as well as confident, self-controlled behavior.
- Children are far more likely to comply with and internalize control that appears fair and reasonable, not arbitrary.
- By making demands and engaging in autonomy granting that matches children's ability to take responsibility for their own behavior, authoritative parents let children know that they are competent individuals who can do things successfully for themselves. In this way, parents foster favorable self-esteem and cognitive and social maturity.
- Supportive aspects of the authoritative style, including parental acceptance, involvement, and rational control, are a powerful source of *resilience,* protecting children from the negative effects of family stress and poverty (Beyers et al., 2003).

Over time, the relationship between parenting and children's attributes becomes increasingly bidirectional (Kuczynski, 2003). When parents intervene patiently but firmly, they promote favorable adjustment, setting the stage for a positive parent–child relationship.

Cultural Variations

Although authoritative parenting is broadly advantageous, ethnic minority parents often have distinct child-rearing beliefs and practices reflecting cultural values. Let's look at some examples.

Compared with Western parents, Chinese parents describe their parenting as more controlling. They are more directive in teaching and scheduling their children's time, as a way of fostering self-control and high achievement. Chinese parents may appear less warm than Western parents because they withhold praise, which they believe results in self-satisfied, poorly motivated children (Chao, 1994; Chen et al., 2001). High control reflects the Confucian belief in strict discipline, respect for elders, and socially desirable behavior, taught by deeply involved parents. Chinese parents report expressing affection and concern and using induction and other reasoning-oriented discipline as much as American parents do, but they more often shame a misbehaving child, withdraw love, and use physical punishment (Cheah et al., 2009; Shwalb et al., 2004; Wu et al., 2002). When these practices become excessive, resulting in an authoritarian style high in psychological or coercive control, Chinese children display the same negative outcomes seen in Western children: poor academic achievement, anxiety, depression, and aggressive behavior (Bradford et al., 2003; Nelson et al., 2005, 2006; Pong, Johnston, & Chen, 2010; Wang, Pomerantz, & Chen, 2007).

In Hispanic families, Asian Pacific Island families, and Caribbean families of African and East Indian origin, firm insistence on respect for parental authority is paired with high parental warmth—a combination suited to promoting competence and strong feelings of family loyalty (Harrison et al., 1994; Roopnarine & Evans, 2007). Hispanic fathers typically spend much time with their children and are warm and sensitive (Cabrera & García Coll, 2004; Jambunathan, Burts, & Pierce, 2000). In Caribbean families that have immigrated to the United States, fathers' authoritativeness—but not mothers'—predicted preschoolers' literacy and math skills, probably because Caribbean fathers take a larger role in guiding their children's academic progress (Roopnarine et al., 2006).

Although wide variation exists, low-SES African-American parents tend to expect immediate obedience, regarding strictness as fostering self-control and a watchful attitude in risky surroundings. Consistent with these beliefs, African-American parents who use more controlling strategies tend to have more cognitively and socially competent children (Brody & Flor, 1998). Recall, also, that a history of mild physical punishment is associated with a reduction in antisocial behavior among African-American youths but with an increase among Caucasian Americans (refer to the Cultural Influences box on page 383). Most African-American parents who use strict, "no-nonsense" discipline use physical punishment sparingly and combine it with warmth and reasoning.

These cultural variations remind us that child-rearing styles must be viewed in their larger context. As we have seen, many factors contribute to good parenting: personal characteristics of the child and parent, SES, access to extended family and community supports, cultural values and practices, and public policies.

As we turn to the topic of child maltreatment, our discussion will underscore, once again, that effective child rearing is sustained not just by the desire of mothers and fathers to be good parents. Almost all want to be. Unfortunately, when vital supports for parenting break down, children—as well as parents—can suffer terribly.

■ In many Caribbean families, parents combine warmth with firm insistence on respect for parental authority, and fathers devote much time to guiding children's academic progress. ■

© TIM DOLAN PHOTOGRAPHY/PHOTOLIBRARY

Child Maltreatment

Child maltreatment is as old as human history, but only recently has the problem been widely acknowledged and research aimed at understanding it. Perhaps public concern has increased because child maltreatment is especially common in large industrialized nations. In the most recently reported year, 770,000 U.S. children (10 out of every 1,000) were identified as victims (U.S. Department of Health and Human Services, 2010a). Most cases go unreported, so the true figures are much higher.

Child maltreatment takes the following forms:

■ *Physical abuse:* Assaults, such as shaking, kicking, biting, punching, or stabbing, that inflict physical injury

- *Sexual abuse:* Fondling, intercourse, exhibitionism, commercial exploitation through prostitution or production of pornography, and other forms of sexual exploitation
- *Neglect:* Failure to meet a child's basic needs for food, clothing, medical attention, education, or supervision
- *Emotional abuse:* Acts that could cause serious mental or behavior disorders, including social isolation, repeated unreasonable demands, ridicule, humiliation, intimidation, or terrorizing

Neglect accounts for about 60 percent of reported cases, physical abuse for 20 percent, emotional abuse for 10 percent, and sexual abuse for 10 percent (U.S. Department of Health and Human Services, 2008b, 2010a). But these figures are only approximate, as many children experience more than one form.

Parents commit more than 80 percent of abusive incidents. Other relatives account for about 7 percent. The remainder are perpetrated by parents' unmarried partners, school officials, camp counselors, and other adults. Mothers engage in neglect more often than fathers, whereas fathers engage in sexual abuse more often than mothers. Maternal and paternal rates of physical and emotional abuse are fairly similar. Infants and young preschoolers are at greatest risk for neglect; preschool and school-age children for physical, emotional, and sexual abuse. But each type occurs at every age (Trocmé & Wolfe, 2002; U.S. Department of Health and Human Services, 2010). Because most sexual abuse victims are identified in middle childhood, we will pay special attention to this form of maltreatment in Chapter 13.

ORIGINS OF CHILD MALTREATMENT   Early findings suggested that child maltreatment was rooted in adult psychological disturbance (Kempe et al., 1962). But although child maltreatment is more common among disturbed parents, it soon became clear that a single "abusive personality type" does not exist. Parents who were abused as children do not necessarily become abusers (Buchanan, 1996; Simons et al., 1991). And sometimes even "normal" parents harm their children!

For help in understanding child maltreatment, researchers turned to *ecological systems theory* (see Chapters 1 and 2). They discovered that many interacting variables—at the family, community, and cultural levels—contribute. The more risks present, the greater the likelihood that abuse or neglect will occur. Table 10.3 summarizes factors associated with child maltreatment.

The Family.   Within the family, children whose characteristics make them more challenging to rear are more likely to become targets of abuse. These include premature or very sick babies and children who are temperamentally difficult, are inattentive and overactive, or have other developmental problems. Child factors, however, only slightly increase the risk of abuse (Jaudes & Mackey-Bilaver, 2008; Sidebotham et al., 2003). Whether such children are maltreated largely depends on parents' characteristics.

TABLE 10.3 Factors Related to Child Maltreatment

FACTOR	DESCRIPTION
Parent characteristics	Psychological disturbance; alcohol and drug abuse; history of abuse as a child; belief in harsh, physical discipline; desire to satisfy unmet emotional needs through the child; unreasonable expectations for child behavior; low educational level
Child characteristics	Premature or very sick baby; difficult temperament; inattentiveness and overactivity; other developmental problems
Family characteristics	Low income or poverty; homelessness; marital instability; social isolation; partner abuse; frequent moves; large families with closely spaced children; overcrowded living conditions; disorganized household; lack of steady employment; other signs of high life stress
Community	Characterized by social isolation; few parks, child-care centers, preschool programs, recreation centers, or churches to serve as family supports
Culture	Approval of physical force and violence as ways to solve problems

Sources: U.S. Department of Health and Human Services, 2010a; Wekerle & Wolfe, 2003; Whipple, 2006.

Maltreating parents are less skillful than other parents in handling discipline confrontations and getting children to cooperate in working toward common goals. They also suffer from biased thinking about their child. For example, they often attribute their baby's crying or their child's misdeeds to a stubborn or bad disposition, evaluate children's transgressions as worse than they are, and feel powerless in parenting—perspectives that lead them to move quickly toward physical force (Bugental & Happaney, 2004; Crouch et al., 2008).

Once abuse begins, it quickly becomes part of a self-sustaining relationship. The small irritations to which abusive parents react—a fussy baby, a preschooler who knocks over her milk, or a child who will not mind immediately—soon become bigger ones. Then the harshness increases. By the preschool years, abusive and neglectful parents seldom interact with their children. When they do, they rarely express pleasure and affection; the communication is almost always negative (Wolfe, 2005).

Most parents have enough self-control not to respond to their children's misbehavior or developmental problems with abuse. Other factors combine with these conditions to prompt an extreme response. Unmanageable parental stress is strongly associated with maltreatment. Abusive parents respond to stressful situations with high emotional arousal. And low income, low education (less than a high school diploma), unemployment, alcohol and drug use, marital conflict, overcrowded living conditions, frequent moves, and extreme household disorganization are common in abusive homes (Wekerle et al., 2007; Wulczyn, 2009). These conditions increase the chances that parents will be too overwhelmed to meet basic child-rearing responsibilities or will vent their frustrations by lashing out at their children.

The Community.   The majority of abusive and neglectful parents are isolated from both formal and informal social supports. Because of their life histories, many have learned to mistrust and avoid others and are poorly skilled at establishing and maintaining positive relationships. Also, maltreating parents are more likely to live in unstable, rundown neighborhoods that provide few links between family and community, such as parks, child-care centers, preschool programs, recreation centers, and religious institutions (Coulton et al., 2007; Zielinski & Bradshaw, 2006). They lack "lifelines" to others and have no one to turn to for help during stressful times.

The Larger Culture.   Cultural values, laws, and customs profoundly affect the chances that child maltreatment will occur when parents feel overburdened. Societies that view violence as an appropriate way to solve problems set the stage for child abuse.

Although the United States has laws to protect children from maltreatment, widespread support exists for use of physical force with children (refer back to page 382). Many countries—including Austria, Croatia, Cyprus, Denmark, Finland, Germany, Israel, Italy, Latvia, Norway, and Sweden—have outlawed physical punishment, a measure that dampens both physical discipline and abuse (Bugental & Grusec, 2006). Furthermore, every industrialized nation except the United States and Canada now prohibits corporal punishment in schools (Center for Effective Discipline, 2005). The U.S. Supreme Court has twice upheld the right of school officials to use corporal punishment. Fortunately, some U.S. states and Canadian provinces have passed laws that ban it.

CONSEQUENCES OF CHILD MALTREATMENT   The family circumstances of maltreated children impair the development of emotional self-regulation, empathy and sympathy, self-concept, social skills, and academic motivation. Over time, these youngsters show serious adjustment problems, including severe depression, aggressive behavior, peer difficulties, substance abuse, and delinquency, including violent crime (Cicchetti & Toth, 2006; Sanchez & Pollak, 2009; Wolfe et al., 2001).

How do these damaging consequences occur? Recall our earlier discussion of hostile cycles of parent–child interaction. For abused children, these are especially severe. Also, a family characteristic strongly associated with child abuse is partner abuse, which predicts similar internalizing and externalizing difficulties (Gewirtz & Edleson, 2004; Kitzmann et al., 2003). Clearly, the home lives of abused children overflow with adult conduct that leads to profound distress, including emotional insecurity (see pages 70–71 in Chapter 2), and to aggression as a way of solving problems.

Furthermore, demeaning parental messages, in which children are ridiculed, humiliated, rejected, or terrorized, result in low self-esteem, high anxiety, self-blame, and efforts to escape from extreme psychological pain—at times severe enough to lead to attempted suicide in adolescence (Wolfe, 2005). At school, maltreated children present serious discipline problems. Their noncompliance, poor motivation, and cognitive immaturity interfere with academic achievement, further undermining their chances for life success (Wekerle & Wolfe, 2003).

Finally, repeated abuse is associated with central nervous system damage, including abnormal EEG brain-wave activity, fMRI-detected reduced size and impaired functioning of the cerebral cortex and corpus callosum, and atypical production of the stress hormone cortisol—initially too high, but after months of abuse, often too low. Over time, the massive trauma of persistent abuse seems to blunt children's normal physiological response to stress (Cicchetti, 2007; Teicher et al., 2004; Watts-English et al., 2006). These effects increase the chances that cognitive and emotional problems will endure.

PREVENTING CHILD MALTREATMENT Because child maltreatment is embedded in families, communities, and society as a whole, efforts to prevent it must be directed at each of these levels. Many approaches have been suggested, including teaching high-risk parents effective child-rearing strategies, providing direct experience with children in high school child development courses, and developing broad social programs aimed at improving economic and neighborhood conditions and community services for at-risk families.

We have seen that providing social supports to families is effective in easing parental stress. This approach sharply reduces child maltreatment as well (Azar & Wolfe, 1998). A trusting relationship with another person is the most important factor in preventing mothers with childhood histories of abuse from repeating the cycle with their own children (Egeland, Jacobvitz, & Sroufe, 1988). Parents Anonymous, a U.S. organization with affiliate programs around the world, helps child-abusing parents learn constructive parenting practices, largely through social supports. Its local chapters offer self-help group meetings, daily phone calls, and regular home visits to relieve social isolation and teach responsible child-rearing skills.

Early intervention aimed at strengthening both child and parent competencies can improve parenting practices, thereby preventing child maltreatment (Howard & Brooks-Gunn, 2009). Healthy Families America, a program that began in Hawaii and has spread to 440 sites across the United States and Canada, identifies families at risk for maltreatment during pregnancy or at birth. Each receives three years of home visitation, in which a trained worker helps parents manage crises, encourages effective child rearing, and puts parents in touch with community services to meet their own and their children's needs (PCA America, 2009). In an evaluation in which over 600 families were randomly assigned to intervention and control groups, Healthy Families home visitation alone reduced only neglect, not abuse (Duggan et al., 2004). But adding a *cognitive component* dramatically increased its impact. When home visitors helped parents change negative appraisals of their children—by countering inaccurate interpretations (for example, that the baby is behaving with malicious intent) and by working on solving child-rearing problems—physical punishment and abuse dropped sharply after one year of intervention (see Figure 10.7) (Bugental et al., 2002).

■ Each year, fourth to sixth graders across Los Angeles County enter a poster contest to celebrate Child Abuse Prevention Month. This recent winner appeals to parents to treat children with warmth and caring. *(Lisa Valicente and Madeline Zauss, 6th Grade, Jefferson Elementary School, Redondo Beach, CA. Courtesy ICAN Associates, Los Angeles County InterAgency Council on Child Abuse & Neglect, ican4kids.org.)* ■

FIGURE 10.7

Impact of a home visitation program with a cognitive component on preventing physical abuse of young children. In an enhanced home visitation condition, home visitors not only provided social support, encouraged effective child rearing, and connected families with community resources but also helped at-risk parents change their negative appraisals of their babies and solve child-rearing problems. After one year of intervention, this cognitive component sharply reduced physical abuse of babies (hitting, shaking, beating, kicking, biting) compared with an unenhanced home visitation condition and a no-intervention control. *(Adapted from Bugental et al., 2002.)*

Still, many experts believe that child maltreatment cannot be eliminated as long as violence is widespread and harsh physical punishment is regarded as acceptable. In addition, combating poverty and its diverse correlates—family stress and disorganization, inadequate food and medical care, teenage parenthood, low-birth-weight babies, and parental hopelessness—would protect many children.

Although more cases reach the courts than in decades past, child maltreatment remains a crime that is difficult to prove. Usually, the only witnesses are the child victims or other loyal family members. And even when the evidence is strong, judges hesitate to impose the ultimate safeguard against further harm: permanently removing the child from the family. There are several reasons for their reluctance. First, in the United States, government intervention into family life is viewed as a last resort. Second, despite destructive family relationships, maltreated children and their parents usually are attached to one another. Usually, neither desires separation. Finally, the U.S. legal system tends to regard children as parental property rather than as human beings in their own right, and this also has stood in the way of court-ordered protection.

Even with intensive treatment, some adults persist in their abusive acts. An estimated 1,700 U.S. children, most of them infants and preschoolers, die from maltreatment each year. About two-thirds suffered from beatings, drownings, suffocation, or *shaken baby syndrome,* in which shaking an infant or young child inflicts brain and neck injuries. And about one-third were severely neglected (Trocmé & Wolfe, 2002; U.S. Department of Health and Human Services, 2010a). When parents are unlikely to change their behavior, the drastic step of separating parent from child and legally terminating parental rights is the only justifiable course of action.

Child maltreatment is a sad note on which to end our discussion of a period of childhood that is so full of excitement, awakening, and discovery. But there is reason to be optimistic. Great strides have been made over the past several decades in understanding and preventing child maltreatment.

ASK YOURSELF

◆ **REVIEW** Summarize findings on ethnic variations in child-rearing styles. Is the concept of authoritative parenting useful for understanding effective parenting across cultures? Explain.

◆ **APPLY** Chandra heard a news report about 10 severely neglected children, living in squalor in an inner-city tenement. She wondered, "Why would parents so mistreat their children?" How would you answer Chandra?

◆ **CONNECT** Which child-rearing style is most likely to be associated with inductive discipline, and why?

◆ **REFLECT** How would you classify your parents' child-rearing styles? What factors might have influenced their approach to parenting?

Summary

Erikson's Theory: Initiative versus Guilt

What personality changes take place during Erikson's stage of initiative versus guilt?

■ Preschoolers develop a new sense of purposefulness as they grapple with Erikson's psychological conflict of **initiative versus guilt.** A healthy sense of initiative depends on exploring the social world through play and experiencing supportive child rearing that fosters a secure (but not overly strict) conscience.

Self-Understanding

Describe preschoolers' self-concepts and the development of autobiographical memory and self-esteem.

■ As preschoolers think more intently about themselves, they construct a **self-concept** that consists largely of observable characteristics and typical emotions and attitudes. Older preschoolers also have an emerging grasp of their own personalities.

■ Securely attached preschoolers have a more positive, coherent self-concept. They experience more elaborative parent–child conversations about past events, which contribute to a clearer, self-image.

■ Preschoolers' **self-esteem** consists of several self-judgments. Their high self-esteem contributes to a mastery-oriented approach to the environment.

Emotional Development

Identify changes in understanding and expressing emotion during early childhood, citing factors that influence those changes.

■ Preschoolers have an impressive understanding of the causes, consequences, and behavioral signs of basic emotions, which is supported by cognitive development, secure attachment, and conversations about feelings. By age 3 to 4, children are aware of various strategies for emotional self-regulation. Temperament, parental modeling, and parental communication about coping strategies influence preschoolers' capacity to handle negative emotion.

■ As their self-concepts become better developed, preschoolers experience self-conscious emotions more often. However, they depend on parental feedback to know when to feel pride, shame, or guilt.

■ Empathy also becomes more common in early childhood. The extent to which empathy leads to **sympathy** and results in **prosocial**, or **altruistic, behavior** depends on temperament and parenting.

© ELLEN B. SENISI PHOTOGRAPHY

Peer Relations

Describe peer sociability, friendship, and social problem solving in early childhood, along with cultural and parental influences on early peer relations.

■ During early childhood, peer interaction increases as children move from **nonsocial activity** to **parallel play** and then to **associative** and **cooperative play.** Nevertheless, both solitary and parallel play remain common.

■ Sociodramatic play seems especially important in societies where child and adult worlds are distinct. In collectivist cultures, play generally occurs in large groups and is highly cooperative.

■ Preschoolers view friendship in concrete, activity-based terms. Their interactions with friends are especially positive and contribute to academic and social adjustment in kindergarten.

■ Social conflicts offer occasions for **social problem solving,** which improves over the preschool and early school years. By kindergarten, each of its information-processing components is related to socially competent behavior.

■ Parents influence early peer relations both directly, through attempts to influence their child's peer relations, and indirectly, through their child-rearing practices.

Foundations of Morality

What are the central features of psychoanalytic, social learning, and cognitive-developmental approaches to moral development?

■ The psychoanalytic perspective emphasizes the emotional side of moral development. Although guilt is an important motivator of moral action, contrary to Freud's theory, discipline promoting fear of punishment and loss of parental love does not foster conscience development. **Induction** is far more effective.

■ Social learning theory focuses on how moral behavior is learned through reinforcement and modeling. Effective adult models of morality are warm and powerful, and they practice what they preach.

■ Alternatives such as **time out** and withdrawal of privileges can help parents avoid the undesirable side effects of harsh punishment. When parents use punishment, they can increase its effectiveness by being consistent, maintaining a warm parent–child relationship, and offering explanations. The most effective discipline encourages good conduct by building a mutually respectful bond with the child.

■ The cognitive-developmental perspective views children as active thinkers about social rules. By age 4, children consider intentions in making moral judgments and distinguish truthfulness from lying. Preschoolers also distinguish **moral imperatives** from **social conventions** and **matters of personal choice,** but they tend to reason rigidly about morality.

■ Through sibling and peer interaction, children work out their first ideas about justice and fairness. Parents who discuss moral issues with their children help them reason about morality.

Describe the development of aggression in early childhood, including family and media influences.

■ During early childhood, **proactive aggression** declines while **reactive aggression** increases. Proactive and reactive aggression come in three forms: **physical aggression** (more common in boys), **verbal aggression,** and **relational aggression.**

■ Ineffective discipline and a conflict-ridden family atmosphere promote children's aggression. Children high in reactive aggression see hostility where it does not exist, making many unprovoked attacks. Those high in proactive aggression callously use it to advance their own goals—a style that predicts severe conduct problems. Media violence also triggers aggression.

- Teaching parents effective child-rearing practices, intervening to enhance children's emotional and social skills, relieving family stress through social supports, and shielding children from violent media reduce aggressive behavior.

Gender Typing

Discuss genetic and environmental influences on preschoolers' gender-stereotyped beliefs and behavior.

- **Gender typing** is well under way in early childhood. Preschoolers acquire a wide range of gender-stereotyped beliefs, which operate as blanket rules rather than flexible guidelines for behavior.

- Prenatal hormones contribute to boys' higher activity level and rowdier play and to children's preference for same-sex playmates. But parents, same-sex older siblings, teachers, peers, and the broader social environment encourage many gender-typed responses. Parents apply more pressure for gender-role conformity to sons, and boys are more gender-typed than girls.

Describe and evaluate major theories that explain the emergence of gender identity.

- Although most people have a traditional **gender identity**, some are **androgynous**, combining both masculine and feminine characteristics. Masculine and androgynous identities are linked to better psychological adjustment.

- According to social learning theory, preschoolers first acquire gender-typed responses through modeling and reinforcement, then organize these into gender-linked ideas about themselves. Cognitive-developmental theory suggests that **gender constancy** must be mastered before children develop gender-typed behavior. However, gender-role behavior is acquired long before gender constancy.

- **Gender schema theory** combines features of social learning and cognitive-developmental perspectives. As children acquire gender-stereotyped preferences and behaviors, they form masculine and feminine categories, or gender schemas, that they apply to themselves and their world.

Child Rearing and Emotional and Social Development

Describe the impact of child-rearing styles on children's development, and explain why authoritative parenting is effective.

- Three features distinguish the major **child-rearing styles:** (1) acceptance and involvement, (2) control, and (3) autonomy granting. Compared with the **authoritarian, permissive, and uninvolved styles,** the **authoritative style** promotes cognitive, emotional, and social competence. Warmth, explanations, and reasonable demands for mature behavior account for the effectiveness of the authoritative style. **Psychological control** is associated with authoritarian parenting and contributes to adjustment problems.

- Certain ethnic groups, including Chinese, Hispanic, Asian Pacific Island, and African-American, combine parental warmth with high levels of control. But when control becomes harsh and excessive, it impairs academic and social competence.

Discuss the multiple origins of child maltreatment, its consequences for development, and prevention strategies.

- Child maltreatment is related to factors within the family, community, and larger culture. Maltreating parents use ineffective discipline and hold a negatively biased view of their child. Unmanageable parental stress and social isolation greatly increase the chances that abuse and neglect will occur. When a society approves of force and violence as a means for solving problems, child abuse is promoted.

- Maltreated children are impaired in emotional self-regulation, empathy and sympathy, self-concept, social skills, and academic motivation. They are also likely to suffer central nervous system damage. Successful prevention of child maltreatment requires efforts at the family, community, and societal levels.

IMPORTANT TERMS AND CONCEPTS

androgyny (p. 395)
associative play (p. 372)
authoritarian child-rearing style (p. 399)
authoritative child-rearing style (p. 398)
child-rearing styles (p. 398)
cooperative play (p. 372)
gender constancy (p. 395)
gender identity (p. 395)
gender schema theory (p. 396)
gender typing (p. 390)
induction (p. 379)

initiative versus guilt (p. 364)
matters of personal choice (p. 384)
moral imperatives (p. 384)
nonsocial activity (p. 372)
parallel play (p. 372)
permissive child-rearing style (p. 399)
physical aggression (p. 385)
proactive aggression (p. 385)
prosocial, or altruistic, behavior (p. 371)
psychological control (p. 399)
reactive aggression (p. 385)

relational aggression (p. 386)
self-concept (p. 365)
self-esteem (p. 366)
social conventions (p. 384)
social problem solving (p. 375)
sympathy (p. 371)
time out (p. 382)
uninvolved child-rearing style (p. 400)
verbal aggression (p. 385)

Milestones

Development in Early Childhood

2 years

PHYSICAL

- Throughout early childhood, height and weight increase more slowly than in toddlerhood. (290)
- Balance improves; walking becomes smooth and rhythmic; running emerges. (308)
- Jumps, hops, throws, and catches with rigid upper body. (308)
- Puts on and removes simple items of clothing. (309)
- Uses spoon effectively. (309)
- First drawings are gestural scribbles. (309–310)

COGNITIVE

- Increasingly uses language as a flexible symbolic tool, to modify existing mental representations. (318)
- Make-believe becomes less dependent on realistic objects, less self-centered, and more complex; sociodramatic play increases. (319)
- Takes the perspective of others in simplified, familiar situations and in face-to-face communication. (328)
- Recognition memory is well developed. (336)

- Shows awareness of the difference between inner mental and outer physical events. (339)
- Begins to count. (344)

LANGUAGE

- Vocabulary increases rapidly. (354)
- Uses a coalition of cues—perceptual and, increasingly, social and linguistic—to figure out word meanings. (356)
- Speaks in simple sentences that follow basic word order of native language. (356)
- Adds grammatical markers. (356–357)
- Displays effective conversational skills. (358–359)

EMOTIONAL/SOCIAL

- Understands causes, consequences, and behavioral signs of basic emotions. (368)
- Begins to develop self-concept and self-esteem. (365, 366)
- Shows early signs of developing moral sense—verbal evaluations of own and others' actions and distress at harmful behaviors. (378)
- May display proactive (or instrumental) aggression. (385)
- Gender-stereotyped beliefs and behavior increase. (391)

3–4 years

PHYSICAL

- May no longer need a daytime nap. (298)

- Running, jumping, hopping, throwing, and catching become more refined, with flexible upper body. (308)

- Galloping and one-foot skipping appear. (308)
- Pedals and steers tricycle. (308)
- Uses scissors. (309)
- Uses fork adeptly. (310)
- Draws first picture of a person, using tadpole image. (310)
- Distinguishes writing from nonwriting. (312)

COGNITIVE

- Understands the symbolic function of drawings and of models of real-world spaces. (320)
- Grasps conservation, reasons about transformations, reverses thinking, and understands cause-and-effect relationships in familiar contexts. (324–326)
- Sorts familiar objects into hierarchically organized categories. (324–326)
- Distinguishes appearance from reality. (327)
- Uses private speech to guide behavior during challenging tasks. (330)
- Sustained attention and planning improve. (334–335)
- Uses scripts to recall familiar experiences. (336)
- Understands that both beliefs and desires determine behavior. (339)
- Knows meaning of numbers up to ten, counts correctly, and grasps cardinality. (344)

LANGUAGE

- Aware of some meaningful features of written language. (343)

- Coins new words based on known words; extends language meanings through metaphor. (356)
- Masters increasingly complex grammatical structures. (357)
- Sometimes overextends grammatical rules to exceptions. (357)
- Adjusts speech to fit the age, sex, and social status of listeners. (323)

EMOTIONAL/SOCIAL

- Describes self in terms of observable characteristics and typical emotions and attitudes. (365)
- Has several self-esteems, such as learning things in school, making friends, and getting along with parents. (366)
- Emotional self-regulation improves. (367)
- Experiences self-conscious emotions more often. (367)
- Relies more on language to express empathy. (371)
- Engages in associative and cooperative play with peers, in addition to parallel play. (372–373)
- Proactive aggression declines, while reactive aggression (verbal and relational) increases. (386)
- Forms first friendships, based on pleasurable play and sharing of toys. (374)

- Distinguishes moral imperatives from social conventions and matters of personal choices. (384)
- Preference for same-sex playmates strengthens. (391–392)

5–6 years

PHYSICAL

- Starts to lose primary teeth. (290)
- Increases running speed, gallops more smoothly, and engages in true skipping. (309)
- Displays mature, flexible throwing and catching patterns. (308)
- Uses knife to cut soft foods. (309)
- Ties shoes. (309)

- Draws more complex pictures. (310)
- Uses an adult pencil grip, writes name, copies some numbers and simple words, and discriminates letters of the alphabet. (312)

COGNITIVE

- Magical beliefs decline. (324)
- Ability to distinguish appearance from reality improves. (327)

- Attention and planning continue to improve. (334–335)

- Recognition, recall, scripted memory, and autobiographical memory improve. (336–337)
- Understanding of false belief strengthens. (339)

LANGUAGE

- Understands that letters and sounds are linked in systematic ways. (343)
- Uses invented spellings. (343)
- By age 6, vocabulary reaches about 10,000 words. (354)
- Uses most grammatical constructions competently. (357)

EMOTIONAL/SOCIAL

- Emotional understanding (ability to interpret, predict, and influence others' emotional reactions) improves. (367–368)
- Becomes better at social problem solving. (376)
- Has acquired many morally relevant rules and behaviors. (378–379)
- Gender-stereotyped beliefs and behavior and preference for same-sex playmates continue to strengthen. (394)

- Understands gender constancy. (395)

"Fun with Wooden Cars"
Gabriel Sambo
10 years, Gabon

Through child-organized games, children develop physically, cognitively, and socially. Chapter 11 takes up the diverse physical attainments of middle childhood and their close connection with other domains of development.

Reprinted with permission from the World Awareness Children's Museum, Glens Falls, New York

Physical Development in Middle Childhood

Body Growth

Worldwide Variations in Body Size • Secular Trends in Physical Growth • Skeletal Growth • Brain Development

Common Health Problems

Nutrition • Overweight and Obesity • Vision and Hearing • Bedwetting • Illnesses • Unintentional Injuries

■ SOCIAL ISSUES: HEALTH
The Obesity Epidemic: How Americans Became the Heaviest People in the World

Health Education

■ SOCIAL ISSUES: EDUCATION
Children's Understanding of Health and Illness

Motor Development and Play

Gross-Motor Development • Fine-Motor Development • Individual Differences in Motor Skills • Games with Rules • Adult-Organized Youth Sports • Shadows of Our Evolutionary Past • Physical Education

■ SOCIAL ISSUES: EDUCATION
School Recess—A Time to Play, a Time to Learn

"**I**'m on my way, Mom!" hollered 10-year-old Joey as he stuffed the last bite of toast into his mouth, slung his book bag over his shoulder, dashed out the door, jumped on his bike, and headed down the street for school. Joey's 8-year-old sister Lizzie followed, kissing her mother goodbye and pedaling furiously until she caught up with Joey. Rena, the children's mother and one of my colleagues at the university, watched from the front porch as her son and daughter disappeared in the distance.

"They're branching out," Rena told me over lunch that day, as she described the children's expanding activities and relationships. Homework, household chores, soccer teams, music lessons, scouting, friends at school and in the neighborhood, and Joey's new paper route were all part of the children's routine. "It seems as if the basics are all there; I don't have to monitor Joey and Lizzie so constantly anymore. Being a parent is still very challenging, but it's more a matter of refinements—helping them become independent, competent, and productive individuals."

Joey and Lizzie have entered middle childhood—the years from 6 to 11. Around the world, children of this age are assigned new responsibilities. For children in industrialized nations, like Joey and Lizzie, middle childhood is often called the "school years" because its onset is marked by the start of formal schooling. In village and tribal cultures, the school may be a field or a jungle. But universally, mature members of society guide children of this age period toward real-world tasks that increasingly resemble those they will perform as adults.

This chapter focuses on physical growth in middle childhood—changes less spectacular than those seen in earlier years. By age 6, the brain has reached 90 percent of its adult weight, and the body continues to grow slowly. In this way, nature gives school-age children the mental powers to master challenging tasks as well as added time—before reaching physical maturity—to acquire the knowledge and skills essential for life in a complex social world.

We begin by reviewing typical growth trends and special health concerns. Then we turn to rapid gains in motor abilities, which support practical everyday activities, athletic skills, and participation in organized games. We will see that each of these achievements is affected by and also contributes to cognitive, emotional, and social development. Our discussion will echo a familiar theme—that all domains are interrelated.

Body Growth

Physical growth during the school years continues at the slow, regular pace of early childhood. At age 6, the average North American child weighs about 45 pounds and is 3½ feet tall. Over the next few years, children will add about 2 to 3 inches in height and 5 pounds in weight each year (see Figure 11.1). Between ages 6 and 8, girls are slightly shorter and lighter than boys. By age 9, this trend reverses. Already, Rena noticed, Lizzie was starting to catch up with Joey in physical size as she approached the dramatic adolescent growth spurt, which occurs two years earlier in girls than in boys.

Because the lower portion of the body is growing fastest, Joey and Lizzie appeared longer-legged than they had in early childhood. They grew out of their jeans more quickly than their

Andy at 8 years

Andy at 6 years

Amy at 8 years

Amy at 6 years

Andy at 9 years

Andy at 10½ years

Amy at 9 years

Amy at 10½ years

PHOTOS COURTESY OF PAT SELFE

FIGURE 11.1

Body growth during middle childhood. Andy and Amy continued the slow, regular pattern of growth that they showed in early childhood (see Chapter 8, page 291). But around age 9, Amy began to grow at a faster rate than Andy. At age 10½, she was taller, heavier, and more mature-looking.

jackets and frequently needed larger shoes. As in early childhood, girls have slightly more body fat and boys more muscle. After age 8, girls begin accumulating fat at a faster rate, and they will add even more during adolescence (Siervogel et al., 2000).

Worldwide Variations in Body Size

TAKE A MOMENT... Glance into any elementary school classroom, and you will see wide individual differences in body growth. Diversity in physical size is especially apparent when we travel to different nations. Worldwide, a 9-inch gap exists between the smallest and the largest 8-year-olds. The shortest children, found in South America, Asia, the Pacific Islands, and parts of Africa, include such ethnic groups as Colombian, Burmese, Thai, Vietnamese, Ethiopian, and Bantu. The tallest children—living in Australia, northern and central Europe, Canada, and the United States—come from Czech, Dutch, Latvian, Norwegian, Swiss, and African populations (Meredith, 1978; Ruff, 2002). These findings remind us that *growth norms* (age-related averages for height and weight) must be applied cautiously, especially in countries with high immigration rates and many ethnic minorities.

What accounts for these vast differences in physical size? Both heredity and environment are involved. Body size sometimes reflects evolutionary adaptations to a particular climate. Long, lean physiques are typical in hot, tropical regions and short, stocky ones in cold, Arctic areas (Katzmarzyk & Leonard, 1998). Also, children who grow tallest usually live in developed countries, where food is plentiful and infectious diseases are largely controlled. Physically small children tend to live in less developed regions, where poverty, hunger, and disease are common (Bogin, 2001). When families move from poor to wealthy nations, their children not only grow taller but also change to a longer-legged body shape. (Recall that during childhood, the legs are growing fastest.) For example, U.S.-born school-age children of immigrant Guatemalan Mayan parents are, on average, 4½ inches taller, with legs nearly 3 inches longer, than their agemates in Guatemalan Mayan villages (Bogin et al., 2002; Varela-Silva et al., 2007).

■ Body size is sometimes the result of evolutionary adaptations to a particular climate. These boys of Tanzania, who gather often to play with homemade cars, live on the hot African plains. They have long, lean physiques, which permit their bodies to cool easily. ■

Secular Trends in Physical Growth

Over the past 150 years, **secular trends in physical growth**—changes in body size from one generation to the next—have occurred in industrialized nations. Joey and Lizzie are taller and heavier than their parents and grandparents were as children. These trends have been found in Australia, Canada, Japan, New Zealand, the United States, and nearly all European countries (Ong, Ahmed, & Dunger, 2006). The secular gain appears early in life, increases over childhood and early adolescence, then declines as mature body size is reached. This pattern suggests that the larger size of today's children is mostly due to a faster rate of physical development.

Once again, improved health and nutrition are largely responsible for these growth gains. Secular trends are smaller for low-income children, who have poorer diets and are more likely to suffer from growth-stunting illnesses. And in regions with widespread poverty, famine, and disease, either no secular change or a secular decrease in body size has occurred (Barnes-Josiah & Augustin, 1995; Cole, 2000). In most industrialized nations, the secular gain in height has slowed in recent decades. Weight gain, however, is continuing. As we will see later, overweight and obesity have reached epic proportions.

■ Although they vary greatly in physical size, these 9-year-olds are generally taller and heavier than previous generations were at the same age. Improved health and nutrition account for this secular trend in physical growth throughout the industrialized world. ■

Skeletal Growth

During middle childhood, the bones of the body lengthen and broaden. However, ligaments are not yet firmly attached to bones. This, combined with increasing muscle strength, gives children unusual flexibility of movement. School-age children often seem like "physical contortionists," turning cartwheels and doing splits and handstands. As their bodies become stronger, many children experience a greater desire for physical exercise. Nighttime "growing pains"—stiffness and aches in the legs—are common as muscles adapt to an enlarging skeleton (Evans, 2008).

Between ages 6 and 12, all 20 primary teeth are lost and replaced by permanent ones, with girls losing their teeth slightly earlier than boys. The first teeth to go are the lower and then upper front teeth, giving many first and second graders a "toothless" smile. For a while, the permanent teeth seem much too large. Gradually, growth of the facial bones, especially those of the jaw and chin, causes the child's face to lengthen and the mouth to widen, accommodating the newly erupting teeth.

Care of the teeth is essential during the school years because dental health affects the child's appearance, speech, and ability to chew properly. Parents need to remind children to brush their teeth thoroughly, and most children need help with flossing until about 9 years of age. More than 50 percent of U.S. school-age children have at least some tooth decay. Low-SES children have especially high levels, with nearly 30 percent untreated (U.S. Department of Health and Human Services, 2007c). Children without health insurance are three times as likely to have unmet dental needs. As decay progresses, they experience pain, embarrassment at damaged teeth, distraction from play and learning, and school absences due to dental-related illnesses.

Malocclusion, a condition in which the upper and lower teeth do not meet properly, occurs in one-third of school-age children. In about 14 percent of cases, serious difficulties in biting and chewing result. Malocclusion can be caused by thumb and finger sucking after permanent teeth erupt. Children who were eager thumb suckers during infancy and early childhood may require gentle but persistent encouragement to give up the habit by school entry (Charchut, Allred, & Needleman, 2003). Another cause of malocclusion is crowding of permanent teeth. In some children, this problem clears up as the jaw grows. Others need braces, a common sight by the end of elementary school.

Brain Development

The weight of the brain increases by only 10 percent during middle childhood and adolescence. Nevertheless, considerable growth occurs in certain brain structures. Using fMRI, researchers can detect the volume of two general types of brain tissue: *white matter,* consisting largely of myelinated nerve fibers, and *gray matter,* consisting mostly of neurons and supportive material. White matter increases steadily throughout childhood and adolescence, especially in the prefrontal cortex (responsible for consciousness, impulse control, integration of information, and strategic thinking), in the parietal lobes (supporting spatial abilities), and in the corpus callosum (leading to improved communication between the two cortical hemispheres) (Barnea-Goraly et al., 2005; Nelson, Thomas, & de Haan, 2006). Because interconnectivity among distant regions of the cerebral cortex increases, the prefrontal cortex becomes a more effective "executive"—coordinating integrated functioning of various areas, yielding more complex, flexible, and adaptive behavior.

As children acquire more complex abilities, stimulated neurons increase in synaptic connections, and their neural fibers become more elaborate and myelinated. As a result, gray matter peaks in middle childhood and then declines as synaptic pruning (reduction of unused synapses) and death of surrounding neurons proceed

© SKIP BROWN/GETTY IMAGES/LIFESIZE

■ In middle childhood, the prefrontal cortex becomes a more effective "executive," coordinating integrated functioning of various brain regions. These changes support more complex, flexible abilities, such as this kayaker's deft maneuvering. ■

(Giedd et al., 1999; Sowell et al., 2002). Recall from Chapter 5 that about 40 percent of synapses are pruned over childhood and adolescence. Pruning and accompanying reorganization and selection of brain circuits contribute greatly to more efficient information processing, including gains in sustained attention, inhibition, response preparation, and working memory capacity (Nelson, Thomas, & de Haan, 2006). These changes yield more optimized functioning of specific brain regions.

Little information is available on how the brain develops in other ways. One idea is that much development takes place at the level of neurotransmitters, chemicals that permit neurons to communicate across synapses (see Chapter 5, page 164). Over time, neurons become increasingly selective, responding only to certain chemical messages. This change may add to school-age children's more efficient and flexible thinking and behavior. Secretions of particular neurotransmitters are related to cognitive performance, social and emotional adjustment, and ability to withstand stress. When neurotransmitters are not present in appropriate balances, children may suffer serious developmental problems, such as inattention and overactivity, emotional disturbance, and epilepsy (an illness involving brain seizures and loss of motor control) (Brooks et al., 2006; Pearl et al., 2005; Weller, Kloos, & Weller, 2006).

Researchers also believe that brain functioning may change in middle childhood because of the influence of hormones. Around age 7 to 8, an increase in androgens (male sex hormones), secreted by the adrenal glands (located on top of the kidneys), occurs in children of both sexes. Androgens will rise further among boys at puberty, when the testes release them in large amounts. Androgens affect brain organization and behavior in many animal species, including humans. Recall from Chapter 10 that androgens contribute to boys' higher activity level. They may also promote social dominance and play-fighting, topics we will take up at the end of this chapter (Azurmendi et al., 2006).

ASK YOURSELF

◆ **REVIEW** What aspects of physical growth account for the long-legged appearance of many 8- to 12-year-olds?

◆ **APPLY** Joey complained to his mother that it wasn't fair that his younger sister Lizzie was almost as tall as he was. He worried that he wasn't growing fast enough. How should Rena respond to Joey's concern?

◆ **CONNECT** Relate secular trends in physical growth to the concept of cohort effects, discussed on page 41 in Chapter 1.

◆ **REFLECT** In your family, how do members of your generation compare with members of your parents' generation in height and weight? How about your grandparents' generation? Do your observations illustrate secular trends?

Common Health Problems

Children from economically advantaged homes, like Joey and Lizzie, are at their healthiest in middle childhood, full of energy and play. The cumulative effects of good nutrition, combined with rapid development of the body's immune system, offer greater protection against disease. At the same time, growth in lung size permits more air to be exchanged with each breath, so children are better able to exercise vigorously without tiring.

Not surprisingly, poverty continues to be a powerful predictor of poor health during middle childhood. Because economically disadvantaged U.S. children often lack health insurance and, if they are publicly insured, generally receive a lower standard of care (see Chapter 8, page 303), many do not have regular access to a doctor. A substantial number also lack such basic necessities as a comfortable home and regular meals.

Nutrition

Children need a well-balanced, plentiful diet to provide energy for successful learning in school and increased physical activity. With their increasing focus on play, friendships, and new activities, many children spend little time at the table. Joey's hurried breakfast, described at the beginning of this chapter, is a common event in middle childhood. The percentage of children who eat meals with their families drops sharply between ages 9 and 14. Family dinnertimes have waned in general over the past quarter century. Yet eating an evening meal with parents leads to a diet higher in fruits and vegetables and lower in fried foods and soft drinks (Fiese & Schwartz, 2008; Neumark-Sztainer et al., 2003).

School-age children report that they "feel better" and "focus better" after eating healthy foods and that they feel sluggish, "like a blob," after eating junk foods. Even mild nutritional deficits can affect cognitive functioning. Among school-age children from middle- to high-SES families, insufficient dietary iron and folate predicted slightly lower mental test performance (Arija et al., 2006). Children say that a major barrier to healthy eating is the ready availability of unhealthy options, even in their homes. As one sixth grader commented, "When I get home from school, I think, 'I should eat some fruit,' but then I see the chips" (O'Dea, 2003, p. 498). Recall from Chapter 8 that food familiarity and food preferences are strongly linked: Children like best foods they have eaten repeatedly in the past. Readily available, healthy between-meal snacks—such as cheese, fruit, raw vegetables, and peanut butter—can help meet school-age children's nutritional needs and increase their liking for healthy foods.

As we have seen in earlier chapters, many poverty-stricken children in developing countries and in North America suffer from serious, prolonged malnutrition. By middle childhood, the effects are apparent in retarded physical growth, low IQ, poor motor coordination, and inattention. The negative impact of malnutrition on learning and behavior may intensify as children encounter new academic and social challenges at school. First, as in earlier years, growth-stunted school-age children respond with greater fear to stressful situations, as indicated by a sharper rise in heart rate and in saliva levels of the stress hormone cortisol (Fernald & Grantham-McGregor, 1998). Second, animal evidence reveals that a deficient diet alters the production of neurotransmitters in the brain—an effect that can disrupt all aspects of psychological functioning (Haller, 2005).

Unfortunately, malnutrition that persists from infancy or early childhood into the school years usually leads to permanent physical and mental damage (Grantham-McGregor, Walker, & Chang, 2000; Liu et al., 2003). Government-sponsored supplementary food programs from the early years through adolescence can prevent these effects. In studies carried out in Egypt, Kenya, and Mexico, quality of food (protein, vitamin, and mineral content) strongly predicted favorable cognitive development in middle childhood (Sigman, 1995; Watkins & Pollitt, 1998).

Overweight and Obesity

Mona, a very heavy child in Lizzie's class, often watched from the sidelines during recess. When she did join in games, she was slow and clumsy, the target of unkind comments: "Move it, Tubs!" Although Mona was a good student, the other children rejected her in the classroom as well. When they chose partners for special activities, Mona was among the last to be selected. Most afternoons, she walked home alone while her schoolmates gathered in groups, talking, laughing, and chasing. At home, Mona sought comfort in high-calorie snacks.

Mona suffers from **obesity,** a greater-than-20-percent increase over healthy weight, based on *body mass index (BMI)*—a ratio of weight to height associated with body fat. A BMI above the 85th percentile for a child's age and sex is considered *overweight,* a BMI above the 95th percentile *obese.* During the past several decades, a rise in overweight and obesity has occurred in many Western nations (see Figure 11.2),

■ Chinese boys attending a weight-loss summer camp get ready for a swim. Lifestyle changes and a culture that equates excess body fat with prosperity have caused a rapid increase in overweight and obesity in China, especially among boys. ■

IMAGINECHINA VIA AP IMAGES

with large increases in Canada, Germany, Israel, Greece, Ireland, New Zealand, United Kingdom, and the United States. Today, 32 percent of U.S. children and adolescents are overweight, more than half extremely so: 17 percent are obese (Ogden et al., 2010; World Health Organization, 2009a, 2010a). Smaller increases have occurred in other industrialized nations, including Australia, Finland, the Netherlands, Norway, and Sweden.

Obesity rates are also increasing rapidly in developing countries, as urbanization shifts the population toward sedentary lifestyles and diets high in meats and energy-dense refined foods (World Health Organization, 2009a, 2010a). In China, for example, where obesity was nearly nonexistent a generation ago, today 20 percent of children are overweight, with 7 percent obese—a nearly fivefold increase over the past twenty-five years, with boys affected more than girls) (Ding, 2008). Childhood obesity in China is especially high in cities, where it has reached 10 percent (Ji & Chen, 2008). In addition to lifestyle changes, a prevailing belief in Chinese culture that excess body fat represents prosperity and health—carried over from a half-century ago, when famine caused millions of deaths—has contributed to this alarming upsurge. High valuing of sons may induce Chinese parents to offer boys especially generous portions of meat, dairy products, and other energy-dense foods that were once scarce but now are widely available.

Overweight rises with age, from 21 percent among U.S. preschoolers to 35 percent among school-age children and adolescents (Ogden et al., 2010). In a longitudinal study of more than 1,000 U.S. children, overweight preschoolers were five times more likely than their normal-weight peers to be overweight at age 12 (Nader et al., 2006). And an estimated 70 percent of affected teenagers become overweight adults (U.S. Department of Health and Human Services, 2007b).

Besides serious emotional and social difficulties, obese children are at risk for lifelong health problems. Symptoms that begin to appear in the early school years—high blood pressure, high cholesterol levels, respiratory abnormalities, and insulin resistance—are powerful predictors of heart disease, circulatory difficulties, type 2 diabetes, gallbladder disease, sleep and digestive disorders, many forms of cancer, and early death (Krishnamoorthy, Hart, & Jelalian, 2006; World Cancer Research Fund, 2007). Furthermore, obesity has caused a dramatic rise in cases of diabetes in children, sometimes leading to early, severe complications, including stroke, kidney failure, and circulatory problems that heighten the risk of eventual blindness and leg amputation (Hannon, Rao, & Arslanian, 2005). As you can see from Table 11.1 on page 418, childhood obesity is a complex physical disorder with multiple causes.

CAUSES OF OBESITY Not all children are equally at risk for excessive weight gain. Overweight children tend to have overweight parents, and identical twins are more likely to share the disorder than fraternal twins. But heredity accounts for only a *tendency* to gain weight (Salbe et al., 2002). The importance of environment is seen in the consistent relationship of low SES to overweight and obesity in industrialized nations, especially among ethnic minorities—in the United States, African-American, Hispanic, and Native-American children and adults (Anand et al., 2001; Ogden et al., 2010). Factors responsible include lack of knowledge about healthy diet; a tendency to buy high-fat, low-cost foods; neighborhoods that lack

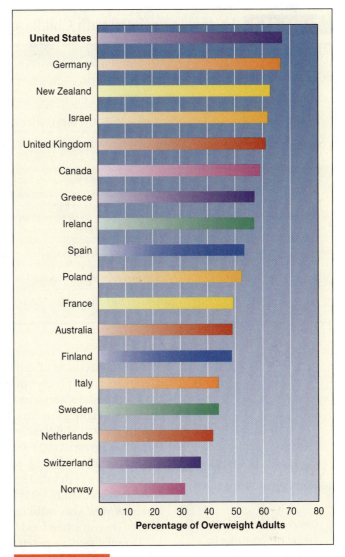

FIGURE 11.2

Overweight adults in eighteen industrialized nations. The United States outranks all other developed nations in pervasiveness of overweight in the adult population, defined here according to the widely accepted adult standard of a BMI greater than 25. *(From World Health Organization, 2010a.)*

TABLE 11.1 Factors Associated with Childhood Obesity

FACTOR	DESCRIPTION
Heredity	Obese children are likely to have at least one obese parent, and concordance for obesity is greater in identical than in fraternal twins.
Socioeconomic status	Obesity is more common in low-SES families.
Early growth pattern	Infants who gain weight rapidly are at greater risk for obesity, probably because their parents promote unhealthy eating habits (see Chapter 5).
Family eating habits	When parents purchase high-calorie fast foods, treats, and junk food; use them as rewards; anxiously overfeed; or control their children's intake, their children are more likely to be obese.
Responsiveness to food cues	Obese children often decide when to eat on the basis of external cues, such as taste, smell, sight, time of day, and food-related words, rather than hunger.
Physical activity	Obese children are less physically active than their normal-weight peers.
Television viewing	Children who spend many hours watching television are more likely to become obese.
Early malnutrition	Early, severe malnutrition that results in growth stunting increases the risk of later obesity.

convenient access to affordable, healthy foods in grocery stores and restaurants; and family stress, which can prompt overeating.

Furthermore, children who were undernourished in their early years are at risk for later excessive weight gain. Studies in many poverty-stricken regions of the world reveal that growth-stunted children are more likely to be overweight than their nonstunted agemates (Branca & Ferrari, 2002). In industrialized nations, many studies confirm that children whose mothers smoked during pregnancy and who therefore are often born underweight (see Chapter 3) are at elevated risk for later overweight and obesity (Rogers, 2009). A malnourished body protects itself by establishing a low basal metabolism rate, which may endure after nutrition improves. Also, malnutrition may disrupt appetite control centers in the brain, causing the child to overeat when food becomes plentiful.

Parental feeding practices also contribute to childhood obesity. Overweight children are more likely to eat larger quantities of high-calorie sugary and fatty foods, perhaps because these foods are prominent in the diets offered by their parents, who also tend to be overweight. Some parents anxiously overfeed, interpreting almost all their child's discomforts as a desire for food. Others pressure their children to eat, a practice common among immigrant parents and grandparents who, as children themselves, survived deadly famines or periods of food deprivation due to poverty. Still other parents are overly controlling, restricting when, what, and how much their child eats and worrying about weight gain (Moens, Braet, & Soetens, 2007). In each case, parents undermine children's ability to regulate their own food intake. Also, parents of overweight children often use high-fat, sugary foods to reinforce other behaviors, leading children to attach great value to treats (Sherry et al., 2004).

Because of these experiences, obese children soon develop maladaptive eating habits. They are more responsive than normal-weight individuals to external stimuli associated with food— taste, sight, smell, time of day, and food-related words—and less responsive to internal hunger cues (Jansen et al., 2003; Temple et al., 2007). They also eat faster and chew their food less thoroughly, a behavior pattern that appears as early as 18 months of age (Drabman et al., 1979).

Another factor implicated in weight gain is insufficient sleep. A follow-up of more than 2,000 U.S. 3- to 12-year-olds revealed that children who got less nightly sleep were more likely to be overweight five years later (Snell, Adam, & Duncan, 2007). Reduced sleep may increase time available for eating, leave children too fatigued for physical activity, or disrupt the brain's regulation of hunger and metabolism.

Overweight children are less physically active than their normal-weight peers. Inactivity is both cause and consequence of excessive weight gain. Research reveals that the rise in childhood obesity is due in part to the many hours U.S. children spend watching television. In a

LOOK AND LISTEN

Observe in the check-out area of a supermarket for an hour on a weekend, recording the percentage of families with children whose carts contain large quantities of high-calorie processed foods and soft drinks. In how many of these families are parents and children overweight?

FIGURE 11.3

Relationship of television viewing to gains in body fat from ages 4 to 11.
Researchers followed more than 100 children from ages 4 to 11, collecting information on hours per day of television viewing and on body fat, measured in millimeters of skinfold thickness at five body sites (upper arms, shoulders, abdomen, trunk, and thighs). The more TV children watched, the greater the gain in body fat. At ages 10 to 11, the difference between children watching fewer than 1¾ hours and those watching more than 3 hours had become large. *(Adapted from M. H. Proctor et al., 2003, "Television Viewing and Change in Body Fat from Preschool to Early Adolescence: The Framingham Children's Study,"* International Journal of Obesity, 27, *p. 831. Reprinted by permission from Macmillan Publishers Ltd.)*

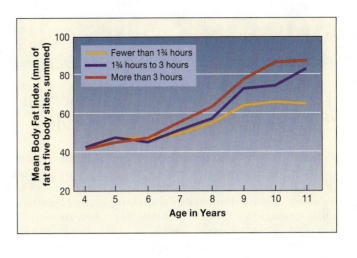

study that tracked children's TV viewing from ages 4 to 11, the more TV children watched, the more body fat they added. Children who devoted more than 3 hours per day to TV accumulated 40 percent more fat than those devoting less than 1¾ hours (see Figure 11.3) (Proctor et al., 2003). Watching TV reduces time devoted to physical exercise, and TV ads encourage children to eat fattening, unhealthy snacks. Children permitted to have a TV in their bedroom—a practice linked to especially high TV viewing—are at even further risk for overweight (Adachi-Mejia et al., 2007).

Finally, the broader food environment affects the incidence of obesity. The Pima Indians of Arizona, who two decades ago changed from a traditional diet of plant foods to a high-fat, typically American diet, have one of the world's highest obesity rates. Compared with descendants of their ancestors living in the remote Sierra Madre region of Mexico, the Arizona Pima have body weights 50 percent greater. Half the population has diabetes (8 times the national average), with many in their twenties and thirties already disabled by the disease—blind, in wheelchairs, and on kidney dialysis. The Pima have a genetic susceptibility to overweight, but it emerges only under Western dietary conditions (Gladwell, 1998; Traurig et al., 2009). Other ethnic groups with a hereditary tendency to gain weight include Pacific Islanders, including native Hawaiians and Samoans (Furusawa et al., 2010). Many now eat an Americanized diet of high-calorie processed and fast foods, and over 80 percent are overweight. Turn to the Social Issues: Health box on pages 420–421 for societal changes that have led Americans to become the heaviest people in the world.

CONSEQUENCES OF OBESITY Unfortunately, physical attractiveness is a powerful predictor of social acceptance. In Western societies, both children and adults rate obese youngsters as unlikable, stereotyping them as lazy, sloppy, dirty, ugly, stupid, and deceitful (Kilpatrick & Sanders, 1978; Penny & Haddock, 2007; Tiggemann & Anesbury, 2000). In school, obese children and adolescents are often socially isolated. They report more emotional, social, and school difficulties, including peer teasing and consequent low self-esteem, depression, and (among obese teenagers) suicidal thoughts and suicide attempts. Because unhappiness and overeating contribute to each other, the child remains overweight (Puhl & Latner, 2007; Zeller & Modi, 2006). Persistent obesity from childhood into adolescence also predicts serious behavior problems, including defiance and aggression (Schwimmer, Burwinkle, & Varni, 2003; Young-Hyman et al., 2006). And overweight girls are more likely to reach puberty early, increasing their risk for early sexual activity and other adjustment problems (Kaplowitz, 2007; Rubin et al., 2009).

The psychological consequences of obesity combine with continuing discrimination to result in reduced life chances. Overweight adults are less likely than their normal-weight agemates to be given financial aid for college, to be rented apartments, to find mates, and to be offered jobs. And they report frequent mistreatment by family members, peers, co-workers, and health-care professionals (Carr & Friedman, 2005; Rogge, Greenwald, & Golden, 2004).

TREATING OBESITY Childhood obesity is difficult to treat because it is a family disorder. In Mona's case, the school nurse suggested that Mona and her

■ This mother and daughter reinforce each other's efforts to lose weight and get in shape. The most effective interventions for childhood obesity focus on changing the whole family's behaviors, emphasizing fitness and healthy eating. ■

SOCIAL ISSUES: HEALTH

The Obesity Epidemic: How Americans Became the Heaviest People in the World

In the late 1980s, obesity in the United States stared to soar. The maps in Figure 11.4 show how quickly it engulfed the nation. Today more than one-third of U.S. school-age children and adolescents and more than two-thirds of adults are overweight or obese (Flegal et al., 2010). No other country matches the United States in prevalence of this life-threatening condition.

A Changing Food Environment and Lifestyle

Several societal factors have encouraged widespread rapid weight gain:

- *Availability of cheap commercial fat and sugar.* The 1970s saw two massive changes in the U.S. food economy: (1) the discovery and mass production of high-fructose corn syrup, a sweetener six times as sweet as ordinary sugar, and therefore far less expensive; and (2) the importing from Malaysia of large quantities of palm oil, which is lower in cost than other vegetable oils and also tastier, because of its high saturated fat content. As food manufacturers relied on corn syrup and palm oil to make soft drinks and calorie-dense convenience foods, the production costs of these items dropped and their variety expanded, launching a new era of "cheap, abundant, and tasty calories" (Critser, 2003). The rise in U.S. fructose consumption (mostly in beverages) closely paralleled population weight gain (Bray, Nielsen, & Popkin, 2004). Currently, fructose constitutes one-sixth of the caloric intake of the average American age 2 and older.

- *Portion supersizing.* Fast-food chains discovered a successful strategy for attracting customers: increasing portion sizes substantially and prices just a little for foods that had become inexpensive to produce. Customers thronged to buy "value meals," jumbo burgers and burritos, pizza "by the foot," and 20-ounce Cokes (Critser, 2003). And they began to view these huge portions as normal and appropriate. Research reveals that when presented with larger portions, individuals 2 years and older increase their intake, on average, by 25 to 30 percent (Fisher, Rolls, & Birch, 2003; Steenhuis & Vermeer, 2009).

- *Increasingly busy lives.* Between the 1970s and the 1990s, women entered the labor force in record numbers, and the average amount of time Americans worked increased by 15 percent, or about 350 hours per year (Higgins & Duxbury, 2002; Schor, 2002). Number of hours employed mothers work increases risk of childhood obesity because as time for meal preparation shrinks, eating out increases (Midlin, Jenkins, & Law, 2009). In addition, Americans have become frequent snackers, tempted by a growing assortment of high-calorie snack foods on supermarket shelves. During this period, the number of calories Americans consumed away from home nearly doubled, and dietary fat increased from 19 to 38 percent. Overall, average daily food intake rose by almost 200 calories—enough to add an extra pound every 20 days (Nielsen & Popkin, 2003).

- *Declining rates of physical activity.* As Americans spent more time working in sedentary jobs, they—and their

© ALEX SEGRE/ALAMY

■ As busy families eat fewer meals at home, fast food has become a regular part of many children's diets. Portion supersizing promotes increased consumption of inexpensive, tasty, high-calorie foods, putting children at risk for excessive weight gain. ■

obese mother enter a weight-loss program together. But Mona's mother, unhappily married for many years, had her own reasons for overeating. She rejected this idea, claiming that Mona would eventually decide to lose weight on her own. In one study, only one-fourth of overweight parents judged their overweight children to have a weight problem (Jeffrey, 2004). Consistent with these findings, fewer than 20 percent of obese children get any treatment. Although many try to slim down in adolescence, they often go on crash diets that make matters worse. Temporary starvation leads to physical stress, discomfort, and fatigue. Soon the child returns to old eating patterns, and weight rebounds to a higher level. Then, to protect itself, the body burns calories more slowly and becomes more resistant to future weight loss.

The most effective interventions are family-based and focus on changing behaviors (Oude et al., 2009). In one program, both parent and child revised eating patterns, exercised daily, and reinforced each other with praise and points for progress, which they exchanged for special activities and times together. The more weight parents lost, the more their children lost

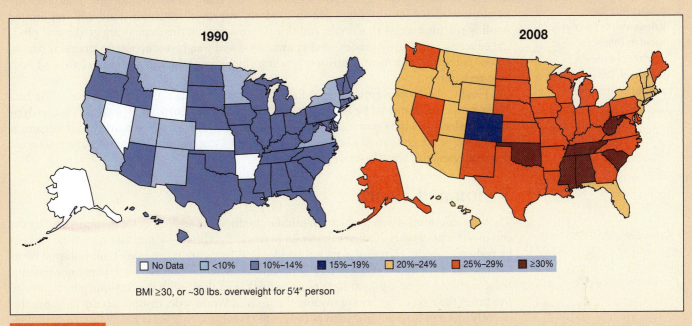

FIGURE 11.4

Obesity trends among Americans, 1990 and 2008. The maps show that obesity has increased sharply. In 2008, only one state (Colorado) had an obesity rate less than 20 percent. Six states (Alabama, Mississippi, Oklahoma, South Carolina, Tennessee, and West Virginia) had rates equal to or greater than 30 percent. *(From U.S. Department of Health and Human Services, 2009g.)*

children—exercised less. At home, TV had become their major leisure pursuit—consuming, on average, about 4 hours per day and linked to weight gain in adults and children alike (Foster, Gore, & West, 2006).

Combating the Obesity Epidemic

Obesity's toll on society is immense. It is responsible for $150 billion in health expenditures and nearly 200,000 premature deaths per year in the United States alone (Finkelstein et al., 2009; Flegal et al., 2007). Besides individual treatment, societal efforts are needed to combat obesity. These include:

- Government funding to support massive public education about healthy eating and physical activity
- A high priority placed on building parks and recreation centers and expanding access to healthy, affordable foods in low-income neighborhoods, where overweight and obesity are highest
- Laws that mandate prominent posting of the calorie, sugar, and fat content of foods sold in restaurants, movie theaters, and convenience stores
- A special tax on foods high in calories, sugar, or fat
- Incentives to schools and workplaces for promoting healthy eating and daily exercise and for offering weight-management programs
- Increased obesity-related medical coverage in government-sponsored health insurance programs for low-income families

(Wrotniak et al., 2004). Follow-ups after five and ten years showed that children maintained their weight loss more effectively than adults—a finding that underscores the importance of intervening at an early age (Epstein, Roemmich, & Raynor, 2001). Treatment programs that focus on both diet and lifestyle can yield substantial, long-lasting weight reduction among children and adolescents. But these interventions work best when parents' and children's weight problems are not severe (Eliakim et al., 2004; Nemet et al., 2005).

Getting obese children to exercise is challenging because they find being sedentary pleasurable. One successful technique is to reinforce them for spending less time inactive. Providing rewards (such as tickets to the zoo or a baseball game) for reducing sedentary time led to greater liking for physical activity and more weight loss among obese children than reinforcing them directly for exercising or punishing them (by loss of privileges) for remaining inactive (Epstein, Saelens, & O'Brien, 1995; Epstein et al., 1997). Rewarding children for giving up inactivity seems to increase their sense of personal control over exercising—a factor linked to sustained physical activity.

LOOK AND LISTEN

Contact your state government to find out about its childhood obesity prevention legislation. Can its policies be improved?

Children consume one-third of their daily energy intake at school. Therefore, schools can help reduce obesity by serving healthier meals and ensuring regular physical activity. Because obesity is expected to rise further without broad prevention strategies, many U.S. states and cities have passed obesity-reduction legislation (Levi et al., 2009). Among measures taken are weight-related school screenings for all children, improved nutrition standards and limited vending machine access in schools, additional recess time in the elementary grades and physical education time in all grades, obesity awareness and weight-reduction programs as part of school curricula, and menu nutrition labeling (including calorie counts) in chain and fast-food restaurants.

Finally, obesity prevention and reduction are becoming U.S. national priorities. The *Let's Move* campaign, launched by First Lady Michelle Obama in 2010, aims to create partnerships among federal and state governments, communities, businesses, schools, and health organizations to solve the childhood obesity problem within a generation. To find out about its goals and strategies, visit *www.letsmove.gov*.

Vision and Hearing

The most common vision problem in middle childhood is *myopia,* or nearsightedness. By the end of the school years, it affects nearly 25 percent of children—a rate that rises to 60 percent by early adulthood. Heredity plays a role: Identical twins are more likely than fraternal twins to share the condition (Pacella et al., 1999). And compared to children with no myopic parents, those with one myopic parent have twice the risk, and those with two myopic parents two to five times the risk, of becoming myopic themselves. Worldwide, myopia occurs far more frequently in Asian than in Caucasian populations (Feldkámper & Schaeffel, 2003). Early biological trauma can also induce myopia. School-age children with low birth weights show an especially high rate, believed to result from immaturity of visual structures, slower eye growth, and a greater incidence of eye disease (O'Connor et al., 2002).

When parents warn their children not to read in dim light or sit too close to the TV or computer screen, their concern ("You'll ruin your eyes!") is well-founded. In diverse cultures, the more time children spend reading, writing, using the computer, and doing other close work, the more likely they are to be myopic (Mutti et al., 2002; Saw et al., 2002). Consequently, myopia is one of the few health conditions to increase with SES, and it has also increased in recent generations. Fortunately, myopia can be overcome easily with corrective lenses.

During middle childhood, the Eustachian tube (canal that runs from the inner ear to the throat) becomes longer, narrower, and more slanted, preventing fluid and bacteria from traveling so easily from the mouth to the ear. As a result, *otitis media* (middle ear infection), common in infancy and early childhood (see Chapter 8), becomes less frequent. Still, about 3 to 4 percent of the school-age population, and as many as 20 percent of low-SES children, develop some hearing loss as a result of repeated infections (Ryding et al., 2002). With regular screening for both vision and hearing, defects can be corrected before they lead to serious learning difficulties.

Bedwetting

One Friday afternoon, Terry called Joey to see if he could sleep over, but Joey refused. "I can't," said Joey anxiously, without offering an explanation.

"Why not? We can take our sleeping bags out in the backyard. Come on, it'll be cool!"

"My mom won't let me," Joey responded, unconvincingly. "I mean, well, I think we're busy. We're doing something tonight."

"Gosh, Joey, this is the third time you've said no. See if I'll ask you again!" snapped Terry as he hung up the phone.

Joey is one of 10 percent of U.S. school-age children who suffer from **nocturnal enuresis, or bedwetting during the night** (Thiedke, 2003). In the overwhelming majority of cases, the problem has biological roots. Heredity is a major contributing factor: Parents with a history of bedwetting are far more likely to have a child with the problem, and identical twins are more likely than fraternal twins to share it (Weaver & Dobson, 2007). Most often, enuresis is caused by a failure of muscular responses that inhibit urination or by a hormonal imbalance that permits too much urine to accumulate during the night. Some children also have difficulty awakening to the sensation of a full bladder (Hjälmäs, 1998). Punishing a school-age child for wetting is only likely to make matters worse.

To treat enuresis, doctors often prescribe antidepressant drugs, which reduce the amount of urine produced. Although medication is a short-term solution for children attending camp or visiting a friend's house, once children stop taking it, they typically begin wetting again. Also, a small number show side effects, such as anxiety, loss of sleep, and personality changes (Diehr, 2003; Harari & Moulden, 2000). The most effective treatment is a urine alarm that wakes the child at the first sign of dampness and works according to conditioning principles. Success rates of about 60 to 70 percent occur after four to six months of treatment. Most children who relapse achieve dryness after trying the alarm a second time (Houts, 2003).

In a study of more than 3,300 U.S. school-age children with nocturnal enuresis, fewer than one-third had seen a health professional about the problem (Butler, Golding, & Heron, 2005). Yet treatment in middle childhood has immediate positive psychological consequences. It leads to gains in parents' evaluation of their child's behavior and in children's self-esteem (Longstaffe, Moffatt, & Whalen, 2000). Although many children outgrow enuresis without intervention, this generally takes years.

Illnesses

Children experience a somewhat higher rate of illness during the first two years of elementary school than later, because of exposure to sick children and an immune system that is still developing. On average, illness causes children to miss about 11 days of school per year, but most absences can be traced to a few students with chronic health problems (Moonie et al., 2006).

About 15 to 20 percent of U.S. children living at home have chronic diseases and conditions (including physical disabilities) (Van Cleave, Gortmaker, & Perrin, 2010). By far the most common—accounting for about one-third of childhood chronic illness and the most frequent cause of school absence and childhood hospitalization—is *asthma,* in which the bronchial tubes (passages that connect the throat and lungs) are highly sensitive (Bonilla et al., 2005). In response to a variety of stimuli, such as cold weather, infection, exercise, allergies, and emotional stress, they fill with mucus and contract, leading to coughing, wheezing, and serious breathing difficulties.

From 1980 to 1997, the prevalence of asthma among U.S. children more than doubled, then stabilized at 9 percent (Akinbami et al., 2009). Although heredity contributes to asthma, researchers believe that environmental factors are necessary to spark the illness. Boys, African-American children, and children who were born underweight, whose parents smoke, and who live in poverty are at greatest risk (Federico & Liu, 2003; Pearlman et al., 2006). The higher rate and greater severity of asthma among African-American and poverty-stricken children may be the result of pollution in inner-city areas (which triggers allergic reactions), stressful home lives, and lack of access to good health care. Childhood obesity is also related to asthma in middle childhood, possibly due to high levels of blood-circulating inflammatory substances associated with body fat and the pressure of excess weight on the chest wall (Story, 2007).

About 2 percent of U.S. children have more severe chronic illnesses, such as sickle cell anemia, cystic fibrosis, diabetes, arthritis, cancer, and acquired immune deficiency syndrome (AIDS). Painful medical treatments, physical discomfort, and changes in appearance often disrupt the sick child's daily life, making it difficult to concentrate in school and separating the child from peers. As the illness worsens, family stress increases (LeBlanc, Goldsmith, & Patel, 2003). For these reasons, chronically ill children are at risk for academic, emotional, and social difficulties. In adolescence, they are more likely than their agemates to suffer from low self-esteem and depression and report more often smoking cigarettes, using illegal drugs, and thinking about and attempting suicide (Erickson et al., 2005).

■ Although heredity contributes to asthma, environmental factors trigger the illness. Pollution may account for higher rates and greater severity of the condition among children living in poverty-stricken, inner-city neighborhoods. ■

© MARK REINSTEIN/THE IMAGE WORKS

A strong link exists between good family functioning and child well-being for chronically ill children, just as it does for physically healthy children (Drotar et al., 2006). Interventions that foster positive family relationships help parent and child cope with the disease and improve adjustment. These include:

- Health education, in which parents and children learn about the illness and get training in how to manage it
- Home visits by health professionals, who offer counseling and social support to enhance parents' and children's strategies for handling the stress of chronic illness
- Schools that accommodate children's special health and education needs
- Disease-specific summer camps, which teach children self-help skills and give parents time off from the demands of caring for an ill youngster
- Parent and peer support groups

Unintentional Injuries

As we conclude our discussion of threats to school-age children's health, let's return to the topic of unintentional injuries (discussed in detail in Chapter 8). As Figure 11.5 shows, injury fatalities increase from middle childhood into adolescence, with rates for boys rising considerably above those for girls. Poverty and either rural or inner-city residence—factors associated with dangerous environments and reduced parental monitoring of children—are also linked to high injury rates (Birken et al., 2006; Schwebel et al., 2004).

Motor vehicle accidents, involving children as passengers or pedestrians, continue to be the leading cause of injury, followed by bicycle accidents (U.S. Department of Health and Human Services, 2008a). Pedestrian injuries most often result from midblock dart-outs, bicycle accidents from disobeying traffic signals and rules. When many stimuli impinge on them at once, young school-age children often fail to think before they act (Tuchfarber, Zins, & Jason, 1997). They need frequent reminders, supervision, and prohibitions against venturing into busy traffic on their own.

As children range farther from home, safety education becomes especially important. Effective school-based prevention programs use extensive modeling and rehearsal of safety practices, give children feedback about their performance along with praise and tangible rewards for acquiring safety skills, and provide occasional booster sessions (Zins et al., 1994).

Parents, who often overestimate their child's safety knowledge and physical abilities, must be educated about children's age-related safety capacities (Schwebel & Bounds, 2003).

One vital safety measure is insisting that children wear protective helmets while bicycling, in-line skating, skateboarding, or using scooters. This simple precaution leads to a 25 percent reduction in head injury, a leading cause of permanent physical disability and death in school-age children (Macpherson & Spinks, 2007; Wesson et al., 2008). Combining helmet use with other prevention strategies is especially effective. In the Harlem Hospital Injury Prevention Program, inner-city children received safety education in classrooms and in a simulated traffic environment. They also attended bicycle safety clinics, during which helmets were distributed. In addition, existing playgrounds were improved and new ones constructed to provide expanded off-street play areas. Finally, more community-sponsored, supervised recreational activities were offered. As a result, motor vehicle and bicycle injuries declined by 36 percent among school-age children (Durkin et al., 1999).

Not all children respond to efforts to increase their safety. By middle childhood, the greatest risk-takers tend to be those whose parents do not act as safety-conscious models, rarely

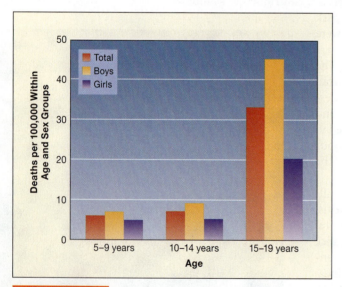

FIGURE 11.5

U.S. rates of injury mortality from middle childhood to adolescence. Injury fatalities increase with age, and the gap between boys and girls expands. Motor vehicle (passenger and pedestrian) accidents are the leading cause, with bicycle injuries next in line. *(From U.S. Department of Health and Human Services, 2008a.)*

supervise their children's activities, or use punitive or inconsistent discipline to enforce rules (Tuchfarber, Zins, & Jason, 1997). These child-rearing tactics, as we saw in Chapter 10, spark children's defiance, reduce their willingness to comply, and actually promote high-risk behavior (Rowe, Maughan, & Goodman, 2004).

Highly active, impulsive children, many of whom are boys, remain particularly susceptible to injury in middle childhood. Although they have just as much safety knowledge as their peers, they are far less likely to implement it. Parents tend to be particularly lax in intervening in the dangerous behaviors of such children (Mori & Peterson, 1995; Schwebel, Hodgens, & Sterling, 2006). Furthermore, compared with girls, boys judge risky play activities as less likely to result in injury, and they pay less attention to injury risk cues, such as a peer who looks hesitant or fearful (Morrongiello & Rennie, 1998). The greatest challenge for injury-control programs is reaching these children, altering high-risk factors in their families, and reducing the dangers to which they are exposed.

■ Unfortunately, parents of these in-line skaters failed to insist that they wear a helmet and use arm and knee protection, placing the children at risk for serious injury. Head injuries are a leading cause of permanent disability and death in school-age children. ■

Health Education

Psychologists, educators, and pediatricians are intensely interested in finding ways to help school-age children understand their bodies, acquire mature conceptions of health and illness, and develop behaviors that foster good health throughout life. Successful health intervention requires information about children's current health-related knowledge. What can they understand? What reasoning processes do they use? What factors influence what they know? The Social Issues: Education box on page 426 summarizes findings on children's concepts of health and illness in middle childhood.

The school-age period may be especially important for fostering healthy lifestyles because of the child's growing independence, increasing cognitive capacities, and rapidly developing self-concept, which includes a sense of physical well-being (Harter, 2006). During middle childhood, children can acquire a wide range of health information—about the structure and functioning of their bodies, about good nutrition, and about the causes and consequences of physical injuries and diseases. Yet most efforts to impart health concepts to school-age children have little impact on behavior (Tinsley, 2003). Several related reasons underlie this gap between knowledge and practice:

■ Health is seldom an important goal for children, who feel good most of the time. They are far more concerned about schoolwork, friends, and play.
■ Children do not yet have an adultlike time perspective that relates past, present, and future. They cannot see the connection between engaging in preventive behaviors now and experiencing later health consequences.
■ Much health information given to children is contradicted by other sources, such as television advertising, and the examples of adults and peers.

Teaching school-age children health-related facts, though important, must be supplemented by other efforts. As we have seen, a powerful means of fostering children's health is to reduce hazards, such as pollution, inadequate medical and dental care, and unhealthy diet. At the same time, because environments will never be totally free of health risks, parents and teachers must coach children in good health practices and must model and reinforce these behaviors. Refer to Applying What We Know on page 427 for ways to foster healthy lifestyles in school-age children.

SOCIAL ISSUES: EDUCATION

Children's Understanding of Health and Illness

izzie lay on the living room sofa with a stuffy nose and sore throat, disappointed that she was missing her soccer team's final game and pizza party. "How'd I get this dumb cold anyhow?" she wondered aloud to Joey. "I probably got it by playing outside when it was freezing cold."

"No, no," Joey contradicted. "Viruses get into your blood and attack, just like an army."

"Gross. I didn't eat any viruses," responded Lizzie.

"You don't eat them, silly, you breathe them in. Somebody probably sneezed them all over you at school. That's how you got sick!"

Lizzie and Joey are at different developmental levels in their understanding of health and illness—due to cognitive development and exposure to biological knowledge. Researchers have asked preschool through high school students questions about the causes of health and of certain illnesses, such as colds, AIDS, and cancer.

During the preschool and early school years, children do not have much biological knowledge to bring to bear on their understanding of health and illness. In research carried out in both the United States and China, 3- to 8-year-olds, who know little about how their internal organs work, generally fell back on their rich knowledge of people's behavior to account for health and illness (Carey, 1995, 1999; Zhu & Liu, 2007). Children of this age regard health as a matter of engaging in specific practices (eating the right foods, getting enough sleep and exercise, wearing warm clothing on cold days), and they regard illness as a matter of failing to follow these rules or coming too close to a sick person.

By age 9 or 10, when children can name many internal organs and view them as an interconnected system, they almost always explain health and illness biologically (Carey, 1999). Joey understands that illness can be caused by contagion—breathing in a harmful substance (a virus), which affects the operation of the body. He also realizes that we eat not just because food tastes good or to stay alive (younger children's explanations) but to build flesh, blood, muscle, and bone (Myant & Williams, 2005; Toyamo, 2000). In early adolescence, explanations become more elaborate and precise, and notions of illness involve clearly

stated ideas about interference in normal biological processes: "You get a cold when your sinuses fill with mucus. Sometimes your lungs do, too, and you get a cough. Colds come from viruses. They get into the bloodstream and make your platelet count go down" (Bibace & Walsh, 1980; Myant & Williams, 2005).

Young school-age children can grasp basic biological ideas that are important for understanding disease. But whether or not they do so depends on information in their environments. When given relevant facts and biological concepts, such as "gene," "germ," and "virus," even 5- and 6-year-olds use the concepts to organize the facts, and their understanding advances (Solomon & Johnson, 2000).

Without such knowledge, children readily generalize from their knowledge of familiar diseases to less familiar ones. As a result, they may conclude that risk factors for colds (sharing a Coke, sneezing on someone) can cause AIDS or that cancer (again, like a cold) is communicable through casual contact (Gonzales-Rivera & Bauermeister, 2007). These incorrect ideas can lead to unnecessary anxiety about getting a serious disease.

Once biological explanations of illness become well-grounded, school-age children (like many adults) seem to combine them with other cultural ideas. For example, children in India, like those in the United States, favor biological explanations of illness. But Indian children tend to suggest moral causes ("Maybe he's being punished by God for his bad behavior") influenced by Hindu notions of karma and retribution—that positive, caring actions lead to positive results, while negative, hurtful actions bring suffering (Raman & Gelman, 2004).

Unfortunately, when certain diseases take on powerfully negative cultural meanings—for example, cancer as a destructive evil or AIDS as a sign of moral

decay—even adults with accurate biological knowledge expect bad things to happen from associating with affected people, and children quickly pick up these attitudes (Bhana, 2008; Gonzales-Rivera & Bauermeister, 2007). This helps explain the severe social rejection experienced by some youngsters with chronic diseases.

Education about the causes of various illnesses leads to an increasingly accurate appreciation of disease transmission and prevention during middle childhood and adolescence. To combat irrational fears and prejudices and foster compassion, teachers can give AIDS, cancer, and other debilitating and deadly illnesses "a human face" by bringing chronically ill people into the classroom or talking about the experiences of people who died of an illness.

© ELLEN B. SENISI PHOTOGRAPHY

■ When school-age children are taught basic biological concepts, such as "germ" and "virus," their understanding of health and disease advances. As a result, they are less likely to harbor incorrect ideas about the causes of illness, which can lead to unnecessary anxiety about getting a serious disease. ■

Applying What We Know

Strategies for Fostering Healthy Lifestyles in School-Age Children

STRATEGY	DESCRIPTION
Increase health-related knowledge and encourage healthy behaviors.	Provide health education that imparts knowledge about healthy lifestyles (including the health risks of overweight and obesity) and that includes modeling, role playing, rehearsal, and reinforcement of good health practices.
Involve parents in supporting health education.	Communicate with parents about health education goals in school, encouraging them to extend these efforts at home. Teach parents about unhealthy feeding practices and how to create healthy food environments at home. Promote proper parental supervision by providing information on children's age-related safety capacities.
Provide healthy environments in schools.	Ask school administrators to ensure that school breakfasts and lunches follow widely accepted dietary guidelines. Limit access to vending machines with junk food. Work for daily recess periods in elementary school and mandatory daily physical education at all grade levels.
Make voluntary screening for risk factors available as part of health education.	Offer periodic measures of height, weight, body mass, blood pressure, and adequacy of diet. Educate children about the meaning of each index, and encourage improvement.
Promote pleasurable physical activity.	Provide opportunities for regular, vigorous physical exercise through activities that de-emphasize competition and stress skill building and personal and social enjoyment.
Teach children to be critical of media advertising.	Besides teaching children to be skeptical of TV ads for unhealthy foods, reduce advertising for such foods in schools.
Work for safer, healthier community environments for children.	Form community action groups to improve child safety, school nutrition, and play environments, and initiate community programs that foster healthy physical activity.

ASK YOURSELF

◆ **REVIEW** Select one of the following health problems of middle childhood: obesity, myopia, bedwetting, asthma, or unintentional injuries. Explain how both genetic and environmental factors contribute to it.

◆ **APPLY** Nine-year-old Talia is afraid to hug and kiss her grandmother, who has cancer. What explains Talia's mistaken belief that the same behaviors that cause colds to spread might lead her to catch cancer? What would you do to change her thinking?

◆ **CONNECT** Children who were undernourished in the early years are more likely to become overweight when their food environments improve. Explain how this finding illustrates epigenesis, described on pages 86–87 in Chapter 2.

◆ **REFLECT** List unintentional injuries that you experienced as a child. Were you injury-prone? Why or why not?

Motor Development and Play

TAKE A MOMENT... Visit a park on a pleasant weekend afternoon, and watch several preschool and school-age children at play. You will see that gains in body size and muscle strength support improved motor coordination during middle childhood. And greater cognitive and social maturity enables older children to use their new motor skills in more complex ways. A major change in children's play takes place at this time.

Gross-Motor Development

During the school years, running, jumping, hopping, and ball skills become more refined. At Joey and Lizzie's school, I watched during the third to sixth graders' recess. Children burst into sprints as they raced across the playground, jumped quickly over rotating ropes, engaged in

TABLE 11.2 Changes in Gross-Motor Skills During Middle Childhood

SKILL	DEVELOPMENTAL CHANGE
Running	Running speed increases from 12 feet per second at age 6 to over 18 feet per second at age 12.
Other gait variations	Skipping improves. Sideways stepping appears around age 6 and becomes more continuous and fluid with age.
Vertical jump	Height jumped increases from 4 inches at age 6 to 12 inches at age 12.
Standing broad jump	Distance jumped increases from 3 feet at age 6 to over 5 feet at age 12.
Precision jumping and hopping (on a mat divided into squares)	By age 7 children can accurately jump and hop from square to square, a performance that improves until age 9 and then levels off.
Throwing	Throwing speed, distance, and accuracy increase for both sexes, but much more for boys than for girls. At age 6, a ball thrown by a boy travels 39 feet per second, one by a girl 29 feet per second. At age 12, a ball thrown by a boy travels 78 feet per second, one by a girl 56 feet per second.
Catching	Ability to catch small balls thrown over greater distances improves with age.
Kicking	Kicking speed and accuracy improve, with boys considerably ahead of girls. At age 6, a ball kicked by a boy travels 21 feet per second, one by a girl 13 feet per second. At age 12, a ball kicked by a boy travels 34 feet per second, one by a girl 26 feet per second.
Batting	Batting motions become more effective with age, increasing in speed and accuracy and involving the entire body.
Dribbling	Style of hand dribbling gradually changes, from awkward slapping of the ball to continuous, relaxed, even stroking.

Sources: Haywood & Getchell, 2005; Malina & Bouchard, 1991.

■ A fancy twist of the rope following each revolution complicates this game of jump rope. Improved physical flexibility, balance, agility, and force, along with more efficient information processing, promote gains in school-age children's gross-motor skills. ■

intricate hopscotch patterns, kicked and dribbled soccer balls, batted at balls pitched by their classmates, and balanced adeptly as they walked heel-to-toe across narrow ledges. Table 11.2 summarizes gross-motor achievements between 6 and 12 years of age. These diverse skills reflect gains in four basic motor capacities:

■ *Flexibility.* Compared with preschoolers, school-age children are physically more pliable and elastic, a difference that is evident as they swing bats, kick balls, jump over hurdles, and execute tumbling routines.
■ *Balance.* Improved balance supports many athletic skills, including running, hopping, skipping, throwing, kicking, and the rapid changes of direction required in many team sports.
■ *Agility.* Quicker and more accurate movements are evident in the fancy footwork of dance and cheerleading and in the forward, backward, and sideways motions used to dodge opponents in tag and soccer.
■ *Force.* Older children can throw and kick a ball harder and propel themselves farther off the ground when running and jumping than they could at earlier ages (Haywood & Getchell, 2005).

Along with body growth, more efficient information processing plays a vital role in improved motor performance. Younger children often have difficulty with skills that require rapid responding, such as dribbling and batting. During middle childhood, the capacity to react only to relevant information increases. And steady gains in reaction time occur, with 11-year-olds responding twice as quickly as 5-year-olds (Band et al., 2000; Kail, 2003; Largo et al., 2001). These differences in speed of reaction have practical implications for physical education. Because 6- and 7-year-olds are seldom successful at batting a thrown ball, T-ball is more appropriate for them than baseball. Similarly, handball, four-square, and kickball should precede instruction in tennis, basketball, and football.

Fine-Motor Development

Fine-motor development also improves over the school years. On rainy afternoons, Joey and Lizzie experimented with yo-yos, built model airplanes, and wove potholders on small looms. Like many children, they took up musical instruments, which demand considerable fine-motor control. And gains in fine-motor skill are especially evident in children's writing and drawing.

By age 6, most children can print the alphabet, their first and last names, and the numbers from 1 to 10 with reasonable clarity. Their writing is large, however, because they make strokes using the entire arm rather than just the wrist and fingers. Children usually master uppercase letters first because their horizontal and vertical motions are easier to control than the small curves of the lowercase alphabet. Legibility of writing gradually increases as children produce more accurate letters with uniform height and spacing. These improvements prepare children for mastering cursive writing by third grade.

Children's drawings show dramatic gains in organization, detail, and representation of depth during middle childhood. By the end of the preschool years, children can accurately copy many two-dimensional shapes, and they integrate these into their drawings. Some depth cues have also begun to appear, such as making distant objects smaller than near ones (Braine et al., 1993). Yet recall from Chapter 8 that before age 8, children have trouble accurately copying a three-dimensional form, such as a cube or cylinder (see page 311). Around 9 to 10 years, the third dimension is clearly evident through overlapping objects, diagonal placement, and converging lines. Furthermore, as Figure 11.6 shows, school-age children not only depict objects in considerable detail but also relate them to one another as part of an organized whole (Case, 1998; Case & Okamoto, 1996).

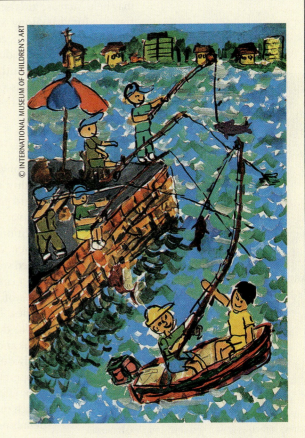

FIGURE 11.6

Increase in organization, detail, and depth cues in school-age children's drawings. TAKE A MOMENT... Compare both drawings to the one by a 6-year-old on page 310. In the drawing on the left, an 8-year-old depicts her family at the dinner table. Notice how all parts are depicted in relation to one another and with greater detail. Integration of depth cues increases dramatically over the school years, as shown in the drawing on the right, by a 10-year-old artist from Singapore. Here, depth is indicated by overlapping objects, diagonal placement, and converging lines, as well as by making distant objects smaller than near ones.

Individual Differences in Motor Skills

As at younger ages, school-age children show marked individual differences in motor capacities that are influenced by both heredity and environment. Body build is one factor: Taller, more muscular children excel at many motor tasks. And children whose parents encourage physical exercise tend to enjoy it more and also to be more skilled.

Family income affects children's access to lessons needed to develop abilities in areas such as ballet, tennis, gymnastics, and instrumental music. For low-SES children, school and community provisions for nurturing athletics and other motor skills by making lessons, equipment, and opportunities for regular practice available and affordable are crucial. When these experiences combine with parental encouragement, many low-SES children become highly skilled.

Sex differences in motor skills that appeared during the preschool years extend into middle childhood and, in some instances, become more pronounced. Girls have an edge in fine-motor skills of handwriting and drawing and in gross-motor capacities that depend on balance and agility, such as hopping and skipping. But boys outperform girls on all other skills listed in Table 11.2, especially throwing and kicking (Cratty, 1986; Haywood & Getchell, 2005).

School-age boys' genetic advantage in muscle mass is not large enough to account for their gross-motor superiority. Rather, the social environment plays a larger role. Research confirms that parents hold higher expectations for boys' athletic performance, and children readily absorb these messages. From first through twelfth grades, girls are less positive than boys about the value of sports and their own sports ability—differences explained in part by parental beliefs (Fredricks & Eccles, 2002). But girls and older school-age children regard boys' advantage in sports as unjust. They indicate, for example, that coaches should spend equal time with children of each sex and that female sports should command just as much media attention as male sports (Solomon & Bredemeier, 1999).

Educating parents about the minimal differences between school-age boys' and girls' physical capacities and sensitizing them to unfair biases against promotion of girls' athletic ability may help increase girls' self-confidence and participation in athletics. Greater emphasis on skill training for girls, along with increased attention to their athletic achievements, is also likely to help. As a positive sign, compared with a generation ago, many more girls now participate in individual and team sports such as gymnastics and soccer (National Council of Youth Sports, 2008). Middle childhood is a crucial time to encourage girls' sports participation because during this period, children start to discover what they are good at and make some definite skill commitments.

Games with Rules

The physical activities of school-age children reflect an important advance in quality of play: Games with rules become common. Children around the world engage in an enormous variety of informally organized games, including variants on popular sports such as soccer, baseball, and basketball. In addition to the best-known childhood games, such as tag, jacks, and hopscotch, children have also invented hundreds of other games, including red rover, statues, leapfrog, kick the can, and prisoner's base (Kirchner, 2000).

Gains in perspective taking—in particular, the ability to understand the roles of several players in a game—permit this transition to rule-oriented games. These play experiences, in turn, contribute greatly to emotional and social development. Child-invented games usually rely on simple physical skills and a sizable element of luck. As a result, they rarely become contests of individual ability. Instead, they permit children to try out different styles of cooperating, competing, winning, and losing with little personal risk. Also, in their efforts to organize a game, children discover why rules are necessary and which ones work well. In fact, they often spend as much time working out the details of how a game should proceed as they do playing the game! As we will see in Chapter 13, these experiences help children form more mature concepts of fairness and justice.

© EITAN SIMANOR/ALAMY

■ Two children in Myanmar play a traditional game with marbles. In middle childhood, child-organized games with rules grow increasingly complex. Through them, children explore different ways of cooperating, competing, winning, and losing. ■

Adult-Organized Youth Sports

Compared with past generations, school-age children today spend less time gathering informally on sidewalks and in playgrounds. In part, this change reflects parental concern about neighborhood safety, as well as competition for children's time from TV, video games, and the Internet. Another factor is the rise in adult-organized sports, such as Little League baseball and soccer and hockey leagues, which fill many hours that children used to devote to spontaneous play. About half of U.S. children—60 percent of boys and 37 percent of girls—participate in organized sports outside of school hours at some time between ages 5 and 18 (National Council of Youth Sports, 2008).

For most children, joining community athletic teams is associated with increased self-esteem and social skills (Daniels & Leaper, 2006; Fletcher, Nickerson, & Wright, 2003). Among shy children, sports participation seems to play a protective role, fostering self-confidence and a decline in social anxiety, perhaps because it provides a sense of group belonging and a basis for communicating with peers (Findlay & Coplan, 2008). And children who view themselves as good at sports are more likely to continue playing on teams in adolescence, which predicts greater participation in sports and other physical fitness activities in early adulthood (Marsh et al., 2007; McHale et al., 2005).

In some cases, though, the arguments of critics—that youth sports overemphasize competition and substitute adult control for children's natural experimentation with rules and strategies—are valid. Children who join teams so early that the necessary skills are beyond their abilities soon lose interest. Coaches and parents who criticize rather than encourage can prompt intense anxiety in some children. And especially among boys—for whom competence at sports is linked to peer admiration—weaker performers generally experience social ostracism when coaches make winning the paramount goal (Stryer, Tofler, & Lapchick, 1998).

Parents, even more than coaches, influence children's athletic attitudes and abilities. At the extreme are parents who value sports so highly that they punish their child for making mistakes, insist that the child keep playing after injury, hold the child back in school to ensure a physical advantage, or even seek medical interventions to improve the child's performance. High parental pressure sets the stage for emotional difficulties and early athletic dropout, not elite performance (Tofler, Knapp, & Drell, 1998; Wall & Côté, 2007).

In most organized youth sports, health and safety rules help ensure that injuries are infrequent and mild. The exception is football, which has a high rate of serious injury (Radelet et al., 2002). But frequent, intense practice in any sport can lead to painful "overuse" injuries and, in extreme cases, to stress-related fractures resulting in premature closure of the epiphyses of the long bones (Frank et al., 2007). When parents and coaches emphasize effort, improvement, participation, and teamwork, young athletes enjoy sports more, exert greater effort to improve their skills, and perceive themselves as more competent at their chosen sport (Ullrich-French & Smith, 2006). See Applying What We Know on page 432 for ways to ensure that athletic leagues provide children with positive learning experiences.

Shadows of Our Evolutionary Past

TAKE A MOMENT... While watching children in your neighborhood park, notice how they occasionally wrestle, roll, hit, and run after one another, alternating roles while smiling and laughing. This friendly chasing and play-fighting is called **rough-and-tumble play.** It emerges in the preschool years and peaks in middle childhood, and children in many cultures engage in it with peers whom they like especially well (Pellegrini, 2004). After a rough-and-tumble episode, children continue interacting rather than separating, as they do after an aggressive encounter.

Children's rough-and-tumble play resembles the social behavior of many other young mammals. It seems to originate in parents' physical play with babies, especially fathers' play with sons (see page 274 in Chapter 7). And it is more common among boys, probably because prenatal exposure

LOOK AND LISTEN

Observe a youth athletic-league game, such as soccer, baseball, or hockey. Do coaches and parents encourage children's effort and skill gains, or are they overly focused on winning? Cite examples of adult and child behaviors.

© PHOTO AND CO./GETTY IMAGES/LIFESIZE

■ The friendly quality of these children's rough-and-tumble play distinguishes it from aggression. In our evolutionary past, rough-and-tumble may have been important for developing fighting skill and establishing dominance hierarchies. ■

Applying What We Know

Providing Developmentally Appropriate Organized Sports in Middle Childhood

STRATEGY	DESCRIPTION
Build on children's interests.	Permit children to select from among appropriate activities the ones that suit them best. Do not push children into sports they do not enjoy.
Teach age-appropriate skills.	For children younger than age 9, emphasize basic skills, such as kicking, throwing, and batting, and simplified games that grant all participants adequate playing time.
Emphasize enjoyment.	Permit children to progress at their own pace and to play for the fun of it, whether or not they become expert athletes.
Limit the frequency and length of practices.	Adjust practice time to children's attention spans and need for unstructured time with peers, with family, and for homework. Two practices a week, each no longer than 30 minutes for younger school-age children and 60 minutes for older school-age children, are sufficient.
Focus on personal and team improvement.	Emphasize effort, skill gains, and teamwork rather than winning. Avoid criticism for errors and defeat, which promotes anxiety and avoidance of athletics.
Discourage unhealthy competition.	Avoid all-star games and championship ceremonies that recognize individuals. Instead, acknowledge all participants.
Permit children to contribute to rules and strategies.	Involve children in decisions aimed at ensuring fair play and teamwork. To strengthen desirable responses, reinforce compliance rather than punishing noncompliance.

to androgens predisposes boys toward active play (see Chapter 10, page 386). Boys' rough-and-tumble largely consists of playful wrestling, restraining, and hitting, whereas girls tend to engage in running and chasing, with only brief physical contact (Boulton, 1996).

In middle childhood, rough-and-tumble accounts for as much as 10 percent of free-play behavior, before declining in adolescence. In our evolutionary past, it may have been important for the development of fighting skill (Power, 2000). It also helps children form a **dominance hierarchy**—a stable ordering of group members that predicts who will win when conflict arises. Observations of arguments, threats, and physical attacks between children reveal a consistent lineup of winners and losers that becomes increasingly stable in middle childhood and adolescence, especially among boys. Once school-age children establish a dominance hierarchy, hostility is rare (Pellegrini & Smith, 1998; Roseth et al., 2007). Children seem to use play-fighting as a safe context to assess the strength of a peer before challenging that peer's dominance.

As children reach puberty, individual differences in strength become apparent, and rough-and-tumble play declines. When it does occur, its meaning changes: Adolescent boys' rough-and-tumble is linked to aggression (Pellegrini, 2003). Unlike children, teenage rough-and-tumble players "cheat," hurting their opponent. In explanation, boys often say that they are retaliating, apparently to reestablish dominance. Thus, a play behavior that limits aggression in childhood becomes a context for hostility in adolescence.

Physical Education

Physical activity supports many aspects of children's development—their health, their sense of self-worth as physically active and capable beings, and the cognitive and social skills necessary for getting along with others. Yet to devote more time to academic instruction, U.S. elementary schools have cut back on recess, despite its contribution all domains of development (see the Social Issues: Education box on the following page). Similarly, only 15 percent of U.S. elementary and middle

© MICHAEL NEWMAN/PHOTOEDIT

■ Cheered by their teacher, fourth through sixth graders participate in an enjoyable ball-carrying race. Many experts believe that physical education classes should emphasize informal games, individual exercise, and personal progress rather than competitive sports. ■

SOCIAL ISSUES: EDUCATION

School Recess—A Time to Play, a Time to Learn

When 7-year-old Whitney's family moved to a new city, she left a school with three daily recess periods for one with just a single 15-minute break per day, which her second-grade teacher cancelled if any child misbehaved. Whitney, who had previously enjoyed school, complained daily of headaches and an upset stomach. Her mother, Jill, thought, "My child is stressing out because she can't move all day!" After Jill and other parents successfully appealed to the school board to add a second recess period, Whitney's symptoms vanished (Rauber, 2006).

In recent years, recess—along with its rich opportunities for child-organized play and peer interaction—has diminished or disappeared in many U.S. elementary schools (Pellegrini, 2005; Pellegrini & Holmes, 2006). Under the assumption that extra time for academics will translate into achievement gains, 7 percent of U.S. schools no longer provide recess to students as young as second grade. And over half of schools that do have recess now schedule it just once a day (U.S. Department of Education, 2010).

Yet rather than subtracting from classroom learning, recess periods boost it! Research dating back more than 100 years confirms that distributing cognitively demanding tasks over a longer time by introducing regular breaks, rather than consolidating intensive effort within one period, enhances attention and performance at all ages. Such breaks are particularly important for young children. In a series of studies, school-age children were more attentive in the classroom after recess than before it—an effect that was greater for second than fourth graders (Pellegrini, Huberty, & Jones, 1995).

Teacher ratings of classroom disruptive behavior also decline for children who have more than 15 minutes of recess a day (Barros, Silver, & Stein, 2009).

In another investigation, kindergartners' and first graders' engagement in peer conversation and games during recess positively predicted later academic achievement, even after other factors that might explain the relationship (such as previous achievement) were controlled (Pellegrini, 1992; Pellegrini et al., 2002). Recall from Chapter 10 that children's social maturity contributes substantially to early academic competence. Recess is one of the few remaining contexts devoted to child-organized games that provide practice in vital social skills—coopera-tion, leadership, followership, and inhibition of aggression—under adult supervision rather than direction. As children transfer these skills to the classroom, they may participate in discussions, collaborate, follow rules, and enjoy academic pursuits more—factors that enhance motivation and achievement.

Finally, children are even more physically active during recess than in gym class (U.S. Department of Education, 2006). School-age girls, especially, engage in more moderate-to-vigorous exercise during recess than at other times of the day (Mota et al., 2005). In sum, regular, unstructured recess fosters children's health and competence—physically, academically, and socially.

TORONTO STAR/FIRSTLIGHT

School-age children, especially girls, are even more physically active during recess than in gym class. By providing regular opportunities for unstructured play and games, recess promotes physical, academic, and social competence. ■

schools provide students with physical education at least three days a week, a figure that drops to 3 percent in high school (Lee et al., 2007). Not surprisingly, physical inactivity among school-age children is pervasive. Only 49 percent of boys and 35 percent of girls are active enough for good health—that is, engage in at least moderate-intensity exercise for one hour or more per day. As children move into adolescence, these rates drop sharply, to just 10 percent of boys and 4 percent of girls (Troiano et al., 2007).

Many experts believe that schools should not only offer more frequent physical education classes but also change the content of these programs. Training in competitive sports, often a high priority, is unlikely to reach the least physically fit youngsters, who avoid activities demanding a high level of skill. Instead, programs should emphasize enjoyable, informal games and individual exercise (walking, running, jumping, tumbling, and climbing)—pursuits most likely to endure. Furthermore, children of varying skill levels are more likely to sustain physical activity when teachers focus on each child's personal progress and contribution to team accomplishment (Connor, 2003). Then physical education fosters a healthy sense of self while satisfying school-age children's need to participate with others.

Physically fit children take great pleasure in their rapidly developing motor skills. As a result, they develop rewarding interests in physical activity and sports and are more likely to become active adolescents and adults who reap many benefits (Janz, Dawson, & Mahoney, 2000; Kjønniksen, Torsheim, & Wold, 2008; Tammelin et al., 2003). These include greater physical strength, resistance to many illnesses (from colds and flu to cancer, diabetes, and heart disease), enhanced psychological well-being, and a longer life.

ASK YOURSELF

◆ **REVIEW** Explain the adaptive value of rough-and-tumble play and dominance hierarchies.

◆ **APPLY** Nine-year-old Allison thinks she isn't good at sports, and she doesn't like physical education class. Suggest some strategies her teacher can use to improve her pleasure and involvement in physical activity.

◆ **CONNECT** On Saturdays, 10-year-old Billy gathers with friends on the driveway of his house to play basketball. Besides improved ball skills, what else is he learning?

◆ **REFLECT** Did you participate in adult-organized sports as a child? If so, what kind of climate for learning did coaches and parents create? What impact do you think your experiences had on your development?

Summary

Body Growth

Describe changes in body size, proportions, and skeletal maturity during middle childhood.

- School-age children's growth is slow and regular, though large individual and ethnic variations exist in physical growth. On average, they add about 2 to 3 inches in height and 5 pounds in weight each year. By age 9, girls overtake boys in physical size.

- **Secular trends in physical growth** have occurred in industrialized nations. Because of improved health and nutrition, many children are growing larger and reaching physical maturity earlier than their ancestors.

- Bones continue to lengthen and broaden, and permanent teeth replace primary teeth. Tooth decay affects over half of U.S. school-age children, with especially high levels among low-SES children. One-third of school-age children suffer from **malocclusion,** making braces common by the end of elementary school.

Describe brain development in middle childhood.

- Only a small gain in brain size occurs during middle childhood. White matter (myelinated nerve fibers) increases steadily. As interconnectivity among distant areas of the cerebral cortex increases, the prefrontal cortex becomes a more effective "executive," yielding more flexible, adaptive behavior. At the same time, gray matter (neurons and supportive material) peaks and then declines as a result of synaptic pruning, and accompanying reorganization and selection of brain circuits result in more efficient information processing.

© SKIP BROWN/GETTY IMAGES/LIFESIZE

Common Health Problems

Describe the causes and consequences of serious nutritional problems in middle childhood, giving special attention to obesity.

- Poverty-stricken children in developing countries and in North America continue to suffer from serious and prolonged malnutrition, which can permanently impair physical and mental development.

- Overweight and **obesity** have increased dramatically in both industrialized and developing nations, especially in the United States. Although heredity contributes to obesity, parental feeding practices, maladaptive eating habits, reduced sleep, lack of exercise, and Western high-fat diets are more powerful influences. Obese children are often socially rejected, are more likely to report feeling depressed, and display more behavior problems than their normal-weight peers.

■ Family-based interventions aimed at changing parents' and children's eating patterns and lifestyles are the most effective approaches to treating childhood obesity. Rewarding obese children for reducing sedentary time is effective in getting them to enjoy and engage in more physical activity. Schools can help by ensuring regular physical activity and serving healthier meals.

What factors contribute to myopia, otitis media, nocturnal enuresis, and asthma, and how can these health problems be reduced?

■ The most common vision problem, myopia, is influenced by heredity, early biological trauma, and time spent reading and doing other close work. It is one of the few health conditions that increases with family education and income. Although ear infections decline during the school years, many low-SES children experience some hearing loss because of chronic, untreated otitis media.

■ Heredity is responsible for most cases of **nocturnal enuresis,** through a failure of muscular responses that inhibit urination or a hormonal imbalance that permits too much urine to accumulate. The most effective treatment is a urine alarm that works according to conditioning principles.

■ Asthma is the most frequent cause of school absence and childhood hospitalization. It occurs more often among African-American and poverty-stricken children, perhaps because of inner-city pollution, stressful home lives, and lack of access to good health care. Childhood obesity is also a factor.

■ Children with severe chronic illnesses are at risk for academic, emotional, and social difficulties, but positive family interactions improve adjustment.

Describe changes in the occurrence of unintentional injuries during middle childhood, and cite effective interventions.

■ Unintentional injuries increase over middle childhood and adolescence, especially for boys, with motor vehicle and bicycle accidents accounting for most of the rise.

■ Effective school-based safety education programs use modeling and rehearsal of safety practices and reward children for good performance. Parents also must be educated about children's age-related safety capacities. One vital safety measure is insisting that children wear protective bicycle helmets, which dramatically reduces the risk of serious head injury.

Health Education

What can parents and teachers do to encourage good health practices in school-age children?

■ Besides providing health-related information, adults must reduce health hazards in children's environments, coach children in good health practices, and model and reinforce these behaviors.

Motor Development and Play

Cite major changes in gross- and fine-motor development during middle childhood.

■ Gross-motor improvements in flexibility, balance, agility, and force occur, and gains in responding only to relevant information and in reaction time also contribute to athletic performance.

■ Fine-motor development also improves. Handwriting becomes more legible, and children's drawings show dramatic increases in organization, detail, and representation of depth.

Describe individual differences in motor performance during middle childhood.

■ Wide individual differences in children's motor capacities are influenced by both heredity and environment, including such factors as body build, parental encouragement, and opportunities to take lessons.

■ Gender stereotypes, which affect parental expectations for children's athletic performance, largely account for school-age boys' superiority on a wide range of gross-motor skills. Greater emphasis on skill training for girls and attention to their athletic achievements can help increase their involvement and performance.

What qualities of children's play are evident in middle childhood?

■ Games with rules become common during the school years, contributing to emotional and social development. Expansion of adult-organized youth sports programs is associated with increased self-esteem and social competence in most players, but for some children, adult overemphasis on competition promotes undue anxiety and avoidance of sports. Encouraging effort, improvement, participation, and teamwork makes organized sports enjoyable and beneficial for self-esteem.

■ Some features of children's physical activity reflect our evolutionary past. **Rough-and-tumble play** may once have been important for the development of fighting skill and may help children establish a **dominance hierarchy.** In middle childhood, dominance hierarchies become increasingly stable, especially among boys, and serve the adaptive function of limiting aggression among group members.

What steps can schools take to promote physical fitness in middle childhood?

■ In addition to providing an opportunity for physical activity, school recess is a rich context for child-organized games and social interaction.

■ Despite cutbacks in U.S. elementary schools, regular physical education classes help ensure that all children have access to the physical, cognitive, and social benefits of exercise and play, which translate into lifelong psychological and physical health benefits.

IMPORTANT TERMS AND CONCEPTS

dominance hierarchy (p. 432)
malocclusion (p. 414)

nocturnal enuresis (p. 422)
obesity (p. 416)

rough-and-tumble play (p. 431)
secular trends in physical growth (p. 413)

chapter

12

"My Favorite Game"
Pabasara Desanjani Wijayawansa
9 years, Sri Lanka

Middle childhood brings dramatic gains in attention, memory, categorization, reasoning, and problem solving. These children use their advancing cognitive skills to play a complex board game.

Reprinted with permission from the International Child Art Foundation, Washington, D.C.

Cognitive Development in Middle Childhood

"Finally!" 6-year-old Lizzie exclaimed the day she entered first grade. "Now I get to go to real school just like Joey!" Lizzie walked into her classroom confidently, pencils, crayons, and writing pad in hand, ready for a more disciplined approach to learning than she had experienced in early childhood. As a preschooler, Lizzie had loved playing school, giving assignments as the "teacher" and pretending to read and write as the "student." Now she was eager to master the tasks that had sparked her imagination as a 4- and 5-year-old.

Lizzie had entered a whole new world of challenging mental activities. In a single morning, she and her classmates wrote in journals, met in reading groups, worked on addition and subtraction, and sorted leaves gathered for a science project. As Lizzie and Joey moved through the elementary school grades, they tackled increasingly complex tasks and became more accomplished at reading, writing, math skills, and general knowledge of the world.

To understand the cognitive attainments of middle childhood, we turn to research inspired by Piaget's theory and the information-processing approach. And we look at expanding definitions of intelligence that help us appreciate individual differences in mental development. We also examine the genetic and environmental roots of IQ scores, which often influence important educational decisions. Our discussion continues with language, which blossoms further in these years. Finally, we consider the role of schools in children's development.

Piaget's Theory: The Concrete Operational Stage

When Lizzie visited my child development class as a 4-year-old, Piaget's conservation problems confused her (see Chapter 9, page 322). For example, when water was poured from a tall, narrow container into a short, wide one, she insisted that

Piaget's Theory: The Concrete Operational Stage

Achievements of the Concrete Operational Stage • Limitations of Concrete Operational Thought • Follow-Up Research on Concrete Operational Thought • Evaluation of the Concrete Operational Stage

Information Processing

Attention • Memory Strategies • The Knowledge Base and Memory Performance • Culture, Schooling, and Memory Strategies • The School-Age Child's Theory of Mind • Cognitive Self-Regulation • Applications of Information Processing to Academic Learning

■ **BIOLOGY AND ENVIRONMENT** *Children with Attention-Deficit Hyperactivity Disorder*

Individual Differences in Mental Development

Defining and Measuring Intelligence • Recent Efforts to Define Intelligence • Explaining Individual and Group Differences in IQ • Reducing Cultural Bias in Testing

■ **SOCIAL ISSUES: EDUCATION** *Emotional Intelligence*

Language Development

Vocabulary • Grammar • Pragmatics • Learning Two Languages

Children's Learning in School

Class Size • Educational Philosophies • Teacher–Student Interaction • Grouping Practices • Computers and Academic Learning • Teaching Children with Special Needs • How Well-Educated Are U.S. Children?

■ **SOCIAL ISSUES: EDUCATION** *Magnet Schools: Equal Access to High-Quality Education*

the amount of water had changed. But when Lizzie returned at age 8, she found these tasks easy. "Of course it's the same!" she exclaimed. "The water's shorter, but it's also wider. Pour it back," she instructed the college student who was interviewing her. "You'll see, it's the same amount!"

Achievements of the Concrete Operational Stage

Lizzie has entered Piaget's **concrete operational stage,** which extends from about 7 to 11 years. Thought is now more logical, flexible, and organized than it was during early childhood.

CONSERVATION The ability to pass *conservation tasks* provides clear evidence of *operations*—mental actions that obey logical rules. Notice how Lizzie is capable of *decentration,* focusing on several aspects of a problem and relating them, rather than centering on just one. She also demonstrates **reversibility,** the capacity to think through a series of steps and then mentally reverse direction, returning to the starting point. Recall from Chapter 9 (page 322) that reversibility is part of every logical operation. It is solidly achieved in middle childhood.

CLASSIFICATION Between ages 7 and 10, children pass Piaget's *class inclusion problem* (see page 322). This indicates that they are more aware of classification hierarchies and can focus on relations between a general category and two specific categories at the same time—that is, on three relations at once (Hodges & French, 1988; Ni, 1998). Collections—stamps, coins, baseball cards, rocks, bottle caps—become common in middle childhood. At age 10, Joey spent hours sorting and resorting his baseball cards, grouping them first by league and team, then by playing position and batting average. He could separate the players into a variety of classes and subclasses and easily rearrange them.

■ An improved ability to categorize underlies children's interest in collecting objects during middle childhood. Here, an 8-year-old sorts and organizes buttons in her extensive collection. ■

SERIATION The ability to order items along a quantitative dimension, such as length or weight, is called **seriation.** To test for it, Piaget asked children to arrange sticks of different lengths from shortest to longest. Older preschoolers can put the sticks in a row to create the series, but they do so haphazardly, making many errors. In contrast, 6- to 7-year-olds create the series efficiently, moving in an orderly sequence from the smallest stick, to the next largest, and so on.

The concrete operational child can also seriate mentally, an ability called **transitive inference.** In a well-known transitive inference problem, Piaget showed children pairings of sticks of different colors. From observing that stick *A* is longer than stick *B* and that stick *B* is longer than stick *C,* children must infer that *A* is longer than *C.* Like Piaget's class inclusion task, transitive inference requires children to integrate three relations at once—in this instance, *A–B, B–C,* and *A–C.* When researchers take steps to ensure that children remember the premises (*A–B* and *B–C*), 7- to 8-year-olds can grasp transitive inference (Andrews & Halford, 1998; Wright, 2006).

SPATIAL REASONING Piaget found that school-age children's understanding of space is more accurate than that of preschoolers. Let's consider children's **cognitive maps**—their mental representations of familiar large-scale spaces, such as their neighborhood or school. Drawing a map of a large-scale space requires considerable perspective-taking skill. Because the entire space cannot be seen at once, children must infer its overall layout by relating its separate parts.

Preschoolers and young school-age children include *landmarks* on the maps they draw, but their arrangement is not always accurate. They do better when asked to place stickers showing the location of desks and people on a map of a single room, such as their classroom. But if the map is rotated to a position other than the orientation of the classroom, they have difficulty (Liben & Downs, 1993). And prior to age 9 to 10, most children have trouble placing stickers on a map to indicate the location of colored flags within a large-scale outdoor environment (Kasten & Liben, 2007). Furthermore, not until the late elementary school years do children fully appreciate that in interpreting map symbols, a mapmaker's assigned meaning supersedes physical resemblance—for example, that green dots (not red dots) may indicate where red fire trucks are hidden in a room (Myers & Liben, 2008).

LOOK AND LISTEN

Ask a 7- to 11-year-old to describe, or show you, how he or she organizes a favorite collection of objects. Does the child's sorting reveal a clear classification hierarchy?

Around age 8 to 10, children's maps become better organized, showing landmarks along an *organized route of travel*. At the same time, children are able to give clear, well-organized instructions for getting from one place to another by using a "mental walk" strategy—imagining another person's movements along a route (Gauvain & Rogoff, 1989b). At the end of middle childhood, children form an *overall view of a large-scale space*. And they readily draw and read maps, even when the orientation of the map and the space it represents do not match (Liben, 2009). Ten- to 12-year-olds also grasp the notion of *scale*—the proportional relation between a space and its map representation (Liben, 2006).

Map-related experiences greatly improve children's map skills. When teachers asked fourth graders to write down the clues they used to decide where stickers (signifying landmark locations) should go on a map of an outdoor space, the accuracy of children's performance improved greatly (Kastens & Liben, 2007). Such self-generated explanations seem to induce learners to reflect on and revise their own thinking, sparking gains in many types of problem solving among students from elementary school through college. And a computer-based curriculum called *Where Are We,* consisting of 12 map-reading and map-making lessons, led to substantial improvements in second to fourth graders' performance on diverse mapping tasks (Liben, Kastens, & Stevenson, 2001).

Cultural frameworks influence children's map making. In many non-Western communities, people rarely use maps for way finding but rely on information from neighbors, street vendors, and shopkeepers. Also, compared to their Western agemates, non-Western children less often ride in cars and more often walk, which results in intimate neighborhood knowledge. When a researcher had older school-age children in small cities in India and in the United States draw maps of their neighborhoods, the Indian children represented a rich array of landmarks and aspects of social life, such as people and vehicles, in a small area surrounding their home. The U.S. children, in contrast, drew a more formal, extended space, highlighting main streets and key directions (north–south, east–west) but including few landmarks (see Figure 12.1)

© ELLEN B. SENISI PHOTOGRAPHY

■ This 6-year-old's drawing of a neighborhood map depicts familiar buildings and other landmarks along an organized route of travel. ■

LOOK AND LISTEN

Ask a 6- to 8-year-old and a 9- to 12-year-old to draw a neighborhood map showing important landmarks, such as the school, a friend's house, or a shopping area. In what ways do the children's maps differ?

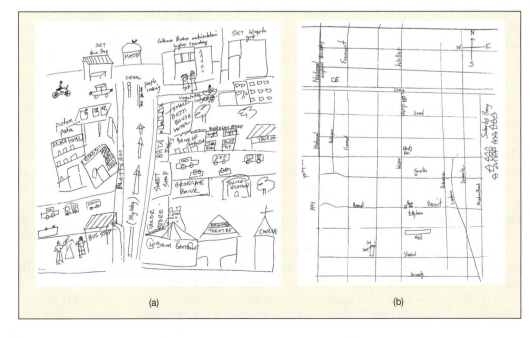

(a)   (b)

FIGURE 12.1

Maps drawn by older school-age children from India and the United States. (a) The Indian child depicted many landmarks and features of social life in a small area near her home. (b) The U.S. child drew a more extended space and highlighted main streets and key directions but included few landmarks and people. *(From G. Parameswaran, 2003, "Experimenter Instructions as a Mediator in the Effects of Culture on Mapping One's Neighborhood," Journal of Environmental Psychology, 23, pp. 415–416. Copyright © 2003, reprinted with permission from Elsevier.)*

(Parameswaran, 2003). Although the U.S. children's maps scored higher in cognitive maturity, this difference reflected cultural interpretations of the task: When asked to create a map to "help people find their way," the Indian children drew spaces as far-reaching and organized as the U.S. children's.

Limitations of Concrete Operational Thought

As the name of this stage suggests, concrete operational thinking suffers from one important limitation: Children think in an organized, logical fashion only when dealing with concrete information they can perceive directly. Their mental operations work poorly with abstract ideas—ones not apparent in the real world. Consider children's solutions to transitive inference problems. When shown pairs of sticks of unequal length, Lizzie easily engaged in transitive inference. But she had great difficulty with a hypothetical version of this task: "Susan is taller than Sally, and Sally is taller than Mary. Who is the tallest?" Not until age 11 or 12 can children solve this problem.

That logical thought is at first tied to immediate situations helps account for a special feature of concrete operational reasoning. Children master concrete operational tasks step by step, not all at once. For example, they usually grasp conservation of number first, followed by length, liquid, and mass, and then weight. This *continuum of acquisition* (or gradual mastery) of logical concepts is another indication of the limitations of concrete operational thinking (Fischer & Bidell, 1991). Rather than coming up with general logical principles that they apply to all relevant situations, children seem to work out the logic of each problem separately.

Follow-Up Research on Concrete Operational Thought

According to Piaget, brain development combined with experience in a rich and varied external world should lead children everywhere to reach the concrete operational stage. Yet recent evidence indicates that specific cultural and school practices have much to do with mastery of Piagetian tasks (Rogoff, 2003). And information-processing research helps explain the gradual mastery of logical concepts in middle childhood.

THE IMPACT OF CULTURE AND SCHOOLING   In tribal and village societies, conservation is often delayed. For example, among the Hausa of Nigeria, who live in small agricultural settlements and rarely send their children to school, even basic conservation tasks—number, length, and liquid—are not understood until age 11 or later (Fahrmeier, 1978). This suggests that taking part in relevant everyday activities helps children master conservation and other Piagetian problems. Joey and Lizzie, for example, think of fairness in terms of equal distribution—a value emphasized in their culture. They frequently divide materials, such as Halloween treats or lemonade, equally among their friends. Because they often see the same quantity arranged in different ways, they grasp conservation early.

The very experience of going to school seems to promote mastery of Piagetian tasks. When children of the same age are tested, those who have been in school longer do better on transitive inference problems (Artman & Cahan, 1993). Opportunities to seriate objects, to learn about order relations, and to remember the parts of complex problems are probably responsible. Yet certain informal, nonschool experiences can also foster operational thought. Brazilian 6- to 9-year-old street vendors, who seldom attend school, do poorly on Piagetian class inclusion tasks. But they perform much better than economically advantaged school-children on versions relevant to street vending—for example, "If you have 4 units of mint chewing gum and 2 units of grape chewing gum, is it better to sell me the mint gum or [all] the gum?" (Ceci & Roazzi, 1994). Similarly, around age 7 to 8, Zinacanteco Indian girls of southern Mexico, who learn to weave elaborately designed fabrics as an alternative to schooling, engage in mental transformations to figure out how a warp strung on will turn out as woven cloth—reasoning expected at the concrete operational stage. North American children of the same age, who do much better than Zinacanteco children on Piagetian tasks, have great difficulty with these weaving problems (Maynard & Greenfield, 2003).

On the basis of such findings, some investigators have concluded that the forms of logic required by Piagetian tasks do not emerge spontaneously in children but, rather, are heavily

■ This Brazilian street vendor might not perform well on Piagetian class inclusion tasks, but he is likely to understand versions relevant to street vending—for example, that "all the chewing gum" represents a larger quantity than the amount of any one flavor. ■

influenced by training, context, and cultural conditions. Does this view remind you of Vygotsky's sociocultural theory, which we discussed in earlier chapters?

AN INFORMATION-PROCESSING VIEW OF CONCRETE OPERATIONAL THOUGHT As we saw in Chapter 9, preschoolers show the beginnings of logical thinking on simplified and familiar tasks. The gradual mastery of logical concepts in middle childhood raises a familiar question about Piaget's theory: Is an abrupt stagewise transition to logical thought the best way to describe cognitive development in middle childhood?

Some *neo-Piagetian theorists* argue that the development of operational thinking can best be understood in terms of gains in information-processing speed rather than a sudden shift to a new stage (Halford & Andrews, 2006). For example, Robbie Case (1996, 1998) proposed that, with practice, cognitive schemes demand less attention and become more automatic. This frees up space in *working memory* (see Chapter 6, page 217) so children can focus on combining old schemes and generating new ones. For instance, the child who sees water poured from one container to another recognizes that the height of the liquid changes. As this understanding becomes routine, the child notices that the width of the water changes as well. Soon children coordinate these observations, and they grasp conservation of liquid. Then, as this logical idea becomes well-practiced, the child transfers it to more demanding situations, such as weight.

Once the schemes of a Piagetian stage are sufficiently automatic, enough working memory is available to integrate them into an improved representation. As a result, children acquire *central conceptual structures*—networks of concepts and relations that permit them to think more effectively in a wide range of situations (Case, 1996, 1998). The central conceptual structures that emerge from integrating concrete operational schemes are broadly applicable principles that result in increasingly complex, systematic reasoning, signifying the transition to formal operational thought.

■ As this 6-year-old practices counting money, she will become a more efficient and effective information processor. Eventually she will coordinate an increasing number of task dimensions into a central conceptual structure—a general representation that she can apply in many situations. ■

Case and his colleagues—along with other information processing researchers—have examined children's performance on a wide variety of tasks, including solving arithmetic word problems, understanding stories, drawing pictures, sight-reading music, handling money, and interpreting social situations. In each task, preschoolers typically focus on only one dimension. In understanding stories, for example, they grasp only a single story line. In drawing pictures, they depict objects separately. By the early school years, children coordinate two dimensions—two story lines in a single plot and drawings that show both the features of objects and their relationships. Around 9 to 11 years, children integrate multiple dimensions (Case, 1998; Halford & Andrews, 2006). They tell coherent stories with a main plot and several subplots. And their drawings follow a set of rules for representing perspective and, therefore, include several points of reference, such as near, midway, and far.

Case's theory helps explain why many understandings appear in specific situations at different times rather than being mastered all at once. First, different forms of the same logical insight, such as the various conservation tasks, vary in their processing demands, with those acquired later requiring more space in working memory. Second, children's experiences vary widely. A child who often listens to and tells stories but rarely draws pictures displays more advanced central conceptual structures in storytelling. Compared with Piaget's, Case's theory better accounts for unevenness in cognitive development. When tasks make similar processing demands, such as Piaget's class inclusion and transitive inference problems (each of which requires children to consider three relations at once), children with relevant experiences master those tasks at about the same time (Halford, Wilson, & Phillips, 1998).

As noted in Chapter 9, young children can be trained to solve many Piagetian problems. Many such tasks can be solved either empirically or logically. In the class inclusion problem shown on page 322 in Chapter 9, children can count the yellow flowers and all the flowers (yellow plus blue) to see that there are more *flowers* than *yellow flowers*—an empirical approach. Or they can take a logical approach, reasoning, "There are more flowers than yellow flowers because yellow flowers are just a type of flower." Younger children, in contrast to older children and adults, often rely on cumbersome empirical strategies, perhaps because they do not realize that certain problems can be solved logically. When 5-year-olds were given logical explanations after failing at class-inclusion tasks, they improved rapidly in performance (Siegler & Svetina, 2006). Relying on logical strategies enhances both accuracy and speed of thinking.

Evaluation of the Concrete Operational Stage

Piaget was correct that school-age children approach many problems in more organized, rational ways than preschoolers. But disagreement continues over whether this difference occurs because of *continuous* improvement in logical skills or *discontinuous* restructuring of children's thinking (as Piaget's stage idea assumes). Many researchers think that both types of change may be involved (Carey, 1999; Case, 1998; Demetriou et al., 2002; Fischer & Bidell, 2006; Halford & Andrews, 2006).

During the school years, children apply logical schemes to many more tasks. In the process, their thought seems to change qualitatively—toward a more comprehensive grasp of the underlying principles of logical thought. Piaget himself seems to have recognized this possibility in evidence for gradual mastery of conservation and other tasks. So perhaps some blend of Piagetian and information-processing ideas holds the greatest promise for explaining cognitive development in middle childhood.

ASK YOURSELF

◆ **REVIEW** Children's performance on conservation tasks illustrates a continuum of acquisition of logical concepts. Review the preceding sections, and list additional examples of gradual development of operational reasoning.

◆ **APPLY** Nine-year-old Adrienne spends many hours helping her father build furniture in his woodworking shop. How might this experience facilitate Adrienne's advanced performance on Piagetian seriation problems?

◆ **CONNECT** Explain how advances in perspective taking contribute to school-age children's improved ability to draw and use maps.

◆ **REFLECT** Which aspects of Piaget's description of the concrete operational child do you accept? Which do you doubt? Explain, citing research evidence.

Information Processing

In contrast to Piaget's focus on overall cognitive change, the information-processing perspective examines separate aspects of thinking. Attention and memory, which underlie every act of cognition, are central concerns in middle childhood, just as they were during infancy and the preschool years. Advances in metacognition and opportunities for self-regulation aid development. Also, increased understanding of how school-age children process information is being applied to their academic learning—in particular, to reading and mathematics.

Researchers believe that brain development contributes to the following basic changes in information processing that facilitate the diverse aspects of thinking we are about to consider:

■ *Increases in information-processing speed and capacity.* Time needed to process information on a wide variety of cognitive tasks declines rapidly between ages 6 and 12 (Kail & Park, 1992, 1994). This suggests a biologically based, age-related gain in speed of thinking, possibly due to myelination and synaptic pruning in the brain. Some researchers believe this greater efficiency contributes to more complex, effective thinking because a faster thinker can hold on to and operate on more information in working memory (Halford & Andrews, 2006; Luna et al., 2004; Nettelbeck & Burns, 2010). Indeed, *digit span,* which assesses the basic capacity of working memory, increases from about five digits at age 7 to seven digits at age 12 (Kail, 2003).

■ *Gains in inhibition.* As indicated in earlier chapters, inhibition— the ability to control internal and external distracting stimuli— improves from infancy on. But additional strides occur in middle childhood as the prefrontal cortex develops further (Luna et al., 2004; Nelson, Thomas, & de Haan, 2006). EEG brain-wave and fMRI measures reveal a steady, age-related increase in activation of diverse cortical regions, especially the prefrontal cortex, in children and adolescents working on tasks that require suppression of inappropriate responses (Bartgis, Lilly, & Thomas, 2003; Luna et al., 2001). Individuals skilled at inhibition can prevent their minds from straying to irrelevant thoughts, an ability that supports many information-processing skills by preserving space in working memory for the task at hand (Dempster & Corkill, 1999; Klenberg, Korkman, & Lahti-Nuuttila, 2001).

■ Gains in processing speed and capacity and in inhibition contribute to the cognitive changes of middle childhood—for example, ability to carry out this complex classroom project, in which third graders study erosion by sprinkling water onto soil and observing the effects of the runoff. ■

Besides brain development, strategy use contributes to more effective information processing. As we have already seen, school-age children think far more strategically than preschoolers. At the same time, neurological change supports gains in strategy use.

Attention

During middle childhood, gains in sustained attention continue. In addition, attention becomes more selective, adaptable, and planful.

SELECTIVITY AND ADAPTABILITY   As Joey and Lizzie moved through elementary school, they became better at deliberately attending to just those aspects of a situation that were relevant to their task goals. Researchers study this increasing selectivity of attention by introducing irrelevant stimuli into a task and seeing how well children attend to its central elements. For example, they might present a stream of numbers on a computer screen and ask children to press a button whenever a particular two-digit sequence (such as "1" followed by "9") appears. Findings show that selective attention improves sharply between ages 6 and 10, with gains continuing through adolescence (Gomez-Perez & Ostrosky-Solis, 2006; Vakil et al., 2009; Tabibi & Pfeffer, 2007).

Older children also flexibly adapt their attention to situational requirements. For example, when asked to sort cards with pictures that vary in both color and shape, children age 5 and older readily switch their basis of sorting from color to shape when asked to do so; younger children have difficulty (Brooks et al., 2003; Zelazo, Frye, & Rapus, 1996). And when studying for a spelling test, 10-year-old Joey was much more likely than Lizzie to devote most attention to the words he knew least well (Masur, McIntyre, & Flavell, 1973).

How do children acquire selective, adaptable attentional strategies? Children's performance on many tasks reveals a predictable, four-step sequence:

1. **Production deficiency.** Preschoolers rarely engage in attentional strategies. In other words, they fail to *produce* strategies when they could be helpful.
2. **Control deficiency.** Young elementary school children sometimes produce strategies, but not consistently. They fail to *control*, or execute, strategies effectively.
3. **Utilization deficiency.** Slightly later, children execute strategies consistently, but their performance either does not improve or improves less than that of older children.
4. **Effective strategy use.** By the mid-elementary school years, children use strategies consistently, and performance improves (Miller, 2000).

As we will soon see, these phases also characterize children's use of memory strategies. Why, when children first use a strategy, does it not work well? A likely reason is that applying a

BIOLOGY AND ENVIRONMENT

Children with Attention-Deficit Hyperactivity Disorder

While the other fifth graders worked quietly at their desks, Calvin squirmed, dropped his pencil, looked out the window, fiddled with his shoelaces, and talked aloud. "Hey Joey," he yelled across the room, "wanna play ball after school?" But the other children weren't eager to play with Calvin, who was physically awkward and failed to follow the rules of the game. He had trouble taking turns at bat. In the outfield, he tossed his mitt up in the air and looked elsewhere when the ball came his way. Calvin's desk was a chaotic mess. He often lost pencils, books, and other school materials, and he had difficulty remembering assignments and due dates.

Symptoms of ADHD

Calvin is one of about 5 percent of U.S. school-age children with **attention-deficit hyperactivity disorder (ADHD),** which involves inattention, impulsivity, and excessive motor activity resulting in academic and social problems (American Psychiatric Association, 2000; Barkley, 2006). Boys are diagnosed about four times as often as girls. However, many girls with ADHD seem to be overlooked, either because their symptoms are less flagrant or because of a gender bias: A difficult, disruptive boy is more likely to be referred for treatment (Abikoff et al., 2002; Biederman et al., 2005).

Children with ADHD cannot stay focused on a task that requires mental effort for more than a few minutes. They often act impulsively, ignoring social rules and lashing out with hostility when frustrated. Many, though not all, are *hyperactive,* exhausting parents and teachers and irritating other children with their excessive motor activity. For a child to be diagnosed with ADHD, these symptoms must have appeared before age 7 as a persistent problem.

Because of their difficulty concentrating, ADHD children score 7 to 15 points lower than other children on intelligence tests (Barkley, 2002b). Researchers agree that deficient executive processing (see page 218 in Chapter 6) underlies ADHD symptoms. According to one view, children with ADHD are impaired in capacity to inhibit action in favor of thought—a basic difficulty that results in wide-ranging inadequacies in strategic thinking and, therefore, in poor self-regulation (Barkley, 2001). Another hypothesis is that ADHD results from a cluster of executive processing problems that interfere with ability to guide one's own behavior (Brown, 2005, 2006). Research confirms that children with ADHD do poorly on tasks requiring sustained attention; find it hard to ignore irrelevant information; have difficulty with memory, planning, reasoning, and problem solving in academic and social situations; and often fail to manage frustration and intense emotion (Barkley, 2003, 2006).

Origins of ADHD

ADHD runs in families and is highly heritable. Identical twins share it more often than fraternal twins (Freitag et al., 2010; Rasmussen et al., 2004). Children with ADHD show abnormal brain functioning, including reduced electrical and blood-flow activity in the prefrontal cortex and in other areas involved in attention, inhibition of behavior, and other aspects of motor control (Mackie et al., 2007; Sowell et al., 2003). Also, the brains of children with ADHD grow more slowly and are about 3 percent smaller in overall volume, with a thinner cerebral cortex, than the brains of unaffected agemates (Narr et al., 2009; Shaw et al., 2007). Several genes that affect neural communication have been implicated in the disorder (Faraone & Mick, 2010).

At the same time, ADHD is associated with environmental factors. Prenatal teratogens—such as tobacco, alcohol, illegal drugs, and environmental pollutants—are linked to inattention and hyperactivity (see Chapter 3). And they can combine with certain genotypes to greatly increase risk of the disorder (see page 87 in Chapter 2). Furthermore, children with ADHD are more likely to come from homes in which

---

new strategy requires so much effort and attention that little remains to perform other parts of the task well (Woody-Dorning & Miller, 2001). Another reason a new strategy may not lead to performance gains is that younger children are not good at monitoring their task performance (Schneider & Bjorklund, 2003). Because they fail to keep track of how well a strategy is working, they do not apply it consistently or refine it in other ways.

PLANNING   School-age children's attentional strategies also become increasingly planful. They scan detailed pictures and written materials for similarities and differences more thoroughly than preschoolers (Vurpillot, 1968). And on tasks with many parts, they make decisions about what to do first and what to do next in an orderly fashion. In one study, 5- to 9-year-olds were given lists of items to obtain from a play grocery store. Older children more often took time to scan the store before shopping. They also paused more often to look for each item before moving to get it. Consequently, they followed shorter routes through the aisles (Gauvain & Rogoff, 1989a; Szepkouski, Gauvain, & Carberry, 1994).

The development of planning illustrates how attention becomes coordinated with other cognitive processes. To solve problems involving multiple steps, children must postpone action in favor of weighing alternatives, organizing task materials (such as items on a grocery list), and remembering the steps of their plan so they can attend to each one in sequence. Along the way,

marriages are unhappy and family stress is high (Bernier & Siegel, 1994). But a stressful home life rarely causes ADHD. Rather, these children's behaviors can contribute to family problems, which intensify the child's preexisting difficulties.

Treating ADHD

Calvin's doctor eventually prescribed stimulant medication, the most common treatment for ADHD. As long as dosage is carefully regulated, these drugs reduce symptoms in 70 percent of children who take them (Greenhill, Halperin, & Abikoff, 1999). Stimulant medication seems to increase activity in the prefrontal cortex, thereby improving the child's capacity to sustain attention and to inhibit off-task behavior.

In 2006, an advisory panel convened by the U.S. Food and Drug Administration warned that stimulants might impair heart functioning, even causing sudden death in a few individuals, and advocated warning labels describing these potential risks. Debate over the safety of medication for ADHD is likely to intensify. In any case, medication is not enough. Drugs cannot teach children to compensate for inattention and impulsivity. The most effective treatment approach combines medication with interventions that model and reinforce appropriate academic and social behavior (American Academy of Pediatrics, 2005b; Smith, Barkley, & Shapiro, 2006).

Family intervention is also important. Inattentive, overactive children strain the patience of parents, who are likely to react punitively and inconsistently—a child-rearing style that strengthens defiant, aggressive behavior. In fact, in 45 to 65 percent of cases, these two sets of behavior problems occur together (Barkley, 2002a).

Some media reports suggest that the number of U.S. children diagnosed with ADHD has increased greatly. But large surveys yielded similar overall prevalence rates 25 years ago and today. Nevertheless, the incidence of ADHD is much higher in some communities than others. At times, children are overdiagnosed and unnecessarily medicated because their parents and teachers are impatient with inattentive, active behavior that is within normal range (Mayes, Bagwell, & Erkulwater, 2008). In Hong Kong, where academic success is particularly prized, children are diagnosed at more than twice the rate in the United States. But in Great Britain, where doctors are hesitant to label a child with ADHD or to prescribe medication, children are underdiagnosed and often do not receive the treatment they need (Taylor, 2004).

ADHD is usually a lifelong disorder. Affected individuals are at risk for persistent antisocial behavior, depression, alcohol and drug abuse, and other problems (Kessler et al., 2005, 2006). Adults with ADHD continue to need help in

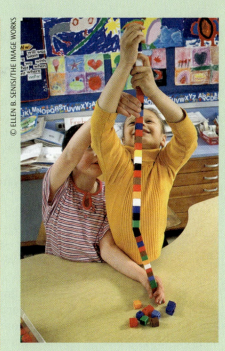

© ELLEN B. SENISI/THE IMAGE WORKS

■ For this 7-year-old with ADHD, a classroom offering many opportunities for active learning and peer collaboration may help her sustain attention and improve in social skills. ■

structuring their environments, regulating negative emotion, selecting appropriate careers, and understanding their condition as a biological deficit rather than a character flaw.

---

they must monitor how well the plan works and revise it if necessary. Clearly, planning places heavy demands on working-memory capacity.

As Chapter 9 revealed, children learn much about planning by collaborating with more expert planners. With age, children take on more responsibility in these joint endeavors, such as organizing task materials and suggesting planning strategies. The demands of school tasks—and teachers' explanations of how to plan—also contribute to gains in planning.

But adult-controlled activities may rob children of opportunities to plan. In one study, researchers videotaped small groups of first and second graders devising plays that they would perform for their class (Baker-Sennett, Matusov, & Rogoff, 2008). Some groups were child-led; others were led by adult volunteers. Child-led groups engaged in extensive planning—brainstorming themes and working out the details of their improvisations. But when adults planned the play in advance, the children spent most of their time in nonplanning pursuits, such as rehearsing lines and making play props. The adults missed a rich opportunity to scaffold learning (see page 331 in Chapter 9) by turning over responsibility for play planning to the children and guiding and supporting, as needed.

The attentional strategies just considered are crucial for success in school. Unfortunately, some children have great difficulty paying attention. See the Biology and Environment box above for a discussion of the serious learning and behavior problems of children with attention-deficit hyperactivity disorder.

Memory Strategies

As attention improves, so do *memory strategies,* the deliberate mental activities we use to store and retain information. During the school years, these techniques for holding information in working memory and transferring it to our long-term knowledge base take a giant leap forward.

REHEARSAL AND ORGANIZATION   When Lizzie had a list of things to learn, such as a phone number, the capitals of the United States, or the names of geometric shapes, she immediately used **rehearsal**—repeating the information to herself. This memory strategy first appears in the early grade school years. Soon after, a second strategy becomes common: **organization**—grouping related items together (for example, all state capitals in the same part of the country), an approach that improves recall dramatically (Schneider, 2002).

Perfecting memory strategies requires time and effort. For example, 8-year-old Lizzie rehearsed in a piecemeal fashion. After being given the word *cat* in a list of items, she said, "Cat, cat, cat." But 10-year-old Joey combined previous words with each new item, saying, "Desk, man, yard, cat, cat"—an approach that greatly increases retention (Kunzinger, 1985). In longitudinal research, younger children organized inconsistently (a *control deficiency*) and, when they did organize, showed little or no memory benefit (a *utilization deficiency*). In contrast, between ages 8 and 10, after realizing how effective organization is, many children suddenly began using it consistently, and their recall improved immediately (Schlagmüller & Schneider, 2002; Weinert & Schneider, 1999). With experience, children organize more skillfully, grouping items into fewer categories. And they apply the strategy to a wider range of memory tasks, including ones with less clearly related materials (Bjorklund et al., 1994).

Furthermore, as children gain in processing capacity and familiarity with strategies, they are more likely to use several memory strategies at once—rehearsing, organizing, and stating category names. And the more strategies they apply simultaneously, the better they remember (Coyle & Bjorklund, 1997; DeMarie et al., 2004). Although younger children's use of multiple strategies has little impact on performance (a *utilization deficiency*), their tendency to experiment is adaptive. By generating a variety of strategies, they discover which ones work best and how to combine them effectively. For example, second to fourth graders know that organizing the items first, next rehearsing category names, and finally rehearsing individual items is a good way to study lists (Hock, Park, & Bjorklund, 1998). Recall from *overlapping-waves theory,* discussed in Chapter 9, that children experiment with strategies when faced with many cognitive challenges—an approach that enables them to gradually "home in" on the most effective techniques (Siegler, 1996, 2007).

ELABORATION   By the end of middle childhood, children start to use **elaboration**—creating a relationship, or shared meaning, between two or more pieces of information that are not members of the same category. For example, if two of the words you must learn are *fish* and *pipe,* you might generate the verbal statement or mental image, "The fish is smoking a pipe." This highly effective memory technique, which requires considerable effort and space in working memory, becomes increasingly common in adolescence and early adulthood (Schneider & Pressley, 1997).

Because organization and elaboration combine items into *meaningful chunks,* they permit children to hold onto much more information and, as a result, further expand working memory. In addition, when children link a new item to information they already know, they can *retrieve* it easily by thinking of other items associated with it. As we will see, this also contributes to improved memory during the school years.

The Knowledge Base and Memory Performance

During middle childhood, the long-term knowledge base grows larger and becomes organized into increasingly elaborate, hierarchically structured networks. This rapid growth of knowledge helps children use strategies and remember (Schneider, 2002). In other words, knowing more about a topic makes new information more meaningful and familiar, so it is easier to store and retrieve.

To test this idea, researchers classified fourth graders as either experts or novices in knowledge of soccer and then gave both groups lists of soccer and nonsoccer items to learn. Experts remembered far more items on the soccer list (but not on the nonsoccer list) than novices. And during recall, the experts' listing of items was better organized, as indicated by clustering of items into categories (Schneider & Bjorklund, 1992). This superior organization at retrieval suggests that highly knowledgeable children organize information in their area of expertise with little or no effort—by rapidly associating new items with the large number they already know. Consequently, experts can devote more working-memory resources to using recalled information to reason and solve problems (Bjorklund & Douglas, 1997).

But knowledge is not the only important factor in children's strategic memory processing. Children who are expert in an area are usually highly motivated. As a result, they not only acquire knowledge more quickly but also *actively use what they know* to add more. In contrast, academically unsuccessful children often fail to ask how previously stored information can clarify new material. This, in turn, interferes with the development of a broad knowledge base (Schneider & Bjorklund, 1998). By the end of the school years, then, extensive knowledge and use of memory strategies support one another.

Culture, Schooling, and Memory Strategies

Rehearsal, organization, and elaboration are techniques that people usually use when they need to remember information for its own sake. On many other occasions, memory occurs as a natural byproduct of participation in daily activities (Rogoff, 2003). For example, Joey can spout a wealth of facts about baseball teams and players—information he picked up from watching ball games, discussing the game, and trading baseball cards with his friends. And without prior rehearsal, he can recount the story line of an exciting movie or novel—narrative material that is already meaningfully organized.

A repeated finding is that people in non-Western cultures who have no formal schooling do not use or benefit from instruction in memory strategies because they see no practical reason to use these techniques (Rogoff & Chavajay, 1995). Tasks that require children to recall isolated bits of information, which are common in classrooms, strongly motivate use of memory strategies. In fact, Western children get so much practice with this type of learning that they do not refine techniques that rely on cues available in everyday life, such as spatial location and arrangement of objects. For example, Guatemalan Mayan 9-year-olds do slightly better than their U.S. agemates when told to remember the placement of 40 familiar objects in a play scene. U.S. children often rehearse object names when it would be more effective to keep track of spatial relations (Rogoff & Wadell, 1982). The development of memory strategies, then, is not just a product of a more competent information-processing system. It also depends on task demands and cultural circumstances.

■ A mother and daughter of the Colombian U'wa people, who have no written tradition, make "cocara" leaf hats, which girls wear from puberty until marriage. Although the child demonstrates keen memory for how to select, cut, and assemble the leaves, she might have difficulty recalling the isolated bits of information that school tasks often require. ■

The School-Age Child's Theory of Mind

During middle childhood, children's *theory of mind*, or set of beliefs about mental activities, becomes much more elaborate and refined. Recall from Chapter 9 that this awareness of thought is often called *metacognition*. School-age children's improved ability to reflect on their own mental life is another reason that their thinking and problem solving advance.

KNOWLEDGE OF COGNITIVE CAPACITIES Unlike preschoolers, who view the mind as a passive container of information, older children regard it as an active, constructive agent that selects and transforms information (Kuhn, 2000). Consequently, they have a much better understanding of cognitive processes and the impact of psychological factors on performance.

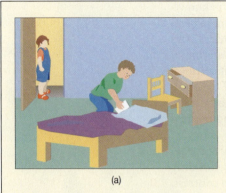 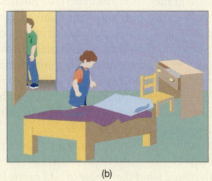 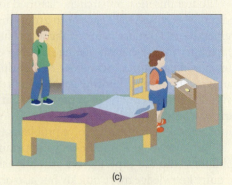

(a)

Jason has a letter from a friend. Lisa wants to read the letter, but Jason doesn't want her to. Jason puts the letter under his pillow.

(b)

Jason leaves the room to help his mother.

(c)

While Jason is gone, Lisa takes the letter and reads it. Jason returns and watches Lisa, but Lisa doesn't see Jason. Then Lisa puts the letter in Jason's desk.

FIGURE 12.2

A second-order false belief task. After relating the story in the sequence of pictures, the researcher asks a second-order false-belief question: "Where does Lisa think Jason will look for the letter? Why?" Around age 7, children answer correctly—that Lisa thinks Jason will look under his pillow because Lisa doesn't know that Jason saw her put the letter in the desk. *(Adapted from Astington, Pelletier, & Homer, 2002.)*

School-age children, for example, know that doing well on a task depends on focusing attention—concentrating and exerting effort (Miller & Bigi, 1979). With age, they also become increasingly aware of effective memory strategies and why they work (Alexander et al., 2003). And they gradually grasp relationships between mental activities—for example, that remembering is crucial for understanding and that understanding strengthens memory (Schwanenflugel, Henderson, & Fabricius, 1998).

Furthermore, school-age children's understanding of sources of knowledge expands. They realize that when two people view the same object, their trains of thought will differ because of variations in their knowledge, experiences, and other characteristics (Eisbach, 2004). And they are aware that people can extend their knowledge not only by directly observing events and talking to others but also by making *mental inferences* (Miller, Hardin, & Montgomery, 2003).

This grasp of inference enables knowledge of false belief to expand. In several studies, researchers told children complex stories involving one character's belief about a second character's belief. Then the children answered questions about what the first character thought the second character would do (see Figure 12.2). By age 6 to 7, children were aware that people form beliefs about other people's beliefs and that these *second-order beliefs* can be wrong! Appreciation of *second-order false belief* enables children to pinpoint the reasons that another person arrived at a certain belief (Astington, Pelletier, & Homer, 2002; Miller, 2009; Naito & Seki, 2009). This assists them greatly in understanding others' perspectives.

fMRI research reveals that from age 6 to 11, children become increasingly selective in the brain regions they recruit when thinking about a character's thoughts. In addition to the prefrontal cortex, they activate an area connecting the right temporal and parietal lobes (known to play a crucial role in theory-of-mind processes), just as adults do (Saxe et al., 2009).

Besides more complex thinking and language, experiences that foster awareness of mental activities contribute to school-age children's more reflective, process-oriented view of the mind. In a study of rural children of Cameroon, Africa, those who attended school performed much better on theory-of-mind tasks (Vinden, 2002). In school, teachers often call attention to the workings of the mind when they remind children to pay attention, remember mental steps, share points of view with peers, and evaluate their own and others' reasoning.

LOOK AND LISTEN

Watch a teacher—in a public school, religious school, recreation center, or other setting—explain a learning activity to 6- to 8-year-olds. How often did the teacher call attention to the workings of the mind?

KNOWLEDGE OF STRATEGIES Consistent with their more active view of the mind, school-age children are far more conscious of mental strategies than preschoolers. When shown video clips depicting two children using different recall strategies and asked which one is likely to produce better memory, kindergarten and young elementary school children knew that rehearsing or organizing is better than looking or naming. Older children were aware of more subtle differences—that organizing is better than rehearsing (Justice, 1986; Schneider, 1986).

Between third and fifth grade, children develop a much better appreciation of how and why strategies work (Alexander et al., 2003). Consequently, fifth graders are considerably better than younger children at discriminating good from bad reasoning. When given examples varying in quality, fifth graders consistently rated "good" reasoning as based on weighing of possibilities (rather than jumping to conclusions) and gathering of evidence (rather than ignoring important facts), even if such reasoning led to an unfavorable result (Amsterlaw, 2006).

Once children become conscious of the many factors that influence mental activity, they combine them into a more effective understanding. By the end of middle childhood, children take account of how *interactions* among multiple variables—age and motivation of the learner, effective use of strategies, and nature and difficulty of the task—affect cognitive performance (Wellman, 1990). In this way, metacognition broadens into a more complex theory.

Cognitive Self-Regulation

Although metacognition expands, school-age children often have difficulty putting what they know about thinking into action. They are not yet good at **cognitive self-regulation,** the process of continuously monitoring progress toward a goal, checking outcomes, and redirecting unsuccessful efforts. For example, Lizzie is aware that she should attend closely to her teacher's directions, group items when memorizing, reread a complicated paragraph to make sure she understands it, and relate new information to what she already knows. But she does not always engage in these activities.

To study cognitive self-regulation, researchers sometimes look at the impact of children's awareness of memory strategies on how well they remember. By second grade, the more children know about memory strategies, the more they recall—a relationship that strengthens over middle childhood (Pierce & Lange, 2000). And when children apply a strategy consistently, their knowledge of strategies strengthens, resulting in a bidirectional relationship between metacognition and strategic processing that enhances self-regulation (Schlagmüller & Schneider, 2002).

Why does cognitive self-regulation develop gradually? Monitoring learning outcomes is cognitively demanding, requiring constant evaluation of effort and progress. Throughout elementary and secondary school, self-regulation predicts academic success (Valiente et al., 2008; Zimmerman & Cleary, 2009). Students who do well in school know when their learning is going well and when it is not. If they encounter obstacles, they take steps to address them—for example, organize the learning environment, review confusing material, or seek support from more expert adults or peers (Zimmerman & Cleary, 2009). This active, purposeful approach contrasts sharply with the passive orientation of students who achieve poorly.

Parents and teachers can foster self-regulation. In one study, researchers observed parents instructing their children on a problem-solving task during the summer before third grade. Parents who patiently pointed out important features of the task and suggested strategies had children who, in the classroom, more often discussed ways to approach problems and monitored their own performance (Stright et al., 2002). Explaining the effectiveness of strategies is particularly helpful because it provides a rationale for future action.

Children who acquire effective self-regulatory skills develop a sense of *academic self-efficacy*—confidence in their own ability, which supports future self-regulation (Schunk & Pajares, 2005). Unfortunately, some children receive messages from parents and teachers that seriously undermine their academic self-esteem and self-regulatory skills. We will consider these *learned-helpless* youngsters, along with ways to help them, in Chapter 13.

■ This fifth grader's capacity for cognitive self-regulation is evident in the convenient way she organizes materials, making sure her textbook glossary and dictionary are handy. When she encounters an unfamiliar word while working on a language arts assignment, she swiftly looks up its definition. ■

Applications of Information Processing to Academic Learning

When Joey entered first grade, he recognized only a handful of written words. By fifth grade, he was a proficient reader. Similarly, at age 6, Joey had an informally acquired knowledge of number concepts. By age 10, he could add, subtract, multiply, and divide with ease and had begun to master fractions and percentages. Fundamental discoveries about the development of information processing have been applied to children's learning of reading and mathematics. Researchers are identifying the cognitive ingredients of skilled performance, tracing their development, and distinguishing good from poor learners by pinpointing differences in cognitive skills. They hope, as a result, to design teaching methods that will improve children's learning.

READING Reading makes use of many skills at once, taxing all aspects of our information-processing systems. We must perceive single letters and letter combinations, translate them into speech sounds, recognize the visual appearance of many common words, hold chunks of text in working memory while interpreting their meaning, and combine the meanings of various parts of a text passage into an understandable whole. And because reading is so demanding, most or all of these skills must be done automatically. If one or more are poorly developed, they will compete for resources in our limited working memories, and reading performance will decline.

As children make the transition from emergent literacy to conventional reading, *phonological awareness*—the ability to reflect on and manipulate the sound structure of spoken language—continues to facilitate their progress (see page 343 in Chapter 9). Other information-processing skills also contribute. Gains in processing speed foster children's rapid conversion of visual symbols into sounds (McBride-Chang & Kail, 2002). Visual scanning and discrimination play important roles and improve with reading experience (Rayner, Pollatsek, & Starr, 2003). Performing all these skills efficiently releases working memory for higher-level activities involved in comprehending the text's meaning.

Until recently, researchers were involved in an intense debate over how to teach beginning reading. Those who took a **whole-language approach** argued that from the beginning, children should be exposed to text in its complete form—stories, poems, letters, posters, and lists—so that they can appreciate the communicative function of written language. According to this view, as long as reading is kept meaningful, children will be motivated to discover the specific skills they need (Watson, 1989). Other experts advocated a **phonics approach,** believing that children should first be coached on *phonics*—the basic rules for translating written symbols into sounds. Only after mastering these skills should they get complex reading material (Rayner & Pollatsek, 1989).

Many studies show that children learn best with a mixture of both approaches. In kindergarten, first, and second grades, teaching that includes phonics boosts reading scores, especially for children who lag behind in reading progress (Stahl & Miller, 2006; Xue & Meisels, 2004). And when teachers combine real reading and writing with teaching of phonics and engage in other excellent teaching practices—encouraging children to tackle reading challenges and integrating reading into all school subjects—first graders show far greater literacy progress (Pressley et al., 2002).

Why might combining phonics with whole language work best? Learning the relationships between letters and sounds enables children to *decode,* or decipher, words they have never seen before. Children who enter school low in phonological awareness make far better reading

© ELLEN B. SENISI PHOTOGRAPHY

■ In this first-grade classroom, teaching of phonics is embedded in captivating stories and challenging writing tasks. Combining instruction in basic skills with whole-language teaching is more effective in promoting children's reading progress than either approach alone. ■

TABLE 12.1   Sequence of Reading Development

GRADE/AGE	DEVELOPMENT	METHOD OF LEARNING
Preschool and kindergarten 2–6 years	"Pretends" to read; recognizes some familiar signs ("ON," "OFF," "PIZZA"); "pretends" to write; prints own name and other words	Informal literacy experiences through literacy-rich physical environments, literacy-related play, and storybook reading (see Chapter 9, page 343)
Grades 1 and 2 6–7 years	Masters letter–sound correspondences; sounds out one-syllable words; reads simple stories; reads about 600 words	Direct teaching, through exposure to many types of texts and the basic rules of decoding written symbols into sounds
Grades 2 and 3 7–8 years	Reads simple stories more fluently; masters basic decoding rules; reads about 3,000 words	Same as above
Grades 4 to 9 9–14 years	Reads to learn new knowledge, usually without questioning the reading material	Reading and studying; participating in classroom discussion; completing written assignments
Grades 10 to 12 15–17 years	Reads more widely, tapping materials with diverse viewpoints	Reading more widely; writing papers
College 18 years and older	Reads with a self-defined purpose; decoding and comprehension skills reach a high level of efficiency	Reading even more widely; writing more sophisticated papers

Source: Chall, 1983.

progress when given training in phonics (Casalis & Cole, 2009). Soon they detect new letter–sound relations while reading on their own, and as their fluency in decoding words increases, they are freer to attend to text meaning. Without early phonics training, such children (many of whom come from poverty-stricken families) are substantially behind their age-mates in text comprehension skills by third grade (Foster & Miller, 2007).

Yet too much emphasis on basic skills may cause children to lose sight of the goal of reading: understanding. Children who read aloud fluently without registering meaning know little about effective reading strategies—for example, that they must read more carefully if they will be tested than if they are reading for pleasure, or that explaining a passage in their own words is a good way to assess comprehension. Providing instruction aimed at increasing knowledge and use of reading strategies enhances reading performance from third grade on (Paris & Paris, 2006; Van Keer, 2004).

Table 12.1 charts the general sequence of reading development. Notice the major shift, around age 7 to 8, from "learning to read" to "reading to learn" (Melzi & Ely, 2009). As decoding and comprehension skills reach a high level of efficiency, older readers become actively engaged with the text. They adjust the way they read to fit their current purpose—sometimes seeking new facts and ideas, sometimes questioning, agreeing with, or disagreeing with the writer's viewpoint.

MATHEMATICS   Mathematics teaching in elementary school builds on and greatly enriches children's informal knowledge of number concepts and counting. Written notation systems and formal computational techniques enhance children's ability to represent numbers and compute. Over the early elementary school years, children acquire basic math facts through a combination of frequent practice, experimentation with diverse computational procedures (through which they discover faster, more accurate techniques), reasoning about number concepts, and teaching that conveys effective strategies. (Return to Chapter 9, page 345, for research supporting the importance of both extended practice and a grasp of concepts.) Eventually children retrieve answers automatically and apply this basic knowledge to more complex problems.

Arguments about how to teach mathematics resemble those about reading, pitting drill in computing against "number sense," or understanding. Again, a blend of both approaches is most beneficial (Fuson, 2009). In learning basic math, poorly performing students use cumbersome techniques or try to retrieve answers from memory too soon. They have not sufficiently experimented with strategies to see which are most effective and to reorganize their observations in logical, efficient ways—for example, noticing that multiplication problems involving 2 (2 × 8) are equivalent to addition doubles (8 + 8). On tasks assessing their grasp of math concepts, their performance is weak (Canobi, 2004; Canobi, Reeve, & Pattison, 2003). This suggests that encouraging students to apply strategies and making sure they know why certain strategies work well are essential for solid mastery of basic math.

A similar picture emerges for more complex skills, such as carrying in addition, borrowing in subtraction, and operating with decimals and fractions. Children taught by rote cannot apply the procedure to new problems. Instead, they persistently make mistakes, following a "math rule" that they recall incorrectly because they do not understand it (Carpenter et al., 1999). Look at the following subtraction errors:

$$
\begin{array}{r} 427 \\ -138 \\ \hline 311 \end{array}
\qquad
\begin{array}{r} 7002 \\ -5445 \\ \hline 1447 \end{array}
$$

In the first problem, the child consistently subtracts a smaller from a larger digit, regardless of which is on top. In the second, the child skips columns with zeros in a borrowing operation and, whenever there is a zero on top, writes the bottom digit as the answer.

Children who are given rich opportunities to experiment with problem solving, to appreciate the reasons behind strategies, and to evaluate solution techniques seldom make such errors. In one study, second graders who were taught in these ways not only mastered correct procedures but even invented their own successful strategies, some of which were superior to standard, school-taught methods! Consider this solution:

$$
\begin{array}{cccc}
3 & 15 & 14 & 12 \\
\cancel{4} & \cancel{6} & \cancel{5} & \cancel{2} \\
-1 & 9 & 6 & 8 \\
\hline
2 & 6 & 8 & 4
\end{array}
$$

In subtracting, the child performed all trades first, flexibly moving either from right to left or from left to right, and then subtracted all four columns—a highly efficient, accurate approach (Fuson & Burghard, 2003).

In a German study, the more teachers emphasized conceptual knowledge, by having children actively construct meanings in word problems before practicing computation and memorizing math facts, the more children gained in math achievement from second to third grade (Staub & Stern, 2002). Children taught in this way draw on their solid knowledge of relationships between operations (for example, that the inverse of division is multiplication) to generate efficient, flexible procedures: To solve the division problem 360/9, they might multiply 9 × 40 = 360. And because such children have been encouraged to estimate answers, if they go down the wrong track in computation, they are usually self-correcting. Furthermore, they appreciate connections between math operations and problem contexts. They can solve a word problem ("Jesse spent $3.45 for bananas, $2.62 for bread, and $3.55 for peanut butter. Can he pay for it all with a $10 bill?") quickly through estimation instead of exact calculation (De Corte & Verschaffel, 2006).

In Asian countries, students receive a variety of supports for acquiring mathematical knowledge and often excel at math computation and reasoning. Use of the metric system helps Asian children grasp place value. The consistent structure of number words in Asian languages (*ten-two* for 12, *ten-three* for 13) also makes this idea clear (Miura & Okamoto, 2003). And because Asian number words are shorter and more quickly pronounced, more digits can be held in working memory at once, increasing speed of thinking. Furthermore, Chinese parents provide their children with extensive everyday practice in counting

■ Children develop math skills through a combination of frequent practice and reasoning about number concepts. The most effective teaching combines both approaches. ■

and computation—experiences that contribute to the superiority of Chinese over U.S. children's math knowledge, even before school entry (Siegler & Mu, 2008; Zhou et al., 2006). Finally, as we will see later in this chapter, compared with lessons in the United States, those in Asian classrooms devote more time to exploring math concepts and less to drill and repetition.

ASK YOURSELF

◆ **REVIEW** Cite evidence indicating that school-age children view the mind as an active, constructive agent.

◆ **APPLY** After viewing a slide show on endangered species, second and fifth graders in Lizzie and Joey's school were asked to remember as many animals as they could. Explain why fifth graders recalled much more than second graders.

◆ **APPLY** Lizzie knows that if you have difficulty learning part of a task, you should devote extra attention to that part. But she plays each of her piano pieces from beginning to end instead of practicing the hard parts. Explain why Lizzie does not engage in cognitive self-regulation.

◆ **REFLECT** In your elementary school math education, how much emphasis was placed on computational drill and how much on understanding concepts? How do you think that balance affected your interest and performance in math?

Individual Differences in Mental Development

Around age 6, IQ becomes more stable than it was at earlier ages, and it correlates moderately well with academic achievement, typically around .50 to .60. And children with higher IQs are more likely when they grow up to attain higher levels of education and enter more prestigious occupations (Brody, 1997; Deary et al., 2007). Because IQ predicts school performance and educational attainment, it often enters into educational decisions. Do intelligence tests accurately assess the school-age child's ability to profit from academic instruction? Let's look closely at this controversial issue.

Defining and Measuring Intelligence

Virtually all intelligence tests provide an overall score (the IQ), which represents *general intelligence* or reasoning ability, along with an array of separate scores measuring specific mental abilities. But intelligence is a collection of many capacities, not all of which are included on currently available tests (Carroll, 2005; Sternberg, 2005). Test designers use a complicated statistical technique called *factor analysis* to identify the various abilities that intelligence tests measure. It identifies which sets of test items cluster together, meaning that test-takers who do well on one item in the cluster tend to do well on the others. Distinct clusters are called *factors*, each of which represents an ability. See Figure 12.3 on page 454 for items typically included in intelligence tests for children.

The intelligence tests given from time to time in classrooms are *group-administered tests.* They permit large numbers of students to be tested at once and are useful for instructional planning and for identifying children who require more extensive evaluation with *individually administered tests.* Unlike group tests, which teachers can give with minimal training, individually administered tests demand considerable training and experience to give well. The examiner not only considers the child's answers but also observes the child's behavior, noting such reactions as attention to and interest in the tasks and wariness of the adult. These observations provide insight into whether the test score accurately reflects the child's abilities. Two individual tests—the Stanford-Binet and the Wechsler—are often used to identify highly intelligent children and to diagnose children with learning problems.

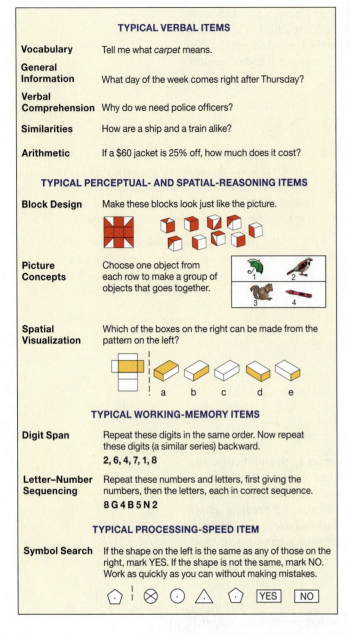

FIGURE 12.3

Test items like those on commonly used intelligence tests for children. The verbal items emphasize culturally loaded, fact-oriented information. The perceptual- and spatial-reasoning, working-memory, and processing-speed items emphasize aspects of information processing and are assumed to assess more biologically based skills.

The contemporary descendent of Alfred Binet's first successful intelligence test is the *Stanford-Binet Intelligence Scales,* Fifth Edition, for individuals from age 2 to adulthood. In addition to general intelligence, it assesses five intellectual factors: general knowledge, quantitative reasoning, visual–spatial processing, working memory, and basic information processing (such as speed of analyzing information). Each factor includes both a verbal mode and a nonverbal mode of testing, yielding 10 subtests in all (Roid, 2003). The nonverbal subtests, which do not require spoken language, are especially useful when assessing individuals with limited English, hearing impairments, or communication disorders. The knowledge and quantitative reasoning factors emphasize culturally loaded, fact-oriented information, such as vocabulary and arithmetic problems. In contrast, the visual–spatial processing, working-memory, and basic information-processing factors are assumed to be less culturally biased because they require little specific information (see the spatial visualization item in Figure 12.3).

The *Wechsler Intelligence Scale for Children–IV (WISC–IV)* is the fourth edition of a widely used test for 6- through 16-year-olds. A downward extension of it, the *Wechsler Preschool and Primary Scale of Intelligence–Revised (WPPSI–III),* is appropriate for children 2 years 6 months through 7 years 3 months (Wechsler, 2002, 2003). The Wechsler tests offered both a measure of general intelligence and a variety of factor scores long before the Stanford-Binet. As a result, many psychologists and educators came to prefer them. The WISC–IV has four broad intellectual factors: verbal reasoning, perceptual (or visual–spatial) reasoning, working memory, and processing speed. Each factor is made up of two or three subtests, yielding 10 separate scores in all. The WISC-IV was designed to downplay culture-dependent information, which is emphasized on only one factor (verbal reasoning). According to the test designers, the result is the most "culture-fair" intelligence test available (Williams, Weis, & Rolfhus, 2003). The WISC was also the first test to be standardized on children representing the total population of the United States, including ethnic minorities.

Recent Efforts to Define Intelligence

As we have seen, intelligence tests now tap important aspects of information processing. In line with this trend, some researchers are combining the mental-testing approach to defining intelligence with the information-processing approach. They believe that once we identify the processing skills that separate individuals who test well from those who test poorly, we will know more about how to intervene to improve performance. These investigators conduct *componential analyses* of children's test scores. This means that they look for relationships between aspects (or components) of information processing and children's intelligence test scores.

Processing speed, measured in terms of reaction time on diverse cognitive tasks, is moderately related to IQ (Deary, 2001; Li et al., 2004). Individuals whose nervous systems function more efficiently, permitting them to take in more information and manipulate it quickly, appear to have an edge in intellectual skills. In support of this interpretation, fast, strong ERPs (EEG brain waves in response to stimulation) predict both speedy cognitive processing and higher mental test scores (Rijsdijk & Boomsma, 1997; Schmid, Tirsch, & Scherb, 2002). And measures of working-memory capacity (such as digit span) correlate well with IQ (de Ribau-pierre & Lecerf, 2006).

But other factors, including flexible attention, memory, and reasoning strategies, are as important as efficient thinking in predicting IQ, and they explain some of the association between response speed and good test performance (Lohman, 2000; Miller & Vernon, 1992). Children who apply strategies effectively acquire more knowledge and can retrieve it rapidly—advantages that carry over to test performance. Similarly, recall from page 443 that available space in working memory depends in part on effective inhibition—keeping irrelevant information from intruding on the task at hand. Inhibition and sustained and selective attention are among a wide array of attentional skills that are good predictors of IQ (Schweizer, Moosbrugger, & Goldhammer, 2006).

The componential approach has one major shortcoming: It regards intelligence as entirely due to causes within the child. Throughout this book, we have seen how cultural and situational factors also affect children's thinking. Robert Sternberg has expanded the componential approach into a comprehensive theory that regards intelligence as a product of inner and outer forces.

STERNBERG'S TRIARCHIC THEORY   As Figure 12.4 shows, Sternberg's (2001, 2005, 2008) **triarchic theory of successful intelligence** is made up of three broad, interacting intelligences: (1) *analytical intelligence,* or information-processing skills; (2) *creative intelligence,* the capacity to solve novel problems; and (3) *practical intelligence,* application of intellectual skills in everyday situations. Intelligent behavior involves balancing all three intelligences to achieve success in life according to one's personal goals and the requirements of one's cultural community.

Analytical Intelligence.   *Analytical intelligence* consists of the information-processing components that underlie all intelligent acts: applying strategies, acquiring task-relevant and metacognitive knowledge, and engaging in self-regulation. But on mental tests, processing skills are used in only a few of their potential ways, resulting in far too narrow a view of intelligent behavior. As we have seen, children in tribal and village societies do not necessarily perform well on measures of "school" knowledge but thrive when processing information in out-of-school situations that most Westerners would find highly challenging.

Creative Intelligence.   In any context, success depends not only on processing familiar information but also on generating useful solutions to new problems. People who are *creative* think more skillfully than others when faced with novelty. Given a new task, they apply their information-processing skills in exceptionally effective ways, rapidly making these skills automatic so that working memory is freed for more complex aspects of the situation. Consequently, they quickly move to high-level performance. Although all of us are capable of some creativity, only a few individuals excel at generating novel solutions.

Practical Intelligence.   Finally, intelligence is a *practical,* goal-oriented activity aimed at *adapting to, shaping,* or *selecting environments.* Intelligent people skillfully *adapt* their thinking to fit with both their desires and the demands

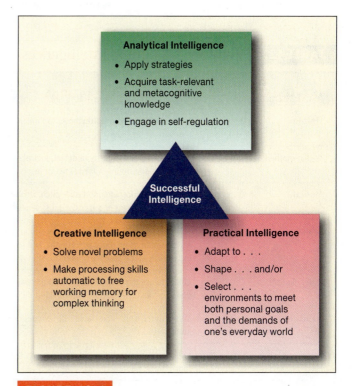

FIGURE 12.4

Sternberg's triarchic theory of successful intelligence. People who behave intelligently balance three interrelated intelligences—analytical, creative, and practical—to achieve success in life, defined by their personal goals and the requirements of their cultural communities.

of their everyday worlds. When they cannot adapt to a situation, they try to *shape*, or change, it to meet their needs. If they cannot shape it, they *select* new contexts that better match their skills, values, or goals. Practical intelligence reminds us that intelligent behavior is never culture-free. Children with certain life histories do well at the behaviors required for success on intelligence tests and adapt easily to the testing conditions and tasks. Others, with different backgrounds, may misinterpret or reject the testing context. Yet such children often display sophisticated abilities in daily life—for example, telling stories, engaging in complex artistic activities, or interacting skillfully with other people.

The triarchic theory emphasizes the complexity of intelligent behavior and the limitations of current intelligence tests in assessing that complexity. For example, out-of-school, practical forms of intelligence are vital for life success and help explain why cultures vary widely in the behaviors they regard as intelligent (Sternberg et al., 2000). When researchers asked ethnically diverse parents for their idea of an intelligent first grader, Caucasian Americans mentioned cognitive traits. In contrast, ethnic minorities (Cambodian, Filipino, Vietnamese, and Mexican immigrants) saw noncognitive capacities—motivation, self-management, and social skills—as particularly important (Okagaki & Sternberg, 1993). According to Sternberg, mental tests can easily underestimate, and even overlook, the intellectual strengths of some children, especially ethnic minorities.

GARDNER'S THEORY OF MULTIPLE INTELLIGENCES   In yet another view of how information-processing skills underlie intelligence behavior, Howard Gardner's (1983, 1993, 2000) **theory of multiple intelligences** defines intelligence in terms of distinct sets of processing operations that permit individuals to engage in a wide range of culturally valued activities. Dismissing the idea of general intelligence, Gardner proposes at least eight independent intelligences (see Table 12.2).

Gardner believes that each intelligence has a unique biological basis, a distinct course of development, and different expert, or "end-state," performances. At the same time, he emphasizes that a lengthy process of education is required to trans-

■ According to Gardner, children are capable of at least eight distinct intelligences. As this child learns pottery skills under the guidance of an expert potter, she enriches her spatial intelligence. ■

© MICHAEL NEWMAN/PHOTOEDIT

TABLE 12.2   Gardner's Multiple Intelligences

INTELLIGENCE	PROCESSING OPERATIONS	END-STATE PERFORMANCE POSSIBILITIES
Linguistic	Sensitivity to the sounds, rhythms, and meaning of words and the functions of language	Poet, journalist
Logico-mathematical	Sensitivity to, and capacity to detect, logical or numerical patterns; ability to handle long chains of logical reasoning	Mathematician
Musical	Ability to produce and appreciate pitch, rhythm (or melody), and aesthetic quality of the forms of musical expressiveness	Instrumentalist, composer
Spatial	Ability to perceive the visual-spatial world accurately, to perform transformations on those perceptions, and to re-create aspects of visual experience in the absence of relevant stimuli	Sculptor, navigator
Bodily-kinesthetic	Ability to use the body skillfully for expressive as well as goal-directed purposes; ability to handle objects skillfully	Dancer, athlete
Naturalist	Ability to recognize and classify all varieties of animals, minerals, and plants	Biologist
Interpersonal	Ability to detect and respond appropriately to the moods, temperaments, motivations, and intentions of others	Therapist, salesperson
Intrapersonal	Ability to discriminate complex inner feelings and to use them to guide one's own behavior; knowledge of one's own strengths, weaknesses, desires, and intelligences	Person with detailed, accurate self-knowledge

Sources: Gardner, 1983, 1993, 2000.

SOCIAL ISSUES: EDUCATION

Emotional Intelligence

During recess, Muriel handed birthday party invitations to every fifth-grade girl except Claire, who looked on sadly as her classmates chattered about the party. But one of Muriel's friends, Jessica, looked troubled. Pulling Muriel aside, she exclaimed, "Why'd you do that? You hurt Claire's feelings—you embarrassed her! If you bring invitations to school, you've got to give everybody one!" And after school, Jessica comforted Claire, saying, "If you aren't invited, I'm not going, either!"

Jessica's IQ is only slightly above average, but she excels at *emotional intelligence*—a term that has captured public attention because of popular books suggesting that it is an overlooked set of skills that can greatly improve life success (Goleman, 1995, 1998). According to one influential definition, **emotional intelligence** refers to a set of emotional abilities that enable individuals to process and adapt to emotional information (Salovey & Pizzaro, 2003). To measure it, researchers have devised items tapping emotional skills that enable people to manage their own emotions and interact competently with others. One test requires people to identify and rate the strength of emotions expressed in photographs of faces (emotional perception), to reason about emotions in social situations (emotional understanding), to identify which emotions promote certain thoughts and activities (emotional facilitation), and to evaluate the effectiveness of strategies for controlling negative emotions (emotion regulation). Factor analyses of the scores of hundreds of test-takers identified several emotional capacities as well as a higher-order general factor (Mayer, Salovey, & Caruso, 2003).

Emotional intelligence is modestly related to IQ. And in school-age children, adolescents, and adults, it is positively associated with self-esteem, empathy, prosocial behavior, cooperation, leadership skills, and life satisfaction and negatively related to drug and alcohol use, dependency, depression, and aggressive behavior (Brackett, Mayer, & Warner, 2004; Mavroveli et al., 2007; Petrides et al., 2006). In adulthood, emotional intelligence predicts many aspects of workplace success, including managerial effectiveness, productive co-worker relationships, and job performance (Mayer, Roberts, & Barsade, 2008; Mayer, Salovey, & Caruso, 2008).

Only a few assessments of emotional intelligence are available for children. These require careful training of teachers in observing and recording children's emotional skills during everyday activities, gathering information from parents, and taking ethnic backgrounds into account (Denham, 2005; Denham & Burton, 2003). As more and better measures are devised, they may help identify children with weak emotional and social competencies who would profit from intervention (Denham, 2006; Stewart-Brown & Edmonds, 2007).

The concept of emotional intelligence has increased teachers' awareness that providing experiences that meet students' emotional and social needs can improve their adjustment. Lessons that teach emotional understanding, respect and caring for others, strategies for regulating emotion, and resistance to unfavorable peer pressure—using active learning techniques that provide skill practice both in and out of the classroom—are becoming more common (Goetz et al., 2005).

© ELLEN B. SENISI PHOTOGRAPHY

■ The 7-year-old on the right displays high emotional intelligence as she accurately interprets her friend's sadness and offers comfort. ■

---

form any raw potential into a mature social role (Connell, Sheridan, & Gardner, 2003). Cultural values and learning opportunities affect the extent to which a child's intellectual strengths are realized and the way they are expressed.

Gardner's list of abilities has yet to be firmly grounded in research. Neurological evidence for the independence of his abilities is weak. Some exceptionally gifted individuals have abilities that are broad rather than limited to a particular domain (Piirto, 2007). And research with mental tests suggests that several of Gardner's intelligences (linguistic, logico-mathematical, and spatial) have at least some features in common. Nevertheless, Gardner calls attention to several intelligences not tapped by IQ scores. For example, his interpersonal and intrapersonal intelligences include a set of capacities for dealing with people and understanding oneself that has become known as *emotional intelligence*. As the Social Issues: Education box above indicates, researchers are attempting to define, measure, and foster the abilities that make up emotional intelligence, which is vital for a satisfying, successful life.

TAKE A MOMENT... Review the *core knowledge perspective*, discussed on page 214 in Chapter 6, and compare it with Gardner's view. Gardner also accepts the existence of innately specified, core domains of thought, present at birth or emerging early in life. Then, as children respond to the demands of their culture, they transform those intelligences to fit the activities they are called on to perform. Gardner's multiple intelligences have been helpful in efforts to understand and nurture children's special talents, a topic we will take up at the end of this chapter.

Explaining Individual and Group Differences in IQ

When we compare individuals in terms of academic achievement, years of education, and occupational status, it is clear that certain sectors of the population are advantaged over others. In trying to explain these differences, researchers have compared the IQ scores of ethnic and SES groups. American black children and adolescents score, on average, 10 to 12 IQ points below American white children. Although the difference has been shrinking over the past several decades, a substantial gap remains (Edwards & Oakland, 2006; Flynn, 2007; Nisbett, 2009). Hispanic children fall midway between black and white children (Ceci, Rosenblum, & Kumpf, 1998).

The IQ gap between middle-SES and low-SES children—about 9 points—accounts for some of the ethnic differences in IQ, but not all. When black children and white children are matched on parental education and income, the black–white IQ gap is reduced by a third to a half (Brooks-Gunn et al., 2003). Of course, considerable IQ variation exists *within* each ethnic and SES group. Still, these group differences are large enough and of serious enough consequence that they cannot be ignored.

In the 1970s, the IQ nature–nurture controversy escalated after psychologist Arthur Jensen (1969) published a controversial monograph entitled, "How Much Can We Boost IQ and Scholastic Achievement?" Jensen's answer was "not much." He claimed—and still maintains—that heredity is largely responsible for individual, ethnic, and SES variations in intelligence (Jensen, 1998, 2001; Rushton & Jensen, 2006, 2010). Jensen's work prompted an outpouring of research studies and responses, including ethical challenges reflecting deep concern that his conclusions would fuel social prejudices. Richard Herrnstein and Charles Murray rekindled the controversy with *The Bell Curve* (1994). Like Jensen, they argued that heredity contributes substantially to individual and SES differences in IQ, and they implied that heredity plays a sizable role in the black–white IQ gap. Let's look closely at some important evidence.

■ Among these second graders at an urban elementary school, differences in IQ scores may correlate with ethnicity and SES. Research aimed at explaining these associations has generated heated controversy. ■

NATURE VERSUS NURTURE   In Chapter 2 we introduced the *heritability estimate*. Recall that heritabilities are obtained from *kinship studies,* which compare family members. The most powerful evidence on the role of heredity in IQ involves twin comparisons. The IQ scores of identical twins (who share all their genes) are more similar than those of fraternal twins (who are genetically no more alike than ordinary siblings). On the basis of this and other kinship evidence, researchers estimate that about half the differences in IQ among children can be traced to their genetic makeup.

Recall, however, that heritabilities risk overestimating genetic influences and underestimating environmental influences. Although these measures offer convincing evidence that genes contribute to IQ, disagreement persists over how large a role heredity plays (Grigorenko, 2000; Plomin, 2003). As we saw in Chapter 2, the heritability of children's intelligence rises with parental education and income—conditions that enable children to realize their genetic potential. And heritability estimates do not reveal the complex processes through which genes and experiences influence intelligence as children develop.

Compared with heritabilities, adoption studies offer a wider range of information. Findings consistently reveal that when young children are adopted into caring, stimulating homes, their IQs rise substantially compared with the IQs of nonadopted children who remain in economically deprived families (van IJzendoorn, Juffer, & Poelhuis, 2005). But adopted children benefit to varying degrees. In one investigation, children of two extreme groups of biological mothers—those with IQs below 95 and those with IQs above 120—were adopted at birth by parents who were well above average in income and education. During the school years, the children of the low-IQ biological mothers scored above average in IQ, indicating that test performance can be greatly improved by an advantaged home life. But they did not do as well as children of high-IQ biological mothers placed in similar adoptive families (Loehlin, Horn, & Willerman, 1997). Adoption research confirms that heredity and environment contribute jointly to IQ.

Adoption research also sheds light on the black–white IQ gap. In two studies, African-American children adopted into economically well-off white homes during the first year of life scored high on intelligence tests, attaining mean IQs of 110 and 117 by middle childhood—20 to 30 points higher than the typical scores of children growing up in low-income black communities (Moore, 1986; Scarr & Weinberg, 1983). In one investigation, the IQs of black adoptees declined in adolescence, perhaps because of the challenges faced by minority teenagers in forming an ethnic identity that blends birth and adoptive backgrounds (DeBerry, Scarr, & Weinberg, 1996). When this process is filled with emotional turmoil, it can dampen motivation on tests and in school. Still, the black adoptees remained above the IQ average for low-SES African Americans. The IQ gains of black children "reared in the culture of the tests and schools" are consistent with a wealth of evidence that poverty severely depresses the intelligence of ethnic minority children (Nisbett, 2009).

Furthermore, a dramatic *secular trend* in mental test performance—a generational rise in average IQ in both industrialized nations and the developing world—supports the role of environmental factors, such as improved nutrition and education, technological advances, and an increase in cognitively demanding leisure activities (Flynn, 1999, 2003; Rodgers & Wänström, 2007). The greatest gains have occurred on tests of spatial reasoning—tasks often assumed to be "culture fair" and, therefore, more genetically based. These show, on average, an increase of 18 points per generation (30 years). The existence of a large, environmentally induced secular trend that exceeds the black–white IQ gap presents another major challenge to the assumption that black–white and other ethnic variations in IQ are mostly genetic (Flynn, 2007; Nisbett, 2009).

CULTURAL INFLUENCES   A controversial question raised about ethnic differences in IQ has to do with whether they result from *test bias.* If a test samples knowledge and skills that not all groups of children have had equal opportunity to learn, or if the testing situation impairs the performance of some groups but not others, the resulting score is a biased, or unfair, measure.

Some experts reject the idea that intelligence tests are biased, claiming that they are intended to represent success in the common culture. According to this view, because IQ predicts academic achievement equally well for majority and minority children, IQ tests are fair to both groups (Edwards & Oakland, 2006; Jensen, 2002). Others believe that lack of exposure to certain communication styles and knowledge, along with negative stereotypes about the test-taker's ethnic group, can undermine children's performance (Ceci & Williams, 1997; Sternberg, 2005). Let's look at the evidence.

Communication Styles. Ethnic minority families often foster unique language skills that do not match the expectations of most classrooms and testing situations. In one study, a researcher spent many hours observing in low-SES black homes in a southeastern U.S. city (Heath, 1990). She found that African-American parents rarely asked their children the types of knowledge-training questions typical of middle-SES white parents ("What color is it?" "What's this story about?"), which resemble the questioning style of tests and classrooms. Instead, the black parents asked only "real" questions, ones that they themselves could not answer. Often these were analogy questions ("What's that like?") or story-starter questions ("Didja hear Miss Sally this morning?") that called for elaborate responses about personal experiences and had no "right" answer.

These experiences led the black children to develop complex verbal skills at home, such as storytelling and exchanging quick-witted remarks. But their language emphasized emotional and social concerns rather than facts about the world. Not surprisingly, when the black children started school, many were unfamiliar with and confused by the "objective" questions they encountered on tests and in classrooms.

■ This Canadian Inuit grandmother and granddaughter communicate collaboratively, smoothly coordinating actions in cleaning freshly caught fish. Many children from ethnic minority families with little education are unfamiliar with the hierarchical communication style typical of classrooms—a reason they may do poorly on tests and assignments. ■

Furthermore, many ethnic minority parents without extensive schooling prefer a *collaborative style of communication* when completing tasks with children. They work together in a coordinated, fluid way, each focused on the same aspect of the problem. This pattern of adult–child engagement has been observed in Native-American, Canadian Inuit, Hispanic, and Guatemalan Mayan cultures (Chavajay & Rogoff, 2002; Crago, Annahatak, & Ningiuruvik, 1993; Delgado-Gaitan, 1994; Paradise & Rogoff, 2009). With increasing education, parents establish a *hierarchical style of communication,* like that of classrooms and tests. The parent directs each child to carry out an aspect of the task, and children work independently (Greenfield, Suzuki, & Rothstein-Fish, 2006). This sharp discontinuity between home and school communication practices may contribute to low-SES minority children's lower IQ and school performance.

Knowledge. Many researchers argue that IQ scores are affected by specific information acquired as part of majority-culture upbringing. Consistent with this view, low-SES African-American children often miss vocabulary words on mental tests that have alternative meanings in their cultural community—for example, interpreting the word *frame* to mean "physique" or *wrapping* as "rapping," referring to the style of music (Champion, 2003a).

Knowledge affects ability to reason effectively. When researchers assessed black and white community college students' familiarity with vocabulary taken from items on an intelligence test, the whites had considerably more knowledge (Fagan & Holland, 2007). But the black students were just as capable as the white students at learning new words, either from dictionary definitions or from their use in sentences. When verbal comprehension, similarities, and analogies test items depended on words and concepts that the white students knew better, the whites scored higher than the blacks. But when the same types of items involved words and concepts that the two groups knew equally well, the two groups did not differ. Prior knowledge, not reasoning ability, fully explained ethnic differences in performance.

Even nonverbal test items, such as spatial reasoning, depend on learning opportunities. For example, using small blocks to duplicate designs and playing video games that require fast responding and mental rotation of visual images increase success on spatial test items (Dirks, 1982; Maynard, Subrahmanyam, & Greenfield, 2005). Low-income minority children, who often grow up in more "people-oriented" than "object-oriented" homes, may lack opportunities to use games and objects that promote certain intellectual skills.

Furthermore, the sheer amount of time a child spends in school predicts IQ. When children of the same age who are in different grades are compared, those who have been in school longer score higher on intelligence tests. Similarly, the earlier young people leave school, the greater their loss of IQ points (Ceci, 1991, 1999). Taken together, these findings indicate that children's exposure to the knowledge and ways of thinking valued in classrooms has a sizable impact on their intelligence test performance.

Stereotypes. **TAKE A MOMENT...** Imagine trying to succeed at an activity when the prevailing attitude is that members of your group are incompetent. What might you be feeling? **Stereotype threat**—the fear of being judged on the basis of a negative stereotype—can trigger anxiety that interferes with performance. Mounting evidence confirms that stereotype threat undermines test taking in children and adults (McKown & Strambler, 2009; Steele, 1997). For

■ School-age children become increasingly conscious of ethnic stereotypes, and those from stigmatized groups are especially mindful of them. Fear of being judged on the basis of a negative stereotype may be behind this child's hands-off attitude toward his schoolwork. ■

FIGURE 12.5

Effect of stereotype threat on performance.
Among African-American and Hispanic-American children who were aware of ethnic stereotypes, being told that verbal tasks were a "test of how good children are at school problems" led to far worse performance than being told that tasks "were not a test." These statements had little impact on the performance of Caucasian-American children. *(Adapted from McKown & Weinstein, 2003.)*

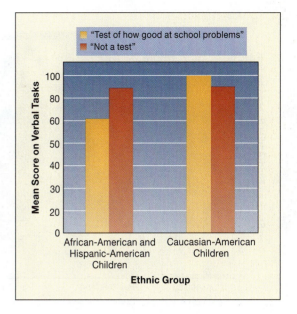

example, researchers gave African-American, Hispanic-American, and Caucasian-American 6- to 10-year-olds verbal tasks. Some children were told that the tasks were "not a test." Others were told that they were "a test of how good children are at school problems"—a statement designed to induce stereotype threat in the ethnic minority children. Among children who were aware of ethnic stereotypes (such as "black people aren't smart"), African Americans and Hispanics performed far worse in the "test" condition than in the "not a test" condition. Caucasian children, in contrast, performed similarly in both conditions (see Figure 12.5) (McKown & Weinstein, 2003).

Over middle childhood, children become increasingly conscious of ethnic stereotypes, and those from stigmatized groups are especially mindful of them. By early adolescence, many low-SES, minority students start to devalue doing well in school, saying it is not important to them (Cooper & Huh, 2008; Major et al., 1998). Self-protective disengagement, sparked by stereotype threat, may be responsible. This weakening of motivation can have serious long-term consequences. Research shows that self-discipline—effort and delay of gratification—predicts academic achievement at least as well as IQ does—and sometimes better (Duckworth & Seligman, 2005).

Reducing Cultural Bias in Testing

Although not all experts agree, many acknowledge that IQ scores can underestimate the intelligence of children from ethnic minority groups. A special concern exists about incorrectly labeling minority children as slow learners and assigning them to remedial classes, which are far less stimulating than regular school experiences. Because of this danger, test scores need to be combined with assessments of children's adaptive behavior—their ability to cope with the demands of their everyday environments. The child who does poorly on an IQ test yet plays a complex game on the playground or figures out how to rewire a broken TV is unlikely to be mentally deficient.

In addition, culturally relevant testing procedures enhance minority children's performance. In an approach called **dynamic assessment,** an innovation consistent with Vygotsky's zone of proximal development, the adult introduces purposeful teaching into the testing situation to find out what the child can attain with social support (Lidz, 2001; Sternberg & Grigorenko, 2002). Dynamic assessment often follows a pretest–intervene–retest procedure. While intervening, the adult seeks the teaching style best suited to the child and communicates strategies that the child can apply in new situations.

Research consistently shows that "static" assessments, such as IQ scores, frequently underestimate how well children do on test items after adult assistance. Children's receptivity to teaching and their capacity to transfer what they have learned to novel problems add considerably to the prediction of future performance (Haywood & Lidz, 2007; Sternberg & Grigorenko, 2002; Tzuriel, 2001). In one study, Ethiopian 6- and 7-year-olds who had recently immigrated to Israel scored well below their Israeli-born agemates on spatial reasoning tasks. The Ethiopian children had little experience with this type of thinking. After several dynamic assessment sessions in which the adult suggested effective strategies, the Ethiopian children's scores rose sharply, nearly equaling those of Israeli-born children (see Figure 12.6 on page 462). They also transferred their learning to new test items (Tzuriel & Kaufman, 1999).

Dynamic assessment is time-consuming and requires extensive knowledge of minority children's cultural values and practices. As yet the approach has not been more effective than traditional tests in predicting academic achievement (Grigorenko & Sternberg, 1998). Better correspondence may emerge in classrooms where teaching interactions resemble the dynamic

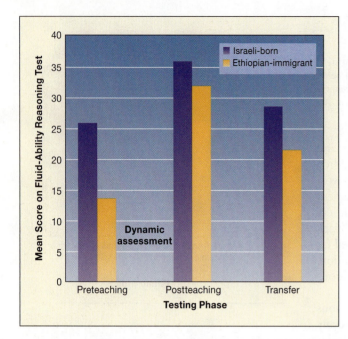

FIGURE 12.6

Influence of dynamic assessment on mental test scores of Ethiopian-immigrant and Israeli-born 6- and 7-year-olds. Each child completed test items in a preteaching phase, a postteaching phase, and a transfer phase, in which they had to generalize their learning to new problems. After dynamic assessment, Ethiopian and Israeli children's scores were nearly equal. Ethiopian children also transferred their learning to new test items, performing much better in the transfer phase than in the preteaching phase. *(Adapted from Tzuriel & Kaufman, 1999.)*

assessment approach—namely, individualized assistance on tasks carefully selected to help the child move beyond her current level of development.

In view of its many problems, should intelligence testing in schools be suspended? Most experts regard this solution as unacceptable. Without testing, important educational decisions would be based only on subjective impressions, perhaps increasing discriminatory placement of minority children. Intelligence tests are useful when interpreted carefully by examiners who are sensitive to cultural influences on test performance. And despite their limitations, IQ scores continue to be valid measures of school learning potential for the majority of Western children.

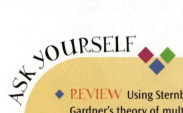

ASK YOURSELF

◆ **REVIEW** Using Sternberg's triarchic theory and Gardner's theory of multiple intelligences, explain the limitations of current mental tests in assessing the diversity of human intelligence.

◆ **APPLY** Josefina, a Hispanic fourth grader, does well on homework assignments. But when her teacher announces, "It's time for a test to see how much you've learned," Josefina usually does poorly. How might stereotype threat explain this inconsistency?

◆ **CONNECT** Explain how dynamic assessment is consistent with Vygotsky's zone of proximal development and with scaffolding (see Chapter 9, pages 330–331).

◆ **REFLECT** Do you think that intelligence tests are culturally biased? What observations and evidence influenced your conclusion?

Language Development

Vocabulary, grammar, and pragmatics continue to develop in middle childhood, though less obviously than at earlier ages. In addition, children's attitude toward language undergoes a fundamental shift. They develop **metalinguistic awareness,** the ability to think about language as a system.

Schooling contributes greatly to these language competencies. Reflecting on language is extremely common during reading instruction. And fluent reading is a major new source of language learning (Ravid & Tolchinsky, 2002). As we will see, an improved ability to reflect on language grows out of literacy and supports many complex language skills.

Vocabulary

During the elementary school years, vocabulary increases fourfold, eventually exceeding 40,000 words. On average, children learn about 20 new words each day—a rate of growth greater than in early childhood. In addition to the word-learning strategies discussed in

Chapter 9, school-age children enlarge their vocabularies by analyzing the structure of complex words. From *happy* and *decide,* they quickly derive the meanings of *happiness* and *decision* (Larsen & Nippold, 2007). They also figure out many more word meanings from context (Nagy & Scott, 2000).

As at earlier ages, children benefit from conversations with more expert speakers, especially when their partners use and explain complex words (Weizman & Snow, 2001). But because written language contains a far more diverse and complex vocabulary than spoken language, reading contributes enormously to vocabulary growth. Children who engage in as little as 21 minutes of independent reading per day are exposed to nearly 2 million words per year (Cunningham & Stanovich, 1998).

As their knowledge becomes better organized, older school-age children think about and use words more precisely: In addition to the verb *fall,* for example, they also use *topple, tumble,* and *plummet* (Berman, 2007). Word definitions also illustrate this change. Five- and 6-year-olds offer concrete descriptions referring to functions or appearance—*knife:* "when you're cutting carrots"; *bicycle:* "it's got wheels, a chain, and handlebars." By the end of elementary school, synonyms and explanations of categorical relationships appear—for example, *knife:* "something you could cut with. A saw is like a knife. It could also be a weapon" (Wehren, De Lisi, & Arnold, 1981). This advance reflects older children's ability to deal with word meanings on an entirely verbal plane. They can add new words to their vocabulary simply by being given a definition.

School-age children's more reflective and analytical approach to language permits them to appreciate the multiple meanings of words—to recognize, for example, that many words, such as *cool* or *neat,* have psychological as well as physical meanings: "Cool shirt!" or "That movie was really neat!" This grasp of double meanings permits 8- to 10-year-olds to comprehend subtle metaphors, such as "sharp as a tack" and "spilling the beans" (Nippold, Taylor, & Baker, 1996; Wellman & Hickling, 1994). It also leads to a change in children's humor. Riddles and puns that alternate between different meanings of a key word are common: "Hey, did you take a bath?" "Why, is one missing?"

■ As part of a fourth-grade field trip, a staff member at a natural history museum discusses features of the teeth and jaws of several animal species. During middle childhood, children can add new words to their vocabulary simply by being given a definition. ■

Grammar

During the school years, mastery of complex grammatical constructions improves. For example, English-speaking children use the passive voice more frequently, and they more often extend it from an abbreviated structure ("It broke") into full statements ("The glass was broken by Mary") (Israel, Johnson, & Brooks, 2000; Tomasello, 2006). Older children also apply their grasp of the passive voice to a wider range of nouns and verbs. Preschoolers comprehend the passive best when the subject of the sentence is an animate being and the verb is an action word: "The boy is *kissed* by the girl." School-age children extend the passive to inanimate subjects *(drum, hat)* and include experiential verbs *(like, know)* (Lempert, 1989; Pinker, Johnson, & Frost, 1987). Although the passive form is challenging, language input makes a difference. When adults speak a language that emphasizes full passives, such as Inuktitut (spoken by the Inuit people of Arctic Canada), children produce them earlier (Allen & Crago, 1996).

Another grammatical achievement of middle childhood is advanced understanding of infinitive phrases—the difference between "John is eager to please" and "John is easy to please" (Chomsky, 1969). Like gains in vocabulary, appreciation of these subtle grammatical distinctions is supported by improved ability to analyze and reflect on language.

Pragmatics

The school years also bring dramatic gains in *pragmatics,* the communicative side of language. Opportunities to communicate in many situations with a variety of people help children refine these skills.

 LOOK AND LISTEN

Record examples of 8- to 10-year-olds' humor, or examine storybooks for humor aimed at second through fourth graders. Does it require a grasp of the multiple meanings of words?

COMMUNICATING CLEARLY   In middle childhood, children can adapt to the needs of listeners in challenging communicative situations, such as describing one object among a group of very similar objects. Whereas preschoolers tend to give ambiguous descriptions ("the red one"), school-age children are precise: "the round red one with stripes on it" (Deutsch & Pechmann, 1982). Because peers challenge unclear messages that adults accept, peer interaction probably contributes greatly to this aspect of conversational competence.

Gains in the ability to evaluate the clarity of others' messages occur as well, and children become better at resolving inconsistencies. Consider the instruction, "Put the frog on the book in the box." Preschoolers cannot make sense of the ambiguity, even though they use similar embedded phrases in their own speech. They respond by attending only to the first prepositional phrase ("on the book") and place a toy frog on a book. School-age children, in contrast, can attend to and integrate two competing representations ("on the book" and "in the box"). They quickly figure out the speaker's meaning and pick up a toy frog resting on a book and place it in a box (Hurewitz et al., 2000).

School-age children are also more sensitive to distinctions between what people say and what they mean (Lee, Torrance, & Olson, 2001). Lizzie, for example, knew that when her mother said, "The garbage is beginning to smell," she really meant, "Take that garbage out!"

NARRATIVES   As a result of improved memory, ability to take the perspective of listeners, and conversations with adults about past experiences, children's narratives increase in organization, detail, and expressiveness. A typical 4- or 5-year-old's narrative states what happened: "We went to the lake. We fished and waited. Paul caught a huge catfish!" Six- and 7-year-olds add orienting information (time, place, participants) and connectives ("next," "then," "so," "finally") that lend coherence to the story. Gradually, narratives lengthen into a *classic form* in which events not only build to a high point but resolve: "After Paul reeled in the catfish, Dad cleaned and cooked it. Then we ate it all up!" And evaluative comments rise dramatically, becoming common by age 8 to 9: "The catfish tasted great. Paul was so proud!" (Melzi & Ely, 2009; Ukrainetz et al., 2005).

Because children pick up the narrative styles of significant adults in their lives, their narratives vary widely across cultures. For example, instead of the *topic-focused style* of most American school-age children, who describe an experience from beginning to end, African-American children often use a *topic-associating style* in which they blend several similar experiences. One 9-year-old related having a tooth pulled, then described seeing her sister's tooth pulled, next told how she had removed one of her baby teeth, and concluded, "I'm a pullin-teeth expert . . . call me, and I'll be over" (McCabe, 1997, p. 164). As a result, African-American children's narratives are usually longer and more complex than those of white children (Champion, 2003b).

© BLICKWINKEL/ALAMY

■ A Vietnamese 8-year-old tells a story to his grandmother, who listens intently. Children's narratives vary widely across cultures, reflecting the styles of significant adults in their lives. ■

The ability to generate clear oral narratives enhances reading comprehension and prepares children for producing longer, more explicit written narratives. In families who regularly eat meals together, children are advanced in language and literacy development, perhaps because mealtimes offer many opportunities to relate personal stories (Snow & Beals, 2006).

Learning Two Languages

Joey and Lizzie speak only one language—English, their native tongue. Yet throughout the world, many children grow up *bilingual,* learning two languages and sometimes more than two. An estimated 20 percent of U.S. children—10 million in all—speak a language other than English at home (U.S. Census Bureau, 2010b).

BILINGUAL DEVELOPMENT   Children can become bilingual in two ways: (1) by acquiring both languages at the same time in early childhood or (2) by learning a second language after mastering the first. Children of bilingual parents who teach them both languages in infancy and early childhood separate the language systems from the start, distinguishing their sounds, mastering equivalent words in each, and attaining early language milestones according to a typical timetable (Conboy & Thal, 2006; Genesee & Nicoladis, 2007; Holowka, Brosseau-Lapré, & Petitto, 2002). Preschoolers acquire normal native ability in the language of their surrounding community and good-to-native ability in the second language, depending on their exposure to it (Genesee, 2001). When school-age children acquire a second language, they generally take 5 to 7 years to attain speaking and writing skills on a par with those of native-speaking agemates (Paradis, 2007).

Like many bilingual adults, bilingual children sometimes engage in *code switching*—producing an utterance in one language that contains one or more "guest" words from the other—without violating the grammar of either language. Children may engage in code switching because they lack the vocabulary to convey a particular thought in one language, so they use the other. But children who code-switch the most are those whose parents often do so. Bilingual adults frequently code-switch to express cultural identity, and children may follow suit—as when a Korean child speaking English switches to Korean on mentioning her piano teacher, as a sign of respect for authority (Chung, 2006). Opportunities to listen to code switching may facilitate bilingual development (Gawlitzek-Maiwald & Tracy, 1996). For example, a child accustomed to hearing French sentences with English guest words may rely on sentence-level cues to figure out English word meanings.

Recall from Chapter 6 that, just as with first-language development, a *sensitive period* for second-language development exists. Although mastery must begin sometime in childhood for full development to occur, a precise age cutoff for a decline in second-language learning has not been established (see page 235).

A large body of research shows that bilingualism has positive consequences for development. Children who become fluent in two languages develop denser gray matter (neurons and connective fibers) in areas of the left hemisphere devoted to language (Mechelli et al., 2004). Bilingual children outperform others on tests of selective attention, analytical reasoning, concept formation, and cognitive flexibility (Bialystok, 2001; Bialystok & Martin, 2004). They are also advanced in certain aspects of metalinguistic awareness, such as detection of errors in grammar, meaning, and conventions of conversation (responding politely, relevantly, and informatively). And children transfer their phonological awareness skills in one language to the other, especially if the two languages share phonological features and letter–sound correspondences, as Spanish and English do (Bialystok, McBride-Chang, & Luk, 2005; Siegal, Iozzi, & Surian, 2009; Snow & Kang, 2006). These capacities, as noted earlier, enhance reading achievement.

BILINGUAL EDUCATION The advantages of bilingualism provide strong justification for bilingual education programs in schools. In Canada, about 7 percent of elementary school students are enrolled in *language immersion programs,* in which English-speaking children are taught entirely in French for several years. This strategy succeeds in developing children who are proficient in both languages and who, by grade 6, achieve as well in reading, writing, and math as their counterparts in the regular English program (Harley & Jean, 1999; Holobow, Genesee, & Lambert, 1991; Turnbull, Hart, & Lapkin, 2003).

In the United States, fierce disagreement exists over the question of how best to educate ethnic minority children with limited English proficiency. Some believe that time spent communicating in the child's native tongue detracts from English-language achievement, which is crucial for success in the worlds of school and work. Other educators, committed to developing minority children's native language while fostering mastery of English, note that providing instruction in the native tongue lets minority children know that their heritage is respected. It also prevents inadequate proficiency in both languages. Minority children who gradually lose their first language as a result of being taught the second end up limited in both languages for a time (Ovando & Collier, 1998). This circumstance leads to serious academic difficulties

■ In this English–Spanish bilingual classroom, children are more involved in learning, participate more actively in class discussions, and acquire the second language more easily than they would in an English-only classroom. ■

and is believed to contribute to the high rates of school failure and dropout among low-SES Hispanic youngsters, who make up nearly 50 percent of the U.S. language-minority population.

At present, public opinion and educational practice favor English-only instruction. Many U.S. states have passed laws declaring English to be their official language, creating conditions in which schools have no obligation to teach minority students in languages other than English. Yet in classrooms where both languages are integrated into the curriculum, minority children are more involved in learning, participate more actively in class discussions, and acquire the second language more easily. In contrast, when teachers speak only in a language that children can barely understand, minority children display frustration, boredom, and withdrawal. Under these conditions, U.S. kindergartners with limited English proficiency quickly fall behind their English-proficient counterparts in reading skills and are likely to struggle academically throughout their elementary school years (Kieffer, 2008). This downward spiral in achievement is greatest in high-poverty schools, where resources to support the needs of language-minority children are especially scarce.

Supporters of U.S. English-only education often point to the success of Canadian language immersion programs, in which classroom lessons are conducted in the second language. But Canadian parents enroll their children in immersion classrooms voluntarily, and both French and English are majority languages that are equally valued in Canada. Furthermore, teaching in the child's native language is merely delayed, not ruled out. For U.S. non-English-speaking minority children, whose native languages are not valued by the larger society, a different strategy seems necessary: one that promotes children's native-language and literacy skills while they learn English.

◆ **REVIEW** Cite examples of how language awareness fosters school-age children's language progress.

◆ **APPLY** Ten-year-old Shana arrived home from soccer practice and remarked, "I'm wiped out!" Megan, her 5-year-old sister, looked puzzled and asked, "What did'ya wipe out, Shana?" Explain Shana's and Megan's different understandings of this expression.

◆ **CONNECT** How can bilingual education promote ethnic minority children's cognitive and academic development?

◆ **REFLECT** Did you acquire a second language at home or study one in school? If so, when did you begin, and how proficient are you in the second language? Considering research on bilingualism, what changes would you make in your second-language learning, and why?

Children's Learning in School

Evidence cited throughout this chapter indicates that schools are vital forces in children's cognitive development. How do schools exert such a powerful influence? Research looking at schools as complex social systems—class size, educational philosophies, teacher–student relationships, and larger cultural context—provides important insights. As you read about these topics, refer to Applying What We Know on the following page, which summarizes characteristics of high-quality education in elementary school.

Class Size

As each school year began, Rena telephoned the principal's office to ask, "How large will Joey's and Lizzie's classes be?" Her concern is well-founded. In a large field experiment, more than 6,000 Tennessee kindergartners were randomly assigned to three class types: "small" (13 to 17 students), "regular" (22 to 25 students) with only a teacher, and regular with a teacher plus a full-time teacher's aide. These arrangements continued into third grade. Small-class students—especially ethnic minority children—scored higher in reading and math achievement each year (Mosteller, 1995). Placing teacher's aides in regular-size classes had no impact.

Applying What We Know

Signs of High-Quality Education in Elementary School

CLASSROOM CHARACTERISTICS	SIGNS OF QUALITY
Class size	Optimum class size is no larger than 18 children.
Physical setting	Space is divided into richly equipped activity centers—for reading, writing, playing math or language games, exploring science, working on construction projects, using computers, and engaging in other academic pursuits. Spaces are used flexibly for individual and small-group activities and whole-class gatherings.
Curriculum	The curriculum helps children both achieve academic standards and make sense of their learning in all subjects, including literacy, mathematics, social studies, art, music, health, and physical education. Subjects are integrated so that children apply knowledge in one area to others. The curriculum is implemented through activities responsive to children's interests, ideas, and everyday lives, including their cultural backgrounds.
Daily activities	Teachers provide challenging activities that include opportunities for small-group and independent work. Groupings vary in size and makeup of children, depending on the activity and on children's learning needs. Teachers encourage cooperative learning and guide children in attaining it.
Interactions between teachers and children	Teachers foster each child's progress and use intellectually engaging strategies, including posing problems, asking thought-provoking questions, discussing ideas, and adding complexity to tasks. They also demonstrate, explain, coach, and assist in other ways, depending on each child's learning needs.
Evaluations of progress	Teachers regularly evaluate children's progress through written observations and work samples, which they use to enhance and individualize teaching. They help children reflect on their work and decide how to improve it. They also seek information and perspectives from parents on how well children are learning and include parents' views in evaluations.
Relationship with parents	Teachers forge partnerships with parents. They hold periodic conferences and encourage parents to visit the classroom anytime, to observe and volunteer.

Source: Copple & Bredekamp, 2009.

Rather, experiencing small classes from kindergarten through third grade predicted substantially higher achievement from fourth through ninth grades, after children had returned to regular-size classes. It also predicted greater likelihood of graduating from high school, particularly for low-income students (Finn, Gerber, & Boyd-Zaharias, 2005; Nye, Hedges, & Konstantopoulos, 2001).

Why is small class size beneficial? With fewer children, teachers spend less time disciplining and more time teaching and giving individual attention. Also, children who learn in smaller groups show better concentration, higher-quality class participation, and more favorable attitudes toward school (Blatchford et al., 2003, 2007; Blatchford, Bassett, & Brown, 2005).

Educational Philosophies

Each teacher brings to the classroom an educational philosophy that plays a major role in children's learning. Two philosophical approaches have received the most research attention. They differ in what children are taught, in the way they are believed to learn, and in how their progress is evaluated.

TRADITIONAL VERSUS CONSTRUCTIVIST CLASSROOMS In a **traditional classroom,** the teacher is the sole authority for knowledge, rules, and decision making and does most of the talking. Students are relatively passive—listening, responding when called on, and completing teacher-assigned tasks. Their progress is evaluated by how well they keep pace with a uniform set of standards for their grade.

A **constructivist classroom,** in contrast, encourages students to *construct* their own knowledge. Although constructivist approaches vary, many are grounded in Piaget's theory, which views children as active agents who reflect on and coordinate their own thoughts, rather than absorbing those of others. A glance inside a constructivist classroom reveals richly equipped learning centers, small groups and individuals solving self-chosen problems, and a teacher who guides and supports in response to children's needs. Students are evaluated by considering their progress in relation to their own prior development.

In the United States, the pendulum has swung back and forth between these two views. In the 1960s and early 1970s, constructivist classrooms gained in popularity. Then, as concern arose over the academic progress of children and youths, a "back-to-basics" movement arose, and classrooms returned to traditional instruction. This style, still prevalent today, has become increasingly pronounced as a result of the U.S. No Child Left Behind Act, signed into law in 2001 (Darling-Hammond, 2010; Ravitch, 2010). Because it places heavy pressure on teachers and school administrators to improve achievement test scores, it has narrowed the curricular focus in many schools to preparing students to take such tests.

Although older elementary school children in traditional classrooms have a slight edge in achievement test scores, constructivist settings are associated with many other benefits—gains in critical thinking, greater social and moral maturity, and more positive attitudes toward school (DeVries, 2001; Rathunde & Csikszentmihalyi, 2005; Walberg, 1986). And as noted in Chapter 9, when teacher-directed instruction is emphasized in preschool and kindergarten, it actually undermines academic motivation and achievement, especially in low-SES children.

The emphasis on knowledge absorption in many kindergarten and primary classrooms has contributed to a growing trend among parents to delay their child's school entry—especially if the child is a boy with a birth date close to the cutoff for kindergarten enrollment. But research reveals no long-term academic or social benefits (Lincove & Painter, 2006; Stipek, 2002). To the contrary, younger first graders reap achievement gains from on-time enrollment, outperforming same-age children a year behind them (Stipek & Byler, 2001). An alternative perspective is that school readiness can be cultivated through classroom experiences that foster children's individual progress.

NEW PHILOSOPHICAL DIRECTIONS   New approaches to education, grounded in Vygotsky's sociocultural theory, capitalize on the rich social context of the classroom to spur children's learning. In these **social-constructivist classrooms,** children participate in a wide range of challenging activities with teachers and peers, with whom they jointly construct understandings. As children *appropriate* (take for themselves) the knowledge and strategies generated through working together, they become competent, contributing members of their classroom community and advance in cognitive and social development (Bodrova & Leong, 2007; Palincsar, 2003). Vygotsky's emphasis on the social origins of complex mental activities has inspired the following educational themes:

- *Teachers and children as partners in learning.* A classroom rich in both teacher–child and child–child collaboration transfers culturally valued ways of thinking to children.
- *Experience with many types of symbolic communication in meaningful activities.* As children master reading, writing, and mathematics, they become aware of their culture's communication systems, reflect on their own thinking, and bring it under voluntary control. **TAKE A MOMENT...** Can you identify research presented earlier in this chapter that supports this theme?
- *Teaching adapted to each child's zone of proximal development.* Assistance that both responds to current understandings and encourages children to take the next step helps ensure that each child makes the best progress possible.

Let's look at two examples of a growing number of programs that have translated these ideas into action.

Reciprocal Teaching.   Originally designed to improve reading comprehension in poorly achieving students, this Vygotsky-inspired teaching method has been extended to other subjects and all schoolchildren (Palincsar & Herrenkohl, 1999). In **reciprocal teaching,** a teacher and two to four students form a cooperative group and take turns leading dialogues on the content of a text passage. Within the dialogues, group members apply four cognitive strategies: questioning, summarizing, clarifying, and predicting.

LOOK AND LISTEN

Ask an elementary school teacher to sum up his or her educational philosophy. Is it closest to a traditional, constructivist, or social-constructivist view? Has the teacher encountered any obstacles to implementing that philosophy? Explain.

The dialogue leader (at first a teacher, later a student) begins by *asking questions* about the content of the text passage. Students offer answers, raise additional questions, and, in case of disagreement, reread the original text. Next, the leader *summarizes* the passage, and children discuss the summary and *clarify* unfamiliar ideas. Finally, the leader encourages students to *predict* upcoming content based on clues in the passage.

Elementary and middle school students exposed to reciprocal teaching show impressive gains in reading comprehension compared to controls taught in other ways (Rosenshine & Meister, 1994; Sporer, Brunstein, & Kieschke, 2009; Takala, 2006). Notice how reciprocal teaching creates a zone of proximal development in which children learn to scaffold one another's progress and assume more responsibility for comprehending text passages (Gillies, 2003). Also, by collaborating with others, children forge group expectations for high-level thinking, more often apply their metacognitive knowledge, and acquire skills vital for learning and success in everyday life.

Communities of Learners. Recognizing that collaboration requires a supportive context to be most effective, another Vygotsky-based innovation makes it a schoolwide value. Classrooms become **communities of learners** where teachers guide the overall process of learning but no other distinction is made between adult and child contributors: All participate in joint endeavors and have the authority to define and resolve problems. This approach is based on the assumption that different people have different expertises that can benefit the community and that students, too, may become experts (Sullivan & Glanz, 2006). Classroom activities are often long-term projects addressing complex, real-world problems. In working toward project goals, children and teachers draw on the expertises of one another and of others within and outside the school.

In one classroom, students studied animal–habitat relationships in order to design an animal of the future, suited to environmental changes. The class formed small research groups, each of which selected a subtopic—for example, defense against predators, protection from the elements, reproduction, or food getting. Each group member assumed responsibility for part of the subtopic, consulting diverse experts and preparing teaching materials. Then group members taught one another, assembled their contributions, and brought them to the community as a whole so the knowledge gathered could be used to solve the problem (Brown, 1997; Stone, 2005). The result was a multifaceted understanding of the topic that would have been too difficult and time-consuming for any learner to accomplish alone.

In communities of learners, collaboration is created from within by teachers and children and supported from without by the culture of the school (Sullivan & Glanz, 2006). As a result, the approach broadens Vygotsky's concept of the zone of proximal development, from a child in collaboration with a more expert partner (adult or peer) to multiple, interrelated zones.

■ A teacher and students form a community of learners to plan, plant, and track the growth of a vegetable garden. During this complex, long-term project, all participants—adults as well as children—may become experts who share knowledge, teaching one another. ■

Teacher–Student Interaction

Elementary and secondary school students describe good teachers as caring, helpful, and stimulating—behaviors associated with gains in motivation, achievement, and positive peer relations (Hughes & Kwok, 2006, 2007; Hughes, Zhang, & Hill, 2006; O'Connor & McCartney, 2007). But too many U.S. teachers emphasize repetitive drill over higher-level thinking, such as grappling with ideas and applying knowledge to new situations (Sacks, 2005). In a longitudinal investigation of a large sample of middle school students, those in more academically demanding classrooms showed better attendance and larger gains in math achievement over the following two years (Phillips, 1997).

Of course, teachers do not interact in the same way with all children. Well-behaved, high-achieving students typically get more support and praise, whereas unruly students have more conflicts with teachers and receive more criticism from them (Henricsson & Rydell, 2004). Caring teacher–student relationships have an especially strong impact on the achievement and social behavior of low-SES minority students and other children at risk for learning difficulties (Baker, 2006; Crosno, Kirkpatrick, & Elder, 2004). But overall, higher-SES students—who tend to be higher-achieving and to have fewer learning and behavior problems—have more sensitive and supportive relationships with teachers (Jerome, Hamre, & Pianta, 2008; Pianta, Hamre, & Stuhlman, 2003).

Unfortunately, once teachers' attitudes toward students are established, they can become more extreme than is warranted by children's behavior. Of special concern are **educational self-fulfilling prophecies:** Children may adopt teachers' positive or negative views and start to live up to them. This effect is particularly strong when teachers emphasize competition and publicly compare children, regularly favoring the best students (Kuklinski & Weinstein, 2001; Weinstein, 2002).

Teacher expectations have a greater impact on low-achieving than high-achieving students (Madom, Jussim, & Eccles, 1997). When a teacher is critical, high achievers can fall back on their history of success. Low-achieving students' sensitivity to self-fulfilling prophecies can be beneficial when teachers believe in them. But biased teacher judgments are usually slanted in a negative direction. In one study, African-American and Hispanic elementary school students taught by high-bias teachers (who expected them to do poorly) showed substantially lower end-of-year achievement than their counterparts taught by low-bias teachers (McKown & Weinstein, 2008). Recall our discussion of *stereotype threat*. A child in the position of confirming a negative stereotype may respond with especially intense anxiety and reduced motivation, amplifying a negative self-fulfilling prophecy.

Grouping Practices

In many schools, students are assigned to *homogeneous* groups or classes, in which children of similar ability levels are taught together. Homogeneous grouping can be a potent source of self-fulfilling prophecies. Low-group students—who as early as first grade are more likely to be low-SES, minority, and male—get more drill on basic facts and skills, engage in less discussion, and progress at a slower pace. Gradually, they decline in self-esteem and motivation and fall further behind in achievement (Chorzempa & Graham, 2006; Condron, 2007; Trautwein et al., 2006). Unfortunately, widespread SES and ethnic segregation in U.S. schools consigns large numbers of low-SES, minority students to a form of school-wide, deleterious homogeneous grouping. Refer to the Social Issues: Education box on the following page to find out how magnet schools foster heterogeneous learning contexts, thereby reducing achievement disparities between SES and ethnic minority groups.

Another way schools can increase the *heterogeneity* of student groups is to combine two or three adjacent grades. In *multigrade classrooms,* academic achievement, self-esteem, and attitudes toward school are usually more favorable than in the single-grade arrangement, perhaps because multigrade classrooms often decrease competition and increase harmony (Lloyd, 1999; Ong, Allison, & Haladyna, 2000). The opportunity that mixed-grade grouping affords for peer tutoring may also contribute to its favorable outcomes. When older or more expert students teach younger or less expert students, both tutors and tutees benefit in achievement and self-esteem, with stronger effects for low-income, minority students and students in grades 1 to 3 than grades 4 to 6 (Ginsburg-Block, Rohrbeck, & Fantuzzo, 2006; Renninger, 1998).

However, small, heterogeneous groups of students working together often engage in poorer-quality inter-

© MARY KATE DENNY/PHOTOEDIT

■ These first through third graders collaborate on a variety of tasks. Compared to children in single-grade classrooms, those in multigrade classrooms are usually advantaged in academic achievement, self-esteem, and attitudes toward school. ■

SOCIAL ISSUES: EDUCATION

Magnet Schools: Equal Access to High-Quality Education

Each school-day morning, Emma leaves her affluent suburban neighborhood, riding a school bus 20 miles to a magnet school in an impoverished, mostly Hispanic inner-city neighborhood. In her sixth-grade class, she settles into a science project with her friend, Maricela, who lives in the local neighborhood. For the first hour of the day, the girls use a thermometer, ice water, and a stopwatch to determine which of several materials is the best insulator, recording and graphing their data. Throughout the school, which specializes in innovative math and science teaching, students diverse in SES and ethnicity learn side-by-side.

Despite the 1954 U.S. Supreme Court *Brown v. Board of Education* decision ordering schools to desegregate, school integration has receded since the late 1980s, as federal courts canceled their integration orders and returned this authority to states and cities. Today, the racial divide in American education is deepening. African-American children are just as likely to attend a school that serves a mostly black population as they were in the 1960s; Hispanic children are even more segregated. And when minority students attend ethnically mixed schools, they typically do so with other minorities (Frankenburg & Orfield, 2007).

U.S. schools in inner-city, low-income neighborhoods are vastly disadvantaged in funding and therefore in educational opportunities, largely because public education is primarily supported by local property taxes. Federal and state grants-in-aid are not sufficient to close this funding gap between rich and poor districts (Darling-Hammond, 2010). Consequently, in inner-city segregated neighborhoods, dilapidated school buildings; inexperienced teachers; out-

dated, poor-quality educational resources; and school cultures that fail to encourage strong teaching are widespread (Kozol, 2005). The negative impact on student achievement is severe.

A promising solution is the establishment of magnet schools. In addition to the usual curriculum, they emphasize a specific area of interest—such as performing arts, math and science, or technology. Families outside the school neighborhood are attracted to magnet schools (hence the name) by their rich academic offerings. Often magnets are located in low-income, minority areas, where they serve the neighborhood student population. Other students, who apply and are admitted by lottery, are bussed in—many from well-to-do city and suburban neighborhoods. In another model, all students—including those in the surrounding neighborhood—must apply. In either case, magnet schools are voluntarily desegregated.

Research confirms that less segregated education enhances minority student achievement (Linn & Welner, 2007). Is this so for magnet schools? A Connecticut study comparing seventh- to tenth-grade students enrolled in magnet schools with those whose lottery numbers were not drawn and who therefore attended other city schools confirmed that the magnets served a far more diverse student population. Although

magnet-school enrollees and nonadmitted applicants were similar in ethnicity, SES, and prior academic achievement, magnet students showed greater gains in reading and math achievement over a two-year period—outcomes especially pronounced for low-SES, ethnic minority students (Bifulco, Cobb, & Bell, 2009).

By high school, the higher-achieving peer environments of ethnically diverse schools encourage more students to pursue higher education (Frankenburg & Orfield, 2007). And as we will see in Chapter 13, a diverse student body also provides opportunities for social learning that can combat racial prejudice. In sum, magnet schools are a promising approach for overcoming the negative forces of SES and ethnic isolation in American schools.

© ELLEN B. SENISI/THE IMAGE WORKS

■ Third graders at a fine arts magnet school jointly create a painting. The ethnically diverse learning environments of many magnet schools enhance academic achievement, especially among low-SES minority students. ■

action (less accurate explanations and answers) than homogeneous groups of above-average students (Webb, Nemer, & Chizhik, 1998). For collaboration between heterogeneous peers to succeed, children need extensive training and guidance in **cooperative learning,** in which small groups of classmates work toward common goals—by resolving differences of opinion, sharing responsibilities, considering one another's ideas, and providing one another with sufficient explanations to correct misunderstandings. When teachers prompt, explain, model, and have children role-play how to work together effectively, cooperative learning among heterogeneous peers results in clearer explanations, greater enjoyment of learning, and achievement gains across a wide range of school subjects (Gillies, 2003; Terwel et al., 2001; Webb et al., 2008). And children readily cooperate in future group activities, building on others' ideas and offering assistance (Gillies, 2002).

Computers and Academic Learning

Virtually all public schools in industrialized nations have integrated computers into their instructional programs and can access the Internet. And, as noted in Chapter 9, most U.S. children have access to a home computer, usually with an Internet connection. Although higher-SES homes are more likely to have computers and Internet access, over 70 percent of U.S. lower-SES families with school-age children and adolescents now have them (Judge, Puckett, & Bell, 2006; Nielsen Company, 2008).

Nongame computer use is associated with academic progress (Calvert et al., 2005). Using the computer for word processing enables children to write freely, experimenting with letters and words without having to struggle with handwriting. Because they can revise their text's meaning and style and also check their spelling, they worry less about making mistakes. As a result, their written products tend to be longer and of higher quality. Often children jointly plan, compose, and revise text, learning from one another (Clements & Sarama, 2003). And as in early childhood, computer programming projects promote problem solving and metacognition and are common classroom contexts for peer collaboration (see page 353 in Chapter 9).

■ At a classroom computer, fifth graders work together on interactive math activities. Schools must ensure that all children have rich opportunities to master the varied aspects of computer technology that enhance academic achievement. ■

As children get older, they increasingly use the computer for schoolwork, mostly to search the Web for information and to prepare written assignments—activities linked to improved academic achievement (Attewell, 2001; Judge, Puckett, & Bell, 2006). In one study, the more low-SES middle-school students used home computers to access the Internet for information gathering (either for school or for personal interests), the better their subsequent reading achievement and school grades (Jackson et al., 2006). Perhaps those who use the Web to find information also devote more time to reading, given that many Web pages are heavily text-based. Nevertheless, a survey of a large, nationally representative sample of U.S. 8- to 18-year-olds revealed that on average, they used the computer only a half-hour a day for schoolwork compared with an hour a day for pleasure—surfing the Web, communicating by e-mail or instant messaging, and accessing music, video, and computer games (Roberts, Foehr, & Rideout, 2005).

The learning advantages of computers raise concerns about a "digital divide" between SES and gender groups. Poverty-stricken children are least likely to have home computers and Internet connections. And low-SES children who do have access devote less time to Internet use than their higher-SES counterparts (Jackson et al., 2006). By the end of elementary school, boys spend more time with computers than girls and use computers somewhat differently. Boys, for example, more often connect to the Internet to download games and music, trade and sell things, and create Web pages. Girls emphasize information gathering, e-mail, and instant messaging (La Ferle, Edwards, & Lee, 2000; Jackson et al., 2008; Lenhart, Rainie, & Lewis, 2001). Furthermore, in a survey of a large, nationally representative sample of Canadian 15- and 16-year-olds, boys more often than girls engaged in writing computer programs, analyzing data, and using spreadsheets and graphics programs. And many more boys than girls rated their computer skills as "excellent" (Looker & Thiessen, 2003). Schools need to ensure that girls and low-SES students have many opportunities to benefit from the cognitively enriching aspects of computers—not just by equipping classrooms with more technology but also by providing the teacher guidance necessary to educate equitably and effectively (Attewell, 2001).

Most parents say they purchased a computer to enrich their child's education; about one-third of American school-age children and adolescents have a computer in their bedroom. At the same time, parents express great concern about the influence of violent computer games (see page 388 in Chapter 10) and the Internet. Yet only 30 percent of U.S. children and youths say their parents have rules about computer use and know what sites they visit on the Web (Rideout & Hamel, 2006; Roberts, Foehr, & Rideout, 2005). Not until ages 10 to 11 do children

FIGURE 12.7

Children's drawings of the Internet, reflecting increased understanding with age.
When elementary school children were asked to describe and draw a picture of the Internet, most children younger than age 10 had either a minimal understanding (viewed it as one computer) or a partial understanding (viewed it as a few connected computers). Most 10- and 11-year-olds had a sophisticated understanding of a networklike system in which computing centers link with many computers. *(From Z. Yan, 2006, "What Influences Children's and Adolescents' Understanding of the Complexity of the Internet?" Developmental Psychology, 42, p. 421. Copyright © 2006 by the American Psychological Association. Reprinted with permission of the American Psychological Association.)*

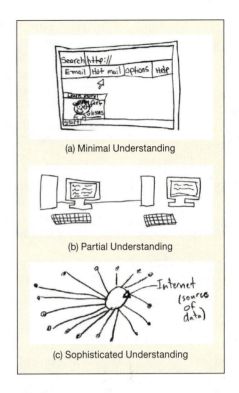

(a) Minimal Understanding

(b) Partial Understanding

(c) Sophisticated Understanding

acquire an adult-level understanding of the technical complexity of the Internet as a networklike system linking a computing center with many computers (see Figure 12.7) (Yan, 2006). This technical grasp precedes and probably contributes to sophisticated knowledge of the Internet's social risks (theft of personal information, virus attacks, exposure to unwanted content), which is attained around age 12 to 13.

Teaching Children with Special Needs

We have seen that effective teachers flexibly adjust their teaching strategies to accommodate students with a wide range of abilities and characteristics. But such adjustments are increasingly difficult at the very low and high ends of the ability distribution. How do schools serve children with special learning needs?

CHILDREN WITH LEARNING DIFFICULTIES U.S. legislation mandates that schools place children who require special supports for learning in the "least restrictive" (as close to normal as possible) environments that meet their educational needs. In **inclusive classrooms,** students with learning difficulties learn alongside typical students in the regular educational setting for part or all of the school day—a practice designed to prepare them for participation in society and to combat prejudices against individuals with disabilities (Kugelmass & Ainscow, 2004). Largely as the result of parental pressures, an increasing number of students experience *full inclusion*—full-time placement in regular classrooms.

Some students in inclusive classrooms have *mild mental retardation:* Their IQs fall between 55 and 70, and they also show problems in adaptive behavior, or skills of everyday living (American Psychiatric Association, 2000). But the largest number—5 to 10 percent of school-age children—have **learning disabilities,** great difficulty with one or more aspects of learning, usually reading. As a result, their achievement is considerably behind what would be expected on the basis of their IQ. Sometimes, deficits express themselves in other ways—for example, as severe inattention (see page 444), which depresses both IQ and achievement test scores. The problems of students with learning disabilities cannot be traced to any obvious physical or emotional difficulty or to environmental disadvantage. Instead, subtle deficits in brain functioning seem to be involved (Berninger, 2006). Some disorders run in families, and in certain cases, specific genes have been identified that contribute to the problem (Miller, Sanchez, & Hynd, 2003; Raskind et al., 2005). In many instances, the cause is unknown.

Although some students benefit academically from inclusion, many do not. Achievement gains depend on both the severity of the disability and the support services available (Klingner et al., 1998). Furthermore, children with disabilities often are rejected by regular-classroom peers. Students with mental retardation are overwhelmed by the social skills of their classmates; they cannot interact adeptly in a conversation or

© ELLEN B. SENISI PHOTOGRAPHY

■ In this inclusive second-grade classroom, a teacher encourages a special-needs child to listen to his classmate read a story. The child is likely to do well if he receives support from a special education teacher and if his classroom teacher minimizes comparisons and promotes cooperative learning. ■

game. And the processing deficits of some learning-disabled students lead to problems in social awareness and responsiveness (Kelly & Norwich, 2004; Sridhar & Vaughn, 2001).

Does this mean that students with special needs cannot be served in regular classrooms? Not necessarily. Often these children do best when they receive instruction in a resource room for part of the day and in the regular classroom for the remainder (Weiner & Tardif, 2004). In the resource room, a special education teacher works with students on an individual and small-group basis. Then, depending on their progress, children join regular classmates for different subjects and amounts of time.

Special steps must be taken to promote positive peer relations in inclusive classrooms. Cooperative learning and peer-tutoring experiences in which teachers guide children with learning difficulties and their classmates in working together lead to friendly interaction, improved peer acceptance, and achievement gains (Fuchs et al., 2002a, 2002b). Teachers also can prepare their class for the arrival of a student with special needs. Under these conditions, inclusion may foster emotional sensitivity and prosocial behavior among regular classmates.

GIFTED CHILDREN   In Joey and Lizzie's school, some children were **gifted,** displaying exceptional intellectual strengths. One or two students in every grade have IQ scores above 130, the standard definition of giftedness based on intelligence test performance (Gardner, 1998). High-IQ children, as we have seen, have keen memories and an exceptional capacity to solve challenging academic problems. Yet recognition that intelligence tests do not sample the entire range of human mental skills, as noted earlier in this chapter, has led to an expanded conception of giftedness.

Creativity and Talent. **Creativity** is the ability to produce work that is *original* yet *appropriate*—something that others have not thought of that is useful in some way (Lubart, 2003; Sternberg, 2003). A child with high potential for creativity can be designated as gifted. Tests of creative capacity tap **divergent thinking**—the generation of multiple and unusual possibilities when faced with a task or problem. Divergent thinking contrasts sharply with **convergent thinking,** which involves arriving at a single correct answer and is emphasized on intelligence tests (Guilford, 1985).

Because highly creative children (like high-IQ children) are often better at some types of tasks than others, a variety of tests of divergent thinking are available (Runco, 1992; Torrance, 1988). A verbal measure might ask children to name uses for common objects (such as a newspaper). A figural measure might ask them to come up with drawings based on a circular motif (see Figure 12.8). A "real-world problem" measure requires students to suggest solutions to everyday problems. Responses can be scored for the number of ideas generated and their originality.

Yet critics point out that these measures are poor predictors of creative accomplishment in everyday life because they tap only one of the complex cognitive contributions to creativity. Also involved are defining new and important problems, evaluating divergent ideas, choosing the most promising, and calling on relevant knowledge to understand and solve problems (Sternberg, 2003b; Lubart, Georgsdottir, & Besançon, 2009).

Consider these ingredients, and you will see why people usually demonstrate expertise and creativity in only one or a few related areas. Even individuals designated as gifted by virtue of their high IQ often show uneven ability across academic subjects. Partly for this reason, definitions of giftedness have been extended to

FIGURE 12.8

Responses of an 8-year-old who scored high on a figural measure of divergent thinking. This child was asked to make as many pictures as she could from the circles on the page. The titles she gave her drawings, from left to right, are as follows: "Dracula," "one-eyed monster," "pumpkin," "Hula-Hoop," "poster," "wheelchair," "earth," "stop-light," "planet," "movie camera," "sad face," "picture," "beach ball," "the letter *O*," "car," "glasses." Tests of divergent thinking tap only one of the complex cognitive contributions to creativity. (Reprinted by permission of Laura Berk.)

include **talent**—outstanding performance in a specific field. Case studies reveal that excellence in such endeavors as creative writing, mathematics, science, music, visual arts, athletics, and leadership have roots in specialized skills that first appear in childhood (Moran & Gardner, 2006; Winner, 2003). Highly talented children are biologically prepared to master their domain of interest, and they display a passion for doing so.

But talent must be nurtured. Studies of the backgrounds of talented children and highly accomplished adults often reveal parents who are warm and sensitive, provide a stimulating home life, are devoted to developing their child's abilities, and provide models of hard work and high achievement. These parents are reasonably demanding but not driving or overambitious (Winner, 1996, 2000). They arrange for caring teachers while the child is young and for more rigorous master teachers as the child's talent develops.

Many gifted children and adolescents are socially isolated, partly because their highly driven, nonconforming, and independent styles leave them out of step with peers and partly because they enjoy solitude, which is necessary to develop their talents. Still, gifted children desire gratifying peer relationships, and some—more often girls than boys—try to become better-liked by hiding

■ These fourth graders collaborate in building a model lighthouse using modular construction materials. Challenging children to generate original solutions to problems helps nurture creativity. ■

their abilities. Compared with their ordinary agemates, gifted youths, especially girls, report more emotional and social difficulties, including low self-esteem and depression (Reis, 2004; Winner, 2000).

Finally, whereas many talented youths become experts in their fields and solve problems in new ways, few become highly creative. Rapidly mastering an existing field and thinking flexibly within it require different skills than innovating in that field. Gifted individuals who are restless with the status quo and daring about changing it are rare. And before these individuals become creative masters, they typically spend a decade or more becoming proficient in their field of interest (Moran & Gardner, 2006; Simonton, 2009). The world, however, needs both experts and creators.

Educating the Gifted. Gifted children thrive in learning environments that permit them to choose topics for extended projects, take intellectual risks, reflect on ideas, and interact with like-minded peers. When not sufficiently challenged, they sometimes lose their drive to excel. And when parents and teachers push them too hard, by adolescence they are likely to ask, "Who am I doing this for?" If the answer is not "myself," they may decide not to pursue their gift (Winner, 1997, 2000, p. 166).

Although many schools offer programs for the gifted, debate about their effectiveness usually focuses on factors irrelevant to giftedness—whether to provide enrichment in regular classrooms, to pull children out for special instruction (the most common practice), or to advance brighter students to a higher grade. Overall, gifted children fare well within each of these models, as long as the special activities provided do not reinforce academic convergent thinking to the detriment of problem solving, critical thinking, and creativity (Guignard & Lubart, 2007).

When gifted students enter selective educational settings, interventions aimed at protecting their self-esteem are crucial. In a study of more than 100,000 students in 26 countries, the more selective the high school, the lower students' academic self-esteem (Marsh & Hau, 2003). A top student in elementary school who enters a selective secondary school may suddenly find herself average or below average, with potentially detrimental effects on motivation and achievement.

Gardner's theory of multiple intelligences has inspired several model programs that provide enrichment to all students in diverse subjects, so any child capable of high-level performance can manifest it. Meaningful activities, each tapping a specific intelligence or set of intelligences, serve as contexts for assessing strengths and weaknesses and, on that basis, teaching new knowledge and original thinking (Gardner, 1993, 2000). For example, linguistic intelligence might be fostered through storytelling or playwriting; spatial intelligence through

Country	Average Math Achievement Score
High-Performing Nations	
Taiwan	549
Finland	548
Hong Kong	547
Korea, Republic of	547
Netherlands	531
Switzerland	530
Canada	527
Macao, China	525
Japan	523
New Zealand	522
Belgium	520
Australia	520
Intermediate-Performing Nations	
Denmark	513
Czech Republic	510
Iceland	506
Austria	505
Germany	504
Sweden	502
Ireland	501
France	496
United Kingdom	495
Poland	495
Hungary	491
Luxembourg	491
Norway	490
Spain	480
United States	**474**
Low-Performing Nations	
Portugal	466
Italy	462
Greece	459
Turkey	424

International Average = 498

FIGURE 12.9

Average mathematics scores of 15-year-olds by country. The Programme for International Student Assessment measured achievement in many nations around the world. The United States performed below the international average in math. Outcomes were similar in science. U.S. performance in reading was at the international average. *(Adapted from Programme for International Student Assessment, 2006.)*

drawing, sculpting, or taking apart and reassembling objects; and kinesthetic intelligence through dance or pantomime.

Evidence is still needed on how effectively these programs nurture children's talents. But so far, they have succeeded in one way—by highlighting the strengths of some students who previously had been considered unexceptional or even at risk for school failure (Kornhaber, 2004). Consequently, they may be especially useful in identifying talented low-SES, ethnic minority children, who are often underrepresented in programs for the gifted (McBee, 2006).

How Well-Educated Are U.S. Children?

Our discussion of schooling has largely focused on how teachers can support the education of children. Yet we have also seen that many factors—both within and outside schools—affect children's learning. Societal values, school resources, quality of teaching, and parental encouragement all play important roles. Nowhere are these multiple influences more apparent than when schooling is examined in cross-cultural perspective.

In international studies of reading, mathematics, and science achievement, young people in Hong Kong, Korea, and Japan are consistently top performers. Among Western nations, Canada, Finland, the Netherlands, and Switzerland are also in the top tier. But U.S. students typically perform at the international average, and sometimes below it (see Figure 12.9) (Programme for International Student Assessment, 2003, 2006).

Why do U.S. children fall behind in academic accomplishments? According to international comparisons, instruction in the United States is less challenging, more focused on absorbing facts, and less focused on high-level reasoning and critical thinking than in other countries. According to a growing number of experts, the U.S. No Child Left Behind Act has contributed to these trends because it mandates severe sanctions for schools whose students do not meet targeted goals on achievement tests—initially, student transfers to higher-performing schools; and ultimately, staff firing, closure, state takeover, or other restructuring (Darling-Hammond, 2010; Noguera, 2010; Ravitch, 2010). Furthermore, compared with top-achieving countries, the United States is far less equitable in the quality of education it provides to its low-income and ethnic minority students. And U.S. teachers vary much more in training, salaries, and teaching conditions.

OLIVIER MORIN/AFP/GETTY IMAGES/NEWSCOM

■ Finnish first graders get to know their teacher and classmates on the first day of school. They will benefit from a national education system designed to cultivate initiative, problem solving, and creativity. In international studies of academic achievement, Finland ranks among the best-performing nations. ■

Finland is a case in point. In the 1980s, it abandoned a national testing system used to ability-group students and replaced it with curricula, teaching practices, and assessments aimed at cultivating initiative, problem solving, and creativity—vital abilities needed for success in the twenty-first century. Finnish teachers are highly trained: They must complete several years of graduate-level education at government expense (Sahlberg, 2010). And Finnish education is grounded in equal opportunity for all—a policy that has nearly eliminated SES variations in achievement, despite an influx of immigrant students from low-income families into Finnish schools over the past decade.

In-depth research on learning environments in Asian nations, such as Japan, Korea, and Taiwan, also highlights social forces that foster strong student learning. Among these is cultural valuing of effort. Whereas American parents and teachers tend to regard native ability as the key to academic success, Japanese, Korean, and Taiwanese parents and teachers believe that all children can succeed academically as long as they try hard. Asian parents devote many more hours to helping their children with homework (Stevenson, Lee, & Mu, 2000). And Asian children, influenced by collectivist values, typically view striving to do well in school as a moral obligation—part of their responsibility to family and community.

As in Finland, all students in Japan, Korea, and Taiwan receive the same nationally mandated, high-quality instruction, delivered by teachers who are well-prepared, highly respected in their society, and far better paid than U.S. teachers (Kang & Hong, 2008; U.S. Department of Education, 2008). Academic lessons are particularly well-organized and presented in ways that capture children's attention and encourage high-level thinking (Grow-Maienza, Hahn, & Joo, 2001). And Japanese teachers are three times as likely as U.S. teachers to work outside class with students who need extra help (Woodward & Ono, 2004).

The Finnish and Asian examples underscore the need for American families, schools, and the larger society to work together to upgrade education. Over the past decade, U.S. international rankings in reading, math, and science achievement have declined. And following several decades of gains, from 1999 on the U.S. National Assessment of Educational Progress—in which challenging achievement tests are given to nationally representative samples of 9-, 13-, and 17-year-olds—showed only slight gains in reading and no improvement in math (U.S. Department of Education, 2008). These disappointing achievement outcomes underscore the need for "a broader, bolder approach to U.S. education." Recommended strategies, verified by research, include:

- providing intellectually challenging, relevant instruction with real-world applications
- strengthening teacher education
- supporting parents in creating stimulating home learning environments, monitoring their children's academic progress, and communicating often with teachers
- investing in high-quality preschool education, so every child arrives at school ready to learn
- vigorously pursuing school improvements that reduce the large inequities in quality of education between SES and ethnic groups (Economic Policy Institute, 2010).

ASK YOURSELF

◆ **REVIEW** List some teaching practices that foster children's academic achievement and some that undermine it. Provide a brief explanation of each practice.

◆ **APPLY** Sandy wonders why her daughter Mira's teacher often has students work on assignments in small, cooperative groups. Explain the benefits of this approach to Sandy. What must Mira's teacher do to ensure that cooperative learning succeeds?

◆ **CONNECT** Review research on child-rearing styles on pages 398–400 in Chapter 10. What style do gifted children who realize their potential typically experience? Explain.

◆ **REFLECT** What grouping practices were used in your elementary education—homogeneous, heterogeneous, or a combination? What impact do you think those practices had on your motivation and achievement?

Summary

Piaget's Theory: The Concrete Operational Stage

What are the major characteristics of concrete operational thought?

- In the **concrete operational stage,** children's thought becomes more logical, flexible, and organized. Mastery of conservation requires decentration and **reversibility** in thinking.

- School-age children are also better at hierarchical classification and **seriation,** including **transitive inference,** the ability to seriate mentally. Their spatial reasoning improves, as indicated by their understanding of **cognitive maps.**

Discuss follow-up research on concrete operational thought.

- Concrete operational children think logically only when dealing with concrete, tangible information, and mastery of concrete operational tasks occurs gradually. Specific cultural practices, especially those associated with schooling, promote mastery of Piagetian tasks.

- Some researchers attribute the gradual development of operational thought to gains in information-processing speed. Case's neo-Piagetian theory proposes that with practice, cognitive schemes demand less attention and become more automatic, freeing up space in working memory for combining old schemes and generating new ones. Eventually, children consolidate schemes into central conceptual structures and are increasingly able to coordinate and integrate multiple dimensions.

Information Processing

Cite basic changes in information processing, and describe the development of attention and memory in middle childhood.

- Brain development contributes to increases in processing speed and capacity and to gains in inhibition, facilitating many aspects of thinking.

- During middle childhood, attention becomes more sustained, selective, and adaptable. Attention (and memory) strategies develop in a four-step sequence: (1) **production deficiency** (failure to use the strategy); (2) **control deficiency** (failure to execute the strategy consistently); (3) **utilization deficiency** (consistent use of the strategy, but with little or no improvement in performance); and finally (4) **effective strategy use.**

- Children become better at planning, particularly when adults turn over responsibility to them and guide and support as needed.

- Deficits in executive processing and inhibition may underlie symptoms of **attention-deficit hyperactivity disorder (ADHD).** ADHD leads to serious academic and social problems.

- Memory strategies also improve. **Rehearsal** appears first, followed by **organization** and then **elaboration.** With age, children use several memory strategies at once.

- Development of the long-term knowledge base facilitates strategic memory processing. Children's motivation to use what they know also contributes. Memory strategies are not used by children in non-Western cultures who have no formal schooling.

Describe the school-age child's theory of mind and capacity to engage in self-regulation.

- Metacognition expands as school-age children view the mind as an active, constructive agent. Consequently, they better understand the process of thinking and factors that influence it. Awareness of the role of mental inferences enables mastery of second-order false belief. By the end of middle childhood, children grasp how interactions among variables—the learner's characteristics, use of strategies, and the task at hand—affect performance.

- **Cognitive self-regulation**—the ability to monitor progress toward a goal and redirect unsuccessful efforts— develops gradually. It improves with adult instruction in effective strategy use and predicts academic success.

Discuss current perspectives on teaching reading and mathematics to elementary school children.

- Skilled reading draws on all aspects of the information-processing system. A combination of **whole-language** and **phonics** is most effective for teaching beginning reading.

- Teaching that combines practice in basic skills with conceptual understanding also is best in mathematics. Students benefit from extensive opportunities to experiment with strategies and reason about number concepts.

Individual Differences in Mental Development

Describe major approaches to defining intelligence.

- During the school years, IQ becomes more stable and correlates moderately with academic achievement. Most intelligence tests yield an overall score as well as scores for separate intellectual factors. The *Stanford-Binet Intelligence Scales,* Fifth Edition, and the *Wechsler Intelligence Scale for Children–IV (WISC–IV)* are widely used individually administered intelligence tests.

- The componential approach to defining intelligence seeks to identify the inner, information- processing skills that contribute to mental test performance. Memory span, speed of thinking, and effective strategy use are positively related to IQ.

- Sternberg's **triarchic theory of successful intelligence** views intelligence as an interaction of analytical intelligence (information-processing skills), creative intelligence (ability to solve novel problems), and practical intelligence (application of intellectual skills in everyday situations).

- Gardner's **theory of multiple intelligences** identifies at least eight mental abilities, each with a distinct biological basis and course of development. It has been helpful in stimulating efforts to define, measure, and foster **emotional intelligence.**

Describe evidence indicating that both heredity and environment contribute to intelligence.

- Heritability estimates and adoption research reveal that intelligence is a product of both heredity and environment. Adoption studies indicate that the black–white IQ gap is substantially determined by environment. A dramatic generational increase in IQ also supports the role of environmental factors.

■ IQ scores are affected by culturally influenced communication styles, knowledge, and by sheer amount of time spent in school. **Stereotype threat** can trigger anxiety that impairs children's test performance. **Dynamic assessment** helps many minority children perform more competently on mental tests.

Language Development

Describe changes in metalinguistic awareness, vocabulary, grammar, and pragmatics during middle childhood.

■ Schooling, especially reading, contributes greatly to **metalinguistic awareness** and other complex language competencies. Vocabulary continues to grow rapidly, and children have a more precise and flexible understanding of word meanings. They also use more complex grammatical constructions and conversational strategies, and their narratives increase in organization, detail, and expressiveness.

What are the advantages of bilingualism in childhood?

■ Children who learn two languages in early childhood acquire each according to a typical timetable. When school-age children acquire a second language, they typically take 5 to 7 years to attain the competence of native-speaking agemates.

■ Bilingual children are advanced in cognitive development and metalinguistic awareness. They transfer their phonological awareness skills in one language to the other, which enhances reading achievement.

■ In Canada, language immersion programs succeed in developing children who are proficient in both English and French. While current public opinion and educational practice favor English-only instruction in the United States, bilingual education that combines instruction in the native language and in English supports non-English-speaking minority children's academic learning.

Children's Learning in School

Describe the impact of class size and educational philosophies on children's motivation and academic achievement.

■ As class size declines, academic achievement improves. Older students in **traditional classrooms** have a slight edge in academic achievement over those in **constructivist classrooms,** who gain in academic motivation, critical thinking, and social and moral maturity.

■ Vygotsky-inspired **social-constructivist classrooms** use the rich social context of the classroom to promote learning, often employing such methods as **reciprocal teaching** and **communities of learners.** Students benefit from working collaboratively and from teaching adapted to each child's zone of proximal development.

Discuss the role of teacher–student interaction and grouping practices in academic achievement.

■ Caring, helpful, and stimulating teaching fosters children's interest, involvement, and academic achievement. **Educational self-fulfilling prophecies** have a greater impact on low achievers and are most likely to occur in homogenous classrooms and ones that emphasize competition and public evaluation.

■ The heterogeneous context of multigrade classrooms promotes academic achievement, self-esteem, and positive school attitudes. To benefit from collaboration with heterogeneous peers, children need extensive training in **cooperative learning.** Ethnically diverse magnet schools are also associated with higher achievement.

Describe educational benefits of computer use as well as concerns about computers.

■ Using the computer for schoolwork, typically to search the Web for information and to prepare written assignments, is linked to improved academic achievement. However, low-SES children are disadvantaged in computer and Internet use, and boys tend to be more skilled at complex computer activities than girls.

Under what conditions is placement of mildly mentally retarded and learning disabled children in regular classrooms successful?

■ Students with mild mental retardation and **learning disabilities** are often placed in **inclusive classrooms** where they learn alongside typical students. Success depends on meeting individual academic needs and promoting positive peer relations.

Describe the characteristics of gifted children and efforts to meet their educational needs.

■ **Giftedness** includes high IQ, **creativity,** and **talent.** Tests of creativity that tap **divergent thinking** rather than **convergent thinking** focus on only one of the complex cognitive ingredients of creativity. Many gifted children, especially girls, report emotional and social difficulties.

■ Gifted children have parents and teachers who nurture their extraordinary ability. They are best served by educational programs that build on their special strengths.

© JEFF MORGAN EDUCATION/ALAMY

How well-educated are U.S. children compared with children in other industrialized nations?

■ In international studies, U.S. students typically display average or below-average performance. Compared with education in top-achieving countries, U.S. instruction is less focused on high-level reasoning and critical thinking. Whereas high-achieving nations emphasize equal opportunity for all, U.S. low-income and ethnic minority students typically attend inferior-quality schools.

IMPORTANT TERMS AND CONCEPTS

attention-deficit hyperactivity disorder (ADHD) (p. 444)
cognitive maps (p. 438)
cognitive self-regulation (p. 449)
communities of learners (p. 469)
concrete operational stage (p. 438)
constructivist classroom (p. 467)
control deficiency (p. 443)
convergent thinking (p. 474)
cooperative learning (p. 471)
creativity (p. 474)
divergent thinking (p. 474)
dynamic assessment (p. 461)

educational self-fulfilling prophecies (p. 470)
effective strategy use (p. 443)
elaboration (p. 446)
emotional intelligence (p. 457)
gifted (p. 474)
inclusive classrooms (p. 473)
learning disabilities (p. 473)
metalinguistic awareness (p. 462)
organization (p. 446)
phonics approach (p. 450)
production deficiency (p. 443)
reciprocal teaching (p. 468)

rehearsal (p. 446)
reversibility (p. 438)
seriation (p. 438)
social-constructivist classroom (p. 468)
stereotype threat (p. 460)
talent (p. 475)
theory of multiple intelligences (p. 456)
traditional classroom (p. 467)
transitive inference (p. 438)
triarchic theory of successful intelligence (p. 455)
utilization deficiency (p. 443)
whole-language approach (p. 450)

Untitled

Sarah Andreassen

12 years, Norway

As this artist's upbeat, imaginative portrayal suggests, school-age children become capable of viewing themselves and others from diverse perspectives—a change that contributes to an improved understanding of one's own and others' traits and competencies, a more flexible grasp of moral obligations, declining racial and ethnic prejudices, and deepening friendships.

Reprinted with permission from the International Museum of Children's Art, Oslo, Norway

Emotional and Social Development in Middle Childhood

*L*ate one afternoon, Rena heard her son Joey burst through the front door, run upstairs, and phone his best friend Terry. "Terry, gotta talk to you," Joey pleaded breathlessly. "Everything was going great until I got that word—*porcupine,*" Joey went on, referring to the fifth-grade spelling bee at school that day. "Just my luck! *P-o-r-k,* that's how I spelled it! I can't believe it. Maybe I'm not so good at social studies," Joey confided, "but I *know* I'm better at spelling than that stuck-up Belinda Brown. I knocked myself out studying those spelling lists. Then *she* got all the easy words. If I *had* to lose, why couldn't it be to a nice person?"

Joey's conversation reflects new emotional and social capacities. By entering the spelling bee, he shows *industriousness,* the energetic pursuit of meaningful achievement in his culture—a major change of middle childhood. Joey's social understanding has also expanded. He can size up strengths, weaknesses, and personality characteristics. Furthermore, friendship means something different to Joey than it did earlier—he counts on his best friend, Terry, for understanding and emotional support.

For an overview of the personality changes of middle childhood, we return to Erikson's theory. Then we look at children's views of themselves and of others, their moral understanding, and their peer relationships. Each increases in complexity as children reason more effectively and spend more time in school and with agemates.

Despite changing parent–child relationships, the family remains powerfully influential in middle childhood. Today, family lifestyles are more diverse than ever before. Through Joey's and his younger sister Lizzie's experiences with parental divorce, we will see that family functioning is far more important than family structure in ensuring children's well-being. Finally, we look at some common emotional problems of middle childhood.

Erikson's Theory: Industry versus Inferiority

Self-Understanding
Self-Concept • Cognitive, Social, and Cultural Influences on Self-Concept • Self-Esteem • Influences on Self-Esteem

Emotional Development
Self-Conscious Emotions • Emotional Understanding • Emotional Self-Regulation

Understanding Others: Perspective Taking

Moral Development
Moral and Social-Conventional Understanding • Understanding Individual Rights • Culture and Moral Understanding • Understanding Diversity and Inequality

■ **CULTURAL INFLUENCES**
Children's Understanding of God

Peer Relations
Peer Groups • Friendships • Peer Acceptance

■ **BIOLOGY AND ENVIRONMENT**
Bullies and Their Victims

Gender Typing
Gender-Stereotyped Beliefs • Gender Identity and Behavior

Family Influences
Parent–Child Relationships • Siblings • Only Children • Gay and Lesbian Families • Never-Married Single-Parent Families • Divorce • Blended Families • Maternal Employment and Dual-Earner Families

Some Common Problems of Development
Fears and Anxieties • Child Sexual Abuse • Fostering Resilience in Middle Childhood

■ **CULTURAL INFLUENCES**
The Impact of Ethnic and Political Violence on Children

■ **SOCIAL ISSUES: HEALTH**
Children's Eyewitness Testimony

Erikson's Theory: Industry versus Inferiority

According to Erikson (1950), children whose previous experiences have been positive enter middle childhood prepared to redirect their energies from the make-believe of early childhood into realistic accomplishment. Erikson believed that the combination of adult expectations and children's drive toward mastery sets the stage for the psychological conflict of middle childhood: **industry versus inferiority,** which is resolved positively when experiences lead children to develop a sense of competence at useful skills and tasks.

In cultures everywhere, adults respond to children's improved physical and cognitive capacities by making new demands, and children are ready to benefit from those challenges. Among the Baka hunters and gatherers of Cameroon, 5- to 7-year-olds fetch and carry water, bathe and mind younger siblings, and accompany adults on food-gathering missions. In a miniature village behind the main camp, children practice hut building, spear shaping, and fire making (Avis & Harris, 1991). The Ngoni of Malawi, Central Africa, believe that when children shed their first teeth, they are mature enough for intensive skill training. Six and 7-year-old boys move out of family huts into dormitories, where they enter a system of male domination and instruction. All children of this age are expected to show independence and are held accountable for irresponsible and disrespectful behavior (Rogoff, 1996).

In industrialized nations, the beginning of formal schooling marks the transition to middle childhood. With it comes literacy training, which prepares children for a vast array of specialized careers. In school, children discover their own and others' unique capacities, learn the value of division of labor, and develop a sense of moral commitment and responsibility. The danger at this stage is *inferiority,* reflected in the pessimism of children who have little confidence in their ability to do things well. This sense of inadequacy can develop when family life has not prepared children for school life or when teachers and peers destroy children's feelings of competence and mastery with negative responses.

Erikson's sense of industry combines several developments of middle childhood: a positive but realistic self-concept, pride in accomplishment, moral responsibility, and cooperative participation with agemates. How do these aspects of self and social relationships change over the school years?

■ The industriousness of middle childhood involves mastery of useful skills and tasks. As they practice bow-hunting skills, these young members of the Pokot people of Kenya develop a sense of competence at an important adult activity in their culture. ■

Self-Understanding

In middle childhood, children become able to describe themselves in terms of psychological traits, to compare their own characteristics with those of their peers, and to speculate about the causes of their strengths and weaknesses. These transformations in self-understanding have a major impact on children's self-esteem.

Self-Concept

During the school years, children refine their self-concept, organizing their observations of behaviors and internal states into general dispositions. A major change takes place between ages 8 and 11, as the following self-description by an 11-year-old illustrates:

My name is A. I'm a human being. I'm a girl. I'm a truthful person. I'm not pretty. I do so-so in my studies. I'm a very good cellist. I'm a very good pianist. I'm a little bit tall for my age. I like several boys. I like several girls. I'm old-fashioned. I play tennis. I am a very good swimmer. I try to be helpful. I'm always ready to be friends with anybody. Mostly I'm good, but I lose my temper. I'm not well liked by some girls and boys. I don't know if I'm liked by boys or not. (Montemayor & Eisen, 1977, pp. 317–318)

Instead of specific behaviors, this child emphasizes competencies: "a very good cellist," "so-so in my studies" (Damon & Hart, 1988). She also describes her personality, mentioning both positive and negative traits: "truthful" but short-tempered. Older school-age children are far less likely than younger children to describe themselves in extreme, all-or-none ways (Harter, 2003, 2006).

These evaluative self-descriptions result from school-age children's frequent **social comparisons**—judgments of their appearance, abilities, and behavior in relation to those of others. For example, Joey observed that he was "better at spelling" than his peers but "not so good at social studies." Whereas 4- to 6-year-olds can compare their own performance to that of a single peer, older children can compare multiple individuals, including themselves (Butler, 1998; Harter, 2006).

Cognitive, Social, and Cultural Influences on Self-Concept

What factors account for these revisions in self-concept? Cognitive development affects the changing *structure* of the self. School-age children, as we saw in Chapter 12, can better coordinate several aspects of a situation in reasoning about their physical world. Similarly, in the social realm, they combine typical experiences and behaviors into stable psychological dispositions, blend positive and negative characteristics, and compare their own characteristics with those of many peers (Harter, 2003, 2006). In middle childhood, children also gain a clearer understanding that traits are linked to specific desires (a "generous" person *wants* to share) and, therefore, are causes of behavior (Yuill & Pearson, 1998).

The changing *content* of self-concept is a product of both cognitive capacities and feedback from others. Sociologist George Herbert Mead (1934) proposed that a well-organized psychological self emerges when children adopt a view of the self that resembles others' attitudes toward the child. Mead's ideas indicate that *perspective-taking skills*—in particular, an improved ability to infer what other people are thinking—are crucial for developing a self-concept based on personality traits. School-age children become better at "reading" others' messages and internalizing their expectations. As they do so, they form an *ideal self* that they use to evaluate their real self. As we will see, a large discrepancy between the two can greatly undermine self-esteem, leading to sadness, hopelessness, and depression.

Parental support for self-development continues to be vitally important. School-age children with a history of elaborative parent–child conversations about past experiences construct a rich, positive narrative about the self and thus have more complex, favorable, and coherent self-concepts (Harter, 2006). In middle childhood, children also look to more people beyond the family for information about themselves as they enter a wider range of settings in school and community. And self-descriptions now include frequent reference to social groups: "I'm a Boy Scout, a paper boy, and a Prairie City soccer player," said Joey. As children move into adolescence, their sources of self-definition become more selective. Although parents and other adults remain influential, self-concept is increasingly vested in feedback from close friends (Oosterwegel & Openheimer, 1993).

But recall that the content of self-concept varies from culture to culture. In earlier chapters, we noted that Asian parents stress harmonious interdependence, whereas Western parents emphasize independence and self-assertion. When asked to recall personally significant past experiences (their last birthday, a time their parent scolded them), U.S. school-age children gave longer accounts including more personal preferences, interests, skills, and opinions. Chinese children, in contrast, more often referred to social interactions and to others rather than themselves. Similarly, in their self-descriptions, U.S. children listed more personal attributes ("I'm smart," "I like hockey"), Chinese children more attributes involving group membership and relationships with others ("I'm in second grade," "My friends are crazy about me") (Wang, 2004, 2006b).

LOOK AND LISTEN

Ask several 8- to 11-year-old children to tell you about themselves. Do their self-descriptions include personality traits (both positive and negative), social comparisons, and references to social groups, as is typical in middle childhood?

Strong collectivist values also exist in many subcultures in Western nations. In one study, Puerto Rican children in a small fishing village described themselves as "polite," "respectful," and "obedient" more often than U.S. small-town children; they justified these social traits by noting others' positive reactions to them (Damon & Hart, 1988).

Self-Esteem

Recall that most preschoolers have extremely high self-esteem. But as children enter school and receive much more feedback about how well they perform compared with their peers, self-esteem differentiates and also adjusts to a more realistic level.

A HIERARCHICALLY STRUCTURED SELF-ESTEEM   Researchers have asked children to indicate the extent to which statements such as "I'm good at reading" or "I'm usually the one chosen for games" are true of themselves. By age 6 to 7, children in diverse Western cultures have formed at least four broad self-evaluations: academic competence, social competence, physical/athletic competence, and physical appearance. Within these are more refined categories that become increasingly distinct with age (Marsh, 1990; Marsh & Ayotte, 2003; Van den Bergh & De Rycke, 2003). Furthermore, the capacity to view the self in terms of stable dispositions permits school-age children to combine their separate self-evaluations into a general psychological image of themselves—an overall sense of self-esteem (Harter, 2003, 2006). As a result, self-esteem takes on the hierarchical structure shown in Figure 13.1.

Children attach greater importance to certain self-evaluations than to others, giving them more weight in the total picture. Although individual differences exist, during childhood and adolescence perceived physical appearance correlates more strongly with overall self-worth than does any other self-esteem factor (Klomsten, Skaalvik, & Espnes, 2004; Shapka & Keating, 2005). Emphasis on appearance—in the media, by parents and peers, and in society—has major implications for young people's overall satisfaction with themselves.

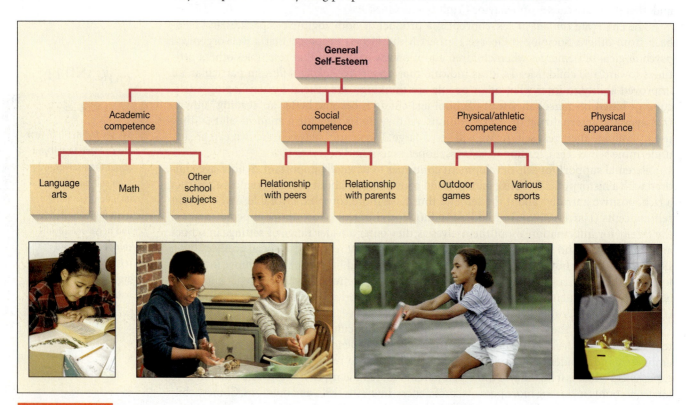

FIGURE 13.1

Hierarchical structure of self-esteem in the mid-elementary school years. From their experiences in different settings, children form at least four separate self-esteems: academic competence, social competence, physical/athletic competence, and physical appearance. These differentiate into additional self-evaluations and combine to form a general sense of self-esteem. *(Photos from left to right: © 2004 Laura Dwight Photography; © George Disario/Corbis; © Mitch Wojnarowicz/The Image Works; © Radius Images/Photolibrary.)*

CHANGES IN LEVEL OF SELF-ESTEEM   Self-esteem declines during the first few years of elementary school as children evaluate themselves in various areas (Marsh, Craven, & Debus, 1998; Wigfield et al., 1997). This decline occurs as children receive more competence-related feedback, as their performances are increasingly judged in relation to those of others, and as they become cognitively capable of social comparison.

To protect their self-worth, children eventually balance social comparisons with personal achievement goals (Ruble & Flett, 1988). Perhaps for this reason, the drop in self-esteem in the early school years usually is not harmful. Then, from fourth grade on, self-esteem rises for the majority of young people, who feel especially good about their peer relationships and athletic capabilities (Cole et al., 2001; Twenge & Campbell, 2001).

Influences on Self-Esteem

From middle childhood on, individual differences in self-esteem become increasingly stable (Trzesniewski, Donnellan, & Robins, 2003). And positive relationships among self-esteem, valuing of various activities, and success at those activities emerge and strengthen with age. Academic self-esteem predicts how important, useful, and enjoyable children judge school subjects to be, their willingness to try hard, and their achievement (Denissen, Zarrett, & Eccles, 2007; Valentine, DuBois, & Cooper, 2004). Children with high social self-esteem are consistently better-liked by classmates (Jacobs et al., 2002). And as we saw in Chapter 11, sense of athletic competence is positively associated with investment and performance in sports.

Furthermore, across age, sex, SES, and ethnic groups, individuals with favorable self-esteem tend to be well-adjusted, sociable, and conscientious. In contrast, a profile of low self-esteem in all areas is linked to anxiety, depression, and antisocial behavior (DuBois et al., 1999; Kim & Cicchetti, 2006; Robins et al., 2001).

CULTURE   Cultural forces profoundly affect self-esteem. An especially strong emphasis on social comparison in school may explain why Chinese and Japanese children, despite their higher academic achievement, score lower than U.S. children in self-esteem—a difference that widens with age (Harter, 2006; Hawkins, 1994; Twenge & Crocker, 2002). In Asian classrooms, competition is tough, and achievement pressure is high. At the same time, because their culture values modesty and social harmony, Asian children rely less on social comparisons to promote their own self-esteem. Rather, they tend to be reserved about judging themselves positively but generous in their praise of others (Falbo et al., 1997).

Gender-stereotyped beliefs also affect self-esteem. In one study, the more 5- to 8-year-old girls talked with friends about they way people look, watched TV shows focusing on physical appearance, and perceived their friends as valuing thinness, the greater their dissatisfaction with their physical self and the lower their overall self-esteem a year later (Dohnt & Tiggemann, 2006). By the end of middle childhood, girls feel less confident than boys about their physical appearance and athletic abilities. With respect to academic self-esteem, boys, again, are somewhat advantaged: Whereas girls score higher in language-arts self-esteem, boys have higher math and science self-esteem—even when children of equal skill levels are compared (Fredricks & Eccles, 2002; Jacobs et al., 2002; Kurtz-Costes et al., 2008). At the same time, girls exceed boys in self-esteem dimensions of close friendship and social acceptance.

Although only a slight difference exists between boys and girls in overall self-esteem, a widely held assumption is that boys' overall sense of self-worth is much higher than girls' (Cole et al., 2001; Marsh & Ayotte, 2003; Young & Mroczek, 2003). Girls may think less well of themselves because they internalize this negative cultural message.

Compared with their Caucasian agemates, African-American children tend to have slightly higher self-esteem, perhaps because of warm extended families and a stronger sense of ethnic pride (Gray-Little & Hafdahl, 2000). Finally, children and adolescents who attend schools or live in neighborhoods

■ An 11-year-old performs a traditional African dance at a community Kwanzaa celebration. A stronger sense of ethnic pride may be partly responsible for African-American children's higher self-esteem relative to their Caucasian agemates. ■

where their SES and ethnic groups are well-represented feel a stronger sense of belonging and have fewer self-esteem problems (Gray-Little & Carels, 1997).

CHILD-REARING PRACTICES   Children whose parents use an *authoritative* child-rearing style (see Chapter 10) feel especially good about themselves (Carolson, Uppal, & Prosser, 2000; Rudy & Grusec, 2006; Wilkinson, 2004). Warm, positive parenting lets children know that they are accepted as competent and worthwhile. And firm but appropriate expectations, backed up with explanations, help them evaluate their own behavior against reasonable standards.

Controlling parents—those who too often help or make decisions for their child—communicate a sense of inadequacy to children. Having parents who are repeatedly disapproving and insulting is also linked to low self-esteem (Kernis, 2002; Pomerantz & Eaton, 2000). Children subjected to such parenting need constant reassurance, and many rely heavily on peers to affirm their self-worth—a risk factor for adjustment difficulties, including aggression and antisocial behavior (Donellan et al., 2005). In contrast, indulgent parenting is correlated with unrealistically high self-esteem, which also undermines development. These children tend to lash out at challenges to their overblown self-images and, as a result, are also likely to be hostile and aggressive (Hughes, Cavell, & Grossman, 1997; Thomaes, Stegge, & Olthof, 2007).

American cultural values have increasingly emphasized a focus on the self that may lead parents to indulge children and boost their self-esteem too much. The self-esteem of U.S. youths rose sharply from the 1970s to the 1990s—a period in which much popular parenting literature advised promoting children's self-esteem (Twenge & Campbell, 2001). Yet compared with previous generations, American youths are achieving less well and displaying more antisocial behavior and other adjustment problems (Berk, 2005). Research confirms that children do not benefit from compliments ("You're terrific") that have no basis in real accomplishment (Damon, 1995). Rather, the best way to foster a positive, secure self-image is to encourage children to strive for worthwhile goals. Over time, a bidirectional relationship emerges: Achievement fosters self-esteem, which contributes to further effort and gains in performance (Gest, Domitrovich, & Welsh, 2005; Marsh et al., 2005).

What can adults do to promote, and to avoid undermining, this mutually supportive relationship between motivation and self-esteem? Some answers come from research on the precise content of adults' messages to children in achievement situations. Let's look first at the meanings children assign to their successes and failures.

ACHIEVEMENT-RELATED ATTRIBUTIONS   *Attributions* are our common, everyday explanations for the causes of behavior—our answers to the question, "Why did I or another person do that?" Notice how Joey, in talking about the spelling bee at the beginning of this chapter, attributes his disappointing performance to *luck* (Belinda got all the easy words) and his usual success to *ability* (he *knows* he's a better speller than Belinda). Joey also appreciates that *effort* matters: "I knocked myself out studying those spelling lists."

The combination of improved reasoning skills and frequent evaluative feedback permits 10- to 12-year-olds to separate all these variables in explaining performance (Dweck, 2002). Those who are high in academic self-esteem and motivation make **mastery-oriented attributions,** crediting their successes to ability—a characteristic they can improve by trying hard and can count on when faced with new challenges. This *incremental view of ability*—that it can increase—influences the way mastery-oriented children interpret negative events. They attribute failure to factors that can be changed and controlled, such as insufficient effort or a difficult task (Heyman &

■ Mastery-oriented children credit their successes to ability, and they seek information on how to increase their ability through effort. As a result, their performance improves over time. ■

© LAURA DWIGHT PHOTOGRAPHY

Dweck, 1998). So whether these children succeed or fail, they take an industrious, persistent approach to learning.

In contrast, children who develop **learned helplessness** attribute their failures, not their successes, to ability. When they succeed, they are likely to conclude that external factors, such as luck, are responsible. Unlike their mastery-oriented counterparts, they hold a *fixed view of ability*—that it cannot be improved by trying hard (Cain & Dweck, 1995). When a task is difficult, these children experience an anxious loss of control—in Erikson's terms, a pervasive sense of inferiority. They give up without really trying.

Children's attributions affect their goals. Mastery-oriented children focus on *learning goals*—seeking information on how best to increase their ability through effort. Hence, their performance improves over time (Blackwell, Trzesniewski, & Dweck, 2007). In contrast, learned-helpless children focus on *performance goals*—obtaining positive and avoiding negative evaluations of their fragile sense of ability. Over time, their ability no longer predicts how well they do. In one study, the more fourth to sixth graders held self-critical attributions, the lower they rated their competence, the less they knew about effective study strategies, the more they avoided challenge, and the poorer their academic performance. These outcomes strengthened their fixed view of ability (Pomerantz & Saxon, 2001). Because learned-helpless children fail to connect effort with success, they do not develop the metacognitive and self-regulatory skills necessary for high achievement (see Chapter 12). Lack of effective learning strategies, reduced persistence, and a sense of loss of control sustain one another in a vicious cycle (Chan & Moore, 2006).

INFLUENCES ON ACHIEVEMENT-RELATED ATTRIBUTIONS   What accounts for the different attributions of mastery-oriented and learned-helpless children? Adult communication plays a key role. When parents hold a fixed view of ability, their perceptions of children's academic competence tend to act as self-fulfilling prophecies (see page 470 in Chapter 12). Their children's self-evaluations and school grades conform more closely to parental ability judgments than do those of children whose parents deny that ability is fixed (Pomerantz & Dong, 2006). Parents who believe that little can be done to improve ability may ignore information that is inconsistent with their perceptions, giving their child little opportunity to counteract a negative parental evaluation.

Indeed, children with a learned-helpless style often have parents who believe that their child is not very capable and must work much harder than others to succeed. When the child fails, the parent might say, "You can't do that, can you? It's OK if you quit" (Hokoda & Fincham, 1995). When the child succeeds, the parent might offer feedback that evaluates the child's traits ("You're so smart"). Such trait statements—even when positive—encourage children to adopt a fixed view of ability, which leads them to question their competence in the face of setbacks and to retreat from challenge (Mueller & Dweck, 1998).

Teachers' messages also affect children's attributions. Teachers who are caring and helpful and who emphasize learning over getting good grades tend to have mastery-oriented students (Anderman et al., 2001). In a study of third to eighth graders, students who viewed their teachers as providing positive, supportive learning conditions worked harder and participated more in class—factors that predicted high achievement, which sustained children's belief in the role of effort. In contrast, students with unsupportive teachers regarded their performance as externally controlled (by their teachers or by luck). This attitude predicted withdrawal from learning activities and declining achievement—outcomes that led children to doubt their ability (Skinner, Zimmer-Gembeck, & Connell, 1998).

For some children, performance is especially likely to be undermined by adult feedback. Despite their higher achievement, girls more often than boys attribute poor performance to lack of ability. When girls do not do well, they tend to receive messages from teachers and parents that their ability is at fault, and negative stereotypes (for example, that girls are weak at math) undermine their interest and performance (Bleeker & Jacobs, 2004; Cole et al., 1999). And as Chapter 12 revealed, low-SES, ethnic-minority students often receive less favorable feedback from teachers, especially when assigned to homogeneous groups of poorly achieving students—conditions that result in a drop in academic self-esteem and achievement (Harris & Graham, 2007; Ogbu, 1997).

LOOK AND LISTEN

Observe a school-age child working on a challenging homework assignment under the guidance of a parent or other adult. What features of the adult's communication likely foster mastery-oriented attributions? How about learned helplessness? Explain.

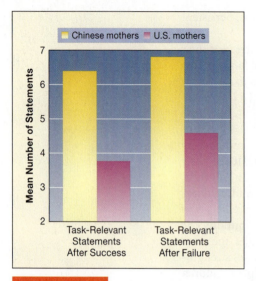

FIGURE 13.2

Chinese and U.S. mothers' task-relevant statements in response to their fourth-grade child's success or failure on puzzle tasks. Observations revealed that regardless of whether their child had just succeeded or failed, Chinese mothers were more likely than U.S. mothers to make task-relevant statements aimed at ensuring that the child exerted high effort. *(Adapted from Ng, Pomerantz, & Lam, 2007.)*

Finally, cultural values affect the likelihood that children will develop learned helplessness. Asian parents and teachers are more likely than their American counterparts to hold an incremental view of ability (see page 476 in Chapter 12). Because of the high value they place on effort and self-improvement, Asians attend more to failure than to success because failure indicates where corrective action is needed. Americans, in contrast, focus more on success because it enhances self-esteem. Observations of U.S. and Chinese mothers' responses to their fourth and fifth graders' puzzle solutions revealed that the U.S. mothers offered more praise after success, whereas the Chinese mothers more often pointed out the child's inadequate performance. And regardless of success or failure, Chinese mothers made more task-relevant statements aimed at ensuring that children exerted sufficient effort to do well ("You concentrated on it"; "You got only 6 out of 12") (see Figure 13.2). When children continued with the task after mothers left the room, the Chinese children showed greater gains in performance (Ng, Pomerantz, & Lam, 2007).

FOSTERING A MASTERY-ORIENTED APPROACH Attribution research suggests that well-intended messages from adults sometimes undermine children's competence. An intervention called **attribution retraining** encourages learned-helpless children to believe they can overcome failure by exerting more effort. Children are given tasks difficult enough that they will experience some failure, followed by repeated feedback that helps them revise their attributions: "You can do it if you try harder." After they succeed, children are given additional feedback—"You're really good at this" or "You really tried hard on that one"—so that they attribute their success to both ability and effort, not chance. Another approach is to encourage low-effort children to focus less on grades and more on mastering a task for its own sake (Hilt, 2004; Horner & Gaither, 2004). Instruction in effective strategies and self-regulation is also vital, to compensate for development lost in this area and to ensure that renewed effort pays off (Wigfield et al., 2006).

Attribution retraining is best begun in middle childhood, before children's views of themselves become hard to change. School-age children with low academic self-esteem whose parents regularly used mastery-oriented practices while helping with homework had gained in sense of academic competence, willingness to try hard on difficult tasks, and positive emotion six months later (Pomerantz, Ng, & Wang, 2006). An even better approach is to prevent learned helplessness, using strategies summarized in Applying What We Know on the following page.

ASK YOURSELF

◆ **REVIEW** How does level of self-esteem change in middle childhood, and what accounts for these changes?

◆ **APPLY** Should parents promote children's self-esteem by telling them they're "smart" or "wonderful"? Are children harmed if they do not feel good about everything they do? Why or why not?

◆ **CONNECT** What cognitive changes, described in Chapter 12 (page 441), support the transition to a self-concept emphasizing competencies, personality traits, and social comparisons?

◆ **REFLECT** Recall your own attributions for academic successes and failures when you were in elementary school. What are those attributions like now? What messages from others may have contributed to your attributions?

Applying What We Know

Fostering a Mastery-Oriented Approach to Learning

STRATEGY	DESCRIPTION
Provision of tasks	Select tasks that are meaningful, responsive to a diversity of student interests, and appropriately matched to current competence so that the child is challenged but not overwhelmed.
Parent and teacher encouragement	Communicate warmth, confidence in the child's abilities, the value of achievement, and the importance of effort in success. Model high effort in overcoming failure. (For teachers) Communicate often with parents, suggesting ways to foster children's effort and progress. (For parents) Monitor schoolwork; provide scaffolded assistance that promotes knowledge of effective strategies and self-regulation.
Performance evaluations	Make evaluations private; avoid publicizing success or failure through wall posters, stars, privileges to "smart" children, and prizes for "best" performance. Emphasize individual progress and self-improvement.
School environment	Offer small classes, which permit teachers to provide individualized support for mastery. Provide for cooperative learning (see page 470 in Chapter 12) and peer tutoring, in which children assist one another; avoid ability grouping, which makes evaluations of children's progress public. Accommodate individual and cultural differences in styles of learning. Create an atmosphere that sends a clear message that all pupils can learn.

Sources: Hilt, 2004; Wigfield et al., 2006.

Emotional Development

Greater self-awareness and social sensitivity support gains in emotional competence in middle childhood. Gains take place in experience of self-conscious emotions, emotional understanding, and emotional self-regulation.

Self-Conscious Emotions

As children integrate social expectations into their self-concepts, self-conscious emotions of pride and guilt become clearly governed by personal responsibility. Unlike preschoolers, school-age children experience pride in a new accomplishment and guilt over a transgression even when no adult is present (Harter & Whitesell, 1989). Also, children no longer report guilt for any mishap, as they did earlier, but only for intentional wrongdoing, such as ignoring responsibilities, cheating, or lying (Ferguson, Stegge, & Damhuis, 1991). These changes reflect the older child's more mature sense of morality, a topic addressed later in this chapter.

When school-age children feel pride or guilt, they view specific aspects of the self as leading to success or failure: "I tried hard on that difficult task, and it paid off" (pride) or "I made a mistake, and now I have to deal with it" (guilt). They tend to feel shame when their violation of a standard is not under their control (Lewis & Ramsay, 2002; Saarni et al., 2006). For example, Lizzie felt ashamed when she dropped a spoonful of spaghetti and had a large spot on her shirt for the rest of the school day. But as children develop an overall sense of self-esteem, they may also experience shame after a controllable breach of standards if someone blames them for it (Harter, 1999, 2006; Mascolo & Fischer, 1995). For example, the child who does poorly on a test and whose teacher or

■ If this child reacts with guilt to wrongdoing, he is likely to make amends. But adult blame and criticism may cause him to experience intense shame, leading to depression, anger, and a sharp drop in self-esteem. ■

parent reprimands him ("Everyone else can do it! Why can't you?") may hang his head in shame while repeating to himself, "I'm stupid! I'm a terrible kid!"

Pride motivates children to take on further challenges, whereas guilt prompts them to make amends and to strive for self-improvement. But profound feelings of shame (as noted in Chapter 10) are particularly destructive. A sharp, shame-induced drop in self-esteem can trigger withdrawal and depression or intense anger at those who participated in the shame-evoking situation (Lindsay-Hartz, de Rivera, & Mascolo, 1995; Mills, 2005).

Emotional Understanding

School-age children's understanding of mental activity means that, unlike preschoolers, they are likely to explain emotion by referring to internal states, such as happy or sad thoughts, rather than to external events (Flavell, Flavell, & Green, 2001). Also, between ages 6 and 12, children become more aware of circumstances likely to spark mixed emotions, each of which

may be positive or negative and may differ in intensity, and they increasingly report experiencing more than one emotion at a time (Larsen, To, & Fireman, 2007; Pons et al., 2003). For example, recalling the birthday present he received from his grandmother, Joey reflected, "I was very happy I got something but a little sad that I didn't get just what I wanted."

Appreciating mixed emotions helps children realize that people's expressions may not reflect their true feelings (Misailidi, 2006; Saarni, 1999). It also fosters awareness of self-conscious emotions. For example, between ages 6 and 7, children improve sharply in ability to distinguish pride from happiness and surprise (Tracy, Robins, & Lagattuta, 2005). And 8- and 9-year-olds understand that pride combines two sources of happiness—joy in accomplishment and joy that a significant person recognized that accomplishment (Harter, 1999).

■ Detroit-area school-age children prepare meal packages for families in need. Gains in emotional understanding and perspective taking enable children to respond with empathy to people's general life condition. ■

Furthermore, children of this age can reconcile contradictory facial and situational cues in figuring out another's feelings. And they can use information about "what might have happened" to predict how people will feel in a new situation—realizing, for example, that someone will feel a sense of relief when an actual outcome is more favorable than what might have occurred (Guttentag & Ferrell, 2004).

As with self-understanding, gains in emotional understanding are supported by cognitive development and social experiences, especially adults' sensitivity to children's feelings and willingness to discuss emotions. Together, these factors contribute to a rise in empathy as well. As children move closer to adolescence, advances in perspective taking permit an empathic response not just to people's immediate distress but also to their general life condition (Hoffman, 2000). As at early ages, emotional understanding and empathy are linked to favorable social relationships and prosocial behavior (Schultz et al., 2001). As Joey and Lizzie imagined how people who are chronically ill or hungry feel and evoked those emotions in themselves, they gave part of their allowance to charity and joined in fundraising projects through school, community center, and scouting.

Emotional Self-Regulation

Rapid gains in emotional self-regulation occur in middle childhood. As children engage in social comparison and care more about peer approval, they must learn to manage negative emotion that threatens their self-esteem.

By age 10, most children shift adaptively between two general strategies for managing emotion. In **problem-centered coping,** they appraise the situation as changeable, identify the difficulty, and decide what to do about it. If problem solving does not work, they engage in **emotion-centered coping,** which is internal, private, and aimed at controlling distress when little can be done about an outcome (Kliewer, Fearnow, & Miller, 1996; Lazarus & Lazarus, 1994). For example, when faced with an anxiety-provoking test or an angry friend, older school-age children view problem solving and seeking social support as the best strategies. But when outcomes are beyond their control—for example, after receiving a bad grade—they opt for distraction or try to redefine the situation in ways that help them accept it: "Things could be worse. There'll be another test." School-age children's improved ability to appraise situations and reflect on thoughts and feelings means that, compared with preschoolers, they more often use these internal strategies to manage emotion (Brenner & Salovey, 1997).

Cognitive development and a wider range of social experiences permit children to flexibly vary their coping strategies. Furthermore, through interacting with parents, teachers, and peers, school-age children become more knowledgeable about socially approved ways to display negative emotion. With age, they increasingly prefer verbal strategies ("Please stop pushing and wait your turn") to crying, sulking, or aggression (Shipman et al., 2003). Young school-age children justify these more mature displays of emotion by mentioning avoidance of punishment or disapproval, but by third grade, they begin to emphasize concern for others' feelings. Children with this awareness are rated as especially helpful, cooperative, and socially responsive by teachers and as better-liked by peers (Garner, 1996; McDowell & Parke, 2000).

When emotional self-regulation has developed well, school-age children acquire a sense of *emotional self-efficacy*—a feeling of being in control of their emotional experience (Saarni, 2000). This fosters a favorable self-image and an optimistic outlook, which further help children face emotional challenges. As at younger ages, school-age children whose parents respond sensitively and helpfully when the child is distressed are emotionally well-regulated—generally upbeat in mood and also empathic and prosocial. In contrast, poorly regulated children often experience hostile, dismissive parental reactions to distress (Davidov & Grusec, 2006; Zeman, Shipman, & Suveg, 2002). These children are overwhelmed by negative emotion, a response that interferes with empathy and prosocial behavior.

Finally, culture influences emotional self-regulation. In a striking illustration, researchers studied children in two collectivist subcultures in rural Nepal. In response to stories about emotionally charged situations (such as peer aggression or unjust parental punishment), Hindu children more often said they would feel angry but would try to mask their feelings. Buddhist children, in contrast, interpreted the situation so that they felt just OK, rather than angry. "Why be angry?" they explained. "The event already happened." In line with this difference, Hindu mothers reported that they often teach their children how to control their emotional behavior, whereas Buddhist mothers pointed to the value their religion places on a calm, peaceful disposition (Cole & Tamang, 1998; Cole, Tamang, & Shrestha, 2006). Compared to both Nepalese groups, U.S. children preferred conveying anger verbally in these situations; for example, to an unjust punishment, they answered, "If I say I'm angry, he'll stop hurting me!" (Cole, Bruschi, & Tamang, 2002). Notice how this response fits with the Western individualistic emphasis on personal rights and self-expression.

Understanding Others: Perspective Taking

We have seen that middle childhood brings major advances in **perspective taking,** the capacity to imagine what other people may be thinking and feeling. These changes support self-concept and self-esteem, understanding of others, and a wide variety of social skills. Robert Selman's five-stage sequence describes changes in perspective-taking skill, based on children's and adolescents' responses to social dilemmas in which characters have differing information and opinions about an event.

As Table 13.1 on page 492 indicates, at first children have only a limited idea of others' thoughts and feelings. Over time, they become more aware that people can interpret the same event quite differently. Soon they can "step into another person's shoes" and reflect on how that person might regard their own thoughts, feelings, and behavior, as when they say something like, "I *thought you would think* I was just kidding when I said that." (Note the similarity between this

| TABLE 13.1 | Selman's Stages of Perspective Taking |

STAGE	APPROXIMATE AGE RANGE	DESCRIPTION
Level 0: Undifferentiated perspective taking	3–6	Children recognize that self and other can have different thoughts and feelings, but they frequently confuse the two.
Level 1: Social-informational perspective taking	4–9	Children understand that different perspectives may result because people have access to different information.
Level 2: Self-reflective perspective taking	7–12	Children can "step into another person's shoes" and view their own thoughts, feelings, and behavior from the other person's perspective. They also recognize that others can do the same.
Level 3: Third-party perspective taking	10–15	Children can step outside a two-person situation and imagine how the self and other are viewed from the point of view of an impartial third party.
Level 4: Societal perspective taking	14–adult	Individuals understand that third-party perspective taking can be influenced by one or more systems of broader societal values.

Sources: Selman, 1976; Selman & Byrne, 1974.

level of perspective taking and second-order false belief, described on page 448 in Chapter 12.) Finally, older children and adolescents can evaluate two people's perspectives simultaneously, at first from the vantage point of a disinterested spectator and later by referring to societal values (Gurucharri & Selman, 1982). The following explanation illustrates this ability: "I know why Joey hid the stray kitten in the basement, even though his mom was against keeping it. He believes in not hurting animals. If you put the kitten outside or give it to the pound, it might die."

Experiences in which adults and peers explain their viewpoints contribute greatly to children's perspective taking. Good perspective takers, in turn, are more likely to display empathy and sympathy and to handle difficult social situations effectively—among the reasons they are better-liked by peers (FitzGerald & White, 2003). Children with poor social skills, especially the angry, aggressive styles we discussed in Chapter 10, have great difficulty imagining others' thoughts and feelings. They often mistreat adults and peers without feeling the guilt and remorse prompted by awareness of another's viewpoint. Interventions that provide coaching and practice in perspective taking reduce antisocial behavior and increase empathy and prosocial responding (Chalmers & Townsend, 1990).

Moral Development

Recall from Chapter 10 that preschoolers pick up many morally relevant behaviors through modeling and reinforcement. By middle childhood, they have had time to internalize rules for good conduct: "It's good to help others in trouble" or "It's wrong to take something that doesn't belong to you." This change leads children to become considerably more independent and trustworthy.

In Chapter 10, we also saw that children do not just copy their morality from others. As the cognitive-developmental approach emphasizes, they actively think about right and wrong. An expanding social world, the capacity to consider more information when reasoning, and gains in perspective taking lead moral understanding to advance greatly in middle childhood.

Moral and Social-Conventional Understanding

During the school years, children construct a flexible appreciation of moral rules. By age 7 to 8, they no longer say truth telling is always good and lying is always bad but also consider prosocial and antisocial intentions. They evaluate very negatively certain types of truthfulness, such as bluntly telling a classmate that you don't like her drawing (Bussey, 1999). And although both Chinese and Canadian schoolchildren consider lying about antisocial acts "very naughty," Chinese children—influenced by collectivist values—more often rate lying favorably when the intention is modesty, as when a student who has thoughtfully picked up litter from the playground said, "I didn't do it" (Lee et al., 1997, 2001). Similarly, Chinese children are more likely to favor lying to support the group at the expense of the individual (claiming you're sick so, as a poor singer, you won't harm your class's chances of winning a singing competition). In contrast, Canadian children more often favor lying to support the individual at the expense of the group (asserting that a friend who is a poor speller is actually a good speller because the friend wants to participate in a spelling competition) (Fu et al., 2007).

As children construct more advanced ideas about justice, taking into account an increasing number of variables, they clarify and link moral imperatives and social conventions. School-age children, for example, distinguish social conventions with a clear *purpose* (not running in school hallways to prevent injuries) from ones with no obvious justification (crossing a "forbidden" line on the playground). They regard violations of purposeful conventions as closer to moral transgressions (Buchanan-Barrow & Barrett, 1998). With age, they also realize that people's *intentions* and the *context* of their actions affect the moral implications of violating a social convention. In one study, 8- to 10-year-olds judged that because of a flag's symbolic value, burning it to express disapproval of a country or to start a cooking fire is worse than burning it accidentally. They also stated that public flag burning is worse than private flag burning because it inflicts emotional harm on others. But they recognized that flag burning is a form of freedom of expression, and most agreed that it would be acceptable in a country that treated its citizens unfairly (Helwig & Prencipe, 1999).

In middle childhood, children also realize that people whose *knowledge* differs may not be equally responsible for moral transgressions. Many 7-year-olds tolerate a teacher's decision to give more snack to girls than to boys because she thinks (incorrectly) that girls need more food. But when a teacher gives girls more snack because she holds an *immoral belief* ("it's all right to be nicer to girls than boys"), almost all children judge her actions negatively (Wainryb & Ford, 1998).

■ School-age children recognize that certain social conventions have a clear purpose—such as separating recyclables from trash to reduce waste. They regard violations of these types of conventions as closer to moral transgressions. ■

Understanding Individual Rights

When children challenge adult authority, they typically do so within the personal domain. As their grasp of moral imperatives and social conventions strengthens, so does their conviction that certain choices, such as hairstyle, friends, and leisure activities, are up to the individual (Nucci, 2005).

Notions of personal choice, in turn, enhance children's moral understanding. As early as age 6, children view freedom of speech and religion as individual rights, even if laws exist that deny those rights (Helwig, 2006). And they regard laws that discriminate against individuals—for example, denying certain people access to medical care or education—as wrong and worthy of violating (Helwig & Jasiobedzka, 2001). In justifying their responses, children appeal to personal privileges and, by the end of middle childhood, to the importance of individual rights for maintaining a fair society.

At the same time, older school-age children place limits on individual choice. Fourth graders faced with conflicting moral and personal concerns—such as whether or not to

■ This 10-year-old observes the social convention of respect for his country's flag. He also grasps individual rights such as free speech—for example, the right to destroy a flag in protest against a country that treats its citizens unfairly. ■

befriend a classmate of a different race or gender—typically decide in favor of kindness and fairness (Killen et al., 2002). Partly for this reason, prejudice generally declines in middle childhood.

Culture and Moral Understanding

Children and adolescents in diverse Western and non-Western cultures use similar criteria to reason about moral, social-conventional, and personal concerns (Neff & Helwig, 2002; Nucci, 2005, 2008). For example, Chinese young people, whose culture places a high value on respect for and deference to adult authority, nevertheless say that adults have no right to interfere in children's personal matters, such as how they spend free time (Hasebe, Nucci, & Nucci, 2004; Helwig et al., 2003). A Colombian child illustrated this passionate defense of personal control when asked if a teacher had the right to tell a student where to sit during circle time. In the absence of a moral reason from the teacher, the child declared, "She should be able to sit wherever she wants" (Ardila-Rey & Killen, 2001, p. 249).

Furthermore, American and Korean children alike claim that a child with no position of authority should be obeyed when she gives a directive that is fair and caring, such as telling others to share candy or to return lost money to its owner. And even in Korean culture, which places a high value on deference to authority, 7- to 11-year-olds evaluate negatively an adult's order to engage in immoral acts, such as stealing or refusing to share—a response that strengthens with age (Kim, 1998; Kim & Turiel, 1996). In sum, children everywhere seem to realize that higher principles, independent of rule and authority, must prevail when people's personal rights and welfare are at stake.

As children extend their grasp of moral imperatives, they also contemplate religious and spiritual concepts. Refer to the Cultural Influences box on the following page for current evidence on how children understand the existence of God, the core idea in the vast majority of the world's religions.

Understanding Diversity and Inequality

By the early school years, children associate power and privilege with white people and poverty and inferior status with people of color. They do not necessarily acquire these views directly from parents or friends. In one study, although white children assumed that parents' and friends' racial attitudes would resemble their own, no similarities in attitudes emerged (Aboud & Doyle, 1996). Perhaps many white parents are reluctant to discuss their racial and ethnic views with children, and friends also say little. Given limited or ambiguous information, children may fill in the gaps with information they encounter in the media and elsewhere in their environments and then use their own attitudes as the basis for inferring others'.

Consistent with this idea, research indicates that children pick up much information about group status from implicit messages in their surroundings. In another investigation, 7- to 12-year-olds attending a summer school were randomly assigned to social groups, identified by colored T-shirts (yellow or blue) that the children wore. The researchers hung posters in the classroom depicting yellow-group members as having higher status—for example, as having won more athletic and spelling competitions. When teachers used the groups as the basis for seating arrangements, assignments, and bulletin-board displays, the children in the high-status group evaluated their own group more favorably than the other group, and the children in the low-status group viewed their own group less favorably. But when teachers ignored the social groupings, no prejudice emerged (Bigler, Brown, & Markell, 2001).

These findings reveal that children do not necessarily form stereotypes even when some basis for them exists—in this instance, information on wall posters. But when an authority figure behaves in ways that endorse group status distinctions, children form biased attitudes.

IN-GROUP AND OUT-GROUP BIASES: DEVELOPMENT OF PREJUDICE Studies in diverse Western nations confirm that by age 5 to 7, white children generally evaluate their own racial group favorably and other racial groups less favorably or negatively (Aboud, 2003; Bennett et al., 2004; Nesdale et al., 2004). Many minority children of this age, in a reverse pat-

CULTURAL INFLUENCES

Children's Understanding of God

Here is how several 6- to 9-year-olds responded to the question: "What is God?"

- "You can pray anytime you feel like it, and they [Jesus and God] are sure to hear you because they got it worked out so one of them is on duty at all times."
- "God hears everything, not just prayers, so there must be an awful lot of noise in his ears, unless he has thought of a way to turn it off."
- "God is a spirit who can go anywhere." *What is a spirit?* "It's a ghost, like in the movies." (From Briggs, 2000; Gandy, 2004.)

Ideas about God differ radically from ideas about ordinary experiences because they violate real-world assumptions. Recall from Chapter 9 that between ages 4 and 8, children distinguish magical beings (such as Santa Claus and the Tooth Fairy) from reality (see page 342). At the same time, they embrace other beliefs that are part of their culturally transmitted religion. To avoid confusion, they must isolate their concepts of God from their grasp of human agents, placing God in a separate religious realm governed by superhuman rules (Woolley, 2000). This is a challenging task for preschool and school-age children.

Previous research, strongly influenced by Piaget's theory, led to a uniform conclusion: Children assign *anthropomorphic* (human) characteristics to God, whom they view as a parentlike figure residing in the sky. Not until adolescence does this concrete image of God as "big person" give way to an abstract, mystical view of God as formless, all-knowing (omniscient), all-powerful (omnipotent), and transcending the limits of time.

Consider the responses of children just given, which contain both concrete human images (God as being "on duty in the sky" or as overwhelmed by the "noise in his ears") and a variety of superhuman properties ("a spirit who can go anywhere"). Recent evidence reveals that even preschoolers are not limited to human, parental images of God. The procedures typically used to investigate children's religious knowledge—asking them to respond to open-ended questions—are so cognitively demanding that children often fall back on their highly detailed notions of humans to fill in for their sketchier thoughts about God.

When researchers make tasks less demanding, children recognize that God has supernatural powers not available to humans, such as seeing and hearing everything (Richert & Barrett, 2005). For example, in research in the United States and in a Mexican Mayan village, most 5- to 6-year-olds given a typical false-belief task indicated that their parents might hold a false belief, but God would not (Knight et al., 2004). Children of this age also say that God—but not a humanlike puppet—can see an object in a darkened box (Barrett, Richert, & Driesenga, 2001; Makris & Pnevmatikos, 2007). And with respect to God's omnipotence, even preschoolers state with certainty that God, but not humans, gives life to all natural things (animals, plants, and trees) (Petrovich, 1997).

Indeed, the most striking feature of children's concepts of God is their mix of tangible and intangible features. In this respect, their religious thinking is far more similar to adults' than previously thought. That children's representations of God are not restricted to a "big person" image suggests that religious education strongly influences their thinking.

Indeed, wide cultural variation in children's and adults' ideas exists (Barrett, 2002; Barrett & Van Orman, 1996). In studies in which school-age children drew pictures of God, Mormons, Lutherans, Mennonites, and Catholics, in line with the teachings of their denominations, more often represented God as humanlike than did Unitarians and Jews (Pitts, 1976; Tamminen, 1991). Furthermore, children say some things about God that seem strange or amusing because their culturally relevant knowledge is often incomplete. During the school years, they frequently ask thoughtful questions about God aimed at broadening their understanding: "Does God have parents?" or "Why doesn't God stop bad things from happening?"

Finally, some children are aware that visions of God can provide emotional comfort and guidance, as these comments reveal: "He comes down and helps you when you're sad or lonely or can't get to sleep at night." "In case you forget, he reminds you to act nice" (Berk, 2004). By adolescence, religiosity is linked to psychological well-being and to prosocial attitudes and behavior (Sherrod & Spiewak, 2008).

■ Cognitive development, religious education, and culture combine to influence children's understanding of God. Like adults, this young participant in an interfaith "blessing of the animals" ceremony probably views God as having both humanlike and supernatural powers. ■

---

tern, assign positive characteristics to the privileged white majority and negative characteristics to their own group (Averhart & Bigler, 1997; Corenblum, 2003).

But recall that with age, children pay more attention to inner traits. The capacity to classify the social world in multiple ways enables school-age children to understand that people can be both "the same" and "different"—those who look different need not think, feel, or act

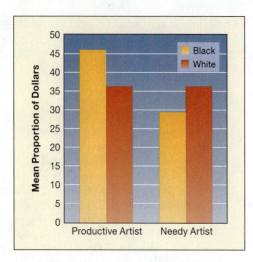

FIGURE 13.3

White fourth graders' racially biased distribution of money to child artists. When dividing money earned from selling children's art among three child artists—two white and one black—the fourth graders gave more money to a productive black artist (who countered a stereotype) than a productive white artist, and less money to a needy black artist (who conformed to a stereotype) than to a needy white artist. In both instances, the fourth graders seemed to engage in subtle, unintentional prejudice. *(From A. V. McGillicuddy-De Lisi, M. Daly, & A. Neal, 2006, "Children's Distributive Justice Judgments: Aversive Racism in Euro-American Children?"* Child Development, 77, *p. 1072. © The Society for Research in Child Development, Inc. Adapted by permission of Blackwell Publishing Ltd.)*

differently (Aboud & Amato, 2001). Consequently, voicing of negative attitudes toward minorities declines. After age 7 or 8, both majority and minority children express *in-group favoritism,* and white children's prejudice against *out-group* members often weakens (Nesdale et al., 2005; Ruble et al., 2004). Most school-age children and adolescents are also quick to verbalize that it is wrong to exclude others from peer-group and learning activities on the basis of skin color—discrimination they evaluate as unfair (Killen et al., 2002).

Yet even in children aware of the injustice of discrimination, prejudice may operate unintentionally and without awareness—as it does in many adults (Dunham, Baron, & Banaji, 2006). Consider a study in which white second and fourth graders were asked to divide fairly among three child artists—two white and one black—money that had been earned from selling the children's art. In each version of the task, one artist was labeled as "productive" (making more artworks), one as "the oldest," and one as "poor and needing money for lunch." By age 8 to 9, most children recognize that special consideration should be given to those who either perform exceptionally or are at a disadvantage. But racial stereotypes interfered with fourth graders' evenhanded application of these principles. They gave more money to a productive black artist (who countered the racial stereotype of "low achiever") than to a productive white artist and less money to a needy black artist (who conformed to the racial stereotype of "poor") than to a needy white artist (see Figure 13.3) (McGillicuddy-De Lisi, Daly, & Neal, 2006).

Nevertheless, the extent to which children hold racial and ethnic biases varies, depending on the following personal and situational factors:

- *A fixed view of personality traits.* Children who believe that people's personality traits are fixed rather than changeable often judge others as either "good" or "bad." Ignoring motives and circumstances, they readily form prejudices on the basis of limited information. For example, they might infer that "a new child at school who tells a lie to get other kids to like her" is simply a bad person (Levy & Dweck, 1999).
- *Overly high self-esteem.* Children (and adults) with very high self-esteem are more likely to hold racial and ethnic prejudices (Baumeister et al., 2003; Bigler, Brown, & Markell, 2001). These individuals seem to belittle disadvantaged individuals or groups to justify their own extremely favorable self-evaluation. Children who say their own ethnicity makes them feel especially "good"—and thus perhaps socially superior—are more likely to display in-group favoritism and out-group prejudice (Pfeifer et al., 2007).
- *A social world in which people are sorted into groups.* The more adults highlight group distinctions for children and the less interracial contact children experience, the more likely white children are to display prejudice (Kowalski & Lo, 1999; McGlothlin & Killen, 2006).

REDUCING PREJUDICE   Research confirms that an effective way to reduce prejudice is through intergroup contact, in which racially and ethnically different children work toward common goals and become personally acquainted (Tropp & Pettigrew, 2005). Children assigned to cooperative learning groups with peers of diverse backgrounds, for example, form more cross-race friendships. Sharing thoughts and feelings with close, cross-race friends, in turn, reduces even subtle, unintentional prejudices (Turner, Hewstone, & Voci, 2007). But the positive effects of cooperative learning seem not to generalize to out-group members who are not part of these learning teams.

Long-term contact and collaboration in neighborhoods, schools, and communities may be the best way to reduce prejudice. Classrooms that expose children to broad ethnic diversity, teach them to understand and value those differences, directly address the damage caused by prejudice, and encourage perspective taking and empathy both prevent children from forming negative biases and reduce already acquired biases (Pfeifer, Brown, & Juvonen, 2007).

Finally, inducing children to view others' traits as changeable, by discussing with them the many possible influences on those traits, is helpful. The more children believe that people can change their personalities, the more they report liking and perceiving themselves as similar to members of disadvantaged groups. Furthermore, children who believe that human attributes are changeable spend more time volunteering to help the needy—for example, by serving meals to the homeless or reading to poverty-stricken preschoolers (Karafantis & Levy, 2004). Volunteering, in turn, may promote changeable views of others by helping children take the perspective of the underprivileged and appreciate the social conditions that lead to disadvantage.

Fourth graders cooperate to figure out how many batteries they need to light a light bulb. Opportunities to work together toward common goals can reduce even subtle, unintentional prejudices as racially and ethnically different children get to know one another. ■

ASK YOURSELF

◆ **REVIEW** How does emotional self-regulation improve in middle childhood? What implications do these advances have for children's self-esteem?

◆ **APPLY** Ten-year-old Marla says her classmate Bernadette will never get good grades because she's lazy. Jane believes that Bernadette tries but can't concentrate because her parents are divorcing. Why is Marla more likely than Jane to develop prejudices?

◆ **CONNECT** Cite examples of how older children's capacity to take more information into account enhances their emotional understanding, perspective taking, and moral understanding.

◆ **REFLECT** Did you attend an integrated elementary school? Why is school integration vital for reducing racial and ethnic prejudice?

Peer Relations

In middle childhood, the society of peers becomes an increasingly important context for development. Peer contact, as we have seen, contributes to perspective taking and understanding of self and others. These developments, in turn, enhance peer interaction. Compared with preschoolers, school-age children resolve conflicts more effectively, using persuasion and compromise (Mayeux & Cillessen, 2003). Sharing, helping, and other prosocial acts also increase. In line with these changes, aggression declines. But the drop is greatest for physical attacks (Côté et al., 2007; Tremblay, 2000). As we will see, verbal and relational aggression continue as children form peer groups.

© DAVID ROTH/GETTY IMAGES/TAXI

■ Peer groups first form in middle childhood. These boys have probably established a social structure of leaders and followers as they gather for joint activities. Their relaxed body language and similar way of dressing suggest a strong sense of group belonging. ■

Peer Groups

TAKE A MOMENT... Watch children in the schoolyard or neighborhood, and notice how they often gather in groups of three to a dozen or more. In what ways are members of the same group noticeably alike?

By the end of middle childhood, children display a strong desire for group belonging. They form **peer groups,** collectives that generate unique values and standards for behavior and a social structure of leaders and followers. Peer groups organize on the basis of proximity (being in the same classroom) and similarity in sex, ethnicity, academic achievement, popularity, and aggression (Rubin, Bukowski, & Parker, 2006). When groups are tracked for 3 to 6 weeks, membership changes very little. When they are followed for a year or longer, substantial change can occur, depending on whether children are reshuffled into different classrooms. For children who remain together, 50 to 70 percent of groups consist mostly of the same children from year to year (Cairns, Xie, & Leung, 1998).

The practices of these informal groups lead to a "peer culture" that typically involves a specialized vocabulary, dress code, and place to "hang out." Joey and three other boys formed a club whose "uniform" was T-shirts, jeans, and sneakers. They met at recess and on Saturdays in the tree house in Joey's backyard. Calling themselves "the pack," the boys devised a secret handshake and chose Joey as their leader. Their activities included improving the clubhouse, trading baseball cards, playing basketball and video games, and—just as important—keeping unwanted peers and adults out!

As children develop these exclusive associations, the codes of dress and behavior that grow out of them become more broadly influential. Peers who deviate—by "kissing up" to teachers, wearing the wrong clothes, or tattling on classmates—are often rebuffed, becoming targets of critical glances and comments. These customs bind peers together, creating a sense of group identity. Within the group, children acquire many social skills—cooperation, leadership, followership, and loyalty to collective goals. Through these experiences, children experiment with and learn about social organizations.

As with other aspects of social reasoning, children evaluate a group's decision to exclude a peer in complex ways. Most view exclusion as wrong, even when they see themselves as different from the excluded child. And with age, children are less likely to endorse excluding someone because of unconventional appearance or behavior. Girls, especially, regard exclusion as unjust, perhaps because they experience it more often than boys (Killen, Crystal, & Watanabe, 2002). But when a peer threatens group functioning, by acting disruptively or by lacking skills to participate in a valued group activity (such as sports), both boys and girls say that exclusion is justified—a perspective that strengthens with age (Killen & Stangor, 2001).

Despite these sophisticated understandings, children do exclude unjustly, often using relationally aggressive tactics. Peer groups—at the instigation of their leaders, who can be skillfully aggressive—frequently oust no longer "respected" children. Some of these cast-outs, whose own previous hostility toward outsiders reduces their chances of being included elsewhere, turn to other low-status peers with poor social skills (Werner & Crick, 2004). Socially anxious children, when ousted, often become increasingly peer-avoidant and thus more isolated (Gazelle & Rudolph, 2004). In either case, opportunities to acquire socially competent behavior diminish.

As excluded children's class participation declines, their academic achievement suffers (Buhs, Ladd, & Herald, 2006). And some aggressive children—especially popular boys—link up with popular, nonaggressive agemates (Bagwell et al., 2000; Farmer et al., 2002). In these groups, mild-mannered children may accept and even support the antisocial acts of their dominant, antisocial associates, who pick fights with other groups or bully weaker children. Consequently, teachers and counselors must target both antisocial and mixed peer groups to reduce peer aggression.

School-age children's desire for group belonging can also be satisfied through formal group ties such as scouting, 4-H, and religious youth groups. Adult involvement holds in check the negative behaviors associated with children's informal peer groups. And through working on joint projects and helping in their communities, children gain in social and moral maturity (Vandell & Shumow, 1999).

Friendships

Whereas peer groups provide children with insight into larger social structures, friendships contribute to the development of trust and sensitivity. During the school years, friendship becomes more complex and psychologically based. Consider the following 8-year-old's ideas:

> *Why is Shelly your best friend?* Because she helps me when I'm sad, and she shares. . . . *What makes Shelly so special?* I've known her longer, I sit next to her and got to know her better. . . . *How come you like Shelly better than anyone else?* She's done the most for me. She never disagrees, she never eats in front of me, she never walks away when I'm crying, and she helps me on my homework. . . . *How do you get someone to like you?* . . . If you're nice to [your friends], they'll be nice to you. (Damon, 1988, pp. 80–81)

As these responses show, friendship has become a mutually agreed-on relationship in which children like each other's personal qualities and respond to one another's needs and desires. And once a friendship forms, *trust* becomes its defining feature. School-age children state that a good friendship is based on acts of kindness, signifying that each person can be counted on to support the other (Hartup & Abecassis, 2004). Consequently, older children regard violations of trust, such as not helping when others need help, breaking promises, and gossiping behind the other's back, as serious breaches of friendship.

Because of these features, school-age children's friendships are more selective. Whereas preschoolers say they have lots of friends, by age 8 or 9, children name only a handful of good friends. Girls, who demand greater closeness than boys, are more exclusive in their friendships (Markovits, Benenson, & Dolensky, 2001). In addition, children tend to select friends similar to themselves in age, sex, race, ethnicity, and SES. Friends also resemble one another in personality (sociability, inattention/hyperactivity, aggression, depression), peer popularity, academic achievement, and prosocial behavior (Hartup, 2006; Mariano & Harton, 2005). But friendship opportunities offered by children's environments also affect their choices. As noted earlier, in integrated classrooms with mixed-race collaborative learning groups, students form more cross-race friendships.

Over middle childhood, high-quality friendships remain fairly stable, with about 50 to 70 percent enduring over a school year, and some for several years (Berndt, 2004). Through them, children learn the importance of emotional commitment. They come to realize that close relationships can survive disagreements if both parties are secure in their liking for one another (Rose & Asher, 1999). Friendship provides an important context in which children learn to tolerate criticism and resolve disputes in ways that meet both partners' needs.

Yet the impact of friendships on children's development depends on the nature of their friends. Children who bring kindness and compassion to their friendships strengthen each other's prosocial tendencies. But when aggressive children make friends, the relationship is often riddled with hostile interaction and is at risk for breakup, especially when just one member of the pair is aggressive (Ellis & Zarbatany, 2007). Aggressive girls' friendships are high in exchange of private feelings but also full of relational hostility, including jealousy, conflict, and betrayal (Werner & Crick, 2004).

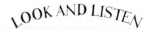

Ask an 8- to 11-year-old to tell you what he or she looks for in a best friend. Is *trust* centrally important? Does the child mention personality traits, just as school-age children do in describing themselves (see page 483)?

■ School-age children tend to select friends similar to themselves in age, sex, race, ethnicity, and SES. However, in integrated classrooms with mixed-race collaborative learning groups, students form more cross-race friendships. ■

Aggressive boys' friendships involve frequent expressions of anger, coercive statements, physical attacks, and enticements to rule-breaking behavior, as well as relational aggression (Bagwell & Coie, 2004; Crick & Nelson, 2002; Dishion, Andrews, & Crosby, 1995). These findings indicate that the social problems of aggressive children operate within their closest peer ties. As we will see next, these children often acquire negative reputations in the wider world of peers.

Peer Acceptance

Peer acceptance refers to likability—the extent to which a child is viewed by a group of age-mates, such as classmates, as a worthy social partner. Unlike friendship, likability is not a mutual relationship but a one-sided perspective, involving the group's view of an individual. Nevertheless, certain social skills that contribute to friendship also enhance peer acceptance. Better-accepted children tend to have more friends and more positive relationships with them (Lansford et al., 2006; Pedersen et al., 2007).

To assess peer acceptance, researchers usually use self-reports that measure *social preferences*—for example, asking children to identify classmates whom they "like very much" or "like very little" (Hymel et al., 2004). Another approach assesses *social prominence*—children's judgments of whom most of their classmates admire. Only moderate correspondence exists between the classmates children identify as prominent (looked up to by many others) and those they say they personally prefer (Prinstein & Cillessen, 2003).

Children's self-reports yield four general categories of peer acceptance:

- **Popular children,** who get many positive votes (are well-liked)
- **Rejected children,** who get many negative votes (are disliked)
- **Controversial children,** who receive many votes, both positive and negative (are both liked and disliked)
- **Neglected children,** who are seldom mentioned, either positively or negatively

About two-thirds of students in a typical elementary school classroom fit one of these categories (Coie, Dodge, & Coppotelli, 1982). The remaining one-third, who do not receive extreme scores, are *average* in peer acceptance.

Peer acceptance is a powerful predictor of current as well as later psychological adjustment. Rejected children, especially, are anxious, unhappy, disruptive, and low in self-esteem. Both teachers and parents rate them as having a wide range of emotional and social problems. Peer rejection in middle childhood is also strongly associated with poor school performance, absenteeism, dropping out, substance use, depression, antisocial behavior, and delinquency in adolescence and with criminality in adulthood (Laird et al., 2001; Parker et al., 1995; Rubin, Bukowski, & Parker, 2006).

However, earlier influences—children's characteristics combined with parenting practices—may largely explain the link between peer acceptance and adjustment. School-age children with peer-relationship problems are more likely to have preexisting, weak emotional self-regulation skills and to have experienced family stress due to low income, insensitive child rearing, and coercive discipline (Cowan & Cowan, 2004; Trentacosta & Shaw, 2009). Nevertheless, as we will see, rejected children evoke reactions from peers that contribute to their unfavorable development.

DETERMINANTS OF PEER ACCEPTANCE Why is one child liked while another is rejected? A wealth of research reveals that social behavior plays a powerful role.

Popular Children. The majority of **popular-prosocial children** combine academic and social competence. They perform well in school, communicate with peers in friendly and cooperative ways, and solve social problems constructively (Cillessen & Bellmore, 2004).

But other popular children are admired for their socially adept yet belligerent behavior. This smaller subtype, **popular-antisocial children,** includes "tough" boys—athletically skilled but poor students who cause trouble and defy adult authority—and relationally aggressive boys and girls who enhance their own status by ignoring, excluding, and spreading rumors about other children (Rodkin et al., 2000; Rose, Swenson, & Waller, 2004). Despite their aggressiveness, peers view these youths as "cool," perhaps because of their athletic ability and sophisticated but devious social skills. Although peer admiration gives these children some protection against lasting adjustment difficulties, their antisocial acts require intervention (Prinstein & La Greca, 2004; Rodkin et al., 2006). With age, peers like these high-status, aggressive youths less and less, a trend that is stronger for relationally aggressive girls. The more socially prominent and controlling these girls become, the more they engage in relational aggression (Cillessen & Mayeux, 2004). Eventually peers condemn their nasty tactics and reject them.

Rejected Children. Rejected children display a wide range of negative social behaviors. The largest subtype, **rejected-aggressive children,** show high rates of conflict, physical and relational aggression, and hyperactive, inattentive, and impulsive behavior. They are usually deficient in perspective taking, and they tend to misinterpret the innocent behaviors of peers as hostile and to blame others for their social difficulties (Crick, Casas, & Nelson, 2002; Dodge, Coie, & Lynam, 2006; Hoza et al., 2005). Compared with popular-aggressive children, they are more extremely antagonistic.

■ Schoolgirls in Beijing, China, gather around a popular classmate. Most popular children are *prosocial*—academically successful, socially sensitive, and cooperative. But some are *antisocial,* admired for their skill at controlling peer relationships through relational aggression. Over time, their popularity declines, and they may experience rejection. ■

In contrast, **rejected-withdrawn children** are passive and socially awkward. These timid children are overwhelmed by social anxiety, hold negative expectations for treatment by peers, and worry about being scorned and attacked. Like their aggressive counterparts, they typically feel like retaliating rather than compromising in conflicts with peers, although they less often act on those feelings (Hart et al., 2000; Ladd & Burgess, 1999; Troop-Gordon & Asher, 2005).

Rejected children are excluded by peers as early as kindergarten. Rejection, in turn, further impairs these children's biased social information processing, heightening their hostility (Dodge et al., 2003). Soon their classroom participation declines, their feelings of loneliness rise, their academic achievement falters, and they want to avoid school (Buhs & Ladd, 2001). Most have few friends, and some have none—a circumstance that compounds their adjustment difficulties (Ladd & Troop-Gordon, 2003; Pedersen et al., 2007).

Both types of rejected children are at risk for peer harassment. But as the Biology and Environment box on page 502 reveals, rejected-aggressive children also act as bullies, and rejected-withdrawn children are especially likely to be victimized (Putallaz et al., 2007; Sandstrom & Cillessen, 2003).

Controversial and Neglected Children. Consistent with the mixed peer opinion they engender, controversial children display a blend of positive and negative social behaviors. They are hostile and disruptive, but they also engage in positive, prosocial acts. Even though some peers dislike them, they have qualities that protect them from exclusion. They have as many friends as popular children and are happy with their peer relationships (Newcomb, Bukowski, & Pattee, 1993). But like their popular-antisocial counterparts, they often bully others and engage in calculated relational aggression to sustain their dominance (DeRosier & Thomas, 2003; Putallaz et al., 2007).

Perhaps the most surprising finding is that neglected children, once thought to be in need of treatment, are usually well-adjusted. Although they engage in low rates of interaction, most are just as socially skilled as average children. They do not report feeling unhappy about their social life, and when they want to, they can break away from their usual, preferred pattern of playing alone (Harrist et al., 1997; Ladd & Burgess, 1999). Largely for this reason, neglected status (like controversial status) is often temporary. Neglected, socially competent children remind us that an outgoing, gregarious personality style is not the only path to emotional well-being. Nevertheless, a few neglected children are socially anxious and poorly skilled and, thus, at risk for peer rejection.

BIOLOGY AND ENVIRONMENT

Bullies and Their Victims

Follow the activities of aggressive children over a school day, and you will see that they reserve their hostilities for certain peers. A particularly destructive form of interaction is **peer victimization,** in which certain children become targets of verbal and physical attacks or other forms of abuse. What sustains these repeated assault–retreat cycles between pairs of children?

About 10 to 20 percent of children are bullies, while 15 to 30 percent are repeatedly victimized. Most bullies are boys who use both physical and verbal attacks, but girls sometimes bombard a vulnerable classmate with verbal and relational hostility (Rigby, 2004). As bullies move into adolescence, many amplify their attacks through electronic means (Twyman et al., 2010). About 20 to 40 percent of youths have experienced "cyberbullying" through text messages, e-mail, chat rooms, or other electronic tools (Tokunaga, 2010). They often do not report it to parents or adults at school.

Some bullies are high-status youngsters who may be liked for their leadership or athletic abilities. But most are disliked, or become so, because of their cruelty (Vaillancourt, Hymel, & McDougall, 2003). Nevertheless, peers rarely intervene to help victims, and about 20 to 30 percent of onlookers actually encourage bullies, even joining in (Salmivalli & Voeten, 2004).

Chronic victims tend to be passive when active behavior is expected. On the playground, they hang around chatting or wander on their own. When bullied, they give in, cry, and assume defensive postures (Boulton, 1999). Biologically based traits—an inhibited temperament and a frail physical appearance—contribute to victimization. But victims also have histories of resistant attachment, overly controlling child rearing, and maternal overprotection—parenting that prompts anxiety, low self-esteem, and dependency, resulting in a fearful demeanor that marks these children

as vulnerable (Snyder et al., 2003). Victims' adjustment problems include depression, loneliness, poor school performance, disruptive behavior, and school avoidance (Paul & Cillessen, 2003).

Aggression and victimization are not polar opposites. One-third to one-half of victims are also aggressive, meeting out physical, relational, or cyber-hostilities. Occasionally, they retaliate against powerful bullies, who respond by abusing them again—a cycle that sustains their victim status (Kochenderfer-Ladd, 2003). Among rejected children, these bully/victims are the most despised. They often have histories of extremely maladaptive parenting, including child abuse. This combination of highly negative home and peer experiences places them at severe risk for maladjustment (Kowalski, Limber, & Agatston, 2008; Schwartz, Proctor, & Chien, 2001).

Interventions that change victimized children's negative opinions of themselves and that teach them to respond in nonreinforcing ways to their attackers are helpful. Another way to assist victimized children is to help them acquire the social skills needed to form and maintain a gratifying friendship. When children have a friend to whom they can turn for help, bullying episodes usually end quickly. Anxious, withdrawn children with a close friend have fewer adjustment problems than those with no friends (Fox & Boulton, 2006; Laursen et al., 2007).

Although modifying victimized children's behavior can help, this does not mean

they are to blame. The best way to reduce bullying is to change youth environments (including school, sports programs, recreation centers, and neighborhoods), promoting prosocial attitudes and behaviors. Effective approaches include developing school and community codes against both "traditional" and "cyber" bullying, teaching child bystanders to intervene, enlisting parents' assistance in changing bullies' behaviors, and (if necessary) moving socially prominent bullies to another class or school (Kiriakidis & Kavoura, 2010; Leadbeater & Hoglund, 2006).

The U.S. Department of Health and Human Services has launched a media campaign, Stop Bullying Now, *www.stopbullyingnow.hrsa.gov,* which raises awareness of the harmfulness of bullying through TV and radio public service announcements. It also provides parents, teachers, and students with information on prevention.

© PAUL BALDESARE/PHOTOFUSION

■ Some bullies are high-status youngsters, but most are disliked, or become so, because of their cruelty. And chronic victims are often easy targets—physically weak, passive, and rejected by peers. ■

HELPING REJECTED CHILDREN   A variety of interventions exist to improve the peer relations and psychological adjustment of rejected children. Most involve coaching, modeling, and reinforcing positive social skills, such as how to initiate interaction with a peer, cooperate in play, and respond to another child with friendly emotion and approval. Several of these programs have produced gains in social competence and peer acceptance still present from several weeks to a year later (Asher & Rose, 1997; DeRosier, 2007). Combining social-skills training with other treatments increases their effectiveness. Rejected children are often poor students, whose low academic self-esteem magnifies their negative reactions to teachers and classmates. Intensive academic tutoring improves both school achievement and social acceptance (O'Neil et al., 1997).

Still another approach focuses on training in perspective taking and social problem solving. But many rejected-aggressive children are unaware of their poor social skills and do not take responsibility for their social failures (Mrug, Hoza, & Gerdes, 2001). Rejected-withdrawn children, in contrast, are likely to develop a *learned-helpless* approach to peer acceptance—concluding, after repeated rebuffs, that they will never be liked (Wichmann, Coplan, & Daniels, 2004). Both types of rejected children need help attributing their peer difficulties to internal, changeable causes.

Finally, because rejected children's socially incompetent behaviors often originate in a poor fit between the child's temperament and parenting practices, interventions focusing on the child may not be sufficient (Bierman & Powers, 2009). As early as the preschool years, rejected children engage in similarly inept communication with parents and with peers (Black & Logan, 1995; Guralnick et al., 2007). Without interventions directed at improving the quality of parent–child interaction, rejected children will continue to practice poor interpersonal skills at home and, as a result, may soon return to their old behavior patterns.

LOOK AND LISTEN

Contact a nearby elementary school or a school district office to find out what practices are in place to prevent bullying. Inquire about a written antibullying policy, and request a copy.

Gender Typing

Children's understanding of gender roles broadens in middle childhood, and their gender identities (views of themselves as relatively masculine or feminine) change as well. We will see that development differs for boys and girls, and it can vary considerably across cultures.

Gender-Stereotyped Beliefs

By age 5, gender stereotyping of activities and occupations is well-established. During the school years, knowledge of stereotypes increases in the less obvious areas of personality traits and achievement.

PERSONALITY TRAITS   Research in many cultures reveals that stereotyping of personality traits increases steadily in middle childhood, becoming adultlike around age 11 (Best, 2001; Heyman & Legare, 2004). For example, children regard "tough," "aggressive," "rational," and "dominant" as masculine and "gentle," "affectionate," and "dependent" as feminine (Serbin, Powlishta, & Gulko, 1993).

Children derive these distinctions from observing sex differences in behavior as well as from adult treatment. When helping a child with a task, for example, parents (especially fathers) behave in a more mastery-oriented fashion with sons, setting higher standards, explaining concepts, and pointing out important features of tasks—particularly during gender-typed pursuits, such as science activities (Tenenbaum & Leaper, 2003; Tenenbaum et al., 2005). Furthermore, parents less often encourage girls to make their own decisions. And both parents and teachers more often praise boys for knowledge and accomplishment, girls for obedience (Good & Brophy, 2003; Leaper, Anderson, & Sanders, 1998; Pomerantz & Ruble, 1998).

ACHIEVEMENT AREAS   Shortly after entering elementary school, school-age children quickly figure out which academic subjects and skill areas are "masculine" and which are "feminine." They often regard reading, spelling, art, and music as more for girls and mathematics, athletics, and mechanical skills as more for boys (Eccles, Jacobs, & Harold, 1990; Jacobs & Weisz, 1994). These stereotypes—and the attitudes and behaviors of parents and teachers that promote them—influence children's preferences for and sense of competence at certain subjects. As we saw in our discussion of self-esteem, boys tend to feel more competent than girls

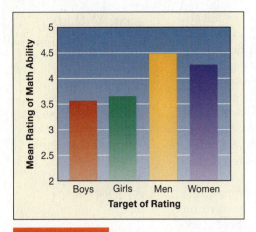

FIGURE 13.4

School-age girls' ratings of the math ability of children and adults. The girls regarded children of each gender as equally good at math. Their ratings of adults, however, reverted to the stereotype that men were better at math than women. *(Adapted from Steele, 2003.)*

at math, science, and athletics, whereas girls feel more competent than boys at language arts (see page 485).

Adults' gender-typed judgments of children's competence can have lasting consequences. In one study, mothers' early perceptions of their children's competence at math continued to predict daughters' self-perceptions and also career choices in their mid-twenties. Young women whose mothers had regarded them as highly capable at math were far more likely to choose a physical science career (Bleeker & Jacobs, 2004). Yet mothers rarely made such optimistic judgments about girls.

Furthermore, girls often adopt a more general stereotype of males as smarter than females, which they apply to themselves. In a study of over 2,000 second to sixth graders from diverse cultures (Eastern and Western Europe, Japan, Russia, and the United States), girls consistently had higher school grades than boys. Yet despite awareness of their better performance, girls did not report stronger beliefs in their own ability but, compared with boys, discounted their talent (Stetsenko et al., 2000). Apparently, gender stereotyping of mental ability occurs in many parts of the world.

One encouraging sign is that some children's gender-stereotyped beliefs about achievement may be changing. In a recent investigation, U.S. elementary school girls from economically advantaged homes regarded children of each gender as equally good at math. But when asked about adults, the girls reverted to the stereotype, saying that men were better than women (see Figure 13.4). Boys, in contrast, held stereotyped views of math ability for both children and adults (Steele, 2003).

TOWARD GREATER FLEXIBILITY   Although school-age children are aware of many gender stereotypes, they also develop a more flexible, open-minded view of what males and females *can do,* a trend that continues into adolescence. As they develop the capacity to integrate conflicting social cues, children realize that a person's sex is not a certain predictor of his or her personality traits, activities, and behaviors (Trautner et al., 2005). By the end of the school years, children regard gender typing as socially rather than biologically influenced (Taylor, 1996).

But acknowledging that people *can* cross gender lines does not mean that children always *approve* of doing so. In one longitudinal study, between ages 7 and 13, children generally became more open-minded about girls being offered the same opportunities as boys (Crouter et al., 2007). But the change was less pronounced for boys than girls, and for children whose parents held more traditional gender attitudes.

Furthermore, many school-age children take a harsh view of certain violations—boys playing with dolls and wearing girls' clothing, girls acting noisily and roughly. They are especially intolerant when boys engage in these "cross-gender" acts, which children regard as nearly as bad as moral transgressions (Blakemore, 2003; Levy, Taylor, & Gelman, 1995). When asked for open-ended descriptions of boys and girls, children most often mention girls' physical appearance ("is pretty," "wears dresses") and boys' activities and personality traits ("likes trucks," "is rough") (Miller et al., 2009). The salience of these stereotypes helps explain why, when children of the other sex display the behaviors just mentioned, they are likely to experience severe peer disapproval.

Nevertheless, school-age children do extend more flexible gender attitudes to the peer context to some degree. As with ethnicity, the majority regard excluding an agemate from peer group activities on the basis of gender as unfair. But between fourth and seventh grades, more young people—again, especially boys—say it is OK to exclude on the basis of gender than ethnicity (see Figure 13.5). When asked to explain, they point to concerns about group functioning related to sex differences in interests and communication styles—boys' preference for active pursuits and commanding forceful behavior, girls' preference for quiet activities, politeness, and compromise (Killen et al., 2002, p. 56). Indeed, sex-segregated peer associations strengthen during middle childhood and continue to contribute powerfully to gender typing (see Chapter 10, page 394).

Percentage of children and adolescents saying "It's OK" to exclude an agemate from a peer-group activity on the basis of gender and ethnicity. When asked about excluding an other-sex or other-ethnicity peer from a peer-group activity (a music club in which members trade CDs), many more young people said that it is OK to do so on the basis of gender than on the basis of ethnicity. Willingness to exclude on the basis of gender increased with age, with many participants justifying their decision by pointing to sex differences in interests and communication styles. *(Adapted from Killen et al., 2002.)*

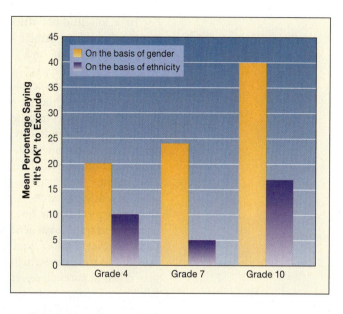

Gender Identity and Behavior

Children who were more strongly gender-typed relative to their agemates in early childhood usually remain so in middle childhood (Golombok et al., 2008). Nevertheless, overall changes do occur, with boys' and girls' gender identities following different paths.

From third to sixth grade, boys tend to strengthen their identification with "masculine" personality traits, whereas girls' identification with "feminine" traits declines. Girls often describe themselves as having some "other-gender" characteristics (Serbin, Powlishta, & Gulko, 1993). And whereas boys usually stick to "masculine" pursuits, many girls experiment with a wider range of options—from cooking and sewing to sports and science projects—and more often consider traditionally male future work roles, such as firefighter or astronomer (Liben & Bigler, 2002).

These changes reflect a mixture of cognitive and social forces. School-age children of both sexes are aware that society attaches greater prestige to "masculine" characteristics. For example, they rate "masculine" occupations as having higher status than "feminine" occupations (Liben, Bigler, & Krogh, 2001). Messages from adults and peers are also influential. In Chapter 10, we saw that parents (especially fathers) are far less tolerant when sons, as opposed to daughters, cross gender lines. Similarly, a tomboyish girl can make her way into boys' activities without losing the approval of her female peers, but a boy who hangs out with girls is likely to be ridiculed and rejected.

As school-age children characterize themselves in terms of general dispositions, their gender identity expands to include the following self-evaluations, which greatly affect their adjustment:

- *Gender typicality*—the degree to which the child feels similar to others of the same gender. Although children need not be highly gender typed to view themselves as gender-typical, their psychological well-being depends, to some degree, on feeling that they "fit in" with their same-sex peers.
- *Gender contentedness*—the degree to which the child feels comfortable with his or her gender assignment, which also promotes happiness.
- *Felt pressure to conform to gender roles*—the degree to which the child feels parents and peers disapprove of his or her gender-related traits. Because such pressure reduces the likelihood that children will explore options related to their interests and talents, children who feel strong gender-typed pressure are often distressed.

■ This 9-year-old girl enjoys karate lessons. Whereas school-age boys usually stick to "masculine" pursuits, girls experiment with a wider range of options. ■

In a longitudinal study of third through seventh graders, *gender-typical* and *gender-contented* children gained in self-esteem over the following year. In contrast, children who were *gender-atypical* and *gender-discontented* declined in self-worth. Furthermore, gender-atypical children who reported *intense pressure to conform to gender roles* experienced serious difficulties—withdrawal, sadness, disappointment, and anxiety (Yunger, Carver, & Perry, 2004).

Clearly, how children feel about themselves in relation to their gender group becomes vitally important in middle childhood and adolescence, and those who experience rejection because of their gender-atypical traits suffer profoundly. **TAKE A MOMENT...** Return to the case of David, the boy who was reared as a girl, on page 392 in Chapter 10. Note how David's dissatisfaction with his gender assignment joined with severe peer condemnation to impair his adjustment.

Currently, researchers and therapists are debating how best to help children who feel gender-atypical. Some favor providing these children with therapy that reinforces them for engaging in traditional gender-role activities, so they will feel more compatible with same-sex peers (Zucker, 2006). Others oppose this approach on grounds that it is likely to heighten felt pressure to conform (which predicts maladjustment) and—for children who fail to change—may result in parental rejection. These experts advocate intervening with parents and peers to help them become more accepting of children's gender-atypical interests and behaviors (Bigler, 2007; Conway, 2007; Crawford, 2003). **TAKE A MOMENT...** In view of what you have learned about the development of children's gender typing in Chapter 10 and this chapter, which approach to you think would be more successful, and why?

◆ **REVIEW** How does friendship change in middle childhood?

◆ **APPLY** What changes in parent–child relationships are probably necessary to help rejected children?

◆ **CONNECT** Return to page 395 in Chapter 10, and review the concept of androgyny. Which of the two sexes is more androgynous in middle childhood, and why?

◆ **REFLECT** As a school-age child, did you have classmates you would classify as popular-aggressive? What were they like, and why do you think peers admired them?

Family Influences

As children move into school, peer, and community contexts, the parent–child relationship changes. We will see that gradual lessening of direct control supports development as long as parental warmth and involvement are sustained. Our discussion will also reveal that families in industrialized nations have become more diverse. Today, there are fewer births per family unit, more lesbian and gay parents who are open about their sexual orientation, and more never-married parents. Further, high rates of divorce, remarriage, and maternal employment have reshaped the family system. **TAKE A MOMENT...** As you consider this array of family forms, note how children's well-being, in each instance, depends on the quality of family interaction, which is sustained by supportive ties to kin and community and by favorable public policies.

Parent–Child Relationships

In middle childhood, the amount of time children spend with parents declines dramatically. Children's growing independence means that parents must deal with new issues. "I've struggled with how many chores to assign, how much allowance to give, whether their friends are good influences, and what to do about problems at school," Rena remarked. "And then there's the challenge of keeping track of them when they're out—or even when they're home and I'm not there to see what's going on."

Despite these new concerns, child rearing becomes easier for parents who established an authoritative style during the early years. Reasoning is more effective with school-age children because of their greater capacity for logical thinking and their increased respect for parents' expert knowledge (Collins, Madsen, & Susman-Stillman, 2002). When parents communicate openly with children and engage in joint decision making when possible, children are more likely to listen to parents' perspectives in situations where compliance is vital (Kuczynski & Lollis, 2002; Russell, Mize, & Bissaker, 2004).

As children demonstrate that they can manage daily activities and responsibilities, effective parents gradually shift control from adult to child. They do not let go entirely but, rather, engage in **coregulation,** a form of supervision in which they exercise general oversight while letting children take charge of moment-by-moment decision making. Coregulation grows out of a warm, cooperative relationship between parent and child based on give-and-take and mutual respect. Parents must guide and monitor from a distance and effectively communicate expectations when they are with their children. And children must inform parents of their whereabouts, activities, and problems so parents can intervene when necessary (Maccoby, 1984). Coregulation supports and protects children while preparing them for adolescence, when they will make many important decisions themselves.

As at younger ages, mothers spend more time than fathers with school-age children and know more about children's everyday activities, although many fathers are highly involved (see pages 274–275 in Chapter 7). Both parents, however, tend to devote more time to children of their own sex (Crouter et al., 1999; Lamb & Lewis, 2004). In parents' separate activities with children, mothers are more concerned with caregiving and ensuring that children meet responsibilities for homework, after-school lessons, and chores. Fathers, especially those with sons, focus on achievement-related and recreational pursuits (Collins & Russell, 1991). But when both parents are present, fathers engage in as much caregiving as mothers.

Although children often press for greater independence, they also know how much they need their parents' support. In one study, fifth and sixth graders described parents as the most influential people in their lives, often turning to them for affection, advice, enhancement of self-worth, and assistance with everyday problems (Furman & Buhrmester, 1992). A strong sense of attachment security to both parents is positively related to school-age children's academic and social self-esteem (Diener et al., 2008). And in a longitudinal survey of more than 13,000 nationally representative U.S. parents, those who were warm and involved, monitored their child's activities, and avoided coercive discipline were more likely to have academically and socially competent children. Using these authoritative strategies in middle childhood predicted reduced engagement in antisocial behavior when children reached adolescence (Amato & Fowler, 2002).

Siblings

In addition to parents and friends, siblings continue to be important sources of support. Yet sibling rivalry tends to increase in middle childhood. As children participate in a wider range of activities, parents often compare siblings' traits and accomplishments. The child who gets less parental affection, more disapproval, or fewer material resources is likely to be resentful and show poorer adjustment over time (Dunn, 2004; Tamrouti-Makkink et al., 2004).

For same-sex siblings who are close in age, parental comparisons are more frequent, resulting in more quarreling and antagonism and in poorer adjustment. This effect is particularly strong when parents are under stress as a result of financial worries, marital conflict, single parenthood, or child negativity (Jenkins, Rasbash, & O'Connor, 2003). Parents whose energies are drained become less careful about being fair. Perhaps because fathers, overall, spend less time with children than mothers, children react especially intensely when fathers prefer one child (Brody, Stoneman, & McCoy, 1992).

To reduce this rivalry, siblings often strive to be different from one another. For example, two brothers I know deliberately selected different athletic pursuits and musical instruments. If the older one did especially well at an activity, the younger one did not want to try it. Parents can limit these effects by making an effort not to compare children, but some feedback about

© BRUCE LAURANCE/GETTY IMAGES/BLEND IMAGES

■ Although sibling rivalry tends to increase in middle childhood, siblings also provide each other with emotional support and, sometimes, patient help with difficult tasks. ■

their competencies is inevitable. As siblings attempt to win recognition for their own uniqueness, they shape important aspects of each other's development.

Although conflict rises, many siblings continue to rely on each other for companionship, assistance, and emotional support (Siebert & Kerns, 2009). When researchers asked siblings about shared daily activities, children mentioned that older siblings often helped younger siblings with academic and peer challenges. And both offered each other help with family issues (Tucker, McHale, & Crouter, 2001). But for siblings to reap these benefits, parental encouragement of warm, considerate sibling ties is vital. Providing parents with training in mediation—how to get siblings to lay down ground rules, clarify their points of disagreement and common ground, and discuss possible solutions—increases siblings' awareness of each other's perspectives and reduces animosity (Smith & Ross, 2007).

When siblings get along well, the older sibling's academic and social competence tends to "rub off on" the younger sibling, fostering more favorable achievement and peer relations (Brody & Murry, 2001; Lamarche et al., 2006). But older siblings with conflict-ridden peer relations tend to transmit their physically or relationally aggressive styles to their younger brothers and sisters (Ostrov, Crick, & Stauffacher, 2006).

Only Children

Although sibling relationships bring many benefits, they are not essential for normal development. Contrary to popular belief, only children are not spoiled, and, in some respects, they are advantaged. U.S. children growing up in one-child and multichild families do not differ in self-rated personality traits (Mottus, Indus, & Allik, 2008). And compared to children with siblings, only children are higher in self-esteem and achievement motivation, do better in school, and attain higher levels of education. One reason may be that only children have somewhat closer relationships with parents, who may exert more pressure for mastery and accomplishment (Falbo, 1992). Furthermore, only children have just as many close, high-quality friends as children with siblings. However, they tend to be less well-accepted in the peer group, perhaps because they have not had opportunities to learn effective conflict-resolution strategies through sibling interaction (Kitzmann, Cohen, & Lockwood, 2002).

Favorable development also characterizes only children in China, where a one-child family policy has been strictly enforced in urban areas for more than two decades to control population growth (Yang, 2008). Compared with agemates who have siblings, Chinese only children are advanced in cognitive development and academic achievement. They also feel more emotionally secure, perhaps because government disapproval promotes tension in families with more than one child (Falbo & Poston, 1993; Jiao, Ji, & Jing, 1996; Yang et al., 1995). Chinese mothers usually ensure that their children have regular contact with first cousins (who are considered siblings). Perhaps as a result, Chinese only children do not differ from agemates with siblings in social skills and peer acceptance (Hart, Newell, & Olsen, 2003). The next generation of Chinese only children, however, will have no first cousins.

Gay and Lesbian Families

Several million American gay men and lesbians are parents, most through previous heterosexual marriages, some through adoption, and a growing number through reproductive technologies (Ambert, 2005; Patterson, 2002). In the past, because of laws assuming that homosexuals could not be adequate parents, those who divorced a heterosexual partner lost custody of their children. Today, some U.S. states hold that sexual orientation in itself is irrelevant to custody. A few U.S. states, however, ban gay and lesbian couples from adopting children. Among other countries, gay and lesbian adoptions are legal in Argentina, Belgium, Canada, Mexico, the Netherlands, Norway, Spain, Sweden, the United Kingdom, and Uruguay.

Most research on homosexual parents and children is limited to volunteer samples. Findings of these investigations indicate that gay and lesbian parents are as committed to and effective at child rearing as heterosexual parents and sometimes more so (Bos, van Balen, & van den Boom, 2007; Tasker, 2005). Also, whether born to or adopted by their parents or conceived through donor insemination, children in gay and lesbian families did not differ from the children of heterosexuals in mental health, peer relations, or gender identity (Allen & Burrell, 1996; Farr, Forssell, & Patterson, 2010; Golombok & Tasker, 1996). Two additional studies, which surmounted the potential bias associated with volunteer samples by including all lesbian-mother families who had conceived children at a fertility clinic, also reported that children were developing favorably (Brewaeys et al., 1997; Chan, Raboy, & Patterson, 1998). Likewise, among participants drawn from a representative sample of British mothers and their 7-year-olds, children reared in lesbian-mother families did not differ from children reared in heterosexual families in adjustment and gender-role preferences (Golombok et al., 2003).

■ Gay and lesbian parents are as committed to and as effective at child rearing as heterosexual parents. Their children are well-adjusted, and the large majority develop a heterosexual orientation. ■

Furthermore, children of gay and lesbian parents do not differ from other children in sexual orientation: The large majority are heterosexual (Tasker, 2005). But some evidence suggests that more adolescents from homosexual families experiment for a time with partners of both sexes, perhaps as a result of being reared in families and communities highly tolerant of nonconformity and difference (Bos, van Balen, & van den Boom, 2004; Stacey & Biblarz, 2001).

A major concern of gay and lesbian parents is that their children will be stigmatized by their parents' sexual orientation. Most studies indicate that incidents of teasing or bullying are rare because parents and children carefully manage the information they reveal to others (Tasker, 2005). But in an Australian study, even though most third to tenth graders were guarded about discussing their parents' relationship with peers, nearly half reported harassment (Ray & Gregory, 2001). Overall, children of gay and lesbian parents can be distinguished from other children mainly by issues related to living in a nonsupportive society.

Never-Married Single-Parent Families

About 10 percent of U.S. children live with a single parent who has never married and does not have a partner. Of these parents, about 85 percent are mothers, 15 percent fathers (U.S. Census Bureau, 2010b). In recent years, more single women over age 30 in high-status occupations have become parents. But they are still few in number, and little is known about their children's development.

In the United States, African-American young women make up the largest group of never-married parents. About 64 percent of births to black mothers in their twenties are to women without a partner, compared with 28 percent of births to white women (U.S. Census Bureau, 2010b). African-American women postpone marriage more and childbirth less than women in other U.S. ethnic groups. Job loss, persisting unemployment, and consequent inability of many black men to support a family have contributed to the number of African-American never-married, single-mother families.

Never-married black mothers tap the extended family, especially their own mothers and sometimes male relatives, for help in rearing their children (Gasden, 1999; Jayakody & Kalil, 2002). For about one-third, marriage—not necessarily to the child's biological father—occurs within nine years after birth of the first child (Wu, Bumpass, & Musick, 2001). These couples function much like other first-marriage parents. Their children often are unaware that the father is a stepfather, and parents do not report the child-rearing difficulties typical of blended families (Ganong & Coleman, 1994).

Still, for low-SES women, never-married parenthood generally increases financial hardship. Nearly 50 percent of white mothers and 60 percent of black mothers have a second child while unmarried. And they are far less likely than divorced mothers to receive paternal child support payments, although child support enforcement both reduces financial stress and increases father involvement (Huang, 2006).

Children in single-mother homes display adjustment problems associated with economic hardship and living in run-down neighborhoods (Kotchick, Dorsey, & Heller, 2005). Furthermore, children of never-married mothers who lack a father's warmth and involvement achieve less well in school and engage in more antisocial behavior than children in low-SES, first-marriage families (Coley, 1998). But marriage to the child's biological father benefits children only when the father is a reliable source of economic and emotional support. When a mother pairs up with an antisocial father, her child is at far greater risk for conduct problems than if she had reared the child alone (Jaffee et al., 2003). Strengthening social support, education, and employment opportunities for low-SES parents would greatly enhance the well-being of unmarried mothers and their children.

Divorce

Children's interactions with parents and siblings are affected by other aspects of family life. Joey and Lizzie's relationship, Rena told me, had been particularly negative only a few years before. Joey pushed, hit, taunted, and called Lizzie names. Although she tried to retaliate, Lizzie was no match for Joey's larger size. The arguments usually ended with Lizzie running in tears to her mother. Joey and Lizzie's fighting coincided with their parents' growing marital unhappiness. When Joey was 8 and Lizzie 5, their father, Drake, moved out.

Between 1960 and 1985, divorce rates in Western nations rose dramatically before stabilizing in most countries. The United States has experienced a decline in divorces over the past decade, largely due to a rise in age at first marriage (couples marrying at older ages have a lower divorce rate) (Amato & Dorius, 2010). Nevertheless, the United States continues to have the highest divorce rate in the world (see Figure 13.6). Of the 45 percent of American marriages that end in divorce, half involve children. At any given time, one-fourth of U.S. children live in single-parent households. Although most reside with their mothers, the percentage in father-headed households has increased steadily, to about 12 percent (Federal Interagency Forum on Child and Family Statistics, 2008).

Children of divorce spend an average of five years in a single-parent home—almost a third of childhood. For many, divorce leads to new family relationships. About two-thirds of divorced parents marry again. Half their children eventually experience a third major change—the end of their parent's second marriage (Hetherington & Kelly, 2002).

These figures reveal that divorce is not a single event in the lives of parents and children. Instead, it is a transition that leads to a variety of new living arrangements, accompanied by changes in housing, income, and family roles and responsibilities. Since the 1960s, many studies have reported that marital breakup is stressful for children. But research also reveals great individual differences (Hetherington, 2003). How well children fare depends on many factors: the custodial parent's psychological health, the child's characteristics, and social supports within the family and surrounding community.

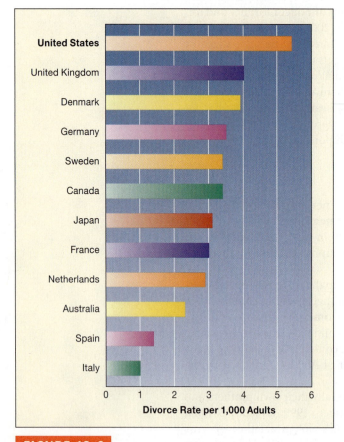

Divorce Rate per 1,000 Adults

FIGURE 13.6

Divorce rates in 12 industrialized nations. The U.S. divorce rate is the highest in the world, far exceeding divorce rates in other countries. *(Adapted from U.S. Census Bureau, 2010b.)*

IMMEDIATE CONSEQUENCES "Things were worst during the period when Drake and I decided to separate," Rena reflected. "We fought over division of our belongings and the custody of the children, and the kids suffered. Sobbing, Lizzie told me she was 'sorry she made Daddy go away.' Joey kicked and threw things at home and didn't do his work at school. In the midst of everything, I could hardly deal with their problems. We had to sell the house; I couldn't afford it alone. And I needed a better-paying job."

Family conflict often rises in newly divorced households as parents try to settle disputes over children and possessions. Once one parent moves out, additional events threaten supportive interactions between parents and children. Mother-headed households typically experience a sharp drop in income. In the United States, the majority of divorced mothers with young children live in poverty, getting less than the full amount of child support from the absent father or none at all (Children's Defense Fund, 2009). They often have to move to lower-cost housing, reducing supportive ties to neighbors and friends.

When parents divorce, young children often blame themselves and respond with both fear and anger. This father's soothing words help his daughter understand that she is not responsible for the marital breakup. ■

The transition from marriage to divorce typically leads to high maternal stress, depression, and anxiety and to a disorganized family situation. Declines in well-being are greatest for mothers of young children (Williams & Dunne-Bryant, 2006). "Meals and bedtimes were at all hours, the house didn't get cleaned, and I stopped taking Joey and Lizzie on weekend outings," said Rena. As children react with distress and anger to their less secure home lives, discipline may become harsh and inconsistent. Contact with noncustodial fathers often decreases over time (Hetherington & Kelly, 2002). Fathers who see their children only occasionally are inclined to be permissive and indulgent, making the mother's task of managing the child even more difficult.

The more parents argue and fail to provide children with warmth, involvement, and consistent guidance, the poorer children's adjustment. About 20 to 25 percent of children in divorced families display severe problems, compared with about 10 percent in nondivorced families (Lansford, 2009; Noller et al., 2008). At the same time, reactions vary with children's age, temperament, and sex.

Children's Age. Five-year-old Lizzie's fear that she had caused her father to leave home is not unusual. Preschool and young school-age children often blame themselves for a marital breakup and fear that both parents may abandon them (Lansford et al., 2006). Hence, they are more likely to display both anxious, fearful and angry, defiant reactions than older children and adolescents with the cognitive maturity to understand that they are not responsible for their parents' divorce.

Still, many school-age and adolescent youngsters also react strongly, experiencing depressed mood, declining in school performance, becoming unruly, and escaping into undesirable peer activities, such as running away, truancy, and early sexual activity, particularly when family conflict is high and parental supervision is low (D'Onofrio et al., 2006; Lansford et al., 2006). Some older children—especially the oldest child in the family—display more mature behavior, willingly taking on extra household tasks, care of younger siblings, and emotional support of a depressed, anxious mother. But if these demands are too great, these children may eventually become resentful, withdraw from the family, and engage in angry, acting-out behavior (Hetherington, 1999).

Children's Temperament and Sex. Exposure to stressful life events and inadequate parenting magnifies the problems of temperamentally difficult children (Lengua et al., 2000). In contrast, easy children are less often targets of parental anger and also cope more effectively with adversity.

These findings help explain sex differences in response to divorce. Girls sometimes respond as Lizzie did, with internalizing reactions such as crying, self-criticism, and withdrawal. More often, children of both sexes show demanding, attention-getting behavior. But in mother-custody families, boys are at slightly greater risk for serious adjustment problems

(Amato, 2001, 2010). Recall from Chapter 10 that boys are more active and noncompliant—behaviors that increase with exposure to parental conflict and inconsistent discipline. Research reveals that long before the marital breakup, sons of divorcing couples display higher rates of impulsivity, defiance, and aggression—behaviors that may have been caused by their parents' marital problems while also contributing to them (Hetherington, 1999; Shaw, Winslow, & Flanagan, 1999; Strohschein, 2005). As a result, more boys enter the period of turmoil surrounding divorce with reduced capacity to cope with family stress.

Perhaps because their behavior is more unruly, boys of divorcing parents receive less emotional support from mothers, teachers, and peers. And as Joey's behavior toward Lizzie illustrates, the coercive cycles of interaction between distressed children and their divorced mothers soon spread to sibling relations (Hetherington & Kelly, 2002; Sheehan et al., 2004). After divorce, children who are challenging to rear generally get worse.

LONG-TERM CONSEQUENCES   Rena eventually found better-paying work and gained control over the daily operation of the household. Her own feelings of anger and rejection also declined. And after several meetings with a counselor, Rena and Drake realized the harmful impact of their quarreling on Joey and Lizzie. Drake visited regularly and handled Joey's disruptiveness with firmness and consistency. Soon Joey's school performance improved, his behavior problems subsided, and both children seemed calmer and happier.

Most children show improved adjustment by two years after divorce. Yet overall, children and adolescents of divorced parents continue to score slightly lower than children of continuously married parents in academic achievement, self-esteem, social competence, and emotional and behavioral adjustment (Amato, 2001; Lansford, 2009). Children with difficult temperaments are more likely to drop out of school, to be depressed, and to engage in antisocial behavior in adolescence. And divorce is linked to problems with adolescent sexuality and development of intimate ties. Young people who experienced parental divorce—especially more than once—display higher rates of early sexual activity and adolescent parenthood (Wolfinger, 2000). Some experience other lasting difficulties—reduced educational attainment, troubled romantic relationships and marriages, divorce in adulthood, and unsatisfying parent–child relationships (Amato, 2006, 2010; Lansford, 2009). Thus, divorce can have consequences for subsequent generations.

© FLYNN LARSEN/CORBIS

■ Regular contact with fathers as well as mothers is an important factor in children's adjustment after divorce. In fact, some evidence indicates that sons do better when the father is the custodial parent. ■

The overriding factor in positive adjustment following divorce is effective parenting—how well the custodial parent handles stress and shields the child from family conflict, and the extent to which each parent uses authoritative child rearing (Leon, 2003; Wolchik et al., 2000). Where the custodial parent is the mother, regular contact with fathers is also important. In the United States, paternal contact has risen over the past three decades, with about one-third of children today experiencing at least weekly visits (Amato & Dorius, 2010).

The more paternal contact and the warmer the relationship, the less children react with defiance and aggression (Dunn et al., 2004). For girls, a good father–child relationship protects against early sexual activity and unhappy romantic involvements. For boys, it seems to affect overall psychological well-being. In fact, several studies report that outcomes for sons are better when the father is the custodial parent (Clarke-Stewart & Hayward, 1996; McLanahan, 1999). Fathers' greater economic security and image of authority seem to help them engage in effective parenting with sons. And boys in father-custody families may benefit from greater involvement of both parents because noncustodial mothers participate more in their children's lives than noncustodial fathers.

Although divorce is painful for children, remaining in an intact but high-conflict family is much worse than making the transition to a low-conflict, single-parent household (Greene et al., 2003; Strohschein, 2005). However, more parents today are divorcing because they are moderately (rather than extremely) dissatisfied with their relationship. Research suggests that children in these low-discord homes are especially puzzled and upset. Perhaps these youngsters' inability to understand the marital breakup and grief over the loss of a seemingly happy home life explain why the adjustment problems of children of divorce have intensified over time (Amato, 2001; Lansford, 2009).

Regardless of the extent of their friction, parents who set aside their disagreements and engage in *coparenting* (see page 70 in Chapter 2), supporting each other in their child-rearing roles, greatly improve their children's chances of growing up competent, stable, and happy. Caring extended-family members, teachers, siblings, and friends also reduce the likelihood that divorce will result in long-term difficulties (Hetherington, 2003; Lussier et al., 2002).

DIVORCE MEDIATION, JOINT CUSTODY, AND CHILD SUPPORT Awareness that divorce is highly stressful for children and families has led to community-based services aimed at helping them through this difficult time. One such service is **divorce mediation,** a series of meetings between divorcing adults and a trained professional aimed at reducing family conflict, including legal battles over property division and child custody. Research reveals that mediation increases out-of-court settlements, cooperation and involvement of both parents in child rearing, and parents' and children's feelings of well-being (Douglas, 2006; Emery, Sbarra, & Grover, 2005).

To further encourage parents to resolve their disputes, parent education programs are becoming common. During a series of weekly sessions over several months, professionals teach parents about the positive impact of constructive conflict resolution and of coparenting on children's well-being (Braver et al., 2005; Cookston et al., 2006; Wolchik et al., 2002). Because of the demonstrated impact of parent education on parental cooperation, courts in many U.S. states may require parents to attend a program.

Joint custody, which grants each parent an equal say in important decisions about the child's upbringing, is becoming increasingly common. Children usually reside with one parent and see the other on a fixed schedule, similar to the typical sole-custody situation. In other cases, parents share physical custody, and children move between homes and sometimes between schools and peer groups. These transitions can be especially hard on some children. Joint-custody parents usually report little conflict—fortunately so, since the success of the arrangement depends on coparenting. And their children, regardless of living arrangements, tend to be better-adjusted than children in sole-maternal-custody homes (Bauserman, 2002).

Finally, many single-parent families depend on child support from the absent parent to relieve financial strain. All U.S. states have procedures for withholding wages from parents who fail to make these payments. Although child support is usually not enough to lift a single-parent family out of poverty, it can ease its burdens substantially. Noncustodial fathers who have generous visitation schedules and who often see their children are more likely to pay child support regularly (Amato & Sobolewski, 2004). Applying What We Know on page 514 summarizes ways to help children adjust to their parents' divorce.

Blended Families

"If you get married to Wendell and Daddy gets married to Carol," Lizzie wondered aloud to Rena, "then I'll have two sisters and one more brother. And let's see, how many grandmothers and grandfathers? A lot!" exclaimed Lizzie.

About 60 percent of divorced parents remarry within a few years. Others *cohabit,* or share a sexual relationship and a residence with a partner outside of marriage. Parent, stepparent, and children form a new family structure called a **blended,** or **reconstituted, family.** For some children, this expanded family network is positive, bringing greater adult attention. But overall, they have more adjustment problems—including internalizing and externalizing symptoms and poor school performance—than children in stable, first-marriage families (Jeynes, 2007; Nicholson et al., 2008). Switching to stepparents' new rules and expectations can be stressful, and children often regard steprelatives as intruders. How well they adapt is, again, related to the quality of family functioning (Hetherington & Kelly, 2002). This depends on which parent forms a new relationship, the child's age and sex, and the complexity of blended-family relationships. As we will see, older children and girls seem to have the hardest time.

Applying What We Know

Helping Children Adjust to Their Parents' Divorce

SUGGESTION	EXPLANATION
Shield children from conflict.	Witnessing intense parental conflict is very damaging to children. If one parent insists on expressing hostility, children fare better if the other parent does not respond in kind.
Provide children with as much continuity, familiarity, and predictability as possible.	Children adjust better during the period surrounding divorce when their lives have some stability—for example, the same school, bedroom, babysitter, playmates, and daily schedule.
Explain the divorce and tell children what to expect.	Children are more likely to develop fears of abandonment if they are not prepared for their parents' separation. They should be told that their parents will not be living together anymore, which parent will be moving out, and when they will be able to see that parent. If possible, parents should explain the divorce together, providing a reason that the child can understand and assure the child that he is not to blame.
Emphasize the permanence of the divorce.	Fantasies of parents getting back together can prevent children from accepting the reality of their current life. Children should be told that the divorce is final and that they cannot change this fact.
Respond sympathetically to children's feelings.	Children need a supportive and understanding response to their feelings of sadness, fear, and anger. For children to adjust well, their painful emotions must be acknowledged, not denied or avoided.
Engage in authoritative parenting.	Parents who engage in authoritative parenting—providing affection and acceptance, reasonable demands for mature behavior, and consistent, rational discipline—greatly reduce their children's risk of maladjustment following divorce.
Promote a continuing relationship with both parents.	When parents disentangle their lingering hostility toward the former spouse from the child's need for a continuing relationship with the other parent, children adjust well. Grandparents and other extended-family members can help by not taking sides.

Source: Teyber, 2001.

MOTHER–STEPFATHER FAMILIES Since mothers generally retain custody of children, the most common form of blended family is a mother–stepfather arrangement. Boys tend to adjust quickly, welcoming a stepfather who is warm, who refrains from exerting his authority too quickly, and who offers relief from coercive cycles of mother–son interaction. Mothers' friction with sons also declines as a result of greater economic security, another adult to share household tasks, and an end to loneliness (Visher, Visher, & Pasley, 2003). Stepfathers who marry rather than cohabit are more involved in parenting, perhaps because men who choose to marry a mother with children are more interested in and skilled at child rearing (Hofferth & Anderson, 2003). Girls, however, often have difficulty with their custodial mother's remarriage. Stepfathers disrupt the close ties many girls have established with their mothers, and girls often react with sulky, resistant behavior (Bray, 1999).

But age affects these findings. Older school-age children and adolescents of both sexes display more irresponsible, acting-out behavior than their peers not in stepfamilies (Hetherington & Stanley-Hagan, 2000; Robertson, 2008). If parents are warmer and more involved with their biological children than with their stepchildren, older children are more likely to notice and challenge unfair treatment. And adolescents often view the new stepparent as a threat to their freedom, especially if they experienced little parental monitoring in the single-parent family. But when teenagers have affectionate, cooperative relationships with their mothers, many eventually develop good relationships with their stepfathers—a circumstance linked to more favorable adolescent well-being (Yuan & Hamilton, 2006).

© ARIEL SKELLEY/GETTY IMAGES/BLEND IMAGES

■ When stepparents move into their new roles gradually, first building warm relationships with stepchildren, they ease adjustment to life in a blended family. ■

FATHER–STEPMOTHER FAMILIES   Remarriage of noncustodial fathers often leads to reduced contact with their biological children, especially when fathers remarry quickly, before they have established post-divorce parent–child routines (Dunn, 2002; Juby et al., 2007). When fathers have custody, children typically react negatively to remarriage. One reason is that children living with fathers often start out with more problems. Perhaps the biological mother could no longer handle the difficult child (usually a boy), so the father and his new partner are faced with a youngster who has behavior problems. In other instances, the father has custody because of a very close relationship with the child, and his remarriage disrupts this bond (Buchanan, Maccoby, & Dornbusch, 1996).

Girls, especially, have a hard time getting along with their stepmothers, either because the remarriage threatens the girl's bond with her father or because she becomes entangled in loyalty conflicts between the two mother figures. But the longer children live in father–stepmother households, the closer they feel to their stepmothers and the more positive their interaction with them becomes (Hetherington & Jodl, 1994; King, 2007). With time and patience, children of both genders benefit from the support of a second mother figure.

SUPPORT FOR BLENDED FAMILIES   Parenting education and couples counseling can help parents and children adapt to the complexities of blended families. Effective approaches encourage stepparents to move into their new roles gradually by first building a warm relationship with the child. Only when a warm bond has formed between stepparents and stepchildren is more active parenting possible (Nicholson et al., 2008). Counselors can offer couples guidance in coparenting to limit loyalty conflicts and provide consistency in child rearing. This allows children to benefit from the increased diversity that stepparent relationships bring to their lives.

Unfortunately, the divorce rate for second marriages is even higher than for first marriages. Parents with antisocial tendencies and poor child-rearing skills are particularly likely to have several divorces and remarriages. The more marital transitions children experience, the greater their adjustment difficulties (Amato, 2010). These families usually require prolonged, intensive therapy.

Maternal Employment and Dual-Earner Families

Today, U.S. single and married mothers are in the labor market in nearly equal proportions, and more than three-fourths of those with school-age children are employed (U.S. Census Bureau, 2010b). In Chapter 7, we saw that the impact of maternal employment on early development depends on the quality of child care and the continuing parent–child relationship. The same is true in middle childhood.

MATERNAL EMPLOYMENT AND CHILD DEVELOPMENT   When mothers enjoy their work and remain committed to parenting, children show favorable adjustment—higher self-esteem, more positive family and peer relations, less gender-stereotyped beliefs, and better grades in school. Girls, especially, profit from the image of female competence. Regardless of SES, daughters of employed mothers perceive women's roles as involving more freedom of choice and satisfaction and are more achievement- and career-oriented (Hoffman, 2000).

Parenting practices contribute to these benefits. Employed mothers who value their parenting role are more likely to use authoritative child rearing and coregulation. Also, children in dual-earner households devote more daily hours to doing homework under parental guidance and participate more in household chores. And maternal employment leads fathers—especially those who believe in the importance of the paternal role and who feel successful at parenting—to take on greater child-rearing responsibilities, with a small but increasing number staying home full-time (Gottfried, Gottfried, & Bathurst, 2002; Jacobs & Kelley, 2006). Paternal involvement is associated with higher intelligence and achievement, more mature social behavior, and a flexible view of gender

© SIMON JARRATT/CORBIS

■ Employed mothers who enjoy their work while also valuing the parenting role tend to have children who show higher self-esteem, more positive family and peer relations, less gender-stereotyped beliefs, and better school performance. ■

roles in childhood and adolescence, and with generally better mental health in adulthood (Coltrane, 1996; Pleck & Masciadrelli, 2004).

But when employment places heavy demands on the mother's schedule or is stressful for other reasons, children are at risk for ineffective parenting. Working many hours or experiencing a negative workplace atmosphere is associated with reduced parental sensitivity, fewer joint parent–child activities, and poorer cognitive development throughout childhood and adolescence (Brooks-Gunn, Han, & Waldfogel, 2002; Bumpus, Crouter, & McHale, 2006; Strazdins et al., 2006). Negative consequences are magnified when low-SES mothers spend long days at low-paying, physically exhausting jobs—conditions linked to maternal depression and to harsh, inconsistent discipline (Raver, 2003). In contrast, part-time employment and flexible work schedules are associated with good child adjustment (Frederiksen-Goldsen & Sharlach, 2000; Hill et al., 2006). By preventing work–family life conflict, these arrangements help parents meet children's needs.

SUPPORT FOR EMPLOYED PARENTS AND THEIR FAMILIES

In dual-earner families, the father's willingness to share responsibilities is a crucial factor. If he helps little or not at all, the mother carries a double load, at home and at work, leading to fatigue, distress, and little time and energy for children. Fortunately, compared to three decades ago, today's U.S. fathers are far more involved in child care (see page 275 in Chapter 7). But their increased participation has resulted in a growing number of fathers who also report work–family life conflict (Galinsky, Aumann, & Bond, 2009).

Employed parents need assistance from work settings and communities in their child-rearing roles. Part-time employment, flexible schedules, job sharing, and paid leave when children are ill help parents juggle the demands of work and child rearing. Equal pay and employment opportunities for women are also important. Because these policies enhance financial status and morale, they improve the way mothers feel and behave when they arrive home at the end of the working day.

CHILD CARE FOR SCHOOL-AGE CHILDREN

High-quality child care is vital for parents' peace of mind and children's well-being, even during middle childhood. An estimated 7 million 5- to 13-year-olds in the United States are **self-care children,** who regularly look after themselves for some period of time during after-school hours (Durlak & Weissberg, 2007). Self-care increases with age and also with SES, perhaps because of the greater safety of higher-income neighborhoods. But when lower-SES parents lack alternatives to self-care, their children spend more hours on their own (Casper & Smith, 2002).

Some studies report that self-care children suffer from low self-esteem, antisocial behavior, poor academic achievement, and fearfulness. Others show no such effects. Children's maturity and the way they spend their time seem to explain these contradictions. Among younger school-age children, those who spend more hours alone have more adjustment difficulties (Vandell & Posner, 1999). As children become old enough to look after themselves, those who have a history of authoritative child rearing, are monitored by parental telephone calls, and have regular after-school chores appear responsible and well-adjusted. In contrast, children left to their own devices are more likely to bend to peer pressures and engage in antisocial behavior (Coley, Morris, & Hernandez, 2004; Vandell et al., 2006).

Before age 8 or 9, most children need supervision because they are not yet competent to handle emergencies (Galambos & Maggs, 1991). But throughout middle childhood and early adolescence, attending after-school programs with well-trained staffs, generous adult–child ratios, and skill-building activities is linked to good school performance and emotional and social adjustment (Durlak & Weissberg, 2007; Granger, 2008). Low-SES children who participate in "after-care" programs offering academic assistance and enrichment activities (scouting, music and art lessons, clubs) show special benefits. They exceed their

■ In this after-school program, children learn about fossils from an AmeriCorps volunteer. Attending high-quality after-school programs is linked to good school performance and emotional and social adjustment. ■

© BOB DAEMMRICH/PHOTOEDIT

self-care counterparts in classroom work habits, academic achievement, and prosocial behavior and display fewer behavior problems (Lauer et al., 2006; Vandell et al., 2006).

Unfortunately, good after-care is in especially short supply in low-income neighborhoods, and children from the very poorest families are least likely to participate in enrichment activities (Afterschool Alliance, 2004; Dearing et al., 2009). A special need exists for well-planned programs in poverty-stricken areas—ones that provide safe environments, warm relationships with adults, and enjoyable, goal-oriented activities.

ASK YOURSELF

◆ **REVIEW** Describe and explain changes in sibling relationships during middle childhood.

◆ **APPLY** Steve and Marissa are in the midst of an acrimonious divorce. Their 9-year-old son Dennis has become hostile and defiant. How can Steve and Marissa help Dennis adjust?

◆ **CONNECT** How does each level in Bronfenbrenner's ecological systems theory—microsystem, mesosystem, exosystem, and macrosystem—contribute to the effects of maternal employment on children's development?

◆ **REFLECT** What after-school child-care arrangements did you experience in elementary school? How do you think they influenced your development?

Some Common Problems of Development

We have considered a variety of stressful experiences that place children at risk for future problems. Next, we address two more areas of concern: school-age children's fears and anxieties and the consequences of child sexual abuse. Finally, we sum up factors that help school-age children cope effectively with stress.

Fears and Anxieties

Although fears of the dark, thunder and lightning, and supernatural beings persist into middle childhood, older children's anxieties are also directed toward new concerns. As children begin to understand the realities of the wider world, the possibility of personal harm (being robbed, stabbed, or shot) and media events (war and disasters) often trouble them. Other common worries include academic failure, separation from parents, parents' health, physical injuries, the possibility of dying, and peer rejection (Muris et al., 2000; Weems & Costa, 2005). Because children often mull over frightening thoughts at bedtime, nighttime fears actually increase between ages 7 and 9 (Muris et al., 2001).

Children in Western nations mention exposure to negative information in the media as the most common source of their fears, followed by direct exposure to frightening events (Muris et al., 2001). Nevertheless, as we saw in Chapters 10 and 12, many parents have no rules about their children's TV viewing or computer use, including Internet access.

As long as fears are not too intense, most children handle them constructively, using the more sophisticated emotional self-regulation strategies that develop in middle childhood. Consequently, fears decline with age, especially for girls, who express more fears than boys throughout childhood and adolescence (Gullone, 2000). But about 5 percent of school-age children develop an intense, unmanageable fear, called a **phobia.** Children with inhibited temperaments are at high risk, displaying phobias five to six times as often as other children (Ollendick, King, & Muris, 2002).

For example, in *school phobia,* children feel severe apprehension about attending school, often accompanied by physical complaints (dizziness, nausea, stomachaches, and vomiting). About one-third of children with school phobia are 5- to 7-year-olds for whom the real fear is maternal separation. Family therapy helps these children, whose difficulty can often be traced to parental overprotection (Elliott, 1999).

CULTURAL INFLUENCES

Impact of Ethnic and Political Violence on Children

Around the world, many children live with armed conflict, terrorism, and other acts of violence stemming from ethnic and political tensions. Some children may participate in fighting, either because they are forced or because they want to please adults. Others are kidnapped, assaulted, and tortured. Those who are bystanders often come under direct fire and may be killed or physically maimed. And many watch in horror as family members, friends, and neighbors flee, are wounded, or die. In the past decade, wars have left 6 million children physically disabled, 20 million homeless, and more than 1 million separated from their parents (Ursano & Shaw, 2007; Wexler, Branski, & Kerem, 2006).

When war and social crises are temporary, most children can be comforted and do not show long-term emotional difficulties. But chronic danger requires children to make substantial adjustments that can seriously impair their psychological functioning. Many children of war lose their sense of safety, become desensitized to violence, are haunted by terrifying intrusive memories, are impaired in moral reasoning, and build a pessimistic view of the future. Anxiety and depression increase, as do aggression and antisocial behavior (Joshi et al., 2006; Klingman, 2006). These outcomes appear to be culturally universal, appearing among children from every war zone studied—from Bosnia, Angola, Rwanda, and the Sudan to the West Bank, Afghanistan, and Iraq (Barenbaum, Ruchkin, & Schwab-Stone, 2004).

Parental affection and reassurance are the best protection against lasting problems. When parents offer security, discuss traumatic experiences with children sympathetically, and serve as role models of calm emotional strength, most

children can withstand even extreme war-related violence (Gewirtz, Forgatch, & Wieling, 2008; Smith et al., 2001). Children who are separated from parents must rely on help from their communities. Orphans in Eritrea who were placed in residential settings where they could form close emotional ties with an adult showed less emotional stress five years later than orphans placed in impersonal settings (Wolff & Fesseha, 1999). Education and recreation programs are powerful safeguards, too, providing children with consistency in their lives along with teacher and peer supports.

With the September 11, 2001, terrorist attacks on the World Trade Center, some U.S. children experienced extreme wartime violence firsthand. Children in Public School 31 in Brooklyn, New York, for example, watched through classroom windows as the planes struck the towers and were engulfed in flames and as the towers crumbled. Many worried about the safety of family members, and some lost them. In the aftermath, most expressed intense fears—for example, that terrorists were infiltrating their neighborhoods and that planes flying overhead might smash into nearby buildings.

Unlike many war-traumatized children in the developing world, Public School 31 students

received immediate intervention—a "trauma curriculum" in which they expressed their emotions through writing, drawing, and discussion and participated in experiences aimed at restoring trust and tolerance (Lagnado, 2001). Older children learned about the feelings of their Muslim classmates, the dire condition of children in Afghanistan, and ways to help victims as a means of overcoming a sense of helplessness.

When wartime drains families and communities of resources, international organizations must step in and help children. Efforts to preserve children's physical, psychological, and educational well-being may be the best way to stop the transmission of violence to the next generation.

AP IMAGES/ANJA NIEDRINGHAUS

■ A trauma counselor comforts a child standing amid the rubble of her neighborhood in the Gaza Strip. Many children of war lose their sense of safety. Without special support from caring adults, they are likely to have lasting emotional problems. ■

Most cases of school phobia appear around age 11 to 13, in children who usually find a particular aspect of school frightening—an overcritical teacher, a school bully, or too much parental pressure to achieve. A change in school environment or parenting practices may be needed. Firm insistence that the child return to school, along with training in how to cope with difficult situations, is also helpful (Silverman & Pina, 2008).

Severe childhood anxieties may also arise from harsh living conditions. In inner-city ghettos and in war-torn areas of the world, many children live in the midst of constant danger, chaos, and deprivation. As the Cultural Influences box above reveals, they are at risk for long-term emotional distress and behavior problems. Finally, as we saw in our discussion of child abuse in Chapter 10, too often violence and other destructive acts become part of adult–child relationships. During middle childhood, child sexual abuse increases.

Child Sexual Abuse

Until recently, child sexual abuse was considered rare, and adults often dismissed children's claims of abuse. In the 1970s, efforts by professionals and media attention led to recognition of child sexual abuse as a serious and widespread problem. About 60,000 cases in the United States were confirmed in the most recently reported year (U.S. Department of Health and Human Services, 2009c). But this figure greatly underestimates the extent of sexual abuse, since most victims either delay disclosure for a long time or remain silent (London et al., 2005).

CHARACTERISTICS OF ABUSERS AND VICTIMS   Sexual abuse is committed against children of both sexes, but more often against girls. Most cases are reported in middle childhood, but for some victims, abuse begins early in life and continues for many years (Hoch-Espada, Ryan, & Deblinger, 2006; Trickett & Putnam, 1998).

Typically, the abuser is a male, either a parent or someone the parent knows well—a father, stepfather, or live-in boyfriend or, somewhat less often, an uncle or older brother. But in about 25 percent of cases, mothers are the offenders, more often with sons (Boroughs, 2004). If the abuser is a nonrelative, the person is usually someone the child has come to know and trust. However, the Internet and mobile phones have become avenues through which other adults commit sexual abuse—for example, by exposing children and adolescents to pornography and online sexual advances as a way of "grooming" them for sexual acts offline (Wolak et al., 2008).

Abusers make the child comply in a variety of distasteful ways, including deception, bribery, verbal intimidation, and physical force. You may wonder how any adult—especially a parent or close relative—could violate a child sexually. Many offenders deny their own responsibility, blaming the abuse on the willing participation of a seductive youngster. Yet children are not capable of making a deliberate, informed decision to enter into a sexual relationship! Even older children and adolescents are not free to say yes or no. Rather, the responsibility lies with abusers, who tend to have characteristics that predispose them toward sexual exploitation of children. They have great difficulty controlling their impulses and may suffer from psychological disorders, including alcohol and drug abuse. Often they pick out children who are unlikely to defend themselves or to be believed—those who are physically weak, emotionally deprived, socially isolated, or affected by disabilities (Bolen, 2001).

Reported cases of child sexual abuse are linked to poverty, marital instability, and resulting weakening of family ties. Children who live in homes with a constantly changing cast of characters—repeated marriages, separations, and new partners—are especially vulnerable. But children in economically advantaged, stable homes are also victims, although their abuse is more likely to escape detection (Putnam, 2003).

CONSEQUENCES OF SEXUAL ABUSE   The adjustment problems of child sexual abuse victims—including anxiety, depression, low self-esteem, mistrust of adults, and anger and hostility—are often severe and can persist for years after the abusive episodes. Younger children frequently react with sleep difficulties, loss of appetite, and generalized fearfulness. Adolescents may run away and show suicidal reactions, substance abuse, and delinquency. At all ages, persistent abuse accompanied by force, violence, and a close relationship to the perpetrator (incest) has a more severe impact (Feiring, Taska, & Lewis, 1999; Wolfe, 2006). And repeated sexual abuse, like physical abuse, is associated with central nervous system damage (Cichetti, 2007).

Sexually abused children frequently display precocious sexual knowledge and behavior. In adolescence, abused young people often become promiscuous, and as adults, they show increased arrest rates for sex crimes (mostly against children) and prostitution (Salter et al., 2003; Whipple, 2006). Furthermore,

ENOUGH ABUSE CAMPAIGN © 2005, MASSACHUSETTS CITIZENS FOR CHILDREN

■ This public service announcement asks concerned adults to join in a "show of hands" to send a clear, simple message—"Enough"—about the reality of child sexual abuse and the urgent need for prevention. ■

■ In Keeping Ourselves Safe, New Zealand's national, school-based child abuse prevention program, teachers and police officers collaborate in teaching children to recognize abusive adult behaviors so they can take steps to protect themselves. Parents are encouraged to support and extend these learning experiences at home. ■

women who were sexually abused are likely to choose partners who abuse them and their children. As mothers, they often engage in irresponsible and coercive parenting, including child abuse and neglect (Pianta, Egeland, & Erickson, 1989). In these ways, the harmful impact of sexual abuse is transmitted to the next generation.

PREVENTION AND TREATMENT Treating child sexual abuse is difficult. The reactions of family members—anxiety about harm to the child, anger toward the abuser, and sometimes hostility toward the victim for telling—can increase children's distress. Because sexual abuse typically appears in the midst of other serious family problems, long-term therapy with both children and parents is usually needed (Olafson & Boat, 2000). The best way to reduce the suffering of victims is to prevent sexual abuse from continuing. Today, courts are prosecuting abusers more vigorously and taking children's testimony more seriously (see the Social Issues: Health box on the following page).

Educational programs that teach children to recognize inappropriate sexual advances and whom to turn to for help reduce the risk of abuse (Hebert & Tourigny, 2004). Yet because of controversies over educating children about sexual abuse, few schools offer these interventions. New Zealand is the only country with a national, school-based prevention program targeting sexual abuse. In Keeping Ourselves Safe, children and adolescents learn that abusers are generally not strangers. Parent involvement ensures that home and school work together in teaching children self-protection skills. Evaluations reveal that virtually all New Zealand parents and children support the program and that it has helped many children avoid or report abuse (Sanders, 2006).

Fostering Resilience in Middle Childhood

Throughout middle childhood—and other periods of development—children are confronted with challenging and sometimes threatening situations that require them to cope with psychological stress. In this trio of chapters, we have considered such topics as chronic illness, learning disabilities, achievement expectations, divorce, harsh living conditions and wartime trauma, and sexual abuse. Each taxes children's coping resources, creating serious risks for development.

Nevertheless, only a modest relationship exists between stressful life experiences and psychological disturbance in childhood (Masten & Reed, 2002). In our discussion in Chapter 4 of the long-term consequences of birth complications, we noted that some children overcome the combined effects of birth trauma, poverty, and a troubled family life. The same is true for school difficulties, family transitions, children of war, and child maltreatment. Refer to Applying What We Know on page 522 for an overview of factors that promote *resilience*—the capacity to overcome adversity—during middle childhood.

Often just one or a few of these ingredients account for why one child is "stress-resilient" and another is not. Usually, however, personal and environmental factors are interconnected: Each resource favoring resilience strengthens others. For example, safe, stable neighborhoods with family-friendly community services reduce parents' daily hassles and stress, thereby promoting good parenting (Pinderhughes et al., 2001). In contrast, unfavorable home and neighborhood experiences increase the chances that children will act in ways that expose them to further hardship. And when negative conditions pile up, such as marital discord, poverty, crowded living conditions, neighborhood violence, and abuse and neglect, the rate of maladjustment multiplies (Wright & Masten, 2005).

Of great concern are children's violent acts. Violence committed in schools and communities by U.S. children and adolescents with troubled lives has at times reached the level of atrocities—maimings and murders of adults and peers. Because children spend a great deal of

SOCIAL ISSUES: HEALTH

Children's Eyewitness Testimony

Increasingly, children are being called on to testify in court cases involving child abuse and neglect, child custody, and other matters. The experience can be difficult and traumatic, requiring children to report on highly stressful events and sometimes to speak against a parent or other relative to whom they feel loyal. In some family disputes, they may fear punishment for telling the truth. In addition, child witnesses are faced with an unfamiliar situation—at the very least an interview in the judge's chambers and at most an open courtroom with judge, jury, spectators, and the possibility of unsympathetic cross-examination. Not surprisingly, these conditions can compromise the accuracy of children's recall.

Age Differences

Until recently, children younger than age 5 were rarely asked to testify, and not until age 10 were they assumed fully competent to do so. As a result of societal reactions to rising rates of child abuse and the difficulty of prosecuting perpetrators, legal requirements for child testimony have been relaxed in the United States (Sandler, 2006). Children as young as age 3 frequently serve as witnesses.

Compared with preschoolers, school-age children are better at giving accurate, detailed narrative accounts of past experiences and correctly inferring others' motives and intentions. Older children are also generally more resistant to misleading questions that attorneys may ask when probing for more information or, in cross-examination, trying to influence the child's response (Roebers & Schneider, 2001). Inhibition (ability to suppress impulses and focus on a competing goal), which improves from early to middle childhood, predicts children's resistance to suggestion (Melinder, Endestad, & Magnussen, 2006).

Nevertheless, when properly questioned, even 3-year-olds can recall recent events accurately (Peterson & Rideout, 1998). And in the face of biased interviewing, adolescents and adults often form elaborate, false memories of events (Ceci et al., 2007).

Suggestibility

Court testimony often involves repeated interviews. When adults lead witnesses by suggesting incorrect "facts," interrupt their denials, reinforce them for giving desired answers, or use a confrontational questioning style, they increase the likelihood of incorrect reporting by children and adolescents alike (Bruck & Ceci, 2004; Owen-Kostelnik, Reppucci, & Meyer, 2006).

In one study, 4- to 7-year-olds were asked to recall details about a visitor who had come to their classroom a week earlier. Half the children received a low-pressure interview containing leading questions that implied abuse ("He took your clothes off, didn't he?"). The other half receive a high-pressure interview in which an adult told the child that her friends had said "yes" to the leading questions, praised the child for agreeing ("You're doing great"), and, if the child did not agree, repeated the question. Children were far more likely to give false information—even to fabricate quite fantastic events—in the high-pressure condition (Finnilä et al., 2003).

By the time children appear in court, weeks, months, or even years have passed since the target events. When a long delay is combined with biased interviewing and with stereotyping of the accused ("He's in jail because he's been bad"), children can easily be misled into giving false information (Gilstrap & Ceci, 2005; Quas et al., 2007). The more distinctive and personally relevant an event is, the more likely children are to recall it accurately over time. For example, a year later, even when exposed to misleading information, children correctly reported details of an injury that required emergency room treatment (Peterson, Parsons, & Dean, 2004).

In many sexual abuse cases, anatomically correct dolls are used to prompt children's recall. Although this method helps older children provide more detail about experienced events, it increases the suggestibility of preschoolers, who report physical and sexual contact that never happened (Goodman & Melinder, 2007).

Interventions

Adults must prepare child witnesses so that they understand the courtroom process and know what to expect. In some places, "court schools" take children through the setting and give them an opportunity to role-play court activities. Practice interviews—in which children learn to provide the most accurate, detailed information possible and to admit not knowing rather than agreeing or guessing—are helpful (Saywitz, Goodman, & Lyon, 2002).

At the same time, legal professionals must use interviewing procedures that increase children's accurate reporting. Unbiased, open-ended questions that prompt children to disclose details—"Tell me what happened" or "You said there was a man; tell me about the man"—reduce suggestibility (Goodman & Melinder, 2007). Also, a warm, supportive interview tone fosters accurate recall, perhaps by easing children's anxiety so they feel freer to disagree with an interviewer's false suggestions (Ceci, Bruck, & Battin, 2000).

If children are likely to experience emotional trauma or later punishment (as in a family dispute), courtroom procedures can be adapted to protect them. For example, children can testify over closed-circuit TV so they do not have to face an abuser. When it is not wise for a child to participate directly, impartial expert witnesses can provide testimony that reports on the child's psychological condition and includes important elements of the child's story.

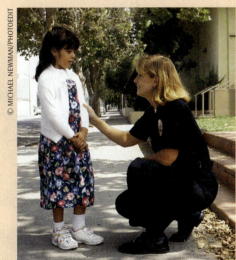

■ School-age eyewitnesses are better able than preschoolers to give accurate, detailed descriptions and correctly infer others' motives and intentions. This police officer can promote accurate recall by using a warm, supportive tone and avoiding leading questions. ■

Applying What We Know

Resources That Foster Resilience in Middle Childhood

TYPE OF RESOURCE	DESCRIPTION
Personal	• Easygoing, sociable temperament • Above-average intelligence • Favorable self-esteem • Persistence in the face of challenge and pleasure in mastery • Good emotional self-regulation and flexible coping strategies
Family	• Warm, trusting relationship with at least one parent • Authoritative child-rearing style • Positive discipline, avoidance of coercive tactics • Warm, supportive sibling relationships
School	• Teachers who are warm, helpful, and stimulating, who encourage students to collaborate, and who emphasize effort and self-improvement • Lessons in tolerance and respect and codes against bullying, which promote positive peer relationships and gratifying friendships • Extracurricular activities, including sports and social service pursuits, that strengthen physical, cognitive, and social skills • High-quality after-school programs that protect children's safety and offer stimulating, skill-building activities
Community	• High-quality after-school programs that protect children's safety and offer stimulating, skill-building activities • An adult—such as an extended-family member, teacher, or neighbor—who provides warmth and social support and is a positive coping model • Stability of neighborhood residents and services—safe outdoor play areas, community centers, and religious organizations—that relieve parental stress and encourage families and neighbors to share leisure time • Youth groups—scouting, clubs, religious youth groups, and other organized activities—that promote positive peer relationships and prosocial behavior

Note: One or a few resources may be sufficient to foster resilience, since each resource strengthens others.
Sources: Commission on Children at Risk, 2008; Wright & Masten, 2005.

© TONY FREEMAN/PHOTOEDIT

■ Personal and environmental factors work together to foster resilience. In the safe, stimulating environment of an after-school workshop in their community, these children acquire new skills, collaborate with peers, and develop gratifying friendships. ■

time in school, the quality of their relationships with teachers and classmates strongly influences their development, academically and socially (Elias, Parker, & Rosenblatt, 2005).

Several highly effective school-based *social and emotional learning programs* reduce violence (including bullying and gang involvement) and other antisocial acts and increase academic motivation by fostering social competence and supportive relationships. Among these is the Resolving Conflict Creatively Program (RCCP), used in more than 400 schools throughout the United States (Lantieri, 2003). RCCP provides children and adolescents with up to 51 hour-long lessons in emotional and social understanding and skills. Topics include expressing feelings, regulating anger, resolving social conflicts, cooperating, appreciating diversity, identifying and standing up against prejudice and bullying, and making decisions based on long- rather than short-term goals. In New York City, RCCP is integrated with language arts: High-quality children's literature, selected for relevance to program themes, complements each lesson. Discussion, writing, and role play of the stories deepen student's understanding of conflict, emotions, relationships, and community.

Compared with students receiving few or no lessons, second to sixth graders receiving substantial RCCP instruction less often misinterpreted others' acts as hostile, less often behaved aggressively, more often engaged in prosocial behavior, and more often gained in academic achievement. Two years of intervention, as opposed to just one, strengthened these outcomes (Brown et al., 2004; Jones, Brown, & Aber, 2008). In unsafe neighborhoods, the program transforms schools into places of safety and mutual respect, where learning can occur.

RCCP and other similar programs recognize that resilience is not a preexisting attribute but rather a capacity that *develops,* enabling children to use internal and external resources to cope with adversity (Dessel, 2010; Roberts & Masten, 2004). Throughout our discussion, we have seen how families, schools, communities, and society as a whole can enhance or undermine the school-age child's developing sense of competence. As the next three chapters reveal, young people whose childhood experiences helped them learn to control impulses, overcome obstacles, strive for self-direction, and respond considerately and sympathetically to others meet the challenges of the next period—adolescence—quite well.

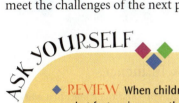

♦ REVIEW When children must testify in court cases, what factors increase the chances of accurate reporting?

♦ APPLY Claire told her 6-year-old daughter to be very careful never to talk to or take candy from strangers. Why will Claire's warning not protect her daughter from sexual abuse?

♦ CONNECT Explain how factors that promote resilience, listed on the previous page, contribute to favorable adjustment following divorce.

♦ REFLECT Describe a challenging time during your childhood. What aspects of the experience increased stress? What resources helped you cope with adversity?

Summary

Erikson's Theory: Industry versus Inferiority

What personality changes take place during Erikson's stage of industry versus inferiority?

■ According to Erikson, children who successfully resolve the psychological conflict of **industry versus inferiority** develop a sense of competence at useful skills and tasks, learn the value of division of labor, and develop a sense of moral commitment and responsibility.

Self-Understanding

Describe school-age children's self-concept and self-esteem, and discuss factors that affect their achievement-related attributions.

■ During middle childhood, children's self-concepts include personality traits (both positive and negative), competencies, and **social comparisons.**

■ Self-esteem differentiates further and becomes hierarchically organized and more realistic, declining as children get more competence-related feedback and compare their performance to that of others. Cultural forces and child-rearing practices affect self-esteem. Warm extended families and strong ethnic pride may contribute to the slight self-esteem advantage of African-American over Caucasian children. The authoritative child-rearing style is linked to favorable self-esteem.

■ Children with **mastery-oriented attributions** hold an incremental view of ability, believing that it can be improved by trying hard, and attribute failure to insufficient effort. In contrast, children with **learned helplessness** attribute success to external factors, such as luck, and hold a fixed view of ability. They believe their failures are due to low ability, which cannot be modified.

■ Supportive parents and teachers and cultural valuing of effort increase the likelihood of a mastery-oriented approach. **Attribution retraining** encourages learned-helpless children to believe they can overcome failure by exerting more effort.

Emotional Development

Cite changes in the expression and understanding of emotion in middle childhood.

■ Self-conscious emotions of pride and guilt become clearly governed by personal responsibility. Intense shame can shatter self-esteem.

■ School-age children recognize that people can experience more than one emotion at a time and that emotional expressions may not reflect people's true feelings. They also reconcile contradictory cues in interpreting another's feelings. Empathy increases and includes sensitivity to both people's immediate distress and their general life condition.

- By age 10, most children can shift adaptively between **problem-centered** and **emotion-centered coping** in regulating emotion. Emotionally well-regulated children develop a sense of emotional self-efficacy and are optimistic, prosocial, and well-liked by peers.

Understanding Others: Perspective Taking

How does perspective taking change in middle childhood?

- As Selman's five-stage sequence indicates, **perspective taking**—the capacity to imagine others' thoughts and feelings—improves greatly, supported by cognitive maturity and experiences in which adults and peers explain their viewpoints. Good perspective takers show more empathy, sympathy, and positive social skills.

Moral Development

Describe changes in moral understanding during middle childhood, including children's understanding of diversity and inequality.

- By middle childhood, children have internalized rules for good conduct. They clarify and link moral imperatives and social conventions, considering the purpose of the rule; people's intentions, knowledge, and beliefs; and the context of their actions. They also better understand individual rights. But when moral and personal concerns conflict, older school-age children typically emphasize fairness. Children in diverse cultures use similar criteria to reason about moral, social-conventional, and personal concerns.

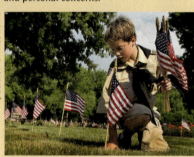

© SYRACUSE NEWSPAPERS/ J. BERRY/THE IMAGE WORKS

- Children of all races pick up prevailing societal attitudes about race and ethnicity. With age, school-age children understand that people who look different need not think, feel, or act differently, and prejudice typically declines. Children most likely to hold racial and ethnic biases are those who believe that personality traits are fixed, who have inflated self-esteem, and who live among adults who highlight group differences. Long-term, intergroup contact may be most effective at reducing prejudice.

Peer Relations

How do peer sociability and friendship change in middle childhood?

- Peer interaction becomes more prosocial, and physical aggression declines. By the end of middle childhood, children organize themselves into **peer groups.**
- Friendships develop into mutual relationships based on trust and become more selective. Children tend to select friends who resemble themselves in age, sex, race, ethnicity, SES, personality, popularity, academic achievement, and prosocial behavior. Girls form closer, more exclusive friendships than boys.

Describe major categories of peer acceptance and ways to help rejected children.

- On measures of **peer acceptance, popular children** are well-liked by many agemates; **rejected children** are actively disliked; **controversial children** are both liked and disliked; and **neglected children** arouse little reaction, positive or negative, but are usually well-adjusted.
- **Popular-prosocial children** are academically and socially competent, while **popular-antisocial children** are aggressive but admired, perhaps for their athletic ability and sophisticated but devious social skills. Rejected children also divide into two subtypes: **rejected-aggressive children,** who are especially high in conflict and hostility, and **rejected-withdrawn children,** who are passive, socially awkward, and frequent targets of **peer victimization.**
- Coaching in social skills, academic tutoring, and training in perspective taking and social problem solving have been used to help rejected youngsters. To produce lasting change, intervening in parent–child interaction is often necessary.

Gender Typing

What changes in gender-stereotyped beliefs and gender identity occur during middle childhood?

- School-age children extend their awareness of gender stereotypes to personality traits and academic subjects. But they also develop a more flexible, open-minded view of what males and females can do.

- Boys strengthen their identification with the masculine role, whereas girls feel free to experiment with "cross-gender" activities. Gender identity includes self-evaluations of gender typicality, contentedness, and felt pressure to conform to gender roles—each of which affects adjustment.

© PETER HVIZDAK/THE IMAGE WORKS

Family Influences

How do parent–child communication and sibling relationships change in middle childhood?

- Despite declines in time spent with parents, **coregulation** allows parents to exercise general oversight over children, who increasingly make their own decisions.
- Sibling rivalry tends to increase with greater participation in diverse activities and more frequent parental comparisons. Siblings often try to reduce this rivalry by striving to be different from one another. Only children do not differ from children with siblings in self-rated personality traits and are higher in self-esteem, school performance, and educational attainment.

How do children fare in gay and lesbian families and in single-parent, never-married families?

- Gay and lesbian parents are as committed to and effective at child rearing as heterosexuals. Their children do not differ from the children of heterosexual parents in adjustment and gender-role preferences.
- Never-married parenthood generally increases economic hardship for low-SES mothers and their children. Children of never-married mothers who lack a father's warmth and involvement achieve less well in school and engage in more antisocial behavior than children in low-SES, first-marriage families.

What factors influence children's adjustment to divorce and blended family arrangements?

■ Although marital breakup is often quite stressful for children, individual differences exist based on parental psychological health, child characteristics (age, temperament, and sex), and social supports. Children with difficult temperaments are at greater risk for adjustment problems. In both sexes, divorce is linked to early sexual activity, adolescent parenthood, and long-term relationship difficulties.

■ The overriding factor in positive adjustment following divorce is effective parenting. Positive father–child relationships have protective value, as do caring extended family members, teachers, siblings, and friends.

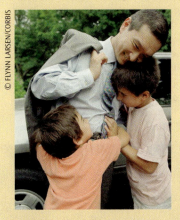

■ **Divorce mediation** and parent education programs can foster parental conflict resolution and cooperation in the period surrounding divorce. The success of joint custody depends on coparenting.

■ When divorced parents enter new relationships and form **blended,** or **reconstituted, families**, girls, older children, and children in father–stepmother families tend to have more adjustment problems. Stepparents who move into their roles gradually help children adjust.

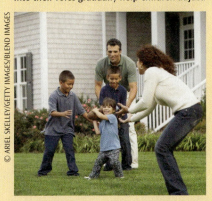

How do maternal employment and life in dual-earner families affect children's development?

■ When employed mothers enjoy their work and remain committed to parenting, their children benefit from higher self-esteem, more positive family and peer relations, less gender-stereotyped beliefs, and better school grades. In dual-earner families, the father's willingness to share household responsibilities is linked to many positive child outcomes. Workplace supports help parents meet the demands of work and child rearing.

■ Authoritative child rearing, parental monitoring, and regular after-school chores lead **self-care children** to be responsible and well-adjusted. Good "after-care" programs also aid school performance and emotional and social adjustment, with low-SES children showing special benefits.

Some Common Problems of Development

Cite common fears and anxieties in middle childhood.

■ School-age children's fears are directed toward new concerns, including physical harm, media events, academic failure, parents' health, the possibility of dying, and peer rejection. Children with inhibited temperaments are at high risk for developing **phobias.** Harsh living conditions, presenting constant danger, chaos, and deprivation, can result in long-term emotional stress and behavior problems.

Discuss factors related to child sexual abuse, its consequences for children's development, and its prevention and treatment.

■ Child sexual abuse is generally committed by male family members, more often against girls than against boys. Abusers have characteristics that predispose them toward sexual exploitation of children. Reported cases are strongly associated with poverty and marital instability.

■ Abused children often have severe adjustment problems. Treatment typically requires long-term therapy with both children and parents. Educational programs that teach children to recognize inappropriate sexual advances and whom to turn to for help reduce the risk of sexual abuse.

Cite factors that foster resilience in middle childhood.

■ Overall, a modest relationship exists between stressful life experiences and psychological disturbance in childhood. Children's personal characteristics, a warm family life that includes authoritative parenting, and school and community resources predict resilience.

IMPORTANT TERMS AND CONCEPTS

attribution retraining (p. 488)
blended, or reconstituted, family (p. 513)
controversial children (p. 500)
coregulation (p. 507)
divorce mediation (p. 513)
emotion-centered coping (p. 490)
industry versus inferiority (p. 482)
learned helplessness (p. 487)

mastery-oriented attributions (p. 486)
neglected children (p. 500)
peer acceptance (p. 500)
peer groups (p. 498)
peer victimization (p. 502)
perspective taking (p. 491)
phobia (p. 517)
popular children (p. 500)

popular-antisocial children (p. 500)
popular-prosocial children (p. 500)
problem-centered coping (p. 490)
rejected children (p. 500)
rejected-aggressive children (p. 501)
rejected-withdrawn children (p. 501)
self-care children (p. 516)
social comparisons (p. 483)

Milestones

Development in Middle Childhood

6–8 years

PHYSICAL

- Slow gains in height and weight continue until adolescent growth spurt. (412)
- Permanent teeth gradually replace primary teeth. (414)
- Legibility of writing increases, preparing children to master cursive writing. (429)
- Drawings become more organized and detailed and include some depth cues. (429)
- Games with rules and rough-and-tumble play become common. (430, 431–432)

COGNITIVE

- Thought becomes more logical, as shown by the ability to pass Piagetian conservation, class inclusion, and seriation problems. (438)
- Attention becomes more selective, adaptable, and planful. (443–445)
- Uses memory strategies of rehearsal and then organization. (446)
- Views the mind as an active, constructive agent, capable of transforming information. (447)

- Awareness of memory strategies and the impact of psychological factors (such as focusing attention) on task performance improves. (448–449)
- Appreciates second-order false beliefs. (448)
- Uses informal knowledge of number concepts and counting to master more complex mathematical skills. (451–453)

LANGUAGE

- Vocabulary increases rapidly as children learn about 20 new words a day. (462)
- Word definitions are concrete, referring to functions and appearance. (463)
- Narratives increase in organization, detail, and expressiveness. (464)
- Transitions from "learning to read" to "reading to learn." (451)

- Metalinguistic awareness improves. (462, 465)
- Conversational strategies become more refined. (464)

EMOTIONAL/SOCIAL

- Self-concept begins to include personality traits and social comparisons. (482–483)
- Self-esteem differentiates, is hierarchically organized, and declines to a more realistic level. (484–485)
- Self-conscious emotions of pride and guilt are governed by personal responsibility. (489–490)
- Understands that people may have different perspectives because they have access to different information. (493)
- Recognizes that people can experience more than one emotion at a time and that their expressions may not reflect their true feelings. (490)

- Empathy increases. (490)
- Attends to more cues (facial, situational, and past experiences) in interpreting another's feelings. (490)
- Becomes more independent and trustworthy. (492)
- Constructs a flexible appreciation of moral rules, taking prosocial and antisocial intentions into account. (492–493)
- Physical aggression declines; verbal and relational aggression continue. (497)

NOTE: Numbers in parentheses indicate the page or pages on which each milestone is discussed.

9–11 years

PHYSICAL

- Adolescent growth spurt begins two years earlier in girls than in boys. (412)
- Executes gross motor skills of running, jumping, throwing, catching, kicking, batting, and dribbling more quickly and with better coordination. (427–428)
- Steady gains in reaction time contribute to improved motor performance. (428)
- Representation of depth in drawings expands. (429)
- Dominance hierarchies become more stable, especially among boys. (432)

COGNITIVE

- Continues to master Piagetian tasks in a step-by-step fashion. (440)
- Spatial reasoning improves, as illustrated by more sophisticated map-reading and drawing skills, including an overall view of space and understanding of scale. (438–439)

- Selective attention and planning improve further. (443–445)
- Uses memory strategies of rehearsal and organization more effectively. (446)
- Applies several memory strategies simultaneously; begins to use elaboration. (446)
- Long-term knowledge base grows larger and becomes better organized. (446)
- Theory of mind becomes more elaborate and refined. (447)
- Cognitive self-regulation improves. (449)

LANGUAGE

- Thinks about and uses words more precisely; word definitions emphasize synonyms and categorical relations. (463)
- Grasps double meanings of words, as reflected in comprehension of metaphors and humor. (463)
- Continues to master complex grammatical constructions, such as passive voice and infinitive phrases. (463)
- Continues to refine conversational strategies. (464)
- Narratives lengthen and increase in organization, detail, and expressiveness. (464)

EMOTIONAL/SOCIAL

- Continues to refine self-concept to include competencies, positive and negative personality traits, and more sophisticated social comparisons. (483)
- Self-esteem tends to rise, as children balance social comparisons with personal achievement goals. (485)
- Distinguishes ability, effort, and luck in attributions for success and failure. (486–487)

- Empathic responding extends to general life conditions. (490)

- Shifts adaptively between problem-centered and emotion-centered strategies in regulating emotion. (490–491)
- Can "step into another's shoes" and view the self from that person's perspective; later, can view the relationship between self and other from the perspective of a third, impartial party. (491)
- Clarifies and links moral rules and social conventions. (493)
- Convictions about matters of personal choice strengthen, and understanding of individual rights expands. (493–494)
- Friendships become more selective and are based on mutual trust. (499)
- Peer groups emerge. (498)

- Becomes aware of more gender stereotypes, including personality traits and achievement, but has a flexible appreciation of what males and females can do. (503–504)
- Gender identity expands to include self-evaluations of typicality, contentedness, and pressure to conform. (504–505)
- Sibling rivalry tends to increase. (507–508)

GLOSSARY

A

academic programs Preschool and kindergarten programs in which teachers structure children's learning, teaching academic skills through formal lessons that often involve repetition and drill. Distinguished from *child-centered programs.* (p. 348)

accommodation In Piaget's theory, that part of adaptation in which new schemes are created and old ones adjusted to produce a better fit with the environment. Distinguished from *assimilation.* (p. 204)

adaptation In Piaget's theory, the process of building schemes through direct interaction with the environment. Consists of two complementary activities: *assimilation* and *accommodation.* (p. 204)

affordances The action possibilities that a situation offers an organism with certain motor capabilities. Discovering affordances plays a major role in perceptual differentiation. (p. 199)

age of viability The age at which the fetus can first survive if born early. Occurs sometime between 22 and 26 weeks. (p. 100)

alcohol-related neurodevelopmental disorder (ARND) The least severe form of fetal alcohol spectrum disorder, involving brain injury but with typical physical growth and absence of facial abnormalities. Distinguished from *fetal alcohol syndrome (FAS)* and *partial fetal alcohol syndrome (p-FAS).* (p. 109)

allele Each of two or more forms of a gene located at the same place on corresponding pairs of chromosomes. (p. 56)

amnion The inner membrane that forms a protective covering around the prenatal organism. (p. 98)

amniotic fluid The fluid that fills the amnion, which helps keep temperature constant and provides a cushion against jolts caused by the mother's movements. (p. 98)

amodal sensory properties Information that overlaps two or more sensory systems, such as common rate, rhythm, duration, and intensity in visual and auditory input. (p. 197)

amygdala An inner-brain structure that plays a central role in processing emotional information. (p. 295)

androgyny The gender identity held by individuals who score high on both traditionally masculine and traditionally feminine personality characteristics. (p. 395)

animistic thinking The belief that inanimate objects have lifelike qualities, such as thoughts, wishes, feelings, and intentions. (p. 321)

A-not-B search error The error made by 8- to 12-month-olds who, after seeing an object moved from one hiding place (A) to another (B), still search for it only in the first hiding place (A). (p. 207)

anoxia Inadequate oxygen supply. (p. 135)

Apgar Scale A rating system used to assess the newborn baby's physical condition immediately after birth. (p. 128)

assimilation That part of adaptation in which the external world is interpreted in terms of current schemes. Distinguished from *accommodation.* (p. 204)

associative play A form of true social interaction in which children engage in separate activities but interact by exchanging toys and commenting on one another's behavior. Distinguished from *nonsocial activity, parallel play,* and *cooperative play.* (p. 372)

attachment The strong affectionate tie that humans have with special people in their lives, which leads them to feel pleasure when interacting with those people and to be comforted by their nearness in times of stress. (p. 264)

Attachment Q-Sort A method of assessing the quality of attachment in children between 1 and 4 years of age through home observations of a variety of attachment-related behaviors. (p. 267)

attention-deficit hyperactivity disorder A childhood disorder involving inattentiveness, impulsivity, and excessive motor activity, often leading to academic and social problems. (p. 444)

attribution retraining An intervention that encourages learned-helpless children to believe they can overcome failure by exerting more effort. (p. 488)

authoritarian child-rearing style A child-rearing style that is low in acceptance and involvement, high in coercive and psychological control, and low in autonomy granting. Distinguished from *authoritative, permissive,* and *uninvolved child-rearing styles.* (p. 399)

authoritative child-rearing style A child-rearing style that is high in acceptance and involvement, emphasizes adaptive control techniques, and includes gradual, appropriate autonomy granting. Distinguished from *authoritarian, permissive,* and *uninvolved child-rearing styles.* (p. 398)

autobiographical memory Long-lasting representations of personally meaningful one-time events from both the recent and the distant past. (p. 221)

autonomy versus shame and doubt In Erikson's theory, the psychological conflict of toddlerhood, which is resolved favorably when parents provide young children with suitable guidance and reasonable choices. (p. 249)

autosomes The 22 matching chromosome pairs in each human cell. (p. 54)

avoidant attachment The attachment pattern characterizing infants who seem unresponsive to the parent when she is present, are usually not distressed by parental separation, and avoid or are slow to greet the parent when she returns. Distinguished from secure, resistant, and disorganized/disoriented attachment. (p. 267)

B

babbling Repetition of consonant–vowel combinations in long strings, beginning around 6 months of age. (p. 236)

basic emotions Emotions such as happiness, interest, surprise, fear, anger, sadness, and disgust that are universal in humans and other primates and have a long evolutionary history of promoting survival. (p. 250)

basic trust versus mistrust In Erikson's theory, the psychological conflict of infancy, which is resolved positively when the balance of care is sympathetic and loving. (p. 248)

behavioral genetics A field devoted to uncovering the contributions of nature and nurture to the diversity in human traits and abilities. (p. 82)

behaviorism An approach that regards directly observable events—stimuli and responses—as the appropriate focus of study and views the development of behavior as taking place through classical and operant conditioning. (p. 17)

behavior modification Procedures that combine conditioning and modeling to eliminate undesirable behaviors and increase desirable responses. (p. 18)

blastocyst The zygote four days after fertilization, when the tiny mass of cells forms a hollow, fluid-filled ball. (p. 98)

blended, or **reconstituted, family** A family structure formed through cohabitation or remarriage that includes parent, child, and steprelatives. (p. 513)

bonding Parents' feelings of affection and concern for the newborn baby. (p. 143)

brain plasticity The capacity of various parts of the cerebral cortex to take over functions of damaged regions. Declines as hemispheres of the cerebral cortex lateralize. (p. 168)

breech position A position of the baby in the uterus that would cause the buttocks or feet to be delivered first. (p. 134)

C

canalization The tendency of heredity to restrict the development of some characteristics to just one or a few outcomes. (p. 84)

cardinality The mathematical principle stating that the last number in a counting sequence indicates the quantity of items in the set. (p. 344)

carrier A heterozygous individual who can pass a recessive trait to his or her children. (p. 56)

central executive In information processing, the conscious part of working memory that directs the flow of information through the mental system by deciding what to attend to, coordinating incoming information with information already in the system, and selecting, applying, and monitoring strategies. (p. 218)

centration In Piaget's theory, the tendency of preoperational children to focus on one aspect of a situation while neglecting other important features. (p. 322)

cephalocaudal trend An organized pattern of physical growth in which the head develops more rapidly than the lower part of the body ("head to tail"). Distinguished from *proximodistal trend*. (p. 162)

cerebellum A structure at the rear and base of the brain that aids in balance and control of body movement. (p. 294)

cerebral cortex The largest, most complex structure of the human brain, containing the greatest number of neurons and synapses, which accounts for the highly developed intelligence of the human species. (p. 167)

cesarean delivery A surgical delivery in which the doctor makes an incision in the mother's abdomen and lifts the baby out of the uterus. (p. 134)

child-centered programs Preschool and kindergarten programs in which teachers provide a variety of activities from which children select, and much learning takes place through play. Distinguished from *academic programs*. (p. 348)

child development An area of study devoted to understanding constancy and change from conception through adolescence and emerging adulthood. (p. 4)

child-directed speech (CDS) A form of language adults use to speak to infants and toddlers, consisting of short sentences with high-pitched, exaggerated expression, clear pronunciation, distinct pauses between speech segments, clear gestures to support verbal meaning, and repetition of new words in a variety of contexts. (p. 241)

child-rearing styles Combinations of parenting behaviors that occur over a wide range of situations, creating an enduring child-rearing climate. (p. 398)

chorion The outer membrane that forms a protective covering around the prenatal organism. It sends out tiny hairlike villi, from which the placenta begins to develop. (p. 98)

chromosomes Rodlike structures in the cell nucleus that store and transmit genetic information. (p. 52)

chronosystem In ecological systems theory, temporal changes in environments, either externally imposed or arising from within the child, that produce new conditions affecting development. Distinguished from *microsystem, mesosystem, exosystem,* and *macrosystem*. (p. 27)

circular reaction In Piaget's theory, a means of building schemes in which infants try to repeat a chance event caused by their own motor activity. (p. 205)

classical conditioning A form of learning that involves associating a neutral stimulus with a stimulus that leads to a reflexive response. Once the nervous system makes the connection between the two stimuli, the neutral stimulus alone will produce the response. (p. 179)

clinical interview An interview method in which the researcher uses a flexible, conversational style to probe for the participant's point of view. Distinguished from *structured interview*. (p. 33)

clinical, or **case study, method** A research method in which the aim is to obtain as complete a picture as possible of one individual's psychological functioning by bringing together interview data, observations, and sometimes test scores. (p. 34)

cognitive-developmental theory An approach introduced by Piaget that views children as actively constructing knowledge as they manipulate and explore their world, and in which cognitive development takes place in stages. (p. 19)

cognitive maps Mental representations of familiar large-scale spaces, such as neighborhood or school. (p. 438)

cognitive self-regulation The process of continuously monitoring progress toward a goal, checking outcomes, and redirecting unsuccessful efforts. (p. 449)

cohort effects The effects of cultural-historical change on the accuracy of longitudinal and cross-sectional research findings. Results based on one cohort—individuals developing in the same time period, who are influenced by particular historical and cultural conditions—may not apply to other cohorts. (p. 41)

collectivist societies Societies in which people define themselves as part of a group and stress group goals over individual goals. Distinguished from *individualistic societies*. (p. 78)

communities of learners An educational approach inspired by Vygotsky's theory, in which teachers guide the overall process of learning, but otherwise, no distinction is made between adult and child contributors. All participate in joint endeavors, and students have the authority to define and resolve problems as they work toward project goals, which often address complex real-world issues. (p. 469)

compliance Voluntary obedience to requests and commands. (p. 282)

comprehension In language development, the words and word combinations that children understand. Distinguished from *production*. (p. 240)

concrete operational stage Piaget's third stage, extending from about 7 to 11 years of age, during which thought becomes logical, flexible, and organized in its application to concrete information, but the capacity for abstract thinking is not yet present. (p. 438)

conditioned response (CR) In classical conditioning, a new response produced by a conditioned stimulus (CS) that is similar to the unconditioned, or reflexive, response (UCR). (p. 179)

conditioned stimulus (CS) In classical conditioning, a neutral stimulus that, through pairing with an unconditioned stimulus (UCS), leads to a new, conditioned response (CR). Distinguished from *unconditioned stimulus*. (p. 179)

conservation The understanding that certain physical characteristics of objects remain the same, even when their outward appearance changes. (p. 321)

constructivist classroom A classroom grounded in Piaget's view of children as active learners who construct their own knowledge. Features include richly equipped learning centers, small groups and individuals solving self-chosen problems, a teacher who guides and supports in response to children's needs, and evaluation based on individual students' progress in relation to their own prior development. Distinguished from *traditional classroom* and *social-constructivist classroom*. (pp. 467–468)

contexts Unique combinations of personal and environmental circumstances that can result in different paths of development. (p. 8)

continuous development The view that development is a process of gradually adding more of the same types of skills that were there to begin with. Distinguished from *discontinuous development*. (p. 7)

contrast sensitivity A general principle accounting for early pattern preferences, which states that if babies can detect a difference in contrast between two patterns, they will prefer the pattern with more visual contrast. (p. 193)

control deficiency The inability to control, or execute, a mental strategy consistently. Distinguished from *production deficiency, utilization deficiency,* and *effective strategy use*. (p. 443)

controversial children Children who receive many votes, both positive and negative, on self-report measures of peer acceptance, indicating that they are both liked and disliked. Distinguished from *popular, rejected,* and *neglected children*. (p. 500)

convergent thinking The type of thinking emphasized on intelligence tests, which involves arriving at a single correct answer to a problem. Distinguished from *divergent thinking*. (p. 474)

cooing Pleasant vowel-like noises made by infants, beginning around 2 months of age. (p. 236)

cooperative learning Collaboration on a task by a small group of classmates who work toward common goals by resolving differences of opinion, sharing responsibilities, and providing one another with sufficient explanation to correct misunderstandings. (p. 471)

cooperative play A form of social interaction in which children orient toward a common goal, such as acting out a make-believe theme. Distinguished from *nonsocial activity, parallel play,* and *associative play*. (p. 372)

coparenting An approach in which parents mutually support each other's parenting behaviors. (p. 70)

coregulation A form of supervision in which parents exercise general oversight while permitting children to take charge of moment-by-moment decision making. (p. 507)

core knowledge perspective A perspective that states that infants are born with a set of innate knowledge systems, or core domains of thought, each of which permits a ready grasp of new, related information and therefore supports early, rapid development of certain aspects of cognition. (p. 214)

corpus callosum The large bundle of fibers connecting the two hemispheres of the cerebral cortex. (p. 295)

correlational design A research design in which the investigator gathers information on individuals without altering their experiences and then examines relationships between participants' characteristics and their behavior or development. Does not permit inferences about cause and effect. (p. 37)

correlation coefficient A number, ranging from +1.00 to −1.00, that describes the strength and direction of the relationship between two variables. (p. 37)

creativity The ability to produce work that is original yet appropriate—something others have not thought of that is useful in some way. (p. 474)

crossing over During meiosis, the exchange of genes between chromosomes next to each other. (p. 53)

cross-sectional design A research design in which groups of participants of different ages are studied at the same point in time. Distinguished from *longitudinal design*. (p. 41)

D

deferred imitation The ability to remember and copy the behavior of models who are not present. (p. 207)

delay of gratification The ability to wait for an appropriate time and place to engage in a tempting act. (p. 283)

deoxyribonucleic acid (DNA) Long, double-stranded molecules that make up chromosomes. (p. 52)

dependent variable The variable the investigator expects to be influenced by the independent variable in an experiment. Distinguished from *independent variable*. (p. 37)

developmental cognitive neuroscience An area of investigation that brings together researchers from psychology, biology, neuroscience, and medicine to study the relationship between changes in the brain and the developing child's cognitive processing and behavior patterns. (p. 23)

developmentally appropriate practice A set of standards devised by the National Association for the Education of Young Children, specifying program characteristics that meet the developmental and individual needs of young children of varying ages, based on current research and the consensus of experts. (p. 230)

developmental quotient (DQ) A score on an infant intelligence test, computed in the same manner as an IQ but labeled more conservatively because it does not tap the same dimensions of intelligence measured in older children. (p. 228)

developmental science An interdisciplinary field devoted to the study of all changes humans experience throughout the lifespan. (p. 4)

differentiation theory The view that perceptual development involves the detection of increasingly fine-grained, invariant features in the environment. (p. 198)

difficult child A child whose temperament is characterized by irregular daily routines, slow acceptance of new experiences, and a tendency to react negatively and intensely. Distinguished from *easy child* and *slow-to-warm-up child*. (p. 256)

dilation and effacement of the cervix Widening and thinning of the cervix during the first stage of labor. (p. 126)

discontinuous development A view of development as a process in which new ways of understanding and responding to the world emerge at specific times. Distinguished from *continuous development*. (p. 8)

disorganized/disoriented attachment The attachment pattern reflecting the greatest insecurity, characterizing infants who show confused, contradictory behaviors when reunited with the parent after a separation. Distinguished from secure, *avoidant,* and *resistant attachment*. (p. 267)

displaced reference The realization that words can be used to cue mental images of things that are not physically present. (p. 211)

divergent thinking The type of thinking associated with creativity, which involves generating multiple and unusual possibilities when faced with a task or problem. Distinguished from *convergent thinking*. (p. 474)

divorce mediation A series of meetings between divorcing adults and a trained professional that are aimed at reducing family conflict, including legal battles over property division and child custody. (p. 513)

dominance hierarchy A stable ordering of group members that predicts who will win when conflict arises. (p. 432)

dominant cerebral hemisphere The hemisphere of the cerebral cortex responsible for skilled motor action and other important abilities. In right-handed individuals, the left hemisphere is dominant; in left-handed individuals, motor and language skills are often shared between the hemispheres. (p. 293)

dominant–recessive inheritance A pattern of inheritance in which, under heterozygous conditions, the influence of only one allele is apparent. (p. 56)

dual representation The ability to view a symbolic object as both an object in its own right and a symbol. (p. 320)

dynamic assessment An approach to testing consistent with Vygotsky's zone of proximal development, in which purposeful teaching is introduced into the testing situation to find out what the child can attain with social support. (p. 461)

dynamic systems perspective A view that regards the child's mind, body, and physical and social worlds as a dynamic, integrated system. A change in any part of the system leads the child to reorganize his or her behavior so the various components of the system work together again but in a more complex, effective way. (p. 28)

dynamic systems theory of motor development A theory that views new motor skills as reorganizations of previously mastered skills, which lead to more effective ways of exploring and controlling the environment. Each new skill is a joint product of central nervous system development, the body's movement possibilities, environmental supports for the skill, and the child's goals. (pp. 184–185)

E

easy child A child whose temperament is characterized by establishment of regular routines in infancy, general cheerfulness, and easy adaptation to new experiences. Distinguished from *difficult child* and *slow-to-warm-up child*. **(p. 256)**

ecological systems theory Bronfenbrenner's approach, which views the child as developing within a complex system of relationships affected by multiple levels of the surrounding environment, from immediate settings of family and school to broad cultural values, laws, customs, and resources. (pp. 25–26)

educational self-fulfilling prophecies Teachers' positive or negative views of individual children, who tend to adopt and start to live up to those views. (p. 470)

effective strategy use Consistent use of a mental strategy that leads to improvement in performance. Distinguished from *production deficiency, control deficiency,* and *utilization deficiency.* (p. 443)

effortful control The self-regulatory dimension of temperament, involving voluntary suppression of a dominant response in order to plan and execute a more adaptive response. (pp. 257–258)

egocentrism Failure to distinguish the symbolic viewpoints of others from one's own. (p. 321)

elaboration A memory strategy that involves creating a relationship, or shared meaning, between two or more items of information that are not members of the same category. (p. 446)

embryo The prenatal organism from 2 to 8 weeks after conception—the period when the groundwork for all body structures and internal organs is laid down. (p. 99)

embryonic disk A small cluster of cells on the inside of the blastocyst, from which the new organism will develop. (p. 98)

emergent literacy Children's active efforts to construct literacy knowledge through informal experiences. (p. 343)

emotional intelligence A set of emotional abilities that enable individuals to process and adapt to emotional information. Measured by tapping the emotional skills people use to manage their own emotions and interact competently with others. (p. 457)

emotional self-regulation Strategies for adjusting our emotional state to a comfortable level of intensity so we can accomplish our goals. (p. 254)

emotion-centered coping A strategy for managing emotion that is internal, private, and aimed at controlling distress when little can be done to change an outcome. Distinguished from *problem-centered coping.* (p. 490–491)

empathy The ability to understand another's emotional state and to *feel with* that person, or respond emotionally in a similar way. (p. 282)

epigenesis Development resulting from ongoing, bidirectional exchanges between heredity and all levels of the environment. (p. 86)

epiphyses Growth centers at the ends of the long bones of the body, where new cartilage cells are produced and gradually harden. (p. 163)

episodic memory Memory for everyday experiences. (p. 336)

ethnography A research method in which an investigator attempts to understand the unique values and social processes of a culture or a distinct social group through participant observation—living with members of the cultural community and taking field notes over an extended period of time. (pp. 34–35)

ethological theory of attachment Bowlby's theory, the most widely accepted view of attachment, which regards the infant's emotional tie to the caregiver as an evolved response that promotes survival. (p. 265)

ethology An approach concerned with the adaptive, or survival, value of behavior and its evolutionary history. (p. 23)

evolutionary developmental psychology An approach that seeks to understand the adaptive value of species-wide cognitive, emotional, and social competencies as those competencies change with age. (p. 24)

exosystem In ecological systems theory, social settings that do not contain children but nevertheless affect children's experiences—for example, parents' workplaces, religious institutions, health and welfare services in the community, and parents' social networks. Distinguished from *microsystem, mesosystem, macrosystem,* and *chronosystem.* (p. 27)

expansions Adult responses that elaborate on children's speech, increasing its complexity. (p. 359)

experience-dependent brain growth Growth and refinement of established brain structures as a result of specific learning experiences that vary widely across individuals and cultures. Distinguished from *experience-expectant brain growth.* (p. 172)

experience-expectant brain growth The young brain's rapidly developing organization, which depends on ordinary experiences—opportunities to see and touch objects, to hear language and other sounds, and to move about and explore the environment. Distinguished from *experience-dependent brain growth.* (p. 172)

experimental design A research design in which the investigator randomly assigns participants to two or more treatment conditions and studies the effect that manipulating an independent variable has on a dependent variable. Permits inferences about cause and effect. (p. 37)

expressive style A style of early language learning in which toddlers use language mainly to talk about their own feelings and needs and those of others, with an initial vocabulary emphasizing social formulas and pronouns. Distinguished from *referential style.* (p. 240)

extended-family household A household in which parent and child live with one or more adult relatives. (p. 78)

F

fast mapping Children's ability to connect new words with their underlying concepts after only a brief encounter. (p. 354)

fetal alcohol spectrum disorder (FASD) A range of physical, mental, and behavioral outcomes caused by prenatal alcohol exposure, including *fetal alcohol syndrome (FAS), partial fetal alcohol syndrome (p-FAS),* and *alcohol-related neurodevelopmental disorder (ARND).* (p. 108)

fetal alcohol syndrome (FAS) The most severe form of fetal alcohol spectrum disorder, distinguished by slow physical growth, facial abnormalities, and brain injury. Usually affects children whose mothers drank heavily during most or all of pregnancy. Distinguished from *partial fetal alcohol syndrome (p-FAS)* and *alcohol-related neurodevelopmental disorder (ARND).* (p. 108)

fetal monitors Electronic instruments that track the baby's heart rate during labor. (p. 132)

fetus The prenatal organism from the ninth week to the end of pregnancy—the period during which body structures are completed and dramatic growth in size occurs. (p. 100)

fontanels Six gaps, or "soft spots," separating the bones of the skull at birth. (p. 164)

fraternal, or dizygotic, twins Twins resulting from the release and fertilization of two ova. They are genetically no more alike than ordinary siblings. Distinguished from *identical*, or *monozygotic, twins*. (p. 55)

G

gametes Sex cells, or sperm and ova, which contain half as many chromosomes as regular body cells. (p. 53)

gender constancy A full understanding of the biologically based permanence of one's gender, including the realization that sex remains the same over time even if clothing, hairstyle, and play activities change. (p. 395)

gender identity An image of oneself as relatively masculine or feminine in characteristics. (p. 395)

gender schema theory An information-processing approach to gender typing that explains how environmental pressures and children's cognitions work together to shape gender-role development. (p. 396)

gender typing Any association of objects, activities, roles, or traits with one sex or the other in ways that conform to cultural stereotypes. (p. 390)

gene A segment of a DNA molecule that contains instructions for production of various proteins that contribute to the body's growth and functioning. (p. 52)

genetic counseling A communication process designed to help couples assess their chances of giving birth to a baby with a hereditary disorder and choose the best course of action in view of risks and family goals. (p. 63)

genetic–environmental correlation The idea that heredity influences the environments to which individuals are exposed. (p. 85)

genomic imprinting A pattern of inheritance in which alleles are imprinted, or chemically marked, in such a way that one pair member is activated, regardless of its makeup. (p. 59)

genotype An individual's genetic makeup. Distinguished from *phenotype*. (p. 51)

gifted Displaying exceptional intellectual strengths, including high IQ, creativity, and specialized talent. (p. 474)

glial cells Cells that are responsible for myelination of neural fibers, improving the efficiency of message transfer and, in certain instances, also participate directly in neural communication. (p. 165)

goodness-of-fit model A model that describes how favorable adjustment depends on an effective match, or good fit, between a child's temperament and the child-rearing environment. (p. 262)

growth faltering Failure of an infant to grow normally, characterized by weight, height, and head circumference substantially below age-related norms and by withdrawn, apathetic behavior, with a disturbed parent–infant relationship often a contributing factor. (p. 178)

growth hormone (GH) A pituitary hormone that affects the development of all body tissues except the central nervous system and the genitals. (p. 297)

guided participation Shared endeavors between more expert and less expert participants, without specifying the precise features of communication, thereby allowing for variations across situations and cultures. A broader concept than *scaffolding*. (p. 331)

H

habituation A gradual reduction in the strength of a response due to repetitive stimulation. (pp. 180–181)

heritability estimate A measure of the extent to which individual differences in complex traits, such as intelligence or personality, in a specific population are due to genetic factors. (p. 82)

heterozygous Having two different alleles at the same place on a pair of chromosomes. Distinguished from *homozygous*. (p. 56)

hierarchical classification The organization of objects into classes and subclasses on the basis of similarities and differences between the groups. (p. 322)

hippocampus An inner-brain structure that plays a vital role in memory and in images of space we use to help us find our way. (p. 294)

Home Observation for Measurement of the Environment (HOME) A checklist for gathering information about the quality of children's home lives through observation and parental interview. (p. 229)

homozygous Having two identical alleles at the same place on a pair of chromosomes. Distinguished from *heterozygous*. (p. 56)

I

identical, or monozygotic, twins Twins that result when a zygote, during early cell duplication, separates into two clusters of cells that have the same genetic makeup. Distinguished from *fraternal*, or *dizygotic, twins*. (p. 55)

imitation Learning by copying the behavior of another person. Also known as *modeling* or *observational learning*. (p. 181)

implantation Attachment of the blastocyst to the uterine lining, which occurs 7 to 9 days after fertilization. (p. 98)

inclusive classrooms Classrooms in which students with learning difficulties learn alongside typical students in a regular educational setting for part or all of the school day. (p. 473)

incomplete dominance A pattern of inheritance in which both alleles are expressed in the phenotype, resulting in a combined trait, or one that is intermediate between the two. (p. 57)

independent variable In an experiment, the variable the researcher expects to cause changes in another variable and that the researcher manipulates by randomly assigning participants to treatment conditions. Distinguished from *dependent variable*. (p. 37)

individualistic societies Societies in which people think of themselves as separate entities and are largely concerned with their own personal needs. Distinguished from *collectivist societies*. (p. 78)

induced labor A labor started artificially by breaking the amnion and giving the mother a hormone that stimulates contractions. (p. 134)

induction A type of discipline in which an adult helps the child notice feelings by pointing out the effects of the child's misbehavior on others. (p. 379)

industry versus inferiority In Erikson's theory, the psychological conflict of middle childhood, which is resolved positively when experiences lead children to develop a sense of competence at useful skills and tasks. (p. 482)

infantile amnesia The inability of most people to remember events that happened to them before age 3. (p. 221)

infant mortality The number of deaths in the first year of life per 1,000 live births. (p. 140)

information processing An approach that views the human mind as a symbol-manipulating system through which information flows and that regards cognitive development as a continuous process. (p. 21)

inhibited, or shy, child A child whose temperament is such that he or she displays negative reaction to and withdrawal from novel stimuli. Distinguished from *uninhibited*, or *sociable, child*. (p. 258)

initiative versus guilt In Erikson's theory, the psychological conflict of early childhood, which is resolved positively through play experiences that foster a healthy sense of purposefulness and through the development of a superego, or conscience, that is not overly strict or guilt-ridden. (p. 364)

intelligence quotient (IQ) A score that permits an individual's performance on an intelligence test to be compared to the performances of other individuals of the same age. (p. 227)

intentional, or **goal-directed, behavior** A sequence of actions in which schemes are deliberately coordinated to solve a problem. (p. 206)

interactional synchrony A form of communication in which the caregiver responds to infant signals in a well-timed, rhythmic, appropriate fashion and both partners match emotional states, especially positive ones. (p. 270)

intermodal perception Perception that combines information from more than one modality, or sensory system, resulting in an integrated whole. (p. 197)

internal working model A set of expectations derived from early caregiving experiences concerning the availability of attachment figures, their likelihood of providing support during times of stress, and the self's interaction with those figures. Becomes a model, or guide, for all future close relationships. (p. 266)

intersubjectivity The process by which two participants who begin a task with different understandings arrive at a shared understanding. (p. 331)

irreversibility The inability to mentally go through a series of steps in a problem and then reverse direction, returning to the starting point. Distinguished from *reversibility*. (p. 322)

J

joint attention A state in which the child and caregiver attend to the same object or event and the caregiver labels what the child sees. Supports language development. (p. 238)

K

kinship studies Studies comparing the characteristics of family members to determine the importance of heredity in complex human characteristics. (p. 82)

kwashiorkor A disease caused by an unbalanced diet very low in protein, which usually appears after weaning, between 1 and 3 years of age. Symptoms include an enlarged belly, swollen feet, hair loss, skin rash, and irritable, listless behavior. (p. 177)

L

language acquisition device (LAD) In Chomsky's theory, an innate system containing a universal grammar, or set of rules common to all languages, that enables children, no matter which language they hear, to understand and speak in a rule-oriented fashion as soon as they have learned enough words. (p. 234)

lanugo White, downy hair that covers the entire body of the fetus, helping the vernix stick to the skin. (p. 100)

lateralization Specialization of functions in the two hemispheres of the cerebral cortex. (p. 168)

learned helplessness Attribution of success to external factors such as luck, and failure to low ability, which cannot be improved through effort. Distinguished from *mastery-oriented attributions*. (p. 487)

learning disabilities Great difficulty with one or more aspects of learning, usually reading, resulting in achievement considerably behind what would be expected on the basis of a child's IQ. (p. 473)

longitudinal design A research design in which participants are studied repeatedly at different ages, and changes are noted as they get older. Distinguished from *cross-sectional design*. (p. 40)

long-term memory In information processing, the largest storage area in the mental system, containing our permanent knowledge base. (p. 218)

M

macrosystem In ecological systems theory, cultural values, laws, customs, and resources that influence experiences and interactions at inner levels of the environment. Distinguished from *microsystem*, *mesosystem*, *exosystem*, and *chronosystem*. (p. 27)

make-believe play A type of play in which children act out everyday and imaginary activities. (p. 207)

malocclusion A condition in which the upper and lower teeth do not meet properly. (p. 414)

marasmus A disease caused by a diet low in all essential nutrients that usually appears in the first year of life and leads to a wasted condition of the body. (p. 177)

mastery-oriented attributions Attributions that credit success to ability, which can be improved by trying hard, and failure to insufficient effort. Distinguished from *learned helplessness*. (p. 486)

matters of personal choice Concerns that do not violate the rights or welfare of others and, therefore, are up to each individual, such as choice of friends, hairstyle, and leisure activities. Distinguished from *moral imperatives* and *social conventions*. (p. 384)

maturation A genetically determined, naturally unfolding course of growth. (p. 13)

meiosis The process of cell division through which gametes are formed and in which the number of chromosomes in each cell is halved. (p. 53)

memory strategies Deliberate mental activities that improve the likelihood of remembering. (p. 336)

mental representation An internal depiction of information that the mind can manipulate. (p. 207)

mental strategies In information processing, procedures that operate on and transform information, thereby increasing the efficiency and flexibility of thinking and the chances that information will be retained. (p. 217)

mesosystem In ecological systems theory, connections between children's microsystems, or immediate settings. Distinguished from *microsystem, exosystem, macrosystem,* and *chronosystem*. (p. 26)

metacognition Thinking about thought; awareness of mental activities. (p. 338)

metalinguistic awareness The ability to think about language as a system. (p. 462)

microgenetic design A research design in which investigators present children with a novel task and follow their mastery over a series of closely spaced sessions. (p. 43)

microsystem In ecological systems theory, the innermost level of the environment, consisting of activities and interaction patterns in the child's immediate surroundings. Distinguished from *mesosystem, exosystem, macrosystem,* and *chronosystem*. (p. 26)

mirror neurons Specialized cells in many areas of the cerebral cortex in primates that underlie the ability to imitate by firing identically when a primate hears or sees an action and when it carries out that action on its own. (p. 182)

mitosis The process of cell duplication, in which each new cell receives an exact copy of the original chromosomes. (p. 53)

modifier genes Genes that enhance or dilute the effects of other genes. (p. 57)

moral imperatives Rules and standards that protect people's rights and welfare. Distinguished from *social conventions* and *matters of personal choice*. (p. 384)

mutation A sudden but permanent change in a segment of DNA. (p. 60)

mutual exclusivity bias Early in vocabulary growth, children's assumption that words refer to entirely separate, nonoverlapping categories. (p. 355)

myelination The coating of neural fibers with *myelin,* an insulating fatty sheath that improves the efficiency of message transfer. (p. 165)

N

naturalistic observation A research method in which the researcher goes into the natural environment to observe the behavior of interest. Distinguished from *structured observation.* (p. 31)

natural, or **prepared, childbirth** A group of techniques designed to reduce pain and medical intervention and to make childbirth as rewarding an experience as possible. (p. 130)

nature–nurture controversy Debate among theorists about whether genetic or environmental factors are more important influences on development. (p. 9)

neglected children Children who are seldom mentioned, either positively or negatively, on self-report measures of peer acceptance. Distinguished from *popular, controversial,* and *rejected children.* (p. 500)

Neonatal Behavioral Assessment Scale (NBAS) A test developed to assess a newborn infant's behavior in terms of reflexes, muscle tone, state changes, and responsiveness to physical and social stimuli. (p. 152)

neonatal mortality The number of deaths in the first month of life per 1,000 live births. (p. 140)

neural tube During the period of the embryo, the primitive spinal cord that develops from the ectoderm, the top of which swells to form the brain. (p. 99)

neurons Nerve cells that store and transmit information. (p. 164)

neurotransmitters Chemicals released by neurons that cross the synapse to send messages to other neurons. (p. 164)

niche-picking A type of genetic–environmental correlation in which individuals actively choose environments that complement their heredity. (p. 85)

nocturnal enuresis Bedwetting during the night. (p. 422)

non-rapid-eye-movement (NREM) sleep A "regular" sleep state in which the body is almost motionless and heart rate, breathing, and brain-wave activity are slow and even. Distinguished from *rapid-eye-movement (REM) sleep.* (p. 146)

nonsocial activity Unoccupied, onlooker behavior and solitary play. Distinguished from *parallel play, associative play,* and *cooperative play.* (p. 372)

normal distribution The bell-shaped distribution that results when individual differences are measured in large samples. Most scores cluster around the mean, or average, with progressively fewer falling toward the extremes. (p. 228)

normative approach An approach to development in which measures of behavior are taken on large numbers of individuals and age-related averages are computed to represent typical development. (p. 13)

O

obesity A greater-than-20-percent increase over healthy weight, based on body mass index, a ratio of weight to height associated with body fat. (p. 416)

object permanence The understanding that objects continue to exist when they are out of sight. (p. 207)

operant conditioning A form of learning in which a spontaneous behavior is followed by a stimulus that influences the probability that the behavior will occur again. (p. 180)

ordinality The mathematical principle specifying order relationships (more than and less than) between quantities. (p. 344)

organization In Piaget's theory, the internal rearrangement and linking together of schemes so that they form a strongly interconnected cognitive system. In information processing, a memory strategy that involves grouping related items together to improve recall. (pp. 205, 446)

overextension An early vocabulary error in which a word is applied too broadly, to a wider collection of objects and events than is appropriate. Distinguished from *underextension.* (p. 239)

overlapping-waves theory A theory of problem solving, which states that when given challenging problems, children try out various strategies and gradually select those that are fastest and most accurate. (p. 338)

overregularization Extension of regular grammatical rules to words that are exceptions. (p. 357)

P

parallel play A form of limited social participation in which a child plays near other children with similar materials but does not interact with them. Distinguished from *nonsocial activity, associative play,* and *cooperative play.* (p. 372)

partial fetal alcohol syndrome (p-FAS) A form of fetal alcohol spectrum disorder characterized by facial abnormalities and brain injury, but less severe than fetal alcohol syndrome; usually seen in children whose mothers drank alcohol in smaller quantities during pregnancy. (p. 108)

peer acceptance Likability, or the extent to which a child is viewed by a group of agemates as a worthy social partner. (p. 500)

peer groups Collectives of peers who generate unique values and standards for behavior and a social structure of leaders and followers. (p. 498)

peer victimization A destructive form of peer interaction in which certain children become frequent targets of verbal and physical attacks or other forms of abuse. (p. 502)

permissive child-rearing style A child-rearing style that is high in acceptance but either overindulgent or inattentive, low in control, and inappropriately lenient in autonomy granting. Distinguished from *authoritative, authoritarian,* and *uninvolved child-rearing styles.* (p. 399)

perspective taking The capacity to imagine what other people may be thinking and feeling. (p. 491)

phenotype An individual's directly observable physical and behavioral characteristics, which are determined by both genetic and environmental factors. Distinguished from *genotype.* (p. 51)

phobia An intense, unmanageable fear that leads to persistent avoidance of the feared situation. (p. 517)

phonics approach An approach to beginning reading instruction that emphasizes coaching children on phonics—the basic rules for translating written symbols into sounds—before exposing them to complex reading material. Distinguished from *whole-language approach.* (p. 450)

phonological awareness The ability to reflect on and manipulate the sound structure of spoken language, as indicated by sensitivity to changes in sounds within words, to rhyming, and to incorrect pronunciation. A strong predictor of emergent literacy. (p. 343)

physical aggression A form of aggression that harms others through physical injury to themselves or their property. Distinguished from *verbal aggression* and *relational aggression.* (p. 385)

pincer grasp The well-coordinated grasp that emerges at the end of the first year, involving thumb and index finger opposition. (p. 188)

pituitary gland A gland located at the base of the brain that releases hormones affecting physical growth. (p. 297)

placenta The organ that permits exchange of nutrients and waste products between the bloodstreams of the mother and the embryo, while also preventing the mother's and embryo's blood from mixing directly. (p. 98)

planning Thinking out a sequence of acts ahead of time and allocating attention accordingly to reach a goal. (p. 335)

plasticity Openness of human development to change in response to influential experiences throughout life. (p. 9)

polygenic inheritance A pattern of inheritance in which many genes affect the characteristic in question. (p. 60)

popular-antisocial children A subtype of popular children who are admired for their socially adept yet belligerent behavior. Includes "tough" boys who are athletically skilled, aggressive, and poor students, as well as relationally aggressive boys and girls. Distinguished from *popular-prosocial children*. (p. 500)

popular children Children who receive many positive votes on self-report measures of peer acceptance, indicating they are well-liked. Distinguished from *rejected, controversial,* and *neglected children*. (p. 500)

popular-prosocial children A subtype of popular children who combine academic and social competence. Distinguished from *popular-antisocial children*. (p. 500)

pragmatics The practical, social side of language, concerned with how to engage in effective and appropriate communication. (p. 358)

prefrontal cortex The region of the cerebral cortex, lying in front of areas controlling body movement, that is responsible for thought—in particular, for consciousness, inhibition of impulses, integration of information, and use of memory, reasoning, planning, and problem-solving strategies. (p. 168)

prenatal diagnostic methods Medical procedures that permit detection of developmental problems before birth. (p. 63)

preoperational stage Piaget's second stage, extending from about 2 to 7 years of age, in which children undergo an extraordinary increase in representational, or symbolic, activity, although thought is not yet logical. (p. 318)

prereaching The poorly coordinated, primitive reaching movements of newborn babies. (p. 187)

preterm infants Infants born several weeks or more before their due date. (p. 137)

private speech Self-directed speech that children use to plan and guide their own behavior. (p. 330)

proactive aggression A type of aggression in which children act to fulfill a need or desire—to obtain an object, privilege, space, or social reward, such as adult attention—and unemotionally attack a person to achieve their goal. Also called *instrumental aggression*. Distinguished from *reactive aggression*. (p. 385)

problem-centered coping A strategy for managing emotion in which the individual appraises the situation as changeable, identifies the difficulty, and decides what to do about it. Distinguished from *emotion-centered coping*. (p. 490)

production In language development, the words and word combinations that children use. Distinguished from *comprehension*. (p. 240)

production deficiency The failure to produce a mental strategy when it could be helpful. Distinguished from *control deficiency, utilization deficiency,* and *effective strategy use*. (p. 443)

Project Head Start The most extensive federally funded preschool intervention program in the United States, which provides low-income children with a year or two of preschool education, along with nutritional and health services, and encourages parent involvement in children's learning and development. (p. 349)

prosocial, or altruistic, behavior Actions that benefit another person without any expected reward for the self. (p. 371)

proximodistal trend An organized pattern of physical growth that proceeds from the center of the body outward. Distinguished from *cephalocaudal trend*. (p. 162)

psychoanalytic perspective An approach to personality development introduced by Freud that assumes children move through a series of stages in which they confront conflicts between biological drives and social expectations. How these conflicts are resolved determines the person's ability to learn, to get along with others, and to cope with anxiety. (p. 15)

psychological control Parental behaviors that intrude on and manipulate children's verbal expression, individuality, and attachments to parents. (p. 399)

psychosexual theory Freud's theory, which emphasizes that how parents manage children's sexual and aggressive drives in the first few years of life is crucial for healthy personality development. (p. 15)

psychosocial dwarfism A growth disorder, usually appearing between 2 and 15 years of age, caused by extreme emotional deprivation. It is characterized by decreased GH secretion, very short stature, immature skeletal age, and serious adjustment problems, which help distinguish it from normal shortness. (p. 297)

psychosocial theory Erikson's theory, which emphasizes that at each Freudian stage, individuals not only develop a unique personality but also acquire attitudes and skills that help them become active, contributing members of their society. (p. 15)

public policies Laws and government programs designed to improve current conditions. (pp. 78–79)

punishment In operant conditioning, removal of a desirable stimulus or presentation of an unpleasant stimulus, either of which decreases the occurrence of a response. (p. 180)

R

random assignment An evenhanded procedure for assigning participants to treatment conditions in an experiment, such as drawing numbers out of a hat or flipping a coin. It increases the chances that participants' characteristics will be equally distributed across treatment groups. (p. 38)

range of reaction Each person's unique, genetically determined response to a range of environmental conditions. (p. 84)

rapid-eye-movement (REM) sleep An "irregular" sleep state in which brain-wave activity is similar to that of the waking state. Distinguished from *non-rapid-eye-movement (NREM) sleep*. (p. 146)

reactive aggression An angry, defensive response to provocation or a blocked goal that is intended to hurt another person. Also called *hostile aggression*. Distinguished from *proactive aggression*. (p. 385)

recall The form of memory that involves remembering something without perceptual support, by generating a mental image of a past experience. Distinguished from *recognition*. (p. 220)

recasts Adult responses that restructure children's grammatically inaccurate speech into correct form. (p. 359)

reciprocal teaching A teaching method in which a teacher and two to four students form a cooperative group and take turns leading dialogues, creating a zone of proximal development in which children scaffold one another's progress. (p. 468)

recognition The form of memory that involves noticing whether a new experience is identical or similar to a previous one. Distinguished from *recall*. (p. 220)

recovery Following habituation, an increase in responsiveness to a new stimulus. (p. 181)

referential style A style of early language learning in which toddlers use language mainly to label objects. Distinguished from *expressive style*. (p. 240)

reflex An inborn, automatic response to a particular form of stimulation. (p. 143)

rehearsal A memory strategy that involves repeating information to oneself to improve recall. (p. 446)

reinforcer In operant conditioning, a stimulus that increases the occurrence of a response. (p. 180)

rejected-aggressive children A subtype of rejected children who show high rates of conflict, physical and relational aggression, and hyperactive, inattentive, and impulsive behavior. Distinguished from *rejected-withdrawn children*. (p. 501)

rejected children Children who receive many negative votes on self-report measures of peer acceptance, indicating they are actively disliked. Distinguished from *popular, controversial,* and *neglected children*. (p. 500)

rejected-withdrawn children A subtype of rejected children who are passive, socially awkward, and overwhelmed by social anxiety. Distinguished from *rejected-aggressive children*. (p. 501)

relational aggression A form of aggression that damages another's peer relationships through social exclusion, malicious gossip, or friendship manipulation. Distinguished from *physical aggression* and *verbal aggression*. (p. 386)

resilience The ability to adapt effectively in the face of threats to development. (p. 10)

resistant attachment The attachment pattern characterizing infants who seek closeness to the parent before her departure, are usually distressed when she leaves, and combine clinginess with angry, resistive behavior when she returns. Distinguished from *secure, avoidant,* and *disorganized/disoriented attachment*. (p. 267)

reticular formation A structure in the brain stem that maintains alertness and consciousness. (p. 294)

reversibility The ability to think through a series of steps in a problem and then mentally reverse direction, returning to the starting point. Distinguished from *irreversibility*. (p. 438)

Rh factor incompatibility A condition that arises when the Rh protein is present in the fetus's blood but not in the mother's, causing the mother to build up antibodies. If these enter the fetus's system, they destroy red blood cells, reducing the oxygen supply to organs and tissues. (p. 115)

rooming in An arrangement in which the newborn baby stays in the mother's hospital room all or most of the time. (p. 143)

rough-and-tumble play A form of peer interaction involving friendly chasing and play-fighting that emerges in the preschool years and peaks in middle childhood. In our evolutionary past, it may have been important for the development of fighting skill. (p. 431)

S

scaffolding Adjusting the support offered during a teaching session to fit the child's current level of performance. As competence increases, the adult gradually and sensitively withdraws support, turning responsibility over to the child. (p. 331)

scale errors Toddlers' attempts to do things that their body size makes impossible, such as trying to put on dolls' clothes, fit themselves into a doll-sized chair, or walk through a door too narrow to pass through. Reflects a lack of objective understanding of one's own body dimensions. (p. 281)

scheme In Piaget's theory, a specific psychological structure, or organized way of making sense of experience, that changes with age. (p. 204)

scripts General descriptions of what occurs and when it occurs in a particular situation, used to organize, interpret, and predict everyday experiences. (p. 336)

secular trends in physical growth Changes in body size from one generation to the next. (p. 413)

secure attachment The attachment pattern characterizing infants who use the parent as a secure base from which to explore and may be distressed by parental separation but actively seek contact and are easily comforted by the parent when she returns. Distinguished from *avoidant, resistant,* and *disorganized/disoriented attachment*. (p. 266)

secure base Role of the familiar caregiver as a point from which the infant explores, venturing into the environment and then returning for emotional support. (p. 252)

self-care children Children who are without adult supervision for some period of time after school. (p. 516)

self-concept The set of attributes, abilities, attitudes, and values that an individual believes defines who he or she is. (p. 365)

self-conscious emotions Emotions involving injury to or enhancement of the sense of self, such as guilt, shame, embarrassment, envy, and pride. (p. 253)

self-esteem An aspect of self-concept that involves judgments about one's own worth and the feelings associated with those judgments. (p. 366)

semantic bootstrapping Using semantics, or word meanings, to figure out grammatical rules. (p. 357)

sensitive caregiving Caregiving that involves responding promptly, consistently, and appropriately to infants and holding them tenderly and carefully. (p. 270)

sensitive period A time that is biologically optimal for certain capacities to emerge and in which the individual is especially responsive to environmental influences. (pp. 23–24)

sensorimotor stage Piaget's first stage, spanning the first two years of life, during which infants and toddlers "think" with their eyes, ears, hands, and other sensorimotor equipment. (p. 204)

sensory register In information processing, the part of the mental system in which sights and sounds are represented directly and stored briefly before they either decay or are transferred to working memory. (p. 217)

separation anxiety An infant's distressed reaction to the departure of the familiar caregiver. (p. 265)

sequential design A research design in which several similar cross-sectional or longitudinal studies (called sequences) are conducted at varying times. (p. 42)

seriation The ability to order items along a quantitative dimension, such as length or weight. (p. 438)

sex chromosomes The twenty-third pair of chromosomes—called XX in females, XY in males—which determines the sex of the individual. (p. 54)

shape constancy Perception of an object's shape as the same, despite changes in the shape projected on the retina. (p. 196)

size constancy Perception of an object's size as the same, despite changes in the size of its retinal image. (p. 196)

skeletal age An estimate of physical maturity based on development of the bones of the body. (p. 163)

slow-to-warm-up child A child whose temperament is characterized by inactivity; mild, low-key reactions to environmental stimuli; negative mood; and slow adjustment to new experiences. Distinguished from *easy child* and *difficult child*. (p. 257)

small-for-date infants Infants whose birth weight is below their expected weight considering the length of the pregnancy. (p. 137)

social comparisons Judgments of one's own appearance, abilities, and behavior in relation to those of others. (p. 483)

social-constructivist classroom A classroom grounded in Vygotsky's sociocultural theory, in which children participate in a wide range of challenging activities with teachers and peers, with whom they jointly construct understandings. Distinguished from *traditional classroom* and *constructivist classroom*. (p. 468)

social conventions Customs determined by consensus within a society, such as table manners and politeness rituals. Distinguished from *moral imperatives* and *matters of personal choice*. (p. 384)

social learning theory An approach that emphasizes the role of modeling, also known as imitation or observational learning, in the development of behavior. (p. 18)

social problem solving Generating and applying strategies that prevent or resolve disagreements, resulting in outcomes that are both acceptable to others and beneficial to the self. (p. 375)

social referencing Actively seeking emotional information from a trusted person in an uncertain situation. (p. 253)

social smile The infant's broad grin evoked by the parent's communication, first appearing between 6 and 10 weeks of age. (p. 251)

sociocultural theory Vygotsky's theory, in which children acquire the ways of thinking and behaving that make up a community's culture through social interaction, especially cooperative dialogues with more knowledgeable members of their society. (pp. 24–25)

sociodramatic play The make-believe play with others that is under way by the end of the second year and increases rapidly in complexity during early childhood. (p. 319)

socioeconomic status (SES) A measure of an individual's social position and economic well-being that combines three related variables: years of education, the prestige of one's job and the skill it requires, and income. (p. 71)

stage A qualitative change in thinking, feeling, and behaving that characterizes a specific period of development. (p. 8)

standardization The practice of giving an intelligence test to a large, representative sample and using the results as the standard for interpreting individual scores. (p. 227)

states of arousal Degrees of sleep and wakefulness. (p. 145)

statistical learning capacity The capacity to analyze the speech stream for repeatedly occurring sequences of sounds, through which infants acquire a stock of speech structures for which they will later learn meanings. (p. 190)

stereotype threat The fear of being judged on the basis of a negative stereotype, which can trigger anxiety that interferes with performance. (p. 460)

stranger anxiety The infant's expression of fear in response to unfamiliar adults, which appears in many babies in the second half of the first year. (p. 252)

Strange Situation A laboratory procedure used to assess the quality of attachment between 1 and 2 years of age by observing the baby's responses to eight short episodes involving brief separations from and reunions with the caregiver in an unfamiliar playroom. (p. 266)

structured interview An interview method in which each participant is asked the same questions in the same way. Distinguished from *clinical interview*. (p. 33)

structured observation A research method in which the investigator sets up a laboratory situation that evokes the behavior of interest so that every participant has an equal opportunity to display the response. Distinguished from *naturalistic observation*. (pp. 31–32)

subculture A group of people with beliefs and customs that differ from those of the larger culture. (p. 78)

sudden infant death syndrome (SIDS) The unexpected death, usually during the night, of an infant under 1 year of age that remains unexplained after thorough investigation. (p. 147)

sympathy Feelings of concern or sorrow for another's plight. (p. 371)

synapses The gaps between neurons, across which chemical messages are sent. (p. 164)

synaptic pruning Loss of synapses by seldom-stimulated neurons, a process that returns them to an uncommitted state so they can support future development. (p. 165)

syntactic bootstrapping Figuring out word meanings by observing how words are used in syntax, or the structure of sentences. (p. 355)

T

talent Outstanding performance in a specific field. (p. 474)

telegraphic speech Toddlers' two-word utterances that, like a telegram, focus on high-content words while omitting smaller, less important ones. (p. 239)

temperament Early-appearing, stable individual differences in reactivity (quickness and intensity of emotional arousal, attention, and motor activity) and self-regulation (strategies that modify reactivity). (p. 256)

teratogen Any environmental agent that causes damage during the prenatal period. (p. 102)

theory An orderly, integrated set of statements that describes, explains, and predicts behavior. (p. 7)

theory of multiple intelligences Gardner's theory, which proposes at least eight independent intelligences, defined in terms of distinct sets of processing operations that permit individuals to engage in a wide range of culturally valued activities. (p. 456)

thyroid-stimulating hormone (TSH) A pituitary hormone that stimulates the thyroid gland to release thyroxine, which is necessary for brain development and for growth hormone to have its full impact on body size. (p. 297)

time out A form of mild punishment in which children are removed from the immediate setting until they are ready to act appropriately. (p. 382)

traditional classroom A classroom in which the teacher is the sole authority for knowledge, rules, and decision making and students are relatively passive learners who are evaluated in relation to a uniform set of standards for their grade. Distinguished from *constructivist classroom* and *social-constructivist classroom*. (p. 467)

transition Climax of the first stage of labor, in which the frequency and strength of contractions are at their peak and the cervix opens completely. (p. 126)

transitive inference The ability to seriate, or order items along a quantitative dimension, mentally. (p. 438)

triarchic theory of successful intelligence Sternberg's theory, which identifies three broad, interacting intelligences—analytical, creative, and practical—that must be balanced to achieve success according to one's personal goals and the requirements of one's cultural community. (p. 455)

trimesters Three equal time periods, each lasting three months, into which prenatal development is divided. (p. 100)

trophoblast The thin outer ring of cells of the blastocyst, which will become the structures that provide protective covering and nourishment to the new organism. (p. 98)

U

ulnar grasp The clumsy grasp of the young infant, in which the fingers close against the palm. (p. 187)

umbilical cord The long cord connecting the prenatal organism to the placenta that delivers nutrients and removes waste products. (pp. 98–99)

unconditioned response (UCR) In classical conditioning, a reflexive response that is produced by an unconditioned stimulus (UCS). Distinguished from *conditioned response*. (p. 179)

unconditioned stimulus (UCS) In classical conditioning, a stimulus that leads to a reflexive response. Distinguished from *conditioned stimulus*. (p. 179)

underextension An early vocabulary error in which a word is applied too narrowly, to a smaller number of objects and events than is appropriate. Distinguished from *overextension.* (p. 239)

uninhibited, or **sociable, child** A child whose temperament is such that he or she displays positive emotion to and approaches novel stimuli. Distinguished from *inhibited,* or *shy, child.* (p. 258)

uninvolved child-rearing style A child-rearing style that combines low acceptance and involvement with little control and general indifference to issues of autonomy. Distinguished from *authoritative, authoritarian,* and *permissive child-rearing styles.* (p. 400)

utilization deficiency The inability to improve performance even with consistent use of a mental strategy. Distinguished from *control deficiency, production deficiency,* and *effective strategy use.* (p. 443)

V

verbal aggression A form of aggression that harms others through threats of physical aggression, name-calling, or hostile teasing. Distinguished from *physical* and *relational aggression.* (p. 385)

vernix A white, cheeselike substance that covers the fetus, protecting the skin from chapping due to constant exposure to amniotic fluid. (p. 100)

video deficit effect In toddlers, poorer performance on tasks after watching a video than a live demonstration. (p. 213)

violation-of-expectation method A method in which researchers show babies an expected event (one that is consistent with reality) and an unexpected event (a variation of the first event that violates reality). Heightened attention to the unexpected event suggests that the infant is "surprised" by a deviation from physical reality and, therefore, is aware of that aspect of the physical world. (p. 208)

visual acuity Fineness of visual discrimination. (p. 151)

W

whole-language approach An approach to beginning reading instruction in which, from the start, children are exposed to text in its complete form, using reading materials that are whole and meaningful to promote appreciation of the communicative function of written language. Distinguished from *phonics approach.* (p. 450)

working, or **short-term, memory** The part of the mental system where we actively "work" on a limited amount of information, actively applying mental strategies so the information will be retained and used effectively. (p. 217)

X

X-linked inheritance A pattern of inheritance in which a recessive gene is carried on the X chromosome, so that males are more likely than females to be affected. (p. 57)

Z

zone of proximal development In Vygotsky's theory, a range of tasks too difficult for a child to do alone but possible with the help of more skilled partners. (p. 224)

zygote The newly fertilized cell formed by the union of sperm and ovum at conception. (p. 53)

References

A

Aarnoudse-Moens, C. S., Weisglas-Kuperus, N., & van Goudoever, J. B. (2009). Meta-analysis of neurobehavioral outcomes in very preterm and/or very low birth weight children. *Pediatrics, 124,* 717–728.

Aber, J. L., Jones, S. M., & Raver, C. C. (2007). Poverty and life development: New perspectives on a defining issue. In J. L. Aber, S. J. Bishop-Josef, S. M. Jones, K. T. McLearn, & D. A. Phillips (Eds.), *Child development and social policy: Knowledge for action* (pp. 149–166). Washington, DC: American Psychological Association.

Abikoff, H. B., Jensen, P. S., Arnold, L. L., Hoza, B., Hechtman, L., et al. (2002). Observed classroom behavior of children with ADHD: Relationship to gender and comorbidity. *Journal of Abnormal Child Psychology, 30,* 349–359.

Aboud, F. E. (2003). The formation of in-group favoritism and out-group prejudice in young children: Are they distinct attitudes? *Developmental Psychology, 39,* 48–60.

Aboud, F. E., & Amato, M. (2001). Developmental and socialization influences on intergroup bias. In R. Brown & S. Gaertner (Eds.), *Blackwell handbook of social psychology: Intergroup processes.* Oxford, UK: Blackwell.

Aboud, F. E., & Doyle, A. (1996). Parental and peer influences on children's racial attitudes. *International Journal of Intercultural Relations, 20,* 371–383.

Achenbach, T. M., Howell C. T., & Aoki, M. F. (1993). Nine-year outcome of the Vermont Intervention Program for low-birthweight infants, *Pediatrics, 91,* 45–55.

Acker, M. M., & O'Leary, S. G. (1996). Inconsistency of mothers' feedback and toddlers' misbehavior and negative affect. *Journal of Abnormal Child Psychology, 24,* 703–714.

Adachi-Mejia, A. M., Longacre, M. R., Gibson, J. J., Beach, M. L., Titus-Ernstoff, L. T., & Dalton, M. A. (2007). Children with a TV in their bedroom at higher risk for being overweight. *International Journal of Obesity, 31,* 644–651

Adams, R. J., & Courage, M. L. (1998). Human newborn color vision: Measurement with chromatic stimuli varying in excitation purity. *Journal of Experimental Child Psychology, 68,* 22–34.

Adamson, D. (2005). Regulation of assisted reproductive technologies in the United States. *Family Law Quarterly, 39,* 727–744.

Adolph, K. E. (2002). Learning to keep balance. In R. V. Kail (Ed.), *Advances in child development and behavior* (Vol. 30, pp. 1–40). Boston: Academic Press.

Adolph, K. E. (2008). Learning to move. *Current Directions in Psychological Science, 17,* 213–218.

Adolph, K. E., & Berger, S. E. (2006). Motor development. In D. Kuhn & R. Siegler (Eds.), *Handbook of child psychology: Vol. 2. Cognition, perception, and language* (6th ed., pp. 161–213). Hoboken, NJ: Wiley.

Adolph, K. E., & Joh, A. S. (2009). Multiple learning mechanisms in the development of action. In A. Woodward & A. Needham (Eds.), *Learning and the infant mind* (pp. 172–207). New York: Oxford University Press.

Adolph, K. E., Karasik, L. B., & Tamis-LeMonda, C. S. (2010). Motor skill. In M. H. Bornstein (Ed.), *Handbook of cultural developmental science* (pp. 61–88). New York: Psychology Press.

Adolph, K. E., Tamis-LeMonda, C. S., Ishak, S., Karasik, L. B., & Lobo, S. A. (2008). Locomotor experience and use of social information are posture specific. *Developmental Psychology, 44,* 1705–1714.

Adolph, K. E., Vereijken, B., & Shrout, P. E. (2003). What changes in infant walking and why. *Child Development, 74,* 475–497.

Afifi, T. O., Brownridge, D. A., Cox, B. J., & Sareen J. (2006). Physical punishment, childhood abuse and psychiatric disorders. *Child Abuse and Neglect, 30,* 1093–1103.

Afterschool Alliance. (2004). *America after 3 PM: A household survey on afterschool in America.* Retrieved from www.afterschoolalliance.org /researchFactSheets.cfm

Aggarwal, R., Sentz, J., & Miller, M. A. (2007). Role of zinc administration in prevention of childhood diarrhea and respiratory illnesses: A meta-analysis. *Pediatrics, 119,* 1120–1130.

Aguiar, A., & Baillargeon, R. (2002). Developments in young infants' reasoning about occluded objects. *Cognitive Psychology, 45,* 267–336.

Ahlgren, M., Melbye, M., Wohlfahrt, J., & Sørensen, T. I. (2004). Growth patterns and the risk of breast cancer in women. *New England Journal of Medicine, 351,* 1619–1626

Ainsworth, M. D. S., Blehar, M. C., Waters, E., & Wall, S. (1978). *Patterns of attachment.* Hillsdale, NJ: Erlbaum.

Akhtar, N., & Montague, L. (1999). Early lexical acquisition: The role of cross-situational learning. *First Language, 19,* 347–358.

Akimoto, S. A., & Sanbinmatsu, D. M. (1999). Differences in self-effacing behavior between European and Japanese Americans: Effect on competence evaluations. *Journal of Cross-Cultural Psychology, 30,* 159–177.

Akinbami, L. J., Moorman, J. E., Garbe, P. L., & Sondik, E. J. (2009). Status of childhood asthma in the United States, 1980–2007. *Pediatrics, 123,* S123–S145.

Aksan, N., & Kochanska, G. (2004). Heterogeneity of joy in infancy. *Infancy, 6,* 79–94.

Akshoomoff, N. A., Feroleto, C. C., Doyle, R. E., & Stiles, J. (2002). The impact of early unilateral brain injury on perceptual organization and visual memory. *Neuropsychologia, 40,* 539–561.

Albers, C. A., & Grieve, A. J. (2007). Test review: Bayley, N. (2006). Bayley Scales of Infant and Toddler Development—Third Edition. San Antonio, TX: Harcourt Assessment. *Journal of Psychoeducational Assessment, 25,* 180–190.

Aldridge, M. A., Stillman, R. D., & Bower, T. G. R. (2001). Newborn categorization of vowel-like sounds. *Developmental Science, 4,* 220–232.

Alexander, J. M., Fabricius, W. V., Fleming, V. M., Zwahr, M., & Brown, S. A. (2003). The development of metacognitive causal explanations. *Learning and Individual Differences, 13,* 227–238.

Alexandre-Bidon, D., & Lett, D. (1997). *Les enfants au Moyen Age, Ve–XVe siecles.* Paris: Hachette.

Alhusen, J. L. (2008). A literature update on maternal–fetal attachment. *Journal of Obstetric, Gynecologic, and Neonatal Nursing, 37,* 315–328.

Ali, U. A., & Norwitz, E. R. (2009). Vacuum-assisted vaginal delivery. *Reviews in Obstetrics and Gynecology, 2,* 5–17.

Alibali, M. W., Phillips, K. M. O., & Fischer, A. D. (2009). Learning new problem-solving strategies leads to changes in problem representation. *Cognitive Development, 24,* 89–101.

Aligne, C. A., Moss, M. E., Auinger, P., & Weitzman, M. (2003). Association of pediatric dental caries with passive smoking. *Journal of the American Medical Association, 289,* 1258–1264.

Alink, L. R. A., Mesman, J., van Zeijl, J., Stolk, M. N., Juffer, F., & Koot, H. M. (2006). The early childhood aggression curve: Development of physical aggression in 10- to 50-month-old children. *Child Development, 77,* 954–966.

Allen, M., & Burrell, N. (1996). Comparing the impact of homosexual and heterosexual parents on children: Meta-analysis of existing research. *Journal of Homosexuality, 32,* 19–35.

Allen, S. E. M., & Crago, M. B. (1996). Early passive acquisition in Inukitut. *Journal of Child Language, 23,* 129–156.

Al-Namlah, A. S., Fernyhough, C., & Meins, E. (2006). Sociocultural influences on the development of verbal mediation: Private speech and phonological recoding in Saudi Arabian and British samples. *Developmental Psychology, 42,* 117–131.

Alter, J. (2008, September 29). It's not just about the boys. Get girls into school. *Newsweek,* pp. 50–51.

Althaus, J., & Wax, J. (2005). Analgesia and anesthesia in labor. *Obstetrics and Gynecology Clinics of North America, 32,* 231–244.

Alwan, S., & Friedman, J. M. (2009). Safety of selective serotonin reuptake inhibitors in pregnancy. *CNS Drugs, 23,* 493–509.

Amato, P. R. (2001). Children of divorce in the 1990s: An update of the Amato and Keith (1991) meta-analysis. *Journal of Family Psychology, 15,* 355–370.

Amato, P. R. (2006). Marital discord, divorce, and children's well-being: Results from a 20-year longitudinal study of two generation. In A. Clarke-Stewart & J. Dunn (Eds.), *Families count: Effects on child and adolescent development* (pp. 179–202). New York: Cambridge University Press.

Amato, P. R. (2010). Research on divorce: Continuing trends and new developments. *Journal of Marriage and Family, 72,* 650–666.

Amato, P. R., & Dorius, C. (2010). Fathers, children, and divorce. In M. E. Lamb (Ed.), *The role of the father in child development* (5th ed., pp. 177–200). Hoboken, NJ: Wiley.

Amato, P. R., & Fowler, F. (2002). Parenting practices, child adjustment, and family diversity. *Journal of Marriage and the Family, 64,* 703–716.

Amato, P. R., Landale, N. S., Havasevich-Brooks, T. C., Booth, A., Eggebeen, D. J., Schoen, R., & McHale, S. M. (2008). Precursors of young women's family formation pathways. *Journal of Marriage and Family, 70,* 1271–1286.

Amato, P. R., & Sobolewski, J. M. (2004). The effects of divorce on fathers and children: Nonresidential fathers and stepfathers. In M. E. Lamb (Ed.), *The role of the father in child development* (4th ed., pp. 341–367). Hoboken, NJ: Wiley.

Ambert, A.-M. (2005). *Same-sex couples and same-sex parent families: Relationships, parenting, and issues of marriage.* Ontario: Vanier Institute of the Family. Retrieved from www.vifamily.ca/library /publications/samesexd.html

Ambert, A.-M. (2006). *One-parent families: Characteristics, causes, consequences, and issues.* Ontario, Canada: Vanier Institute of the Family.

American Academy of Pediatrics. (2001). Committee on Public Education: Children, adolescents, and television. *Pediatrics, 104,* 341–343.

American Academy of Pediatrics. (2005a). Breastfeeding and the use of human milk. *Pediatrics, 115,* 496–506.

American Academy of Pediatrics, Subcommittee on Attention-Deficit Hyperactivity Disorder. (2005b). Treatment of attention-deficit hyperactivity disorder. *Pediatrics, 115,* e749–e757.

American Academy of Pediatrics. (2006). Folic acid for the prevention of neural tube defects. *Pediatrics, 104,* 325–327.

American Diabetes Association. (2010). Diabetes statistics. Retrieved from www.diabetes.org/diabetes-basics/diabetes-statistics

American Psychiatric Association. (2000). *DSM-IV-TR: Diagnostic and statistical manual of mental disorders—Text revision* (4th ed.). Washington, DC: American Psychiatric Association.

American Psychological Association. (2002). Ethical principles of psychologists and code of conduct. *American Psychologist, 57,* 1060–1073.

Amso, D., & Johnson, S. P. (2006). Learning by selection: Visual search and object perception in young infants. *Developmental Psychology, 42,* 1236–1245.

Amsterlaw, J. (2006). Children's beliefs about everyday reasoning. *Child Development, 77,* 443–464.

Amsterlaw, J., & Wellman, H. M. (2006). Theories of mind in transition: A micro-genetic study of the development of false belief understanding. *Journal of Cognition and Development, 7,* 139–172.

Anand, S. S., Yusuf, S., Jacobs, R., Davis, A. D., Yi, Q., & Gerstein, H. (2001). Risk factors, arteriosclerosis, and cardiovascular disease among Aboriginal people in Canada: The study of health assessment and risk evaluation in Aboriginal peoples (SHARE-AP). *Lancet, 358,* 1147–1153.

Anderman, E. M., Eccles, J. S., Yoon, K. S., Roeser, R., Wigfield, A., & Blumenfeld, P. (2001). Learning to value mathematics and reading: Relations to mastery and performance-oriented instructional practices. *Contemporary Educational Psychology, 26,* 76–95.

Andersen, E. (2000). Exploring register knowledge: The value of "controlled improvisation." In L. Menn & N. B. Ratner (Eds.), *Methods for studying language production* (pp. 225–248). Mahwah, NJ: Erlbaum.

Anderson, C. A. (2004). An update on the effects of violent video games. *Journal of Adolescence, 27,* 113–122.

Anderson, C. A., Berkowitz, L., Donnerstein, E., Huesmann, R., Johnson, J. D., Linz, D., Malamuth, N. M., & Wartella, E. (2003). The influence of media violence on youth. *Psychological Science in the Public Interest, 4*(3), 81–106.

Anderson, C. A., Sakamoto, A., Gentile, D. A., Ihori, N., Shibuya, A., Yukawa, S., et al. (2008). Longitudinal effects of violent video games on aggression in Japan and the United States. *Pediatrics, 122,* e1067–e1072.

Anderson, D. M., Huston, A. C., Schmitt, K. L., Linebarger, D. L., & Wright, J. C. (2001). Early childhood television viewing and adolescent behavior. *Monographs of the Society for Research in Child Development, 66*(1, Serial No. 264).

Anderson, D. R. (2004). Watching children watch television and the creation of Blues Clues. In H. Hendershot (Ed.), *Nickelodeon nation: The history, politics, and economics of America's only TV channel for kids* (pp. 241–268). New York: New York University Press.

Anderson, L. L., Morgan, J. L., & White, K. S. (2003). A statistical basis for speech sound discrimination. *Language and Speech, 46,* 155–182.

Anderson, M. E., Johnson, D. C., & Batal, H. A. (2005). Sudden infant death syndrome and prenatal maternal smoking: Rising attributed risk in the Back to Sleep era. *BMC Medicine, 3,* 4.

Anderson, P. J., Wood, S. J., Francis, D. E., Coleman, L., Anderson, V., & Boneh, A. (2007). Are neuropsychological impairments in children with early-treated phenylketonuria (PKU) related to white matter abnormalities or elevated phenylalanine levels? *Developmental Neuropsychology, 32,* 645–668.

Anderson, V. A., Catroppa, C., Dudgeon, P., Morse, S. A., Haritou, F., & Rosenfeld, J. V. (2006). Understanding predictors of functional recovery and outcome 30 months following early childhood head injury. *Neuropsychology, 20,* 42–57.

Andersson, B.-E. (1989). Effects of public day care—A longitudinal study. *Child Development, 60,* 857–866.

Andersson, B.-E. (1992). Effects of day care on cognitive and socioemotional competence of thirteen-year-old Swedish schoolchildren. *Child Development, 63,* 20–36.

Andrews, G., & Halford, G. S. (1998). Children's ability to make transitive inferences: The importance of premise integration and structural complexity. *Cognitive Development, 13,* 479–513.

Andrews, G., & Halford, G. S. (2002). A cognitive complexity metric applied to cognitive development. *Cognitive Psychology, 45,* 475–506.

Anisfeld, M., Turkewitz, G., Rose, S. A., Rosenberg, F. R., Shelber, F. J., Couturier-Fagan, D. A., Ger, J. S., & Sommer I. (2001). No compelling evidence that newborns imitate oral gestures. *Infancy, 2,* 111–122.

Annett, M. (2002). *Handedness and brain asymmetry: The right shift theory.* Hove, U.K.: Psychology Press.

Apgar, V. (1953). A proposal for a new method of evaluation in the newborn infant. *Current Research in Anesthesia and Analgesia, 32,* 260–267.

Aram, D., & Levin, I. (2001). Mother–child joint writing in low SES: Sociocultural factors, maternal mediation, and emergent literacy. *Cognitive Development, 16,* 831–852.

Aram, D., & Levin, I. (2002). Mother–child joint writing and storybook reading: Relations with literacy among low SES kindergartners. *Merrill-Palmer Quarterly, 48,* 202–224.

Arcus, D., & Chambers, P. (2008). Childhood risks associated with adoption. In T. P. Gullotta & G. M. Blau (Eds.), *Family influences on childhood behavior and development* (pp. 117–142). New York: Routledge.

Ardila-Rey, A., & Killen, M. (2001). Middle-class Colombian children's evaluations of personal, moral, and social-conventional interactions in the classroom. *International Journal of Behavioral Development, 25,* 246–255.

Arija, V., Esparó, G., Fernández-Ballart, J., Murphy, M. M., Biarnés, E., & Canals, J. (2006). Nutritional status and performance in test of verbal and nonverbal intelligence in 6 year old children. *Intelligence, 34,* 141–149.

Arnett, J. J. (2003). Conceptions of the transition to adulthood among emerging adults in American ethnic groups. In J. J. Arnett & N. L. Galambos (Eds.), *Exploring cultural conceptions of the transitions to adulthood* (*New directions for child and adolescent development,* No. 100, pp. 63–75). San Francisco: Jossey-Bass.

Arnett, J. J. (2004). *Emerging adulthood: The winding road from the late teens through the twenties.* New York: Oxford University Press.

Arnett, J. J., & Tanner, J. L. (Eds.). (2006). *Emerging adults in America: Coming of age in the 21st century.* Washington, DC: American Psychological Association.

Arnold, D. H., McWilliams, L., & Harvey-Arnold, E. (1998). Teacher discipline and child misbehavior in daycare: Untangling causality with correlational data. *Developmental Psychology, 34,* 276–287.

Arnold, P. (1999). Emotional disorders in deaf children. In V. L. Schwean & D. H. Saklofske (Eds.), *Handbook of psychosocial characteristics of exceptional children* (pp. 493–522). New York: Kluwer.

Arnon, S., Shapsa, A., Forman, L., Regev, R., Bauer, S., & Litmanovitz, I. (2006). Live music is beneficial to preterm infants in the neonatal intensive care unit. *Birth, 33,* 131–136.

Aronson, A. A., & Henderson, S. O. (2006). Pediatrics, otitis media. *eMedicine Specialties, Pediatrics.* Retrieved from www.emedicine.com/emerg/topic393.htm

Arsenio, W. F. (2010). Integrating emotion attributions, morality, and aggression: Research and theoretical foundations. In W. F. Arsenio & E. A. Lemerise (Eds.), *Emotions, aggression, and morality in children: Bridging development and psychopathology* (pp. 75–94). Washington, DC: American Psychological Association.

Arsenio, W. F., & Lemerise, E. A. (2001). Varieties of childhood bullying: Values, emotion processes, and social competence. *Social Development, 10,* 59–73.

Arterberry, M. E. (2008). Infants' sensitivity to the depth cue of height-in-the-picture-plane. *Infancy, 13,* 544–555.

Arterberry, M. E., Craton, L. G., & Yonas, A. (1993). Infants' sensitivity to motion-carried information for depth and object properties. In C. E. Granrud (Ed.), *Visual perception and cognition in infancy* (pp. 215–234). Hillsdale, NJ: Erlbaum.

Artman, L., & Cahan, S. (1993). Schooling and the development of transitive inference. *Developmental Psychology, 29,* 753–759.

Asakawa, K. (2001). Family socialization practices and their effects on the internationalization of educational values for Asian and white American adolescents. *Applied Developmental Science, 5,* 184–194.

Asbjornsen, A. E., Obrzut, J. E., Boliek, C. A., Myking, E., Holmefjord, A., & Reisaeter, S. (2005). Impaired auditory attention skills following middle-ear infections. *Child Neuropsychology, 11,* 121–133.

Asher, S. R., & Rose, A. J. (1997). Promoting children's social-emotional adjustment with peers. In P. Salovey & D. J. Sluyter (Eds.), *Emotional development and emotional intelligence* (pp. 193–195). New York: Basic Books.

Aslin, R. N., Jusczyk, P. W., & Pisoni, D. B. (1998). Speech and auditory processing during infancy: Constraints on and precursors to language. In D. Kuhn & R. S. Siegler (Eds.), *Handbook of child psychology: Vol. 2. Cognition, perception, and language* (5th ed., pp. 147–198). New York: Wiley.

Aslin, R. N., & Newport, E. L. (2009). What statistical learning can and can't tell us about language acquisition. In J. Colombo, P. McCardle, & L. Freund (Eds.), *Infant pathways to language: Methods, models, and research directions* (pp. 15–29). New York: Psychology Press.

Astington, J. W., & Jenkins, J. M. (1995). Theory of mind development and social understanding. *Cognition and Emotion, 9,* 151–165.

Astington, J. W., & Pelletier, J. (2005). Theory of mind, language, and learning in the early years: Developmental origins of school readiness. In B. D. Homer & C. S. Tamis-LeMonda (Eds.), *The development of social cognition and communication* (pp. 205–230). Mahwah, NJ: Erlbaum.

Astington, J. W., Pelletier, J., & Homer, B. (2002). Theory of mind and epistemological development: The relation between children's second-order false belief understanding and their ability to reason about evidence. *New Ideas in Psychology, 20,* 131–144.

Atance, C. M., & Meltzoff, A. N. (2005). My future self: Young children's ability to anticipate and explain future states. *Cognitive Development, 20,* 341–361.

Atkinson, R. C., & Shiffrin, R. M. (1968). Human memory: A proposed system and its control processes. In K. W. Spence & J. T. Spence (Eds.), *Advances in the psychology of learning and motivation* (Vol. 2, pp. 90–195). New York: Academic Press.

Attewell, P. (2001). The first and second digital divides. *Sociology of Education, 74,* 252–259.

Au, T. K., Sidle, A. L., & Rollins, K. B. (1993). Developing an intuitive understanding of conservation and contamination: Invisible particles as a plausible mechanism. *Developmental Psychology, 29,* 286–299.

Aunola, K., Stattin, H., & Nurmi, J.-E. (2000). Parenting styles and adolescents' achievement strategies. *Journal of Adolescence, 23,* 205–222.

Averhart, C. J., & Bigler, R. S. (1997). Shades of meaning: Skin tone, racial attitudes, and constructive memory in African-American children. *Journal of Experimental Child Psychology, 67,* 368–388.

Avis, J., & Harris, P. L. (1991). Belief–desire reasoning among Baka children: Evidence for a universal conception of mind. *Child Development, 62,* 460–467.

AWC (American Women's Club) Oslo. (2005). *Health care in Norway.* Retrieved from www.awcoslo.org/Sections/LivingInOslo/health_care_in_norway.htm

Axelin, A., Salantera, S., & Lehtonen, L. (2006). 'Facilitated tucking by parents' in pain management of preterm infants—a randomized crossover trial. *Early Human Development, 82,* 241–247.

Azar, S. T., & Wolfe, D. A. (2006). Child physical abuse and neglect. In E. J. Mash & R. A. Barkley (Eds.), *Treatment of childhood disorders* (2nd ed., pp. 501–544). New York: Guilford.

Azurmendi, A., Braza, F., Garcia, A., Braza, P., Munoz, J. M., & Sanchez-Martin, J. R. (2006). Aggression, dominance, and affiliation: Their relationships with androgen levels and intelligence in 5-year-old children. *Hormones and Behavior, 50,* 132–140.

B

Bacallao, M. L., & Smokowski, P. R. (2007). The costs of getting ahead: Mexican family system changes after immigration. *Family Relations, 56,* 52–66.

Baddeley, A. (2000). Short-term and working memory. In E. Tulving & R. I. M. Craik (Eds.), *The Oxford handbook of memory* (pp. 77–92). New York: Oxford University Press.

Bader, A. P. (1995). Engrossment revisited: Fathers are still falling in love with their newborn babies. In J. L. Shapiro, M. J. Diamond, & M. Greenberg (Eds.), *Becoming a father* (pp 224–233). New York: Springer.

Bader, A. P., & Phillips, R. D. (2002). Fathers' recognition of their newborns by visual-facial and olfactory cues. *Psychology of Men and Masculinity, 3,* 79–84.

Baer, J. (2002). Is family cohesion a risk or protective factor during adolescent development? *Journal of Marriage and Family, 64,* 668–675.

Bagwell, C. L., & Coie, J. D. (2004). The best friendships of aggressive boys: Relationship quality, conflict management, and rule-breaking behavior. *Journal of Experimental Child Psychology, 88,* 5–24.

Bagwell, C. L., Coie, J. D., Terry, R. A., & Lochman, J. E. (2000). Peer clique participation and social status in preadolescence. *Merrill-Palmer Quarterly, 46,* 280–305.

Bahrick, L. E., Gogate, L. J., & Ruiz, I. (2002). Attention and memory for faces and actions in infancy: The salience of actions over faces in dynamic events. *Child Development, 73,* 1629–1643.

Bahrick, L. E., Hernandez-Reif, M., & Flom, R. (2005). The development of infant learning about specific face–voice relations. *Developmental Psychology, 41,* 541–552.

Bahrick, L. E., Hernandez-Reif, M., & Pickens, J. N. (1997). The effect of retrieval cues on visual preferences and memory in infancy: Evidence for a four-phase attention function. *Journal of Experimental Child Psychology, 67,* 1–20.

Bahrick, L. E., Lickliter, R., & Flom, R. (2004). Intersensory redundancy guides the development of selective attention, perception, and cognition in infancy. *Current Directions in Psychological Science, 13,* 99–102.

Bahrick, L. E., Netto, D., & Hernandez-Reif, M. (1998). Intermodal perception of adult and child faces and voices by infants. *Child Development, 69,* 1263–1275.

Bahrick, L. E., & Pickens, J. N. (1995). Infant memory for object motion across a period of three months: Implications for a four-phase attention function. *Journal of Experimental Child Psychology, 59,* 343–371.

Bai, D. L., & Bertenthal, B. I. (1992). Locomotor status and the development of spatial search skills. *Child Development, 63,* 215–226.

Bailey, R. C. (1991). The comparative growth of Efe pygmies and African farmers from birth to age 5 years. *Annals of Human Biology, 18,* 113–120.

Baillargeon, R. (2004). Infants' reasoning about hidden objects: Evidence for event-general and event-specific expectations. *Developmental Science, 7,* 391–424.

Baillargeon, R., & DeVos, J. (1991). Object permanence in young infants: Further evidence. *Child Development, 62,* 1227–1246.

Baillargeon, R., Scott, R. M., & He, Z. (2010). False-belief understanding in infants. *Trends in Cognitive Sciences, 14,* 110–118.

Baillargeon, R. H., Zoccolillo, M., Keenan, K., Côté, S., Pérusse, D., Wu, H.-X., & Boivin, M. (2007). Gender differences in physical aggression: A prospective population-based survey of children before and after 2 years of age. *Developmental Psychology, 43,* 13–26.

Baker, J. A. (2006). Contributions of teacher–child relationships to positive school adjustment during elementary school. *Journal of School Psychology, 44,* 211–229.

Bakermans-Kranenberg, M. J., van IJzendoorn, M. H., Mesman, J., Alink, L. R. A., & Juffer, F. (2008a). Effects of an attachment-based intervention on daily cortisol moderated by dopamine receptor D4: A randomized control trial on 1- to 3-year-olds screened for externalizing behavior. *Development and Psychopathology, 20,* 805–820.

Bakermans-Kranenburg, M. J., van IJzendoorn, M. H., Pijlman, F. T. A., Mesman, J., & Juffer, F. (2008b). Experimental evidence for differential susceptibility: Dopamine D4 receptor polymorphism (DRD4 VNTR) moderates intervention effects on toddlers' externalizing behavior in a randomized control trial. *Developmental Psychology, 44,* 293–300.

Baker-Sennett, J., Matusov, E., & Rogoff, B. (2008). Children's planning of classroom plays with adult or child direction. *Social Development, 17,* 998–1018.

Balaban, M. T., & Waxman, S. R. (1997). Do words facilitate object categorization in 9-month-old infants? *Journal of Experimental Child Psychology, 64,* 3–26.

Ball, H. (2006). Parent–infant bed-sharing behavior: Effects of feeding type and presence of father. *Human Nature, 17,* 301–318.

Baltes, P. B., Lindenberger, U., & Staudinger, U. M. (2006). Life span theory in developmental psychology. In R. M. Lerner & W. Damon (Eds.), *Handbook of child psychology: Vol. 1. Theoretical models of human development* (6th ed., pp. 569–664). Hoboken, N.J.: Wiley.

Band, G. P. H., van der Molen, M. W., Overtoom, C. C. E., & Verbaten, M. N. (2000). The ability to activate and inhibit speeded responses: Separate developmental trends. *Journal of Experimental Child Psychology, 75,* 263–290.

Bandura, A. (1977). *Social learning theory.* Englewood Cliffs, NJ: Prentice-Hall.

Bandura, A. (1992). Perceived self-efficacy in cognitive development and functioning. *Educational Psychologist, 28,* 117–148.

Bandura, A. (1999). Social cognitive theory of personality. In L. A. Pervin (Ed.), *Handbook of personality: Theory and research* (2nd ed., pp. 154–196). New York: Guilford.

Bandura, A. (2001). Social cognitive theory: An agentic perspective. *Annual Review of Psychology, 52,* 1–26.

Banish, M. T., & Heller, W. (1998). Evolving perspectives on lateralization of function. *Current Directions in Psychological Science, 7,* 1–2.

Banks, M. S. (1980). The development of visual accommodation during early infancy. *Child Development, 51,* 157–173.

Banks, M. S., & Ginsburg, A. P. (1985). Early visual preferences: A review and new theoretical treatment. In H. W. Reese (Ed.), *Advances in child development and behavior* (Vol. 19, pp. 207–246). New York: Academic Press.

Barber, B. K., & Olsen, J. A. (1997). Socialization in context: Connection, regulation, and autonomy in the family, school, and neighborhood, and with peers. *Journal of Adolescent Research, 12,* 287–315.

Barber, B. K., Stolz, H. E., & Olsen, J. A. (2005). Parental support, psychological control, and behavioral control: Assessing relevance across time, culture, and method. *Monographs of the Society for Research in Child Development, 70*(4, Serial No. 282).

Bard, K. A., Todd, B. K., Bernier, C., Love, J., & Leavens, D. A. (2006). Self-awareness in human and chimpanzee infants: What is measured and what is meant by the mark and mirror test? *Infancy, 9,* 191–219.

Barenbaum, J., Ruchkin, V., & Schwab-Stone, M. (2004). The psychosocial aspects of children exposed to war: Practice and policy initiatives. *Journal of Child Psychology and Psychiatry, 45,* 41–62.

Bar-Haim, Y., Ziv, T., Lamy, D., & Hodes, R. M. (2006). Nature and nurture in own-race face processing. *Psychological Science, 17,* 159–163.

Barker, D. J. (2008). Human growth and cardiovascular disease. *Nestlé Nutrition Workshop Series, 61,* 21–38.

Barker, D. J., Osmond, C., Thornburg, K. L., Kajantie, E., Forsen, T., & Eriksson, J. G. (2008). A possible link between the pubertal growth of girls and breast cancer in their daughters. *American Journal of Human Biology, 20,* 127–131.

Barkley, R. A. (2001). Executive functions and self-regulation : An evolutionary neuropsychological perspective. *Neuropsychology Review, 11,* 1–29.

Barkley, R. A. (2002a). Psychosocial treatments of attention-deficit/hyperactivity disorder in children. *Journal of Clinical Psychology, 63*(Suppl. 12), 36–43.

Barkley, R. A. (2002b). Major life activity and health outcomes associated with attention-deficit/ hyperactivity disorder. *Journal of Clinical Psychiatry, 63*(Suppl. 12), 10–15.

Barkley, R. A. (2003). Attention-deficit/hyperactivity disorder. In E. J. Mash & R. A. Barkley (Eds.), *Child psychopathology* (2nd ed., pp. 75–143). New York: Guilford.

Barkley, R. A. (2006). Attention-deficit/hyperactivity disorder. In R. A. Barkley, D. A. Wolfe, & E. J. Mash (Eds.), *Behavioral and emotional disorders in adolescents: Nature, assessment, and treatment* (pp. 91–152). New York: Guilford.

Barnea-Goraly, N., Menon, V., Eckert, M., Tamm, L., Bammer, R., & Karchemskiy, A. (2005). White matter development during childhood and adolescence: A cross-sectional diffusion tensor imaging study. *Cerebral Cortex, 15,* 1848–1854.

Barnes, G. M., Hoffman, J. H., Welte, J. W., Farrell, M. P., & Dintcheff, B. A. (2007). Adolescents' time use: Effects on substance use, delinquency and sexual activity. *Journal of Youth and Adolescence, 36,* 697–710.

Barnes-Josiah, D., & Augustin, A. (1995). Secular trend in the age at menarche in Haiti. *American Journal of Human Biology, 7,* 357–362.

Barnett, S., & Vondra, J. I. (1999). Atypical patterns of early attachment: Theory, research, and current directions. In J. I. Vondra & D. Barnett (Eds.), *Atypical attachment in infancy and early childhood among children at developmental risk. Monographs of the Society for Research in Child Development, 64*(3, Serial No. 258), pp. 1–24.

Barnett, W. S. (2004). Does Head Start have lasting cognitive effects? The myth of fade-out. In E. Zigler & S. J. Styfco (Eds.), *The Head Start debates* (pp. 221–250). Baltimore: Brookes.

Baron-Cohen, S., & Belmonte, M. K. (2005). Autism: A window onto the development of the social and the analytic brain. *Annual Review of Neuroscience, 28,* 109–126.

Baron-Cohen, S., Baldwin, D. A., & Crowson, M. (1997). Do children with autism use the speaker's direction of gaze strategy to crack the code of language? *Child Development, 68,* 48–57.

Barr, H. M., Bookstein, F. L., O'Malley, K. D., Connor, P. D., Huggins, J. E., & Streissguth, A. P. (2006). Binge drinking during pregnancy as a predictor of psychiatric disorders on the structured clinical interview for DSM-IV in young adult offspring. *American Journal of Psychiatry, 163,* 1061–1065.

Barr, H. M., Streissguth, A. P., Darby, B. L., & Sampson, P. D. (1990). Prenatal exposure to alcohol, caffeine, tobacco, and aspirin: Effects on fine and gross motor performance in 4-year-old children. *Developmental Psychology, 26,* 339–348.

Barr, R., & Hayne, H. (2003). It's not what you know, it's who you know: Older siblings facilitate imitation during infancy. *International Journal of Early Years Education, 11,* 7–21.

Barr, R., Marrott, H., & Rovee-Collier, C. (2003). The role of sensory preconditioning in memory retrieval by preverbal infants. *Learning and Behavior, 31,* 111–123.

Barr, R., Muentener, P., & Garcia, A. (2007). Age-related changes in deferred imitation from television by 6- to 18-month-olds. *Developmental Science, 10,* 910–921.

Barr, R. G. (2001). "Colic" is something infants do, rather than a condition they "have": A developmental approach to crying phenomena patterns, pacification and (patho)genesis. In R. G. Barr, I. St James-Roberts, & M. R. Keefe (Eds), *New evidence on unexplained infant crying* (pp. 87–104). St. Louis: Johnson & Johnson Pediatric Institute.

Barr, R. G., Paterson, J. A., MacMartin, L. M., & Lehtonen, L. (2005). Prolonged and unsoothable crying bouts in infants with and without colic. *Journal of Developmental and Behavioral Pediatrics, 26,* 14–23.

Barratt, M. S., Roach, M. A., & Leavitt, L. A. (1996). The impact of low-risk prematurity on maternal behaviour and toddler outcomes. *International Journal of Behavioral Development, 19,* 581–602.

Barrett, J. L. (2002). Do children experience God as adults do? In J. Andresen (Ed.), *Religion in mind* (pp. 173–190). New York: Cambridge University Press.

Barrett, J. L., Richert, R. A., & Driesenga, A. (2001). God's beliefs versus mother's: The development of nonhuman agent concepts. *Child Development, 72,* 50–65.

Barrett, J. L., & Van Orman, B. (1996). The effects of the use of images in worship on God concepts. *Journal of Psychology and Christianity, 15,* 38–45.

Barrett, K. C. (2005). The origins of social emotions and self-regulation in toddlerhood: New evidence. *Cognition and Emotion, 19,* 953–979.

Barrett, T. M., Traupman, E., & Needham, A. (2008). Infants' visual anticipation of object structure in grasp planning. *Infant Behavior and Development, 31,* 1–9.

Barros, R. M., Silver, E. J., & Stein, R. E. K. (2009). School recess and group classroom behavior. *Pediatrics, 123,* 431–436.

Bartgis, J., Lilly, A. R., & Thomas, D. G. (2003). Event-related potential and behavioral measures of attention in 5-, 7-, and 9-year-olds. *Journal of General Psychology, 130,* 311–335.

Bartocci, M., Berggvist, L. L., Lagercrantz, H., & Anand, K. J. (2006). Pain activates cortical areas in the preterm newborn brain. *Pain, 122,* 109–117.

Barton, M. E., & Strosberg, R. (1997). Conversational patterns of two-year-old twins in mother–twin– twin triads. *Journal of Child Language, 24,* 257–269.

Barton, M. E., & Tomasello, M. (1991). Joint attention and conversation in mother–infant–sibling triads. *Child Development, 62,* 517–529.

Bartrip, J., Morton, J., & de Schonen, S. (2001). Responses to mother's face in 3-week to 3-month-old infants. *British Journal of Developmental Psychology, 19,* 219–232.

Bartsch, K., & Wellman, H. M. (1995). *Children talk about the mind.* New York: Oxford University Press.

Bass, J. L., Corwin, M., Gozal, D., Moore, C., Nishida, H., Parker, S., Schonwald, A., Wilker, R. E., Stehle, S., & Kinane, T. B. (2004). The effect of chronic or intermittent hypoxia on cognition in childhood: A review of the evidence. *Pediatrics, 114,* 805–816.

Batchelor, J. (2008). 'Failure to thrive' revisited. *Child Abuse Review, 17,* 147–159.

Bates, E. (2004). Explaining and interpreting deficits in language development across clinical groups: Where do we go from here? *Brain and Language, 88,* 248–253.

Bates, E., & MacWhinney, B. (1987). Competition, variation, and language learning. In B. MacWhinney (Ed.), *Mechanisms of language acquisition* (pp. 157–193). Hillsdale, NJ: Erlbaum.

Bates, E., Marchman, V., Thal, D., Fenson, L., Dale, P., Reznick, J. S., Reilly, J., & Hartung, J. (1994). Developmental and stylistic variation in the composition of early vocabulary. *Journal of Child Language, 21,* 85–123.

Bates, E., Wilson, S. M., Saygin, A. P., Dick, F., Sereno, M. I., Knight, R. T., & Dronkers, N. F. (2003). Voxel-based lesion-symptom mapping. *Nature Neuroscience, 6,* 448–450.

Bates, J. E., Wachs, T. D., & Emde, R. N. (1994). Toward practical uses for biological concepts. In J. E. Bates & T. D. Wachs (Eds.), *Temperament: Individual differences at the interface of biology and behavior* (pp. 275–306). Washington, DC: American Psychological Association.

Bauer, C. R., Langer, J. C., Shakaran, S., Bada, H. S., & Lester, B. (2005). Acute neonatal effects of cocaine exposure during pregnancy. *Archives of Pediatrics and Adolescent Medicine, 159,* 824–834.

Bauer, P. J. (2002). Early memory development. In U. Goswami (Ed.), *Blackwell handbook of child cognitive development* (pp. 127–150). Malden, MA: Blackwell.

Bauer, P. J. (2006). Event memory. In D. Kuhn & R. Siegler (Eds.), *Handbook of child psychology: Vol. 2. Cognition, perception, and language* (6th ed., pp. 373–425). Hoboken, NJ: Wiley.

Bauer, P. J. (2007). Recall in infancy: A neurodevelopmental account. *Current Directions in Psychological Science, 16,* 142–146.

Bauer, P. J. (2009). Learning and memory: Like a horse and carriage. In A. Woodward & A. Needham (Eds.), *Learning and the infant mind* (pp. 3–28). New York: Oxford University Press.

Bauer, P. J., Wiebe, S. A., Carver, L. J., Lukowski, A. F., Haight, J. C., Waters, J. M., & Nelson, C. A. (2006). Electrophysiological indexes of encoding and behavioral indexes of recall: Examining relations and developmental change late in the first year of life. *Developmental Neuropsychology, 29,* 293–320.

Baughman, F. D., & Cooper, R. P. (2006). Inhibition and young children's performance on the Tower of London task. In *Proceedings of the 7th International Conference on Cognitive Modeling* (pp. 26–31). Trieste, Italy.

Baumeister, R. F. (1998). Inducing guilt. In J. Bybee (Ed.), *Guilt and children* (pp. 185–213). San Diego: Academic Press.

Baumeister, R. F., Campbell, J. D., Krueger, J. I., & Vohs, K. D. (2003). Does high self-esteem cause better performance, interpersonal success, happiness, or healthier lifestyles? *Psychological Science in the Public Interest, 4*(1), 1–44.

Baumrind, D. (1971). Current patterns of parental authority. *Developmental Psychology Monograph, 4* (No. 1, Pt. 2).

Baumwell, L., Tamis-LeMonda, C. S., & Bornstein, M. H. (1997). Maternal verbal sensitivity and child language comprehension. *Infant Behavior and Development, 20,* 247–258.

Bauserman, R. (2002). Child adjustment in joint-custody versus sole-custody arrangements: A meta-analytic review. *Journal of Family Psychology, 16,* 91–102.

Baydar, N., Greek, A., & Brooks-Gunn, J. (1997). A longitudinal study of the effects of the birth of a sibling during the first 6 years of life. *Journal of Marriage and the Family, 59,* 939–956.

Bayless, S., & Stevenson, J. (2007). Executive functions in school-age children born very prematurely. *Early Human Development, 83,* 247–254.

Bayley, N. (1969). *Bayley Scales of Infant Development.* New York: Psychological Corporation.

Bayley, N. (1993). *Bayley Scales of Infant Development* (2nd ed.). New York: Psychological Corporation.

Bayley, N. (2005). *Bayley Scales of Infant and Toddler Development* (3rd ed.). (Bayley III). San Antonio, TX: Harcourt Assessment.

Baynes, K., & Gazzaniga, M. S. (1988). Right hemisphere language: Insights into normal language mechanisms. In F. Plum (Ed.), *Language, communication, and the brain* (pp. 117–126). New York: Raven.

Becker, G., Beyene, Y., Newsome, E., & Mayen, N. (2003). Creating continuity through mutual assistance: Intergenerational reciprocity in four ethnic groups. *Journal of Gerontology, 38B,* S151–S159.

Becker, K., El-Faddagh, M., Schmidt, M. H., Esser, G., & Laucht, M. (2008). Interaction of dopamine transporter genotype with prenatal smoke exposure on ADHD symptoms. *Journal of Pediatrics, 152,* 263–269.

Beckett, C., Maughan, B., Rutter, M., Castle, J., Colvert, E., & Groothues, C. (2006). Do the effects of early severe deprivation on cognition persist into early adolescence? Findings from the English and Romanian adoptees study. *Child Development, 77,* 696–711.

Bedford, O. A. (2004). The individual experience of guilt and shame in Chinese culture. *Culture and Psychology, 10,* 29–52.

Behnke, M., Eyler, F. D., Garvan, C. W., & Wobie, K. (2001). The search for congenital malformations in newborns with fetal cocaine exposure. *Pediatrics, 107,* e74.

Behnke, M., Eyler, F. D., Warner, T. D., Garvan, C. W., Hou, W., & Wobie, K. (2006). Outcome from a prospective, longitudinal study of prenatal cocaine use: Preschool development at 3 years of age. *Journal of Pediatric Psychology, 31,* 41–49.

Beilin, H. (1992). Piaget's enduring contribution to developmental psychology. *Developmental Psychology, 28,* 191–204.

Beitel, A. H., & Parke, R. D. (1998). Paternal involvement in infancy: The role of maternal and paternal attitudes. *Journal of Family Psychology, 12,* 268–288.

Bell, M. A. (1998). Frontal lobe function during infancy: Implications for the development of cognition and attention. In J. E. Richards (Ed.), *Cognitive neuroscience of attention: A developmental perspective* (pp. 327–362). Mahwah, NJ: Erlbaum.

Bell, M. A., & Fox, N. A. (1996). Crawling experience is related to changes in cortical organization during infancy: Evidence from EEG coherence. *Developmental Psychobiology, 29,* 551–561.

Bellagamba, F., Camaioni, L., & Colonnesi, C. (2006). Change in children's understanding of others' intentional actions. *Developmental Science, 9,* 182–188.

Bellamy, C. (2004). *The state of the world's children: 2004.* New York: UNICEF.

Bellinger, D. C. (2005). Teratogen update: Lead and pregnancy. *Birth Defects Research: Part A, Clinical and Molecular Teratology, 73,* 409–420.

Bellinger, D. C., Leviton, A., & Sloman, J. (1990). Antecedents and correlates of improved cognitive performance in children exposed in utero to low levels of lead. *Environmental Health Perspectives, 89,* 5–11.

Belsky, J. (2001). Emanuel Miller Lecture: Developmental risks (still) associated with early child care. *Journal of Child Psychology and Psychiatry, 42,* 845–859.

Belsky, J. (2005). Attachment theory and research in ecological perspective: Insights from the Pennsylvania Infant and Family Development Project and the NICHD Study of Early Child Care. In K. E. Grossmann, K. Grossmann, & E. Waters (Eds.), *Attachment from infancy to adulthood: The major longitudinal studies* (pp. 71–97). New York: Guilford.

Belsky, J. (2006). Early child care and early child development: Major findings of the NICHD Study of Early Child Care. *European Journal of Developmental Psychology, 3,* 95–110.

Belsky, J., Campbell, S. B., Cohn, J. F., & Moore, G. (1996). Instability of infant–parent attachment security. *Developmental Psychology, 32,* 921–924.

Belsky, J., & Fearon, R. M. P. (2002a). Early attachment security, subsequent maternal sensitivity, and later child development: Does continuity in development depend on caregiving? *Attachment and Human Development, 4,* 361–387.

Belsky, J., & Fearon, R. M. P. (2002b). Infant–mother attachment security, contextual risk, and early development: A moderated analysis. *Development and Pathology, 14,* 293–310.

Belsky, J., Vandell, D. L., Burchinal, M., Clarke-Stewart, K. A., McCartney, K., & Owen, M. T. (2007). Are there long-term effects of early child care? *Child Development, 78,* 681–701.

Bemmels, H. R., Burt, A., Legrand, L. N., Iacono, W. G., & McGue, M. (2008). The heritability of life events: An adolescent twin and adoption study. *Twin Research and Human Genetics, 11,* 257–265.

Benarroch, F., Hirsch, H. J., Genstil, L., Landau, Y. E., & Gross-Tsur, V. (2007). Prader-Willi syndrome: Medical prevention and behavioral challenges. *Child and Adolescent Psychiatric Clinics of North America, 16,* 695–708.

Bender, H. L., Allen, J. P., McElhaney, K. B., Antonishak, J., Moore, C. M., Kelly, H. L., & Davis, S. M. (2007). Use of harsh physical discipline and developmental outcomes in adolescence. *Development and Psychopathology, 19,* 227–242.

Bengtson, H. (2005). Children's cognitive appraisal of others' distressful and positive experiences. *International Journal of Behavioral Development, 29,* 457–466.

Bennett, K. E., Haggard, M. P., Silva, P. A., & Stewart, I. A. (2001). Behaviour and developmental effects of otitis media with effusion into the teens. *Archives of Disease in Childhood, 85,* 91–95.

Bennett, M., Barrett, M., Karakozov, R., Kipiani, G., Lyons, E., Pavlenko, V., & Riazanova, T. (2004). Young children's evaluations of the ingroup and outgroups: A multinational study. *Social Development, 13,* 124–141.

Benson, P. L., Scales, P. C., Hamilton, S. F., & Sesma, A., Jr. (2006). Positive youth development: Theory, research, and applications. In R. M. Lerner (Ed.), *Handbook of child psychology: Vol. 1. Theoretical models of human development* (6th ed., pp. 894–941). Hoboken, NJ: Wiley.

Bergen, D., & Mauer, D. (2000). Symbolic play, phonological awareness, and literacy skills at three age levels. In K. A. Roskos & J. F. Christie (Eds.), *Play and literacy in early childhood: Research from multiple perspectives* (pp. 45–62). Mahwah, NJ: Erlbaum.

Berger, A., Tzur, G., & Posner, M. I. (2006). Infant brains detect arithmetic errors. *Proceedings of the National Academy of Sciences, 103*, 12649–12653.

Berger, L. M., Paxson, C., & Waldfogel, J. (2009). Income and child development. *Children and Youth Services Review, 31*, 978–989.

Berger, S. E., Theuring, C., & Adolph, K. E. (2007). How and when infants learn to climb stairs. *Infant Behavior and Development, 30*, 36–49.

Berk, L. E. (2001a). *Awakening children's minds: How parents and teachers can make a difference.* New York: Oxford University Press.

Berk, L. E. (2001b). Private speech and self-regulation in children with impulse-control difficulties: Implications for research and practice. *Journal of Cognitive Education and Psychology, 2*(1), 1–21.

Berk, L. E. (2004). *Conversations with children.* Normal, IL: Illinois State University.

Berk, L. E. (2005). Why parenting matters. In S. Olfman (Ed.), *Childhood lost: How American culture is failing our kids* (pp. 19–53). New York: Guilford.

Berk, L. E. (2006). Looking at kindergarten children. In D. Gullo (Ed.), *K today: Teaching and learning in the kindergarten year* (pp. 11–25). Washington, DC: National Association for the Education of Young Children.

Berk, L. E., & Harris, S. (2003). Vygotsky, Lev. In L. Nadel (Ed.), *Encyclopedia of cognitive science.* London: Macmillan.

Berk, L. E., Mann, T., & Ogan, A. (2006). Make-believe play: Wellspring for development of self-regulation. In D. Singer, K. Hirsh-Pasek, & R. Golinkoff (Eds.), *Play=learning* (pp. 74–100). New York: Oxford University Press.

Berk, L. E., & Spuhl, S. T. (1995). Maternal interaction, private speech, and task performance in preschool children. *Early Childhood Research Quarterly, 10*, 145–169.

Berkowitz, R. L., Roberts, J., & Minkoff, H. (2006). Challenging the strategy of maternal age-based prenatal genetic counseling. *Journal of the American Medical Association, 295*, 1446–1448.

Berlin, L. J., Ipsa, J. M., Fine, M. A., Malone, P. S., Brooks-Gunn, J., Brady-Smith, C., et al. (2009). Correlates and consequences of spanking and verbal punishment for low-income white, African-American, and Mexican-American toddlers. *Child Development, 80*, 1403–1420.

Berman, P. W. (1980). Are women more responsive than men to the young? A review of developmental and situational variables. *Psychological Bulletin, 88*, 668–695.

Berman, R. A. (2007). Developing linguistic knowledge and language use across adolescence. In K. Hirsh-Pasek & R. M. Golinkoff (Eds.), *Action meets word: How children learn verbs* (pp. 347–367). New York: Oxford University Press.

Berndt, T. J. (2004). Children's friendships: Shifts over a half-century in perspectives on their development and effects. *Merrill-Palmer Quarterly, 50*, 206–223.

Bernier, J. C., & Siegel, D. H. (1994). Attention-deficit hyperactivity disorder: A family ecological systems perspective. *Families in Society, 75*, 142–150.

Berninger, V. W. (2006). A developmental approach to learning disabilities. In K. A. Renninger & I. E. Sigel (Eds.), *Handbook of child psychology: Vol. 4. Child psychology in practice* (6th ed., pp. 420–452). Hoboken, NJ: Wiley.

Bertenthal, B. I., & Longo, M. R. (2007). Is there evidence of a mirror neuron system from birth? *Developmental Science, 10*, 513–523.

Bertenthal, B. I., Longo, M. R., & Kenny, S. (2007). Phenomenal permanence and the development of predictive tracking in infancy. *Child Development, 78*, 350–363.

Best, D. L. (2001). Gender concepts: Convergence in cross-cultural research and methodologies. *Cross-cultural Research: The Journal of Comparative Social Science, 35*, 23–43.

Betrán, A. P., Merialdi, M., Lauer, J. A., Bing-Shun, W., Thomas, J., et al. (2007). Rates of caesarean section: Analysis of global, regional, and national estimates. *Paediatric and Perinatal Epidemiology, 21*, 98–113.

Beyers, J. M., Bates, J. E., Pettit, G. S., & Dodge, K. A. (2003). Neighborhood structure, parenting processes, and the development of youths' externalizing behaviors: A multilevel analysis. *American Journal of Community Psychology, 31*, 35–53.

Bhagavath, B., & Layman, L. C. (2007). The genetics of hypogonadotropic hypogonadism. *Seminars in Reproductive Medicine, 25*, 272–286.

Bhana, D. (2008). Beyond stigma? Young children's responses to HIV and AIDS. *Culture, Health and Sexuality, 10*, 725–738.

Bhat, A., Heathcock, J., & Galloway, J. C. (2005). Toy-oriented changes in hand and joint kinematics during the emergence of purposeful reaching. *Infant Behavior and Development, 28*, 445–465.

Bhatt, R. S., Rovee-Collier, C., & Weiner, S. (1994). Developmental changes in the interface between perception and memory retrieval. *Developmental Psychology, 30*, 151–162.

Bhatt, R. S., Wilk, A., Hill, D., & Rovee-Collier, C. (2004). Correlated attributes and categorization in the first half-year of life. *Developmental Psychobiology, 44*, 103–115.

Bialystok, E. (2001). *Bilingualism in development: Language, literacy, and cognition.* New York: Cambridge University Press.

Bialystok, E., & Martin, M. M. (2003). Notation to symbol: Development in children's understanding of print. *Journal of Experimental Child Psychology, 86*, 223–243.

Bialystok, E., & Martin, M. M. (2004). Attention and inhibition in bilingual children: Evidence from the dimensional change card sort task. *Developmental Science, 7*, 325–339.

Bialystok, E., McBride-Chang, C., & Luk, G. (2005). Bilingualism, language proficiency, and learning to read in two writing systems. *Journal of Educational Psychology, 97*, 580–590.

Bialystok, E., & Senman, L. (2004). Executive processes in appearance–reality tasks: The role of inhibition of attention and symbolic representation. *Child Development, 75*, 562–579.

Bianco, A., Stone, J., Lynch, L., Lapinski, R., Berkowitz, G., & Berkowitz, R. L. (1996). Pregnancy outcome at age 40 and older. *Obstetrics and Gynecology, 87*, 917–922.

Bibace, R., & Walsh, M. E. (1980). Development of children's concepts of illness. *Pediatrics, 66*, 912–917.

Biederman, J., Kwon, A., Aleardi, M., Chouinard, V.-A., Marino, T., & Cole, H. (2005). Absence of gender effects on attention-deficit hyperactivity disorder: Findings in nonreferred subjects. *American Journal of Psychiatry, 162*, 1083–1089.

Bielawska-Batorowicz, E., & Kossakowska-Petrycka, K. (2006). Depressive mood in men after the birth of their offspring in relation to a partner's depression, social support, fathers' personality and prenatal expectations. *Journal of Reproductive and Infant Psychology, 24*, 21–29.

Bierman, K. L., Domitrovich, C. E., Nix, R. L., Gest, S. D., Welsh, J. A., Greenberg, M. T., et al. (2008). Promoting academic and social-emotional school readiness: The Head Start REDI program. *Child Development, 79*, 1802–1817.

Bierman, K. L., & Powers, C. J. (2009). Social skills training to improve peer relations. In K. H. Rubin, W. M. Bukowski, & B. Laursen (Eds.), *Handbook of peer interactions, relationships, and groups* (pp. 603–621). New York: Guilford.

Bifulco, R., Cobb, C. D., & Bell, C. (2009). Can interdistrict choice boost student achievement? The case of Connecticut's interdistrict magnet school program. *Educational Evaluation and Policy Analysis, 31*, 323–345.

Bigelow, A. E. (1992). Locomotion and search behavior in blind infants. *Infant Behavior and Development, 15*, 179–189.

Bigelow, A. E. (2003). The development of joint attention in blind infants. *Development and Psychopathology, 15*, 259–275.

Bigelow, A. E., MacLean, K., Proctor, J., Myatt, T., Gillis, R., & Power, M. (2010). Maternal sensitivity throughout infancy: Continuity and relation to attachment security. *Infant Behavior and Development, 33*, 50–60.

Bigler, R. S. (2007, June). Personal communication.

Bigler, R. S., Brown, C. S., & Markell, M. (2001). When groups are not created equal: Effects of group status on the formation of intergroup attitudes in children. *Child Development, 72*, 1151–1162.

Bimmel, N., Juffer, F., van IJzendoorn, M. H., & Bakermans-Kranenburg, M. J. (2003). Problem behavior of internationally adopted adolescents: A review and meta-analysis. *Harvard Review of Psychiatry, 11*, 64–77.

Bioethics Consultative Committee. (2003). *Comparison of ethics legislation in Europe.* Retrieved from www.synapse.net.mt/bioethics/euroleg1.htm

Birch, E. E. (1993). Stereopsis in infants and its developmental relation to visual acuity. In K. Simons (Ed.), *Early visual development: Normal and abnormal* (pp. 224–236). New York: Oxford University Press.

Birch, L. L. (1999). Development of food preferences. *Annual Review of Nutrition, 19*, 41–62.

Birch, L. L., & Fisher, J. A. (1995). Appetite and eating behavior in children. *Pediatric Clinics of North America, 42*, 931–953.

Birch, L. L., Fisher, J. O., & Davison, K. K. (2003). Learning to overeat: Maternal use of restrictive feeding practices promotes girls' eating in the absence of hunger. *American Journal of Clinical Nutrition, 78*, 215–220.

Birch, L. L., Zimmerman, S., & Hind, H. (1980). The influence of social-affective context on preschool children's food preferences. *Child Development, 51*, 856–861.

Birch, S. A. J., & Bloom, P. (2003). Children are cursed: An asymmetric bias in mental-state attribution. *Psychological Science, 14*, 283–285.

Birch, S. H., & Ladd, G. W. (1998). Children's interpersonal behaviors and the teacher–child relationship. *Developmental Psychology, 34*, 934–946.

Bird, A., & Reese, E. (2006). Emotional reminiscing and the development of an autobiographical self. *Developmental Psychology, 42*, 613–626.

Biringen, Z., Emde, R. N., Campos, J. J., & Appelbaum, M. I. (1995). Affective reorganization in the infant, the mother, and the dyad: The role of upright locomotion and its timing. *Child Development, 66*, 499–514.

Birken, C. S., Parkin, P. C., To, T., & Macarthur, C. (2006). Trends in rates of death from unintentional injury among Canadian children in urban areas: Influence of socioeconomic status. *Canadian Medical Association Journal, 175*, 867–868.

Birney, D. P., Citron-Pousty, J. H., Lutz, D. J., & Sternberg, R. J. (2005). The development of cognitive and intellectual abilities. In M. H. Bornstein & M. E. Lamb (Eds.), *Developmental science: An advanced textbook* (5th ed., pp. 327–358). Mahwah, NJ: Erlbaum.

Bjorklund, D. F. (2004). *Children's thinking* (4th ed.). Belmont, CA: Wadsworth.

Bjorklund, D. F., & Douglas, R. N. (1997). The development of memory strategies. In N. Cowan (Ed.), *The development of memory in childhood* (pp. 83–111). Hove, U.K.: Psychology Press.

Bjorklund, D. F., Schneider, W., Cassel, W. S., & Ashley, E. (1994). Training and extension of a memory strategy: Evidence for utilization deficiencies in high- and low-IQ children. *Child Development, 65*, 951–965.

Black, B., & Logan, A. (1995). Links between communication patterns in mother–child, father–child, and child–peer interactions and children's social status. *Child Development, 66*, 255–271.

Black, M. M. (2005). Failure to thrive. In M. C. Roberts (Ed.), *Handbook of pediatric psychology and psychiatry* (3rd ed., pp. 499–511). New York: Guilford.

Black, M. M., Dubowitz, H., Krishnakumar, A., & Starr, R. H., Jr. (2007). Early intervention and recovery among children with failure to thrive: Follow-up at age 8. *Pediatrics, 120,* 59–69.

Black, R. E., Williams, S. M., Jones, I. E., & Goulding, A. (2002). Children who avoid drinking cow milk have low dietary calcium intakes and poor bone health. *American Journal of Clinical Nutrition, 76,* 675–680.

Blackwell, L. S., Trzesniewski, K. H., & Dweck, C. S. (2007). Implicit theories of intelligence predict achievement across an adolescent transition: A longitudinal study and an intervention. *Child Development, 78,* 246–263.

Blaga, O. M., & Colombo, J. (2006). Visual processing and infant ocular latencies in the overlap paradigm. *Developmental Psychology, 42,* 1069–1076.

Blair, C., & Razza, R. P. (2007). Relating effortful control, executive function, and false belief understanding to emerging math and literacy ability in kindergarten. *Developmental Psychology, 78,* 647–663.

Blakemore, J. E. O. (2003). Children's beliefs about violating gender norms: Boys shouldn't look like girls, and girls shouldn't act like boys. *Sex Roles, 48,* 411–419.

Blasi, C. H., & Bjorklund, D. F. (2003). Evolutionary developmental psychology: A new tool for better understanding human ontogeny. *Human Development, 46,* 259–281.

Blass, E. M., Ganchrow, J. R., & Steiner, J. E. (1984). Classical conditioning in newborn humans 2–48 hours of age. *Infant Behavior and Development, 7,* 223–235.

Blatchford, P., Bassett, P., & Brown, P. (2005). Teachers' and pupils' behavior in large and small classes: A systematic observation study of pupils aged 10 and 11 years. *Journal of Educational Psychology, 97,* 454–467.

Blatchford, P., Bassett, P., Goldstein, H., & Martin, C. (2003). Are class size differences related to pupils' educational progress and classroom processes? Findings from the Institute of Education Class Size Study of children aged 5–7 years. *British Educational Research Journal, 29,* 709–730.

Blatchford, P., Russell, A., Bassett, P., Brown, P., & Martin, C. (2007). The effect of class size on the teaching of pupils aged 7–11 years. *School Effectiveness and School Improvement, 18,* 147–172.

Bleeker, M. M., & Jacobs, J. E. (2004). Achievement in math and science: Do mothers' beliefs matter 12 years later? *Journal of Educational Psychology, 96,* 97–109.

Bloom, L. (1998). Language acquisition in its developmental context. In D. Kuhn & R. S. Siegler (Eds.), *Handbook of child psychology: Vol. 2. Cognition, perception, and language* (5th ed., pp. 309–370). New York: Wiley.

Bloom, L. (2000). The intentionality model of language development: How to learn a word, any word. In R. Golinkoff, K. Hirsh-Pasek, N. Akhtar, L. Bloom, G. Hollich, L. Smith, M. Tomasello, & A. Woodward (Eds.), *Becoming a word learner: A debate on lexical acquisition.* New York: Oxford University Press.

Bloom, P. (1999). The role of semantics in solving the bootstrapping problem. In R. Jackendoff & P. Bloom (Eds.), *Language, logic, and concepts* (pp. 285–309). Cambridge, MA: MIT Press.

Blumberg, M. S., & Lucas, D. E. (1996). A developmental and component analysis of active sleep. *Developmental Psychobiology, 29,* 1–22.

Blumenfeld, P. C., Marx, R. W., & Harris, C. J. (2006). Learning environments. In K. A. Renninger & I. E. Sigel (Eds.), *Handbook of child psychology: Vol. 4. Child psychology in practice* (6th ed., pp. 297–342). Hoboken, NJ: Wiley.

Boardman, J. D. (2004). Stress and physical health: The role of neighborhoods as mediating and moderating mechanisms. *Social Science and Medicine, 58,* 2473–2483.

Bodrova, E., & Leong, D. J. (2007). *Tools of the mind: The Vygotskian approach to early childhood education* (2nd ed.). Upper Saddle River, NJ: Merrill Prentice Hall.

Bogartz, R. S., Shinskey, J. L., & Schilling, T. H. (2000). Object permanence in five-and-a-half-month-old infants. *Infancy, 1,* 403–428.

Bogin, B. (2001). *The growth of humanity.* New York: Wiley-Liss.

Bogin, B., Smith, P., Orden, A. B., Varela, S., & Loucky, J. (2002). Rapid change in height and body proportions of Maya American children. *American Journal of Human Biology, 14,* 753–761.

Bohannon, J. N., III, & Bonvillian, J. D. (2009). Theoretical approaches to language acquisition. In J. B. Gleason & B. Ratner (Ed.), *The development of language* (7th ed., pp. 227–284). Boston: Allyn and Bacon.

Bohannon, J. N., III, & Stanowicz, L. (1988). The issue of negative evidence: Adult responses to children's language errors. *Developmental Psychology, 24,* 684–689.

Boldizar, J. P. (1991). Assessing sex typing and androgyny in children: The children's sex role inventory. *Developmental Psychology, 27,* 505–515.

Bolen, R. M. (2001). *Child sexual abuse.* New York: Kluwer Academic.

Bolisetty, S., Bajuk, B., Me, A.-L., Vincent, T., Sutton, L., & Lui, K. (2006). Preterm outcome table (POT): A simple tool to aid counselling parents of very preterm infants. *Australian and New Zealand Journal of Obstetrics and Gynaecology, 46,* 189–192.

Bolzani, L. H., Messinger, D. S., Yale, M., & Dondi, M. (2002). Smiling in infancy. In M. H. Abel (Ed.), *An empirical reflection on the smile* (pp. 111–136). Lewiston, NY: Edwin Mellen Press.

Bonilla, S., Kehl, S., Kwong, K. Y., Morphew, T., Kachru, R., & Jones, C. A. (2005). School absenteeism in children with asthma in a Los Angeles inner-city school. *Journal of Pediatrics, 147,* 802–806.

Bono, M. A., & Stifter, C. A. (2003). Maternal attention-directing strategies and infant focused attention during problem solving. *Infancy, 4,* 235–250.

Borke, H. (1975). Piaget's mountains revisited: Changes in the egocentric landscape. *Developmental Psychology, 11,* 240–243.

Bornstein, M. H. (1989). Sensitive periods in development: Structural characteristics and causal interpretations. *Psychological Bulletin, 105,* 179–197.

Bornstein, M. H. (2002). Parenting infants. In M. H. Bornstein (Ed.), *Handbook of parenting: Vol. 1* (2nd ed., pp. 3–44). Mahwah, NJ: Erlbaum.

Bornstein, M. H. (2006). Parenting science and practice. In K. Renninger & I. E. Sigel (Eds.), *Handbook of child psychology: Vol. 4. Child psychology in practice* (6th ed., pp. 893–949). Hoboken, NJ: Wiley.

Bornstein, M. H., & Arterberry, M. E. (1999). Perceptual development. In M. H. Bornstein & M. E. Lamb (Eds.), *Developmental psychology: An advanced textbook* (pp. 231–274). Mahwah, NJ: Erlbaum.

Bornstein, M. H., & Arterberry, M. E. (2003). Recognition, discrimination, and categorization of smiling by 5-month-old infants. *Developmental Science, 6,* 585–599.

Bornstein, M. H., Arterberry, M. E., & Mash, C. (2010). Infant object categorization transcends object–context relations. *Infant Behavior and Development, 33,* 7–15.

Bornstein, M. H., Haynes, O. M., Pascual, L., Painter, K. M., & Galperin, C. (1999a). Play in two societies: Pervasiveness of process, specificity of structure. *Child Development, 70,* 317–331.

Bornstein, M. H., Selmi, A. M., Haynes, O. M., Painter, K. M., & Marx, E. S. (1999b). Representational abilities and the hearing status of child/mother dyads. *Child Development, 70,* 833–852.

Bornstein, M. H., Vibbert, M., Tal, J., & O'Donnell, K. (1992). Toddler language and play in the second year: Stability, covariation, and influences of parenting. *First Language, 12,* 323–338.

Boroughs, D. S. (2004). Female sexual abusers of children. *Children and Youth Services Review, 26,* 481–487.

Borst, C. G. (1995). *Catching babies: The professionalization of childbirth, 1870–1920.* Cambridge, MA: Harvard University Press.

Bos, H. M. W., van Balen, F., & van den Boom, D. C. (2004). Experience of parenthood, couple relationship, social support, and child-rearing goals in planned lesbian mother families. *Journal of Child Psychology and Psychiatry, 25,* 755–764.

Bos, H. M. W., van Balen, F., & van den Boom, D. C. (2007). Child adjustment and parenting in planned lesbian-parent families. *American Journal of Orthopsychiatry, 77,* 38–48.

Bosacki, S. L., & Moore, C. (2004). Preschoolers' understanding of simple and complex emotions: Links with gender and language. *Sex Roles, 50,* 659–675.

Bost, K. K., Shin, N., McBride, B. A., Brown, G. L., Vaughn, B. E., & Coppola, G. (2006). Maternal secure base scripts, children's attachment security, and mother–child narrative styles. *Attachment and Human Development, 8,* 241–260.

Botton, J., Heude, B., Maccario, J., Ducimetiére, P., & Charles, M. A. (2008). Postnatal weight and height growth velocities at different ages between birth and 5y and body composition in adolescent boys and girls. *American Journal of Clinical Nutrition, 87,* 1760–1768

Bouchard, T. J. (2004) Genetic influence on human psychological traits: A survey. *Current Directions in Psychological Science, 13,* 148–151.

Bouchard, T. J., & Loehlin, J. C. (2001). Genes, evolution, and personality. *Behavior Genetics, 31,* 243–274.

Boucher, O., Muckle, G., & Bastien, C. H. (2009). Prenatal exposure to polychlorinated biphenyls: A neuropsychologic analysis. *Environmental Health Perspectives, 117,* 7–16.

Boukydis, C. F. Z., & Lester, B. M. (1998). Infant crying, risk status and social support in families of preterm and term infants. *Early Development and Parenting, 7,* 31–39.

Bouldin, P. (2006). An investigation of the fantasy predisposition and fantasy style of children with imaginary companions. *Journal of Genetic Psychology, 167,* 17–29.

Boulton, M. J. (1996). A comparison of 8- and 11-year-old girls' and boys' participation in specific types of rough-and-tumble play and aggressive fighting: Implications for functional hypotheses. *Aggressive Behavior, 22,* 271–287.

Boulton, M. J. (1999). Concurrent and longitudinal relations between children's playground behavior and social preference, victimization, and bullying. *Child Development, 70,* 944–954.

Bower-Russa, M. E., Knutson, J. F., & Winebarger, A. (2001). Disciplinary history, adult disciplinary attitudes, and risk for abusive parenting. *Journal of Community Psychology, 29,* 219–240.

Bowlby, J. (1980). *Attachment and loss: Vol. 3. Loss.* New York: Basic Books.

Boyatzis, C. J. (2000). The artistic evolution of mommy: A longitudinal case study of symbolic and social processes. In C. J. Boyatzis & M. W. Watson (Eds.), *Symbolic and social constraints on the development of children's artistic style* (pp. 5–29). San Francisco: Jossey-Bass.

Boyd-Franklin, N. (2006). *Black families in therapy* (2nd ed.). New York: Guilford.

Boyer, K., & Diamond, A. (1992). Development of memory for temporal order in infants and young children. In A. Diamond (Ed.), *Development and neural bases of higher cognitive function* (pp. 267–317). New York: New York Academy of Sciences.

Boyle, M. H., & Lipman, E. L. (2002). Do places matter? Socioeconomic disadvantage and behavioral problems of children in Canada. *Journal of Consulting and Clinical Psychology, 70,* 378–389.

Boysson-Bardies, B. de, & Vihman, M. M. (1991). Adaptation to language: Evidence from babbling and first words in four languages. *Language, 67,* 297–319.

Bracci, R., Perrone, S., & Buonocore, G. (2006). The timing of neonatal brain damage. *Biology of the Neonate, 90,* 145–155.

Brackbill, Y., McManus, K., & Woodward, L. (1985). Medication in maternity: Infant exposure and maternal *information.* Ann Arbor: University of Michigan Press.

Bracken, B. A. (2000). *The psychoeducational assessment of preschool children.* Boston: Allyn and Bacon.

Brackett, M. A., Mayer, J. D., & Warner, R. M. (2004). Emotional intelligence and its relation to everyday behaviour. *Personality and Individual Differences, 36,* 1387–1402.

Bradford, K., Barber, B. K., Olsen, J. A., Maughan, S. L., Erickson, L. D., Ward, D., & Stolz, H. E. (2003). A multinational study of interparental conflict, parenting, and adolescent functioning: South Africa, Bangladesh, China, India, Bosnia, Germany, Palestine, Colombia, and the United States. *Marriage and Family Review, 35,* 107–137.

Bradley, P. J., & Bray, K. H. (1996). The Netherlands' Maternal-Child Health Program: Implications for the United States. *Journal of Obstetric, Gynecologic, and Neonatal Nursing, 25,* 471–475.

Bradley, R. H. (1994). The HOME Inventory: Review and reflections. In H. W. Reese (Ed.), *Advances in child development and behavior* (Vol. 25, pp. 241–288). San Diego: Academic Press.

Bradley, R. H., & Caldwell, B. M. (1982). The consistency of the home environment and its relation to child development. *International Journal of Behavioral Development, 5,* 445–465.

Bradley, R. H., & Corwyn, R. F. (2003). Age and ethnic variations in family process mediators of SES. In M. H. Bornstein & R. H. Bradley (Eds.), *Socioeconomic status, parenting, and child development* (pp. 161–188). Mahwah, NJ: Erlbaum.

Bradley, R. H., Corwyn, R. F., McAdoo, H. P., & García-Coll, C. (2001). The home environments of children in the United States. Part I: Variations by age, ethnicity, and poverty status. *Child Development, 72,* 1844–1867.

Bradley, R. H., Whiteside, L., Mundfrom, D. J., Casey, P. H., Kelleher, K. J., & Pope, S. K.(1994). Contribution of early intervention and early caregiving experiences to resilience in low-birthweight, premature children living in poverty. *Journal of Clinical Child Psychology, 23,* 425–434.

Braine, L. G., Schauble, L., Kugelmass, S., & Winter, A. (1993). Representation of depth by children: Spatial strategies and lateral biases. *Developmental Psychology, 29,* 466–479.

Braine, M. D. S. (1994). Is nativism sufficient? *Journal of Child Language, 21,* 1–23.

Brainerd, C. J. (2003). Jean Piaget, learning, research, and American education. In B. J. Zimmerman (Ed.), *Educational psychology: A century of contributions* (pp. 251–287). Mahwah, NJ: Erlbaum.

Branca, F., & Ferrari, M. (2002). Impact of micronutrient deficiencies on growth: The stunting syndrome. *Annals of Nutrition and Metabolism, 46*(Suppl. 1), 8–17.

Brand, S. R., Engel, S. M., Canfield, R. L., & Yehuda, R. (2006). The effect of maternal PTSD following in utero trauma exposure on behavior and temperament in the 9-month-old infant. *Annals of the New York Academy of Sciences, 1071,* 454–458.

Branje, S. J. T., van Lieshout, C. F. M., van Aken, M. A. G., & Haselager, G. J. T. (2004). Perceived support in sibling relationships and adolescent adjustment. *Journal of Child Psychology and Psychiatry, 45,* 1385–1396.

Braswell, G. S. (2006). Sociocultural contexts for the early development of semiotic production. *Psychological Bulletin, 132,* 877–894.

Braswell, G. S., & Callanan, M. A. (2003). Learning to draw recognizable graphic representations during mother–child interactions. *Merrill-Palmer Quarterly, 49,* 471–494.

Bratt, R. G. (2002). Housing: The foundation of family life. In F. Jacobs, D. Wertlieb, & R. M. Lerner (Eds.), *Handbook of applied developmental science* (Vol. 2, pp. 445–468). Thousand Oaks, CA: Sage.

Braver, S. L., Griffin, W. A., Cookston, J. T., Sandler, I. N., & Williams, J. (2005). Promoting better fathering among divorced non-resident fathers. In W. M. Pinsof & J. Lebow (Eds.), *Family psychology: The art of the science* (pp. 295–325). New York: Oxford University Press.

Bray, G. A., Nielsen, J., & Popkin, B. M. (2004). Consumption of high-fructose corn syrup in beverages may play a role in the epidemic of obesity. *American Journal of Clinical Nutrition, 79,* 537–543.

Bray, J. H. (1999). From marriage to remarriage and beyond: Findings from the Developmental Issues in Stepfamilies Research Project. In E. M. Hetherington (Ed.), *Coping with divorce, single parenting, and remarriage: A risk and resiliency perspective* (pp. 295–319). Mahwah, NJ: Erlbaum.

Brazelton, T. B., Koslowski, B., & Tronick, E. (1976). Neonatal behavior among urban Zambians and Americans. *Journal of the American Academy of Child Psychiatry, 15,* 97–107.

Brazelton, T. B., & Nugent, J. K. (1995). *Neonatal Behavioral Assessment Scale.* London: Mac Keith Press.

Brazelton, T. B., Nugent, J. K., & Lester, B. M. (1987). Neonatal Behavioral Assessment Scale. In J. D. Osofsky (Ed.), *Handbook of infant development* (2nd ed., pp. 780–817). New York: Wiley.

Brazelton, T. B., & Sparrow, J. D. (2004). Toilet learning: The child's role. In T. B. Brazelton (Ed.), *Toilet training the Brazelton way.* Cambridge, MA: Da Capo Press.

Bremner, A. J., & Mareschal, D. (2004). Reasoning . . . what reasoning? *Developmental Science, 7,* 419–421.

Brennan, W. M., Ames, E. W., & Moore, R. W. (1966). Age differences in infants' attention to patterns of different complexities. *Science, 151,* 354–356.

Brenner, E., & Salovey, P. (1997). Emotional regulation during childhood: Developmental, interpersonal, and individual considerations. In P. Salovey & D. Sluyter (Eds.), *Emotional literacy and emotional development* (pp. 168–192). New York: Basic Books.

Brenner, R. A., & Committee on Injury, Violence, and Poison Prevention. (2003). Prevention of drowning in infants, children, and adolescents. *Pediatrics, 112,* 440–445.

Bretherton, I., Fritz, J., Zahn-Waxler, C., & Ridgeway, D. (1986). Learning to talk about emotions: A functionalist perspective. *Child Development, 57,* 529–548.

Bretherton, I., & Munholland, K. A. (1999). Internal working models in attachment relationships: A construct revisited. In J. Cassidy & P. R. Shaver (Eds.), *Handbook of attachment* (pp. 89–111). New York: Guilford.

Brewaeys, A., Ponjaert, I., Van Hall, E. V., & Golombok, S. (1997). Donor insemination: Child development and family functioning in lesbian mother families. *Human Reproduction, 12,* 1349–1359.

Bridgett, D. J., Gartstein, M. A., Putnam, S. P., McKay, T., Iddins, R., Robertson, C., et al. (2009). Maternal and contextual influences and the effect of temperament development during infancy on parenting in toddlerhood. *Infant Behavior and Development, 32,* 103–116.

Briefel, R. R., Reidy, K., Karwe, V., & Devaney, B. (2004). Feeding Infants and Toddlers study: Improvements needed in meeting infant feeding recommendations. *Journal of the American Dietetic Association, 104*(Suppl. 1), s31–s37.

Briggs, F. (2000). *Children's views of the world.* Magill, Australia: University of South Australia.

Bright, G. M., Mendoza, J. R., & Rosenfeld, R. G. (2009). Recombinant human insulin-like growth factor-1 treatment: Ready for primetime. *Endocrinology and Metabolism Clinics of North America, 38,* 625–638.

Broberg, A. G., Wessels, H., Lamb, M. E., & Hwang, C. P. (1997). Effects of day care on the development of cognitive abilities in 8-year-olds : A longitudinal study. *Developmental Psychology, 33,* 62–69.

Brody, G. H., & Flor, D. L. (1998). Maternal resources, parenting practices, and child competence in rural, single-parent African American families. *Child Development, 69,* 803–816.

Brody, G. H., Ge, X., Kim, S. Y., Murry, V. M., Simons, R. L., & Gibbons, F. X. (2003). Neighborhood disadvantage moderates associations of parenting and older sibling problem attitudes and behavior with conduct disorders in African American children. *Journal of Consulting and Clinical Psychology, 71,* 211–222.

Brody, G. H., & Murry, V. M. (2001). Sibling socialization of competence in rural, single-parent African American families. *Journal of Marriage and the Family, 63,* 996–1008.

Brody, G. H., Stoneman, Z., & McCoy, J. K. (1994). Forecasting sibling relationships in early adolescence from child temperament and family processes in middle childhood. *Child Development, 65,* 771–784.

Brody, L. (1999). *Gender, emotion, and the family.* Cambridge, MA: Harvard University Press.

Brody, N. (1997). Intelligence, schooling, and society. *American Psychologist, 52,* 1046–1050.

Bronfenbrenner, U. (Ed.). (2005). *Making human beings human.* Thousand Oaks, CA: Sage.

Bronfenbrenner, U., & Morris, P. A. (2006). The bioecological model of human development. In R. M. Lerner (Ed.), *Handbook of child psychology: Vol. 1. Theoretical models of human development* (6th ed., pp. 793–828). Hoboken, NJ: Wiley.

Bronson, G. W. (1994). Infant's transitions toward adult-like scanning. *Child Development, 65,* 1243–1261.

Bronstein, P. (2006). The family environment: Where gender role socialization begins. In J. Worell & C. D. Goodheart (Eds.), *Handbook of girls' and women's psychological health: Gender and well-being across the life span* (pp. 262–271). New York: Oxford University Press.

Brooks, K., Xu, X., Chen, W., Zhou, K., Neale, B., & Lowe, N. (2006). The analysis of 51 genes in DSM-IV combined type attention deficit hyperactivity disorder: Association signals in DRD4, DAT1, and 16 other genes. *Molecular Psychiatry, 11,* 935–953.

Brooks, P. J., Hanauere, J. B., Padowska, B., & Rosman, H. (2003). The role of selective attention in preschoolers' rule use in a novel dimensional card sort. *Cognitive Development, 18,* 195–215.

Brooks, R., & Meltzoff, A. N. (2002). The importance of eyes: How infants interpret looking behavior. *Developmental Psychology, 38,* 958–966.

Brooks, R., & Meltzoff, A. N. (2005). The development of gaze following and its relation to language. *Developmental Science, 8,* 535–543.

Brooks, R., & Meltzoff, A. N. (2008). Infant gaze following and pointing predict accelerated vocabulary growth through two years of age: A longitudinal, growth curve modeling study. *Journal of Child Language, 35,* 207–220.

Brooks-Gunn, J. (2003). Do you believe in magic? What we can expect from early childhood intervention programs. *Social Policy Report of the Society for Research in Child Development, 27*(1).

Brooks-Gunn, J. (2004). Intervention and policy as change agents for young children. In P. L. Chase-Lansdale, K. Kiernan, & R. J. Friedman (Eds.), *Human development across lives and generations: The potential for change* (pp. 293–340). New York: Cambridge University Press.

Brooks-Gunn, J., Han, W.-J., & Waldfogel, J. (2002). Maternal employment and child cognitive outcomes in the first three years of life: The NICHD study of early child care. *Child Development, 73,* 1052–1072.

Brooks-Gunn, J., Klebanov, P. K., Smith, J., Duncan, G. J., & Lee, K. (2003). The black-white test score gap in young children. Contributions of test and family characteristics. *Applied Developmental Science, 7,* 239–252.

Brown, A. L. (1997). Transforming schools into communities of thinking and learning about serious matters. *American Psychologist, 52,* 399–413.

Brown, A. M., & Miracle, J. A. (2003). Early binocular vision in human infants: Limitations on the generality of the Superposition Hypothesis. *Vision Research, 43,* 1563–1574.

Brown, A. S. (2006). Prenatal infection as a risk factor for schizophrenia. *Schizophrenia Bulletin, 32,* 200–202.

Brown, C. S., & Bigler, R. S. (2004). Children's perceptions of gender discrimination. *Developmental Psychology, 40,* 714–726.

Brown, G. L., Mangelsdorf, S. C., Agathen, J. M., & Ho, M.-H. (2008). Young children's psychological selves: Convergence with maternal reports of child personality. *Social Development, 17,* 161–182.

Brown, G. L., Schoppe-Sullivan, S. J., Mangelsdorf, S. C., & Neff, C. (2010). Observed and reported supportive coparenting as predictors of infant–mother and infant–father attachment security. *Early Child Development and Care, 180,* 121–137.

Brown, J. L., Roderick, T., Lantieri, L., & Aber, J. L. (2004). The Resolving Conflict Creatively Program: A school-based social and emotional learning program. In J. E. Zins, R. P. Weissberg, M. C. Wang, & H. J. Walberg (Eds.), *Building academic success on social and emotional learning: What does the research say?* (pp. 151–169). New York: Teachers College Press.

Brown, J. R., Donelan-McCall, N., & Dunn, J. (1996). Why talk about mental states? The significance of children's conversations with friends, siblings, and mothers. *Child Development, 67,* 836–849.

Brown, J. R., & Dunn, J. (1996). Continuities in emotion understanding from 3 to 6 years. *Child Development, 67,* 789–802.

Brown, R. W. (1973). *A first language: The early stages.* Cambridge, MA: Harvard University Press.

Brown, T. E. (2005). *Attention deficit disorder: The unfocused mind in children and adults.* New Haven, CT: Yale University Press.

Brown, T. E. (2006). Executive functions and attention deficit hyperactivity disorder: Implications of two conflicting views. *International Journal of Disability, Development and Education, 53,* 35–46.

Browne, C. A., & Woolley, J. D. (2004). Preschoolers' magical explanations for violations of physical, social, and mental laws. *Journal of Cognition and Development, 5,* 239–260.

Browne, J. V., & Talmi, A. (2005). Family-based intervention to enhance infant–parent relationships in the neonatal intensive care unit. *Journal of Pediatric Psychology, 30,* 667–677.

Brownell, C. A., & Kopp, C. B. (2007). Transitions in toddler socioemotional development: Behavior, understanding, relationships. In C. A. Brownell & C. B. Kopp (Eds.), *Socioemotional development in the toddler years: Transitions and transformations* (pp. 1–40). New York: Guilford.

Brownell, C. A., Zerwas, S., & Ramani, G. B. (2007). "So big": The development of body self-awareness in toddlers. *Child Development, 78,* 1426–1440.

Bruce, D., Dolan, A., & Phillips-Grant, K. (2000). On the transition from childhood amnesia to recall of personal memories. *Psychological Science, 11,* 360–364.

Bruck, M., & Ceci, S. J. (2004). Forensic developmental psychology: Unveiling four common misconceptions. *Current Directions in Psychological Science, 13,* 229–232.

Bruer, J. T. (1999). *The myth of the first three years.* New York: Free Press.

Bruschweiler-Stern, N. (2004). A multifocal neonatal intervention. In A. J. Sameroff, S. C. McDonough, & K. L. Rosenblum (Eds.), *Treating parent–infant relationship problems* (pp. 188–212). New York: Guilford.

Bruzzese, J., & Fisher, C. B. (2003). Assessing and enhancing the research consent capacity of children and youth. *Applied Developmental Science, 7,* 13–26.

Bryan, A. E., & Dix, T. (2009). Mothers' emotions and behavioral support during interactions with toddlers: The role of child temperament. *Social Development, 18,* 647–670.

Bryant, P., & Nunes, T. (2002). Children's understanding of mathematics. In U. Goswami (Ed.), *Blackwell handbook of childhood cognitive development* (pp. 412–439). Malden, MA: Blackwell.

Buchanan, A. (1996). *Cycles of child maltreatment.* Chichester, U.K.: Wiley.

Buchanan, C. M., Maccoby, E. E., & Dornbusch, S. M. (1996). *Adolescents after divorce.* Cambridge, MA: Harvard University Press.

Buchanan-Barrow, E., & Barrett, M. (1998). Children's rule discrimination within the context of the school. *British Journal of Developmental Psychology, 16,* 539–551.

Buckhalt, J. A., El-Sheikh, M., Keller, P. S., & Kelly, R. J. (2009). Concurrent and longitudinal relations between children's sleep and cognitive functioning:

The moderating role of parent education. *Child Development, 80,* 875–892.

Buescher, E. S. (2001). Anti-inflammatory characteristics of human milk: How, where, why. *Advances in Experimental Medicine and Biology, 501,* 207–222.

Bugental, D. B., Ellerson, P. C., Lin, E. K., Rainey, B., & Kokotovic, A. (2002). A cognitive approach to child abuse prevention. *Journal of Family Psychology, 16,* 243–258.

Bugental, D. B., & Grusec, J. E. (2006). Socialization processes. In N. Eisenberg (Ed.), *Handbook of child psychology: Vol. 3. Social, emotional, and personality development* (6th ed., pp. 366–428). Hoboken, NJ: Wiley.

Bugental, D. B., & Happaney, K. (2004). Predicting infant maltreatment in low-income families: The interactive effects of maternal attributions and child status at birth. *Developmental Psychology, 40,* 234–243.

Buhrmester, D., & Furman, W. (1990). Perceptions of sibling relationships during middle childhood and adolescence. *Child Development, 61,* 1387–1398.

Buhs, E. S., & Ladd, G. W. (2001). Peer rejection as antecedent of young children's school adjustment: An examination of mediating processes. *Developmental Psychology, 37,* 550–560.

Buhs, E. S., Ladd, G. W., & Herald, S. L. (2006). Peer exclusion and victimization: Processes that mediate the relation between peer group rejection and children's classroom engagement and achievement. *Journal of Educational Psychology, 98,* 1–13.

Bullock, M., & Lutkenhaus, P. (1990). Who am I? The development of self-understanding in toddlers. *Merrill-Palmer Quarterly, 36,* 217–238.

Bumpus, M. F., Crouter, A. C., & McHale, S. M. (2006). Linkages between negative work-to-family spillover and mothers' and fathers' knowledge of their young adolescents' daily lives. *Journal of Early Adolescence, 26,* 36–59.

Bunge, S. A., & Wright, S. B. (2007). Neurodevelopmental changes in working memory and cognitive control. *Current Opinion in Neurobiology, 17,* 243–250.

Burden, M. J., Jacobson, S. W., & Jacobson, J. L. (2005). Relation of prenatal alcohol exposure to cognitive processing speed and efficiency in childhood. *Alcoholism: Clinical and Experimental Research, 29,* 1473–1483.

Burhans, K. K., & Dweck, C. S. (1995). Helplessness in early childhood: The role of contingent worth. *Child Development, 66,* 1719–1738.

Burns, C. E. (2000). *Pediatric primary care: A handbook for nurse practitioners.* Philadelphia: Saunders.

Burts, D. C., Hart, C. H., Charlesworth, R., Fleege, P. O., Mosley, J., & Thomasson, R. H. (1992). Observed activities and stress behaviors of children in developmentally appropriate and inappropriate kindergarten classrooms. *Early Childhood Research Quarterly, 7,* 297–318.

Bush, K. R., & Peterson, G. W. (2008). Family influences on child development. In T. P. Gullotta & G. M. Blau (Eds.), *Handbook of child behavioral issues: Evidence-based approaches to prevention and treatment* (pp. 43–67). New York: Routledge.

Bushman, B. J., & Huesmann, L. R. (2001). Effects of televised violence of aggression. In D. G. Singer & J. L. Singer (Eds.), *Handbook of children and the media* (pp. 223–254). Thousand Oaks, CA: Sage.

Bushnell, E. W., & Boudreau, J. P. (1993). Motor development and the mind: The potential role of motor abilities as a determinant of aspects of perceptual development. *Child Development, 64,* 1005–1021.

Bussey, K. (1992). Lying and truthfulness: Children's definitions, standards, and evaluative reactions. *Child Development, 63,* 129–137.

Bussey, K. (1999). Children's categorization and evaluation of different types of lies and truths. *Child Development, 70,* 1338–1347.

Buswell, S. D., & Spatz, D. L. (2007). Parent–infant co-sleeping and its relationship to breastfeeding. *Journal of Pediatric Health Care, 21,* 22–28.

Butler, M., & Meaney, J. (Eds.). (2005). *Genetics of developmental disabilities.* Boca Raton, FL: Taylor & Francis.

Butler, R. (1998). Age trends in the use of social and temporal comparison for self-evaluation : Examination of a novel developmental hypothesis. *Child Development, 69,* 1054–1073.

Butler, R. J., Golding, J., & Heron, J. (2005). Nocturnal enuresis: A survey of parental coping strategies at 7½ years. *Child: Care, Health and Development, 31,* 659–667.

Buttelmann, D., Carpenter, M., & Tomasello, M. (2009). Eighteen-month-old infants show false belief understanding in an active helping paradigm. *Cognition, 112,* 337–342.

Bybee, J., Merisca, R., & Velasco, R. (1998). The development of reactions to guilt-producing events. In J. Bybee (Ed.), *Guilt and children* (pp. 185–213). San Diego: Academic Press.

C

Cabrera, N. J., Fitzgerald, H. E., Bradley, R. H., & Roggman, L. (2007). Modeling the dynamics of paternal influence on children over the life course. *Applied Developmental Science, 11,* 185–189.

Cabrera, N. J., & García-Coll, C. (2004). Latino fathers: Uncharted territory in need of much exploration. In M. E. Lamb (Ed.), *The role of the father in child development* (4th ed., pp. 98–120). Hoboken, NJ: Wiley.

Cabrera, N. J., Shannon, J. D., & Tamis-LeMonda, C. (2007). Fathers' influence on their children's cognitive and emotional development: From toddlers to pre-K. *Applied Developmental Science, 11,* 208–213.

Cabrera, N. J., Tamis-LeMonda, C. S., Bradley, R. H., Hoferth, S., & Lamb, M. E. (2000). Fatherhood in the twenty-first century. *Child Development, 71,* 127–136.

Cahill, A. G., & Macones, G. A. (2007). Vaginal birth after cesarean delivery: Evidence-based practice. *Clinical Obstetrics and Gynecology, 50,* 518–525.

Cain, K. M., & Dweck, C. S. (1995). The relation between motivational patterns and achievement cognitions through the elementary school years. *Merrill-Palmer Quarterly, 41,* 25–52.

Cairns, R. B., & Cairns, B. D. (2006). The making of developmental psychology. In R. M. Lerner (Ed.), *Handbook of child psychology: Vol. 1. Theoretical models of human development* (6th ed., pp. 89–165). Hoboken, NJ: Wiley.

Cairns, R. B., Xie, H., & Leung, M.-C. (1998). The popularity of friendship and the neglect of social networks: Toward a new balance. In W. M. Bukowski & A. H. Cillessen (Eds.), *Sociometry then and now: Building on six decades of measuring children's experiences with the peer group* (pp. 25–53). San Francisco: Jossey-Bass.

Caldera, Y. M., & Lindsey, E. W. (2006). Coparenting, mother–infant interaction, and infant–parent attachment relationships in two-parent families. *Journal of Family Psychology, 20,* 275–283.

Caldwell, B. M., & Bradley, R. H. (1994). Environmental issues in developmental follow-up research. In S. L. Friedman & H. C. Haywood (Eds.), *Developmental follow-up* (pp. 235–256). San Diego: Academic Press.

Callaghan, T. C. (1999). Early understanding and production of graphic symbols. *Child Development, 70,* 1314–1324.

Callaghan, T. C., & Rankin, M. P. (2002). Emergence of graphic symbol functioning and the question of domain specificity: A longitudinal training study. *Child Development, 73,* 359–376.

Callaghan, T., Rochat, P., Lillard, A., Claux, M. L., Odden, H., Itakura, S., Tapanya, S., & Singh, S. (2005). Synchrony in the onset of mental-state reasoning: Evidence from five cultures. *Psychological Science, 16,* 378–384.

Callanan, M. A., & Oakes, L. M. (1992). Preschoolers' questions and parents' explanations: Causal thinking in everyday activity. *Cognitive Development, 7,* 213–233.

Callanan, M. A., & Sabbagh, M. A. (2004). Multiple labels for objects in conversations with young children: Parents' language and children's developing expectations about word meanings. *Developmental Psychology, 40,* 746–763.

Callen, J., & Pinelli, J. (2005). A review of the literature examining the benefits and challenges, incidence and duration, and barriers to breastfeeding in preterm infants. *Advances in Neonatal Care, 5,* 72–88.

Calvert, S. L., Rideout, V. J., Woolard, J. L., Barr, R. F., & Strouse, G. A. (2005). Age, ethnicity, and socioeconomic patterns in early computer use. *American Behavioral Scientist, 48,* 590–607.

Calvert, S. L., Strong, B. L., & Gallagher, L. (2005). Control as an engagement feature for young children's attention to, and learning of, computer content. *American Behavioral Scientist, 48,* 578–589.

Cameron, C. A., & Lee, K. (1997). The development of children's telephone communication. *Journal of Applied Developmental Psychology, 18,* 55–70.

Cameron, P. A., & Gallup, G. G. (1988). Shadow recognition in human infants. *Infant Behavior and Development, 11,* 465–471.

Cameron-Faulkner, T., Lieven, E., & Tomasello, M. (2003). A construction based analysis of child-directed speech. *Cognitive Science, 27,* 843–873.

Cammu, H., Martens, G., Ruyssinck, G., & Amy, J. J. (2002). Outcome after elective labor induction in nulliparous women: A matched cohort study. *American Journal of Obstetrics and Gynecology, 186,* 240–244.

Campbell, A., Shirley, L., & Candy, J. (2004). A longitudinal study of gender-related cognition and behaviour. *Developmental Science, 7,* 1–9.

Campbell, D. A., Lake, M. F., Falk, M., & Backstrand, J. R. (2006). A randomized control trial of continuous support in labor by a lay doula. *Journal of Obstetrics and Gynecology and Neonatal Nursing, 35,* 456–464.

Campbell, D., Scott, K. D., Klaus, M. H., & Falk, M. (2007). Female relatives or friends trained as labor doulas: Outcomes at 6 to 8 weeks postpartum. *Birth, 34,* 220–227.

Campbell, F. A., Pungello, E. P., Miller-Johnson, S., Burchinal, M., & Ramey, C. T. (2001). The development of cognitive and academic abilities: Growth curves from an early childhood educational experiment. *Developmental Psychology, 37,* 231–242.

Campbell, F. A., Ramey, C. T., Pungello, E., Sparling, J., & Miller-Johnson, S. (2002). Early childhood education: Young adult outcomes from the Abecedarian Project. *Applied Developmental Science, 6,* 42–57.

Campbell, S. B., Brownell, C. A., Hungerford, A., Spieker, S. J., Mohan, R., & Blessing, J. S. (2004). The course of maternal depressive symptoms and maternal sensitivity as predictors of attachment security at 36 months. *Development and Psychopathology, 16,* 231–252.

Campbell, S. B., Spieker, S., Burchinal, M., Poe, M. D., & the NICHD Early Child Care Research Network. (2006). Trajectories of aggression from toddlerhood to age 9 predict academic and social functioning through age 12. *Journal of Child Psychology and Psychiatry, 47,* 791–800.

Campos, J. J., Anderson, D. I., Barbu-Roth, M. A., Hubbard, E. M., Hertenstein, J. J., & Witherington, D. (2000). Travel broadens the mind. *Infancy, 1,* 149–219

Campos, J. J., Frankel, C. B., & Camras, L. (2004). On the nature of emotion regulation. *Child Development, 75,* 377–394.

Campos, J. J., Witherington, D., Anderson, D. I., Frankel, C. I., Uchiyama, I., & Barbu-Roth, M. (2008). Rediscovering development in infancy. *Child Development, 79,* 1625–1632.

Campos, R. G. (1989). Soothing pain-elicited distress in infants with swaddling and pacifiers. *Child Development, 60,* 781–792.

Camras, L. A. (1992). Expressive development and basic emotions. *Cognition and Emotion, 6,* 267–283.

Camras, L. A., Oster, H., Campos, J. J., & Bakeman, R. (2003). Emotional facial expressions in European-American, Japanese, and Chinese infants. *Annals of the New York Academy of Sciences, 1000,* 1–17

Camras, L. A., Oster, H., Campos, J. J., Campos, R., Ujie, T., Miyake, K., Wang, L., & Meng, Z. (1998).

Production of emotional and facial expressions in European American, Japanese, and Chinese infants. *Developmental Psychology, 34,* 616–628.

Camras, L. A., Oster, H., Campos, J. J., Miyake, K., & Bradshaw, D. (1992). Japanese and American infants' responses to arm restraint. *Developmental Psychology, 28,* 578–583.

Canada Campaign 2000. (2009). 2009 Report Card on Child and Family Poverty in Canada: 1989–2009. Retrieved from www.campaign2000.ca/reportcards .html

Canobi, K. H. (2004). Individual differences in children's addition and subtraction knowledge. *Cognitive Development, 19,* 81–93.

Canobi, K. H., Reeve, R. A., & Pattison, P. E. (2003). The role of conceptual understanding in children's addition problem solving. *Developmental Psychology, 39,* 521–534.

Capirci, O., Contaldo, A., Caselli, M. C., & Volterra, V. (2005). From action to language through gesture. *Gesture, 5,* 155–177.

Card, N. A., Stucky, B. D., Sawalani, G. M., & Little, T. D. (2008). Direct and indirect aggression during childhood and adolescence: A meta-analytic review of gender differences, intercorrelations, and relations to maladjustment. *Child Development, 79,* 1185–1229.

CARE Study Group. (2008). Maternal caffeine intake during pregnancy and risk of fetal growth restriction: A large prospective observational study. *British Medical Journal, 337,* a2337.

Carey, S. (1995). On the origins of causal understanding. In D. Sperber, D. Premack, & A. J. Premack (Eds.), *Causal cognition* (pp. 268–308). Oxford, U.K.: Clarendon Press.

Carey, S. (1999). Sources of conceptual change. In E. K. Scholnick, K. Nelson, S. A. Gelman, & P. H. Miller (Eds.), *Conceptual development: Piaget's legacy* (pp. 293–326). Mahwah, NJ: Erlbaum.

Carey, S., & Markman, E. M. (1999). Cognitive development. In B. M. Bly & D. E. Rumelhart (Eds.), *Cognitive science* (pp. 201–254). San Diego: Academic Press.

Carlson, C., Uppal, S., & Prosser, E. (2000). Ethnic differences in processes contributing to the self-esteem of early adolescent girls. *Journal of Early Adolescence, 20,* 44–67.

Carlson, M., & Earls, F. (1997). Psychological and neuroendocrinological sequelae of early social deprivation in institutionalized children in Romania. *Annals of the New York Academy of Sciences, 807,* 419–428.

Carlson, S. M., Moses, L. J., & Claxton, S. J. (2004). Individual differences in executive functioning and theory of mind: An investigation of inhibitory control and planning ability. *Journal of Experimental Child Psychology, 87,* 299–319.

Carlson, V. J., & Harwood, R. L. (2003). Attachment, culture, and the caregiving system: The cultural patterning of everyday experiences among Anglo and Puerto Rican mother–infant pairs. *Infant Mental Health Journal, 24,* 53–73.

Carmichael, S. L., & Shaw, G. M. (2000). Maternal life stress and congenital anomalies. *Epidemiology, 11,* 30–35.

Carpenter, M., Akhtar, N., & Tomasello, M. (1998). Fourteen- through eighteen-month-old infants differentially imitate intentional and accidental actions. *Infant Behavior and Development, 21,* 315–330.

Carpenter, M., Nagel, K., & Tomasello, M. (1998). Social cognition, joint attention, and communicative competence. *Monographs of the Society for Research in Child Development, 63*(4, Serial No. 255).

Carpenter, T. P., Fennema, E., Fuson, K., Hiebert, J., Human, P., & Murray, H. (1999). Learning basic number concepts and skills as problem solving. In E. Fennema & T. A. Romberg (Eds.), *Mathematics classrooms that promote understanding: Studies in mathematical thinking and learning series* (pp. 45–61). Mahwah, NJ: Erlbaum.

Carr, D., & Friedman, M. A. (2005). Is obesity stigmatizing? Body weight, perceived discrimination,

and psychological well-being in the United States. *Journal of Health and Social Behavior, 46,* 244–256.

Carr, J. (2002). Down syndrome. In P. Howlin & O. Udwin (Eds.), *Outcomes in neurodevelopmental and genetic disorders* (pp. 169–197). New York: Cambridge University Press.

Carroll, J. B. (2005). The three-stratum theory of cognitive abilities. In D. P. Flanagan & P. L. Harrison (Eds.), *Contemporary intellectual assessment: Theories, tests, and issues* (2nd ed., pp. 69–76). New York: Guilford.

Casalis, S., & Cole, P. (2009). On the relationship between morphological and phonological awareness: Effects of training in kindergarten and in first-grade reading. *First Language, 29,* 113–142.

Casasola, M., Bhagwat, J., & Burke, A. S. (2009). Learning to form a spatial category of tight-fit relations: How experience with a label can give a boost. *Developmental Psychology, 45,* 711–723.

Casasola, M., Cohen, L. B., & Chiarello, E. (2003). Six-month-old infants' categorization of containment spatial relations. *Child Development, 74,* 679–693.

Casby, M. W. (2001). Otitis media and language development: A meta-analysis. *American Journal of Speech-Language Pathology, 10,* 65–80.

Case, R. (1996). Introduction: Reconceptualizing the nature of children's conceptual structures and their development in middle childhood. In R. Case & Y. Okamoto (Eds.), The role of central conceptual structures in the development of children's thought. *Monographs of the Society for Research in Child Development, 246*(61, Serial No. 246), pp. 1–26.

Case, R. (1998). The development of conceptual structures. In D. Kuhn & R. S. Siegler (Eds.), *Handbook of child psychology: Vol. 2. Cognition, perception, and language* (pp. 745–800). New York: Wiley.

Case, R., & Okamoto, Y. (Eds.). (1996). The role of central conceptual structures in the development of children's thought. *Monographs of the Society for Research in Child Development, 61*(1–2, Serial No. 246).

Casey, B. J., Thomas, K. M., Davidson, M. C., Kunz, K., & Franzen, P. L. (2002). Dissociating striatal and hippocampal function developmentally with a stimulus-response compatibility task. *Journal of Cognitive Neuroscience, 22,* 8647–8652.

Casey, B. M. (1986). Individual differences in selective attention among prereaders: A key to mirror-image confusions. *Developmental Psychology, 22,* 824–831.

Cashon, C. H., & Cohen, L. B. (2000). Eight-month-old infants' perceptions of possible and impossible events. *Infancy, 1,* 429–446.

Casper, L. M., & Smith, K. E. (2002). Dispelling the myths: Self-care, class, and race. *Journal of Family Issues, 23,* 716–727.

Caspi, A. (2000). The child is father of the man: Personality continuities from childhood to adulthood. *Journal of Personality and Social Psychology, 78,* 158–172.

Caspi, A., Elder, G. H., Jr., & Bem, D. J. (1987). Moving against the world: Life-course patterns of explosive children. *Developmental Psychology, 23,* 308–313.

Caspi, A., Elder, G. H., Jr., & Bem, D. J. (1988). Moving away from the world: Life-course patterns of shy children. *Developmental Psychology, 24,* 824–831.

Caspi, A., Harrington, H., Milne, B., Amell, J. W., Theodore, R. F., & Moffitt, T. E. (2003). Children's behavioral styles at age 3 are linked to their adult personality traits at age 26. *Journal of Personality, 71,* 495–513.

Caspi, A., McClay, J., Moffitt, T. E., Mill, J., Martin, J., & Craig, I. W. (2002). Role of genotype in the cycle of violence in maltreated children. *Science, 297,* 851–854.

Caspi, A., Moffitt, T. E., Morgan, J., Rutter, M., Taylor, A., Kim-Cohen, J., & Polo-Tomas, M. (2004). Maternal expressed emotion predicts children's antisocial behavior problems: Using monozygotic-twin differences to identify environmental effects on behavioral development. *Developmental Psychology, 40,* 149–161.

Caspi, A., & Roberts, B. W. (2001). Personality development across the life course: The argument for change and continuity. *Psychological Inquiry, 12,* 49–66.

Caspi, A., & Shiner, L. (2006). Personality development. In N. Eisenberg (Ed.), *Handbook of child psychology: Vol. 3. Social, emotional, and personality development* (6th ed., pp. 300–365). Hoboken, NJ: Wiley.

Cassia, V. M., Simion, F., & Umiltá, C. (2001). Face preference at birth: The role of an orienting mechanism. *Developmental Science, 4,* 101–108.

Cassia, V. M., Turati, C., & Simion, F. (2004). Can a nonspecific bias toward top-heavy patterns explain newborns' face preference? *Psychological Science, 15,* 379–383.

Cassidy, J., & Berlin, L. J. (1994). The insecure/ambivalent pattern of attachment: Theory and research. *Child Development, 65,* 971–991.

Catalano, R. A. (2003). Sex ratios in the two Germanies: A test of the economic stress hypothesis. *Human Reproduction, 18,* 1972–1975.

Catalano, R., Ahern, J., Bruckner, T., Anderson, E., & Saxton, K. (2009). Gender-specific selection in utero among contemporary human birth cohorts. *Paediatric and Perinatal Epidemiology, 23,* 273–278.

Catalano, R., Bruckner, T., Anderson, E., & Gould, J. B. (2005). Fetal death sex ratios: A test of the economic stress hypothesis. *International Journal of Epidemiology, 34,* 944–948.

Caton, D., Corry, M. P., Frigoletto, F. D., Hopkins, D. P., Liberman, E., & Mayberry, L. (2002). The nature and management of labor pain: Executive summary. *American Journal of Obstetrics and Gynecology, 186,* S1–S15.

Caughey, R. W., & Michels, K. B. (2009). Birth weight and childhood leukemia: A meta-analysis and review of the current evidence. *International Journal of Cancer, 124,* 2658–2670.

Ceci, S. J. (1991). How much does schooling influence general intelligence and its cognitive components? A reassessment of the evidence. *Developmental Psychology, 27,* 703–722.

Ceci, S. J. (1999). Schooling and intelligence. In S. J. Ceci & W. M. Williams (Eds.), *The nature–nurture debate: The essential readings* (pp. 168–175). Oxford: Blackwell.

Ceci, S. J., Bruck, M., & Battin, D. (2000). The suggestibility of children's testimony. In Bjorklund, D. (Ed), *False-memory creation in children and adults* (pp. 169–201) Mahwah, NJ: Erlbaum.

Ceci, S. J., Kulkofsky, S., Klemfuss, J. Z., Sweeney, C. D., & Bruck, M. (2007). Unwarranted assumptions about children's testimonial accuracy. *Annual Review of Clinical Psychology, 3,* 311–328.

Ceci, S. J., & Roazzi, A. (1994). The effects of context on cognition: Postcards from Brazil. In R. J. Sternberg (Ed.), *Mind in context* (pp. 74–101). New York: Cambridge University Press.

Ceci, S. J., Rosenblum, T. B., & Kumpf, M. (1998). The shrinking gap between high- and low-scoring groups: Current trends and possible causes. In U. Neisser (Ed.), *The rising curve: Long-term gains in IQ and related measures* (pp. 287–302). Washington, DC: American Psychological Association.

Ceci, S. J., & Williams, W. M. (1997). Schooling, intelligence, and income. *American Psychologist, 52,* 1051–1058.

Cecil, J. E., Watt, P., Murrie, I. S. L., Wrieden, W., Wallis, D. J., Hetherington, M. M., Bolton-Smith, C., & Palmer, C. N. A. (2005). Childhood obesity and socioeconomic status: A novel role for height growth limitation. *International Journal of Obesity, 29,* 1199–1203.

Center for Communication and Social Policy. (Ed.). (1998). *National Television Violence Study* (Vol. 2). Newbury Park, CA: Sage.

Center for Effective Discipline. (2005). *Worldwide bans on corporal punishment.* Retrieved from www.stophitting.com/disatschool/facts.php

Cernoch, J. M., & Porter, R. H. (1985). Recognition of maternal axillary odors by infants. *Child Development, 56,* 1593–1598.

Cervantes, C. A., & Callanan, M. A. (1998). Labels and explanations in mother–child emotion talk: Age and gender differentiation. *Developmental Psychology, 34,* 88–98.

Chall, J. S. (1983). *Stages of reading development.* New York: McGraw-Hill.

Chalmers, J. B., & Townsend, M. A. R. (1990). The effects of training in social perspective taking on socially maladjusted girls. *Child Development, 61,* 178–190.

Champion, T. B. (2003a). "A matter of vocabulary": Performances of low-income African-American Head Start children on the Peabody Picture Vocabulary Test. *Communication Disorders Quarterly, 24,* 121–127.

Champion, T. B. (2003b). *Understanding storytelling among African-American children: A journey from Africa to America.* Mahwah, NJ: Erlbaum.

Chan, L. K. S., & Moore, P. J. (2006). Development of attributional beliefs and strategic knowledge in years 5–9: A longitudinal analysis. *Educational Psychology, 26,* 161–185.

Chan, R. W., Raboy, B., & Patterson, C. J. (1998). Psychosocial adjustment among children conceived via donor insemination by lesbian and heterosexual mothers. *Child Development, 69,* 443–457.

Chandra, R. K. (1991). Interactions between early nutrition and the immune system. In *Ciba Foundation Symposium No. 156* (pp. 77–92). Chichester, U.K.: Wiley.

Chang, F., Dell, G. S., & Bock, K. (2006). Becoming syntactic. *Psychological Review, 113,* 234–272.

Chang, L., Schwartz, D., Dodge, D. A., & McBride-Chang, C. (2003). Harsh parenting in relation to child emotion regulation and aggression. *Journal of Family Psychology, 17,* 598–606.

Chao, R. K. (1994). Beyond parental control and authoritarian parenting style: Understanding Chinese parenting through the cultural notion of training. *Child Development, 65,* 1111–1119.

Chapman, R. S. (2000). Children's language learning: An interactionist perspective. *Journal of Child Psychology and Psychiatry, 41,* 33–54.

Chapman, R. S. (2006). Children's language learning: An interactionist perspective. In R. Paul (Ed.), *Language disorders from a developmental perspective* (pp. 1–53). Mahwah, NJ: Erlbaum.

Charchut, S. W., Allred, E. N., & Needleman, H. L. (2003). The effects of infant feeding patterns on the occlusion of the primary dentition. *Journal of Dentistry for Children, 70,* 197–203.

Charman, T., Baron-Cohen, S., Swettenham, J., Baird, G., Cox, A., & Drew, A. (2001). Testing joint attention, imitation, and play as infancy precursors to language and theory of mind. *Cognitive Development, 15,* 481–49.

Charpak, N., Ruiz-Peláez, J. G., & Figueroa, Z. (2005). Influence of feeding patterns and other factors on early somatic growth of healthy, preterm infants in home-based kangaroo mother care: A cohort study. *Journal of Pediatric Gastroenterology and Nutrition, 41,* 430–437.

Chase-Lansdale, P. L., Brooks-Gunn, J., & Zamsky, E. S. (1994). Young African-American multigenerational families in poverty: Quality of mothering and grandmothering. *Child Development, 65,* 373–393.

Chase-Lansdale, P. L., Gordon, R., Brooks-Gunn, J., & Klebanov, P. K. (1997). Neighborhood and family influences on the intellectual and behavioral competence of preschool and early school-age children. In J. Brooks-Gunn, G. Duncan, & J. L. Aber (Eds.), *Neighborhood poverty: Context and consequences for development* (pp. 79–118). New York: Russell Sage Foundation.

Chauhan, G. S., Shastri, J., & Mohite, P. (2005). Development of gender constancy in preschoolers. *Psychological Studies, 50,* 62–71.

Chavajay, P., & Rogoff, B. (1999). Cultural variation in management of attention by children and their caregivers. *Developmental Psychology, 35,* 1079–1090.

Chavajay, P., & Rogoff, B. (2002). Schooling and traditional collaborative social organization of problem solving by Mayan mothers and children. *Developmental Psychology, 38,* 55–66.

Chawarska, K., & Shic, F. (2009). Looking but not seeing: Atypical visual scanning and recognition of faces in 2- and 4-year-old children with autism

spectrum disorder. *Journal of Autism and Developmental Disorders, 39,* 1663–1672.

Cheah, C. S. L., Leung, C. Y. Y., Tahseen, M., & Schultz, D. (2009). Authoritative parenting among immigrant Chinese mothers of preschoolers. *Journal of Family Psychology, 23,* 311–320.

Checkley, W., Epstein, L. D., Gilman, R. H., Cabrera, L., & Black, R. E. (2003). Effects of acute diarrhea on linear growth in Peruvian children. *American Journal of Epidemiology, 157,* 166–175.

Chen, D. W., Fein, G. G., Killen, M., & Tam, H.-P. (2001). Peer conflicts of preschool children: Issues, resolution, incidence, and age-related patterns. *Early Education and Development, 12,* 523–544.

Chen, L.-C., Metcalfe, J. S., Jeka, J. J., & Clark, J. E. (2007). Two steps forward and one back: Learning to walk affects infants' sitting posture. *Infant Behavior and Development, 30,* 16–25.

Chen, M. (2003). Wombs for rent: An examination of prohibitory and regulatory approaches to governing preconception arrangements. *Health Law in Canada, 23,* 33–50.

Chen, X., Cen, G., Li, D., & He, Y. (2005). Social functioning and adjustment in Chinese children: The imprint of historical time. *Child Development, 76,* 182–195.

Chen, X., DeSouza, A. T., Chen, H., & Wang, L. (2006). Reticent behavior and experiences in peer interactions in Chinese and Canadian children. *Developmental Psychology, 42,* 656–665.

Chen, X., & French, D. C. (2008). Children's social competence in cultural context. *Annual Review of Psychology, 59,* 591–616.

Chen, X., Hastings, P. D., Rubin, K. H., Chen, H., Cen, G., & Stewart, S. L. (1998). Child-rearing attitudes and behavioral inhibition in Chinese and Canadian toddlers: A cross-cultural study. *Developmental Psychology, 34,* 677–686.

Chen, X., Rubin, K. H., & Li, Z. (1995). Social functioning and adjustment in Chinese children: A longitudinal study. *Developmental Psychology, 31,* 531–539.

Chen, X., Wang, L., & DeSouza, A. (2006). Temperament, socioemotional functioning, and peer relationships in Chinese and North American children. In X. Chen, D. C. French, & B. H. Schneider (Eds.), *Peer relationships in cultural context* (pp. 123–147). New York: Cambridge University Press.

Chen, Y.-C., Yu, M.-L., Rogan, W., Gladen, B., & Hsu, C.-C. (1994). A 6-year follow-up of behavior and activity disorders in the Taiwan Yu-cheng children. *American Journal of Public Health, 84,* 415–421.

Chen, Y.-J., & Hsu, C.-C. (1994). Effects of prenatal exposure to PCBs on the neurological function of children: A neuropsychological and neurophysiological study. *Developmental Medicine and Child Neurology, 36,* 312–320.

Chen, Z., Sanchez, R. P., & Campbell, T. (1997). From beyond to within their grasp: The rudiments of analogical problem solving in 10- to 13-month-olds. *Developmental Psychology, 33,* 790–801.

Chen, Z., & Siegler, R. S. (2000). Across the great divide: Bridging the gap between understanding of toddlers' and older children's thinking. *Monographs of the Society for Research in Child Development, 65*(2, Serial No. 261).

Chess, S., & Thomas, A. (1984). *Origins and evolution of behavior disorders.* New York: Brunner/Mazel.

Child Trends. (2007). *Late or no prenatal care.* Retrieved from www.childtrendsdatabank.org/indicators/25PrenatalCare.cfm

Children's Defense Fund. (2008). *Annual Report 2007.* Washington, DC: Author.

Children's Defense Fund. (2009). *State of America's children: 2008.* Washington, DC: Author.

Chisholm, K. (1998). Attachment security and indiscriminately friendly behavior in children adopted from Romanian orphanages. *Development and Psychopathology, 7,* 283–294.

Choby, B. A., & George, S. (2008). Toilet training. *American Family Physician, 78,* 1059–1064.

Choi, S., & Gopnik, A. (1995). Early acquisition of verbs in Korean: A cross-linguistic study. *Journal of Child Language, 22,* 497–529.

Choi, S., McDonough, L., Bowerman, M., & Mandler, J. M. (1999). Early sensitivity to language-specific spatial categories in English and Korean. *Cognitive Development, 14,* 241–268.

Chomsky, C. (1969). *The acquisition of syntax in children from five to ten.* Cambridge, MA: MIT Press.

Chomsky, N. (1957). *Syntactic structures.* The Hague: Mouton.

Chomtho, S., Wells, J. C., Williams, J. E., Davies, P. S., Lucas, A., & Fewtrell, M. S. (2008). Infant growth and later body composition: Evidence from the 4-component model. *American Journal of Clinical Nutrition, 87,* 1776–1784.

Chorzempa, B. F., & Graham, S. (2006). Primary-grade teachers' use of within-class ability grouping in reading. *Journal of Educational Psychology, 98,* 529–541.

Chouinard, M. M. (2007). Children's questions: A mechanism for cognitive development. *Monographs of the Society for Research in Child Development, 72*(1, Serial No. 286).

Chouinard, M. M., & Clark, E. V. (2003). Adult reformulations of child errors as negative evidence. *Journal of Child Language, 30,* 637–669.

Christ, S. E., Steiner, R. D., Grange, D. K., Abrams, R. A., & White, D. A. (2006). Inhibitory control in children with phenylketonuria. *Developmental Neuropsychology, 30,* 845–864.

Christakis, D. A., Zimmerman, F. J., DiGiuseppe, D. L., & McCarty, C. A. (2004). Early television exposure and subsequent attentional problems in children. *Pediatrics, 113,* 708–713.

Christiansen, M. H., & Chater, N. (2008). Language as shaped by the brain. *Behavioral and Brain Sciences, 31,* 489–558.

Christophersen, E. R., & Mortweet, S. L. (2003). *Parenting that works: Building skills that last a lifetime.* Washington, DC: American Psychological Association.

Chudley, A. E., Conry, J., Cook, J. L., Loock, C., Rosales, T., & LeBlanc, N. (2005). Fetal alcohol spectrum disorder: Canadian guidelines for diagnosis. *Canadian Medical Association Journal, 172,* S1–S21.

Chung, H. H. (2006). Code switching as a communicative strategy: A case study of Korean–English bilinguals. *Bilingual Research Journal, 30,* 293–307.

Cicchetti, D. (2007). Intervention and policy implications of research on neurobiological functioning in maltreated children. In J. L. Aber, S. J. Bishop-Josef, S. M. Jones, K. T. McLearn, & D. A. Phillips (Eds.), *Child development and social policy* (pp. 167–184). Washington, DC: American Psychological Association.

Cicchetti, D., & Toth, S. L. (2006). Developmental psychopathology and preventive intervention. In K. A. Renninger & I. E. Sigel (Eds.), *Handbook of child psychology: Vol. 4. Child psychology in practice* (6th ed., pp. 497–547). Hoboken, NJ: Wiley.

Cillessen, A. H. N., & Bellmore, A. D. (2004). Social skills and interpersonal perception in early and middle childhood. In P. K. Smith & C. H. Hart (Eds.), *Blackwell handbook of childhood social development* (pp. 355–374). Malden, MA: Blackwell.

Cillessen, A. H. N., & Mayeux, L. (2004). From censure to reinforcement: Developmental changes in the association between aggression and social status. *Child Development, 75,* 147–163.

Clapp, J. F., III, Kim, H., Burciu, B., Schmidt, S., Petry, K., & Lopez, B. (2002). Continuing regular exercise during pregnancy: Effect of exercise volume on fetoplacental growth. *American Journal of Obstetrics and Gynecology, 186,* 142–147.

Clark, C. A., Woodward, L. J., Horwood, L. J., & Moor, S. (2008). Development of emotional and behavioral regulation in children born extremely preterm and very preterm: Biological and social influences. *Child Development, 79,* 1444–1462.

Clark, E. V. (1990). On the pragmatics of contrast. *Journal of Child Language, 17,* 417–431.

Clark, E. V. (2007). Young children's uptake of new words in conversation. *Language in Society, 36,* 157–182.

Clark, K. E., & Ladd, G. W. (2000). Connectedness and autonomy support in parent–child relationships: Links to children's socioemotional orientation and peer relationships. *Developmental Psychology, 36,* 485–498.

Clark, S. L., Miller, D. D., Belfort, M. A., Dildy, G. A., Frye, D. K., & Meyers, J. A. (2009). Neonatal and maternal outcomes associated with elective term delivery. *American Journal of Obstetrics and Gynecology, 200,* 156.e1–e4.

Clark, S. M., Ghulmiyyah, L. M., & Hankins, G. D. (2008). Antenatal antecedents and the impact of obstetric care in the etiology of cerebral palsy. *Clinical Obstetrics and Gynecology, 51,* 775–786.

Clarke-Stewart, K. A. (1998). Historical shifts and underlying themes in ideas about rearing young children in the United States: Where have we been? Where are we going? *Early Development and Parenting, 7,* 101–117.

Clarke-Stewart, K. A., Allhusen, V., & Goossens, F. (2001). Day care and the Strange Situation. In A. Göncü & E. L., Klein (Eds.), *Children in play, story, and school* (pp. 241–266). New York: Guilford.

Clarke-Stewart, K. A., & Hayward, C. (1996). Advantages of father custody and contact for the psychological well-being of school-age children. *Journal of Applied Developmental Psychology, 17,* 239–270.

Clarkson, T. W., Magos, L., & Myers, G. J. (2003). The toxicology of mercury—current exposures and clinical manifestations. *New England Journal of Medicine, 349,* 1731–1737.

Claxton, L. J., Keen, R., & McCarty, M. E. (2003). Evidence of motor planning in infant reaching behavior. *Psychological Science, 14,* 354–356.

Clearfield, M. W., & Nelson, N. M. (2006). Sex differences in mothers' speech and play behavior with 6-, 9-, and 14-month-old infants. *Sex Roles, 54,* 127–137.

Clearfield, M. W., Osborn, C. N., & Mullen, M. (2008). Learning by looking: Infants' social looking behavior across the transition from crawling to walking. *Journal of Experimental Child Psychology, 100,* 297–307.

Clements, D. H., & Sarama, J. (2003). Young children and technology: What does the research say? *Young Children, 58*(6), 34–40.

Clements, D. H., & Sarama, J. (2008). Experimental evaluation of the effects of a research-based preschool mathematics curriculum. *American Educational Research Journal, 45,* 443–494.

Cleveland, E. S., & Reese, E. (2005). Maternal structure and autonomy support in conversations about the past: Contributions to children's autobiographical memory. *Developmental Psychology, 41,* 376–388.

Clifford, R. M., Barbarin, O., Chang, F., Early, D., Bryant, D., Howes, C., Burchinal, M., & Pianta, R. (2005). What is pre-kindergarten? Characteristics of public prekindergarten programs. *Applied Developmental Science, 9,* 126–143.

Clifton, R. K., Rochat, P., Robin, D. J., & Berthier, N. E. (1994). Multimodal perception in the control of infant reaching. *Journal of Experimental Psychology: Human Perception and Performance, 20,* 876–886.

Cluett, E. R., & Burns, E. (2009). Immersion in water in labour and birth. *Cochrane Database of Systematic Reviews,* Issue 2. Art. No. CD000111.

Cnattingius, S., Lundberg, F., Sandin, S., Grönberg, H., & Iliadou, A. (2009). Birth characteristics and risk of prostate cancer: The contribution of genetic factors. *Cancer Epidemiology, 18,* 2422–2466.

Cohen, L. B. (2003). Commentary on Part I: Unresolved issues in infant categorization. In D. H. Rakison & L. M. Oakes (Eds.), *Early category and concept development: Making sense of the blooming, buzzing confusion* (pp. 193–209). New York: Oxford University Press.

Cohen, L. B. (2009). The evolution of infant cognition: A personal account. *Infancy, 14,* 403–413.

Cohen, L. B. (2010). A bottom-up approach to infant perception and cognition: A summary of evidence and discussion of issues. In S. P. Johnson (Ed.), *Neoconstructivism: The new science of cognitive development* (pp. 335–346). New York: Oxford University Press.

Cohen, L. B., & Brunt, J. (2009). Early word learning and categorization: Methodological issues and recent empirical evidence. In J. Colombo, P. McCardle, & L. Freund (Eds.), *Infant pathways to language: Methods, models, and research disorders* (pp. 245–266). New York: Psychology Press.

Cohen, L. B., & Cashon, C. H. (2001). Infant object segregation implies information integration. *Journal of Experimental Child Psychology, 78,* 75–83.

Cohen, L. B., & Cashon, C. H. (2006). Infant cognition. In D. Kuhn & R. Siegler (Eds.), *Handbook of child psychology: Vol. 2. Cognition, perception, and language* (6th ed., pp. 214–251). Hoboken, NJ: Wiley.

Cohen, L. B., & Marks, K. S. (2002). How infants process addition and subtraction events. *Developmental Science, 5,* 186–201.

Cohen, S., & Herbert, T. B. (1996). Health psychology: Psychological factors and physical disease from the perspective of human psychoneuroimmunology. *Annual Review of Psychology, 47,* 113–142.

Cohen-Bendahan, C. C. C., van de Beek, C., & Berenbaum, S. A. (2005). Prenatal sex hormones effects on child and adult sex-typed behavior: Methods and findings. *Neuroscience and Biobehavioral Reviews, 29,* 353–384.

Coie, J. D., Dodge, K. A., & Coppotelli, H. (1982). Dimensions and types of social status: A cross-age perspective. *Developmental Psychology, 18,* 557–570.

Colapinto, J. (2001). *As nature made him: The boy who was raised as a girl.* New York: Perennial.

Cole, D. A., Martin, J. M., Peeke, L. A., Seroczynski, A. D., & Fier, J. (1999). Children's over- and underestimation of academic competence: A longitudinal study of gender differences, depression, and anxiety. *Child Development, 70,* 459–473.

Cole, D. A., Maxwell, S. E., Martin, J. M., Peeke, L. G., Seroczynski, A. D., & Tram, J. M. (2001). The development of multiple domains of child and adolescent self-concept : A cohort sequential longitudinal design. *Child Development, 72,* 1723–1746.

Cole, M. (2006). Culture and cognitive development in phylogenetic, historical, and ontogenetic perspective. In D. Kuhn & R. S. Siegler (Eds.), *Handbook of child psychology: Vol. 2. Cognition, perception, and language* (6th ed., pp. 636–685). Hoboken, NJ: Wiley.

Cole, P. M., Armstrong, L. M., & Pemberton, C. K. (2010). The role of language in the development of emotion regulation. In S. D. Calkins & M. A. Bell (Eds.), *Child development at the intersection of emotion and cognition* (pp. 59–77). Washington, DC: American Psychological Association.

Cole, P. M., Bruschi, C. J., & Tamang, B. L. (2002). Cultural differences in children's emotional reactions to difficult situations. *Child Development, 73,* 983–996.

Cole, P. M., & Tamang, B. L. (1998). Nepali children's ideas about emotional displays in hypothetical challenges. *Developmental Psychology, 34,* 640–648.

Cole, P. M., Tamang, B. L., & Shrestha, S. (2006). Cultural variations in the socialization of young children's anger and shame. *Child Development, 77,* 1237–1251.

Cole, S. A. (2006). Building secure relationships: Attachment in kin and unrelated foster caregiver–infant relationships. *Families in Society, 87,* 497–508.

Cole, T. J. (2000). Secular trends in growth. *Proceedings of the Nutrition Society, 59,* 317–324.

Coley, R. L. (1998). Children's socialization experiences and functioning in single-mother households: The importance of fathers and other men. *Child Development, 69,* 219–230.

Coley, R. L., Morris, J. E., & Hernandez, D. (2004). Out-of-school care and problem behavior trajectories among low-income adolescents: Individual, family, and neighborhood characteristics as added risks. *Child Development, 75,* 948–965.

Collins, W. A., Maccoby, E. E., Steinberg, L., Hetherington, E. M., & Bornstein, M. H. (2000). Contemporary research on parenting: The case for nature and nurture. *American Psychologist, 52,* 218–232.

Collins, W. A., Madsen, S. D., & Susman-Stillman, A (2002). Parenting during middle childhood. In M. H. Bornstein (Ed.), *Handbook of parenting: Vol. 1. Children and parenting* (2nd ed., pp. 73–101). Mahwah, NJ: Erlbaum.

Collins, W. A., & Russell, G. (1991). Mother–child and father–child interactions in middle childhood and adolescence. *Developmental Review, 11,* 99–136.

Colman, L. L., & Colman, A. D. (1991). *Pregnancy: The psychological experience.* Noonday Press.

Colman, R. A., Hardy, S. A., Albert, M., Raffaelli, M., & Crockett, L. (2006). Early predictors of self-regulation in middle childhood. *Infant and Child Development, 15,* 421–437.

Colombo, J. (1995). On the neural mechanisms underlying developmental and individual differences in visual fixation in infancy. *Developmental Review, 15,* 97–135.

Colombo, J. (2002). Infant attention grows up: The emergence of a developmental cognitive neuroscience perspective. *Current Directions in Psychological Science, 11,* 196–199.

Coltrane, S. (1996). *Family man.* New York: Oxford University Press.

Commission on Children at Risk. (2008). Hardwired to connect: The new scientific case for authoritative communities. In K. K. Kline (Ed.), *Authoritative communities: The scientific case for nurturing the whole child* (pp. 3–68). New York: Springer.

Comstock, G., & Scharrer, E. (2006). Media and popular culture. In K. A. Renninger & I. E. Sigel (Eds.), *Handbook of child psychology: Vol. 4. Child psychology in practice* (6th ed., pp. 817–863). Hoboken, NJ: Wiley.

Conboy, B. T., & Thal, D. J. (2006). Ties between the lexicon and grammar: Cross-sectional and longitudinal studies of bilingual toddlers. *Child Development, 77,* 712–735.

Condron, D. J. (2007). Stratification and educational sorting: Explaining ascriptive inequalities in early childhood reading group placement. *Social Problems, 54,* 139–160.

Conger, R. D., & Conger, K. J. (2002). Resilience in Midwestern families: Selected findings from the first decade of a prospective, longitudinal study. *Journal of Marriage and the Family, 64,* 361–373.

Conger, R. D., & Donnellan, M. B. (2007). An interactionist perspective on the socioeconomic context of human development. *Annual Review of Psychology, 58,* 175–199.

Connell, M. W., Sheridan, K., & Gardner, H. (2003). On abilities and domains. In R. J. Sternberg & E. Grigorenko (Eds.), *Perspectives on the psychology of abilities, competencies, and expertise* (pp. 126–155). New York: Cambridge University Press.

Conner, D. B., & Cross, D. R. (2003). Longitudinal analysis of the presence, efficacy, and stability of maternal scaffolding during informal problem-solving interactions. *British Journal of Developmental Psychology, 21,* 315–334.

Connolly, J. A., & Doyle, A. B. (1984). Relations of social fantasy play to social competence in preschoolers. *Developmental Psychology, 20,* 797–806.

Connor, J. M. (2003). Physical activity and well-being. In M. H. Bornstein, L. Davidson, C. L. M. Keyes, K. A. Moore, & the Center for Child Well-Being (Eds.), *Well-being: Positive development across the life course* (pp. 65–79). Mahwah, NJ: Erlbaum.

Conti-Ramsden, G., & Pérez-Pereira, M. (1999). Conversational interactions between mothers and their infants who are congenitally blind, have low vision, or are sighted. *Journal of Visual Impairment and Blindness, 93,* 691–703.

Conway, L. (2007, April 5). Drop the Barbie: Ken Zucker's reparatist treatment of gender-variant children. *Trans News Updates.* Retrieved from ai.eecs.umich.edu/people/conway/TS/News/Drop%20the %20Barbie.htm

Conyers, C., Miltenberger, R., Maki, A., Barenz, R., Jurgens, M., Sailer, A., Haugen, M., & Kopp, B. (2004). A comparison of response cost and differential reinforcement of other behaviors to reduce disruptive behavior in a preschool classroom. *Journal of Applied Behavior Analysis, 37,* 411–415.

Cookston, J. T., Braver, S. L., Griffin, W. A., De Lusé, S. R., & Miles, J. C. (2006). Effects of the Dads for Life intervention on interparental conflict and coparenting in the two years after divorce. *Family Process, 46,* 123–137.

Cooper, R., & Huh, C. R. (2008). Improving academic possibilities of students of color during the middle school to high school transition: Conceptual and strategic considerations in a U.S. context. In J. K. Asamen, M. L. Ellis, & G. L. Berry (Eds.), *Sage handbook of child development, multiculturalism, and media* (pp. 143–162). Thousand Oaks, CA: Sage.

Coplan, R. J., & Arbeau, K. A. (2008). The stresses of a "brave new world": Shyness and school adjustment in kindergarten. *Journal of Research in Childhood Education, 22,* 377–389.

Coplan, R. J., & Armer, M. (2007). A "multitude" of solitude: A closer look at social withdrawal and nonsocial play in early childhood. *Child Development Perspectives, 1,* 26–32.

Coplan, R. J., Gavinsky-Molina, M. H., Lagace-Seguin, D., & Wichmann, C. (2001). When girls versus boys play alone: Nonsocial play and adjustment in kindergarten. *Developmental Psychology, 37,* 464–474.

Coplan, R. J., Prakash, K., O'Neil, K., & Armer, M. (2004). Do you "want" to play? Distinguishing between conflicted shyness and social disinterest in early childhood. *Developmental Psychology, 40,* 244–258.

Copple, C., & Bredekamp, S. (2009). *Developmentally appropriate practice in early childhood programs* (3rd ed.). Washington, DC: National Association for the Education of Young Children.

Corapci, F., Radan, A. E., & Lozoff, B. (2006). Iron deficiency in infancy and mother–child interaction at 5 years. *Journal of Developmental and Behavioral Pediatrics, 27,* 371–378.

Corenblum, B. (2003). What children remember about ingroup and outgroup peers: Effects of stereotypes on children's processing of information about group members. *Journal of Experimental Child Psychology, 86,* 32–66.

Cornish, A. M., McMahon, C. A., Ungerer, J. A., Barnett, B., Kowalenko, N., & Tennant, C. (2005). Postnatal depression and infant cognitive and motor development in the second postnatal year: The impact of depression chronicity and infant gender. *Infant Behavior and Development, 28,* 407–417.

Cornwell, A. C., & Feigenbaum, P. (2006). Sleep biological rhythms in normal infants and those at high risk for SIDS. *Chronobiology International, 23,* 935–961.

Correa-Chavez, M., Rogoff, B., & Arauz, R. M. (2005). Cultural patterns in attending to two events at once. *Child Development, 76,* 664–678.

Cosden, M., Peerson, S., & Elliott, K. (1997). Effects of prenatal drug exposure on birth outcomes and early child development. *Journal of Drug Issues, 27,* 525–539.

Côté, S. M., Vaillancourt, T., Barker, E. D., Nagin, D., & Tremblay, R. E. (2007). The joint development of physical and indirect aggression: Predictors of continuity and change during childhood. *Development and Psychopathology, 19,* 37–55.

Coulton, C. J., Crampton, D. S., Irwin, M., Spilsbury, J. C., & Korbin, J. E. (2007). How neighborhoods influence child maltreatment: A review of the literature and alternative pathways. *Child Abuse and Neglect, 31,* 1117–1142.

Courage, M. L., & Howe, M. L. (1998). The ebb and flow of infant attentional preferences: Evidence for long-term recognition memory in 3-month-olds. *Journal of Experimental Child Psychology, 18,* 98–106.

Courage, M. L., & Howe, M. L. (2002). From infant to child: The dynamics of cognitive change in the second year of life. *Psychological Bulletin, 128,* 250–277.

Courchesne, E., Carper, R., & Akshoomoff, N. (2003). Evidence of brain overgrowth in the first year of life in autism. *Journal of the American Medical Association, 290,* 337–344.

Covington, C. Y., Nordstrom-Klee, B., Ager, J., Sokol, R., & Delaney-Black, V. (2002). Birth to age 7 growth of children prenatally exposed to drugs: A prospective cohort study. *Neurotoxicology and Teratology, 24,* 489–496.

Cowan, C. P., & Cowan, P. A. (1997). Working with couples during stressful transitions. In S. Dreman (Ed.), *The family on the threshold of the 21st century* (pp. 17–47). Mahwah, NJ: Erlbaum.

Cowan, C. P., & Cowan, P. A. (2000). *When partners become parents.* Mahwah, NJ: Erlbaum.

Cowan, P. A., & Cowan, C. P. (2004). From family relationships to peer rejection to antisocial behavior in middle childhood. In J. B. Kupersmidt & K. A. Dodge (Eds.), *Children's peer relations: From development to intervention* (pp. 159–177). Washington, DC: American Psychological Association.

Cox, M., & Littlejohn, K. (1995). Children's use of converging obliques in their perspective drawings. *Educational Psychology, 15,* 127–139.

Cox, M. J., Owen, M. T., Henderson, V. K., & Margand, N. A. (1992). Prediction of infant–father and infant–mother attachment. *Developmental Psychology, 28,* 474–483.

Cox, S. M., Hopkins, J., & Hans, S. L. (2000). Attachment in preterm infants and their mothers: Neonatal risk status and maternal representations. *Infant Mental Health Journal, 21,* 464–480.

Coyle, T. R., & Bjorklund, D. F. (1997). Age differences in, and consequences of, multiple- and variable-strategy use on a multitrial sort-recall task. *Developmental Psychology, 33,* 372–380.

Crago, M. B., Annahatak, B., & Ningiuruvik, L. (1993). Changing patterns of language socialization in Inuit homes. *Anthropology and Education Quarterly, 24,* 205–223.

Craig, C. M., & Lee, D. N. (1999). Neonatal control of sucking pressure: Evidence for an intrinsic τ-guide. *Experimental Brain Research, 124,* 371–382.

Craig, W. M., Pepler, D., & Atlas, R. (2000). Observations of bullying in the playground and in the classroom. *School Psychology International, 21,* 22–36.

Crain, W. (2005). *Theories of development* (5th ed.). Upper Saddle River, NJ: Prentice-Hall.

Crair, M. C., Gillespie, D. C., & Stryker, M. P. (1998). The role of visual experience in the development of columns in the cat visual cortex. *Science, 279,* 566–570.

Cratty, B. J. (1986). *Perceptual and motor development in infants and children* (3rd ed.). Englewood Cliffs, NJ: Prentice-Hall.

Crawford, N. (2003, September). Understanding children's atypical gender behavior. *APA Monitor,* p. 40.

Creasey, G. L., Jarvis, P. A., & Berk, L. E. (1998). Play and social competence. In O. N. Saracho & B. Spodek (Eds.), *Multiple perspectives on play in early childhood education* (pp. 116–143). Albany: State University of New York Press.

Crick, N. R., Casas, J. F., & Nelson, D. A. (2002). Toward a more comprehensive understanding of peer maltreatment: Studies of relational victimization. *Current Directions in Psychological Science, 11,* 98–101.

Crick, N. R., & Dodge, K. A. (1994). A review and reformulation of social information-processing mechanisms in children's social adjustment. *Psychological Bulletin, 115,* 74–101.

Crick, N. R., & Nelson, D. A. (2002). Relational and physical victimization within friendships: Nobody told me there'd be friends like these. *Journal of Abnormal Child Psychology, 30,* 599–607.

Crick, N. R., Ostrov, J. M., Appleyard, K., Jansen, E., & Casas, J. F. (2004). Relational aggression in early childhood: You can't come to my birthday party unless. . . . In M. Putallaz & K. Bierman (Eds.), *Duke series in child development and public policy: Aggressive antisocial behavior and violence among girls: A developmental perspective* (Vol. 1, pp. 71–89). New York: Guilford.

Crick, N. R., Ostrov, J. M., & Werner, N. E. (2006). A longitudinal study of relational aggression, physical aggression, and social-psychological adjustment. *Journal of Abnormal Child Psychology, 34,* 131–142.

Critser, G. (2003). *Fat land.* Boston: Houghton Mifflin.

Crockenberg, S., & Leerkes, E. M. (2000). Infant social and emotional development in family context. In C. H. Zeanah, Jr. (Ed.), *Handbook of infant mental health* (2nd ed., pp. 60–90). New York: Guilford.

Crockenberg, S., & Leerkes, E. M. (2003a). Infant negative emotionality, caregiving, and family relationships. In A. C. Crouter & A. Booth (Eds.), *Children's influence on family dynamics* (pp. 57–78). Mahwah, NJ: Erlbaum

Crockenberg. S. C., & Leerkes, E. M. (2003b). Parental acceptance, postpartum depression, and maternal sensitivity: Mediating and moderating processes. *Journal of Family Psychology, 17,* 80–93.

Crockenberg, S. C., & Leerkes, E. M. (2004). Infant and maternal behaviors regulate infant reactivity to novelty at 6 months. *Developmental Psychology, 40,* 1123–1132.

Crosby, B., LeBourgeois, M. K., & Harsh, J. (2005). Racial differences in reported napping and nocturnal sleep in 2- to 8-year-old children. *Pediatrics, 115,* 225–232.

Crosno, R., Kirkpatrick, M., & Elder, G. H., Jr. (2004). Intergenerational bonding in school: The behavioral and contextual correlates of student–teacher relationships. *Sociology of Education, 77,* 60–81.

Crouch, J. L., Skowronski, J. J., Milner, J. S., & Harris, B. (2008). Parental responses to infant crying: The influence of child physical abuse risk and hostile priming. *Child Abuse and Neglect, 32,* 702–710.

Crouter, A. C., Helms-Erikson, H., Updegraff, K., & McHale, S. M. (1999). Conditions underlying parents' knowledge about children's daily lives in middle childhood: Between- and within-family comparisons. *Child Development, 70,* 246–259.

Crouter, A. C., Whiteman, S. D., McHale, S. M., & Osgood, D. W. (2007). Development of gender attitude traditionality across middle childhood and adolescence. *Child Development, 78,* 911–926.

Culnane, M., Fowler, M. G., Lee, S. S., McSherry, G., Brady, M., & O'Donnell, K. (1999). Lack of long-term effects of in utero exposure to zidovudine among uninfected children born to HIV-infected women. *Journal of the American Medical Association, 281,* 151–157.

Cummings, E. M., Goeke-Morey, M. C., & Papp, L. M. (2004). Everyday marital conflict and child aggression. *Journal of Abnormal Child Psychology, 32,* 191–202.

Cummings, E. M., & Merrilees, C. E. (2010). Identifying the dynamic processes underlying links between marital conflict and child adjustment. In M. S. Schulz, M. K. Pruett, P. K. Kerig, & R. D. Parke (Eds.), *Strengthening couple relationships for optimal child development* (pp. 27–40). Washington, DC: American Psychological Association.

Cunningham, A. E., & Stanovich, K. E. (1998). What reading does for the mind. *American Educator,* Spring/Summer, 8–15.

Curby, T. W., LoCasale-Crouch, J., Konold, T. R., Pianta, R. C., Howes, C., Burchinal, M., et al. (2009). The relations of observed pre-K classroom quality profiles to children's achievement and social competence. *Early Education and Development, 20,* 346–372.

Curran, M., Hazen, N., Jacobvitz, D., & Feldman, A. (2005). Representations of early family relationships predict marital maintenance during the transition to parenthood. *Journal of Family Psychology, 19,* 189–197.

Cutter, W. J., Daly, E. M., Robertson, D. M. W., Chitnis, X. A., van Amelsvoort, T. A. M. J., Simmons, A., et al. (2006). Influence of X chromosome and hormones on human brain development: A magnetic resonance imaging and proton magnetic resonance spectroscopy study of Turner syndrome. *Biological Psychiatry, 59,* 273–283.

D

Dabrowska, E. (2000). From formula to schema: The acquisition of English questions. *Cognitive Linguistics, 11,* 1–20.

Dahl, R. E., Scher, M. S., Williamson, D. E., Robles, N., & Day, N. (1995). A longitudinal study of prenatal marijuana use: Effects on sleep and arousal at age 3 years. *Archives of Pediatric and Adolescent Medicine, 149,* 145–150.

Dal Santo, J. A., Goodman, R. M., Glik, D., & Jackson, K. (2004). Childhood unintentional injuries: Factors predicting injury risk among preschoolers. *Journal of Pediatric Psychology, 29,* 273–283.

Dales, L., Hammer, S. J., & Smith, N. J. (2001). Time trends in autism and MMR immunization coverage in California. *Journal of the American Medical Association, 285,* 1183–1185.

Damashek, A., & Peterson, L. (2002). Unintentional injury prevention efforts for young children: Levels, methods, types, and targets. *Developmental and Behavioral Pediatrics, 23,* 443–455.

Damon, W. (1988). *The moral child.* New York: Free Press.

Damon, W. (1995). *Greater expectations: Overcoming the culture of indulgence in America's homes and schools.* New York: Free Press.

Damon, W., & Hart, D. (1988). *Self-understanding in childhood and adolescence.* New York: Cambridge University Press.

Daniels, E., & Leaper, C. (2006). A longitudinal investigation of sport participation, peer acceptance, and self-esteem among adolescent girls and boys. *Sex Roles, 55,* 875–880.

Daniels, P., Noe, G. F, & Mayberry, R. (2006). Barriers to prenatal care among Black women of low socioeconomic status. *American Journal of Health Behavior, 30,* 188–198.

Dannemiller, J. L., & Stephens, B. R. (1988). A critical test of infant pattern preference models. *Child Development, 59,* 210–216.

Dapretto, M., & Bjork, E. L. (2000). The development of word retrieval abilities in the second year and its relation to early vocabulary growth. *Child Development, 71,* 635–648.

Darling, N., & Steinberg, L. (1997). Community influences on adolescent achievement and deviance. In J. Brooks-Gunn, G. Duncan, & L. Aber (Eds.), *Neighborhood poverty: Context and consequences for children: Conceptual, ethological, and policy approaches to studying neighborhoods* (Vol. 2, pp. 120–131). New York: Russell Sage Foundation.

Darling-Hammond, L. (2010). *The flat world and education: How America's commitment to equity will determine our future.* New York: Teachers College Press.

Das, D. A., Grimmer, D. A., Sparnon, A. L., McRae, S. E., & Thomas, B. H. (2005). The efficacy of playing a virtual reality game in modulating pain for children with acute burn injuries: A randomized controlled trial. *BMC Pediatrics, 5*(1), 1–10.

Davidov, M., & Grusec, J. E. (2006). Untangling the links of parental responsiveness to distress and warmth to child outcomes. *Child Development, 77,* 44–58.

Davidson, R. J. (1994). Asymmetric brain function, affective style, and psychopathology: The role of early experience and plasticity. *Development and Psychopathology, 6,* 741–758.

Davies, P. T., & Lindsay, L. L. (2004). Interparental conflict and adolescent adjustment: Why does gender moderate early adolescent vulnerability? *Journal of Family Psychology, 18,* 160–170.

Davis, K. F., Parker, K. P., & Montgomery, G. L. (2004). Sleep in infants and young children. Part 1: Normal sleep. *Journal of Pediatric Health Care, 18,* 65–71.

Dawley, K., Loch, J., & Bindrich, I. (2007). The Nurse–Family Partnership. *American Journal of Nursing, 107,* 60–67.

De Corte, E., & Verschaffel, L. (2006). Mathematical thinking and learning. In K. A. Renninger & I. E. Sigel (Eds.), *Handbook of child psychology: Vol. 4. Child psychology in practice* (6th ed., pp. 103–152). Hoboken, NJ: Wiley.

de Haan, M., & Johnson, M. H. (2003). Mechanisms and theories of brain development. In M. de Haan &

M. H. Johnson (Eds.), *The cognitive neuroscience of development* (pp. 1–18). Hove, UK: Psychology Press.

de Haan, M., & Matheson, A. (2009). The development and neural bases of processing emotion in faces and voices. In M. de Haan & M. R. Gunnar (Eds.), *Handbook of developmental social science* (pp. 107–121). New York: Guilford.

De Lisi, R., & Gallagher, A. M. (1991). Understanding gender stability and constancy in Argentinean children. *Merrill-Palmer Quarterly, 37,* 483–502.

de Pree-Geerlings, B., de Pree, I. M., & Bulk-Bunschoten, A. M. (2001). 1901–2001: 100 years of physicians of infant and toddler welfare centers in the Netherlands. *Netherlands Tijdschrift Voor Geneeskunde, 145,* 2461–2465.

de Ribaupierre, A., & Lecerf, T. (2006). Relationships between working memory and intelligence from a developmental perspective: Convergent evidence from a neo-Piagetian and a psychometric approach. *European Journal of Cognitive Psychology, 18,* 109–137.

de Rosnay, M., & Hughes, C. (2006). Conversation and theory of mind: Do children talk their way to socio-cognitive understanding? *British Journal of Developmental Psychology, 24,* 7–37.

De Schipper, J. C., Tavecchio, L. W. C., van IJzendoorn, M. H., & van Zeijl, J. (2004). Goodness-of-fit in center day care: Relations of temperament, stability, and quality of care with the child's adjustment. *Early Childhood Research Quarterly, 19,* 257–272.

De Schipper, J. C., van IJzendoorn, M. H., & Tavecchio, L. W. C. (2004). Stability in center day care: Relations with children's well-being and problem behavior in day care. *Social Development, 13,* 531–550.

De Souza, E., Alberman, E., & Morris, J. K. (2009). Down syndrome and paternal age, a new analysis of case-control data collected in the 1960s. *American Journal of Medical Genetics, 149A,* 1205–1208.

de Villiers, J. G., & de Villiers, P. A. (1973). A cross-sectional study of the acquisition of grammatical morphemes in child speech. *Journal of Psycholinguistic Research, 2,* 267–278.

de Villiers, J. G., & de Villiers, P. A. (2000). Linguistic determinism and the understanding of false beliefs. In P. Mitchell & K. J. Riggs (Eds.), *Children's reasoning and the mind* (pp. 87–99). Hove, U.K.: Psychology Press.

de Waal, F. B. M. (1993). Sex differences in chimpanzee (and human) behavior: A matter of social values? In M. Hechter, L. Nadel, & R. E. Michod (Eds.), *The origin of values* (pp. 285–303). New York: Aldine de Gruyter.

de Waal, F. B. M. (2001). *Tree of origin.* Cambridge, MA: Harvard University Press.

de Weerd, A. W., & van den Bossche, A. S. (2003). The development of sleep during the first months of life. *Sleep Medicine Reviews, 7,* 179–191.

de Weerth, C., & Buitelaar, J. K. (2005). Physiological stress reactivity in human pregnancy—a review. *Neuroscience and Biobehavioral Reviews, 29,* 295–312.

de Winter, M., Balledux, M., & de Mare, J. (1997). A critical evaluation of Dutch preventive child health care. *Child: Care, Health and Development, 23,* 437–446.

De Wolff, M. S., & van IJzendoorn, M. H. (1997). Sensitivity and attachment: A meta-analysis on parental antecedents of infant attachment. *Child Development, 68,* 571–591.

Deafness Research Foundation. (2010). *Hearing statistics.* Retrieved from www.drf.org/statistics

Deák, G. O. (2000). Hunting the fox of word learning: Why "constraints" fail to capture it. *Developmental Review, 20,* 29–80.

Deák, G. O., Ray, S. D., & Brenneman, K. (2003). Children's perseverative appearance–reality errors are related to emerging language skills. *Child Development, 74,* 944–964.

Deák, G. O., Yen, L., & Pettit, J. (2001). By any other name: When will preschoolers produce several labels for a reference? *Journal of Child Language, 28,* 787–804.

Dearing, E. (2008). The psychological costs of growing up poor. *Annals of the New York Academy of Sciences, 1136,* 324–332.

Dearing, E., Wimer, C., Simpkins, S. D., Lund, T., Bouffard, S. M., Caronongan, P., & Kreider, H. (2009). Do neighborhood and home contexts help explain why low-income children miss opportunities to participate in activities outside of school? *Developmental Psychology, 45*, 1545–1562.

Deary, I. J. (2001). *g* and cognitive elements of information progressing: An agnostic view. In R. J. Sternberg & E. L. Grigorenko (Eds.), *The general factor of intelligence: How general is it?* (pp. 447–479). Mahwah, NJ: Erlbaum.

Deary, I. J., Strand, S., Smith, P., & Fernandes, C. (2007). Intelligence and educational achievement. *Intelligence, 35*, 13–21.

Deater-Deckard, K., Lansford, J. E., Dodge, K. A., Pettit, G. S., & Bates, J. E. (2003). The development of attitudes about physical punishment: An 8-year longitudinal study. *Journal of Family Psychology, 17*, 351–360.

Deater-Deckard, K., Pike, A., Petrill, S. A., Cutting, A. L., Hughes, C., & O'Connor, T. G. (2001). Nonshared environmental processes in social-emotional development: An observational study of identical twin differences in the preschool period. *Developmental Science, 4*, F1–F6.

Deater-Deckard, K., Scarr, S., McCartney, K., & Eisenberg, M. (1994). Paternal separation anxiety: Relationships with parenting stress, child-rearing attitudes, and maternal anxieties. *Psychological Science, 5*, 341–346.

DeBerry, K. M., Scarr, S., & Weinberg, R. (1996). Family racial socialization and ecological competence: Longitudinal assessments of African-American transracial adoptees. *Child Development, 67*, 2375–2399.

DeBoer, T., Scott, L. S., & Nelson, C. A. (2007). Methods for acquiring and analyzing infant event-related potentials. In M. de Haan (Ed.), *Infant EEG and event-related potentials* (pp. 5–37). New York: Psychology Press.

DeCasper, A. J., & Spence, M. J. (1986). Prenatal maternal speech influences newborns' perception of speech sounds. *Infant Behavior and Development, 9*, 133–150.

DeCasper, A. J., & Spence, M. J. (1988). Prenatal maternal speech influences newborns' perception of speech sounds. In S. Chess, A. Thomas, & M. Hertzig (Eds.), *Annual progress in child psychiatry and child development, 1987* (pp. 5–25). Philadelphia: Brunner/Mazel.

Deković, M., & Buist, K. L. (2005). Multiple perspectives within the family: Family relationship patterns. *Journal of Family Issues, 26*, 467–490.

Delahunty, K. M., McKay, D. W., Noseworthy, D. E., & Storey, A. E. (2007). Prolactin responses to infant cues in men and women: Effects of parental experience and recent infant contact. *Hormones and Behavior, 51*, 213–220.

Delgado-Gaitan, C. (1994). Socializing young children in Mexican-American families: An intergenerational perspective. In P. Greenfield & R. Cocking (Eds.), *Cross-cultural roots of minority child development* (pp. 55–86). Hillsdale, NJ: Erlbaum.

DeLoache, J. S. (1987). Rapid change in symbolic functioning of very young children. *Science, 238*, 1556–1557.

DeLoache, J. S. (2000). Dual representation and children's use of scale models. *Child Development, 71*, 329–338.

DeLoache, J. S. (2002). The symbol-mindedness of young children. In W. Hartup & R. A. Weinberg (Eds.), *Minnesota symposia on child psychology* (Vol. 32, pp. 73–101). Mahwah, NJ: Erlbaum.

DeLoache, J. S., & Ganea, P. A. (2009). Symbol-based learning in infancy. In A. Woodward & A. Needham (Eds.), *Learning and the infant mind* (pp. 263–285). New York: Oxford University Press.

DeLoache, J. S., Pierroutsakos, S. L., Uttal, D. H., Rosengren, K. S., & Gottlieb, A. (1988). Grasping the nature of pictures. *Psychological Science, 9*, 205–210.

DeLoache, J. S., & Todd, C. M. (1988). Young children's use of spatial categorization as a mnemonic strategy. *Journal of Experimental Child Psychology, 46*, 1–20.

DeLoache, J. S., Uttal, D., & Rosengren, K. (2004). Scale errors offer evidence for a perception–action dissociation early in life. *Science, 304*, 1027–1029.

Delobel-Ayoub, M., Arnaud, C., White-Koning, M., Casper, C., Pierrat, V., Garel, M., et al. (2009). Behavioral problems and cognitive performance at 5 years of age after very preterm birth: The EPIPAGE Study. *Pediatrics, 123*, 1485–1492.

Deltondo, J., Por, I., Hu, W., Merchenthaler, I., Semeniken, K., Jojart, J., & Dudas, B. (2008). Associations between the human growth hormone-releasing hormone and neuropeptide-Y-immunoreactive systems in the human diencephalons: A possible morphological substrate of the impact of stress on growth. *Neuroscience, 153*, 1146–1152.

DeMarie, D., Miller, P. H., Ferron, J., & Cunningham, W. R. (2004). Path analysis tests of theoretical models of children's memory performance. *Journal of Cognition and Development, 5*, 461–492.

Demetriou, A., Christou, C., Spanoudis, G., & Platsidou, M. (2002). The development of mental processing: Efficiency, working memory, and thinking. *Monographs of the Society for Research in Child Development, 67*(1, Serial No. 268).

Dempster, F. N., & Corkill, A. J. (1999). Interference and inhibition in cognition and behavior: Unifying themes for educational psychology. *Educational Psychology Review, 11*, 1–88.

Denham, S. (1998). *Emotional development in young children.* New York: Guilford.

Denham, S. A. (2005). Emotional competence counts: Assessment as support for school readiness. In K. Hirsh-Pasek, A. Kochanoff, N. S. Newcombe, & J. de Villiers (Eds.), Using scientific knowledge to inform preschool assessment. *Social Policy Report of the Society for Research in Child Development, 19*(No.1), 12.

Denham, S. A. (2006). Emotional competence: Implications for social functioning. In J. L. Luby (Ed.), *Handbook of preschool mental health: Development, disorders, and treatment* (pp. 23–44). New York: Guilford.

Denham, S. A., & Burton, R. (2003). *Social and emotional prevention and intervention programming for preschoolers.* New York: Kluwer-Plenum.

Denham, S. A., & Kochanoff, A. T. (2002). Parental contributions to preschoolers' understanding of emotion. *Marriage and Family Review, 34*, 311–343.

Denissen, J. J. A., Zarrett, N. R., & Eccles, J. S. (2007). I like to do it, I'm able, and I know I am: Longitudinal couplings between domain-specific achievement, self-concept, and interest. *Child Development, 78*, 430–447.

Dennis, T., Bendersky, M., Ramsay, D., & Lewis, M. (2006). Reactivity and regulation in children prenatally exposed to cocaine. *Developmental Psychology, 42*, 688–697.

Dennis, W. (1960). Causes of retardation among institutionalized children: Iran. *Journal of Genetic Psychology, 96*, 47–59.

Deocampo, J. A. (2003, April). *Tools on TV: A new paradigm for testing dual representational understanding.* Poster presented at the biennial meeting of the Society for Research in Child Development, Tampa, FL.

Der, G., Batty, G. D., & Deary, I. J. (2006). Effect of breastfeeding on intelligence in children: Prospective study, sibling pairs analysis, and meta-analysis. *British Medical Journal, 333*, 945.

deRegnier, R. A. (2005). Neurophysiologic evaluation of early cognitive development in high-risk infants and toddlers. *Mental Retardation and Developmental Disabilities, 11*, 317–324.

deRegnier, R. A., Long, J. D., Georgieff, M. K., & Nelson, C. A. (2007). Using event-related potentials and brain development in infants of diabetic mothers. *Developmental Neuropsychology, 31*, 379–396.

DeRoche, K., & Welsh, M. (2008). Twenty-five years of research on neurocognitive outcomes in early-treated phenylketonuria: Intelligence and executive function. *Developmental Neuropsychology, 33*, 474–504.

Derom, C., Thiery, E., Vlietinck, R., Loos, R., & Derom, R. (1996). Handedness in twins according to

zygosity and chorion type: A preliminary report. *Behavior Genetics, 26*, 407–408.

DeRosier, M. E. (2007). Peer-rejected and bullied children: A safe schools initiative for elementary school students. In J. E. Zins, M. J. Elias, & C. A. Maher (Eds.), *Bullying, victimization, and peer harassment* (pp. 257–276). New York: Haworth.

DeRosier, M. E., & Thomas, J. M. (2003). Strengthening sociometric prediction: Scientific advances in the assessment of children's peer relations. *Child Development, 75*, 1379–1392.

Desrochers, S. (2008). From Piaget to specific Genevan developmental models. *Child Development Perspectives, 2*, 7–12.

Dessel, A. (2010). Prejudice in schools: Promotion of an inclusive culture and climate. *Education and Urban Society, 42*, 407–429.

deUngria, M., Rao, R., Wobken, J. D., Luciana, M., & Georgieff, M. K. (2000). Neurophysiologic evaluation of auditory recognition memory in healthy newborn infants and infants of diabetic mothers. *Journal of Pediatrics, 137*, 777–784.

Deutsch, F. M., Ruble, D. N., Fleming, A., Brooks-Gunn, J., & Stangor, C. (1988). Information-seeking and maternal self-definition during the transition to motherhood. *Journal of Personality and Social Psychology, 55*, 420–431.

Deutsch, W., & Pechmann, T. (1982). Social interaction and the development of definite descriptions. *Cognition, 11*, 159–184.

Devi, N. P. G., Shenbagvalli, R., Ramesh, K., & Rathinam, S. N. (2009). Rapid progression of HIV infection in infancy. *Indian Pediatrics, 46*, 53–56.

DeVries, R. (2001). Constructivist education in preschool and elementary school: The sociomoral atmosphere as the first educational goal. In S. L. Golbeck (Ed.), *Psychological perspectives on early childhood education* (pp. 153–180). Mahwah, NJ: Erlbaum.

Deynoot-Schaub, M. J. G., & Riksen-Walraven, J. M. (2006a). Peer contacts of 15-month-olds in childcare: Links with child temperament, parent–child interaction and quality of childcare. *Social Development 15*, 709–729.

Deynoot-Schaub, M. J. G., & Riksen-Walraven, J. M. (2006b). Peer interaction in child care centres at 15 and 23 months: Stability and links with children's socioemotional adjustment. *Infant Behavior and Development, 29*, 276–288.

Diamond, A. (2000). Close interrelation of motor development and cognitive development and of the cerebellum and prefrontal cortex. *Child Development, 71*, 44–56.

Diamond, A. (2004). Normal development of prefrontal cortex from birth to young adulthood: Cognitive functions, anatomy, and biochemistry. In D. T. Stuss & R. T. Knight (Eds.), *Principles of frontal lobe function* (pp. 466–503). New York: Oxford University Press.

Diamond, A. (2009). The interplay of biology and the environment broadly defined. *Developmental Psychology, 45*, 1–8.

Diamond, A., Barnett, W. S., Thomas, J., & Munro, S. (2007). Preschool program improves cognitive control. *Science, 318*, 1387–1388.

Diamond, A., Cruttenden, L., & Neiderman, D. (1994). AB with multiple wells: 1. Why are multiple wells sometimes easier than two wells? 2. Memory or memory + inhibition. *Developmental Psychology, 30*, 192–205.

Diamond, M., & Sigmundson, H. K. (1999). Sex reassignment at birth. In S. J. Ceci & W. M. Williams (Eds.), *The nature–nurture debate* (pp. 55–75). Malden, MA: Blackwell.

Dick, F., Dronkers, N. F., Pizzamiglio, L., Saygin, A. P., Small, S. L., Wilson, S. (2004). Language and the brain. In M. Tomasello & D. I Slobin (Eds.), *Beyond nature–nurture: Essays in honor of Elizabeth Bates* (pp. 237–260). Mahwah, NJ: Erlbaum.

Dickinson, D. K., & McCabe, A. (2001). Bringing it all together: The multiple origins, skills, and environmental supports of early literacy. *Learning Disabilities Research and Practice, 16*, 186–202.

Dickinson, D. K., McCabe, A., Anastasopoulos, L., Peisner-Feinberg, E. S., & Poe, M. D. (2003). The comprehensive language approach to early literacy: The interrelationships among vocabulary, phonological sensitivity, and print knowledge among preschool-age children. *Journal of Educational Psychology, 95,* 465–481.

Dickinson, D. K., & Sprague, K. E. (2001). The nature and impact of early childhood care environments on the language and early literacy development of children from low-income families. In S. B. Neuman & D. K. Dickinson (Eds.), *Handbook of early literacy research.* New York: Guilford.

Dick-Read, G. (1959). *Childbirth without fear.* New York: Harper & Brothers.

Dickson, K. L., Fogel, A., & Messinger, D. (1998). The development of emotion from a social process view. In M. F. Mascolo (Ed.), *What develops in emotional development?* (pp. 253–271). New York: Plenum.

Diehr, S. (2003). How effective is desmopressin for primary nocturnal enuresis? *Journal of Family Practice, 52,* 568–569.

Diener, M. L., Isabella, R., Behunin, M. G., & Wong, M. S. (2008). Attachment to mothers and fathers during middle childhood: Associations with child gender, grade, and competence. *Social Development, 17,* 84–101.

Dietrich, K. N., Ware, J. H., Salganik, M., Radcliffe, J., Rogan, W. J., & Rhoads, G. C. (2004). Effect of chelation therapy on the neuropsychological and behavioral development of lead-exposed children after school entry. *Pediatrics, 114,* 19–26.

Dietrich, K. N., Ris, M. D., Succop, P. A., Berger, O. G., & Bornschein, R. L. (2001). Early exposure to lead and juvenile delinquency. *Neurotoxicology and Teratology, 23,* 511–518.

Dildy, G. A., Jackson, G. M., Fowers, G. K., Oshiro, B. T., Varner, M. W., & Clark, S. L. (1996). Very advanced maternal age: Pregnancy after age 45. *American Journal of Obstetrics and Gynecology, 175,* 668–674.

DiMatteo, M. R., & Kahn, K. L. (1997). Psychosocial aspects of childbirth. In S. J. Gallant, G. P. Keita, & R. Royak-Schaler (Eds.), *Health care for women: Psychological, social, and behavioral influences* (pp. 175–186). Washington, DC: American Psychological Association.

Ding, Z. Y. (2008). National epidemiological survey on childhood obesity, 2006. *Chinese Journal of Pediatrics, 46,* 179–184.

DiPietro, J. A., Bornstein, M. H., Costigan, K. A., Pressman, E. K., Hahn, C.-S., & Painter, K. (2002). What does fetal movement predict about behavior during the first two years of life? *Developmental Psychobiology, 40,* 358–371.

DiPietro, J. A., Hodgson, D. M., Costigan, K. A., & Hilton, S. C. (1996). Fetal neurobehavioral development. *Child Development, 67,* 2553–2567.

DiPietro, J. A., Novak, M. F. S. X., Costigan, K. A., Atella, L. D., & Reusing, S. P. (2006). Maternal psychological distress during pregnancy in relation to child development at age two. *Child Development, 77,* 573–587.

Dirix, C. E. H., Nijhuis, J. G., Jongsma, H. W., & Hornstra, G. (2009). Aspects of fetal learning and memory. *Child Development, 80,* 1251–1258.

Dirks, J. (1982). The effect of a commercial game on children's Block Design scores on the WISC–R test. *Intelligence, 6,* 109–123.

Dishion, T. J., Andrews, D. W., & Crosby, L. (1995). Antisocial boys and their friends in early adolescence: Relationship characteristics, quality, and interactional processes. *Child Development, 66,* 139–151.

Dishion, T. J., Shaw, D., Connell, A., Gardner, F., Weaver, C., & Wilson, M. (2008). The family check-up with high-risk indigent families: Preventing problem behavior by increasing parents' positive behavior support in early childhood. *Child Development, 79,* 1395–1414.

Dix, T., Stewart, A. D., Gershoff, E. T., & Day, W. H. (2007). Autonomy and children's reactions to being controlled: Evidence that both compliance and defiance may be positive markers in early development. *Child Development, 78,* 1204–1221.

Dmitrieva, J., Steinberg, L., & Belsky, J. (2007). Child-care history, classroom composition and children's functioning in kindergarten. *Psychological Science, 18,* 1032–1039.

Dodd, V. L. (2005). Implications of kangaroo care for growth and development in preterm infants. *JOGNN, 34,* 218–232.

Dodge, K. A., Coie, J. D., & Lynam, D. (2006). Aggression and antisocial behavior in youth. In N. Eisenberg (Ed.), *Handbook of child psychology: Vol. 3. Social, emotional, and personality development* (6th ed., pp. 719–788). Hoboken, NJ: Wiley.

Dodge, K. A., Lansford, J. E., Burks, V. S., Bates, J. E., Pettit, G. S., Fontaine, R., & Price, J. M. (2003). Peer rejection and social information-processing factors in the development of aggressive behavior problems in children. *Child Development, 74,* 374–393.

Dodge, K. A., Lochman, J. E., Harnish, J. D., Bates, J. E., & Pettit, G. S. (1997). Reactive and proactive aggression in school children and psychiatrically impaired chronically assaultive youth. *Journal of Abnormal Psychology, 106,* 37–51.

Dodge, K. A., McLoyd, V. C., & Lansford, J. E. (2006). The cultural context of physically disciplining children. In V. C. McLoyd, N. E. Hill, & K A. Dodge (Eds.), *African-American family life: Ecological and cultural diversity* (pp. 245–263). New York: Guilford.

Dodge, K. A., Pettit, G. S., McClaskey, C. L., & Brown, M. M. (1986). Social competence in children. *Monographs of the Society for Research in Child Development, 51*(2, Serial No. 213).

Doherty, N. N., & Hepper, P. G. (2000). Habituation in fetuses of diabetic mothers. *Early Human Development, 59,* 85–93.

Dohnt, H., & Tiggemann, M. (2006). The contribution of peer and media influences to the development of body satisfaction and self-esteem in young girls: A prospective study. *Developmental Psychology, 42,* 929–936.

Dombrowski, K. J., Lantz, P. M., & Freed, G. L. (2004). Risk factors for delay in age-appropriate vaccination. *Public Health Reports, 119,* 144–155.

Dombrowski, S. C., Noonan, K., & Martin, R. P. (2007). Low birth weight and cognitive outcomes: Evidence for a gradient relationship in an urban, poor, African American birth cohort. *School Psychology Quarterly, 22,* 26–43.

Domitrovich, C. E., Cortes, R. C., & Greenberg, M. T. (2007). Improving young children's social and emotional competence: A randomized trial of the preschool "PATHS" curriculum. *The Journal of Primary Prevention, 28,* 67–91.

Dondi, M., Simion, F., & Caltran, G. (1999). Can newborns discriminate between their own cry and the cry of another newborn infant? *Developmental Psychology, 35,* 418–426.

Donnellan, M. B., Trzesniewski, K. H., Robins, R. W., Moffitt, T. E., & Caspi, A. (2005). Low self-esteem is related to aggression, antisocial behavior, and delinquency. *Psychological Science, 16,* 328–335.

Donnerstein, E., Slaby, R. G., & Eron, L. D. (1994). The mass media and youth aggression. In L. D. Eron, J. H. Gentry, & P. Schlegel (Eds.), *Reason to hope: A psychosocial perspective on violence and youth* (pp. 219–250). Washington, DC: American Psychological Association.

D'Onofrio, B. M., Turkheimer, E., Emery, R. E., Slutske, W. S., Heath, A. C., Madden, P. A., & Martin, N. G. (2006). A genetically informed study of the processes underlying the association between parental marital instability and offspring adjustment. *Developmental Psychology, 42,* 486–499.

Dorris, M. (1989). *The broken cord.* New York: Harper & Row.

dos Santos Silva, I., De Stavola, B. L., Hardy, R. J., Kuh, D. J., McCormack, V. A., & Wadsworth, M. E. J. (2004). Is the association of birth weight with premenopausal breast cancer risk mediated through childhood growth? *British Journal of Cancer, 91,* 519–524.

Doss, B. D., Rhoades, G. K., & Stanley, S. M. (2009). The effect of the transition to parenthood on relationship quality: An 8-year prospective study. *Journal of Personality and Social Psychology, 96,* 601–619.

Douglas, E. M. (2006). *Mending broken families: Social policies for divorced families.* Lanham, MD: Rowman & Littlefield.

Dowker, A. (2003). Younger children's estimates for addition: The zone of partial knowledge and understanding. In A. J. Baroody & A. Dowker (Eds.), *The development of arithmetic concepts and skills: Constructing adaptive expertise* (pp. 243–265). Mahwah, NJ: Erlbaum.

Downe, S., Finlayson, K., Walsh, D., & Lavender, T. (2009). "Weighing up and balancing out": A meta-synthesis of barriers to antenatal care for marginalized women in high-income countries. *BJOG, 116,* 518–529.

Dozier, M., Stovall, K. C., Albus, K. E., & Bates, B. (2001). Attachment for infants in foster care: The role of caregiver state of mind. *Child Development, 72,* 1467–1477.

Drabman, R. S., Cordua, G. D., Hammer, D., Jarvie, G. J., & Horton, W. (1979). Developmental trends in eating rates of normal and overweight preschool children. *Child Development, 50,* 211–216.

Drewett, R. F., Corbett, S. S., & Wright, C. M. (2006). Physical and emotional development, appetite and body image in adolescents who failed to thrive as infants. *Journal of Child Psychology and Psychiatry, 47,* 524–531.

Driscoll, M. C. (2007). Sickle cell disease. *Pediatrics in Review, 28,* 259–268.

Drotar, D., Witherspoon, D. O., Zebracki, K., & Peterson, C. C. (2006). *Psychological interventions in childhood chronic illness.* Washington, DC: American Psychological Association.

DuBois, D. L., Felner, R. D., Brand, S., & George, G. R. (1999). Profiles of self-esteem in early adolescence: Identification and investigation of adaptive correlates. *American Journal of Community Psychology, 27,* 899–932.

Duckworth, A. L., & Seligman, M. E. P. (2005). Self-discipline outdoes IQ in predicting academic performance of adolescents. *Psychological Science, 12,* 939–944.

Dueker, G. L., Modi, A., & Needham, A. (2003). 4.5-month-old infants' learning, retention and use of object boundary information. *Infant Behavior and Development, 26,* 588–605.

Duggan, A., McFarlane, E., Fuddy, L., Burrell, L., Higman, S. M., Windham, A., & Sia, C. (2004). Randomized trial of a statewide home visiting program: Impact in preventing child abuse and neglect. *Child Abuse and Neglect, 28,* 597–622.

Duncan, G. J., & Magnuson, K. A. (2003). Off with Hollingshead: Socioeconomic resources, parenting, and child development. In M. H. Bornstein & R. H. Bradley (Eds.), *Socioeconomic status, parenting, and child development* (pp. 83–106). Mahwah, NJ: Erlbaum.

Duncan, G. J., Dowsett, C. J., Claessens, A., Magnuson, K., Huston, A. C., Klebanov, P., et al. (2007). School readiness and later achievement. *Developmental Psychology, 43,* 1428–1446.

Duncan, S. R., Paterson, D. S., Hoffman, J. M., Mokler, D. J., et. al. (2010). Brainstem serotonergic deficiency in sudden infant death syndrome. *Journal of the American Medical Association, 303,* 430–437.

Dundek, L. H. (2006) Establishment of a Somali doula program at a large metropolitan hospital. *Journal of Perinatal and Neonatal Nursing, 20,* 128–137.

Dunham, Y., Baron, A. S., & Banaji, M. R. (2006). From American city to Japanese village: A cross-cultural investigation of implicit race attitudes. *Child Development, 77,* 1129–1520.

Dunifon, R., Kalil, A., & Danziger, S. K. (2003). Maternal work behavior under welfare reform: How does the transition from welfare to work affect child development? *Children and Youth Services Review, 25,* 55–82.

Dunn, J. (1989). Siblings and the development of social understanding in early childhood. In P. G. Zukow (Ed.), *Sibling interaction across cultures* (pp. 106–116). New York: Springer-Verlag.

Dunn, J. (1994). Temperament, siblings, and the development of relationships. In W. B. Carey & S. C.

McDevitt (Eds.), *Prevention and early intervention* (pp. 50–58). New York: Brunner/Mazel.

Dunn, J. (2002). The adjustment of children in stepfamilies: Lessons from community studies. *Child and Adolescent Mental Health, 7,* 154–161.

Dunn, J. (2004). Sibling relationships. In P. K. Smith & C. H. Hart (Eds.), *Handbook of childhood social development* (pp. 223–237). Malden, MA: Blackwell.

Dunn, J. (2005). Moral development in early childhood and social interaction in the family. In M. Killen & J. G. Smetana (Eds.), *Handbook of moral development* (pp. 331–350). Mahwah, NJ: Erlbaum.

Dunn, J., Brown, J. R., & Maguire, M. (1995). The development of children's moral sensibility: Individual differences and emotion understanding. *Developmental Psychology, 31,* 649–659.

Dunn, J., Cheng, H., O'Connor, T. G., & Bridges, L. (2004). Children's perspectives on their relationships with their nonresident fathers: Influences, outcomes and implications. *Journal of Child Psychology and Psychiatry, 45,* 553–566.

Dunn, J. R., Schaefer-McDaniel, N. J., & Ramsay, J. T. (2010). Neighborhood chaos and children's development: Question and contradictions. In G. W. Evans & T. D. Wachs (Eds.), *Chaos and its influence on children's development: An ecological perspective,* (pp. 173–189.). Washington, DC: American Psychological Association.

Dunphy-Lelii, S., & Wellman, H. M. (2004). Infants' understanding of occlusion of others' line of sight: Implications for an emerging theory of mind. *European Journal of Developmental Psychology, 1,* 49–66.

Durkin, M. S., Laraque, D., Lubman, I., & Barlow, B. (1999). Epidemiology and prevention of traffic injuries to urban children and adolescents. *Pediatrics, 103,* e74.

Durlach, J. (2004). New data on the importance of gestational Mg deficiency. *Journal of the American College of Nutrition, 23,* 694S-700S.

Durlak, J. A., & Weissberg, R. P. (2007). *The impact of after-school programs that promote personal and social skills.* Chicago: Collaborative for Academic, Social, and Emotional Learning.

Durston, S., & Conrad, K. (2007). Integrating genetic, psychopharmacological and neuroimaging studies: A converging methods approach to understanding the neurobiology of ADHD. *Developmental Review, 27,* 374–395.

Durston, S., & Casey, B. J. (2006). What have we learned about cognitive development from neuroimaging? *Neuropsychologia, 44,* 2149–2157.

Duszak, R. S. (2009). Congenital rubella syndrome—major review. *Optometry, 80,* 36–43.

Dweck, C. S. (2002). Messages that motivate: How praise molds students' beliefs, motivation, and performance (in surprising ways). In J. Aronson (Ed.), *Improving academic achievement: Impact of psychological factors on education* (pp. 37–60). San Diego, CA: Academic Press.

Dynarski, M., James-Burdumy, S., Moore, M., Rosenberg, L., Deke, J., & Mansfield, W. (2004). *When schools stay open late: The national evaluation of the 21st Century Community Learning Centers Program: New findings.* Washington DC: U.S. Department of Education.

Dzurova, D., & Pikhart, H. (2005). Down syndrome, paternal age and education: Comparison of California and the Czech Republic. *BMC Public Health, 5,* 69.

E

Ebeling, K. S., & Gelman, S. A. (1994). Children's use of context in interpreting "big" and "little." *Child Development, 65,* 1178–1192.

Eberhard, J., Stein, S., & Geissbuehler, V. (2005). Experience of pain and analgesia with water and land births. *Journal of Psychosomatic Obstetrics and Gynecology, 26,* 127–133.

Eccles, J. S., Jacobs, J., & Harold, R. D. (1990). Gender-role stereotypes, expectancy effects, and parents' role in the socialization of gender differences in self-perceptions and skill acquisition. *Journal of Social Issues, 46,* 183–201.

Eckerman, C. O., & Peterman, K. (2001). Peers and infant social/communicative development. In G. Bremner & A. Fogel (Eds.), *Blackwell handbook of infant development* (pp. 326–350). Malden, MA: Blackwell.

Eckerman, C. O., & Whitehead, H. (1999). How toddler peers generate coordinated action: A cross-cultural exploration. *Early Education and Development, 10,* 241–266.

Economic Policy Institute. (2010). *A broader, bolder approach to education.* Retrieved from www .boldapproach.org

Eder, R. A., & Mangelsdorf, S. C. (1997). The emotional basis of early personality development: Implications for the emergent self-concept. In R. Hogan, J. Johnson, & S. Briggs (Eds.), *Handbook of personality psychology* (pp. 209–240). San Diego, CA: Academic Press.

Edmondson, P. (2006). Deaf children's understanding of other people's thought processes. *Educational Psychology in Practice, 22,* 159–169.

Edwards, O. W., & Oakland, T. D. (2006). Factorial invariance of Woodcock-Johnson III scores for African Americans and Caucasian Americans. *Journal of Psychoeducational Assessment, 24,* 358–366.

Egeland, B., Jacobvitz, D., & Sroufe, L. A. (1988). Breaking the cycle of abuse. *Child Development, 59,* 1080–1088.

Ehri, L. C., & Roberts, T. (2006). The roots of learning to read and write: Acquisition of letters and phonemic awareness. In D. K. Dickinson & S. B. Neuman (Eds.), *Handbook of early literacy research* (Vol. 2, pp. 113–131). New York: Guilford.

Eichstedt, J. A., Serbin, L. A., Poulin-Dubois, D., & Sen, M. G. (2002). Of bears and men: Infants' knowledge of conventional and metaphorical gender stereotypes. *Infant Behavior and Development, 25,* 296–310.

Einspieler, C., Marschik, P. B., & Prechtl, H. F. R. (2008). Human motor behavior: Prenatal origin and early postnatal development. *Zeitschrift für Psychologie, 216,* 147–153.

Eisbach, A. O. (2004). Children's developing awareness of diversity in people's trains of thought. *Child Development, 75,* 1694–1707.

Eisenberg, N. (2003). Prosocial behavior, empathy, and sympathy. In M. H. Bornstein & L. Davidson (Eds.), *Well-being : Positive development across the life course* (pp. 253–265). Mahwah, NJ: Erlbaum.

Eisenberg, N. (2010). Empathy-related responding: Links with self-regulation, moral judgment, and moral behavior. In M. Mikulincer & P. R. Shaver (Eds.), *Prosocial motives, emotions, and behavior: The better angels of our nature* (pp. 129-148). Washington, D. C.: American Psychological Association.

Eisenberg, N., Eggum, N. D., & Edwards, A. (2010). Empathy-related responding and moral development. In W. F. Arsenio & E. A. Lemerise (Eds.), *Emotions, aggression, and morality in children: Bridging development and psychopathology* (pp. 115–135). Washington, DC: American Psychological Association.

Eisenberg, N., Fabes, R. A., Shepard, S. A., Murphy, B. C., Jones, S., & Guthrie, I. K. (1998). Contemporaneous and longitudinal prediction of children's sympathy from dispositional regulation and emotionality. *Developmental Psychology, 34,* 910–924.

Eisenberg, N., Fabes, R. A., & Spinrad, T. L. (2006). Prosocial development. In N. Eisenberg (Ed.), *Handbook of child psychology: Vol. 3. Social, emotional, and personality development* (6th ed., pp. 646–718). Hoboken, NJ: Wiley.

Eisenberg, N., Sadovsky, A., Spinrad, T. L., Fabes, R. A., Losoya, S., & Valiente, C. (2005). The relations of problem behavior status to children's negative emotionality, effortful control, and impulsivity: Concurrent relations and prediction of change. *Developmental Psychology, 41,* 193–211.

Eisenberg, N., Smith, C. L., Sadovsky, A., & Spinrad, T. L. (2004a). Effortful control: Relations with emotion regulation, adjustment, and socialization in childhood. In R. Baumeister & K. D. Vohs (Eds.), *Handbook of self-regulation : Research, theory, and applications* (pp. 259–282). New York: Guilford.

Eisenberg, N., & Spinrad, T. L. (2004). Emotion-related regulation: Sharpening the definition. *Child Development, 75,* 334–339.

Eisenberg, N., Spinrad, T., Fabes, R., Reiser, M., Cumberland, A., & Shepard, S. (2004b). The relations of effortful control and impulsivity to children's resiliency and adjustment. *Child Development, 75,* 25–46.

Ekeus, C., Christensson, K., & Hjern, A. (2003). Unintentional and violent injuries among preschool children of teenage mothers in Sweden: A national cohort study. *Journal of Epidemiology and Community Health, 58,* 680–685.

Ekman, P. (2003). *Emotions revealed.* New York: Times Books.

Ekman, P., & Friesen, W. (1972). Constants across culture in the face and emotion. *Journal of Personality and Social Psychology, 17,* 124–129.

Eliakim, A., Friedland, O., Kowen, G., Wolach, B., & Nemet, D. (2004). Parental obesity and higher pre-intervention BMI reduce the likelihood of a multidisciplinary childhood obesity program to succeed: A clinical observation. *Journal of Pediatric Endocrinology and Metabolism, 17,* 1055–1061.

Elias, C. L., & Berk, L. E. (2002). Self-regulation in young children: Is there a role for sociodramatic play? *Early Childhood Research Quarterly, 17,* 1–17.

Elias, M. J., Parker, S., & Rosenblatt, J. L. (2005). Building educational opportunity. In S. Goldstein & R. B. Brooks (Eds.), *Handbook of resilience in children* (pp. 315–336). New York: Kluwer Academic.

Elicker, J., Englund, M., & Sroufe, L. A. (1992). Predicting peer competence and peer relationships in childhood from early parent–child relationships. In R. D. Parke & G. W. Ladd (Eds.), *Family–peer relationships: Modes of linkage* (pp. 77–106). Hillsdale, NJ: Erlbaum.

Elliott, J. G. (1999). School refusal: Issues of conceptualization, assessment, and treatment. *Journal of Child Psychology and Psychiatry and Allied Disciplines, 40,* 1001–1012.

Ellis, A. E., & Oakes, L. M. (2006). Infants flexibly use different dimensions to categorize objects. *Developmental Psychology, 42,* 1000–1011.

Ellis, W. E., & Zarbatany, L. (2007). Explaining friendship formation and friendship stability: The role of children's and friends' aggression and victimization. *Merrill-Palmer Quarterly, 53,* 79–104.

Elman, J. L. (2001). Connectionism and language acquisition. In M. Tomasello & E. Bates (Eds.), *Language development* (pp. 295–306). Oxford, U.K.: Blackwell.

Else-Quest, N. M., Hyde, J. S., Goldsmith, H. H., & Van Hulle, C. A. (2006). Gender differences in temperament: A meta-analysis. *Psychological Bulletin, 132,* 33–72.

El-Sheikh, M., Cummings, E. M., & Reiter, S. (1996). Preschoolers' responses to ongoing interadult conflict: The role of prior exposure to resolved versus unresolved arguments. *Journal of Abnormal Child Psychology, 24,* 665–679.

Eltzschig, H. K., Lieberman, E. S., & Camann, W. R. (2003). Regional anesthesia and analgesia for labor and delivery. *New England Journal of Medicine, 384,* 319–332.

Eluvathingal, T. J., Chugani, H. T., Behen, M. E., Juhasz, C., Muzik, O., Maqbook, M., et al. (2006). Abnormal brain connectivity in children after early severe socioemotional deprivation: A diffusion tensor imaging study. *Pediatrics, 117,* 2093–2100.

Emery, R. E., Sbarra, D., & Grover, T. (2005). Divorce mediation: Research and reflections. *Family Court Review, 43,* 22–37.

Emory, E., Schlackman, L. J., & Fiano, K. (1996). Drug–hormone interactions on neurobehavioral responses in human neonates. *Infant Behavior and Development, 19,* 213–220.

Ennemoser, M., & Schneider, W. (2007). Relations of television viewing and reading: Findings from a 4-year longitudinal study. *Journal of Educational Psychology, 99,* 349–368.

Epstein, L. H., Roemmich, J. N., & Raynor, H. A. (2001). Behavioral therapy in the treatment of pediatric obesity. *Pediatric Clinics of North America, 48,* 981–983.

Epstein, L. H., Saelens, B. E., Myers, M. D., & Vito, D. (1997). Effects of decreasing sedentary behaviors on activity choice in obese children. *Health Psychology, 16,* 107–113.

Epstein, L. H., Saelens, B. E., & O'Brien, J. G. (1995). Effects of reinforcing increases in active versus decreases in sedentary behavior for obese children. *International Journal of Behavioral Medicine, 2,* 41–50.

Erath, S. A., Bierman, K. L., & the Conduct Problems Prevention Research Group. (2006). Aggressive marital conflict, maternal harsh punishment, and child aggressive-disruptive behavior: Evidence for direct and mediate relations. *Journal of Family Psychology, 20,* 217–226.

Erden, F., & Wolfgang, C. H. (2004). An exploration of the differences in prekindergarten, kindergarten, and first-grade teachers' beliefs related to discipline when dealing with male and female students. *Early Child Development and Care, 174,* 3–11.

Erickson, J. D., Patterson, J. M., Wall, M., & Neumark-Sztainer, D. (2005). Risk behaviors and emotional well-being in youth with chronic health conditions. *Children's Health Care, 34,* 181–192.

Erikson, E. H. (1950). *Childhood and society.* New York: Norton.

Ernst, M., Moolchan, E. T., & Robinson, M. L. (2001). Behavioral and neural consequences of prenatal exposure to nicotine. *Journal of the American Academy of Child and Adolescent Psychiatry, 40,* 630–641.

Espy, K. A., Molfese, V. J., & DiLalla, L. F. (2001). Effects of environmental measures on intelligence in young children: Growth curve modeling of longitudinal data. *Merrill-Palmer Quarterly, 47,* 42–73.

Estourgie-van Burk, G. F., Bartels, M., van Beijsterveldt, T. C., Delemarre-van de Waal, H. A., & Boomsma, D. I. (2006). Body size in five-year-old twins: Heritability and comparison to singleton standards. *Twin Research and Human Genetics, 9,* 646–655.

Evanoo, G. (2007). Infant crying: A clinical conundrum. *Journal of Pediatric Health Care, 21,* 333–338.

Evans, A. M. (2008). Growing pains: Contemporary knowledge and recommended practice. *Journal of Foot and Ankle Research, 1,* 4.

Evans, G. W. (2006). Child development and the physical environment. *Annual Review of Psychology, 57,* 424–451.

Evans, G. W., Maxwell, L. E., & Hart, B. (1999). Parental language and verbal responsiveness to children in crowded homes. *Developmental Psychology, 35,* 1020–1023.

Everman, D. B., & Cassidy, S. B. (2000). Genetics of childhood disorders: XII. Genomic imprinting: Breaking the rules. *Journal of the American Academy of Child and Adolescent Psychiatry, 38,* 386–389.

F

Fabes, R. A., Eisenberg, N., Hanish, L. D., & Spinrad, T. L. (2001). Preschoolers' spontaneous emotion vocabulary: Relations to likability. *Early Education and Development, 12,* 11–27.

Fabes, R. A., Eisenberg, N., McCormick, S. E., & Wilson, M. S. (1988). Preschoolers' attributions of the situational determinants of others' naturally occurring emotions. *Developmental Psychology, 24,* 376–385.

Fabes, R. A., Martin, C. L., & Hanish, L. D. (2003). Young children's play qualities in same-, other-, and mixed-sex peer groups. *Child Development, 74,* 921–932.

Fagan, J. F., & Holland, C. R. (2007). Racial equality in intelligence: Predictions from a theory of intelligence as processing. *Intelligence, 35,* 319–334.

Fagan, J. F., Holland, C. R., & Wheeler, K. (2007). The prediction, from infancy, of adult IQ and achievement. *Intelligence, 35,* 225–231.

Fagan, J. F., III. (1973). Infants' delayed recognition memory and forgetting. *Journal of Experimental Child Psychology, 16,* 424–450.

Fagard, J., & Pezé, A. (1997). Age changes in interlimb coupling and the development of bimanual coordination. *Journal of Motor Behavior, 29,* 199–208.

Fagard, J., Spelke, E., & von Hofsten, C. (2009). Reaching and grasping a moving object in 6-, 8-, and 10-month-old infants: Laterality and performance. *Infant Behavior and Development, 32,* 137–146.

Fagot, B. I. (1984). The child's expectations of differences in adult male and female interactions. *Sex Roles, 11,* 593–600.

Fagot, B. I. (1985). Changes in thinking about early sex role development. *Developmental Review, 5,* 83–98.

Fagot, B. I., & Hagan, R. I. (1991). Observations of parent reactions to sex-stereotyped behaviors: Age and sex effects. *Child Development, 62,* 617–628.

Fagot, B. I., & Leinbach, M. D. (1989). The young child's gender schema: Environmental input, internal organization. *Child Development, 60,* 663–672.

Fahrmeier, E. D. (1978). The development of concrete operations among the Hausa. *Journal of Cross-Cultural Psychology, 9,* 23–44.

Falbo, T. (1992). Social norms and the one-child family: Clinical and policy implications. In F. Boer & J. Dunn (Eds.), *Children's sibling relationships* (pp. 71–82). Hillsdale, NJ: Erlbaum.

Falbo, T., & Poston, D. L., Jr. (1993). The academic, personality, and physical outcomes of only children in China. *Child Development, 64,* 18–35.

Falbo, T., Poston, D. L., Jr., Triscari, R. S., & Zhang, X. (1997). Self-enhancing illusions among Chinese schoolchildren. *Journal of Cross-Cultural Psychology, 28,* 172–191.

Falk, D. (2005). Brain lateralization in primates and its evolution in hominids. *American Journal of Physical Anthropology, 30,* 107–125.

Fantz, R. L. (1961, May). The origin of form perception. *Scientific American, 204*(5), 66–72.

Faraone, S. V. (2008). Statistical and molecular genetic approaches to developmental psychopathology: The pathway forward. In J. J. Hudziak (Ed.), *Developmental psychology and wellness: Genetic and environmental influences* (pp. 245–265). Washington, DC: American Psychiatric Publishing.

Faraone, S. V., & Mick, E. (2010). Molecular genetics of attention deficit hyperactivity disorder. *Psychiatric Clinics of North America, 33,* 159–180.

Farmer, T. W., Leung, M., Pearl, R., Rodkin, P. C., Cadwallader, T. W., & Van Acker, R. (2002). Deviant or diverse peer groups? The peer affiliations of aggressive elementary students. *Journal of Educational Psychology, 94,* 611–620.

Farr, R. H., Forssell, S. L., & Patterson, C. J. (2010). Parenting and child development in adoptive families: Does parental sexual orientation matter? *Applied Developmental Science, 14,* 164–178.

Farrant, K., & Reese, E. (2000). Maternal style and children's participation in reminiscing: Stepping stones in children's autobiographical memory development. *Journal of Cognition and Development, 1,* 193–225.

Farroni, T., Csibra, G., Simion, F., & Johnson, M. H. (2002). Eye contact detection in humans from birth. *Proceedings of the National Academy of Sciences, 99,* 9602–9605.

Farroni, T., Massaccesi, S., Menon, E., & Johnson, M. H. (2007). Direct gaze modulates face recognition in young infants. *Cognition, 102,* 396–404.

Farver, J. M., & Branstetter, W. H. (1994). Preschoolers' prosocial responses to their peers' distress. *Developmental Psychology, 30,* 334–341.

Farver, J. M., Kim, Y. K., & Lee, Y. (1995). Cultural differences in Korean- and Anglo-American preschoolers' social interaction and play behaviors. *Child Development, 66,* 1099–1099.

Farver, J. M., & Wimbarti, S. (1995). Indonesian children's play with their mothers and older siblings. *Child Development, 66,* 1493–1503.

Fasolo, M., Majorano, M., & D'Odorico, L. (2008). Babbling and first words in children with slow expressive development. *Clinical Linguistics and Phonetics, 22,* 83–94.

Fattibene, P., Mazzei, F., Nuccetelli, C., & Risica, S. (1999). Prenatal exposure to ionizing radiation: Sources, effects, and regulatory aspects. *Acta Paediatrica, 88,* 693–702.

Fearon, R. P., Bakermans-Kranenburg, M. J., Lapsley, A., & Roisman, G. I. (2010). The significance of insecure attachment and disorganization in the development of children's externalizing behavior: A meta-analytic study. *Child Development, 81,* 435–456.

Federal Interagency Forum on Child and Family Statistics. (2008). *America's children: Key national indicators of well-being, 2008.* Retrieved from www .childstats.gov/americaschildren/tables.asp

Federal Interagency Forum on Child and Family Statistics. (2009). *America's children: Key national indicators of well-being, 2009.* Washington, DC: U.S. Government Printing Office.

Federico, M. J., & Liu, A. H. (2003). Overcoming childhood asthma disparities of the inner-city poor. *Pediatric Clinics of North America, 50,* 655–675.

Feeney, J. A., Hohaus, L., Noller, P., & Alexander, R. P. (2001). *Becoming parents: Exploring the bonds between mothers, fathers, and their infants.* New York: Cambridge University Press.

Feiring, C., Taska, L., & Lewis, M. (1999). Age and gender differences in children's and adolescents' adaptation to sexual abuse. *Child Abuse and Neglect, 23,* 115–128.

Feldkämper, M., & Schaeffel, F. (2003). Interactions of genes and environment in myopia. *Developmental Ophthalmology, 37,* 34–49.

Feldman, D. H. (2004). Piaget's stages: The unfinished symphony of cognitive development. *New Ideas in Psychology, 3,* 175–231.

Feldman, R. (2003). Infant–mother and infant–father synchrony: The coregulation of positive arousal. *Infant Mental Health Journal, 24,* 1–23.

Feldman, R. (2006). From biological rhythms to social rhythms: Physiological precursors of mother–infant synchrony. *Developmental Psychology, 42,* 175–188.

Feldman, R. (2007a). Maternal–infant contact and child development: Insights from the kangaroo intervention. In L. L'Abate (Ed.), *Low-cost approaches to promote physical and mental health: Theory, research, and practice* (pp. 323–351). New York: Springer.

Feldman, R., & Eidelman, A. I. (2003). Skin-to-skin contact (kangaroo care) accelerates autonomic and neurobehavioral maturation in preterm infants. *Developmental Medicine and Child Neurology, 45,* 274–281.

Feldman, R. (2007b). Maternal versus child risk and the development of parent–child and family relationships in five high-risk populations. *Development and Psychopathology, 19,* 293–312.

Feldman, R., Eidelman, A. I., & Rotenberg, N. (2004). Parenting stress, infant emotion regulation, maternal sensitivity, and the cognitive development of triplets: A model for parent and child influences in a unique ecology. *Child Development, 75,* 1774–1791.

Feldman, R., Eidelman, A., Sirota, L., & Weller, A. (2002). Comparison of skin-to-skin (kangaroo) and traditional care: Parenting outcomes and preterm infant development. *Pediatrics, 110,* 16–26.

Feldman, R., Greenbaum, C. W., & Yirmiya, N. (1999). Mother–infant affect synchrony as an antecedent of the emergence of self-control. *Developmental Psychology, 35,* 223–231.

Feldman, R., & Klein, P. S. (2003). Toddlers' self-regulated compliance to mothers, caregivers, and fathers: Implications for theories of socialization. *Developmental Psychology, 39,* 680–692.

Feldman, R., Sussman, A. L., & Zigler, E. (2004). Parental leave and work adaptation at the transition to parenthood: Individual, marital, and social correlates. *Journal of Applied Developmental Psychology, 25,* 459–479.

Feldman, R., Weller, A., Sirota, L., & Eidelman, A. I. (2003). Testing a family intervention hypothesis: The contribution of mother–infant skin-to-skin contact (kangaroo care) to family interaction, proximity, and touch. *Journal of Family Psychology, 17,* 94–107.

Feng, Q. (2005). Postnatal consequences of prenatal cocaine exposure and myocardial apoptosis: Does cocaine in utero imperil the adult heart? *British Journal of Pharmacology, 144,* 887–888.

Fenson, L., Dale, P. S., Reznick, J. S., Bates, E., Thal, D. J., & Pethick, S. J. (1994). Variability in early communicative development. *Monographs of the Society for Research in Child Development, 59*(5, Serial No. 242).

Ferguson, T. J., Stegge, H., & Damhuis, I. (1991). Children's understanding of guilt and shame. *Child Development, 62,* 827–839.

Fergusson, D. M., & Horwood, J. (2003). Resilience to childhood adversity: Results of a 21-year study. In S. S. Luthar (Ed.), *Resilience and vulnerability* (pp. 130–155). New York: Cambridge University Press.

Fergusson, D. M., & Woodward, L. J. (1999). Breast-feeding and later psychosocial adjustment. *Paediatric and Perinatal Epidemiology, 13,* 144–157.

Fernald, A., & Morikawa, H. (1993). Common themes and cultural variations in Japanese and American mothers' speech to infants. *Child Development, 64,* 637–656.

Fernald, A., Perfors, A., & Marchman, V. A. (2006). Picking up speed in understanding: Speech processing efficiency and vocabulary growth across the 2nd year. *Developmental Psychology, 42,* 98–116.

Fernald, A., Taeschner, T., Dunn, J., Papousek, M., Boysson-Bardies, B., & Fukui, I. (1989). A cross-language study of prosodic modifications in mothers' and fathers' speech to preverbal infants. *Journal of Child Language, 16,* 477–502.

Fernald, L. C., & Grantham-McGregor, S. M. (1998). Stress response in school-age children who have been growth-retarded since early childhood. *American Journal of Clinical Nutrition, 68,* 691–698.

Fernyhough, C., & Fradley, E. (2005). Private speech on an executive task: Relations with task difficulty and task performance. *Cognitive Development, 20,* 103–120.

Ficca, G., Fagioli, I., Giganti, F., & Salzarulo, P. (1999). Spontaneous awakenings from sleep in the first year of life. *Early Human Development, 55,* 219–228.

Field, T. M. (1998). Massage therapy effects. *American Psychologist, 53,* 1270–1281.

Field, T. (2001). Massage therapy facilitates weight gain in preterm infants. *Current Directions in Psychological Science, 10,* 51–54.

Field, T., Diego, M., Hernandez-Reif, M., Figueiredo, B., Schanberg, S., & Kuhn, C. (2007). Sleep disturbances in depressed pregnant women and their newborns. *Infant Behavior and Development, 30,* 127–133.

Field, T., Hernandez-Reif, M., & Freedman, J. (2004) Stimulation programs for preterm infants. *Social Policy Report of the Society for Research in Child Development, 18*(1).

Field, T, Hernandez-Reif, M., Feijo, L., & Freedman, J. (2006). Prenatal, perinatal and neonatal stimulation: A survey of neonatal nurseries. *Infant Behavior and Development, 29,* 24–31.

Fiese, B. H., & Schwartz, M. (2008). Reclaiming the family table: Mealtimes and child health and wellbeing. *Social Policy Report of the Society for Research in Child Development, 22*(4), 3–18.

Findlay, L. C., & Coplan, R. J. (2008). Come out and play: Shyness in childhood and the benefits of organized sports participation. *Canadian Journal of Behavioural Science, 40,* 153–161.

Finger, B., Hans, S. L., Bernstein, V. J., & Cox, S. M. (2009). Parent relationship quality and infant–mother attachment. *Attachment and Human Development, 11,* 285–306.

Finkelstein, E. A., Trogdon, J. G., Cohen, J. W., & Dietz, W. (2009). Annual medical spending attributable to obesity: Payer- and service-specific estimates. *Health Affairs, 28,* w822–w831.

Finn, J. D., Gerber, S. B., & Boyd-Zaharias, J. (2005). Small classes in the early grades, academic achievement, and graduating from high school. *Journal of Educational Psychology, 97,* 214–233.

Finnilä, K., Mahlberga, N., Santtilia, P., & Niemib, P. (2003). Validity of a test of children's suggestibility for predicting responses to two interview situations differing in degree of suggestiveness. *Journal of Experimental Child Psychology, 85,* 32–49.

Fischer, K. W., & Bidell, T. (1991). Constraining nativisit inferences about cognitive capacities. In S. Carey & R. Gelman (Eds.), *The epigenesis of mind: Essays on biology and cognition* (pp. 199–235). Hillsdale, NJ: Erlbaum.

Fischer, K. W., & Bidell, T. R. (2006). Dynamic development of action and thought. In R. M. Lerner (Ed.), *Handbook of child psychology: Vol. 1. Theoretical models of human development* (6th ed., pp. 313–399). Hoboken, NJ: Wiley.

Fischman, M. G., Moore, J. B., & Steele, K. H. (1992). Children's one-hand catching as a function of age, gender, and ball location. *Research Quarterly for Exercise and Sport, 63,* 349–355.

Fish, M. (2004). Attachment in infancy and preschool in low socioeconomic status rural Appalachian children: Stability and change and relations to preschool and kindergarten competence. *Development and Psychopathology, 16,* 293–312.

Fisher, C. B. (1993, Winter). Integrating science and ethics in research with high-risk children and youth. *Social Policy Report of the Society for Research in Child Development, 4*(4).

Fisher, C. B., Hoagwood, K., Boyce, C., Duster, T., Frank, D. A., & Grisso, T. (2002). Research ethics for mental health science involving ethnic minority children and youths. *American Psychologist, 57,* 1024–1040.

Fisher, J. O., & Birch, L. L. (1999). Restricting access to palatable foods affects children's behavioral response, food selection, and intake. *American Journal of Clinical Nutrition, 69,* 1264–1272.

Fisher, J. O., Mitchell, D. S., Smiciklas-Wright, H., & Birch, L. L. (2001). Maternal milk consumption predicts the tradeoff between milk and soft drinks in young girls' diets. *Journal of Nutrition, 131,* 246–250.

Fisher, J. O., Rolls, B. J., & Birch, L. L. (2003). Children's bite size and intake of an entré are greater with large portions than with age-appropriate or self-selected portions. *American Journal of Clinical Nutrition, 77,* 1164–1170.

Fisher, L., Ames, E. W., Chisholm, K., & Savoie, L. (1997). Problems reported by parents of Romanian orphans adopted to British Columbia. *International Journal of Behavioral Development, 20,* 67–82.

Fisher, S. E., Francks, C., McCracken, J. T., McGough, J. J., Marlow, A. J., & MacPhie, I. L. (2002). A genomewide scan for loci involved in attention-deficit/hyperactivity disorder. *American Journal of Human Genetics, 70,* 1183–1196.

Fite, P. J., Stauffacher, K., Ostrov, J. M., & Colder, C. R. (2008). Replication and extension of Little et al.'s (2003) forms and functions of aggression measure. *International Journal of Behavioral Development, 32,* 238–242.

FitzGerald, D. P., & White, K. J. (2003). Linking children's social worlds: Perspective-taking in parent–child and peer contexts. *Social Behavior and Personality, 31,* 509–522.

Fivush, R. (2001). Owning experience: Developing subjective perspective in autobiographical narratives. In C. Moore & K. Lemmon (Eds.), *The self in time: Developmental perspectives* (pp. 35–52). Mahwah, NJ: Erlbaum.

Fivush, R., & Haden, C. A. (2005). Parent–child reminiscing and the construction of a subjective self. In B. D. Homer & C. S. Tamis-LeMonda (Eds.), *The development of social cognition and communication* (pp. 315–336). Mahwah, NJ: Erlbaum.

Fivush, R., & Wang, Q. (2005). Emotion talk in mother–child conversations of the shared past: The effects of culture, gender, and event valence. *Journal of Cognition and Development, 6,* 489–506.

Flannery, K. A., & Liederman, J. (1995). Is there really a syndrome involving the co-occurrence of neurodevelopmental disorder, talent, non-right handedness and immune disorder among children? *Cortex, 31,* 503–515.

Flavell, J. H. (2000). Development of children's knowledge about the mental world. *International Journal of Behavioral Development, 24,* 15–23.

Flavell, J. H., Flavell, E. R., & Green, F. L. (2001). Development of children's understanding of connections between thinking and feeling. *Psychological Science, 12,* 430–432.

Flavell, J. H., Green, F. L., & Flavell, E. R. (1987). Development of knowledge about the appearance–reality distinction. *Monographs of the Society for Research in Child Development, 51*(1, Serial No. 212).

Flavell, J. H., Green, F. L., & Flavell, E. R. (1993). Children's understanding of the stream of consciousness. *Child Development, 64,* 387–398.

Flavell, J. H., Green, F. L., & Flavell, E. R. (1995). Young children's knowledge about thinking. *Monographs of the Society for Research in Child Development, 60*(1, Serial No. 243).

Flavell, J. H., Green, F. L., Flavell, E. R., & Grossman, J. B. (1997). The development of children's knowledge about inner speech. *Child Development, 68,* 39–47.

Flegal, K. M., Carroll, M. D., Ogden, C. L., & Curtin, L. R. (2010). Prevalence and trends in obesity among U.S. adults, 1999–2008. *Journal of the American Medical Association, 303,* 235–241.

Flegal, K. M., Graubard, B. I., Williamson, D. F., & Gail, M. H. (2007). Cause-specific excess deaths associated with underweight, overweight, and obesity. *Journal of the American Medical Association, 299,* 1260–1261.

Fletcher, A. C., Nickerson, P., & Wright, K. L. (2003). Structured leisure activities in middle childhood: Links to well-being. *Journal of Community Psychology, 31,* 641–659.

Floccia, C., Christophe, A., & Bertoncini, J. (1997). High-amplitude sucking and newborns: The quest for underlying mechanisms. *Journal of Experimental Child Psychology, 64,* 175–198.

Flom, R., & Pick, A. D. (2003). Verbal encouragement and joint attention in 18-month-old infants. *Infant Behavior and Development, 26,* 121–134.

Flynn, E. (2006). A microgenetic investigation of stability and continuity in theory of mind development. *British Journal of Developmental Psychology, 24,* 631–654.

Flynn, E., & Siegler, R. (2007). Measuring change: Current trends and future directions in microgenetic research. *Infant and Child Development, 16,* 135–149.

Flynn, J. R. (1999). Searching for justice: The discovery of IQ gains over time. *American Psychologist, 54,* 5–20.

Flynn, J. R. (2003). Movies about intelligence: The limitations of *g. Current Directions in Psychological Science, 12,* 95–99.

Flynn, J. R. (2007). *What is intelligence? Beyond the Flynn effect.* New York: Cambridge University Press.

Fogel, A. (1993). *Developing through relationships: Origins of communication, self and culture.* New York: Harvester Wheatsheaf.

Fogel, A., & Garvey, A. (2007). Alive communication. *Infant Behavior and Development, 30,* 251–257.

Fomon, S. J., & Nelson, S. E. (2002). Body composition of the male and female reference infants. *Annual Review of Nutrition, 22,* 1–17.

Fordham, K., & Stevenson-Hinde, J. (1999). Shyness, friendship quality, and adjustment during middle childhood. *Journal of Child Psychology and Psychiatry, 40,* 757–768.

Forman, D. R., Aksan, N., & Kochanska, G. (2004). Toddlers' responsive imitation predicts preschool-age conscience. *Psychological Science, 15,* 699–704.

Forman, D. R., O'Hara, M. W., Stuart, S., Gorman, L. L., Larsen, K. E., & Coy, K. C. (2007). Effective treatment for postpartum depression is not sufficient to improve the developing mother–child relationship. *Development and Psychopathology, 19,* 585–602.

Foster, J. A., Gore, S. A., & West, D. S. (2006). Altering TV viewing habits: An unexplored strategy for adult obesity intervention? *American Journal of Health Behavior, 30,* 3–14.

Foster, M. A., Lambert, R., Abbott-Shim, M., McCarty, F., & Franze, S. (2005). A model of home learning environment and social risk factors in relation to children's emergent literacy and social outcomes. *Early Childhood Research Quarterly, 20,* 13–36.

Foster, W. A., & Miller, M. (2007). Development of the literacy achievement gap: A longitudinal study of kindergarten through third grade. *Language, Speech, and Hearing Services in Schools, 38,* 173–181.

Fox, C. L., & Boulton, M. J. (2006). Friendship as a moderator of the relationship between social skills problems and peer victimization. *Aggressive Behavior, 32,* 110–121.

Fox, N. A. (1991). If it's not left, it's right: Electroencephalograph asymmetry and the development of emotion. *American Psychologist, 46,* 863–872.

Fox, N. A., & Calkins, S. D. (2003). The development of self-control of emotion: Intrinsic and extrinsic influences. *Motivation and Emotion, 27,* 7–26.

Fox, N. A., & Davidson, R. J. (1986). Taste-elicited changes in facial signs of emotion and the asymmetry of brain electrical activity in newborn infants. *Neuropsychologia, 24,* 417–422.

Foy, J. G., & Mann, V. (2003). Home literacy environment and phonological awareness in preschool children: Differential effects for rhyme and phoneme awareness. *Applied Psycholinguistics, 24,* 59–88.

Fraiberg, S. (1971). *Insights from the blind.* New York: Basic Books.

Franco, P., Danias, A. P., Akamine, E. H., Kawamoto, E. M., Fortes, Z. B., Scavone, C., & Tostes, R. C. (2002). Enhanced oxidative stress as a potential mechanism underlying the programming of hypertension in utero. *Journal of Cardiovascular Pharmacology, 40,* 501–509.

Frank, D. A., Rose-Jacobs, R., Beeghly, M., Wilbur, M., Bellinger, D., & Cabral, H. (2005). Level of prenatal cocaine exposure and 48-month IQ: Importance of preschool enrichment. *Neurotoxicology and Teratology, 27,* 15–28.

Frank, J. B., Jarit, G. J., Bravman, J. T., & Rosen, J. E. (2007). Lower extremity injuries in the skeletally immature athlete. *Journal of the American Academy of Orthopaedic Surgeons, 15,* 356–366.

Frankenburg, E., & Orfield, G. (2007). *Lessons in integration: Realizing the promise of racial diversity in American schools.* Charlottesville, VA: University of Virginia Press.

Frederiksen-Goldsen, K. I., & Sharlach, A. E. (2000). *Families and work: New directions in the twenty-first century.* New York: Oxford University Press.

Fredricks, J. A., & Eccles, J. S. (2002). Children's competence and value beliefs from childhood through adolescence: Growth trajectories in two male-sex-typed domains. *Developmental Psychology, 38,* 519–533.

Freeman, H., & Newland, L. A. (2010). New directions in father attachment. *Early Child Development and Care, 180,* 1–8.

Freitag, C. M., Rohde, L. A., Lempp, T., & Romanos, M. (2010). Phenotypic and measurement influences on heritability estimates in childhood ADHD. *European Child and Adolescent Psychiatry, 19,* 311–323.

Freud, S. (1973). *An outline of psychoanalysis.* London: Hogarth. (Original work published 1938)

Freud, S. (1974). *The ego and the id.* London: Hogarth. (Original work published 1923)

Fried, P. A. (1993). Prenatal exposure to tobacco and marijuana: Effects during preganancy, infancy, and early childhood. *Clinical Obstetrics and Gynecology, 36,* 319–337.

Friedman, S. L., & Scholnick, E. K. (1997). An evolving "blueprint" for planning: Psychological requirements, task characteristics, and social–cultural influences. In S. L. Friedman & E. K. Scholnick (Eds.), *The developmental psychology of planning: Why, how, and when do we plan?* (pp. 3–22). Mahwah, NJ: Erlbaum.

Fries, A. B. W., & Pollak, S. D. (2004). Emotion understanding in postinstitutionalized Eastern European children. *Development and Psychopathology, 16,* 355–369.

Fries, A. B. W., Ziegler, T. E., Kurian, J. R., Jacoris, S., & Pollak, S. D. (2005). Early experience in humans is associated with changes in neuropeptides critical for regulating social behavior. *Proceedings of the National Academy of Sciences, 102,* 17237–17240.

Frith, L. (2001). Gamete donation and anonymity: The ethical and legal debate. *Human Reproduction, 16,* 818–824.

Frith, U. (2003). *Autism: Explaining the enigma* (2nd ed.). Malden, MA: Blackwell.

Fryer, S. L., Crocker, N. A., & Mattson, S. N. (2008). Exposure to teratogenic agents as a risk factor for psychopathology. In T. P. Beauchaine & S. P. Hinshaw (Eds.), *Child and adolescent psychopathology* (pp. 180–207). Hoboken, NJ: Wiley.

Fu, G., Xu, F., Cameron, C. A., Heyman, G., & Lee, K. (2007). Cross-cultural differences in children's choices, categorizations, and evaluations of truths and lies. *Developmental Psychology, 43,* 278–293.

Fuchs, D., Fuchs, L. S., Mathes, P. G., & Martinez, E. A. (2002a). Preliminary evidence on the standing of students with learning disabilities in PALS and No-PALS classrooms. *Learning Disabilities Research and Practice, 17,* 205–215.

Fuchs, L. S., Fuchs, D., Yazdian, L., & Powell, S. R. (2002b). Enhancing first-grade children's mathematical development with peer-assisted learning strategies. *School Psychology Review, 31,* 569–583.

Fuligni, A. J. (1998). Authority, autonomy, and parent–adolescent conflict and cohesion: A study of adolescents from Mexican, Chinese, Filipino, and European backgrounds. *Developmental Psychology, 34,* 782–792.

Fuligni, A. J. (2004). The adaptation and acculturation of children from immigrant families. In U. P. Gielen & J. Roopnarine (Eds.), *Childhood and adolescence: Cross-cultural perspectives* (pp. 297–318). Westport, CT: Praeger.

Fuligni, A. J., Yip, T., & Tseng, V. (2002). The impact of family obligation on the daily activities and psychological well-being of Chinese-American adolescents. *Child Development, 73,* 302–314.

Fuligni, A. J., & Yoshikawa, H. (2003). Socioeconomic resources, parenting, and child development among immigrant families. In M. H. Bornstein & R. H. Bradley (Eds.), *Socioeconomic status, parenting, and child development* (pp. 107–124). Mahwah, NJ: Erlbaum.

Fuligni, A. S., Han, W.-J., & Brooks-Gunn, J. (2004). The Infant-Toddler HOME in the 2nd and 3rd years of life. *Parenting: Science and Practice, 4,* 139–159.

Fuller, C., Keller, L., Olson, J., Plymale, A., & Gottesman, M. (2005). Helping preschoolers become healthy eaters. *Journal of Pediatric Health Care, 19,* 178–182.

Fuller-Thomson, E., & Minkler, M. (2005). Native American grandparents raising grandchildren: Findings from the Census 2000 Supplementary Survey and implications for social work practice. *Social Work, 50,* 131–139.

Fuller-Thomson, E., & Minkler, M. (2007). Mexican American grandparents raising grandchildren: Findings from the Census 2000 American Community Survey. *Families in Society, 88,* 567–574.

Fullerton, J. T., Navarro, A. M., & Young, S. H. (2007). Outcomes of planned home birth: An integrative review. *Journal of Midwifery and Women's Health, 52,* 323–333.

Furman, W., & Buhrmester, D. (1992). Age and sex differences in perceptions of networks of personal relationships. *Child Development, 63,* 103–115.

Furusawa, T., Naka, I., Yamauchi, T., Natsuhara, K., Kimura, R., Nakazawa, M., et al. (2010). The Q223r polymorphism in LEPR is associated with obesity in Pacific Islanders. *Human Genetics, 127,* 287–294.

Fuson, K. C. (2009). Avoiding misinterpretations of Piaget and Vygotsky: Mathematical teaching without learning, learning without teaching, or helpful learning-path teaching? *Cognitive Development, 24,* 343–361.

Fuson, K. C., & Burghard, B. H. (2003). Multidigit addition and subtraction methods invented in small groups and teacher support of problem solving and reflection. In A. J. Baroody & A. Dowker (Eds.), *The development of arithmetic concepts and skills* (pp. 267–304). Mahwah, NJ: Erlbaum.

Fussell, E., & Gauthier, A. H. (2005). American women's transition to adulthood in comparative perspective. In R. A. Settersten, Jr., F. F. Furstenberg, Jr., & R. G. Rumbaut (Eds.), *On the frontier of adulthood: Theory, research, and public policy* (pp. 76–109). Chicago: University of Chicago Press.

G

Galambos, S. J., & Maggs, J. L. (1991). Children in self-care: Figures, facts and fiction. In J. V. Lerner & N. L. Galambos (Eds.), *Employed mothers and their children* (pp. 131–157). New York: Garland.

Galinsky, E., Aumann, K., & Bond, J. T. (2009). *Times are changing: Gender and generation at work and at home.* New York: Families and Work Institute.

Galler, J. R., Ramsey, C. F., Morley, D. S., Archer, E., & Salt, P. (1990). The long-term effects of early kwashiorkor compared with marasmus. IV. Performance on the National High School Entrance Examination. *Pediatric Research, 28,* 235–239.

Galloway, J. C., & Thelen, E. (2004). Feet first. Object exploration in young infants. *Infant Behavior and Development, 27,* 107-112

Gandy, J. (2004). *Children explain God.* Retrieved from http://www.geocities.com/jonathangandy.geo/chilrendescribeGod.html

Ganea, P. A., Allen, M. L., Butler, L., Carey, S., & DeLoache, J. S. (2009). Toddlers' referential understanding of pictures. *Journal of Experimental Child Psychology, 104,* 283–295.

Ganea, P. A., & Harris, P. A. (2010). Not doing what you are told: Early perseverative errors in updating mental representations via language. *Child Development, 81,* 457–463.

Ganea, P. A., Pickard, M. B., & DeLoache, J. S. (2008). Transfer between picture books and the real world by very young children. *Journal of Cognition and Development, 9,* 46–66.

Ganea, P. A., Shutts, K., Spelke, E., & DeLoache, J. S. (2007). Thinking of things unseen: Infants' use of language to update object representations. *Psychological Science, 8,* 734–739.

Ganger, J., & Brent, M. R. (2004). Reexamining the vocabulary spurt. *Developmental Psychology, 40,* 621–632.

Ganji, V., Hampl, J. S., & Betts, N. M. (2003). Race-, gender-, and age-specific differences in dietary micronutrient intakes of U.S. children. *International Journal of Food Sciences and Nutrition, 54,* 485–490.

Ganong, L. H., & Coleman, M. (1994). *Remarried family relationships.* Thousand Oaks, CA: Sage.

Garces, E., Thomas, D., & Currie, J. (2002). Longer-term effects of Head Start. *American Economic Review, 92,* 999–1012.

Garcia, M. M., Shaw, D. S., Winslow, E. B., & Yaggi, K. E. (2000). Destructive sibling conflict and the development of conduct problems in young boys. *Developmental Psychology, 36,* 44–53.

Garcia-Bournissen, F., Tsur, L., Goldstein, L. H., Staroselsky, A., Avner, M., & Asrar, F. (2008). Fetal exposure to isotretinoin—an international problem. *Reproductive Toxicology, 25,* 124–128.

Gardner, H. (1983). *Frames of mind: The theory of multiple intelligences.* New York: Basic Books.

Gardner, H. (1993). *Multiple intelligences: The theory in practice.* New York: Basic Books.

Gardner, H. (1998). Extraordinary cognitive achievements (ECA): A symbol systems approach. In R. M. Learner (Ed.), *Handbook of child psychology: Vol. 1. Theoretical models of human development* (5th ed., pp. 415–466). New York: Wiley.

Gardner, H. (2000). *Intelligence reframed: Multiple intelligences for the twenty-first century.* New York: Basic Books.

Garner, P. W. (1996). The relations of emotional role taking, affective/moral attributions, and emotional display rule knowledge to low-income school-age children's social competence. *Journal of Applied Developmental Psychology, 17,* 19–36.

Garner, P. W. (2003). Child and family correlates of toddlers' emotional and behavioral responses to a mishap. *Infant Mental Health Journal, 24,* 580–596.

Garner, P. W., & Estep, K. (2001). Emotional competence, emotion socialization, and young children's peer-related social competence. *Early Education and Development, 12*, 29–48.

Garrison, M. M., & Christakis, D. A. (2005). *A teacher in the living room? Educational media for babies, toddlers, and preschoolers.* Menlo Park, CA: Henry J. Kaiser Family Foundation.

Gartstein, M. A., & Rothbart, M. K. (2003). Studying infant temperament via the revised infant behavior questionnaire. *Infant Behavior and Development, 26*, 64–86.

Gartstein, M. A., Slobodskaya, H. R., & Kinsht, I. A. (2003). Cross-cultural differences in temperament in the first year of life: United States of America (U.S.) and Russia. *International Journal of Behavioral Development, 27*, 316–328.

Gasden, V. (1999). Black families in intergenerational and cultural perspective. In M. E. Lamb (Ed.), *Parenting and child development in "nontraditional" families* (pp. 221–246). Mahwah, NJ: Erlbaum.

Gaskins, S. (1999). Children's daily lives in a Mayan village: A case study of culturally constructed roles and activities. In R. Göncü (Ed.), *Children's engagement in the world: Sociocultural perspectives* (pp. 25–61). Cambridge, U.K.: Cambridge University Press.

Gaskins, S. (2000). Children's daily activities in a Mayan village: A culturally grounded description. *Cross-Cultural Research, 34*, 375–389.

Gaskins, S., Haight, W., & Lancy, D. F. (2007). The cultural construction of play. In A. Göncü & S. Gaskins (Eds.), *Play and development: Evolutionary, sociocultural, and functional perspectives* (pp. 179–202). Mahwah, NJ: Erlbaum.

Gathercole, S. E., Adams, A.-M., & Hitch, G. (1994). Do young children rehearse? An individual-differences analysis. *Memory and Cognition, 22*, 201–207.

Gathercole, V., Sebastián, E., & Soto, P. (1999). The early acquisition of Spanish verbal morphology: Across-the-board or piecemeal knowledge? *International Journal of Bilingualism, 3*, 133–182.

Gauvain, M. (2004). Bringing culture into relief: Cultural contributions to the development of children's planning skills. In R. V. Kail (Ed.), *Advances in child development and behavior* (pp. 39–71). San Diego, CA: Elsevier.

Gauvain, M., de la Ossa, J. L., & Hurtado-Ortiz, M. T. (2001). Parental guidance as children learn to use cultural tools: The case of pictorial plans. *Cognitive Development, 16*, 551–575.

Gauvain, M., & Rogoff, B. (1989a). Collaborative problem solving and children's planning skills. *Developmental Psychology, 25*, 139–151.

Gauvain, M., & Rogoff, B. (1989b). Ways of speaking about space: The development of children's skill in communicating spatial knowledge. *Cognitive Development, 4*, 295–307.

Gawlitzek-Maiwald, I., & Tracy, R. (1996). Bilingual bootstrapping. *Linguistics, 34*, 901–926.

Gaylor, E. E., Burnham, M. M., Goodlin-Jones, B. L., & Anders, T. (2005). A longitudinal follow-up study of young children's sleep patterns using a developmental classification system. *Behavioral Sleep Medicine, 3*, 44–61.

Gazelle, H., & Rudolph, K. D. (2004). Moving toward and away from the world: Social approach and avoidance trajectories in anxious and solitary youth. *Child Development, 75*, 829–849.

Geary, D. C. (1999). Evolution and developmental sex differences. *Current Directions in Psychological Science, 8*, 115–120.

Geary, D. C. (2006a). Development of mathematical understanding. In D. Kuhn & R. Siegler (Eds.), *Handbook of child psychology: Vol. 2. Cognition, perception, and language* (6th ed., pp. 777–810). Hoboken, NJ: Wiley.

Geary, D. C. (2006b). Evolutionary developmental psychology: Current status and future directions. *Developmental Review, 26*, 113–119.

Geerts, M., Steyaert, J., & Fryns, J. P. (2003). The XYY syndrome: A follow-up study on 38 boys. *Genetic Counseling, 14*, 267–279.

Gelman, R. (1972). Logical capacity of very young children: Number invariance rules. *Child Development, 43*, 75–90.

Gelman, R., & Shatz, M. (1978). Appropriate speech adjustments: The operation of conversational constraints on talk to two-year-olds. In M. Lewis & L. A. Rosenblum (Eds.), *Interaction, conversation, and the development of language* (pp. 27–61). New York: Wiley.

Gelman, S. A. (2003). *The essential child.* New York: Oxford University Press.

Gelman, S. A. (2006). Early conceptual development. In K. McCartney & D. Phillips (Eds.), *Blackwell handbook of early childhood development* (pp. 149–166). Malden, MA: Blackwell.

Gelman, S. A., & Kalish, C. W. (2006). Conceptual development. In D. Kuhn & R. Siegler (Eds.), *Handbook of child psychology: Vol. 2. Cognition, perception, and language* (6th ed., 687–733). New York: Wiley.

Gelman, S. A., & Koenig, M. A. (2003). Theory-based categorization in early childhood. In D. H. Rakison & L. M. Oakes (Ed.), *Early category and concept development* (pp. 330–359). New York: Oxford University Press.

Gelman, S. A., Taylor, M. G., & Nguyen, S. P. (2004). Mother–child conversations about gender. *Monographs of the Society for Research in Child Development, 69*(1, Serial No. 275), pp. 1–127.

Gendler, M. N., Witherington, D. C., & Edwards, A. (2008). The development of affect specificity in infants' use of emotion cues. *Infancy, 13*, 456–468.

Genesee, F. (2001). Portrait of the bilingual child. In V. Cook (Ed.), *Portraits of the second language user* (pp. 170–196). Clevedon, U.K.: Multilingual Matters.

Genesee, F., & Nicoladis, E. (2007). Bilingual first language acquisition. In E. Hoff & M. Shatz (Eds.), *Blackwell handbook of language development* (pp. 324–342). Malden, MA: Blackwell.

Gennetian, L. A., & Morris, P. A. (2003). The effects of time limits and make-work-pay strategies on the well-being of children: Experimental evidence from two welfare reform programs. *Children and Youth Services Review, 25*, 17–54.

Gentner, D., & Namy, L. L. (2004). The role of comparison in children's early word learning. In D. G. Hall & S. R. Waxman (Eds.), *Weaving a lexicon* (pp. 533–568). Cambridge, MA: MIT Press.

Gerardi-Caulton, G. (2000). Sensitivity to spatial conflict and the development of self-regulation in children 24–36 months of age. *Developmental Science, 3*, 397–404.

Gergely, G., & Watson, J. (1996). The social biofeedback theory of parental affect-mirroring : The development of emotional self-awareness and self-control in infancy. *International Journal of Psychoanalysis, 77*, 1181–1212.

Gergely, G., & Watson, J. (1999). Early socio-emotional development: Contingency perception and the social-biofeedback model. In P. Rochat (Ed.), *Early social cognition: Understanding others in the first months of life* (pp. 101–136). Mahwah, NJ: Erlbaum.

Gershoff, E. T. (2002). Corporal punishment, physical abuse, and the burden of proof: Reply to Baumrind, Larzelere, and Cowan (2002), Holden (2002), and Parke (2002). *Psychological Bulletin, 128*, 602–611.

Gershoff, E. T., & Aber, J. L. (2006). Neighborhoods and schools: Contexts and consequences for the mental health and risk behaviors of children and youth. In L. Balter & C. S. Tamis-LeMonda (Eds.), *Child psychology: A handbook of contemporary issues* (2nd ed., pp. 611–645). New York: Psychology Press.

Gershoff-Stowe, L., & Hahn, E. R. (2007). Fast mapping skills in the developing lexicon. *Journal of Speech, Language, and Hearing Research, 50*, 682–697.

Gerson, S., & Woodward, A. L. (2010). Building intentional action knowledge with one's hands. In S. P. Johnson (Ed.), *Neoconstructivism: The new science of cognitive development* (pp. 295–313). New York: Oxford University Press.

Gesell, A. (1933). Maturation and patterning of behavior. In C. Murchison (Ed.), *A handbook of child psychology.* Worcester, MA: Clark University Press.

Gest, S. D., Domitrovich, C. E., & Welsh, J. A. (2005). Peer academic reputation in elementary school: Associations with changes in self-concept and academic skills. *Journal of Educational Psychology, 97*, 337–346.

Gewirtz, A., & Edleson, J. L. (2004). Young children's exposure to adult domestic violence: Toward a developmental risk and resilience framework for research and intervention. In S. Schechter (Ed.), *Early childhood, domestic violence, and poverty: Helping young children and their families*, Series Paper 6. Iowa City: University of Iowa School of Social Work

Gewirtz, A., Forgatch, M., & Weiling, E. (2008). Parenting practices as potential mechanisms for child adjustment following mass trauma. *Journal of Marital and Family Therapy, 34*, 177–192.

Ghim, H. R. (1990). Evidence for perceptual organization in infants: Perception of subjective contours by young infants. *Infant Behavior and Development, 13*, 221–248.

Gibbons, A. (1998). Which of our genes make us human? *Science, 281*, 1432–1434.

Gibbons, R., Dugaiczyk, L. J., Girke, T., Duistermars, B., Zielinski, R., & Dugaiczyk, A. (2004). Distinguishing humans from great apes with AluYb8 repeats. *Journal of Molecular Biology, 339*, 721–729.

Gibbs, J. C. (2010). Beyond the conventionally moral. *Journal of Applied Developmental Psychology, 31*, 106–108.

Gibson, E. J. (1970). The development of perception as an adaptive process. *American Scientist, 58*, 98–107.

Gibson, E. J. (2000). Perceptual learning in development: Some basic concepts. *Ecological Psychology, 12*, 295–302.

Gibson, E. J. (2003). The world is so full of a number of things: On specification and perceptual learning. *Ecological Psychology, 15*, 283–287.

Gibson, E. J., & Walk, R. D. (1960). The "visual cliff." *Scientific American, 202*, 64–71.

Gibson, J. J. (1979). *The ecological approach to visual perception.* Boston: Houghton Mifflin.

Giedd, J. N., Blumenthal, J., Jeffries, N. O., Rajapakse, J. C., et al. (1999). Development of the human corpus callosum during childhood and adolescence: A longitudinal MRI study. *Progress in Neuro-Psychology and Biological Psychiatry, 23*, 571-588.

Giles, J. W., & Heyman, G. D. (2005). Young children's beliefs about the relationship between gender and aggressive behavior. *Child Development, 76*, 107–121.

Giles-Sims, J., Straus, M. A., & Sugarman, D. B. (1995). Child, maternal, and family characteristics associated with spanking. *Family Relations, 44*, 170–176.

Gill, M., Daly, G., Heron, S., Hawi, Z., & Fitzgerald, M. (1997). Confirmation of association between attention deficit hyperactivity disorder and a dopamine transporter polymorphism. *Molecular Psychiatry, 2*, 311–313.

Gillet, J.-P., Macadangdang, B., Rathke, R. L., Gottesman, M. M., & Kimchi-Sarfaty, C. (2009). The development of gene therapy: From monogenic recessive diseases to complex diseases such as cancer. *Methods in Molecular Biology, 542*, 5–54.

Gillies, R. M. (2002). The residual effects of cooperative-learning experiences: A two-year follow-up. *Journal of Educational Research, 96*, 15–20.

Gillies, R. M. (2003). Structuring co-operative learning experiences in primary school. In R. M. Gillies & A. F. Ashman (Eds.), *Co-operative learning: The social and intellectual outcomes of learning in groups* (pp. 36–53). New York: Routledge.

Gilliom, M., Shaw, D. S., Beck, J. E., Schonberg, M. A., & Lukon, J. L. (2002). Anger regulation in disadvantaged preschool boys: Strategies, antecedents, and the development of self-control. *Developmental Psychology, 38*, 222–235.

Gilstrap, L. L., & Ceci, S. J. (2005). Reconceptualizing children's suggestibility: Bidirectional and temporal properties. *Child Development, 76*, 40–53.

Ginsburg, H. P., Lee, J. S., & Boyd, J. S. (2008). Mathematics education for young children: What it is and how to promote it. *Social Policy Report of the Society for Research in Child Development, 12*(1).

Ginsburg-Block, M. D., Rohrbeck, C. A., & Fantuzzo, J. W. (2006). A meta-analytic review of social, self-concept, and behavioral outcomes of peer-assisted learning. *Journal of Educational Psychology, 98*, 732–749.

Giuliani, A., Schöll, W. M., Basver, A., & Tasmussino, K. F. (2002). Mode of delivery and outcome of 699 term singleton breech deliveries at a single center. *American Journal of Obstetrics and Gynaecology, 187,* 1694–1698.

Glade, A. C., Bean, R. A., & Vira, R. (2005). A prime time for marital/relational intervention: A review of the transition to parenthood literature with treatment recommendations. *American Journal of Family Therapy, 33,* 319–336.

Gladstone, I. M., & Katz, V. L. (2004). The morbidity of the 34- to 35-week gestation: Should we reexamine the paradigm? *American Journal of Perinatology, 21,* 9–13.

Gladwell, M. (1998, February 2). The Pima paradox. *The New Yorker,* pp. 44–57.

Gleason, J. B. (2009). The development of language. In J. B. Gleason (Ed.), *The development of language* (7th ed., pp. 1–33). Boston: Allyn and Bacon.

Gleason, T. R. (2002). Social provisions of real and imaginary relationships in early childhood. *Developmental Psychology, 38,* 979–992.

Gleason, T. R., & Hohmann, L. M. (2006). Concepts of real and imaginary friendships in early childhood. *Social Development, 15,* 128–144.

Gleason, T. R., Sebanc, A. M., & Hartup, W. W. (2000). Imaginary companions of preschool children. *Developmental Psychology, 36,* 419–428.

Gleitman, L. R., Cassidy, K., Nappa, R., Papfragou, A., & Trueswell, J. C. (2005). Hard words. *Language Learning and Development, 1,* 23–64.

Gleitman, L. R., & Newport, E. (1996). *The invention of language by children.* Cambridge, MA: MIT Press.

Glover, V., Bergman, K., & O'Connor, T. G. (2008). The effects of maternal stress, anxiety, and depression during pregnancy on the neurodevelopment of the child. In S. D. Stone & A. E. Menken (Eds.), *Perinatal and postpartum mood disorders: Perspectives and treatment guide for the health care practitioner* (pp. 3–15). New York: Springer.

Gluckman, P. D., Sizonenko, S. V., & Bassett, N. S. (1999). The transition from fetus to neonate— an endocrine perspective. *Acta Paediatrica Supplement, 88*(428), 7–11.

Gnepp, J. (1983). Children's social sensitivity: Inferring emotions from conflicting cues. *Developmental Psychology, 19,* 805–814.

Godfrey, K. M., & Barker, D. J. (2000). Fetal nutrition and adult disease. *American Journal of Clinical Nutrition, 71,* 1344S–1352S.

Goering, J. (Ed.). (2003). Choosing a better life? *How public housing tenants selected a HUD experiment to improve their lives and those of their children: The Moving to Opportunity Demonstration Program.* Washington, DC: Urban Institute Press.

Goetz, T., Frenzel, A. C., Pekrun, R., & Hall, N. (2005). Emotional intelligence in the context of learning and achievement. In R. Schulze & R. D. Roberts (Eds.), *Emotional intelligence: An international handbook* (pp. 233–253). Göttingen, Germany: Hogrefe & Huber.

Gogate, L. J., & Bahrick, L. E. (1998). Intersensory redundancy facilitates learning of arbitrary relations between vowel sounds and objects in seven-month-old infants. *Journal of Experimental Child Psychology, 69,* 133–149.

Gogate, L. J., & Bahrick, L. E. (2001). Intersensory redundancy and 7-month-old infants' memory for arbitrary syllable–object relations. *Infancy, 2,* 219–231.

Goh, Y. I., & Koren, G. (2008). Folic acid in pregnancy and fetal outcomes. *Journal of Obstetrics and Gynaecology, 28,* 3–13.

Goldberg, A. E., & Perry-Jenkins, M. (2003). Division of labor and working-class women's well-being across the transition to parenthood. *Journal of Family Psychology, 18,* 225–236.

Goldenberg, C., Gallimore, R., Reese, L., & Garnier, H. (2001). Cause or effect? Immigrant Latino parents' aspirations and expectations, and their children's school performance. *American Educational Research Journal, 38,* 547–582.

Goldfield, B. A. (1987). Contributions of child and caregiver to referential and expressive language. *Applied Psycholinguistics, 8,* 267–280.

Goldin-Meadow, S., & Butcher, S. (2003). Pointing toward two-word speech in young children. In S. Kita (Ed.), *Pointing: Where language, culture, and cognition meet* (pp. 85–107). Mahwah, NJ: Erlbaum.

Goldschmidt, L., Richardson, G. A., Cornelius, M. D., & Day, N. L. (2004). Prenatal marijuana and alcohol exposure and academic achievement at age 10. *Neurotoxicology and Teratology, 26,* 521–532.

Goldstein, M. H., & Schwade, J. A. (2008). Social feedback to infants' babbling facilitates rapid phonological learning. *Psychological Science, 19,* 515–523.

Goldstein, S. E., & Tisak, M. S. (2004). Adolescents' outcome expectancies about relational aggression within acquaintanceships, friendships, and dating relationships. *Journal of Adolescence, 27,* 283–302.

Goleman, D. (1995). *Emotional intelligence.* New York: Bantam.

Goleman, D. (1998). *Working with emotional intelligence.* New York: Bantam.

Golfier, F., Vaudoyer, F., Ecochard, R., Champion, F., Audra, P., & Raudrant, D. (2001). Planned vaginal delivery versus elective caesarean section in singleton term breech presentation: A study of 1116 cases. *European Journal of Obstetrics and Gyncecology, 98,* 186–192.

Golinkoff, R. M., & Hirsh-Pasek, K. (2006). Baby wordsmith: From associationist to social sophisticate. *Current Directions in Psychological Science, 15,* 30–33.

Golinkoff, R. M., & Hirsh-Pasek, K. (2008). How toddlers begin to learn verbs. *Trends in Cognitive Sciences, 12,* 397–403.

Golomb, C. (2004). *The child's creation of a pictorial world* (2nd ed.). Mahwah, NJ: Erlbaum.

Golombok, S., Lycett, E., MacCallum, F., Jadva, V., Murray, C., Rust, J., Abdalla, H., Jenkins, J., & Margar, R. (2004). Parenting of infants conceived by gamete donation. *Journal of Family Psychology, 18,* 443–452.

Golombok, S., Perry, B., Burston, A., Murray, C., Mooney-Somers, J., Stevens, M., & Golding, J. (2003). Children with lesbian parents: A community study. *Developmental Psychology, 39,* 20–33.

Golombok, S., Rust, J., Zervoulis, K., Croudace, T., Golding, J., & Hines, M. (2008). Developmental trajectories of sex-typed behavior in boys and girls: A longitudinal general population study of children aged 2.5–8 years. *Child Development, 79,* 1583–1593.

Golombok, S., & Tasker, F. L. (1996). Do parents influence the sexual orientation of their children? Findings from a longitudinal study of lesbian families. *Developmental Psychology, 32,* 3–11.

Gomez-Perez, E., & Ostrosky-Solis, F. (2006). Attention and memory evaluation across the life span: Heterogeneous effects of age and education. *Journal of Clinical and Experimental Neuropsychology, 28,* 477–494.

Göncü, A., Patt, M. B., & Kouba E. (2004). Understanding young children's pretend play in context. In P. K. Smith & C. H. Hart (Eds.), *Blackwell handbook of childhood social development* (pp. 418–437). Malden, MA: Blackwell.

Gonzales, N. A., Cauce, A. M., Friedman, R. J., & Mason, C. A. (1996). Family, peer, and neighborhood influences on academic achievement among African-American adolescents: One-year prospective effects. *American Journal of Community Psychology, 24,* 365–387.

Gonzalez, A.-L., & Wolters, C. A. (2006). The relation between perceived parenting practices and achievement motivation in mathematics. *Journal of Research in Childhood Education, 21,* 203–217.

Gonzalez-Rivera, M., & Bauermeister, J. A. (2007). Children's attitudes toward people with AIDS in Puerto Rico: Exploring stigma through drawings and stories. *Qualitative Health Research, 17,* 250–263.

Good, T. L., & Brophy, J. (2003). *Looking in classrooms* (9th ed.). Boston: Allyn and Bacon.

Goodlin-Jones, B. L., Burnham, M. M., & Anders, T. F. (2000). Sleep and sleep disturbances: Regulatory processes in infancy. In A. J. Sameroff, M. Lewis, &

S. M. Miller (Eds.), *Handbook of developmental psychology* (2nd ed., pp. 309–325). New York: Kluwer.

Goodman, G. S., & Melinder, A. (2007). Child witness research and forensic interviews of young children: A review. *Legal and Criminological Psychology, 12,* 1–19.

Goodman, S. H., Gravitt, G. W., Jr., & Kaslow, N. J. (1995). Social problem solving: A moderator of the relation between negative life stress and depression symptoms in children. *Journal of Abnormal Child Psychology, 23,* 473–485.

Goodnow, J. J. (2010). Culture. In M. H. Bornstein (Ed.), *Handbook of cultural developmental science* (pp. 3–20). New York: Psychology Press.

Goodvin, R., Meyer, S., Thompson, R. A., & Hayes, R. (2008). Self-understanding in early childhood: Associations with child attachment security and maternal negative affect. *Attachment and Human Development, 10,* 433–450.

Goodwin, M. H. (1998). Games of stance: Conflict and footing in hopscotch. In S. Hoyle & C. T. Adger (Eds.), *Language practices of older children* (pp. 23–46). New York: Oxford University Press.

Gopnik, A., & Choi, S. (1990). Do linguistic differences lead to cognitive differences? A cross-linguistic study of semantic and cognitive development. *First Language, 11,* 199–215.

Gopnik, A., & Nazzi, T. (2003). Words, kinds, and causal powers: A theory theory perspective on early naming and categorization. In D. H. Rakison & L. M. Oakes (Eds.), *Early category and concept development* (pp. 303–329). New York: Oxford University Press.

Gordon, R. A., Chase-Lansdale, P. L., & Brooks-Gunn, J. (2004). Extended households and the life course of young mothers: Understanding the associations using a sample of mothers with premature, low-birth-weight babies. *Child Development, 75,* 1013–1038.

Gormally, S., Barr, R. G., Wertheim, L., Alkawaf, R., Calinoiu, N., & Young, S. N. (2001). Contact and nutrient caregiving effects on newborn infant pain responses. *Developmental Medicine and Child Neurology, 43,* 28–38.

Goswami, U. (1996). Analogical reasoning and cognitive development. In H. Reese (Ed.), *Advances in child development and behavior* (Vol. 26, pp. 91–138). New York: Academic Press.

Gottesman, I. I. (1963). Genetic aspects of intelligent behavior. In N. Ellis (Ed.), *Handbook of mental deficiency* (pp. 253–296). New York: McGraw-Hill.

Gottfried, A. E., Gottfried, A. W., & Bathurst, K. (2002). Maternal and dual-earner employment status and parenting. In M. H. Bornstein (Ed.), *Handbook of parenting: Vol. 3. Being and becoming a parent* (2nd ed., pp. 207–230). Mahwah, NJ: Erlbaum.

Gottlieb, G. (1998). Normally occurring environmental and behavioral influences on gene activity: From central dogma to probabilistic epigenesis. *Psychological Review, 105,* 792–802.

Gottlieb, G. (2003). On making behavioral genetics truly developmental. *Human Development, 46,* 337–355.

Gottlieb, G. (2007). Probabilistic epigenesis. *Developmental Science, 10,* 1–11.

Gottlieb, G., Wahlsten, D., & Lickliter, R. (2006). The significance of biology for human development: A developmental psychobiological systems of view. In R. M. Lerner (Ed.), *Handbook of child psychology: Vol. 1. Theoretical models of human development* (6th ed., pp. 210–257). Hoboken, NJ: Wiley.

Gould, J. L., & Keeton, W. T. (1996). *Biological science* (6th ed.). New York: Norton.

Govaerts, P. J., De Beukelaer, C., Daemers, K., De Ceulaer, G., Yperman, M., Somers, T., Schatteman, I., & Offeciers, F. E. (2002). Outcome of cochlear implantation at different ages from 0 to 6 years. *Otology and Neurotology, 23,* 885–890.

Graber, J. A., Nichols, T., Lynne, S. D., Brooks-Gunn, J., & Botwin, G. J. (2006). A longitudinal examination of family, friend, and media influences on competent versus problem behaviors among urban minority youth. *Applied Developmental Science, 10,* 75–85.

Gralinski, J. H., & Kopp, C. B. (1993). Everyday rules for behavior: Mothers' requests to young children. *Developmental Psychology, 29,* 573–584.

Granger, R. C. (2008). After-school programs and academics: Implications for policy, practice, and research. *Social Policy Report of the Society for Research in Child Development, 22*(2), 3–11.

Granic, I., Hollenstein, T., Dishion, T. J., & Patterson, G. R. (2003). Longitudinal analysis of flexibility and reorganization in early adolescence: A dynamic systems study of family interactions. *Developmental Psychology, 39*, 606–617.

Granier-Deferre, C., Bassereau, S., Ribeiro, A., Jacquet, A. Y., & Lecanuet, J.-P. (2003). *Cardiac "orienting" response in fetuses and babies following in utero melody-learning.* Paper presented at the 11th European Conference on Developmental Psychology, Milan, Italy.

Grant, K. B., & Ray, J. A. (2010). *Home, school, and community collaboration: Culturally responsive family involvement.* Thousand Oaks, CA: Sage Publications.

Grant, K. E., O'Koon, J., Davis, T., Roache, N., Poindexter, L., & Armstrong, M. (2000). Protective factors affecting low-income urban African American youth exposed to stress. *Journal of Early Adolescence, 20*, 388–418.

Grantham-McGregor, S., & Ani, C. (2001). A review of studies on the effect of iron deficiency on cognitive development in children. *Journal of Nutrition, 131*, 649S–668S.

Grantham-McGregor, S., Powell, C., Walker, S., Chang, S., & Fletcher, P. (1994). The long-term follow-up of severely malnourished children who participated in an intervention program. *Child Development, 65*, 428–439.

Grantham-McGregor, S., Schofield, W., & Powell, C. (1987). Development of severely malnourished children who received psychosocial stimulation: Six-year follow-up. *Pediatrics, 79*, 247–254.

Grantham-McGregor, S., Walker, S. P., & Chang, S. (2000). Nutritional deficiencies and later behavioral development. *Proceedings of the Nutrition Society, 59*, 47–54.

Grattan, M. P., De Vos, E., Levy, J., & McClintock, M. K. (1992). Asymmetric action in the human newborn: Sex differences in patterns of organization. *Child Development, 63*, 273–289.

Gray, K. A., Day, N. L., Leech, S., & Richardson, G. A. (2005). Prenatal marijuana exposure: Effect on child depressive symptoms at ten years of age. *Neurotoxicology and Teratology, 27*, 439–448.

Gray, M. R., & Steinberg, L. (1999). Unpacking authoritative parenting: Reassessing a multidimensional construct. *Journal of Marriage and the Family, 61*, 574–587.

Gray-Little, B., & Carels, R. (1997). The effects of racial and socioeconomic consonance on self-esteem and achievement in elementary, junior high, and high school students. *Journal of Research on Adolescence, 7*, 109–131.

Gray-Little, B., & Hafdahl, A. R. (2000). Factors influencing racial comparisons of self-esteem: A quantitative review. *Psychological Bulletin, 126*, 26–54.

Green, G. E., Irwin, J. R., & Gustafson, G. E. (2000). Acoustic cry analysis, neonatal status and long-term developmental outcomes. In R. G. Barr, B. Hopkins, & J. A. Green (Eds.), *Crying as a sign, a symptom, and a signal* (pp. 137–156). Cambridge, U.K.: Cambridge University Press.

Greenberg, D., Hoffman, S., Leibovitz, E., & Dagan, R. (2008). Acute otitis media in children: Association with day care centers—Antibacterial resistance, treatment, and prevention. *Pediatric Drugs, 10*, 75–83.

Greenberger, E., O'Neil, R., & Nagel, S. K. (1994). Linking workplace and homeplace: Relations between the nature of adults' work and their parenting behaviors. *Developmental Psychology, 30*, 990–1002.

Greendorfer, S. L., Lewko, J. H., & Rosengren, K. S. (1996). Family and gender-based socialization of children and adolescents. In F. L. Smoll & R. E. Smith (Eds.), *Children and youth in sport: A biopsychological perspective* (pp. 89–111). Dubuque, IA: Brown & Benchmark.

Greene, S. M., Anderson, E., Hetherington, E. M., Forgath, M. S., & DeGarmo, D. S. (2003). Risk and resilience after divorce. In R. Walsh (Ed.), *Normal family processes* (pp. 96–120). New York: Guilford.

Greenfield, P. M. (1992, June). *Notes and references for developmental psychology.* Conference on Making Basic Texts in Psychology More Culture-Inclusive and Culture-Sensitive, Western Washington University, Bellingham, WA.

Greenfield, P. M. (2004). *Weaving generations together: Evolving creativity in the Maya of Chiapas.* Santa Fe, NM: School of American Research.

Greenfield, P. M., Keller, H., Fuligni, A., & Maynard, A. (2003). Cultural pathways through universal development. *Annual Review of Psychology, 54*, 461–490.

Greenfield, P. M., Maynard, A. E., & Childs, C. P. (2000). History, culture, learning, and development. *Cross-Cultural Research, 34*, 351–374.

Greenfield, P. M., Suzuki, L. K., & Rothstein-Fish, C. (2006). Cultural pathways through human development. In K. A. Renninger & I. E. Sigel (Eds.), *Handbook of child psychology: Vol. 4. Child psychology in practice* (6th ed., pp. 655–699). Hoboken, NJ: Wiley.

Greenhill, L. L., Halperin, J. M., & Abikoff, H. (1999). Stimulant medications. *Journal of the American Academy of Child and Adolescent Psychiatry, 38*, 503–512.

Greenough, W. T., & Black, J. E. (1992). Induction of brain structure by experience: Substrates for cognitive development. In M. Gunnar & C. A. Nelson (Eds.), *Minnesota symposia on child psychology* (pp. 155–200). Hillsdale, NJ: Erlbaum.

Greer, T., & Lockman, J. J. (1998). Using writing instruments: Invariances in young children and adults. *Child Development, 69*, 888–902.

Gregory, A. M., Eley, T. C., O'Connor, T. G., & Plomin, R. (2004). Etiologies of associations between childhood sleep and behavioral problems in a large twin sample. *Journal of the American Academy of Child and Adolescent Psychiatry, 43*, 744–751.

Grigorenko, E. L. (2000). Heritability and intelligence. In R. J. Sternberg (Ed.), *Handbook of intelligence* (pp. 53–91). Cambridge, U.K.: Cambridge University Press.

Grigorenko, E. L., & Sternberg, R. J. (1998). Dynamic testing. *Psychological Bulletin, 124*, 75–111.

Groome, L. J., Swiber, M. J., Holland, S. B., Bentz, L. S., Atterbury, J. L., & Trimm, R. F., III. (1999). Spontaneous motor activity in the perinatal infant before and after birth: Stability in individual differences. *Developmental Psychobiology, 35*, 15–24.

Grossmann, K., Grossmann, K. E., Fremmer-Bombik, E., Kindler, H., Scheuerer-Englisch, H., & Zimmermann, P. (2002). The uniqueness of the child–father attachment relationship: Fathers' sensitive and challenging play as a pivotal variable in a 16-year longitudinal study. *Social Development, 11*, 307–331.

Grossmann, K., Grossmann, K. E., Kindler, H., & Zimmermann, P. (2008). A wider view of attachment and exploration: The influence of mothers and fathers on the development of psychological security from infancy to young adulthood. In J. Cassidy & P. R. Shaver (Eds.), *Handbook of attachment: Theory, research, and clinical applications* (2nd ed., pp. 880–905). New York: Guilford.

Grossmann, K., Grossmann, K. E., Spangler, G., Suess, G., & Unzner, L. (1985). Maternal sensitivity and newborns' orientation responses as related to quality of attachment in Northern Germany. In I. Bretherton & E. Waters (Eds.), Growing points of attachment theory and research. *Monographs of the Society for Research in Child Development, 50*(1–2, Serial No. 209).

Grossmann, T., Striano, T., & Friederici, A. D. (2007). Developmental changes in infants' processing of happy and angry facial expressions: A neurobehavioral study. *Brain and Cognition, 64*, 30–41.

Grotuss, J., Bjorklund, D. F., & Csinady, A. (2007). Evolutionary developmental psychology: Developing human nature. *Acta Psychologica Sinica, 39*, 439–453.

Grow-Maienza, J., Hahn, D.-D., & Joo, C.-A. (2001). Mathematics instruction in Korean primary schools: Structures, processes, and a linguistic analysis of questioning. *Journal of Educational Psychology, 93*, 363–376.

Gruendel, J., & Aber, J. L. (2007). Bridging the gap between research and child policy change: The role of strategic communications in policy advocacy. In J. L. Aber, S. J. Bishop-Josef, S. M. Jones, K. T. McLearn, & D. A. Phillips (Eds.), *Child development and social policy: Knowledge for action* (pp. 43–58). Washington, DC: American Psychological Association.

Grusec, J. E. (1988). *Social development: History, theory, and research.* New York: Springer-Verlag.

Grusec, J. E. (2006). The development of moral behavior and conscience from a socialization perspective. In M. Killen & J. Smetana (Eds.), *Handbook of moral development* (pp. 243–265). Philadelphia: Erlbaum.

Grusec, J. E., & Goodnow, J. J. (1994). Impact of parental discipline methods on the child's internalization of values: A reconceptualization of current points of view. *Developmental Psychology, 30*, 4–19.

Grych, J. H., & Clark, R. (1999). Maternal employment and development of the father–infant relationship in the first year. *Developmental Psychology, 35*, 893–903.

Guignard, J.-H., & Lubart, T. I. (2007). A comparative study of convergent and divergent thinking in intellectually gifted children. *Gifted and Talented International, 22*(1), 9–15.

Guilford, J. P. (1985). The structure-of-intellect model. In B. B. Wolman (Ed.), *Handbook of intelligence* (pp. 225–266). New York: Wiley.

Guilleminault, C., Palombini, L., Pelayo, R., & Chervin, R. D. (2003). Sleepwalking and sleep terrors in prepubertal children: What triggers them? *Pediatrics, 111*, e17–e25.

Gullone, E. (2000). The development of normal fear: A century of research. *Clinical Psychology Review, 20*, 429–451.

Gulotta, T. P. (2008). How theory influences treatment and prevention practice within the family. In T. P. Gulotta (Ed.), *Family influences on child behavior and development: Evidence-based prevention and treatment approaches* (pp. 1–20). New York: Routledge.

Gunnar, M. R., & Cheatham, C. L. (2003). Brain and behavior interfaces: Stress and the developing brain. *Infant Mental Health Journal, 24*, 195–211.

Gunnar, M. R., Morison, S. J., Chisholm, K., & Schuder, M. (2001). Salivary cortisol levels in children adopted from Romanian orphanages. *Development and Psychopathology, 13*, 611–628.

Gunnar, M. R., & Vasquez, D. M. (2001). Low cortisol and a flattening of expected daytime rhythm: Potential indices of risk in human development. *Development and Psychopathology, 13*, 515–538.

Gunnarsdottir, I., Schack-Nielsen, L., Michaelson, K. F., Sørensen, T. I., & Thorsdottir, I. (2010). Infant weight gain, duration of exclusive breast-feeding, and childhood BMI—two similar follow-up cohorts. *Public Health Nutrition, 13*, 201–207.

Gunnoe, M. L., & Mariner, C. L. (1997). Toward a developmental-contextual model of the effects of parental spanking on children's aggression. *Archives of Pediatrics and Adolescent Medicine, 151*, 768–775.

Gunstad, J., Spitznagel, M. B., Luyster, F., Cohen, R. A., & Paul, R. H. (2007). Handedness and cognition across the healthy lifespan. *International Journal of Neuroscience, 117*, 477–485.

Guo, G., & VanWey, L. K. (1999). Sibship size and intellectual development: Is the relationship causal? *American Sociological Review, 64*, 169–187.

Guralnick, M. J., Neville, B., Hammond, M. A., & Connor, R. T. (2007). Linkages between delayed children's social interactions with mothers and peers. *Child Development, 78*, 459–473.

Gurucharri, C., & Selman, R. L. (1982). The development of interpersonal understanding during childhood, preadolescence, and adolescence: A longitudinal follow-up study. *Child Development, 53*, 924–927.

Gustafson, G. E., Green, J. A., & Cleland, J. W. (1994). Robustness of individual identity in the cries of human infants. *Developmental Psychobiology, 27,* 1–9.

Gustafson, G. E., Wood, R. M., & Green, J. A. (2000). Can we hear the causes of infants' crying? In R. G. Barr & B. Hopkins (Eds.), *Crying as a sign, a symptom, and a signal: Clinical, emotional, and developmental aspects of infant and toddler crying* (pp. 8–22). New York: Cambridge University Press.

Gutman, L. M., Sameroff, A. J., & Cole, R. (2003). Academic growth curve trajectories from 1st grade to 12th grade: Effects of multiple social risk factors and preschool child factors. *Developmental Psychology, 39,* 777–790.

Gutteling, B. M., de Weerth, C., Zandbelt, N., Mulder, E. J. H., Visser, G. H. A., & Buitelaar, J. K. (2006). Does maternal prenatal stress adversely affect the child's learning and memory at age six? *Journal of Abnormal Child Psychology, 34,* 789–798.

Guttentag, R., & Ferrell, J. (2004). Reality compared with its alternatives: Age differences in judgments of regret and relief. *Developmental Psychology, 40,* 764–775.

Gwiazda, J., & Birch, E. E. (2001). Perceptual development: Vision. In E. B. Goldstein (Ed.), *Blackwell handbook of perception* (pp. 636–668). Oxford, U.K.: Blackwell.

H

Hack, M., & Klein, N. (2006). Young adult attainments of preterm infants. *Journal of the American Medical Association, 295,* 695–696.

Hagerman, R. J., Berry-Kravis, E., Kaufmann, W. E., Ono, M. Y., Tartaglia, N., & Lachiewicz, A. (2009). Advances in the treatment of fragile X syndrome. *Pediatrics, 123,* 378–390.

Hahn, S., & Chitty, L. S. (2008). Noninvasive prenatal diagnosis: Current practice and future perspectives. *Current Opinion in Obstetrics and Gynecology, 20,* 146–151.

Haight, W. L., & Miller, P. J. (1993). *Pretending at home: Early development in a sociocultural context.* Albany: State University of New York Press.

Hainline, L. (1998). The development of basic visual abilities. In A. Slater (Ed.), *Perceptual development: Visual, auditory, and speech perception in infancy* (pp. 37–44). Hove, U.K.: Psychology Press.

Hakuta, K., Bialystok, E., & Wiley, E. (2003). Critical evidence: A test of the critical period hypothesis for second-language acquisition. *Psychological Science, 14,* 31–38.

Halberstadt, A. G., Denham, S. A., & Dunsmore, J. C. (2001). Affective social competence. *Social Development, 10,* 79–119.

Hale, C. M., & Tager-Flusberg, H. (2003). The influence of language on theory of mind: A training study. *Developmental Science, 6,* 346–359.

Hales, V. N., & Ozanne, S. E. (2003). The dangerous road of catch-up growth. *Journal of Physiology, 547,* 5–10.

Halfon, N., & McLearn, K. T. (2002). Families with children under 3: What we know and implications for results and policy. In N. Halfon & K. T. McLearn (Eds.), *Child rearing in America: Challenges facing parents with young children* (pp. 367–412). New York: Cambridge University Press.

Halford, G. S. (2002). Information-processing models of cognitive development. In U. Goswami (Ed.), *Blackwell handbook of childhood cognitive development* (pp. 555–574). Malden, MA: Blackwell.

Halford, G. S. (2005). Development of thinking. In K. J. Holyoak & R. G. Morrison (Eds.), *The Cambridge handbook of thinking and reasoning* (pp. 529–558). New York: Cambridge University Press.

Halford, G. S., & Andrews, G. (2006). Reasoning and problem solving. In D. Kuhn & R. Siegler (Eds.), *Handbook of child psychology: Vol. 2. Cognition, perception, and language* (6th ed., pp. 557–608). Hoboken, NJ: Wiley.

Halford, G. S., Wilson, W. H., Phillips, S. (1998). Processing capacity defined by relational complexity: Implications for comparative, developmental, and cognitive psychology. *Behavioral and Brain Sciences, 21,* 803–864.

Hall, D. G., & Graham, S. A. (1999). Lexical form class information guides word-to-object mapping in preschoolers. *Child Development, 70,* 78–91.

Hall, D. G., Burns, T., & Pawluski, J. (2003). Input and word learning: Caregivers' sensitivity to lexical category distinctions. *Journal of Child Language, 30,* 711–729.

Hall, G. S. (1904). *Adolescence.* New York: Appleton-Century-Crofts.

Hall, J. G. (2003). Twinning. *Lancet, 362,* 735–743.

Halle, T. G. (2003). Emotional development and well-being. In M. H. Bornstein, L. Davidson, C. L. M. Keyes, K. A. Moore, & the Center for Child Well-Being (Eds.), *Well-being: Positive development across the life course* (pp. 125–138). Mahwah, NJ: Erlbaum.

Haller, J. (2005). Vitamins and brain function. In H. R. Lieberman, R. B. Kanarek, & C. Prasad (2005). *Nutritional neuroscience* (pp. 207–233). Philadelphia: Taylor & Francis.

Hamilton, H. A. (2005). Extended families and adolescent well-being. *Journal of Adolescent Health, 36,* 260–266.

Hamlin, J. K., Wynn, K., & Bloom, P. (2007). Social evaluation by preverbal infants. *Nature, 450,* 557–559.

Hammes, B., & Laitman, C. J. (2003). Diethylstilbestrol (DES) update: Recommendations for the identification and management of DES-exposed individuals. *Journal of Midwifery and Women's Health, 48,* 19–29.

Hanawalt, B. A. (1993). *Growing up in medieval London: The experience of childhood in history.* New York: Oxford University Press.

Hanawalt, B. A. (2003). The child in the Middle Ages and the Renaissance. In W. Koops & M. Zuckerman (Eds.), *Beyond the century of childhood: Cultural history and developmental psychology.* Philadelphia: University of Pennsylvania Press.

Hane, A. A., Cheah, C., Rubin, K. H., & Fox, N. A. (2008). The role of maternal behavior in the relation between shyness and social reticence in early childhood and social withdrawal in middle childhood. *Social Development, 17,* 795–811.

Hanke, W., Sobala, W., & Kalinka, J. (2004). Environmental tobacco smoke exposure among pregnant women: Impact on fetal biometry at 20–24 weeks of gestation and newborn child's birth weight. *International Archives of Occupational and Environmental Health, 77,* 47–52.

Hannon, E. E., & Johnson, S. P. (2004). Infants use meter to categorize rhythms and melodies: Implications for musical structure learning. *Cognitive Psychology, 50,* 354–377.

Hannon, E. E., & Trehub, S. E. (2005a). Metrical categories in infancy and adulthood. *Psychological Science, 16,* 48–55.

Hannon, E. E., & Trehub, S. E. (2005b). Tuning in to musical rhythms: Infants learn more readily than adults. *Proceedings of the National Academy of Sciences, 102,* 12639–12643.

Hannon, T. S., Rao, G., & Arslanian, S. A. (2005). Childhood obesity and type 2 diabetes mellitus. *Pediatrics, 116,* 473–480.

Hans, S. L., & Jeremy, R. J. (2001). Postneonatal mental and motor development of infants exposed in utero to opiate drugs. *Infant Mental Health Journal, 22,* 300–315.

Hansen, M. B., & Markman, E. M. (2009). Children's use of mutual exclusivity to learn labels for parts of objects. *Developmental Psychology, 45,* 592–596.

Happé, F., & Frith, U. (2006). The weak coherence account: Detail-focused cognitive style in autism spectrum disorders. *Journal of Autism and Developmental Disorders, 1,* 1–21.

Harari, M. D., & Moulden, A. (2000). Nocturnal enuresis: What is happening? *Journal of Paediatrics and Child Health, 36,* 78–81.

Harley, B., & Jean, G. (1999). Vocabulary skills of French immersion students in their second language. *Zeitschrift für Interkulturellen Fremdsprachenunterricht, 4*(2). Retrieved from www.ualberta.ca

Harley, K., & Reese, E. (1999). Origins of autobiographical memory. *Developmental Psychology, 35,* 1338–1348.

Harlow, H. F., & Zimmerman, R. (1959). Affectional responses in the infant monkey. *Science, 130,* 421–432.

Harris, G. (1997). Development of taste perception and appetite regulation. In G. Bremner, A. Slater, & G. Butterworth (Eds.), *Infant development: Recent advances* (pp. 9–30). East Sussex, U.K.: Erlbaum.

Harris, P. L., Brown, E., Marriott, C., Whitall, S., & Harmer, S. (1991). Monsters, ghosts and witches: Testing the limits of the fantasy–reality distinction in young children. *British Journal of Developmental Psychology, 9,* 105–123.

Harris, R. C., Robinson, J. B., Chang, F., & Burns, B. M. (2007). Characterizing preschool children's attention regulation in parent–child interactions: The roles of effortful control and motivation. *Journal of Applied Developmental Psychology, 28,* 25–39.

Harris, S., & Berk, L. E. (2011, March). *Impact of individualized, supplementary preschool intervention on literacy, school readiness, and socioemotional skills.* Poster presented at the biennial meeting of the Society for Research in Child Development, Montreal, Canada.

Harris, Y. R., & Graham, J. A. (2007). *The African American child: Development and challenges.* New York: Springer.

Harrison, A. O., Wilson, M. N., Pine, C. J., Chan, S. Q., & Buriel, R. (1994). Family ecologies of ethnic minority children. In G. Handel & G. G. Whitchurch (Eds.), *The psychosocial interior of the family* (pp. 187–210). New York: Aldine De Gruyter.

Harrison, Y. (2004). The relationship between daytime exposure to light and night-time sleep in 6–12-week-old infants. *Journal of Sleep Research, 13,* 345–352.

Harrist, A. W., Zaia, A. F., Bates, J. E., Dodge, K. A., & Pettit, G. S. (1997). Subtypes of social withdrawal in early childhood: Sociometric status and social-cognitive differences across four years. *Child Development, 68,* 278–294.

Hart, B. (2004). What toddlers talk about. *First Language, 24,* 91–106.

Hart, B., & Risley, T. R. (1995). *Meaningful differences in the everyday experience of young American children.* Baltimore: Paul H. Brookes.

Hart, C. H., Burts, D. C., Durland, M. A., Charlesworth, R., DeWolf, M., & Fleege, P. O. (1998). Stress behaviors and activity type participation of preschoolers in more and less developmentally appropriate classrooms: SES and sex differences. *Journal of Research in Childhood Education, 13.*

Hart, C. H., Newell, L. D., & Olsen, S. F. (2003). Parenting skills and social–communicative competence in childhood. In J. O. Greene & B. R. Burleson (Eds.), *Handbook of communication and social interaction skills* (pp. 753–797). Mahwah, NJ: Erlbaum.

Hart, C. H., Yang, C., Charlesworth, R., & Burts, D. C. (2003, April). *Kindergarten teaching practices: Associations with later child academic and social/emotional adjustment to school.* Paper presented at the biennial meeting of the Society for Research in Child Development, Tampa, FL.

Hart, C. H., Yang, C., Nelson, L. J., Robinson, C. C., Olsen, J. A., Nelson, D. A., et al. (2000). Peer acceptance in early childhood and subtypes of socially withdrawn behavior in China, Russia and the United States. *International Journal of Behavioral Development, 24,* 73–81.

Hart, D., Atkins, R., & Matsuba, M. K. (2008). The association of neighborhood poverty with personality change in childhood. *Journal of Personality and Social Psychology, 94,* 1048–1061.

Harter, S. (1999). *The construction of self: A developmental perspective.* New York: Guilford.

Harter, S. (2003). The development of self-representations during childhood and adolescence. In M. R. Leary & J. P. Tangney (Eds.), *Handbook of self and identity* (pp. 610–642). New York: Guilford.

Harter, S. (2006). The self. In N. Eisenberg (Ed.), *Handbook of child psychology: Vol. 3. Social, emotional, and personality development* (6th ed., pp. 505–570). Hoboken, NJ: Wiley.

Harter, S., & Whitesell, N. (1989). Developmental changes in children's understanding of simple, multiple, and blended emotion concepts. In C. Saarni & P. Harris (Eds.), *Children's understanding of emotion* (pp. 81–116). Cambridge, U.K.: Cambridge University Press.

Hartshorn, K. (2003). Reinstatement maintains a memory in human infants for 1½ years. *Developmental Psychobiology, 42,* 269–282.

Hartshorn, K., Rovee-Collier, C., Gerhardstein, P., Bhatt, R. S., Klein, P. J., Aaron, F., Wondoloski, T. L., & Wurtzel, N. (1998a). Developmental changes in the specificity of memory over the first year of life. *Developmental Psychobiology, 33,* 61–78.

Hartshorn, K., Rovee-Collier, C., Gerhardstein, P., Bhatt, R. S., Wondoloski, T. L., Klein, P., Gilch, J., Wurtzel, N., & Campos-deCarvalho, M. (1998b). The ontogeny of long-term memory over the first year-and-a-half of life. *Developmental Psychobiology, 32,* 69–89.

Hartup, W. W. (1999). Peer experience and its developmental significance. In M. Bennett (Ed.), *Developmental psychology: Achievements and prospects* (pp. 106–125). Philadelphia, PA: Psychology Press.

Hartup, W. W. (2006). Relationships in early and middle childhood. In A. L. Vangelisti & D. Perlman (Eds.), *Cambridge handbook of personal relationships* (pp. 177–190). New York: Cambridge University Press.

Hartup, W. W., & Abecassis, M. (2004). Friends and enemies. In P. K. Smith & C. H. Hart (Eds.), *Blackwell handbook of childhood social development* (pp. 285–306). Malden, MA: Blackwell.

Harwood, M. D., & Farrar, M. J. (2006). Conflicting emotions: The connection between affective perspective taking and theory of mind. *British Journal of Developmental Psychology, 24,* 401–418.

Harwood, R., Leyendecker, B., Carlson, V., Asencio, M., & Miller, A. (2002). Parenting among Latino families in the U.S. In M. H. Bornstein (Ed.), *Handbook of Parenting: Vol. 4. Social conditions and applied parenting* (2nd ed., pp. 21–46). Mahwah, NJ: Lawrence Erlbaum Associates.

Hasebe, Y., Nucci, L., & Nucci, M. S. (2004). Parental control of the personal domain and adolescent symptoms of psychopathology: A cross-national study in the United States and Japan. *Child Development, 75,* 815–828.

Hatton, D. D., Bailey, D. B., Jr., Burchinal, M. R., & Ferrell, K. A. (1997). Developmental growth curves of preschool children with vision impairments. *Child Development, 68,* 788–806.

Hausenblas, H. A., & Downs, D. S. (2005). Prospective examination of leisure-time exercise behavior during pregnancy. *Journal of Applied Psychology, 17,* 240–246.

Hauser-Cram, P., Warfield, M. E., Stadler, J., & Sirin, S. R. (2006). School environments and the diverging pathways of students living in poverty. In A. C. Huston & M. N. Ripke (Eds.), *Developmental contexts in middle childhood* (pp. 198–216). New York: Cambridge University Press.

Hausfather, A., Toharia, A., LaRoche, C., & Engelsmann, F. (1997). Effects of age of entry, day-care quality, and family characteristics on preschool behavior. *Journal of Child Psychology and Psychiatry, 38,* 441–448.

Hawke, S., & Knox, D. (1978). The one-child family: A new life-style. *The Family Coordinator, 27,* 215–219.

Hawkins, J. N. (1994). Issues of motivation in Asian education. In H. F. O'Neil, Jr., & M. Drillings (Eds.), *Motivation: Theory and research* (pp. 101–115). Hillsdale, NJ: Erlbaum.

Haws, R. A., Yakoob, M. Y., Soomro, T., Menezes, E. V., Darmstadt, G. L., & Bhutta, Z. A. (2009). Reducing stillbirths: Screening and monitoring during pregnancy and labour. *BMC Pregnancy and Childbirth, 9*(Suppl. S1).

Hay, D. F., Pawlby, S., Waters, C. S., Perra, O., & Sharp, D. (2010). Mothers' antenatal depression and their children's antisocial outcomes. *Child Development, 81,* 149–165.

Hay, D. F., Payne, A., & Chadwick, A. (2004). Peer relations in childhood. *Journal of Child Psychology and Psychiatry, 45,* 84–108.

Hayne, H. (2002). Thoughts from the crib: Meltzoff and Moore (1994) alter our views of mental representation during infancy. *Infant Behavior and Development, 25,* 62–64.

Hayne, H. (2004). Infant memory development: Implications for childhood amnesia. *Developmental Review, 24,* 33–73.

Hayne, H., Boniface, J., & Barr, R. (2000). The development of declarative memory in human infants: Age-related changes in deferred imitation. *Behavioral Neuroscience, 114,* 77–83.

Hayne, H., Herbert, J., & Simcock, G. (2003). Imitation from television by 24- and 30-month-olds. *Developmental Science, 6,* 254–261.

Hayne, H., & Rovee-Collier, C. K. (1995). The organization of reactivated memory in infancy. *Child Development, 66,* 893–906.

Hayne, H., Rovee-Collier, C., & Perris, E. E. (1987). Categorization and memory retrieval by three-month-olds. *Child Development, 58,* 750–767.

Hayslip, B., Emick, M. A., Henderson, C. E., & Elias, K. (2002). Temporal variations in the experiences of custodial grandparenting: A short-term longitudinal study. *Journal of Applied Gerontology, 21,* 139–156.

Haywood, H. C., & Lidz, C. (2007). *Dynamic assessment in practice.* New York: Cambridge University Press.

Haywood, K. M., & Getchell, N. (2005). *Life span motor development* (4th ed.). Champaign, IL: Human Kinetics.

Hazen, N. L., McFarland, L., Jacobvitz, D., & Boyd-Soisson, E. (2010). Fathers' frightening behavours and sensitivity with infants: Relations with fathers' attachment representations, father–infant attachment, and children's later outcomes. *Early Child Development and Care, 180,* 51–69.

Head Start Bureau. (2008) *Head Start fact sheet.* Retrieved from www.acf.hhs.gov/programs/ohs /about/fy2008.html

Heath, S. B. (1990). The children of Trackton's children: Spoken and written language in social change. In J. Stigler, G. Herdt, & R. A. Shweder (Eds.), *Cultural psychology: Essays on comparative human development* (pp. 496–519). New York: Cambridge University Press.

Hebert, M., & Tourigny, M. (2004). Child sexual abuse prevention: A review of evaluative studies and recommendations for program development. In S. P. Serge (Eds.), *Advances in psychology research* (Vol. 29, pp. 123–155). Hauppauge, NY: Nova Science Publishers.

Heckman, J. J., & Masterov, D. V. (2004). *The productivity argument for investing in young children.* Working Paper 5, Invest in Kids Working Group, Committee for Economic Development. Retrieved from jenni.uchicago.edu/Invest

Hediger, M. L., Overpeck, M. D., Ruan, W. J., & Troendle, J. F. (2002). Birthweight and gestational age effects on motor and social development. *Paediatric and Perinatal Epidemiology, 16,* 33–46.

Helburn, S. W. (Ed.). (1995). *Cost, quality and child outcomes in child care centers.* Denver: University of Colorado.

Helwig, C. C. (2006). Rights, civil liberties, and democracy across cultures. In M. Killen & J. G. Smetana (Eds.), *Handbook of moral development* (pp. 185–210). Philadelphia: Erlbaum.

Helwig, C. C., Arnold, M. L., Tan, D., & Boyd, D. (2003). Chinese adolescents' reasoning about democratic and authority-based decision making in peer, family, and school contexts. *Child Development, 74,* 783–800.

Helwig, C. C., & Jasiobedzka, U. (2001). The relation between law and morality: Children's reasoning about socially beneficial and unjust laws. *Child Development, 72,* 1382–1393.

Helwig, C. C., & Prencipe, A. (1999). Children's judgments of flags and flag-burning. *Child Development, 70,* 132–143.

Helwig, C. C., & Turiel, E. (2004). Children's social and moral reasoning. In P. K. Smith & C. H. Hart (Eds.), *Blackwell handbook of childhood social development* (pp. 476–490). Malden, MA: Blackwell.

Helwig, C. C., Zelazo, P. D., & Wilson, M. (2001). Children's judgments of psychological harm in normal and canonical situations. *Child Development, 72,* 66–81.

Henderson, H. A., Marshall, P. J., Fox, N. A., & Rubin, K. H. (2004). Psychophysiological and behavioral evidence for varying forms and functions of nonsocial behavior in preschoolers. *Child Development, 75,* 251–263.

Henricsson, L., & Rydell, A.-M. (2004). Elementary school children with behavior problems: Teacher–child relations and self-perception. A prospective study. *Merrill-Palmer Quarterly, 50,* 111–138.

Hepper, P. G., McCartney, G. R., & Shannon, E. A. (1998). Lateralised behaviour in first trimester human foetuses. *Neuropsychologia, 43,* 313–315.

Heraghty, J. L., Hilliard, T. N., Henderson, A. J., & Fleming, P. J. (2008). The physiology of sleep in infants. *Archives of Disease in Childhood, 93,* 982–985.

Herbert, J., & Hayne, H. (2000). The ontogeny of long-term retention during the second year of life. *Developmental Science, 3,* 50–56.

Hernandez, D. J., Denton, N. A., & Macartney, S. E. (2008). Children in immigrant families: Looking to America's future. *Social Policy Report of the Society for Research in Child Development, 12*(11).

Herrera, E., Reissland, N., & Shepherd, J. (2004). Maternal touch and maternal child-directed speech: Effects of depressed mood in the postnatal period. *Journal of Affective Disorders, 81,* 29–39.

Herrnstein, R. J., & Murray, C. (1994). *The bell curve.* New York: Free Press.

Hertenstein, M. J., & Campos, J. J. (2004). The retention effects of an adult's emotional displays on infant behavior. *Child Development, 75,* 595–613.

Hesketh, K., Ball, K., Crawford, D., Campbell, K., & Salmon, J. (2007). Mediators of the relationship between maternal education and children's TV viewing. *American Journal of Preventive Medicine, 33,* 41–47.

Hespos, S. J., & Baillargeon, R. (2001). Reasoning about containment events in very young infants. *Cognition, 78,* 207–245.

Hespos, S. J., Ferry, A. L., Cannistraci, C. J., Gore, J., & Park, S. (2010). Using optical imaging to investigate functional cortical activity in human infants. In A. W. Roe (Ed.), *Imaging the brain with optical methods* (pp. 159–176). New York: Springer Science + Business Media.

Hesse, E., & Main, M. (2000). Disorganized infant, child, and adult attachment: Collapse in behavioral and attentional strategies. *Journal of the American Psychoanalytic Association, 48,* 1097–1127.

Hetherington, E. M. (1999). Should we stay together for the sake of the children? In E. M. Hetherington (Ed.), *Coping with divorce, single parenting, and remarriage: A risk and resiliency perspective* (pp. 93–116). Hillsdale, NJ: Erlbaum.

Hetherington, E. M. (2003). Social support and the adjustment of children in divorced and remarried families. *Childhood, 10,* 237–254

Hetherington, E. M., & Jodl, K. M. (1994). Stepfamilies as settings for child development. In A. Booth & J. Dunn (Eds.) *Stepfamilies: Who benefits? Who does not?* (pp. 55–79). Hillsdale, NJ: Erlbaum.

Hetherington, E. M., & Kelly, J. (2002). *For better or for worse: Divorce reconsidered.* New York: Norton.

Hetherington, E. M., & Stanley-Hagan, M. (2000). Diversity among stepfamilies. In D. H. Demo, K. R. Allen, & M. A. Fine (Eds.), *Handbook of family diversity* (pp. 173–196). New York: Oxford University Press.

Hewlett, B. S. (1992). Husband–wife reciprocity and the father–infant relationship among Aka pygmies. In B. S. Hewlett (Ed.), *Father–child relations: Cultural and biosocial contexts* (pp. 153–176). New York: Aldine De Gruyter.

Hewlett, B. S. (2004). Fathers in forager, farmer, and pastoral cultures. In M. E. Lamb (Ed.), *The role of the father in child development* (4th ed., pp. 182–195). Hoboken, NJ: Wiley.

Hewlett, S. (2003). *Creating a life.* New York: Miramax.

Heyes, C. (2005). Imitation by association. In S. Hurley & N. Chater (Eds.), *Perspectives on imitation: From neuroscience to social science: Vol. 1. Mechanisms of imitation and imitation in animals* (pp. 157–177). Cambridge, MA: MIT Press.

Heyman, G. D., & Dweck, C. S. (1998). Children's thinking about traits: Implications for judgments of the self and others. *Child Development, 69,* 391–403.

Heyman, G. D., Dweck, C. S., & Cain, K. M. (1992). Young children's vulnerability to self-blame and helplessness: Relationship to beliefs about goodness. *Child Development, 63,* 401–415.

Heyman, G. D., & Gelman, S. A. (1999). The use of trait labels in making psychological inferences. *Child Development, 70,* 604–619.

Heyman, G. D., & Gelman, S. A. (2000). Preschool children's use of trait labels to make inductive inferences. *Journal of Experimental Child Psychology, 77,* 1–19.

Heyman, G. D., & Legare, C. H. (2004). Children's beliefs about gender differences in the academic and social domains. *Sex Roles, 50,* 227–239.

Hickling, A. K., & Wellman, H. M. (2001). The emergence of children's causal explanations and theories: Evidence from everyday conversation. *Developmental Psychology, 37,* 668–683.

Hicks, J. H., & Goedereis, E. A. (2009). The importance of context and the gain-loss dynamic for understanding grandparent caregivers. In K. Shifren (Ed.), *How caregiving affects development: Psychological implications for child, adolescent, and adult caregivers* (pp. 169–190). Washington, DC: American Psychological Association.

Higginbottom, G. M. A. (2006). 'Pressure of life': Ethnicity as a mediating factor in mid-life and older peoples' experience of high blood pressure. *Sociology of Health and Illness, 28,* 583–610.

Higgins, C., & Duxbury, L. (2002). *The 2001 National Work-Life Conflict Study: Report One.* Retrieved from www.phac-aspc.gc.ca/publicat/worktravail/report1/index.html

High, P. C., LaGasse, L., Becker, S., Ahlgren, I., & Gardner, A. (2000). Literacy promotion in primary care pediatrics: Can we make a difference? *Pediatrics, 105,* 927–934.

Hildreth, K., & Rovee-Collier, C. (2002). Forgetting functions of reactivated memories over the first year of life. *Developmental Psychobiology, 41,* 277–288.

Hildreth, K., Sweeney, B., & Rovee-Collier, C. (2003). Differential memory-preserving effects of reminders at 6 months. *Journal of Experimental Child Psychology, 84,* 41–62.

Hilgers, K. K., Akridge, M., Scheetz, J. P., & Kinance, D. E. (2006). Childhood obesity and dental development. *Pediatric Dentistry, 28,* 18–22.

Hill, A. L., Degnan, K. A., Calkins, S. D., & Keane, S. P. (2006). Profiles of externalizing behavior problems for boys and girls across preschool: The roles of emotion regulation and inattention. *Developmental Psychology, 42,* 913–928.

Hill, E. J., Mead, N. T., Dean, L. R., Hafen, D. M., Gadd, R., Palmer, A. A., & Ferris, M. S. (2006). Researching the 60-hour dual-earner workweek: An alternative to the "opt-out revolution." *American Behavioral Scientist, 49,* 1184–1203.

Hill, J. L., Brooks-Gunn, J., & Waldfogel, J. (2003). Sustained effects of high participation in an early intervention for low-birth-weight premature infants. *Developmental Psychology, 39,* 730–744.

Hilt, L. M. (2004). Attribution retaining for therapeutic change: Theory, practice, and future directions. *Imagination, Cognition, and Personality, 23,* 289–307.

Hinojosa, T., Sheu, C.-F., & Michael, G. F. (2003). Infant hand-use preference for grasping objects contributes to the development of a hand-use preference for manipulating objects. *Developmental Psychobiology, 43,* 328–334.

Hirsh-Pasek, K., & Burchinal, M. (2006). Mother and caregiver sensitivity over time: Predicting language and academic outcomes with variable- and person-centered approaches. *Merill-Palmer Quarterly, 52,* 449-485.

Hirsh-Pasek, K., & Golinkoff, R. M. (2003). *Einstein never used flash cards.* New York: Rodale.

Hirsh-Pasek, K., Golinkoff, R. M., Berk, L. E., & Singer, D. G. (2009). *A mandate for playful learning in preschool: Presenting the evidence.* New York: Oxford University Press.

Hjälmäs, K. (1998). Nocturnal enuresis: Basic facts and new horizons. *European Urology, 33*(Suppl. 3), 53–57.

Hoch-Espada, A., Ryan, E., & Deblinger, E. (2006). Child sexual abuse. In J. E. Fisher & W. T. O'Donohue (Eds.), *Practitioner's guide to evidence-based psychotherapy* (pp. 177–188). New York: Springer.

Hock, H. S., Park, C. L., & Bjorklund, D. F. (1998). Temporal organization in children's strategy formation. *Journal of Experimental Child Psychology, 70,* 187–206.

Hodges, J., & Tizard, B. (1989). Social and family relationships of ex-institutional adolescents. *Journal of Child Psychology and Psychiatry, 30,* 77–97.

Hodges, R. M., & French, L. A. (1988). The effect of class and collection labels on cardinality, class-inclusion, and number conservation tasks. *Child Development, 59,* 1387–1396.

Hodnett, E. D., Gates, S., Hofmeyr, G. J., & Sakala, C. (2003). Continuous support for women during childbirth. *Cochrane Database of Systematic Reviews, 3,* CD003766.

Hoehn, T., Hansmann, G., Bührer, C., Simbruner, G., Gunn, A. J., Yager, J., et al. (2008). Therapeutic hypothermia in neonates: Review of current clinical data, ILCOR recommendations and suggestions for implementation in neonatal intensive care units. *Resuscitation, 78,* 7–12.

Hoekstra, R. A., Bartels, M., Hudziak, J. J., Van Beijsterveldt, T. C., & Boomsma, D. I. (2008). Genetic and environmental influences on the stability of withdrawn behavior in children: A longitudinal, multi-informant twin study. *Behavior Genetics, 38,* 447–461.

Hoff, E. (2003). The specificity of environmental influence: Socioeconomic status affects early vocabulary development via maternal speech. *Child Development, 74,* 1368–1378.

Hoff, E. (2006). How social contexts support and shape language development. *Developmental Review, 26,* 55–88.

Hoff, E., Laursen, B., & Tardif, T. (2002). Socioeconomic status and parenting. In M. H. Bornstein (Ed.), *Handbook of parenting: Vol. 2. Biology and ecology of parenting* (pp. 231–252). Mahwah, NJ: Erlbaum.

Hoff, E. V. (2005). A friend living inside me: The forms and functions of imaginary companions. *Imagination, Cognition and Personality, 24,* 151–189.

Hofferth, S. L., & Anderson, K. G. (2003). Are all dads equal? Biology versus marriage as a basis for paternal investment. *Journal of Marriage and the Family, 65,* 213–232.

Hoffman, L. W. (2000). Maternal employment: Effects of social context. In R. D. Taylor & M. C. Wang (Eds.), *Resilience across contexts: Family, work, culture, and community* (pp. 147–176). Mahwah, NJ: Erlbaum.

Hoffman, M. K., Vahratian, A., Sciscione, A. C., Troendle, J. F., & Zhang, J. (2006). Comparison of labor progression between induced and noninduced multiparous women. *Obstetrics and Gynecology, 107,* 1029–1034.

Hoffman, M. L. (2000). *Empathy and moral development.* New York: Cambridge University Press.

Hoffmann, W. (2001). Fallout from the Chernobyl nuclear disaster and congenital malformations in Europe. *Archives of Environmental Health, 56,* 478–483.

Hoffner, C., & Badzinski, D. M. (1989). Children's integration of facial and situational cues to emotion. *Child Development, 60,* 411–422.

Hokoda, A., & Fincham, F. D. (1995). Origins of children's helpless and mastery achievement patterns in the family. *Journal of Educational Psychology, 87,* 375–385.

Holden, G. W., Coleman, S. M., & Schmidt, K. L. (1995). Why 3-year-old children get spanked: Determinants as reported by college-educated mothers. *Merill-Palmer Quarterly, 41,* 431–452.

Holditch-Davis, D., Belyea, M., & Edwards, L. J. (2005). Prediction of 3-year developmental outcomes from sleep development over the preterm period. *Infant Behavior and Development, 79,* 49–58.

Holland, A. L. (2004). Plasticity and development. *Brain and Language, 88,* 254–255.

Hollich, G. J., Hirsh-Pasek, K., & Golinkoff, R. M. (2000). Breaking the language barrier: An emergentist coalition model for the origins of word learning. *Monographs of the Society for Research in Child Development, 65*(3, Serial No. 262).

Holobow, N., Genesee, F., & Lambert, W. (1991). The effectiveness of a foreign language immersion program for children from different ethnic and social class backgrounds: Report 2. *Applied Psycholinguistics, 12,* 179–198.

Holowka, S., Brosseau-Lapré, F., & Petitto, L. A. (2002). Semantic and conceptual knowledge underlying bilingual babies' first signs and words. *Language Learning, 52,* 205–262.

Honein, M. A., Paulozzi, L. J., & Erickson, J. D. (2001). Continued occurrence of Accutane-exposed pregnancies. *Teratology, 64,* 142–147.

Hood, B. M. (2004). Is looking good enough or does it beggar belief? *Developmental Science, 7,* 415–417.

Hood, M., Conlon, E., & Andrews, G. (2008). Preschool home literacy practices and children's literacy development: A longitudinal analysis. *Journal of Educational Psychology, 100,* 252–271.

Hopkins, B., & Westra, T. (1988). Maternal handling and motor development: An intracultural study. *Genetic, Social and General Psychology Monographs, 14,* 377–420.

Hopkins-Golightly, T., Raz, S., & Sander, C. J. (2003). Influence of slight to moderate risk for birth hypoxia on acquisition of cognitive and language function in the preterm infant: A cross-sectional comparison with preterm-birth controls. *Neuropsychology, 17,* 3–13.

Horgan, D. (1978). The development of the full passive. *Journal of Child Language, 5,* 65–80.

Horner, S. L., & Gaither, S. M. (2004). Attribution retraining instruction with a second-grade class. *Early Childhood Education Journal, 31,* 165–170.

Horner, T. M. (1980). Two methods of studying stranger reactivity in infants: A review. *Journal of Child Psychology and Psychiatry, 21,* 203–219.

Horst, J. S., Oakes, L. M., & Madole, K. L. (2005). What does it look like and what can it do? Category structure influences how infants categorize. *Child Development, 76,* 614–631.

Houlihan, J., Kropp. T., Wiles, R., Gray, S., & Campbell, C. (2005). *Body burden: The pollution in newborns.* Washington, DC: Environmental Working Group.

Houts, A. C. (2003). Behavioral treatment for enuresis. In A. E. Kazdin (Ed.), *Evidence-based psychotherapies for children and adolescents* (pp. 389–406). New York: Guilford.

Hoven, C. W., Duarte, C. S., Lucas, C. P., Wu, P., Mandell, D. J., Goodwin, R. D., et al. (2005). Psychopathology among New York City public school children 6 months after September 11. *Archives of General Psychiatry, 62,* 545–552.

Howard, B. J., & Wong, J. (2001). Sleep disorders. *Pediatrics in Review, 22,* 327–342.

Howard, K. S., & Brooks-Gunn, J. (2009). The role of home-visiting programs in preventing child abuse and neglect. *Future of Children, 19,* 119–146.

Howell, K. K., Coles, C. D., & Kable, J. A. (2008). The medical and developmental consequences of prenatal drug exposure. In J. Brick (Ed.), *Handbook of the medical consequences of alcohol and drug abuse* (2nd ed., pp. 219–249). New York: Haworth Press.

Howell, K. K., Lynch, M. E., Platzman, K. A., Smith, G. H., & Coles, C. D. (2006). Prenatal alcohol exposure and ability, academic achievement, and school functioning in adolescence: A longitudinal follow-up. *Journal of Pediatric Psychology, 31,* 116–126.

Howes, C., & Matheson, C. C. (1992). Sequences in the development of competent play with peers: Social and social pretend play. *Developmental Psychology, 28,* 961–974.

Hoza, B., Gerdes, A. C., Hinshaw, S. P., Bukowski, W. M., Gold, J. A., Kraemer, H. C., Pelham, W. E., Jr., Wigal, T., & Arnold, L. E. (2005). What aspects of peer relationships are impaired in children with attention-deficit/hyperactivity disorder? *Journal of Consulting and Clinical Psychology, 73,* 411–423.

Huang, C.-C. (2006). Child support enforcement and father involvement for children in never-married mother families. *Fathering, 4,* 97–111.

Hubbs-Tait, L., Nation, J. R., Krebs, N. F., & Bellinger, D. C. (2005). Neurotoxicants, micronutrients, and social environments: Individual and combined effects on children's development. *Psychological Science in the Public Interest, 6,* 57–121.

Hudson, J. A., Fivush, R., & Kuebli, J. (1992). Scripts and episodes: The development of event memory. *Applied Cognitive Psychology, 6,* 483–505.

Hudson, J. A., Sosa, B. B., & Shapiro, L. R. (1997). Scripts and plans: The development of preschool children's event knowledge and event planning. In S. L. Friedman & E. K. Scholnick (Eds.), *The developmental psychology of planning* (pp. 77–102). Mahwah, NJ: Erlbaum.

Hudziak, J. J., & Rettew, D. C. (2009). Genetics of ADHD. In T. E. Brown (Ed.), *ADHD comorbidties: Handbook for ADHD complications in children and adults* (pp. 23–36). Arlington, VA: American Psychiatric Publishing.

Huesmann, L. R. (1986). Psychological processes promoting the relation between exposure to media violence and aggressive behavior by the viewer. *Journal of Social Issues, 42,* 125–139.

Huesmann, L. R., Moise-Titus, J., Podolski, C., & Eron, L. D. (2003). Longitudinal relations between children's exposure to TV violence and their aggressive and violent behavior in young adulthood: 1977–1992. *Developmental Psychology, 39,* 201–221.

Hueston, W. J., Geesey, M. E., & Diaz, V. (2008). Prenatal care initiation among pregnant teens in the United States: An analysis over 25 years. *Journal of Adolescent Health, 42,* 243–248.

Hughes, C. (1998). Finding your marbles: Does preschoolers' strategic behavior predict later understanding of mind? *Developmental Psychology, 34,* 1326–1339.

Hughes, C., & Dunn, J. (1998). Understanding mind and emotion: Longitudinal associations with mental-state talk between young friends. *Developmental Psychology, 34,* 1026–1037.

Hughes, D. C., & Ng, S. (2003). Reducing health disparities among children. *Future of Children, 13,* 153–167.

Hughes, J. N., Cavell, T. A., & Grossman, P. B. (1997). A positive view of self: Risk or protection for aggressive children? *Development and Psychopathology, 9,* 75–94.

Hughes, J. N., & Kwok, O. (2006). Classroom engagement mediates the effect of teacher–student support on elementary students' peer acceptance. *Journal of School Psychology, 43,* 465–480.

Hughes, J. N., & Kwok, O. (2007). Influence of student–teacher and parent–teacher relationships on lower achieving readers' engagement and achievement in the primary grades. *Journal of Educational Psychology, 99,* 39–51.

Hughes, J. N., Zhang, D., & Hill, C. R. (2006). Peer assessments of normative and individual teacher–student support predict social acceptance and engagement among low-achieving children. *Journal of School Psychology, 43,* 447–463.

Huizink, A. C., & Mulder, E. J. H. (2006). Maternal smoking, drinking or cannabis use during pregnancy and neurobehavioral and cognitive functioning in human offspring. *Neuroscience and Biobehavioral Reviews, 30,* 24–41.

Huizink, A. C., Mulder, E. J. H., & Buitelaar, J. K. (2004). Prenatal stress and risk for psychopathology: Specific effects or induction of general susceptibility? *Psychological Bulletin, 130,* 115–142.

Human Genome Program. (2008). *How many genes are in the human genome?* Retrieved from www.ornl.gov/sci/techresources/Human_Genome/faq/genenumber.shtml

Humphrey, T. (1978). Function of the nervous system during prenatal life. In U. Stave (Ed.), *Perinatal physiology* (pp. 651–683). New York: Plenum.

Hunnius, S., & Geuze, R. H. (2004a). Developmental changes in visual scanning of dynamic faces and abstract stimuli in infants: A longitudinal study. *Infancy, 6,* 231–255.

Hunnius, S., & Geuze, R. H. (2004b). Gaze shifting in infancy: A longitudinal study using dynamic faces and abstract stimuli. *Infant Behavior and Development, 27,* 397–416.

Hunt, C. E., & Hauck, F. R. (2006). Sudden infant death syndrome. *Canadian Medical Association Journal, 174,* 1861–1869.

Huotilainen, M., Kujala, A., Hotakainen, M., Parkkonen, L., Taulu, S., & Simola, J. (2005). Short-term memory functions of the human fetus recorded with magnetoencephalography. *Neuroreport, 16,* 81–84.

Hurewitz, F., Brown-Schmidt, S., Thorpe, K., Gleitman, L. R., & Trueswell, J. C. (2000). One frog, two frog, red frog, blue frog: Factors affecting children's syntactic choices in production and comprehension. *Journal of Psycholinguistic Research, 29,* 597–626.

Hursti, U.-K. (1999). Factors influencing children's food choice. *Annals of Medicine, 31,* 26–32.

Hurt, H., Brodsky, N. L., Roth, H., Malmud, E., & Giannetta, J. M. (2005). School performance of children with gestational cocaine exposure. *Neurotoxicology and Teratology, 27,* 203–211.

Huston, A. C., Wright, J. C., Marquis, J., & Green, S. B. (1999). How young children spend their time: Television and other activities. *Developmental Psychology, 35,* 912–925.

Hutinger, P. L., Bell, C., Beard, M., Bond, J., Johanson, J., & Terry, C. (1998). *The early childhood emergent literacy technology research study: Final report.* Macomb, IL: Western Illinois University. ERIC ED418545.

Huttenlocher, P. R. (2002). *Neural plasticity: The effects of environment on the development of the cerebral cortex.* Cambridge, MA: Harvard University Press.

Huyck, M. H. (1996). Continuities and discontinuities in gender identity in midlife. In V. L. Bengtson (Ed.), *Adulthood and aging* (pp. 98–121). New York: Springer-Verlag.

Hyde, J. S., Essex, M. J., Clark, R., & Klein, M. H. (2001). Maternity leave, women's employment, and marital incompatibility. *Journal of Family Psychology, 15,* 476–491.

Hymel, S., Vaillancourt, T., McDougall, P., & Renshaw, P. D. (2004). Peer acceptance and rejection in childhood. In P. K. Smith & C. H. Hart (Eds.), *Blackwell handbook of childhood social development* (pp. 265–284). Malden, MA: Blackwell.

Hyppönen, E., Power, C., & Smith, G. D. (2003). Prenatal growth, BMI, and risk of type 2 diabetes by early midlife. *Diabetes Care, 26,* 2512–2517.

Iglowstein, I., Jenni, O. G., Molinari, L., & Largo, R. H. (2003). Sleep duration from infancy to adolescence: Reference values and generational trends. *Pediatrics, 111,* 302–307.

Imai, M., & Haryu, E. (2004). The nature of word-learning biases and their roles for lexical development: From a cross-linguistic perspective. In D. G. Hall & S. R. Waxman (Eds.), *Weaving a lexicon* (pp. 411–444). Cambridge, MA: MIT Press.

Imai, M., Li, L., Haryu, E., Okada, H., Hirsh-Pasek, K., Golinkoff, R. M., & Shigematsu, J. (2008). Novel noun and verb learning in Chinese-, English-, and Japanese-speaking children. *Child Development, 79,* 979–1000.

Iocaboni, M., Molnar-Szakacs, I., Gallese, V., Buccino, G., & Mazziotta, J. C. (2005). Grasping the intentions of others with one's own mirror neuron system. *Public Library of Science: Biology, 3*(3), e79.

Isabella, R. (1993). Origins of attachment: Maternal interactive behavior across the first year. *Child Development, 64,* 605–621.

Isabella, R., & Belsky, J. (1991). Interactional synchrony and the origins of infant–mother attachment: A replication study. *Child Development, 62,* 373–384.

Isasi, R. M., Nguyen, T. M., & Knoppers, B. M. (2006). *National regulatory frameworks regarding human genetic modification technologies (somatic and germline modification).* Montréal, Québec: Centre de Recherche en Droit Public (CRDP), Université de Montréal.

Ishihara, K., Warita, K., Tanida, T., Sugawara, T., Kitagawa, H., & Hoshi, N. (2007). Does paternal exposure to 2,3,7,8-tetrachlorodibenzo-p-dioxin (TCDD) affect the sex ratio of offspring? *Journal of Veterinary Medical Science, 69,* 347–352.

Israel, M. Johnson, C., & Brooks, P. J. (2000). From states to events: The acquisition of English passive participles. *Cognitive Linguistics, 11,* 103–129.

Itti, E., Gaw, G. I. T., Pawlikowska-Haddal, A., Boone, K. B., Mlikotic, A., & Itti, L. (2006). The structural brain correlates of cognitive deficits in adults with Klinefelter's syndrome. *Journal of Clinical Endocrinology and Metabolism, 91,* 1423–1427.

Izard, C. E., & Ackerman, B. P. (2000). Motivational, organizational, and regulatory functions of discrete emotions. In M. Lewis & J. M. Haviland-Jones (Eds.), *Handbook of emotions* (2nd ed., pp. 253–264). New York: Guilford.

Izard, C. E., Trentacosta, C. J., King, K. A., & Mostow, A. J. (2004). An emotion-based prevention program for Head Start children. *Early Education and Development, 15,* 407–422.

J

Jaakkola, J. J., & Gissler, M. (2004). Maternal smoking in pregnancy, fetal development, and childhood asthma. *American Journal of Public Health, 94,* 136–140.

Jackson, A. P., Bentler, P. M., & Franke, T. M. (2006). Employment and parenting among current and former welfare recipients. *Journal of Social Service Research, 33,* 13–25.

Jackson, L. A., von Eye, A., Biocca, F. A., Barbatsis, G., Zhao, Y., & Fitzgerald, H. E. (2006). Does home Internet use influence the academic performance of low-income children? *Developmental Psychology, 42,* 429–435.

Jackson, L. A., Zhao, Y., Kolenic, A., III, Fitzgerald, H. E., Harold, R., & von Eye, A. (2008). Race, gender, and information technology use: The new digital divide. *CyberPsychology and Behavior, 11,* 437–442.

Jackson, R. A., Gibson, K. A., & Wu, Y. W. (2004). Perinatal outcomes in singletons following in vitro fertilization: A meta-analysis. *Obstetrics and Gynecology, 103,* 551–563.

Jacobs, J. A., & Gerson, K. (2004). *The time divide: Work, family, and gender inequality.* Cambridge, MA: Harvard University Press.

Jacobs, J. E., Lanza, S., Osgood, D. W., Eccles, J. S., & Wigfield, A. (2002). Changes in children's self-competence and values: Gender and domain differences across grades one through twelve. *Child Development, 73,* 509–527.

Jacobs, J. E., & Weisz, V. (1994). Gender stereotypes: Implications for gifted education. *Roeper Review, 16,* 152–155.

Jacobs, J. N., & Kelley, M. L. (2006). Predictors of paternal involvement in childcare in dual-earner families with young children. *Fathering, 4,* 23–47.

Jacobson, J. L., & Jacobson, S. W. (2003). Prenatal exposure to polychlorinated biphenyls and attention at school age. *Journal of Pediatrics, 143,* 780–788.

Jacobson, S. W., Jacobson, J. L., Sokol, R. J., Chiodo, L. M., & Corobana, R. (2004). Maternal age, alcohol abuse history, and quality of parenting as moderators of the effects of prenatal alcohol exposure on 7.5-year intellectual function. *Alcoholism, Clinical and Experimental Research, 28,* 1732–1745.

Jacquet, P. (2004). Sensitivity of germ cells and embryos to ionizing radiation. *Journal of Biological Regulators and Homeostatic Agents, 18,* 106–114.

Jaffe, J., Beebe, B., Feldstein, S., Crown, C. L., & Jasnow, M. D. (2001). Rhythms of dialogue in infancy. *Monographs of the Society for Research in Child Development, 66*(2, Serial No. 265).

Jaffee, S. R., Moffitt, T. E., Caspi, A., & Taylor, A. (2003). Life with (or without) father: The benefits of living with two biological parents depend on the father's antisocial behavior. *Child Development, 74,* 109–126.

Jambunathan, S., Burts, D. C., & Pierce, S. (2000). Comparisons of parenting attitudes among five ethnic groups in the United States. *Journal of Comparative Family Studies, 31,* 395–406.

Jamieson, J. R. (1995). Interactions between mothers and children who are deaf. *Journal of Early Intervention, 19,* 108–117.

Jansen, A., Theunissen, N., Slechten, K., Nederkoorn, C., Boon, B., Mulkens, S., & Roefs, A. (2003). Overweight children overeat after exposure to food cues. *Eating Behaviors, 4,* 197–209.

Jansen, J., de Weerth, C., & Riksen-Walraven, J. M. (2008). Breastfeeding and the mother–infant relationship. *Developmental Review, 28,* 503–521.

Janssens, J. M. A. M., & Deković, M. (1997). Child rearing, prosocial moral reasoning, and prosocial behavior. *International Journal of Behavioral Development, 20,* 509–527.

Janz, K. F., Dawson, J. D., & Mahoney, L. T. (2000). Tracking physical fitness and physical activity from childhood to adolescence: The Muscatine study. *Medicine and Science in Sports and Exercise, 32,* 1250–1257.

Jaudes, P. K., & Mackey-Bilaver, L. (2008). Do chronic conditions increase young children's risk of being maltreated? *Child Abuse and Neglect, 32,* 671–681.

Jayakody, R., & Kalil, A. (2002). Social fathering in low-income, African-American families with preschool children. *Journal of Marriage and the Family, 64,* 504–516.

Jeffrey, J. (2004, November). Parents often blind to their kids' weight. *British Medical Journal Online.* Retrieved from content.health.msn.com/content/article/97/104292.htm

Jenkins, J. M., Rasbash, J., & O'Connor, T. G. (2003). The role of the shared family context in differential parenting. *Developmental Psychology, 39,* 99–113.

Jenkins, J. M., Turrell, S. L., Kogushi, Y., Lollis, S., & Ross, H. S. (2003). A longitudinal investigation of the dynamics of mental state talk in families. *Child Development, 74,* 905–920.

Jenni, O. G., Molinari, L., Caflisch, J. A., & Largo, R. H. (2007). Sleep duration from ages 1 to 10 years: Variability and stability in comparison with growth. *Pediatrics, 120,* e769–e776.

Jenni, O. G., & O'Connor, B. B. (2005). Children's sleep: An interplay between culture and biology. *Pediatrics, 115,* 204–216.

Jensen, A. R. (1969). How much can we boost IQ and scholastic achievement? *Harvard Educational Review, 39,* 1–123.

Jensen, A. R. (1998). *The g factor: The science of mental ability.* New York: Praeger.

Jensen, A. R. (2001). Spearman's hypothesis. In J. M. Collis & S. Messick (Eds.), *Intelligence and personality: Bridging the gap in theory and measurement* (pp. 3–24). Mahwah, NJ: Erlbaum.

Jensen, A. R. (2002). Galton's legacy to research on intelligence. *Journal of Biosocial Science, 34,* 145–172.

Jerome, E. M., Hamre, B. K., & Pianta, R. C. (2009). Teacher-child relationships from kindergarten to sixth grade: Early childhood predictors of teacher-perceived conflict and closeness. *Social Development, 18,* 915–945.

Jeynes, W. H. (2005). A meta-analysis of the relation of parental involvement to urban elementary school student academic achievement. *Urban Education, 40,* 237–269.

Jeynes, W. H. (2007). The impact of parental remarriage on children: A meta-analysis. *Marriage and Family Review, 40,* 75–102.

Ji, C. Y., & Cheng, T. O. (2008). Prevalence and geographic distribution of childhood obesity in China in 2005. *International Journal of Cardiology, 131,* 1–8.

Jiao, S., Ji, G., & Jing, Q. (1996). Cognitive development of Chinese urban only children and children with siblings. *Child Development, 67,* 387–395.

Jipson, J. L., & Gelman, S. A. (2007). Robots and rodents: Children's inferences about living and nonliving kinds. *Child Development, 78,* 1675–1688.

Joh, A. S., & Adolph, K. E. (2006). Learning from falling. *Child Development, 77,* 89–102.

Johnson, D. E. (2000). Medical and developmental sequelae of early childhood institutionalization in Eastern European adoptees. In C. A. Nelson (Ed.), *Minnesota symposia on child psychology* (Vol. 31, pp. 113–162). Mahwah, NJ: Erlbaum.

Johnson, E. K., & Seidl, A. (2008). Clause segmentation by 6-month-old infants: A crosslinguistic perspective. *Infancy, 13,* 440–455.

Johnson, J., Im-Bolter, N., & Pascual-Leone, J. (2003). Development of mental attention in gifted and mainstream children: The role of mental capacity, inhibition, and speed of processing. *Child Development, 74,* 1594–1614.

Johnson, J. G., Cohen, P., Smailes, E. M., Kasen, S., & Brook, J. S. (2002). Television viewing and aggressive behavior during adolescence and adulthood. *Science, 295,* 2468–2471.

Johnson, K. C., & Daviss, B.-A. (2005). Outcomes of planned home births with certified professional midwives: Large prospective study in North America. *British Medical Journal, 330,* 1416.

Johnson, M. H. (1999). Ontogenetic constraints on neural and behavioral plasticity: Evidence from imprinting and face processing. *Canadian Journal of Experimental Psychology, 55,* 77–90.

Johnson, M. H. (2001a). The development and neural basis of face recognition: Comment and speculation. *Infant and Child Development, 10,* 31–33.

Johnson, M. H. (2001b). Infants' initial "knowledge" of the world: A cognitive neuroscience perspective. In F. Lacerda, C. von Hofsten, & M. Heimann (Eds.), *Emerging cognitive abilities in early infancy* (pp. 53–72). Mahwah, NJ: Erlbaum.

Johnson, M. H. (2005). Developmental neuroscience, psychophysiology, and genetics. In M. H. Bornstein & M. E. Lamb (Eds.), *Developmental science: An advanced textbook* (5th ed., pp. 187–222). Mahwah, NJ: Erlbaum.

Johnson, S. C., Dweck, C. S., & Chen, F. S. (2007). Evidence for infants' internal working models of attachment. *Psychological Science, 18,* 501–502.

Johnson, S. P. (1997). Young infants' perception of object unity: Implications for development of attentional and cognitive skills. *Current Directions in Psychological Science, 6,* 5–11.

Johnson, S. P. (2009). Developmental origins of object perception. In A. Woodward & A. Needham (Eds.), *Learning and the infant mind* (pp. 47–65). New York: Oxford University Press.

Johnson, S. P., Bremner, J. G., Slater, A., Mason, U., Foster, K., & Cheshire, A. (2003). Infants' perception of object trajectories. *Child Development, 74,* 94–108.

Johnson, S. P., Slemmer, J. A., & Amso, D. (2004). Where infants look determines how they see: Eye movements and object perception performance in 3-month-olds. *Infancy, 6,* 185–201.

Johnston, M. V., Nishimura, A., Harum, K., Pekar, J., & Blue, M. E. (2001). Sculpting the developing brain. *Advances in Pediatrics, 48,* 1–38.

Jones, E. F., & Thompson, N. R. (2001). Action perception and outcome valence: Effects on children's inferences of intentionality and moral and liking judgments. *Journal of Genetic Psychology, 162,* 154–166.

Jones, H. E. (2006). Drug addiction during pregnancy: Advances in maternal treatment and understanding child outcomes. *Current Directions in Psychological Science, 15,* 126–130.

Jones, J., Lopez, A., & Wilson, M. (2003). Congenital toxoplasmosis. *American Family Physician, 67,* 2131–2137.

Jones, N. A., Field, T., & Davalos, M. (2000). Right frontal EEG asymmetry and lack of empathy in preschool children of depressed mothers. *Child Psychiatry and Human Development, 30,* 189–204.

Jones, R. L., Homa, D. M., Meyer, P. A., Brody, D. J., Caldwell, K. L., Pirkle J. L., et al. (2009). Trends in blood lead levels and blood lead testing among U.S. children aged 1 to 5 years: 1998–2004. *Pediatrics, 123,* e376–385.

Jones, S. M., Brown, J. L., & Aber, J. L. (2008). Classroom settings as targets of intervention and research. In M. Shinn & H. Yoshikawa (Eds.), *Toward positive youth development: Transforming schools and community programs* (pp. 58–77). New York: Oxford University Press.

Jones, S. S. (2006). Exploration or imitation? The effect of music on 4-week-old infants' tongue protrusions. *Infant Behavior and Development, 29,* 126–130.

Jongbloet, P. H., Zielhuis, G. A., Groenewoud, H. M., & Pasker-De Jong, P. C. (2001). The secular trends in male:female ratio at birth in postwar industrialized countries. *Environmental Health Perspectives, 109,* 749–752.

Jordan, B. (1993). *Birth in four cultures.* Prospect Heights, IL: Waveland.

Joseph, R. M., & Tager-Flusberg, H. (2004). The relationship of theory of mind and executive functions to symptom type and severity in children with autism. *Development and Psychopathology, 16,* 137–155.

Joshi, P. T., O'Donnell, D. A., Cullins, L. M., & Lewin, S. (2006). Children exposed to war and terrorism. In M. M. Feerick & G. B. Silverman (Eds.), *Children exposed to violence* (pp. 53–84). Baltimore: Paul H. Brookes.

Juby, H., Billette, J.-M., Laplante, B., & Le Bourdais, C. (2007). Nonresident fathers and children: Parents' new unions and frequency of contact. *Journal of Family Issues, 28,* 1220–1245.

Judge, S., Puckett, K., & Bell, S. M. (2006). Closing the digital divide: Update from the Early Childhood Longitudinal Study. *Journal of Educational Research, 100,* 52–60.

Jumpstart Evaluation Team. (2008, April). *Influence of Jumpstart implementation quality on child outcomes.* Paper presented at the annual meeting of the American Educational Research Association, New York.

Jürgensen, M., Hiort, O., Holterhus, P.-M., & Thyen, U. (2007). Gender role behavior in children with XY karyotype and disorders of sex development. *Hormones and Behavior, 51,* 443–453.

Jusczyk, P. W. (2001). In the beginning was the word . . . In F. Lacerda & C. von Hofsten (Eds.), *Emerging cognitive abilities in early infancy* (pp. 173–192). Mahwah, NJ: Erlbaum.

Jusczyk, P. W. (2002). Some critical developments in acquiring native language sound organization. *Annals of Otology, Rhinology and Laryngology, 189,* 11–15.

Jusczyk, P. W., & Hohne, E. A. (1997). Infants' memory for spoken words. *Science, 277,* 1984–1986.

Jusczyk, P. W., Johnson, S. P., Spelke, E. S., & Kennedy, L. J. (1999). Synchronous change and perception of object unity: Evidence from adults and infants. *Cognition, 71,* 257–288.

Jusczyk, P. W., & Luce, P. A. (2002). Speech perception. In H. Pashler & S. Yantis (Eds.), *Steven's handbook of experimental psychology: Vol. 1. Sensation and perception* (3rd ed., pp. 493–536). New York: Wiley.

Justice, E. M. (1986). Developmental changes in judgments of relative strategy effectiveness. *British Journal of Developmental Psychology, 4,* 75–81.

K

Kagan, J. (1998). Biology and the child. In N. Eisenberg (Ed.), *Handbook of child psychology: Vol. 3. Social, emotional, and personality development* (5th ed., pp. 177–236). New York: Wiley.

Kagan, J. (2003). Behavioral inhibition as a temperamental category. In R. J. Davidson, K. R. Scherer, & H. H. Goldsmith (Eds.), *Handbook of affective sciences* (pp. 320–331). New York: Oxford University Press.

Kagan, J. (2008). Behavioral inhibition as a risk factor for psychopathology. In T. P. Beauchaine & S. P. Hinshaw (Eds.), *Child and adolescent psychopathology* (pp. 157–179). Hoboken, NJ: Wiley.

Kagan, J. (2010). Emotions and temperament. In M. H. Bornstein (Ed.), *Handbook of cultural developmental science* (pp 175–194). New York: Psychology Press.

Kagan, J., Arcus, D., Snidman, N., Feng, W. Y., Hendler, J., & Greene, S. (1994). Reactivity in infants: A cross-national comparison. *Developmental Psychology, 30,* 342–345.

Kagan, J., & Fox, N. A. (2006). Biology, culture, and temperamental biases. In N. Eisenberg (Ed.),

Handbook of child psychology: Vol. 3. Social, emotional, and personality development (6th ed., pp. 167–225). Hoboken, NJ: Wiley.

Kagan, J., & Saudino, K. J. (2001). Behavioral inhibition and related temperaments. In R. N. Emde & J. K. Hewitt (Eds.), *Infancy to early childhood: Genetic and environmental influences on developmental change* (pp. 111–119). New York: Oxford University Press.

Kagan, J., & Snidman, N. (2004). *The long shadow of temperament.* Cambridge, MA: Belknap Press.

Kagan, J., Snidman, N., Kahn, V., & Towsley, S. (2007). The preservation of two infant temperaments into adolescence. *Monographs of the Society for Research in Child Development, 72*(2, Serial No. 287).

Kagan, J., Snidman, N., Zentner, M., & Peterson, E. (1999). Infant temperament and anxious symptoms in school-age children. *Development and Psychopathology, 11,* 209–224.

Kahn, R. S., Khoury, J., Nichols, W. C., & Lanphear, B. M. (2003). Role of dopamine transporter genotype and maternal prenatal smoking in childhood hyperactive–impulsive, inattentive, and oppositional behaviors. *Journal of Pediatrics, 143,* 104–110.

Kaijser, M., Bonamy, A. K., Akre, O., Cnattingius, S., Granath, F., Norman, M., et al. (2009). Perinatal risk factors for diabetes in later life. *Diabetes, 58,* 523–526.

Kail, R., & Park, Y. (1992). Global developmental change in processing time. *Merrill-Palmer Quarterly, 38,* 525–541.

Kail, R., & Park, Y. (1994). Processing time, articulation time, and memory span. *Journal of Experimental Child Psychology, 57,* 281–291.

Kail, R. V. (2003). Information processing and memory. In M. H. Bornstein, L. Davidson, C. L. M. Keyes, K. A. Moore, and the Center for Child Well-Being (Eds.), *Well-being: Positive development across the life course* (pp. 269–280). Mahwah, NJ: Erlbaum.

Kaiser Commission on Medicaid and the Uninsured. (2009). *Children's Health Insurance Program Reauthorization Act of 2009.* Washington, DC: Henry J. Kaiser Family Foundation.

Kaitz, M., Good, A., Rokem, A. M., & Eidelman, A. I. (1987). Mothers' recognition of their newborns by olfactory cues. *Developmental Psychobiology, 20,* 587–591.

Kaitz, M., Good, A., Rokem, A. M., & Eidelman, A. I. (1988). Mothers' and fathers' recognition of their newborns' photographs during the postpartum period. *Journal of Developmental and Behavioral Pediatrics, 9,* 223–226.

Kaitz, M., Meirov, H., Landman, I., & Eidelman, A. I. (1993a). Infant recognition by tactile cues. *Infant Behavior and Development, 16,* 333–341.

Kaitz, M., Shiri, S., Danziger, S., Hershko, Z., & Eidelman, A. I. (1993b). Fathers can also recognize their newborns by touch. *Infant Behavior and Development, 17,* 205–207.

Kaller, C. P., Rahm, B., Spreer, J., Mader, I., & Unterrainer, J. M. (2008). Thinking around the corner: The development of planning abilities. *Brain and Cognition, 67,* 360–370.

Kalra, L., & Ratan, R. (2007). Recent advances in stroke rehabilitation. *Stroke, 38,* 235–237.

Kane, C. M. (2000). African-American family dynamics as perceived by family members. *Journal of Black Studies, 30,* 691–702.

Kane, P., & Garber, J. (2004). The relations among depression in fathers, children's psychopathology, and father–child conflict: A meta-analysis. *Clinical Psychology Review, 24,* 339–360.

Kang, N. H., & Hong, M. (2008). Achieving excellence in teacher workforce and equity in learning opportunities in South Korea. *Educational Researcher, 37,* 200–207.

Kaplowitz, P. B. (2007). Link between body fat and the timing of puberty. *Pediatrics, 121,* S208–S217.

Karafantis, D. M., & Levy, S. R. (2004). The role of children's lay theories about the malleability of human attributes in beliefs about and volunteering for disadvantaged groups. *Child Development, 75,* 236–250.

Karrass, J., & Braungart-Rieker, J. M. (2005). Effects of shared parent–infant book reading on early language acquisition. *Applied Developmental Psychology, 26,* 133–148.

Kastens, K. A., & Liben, L. S. (2007). Eliciting self-explanations improves children's performance on a field-based map skills task. *Cognition and Instruction, 25,* 45–74.

Kato, I., Franco, P., Groswasser, J., Scaillet, S., Kelmanson, I., Togari, H., & Kahn, A. (2003). Incomplete arousal processes in infants who were victims of sudden death. *American Journal of Respiratory and Critical Care, 168,* 1298–1303.

Katz, L. F., & Windecker-Nelson, B. (2004). Parental meta-emotion philosophy in families with conduct-problem children: Links with peer relations. *Journal of Abnormal Child Psychology, 32,* 385–398.

Katzmarzyk, P. T., & Leonard, W. R. (1998). Climatic influences on human body size and proportions: Ecological adaptations and secular trends. *American Journal of Physical Anthropology, 106,* 483–503.

Kaufman, J., Csibra, G., & Johnson, M. H. (2005). Oscillatory activity in the infant brain reflects object maintenance. *Proceedings of the National Academy of Sciences, 102,* 15271–15274.

Kavanaugh, R. D. (2006a). Pretend play. In B. Spodek & O. N. Saracho (Eds.), *Handbook of research on the education of young children* (2nd ed., pp. 269–278). Mahwah, NJ: Erlbaum.

Kavanaugh, R. D. (2006b). Pretend play and theory of mind. In L. Balter & C. S. Tamis-LeMonda (Eds.), *Child psychology: A handbook of contemporary issues* (2nd ed., pp. 153–166). New York: Psychology Press.

Kavsek, M. (2004). Predicting later IQ from infant visual habituation and dishabituation: A meta-analysis. *Journal of Applied Developmental Psychology, 25,* 369–393.

Kaye, K., & Marcus, J. (1981). Infant imitation: The sensory-motor agenda. *Developmental Psychology, 17,* 258–265.

Kazdin, A. E. (2003). Problem-solving skills training and parent management training for conduct disorder. In A. E. Kazdin & J. R. Weisz (Eds.), *Evidence-based psychotherapies for children and adolescents* (pp. 241–262). New York: Guilford.

Kazdin, A. E., & Whitley, M. E. (2003). Treatment of parental stress to enhance therapeutic change among children referred for aggressive and antisocial behavior. *Journal of Consulting and Clinical Psychology, 71,* 504–515.

Keating-Lefler, R., Hudson, D. B., Campbell-Grossman, C., Fleck, M. O., & Westfall, J. (2004). Needs, concerns, and social support of single, low-income mothers. *Issues in Mental Health Nursing, 25,* 381–401.

Keefe, M. R., Barbosa, G. A., Froese-Fretz, A., Kotzer, A. M., & Lobo, M. (2005). An intervention program for families with irritable infants. *American Journal of Maternal/Child Nursing, 30,* 230–236.

Keil, F. C. (1986). Conceptual domains and the acquisition of metaphor. *Cognitive Development, 1,* 72–96.

Keil, F. C., & Lockhart, K. L. (1999). Explanatory understanding in conceptual development. In E. K. Scholnick, K. Nelson, S. A. Gelman, & P. H. Miller (Eds.), *Conceptual development: Piaget's legacy* (pp. 103–130). Mahwah, NJ: Erlbaum.

Keller, H., Borke, Y. J., Kärtner, J., Jensen, H., & Papaligoura, Z. (2004). Developmental consequences of early parenting experiences: Self-recognition and self-regulation in three cultural communities. *Child Development, 75,* 1745–1760.

Keller, H., Kärtner, J., Borke, J., Yovsi, R., & Kleis, A. (2005). Parenting styles and the development of the categorical self: A longitudinal study on mirror self-recognition in Cameroonian Nso and German families. *International Journal of Behavioral Development, 29,* 496–504.

Keller, S. S., Crow, T., Foundas, A., Amunts, K., & Roberts, N. (2009). Broca's area: Nomenclature, anatomy, typology and symmetry. *Brain and Language, 109,* 29–48.

Kelley, S. A., Brownell, C. A., & Campbell, S. B. (2000). Mastery motivation and self-evaluative affect in toddlers: Longitudinal relations with maternal behavior. *Child Development, 71,* 1061–1071.

Kellman, P. J., & Arterberry, M. E. (2006). Infant visual perception. In D. Kuhn & R. Siegler (Eds.), *Handbook*

of child psychology: Vol. 2. Cognition, perception, and language (6th ed., pp. 109–160). Hoboken, NJ: Wiley.

Kelly, D. J., Liu, S., Ge, L., Quinn, P. C., Slater, A. M., Lee, K., et al. (2007a). Cross-race preferences for same-race faces extend beyond the African versus Caucasian contrast in 3-month-old infants. *Infancy, 11,* 87–95.

Kelly, D. J., Quinn, P. C., Slater, A. M., Lee, K., Ge, L., & Pascalis, O. (2007b). The other-race effect develops during infancy: Evidence of perceptual narrowing. *Psychological Science, 18,* 1084–1089.

Kelly, N., & Norwich, B. (2004). Pupils' perceptions of self and of labels: Moderate learning difficulties in mainstream and special schools. *British Journal of Educational Psychology, 74,* 411–435.

Kemeny, M. E. (2003). The psychobiology of stress. *Current Directions in Psychological Science, 12,* 124–129.

Kempe, C. H., Silverman, B. F., Steele, P. W., Droegemueller, P. W., & Silver, H. K. (1962). The battered-child syndrome. *Journal of the American Medical Association, 181,* 17–24.

Kendall, G., & Peebles, D. (2005). Acute fetal hypoxia: The modulating effect of infection. *Early Human Development, 81,* 27–34.

Kendrick, D., Barlow, J., Hampshire, A., Stewart-Brown, S., & Polnay, L. (2008). Parenting interventions and the prevention of unintentional injuries in childhood: Systematic review and meta-analysis. *Child: Care, Health and Development, 34,* 682–695.

Kennedy, A. M., & Gust, D. A. (2008). Measles outbreak associated with a church congregation: A study of immunization attitudes of congregation members. *Public Health Reports, 123,* 126–134.

Kennell, J. H., Klaus, M., McGrath, S., Robertson, S., & Hinkley, C. (1991). Continuous emotional support during labor in a U.S. hospital. *Journal of the American Medical Association, 265,* 2197–2201.

Kenney, G. M., Lynch, V., & Cook, A. (2010). Who and where are the children yet to enroll in Medicaid and the Children's Health Insurance Program? *Health Affairs, 29,* 1920–1929.

Keren, M., Feldman, R., Namdari-Weinbaum, I., Spitzer, S., & Tyano, S. (2005). Relations between parents' interactive style in dyadic and triadic play and toddlers' symbolic capacity. *American Journal of Orthopsychiatry, 75,* 599–607.

Kern, S. (2007). Lexicon development in French-speaking infants. *First Language, 27,* 227–250.

Kernis, M. H. (2002). Self-esteem as a multifaceted construct. In T. M. Brinthaupt & R. P. Lipka (Eds.), *Understanding early adolescent self and identity* (pp. 57–88). Albany, NY: State University of New York Press.

Kerr, D. C. R., Lopez, N. L., Olson, S. L., & Sameroff, A. J. (2004). Parental discipline and externalizing behavior problems in early childhood: The roles of moral regulation and child gender. *Journal of Abnormal Child Psychology, 32,* 369–383.

Kesler, S. R. (2007). Turner syndrome. *Child and Adolescent Psychiatric Clinics of North America, 16,* 709–722.

Kessen, W. (1967). Sucking and looking: Two organized congenital patterns of behavior in the human newborn. In H. W. Stevenson, E. H. Hess, & H. L. Rheingold (Eds.), *Early behavior: Comparative and developmental approaches* (pp. 147–179). New York: Wiley.

Kessler, R. C., Adler, L. A., Barkley, R., Biederman, J., Conners, C. K., & Demler, O. (2006). The prevalence and correlates of adult ADHD in the United States: Results from the National Comorbidity Survey Replication. *American Journal of Psychiatry, 163,* 716–723.

Kessler, R. C., Adler, L. A., Barkley, R., Biederman, J., Conners, C. K., & Faraone, S. V. (2005). Patterns and predictors of attention-deficit/hyperactivity disorder persistence into adulthood: Results from the National Comorbidity Survey Replication. *Biological Psychiatry, 57,* 1442–1451.

Kieffer, M. J. (2008). Catching up or falling behind? Initial English proficiency, concentrated poverty, and the reading growth of language minority learners in the United States. *Journal of Educational Psychology, 100,* 851–868.

Kieras, J. E., Tobin, R. M., Graziano, W. G., & Rothbart, M. K. (2005). You can't always get what you want: Effortful control and children's responses to undesirable gifts. *Psychological Science, 16,* 391–396.

Killen, M., Crystal, D., & Watanabe, H. (2002). The individual and the group: Japanese and American children's evaluations of peer exclusion, tolerance of difference, and prescriptions for conformity. *Child Development, 73,* 1788–1802.

Killen, M., Lee-Kim, J., McGlothlin, H., & Stangor, C. (2002). How children and adolescents evaluate gender and racial exclusion. *Monographs of the Society for Research in Child Development, 67*(4, Serial No. 271).

Killen, M., Margie, N. G., & Sinno, S. (2006). Morality in the context of intergroup relationships. In M. Killen & J. G. Smetana (Eds.), *Handbook of moral development* (pp. 155–183). Mahwah, NJ: Erlbaum.

Killen, M., & Stangor, M. (2001). Children's social reasoning about inclusion and exclusion in gender and race peer group contexts. *Child Development, 72,* 174–186.

Kilpatrick, S. W., & Sanders, D. M. (1978). Body image stereotypes: A developmental comparison. *Journal of Genetic Psychology, 132,* 87–95.

Kim, J., & Cicchetti, D. (2006). Longitudinal trajectories of self-system processes and depressive symptoms among maltreated and nonmaltreated children. *Child Development, 77,* 624–639.

Kim, J., McHale, S. M., Osgood, D. W., & Crouter, A. C. (2006). Longitudinal course and family correlates of sibling relationships from childhood through adolescence. *Child Development, 77,* 1746–1761.

Kim, J. M. (1998). Korean children's concepts of adult and peer authority and moral reasoning. *Developmental Psychology, 34,* 947–955.

Kim, J. M., & Turiel, E. (1996). Korean children's concepts of adult and peer authority. *Social Development, 5,* 310–329.

Kim, M., McGregor, K. K., & Thompson, C. K. (2000). Early lexical development in English- and Korean-speaking children: Language-general and language-specific patterns. *Journal of Child Language, 27,* 225–254.

Kimbro, R. T. (2006). On-the-job moms: Work and breastfeeding initiation and duration for a sample of low-income women. *Maternal and Child Health Journal, 10,* 19–26.

King, E. M., & Mason, A. D. (2001). *Engendering development: Through gender equality in rights, resources, and voice.* Washington, DC: UNICEF.

King, V. (2007). When children have two mothers: Relationships with nonresident mothers, stepmothers, and fathers. *Journal of Marriage and Family, 69,* 1178–1193.

Kinney, H. C. (2009). Brainstem mechanisms underlying the sudden infant death syndrome: Evidence from human pathologic studies. *Developmental Psychobiology, 51,* 223–233.

Kinnunen, M.-L., Pietilainen, K., & Rissanen, A. (2006). Body size and overweight from birth to adulthood. In L. Pulkkinen & J. Kaprio (Eds.), *Socioemotional development and health from adolescence to adulthood* (pp. 95–107). New York: Cambridge University Press.

Kirchner, G. (2000). *Children's games from around the world.* Boston: Allyn and Bacon.

Kiriakidis, S. P., & Kavoura, A. (2010). Cyberbullying: A review of the literature on harassment through the Internet and other electronic means. *Family and Community Health, 33,* 82–93.

Kirkham, N. Z., Cruess, L., & Diamond, A. (2003). Helping children apply their knowledge to their behavior on a dimension-switching task. *Developmental Science, 6,* 449–476.

Kisilevsky, B. S., Hains, S. M. J., Lee, K., Muir, D. W., Xu, F., Fu, G., Zhao, Z. Y., & Yang, R. L. (1998). The still-face effect in Chinese and Canadian 3- to 6-month-old infants. *Developmental Psychology, 34,* 629–639.

Kisilevsky, B. S., Hains, S. M. J., Lee, K., Xie, X., Huang, H., Ye, H. H., Zhang, K., & Wang, Z. (2003).

Effects of experience on fetal voice recognition. *Psychological Science, 14,* 220–224.

Kisilevsky, B. S., Hains, S. M. J., Brown, C. A., Lee, C. T., Cowperthwaite, B., & Stutzman, S. S. (2009). Fetal sensitivity to properties of maternal speech and language. *Infant Behavior and Development, 32,* 59–71.

Kisilevsky, B. S., & Low, J. A. (1998). Human fetal behavior: 100 years of study. *Developmental Review, 18,* 1–29.

Kitzmann, K. M., Cohen, R., & Lockwood, R. L. (2002). Are only children missing out? Comparison of the peer-related social competence of only children and siblings. *Journal of Social and Personal Relationships, 19,* 299–316.

Kitzmann, K. M., Gaylord, N. K., Holt, A. R., & Kenny, E. D. (2003). Child witnesses to domestic violence: A meta-analytic review. *Journal of Consulting and Clinical Psychology, 71,* 339–352.

Kjønniksen, L., Torsheim, T., & Wold, B. (2008). Tracking of leisure-time physical activity during adolescence and young adulthood: A 10-year longitudinal study. *International Journal of Behavioral Nutrition and Physical Activity, 5,* 69.

Klahr, D., & MacWhinney, B. (1998). Information processing. In D. Kuhn & R. S. Siegler (Eds.), *Handbook of child psychology: Vol. 2. Cognition, perception, and language* (5th ed., pp. 631–678). New York: Wiley.

Klahr, D., & Nigam, M. (2004). The equivalence of learning paths in early science instruction: Effects of direct instruction and discovery learning. *Psychological Science, 15,* 661–667.

Klaus, M. H., & Kennell, J. H. (1982). *Parent–infant bonding.* St. Louis: Mosby.

Klebanov, P. K., Brooks-Gunn, J., McCarton, C., & McCormick, M. C. (1998). The contribution of neighborhood and family income to developmental test scores over the first three years of life. *Child Development, 69,* 1420–1436.

Klein, M. C. (2006). Does epidural analgesia increase rate of cesarean section? *Canadian Family Physician, 52,* 419–421.

Klein, P. J., & Meltzoff, A. N. (1999). Long-term memory, forgetting, and deferred imitation in 12-month-old infants. *Developmental Science, 2,* 102–113.

Klenberg, L., Korkman, M., & Lahti-Nuuttila, P. (2001). Differential development of attention and executive functions in 3- to 12-year-old Finnish children. *Developmental Neuropsychology, 20,* 407–428.

Klesges, L. M., Johnson, K. C., Ward, K. D., & Barnard, M. (2001). Smoking cessation in pregnant women. *Obstetrics and Gynecology Clinics of North America, 28,* 269–282.

Klibanoff, R. S., Levine, S. C., Huttenlocher, J., Vasilyeva, M., & Hedges, L. V. (2006). Preschool children's mathematical knowledge: The effect of teacher "math talk." *Developmental Psychology, 42,* 59–69.

Kliegman, R. M., Behrman, R. E., Jenson, H. B., & Stanton, B. F. (Eds.). (2008). *Nelson textbook of pediatrics e-dition* (18th ed. text with continually updated online references.) Philadelphia: Saunders.

Kliewer, W., Fearnow, M. D., & Miller, P. A. (1996). Coping socialization in middle childhood: Tests of maternal and paternal influences. *Child Development, 67,* 2339–2357.

Klimes-Dougan, B., & Kistner, J. (1990). Physically abused preschoolers' responses to peers' distress. *Developmental Psychology, 26,* 599–602.

Klingman, A. (2006). Children and war trauma. In K. A. Renninger & I. E. Sigel (Eds.), *Handbook of child psychology: Vol. 4. Child psychology in practice* (6th ed., pp. 619–652). Hoboken, NJ: Wiley.

Klingner, J. K., Vaughn, S., Hughes, M. T., Schumm, J. S., & Elbaum, B. (1998). Outcomes for students with and without learning disabilities in inclusive classrooms. *Learning Disabilities Research and Practice, 13,* 153–161.

Klitzing, K. von, Simoni, H., Amsler, F., & Buergin, D. (1999). The role of the father in early family interactions. *Infant Mental Health Journal, 20,* 222–237.

Klomsten, A. T., Skaalvik, E. M., & Espnes, G. A. (2004). Physical self-concept and sports: Do gender differences exist? *Sex Roles, 50,* 119–127.

Knafo, A., & Plomin, R. (2006). Parental discipline and affection and children's prosocial behavior: Genetic and environmental links. *Journal of Personality and Social Psychology, 90,* 147–164.

Knickmeyer, R. C., Gouttard, S., Kang, C., Evans, D., Wilber, K., Smith, J. K., et al. (2008). A structural MRI study of human brain development from birth to 2 years. *Journal of Neuroscience, 28,* 12176–12182.

Knight, N., Sousa, P., Barrett, J. L., & Atran, S. (2004). Children's attributions of beliefs to humans and God: Cross-cultural evidence. *Cognitive Science, 28,* 117–126.

Knobloch, H., & Pasamanick, B. (Eds.). (1974). *Gesell and Amatruda's Developmental Diagnosis.* Hagerstown, MD: Harper & Row.

Knopf, M., Kraus, U., & Kressley-Mba, R. A. (2006). Relational information processing of novel unrelated actions by infants. *Infant Behavior and Development, 29,* 44–53.

Kobayashi, T., Hiraki, K., & Hasegawa, T. (2005). Auditory-visual intermodal matching of small numerosities in 6-month-old infants. *Developmental Science, 8,* 409–419.

Kobayashi, T., Kazuo, H., Ryoko, M., & Hasegawa, T. (2004). Baby arithmetic: One object plus one tone. *Cognition, 91,* B23–B34.

Kobayashi, Y. (1994). Conceptual acquisition and change through social interaction. *Human Development, 37,* 233–241.

Kochanska, G. (1991). Socialization and temperament in the development of guilt and conscience. *Child Development, 62,* 1379–1392.

Kochanska, G., & Aksan, N. (2006). Children's conscience and self-regulation. *Journal of Personality, 74,* 1587–1617.

Kochanska, G., Aksan, N., & Carlson, J. J. (2005). Temperament, relationships, and young children's receptive cooperation with their parents. *Developmental Psychology, 41,* 648–660.

Kochanska, G., Aksan, N., & Joy, M. E. (2007). Children's fearfulness as a moderator of parenting in early socialization: Two longitudinal studies. *Developmental Psychology, 43,* 222–237.

Kochanska, G., Aksan, N., & Nichols, K. E. (2003). Maternal power assertion in discipline and moral discourse contexts: Commonalities, differences, and implications for children's moral conduct and cognition. *Developmental Psychology, 39,* 949–963.

Kochanska, G., Aksan, N., Prisco, T. R., & Adams, E. E. (2008). Mother–child and father–child mutually responsive orientation in the first 2 years and children's outcomes at preschool age: Mechanisms of influence. *Child Development, 79,* 30–44.

Kochanska, G., Casey, R. J., & Fukumoto, A. (1995). Toddlers' sensitivity to standard violations. *Child Development, 66,* 643–656.

Kochanska, G., Forman, D. R., Aksan, N., & Dunbar, S. B. (2005). Pathways to conscience: Early mother–child mutually responsive orientation and children's moral emotion, conduct, and cognition. *Journal of Child Psychology and Psychiatry, 46,* 19–34.

Kochanska, G., Gross, J. N., Lin, M.-H., & Nichols, K. E. (2002). Guilt in young children: Development, determinants, and relations with broader system standards. *Child Development, 73,* 461–482.

Kochanska, G., & Knaack, A. (2003). Effortful control as a personality characteristic of young children: Antecedents, correlates, and consequences. *Journal of Personality, 71,* 1087–1112.

Kochanska, G., Murray, K. T., & Harlan, E. T. (2000). Effortful control in early childhood: Continuity and change, antecedents, and implications for social development. *Developmental Psychology, 36,* 220–232.

Kochenderfer-Ladd, B. (2003). Identification of aggressive and asocial victims and the stability of their peer victimization. *Merrill-Palmer Quarterly, 49,* 401–425.

Koelsch, S., Gunter, T., von Cramon, D., Zysset, S., Lohmann, G., & Friederici, A. (2002). Bach speaks: A cortical "language-network " serves the processing of music. *NeuroImage, 17,* 956–966.

Koestner, R., Franz, C., & Weinberger, J. (1990). The family origins of empathic concern: A 26-year longitudinal study. *Journal of Personality and Social Psychology, 58,* 709–717.

Kohen, D. E., Leventhal, T., Dahinten, V. S., & McIntosh, C. N. (2008). Neighborhood disadvantage: Pathways of effects for young children. *Child Development, 79,* 156–169.

Kohlberg, L. (1966). A cognitive-developmental analysis of children's sex-role concepts and attitudes. In E. E. Maccoby (Ed.), *The development of sex differences* (pp. 82–173). Stanford, CA: Stanford University Press.

Kolomer, S. R., & McCallion, P. (2005). Depression and caregiver mastery in grandfathers caring for their grandchildren. *International Journal of Aging and Human Development, 60,* 283–294.

Komsi, N., Räikkönen, K., Pesonen, A.-K., Heinonen, K., Keskivaara, P., Järvenpää, A.-L., & Strandberg, T. E. (2006). Continuity of temperament from infancy to middle childhood. *Infant Behavior and Development, 29,* 494–508.

Konner, M. J. (1977). Infancy among the Kalahari Desert San. In P. H. Leiderman, S. R. Tulkin, & A. Rosenfield (Eds.), *Culture and infancy: Variations in the human experience* (pp. 287–328). New York: Academic Press.

Konold, T. R., & Pianta, R. C. (2005). Empirically-derived, person-oriented patterns of school readiness in typically developing children: Description and prediction to first-grade achievement. *Applied Developmental Science, 9,* 174–187.

Kontic-Vucinic, O., Sulovic, N., & Radunovic, N. (2006). Micronutrients in women's reproductive health: II. Minerals and trace elements. *International Journal of Fertility and Women's Medicine, 51,* 116–124.

Kooijman, V., Hagoort, P., & Cutler, A. (2009). Prosodic structure in early word segmentation: ERP evidence from Dutch ten-month-olds. *Infancy, 14,* 591–612.

Kopp, C. B., & Neufeld, S. J. (2003). Emotional development during infancy. In R. Davidson, K. R. Scherer, & H. H. Goldsmith (Eds.), *Handbook of affective sciences* (pp. 347–374). Oxford, UK: Oxford University Press.

Korkman, M., Kettunen, S., & Autti-Raemoe, I. (2003). Neurocognitive impairment in early adolescence following prenatal alcohol exposure of varying duration. *Child Neurology, 9,* 117–128.

Kornhaber, M. L. (2004). Using multiple intelligences to overcome cultural barriers to identification for gifted education. In D. Boothe & J. C. Stanley (Eds.), *In the eyes of the beholder: Critical issues for diversity in gifted education* (pp. 215–225). Waco, TX: Prufrock Press.

Kotchick, B. A., Dorsey, S., & Heller, L. (2005). Predictors of parenting among African-American single mothers: Personal and contextual factors. *Journal of Marriage and Family, 67,* 448–460.

Kowalski, K., & Lo, Y. (1999, April). *The influence of perceptual features and sociocultural information on the development of ethnic/racial bias in young children.* Paper presented at the biennial meeting of the Society for Research in Child Development, Albuquerque, NM.

Kowalski, R. M., Limber, S. P., & Agatston, P. W. (2008). *Cyber bullying: Bullying in the digital age.* Malden, MA: Blackwell.

Kozer, E., Costei, A. M., Boskovic, R., Nulman, I., Nikfar, S., & Koren, G. (2003). Effects of aspirin consumption during pregnancy on pregnancy outcomes: Meta-analysis. *Birth Defects Research: Part B, Developmental and Reproductive Toxicology, 68,* 70–84.

Kozol, J. (2005). *The shame of the nation: The restoration of apartheid schooling in America.* New York: Three Rivers Press.

Kozulin, A. (Ed.). (2003). *Vygotsky's educational theory in cultural context.* Cambridge, U.K.: Cambridge University Press.

Krafft, K., & Berk, L. E. (1998). Private speech in two preschools: Significance of open-ended activities and make-believe play for verbal self-regulation. *Early Childhood Research Quarterly, 13,* 637–658.

Krascum, R. M., & Andrews, S. (1998). The effects of theories on children's acquisition of family-resemblance categories. *Child Development, 69,* 333–346.

Krcmar, M., Grela, B., & Linn, K. (2007). Can toddlers learn vocabulary from television? An experimental approach. *Media Psychology, 10,* 41–63.

Kreppner, J., Kumsta, R., Rutter, M., Beckett, C., Castle, J., Stevens, S., et al. (2010). Developmental course of deprivation-specific psychological patterns: Early manifestations, persistence to age 15, and clinical features. *Monographs of the Society for Research in Child Development, 75*(1, Serial No. 295), 79–101.

Kreppner, J., Rutter, M., Beckett, C., Castle, J., Colvert, E., Groothues, C., et al. (2007). Normality and impairment following profound early institutional deprivation: A longitudinal follow-up into early adolescence. *Developmental Psychology, 43,* 931–946.

Krevans, J., & Gibbs, J. C. (1996). Parents' use of inductive discipline: Relations to children's empathy and prosocial behavior. *Child Development, 67,* 3263–3277.

Krieg, D. B. (2007). Does motherhood get easier the second-time around? Examining parenting stress and marital quality among mothers having their first or second child. *Parenting: Science and Practice, 7,* 149–175.

Krishnamoorthy, J. S., Hart, C., & Jelalian, E. (2006). The epidemic of childhood obesity: Review of research and implications for public policy. *Social Policy Report of the Society for Research in Child Development, 9*(2).

Krumhansl, C. L., & Jusczyk, P. W. (1990). Infants' perception of phrase structure in music. *Psychological Science, 1,* 70–73.

Kuchner, J. (1989). *Chinese-American and European-American mothers and infants: Cultural influences in the first three months of life.* Paper presented at the biennial meeting of the Society for Research in Child Development, Kansas City, MO.

Kuczynski, L. (1984). Socialization goals and mother–child interaction: Strategies for long-term and short-term compliance. *Developmental Psychology, 20,* 1061–1073.

Kuczynski, L. (2003). Beyond bidirectionality. In L. Kuczynski (Ed.), *Handbook of dynamics in parent–child relations* (pp. 3–24). Thousand Oaks, CA: Sage.

Kuczynski, L., & Lollis, S. (2002). Four foundations for a dynamic model of parenting. In J. R. M. Gerris (Ed.), *Dynamics of parenting.* Hillsdale, NJ: Erlbaum.

Kuebli, J., Butler, S., & Fivush, R. (1995). Mother–child talk about past emotions: Relations of maternal language and child gender over time. *Cognition and Emotion, 9,* 265–283.

Kugelmass, J., & Ainscow, M. (2004). Leadership for inclusion: A comparison of international practices. *Journal of Research in Special Educational Needs, 4,* 133–141.

Kuhl, P. K., Tsao, F.-M., & Liu, H.-M. (2003). Foreign-language experience in infancy: Effects of short-term exposure and social interaction on phonetic learning. *Proceedings of the National Academy of Sciences, 100,* 9096–9101.

Kuhn, D. (1995). Microgenetic study of change: What has it told us? *Psychological Science, 6,* 133–139.

Kuhn, D. (2000). Theory of mind, metacognition, and reasoning: A life-span perspective. In P. Mitchell & K. J. Riggs (Eds.), *Children's reasoning and the mind* (pp. 301–326). Hove, U.K.: Psychology Press.

Kuhn, D. (2008). Formal operations from a twenty-first century perspective. *Human Development, 51,* 48–55.

Kuklinski, M. R., & Weinstein, R. S. (2001). Classroom and developmental differences in a path model of teacher expectancy effects. *Child Development, 72,* 1554–1578.

Kumar, S., & O'Brien, A. (2004). Recent developments in fetal medicine. *British Medical Journal, 328,* 1002–1006.

Kunisaki, S. M., & Jennings, R. W. (2008). Fetal surgery. *Journal of Intensive Care Medicine, 23,* 33–51.

Kunzinger, E. L., III. (1985). A short-term longitudinal study of memorial development during early grade school. *Developmental Psychology, 21,* 642–646.

Kuppens, S., Grietens, H., Onghena, P., & Michiels, D. (2009). Associations between parental control and children's overt and relational aggression. *British Journal of Developmental Psychology, 27,* 607–623.

Kurdek, L. A., & Fine, M. A. (1994). Family acceptance and family control as predictors of adjustment in young adolescents: Linear, curvilinear, or interactive effects? *Child Development, 65,* 1137–1146.

Kurtz-Costes, B., Rowley, S. J., Harris-Britt, A., & Woods, T. A. (2008). Gender stereotypes about mathematics and science and self-perceptions of ability in late childhood and early adolescence. *Merrill-Palmer Quarterly, 54,* 386–409.

Kyratzis, A., & Guo, J. (2001). Preschool girls' and boys' verbal conflict strategies in the United States and China. *Research on Language and Social Interaction, 34,* 45–74.

L

La Ferle, C., Edwards, S. M., & Lee, W. N. (2000). Teens' use of traditional media and the Internet. *Journal of Advertising Research, 40,* 55–65.

Ladd, G. W., Birch, S. H., & Buhs, E. S. (1999). Children's social and scholastic lives in kindergarten: Related spheres of influence? *Child Development, 70,* 1373–1400.

Ladd, G. W., Buhs, E. S., & Seid, M. (2000). Children's initial sentiments about kindergarten: Is school liking an antecedent of early classroom participation and achievement? *Merrill-Palmer Quarterly, 46,* 255–279.

Ladd, G. W., & Burgess, K. B. (1999). Charting the relationship trajectories of aggressive, withdrawn, and aggressive/withdrawn children during early grade school. *Child Development, 70,* 910–929.

Ladd, G. W., Herald, S. L., & Kochel, K. P. (2006). School readiness: Are there social prerequisites? *Early Education and Development, 17,* 115–150.

Ladd, G. W., LeSieur, K., & Profilet, S. M. (1993). Direct parental influences on young children's peer relations. In S. Duck (Ed.), *Learning about relationships* (Vol. 2, pp. 152–183). London: Sage.

Ladd, G. W., & Pettit, G. S. (2002). Parenting and the development of children's peer relationships. In M. Bornstein (Ed.), *Handbook of parenting: Vol. 5. Practical issues in parenting* (2nd ed., pp. 269–309). Mahwah, NJ: Erlbaum.

Ladd, G. W., & Price, J. M. (1987). Predicting children's social and school adjustment following the transition from preschool to kindergarten. *Child Development, 58,* 1168–1189.

Ladd, G. W., & Troop-Gordon, W. (2003). The role of chronic peer difficulties in the development of children's psychological adjustment problems. *Child Development, 74,* 1344–1367.

Lagattuta, K. H., Wellman, H. M., & Flavell, J. H. (1997). Preschoolers' understanding of the link between thinking and feeling: Cognitive cuing and emotional change. *Child Development, 68,* 1081–1104.

Lagnado, L. (2001, November 2). Kids confront Trade Center trauma. *Wall Street Journal,* pp. B1, B6.

Laible, D. (2004). Mother–child discourse in two contexts: Links with child temperament, attachment security, and socioemotional competence. *Developmental Psychology, 40,* 979–992.

Laible, D. (2007). Attachment with parents and peers in late adolescence: Links with emotional competence and social behavior. *Personality and Individual Differences, 43,* 1185–1197.

Laible, D., & Song, J. (2006). Constructing emotional and relational understanding: The role of affect and mother–child discourse. *Merrill-Palmer Quarterly, 52,* 44–69.

Laible, D., & Thompson, R. A. (2002). Mother–child conflict in the toddler years: Lessons in emotion, morality, and relationships. *Child Development, 73,* 1187–1203.

Laird, R. D., Jordan, K. Y., Dodge, K. A., Pettit, G. S., & Bates, J. E. (2001). Peer rejection in childhood, involvement with antisocial peers in early adolescence, and the development of externalizing behavior problems. *Development and Psychopathology, 13,* 337–354.

Laird, R. D., Pettit, G. S., Mize, J., & Lindsey, E. (1994). Mother–child conversations about peers: Contributions to competence. *Family Relations, 43,* 425–432.

Lalonde, C. E., & Chandler, M. J. (1995). False-belief understanding goes to school: On the social-emotional consequences of coming early or late to a first theory of mind. *Cognition and Emotion, 9,* 167–185.

Lamarche, V., Brendgen, M., Boivin, M., Vitaro, F., Perusse, D., & Dionne, G. (2006). Do friendships and sibling relationships provide protection against peer victimization in a similar way? *Social Development, 15,* 373–393.

Lamaze, F. (1958). *Painless childbirth.* London: Burke.

Lamb, M. (1994). Infant care practices and the application of knowledge. In C. B. Fisher & R. M. Lerner (Eds.), *Applied developmental psychology* (pp. 23–45). New York: McGraw-Hill.

Lamb, M. E., & Ahnert, L. (2006). Nonparental child care: Context, concepts, correlates, and consequences. In K. A. Renninger & I. E. Sigel (Eds.), *Handbook of child psychology: Vol. 4. Child psychology in practice* (6th ed., pp. 700–778). Hoboken, NJ: Wiley.

Lamb, M. E., & Lewis, C. (2004). The development and significance of father–child relationships in two-parent families. In M. E. Lamb (Ed.), *The role of the father in child development* (4th ed., pp. 272–306). Hoboken, NJ: Wiley.

Lamb, M. E., & Oppenheim, D. (1989). Fatherhood and father–child relationships: Five years of research. In S. H. Cath, A. Gurwitt, & L. Gunsberg (Eds.), *Fathers and their families* (pp. 11–26). Hillsdale, NJ: Erlbaum.

Lamb, M. E., Sternberg, K. J., & Prodromidis, M. (1992). Nonmaternal care and the security of infant–mother attachment: A reanalysis of the data. *Infant Behavior and Development, 15,* 71–83.

Lamb, M. E., Thompson, R. A., Gardner, W., Charnov, E. L., & Connell, J. P. (1985). Infant–mother attachment: The origins and developmental significance of individual differences in the Strange Situation: Its study and biological interpretation. *Behavioral and Brain Sciences, 7,* 127–147.

Lambert, S. M., Masson, P., & Fisch, H. (2006). The male biological clock. *World Journal of Urology, 24,* 611–617.

Lamphear, B. P., Hornung, R., Khoury, J., Yolton, K., Baghurst, P., & Bellinger, D. C. (2005). Low-level environmental lead exposure and children's intellectual function: An international pooled analysis. *Environmental Health Perspectives, 113,* 894–899.

Lampl, M. (1993). Evidence of saltatory growth in infancy. *American Journal of Human Biology, 5,* 641–652.

Lampl, M., Veldhuis, J. D., & Johnson, M. L. (1992). Saltation and stasis: A model of human growth. *Science, 258,* 801–803.

Landry, S. H., Smith, K. E., Swank, P. R., & Miller-Loncar, C. L. (2000). Early maternal and child influences on children's later independent cognitive and social functioning. *Child Development, 71,* 358–375.

Langdridge, D., Connolly, K., & Sheeran, P. (2000). Reasons for wanting a child: A network analytic study. *Journal of Reproductive and Infant Psychology, 18,* 321–338.

Langer, J., Gillette, P., & Arriaga, R. I. (2003). Toddlers' cognition of adding and subtracting objects in action and in perception. *Cognitive Development, 18,* 233–246.

Lansford, J. E. (2009). Parental divorce and children's adjustment. *Perspectives on Psychological Science, 4,* 140–152.

Lansford, J. E., Criss, M. M., Dodge, K. A., Shaw, D. S., Pettit, G. S., & Bates, J. E. (2009). Trajectories of physical discipline: Early childhood antecedents and developmental outcomes. *Child Development, 80,* 1385–1402.

Lansford, J. E., Deater-Deckard, K., Dodge, K. A., Bates, J. E., & Pettit, G. S. (2004a). Ethnic differences in the link between physical discipline and later adolescent externalizing behaviors. *Journal of Child Psychology and Psychiatry, 45,* 801–812.

Lansford, J. E., Deater-Deckard, K., Dodge, K. A., Bates, J. E., & Pettit, G. S. (2004b). Ethnic differences in the link between physical punishment by parents: An updated literature review. *Clinical Child and Family Psychology Review, 3,* 199–221.

Lansford, J. E., Malone, P. S., Castellino, D. R., Dodge, K. A., Pettit, G., & Bates, J. E. (2006). Trajectories of internalizing, externalizing, and grades for children who have and have not experienced their parents' divorce or separation. *Journal of Family Psychology, 20,* 292–301.

Lantieri, L. (2003). Waging peace in our schools: The Resolving Conflict Creatively Program. In M. J. Elias & H. Arnold (Eds.), *EQ + IQ = best leadership practices for caring and successful schools* (pp. 76–88). Thousand Oaks, CA: Corwin.

Largo, R. H., Caflisch, J. A., Hug, F., Muggli, K., Molnar, A. A., & Molinari, L. (2001). Neuromotor development from 5 to 18 years. Part 1: Timed performance. *Developmental Medicine and Child Neurology, 43,* 436–443.

Larroque, B., Ancel, P.-Y., Marret, S., Marchand, L., André, M., Arnaud, C., et al. (2008). Neurodevelopmental disabilities and special care of 5-year-old children born before 33 weeks of gestation (the EPIPAGE study): A longitudinal cohort study. *Lancet, 371,* 813–820.

Larsen, J. A., & Nippold, M. A. (2007). Morphological analysis in school-age children: Dynamic assessment of a word learning strategy. *Language, Speech, and Hearing Services in Schools, 38,* 201–212.

Larsen, J. T., To, Y. M., & Fireman, G. (2007). Childen's understanding and experience of mixed emotions. *Psychological Science, 18,* 186–191.

Larzelere, R. E., Schneider, W. N., Larson, D. B., & Pike, P. L. (1996). The effects of discipline responses in delaying toddler misbehavior recurrences. *Child and Family Behavior Therapy, 18,* 35–7.

Lashley, F. R. (2007). *Essentials of clinical genetics in nursing practice.* New York: Springer.

Latz, S., Wolf, A. W., & Lozoff, B. (1999). Sleep practices and problems in young children in Japan and the United States. *Archives of Pediatric and Adolescent Medicine, 153,* 339–346.

Laucht, M., Esser, G., & Schmidt, M. H. (1997). Developmental outcome of infants born with biological and psychosocial risks. *Journal of Child Psychology and Psychiatry, 38,* 843–853.

Lauer, J. A., Betrán, A. P., Victora, C. G., de Onís, M., & Barros, A. J. D. (2004). Breastfeeding patterns and exposure to suboptimal breastfeeding among children in developing countries: Review and analysis of nationally representative surveys. *BMC Medicine, 2,* 26.

Lauer, P. A., Akiba, M., Wilkerson, S. B., Apthorp, H. S., Snow, D., & Martin-Glenn, M. (2006). Out-of-school time programs: A meta-analysis of effects for at-risk students. *Review of Educational Research, 76,* 275–313.

Laurent, H., Kim, H., & Capaldi, D. (2008). Prospective effects of interparental conflict on child attachment security and the moderating role of parents' romantic attachment. *Journal of Family Psychology, 22,* 377–388.

Laursen, B., Bukowski, W. M., Aunola, K., & Nurmi, J.-E. (2007). Friendship moderates prospective associations between social isolation and adjustment problems in young children. *Child Development, 78,* 1395–1404.

Lavelli, M., & Fogel, A. (2005). Developmental changes in the relationship between the infant's attention and emotion during early face-to-face communication: The 2-month transition. *Developmental Psychology, 41,* 265–280.

Lavigne, J. V., Arend, R., Rosenbaum, D., Smith, A., Weissbluth, M., Binns, H. J., et al. (1999). Sleep and behavior problems among preschoolers. *Journal of Developmental and Behavioral Pediatrics, 20,* 164–169.

Law, K. L., Stroud, L. R., Niaura, R., LaGasse, L. L., Liu, J., & Lester, B. M. (2003). Smoking during pregnancy and newborn neurobehavior. *Pediatrics, 111,* 1318–1323.

Lawrence, K., Kuntsi, J., Coleman, M., Campbell, R., & Skuse, D. (2003). Face and emotion recognition deficits in Turner syndrome: A possible role for X-linked genes in amygdala development. *Neuropsychology, 17,* 39–49.

Lawson, K. R., & Ruff, H. A. (2004). Early attention and negative emotionality predict later cognitive and behavioral function. *International Journal of Behavioral Development, 28,* 157–165.

Lazar, I., & Darlington, R. (1982). Lasting effects of early education: a report from the Consortium for Longitudinal Studies. *Monographs of the Society for Research in Child Development, 47*(2–3, Serial No. 195).

Lazarus, R. S., & Lazarus, B. N. (1994). *Passion and reason.* New York: Oxford University Press.

Lazinski, M. J., Shea, A. K., & Steiner, M. (2008). Effects of maternal prenatal stress on offspring development: A commentary. *Archives of Women's Mental Health, 11,* 363–375.

Le Grand, R., Mondloch, C. J., Maurer, D., & Brent, H. P. (2001). Early visual experience and face processing. *Nature, 410,* 890.

Le Grand, R., Mondloch, C. J., Maurer, D., & Brent, H. P. (2003). Expert face processing requires input to the right hemisphere during infancy. *Nature Neuroscience, 6,* 1108–1112.

Leadbeater, B., & Hoglund, W. (2006). Changing the social texts of peer victimization. *Journal of the Canadian Academy of Child and Adolescent Psychiatry, 15,* 21–26.

Leaper, C. (1994). Exploring the correlates and consequences of gender segregation: Social relationships in childhood, adolescence, and adulthood. In C. Leaper (Ed.), *New directions for child development* (No. 65, pp. 67–86). San Francisco: Jossey-Bass.

Leaper, C. (2000). Gender, affiliation, assertion, and the interactive context of parent–child play. *Developmental Psychology, 36,* 381–393.

Leaper, C., Anderson, K. J., & Sanders, P. (1998). Moderators of gender effects on parents' talk to their children: A meta-analysis. *Developmental Psychology, 34,* 3–27.

Leaper, C., & Friedman, C. K. (2007). The socialization of gender. In J. E. Grusec & P. D. Hastings (Eds.), *Handbook of socialization: Theory and research* (pp. 561–587). New York: Guilford.

Leaper, C., Leve, L., Strasser, T., & Schwartz, R. (1995). Mother–child communication sequences: Play activity, child gender, and marital status effects. *Merrill-Palmer Quarterly, 41,* 307–327.

Leaper, C., Tenenbaum, H. R., & Shaffer, T. G. (1999). Communication patterns of African-American girls and boys from low-income, urban backgrounds. *Child Development, 70,* 1489–1503.

LeBlanc, L. A., Goldsmith, T., & Patel, D. R. (2003). Behavioral aspects of chronic illness in children and adolescents. *Pediatric Clinics of North America, 50,* 859–878.

Lecanuet, J.-P., Granier-Deferre, C., & DeCasper, A. (2005). Are we expecting too much from prenatal sensory experiences? In B. Hopkins & S. P. Johnson (Eds.), *Prenatal development of postnatal functions* (pp. 31–49). Westport, CT: Praeger.

Lecanuet, J.-P., Granier-Deferre, C., Jacquet, A.-Y., Capponi, I., & Ledru, L. (1993). Prenatal discrimination of a male and female voice uttering the same sentence. *Early Development and Parenting, 2,* 217–228.

Lecuyer, E., & Houck, G. M. (2006). Maternal limit-setting in toddlerhood: Socialization strategies for the development of self-regulation. *Infant Mental Health Journal, 27,* 344–370.

Lee, C.-Y. S., & Doherty, W. J. (2007). Marital satisfaction and father involvement during the transition to parenthood. *Fathering, 5,* 75–96.

Lee, E. A., Torrance, N., & Olson, D. R. (2001). Young children and the say/mean distinction: Verbatim and paraphrase recognition in narrative and nursery rhyme contexts. *Journal of Child Language, 28,* 531–543.

Lee, K., Cameron, C., Xu, F., Fu, G., & Board, J. (1997). Chinese and Canadian children's evaluations of lying and truth telling: Similarities and differences in the context of pro- and antisocial behaviors. *Child Development, 68,* 924–934.

Lee, K., Xu, F., Fu, G., Cameron, C. A., & Chen, S. (2001). Taiwan and Mainland Chinese and Canadian children's categorization and evaluation of lie- and truth-telling : A modesty effect. *British Journal of Developmental Psychology, 19,* 525–542.

Lee, S. (2001). More than "model minorities" or "delinquents": A look at Hmong American high school students. *Harvard Educational Review, 71,* 505–528.

Lee, S. J., Ralston, H. J., Partridge, J. C., & Rosen, M. A. (2005). Fetal pain: A systematic multidisciplinary review of the evidence. *Journal of the American Medical Association, 294,* 947–954.

Lee, S. M., Burgeson, C. R., Fulton, J. E., & Spain, C. G. (2007). Physical education and physical activity: Results from the School Health Policies and Programs Study, 2006. *Journal of School Health, 77,* 435–463.

Lee, V. E., & Burkam, D. T. (2002). *Inequality at the starting gate.* Washington, DC: Economic Policy Institute.

Leet, T., & Flick, L. (2003). Effect of exercise on birth weight. *Clinical Obstetrics and Gynecology, 46,* 423–431.

Lehr, V. T., Zeskind, P. S., Ofenstein, J. P., Cepeda, E., Warrier, I., & Aranda, J. V. (2007). Neonatal facial coding system scores and spectral characteristics of infant crying during newborn circumcision. *Clinical Journal of Pain, 23,* 417–424.

Leiferman, J. A., & Evenson, K. R. (2003). The effect of regular leisure physical activity on birth outcomes. *Maternal and Child Health Journal, 7,* 59–64.

Lemche, E., Lennertz, I., Orthmann, C., Ari, A., Grote, K., Hafker, J., & Klann-Delius, G. (2003). Emotion-regulatory process in evoked play narratives: Their relation with mental representations and family interactions. *Praxis der Kinderpsychologie und Kinderpsychiatrie, 52,* 156–171.

Lempert, H. (1989). Animacy constraints on preschoolers' acquisition of syntax. *Child Development, 60,* 237–245.

Lempert, H. (1990). Acquisition of passives: The role of patient animacy, salience, and lexical accessibility. *Journal of Child Language, 17,* 677–696.

Lengua, L. J., Wolchik, S., Sandler, I. N., & West, S. G. (2000). The additive and interactive effects of parenting and temperament in predicting problems of children of divorce. *Journal of Clinical Psychology, 29,* 232–244.

Lenhart, A. (2010). Teens, cell phones and texting. Washington, DC: Pew Internet and American Life Project. Retrieved from pewresearch.org/pubs/1572/teens-cell-phones-text-messages

Lenhart, A., Rainie, L., & Lewis, O. (2001). *Teenage life online: The rise of the instant-message generation and the Internet's impact on friendships and family relationships.* Washington, DC: Pew Internet & American Life Project. Retrieved from www.pewinternet.org/reports/toc?aspReport=36

Leon, K. (2003). Risk and protective factors in young children's adjustment to parental divorce: A review of the research. *Family Relations, 52,* 258–270.

Lepage, J.-F., & Théoret, H. (2007). The mirror neuron system: Grasping others' actions from birth? *Developmental Science, 10,* 513–523.

Lerner, R. M. (2006). Developmental science, developmental systems, and contemporary theories of human development. In R. M. Lerner (Ed.), *Handbook of child psychology: Vol. 1. Theoretical models of human development* (6th ed., pp. 1–17). Hoboken, NJ: Wiley.

Lerner, R. M., & Overton, W. F. (2008). Exemplifying the integrations of the relational developmental system. *Journal of Adolescent Research, 23,* 245–255.

Lerner, R. M., Rothbaum, F., Boulos, S., & Castellino, D. R. (2002). Developmental systems perspective on parenting. In M. H. Bornstein (Ed.), *Handbook of parenting: Vol. 2. Biology and ecology of parenting* (2nd ed., pp. 315–344). Mahwah, NJ: Erlbaum.

Leslie, A. M. (2004). Who's for learning? *Developmental Science, 7,* 417–419.

Lester, B. M. (1985). Introduction: There's more to crying than meets the ear. In B. M. Lester & C. F. Z. Boukydis (Eds.), *Infant crying* (pp. 1–27). New York: Plenum.

Lester, B. M., LaGasse, L., Seifer, R., Tronick, E. Z., Bauer, C., & Shankaran, S. (2003). The maternal lifestyle study (MLS): Effects of prenatal cocaine and/or opiate exposure on auditory brain response at one month. *Journal of Pediatrics, 142,* 279–285.

Lester, B. M., Masten, A. S., & McEwen, B. (2006). Resilience in children. *Annals of the New York Academy of Sciences, 1094.*

Lester, B. M., & Tronick, E. Z. (2004). *NICU Network Neurobehavioral Scale (NNNS).* Baltimore, MD: Brookes.

Lett, D. (1997). *L'enfant des miracles: Enfance et société au Moyen Age (XIIe–XIIIe siecle).* Paris: Aubier.

Leventhal, T., & Brooks-Gunn, J. (2003). Children and youth in neighborhood contexts. *Current Directions in Psychological Science, 12,* 27–31.

Levi, J., Vinter, S., Richardson, L., St. Laurent, R., & Segal, L. M. (2009). *F as in fat: How obesity policies are failing in America.* Washington, DC: Trust for America's Health.

Levin, I., & Bus, A. G. (2003). How is emergent writing based on drawing? Analyses of children's products and their sorting by children and mothers. *Developmental Psychology, 39,* 891–905.

Levine, L. J. (1995). Young children's understanding of the causes of anger and sadness. *Child Development, 66,* 697–709.

LeVine, R. A., Dixon, S., LeVine, S., Richman, A., Leiderman, P. H., Keefer, C. H., & Brazelton, T. B. (1994). *Child care and culture: Lessons from Africa.* New York: Cambridge University Press.

LeVine, R. A., LeVine, S., Richman, A., Tapia Uribe, M. R., Sunderland Correa, C., & Miller, P. (1991). Women's schooling and child care in the demographic transition: A Mexican case study. *Population and Development Review, 17,* 459–496.

LeVine, R. A., LeVine, S. E., Rowe, M. L., & Schnell-Anzola, B. (2004). Maternal literacy and health behavior: A Nepalese case study. *Social Science and Medicine, 58,* 863–877.

LeVine, R. A., LeVine, S. E., & Schnell, B. (2001). "Improve the women": Mass schooling, female literacy, and worldwide social change. *Harvard Educational Review, 71,* 1–50.

Levtzion-Korach, O., Tennenbaum, A., Schnitzer, R., & Ornoy, A. (2000). Early motor development of blind children. *Journal of Paediatric and Child Health, 36,* 226–229.

Levy, G. D., Taylor, M. G., & Gelman, S. A. (1995). Traditional and evaluative aspects of flexibility in gender roles, social conventions, moral rules, and physical laws. *Child Development, 66,* 515–531.

Levy, S. R., & Dweck, C. S. (1999). The impact of children's static vs. dynamic conceptions of people on stereotype information. *Child Development, 70,* 1163–1180.

Levy-Shiff, R., & Israelashvili, R. (1988). Antecedents of fathering: Some further exploration. *Developmental Psychology, 24,* 434–440.

Lewis, C., Freeman, N. H., Kyriadidou, C., Maridakikassotaki, K., & Berridge, D. M. (1996). Social influences on false belief access—specific sibling influences or general apprenticeship? *Child Development, 67,* 2930–2947.

Lewis, M. (1992). *Shame: The exposed self.* New York: Free Press.

Lewis, M. (1995). Embarrassment: The emotion of self-exposure and evaluation. In J. P. Tangney & K. W. Fischer (Eds.), *Self-conscious emotions* (pp. 198–218). New York: Guilford.

Lewis, M. (1998). Emotional competence and development. In D. Pushkar, W. M. Bukowski, A. E. Schwartzman, E. M. Stack, & D. R. White (Eds.), *Improving competence across the lifespan* (pp. 27–36). New York: Plenum.

Lewis, M., & Brooks-Gunn, J. (1979). *Social cognition and the acquisition of self.* New York: Plenum.

Lewis, M., & Ramsay, D. (2002). Cortisol response to embarrassment and shame. *Child Development, 73,* 1034–1045.

Lewis, M., & Ramsay, D. (2004). Development of self-recognition, personal pronoun use, and pretend play during the 2nd year. *Child Development, 75,* 1821–1831.

Lewis, M., Ramsay, D. S., & Kawakami, K. (1993). Differences between Japanese infants and Caucasian American infants in behavioral and cortisol response to inoculation. *Child Development, 64,* 1722–1731.

Lewis, M., Sullivan, M. W., Stanger, C., & Weiss, M. (1989). Self development and self-conscious emotions. *Child Development, 60,* 146–156.

Lewis, M. D. (2000). The promise of dynamic systems approaches for an integrated account of human development. *Child Development, 71,* 36–43.

Lewis, M. D. (2008). Emotional habits in brain and behavior: A window on personality development. In A. Fogel, B. J. King, & S. G. Shanker (Eds.), *Human development in the twenty-first century* (pp. 72–80). New York: Cambridge University Press.

Lewis, T. L., & Maurer, D. (2005). Multiple sensitive periods in human visual development: Evidence from visually deprived children. *Developmental Psychobiology, 46,* 163–183.

Li, D.-K., Willinger, M., Petitti, D. B., Odouli, R., Liu, L., & Hoffman, H. J. (2006). Use of a dummy (pacifier) during sleep and risk of sudden infant death syndrome (SIDS): Population based case-control study. *British Medical Journal, 332,* 18–21.

Li, S.-C., Lindenberger, U., Hommel, B., Aschersleben, G., Prinz, W., & Baltes, P. B. (2004). Transformation in the couplings among intellectual abilities and constituent cognitive processes across the life span. *Psychological Science, 15,* 155–163.

Liben, L. S. (2006). Education for spatial thinking. In K. A. Renninger & I. E. Sigel (Eds.), *Handbook of child psychology: Vol. 4. Child psychology in practice* (6th ed., pp. 197–247). Hoboken, NJ: Wiley.

Liben, L. S. (2009). The road to understanding maps. *Current Directions in Psychological Science, 18,* 310–315.

Liben, L. S., & Bigler, R. S. (2002). The developmental course of gender differentiation: Conceptualizing, measuring, and evaluating constructs and pathways. *Monographs of the Society for Research in Child Development, 67*(2, Serial No. 269).

Liben, L. S., Bigler, R. S., & Krogh, H. R. (2001). Pink and blue collar jobs: Children's judgments of job status and job aspirations in relation to sex of worker. *Journal of Experimental Child Psychology, 79,* 346–363.

Liben, L. S., & Downs, R. M. (1993). Understanding person-space-map relations: Cartographic and developmental perspectives. *Developmental Psychology, 29,* 739–752.

Liben, L. S., Kastens, K. A., & Stevenson, L. M. (2002). Real-world knowledge through real-world maps: A developmental guide for navigating the educational terrain. *Developmental Review, 22,* 267–322.

Liben, L. S., & Signorella, M. L. (1993). Gender-schematic processing in children: The role of initial interpretations of stimuli. *Developmental Psychology, 29,* 141–149.

Lickliter, R., & Bahrick, L. E. (2000). The development of infant intersensory perception: Advantages of a comparative convergent-operations approach. *Psychological Bulletin, 126,* 260–280.

Lidz, C. S. (2001). Multicultural issues and dynamic assessment. In L. A. Suzuki & J. G. Ponterotto (Eds.), *Handbook of multicultural assessment: Clinical, psychological, and educational applications* (2nd ed., pp. 523–539). San Francisco: Jossey-Bass.

Lidz, J. (2007). The abstract nature of syntactic representations. In E. Hoff & M. Shatz (Eds.), *Blackwell handbook of language development* (pp. 277–303). Malden, MA: Blackwell.

Lidz, J., Gleitman, H., & Gleitman, L. (2004). Kidz in the 'hood: Syntactic bootstrapping and the mental lexicon. In D. G. Hall & S. R. Waxman (Eds.),

Weaving a lexicon (pp. 603–636). Cambridge, MA: MIT Press.

Lieven, E., Pine, J., & Baldwin, G. (1997). Lexically based learning and early grammatical development. *Journal of Child Language, 24,* 187–220.

Li-Grining, C. P. (2007). Effortful control among low-income preschoolers in three cities: Stability, change, and individual differences. *Developmental Psychology, 43,* 208–221.

Lillard, A. S. (2003). Pretend play and cognitive development. In U. Goswami (Ed.), *Blackwell handbook of childhood cognitive development* (pp. 189–205). Malden, MA: Blackwell.

Lillard, A. (2007). *Montessori: The science behind the genius.* New York: Oxford University Press.

Lillard, A., & Else-Quest, N. (2006). Evaluating Montessori education. *Science, 313,* 1893–1894.

Lillard, A. S., Nishida, T., Massaro, D., Vaish, A., Ma, L., & McRoberts, G. (2007). Signs of pretense across age and scenario. *Infancy, 11,* 130.

Lillard, A. S., & Witherington, D. (2004). Mothers' behavior modifications during pretense snacks and their possible signal value for toddlers. *Developmental Psychology, 40,* 95–113.

Lin, Z. L., Yu, H. M., Chen, S. Q., Liang, Z. Q., & Zhang, Z. Y. (2006). Mild hypothermia via selective head cooling as neuroprotective therapy in term neonates with perinatal asphyxia: An experience from a single neonatal intensive care unit. *Journal of Perinatology, 26,* 180–184.

Linares, T. J., Singer, L. T., Kirchner, H., Lester, H., Short, E. J., & Minn, M. O. (2006). Mental health outcomes of cocaine-exposed children at 6 years of age. *Journal of Pediatric Psychology, 31,* 85–97.

Lincove, J. A., & Painter, G. (2006). Does the age that children start kindergarten matter? Evidence of long-term educational and social outcomes. *Educational Evaluation and Policy Analysis, 28,* 153–179.

Lindsay-Hartz, J., de Rivera, J., & Mascolo, M. F. (1995). Differentiating guilt and shame and their effects on motivation. In J. P. Tangney & K. W. Fischer (Eds.), *Self-conscious emotions* (pp. 274–300). New York: Guilford.

Lindsey, E. W., & Colwell, M. J. (2003). Preschoolers' emotional competence: Links to pretend and physical play. *Child Study Journal, 33,* 39–52.

Lindsey, E. W., & Mize, J. (2000). Parent–child physical and pretense play: Links to children's social competence. *Merrill-Palmer Quarterly, 46,* 565–591.

Linebarger, D. L., Kosanic, A. Z., Greenwood, C. R., & Doku, N. S. (2004). Effects of viewing the television program *Between the Lions* on the emergent literacy skills of young children. *Journal of Educational Psychology, 96,* 297–308.

Linn, R. L., & Welner, K. G. (2007). *Race-conscious policies for assigning students to schools: Social science research and the Supreme Court cases.* Washington, DC: National Academy Press.

Lino, M., & Carlson, A. (2009). *Expenditures on children by families, 2008.* Miscellaneous Publication Number 1528–2008. Washington, DC: U.S. Department of Agriculture.

Linscheid, T. R., Budd, K. S., & Rasnake, L. K. (2005). Pediatric feeding problems. In M. C. Roberts (Ed.), *Handbook of pediatric psychology and psychiatry* (3rd ed., pp. 481–488). New York: Guilford.

Linver, M. R., Martin, A., & Brooks-Gunn, J. (2004). Measuring infants' home environment: The IT-HOME for infants between birth and 12 months in four national data sets. *Parenting: Science and Practice, 4,* 115–137.

Lipsitt, L. P. (2003). Crib death: A biobehavioral phenomenon? *Psychological Science, 12,* 164–170.

Lipton, J. S., & Spelke, E. S. (2003). Origins of number sense: Large-number discrimination in human infants. *Psychological Science, 14,* 396–401.

Liszkowski, U., Carpenter, M., & Tomasello, M. (2007). Pointing out new news, old news, and absent referents at 12 months of age. *Developmental Science, 10,* F1–F7.

Liszkowski, U., Carpenter, M., & Tomasello, M. (2008). Twelve-month-olds communicate helpfully and appropriately for knowledgeable and ignorant partners. *Cognition, 108,* 732–739.

Litovsky, R. Y., & Ashmead, D. H. (1997). Development of binaural and spatial hearing in infants and children. In R. H. Gilkey & T. R. Anderson (Eds.), *Binaural and spatial hearing in real and virtual environments* (pp. 571–592). Mahwah, NJ: Erlbaum.

Little, C., & Carter, A. S. (2005). Negative emotional reactivity and regulation in 12-month-olds following emotional challenge: Contributions of maternal–infant emotional availability in a low-income sample, *Infant Mental Health Journal, 26,* 354–368.

Little, T. D., Jones, S. M., Henrich, C. C., & Hawley, P. H. (2003). Disentangling the "whys" from the "whats" of aggressive behavior. *International Journal of Behavioral Development, 27,* 122–133.

Liu, D., Sabbagh, M. A., Gehring, W. J., & Wellman, H. M. (2009). Neural correlates of children's theory of mind development. *Child Development, 80,* 318–326.

Liu, J., Raine, A., Venables, P. H., Dalais, C., & Mednick, S. A. (2003). Malnutrition at age 3 years and lower cognitive ability at age 11 years. *Archives of Paediatric and Adolescent Medicine, 157,* 593–600.

Liu, J., Raine, A., Venables, P. H., & Mednick, S. A. (2004). Malnutrition at age 3 years and externalizing behavior problems at ages 8, 11, and 17 years. *American Journal of Psychiatry, 161,* 2005–2013.

Lloyd, L. (1999). Multi-age classes and high ability students. *Review of Educational Research, 69,* 187–212.

Lochman, J. E., & Dodge, K. A. (1998). Distorted perceptions in dyadic interactions of aggressive and nonaggressive boys: Effects of prior expectations, context, and boys' age. *Development and Psychopathology, 10,* 495–512.

Locke, J. (1892). Some thoughts concerning education. In R. H. Quick (Ed.), *Locke on education* (pp. 1–236). Cambridge, U.K.: Cambridge University Press. (Original work published 1690).

Lockhart, R. S., & Craik, F. I. M. (1990). Levels of processing: A retrospective commentary on a framework for memory research. *Canadian Journal of Psychology, 44,* 87–112.

Loeb, S., Fuller, B., Kagan, S. L., & Carrol, B. (2004). Child care in poor communities: Early learning effects of type, quality, and stability. *Child Development, 75,* 47–65.

Loehlin, J. C., & Martin, N. G. (2001). Age changes in personality traits and their heritabilities during the adult years: Evidence from Australian twin registry samples *Personality and Individual Differences, 30,* 1147–1160.

Loehlin, J. C., Horn, J. M., & Willerman, L. (1997). Heredity, environment, and IQ in the Texas Adoption Project. In R. J. Sternberg & E. L. Grigorenko (Eds.), *Intelligence, heredity, and environment* (pp. 105–125). New York: Cambridge University Press.

Loganovskaja, T. K., & Loganovsky, K. N. (1999). EEG, cognitive and psychopathological abnormalities in children irradiated in utero. *International Journal of Psychophysiology, 34,* 213–224.

Loganovsky, K. N., Loganovskaja, T. K., Nechayev, S. Y., Antipchuk, Y. Y., & Bomko, M. A. (2008). Disrupted development of the dominant hemisphere following prenatal irradiation. *The Journal of Neuropsychiatry and Clinical Neurosciences, 20,* 274–291.

Lohman, D. F. (2000). Measures of intelligence: Cognitive theories. In A. E. Kazdin (Ed.), *Encyclopedia of psychology: Vol. 5* (pp. 147–150). Washington, DC: American Psychological Association.

London, K., Bruck, M., Ceci, S. J., & Shuman, D. (2005). Disclosure of child sexual abuse: What does the research tell us about the ways that children tell? *Psychology and Public Policy Law, 11,* 194–226.

Longstaffe, S., Moffatt, M. E., & Whalen, J. C. (2000). Behavioral and self-concept changes after six months of enuresis treatment: A randomized, controlled trial. *Pediatrics, 105,* 935–940.

Loock, C., Conry, J., Cook, J. L., Chudley, A. E., & Rosales, T. (2005). Identifying fetal alcohol spectrum disorder in primary care. *Canadian Medical Association Journal, 172,* 628–630.

Looker, D., & Thiessen, V. (2003). *The digital divide in Canadian schools: Factors affecting student access to and use of information technology.* Ottawa: Canadian Education Statistics Council.

Loots, G., & Devise, I. (2003). The use of visual-tactile communication strategies by deaf and hearing fathers and mothers of deaf infants. *Journal of Deaf Studies and Deaf Education, 8,* 31–42.

Lorenz, K. Z. (1952). *King Solomon's ring.* New York: Crowell.

LoTurco, J. J. (2000). Neural circuits in the 21st century: Synaptic networks of neurons and glia. *Proceedings of the National Academy of Sciences, 97,* 8196–8197.

Louie, V. (2001). Parents' aspirations and investment: The role of social class in the educational experiences of 1.5- and second-generation Chinese Americans. *Harvard Educational Review, 71,* 438–474.

Louis, J., Cannard, C., Bastuji, H., & Challamel, M. J. (1997). Sleep ontogenesis revisited: A longitudinal 24-hour home polygraphic study on 15 normal infants during the first two years of life. *Sleep, 20,* 323–333.

Lourenco, O. (2003). Making sense of Turiel's dispute with Kohlberg: The case of the child's moral competence. *New Ideas in Psychology, 21,* 43–68.

Love, J. M., Chazan-Cohen, R., & Raikes, H. (2007). Forty years of research knowledge and use: From Head Start to Early Head Start and beyond. In J. L. Aber, S. J. Bishop-Josef, S. M. Jones, K. T. McLearn, & D. Phillips (Eds.), *Child development and social policy: Knowledge for action* (pp. 79–95). Washington, DC: American Psychological Association.

Love, J. M., Harrison, L., Sagi-Schwartz, A., van IJzendoorn, M. H., Ross, C., & Ungerer, J. A. (2003). Child care quality matters: How conclusions may vary with context. *Child Development, 74,* 1021–1033.

Love, J. M., Kisker, E. E., Ross, C., Raikes, H., Constantine, J., Boller, K., & Brooks-Gunn, J. (2005). The effectiveness of early Head Start for 3-year-old children and their parents: Lessons for policy and programs. *Developmental Psychology, 41,* 885–901.

Love, J. M., Tarullo, L. B., Raikes, H., & Chazan-Cohen, R. (2006). Head Start: What do we know about its effectiveness? What do we need to know? In K. McCartney & D. Phillips (Eds.), *Blackwell handbook of early childhood development* (pp. 550–575). Malden, MA: Blackwell.

Lubart, T. I. (2003). In search of creative intelligence. In R. J. Sternberg, J. Lautrey, & T. I. Lubart (Eds.), *Models of intelligence: International perspectives* (pp. 279–292). Washington, DC: American Psychological Association.

Lubart, T. I., Georgsdottir, A., & Besançon, M. (2009). The nature of creative giftedness and talent. In T. Balchin, B. Hymer, & D. J. Matthews (Eds.), *The Routledge international companion to gifted education* (pp. 42–49). New York: Routledge.

Luby, J., Belden, A., Sullivan, J., Hayen, R., McCadney, A., & Spitznagel, E. (2009). Shame and guilt in preschool depression: Evidence for elevations in self-conscious emotions in depression as early as age 3. *Journal of Child Psychology and Psychiatry, 50,* 1156–1166.

Lucas-Thompson, R., & Clarke-Stewart, K. A. (2007). Forecasting friendship: How marital quality, maternal mood, and attachment security are linked to children's peer relationships. *Journal of Applied Developmental Psychology, 28,* 499–514.

Luciana, M. (2007). Special issue: Developmental cognitive neuroscience. *Developmental Review, 27,* 277–282.

Ludemann, P. M. (1991). Generalized discrimination of positive facial expressions by seven- and ten-month-old infants. *Child Development, 62,* 55–67.

Luna, B., Garver, K. E., Urban, T. A., Lazar, N. A., & Sweeney, J. A. (2004). Maturation of cognitive processes from late childhood to adulthood. *Child Development, 75,* 1357–1372.

Luna, B., Thulborn, K. R., Monoz, D. P., Merriam, E. P., Garver, K. E., Minshew, N. J., Keshavan, M. S., Genovese, C. R., Eddy, W. F., & Sweeney, J. A. (2001). Maturation of widely distributed brain function subserves cognitive development. *Neuroimage, 13,* 786–793.

Lund, N., Pedersen, L. H., & Henriksen, T. B. (2009). Selective serotonin reuptake inhibitor exposure in utero and pregnancy outcomes. *Archives of Pediatrics and Adolescent Medicine, 163,* 949–954.

Lundy, B. L. (2002). Paternal socio-psychological factors and infant attachment: The mediating role of synchrony in father–infant interactions. *Infant Behavior and Development, 25,* 221–236.

Lundy, B. L. (2003). Father–and mother–infant face-to-face interactions: Differences in mind-related comments and infant attachment? *Infant Behavior and Development, 26,* 200–212.

Luo, Y., & Baillargeon, R. (2005). When the ordinary seems unexpected: Evidence for incremental physical knowledge in young infants. *Cognition, 95,* 297–328.

Lussier, G., Deater-Deckard, K., Dunn, J., & Davies, L. (2002). Support across two generations: Children's closeness to grandparents following parental divorce and remarriage. *Journal of Family Psychology, 16,* 363–376.

Luthar, S. S., & Becker, B. E. (2002). Privileged but pressured: A study of affluent youth. *Child Development, 73,* 1593–1610.

Luthar, S. S., & Goldstein, A. S. (2008). Substance use and related behaviors among suburban late adolescents: The importance of perceived parent containment. *Development and Psychopathology, 20,* 591–614.

Luthar, S. S., & Latendresse, S. J. (2005a). Children of the affluent: Challenges to well-being. *Current Directions in Psychological Science, 14,* 49–53.

Luthar, S. S., & Latendresse, S. J. (2005b). Comparable "risks" at the socioeconomic status extremes: Preadolescents' perceptions of parenting. *Development and Psychopathology, 17,* 207–230.

Luthar, S. S., & Sexton, C. (2004). The high price of affluence. In R. V. Kail (Ed.), *Advances in child development* (Vol. 32, pp. 126–162). San Diego, CA: Academic Press.

Lynch, S. K., Turkheimer, E., D'Onofrio, B. M., Mendle, J., Emery, R. E., Slutske, W. S., & Martin, N. G. (2006). A genetically informed study of the association between harsh punishment and offspring behavioral problems. *Journal of Family Psychology, 20,* 190–198.

Lyon, T. D., & Flavell, J. H. (1994). Young children's understanding of "remember" and "forget." *Child Development, 65,* 1357–1371.

Lyons-Ruth, K. (1996). Attachment relationships among children with aggressive behavior problems: The role of disorganized early attachment patterns. *Journal of Consulting and Clinical Psychology, 64,* 64–73.

Lyons-Ruth, K., Bronfman, E., & Parsons, E. (1999). Maternal frightened, frightening, or aytpical behavior and disorganized infant attachment patterns. *Monographs of the Society for Research in Child Development, 64*(3, Serial No. 258), 67–96.

Lyons-Ruth, K., Easterbrooks, M. A., & Cibelli, C. (1997). Infant attachment strategies, infant mental lag, and maternal depressive symptoms: Predictors of internalizing and externalizing problems at age 7. *Developmental Psychology, 33,* 681–692.

Lytton, H., & Gallagher, L. (2002). Parenting twins and the genetics of parenting. In M. H. Bornstein (Ed.), *Handbook of parenting: Vol. 1. Children and parenting* (pp. 227–253). Mahwah, NJ: Erlbaum.

M

Ma, L., & Lillard, A. S. (2006). Where is the real cheese? Young children's ability to discriminate between real and pretend acts. *Child Development, 77,* 1762–1777.

Ma, W., Golinkoff, R. M., Hirsh-Pasek, K., McDonough, C., & Tardif, T. (2009). Imageability predicts the age of acquisition of verbs in Chinese children. *Journal of Child Language, 36,* 405–423.

Maas, F. K. (2008). Children's understanding of promising, lying, and false belief. *Journal of General Psychology, 13,* 301–321.

Maas, F. K., & Abbeduto, L. J. (2001). Children's judgments about intentionally and unintentionally broken promises. *Journal of Child Language, 28,* 517–529.

Maccoby, E. E. (1984). Middle childhood in the context of the family. In W. A. Collins (Ed.), *Development during middle childhood* (pp. 184–239). Washington, DC: National Academy Press.

Maccoby, E. E. (1998). *The two sexes: Growing up apart, coming together.* Cambridge, MA: Belknap/Harvard University Press.

Maccoby, E. E. (2002). Gender and group process: A developmental perspective. *Current Directions in Psychological Science, 11,* 54–58.

Machin, G. A. (2005). Multiple birth. In H. W. Taeusch, R. A. Ballard, & C. A. Gleason (Eds.), *Avery's diseases of the newborn* (8th ed., pp. 57–62). Philadelphia: Saunders.

Mackey, K., Arnold, M. L., & Pratt, M. W. (2001). Adolescents' stories of decision making in more and less authoritative families: Representing the voices of parents in narrative. *Journal of Adolescent Research, 16,* 243–268.

Mackie, S., Show, P., Lenroot, R., Pierson, R., Greenstein, D. K., & Nugent, T. F., III. (2007). Cerebellar development and clinical outcome in attention deficit hyperactivity disorder. *American Journal of Psychiatry, 164,* 647–655.

Macpherson, A., & Spinks, A. (2007). Bicycle helmet legislation for the uptake of helmet use and prevention of head injuries. *Cochrane Database of Systematic Reviews,* Issue 3. Chichester, UK: Wiley.

MacWhinney, B. (2005). Language development. In M. H. Bornstein & M. E. Lamb (Eds.), *Developmental science: An advanced textbook* (5th ed., pp. 359–387). Mahwah, NJ: Erlbaum.

Madigan, S., Moran, G., & Pederson, D. R. (2006). Unresolved states of mind, disorganized attachment relationships, and disrupted interactions of adolescent mothers and their infants. *Developmental Psychology, 42,* 293–304.

Madom, S., Jussim, L., & Eccles, J. (1997). In search of the powerful self-fulfilling prophecy. *Journal of Personality and Social Psychology, 72,* 791–809.

Madsen, S. A., & Juhl, T. (2007). Paternal depression in the postnatal period assessed with traditional and male depression scales. *Journal of Men's Health and Gender, 4,* 26–31.

Main, M. (2000). The organized categories of infant, child, and adult attachment: Flexible vs. inflexible attention under attachment-related stress. *Journal of the American Psychoanalytic Association, 48,* 1055–1096.

Main, M., & Goldwyn, R. (1998). *Adult attachment classification system.* London: University College.

Main, M., & Solomon, J. (1990). Procedures for identifying infants as disorganized/disoriented during the Ainsworth Strange Situation. In M. Greenberg, D. Cicchetti, & M. Cummings (Eds.), *Attachment in the preschool years: Theory, research, and intervention* (pp. 121–160). Chicago: University of Chicago Press.

Majdandžić, M., & van den Boom, D. C. (2007). Multimethod longitudinal assessment of temperament in early childhood. *Journal of Personality, 75,* 121–167.

Majnemer, A., & Barr, R. G. (2005). Influence of supine sleep positioning on early motor milestone acquisition. *Developmental Medicine and Child Neurology, 47,* 370–376.

Major, B., Spencer, S., Schmader, T., Wolfe, C., & Crocker, J. (1998). Coping with negative stereotypes about intellectual performance: The role of psychological disengagement. *Personality and Social Psychology Bulletin, 24,* 34–50.

Makin, J. E., Fried, P. A., & Watkinson, B. (1991). A comparison of active and passive smoking during pregnancy: Long-term effects. *Neurotoxicology and Teratology, 13,* 5–12.

Makris, N., & Pnevmatikos, D. (2007). Children's understanding of human and super-natural mind. *Cognitive Development, 22,* 365–375.

Malatesta, C. Z., Grigoryev, P., Lamb, C., Albin, M., & Culver, C. (1986). Emotion socialization and expressive development in preterm and full-term infants. *Child Development, 57,* 316–330.

Malina, R. M., & Bouchard, C. (1991). *Growth, maturation, and physical activity.* Champaign, IL: Human Kinetics.

Mandara, J., Varner, F., Greene, N., & Richman, S. (2009). Intergenerational family predictors of the black–white achievement gap. *Journal of Educational Psychology, 101,* 867–878.

Mandler, J. M. (2004). Thought before language. *Trends in Cognitive Sciences, 8,* 508–513.

Mandler, J. M., & McDonough, L. (1998). On developing a knowledge base in infancy. *Developmental Psychology, 34,* 1274–1288.

Mangelsdorf, S. C., Schoppe, S. J., & Buur, H. (2000). The meaning of parental reports: A contextual approach to the study of temperament and behavior problems. In V. J. Molfese & D. L. Molfese (Eds.), *Temperament and personality across the life span* (pp. 121–140). Mahwah, NJ: Erlbaum.

Mao, A., Burnham, M. M., Goodlin-Jones, B. L., Gaylor, E. E., & Anders, T. F. (2004). A comparison of the sleep–wake patterns of cosleeping and solitary-sleeping infants. *Child Psychiatry and Human Development, 35,* 95–105.

Maratsos, M. (2000). More overregularizations after all: New data and discussion on Marcus, Pinker, Ullman, Hollander, Rosen, & Xu. *Journal of Child Language, 27,* 183–212.

Marchman, V. A., & Thal, D. J. (2005). Words and grammar. In M. Tomasello & D. I. Slobin (Eds.), *Beyond nature–nurture: Essays in honor of Elizabeth Bates* (pp. 141–164). Mahwah, NJ: Erlbaum.

Marcon, R. A. (1999a). Differential impact of preschool models on development and early learning of inner-city children: A three-cohort study. *Developmental Psychology, 35,* 358–375.

Marcon, R. A. (1999b). Positive relationships between parent–school involvement and public school inner-city preschoolers' development and academic performance. *School Psychology Review, 28,* 395–412.

Marcus, G. F. (1995). Children's overregularization of English plurals: A quantitative analysis. *Journal of Child Language, 22,* 447–459.

Marcus, G. F., Fernandes, K. J., & Johnson, S. P. (2007). Infant rule learning facilitated by speech. *Psychological Science, 18,* pp. 387–391.

Marcus, G. F., Vijayan, S., Rao, S. B., & Vishton, P. M. (1999). Rule learning by seven-month-old infants. *Science, 283,* 77–80.

Mardh, P. A. (2002). Influence of infection with *Chlamydia trachomatis* on pregnancy outcome, infant health and life-long sequelae in infected offspring. *Best Practices in Clinical Obstetrics and Gynaecology, 16,* 847–964.

Marian, V., Neisser, U., & Rochat, P. (1996). *Can 2-month-old infants distinguish live from videotaped interactions with their mothers* (Emory Cognition Project, Report #33). Atlanta, GA: Emory University.

Mariano, K. A., & Harton, H. C. (2005). Similarities in aggression, inattention/hyperactivity, depression, and anxiety in middle childhood friendships. *Journal of Social and Clinical Psychology, 24,* 471–496.

Markman, E. M. (1992). Constraints on word learning: Speculations about their nature, origins, and domain specificity. In M. R. Gunnar & M. P. Maratsos (Eds.), *Minnesota Symposia on Child Psychology* (Vol. 25, pp. 59–101). Hillsdale, NJ: Erlbaum.

Markova, G., & Legerstee, M. (2006). Contingency, imitation, and affect sharing: Foundations of infants' social awareness. *Developmental Psychology, 42,* 132–141.

Markovits, H., Benenson, J., & Dolenszky, E. (2001). Evidence that children and adolescents have internal models of peer interactions that are gender differentiated. *Child Development, 72,* 879–886.

Marlier, L., & Schaal, B. (2005). Human newborns prefer human milk: Conspecific milk odor is attractive without postnatal exposure. *Child Development, 76,* 155–168.

Marsee, M. A., & Frick, P. J. (2010). Callous-unemotional traits and aggression in youth. In W. F. Arsenio & E. A. Lemerise (Eds.), *Emotions, aggression, and morality in children: Bridging development and psychopathology* (pp. 137–156). Washington, D. C.: American Psychological Association.

Marsh, H. W. (1990). The structure of academic self-concept: The Marsh/Shavelson model. *Journal of Educational Psychology, 82,* 623–636.

Marsh, H. W., & Ayotte, V. (2003). Do multiple dimensions of self-concept become more differentiated with age? The differential distinctiveness hypothesis. *Journal of Educational Psychology, 95,* 687–706.

Marsh, H. W., Craven, R., & Debus, R. (1998). Structure, stability, and development of young children's self-concept: A multicohort–multioccasion study. *Child Development, 69,* 1030–1053.

Marsh, H. W., Ellis, L. A., & Craven, R. G. (2002). How do preschool children feel about themselves? Unraveling measurement and multidimensional self-concept structure. *Developmental Psychology, 38,* 376–393.

Marsh, H. W., Gerlach, E., Trautwein, U., Lüdtke, O., & Brettschneider, W.-D. (2007). Longitudinal study of predadolescent sport self-concept and performance: Reciprocal effects and causal ordering. *Child Development, 78,* 1640–1656.

Marsh, H. W., & Hau, K.-T. (2003). Big-fish–little-pond effect on academic self-concept: A cross-cultural (26-country) test of the negative effects of academically selective schools. *American Psychologist, 58,* 364–376.

Marsh, H. W., Trautwein, U., Lüdtke, O., Koller, O., & Baumert, J. (2005). Academic self-concept, interest, grades, and standardized test scores: Reciprocal effects models of causal ordering. *Child Development, 76,* 397–416.

Marshall-Baker, A., Lickliter, R., & Cooper, R. P. (1998). Prolonged exposure to a visual pattern may promote behavioral organization in preterm infants. *Journal of Perinatal and Neonatal Nursing, 12,* 50–62.

Martin, C. L., Eisenbud, L., & Rose, H. (1995). Children's gender-based reasoning about toys. *Child Development, 66,* 1453–1471.

Martin, C. L., & Fabes, R. A. (2001). The stability and consequences of young children's same-sex peer interactions. *Developmental Psychology, 37,* 431–446.

Martin, C. L., Fabes, R. A., Evans, S. M., & Wyman, H. (1999). Social cognition on the playground: Children's beliefs about playing with girls versus boys and their relations to sex segregated play. *Journal of Social and Personal Relationships, 16,* 751–771.

Martin, C. L., & Halverson, C. F. (1987). The role of cognition in sex role acquisition. In D. B. Carter (Ed.), *Current conceptions of sex roles and sex typing: Theory and research* (pp. 123–137). New York: Praeger.

Martin, C. L., & Ruble, D. (2004). Children's search for gender cues: Cognitive perspectives on gender development. *Current Directions in Psychological Science, 13,* 67–70.

Martin, C. L., Ruble, D. N., & Szkrybalo, J. (2002). Cognitive theories of early gender development. *Psychological Bulletin, 128,* 903–933.

Martin, G. L., & Pear, J. (2007). *Behavior modification: What it is and how to do it* (8th ed.). Upper Saddle River, NJ: Prentice-Hall.

Martin, R. (2008). Meiotic errors in human oogenesis and spermatogenesis. *Reproductive Biomedicine Online, 16,* 523–531.

Martinez-Frias, M. L., Bermejo, E., Rodríguez-Pinilla, E., & Frías, J. L. (2004). Risk for congenital anomalies associated with different sporadic and daily doses of alcohol consumption during pregnancy: A case-control study. *Birth Defects Research, Part A, Clinical and Molecular Teratology, 70,* 194–200.

Martlew, M., & Connolly, K. J. (1996). Human figure drawings by schooled and unschooled children in Papua New Guinea. *Child Development, 67,* 2743–2762.

Martyn, C. N., Barker, D. J. P., & Osmond, C. (1996). Mothers' pelvic size, fetal growth, and death from stroke and coronary heart disease in men in the UK. *Lancet, 348,* 1264–1268.

Marzolf, D. P., & DeLoache, J. S. (1994). Transfer in young children's understanding of spatial representations. *Child Development, 65,* 1–15.

Masataka, N. (1996). Perception of motherese in a signed language by 6-month-old deaf infants. *Developmental Psychology, 32,* 874–879.

Mascolo, M. F., & Fischer, K. W. (1995). Developmental transformations in appraisals for pride, shame, and guilt. In J. P. Tangney & K. W. Fischer (Eds.), *Self-conscious emotions* (pp. 114–139). New York: Guilford.

Mascolo, M. F., & Fischer, K. W. (2007). The codevelopment of self and sociomoral emotions during the toddler years. In C. A. Brownell & C. B. Kopp (Eds.), *Socioemotional development in the toddler years: Transitions and transformations* (pp. 66–99). New York: Guilford.

Mashburn, A. J. (2008). Quality of social and physical environments in preschools and children's development of academic, language, and literacy skills. *Applied Developmental Science, 12,* 113–127.

Mashburn, A. J., Pianta, R. C., Hamre, B. K., Downer, J. T., Barbarin, O. A., Bryant, D., et al. (2008). Measures of classroom quality in prekindergarten and children's development of academic, language, and social skills. *Child Development, 79,* 732–749.

Massey, Z., Rising, S. S., & Ickovics, J. (2006). CenteringPregnancy group prenatal care: Promoting relationship-centered care. *JOGNN, 35,* 286–294.

Masten, A. S., Coatsworth, J. D., Neemann, J., Gest, S. D., Tellegen, A., & Garmezy, N. (1995). The structure and coherence of competence from childhood through adolescence. *Child Development, 66,* 1635–1659.

Masten, A. S., & Gewirtz, A. H. (2006). Vulnerability and resilience in early child development. In K. McCartney & D. Phillips (Eds.), *Blackwell handbook of early childhood development* (pp. 22–43). Malden, MA: Blackwell.

Masten, A. S., & Powell, J. L. (2003). A resilience framework for research, policy, and practice. In S. S. Luthar (Ed.), *Resilience and vulnerability* (pp. 1–25). New York: Cambridge University Press.

Masten, A. S., & Reed, M. J. (2002). Resilience in development. In C. R. Snyder & S. J. Lopez (Eds.), *Handbook of positive psychology* (pp. 74–88). New York: Oxford University Press.

Masten, A. S., & Shaffer, A. (2006). How families matter in child development: Reflections from research on risk and resilience. In A. S. Masten & A. Shaffer (Eds.), *Families count: Effects on child and adolescent development* (pp. 5–25). New York: Cambridge University Press.

Mastropieri, D., & Turkewitz, G. (1999). Prenatal experience and neonatal responsiveness to vocal expressions of emotion. *Developmental Psychobiology, 35,* 204–214.

Masur, E. F., McIntyre, C. W., & Flavell, J. H. (1973). Developmental changes in apportionment of study time among items in a multi-trial free recall task. *Journal of Experimental Child Psychology, 15,* 237–246.

Masur, E. F., & Rodemaker, J. E. (1999). Mothers' and infants' spontaneous vocal, verbal, and action imitation during the second year. *Merrill-Palmer Quarterly, 45,* 392–412.

Mathews, F., Yudkin, P., & Neil, A. (1999). Influence of maternal nutrition on outcome of pregnancy: Prospective cohort study. *British Medical Journal, 319,* 339–343.

Mathews, T. J., & MacDorman, M. F. (2006, May). Infant mortality statistics from the 2003 period linked birth/infant death data set. *National Vital Statistics Reports, 54*(16), 1–29.

Mathews, T. J., & MacDorman, M. F. (2008). Infant mortality statistics from the 2005 period linked birth/infant death data set. *National Vital Statistics Reports from the Centers for Disease Control and Prevention, 57,* 1–32.

Mathiesen, K. S., & Prior, M. (2006). The impact of temperament factors and family functioning on resilience processes from infancy to school age. *European Journal of Developmental Psychology, 3,* 357–387.

Mattson, S. N., Calarco, K. E., & Lang, A. R. (2006). Focused and shifting attention in children with heavy prenatal alcohol exposure. *Neuropsychology, 20,* 361–369.

Maupin, R., Lyman, R., Fatsis, J., Prystowiski, E., Nguyen, A., & Wright, C. (2004). Characteristics of women who deliver with no prenatal care. *Journal of Maternal-Fetal and Neonatal Medicine, 16,* 45–50.

Maurer, D., Lewis, T. L., Brent, H. P., & Levin, A. V. (1999). Rapid improvement in the acuity of infants after visual input. *Science, 286,* 108–110.

Mavroveli, S., Petrides, K. V., Rieffe, C., & Bakker, F. (2007). Trait emotional intelligence, psychological well-being and peer-rated social competence in adolescence. *British Journal of Developmental Psychology, 25,* 263–275.

Mayberry, R. I. (1994). The importance of childhood to language acquisition: Evidence from American Sign Language. In J. C. Goodman & H. C. Nusbaum (Eds.), *The development of speech perception: The transition from speech sounds to spoken words* (pp. 57–90). Cambridge, MA: MIT Press.

Mayeiux, L., & Cillessen, A. H. N. (2003). Development of social problem solving in early childhood: Stability, change, and associations with social competence. *Journal of Genetic Psychology, 164,* 153–173.

Mayer, J. D., Roberts, R. D., & Barsade, S. G. (2008). Human abilities: Emotional intelligence. *Annual Review of Psychology, 59,* 507–536.

Mayer, J. D., Salovey, P., & Caruso, D. R. (2003). *Mayer–Salovey–Caruso Emotional Intelligence Test (MSCEIT): User's manual.* Toronto, Ontario: Multi-Health Systems.

Mayer, J. D., Salovey, P., & Caruso, D. R. (2008). Emotional intelligence: New ability or eclectic traits? *American Psychologist, 63,* 503–517.

Mayes, L. C. (1999). Reconsidering the concept of vulnerability in children using the model of prenatal cocaine exposure. In T. B. Cohen & E. M. Hossein (Eds.), *The vulnerable child* (Vol. 3, pp. 35–54). Madison, CT: International Universities Press.

Mayes, L. C., & Zigler, E. (1992). An observational study of the affective concomitants of mastery in infants. *Journal of Child Psychology and Psychiatry, 33,* 659–667.

Mayes, R., Bagwell, C., & Erkulwater, J. (2008). ADHD and the rise in stimulant use among children. *Harvard Review of Psychiatry, 16,* 151–166.

Maynard, A. E. (2002). Cultural teaching: The development of teaching skills in Maya sibling interactions. *Child Development, 73,* 969–982.

Maynard, A. E., & Greenfield, P. M. (2003). Implicit cognitive development in cultural tools and children: Lessons from Maya Mexico. *Cognitive Development, 18,* 489–510.

Maynard, A. E., Subrahmanyam, K., & Greenfield, P. M. (2005). Technology and the development of intelligence: From the loom to the computer. In R. J. Sternberg & D. D. Preiss (Eds.), *Intelligence and technology: The impact of tools on the nature and development of human abilities* (pp. 29–53). Mahwah, NJ: Erlbaum.

McAlister, A., & Peterson, C. C. (2006). Mental playmates: Siblings, executive functioning and theory of mind. *British Journal of Developmental Psychology, 24,* 733–751.

McAlister, A., & Peterson, C. C. (2007). A longitudinal study of child siblings and theory of mind development. *Cognitive Development, 22,* 258–270.

McBee, M. T. (2006). A descriptive analysis of referral sources for gifted identification screening by race and socioeconomic status. *Journal of Secondary Gifted Education, 17,* 103–111.

McBride-Chang, C., & Kail, R. V. (2002). Cross-cultural similarities in the predictors of reading acquisition. *Child Development, 73,* 1392–1407.

McCabe, A. (1997). Developmental and cross-cultural aspects of children's narration. In M. Bamberg (Ed.), *Narrative development: Six approaches* (pp. 137–174). Mahwah, NJ: Erlbaum.

McCall, R. B. (1993). Developmental functions for general mental performance. In D. K. Detterman (Ed.), *Current topics in human intelligence* (Vol. 3, pp. 3–29). Norwood, NJ: Ablex.

McCall, R. B., & Carriger, M. S. (1993). A meta-analysis of infant habituation and recognition memory performance as predictors of later IQ. *Child Development, 64,* 57–79.

McCartney, K., Dearing, E., Taylor, B., & Bub, K. (2007). Quality child care supports the achievement of low-income children: Direct and indirect pathways through caregiving and the home environment. *Journal of Applied Developmental Psychology, 28,* 411–426.

McCartney, K., Harris, M. J., & Bernieri, F. (1990). Growing up and growing apart: A developmental meta-analysis of twin studies. *Psychological Bulletin, 107,* 226–237.

McCartney, K., Owen, M., Booth, C., Clarke-Stewart, A., & Vandell, D. (2004). Testing a maternal attachment model of behavior problems in early childhood. *Journal of Child Psychology and Psychiatry, 45,* 765–778.

McCarton, C. (1998). Behavioral outcomes in low birth weight infants. *Pediatrics, 102,* 1293–1297.

McCarty, M. E., & Ashmead, D. H. (1999). Visual control of reaching and grasping in infants. *Developmental Psychology, 35,* 620–631.

McCarty, M. E., & Keen, R. (2005). Facilitating problem-solving performance among 9- and 12-month-old infants. *Journal of Cognition and Development, 6,* 209–228.

McClelland, M. M., Cameron, C. E., Wanless, S. B., & Murray, A. (2007). Executive function, behavioral self-regulation, and social-emotional competence: Links to school readiness. In O. Saracho & B. Spodek (Eds.), *Contemporary perspectives on social learning in early childhood education* (pp. 83–107). Charlotte, NC: Information Age Publishing.

McColgan, K. L., & McCormack, T. (2008). Searching and planning: Young children's reasoning about past and future event sequences. *Child Development, 79,* 1477–1479.

McCormack, V. A., dos Santos Silva, I., Koupil, I., Leon, D. A., & Lithell, H. O. (2005). Birth characteristics and adult cancer incidence: Swedish cohort of over 11,000 men and women. *International Journal of Cancer, 115,* 611–617.

McCormick, M. C., Brooks-Gunn, J., Buka, S. L., Goldman, J., Yu, J., Salganik, M., Scott, D. T., et al. (2006). Early intervention in low birth weight premature infants: Results at 18 years of age for the Infant Health and Development Program. *Pediatrics, 117,* 771–780.

McCune, L. (1993). The development of play as the development of consciousness. In M. H. Bornstein & A. O'Reilly (Eds.), *New directions for child development* (No. 59, pp. 67–79). San Francisco: Jossey-Bass.

McDonagh, M. S., Osterweil, P., & Guise, J. M. (2005). The benefits and risks of inducing labour in patients with prior cesarean delivery: A systematic review. *BJOG, 112,* 1007–1015.

McDonough, L. (1999). Early declarative memory for location. *British Journal of Developmental Psychology, 17,* 381–402.

McDowell, D. J., & Parke, R. D. (2000). Differential knowledge of display rules for positive and negative emotions: Influences from parents, influences on peers. *Social Development, 9,* 415–432.

McElwain, N. L., & Booth-LaForce, C. (2006). Maternal sensitivity to infant distress and nondistress as predictors of infant–mother attachment security. *Journal of Family Psychology, 20,* 247–255.

McGee, G. (1997). Legislating gestation. *Human Reproduction, 12,* 407–408.

McGee, L. M., & Richgels, D. J. (2008). *Literacy's beginnings: Supporting young readers and writers* (5th ed.). Boston: Allyn and Bacon.

McGillicuddy-De Lisi, A. V., Daly, M. & Neal, A. (2006). Children's distributive justice judgments: Aversive racism in Euro-American children? *Child Development, 77,* 1063–1080.

McGlothlin, H., & Killen, M. (2006). Intergroup attitudes of European American children attending ethnically homogeneous schools. *Child Development, 77,* 1375–1386.

McGrath, S. K., & Kennell, J. H. (2008). A randomized controlled trial of continuous labor support for middle-class couples: Effect on cesarean delivery rates. *Birth: Issues in Perinatal Care, 35,* 9–97.

McHale, J. P., Kazali, C., Rotman, T., Talbot, J., Carleton, M., & Lieberson, R. (2004). The transition to coparenthood: Parents' prebirth expectations and early coparental adjustment at 3 months postpartum. *Development and Psychopathology, 16,* 711–733.

McHale, J. P., Lauretti, A., Talbot, J., & Pouquette, C. (2002). Retrospect and prospect in the psychological study of coparenting and family group process. In J. P. McHale & W. S. Grolnick (Eds.), *Retrospect and prospect in the psychological study of families* (pp. 127–165). Mahwah, NJ: Erlbaum.

McHale, J. P., & Rotman, T. (2007). Is seeing believing? Expectant parents' outlooks on coparenting and later coparenting solidarity. *Infant Behavior and Development, 30,* 63–81.

McHale, J. P., Vinden, P. G., Bush, L., Richer, D., Shaw, D., & Smith, B. (2005). Patterns of personal and social adjustment among sport-involved and noninvolved urban middle-school children. *Sociology of Sport Journal, 22,* 119–136.

McHale, S. M., Updegraff, K. A., Helms-Erikson, H., & Crouter, A. C. (2001). Sibling influences on gender development in middle childhood and early adolescence: A longitudinal study. *Developmental Psychology, 37,* 115–125.

McKelvie, P., & Low, J. (2002). Listening to Mozart does not improve children's spatial ability: Final curtains for the Mozart effect. *British Journal of Developmental Psychology, 20,* 241–258.

McKenna, J. J. (2001). Why we never ask "Is it safe for infants to sleep alone?" *Academy of Breast Feeding Medicine News and Views, 7*(4), 32, 38.

McKenna, J. J. (2002, September/October). Breastfeeding and bedsharing still useful (and important) after all these years. *Mothering, 114.* Retrieved from www.mothering.com/articles /new_baby/sleep/mckenna.html

McKenna, J. J., & McDade, T. (2005). Why babies should never sleep alone: A review of the co-sleeping controversy in relation to SIDS, bedsharing, and breastfeeding. *Paediatric Respiratory Reviews, 6,* 134–152.

McKenna, J. J., & Volpe, L. E. (2007). Sleeping with baby: An Internet-based sampling of parental experiences, choices, perceptions, and interpretations in a Western industrialized context. *Infant and Child Development, 16,* 359–385.

McKown, C., & Strambler, M. J. (2009). Developmental antecedents and social and academic consequences of stereotype-consciousness in middle childhood. *Child Development, 80,* 1643–1659.

McKown, C., & Weinstein, R. S. (2003). The development and consequences of stereotype consciousness in middle childhood. *Child Development, 74,* 498–515.

McKown, C., & Weinstein, R. S. (2008). Teacher expectations, classroom context, and the achievement gap. *Journal of School Psychology, 46,* 235–261.

McKusick, V. A. (2007). *Online Mendelian inheritance in man.* Retrieved from www.ncbi.nlm.nih.gov /sites/entrez?db=omim

McLanahan, S. (1999). Father absence and the welfare of children. In E. M. Hetherington (Ed.), *Coping with divorce, single parenting, and remarriage: A risk and resiliency perspective* (pp. 117–145). Mahwah, NJ: Erlbaum.

McLoyd, V. C., Aikens, N. L., & Burton, L. M. (2006). Childhood poverty, policy, and practice. In K. A. Renninger & I. E. Sigel (Eds.), *Handbook of child psychology: Vol. 4. Child psychology in practice* (6th ed., pp. 700–778). Hoboken, NJ: Wiley.

McLoyd, V. C., Kaplan, R., Hardaway, C. R., & Wood, D. (2007). Does endorsement of physical discipline matter? Assessing moderating influences on the maternal and child psychological correlates of physical discipline in African-American families. *Journal of Family Psychology, 21,* 165–175.

McLoyd, V. C., & Smith, J. (2002). Physical discipline and behavior problems in African-American, European-American, and Hispanic children: Emotional support as a moderator. *Journal of Marriage and the Family, 64,* 40–53.

McMahon, C. A., Barnett, B., Kowalenko, N. M., & Tennant, C. C. (2006). Maternal attachment state of mind moderates the impact of postnatal depression on infant attachment. *Journal of Child Psychology and Psychiatry and Allied Disciplines, 47,* 660–669.

McManus, I. C., Sik, G., Cole, D. R., Mellon, A. F., Wong, J., & Kloss, J. (1988). The development of handedness in children. *British Journal of Developmental Psychology, 6,* 257–273.

MCR Vitamin Study Research Group. (1991). Prevention of neural tube defects: Results of the Medical Research Council Vitamin Study. *Lancet, 338,* 131–137.

Mead, G. H. (1934). *Mind, self, and society.* Chicago: University of Chicago Press.

Mead, M., & Newton, N. (1967). Cultural patterning of perinatal behavior. In S. Richardson & A. Guttmacher (Eds.), *Childbearing: Its social and psychological aspects* (pp. 142–244). Baltimore: Williams & Wilkins.

Mechelli, A., Crinion, J. T., Noppeney, U., O'Doherty, J., Ashburner, J., Frackowiak, R. S., & Price, C. J. (2004). Structural plasticity in the bilingual brain: Proficiency in a second language and age at acquisition affect grey-matter density. *Nature, 431,* 757.

Meek, J. (2002). Basic principles of optical imaging and application to the study of infant development. *Developmental Science, 5,* 371–380.

Mehlmadrona, L., & Madrona, M. M. (1997). Physician- and midwife-attended home births—effects of breech, twin, and post-dates outcome data on mortality rates. *Journal of Nurse-Midwifery, 42,* 91–98.

Meins, E., Fernyhough, C., Russell, J., & Clark-Carter, D. (1998). Security of attachment as a predictor of symbolic and mentalizing abilities: A longitudinal study. *Social Development, 7,* 1–24.

Meins, E., Fernyhough, C., Wainwright, R., Clark-Carter, D., Gupta, M. D., Fradley, E., & Tucker, M. (2003). Pathways to understanding mind: Construct validity and predictive validity of maternal mind-mindedness. *Child Development, 74,* 1194–1211.

Melby, J. N., Conger, R. D., Fang, S., Wichrama, K. A. S., & Conger, K. J. (2008). Adolescent family experiences and educational attainment during early adulthood. *Developmental Psychology, 44,* 1519-1536.

Melinder, A., Endestad, T., & Magnussen, S. (2006). Relations between episodic memory, suggestibility, theory of mind, and cognitive inhibition in the preschool child. *Scandinavian Journal of Psychology, 47,* 485–495.

Melton, G. B. (2005). Treating children like people: A framework for research and advocacy. *Journal of Clinical Child and Adolescent Psychology, 34,* 646–657.

Meltzoff, A. N. (1995). Understanding the intentions of others: Reenactment of intended acts by 18-month-old children. *Developmental Psychology, 31,* 838–850.

Meltzoff, A. N. (2007). 'Like me': A foundation for social cognition. *Developmental Science, 10,* 126–134.

Meltzoff, A. N., & Kuhl, P. K. (1994). Faces and speech: Intermodal processing of biologically relevant signals in infants and adults. In D. J. Lewkowicz & R. Lickliter (Eds.), *The development of intersensory perception: Comparative perspectives* (pp. 335–369). Hillsdale, NJ: Erlbaum.

Meltzoff, A. N., & Moore, M. K. (1977). Imitation of facial and manual gestures by human neonates. *Science, 198,* 75–78.

Meltzoff, A. N., & Moore, M. K. (1994). Imitation, memory, and the representation of persons. *Infant Behavior and Development, 17,* 83–99.

Meltzoff, A. N., & Moore, M. K. (1999). Persons and representation: Why infant imitation is important for theories of human development. In J. Nadel & G. Butterworth (Eds.), *Imitation in infancy* (pp. 9–35). Cambridge, U.K.: Cambridge University Press.

Melzi, G., & Ely, R. (2009). Language development in the school years. In J. B. Gleason & N. B. Ratner (Eds.), *Development of language* (7th ed., pp. 391–435). Boston: Allyn and Bacon.

Mennella, J. A., & Beauchamp, G. K. (1998). Early flavor experiences: Research update. *Nutrition Reviews, 56,* 205–211.

Ment, L. R., Vohr, B., Allan, W., Katz, K. H., Schneider, K. C., Westerveld, M., Cuncan, C. C., & Makuch, R. W. (2003). Change in cognitive function over time in very low-birth-weight infants. *Journal of the American Medical Association, 289,* 705–711.

Menyuk, P., Liebergott, J. W., & Schultz, M. C. (1995). *Early language development in full-term and premature infants.* Hillsdale, NJ: Erlbaum.

Meredith, N. V. (1978). *Human body growth in the first ten years of life.* Columbia, SC: State Printing.

Mervis, C. B., Pani, J. R., & Pani, A. M. (2003). Transaction of child cognitive-linguistic abilities and adult input in the acquisition of lexical categories at the basic and subordinate levels. In D. H. Rakison & L. M. Oakes (Ed.), *Early category and concept development* (pp. 242–274). New York: Oxford University Press.

Meyer, P. A., Pivetz, T., Dignam, T. A., Hma, D. M., Schoonover, J., & Brody, D. (2003). Surveillance for elevated blood lead levels among children—United States, 1997–2001. *Morbidity and Mortality Weekly Report, 52*(No. SS-10), 1–21.

Meyer, R. (2009). Infant feeding in the first year. 1: Feeding practices in the first six months of life. *Journal of Family Health Care, 19,* 13–16.

Mezulis, A. H., Hyde, J. S., & Clark, R. (2004). Father involvement moderates the effect of maternal depression during a child's infancy on child behavior problems in kindergarten. *Journal of Family Psychology, 18,* 575–588.

Miccio, A. W., Yont, K. M., Clemons, H. L., & Vernon-Feagans, L. (2002). Otitis media and the acquisition of consonants. In F. Windsor & M. L. Kelly (Eds.), *Investigations in clinical phonetics and linguistics* (pp. 429–235). Mahwah, NJ: Erlbaum.

Miceli, P. J., Whitman, T. L., Borkowski, J. G., Braungart-Riekder, J., & Mitchell, D. W. (1998). Individual differences in infant information processing: The role of temperamental and maternal factors. *Infant Behavior and Development, 21,* 119–136.

Michalik, N. M., Eisenberg, N., Spinrad, T. L., Ladd, B., Thompson, M., & Valiente, C. (2007). Longitudinal relations among parental emotional expressivity and sympathy and prosocial behavior in adolescence. *Social Development, 16,* 286–309.

Michels, K. B., Willett, W. C., Graubard, B. I., Vaidya, R. L., Cantwell, M. M., Sansbury, L. B., & Forman, M. R. (2007). A longitudinal study of infant feeding and obesity throughout the life course. *International Journal of Obesity, 31,* 1078–1085.

Michiels, D., Grietens, H., Onghena, P., & Kuppens, S. (2010). Perceptions of maternal and paternal attachment security in middle childhood: Links with positive parental affection and psychological adjustment. *Early Child Development and Care, 180,* 211–225.

Midlin, M., Jenkins, R., & Law, C. (2009). Maternal employment and indicators of child health: A systematic review in pre-school children in OECD countries. *Journal of Epidemiology and Community Health, 63,* 340–350.

Milan, S., Snow, S., & Belay, S. (2007). The context of preschool children's sleep: Racial/ethnic differences in sleep locations, routines, and concerns. *Journal of Family Psychology, 21,* 20–28.

Milevsky, A., Schlechter, M., Netter, S., & Keehn, D. (2007). Maternal and paternal parenting styles in adolescents: Associations with self-esteem, depression, and life satisfaction. *Journal of Child and Family Studies, 16,* 39–47.

Miller, C. F., Lurye, L. E., Zosuls, K. M., & Ruble, D. N. (2009). Accessibility of gender stereotype domains: Developmental and gender differences in children. *Sex Roles, 60,* 870–881.

Miller, C. J., Sanchez, J., & Hynd, G. W. (2003). Neurological correlates of reading disabilities. In H. L. Swanson, K. R. Harris, & S. Graham (Eds.), *Handbook of learning disabilities* (pp. 242–255). New York: Guilford.

Miller, L. T., & Vernon, P. A. (1992). The general factor in short-term memory, intelligence, and reaction time. *Intelligence, 16,* 5–29.

Miller, P. H. (2000). How to best utilize a deficiency. *Child Development, 71,* 1013–1017.

Miller, P. H. (2009). *Theories of developmental psychology* (5th ed.) New York: Worth.

Miller, P. H., & Bigi, L. (1979). The development of children's understanding of attention. *Merrill-Palmer Quarterly, 25,* 235–250.

Miller, P. J., Fung, H., & Koven, M. (2007). Narrative reverberations: How participation in narrative practices co-creates persons and cultures. In S. Kitayama & D. Cohen (Eds.), *Handbook of cultural psychology* (pp. 595–614). New York: Guilford.

Miller, P. J., Fung, H., & Mintz, J. (1996). Self-construction through narrative practices: A Chinese and American comparison of early socialization. *Ethos, 24,* 1–44.

Miller, P. J., Hengst, J. A., & Wang, S. (2003). Ethnographic methods: Applications from developmental cultural psychology. In P. M. Camic & J. E. Rhodes (Eds.), *Qualitative research in psychology* (pp. 219–242). Washington, DC: American Psychological Association.

Miller, P. J., Wang, S., Sandel, T., & Cho, G. E. (2002). Self-esteem among immigrants as folk theory: A comparison of European American and Taiwanese mothers' beliefs. *Parenting: Science and Practice, 2,* 209–239.

Miller, P. J., Wiley, A. R., Fung, H., & Liang, C. H. (1997). Personal storytelling as a medium of socialization in Chinese and American families. *Child Development, 68,* 557–568.

Miller, S. A. (2009). Children's understanding of second-order mental states. *Psychological Bulletin, 135,* 749–773.

Miller, S. A., Hardin, C. A., & Montgomery, D. E. (2003). Young children's understanding of the conditions for knowledge acquisition. *Journal of Cognition and Development, 4,* 325–356.

Milligan, K., Astington, J. W., & Dack, L. A. (2007). Language and theory of mind: Meta-analysis of the relation between language ability and false-belief understanding. *Child Development, 78,* 622–646.

Mills, D., & Conboy, B. T. (2005). Do changes in brain organization reflect shifts in symbolic functioning? In L. Namy (Ed.), *Symbol use and symbolic representation* (pp. 123–153). Mahwah, NJ: Erlbaum.

Mills, D., Plunkett, K., Prat, C., & Schafer, G. (2005). Watching the infant brain learn words: Effects of language and experience. *Cognitive Development, 20,* 19–31.

Mills, R. S. L. (2005). Taking stock of the developmental literature on shame. *Developmental Review, 25,* 26–63.

Mills, R. S. L., & Grusec, J. E. (1989). Cognitive, affective, and behavioral consequences of praising altruism. *Merrill-Palmer Quarterly, 35,* 299–326.

Mills, T. L., Gomez-Smith, Z., & De Leon, J. M. (2005). Skipped generation families: Sources of psychological distress among grandmothers of grandchildren who live in homes where neither parent is present. *Marriage and Family Review, 37,* 191–212.

Mindell, J. A. (2005). *Sleeping through the night.* New York: HarperResource.

Minkler, M., & Fuller-Thomson, E. (2005). African American grandparents raising grandchildren: A national study using the Census 2000 American Community Survey. *Journal of Gerontology, 60B,* S82–S92.

Misailidi, P. (2006). Young children's display rule knowledge: Understanding the distinction between apparent and real emotions and the motives underlying the use of display rules. *Social Behavior and Personality, 34,* 1285–1296.

Mischel, W., & Liebert, R. M. (1966). Effects of discrepancies between observed and imposed reward criteria on their acquisition and transmission. *Journal of Personality and Social Psychology, 3,* 45–53.

Mishna, F., Antle, B. J., & Regehr, C. (2004). Tapping the perspectives of children. *Qualitative Social Work, 3,* 449–468.

Mistry, R. S., Biesanz, J. C., Chien, N., Howes, C., & Benner, A. D. (2008). Socioeconomic status, parental investments, and the cognitive and behavioral outcomes of low-income children from immigrant and native households. *Early Childhood Research Quarterly, 23,* 193–212.

Mitchell, A., & Boss, B. J. (2002). Adverse effects of pain on the nervous systems of newborns and young children: A review of the literature. *Journal of Neuroscience Nursing, 34,* 228–235.

Miura, I. T., & Okamoto, Y. (2003). Language supports for mathematics understanding and performance. In A. J. Baroody & A. Dowker (Eds.), *The development of arithmetic concepts and skills* (pp. 229–242). Mahwah, NJ: Erlbaum.

Mize, J., & Pettit, G. S. (1997). Mothers' social coaching, mother–child relationship style, and children's peer competence: Is the medium the message? *Child Development, 68,* 312–332.

Mocarelli, P., Gerthoux, P., Ferrari, E., Patterson, D. G., Jr., Kieszak, S. M., & Brambilla, P. (2000). Paternal concentrations of dioxin and sex ratio of offspring. *Lancet, 355,* 1858–1862.

Moens, E., Braet, C., & Soetens, B. (2007). Observation of family functioning at mealtime: A comparison between families of children with and without overweight. *Journal of Pediatric Psychology, 32,* 52–63.

Moerk, E. L. (2000). *The guided acquisition of first language skills.* Westport, CT: Ablex.

Moll, H., & Tomasello, M. (2006). Level I perspective-taking at 24 months of age. *British Journal of Developmental Psychology, 24,* 603–613.

Moll, I. (1994). Reclaiming the natural line in Vygotsky's theory of cognitive development. *Human Development, 37,* 333–342.

Moller, K., Hwang, C. P., & Wickberg, B. (2008). Couple relationship and transition to parenthood: Does workload at home matter? *Journal of Reproductive and Infant Psychology, 26,* 57–68.

Möller, O., & Krawinkel, M. (2005). Malnutrition and health in developing countries. *Canadian Medical Association Journal, 173,* 279–286.

Mondloch, C. J., Lewis, T., Budreau, D. R., Maurer, D., Dannemiller, J. L., Stephens, B. R., & Kleiner-Gathercoal, K. A. (1999). Face perception during early infancy. *Psychological Science, 10,* 419–422.

Monk, C., Fifer, W. P., Myers, M. M., Sloan, R. P., Trien, L., & Hurtado, A. (2000). Maternal stress responses and anxiety during pregnancy: Effects on fetal heart rate. *Developmental Psychobiology, 36,* 67–77.

Monk, C., Sloan, R., Myers, M. M., Ellman, L., Werner, E., Jeon, J., Tager, F., & Fifer, W. P. (2004). Fetal heart rate reactivity differs by women's psychiatric status: An early marker for developmental risk? *Journal of the American Academy of Child and Adolescent Psychiatry, 43,* 283–290.

Monk, C. S., Weng, S.-J., Wiggins, J., Kurapati, N., Louro, H. M. C., Carrasco, M., et al. (2010). Neural circuitry of emotional face processing in autism spectrum disorders. *Journal of Psychiatry and Neuroscience, 35,* 105–114.

Montague, D. P. F., & Walker-Andrews, A. S. (2001). Peekaboo: A new look at infants' perception of emotion expressions. *Developmental Psychology, 37,* 826–838.

Montemayor, R., & Eisen, M. (1977). The development of self-conceptions from childhood to adolescence. *Developmental Psychology, 13,* 314–319.

Moon, C., Cooper, R. P., & Fifer, W. P. (1993). Two-day-old infants prefer their native language. *Infant Behavior and Development, 16,* 495–500.

Moon, R. Y., Horne, R. S. C., & Hauck, F. R.(2007). Sudden infant death syndrome. *The Lancet, 370,* 1578–1587.

Moonie, D. A., Sterling, D. A., Figgs, L., & Castro, M. (2006). Asthma status and severity affects missed school days. *Journal of School Health, 76,* 18–24.

Moore, C., Mealiea, J., Garon, N., & Povinelli, D. (2007). The development of body self-awareness. *Infancy, 11,* 157–174.

Moore, E. G. J. (1986). Family socialization and the IQ test performance of traditionally and transracially adopted black children. *Developmental Psychology, 22,* 317–326.

Moore, G. A., Cohn, J. E., & Campbell, S. B. (2001). Infant affective responses to mother's still face at 6 months differentially predict externalizing and internalizing behaviors at 18 months. *Developmental Psychology, 37,* 706–714.

Moore, K. L., & Persaud, T. V. N. (2008). *Before we are born* (7th ed.). Philadelphia: Saunders.

Moore, M. K., & Meltzoff, A. N. (1999). New findings on object permanence: A developmental difference between two types of occlusion. *British Journal of Developmental Psychology, 17,* 563–584.

Moore, M. K., & Meltzoff, A. N. (2004). Object permanence after a 24-hr delay and leaving the locale of disappearance: The role of memory, space, and identity. *Developmental Psychology, 40,* 606–620.

Moore, M. K., & Meltzoff, A. N. (2008). Factors affecting infants' manual search for occluded objects and the genesis of object permanence. *Infant Behavior and Development, 31,* 168–180.

Moran, G., Forbes, L., Evans, E., Tarabulsy, G. M., & Madigan, S. (2008). Both maternal sensitivity and atypical maternal behavior independently predict attachment security and disorganization in adolescent mother–infant relationships. *Infant Behavior and Development, 31,* 321–325.

Moran, G. F., & Vinovskis, M. A. (1986). The great care of godly parents: Early childhood in Puritan New England. *Monographs of the Society for Research in Child Development, 50*(4–5, Serial No. 211).

Moran, S., & Gardner, H. (2006). Extraordinary achievements: A developmental and systems analysis. In D. Kuhn & R. S. Siegler (Eds.), *Handbook of child psychology: Vol. 2. Cognition, perception, and language* (6th ed., pp. 905–949). Hoboken, NJ: Wiley.

Morelli, G. A., Rogoff, B., & Angelillo, C. (2003). Cultural variation in young children's access to work or involvement in specialized child-focused activities. *International Journal of Behavioral Development, 27,* 264–274.

Morelli, G. A., Rogoff, B., Oppenheim, D., & Goldsmith, D. (1992). Cultural variation in infants' sleeping arrangements: Questions of independence. *Developmental Psychology, 28,* 604–613.

Moreno, A. J., Klute, M. M., & Robinson, J. L. (2008). Relational and individual resources as predictors of empathy in early childhood. *Social Development, 17,* 613–637.

Morgan, B., Maybery, M., & Durkin, K. (2003). Weak central coherence, poor joint attention, and low verbal ability: Independent deficits in early autism. *Developmental Psychology, 39,* 646–656.

Morgan, P. L., Farkas, G., Hillemeier, M. M., & Maczuga, S. (2009). Risk factors for learning-related behavior problems at 24 months of age: Population-based estimates. *Journal of Abnormal Child Psychology, 37,* 401–413.

Morgane, P. J., Austin-LaFrance, R., Bronzino, J., Tonkiss, J., Diaz-Cintra, S., Cintra, L., Kemper, T., & Galler, J. R. (1993). Prenatal malnutrition and development of the brain. *Neuroscience and Biobehavioral Reviews, 17,* 91–128.

Mori, L., & Peterson, L. (1995). Knowledge of safety of high and low active–impulsive boys: Implications for child injury prevention. *Journal of Clinical Child Psychology, 24,* 370–376.

Morris, G., & Baker-Ward, L. (2007). Fragile but real: Children's capacity to use newly acquired words to convey preverbal memories. *Child Development, 78,* 448–458.

Morrongiello, B. A., Fenwick, K. D., & Chance, G. (1998). Crossmodal learning in newborn infants: Inferences about properties of auditory-visual events. *Infant Behavior and Development, 21,* 543–554.

Morrongiello, B. A., & Kiriakou, S. (2004). Mothers' home-safety practices for preventing six types of childhood injuries: What do they do, and why? *Journal of Pediatric Psychology, 29,* 285–297.

Morrongiello, B. A., Midgett, C., & Shields, R. (2001). Don't run with scissors: Young children's knowledge of home safety rules. *Journal of Pediatric Psychology, 26,* 105–115.

Morrongiello, B. A., Ondejko, L., & Littlejohn, A. (2004). Understanding toddlers' in-home injuries: I. Context,

correlates, and determinants. *Journal of Pediatric Psychology, 29,* 415–431.

Morrongiello, B. A., & Rennie, H. (1998). Why do boys engage in more risk taking than girls? The role of attributions, beliefs, and risk appraisals. *Journal of Pediatric Psychology, 23,* 33–43.

Morse, S. B., Zheng, H., Tang, Y., & Roth, J., (2009). Early school-age outcomes of late preterm infants. *Pediatrics, 123,* e622–e629.

Mosby, L., Rawls, A. W., Meehan, A. J., Mays, E., & Pettinari, C. J. (1999). Troubles in interracial talk about discipline: An examination of African American child rearing narratives. *Journal of Comparative Family Studies, 30,* 489–521.

Mosely-Howard, G. S., & Evans, C. B. (2000). Relationships and contemporary experiences of the African-American family: An ethnographic case study. *Journal of Black Studies, 30,* 428–451.

Moses, L. J., Baldwin, D. A., Rosicky, J. G., & Tidball, G. (2001). Evidence for referential understanding in the emotions domain at twelve and eighteen months. *Child Development, 72,* 718–735.

Moss, E., Cyr, C., Bureau, J.-F., Tarabulsy, G. M., & Dubois-Comtois, K. (2005). Stability of attachment during the preschool period. *Developmental Psychology, 41,* 773–783.

Moss, E., Cyr, C., & Dubois-Comtois, K. (2004). Attachment at early school age and developmental risk: Examining family contexts and behavior problems of controlling-caregiving, controlling-punitive, and behaviorally disorganized children. *Developmental Psychology, 40,* 519–532.

Moss, E., Smolla, N., Guerra, I., Mazzarello, T., Chayer, D., & Berthiaume, C. (2006). Attachment and self-reported internalizing and externalizing behavior problems in a school period. *Canadian Journal of Behavioural Science, 38,* 142–157.

Mosteller, F. (1995). The Tennessee Study of Class Size in the Early School Grades. *Future of Children, 5*(2), 113–127.

Mota, J., Silva, P., Santos, M. P., Ribeiro, J. C., Oliveira, J., & Duarte, J. A. (2005). Physical activity and school recess time: Differences between the sexes and the relationship between children's playground physical activity and habitual physical activity. *Journal of Sports Sciences, 23,* 269–275.

Mottus, R., Indus, K., & Allik, J. (2008). Accuracy of only children stereotype. *Journal of Research in Personality, 42,* 1047–1052.

Mounts, N. S., Valentiner, D. P., Anderson, K. L., & Boswell, M. K. (2006). Shyness, sociability, and parental support for the college transition: Relation to adolescents' adjustment. *Journal of Youth and Adolescence, 35,* 71–80.

Mrug, S., Hoza, B., & Gerdes, A. C. (2001). Children with attention-deficit/hyperactivity disorder: Peer relationships and peer-oriented interventions. In D. W. Nangle & C. A. Erdley (Eds.), *The role of friendship in psychological adjustment* (pp. 51–77). San Francisco: Jossey-Bass.

Mueller, C. M., & Dweck, C. S. (1998). Intelligence praise can undermine motivation and performance. *Journal of Personality and Social Psychology, 75,* 33–52.

Muenchow, S., & Marsland, K. W. (2007). Beyond baby steps: Promoting the growth and development of U.S. child-care policy. In J. L. Aber, S. J. Bishop-Josef, S. M. Jones, K. T. McLearn, & D. Phillips (Eds.), *Child development and social policy: Knowledge for action* (pp. 97–112). Washington, DC: American Psychological Association.

Mullett-Hume, E., Anshel, D., Guevara, V., & Cloitre, M. (2008). Cumulative trauma and posttraumatic stress disorder among children exposed to the 9/11 World Trade Center attack. *American Journal of Orthopsychiatry, 78,* 103–108.

Mulvaney, M. K., McCartney, K., Bub, K. L., & Marshall, N. L. (2006). Determinants of dyadic scaffolding and cognitive outcomes in first graders. *Parenting: Science and Practice, 6,* 297–310.

Mulvaney, M. K., & Mebert, C. J. (2007). Parental corporal punishment predicts behavior problems in early childhood. *Journal of Family Psychology, 21,* 389–397.

Mumme, D. L., Bushnell, E. W., DiCorcia, J. A., & Lariviere, L. A. (2007). Infants' use of gaze cues to interpret others' actions and emotional reactions. In R. Flom, K. Lee, & D. Muir (Eds.), *Gaze-following : Its development and significance* (pp. 143–170). Mahwah, NJ: Erlbaum.

Munakata, Y. (2001). Task-dependency in infant behavior: Toward an understanding of the processes underlying cognitive development. In F. Lacerda, C. von Hofsten, & M. Heimann (Eds.), *Emerging cognitive abilities in early infancy* (pp. 29–52). Mahwah, NJ: Erlbaum.

Munakata, Y. (2006). Information processing approaches to development. In D. Kuhn & R. S. Siegler (Eds.), *Handbook of child psychology: Vol. 2. Cognition, perception, and language* (6th ed., pp. 426–463). Hoboken, NJ: Wiley.

Munakata, Y., & Stedron, J. M. (2002). Modeling infants' perception of object unity: What have we learned? *Developmental Science, 5,* 176.

Mundy, P., & Stella, J. (2000). Joint attention, social orienting, and nonverbal communication in autism. In A. M. Wetherby & B. M. Prizant (Eds.), *Autism spectrum disorders* (Vol. 9, pp. 55–77). Baltimore, MD: Paul H. Brookes.

Munroe, R. L., & Romney, A. K. (2006). Gender and age differences in same-sex aggregation and social behavior. *Journal of Cross-Cultural Psychology, 37,* 3–19.

Muret-Wagstaff, S., & Moore, S. G. (1989). The Hmong in America: Infant behavior and rearing practices. In J. K. Nugent, B. M. Lester, & T. B. Brazelton (Eds.), *Biology, culture, and development* (Vol. 1, pp. 319–339). Norwood, NJ: Ablex.

Muris, P., Merckelbach, H., Gadet, B., & Moulaert, V. (2000). Fears, worries, and scary dreams in 4- to 12-year-old children: Their content, developmental pattern, and origins. *Journal of Clinical Child Psychology, 29,* 43–52.

Muris, P., Merckelbach, H., Ollendick, T. H., King, N. J., & Bogie, N. (2001). Children's nighttime fears: Parent–child ratings of frequency, content, origins, coping behaviors and severity. *Behaviour Research and Therapy, 39,* 13–28.

Murphy, T. H., & Corbett, D. (2009). Plasticity during recovery: From synapse to behaviour. *Nature Reviews Neuroscience, 10,* 861–872.

Murray, A. D. (1985). Aversiveness is in the mind of the beholder. In B. M. Lester & C. F. Z. Boukydis (Eds.), *Infant crying* (pp. 217–239). New York: Plenum.

Mussen, P., & Eisenberg-Berg, N. (1977). *Roots of caring, sharing, and helping.* San Francisco: Freeman.

Mutti, D. O., Mitchell, G. L., Moeschberger, M. L., Jones, L. A., & Zadnik, K. (2002). Parental myopia, near work, school achievement, and children's refractive error. *Investigative Ophthalmology and Visual Science, 43,* 3633–3640.

Myant, K. A., & Williams, J. M. (2005). Children's concepts of health and illness: Understanding of contagious illnesses, noncontagious illnesses and injuries. *Journal of Health Psychology, 10,* 805–819.

Myers, L. J., & Liben, L. S. (2008). The role of intentionality and iconicity in children's developing comprehension and production of cartographic symbols. *Child Development, 79,* 668–684.

Myowa-Yamakoshi, M., Tomonaga, M., Tanaka, M., & Matsuzawa, T. (2004). Imitation in neonatal chimpanzees (Pan troglodytes). *Developmental Science, 7,* 437–442.

N

Nadel, J., Prepin, K., & Okanda, M. (2005). Experiencing contingency and agency: First step toward self-understanding in making a mind? *Interaction Studies, 6,* 447–462.

Nader, P. R., O'Brien, M., Houts, R., Bradley, R., Belsky, J., Crosnoe, R., et al. (2006). Identifying risk for obesity in early childhood. *Pediatrics, 118,* e594–e601.

Nafstad, P., Hagen, J. A., Öie, L., Magnus, P., & Jaakkola, J. J. K. (1999). Day care centers and respiratory health. *Pediatrics, 103,* 753–758.

Nagy, E., Compagne, H., Orvos, H., Pal, A., Molnar, P., & Janszky, I. (2005). Index finger movement imitation by human neonates: Motivation, learning, and left-hand preference. *Pediatric Research, 58,* 749–753.

Nagy, W. E., & Scott, J. A. (2000). Vocabulary processes. In M. L. Kamil & P. B. Mosenthal (Eds.), *Handbook of reading research* (Vol. 3, pp. 269–284). Mahwah, NJ: Erlbaum.

Naigles, L. R., & Swenson, L. D. (2007). Syntactic supports for word learning. In E. Hoff & M. Shatz (Eds.), *Blackwell handbook of language development* (pp. 212–231). Malden, MA: Blackwell.

Naito, M., & Seki, Y. (2009). The relationship between second-order false belief and display rules reasoning: Integration of cognitive and affective social understanding. *Developmental Science, 12,* 150–164.

Nánez, J., Sr., & Yonas, A. (1994). Effects of luminance and texture motion on infant defensive reactions to optical collision. *Infant Behavior and Development, 17,* 165–174.

Narr, K. L., Woods, R. P., Lin, J., Kim, J., Phillips, O. R., Del'Homme, M., et al. (2009). Widespread cortical thinning is a robust anatomical marker for attention-deficit/hyperactivity disorder. *Journal of the American Academy of Child and Adolescent Psychiatry, 48,* 1014–1022.

Nastasi, B. K., & Clements, D. H. (1994). Effectance motivation, perceived scholastic competence, and higher-order thinking in two cooperative computer environments. *Journal of Educational Computing Research, 10,* 249–275.

Natale, R., & Dodman, N. (2003). Birth can be a hazardous journey: Electronic fetal monitoring does not help. *JOGC, 25,* 1007–1009.

National Association for Sport and Physical Education. (2009). *Active start: A statement of physical activity guidelines for children from birth to age 5* (2nd ed.). Reston, VA: Author.

National Center for Biotechnology Information, National Institutes of Health. (2007). *Genes and disease: Sickle cell anemia.* Retrieved from www.ncbi.nlm.nih.gov/bookshelf/br.fcgi?book=gnd&part=anemiasicklecell

National Coalition for the Homeless. (2008). *Homeless families with children.* Washington, DC: Author.

National Council of Youth Sports. (2008). Report on trends and participation in organized youth sports. Stuart, FL: Author.

National Early Literacy Panel. (2008). *Developing early literacy: A scientific synthesis of early literacy development and implications for intervention.* Jessup, MD: National Institute for Literacy.

National Institutes of Health. (2008). *Genes and disease.* Retrieved from www.ncbi.nlm.nih.gov/books/bv.fcgi?rid=gnd.TOC&depth=2

Navarrete, C., Martinez, I., & Salamanca, F. (1994). Paternal line of transmission in chorea of Huntington with very early onset. *Genetic Counseling, 5,* 175–178.

Needham, A. (2001). Object recognition in 4.5-month-old infants. *Journal of Experimental Child Psychology, 78,* 3–24.

Needleman, H. L., MacFarland, C., Ness, R. B., Reinberg, S., & Tobin, M. J. (2002). Bone lead levels in adjudicated delinquents: A case control study. *Neurotoxicology and Teratology, 24,* 711–717.

Neff, K. D., & Helwig, C. C. (2002). A constructivist approach to understanding the development of reasoning about rights and authority within cultural contexts. *Cognitive Development, 17,* 1429–1450.

Neitzel, C., & Stright, A. D. (2003). Mothers' scaffolding of children's problem solving: Establishing a foundation of academic self-regulatory competence. *Journal of Family Psychology, 17,* 147–159.

Nelson, C. A. (2002). Neural development and lifelong plasticity. In R. M. Lerner, F. Jacobs, & D. Wertlieb (Eds.), *Handbook of applied developmental science* (Vol. 1, pp. 31–60). Thousand Oaks, CA: Sage.

Nelson, C. A. (2007a). A developmental cognitive neuroscience approach to the study of atypical development: A model system involving infants of diabetic mothers. In D. Coch, G. Dawson, & K. W. Fischer (Eds.), *Human behavior, learning, and the developing brain: Atypical development* (2nd ed., pp. 37–59). New York: Guilford.

Nelson, C. A. (2007b). A neurobiological perspective on early human deprivation. *Child Development Perspectives, 1,* 13–18.

Nelson, C. A., & Bosquet, M. (2000). Neurobiology of fetal and infant development: Implications for infant mental health. In C. H. Zeanah, Jr. (Ed.), *Handbook of infant mental health* (2nd ed., pp. 37–59). New York: Guilford.

Nelson, C. A., Thomas, K. M., & de Haan, M. (2006). Neural bases of cognitive development. In D. Kuhn & R. Siegler (Eds.), *Handbook of child psychology: Vol. 2. Cognition, perception, and language* (6th ed., pp. 3–57). Hoboken, NJ: Wiley.

Nelson, C. A., Wewerka, S., Borscheid, A. J., deRegnier, R., & Georgieff, M. K. (2003). Electrophysiologic evidence of impaired cross-modal recognition memory in 8-month-old infants of diabetic mothers. *Journal of Pediatrics, 142,* 575–582.

Nelson, C. A., Wewerka, S., Thomas, K. M., Tribby-Walbridge, S., deRegnier, R., & Georgieff, M. K. (2000). Neurocognitive sequelae of infants of diabetic mothers. *Behavioral Neuroscience, 114,* 950–956.

Nelson, D. A., & Coyne, S. M. (2009). Children's intent attributions and feelings of distress: Associations with maternal and paternal parenting practices. *Journal of Abnormal Child Psychology, 37,* 223–237.

Nelson, D. A., Hart, C. H., Yang, C., Olsen, J. A., & Jin, S. (2006). Aversive parenting in China: Associations with child physical and relational aggression. *Child Development, 77,* 554–572.

Nelson, D. A., Nelson, L. J., Hart, C. H., Yang, C., & Jin, S. (2005). Parenting and peer-group behavior in cultural context. In X. Chen, B. Schneider, & D. French (Eds.), *Peer relations in cultural context.* New York Cambridge University Press.

Nelson, D. A., Robinson, C. C., & Hart, C. H. (2005). Relational and physical aggression of preschool-age children: Peer status linkages across informants. *Early Education and Development, 16,* 115–139.

Nelson, J. (1996). *Positive discipline.* New York: Ballantine.

Nelson, K. (1973). Structure and strategy in learning to talk. *Monographs of the Society for Research in Child Development, 38*(1–2, Serial No. 149).

Nelson, K. (2001). Language and the self: From the "experiencing I" to the "continuing me." In C. Moore & K. Lemmon (Eds.), *The self in time* (pp. 15–33). Mahwah NJ: Erlbaum.

Nelson, K. (2003). Narrative and the emergence of a consciousness of self. In G. D. Fireman & T. E. McVay, Jr. (Eds.), *Narrative and consciousness: Literature, psychology, and the brain* (pp. 17–36). London: Oxford University Press.

Nelson, K. (2007). *Young minds in social worlds: Experience, meaning, and memory.* Cambridge, MA: Harvard University Press.

Nelson, K., & Fivush, R. (2004). The emergence of autobiographical memory: A social cultural developmental theory. *Developmental Review, 111,* 486–511.

Nemet, D., Barkan, S., Epstein, Y., Friedland, O., Kowen, G., & Eliakim, A. (2005). Short- and long-term beneficial effects of a combined dietary–behavioral–physical activity intervention for the treatment of childhood obesity. *Pediatrics, 115,* e443–e449.

Nepomnyaschy, L., & Waldfogel, J. (2007). Paternity leave and fathers' involvement with their young children. *Community, Work and Family, 10,* 427–453.

Neri, Q., Takeuchi, T., & Palermo, G. D. (2008). An update of assisted reproductive technologies in the United States. *Annals of the New York Academy of Sciences, 1127,* 41-48.

Nesdale, D., Durkin, K., Maas, A., & Griffiths, J. (2004). Group status, outgroup ethnicity, and children's ethnic attitudes. *Applied Developmental Psychology, 25,* 237–251.

Nesdale, D., Durkin, K., Maas, A., & Griffiths, J. (2005). Threat, group identification, and children's ethnic prejudice. *Social Development, 14,* 189–205.

Nettelbeck, T., & Burns, N. R. (2010). Processing speed, working memory and reasoning ability from childhood to old age. *Personality and Individual Differences, 48,* 379–384.

Neuman, S. B. (1999). Books make a difference: A study of access to literacy. *Reading Research Quarterly, 34,* 286–311.

Neuman, S. B. (2003). From rhetoric to reality: The case for high-quality compensatory prekindergarten programs. *Phi Delta Kappan, 85*(4), 286–291.

Neuman, S. B. (2006). The knowledge gap: Implications for early education. In D. K. Dickinson & S. B. Neuman (Eds.), *Handbook of early literacy research* (Vol. 2, pp. 29–40). New York: Guilford.

Neuman, S. B., & Celano, D. (2001). Access to print in middle- and low-income communities: An ecological study of four neighborhoods. *Reading Research Quarterly, 36,* 8–26.

Neumark-Sztainer, D., Hannan, P. J., Story, M., Croll, J., & Perry, C. (2003). Family meal patterns: Associations with sociodemographic characteristics and improved dietary intake among adolescents. *Journal of the American Dietetic Association, 103,* 317–322.

Neville, H. J., & Bavelier, D. (2002). Human brain plasticity: Evidence from sensory deprivation and altered language experience. In M. A. Hofman, G. J. Boer, A. J. G. D. Holtmaat, E. J. W. van Someren, J. Berhaagen, & D. F. Swaab (Eds.), *Plasticity in the adult brain: From genes to neurotherapy* (pp. 177–188). Amsterdam: Elsevier Science.

Neville, H. J., & Bruer, J. T. (2001). Language processing: How experience affects brain organization. In D. B. Bailey, Jr., J. T. Bruer, F. J. Symons, & J. W. Lichtman (Eds.), *Critical thinking about critical periods* (pp. 151–172). Baltimore: Paul H. Brookes.

Nevin, R. (2000). How lead exposure relates to temporal changes in IQ, violent crime, and unwed pregnancy. *Environmental Research, 83,* 1–22.

Newachek, P., Hung, Y.-Y., Hochstein, M., & Halfon, N. (2002). Access to health care for disadvantaged young children. *Journal of Early Intervention, 25,* 1–11.

Newcomb, A. F., Bukowski, W. M., & Pattee, L. (1993). Children's peer relations: A meta-analytic review of popular, rejected, neglected, controversial, and average sociometric status. *Psychological Bulletin, 113,* 99–128.

Newcombe, N. S., & Huttenlocher, J. (1992). Children's early ability to solve perspective-taking problems. *Developmental Psychology, 28,* 635–643.

Newcombe, N. S., Sluzenski, J., & Huttenlocher, J. (2005). Preexisting knowledge versus on-line learning: What do young infants really know about spatial location? *Psychological Science, 16,* 222–227.

Newland, L. A., Coyl, D. D., & Freeman, H. (2008). Predicting preschoolers' attachment security from fathers' involvement, internal working models, and use of social support. *Early Child Development and Care, 178,* 785–801.

Newman, A. J., Bavelier, D., Corina, D., Jezzard, P., & Neville, H. J. (2002). A critical period for right hemisphere recruitment in American sign language processing. *Nature Neuroscience, 5,* 76–80.

Newnham, C. A., Milgrom, J., & Skouteris, H. (2009). Effectiveness of a modified mother–infant transaction program on outcomes for preterm infants from 3 to 24 months of age. *Infant Behavior and Development, 32,* 17–26.

Newport, E. L. (1991). Contrasting conceptions of the critical period for language. In S. Carey & R. Gelman (Eds.), *The epigenesis of mind: Essays on biology and cognition* (pp. 111–130). Hillsdale, NJ: Erlbaum.

Newport, E. L., & Aslin, R. N. (2000). Innately constrained learning: Blending old and new approaches to language acquisition. In S. C. Howell, S. A. Fish, & T. Keith-Lucas (Eds.), *Proceedings of the 24th Annual Boston University Conference on Language Development* (pp. 1–21). Somerville, MA: Cascadilla Press.

Newson, J., & Newson, E. (1975). Intersubjectivity and the transmission of culture: On the social origins of symbolic functioning. *Bulletin of the British Psychological Society, 28,* 437–446.

Ng, F. F., Pomerantz, E. M., & Lam, S. (2007). European American and Chinese parents' responses to children's success and failure: Implications for children's responses. *Developmental Psychology, 43,* 1239–1255.

Ni, Y. (1998). Cognitive structure, content knowledge, and classificatory reasoning. *Journal of Genetic Psychology, 159,* 280–296.

NICHD (National Institute for Child Health and Human Development) Early Child Care Research Network. (1997). The effects of infant child care on infant–mother attachment security: Results of the NICHD Study of Early Child Care. *Child Development, 68,* 860–879.

NICHD (National Institute for Child Health and Human Development) Early Child Care Research Network. (1999). Child care and mother–child interaction in the first 3 years of life. *Developmental Psychology, 35,* 1399–1413.

NICHD (National Institute of Child Health and Human Development) Early Child Care Research Network. (2000a). Characteristics and quality of child care for toddlers and preschoolers. *Applied Developmental Science, 4,* 116–135.

NICHD (National Institute of Child Health and Human Development) Early Child Care Research Network. (2000b). The relation of child care to cognitive and language development. *Child Development, 71,* 960–980.

NICHD (National Institute of Child Health and Human Development) Early Child Care Research Network. (2001). Before Head Start: Income and ethnicity, family characteristics, child care experiences, and child development. *Early Education and Development, 12,* 545–575.

NICHD (National Institute of Child Health and Human Development) Early Child Care Research Network. (2002a). Child-care structure → process → outcome: Direct and indirect effects of child-care quality on young children's development. *Psychological Science, 13,* 199–206.

NICHD (National Institute of Child Health and Human Development) Early Child Care Research Network. (2002b). The interaction of child care and family risk in relation to child development at 24 and 36 months. *Applied Developmental Science, 6,* 144–156.

NICHD (National Institute of Child Health and Human Development) Early Child Care Research Network. (2003a). Does amount of time spent in child care predict socioemotional adjustment during the transition to kindergarten? *Child Development, 74,* 976–1005.

NICHD (National Institute of Child Health and Human Development) Early Child Care Research Network. (2003b). Does quality of child care affect child outcomes at age *Developmental Psychology, 39,* 451–469.

NICHD (National Institute of Child Health and Human Development) Early Child Care Research Network. (2004). Type of child care and children's development at 54 months. *Early Childhood Research Quarterly, 19,* 203–230.

NICHD (National Institute of Child Health and Human Development) Early Child Care Research Network. (2006). Child-care effect sizes for the NICHD Study of Early Child Care and Youth Development. *American Psychologist, 61,* 99–116.

Nicholls, A. L., & Kennedy, J. M. (1992). Drawing development: From similarity of features to direction. *Child Development, 63,* 227–241.

Nichols, K. E., Fox, N., & Mundy, P. (2005). Joint attention, self-recognition, and neurocognitive function in toddlers. *Infancy, 7,* 35–51.

Nicholson, C. (2006, September). Thinking it over: fMRI and psychological science. *APS Observer,* pp. 21–25.

Nicholson, J. M., Sanders, M. R., Halford, W. K., Phillips, M., & Whitton, S. W. (2008). The prevention and treatment of children's adjustment problems in stepfamilies. In J. Pryor (Ed.), *International handbook of stepfamilies: Policy and practice in legal, research, and clinical environments* (pp. 485–521). Hoboken, NJ: Wiley.

Nickman, S. L., Rosenfeld, A. A., & Fine, P. (2005). Children in adoptive families: Overview and update. *Journal of the American Academy of Child and Adolescent Psychiatry, 44,* 987–995.

Nickman, S. L., Rosenfeld, A. A., Fine, P., MacIntyre, J. C., Pilowsky, D. J., & Howe, R.-A. (2005). Children in adoptive families: Overview and update. *Journal of the American Academy of Child and Adolescent Psychiatry, 44,* 987–995.

Niehaus, M. D., Moore, S. R., Patrick, P. D., Derr, L. L., Lorntz, B., Lima, A. A., & Gurerrant, R. L. (2002). Early childhood diarrhea is associated with diminished cognitive function 4 to 7 years later in children in a northeast Brazilian shantytown. *American Journal of Tropical Medicine and Hygiene, 66,* 590–593.

Nielsen Company. (2008). *An overview of home Internet access in the U.S.* Retrieved from blog.nielsen.com/nielsenwire/online_mobile/home-internet-access-continuing-to-grow-but-big-differences-among-demographics/

Nielsen, M., & Christie, T. (2008). Adult modeling facilitates young children's generation of novel pretend acts. *Infant and Child Development, 17,* 151–162.

Nielsen, S. J., & Popkin, B. M. (2003). Patterns and trends in food portion sizes. *Journal of the American Medical Association, 289,* 450–453.

Nievar, M. A., & Becker, B. J. (2008). Sensitivity as a privileged predictor of attachment: A second perspective on De Wolff & van IJzendoorn's meta-analysis. *Social Development, 17,* 102–114.

Nigg, J. T., & Breslau, N. (2007). Prenatal smoking exposure, low birth weight, and disruptive behavior disorders. *Journal of the American Academy of Child and Adolescent Psychiatry, 46,* 362–369.

Nippold, M. A., Taylor, C. L., & Baker, J. M. (1996). Idiom understanding in Australian youth: A cross-cultural comparison. *Journal of Speech and Hearing Research, 39,* 442–447.

Nisbett, R. E. (2009). *Intelligence and how to get it.* New York: Norton.

Nishitani, S., Miyamura, T., Tagawa, M., Sumi, M., Takase, R., Doi, H., Moriuchi, H., & Shinohara, K. (2009). The calming effect of a maternal breast milk odor on the human newborn infant. *Neuroscience Research, 63,* 66–71.

Nix, R. L., Pinderhughes, E. E., Dodge, K. A., Bates, J. E., Pettit, G. S., & McFadyen-Ketchum, S. A. (1999). The relation between mothers' hostile attribution tendencies and children's externalizing behavior problems: The mediating role of mothers' harsh discipline practices. *Child Development, 70,* 896–909.

Noguera, P. (2010, June 14). A new vision for school reform. *The Nation,* pp. 11–14.

Noland, J. S., Singer, L. T., Short, E. J., Minnes, S., Arendt, R. E., & Krichner, H. L. (2005). Prenatal drug exposure and selective attention in preschoolers. *Neurotoxicology and Teratology, 27,* 429–438.

Noller, P., Feeney, J. A., Sheehan, G., Darlington, Y., & Rogers, C. (2008). Conflict in divorcing and continuously married families: A study of marital, parent–child and sibling relationships. *Journal of Divorce and Remarriage, 49,* 1–24.

Noonan, C. W., Kathman, S. J., Sarasua, S. M., & White, M. C. (2003). Influence of environmental zinc on the association between environmental and biological measures of lead in children. *Journal of Exposure Analysis and Environmental Epidemiology, 13,* 318–323.

Nord, M., Andrews, M., & Carlson, S. (2009). *Household food security in the United States, 2008.* Washington, DC: U.S. Department of Agriculture.

Norwitz, E. R. (2009). A blood test to predict preterm birth: Don't mess with maternal–fetal stress. *Journal of Clinical Endocrinology and Metabolism, 94,* 1886–1889.

Noterdaeme, M., Mildenberger, K., Minow, F., & Amorosa, H. (2002). Evaluation of neuromotor deficits in children with autism and children with a specific speech and language disorder. *European Child and Adolescent Psychiatry, 11,* 219–225.

Nucci, L. P. (1996). Morality and the personal sphere of action. In E. Reed, E. Turiel, & T. Brown (Eds.), *Values and knowledge* (pp. 41–60). Hillsdale, NJ: Erlbaum.

Nucci, L. P. (2002). The development of moral reasoning. In U. Goswami (Ed.), *Blackwell handbook of childhood cognitive development* (pp. 303–325). Malden, MA: Blackwell.

Nucci, L. (2005). Culture, context, and the psychological sources of human rights concepts. In W. Edelstein & G. Nunner-Winkler (Eds.), *Morality in context* (pp. 365–394). Amsterdam: Elsevier.

Nucci, L. (2008). *Nice is not enough: Facilitating moral development.* Upper Saddle River, NY: Prentice Hall.

Nye, B., Hedges, L. V., & Konstantopoulos, S. (2001). Are effects of small classes cumulative? Evidence from a Tennessee experiment. *Journal of Educational Research, 94,* 336–345.

O

Oakes, L. M., Coppage, D. J., & Dingel, A. (1997). By land or by sea: The role of perceptual similarity in infants' categorization of animals. *Developmental Psychology, 33,* 396–407.

Oakes, L. M., Horst, J. S., & Kovack-Lesh, K. A. (2009). How infants learn categories. In A. Woodward & A. Needham (Eds.), *Learning and the infant mind* (pp. 144–171). New York: Oxford University Press.

Oakes, L. M., & Madole, K. L. (2003). Principles of developmental change in infants' category formation. In D. H. Rakison & L. M. Oakes (Eds.), *Early category and concept development: Making sense of the blooming, buzzing confusion* (pp. 132–158). New York: Oxford University Press.

Oberecker, R., & Friederici, A. D. (2006). Syntactic event-related potential components in 24-month-olds' sentence comprehension. *NeuroReport, 17,* 1017–1021.

Oberecker, R., Friedrich, M., & Friederici, A. D. (2005). Neural correlates of syntactic processing in two-year-olds. *Journal of Cognitive Neuroscience, 17,* 1667–1678.

Oberlander, T. F., Warburton, W., Misri, S., Aghajanian, J., & Hertzman, C. (2006). Neonatal outcomes after prenatal exposure to selective serotonin reuptake inhibitor antidepressants and maternal depression using population-based linked health data. *Archives of General Psychiatry, 63,* 898–906.

Obradović, J., Long, J. D., Cutuli, J. J., Chan, C. K., Hinz, E., Heistad, D., & Masten, A. S. (2009). Academic achievement of homeless and highly mobile children in an urban school district: Longitudinal evidence on risk, growth, and resilience. *Development and Psychopathology, 21,* 493–518.

O'Brien, M. A., Prosser, L. A., Paradise, J., Ray, G. T., et al. (2009). New vaccines against otitis media: Projected benefits and cost-effectiveness. *Pediatrics, 123,* 1452–1463.

O'Callaghan, M. J., Burn, Y. R., Mohay, H. A., Rogers, Y., & Tudehope, D. I. (1993). The prevalence and origins of left hand preference in high risk infants, and its implications for intellectual, motor, and behavioral performance at four and six years. *Cortex, 29,* 617–627.

O'Connor, A. R., Stephenson, T., Johnson, A., Tobin, M. J., Ratib, S., Ng, Y., & Fielder, A. R. (2002). Long-term ophthalmic outcome of low birth weight children with and without retinopathy of prematurity. *Pediatrics, 109,* 12–18.

O'Connor, E., & McCartney, K. (2007). Examining teacher–child relationships and achievement as part of an ecological model of development. *American Educational Research Journal, 44,* 340–369.

O'Connor, T. G., & Croft, C. M. (2001). A twin study of attachment in preschool children. *Child Development, 72,* 1501–1511.

O'Connor, T. G., Marvin, R. S., Rutter, M., Olrich, J. T., Britner, P. A., & the English and Romanian Adoptees Study Team. (2003). Child–parent attachment following early institutional deprivation. *Development and Psychopathology, 15,* 19–38.

O'Connor, T. G., Rutter, M., Beckett, C., Keaveney, L., Dreppner, J. M., & the English and Romanian Adoptees Study Team. (2000). The effects of global severe privation on cognitive competence: Extension and longitudinal follow-up. *Child Development, 71,* 376–390.

O'Dea, J. A. (2003). Why do kids eat healthful food? Perceived benefits of and barriers to healthful eating and physical activity among children and adolescents. *Journal of the American Dietetic Association, 103,* 497–501.

OECD (Organisation for Economic Cooperation and Development). (2006). *Starting strong II: Early childhood education and care.* Paris: OECD Publishing. Retrieved from www.sourceoecd.org /education/9264035451

OECD (Organisation for Economic Cooperation and Development). (2008a). *Education at a glance 2008: OECD indicators.* Paris: Author. Retrieved from www.oecd.org/infobycountry/0,3380,en _2649_33715_1_1_1_1,00.html

OECD (Organisation for Economic Cooperation and Development). (2008b). OECD Health data: 2008. Retrieved from secure.cihi.ca/cihiweb /dispPage.jsp?cw_page=media_ 26jun2008_e

Ogan, A., & Berk, L. E. (2009, April). *Effects of two approaches to make-believe play training on self-regulation in Head Start children.* Paper presented at the biennial meeting of the Society for Research in Child Development, Denver, CO.

Ogbu, J. U. (1997). Understanding the school performance of urban blacks: Some essential background knowledge. In H. J. Walberg, O. Reyes, & R. P. Weissberg (Eds.), *Children and youth: Interdisciplinary perspectives* (pp. 190–222). Thousand Oaks, CA: Sage.

Ogden, C. L., Carroll, M. D., Curtin, L. R., Lamb, M. M., & Flegal, K. M. (2010). Prevalence of high body mass index in U.S. children and adolescents, 2007–2008. *Journal of the American Medical Association, 303,* 242–249.

Ohgi, S., Arisawa, K., Takahashi, T., Kusumoto, T., Goto, Y., Akiyama, T., & Saito, H. (2003a). Neonatal behavioral assessment scale as a predictor of later developmental disabilities of low-birth-weight and/or premature infants. *Brain and Development, 25,* 313–321.

Ohgi, S., Takahashi, T., Nugent, J. K., Arisawa, K., & Akiyama, T. (2003b). Neonatal behavioral characteristics and later behavioral problems. *Clinical Pediatrics, 42,* 679–686.

Ohlsson, G., Buchhave, P., Leandersson, U., Nordstrom, L., Rydhstrom, H., & Sjolin, I. (2001). Warm tub bathing during labor: Maternal and neonatal effects. *Acta Obstetrica et Gynecologica Scandinavica, 80,* 311–314.

Okagaki, L., & Sternberg, R. J. (1993). Parental beliefs and children's school performance. *Child Development, 64,* 36–56.

Okami, P., Weisner, T., & Olmstead, R. (2002). Outcome correlates of parent–child bedsharing: An eighteen-year longitudinal study. *Developmental and Behavioral Pediatrics, 23,* 244–253.

O'Keefe, M. J., O'Callaghan, M., Williams, G. M., Najman, J. M., & Bor, W. (2003). Learning, cognitive, and attentional problems in adolescents born small for gestational age. *Pediatrics, 112,* 301–307.

Olafson, E., & Boat, B. W. (2000). Long-term management of the sexually abused child: Considerations and challenges. In R. M. Reece (Ed.), *Treatment of child abuse: Common ground for mental health, medical, and legal practitioners* (pp. 14–35). Baltimore: Johns Hopkins University Press.

O'Laughlin, E. M., & Anderson, V. N. (2001). Perceptions of parenthood among young adults: Implications for career and family planning. *American Journal of Family Therapy, 29,* 95–108.

Olds, D. L., Kitzman, H., Cole, R., Robinson, J., Sidora, K., Luckey, D. W., et al. (2004). Effects of nurse home–visiting on maternal life course and child development: Age 6 follow-up results of a randomized trial. *Pediatrics, 114,* 1550–1559.

Olds, D. L., Kitzman, H., Hanks, C., Cole, R., Anson, E., Sidora-Arcoleo, K., et al. (2007). Effects of nurse home visiting on maternal and child functioning: Age-9 follow-up of a randomized trial. *Pediatrics, 120,* e832–e845.

Olds, D. L., Robinson, J., O'Brien, R., Luckey, D. W., Pettitt, L. M., Henderson, C. R., Jr., et al. (2002). Home visiting by paraprofessionals and by nurses: A randomized, controlled trial. *Pediatrics, 110,* 486–496.

Olineck, K. M., & Poulin-Dubois, D. (2007). Imitation of intentional actions and internal state language in infancy predict preschool theory of mind skills. *European Journal of Developmental Psychology, 4,* 14–30.

Olineck, K. M., & Poulin-Dubois, D. (2009). Infants' understanding of intention from 10 to 14 months: Interrelations among violation of expectancy and imitation tasks. *Infant Behavior and Development, 32,* 404–415.

Ollendick, T. H., King, N. J., & Muris, P. (2002). Fears and phobias in children: Phenomenology, epidemiology, and aetiology. *Child and Adolescent Mental Health, 7,* 98–106.

Oller, D. K. (2000). *The emergence of the speech capacity.* Mahwah, NJ: Erlbaum.

Olson, D., Sikka, R. S., Hayman, J., Novak, M., & Stavig, C. (2009). Exercise in pregnancy. *Current Sports Medicine Reports, 8,* 147–153.

Olson, S. L., Bates, J. E., Sandy, J. M., & Lantheir, R. (2000). Early development precursors of externalizing behavior in middle childhood and adolescence. *Journal of Abnormal Child Psychology, 28,* 119–133.

Ondrusek, N., Abramovitch, R., Pencharz, P., & Koren, G. (1998). Empirical examination of the ability of children to consent to clinical research. *Journal of Medical Ethics, 24,* 158–165.

O'Neil, R., Welsh, M., Parke, R. D., Wang, S., & Strand, C. (1997). A longitudinal assessment of the academic correlates of early peer acceptance and rejection. *Journal of Clinical Child Psychology, 26,* 290–303.

O'Neill, M., Bard, K. A., Kinnell, M., & Fluck, M. (2005). Maternal gestures with 20-month-old infants in two contexts. *Developmental Science, 8,* 352–359.

Ong, K. K., Ahmed, M. L., & Dunger, D. B. (2006). Lessons from large population studies on timing and tempo of puberty (secular trends and relation to body size): the European trend. *Molecular and Cellular Endocrinology, 254–255,* 8–12.

Ong, W., Allison, J., & Haladyna, T. M. (2000). Student achievement of third graders in comparable single-age and multiage classrooms. *Journal of Research in Childhood Education, 14,* 205–215.

Ontai, L. L., & Thompson, R. A. (2008). Attachment, parent–child discourse and theory-of-mind development. *Social Development, 17,* 47–60.

Oosterwegel, A., & Openheimer, L. (1993). *The self-system: Developmental changes between and within self-concepts.* Hillsdale, NJ: Erlbaum.

O'Rahilly, R., & Müller, F. (2001). *Human embryology and teratology.* New York: Wiley-Liss.

Ordonana, J. R., Caspi, A., & Moffitt, T. E. (2008). Unintentional injuries in a twin study of preschool children: Environmental, not genetic risk factors. *Journal of Pediatric Psychology, 33,* 185–194.

O'Reilly, A. W. (1995). Using representations: Comprehension and production of actions with imagined objects. *Child Development, 66,* 999–1010.

Orobio de Castro, B., Veerman, J. W., Koops, W., Bosch, J. D., & Monshouwer, H. J. (2002). Hostile attribution of intent and aggressive behavior: A meta-analysis. *Child Development, 73,* 916–934.

Oshima-Takane, Y., & Robbins, M. (2003). Linguistic environment of secondborn children. *First Language, 23,* 21–40.

Ostad, S. A., & Sorensen, P. M. (2007). Private speech and strategy-use patterns: Bidirectional comparisons of children with and without mathematical difficulties in a developmental perspective. *Journal of Learning Disabilities, 40,* 2–14.

Ostrov, J. M., Crick, N. R., & Stauffacher, K. (2006). Relational aggression in sibling and peer relationships during early childhood. *Applied Developmental Psychology, 27,* 241–253.

Ostrov, J. M., Gentile, D. A., & Crick, N. R. (2006). Media exposure, aggression, and prosocial behavior during early childhood: A longitudinal study. *Social Development, 15,* 612–627.

Oude, L. H., Baur, L., Jansen, H., Shrewsbury, V. A., O'Malley, C., Stolk, R. P., & Summerbell, C. D. (2009). Interventions for treating obesity in children. *Cochrane Database of Systematic Reviews,* Issue 4. Chichester, UK: Wiley.

Ouko, L. A., Shantikumar, K., Knezovich, J., Haycock, P., Schnugh, D. J., & Ramsay, M. (2009). Effect of alcohol consumption on CpG methylation in the differentially methylated regions of H19 and IG-DMR in male gametes: Implications for fetal alcohol spectrum disorders. *Alcoholism, Clinical and Experimental Research, 33,* 1615–1627.

Ovando, C. J., & Collier, V. P. (1998). *Bilingual and ESL classrooms: Teaching in multicultural contexts.* Boston: McGraw-Hill.

Ovelese, Y., & Ananth, C. V. (2006). Placental abruption. *Obstetrics and Gynecology, 108,* 1005–1016.

Ovelese, Y., & Smulian, J. C. (2006). Placenta previa, placenta accreta, and vasa previa. *Obstetrics and Gynecology, 107,* 927–941.

Owen, C. G., Whincup, P. H., Kaye, S. J., Martin, R. M., Smith, G. D., Cook, D. G., et al. (2008). Does initial breastfeeding lead to lower blood cholesterol in adult life? A quantitative review of the evidence. *American Journal of Clinical Nutrition, 88,* 305–314.

Owen-Kostelnik, J., Reppucci, N. D., & Meyer, J. R. (2006). Testimony and interrogation of minors: Assumptions about maturity and morality. *American Psychologist, 61,* 286–304.

Owens, R. E. (2008). *Language development: An introduction.* Boston: Allyn and Bacon.

Oyserman, D., Bybee, D., Mowbray, C., & Hart-Johnson, T. (2005). When mothers have serious mental health problems: Parenting as a proximal mediator. *Journal of Adolescence, 28,* 443–463.

Ozçaliskan, S., & Goldin-Meadow, S. (2005). Gesture is at the cutting edge of early language development. *Cognition, 96,* B101–B113.

P

Pacella, R., McLellan, M., Grice, K., Del Bono, E. A., Wiggs, J. L., & Gwiazda, J. E. (1999). Role of genetic factors in the etiology of juvenile-onset myopia based on a longitudinal study of refractive error. *Optometry and Vision Science, 76,* 381–386.

Paladino, J. (2006). *Private speech in children with autism: Developmental course and functional utility.* Unpublished doctoral dissertation, Illinois State University.

Palincsar, A. S. (2003). Advancing a theoretical model of learning and instruction. In B. J. Zimmerman (Ed.), *Educational psychology: A century of contributions* (pp. 459–475). Mahwah, NJ: Erlbaum.

Palincsar, A. S., & Herrenkohl, L. R. (1999). Designing collaborative contexts: Lessons from three research programs. In A. M. O'Donnell & A. King (Eds.), *Cognitive perspectives on peer learning. The Rutgers Invitational Symposium on Education Series* (pp. 151–177). Mahwah, NJ: Erlbaum.

Palmer, J. R., Hatch, E. E., Rao, R. S., Kaufman, R. H., Herbst, A. L., & Noller, K. L. (2001). Infertility among women exposed prenatally to diethylstilbestrol. *American Journal of Epidemiology, 154,* 316–321.

Pan, B. A., & Snow, C. E. (1999). The development of conversation and discourse skills. In M. Barrett (Ed.), *The development of language* (pp. 229–249). Hove, U.K.: Psychology Press.

Pan, H. W. (1994). Children's play in Taiwan. In J. L. Roopnarine, J. E. Johnson, & F. H. Hooper (Eds.), *Children's play in diverse cultures* (pp. 31–50). Albany, NY: SUNY Press.

Papousek, M. (2007). Communication in early infancy: An arena of intersubjective learning. *Infant Behavior and Development, 30,* 258–266.

Paquette, D. (2004). Theorizing the father–child relationship: Mechanisms and developmental outcomes. *Human Development, 47,* 193–219.

Paradis, J. (2007). Second language acquisition in childhood. In E. Hoff & M. Shatz (Eds.), *Blackwell handbook of language development* (pp. 387–405). Malden, MA: Blackwell.

Paradise, R., & Rogoff, B. (2009). Side by side: Learning by observing and pitching in. *Ethos, 27,* 102–138.

Parameswaran, G. (2003). Experimenter instructions as a mediator in the effects of culture on mapping one's neighborhood. *Journal of Environmental Psychology, 23,* 409–417.

Paris, S. G., & Paris, A. G. (2006). Assessments of early reading. In K. A. Renninger & I. E. Sigel (Eds.), *Handbook of child psychology: Vol. 4. Child psychology in practice* (6th ed., pp. 48–74). Hoboken, NJ: Wiley.

Parke, R. D. (2002). Fathers and families. In M. H. Bornstein (Ed.), *Handbook of parenting: Vol. 3* (2nd ed., pp. 27–73). Mahwah, NJ: Erlbaum.

Parke, R. D., & Buriel, R. (2006). Socialization in the family: Ethnic and ecological perspectives. In N. Eisenberg (Ed.), *Handbook of child psychology: Vol. 3. Social, emotional, and personality development* (6th ed., pp. 429–504). Hoboken, NJ: Wiley.

Parke, R. D., Coltrane, S., Fabricius, W., Powers, J., & Adams, M. (2004). Assessing father involvement in Mexican-American families. In R. Day & M. E. Lamb (Eds.), *Conceptualizing and measuring paternal involvement* (pp. 17–38). Mahwah, NJ: Erlbaum.

Parke, R. D., Simpkins, S. D., McDowell, D. J., Kim, M., Killian, C., Dennis, J., Flyr, M. L., Wild, M., & Rah, Y. (2004). Relative contributions of families and peers to children's social development. In P. K. Smith & C. H. Hart (Eds.), *Blackwell handbook of childhood social development* (pp. 156–177). Malden, MA: Blackwell.

Parke, R. D., & Tinsley, B. R. (1981). The father's role in infancy: Determinants of involvement in caregiving and play. In M. E. Lamb (Ed.), *The role of the father in child development* (pp. 429–458). New York: Wiley.

Parker, F. L., Boak, A. Y., Griffin, K. W., Ripple, C., & Peay, L. (1999). Parent–child relationship, home learning environment, and school readiness. *School Psychology Review, 28,* 413–425.

Parker, J. G., Rubin, K. H., Price, J., & DeRosier, M. E. (1995). Peer relationships, child development, and adjustment: A developmental psychopathology perspective. In D. Cicchetti & D. Cohen (Eds.), *Developmental psychopathology: Vol. 2. Risk, disorder, and adaptation* (pp. 96–161). New York: Wiley.

Parker, S. W., Nelson, C. A., & the Bucharest Early Intervention Project Core Group. (2005). The impact of early institutional rearing on the ability to discriminate facial expressions of emotion: An event-related potential study. *Child Development, 76,* 54–72.

Parten, M. (1932). Social participation among preschool children. *Journal of Abnormal and Social Psychology, 27,* 243–269.

Pascalis, O., de Haan, M., & Nelson, C. A. (1998). Long-term recognition memory for faces assessed by visual paired comparison in 3- and 6-month-old infants. *Journal of Experimental Psychology: Learning, Memory, and Cognition, 24,* 249–260.

Pascalis, O., de Haan, M., & Nelson, C. A. (2002). Is face processing species-specific during the first year of life? *Science, 296,* 1321–1323.

Pasterski, V. L., Geffner, M. E., Brain, C., Hindmarsh, P., Brook, C., & Hines, M. (2005). Prenatal hormones and postnatal socialization by parents as determinants of male-typical toy play in girls with congenital adrenal hyperplasia. *Child Development, 76,* 264–278.

Paterson, D. S., Trachtenberg, F. L., Thompson, E. G., Belliveau, R. A., Beggs, A. H., & Darnall, R. (2006). Multiple serotonergic brainstem abnormalities in sudden infant death syndrome. *Journal of the American Medical Association, 296,* 2124–2132.

Pattenden, S., Antova, T., Neuberger, M., Nikiforov, B., De Sario, M., Grize, L., & Heinrich, J. (2006). Parental smoking and children's respiratory health: Independent effects of prenatal and postnatal exposure. *Tobacco Control, 15,* 294–301.

Patterson, C. J. (2002). Lesbian and gay parenthood. In M. H. Bornstein (Ed.), *Handbook of parenting: Vol. 3. Being and becoming a parent* (2nd ed., pp. 317–338).

Patterson, G. R., & Fisher, P. A. (2002). Recent developments in our understanding of parenting: Bidirectional effects, causal models, and the search for parsimony. In M. H. Bornstein (Ed.), *Handbook of parenting* (Vol. 5, pp. 59–88). Mahwah, NJ: Erlbaum.

Paul, J. J., & Cillessen, A. H. N. (2003). Dynamics of peer victimization in early adolescence: Results from a four-year longitudinal study. *Journal of Applied School Psychology, 19,* 25–43.

Pauli, S. A., Berga, S. L., Shang, W., & Session, D. R. (2009). Current status of the approach to assisted reproduction. *Pediatric Clinics of North America, 56,* 467–488.

Paulussen-Hoogeboom, M. C., Stams, G. J. J. M., Hermanns, J. M. A., & Peetsma, T. T. D. (2007). Child negative emotionality and parenting from infancy to preschool: A meta-analytic review. *Developmental Psychology, 43,* 438–453.

PCA America. (2009). Healthy Families America FAQ. Retrieved from www.healthyfamiliesamerica.org/about_us/findex.shtml

Pearl, P. L., Capp, P. K., Novotny, E. J., & Gibson, K. M. (2005). Inherited disorders of neurotransmitters in children and adults. *Clinical Biochemistry, 38,* 1051–1058.

Pearlman, D. N., Zierler, S., Meersman, S., Kim, H. K., Viner-Brown, & Caron, C. (2006). Race disparities in childhood asthma: Does where you live matter? *Journal of the National Medical Association, 98,* 239–247.

Pedersen, S., Vitaro, F., Barker, E. D., & Anne, I. H. (2007). The timing of middle-childhood peer rejection and friendship: Linking early behavior to early adolescent adjustment. *Child Development, 78,* 1037–1051.

Pederson, D. R., & Moran, G. (1996). Expressions of the attachment relationship outside of the Strange Situation. *Child Development, 67,* 915–927.

Peirano, P., Algarin, C., & Uauy, R. (2003). Sleep–wake states and their regulatory mechanisms throughout early human development. *Journal of Pediatrics, 143,* S70–S79.

Pellegrini, A. D. (1992). Kindergarten children's social cognitive status as a predictor of first grade success. *Early Childhood Research Quarterly, 7,* 565–577.

Pellegrini, A. D. (2003). Perceptions and functions of play and real fighting in early adolescence. *Child Development, 74,* 1522–1533.

Pellegrini, A. D. (2004). Rough-and-tumble play from childhood through adolescence: Development and possible functions. In P. K. Smith & C. H. Hart (Eds.), *Blackwell handbook of childhood social development* (pp. 438–453). Malden, MA: Blackwell.

Pellegrini, A. D. (2005). *Recess: Its role in development and education.* Mahwah, NJ: Erlbaum.

Pellegrini, A. D., & Holmes, R. M. (2006). The role of recess in primary school. In D. G. Singer, R. M. Golinkoff, & K. Hirsh-Pasek (Eds.), *Play=learning* (pp. 36–53). New York: Oxford University Press.

Pellegrini, A. D., Huberty, P. D., & Jones, I. (1995). The effects of recess timing on children's playground and classroom behaviors. *American Educational Research Journal, 32,* 845–864.

Pellegrini, A. D., Kato, K., Blatchford, P., & Baines, E. (2002). A short-term longitudinal study of children's playground games across the first year of school: Implications for social competence and adjustment to school. *American Educational Research Journal, 39,* 991–1015.

Pellegrini, A. D., & Smith, P. K. (1998). Physical activity play: The nature and function of a neglected aspect of play. *Child Development, 69,* 577–598.

Pellicano, E., Maybery, M., Durkin, K., & Maley, A. (2006). Multiple cognitive capabilities/deficits in children with an autism spectrum disorder: "Weak" central coherence and its relationship to theory of mind and executive control. *Development and Psychopathology, 18,* 77–98.

Peña, R., Wall, S., & Person, L. (2000). The effect of poverty, social inequality, and maternal education on infant mortality in Nicaragua, 1988–1993. *American Journal of Public Health, 90,* 64–69.

Pennington, B. F., Snyder, K. A., & Roberts, R. J., Jr. (2007). Developmental cognitive neuroscience: Origins, issues, and prospects. *Developmental Review, 27,* 428–441.

Penny, H., & Haddock, G. (2007). Anti-fat prejudice among children: The 'mere proximity' effect in 5–10

year olds. *Journal of Experimental Social Psychology, 43,* 678–683.

Peralta de Mendoza, O. A., & Salsa, A. M. (2003). Instruction in early comprehension and use of a symbol–referent relation. *Cognitive Development, 18,* 269–284.

Perelle, I. B., & Ehrman, L. (2009). Handedness: A behavioral laterality manifestation. In Y.-K. Kim (Ed.), *Handbook of behavior genetics* (pp. 331–342). New York: Springer Science + Business Media.

Perlman, M., & Ross, H. S. (1997). The benefits of parent intervention in children's disputes: An examination of concurrent changes in children's fighting styles. *Child Development, 64,* 690–700.

Perlmutter, M. (1984). Continuities and discontinuities in early human memory: Paradigms, processes, and performances. In R. V. Kail, Jr., & N. E. Spear (Eds.), *Comparative perspectives on the development of memory* (pp. 253–287). Hillsdale, NJ: Erlbaum.

Perren, S., von Wyl, A., Burgin, D., Simoni, H., & von Klitzing, K. (2005). Intergenerational transmission of marital quality across the transition to parenthood. *Family Process, 44,* 441–459.

Perry, G. H., & Dominy, N. J. (2009). Evolution of the human pygmy phenotype. *Trends in Ecology and Evolution, 24,* 218–225.

Peshkin, A. (1994). *Growing up American: Schooling and the survival of community.* Prospect Heights, IL: Waveland Press.

Peshkin, A. (1997). *Places of memory: Whiteman's schools and Native American communities.* Mahwah, NJ: Erlbaum.

Pesonen, A.-K., Räikkönen, K., Heinonen, K., & Komsi, N. (2008). A transactional model of temperamental development: Evidence of a relationship between child temperament and maternal stress over five years. *Social Development, 17,* 326–340.

Petch, J., & Halford, W. K. (2008). Psycho-education to enhance couples' transition to parenthood. *Clinical Psychology Review, 28,* 1125–1137.

Peters, R. D. (2005). A community-based approach to promoting resilience in young children, their families, and their neighborhoods. In R. D. Peters, B. Leadbeater, & R. J. McMahon (Eds.), *Resilience in children, families, and communities: Linking context to practice and policy* (pp. 157–176). New York: Kluwer Academic.

Peters, R. D., Petrunka, K., & Arnold, R. (2003). The Better Beginnings, Better Futures Project: A universal, comprehensive, community-based prevention approach for primary school children and their families. *Journal of Clinical Child and Adolescent Psychology, 32,* 215–227.

Peterson, C., Parsons, T., & Dean, M. (2004). Providing misleading and reinstatement information a year after it happened: Effects on long-term memory. *Memory, 12,* 1–13.

Peterson, C., & Rideout, R. (1998). Memory for medical emergencies experienced by 1- and 2-year-olds. *Developmental Psychology, 34,* 1059–1072.

Petinou, K. C., Schwartz, R. G., Gravel, J. S., & Raphael, L. J. (2001). A preliminary account of phonological and morphological perception in young children with and without otitis media. *International Journal of Language and Communication Disorders, 36,* 21–41.

Petitto, L. A., Holowka, S., Sergio, L. E., Levy, B., & Ostry, D. J. (2004). Baby hands that move to the rhythm of language: Hearing babies acquiring sign languages babble silently on the hands. *Cognition, 93,* 43–73.

Petitto, L. A., Holowka, S., Sergio, L. E., & Ostry, D. (2001). Language rhythms in babies' hand movements. *Nature, 413,* 35–36.

Petitto, L. A., & Marentette, P. F. (1991). Babbling in the manual mode: Evidence for the ontogeny of language. *Science, 251,* 1493–1496.

Petrides, K. V., Sangareau, Y., Furnham, A., & Frederickson, N. (2006). Trait emotional intelligence and children's peer relations at school. *Social Development, 15,* 537–547.

Petrill, S. A., & Deater-Deckard, K. (2004). The heritability of general cognitive ability: A within-family adoption design. *Intelligence, 32,* 403–409.

Petrovich, O. (1997). Understanding non-natural causality in children and adults: The case against artificialism. *Psyche en Geloof, 8,* 151–165.

Pettit, G. S., Brown, E. G., Mize, J., & Lindsey, E. (1998). Mothers' and fathers' socializing behaviors in three contexts: Links with children's peer competence. *Merrill-Palmer Quarterly, 44,* 173–193.

Pfeffer, C. R., Altemus, M., Heo, M., & Jiang, H. (2007). Salivary cortisol and psychopathology in children bereaved by the September 11, 2001 terror attacks. *Biological Psychiatry, 61,* 957–965.

Pfeifer, J. H., Brown, C. S., & Juvonen, J. (2007). Fifty years since Brown vs. Board of Education: Lessons learned about the development and reduction of children's prejudice. *Social Policy Report 21*(2), 3–23.

Pfeifer, J. H., Ruble, D. N., Bachman, M. A., Alvarez, J. M., Cameron, J. A., & Fuligni, A. J. (2007). Social identities and intergroup bias in immigrant and nonimmigrant children. *Developmental Psychology, 43,* 496–507.

Philips, S. U. (1983). *The invisible culture: Communication in classroom and community on the Warm Springs Indian Reservation.* Prospect Heights, IL: Waveland.

Phillips, M. (1997). What makes schools effective? A comparison of the relationships of communitarian climate and academic climate to mathematics achievement and attendance during middle school. *American Educational Research Journal, 34,* 633–662.

Piaget, J. (1926). *The language and thought of the child.* New York: Harcourt, Brace & World. (Original work published 1923)

Piaget, J. (1930). *The child's conception of the world.* New York: Harcourt, Brace, & World. (Original work published 1926)

Piaget, J. (1951). *Play, dreams, and imitation in childhood.* New York: Norton. (Original work published 1945)

Piaget, J. (1952). *The origins of intelligence in children.* New York: International Universities Press. (Original work published 1936)

Piaget, J. (1971). *Biology and knowledge.* Chicago: University of Chicago Press.

Pianta, R., Egeland, B., & Erickson, M. F. (1989). The antecedents of maltreatment: Results of the Mother–Child Interaction Research Project. In D. Cicchetti & V. Carlson (Eds.), *Child maltreatment* (pp. 203–253). New York: Cambridge University Press.

Pianta, R. C., Hamre, B., & Stuhlman, M. (2003). Relationships between teachers and children. In W. M. Reynolds & G. E. Miller (Eds.), *Handbook of psychology: Educational psychology* (Vol. 7, pp. 199–234). New York: Wiley.

Pianta, R. C., Howes, C., Burchinal, M., Bryant, D., Clifford, R., Early, D., & Barbarin, O. (2005). Features of prekindergarten programs, classrooms, and teachers: Do they predict observed classroom quality and child–teacher interactions? *Applied Developmental Science, 9,* 144–159.

Pickens, J., Field, T., & Nawrocki, T. (2001). Frontal EEG asymmetry in response to emotional vignettes in preschool age children. *International Journal of Behavioral Development, 25,* 105–112.

Pickett, K. E., Luo, Y., & Lauderdale, D. S. (2005). Widening social inequalities in risk for sudden infant death syndrome. *American Journal of Public Health, 95,* 1976–1981.

Pierce, S. H., & Lange, G. (2000). Relationships among metamemory, motivation and memory performance in young school-age children. *British Journal of Developmental Psychology, 18,* 121–135.

Pierroutsakos, S. L., & Troseth, G. L. (2003). Video verite: Infants' manual investigation of objects on video. *Infant Behavior and Development, 26,* 183–199.

Pierson, L. (1996). Hazards of noise exposure on fetal hearing. *Seminars in Perinatology, 20,* 21–29.

Pietz, J., Peter, J., Graf, R., Rauterberg, R. I., Rupp, A., & Sontheimer, D. (2004). Physical growth and neurodevelopmental outcome of nonhandicapped low-risk children born preterm. *Early Human Development, 79,* 131–143.

Piirto, J. (2007). *Talented children and adults* (3rd ed.). Waco, TX: Prufrock Press.

Pinderhughes, E. E., Dodge, K. A., Bates, J. E., Pettit, G. S., & Zelli, A. (2000). Discipline responses: Influences of parents' socioeconomic status, ethnicity, beliefs about parenting, stress, and cognitive-emotional processes. *Journal of Family Psychology, 14,* 380–400.

Pinderhughes, E. E., Nix, R., Foster, E. M., Jones, D., & the Conduct Problems Prevention Research Group. (2001). Parenting in context: Impact of neighborhood poverty, residential stability, public services, social networks, and danger on parental behaviors. *Journal of Marriage and the Family, 63,* 941–953.

Pine, J. M. (1995). Variation in vocabulary development as a function of birth order. *Child Development, 66,* 272–281.

Ping, R. M., & Goldin-Meadow, S. (2008). Hands in the air: Using ungrounded iconic gestures to teach children conservation of quantity. *Developmental Psychology, 44,* 1277–1287.

Pinker, S. (1989). *Learnability and cognition.* Cambridge, MA: MIT Press.

Pinker, S. (1999). *Words and rules: The ingredients of language.* New York: Basic Books.

Pinker, S., Lebeaux, D. S., & Frost, L. A. (1987). Productivity and constraints in the acquisition of the passive. *Cognition, 26,* 195–267.

Pipp, S., Easterbrooks, M. A., & Brown, S. R. (1993). Attachment status and complexity of infants' self- and other-knowledge when tested with mother and father. *Social Development, 2,* 1–14.

Pipp, S., Easterbrooks, M. A., & Harmon, R. J. (1992). The relation between attachment and knowledge of self and mother in one-year-old infants to three-year-old infants. *Child Development, 63,* 738–750.

Pitts, V. P. (1976). Drawing the invisible: Children's conceptualization of God. *Character Potential, 8,* 12–24.

Pleck, J. H., & Masciadrelli, B. P. (2004). Paternal involvement by U.S. residential fathers: Levels, sources, and consequences. In M. E. Lamb (Ed.), *The role of the father in child development* (4th ed., pp. 222–271). Hoboken, NJ: Wiley

Plomin, R. (1994). *Genetics and experience: The interplay between nature and nurture.* Thousand Oaks, CA: Sage.

Plomin, R. (2003). General cognitive ability. In R. Plomin & J. C. DeFries (Eds.), *Behavioral genetics in the postgenomic era* (pp. 183–201). Washington, DC: American Psychological Association.

Plomin, R. (2005). *Finding genes in child psychology and psychiatry: When are we going to be there?* Unpublished manuscript. London: King's College.

Plomin, R. (2009). The nature of nurture. In K. McCartney & R. A. Weinberg (Eds.), *Experience and development: A festschrift in honor of Sandra Wood Scarr* (pp. 61–80). New York: Psychology Press.

Plomin, R., & Davis, O. S. P. (2009). The future of genetics in psychology and psychiatry: Microarrays, genome-wide association, and non-coding RNA. *Journal of Child Psychology and Psychiatry, 50,* 63–71.

Plomin, R., DeFries, J. C., McClearn, G. E., & McGuffin, P. (2001). *Behavioral genetics* (4th ed.). New York: Worth.

Plomin, R., & Spinath, F. M. (2004). Intelligence: Genetics, genes, and genomics. *Journal of Personality and Social Psychology, 86,* 112–129.

Poehlmann, J. (2003). An attachment perspective on grandparents raising their very young grandchildren: Implications for intervention and research. *Infant Mental Health Journal, 24,* 149–173.

Poehlmann, J., & Fiese, B. H. (2001). The interaction of maternal and infant vulnerabilities on developing attachment relationships. *Development and Psychopathology, 13,* 1–11.

Pohl, R. (2002). *Poverty in Canada.* Ottawa: Innercity Ministries.

Polka, L., & Rvachew, S. (2005). The impact of otitis media with effusion on infant phonetic perception. *Infancy, 8,* 101–117.

Polka, L., & Werker, J. F. (1994). Developmental changes in perception of non-native vowel contrasts. *Journal of Experimental Psychology: Human Perception and Performance, 20,* 421–435.

Pollitt, E. (1996). A reconceptualization of the effects of undernutrition on children's biological, psychosocial, and behavioral development. *Social Policy Report of the Society for Research in Child Development, 10*(5).

Pollitt, E. (2001). The developmental and probabilistic nature of the functional consequences of iron-deficiency anemia in children. *Journal of Nutrition, 131*(Suppl. 2), 669S–675S.

Polman, H., Orobio de Castro, B., Koops, W., van Boxtel, H. W., & Merk, W. W. (2007). A meta-analysis of the distinction between reactive and proactive aggression in children and adolescents. *Journal of Abnormal Child Psychology, 35,* 522–535.

Pomerantz, E. M., & Dong, W. (2006). Effects of mothers' perceptions of children's competence: The moderating role of mothers' theories of competence. *Developmental Psychology, 42,* 950–961.

Pomerantz, E. M., & Eaton, M. M. (2000). Developmental differences in children's conceptions of parental control: "They love me, but they make me feel incompetent." *Merrill-Palmer Quarterly, 46,* 140–167.

Pomerantz, E. M., Ng, F. F., & Wang, Q. (2006). Mothers' mastery-oriented involvement in children's homework: Implications for the well-being of children with negative perceptions of competence. *Journal of Educational Psychology, 98,* 99–111.

Pomerantz, E. M., & Saxon, J. L. (2001). Conceptions of ability as stable and self-evaluative processes: A longitudinal examination. *Child Development, 72,* 152–173.

Pong, S., Johnston, J., & Chen, V. (2010). Authoritarian parenting and Asian adolescent school performance. *International Journal of Behavioral Development, 34,* 62–72.

Pons, F., Lawson, J., Harris, P. L., & de Rosnay, M. (2003). Individual differences in children's emotion understanding: Effects of age and language. *Scandinavian Journal of Psychology, 44,* 347–353.

Portes, A., & Rumbaut, R. G. (2005), Introduction: The second generation and the Children of Immigrants Longitudinal Study. *Ethnic and Racial Studies, 28,* 983–999.

Posada, G., Carbonell, O. A., Alzate, G., & Plata, S. J. (2004). Through Colombian lenses: Ethnographic and conventional analyses of maternal care and their associations with secure base behavior. *Developmental Psychology, 40,* 508–518.

Posada, G., Jacobs, A., Richmond, M. K., Carbonell, O. A., Alzate, G., Bustamante, M. R., & Quiceno, J. (2002). Maternal caregiving and infant security in two cultures. *Developmental Psychology, 38,* 67–78.

Posner, M. I., & Rothbart, M. K. (2007a). *Educating the human brain.* Washington, DC: American Psychological Association.

Posner, M. I., & Rothbart, M. K. (2007b). Temperament and learning. In M. I. Posner & M. K. Rothbart (Eds.), *Educating the human brain* (pp. 121–146). Washington, DC: American Psychological Association.

Poulin-Dubois, D., Brooker, I., & Chow, V. (2009). The developmental origins of naïve psychology in infancy. *Advances in Child Development and Behavior, 37,* 55–104.

Poulin-Dubois, D., Serbin, L. A., Eichstedt, J. A., Sen, M. G., & Beissel, C. F. (2002). Men don't put on make-up: Toddlers' knowledge of the gender stereotyping of household activities. *Social Development, 11,* 166–181.

Povinelli, D. J. (2001). The self—Elevated in consciousness and extended in time. In C. Moore & K. Lemmon (Eds.), *The self in time: Developmental perspectives* (pp. 75–95). Mahwah, NJ: Erlbaum.

Power, T. G. (2000). *Play and exploration in children and animals.* Mahwah, NJ: Erlbaum.

Powlishta, K. K., Serbin, L. A., & Moller, L. C. (1993). The stability of individual differences in gender typing: Implications for understanding gender segregation. *Sex Roles, 29,* 723–737.

Powls, A., Botting, N., Cooke, R. W. I., & Marlow, N. (1996). Handedness in very-low-birthweight (VLBW) children at 12 years of age: Relation to perinatal and outcome variables. *Developmental Medicine and Child Neurology, 38,* 594–602.

Prechtl, H. F. R. (1958). Problems of behavioral studies in the newborn infant. In D. S. Lehrmann, R. A. Hinde, & E. Shaw (Eds.), *Advances in the study of behavior* (Vol. 1, pp. 75–98). New York: Academic Press.

Prechtl, H. F. R., & Beintema, D. (1965). *The neurological examination of the full-term newborn infant.* London: Heinemann Medical.

Preisler, G. M. (1991). Early patterns of interaction between blind infants and their sighted mothers. *Child: Care, Health and Development, 17,* 65–90.

Preisler, G. M. (1993). A descriptive study of blind children in nurseries with sighted children. *Child: Care, Health and Development, 19,* 295–315.

Preissler, M. A., & Carey, S. (2004). Do both pictures and words function as symbols for 18- and 24-month-old children? *Journal of Cognition and Development, 5,* 185–212.

Pressley, M., & Hilden, D. (2006). Cognitive strategies. In D. Kuhn & R. Siegler (Eds.), *Handbook of child psychology: Vol. 2. Cognition, perception, and language* (6th ed., pp. 511–556). Hoboken, NJ: Wiley.

Pressley, M., Wharton-McDonald, R., Raphael, L. M., Bogner, K., & Roehrig, A. (2002). Exemplary first-grade teaching. In B. M. Taylor & P. D. Pearson (Eds.), *Teaching reading: Effective schools, accomplished teachers* (pp. 73–88). Mahwah, NJ: Erlbaum.

Previc, F. H. (1991). A general theory concerning the prenatal origins of cerebral lateralization. *Psychological Review, 98,* 299–334.

Prinstein, M. J., & Cillessen, A. H. N. (2003). Forms and functions of adolescent peer aggression associated with high levels of peer status. *Merrill-Palmer Quarterly, 49,* 310–342.

Prinstein, M. J., & La Greca, A. (2004). Childhood peer rejection and aggression as predictors of adolescent girls' externalizing and health risk behaviors: A 6-year longitudinal study. *Journal of Consulting and Clinical Psychology, 72,* 103–112.

Proctor, M. H., Moore, L. L. Gao, D., Cupples, L. A., Bradlee, M. L., Hood, M. Y., & Ellison, R. C. (2003). Television viewing and change in body fat from preschool to early adolescence: The Framingham Children's Study. *International Journal of Obesity, 27,* 827–833.

Proffitt, D. R., & Bertenthal, B. I. (1990). Converging operations revisited: Assessing what infants perceive using discrimination measures. *Perception and Psychophysics, 47,* 1–11.

Programme for International Student Assessment. (2003). Learning for tomorrow's world: First results from Programme for International Student Assessment 2003. Retrieved from www.pisa.oecd.org

Programme for International Student Assessment. (2006). PISA 2006: Science competencies for tomorrow's world. Retrieved from www.oecd.org

Provins, K. A. (1997). Handedness and speech: A critical reappraisal of the role of genetic and environmental factors in the cerebral lateralization of function. *Psychological Review, 104,* 554–571.

Pruden, S. M., Hirsh-Pasek, K., Golinkoff, R. M., & Hennon, E. A. (2006). The birth of words: Ten-month-olds learn words through perceptual salience. *Child Development, 77,* 266–280.

Prysak, M., Lorenz, R. P., & Kisly, A. (1995). Pregnancy outcome in nulliparous women 35 years and older. *Obstetrics and Gynecology, 85,* 65–70.

Puhl, R. M., & Latner, J. D. (2007). Stigma, obesity, and the health of the nation's children. *Psychological Bulletin, 133,* 557–580.

Pujol, J., Soriano-Mas, C., Ortiz, H., Sebastián-Gallés, N., Losilla, J. M., & Deus, J. (2006). Myelination of language-related areas in the developing brain. *Neurology, 66,* 339–343.

Punamaki, R. L. (2006). Ante- and perinatal factors and child characteristics predicting parenting experience among formerly infertile couples during the child's first year: A controlled study. *Journal of Family Psychology, 20,* 670–679.

Purcell-Gates, V. (1996). Stories, coupons, and the TV guide: Relationships between home literacy experiences and emergent literacy knowledge. *Reading Research Quarterly, 31,* 406–428.

Putallaz, M., Grimes, C. L., Foster, K. J., Kupersmidt, J. B., Coie, J. D., & Dearing, K. (2007). Overt and relational aggression and victimization: Multiple perspectives within the school setting. *Journal of School Psychology, 45,* 523–547.

Putnam, F. W. (2003). Ten-year research update review: Child sexual abuse. *Journal of the American Academy of Child and Adolescent Psychiatry, 42,* 269–278.

Putnam, S. P., Samson, A. V., & Rothbart, M. K. (2000). Child temperament and parenting. In V. J. Molfese & D. L. Molfese (Eds.), *Temperament and personality across the life span* (pp. 255–277). Mahwah, NJ: Erlbaum.

Q

Quas, J. A., Malloy, L. C., Melinder, A., Goodman, G. S., & D'Mello, M. (2007). Developmental differences in the effects of repeated interviews and interviewer bias on young children's event memory and false reports. *Developmental Psychology, 43,* 823–837.

Quinn, P. C. (2008). In defense of core competencies, quantitative change, and continuity. *Child Development, 79,* 1633–1638.

Quinn, P. C., & Intraub, H. (2007). Perceiving "outside the box" occurs early in development: Evidence for boundary extension in three- to seven-month-old infants. *Child Development, 78,* 324–334.

Quinn, P. C., Yahr, J., Kuhn, A., Slater, A. M., & Pascalis, O. (2002). Representation of the gender of human faces by infants: A preference for female. *Perception, 31,* 1109–1121.

Quinn, T. C., & Overbaugh, J. (2005). HIV/AIDS in women: An expanding epidemic. *Science, 308,* 1582–1583.

R

Radelet, M. A., Lephart, S. M., Rubinstein, E. N., & Myers, J. B. (2002). Survey of the injury rate for children in community sports. *Pediatrics, 110,* e28.

Radziszewska, B., & Rogoff, B. (1988). Influence of adult and peer collaboration on the development of children's planning skills. *Developmental Psychology, 24,* 840–848.

Raikes, H. A., & Thompson, R. A. (2005). Links between risk and attachment security: Models of influence. *Journal of Applied Developmental Psychology, 26,* 440–455.

Raikes, H. A., & Thompson, R. A. (2006). Family emotional climate, attachment security, and young children's emotion knowledge in a high-risk sample. *British Journal of Developmental Psychology, 24,* 89–104.

Raikes, H. A., Robinson, J. L., Bradley, R. H., Raikes, H. H., & Ayoub, C. C. (2007). Developmental trends in self-regulation among low-income toddlers. *Social Development, 16,* 128–149.

Rakison, D. H. (2005). Developing knowledge of objects' motion properties in infancy. *Cognition, 96,* 183–214.

Rakison, D. H. (2006). Make the first move: How infants learn about self-propelled objects. *Developmental Psychology, 42,* 900–912.

Rakison, D. H., & Lupyan, G. (2008). Developing object concepts in infancy: An associative learning perspective. *Monographs of the Society for Research in Child Development, 73*(1, Serial No. 289).

Rakoczy, H., Tomasello, M., & Striano, T. (2004). Young children know that trying is not pretending: A test of the "behaving-as-if" construal of children's early concept of pretense. *Developmental Psychology, 40,* 388–399.

Rakoczy, H., Tomasello, M., & Striano, T. (2005). How children turn objects into symbols: A cultural learning account. In L. Namy (Ed.), *Symbol use and symbol representation* (pp. 67–97). New York: Erlbaum.

Raman, L., & Gelman, S. A. (2004). A cross-cultural developmental analysis of children's and adults' understanding of illness in South Asia (India) and the United States. *Journal of Cognition and Culture, 4,* 293–317.

Ramchandani, P. G., Stein, A., O'Connor, T. G., Heron, J., Murray, L., & Evans, J. (2008). Depression in men in the postnatal period and later child psychopathology: A population cohort study. *Journal of the American Academy of Child and Adolescent Psychiatry, 47,* 390–398.

Ramey, C. T., Ramey, S. L., & Lanzi, R. G. (2006). Children's health and education. In K. A. Renninger & I. E. Sigel (Eds.), *Handbook of child psychology: Vol. 4. Child psychology in practice* (6th ed., pp. 864–892). Hoboken, NJ: Wiley.

Ramey, S. L., & Ramey, C. T. (1999). Early experience and early intervention for children "at risk" for developmental delay and mental retardation. *Mental Retardation and Developmental Disabilities, 5,* 1–10.

Ramos, M. C., Guerin, D. W., Gottfried, A. W., Bathurst, K., & Oliver, P. H. (2005). Family conflict and children's behavior problems: The moderating role of child temperament. *Structural Equation Modeling, 12,* 278–298.

Ramus, F. (2002). Language discrimination by newborns: Teasing apart phonotactic, rhythmic, and intonational cues. *Annual Review of Language Acquisition, 2,* 85–115.

Raskind, W. H., Igo, R. P. Jr., Chapman, N. H., Berninger, V. W., Thomson, J. B., Matsushita, M., & Brkanac, Z. (2005). A genome scan in multigenerational families with dyslexia: Identification of a novel locus on chromosome 2q that contributes to phonological decoding efficiency. *Molecular Psychiatry, 10,* 699–711.

Rasmussen, C., Ho, E., & Bisanz, J. (2003). Use of the mathematical principle of inversion in young children. *Journal of Experimental Child Psychology, 85,* 89–102.

Rasmussen, C., Neuman, R. J., Heath, A. C., Levy, F., Hay, D. A., & Todd, R. D. (2004). Familial clustering of latent class and DSM-IV defined attention-deficit hyperactivity disorder (ADHD) subtypes. *Journal of Child Psychology and Psychiatry, 45,* 589–598.

Rathunde, K., & Csikszentmihalyi, M. (2005). The social context of middle school: Teachers, friends, and activities in Montessori and traditional school environments. *Elementary School Journal, 106,* 59–79.

Rauber, M. (2006, May 18). Parents aren't sitting still as recess disappears. *Parents in Action.* Retrieved from www.parentsaction.org/news/parents-in-action/index.cfm?i=410

Rauscher, F. H., Shaw, G. L., & Ky, K. N. (1993). Music and spatial task performance. *Nature, 365,* 611.

Raver, C. C. (2003). Does work pay psychologically as well as economically? The role of employment in predicting depressive symptoms and parenting among low-income families. *Child Development, 74,* 1720–1736.

Ravid, D., & Tolchinsky, L. (2002). Developing linguistic literacy: A comprehensive model. *Journal of Child Language, 29,* 417–447.

Ravitch, D. (2010). *The death and life of the great American school system: How testing and choice are undermining education.* New York: Basic Books.

Ray, N., & Gregory, R. (2001). School experiences of the children of lesbian and gay parents. *Family Matters, 59,* 28–35.

Rayner, K., & Pollatsek, A. (1989). *The psychology of reading.* Englewood Cliffs, NJ: Prentice Hall.

Rayner, K., Pollatsek, A., & Starr, M. S. (2003). Reading. In A. F. Healy & R. W. Proctor (Eds.). (2003). *Handbook of psychology: Experimental psychology* (Vol. 4, pp. 549–574). New York: Wiley.

Raz, S., Shah, F., & Sander, C. J. (1996). Differential effects of perinatal hypoxic risk on early developmental outcome: A twin study. *Neuropsychology, 10,* 429–436.

Reed, R. K. (2005). *Birthing fathers.* New Brunswick, NJ: Rutgers University Press.

Reese, E., & Newcombe, R. (2007). Training mothers in elaborative reminiscing enhances children's autobiographical memory and narrative. *Child Development, 78,* 1153–1170.

Reese, E., Newcombe, R., & Bird, G. M. (2006). The emergence of autobiographical memory:

Cognitive, social, and emotional factors. In C. M. Flinn-Fletcher & G. M. Haberman (Eds.), *Cognition and language: Perspectives from New Zealand* (pp. 177–189). Bowen Hills, Australia: Australian Academic Press.

Reilly, J. S., Bates, E. A., & Marchman, V. A. (1998). Narrative discourse in children with early focal brain injury. *Brain and Language, 61,* 335–375.

Reilly, J., Losh, M., Bellugi, U., & Wulfeck, B. (2004)."Frog, where are you?" Narratives in children with specific language impairment, early focal brain injury, and Williams syndrome. *Brain and Language, 88,* 229–247.

Reis, S. M. (2004). We can't change what we don't recognize: Understanding the special needs of gifted females. In S. Baum (Ed.), *Twice-exceptional and special populations of gifted students* (pp. 67–80). Thousand Oaks, CA: Corwin Press.

Reisman, J. E. (1987). Touch, motion, and proprioception. In P. Salapatek & L. Cohen (Eds.), *Handbook of infant perception: Vol. 1. From sensation to perception* (pp. 265–303). Orlando, FL: Academic Press.

Reiss, D. (2003). Child effects on family systems: Behavioral genetic strategies. In A. C. Crouter & A. Booth (Eds.), *Children's influence on family dynamics* (pp. 3–36). Mahwah, NJ: Erlbaum.

Renninger, K. A. (1998). Developmental psychology and instruction: Issues from and for practice. In I. Sigel & K. A. Renninger (Eds.), *Handbook of child psychology: Vol. 4. Child psychology and practice* (pp. 211–274). New York: Wiley.

Repacholi, B. M. (1998). Infants' use of attentional cues to identify the referent of another person's emotional expression. *Developmental Psychology, 34,* 1017–1025.

Repacholi, B. M., & Gopnik, A. (1997). Early reasoning about desires: Evidence from 14- and 18-month-olds. *Developmental Psychology, 33,* 12–21.

Repacholi, B. M., & Meltzoff, A. N. (2007). Emotional eavesdropping: Infants selectively respond to indirect emotional signals. *Child Development, 78,* 503–521.

Reschly, A. L., & Christenson, S. L. (2009). Parents as essential partners for fostering students' learning outcomes. In R. Gilman & E. Scott Huebner (Eds.), *Handbook of positive psychology in schools* (pp. 257–272). New York: Routledge.

Resnick, M., & Silverman, B. (2005). *Some reflections on designing construction kits for kids.* Proceedings of the Conference on Interaction Design and Children, Boulder, CO.

Resnick, M. B., Gueorguieva, R. V., Carter, R. L., Ariet, M., Sun, Y., Roth, J., Bucciarelli, R. L., Curran, J. S., & Mahan, C. S. (1999). The impact of low birth weight, perinatal conditions, and sociodemographic factors on educational outcome in kindergarten. *Pediatrics, 104,* e74.

Resta, R., Biesecker, B. B., Bennett, R. L., Blum, S., Hahn, S. E., Strecker, M. N., & Williams, J. L. (2006). A new definition of genetic counseling: National Society of Genetic Counselors' Task Force Report. *Journal of Genetic Counseling, 15,* 77–83.

RESULTS. (2006). *The abolition of public school fees.* Retrieved from www.results.org/website /article.asp?id=1718

Reynolds, A. J., & Temple, J. A. (1998). Extended early childhood intervention and school achievement: Age thirteen findings from the Chicago Longitudinal Study. *Child Development, 69,* 231–246.

Rhoades, B. L., Greenberg, M. T., & Domitrovich, C. E. (2009). The contribution of inhibitory control to preschoolers' social-emotional competence. *Journal of Applied Developmental Psychology, 30,* 310–320.

Richardson, H. L., Walker, A. M., & Horne, R. S. C. (2008) Sleep position alters arousal processes maximally at the high-risk age for sudden infant death syndrome. *Journal of Sleep Research, 17,* 450–457.

Richert, R. A., & Barrett, J. L. (2005). Do you see what I see? Young children's assumptions about God's perceptual abilities. *International Journal for the Psychology of Religion, 15,* 283–295.

Richler, J., Luyster, R., Risi, S., Hsu, W.-L., Dawson, G., & Bernier, R. (2006). Is there a 'regressive phenotype' of autism spectrum disorder associated with the

measles-mumps-rubella vaccine? A CPEA study. *Journal of Autism and Developmental Disorders, 36,* 299–316.

Richmond, J., Colombo, M., & Hayne, H. (2007). Interpreting visual preferences in the visual paired-comparison task. *Journal of Experimental Psychology: Learning, Memory, and Cognition, 33,* 823–831.

Ridenour, T. A. (2000). Genetic epidemiology of antisocial behavior. In D. H. Fishbein (Ed.), *The science, treatment, and prevention of antisocial behaviors: Application to the criminal justice system* (pp. 7.1–7.24). Kingston, NJ: Civic Research Institute.

Rideout, V., & Hamel, E. (2006). *The media family: Electronic media in the lives of infants, toddlers, preschoolers and their parents.* Menlo Park, CA: Henry J. Kaiser Family Foundation.

Rideout, V. J., Vandewater, E. A., & Wartella, E. A. (2003). *Zero to six: Electronic media in the lives of infants, toddlers and preschoolers.* Menlo Park, CA: Henry J. Kaiser Family Foundation.

Rigby, K. (2004). Bullying in childhood. In P. K. Smith & C. H. Hart (Eds.), *Blackwell handbook of childhood social development* (pp. 549–568). Malden, MA: Blackwell.

Riggs, K. J., & Peterson, D. M. (2000). Counterfactual thinking in preschool children: Mental state and causal inferences. In P. Mitchell & K. J. Riggs (Eds.), *Children's reasoning and the mind* (pp. 87–99). Hove, U.K.: Psychology Press.

Rijsdijk, F. V., & Boomsma, D. I. (1997). Genetic mediation of the correlation between peripheral nerve conduction velocity and IQ. *Behavior Genetics, 27,* 87–98.

Riley, E. P., McGee, C. L., & Sowell, E. R. (2004). Teratogenic effects of alcohol: A decade of brain imaging. *American Journal of Medical Genetics: Part C, Seminars in Medical Genetics, 127,* 35–41.

Riordan, J., Gross, A., Angeron, J., Drumwiede, B., & Melin, J. (2000). The effect of labor pain relief medication on neonatal suckling and breastfeeding duration. *Journal of Human Lactation, 16,* 7–12.

Ripple, C. H., & Zigler, E. (2003). Research, policy, and the federal role in prevention initiatives for children. *American Psychologist, 58,* 482–490.

Ris, M. D., Dietrich, K. N., Succop, P. A., Berger, O. G., & Bornschein, R. L. (2004). Early exposure to lead and neuropsychological outcome in adolescence. *Journal of the International Neuropsychological Society, 10,* 261–270.

Riva, D., & Giorgi, C. (2000). The cerebellum contributes to higher functions during development: Evidence from a series of children surgically treated for posterior fossa tumors. *Brain, 123,* 1051–1061.

Rivera, S. M., Wakeley, A., & Langer, J. (1999). The drawbridge phenomenon: Representational reasoning or perceptual preference? *Developmental Psychology, 35,* 427–435.

Rivkees, S. A. (2003). Developing circadian rhythmicity in infants. *Pediatrics, 112,* 373–381.

Rizzo, T. A., Metzger, B. E., Dooley, S. L., & Cho, N. H. (1997). Early malnutrition and child neurobehavioral development: Insights from the study of children of diabetic mothers. *Child Development, 68,* 26–38.

Rizzolatti, G., & Craighero, L. (2004). The mirror-neuron system. *Annual Review of Neuroscience, 27,* 169–192.

Roberts, B. W., & DelVecchio, W. F. (2000). The rank-order consistency of personality traits from childhood to old age: A quantitative review of longitudinal studies. *Psychological Bulletin, 126,* 3–25.

Roberts, D. F., Foehr, U. G., & Rideout, V. (2005). *Generation M: Media in the lives of 8–18 year olds.* Menlo Park, CA: Henry J. Kaiser Family Foundation.

Roberts, J. E., Burchinal, M. R., & Durham, M. (1999). Parents' report of vocabulary and grammatical development of American preschoolers: Child and environment associations. *Child Development, 70,* 92–106.

Roberts, J. E., Burchinal, M. R., Zeisel, S. A., Neebe, E. C., Hooper, S. R., Roush, J., Bryant, D., Mundy, M., & Henderson, F. W. (1998). Otitis media, the caregiving environment, and language and cognitive outcomes at 2 years. *Pediatrics, 102,* 346–354.

Roberts, J. M., & Masten, A. S. (2004). Resilience in context. In R. D. Peters, R. McMahon, & B. Leadbeater (Eds.), *Resilience in children, families, and communities: Linking context to practice and policy* (pp. 13–25). New York: Kluwer Academic.

Robertson, J. (2008). Stepfathers in families. In J. Pryor (Ed.), *International handbook of stepfamilies: Policy and practice in legal, research, and clinical environments* (pp. 125–150). Hoboken, NJ: Wiley.

Robin, D. J., Berthier, N. E., & Clifton, R. K. (1996). Infants' predictive reaching for moving objects in the dark. *Developmental Psychology, 32,* 824–835.

Robins, R. W., Tracy, J. L., Trzesniewski, K., Potter, J., & Gosling, S. D. (2001). Personality correlates of self-esteem. *Journal of Research in Personality, 35,* 463–482.

Robinson, C. C., Anderson, G. T., Porter, C. L., Hart, C. H., & Wouden-Miller, M. (2003). Sequential transition patterns of preschoolers' social interactions during child-initiated play: Is parallel-aware play a bidirectional bridge to other play states? *Early Childhood Research Quarterly, 18,* 3–21.

Robinson, J. L., Lee, B. E., Preiksaitis, J. K., Plitt, S., & Tipplies, G. A. (2006). Prevention of congenital rubella syndrome—What makes sense in 2006? *Epidemiologic Reviews, 28,* 81–87.

Robinson, S., Goddard, L., Dritschel, B., Wisley, M., & Howlin, P. (2009). Executive functions in children with autism spectrum disorders. *Brain and Cognition, 71,* 362–368.

Rochat, P. (1989). Object manipulation and exploration in 2- to 5-month-old infants. *Developmental Psychology, 25,* 871–884.

Rochat, P. (1998). Self-perception and action in infancy. *Experimental Brain Research, 123,* 102–109.

Rochat, P. (2001). *The infant's world.* Cambridge, MA: Harvard University Press.

Rochat, P. (2003). Five levels of self-awareness as they unfold early in life. *Consciousness and Cognition, 12,* 717–731.

Rochat, P., & Goubet, N. (1995). Development of sitting and reaching in 5- to 6-month-old infants. *Infant Behavior and Development, 18,* 53–68.

Rochat, P., & Hespos, S. J. (1997). Differential rooting responses by neonates: Evidence for an early sense of self. *Early Development and Parenting, 6,* 105–112.

Rochat, P., Querido, J. G., & Striano, T. (1999). Emerging sensitivity to the timing and structure of protoconversation. *Developmental Psychology, 35,* 950–957.

Rochat, P., & Striano, T. (2002). Who's in the mirror? Self–other discrimination in specular images by four- and nine-month-old infants. *Child Development, 73,* 35–46.

Rochat, P., Striano, T., & Blatt, L. (2002). Differential effects of happy, neutral, and sad still-faces on 2-, 4-, and 6-month-old infants. *Infant and Child Development, 11,* 289–303.

Rodgers, J. L., Cleveland, H. H., van den Oord, E., & Rowe, D. C. (2000). Resolving the debate over birth order, family size, and intelligence. *American Psychologist, 55,* 599–612.

Rodgers, J. L., & Wänström, L. (2007). Identification of a Flynn effect in the NLSY: Moving from the center to the boundaries. *Intelligence, 35,* 187–196.

Rodkin, P. C., Farmer, T. W., Pearl, R., & Van Acker, R. (2000). Heterogeneity of popular boys: Antisocial and prosocial configurations. *Developmental Psychology, 36,* 14–24.

Rodkin, P. C., Farmer, T. W., Pearl, R., & Van Acker, R. (2006). They're cool: Social status and peer group supports for aggressive boys and girls. *Social Development, 15,* 175–204.

Rodriguez, A., & Waldenström, U. (2008). Fetal origins of child non-right-handedness and mental health. *Child Psychology and Psychiatry, 49,* 967–976.

Roebers, C. M., & Schneider, W. (2001). Individual differences in children's eyewitness recall: The influence of intelligence and shyness. *Applied Developmental Science, 5,* 9–20.

Roelfsema, N. M., Hop, W. C., Boito, S. M., & Wladimiroff, J. W. (2004). Three-dimensional sonographic measurement of normal fetal brain volume during the second half of pregnancy.

American Journal of Obstetrics and Gynecology, 190, 275–280.

Rogan, W. J., Dietrich, K. N., Ware, J. H., Dockery, D. W., Salganik, M., & Radcliffe, J. (2001). The effect of chelation therapy with succimer on neuropsychological development in children exposed to lead. *New England Journal of Medicine, 344,* 1421–1426.

Rogers, J. M. (2009). Tobacco and pregnancy. *Reproductive Toxicology, 28,* 152–160.

Rogge, M. M., Greenwald, M., & Golden, A. (2004). Obesity, stigma, and civilized oppression. *Advances in Nursing Science, 27,* 301–315.

Roggman, L. A., Langlois, J. H., Hubbs-Tait, L., & Rieser-Danner, L. A. (1994). Infant day-care, attachment, and the "file drawer problem." *Child Development, 65,* 1429–1443.

Rogoff, B. (1996). Developmental transitions in children's participation in sociocultural activities. In A. J. Sameroff & M. M. Haith (Eds.), *The five to seven year shift: The age of reason and responsibility* (pp. 273–294). Chicago: University of Chicago Press.

Rogoff, B. (1998). Cognition as a collaborative process. In D. Kuhn & R. S. Siegler (Eds.), *Handbook of child psychology: Vol. 2. Cognition, perception, and language* (5th ed., pp. 679–744). New York: Wiley.

Rogoff, B. (2003). *The cultural nature of human development.* New York: Oxford University Press.

Rogoff, B., & Chavajay, P. (1995). What's become of research on the cultural basis of cognitive development? *American Psychologist, 50,* 859–877.

Rogoff, B., Malkin, C., & Gilbride, K. (1984). Interaction with babies as guidance in development. In B. Rogoff & J. V. Wertsch (Eds.), *Children's learning in the "zone of proximal development" (New directions for child development,* No. 23, pp. 31–44). San Francisco: Jossey-Bass.

Rogoff, B., Paradise, R., Arauz, R. M., Correa-Chávez, M., & Angelillo, C. (2003). Firsthand learning through intent participation. *Annual Review of Psychology, 54,* 175–203.

Rogoff, B., & Waddell, K. J. (1982). Memory for information organized in a scene by children from two cultures. *Child Development, 53,* 1224–1228.

Rohner, R. P., & Veneziano, R. A. (2001). The importance of father love: History and contemporary evidence. *Review of General Psychology, 5,* 382–405.

Roid, G. (2003). *The Stanford-Binet Intelligence Scales, Fifth Edition, interpretive manual.* Itasca, IL: Riverside Publishing.

Roisman, R., & Fraley, C. (2006). The limits of genetic influence: A behavior-genetic analysis of infant–caregiver relationship quality and temperament. *Child Development, 77,* 1656–1667.

Romano, A. M., & Lothian, J. A. (2008). Promoting, protecting, and supporting normal birth: A look at the evidence. *Journal of Obstetric, Gynecologic, and Neonatal Nursing, 37,* 94–104.

Rome-Flanders, T., & Cronk, C. (1995). A longitudinal study of infant vocalizations during mother–infant games. *Journal of Child Language, 22,* 259–274.

Rönnqvist, L., & Domellof, E. (2006). Quantitative assessment of right and left reaching movements in infants: A longitudinal study from 6 to 36 months. *Developmental Psychobiology, 48,* 444–459.

Rönnqvist, L., & Hopkins, B. (1998). Head position preference in the human newborn: A new look. *Child Development, 69,* 13–23.

Roopnarine, J. L., & Evans, M. E. (2007). Family structural organization, mother–child and father–child relationships and psychological outcomes in English-speaking African Caribbean and Indo Caribbean families. In M. Sutherland (Ed.), *Psychology of development in the Caribbean.* Kingston, Jamaica: Ian Randle.

Roopnarine, J. L., Hossain, Z., Gill, P., & Brophy, H. (1994). Play in the East Indian context. In J. L. Roopnarine, J. E. Johnson, & F. H. Hooper (Eds.), *Children's play in diverse cultures* (pp. 9–30). Albany, NY: SUNY Press.

Roopnarine, J. L., Krishnakumar, A., Metindogan, A., & Evans, M. (2006). Links between parenting styles, parent–child academic interaction, parent–school interaction, and early academic skills and social

behaviors in young children of English-speaking Caribbean immigrants. *Early Childhood Research Quarterly, 21,* 238–252.

Roopnarine, J. L., Talukder, E., Jain, D., Joshi, P., & Srivastav, P. (1990). Characteristics of holding, patterns of play, and social behaviors between parents and infants in New Delhi, India. *Developmental Psychology, 26,* 667–673.

Rosander, K., & von Hofsten, C. (2002). Development of gaze tracking of small and large objects. *Experimental Brain Research, 146,* 257–264.

Rosander, K., & von Hofsten, C. (2004). Infants' emerging ability to represent occluded object motion. *Cognition, 91,* 1–22.

Rose, A. J., & Asher, S. R. (1999). Children's goals and strategies in response to conflicts within a friendship. *Developmental Psychology, 35,* 69–79.

Rose, A. J., Swenson, L. P., & Waller, E. M. (2004). Overt and relational aggression and perceived popularity: Developmental differences in concurrent and prospective relations. *Developmental Psychology, 40,* 378–387.

Rose, L. (2000). Fathers of full-term infants. In N. Tracey (Ed.), *Parents of premature infants: Their emotional world* (pp. 105–116). London: Whurr.

Rose, S. A., & Feldman, J. F. (1997). Memory and speed: Their role in the relation of infant information processing to later IQ. *Child Development, 68,* 610–620.

Rose, S. A., Feldman, J. F., & Jankowski, J. J. (2001). Attention and recognition memory in the 1st year of life: A longitudinal study of preterm and full-term infants. *Developmental Psychology, 37,* 135–151.

Rose, S. A., Feldman, J. F., & Wallace, I. F. (1992). Infant information processing in relation to six-year cognitive outcomes. *Child Development, 63,* 1126–1141.

Rose, S. A., Jankowski, J. J., & Senior, G. J. (1997). Infants' recognition of contour-deleted figures. *Journal of Experimental Psychology: Human Perception and Performance, 23,* 1206–1216.

Rosen, A. B., & Rozin, P. (1993). Now you see it, now you don't: The preschool child's conception of invisible particles in the context of dissolving. *Developmental Psychology, 29,* 300–311.

Rosenberger, L. R., Zeck, J., Berl, M. M., Moore, E. N., Ritzl, E. K., Shamim, S., et al. (2009). Interhemispheric and intrahemispheric language reorganization in complex partial epilepsy. *Neurology, 72,* 1830–1836.

Rosenbloom, A. L. (2009). Idiopathic short stature: Conundrums of definition and treatment. *International Journal of Pediatric Endocrinology,* Article ID 470378.

Rosengren, K. S., & Hickling, A. K. (2000). The development of children's thinking about possible events and plausible mechanisms. In K. S. Rosengren, C. N. Johnson, & P. L. Harris (Eds.), *Imagining the impossible* (pp. 75–98). Cambridge, U.K.: Cambridge University Press.

Rosenshine, B., & Meister, C. (1994). Reciprocal teaching: A review of nineteen experimental studies. *Review of Educational Research, 64,* 479–530.

Roseth, C. J., Pellegrini, A. D., Bohn, C. M., van Ryzin, M., & Vance, N. (2007). Preschoolers' aggression, affiliation, and social dominance relationships: An observational, longitudinal study. *Journal of School Psychology, 45,* 479–497.

Rosetta, L., & Baldi, A. (2008). On the role of breastfeeding in health promotion and the prevention of allergic diseases. *Advances in Experimental Medicine and Biology, 606,* 467–483.

Ross, H. S., Conant, C., Cheyne, J. A., & Alevizos, E. (1992). Relationships and alliances in the social interactions of kibbutz toddlers. *Social Development, 1,* 1–17.

Rothbart, M. K. (2003). Temperament and the pursuit of an integrated developmental psychology. *Merrill-Palmer Quarterly, 50,* 492–505.

Rothbart, M. K., Ahadi, S. A., & Evans, D. E. (2000). Temperament and personality: Origins and outcome. *Journal of Personality and Social Psychology, 78,* 122–135.

Rothbart, M. K., & Bates, J. E. (2006). Temperament. In N. Eisenberg (Ed.), *Handbook of child psychology: Vol. 3. Social, emotional, and personality development* (6th ed., pp. 99–166). Hoboken, NJ: Wiley.

Rothbart, M. K., & Mauro, J. A. (1990). Questionnaire approaches to the study of infant temperament. In J. W. Fagen & J. Colombo (Eds.), *Individual differences in infancy: Reliability, stability and prediction* (pp. 411–429). Hillsdale, NJ: Erlbaum.

Rothbart, M. K., Posner, M. I., & Kieras, J. (2006). Temperament, attention, and the development of self-regulation. In K. McCartney & D. Phillips (Eds.), *Blackwell handbook of early childhood development* (pp. 338–357). Malden, MA: Blackwell.

Rothbaum, F., Kakinuma, M., Nagaoka, R., & Azuma, H. (2007). Attachment and *amae:* Parent–child closeness in the United States and Japan. *Journal of Cross-Cultural Psychology, 38,* 465–486.

Rothbaum, F., Pott, M., Azuma, H., Miyake, K., & Weisz, J. (2000a). The development of close relationships in Japan and the United States: Paths of symbiotic harmony and generative tension. *Child Development, 71,* 1121–1142.

Rothbaum, F., Weisz, J., Pott, M., Miyake, K., & Morelli, G. (2000b). Attachment and culture: Security in the United States and Japan. *American Psychologist, 55,* 1093–1104.

Rouselle, L., Palmers, E., & Noël, M.-P. (2004). Magnitude comparison in preschoolers: What counts? Influence of perceptual variables. *Journal of Experimental Child Psychology, 87,* 57–84.

Rovee-Collier, C. (1999). The development of infant memory. *Current Directions in Psychological Science, 8,* 80–85.

Rovee-Collier, C., & Barr, R. (2001). Infant learning and memory. In G. Bremner & A. Fogel (Eds.), *Blackwell handbook of infant development* (pp. 139–168). Oxford, U.K.: Blackwell.

Rovee-Collier, C., & Bhatt, R. S. (1993). Evidence of long-term memory in infancy. *Annals of Child Development, 9,* 1–45.

Rovee-Collier, C., & Cuevas, K. (2009). Multiple memory systems are unnecessary to account for infant memory development: An ecological model. *Developmental Psychology, 45,* 160–174.

Rovers, M. M., Numans, M. E., Langenbach, E., Grobbee, D. E., et al. (2008). Is pacifier use a risk factor for acute otitis media? A dynamic cohort study. *Family Practice, 25,* 233–236.

Rowe, D. (1994). *The limits of family influence: Genes, experience, and behavior.* New York: Guilford.

Rowe, M. L. (2008). Child-directed speech: Relation to socioeconomic status, knowledge of child development and child vocabulary skill. *Journal of Child Language, 35,* 185–205.

Rowe, R., Maughan, B., & Goodman, R. (2004). Childhood psychiatric disorder and unintentional injury: Findings from a national cohort study. *Journal of Pediatric Psychology, 29,* 119–130.

Rowland, C. F. (2007). Explaining errors in children's questions. *Cognition, 104,* 106–134.

Rowland, C. F., & Pine, J. M. (2000). Subject-auxiliary inversion errors and wh-question acquisition: "What children do know?" *Journal of Child Language, 27,* 157–181.

Rubin, K. H., Bukowski, W. M., & Parker, J. G. (2006). Peer interactions, relationships, and groups. In N. Eisenberg (Ed.), *Handbook of child psychology: Vol. 3. Social, emotional, and personality development* (6th ed., pp. 571–645). Hoboken, NJ: Wiley.

Rubin, K. H., & Burgess, K. (2002). Parents of aggressive and withdrawn children. In M. Bornstein (Ed.), *Handbook of parenting* (2nd ed., pp. 383–418). Hillsdale, NJ: Erlbaum.

Rubin, K. H., Burgess, K. B., & Coplan, R. (2002). Social withdrawal and shyness. In P. K. Smith & C. H. Hart (Eds.), *Blackwell handbook of child social development* (pp. 329–352). Oxford: Blackwell.

Rubin, K. H., Burgess, K. B., Dwyer, K. M., & Hastings, P. D. (2003). Predicting preschoolers' externalizing behaviors from toddler temperament, conflict, and maternal negativity. *Developmental Psychology, 39,* 164–176.

Rubin, K. H., Burgess, K. B., & Hastings, P. D. (2002). Stability and social-behavioral consequences of toddlers' inhibited temperament and parenting behaviors. *Child Development, 73,* 483–495.

Rubin, K. H., Coplan, R. J., Chen, X., Buskirk, A. A., & Wojslawowicz, J. C. (2005). Peer relationships in childhood. In M. H. Bornstein & M. E. Lamb (Eds.), *Developmental science: An advanced textbook* (pp. 469–512). Mahwah, NJ: Erlbaum.

Rubin, K. H., Fein, G. G., & Vandenberg, B. (1983). Play. In E. M. Hetherington (Ed.), *Handbook of child psychology: Vol. 4. Socialization, personality, and social development* (4th ed., pp. 693–744). New York: Wiley.

Rubin, C., Maisonet, M., Kieszak, S., Monteilh, C., Holmes A., Flanders, D., et al. (2009). Timing of maturation and predictors of menarche in girls enrolled in a contemporary British cohort. *Paediatric and Perinatal Epidemiology, 23,* 492–504.

Rubin, K. H., Stewart, S. L., & Coplan, R. J. (1995). Social withdrawal in childhood: Conceptual and empirical perspectives. In T. H. Ollendick & R. J. Prinz (Eds.), *Advances in clinical child psychology* (Vol. 17, pp. 157–196). New York: Plenum.

Rubin, K. H., Watson, K. S., & Jambor, T. W. (1978). Free-play behaviors in preschool and kindergarten children. *Child Development, 49,* 539–536.

Ruble, D. N., Alvarez, J., Bachman, M., Cameron, J., Fuligni, A., Garcia Coll, C. T., & Rhee, E. (2004). The development of a sense of "we": The emergence and implications of children's collective identity. In M. Bennett & F. Sani (Eds.), *The development of the social self* (pp. 29–76). Hove, U.K.: Psychology Press.

Ruble, D. N., & Flett, G. L. (1988). Conflicting goals in self-evaluative information seeking: Developmental and ability level analyses. *Child Development, 59,* 97–106.

Ruble, D. N., Martin, C. L., & Berenbaum, S. A. (2006). Gender development. In N. Eisenberg (Ed.), *Handbook of child psychology: Vol. 3. Social, emotional, and personality development* (6th ed., pp. 858–932). Hoboken, NJ: Wiley.

Ruble, D. N., Taylor, L. J., Cyphers, L., Greulich, F. K., Lurye, L. E., & Shrout, P. E. (2007). The role of gender constancy in early gender development. *Child Development, 78,* 1121–1136.

Rudolph, K. D., & Heller, T. L. (1997). Interpersonal problem solving, externalizing behavior, and social competence in preschoolers: A knowledge-performance discrepancy? *Journal of Applied Developmental Psychology, 18,* 107–117.

Rudy, D., & Grusec, J. E. (2006). Authoritarian parenting in individualist and collectivist groups: Associations with maternal emotion and cognition and children's self-esteem. *Journal of Family Psychology, 20,* 68–78.

Ruff, C. (2002). Variation in human body size and shape. *Annual Review of Anthropology, 31,* 211–232.

Ruff, H. A., & Capozzoli, M. C. (2003). Development of attention and distractibility in the first 4 years of life. *Developmental Psychology, 39,* 877–890.

Ruff, H. A., & Rothbart, M. K. (1996). *Attention in early development.* New York: Oxford University Press.

Ruffman, J., & Perner, T. (2005). Do infants really understand false belief? *Trends in Cognitive Sciences, 9,* 462–463.

Ruffman, T. (1999). Children's understanding of logical inconsistency. *Child Development, 70,* 872–886.

Ruffman, T., & Langman, L. (2002). Infants' reaching in a multi-well A not B task. *Infant Behavior and Development, 25,* 237–246.

Ruffman, T., Slade, L., Devitt, K., & Crowe, E. (2006). What mothers say and what they do: The relation between parenting, theory of mind, language, and conflict/cooperation. *British Journal of Developmental Psychology, 24,* 105–124.

Runco, M. A. (1992). Children's divergent thinking and creative ideation. *Developmental Review, 12,* 233–264.

Rushton, J. P., & Jensen, A. R. (2005). Thirty years of research on race differences in cognitive ability. *Psychology, Public Policy, and Law, 11,* 235–294.

Rushton, J. P., & Jensen, A. R. (2006). The totality of available evidence shows the race IQ gap still remains. *Psychological Science, 17,* 921–922.

Rushton, J. P., & Jensen, A. R. (2010). The rise and fall of the Flynn effect as a reason to expect a narrowing of the black–white IQ gap. *Intelligence, 38,* 213–219.

Russell, A., Mize, J., & Bissaker, K. (2004). Parent– child relationships. In P. K. Smith & C. H. Hart (Eds.), *Blackwell handbook of childhood social development* (pp. 204–222). Malden, MA: Blackwell.

Russell, J. A. (1990). The preschooler's understanding of the causes and consequences of emotion. *Child Development, 61,* 1872–1881.

Russell, J. A., Douglas, A. J., & Ingram, C. D. (2001). Brain preparations for maternity–Adaptive changes in behavioral and neuroendocrine systems during pregnancy and lactation: An overview. *Progress in Brain Research, 133,* 1–38.

Russell, R. B., Petrini, J. R., Damus, K., Mattison, D. R., & Schwarz, R. H. (2003). The changing epidemiology of multiple births in the United States. *Obstetrics and Gynecology, 101,* 129–135.

Rust, J., Golombok, S., Hines, M., Johnston, K., Golding, J., & the ALSPAC Study Team. (2000). The role of brothers and sisters in the gender development of preschool children. *Journal of Experimental Child Psychology, 77,* 292–303.

Rutter, M. (1996). Maternal deprivation. In M. H. Bornstein (Ed.), *Handbook of parenting: Vol. 4. Applied and practical parenting* (pp. 3–31). Mahwah, NJ: Erlbaum.

Rutter, M. (2002). Nature, nurture, and development: From evangelism through science toward policy and practice. *Child Development, 73,* 1–21.

Rutter, M. (2007a). Gene–environment interdependence. *Developmental Science, 10,* 12–18.

Rutter, M. (2007b). Proceeding from observed correlation to causal inference: The use of natural experiments. *Perspectives on Psychological Science, 2,* 377–395.

Rutter, M., Colvert, E., Kreppner, J., Beckett, C., Castle, J., & Groothues, C. (2007). Early adolescent outcomes for institutionally deprived and non-deprived adoptees. I: Disinhibited attachment. *Journal of Child Psychology and Psychiatry, 48,* 17–30.

Rutter, M., & the English and Romanian Adoptees Study Team. (1998). Developmental catch-up, and deficit, following adoption after severe global early privation. *Journal of Child Psychology and Psychiatry, 39,* 465–476.

Rutter, M., O'Connor, T. G., and the English and Romanian Adoptees Study Team. (2004). Are there biological programming effects for psychological development? Findings from a study of Romanian adoptees. *Developmental Psychology, 40,* 81–94.

Rutter, M., Pickles, A., Murray, R., & Eaves, L. (2001). Testing hypotheses on specific environmental causal effects on behavior. *Psychological Bulletin, 127,* 291–324.

Rutter, M., Sonuga-Barke, E. J, Beckett, C., Castle, J., Kreppner, J., Kumsta, R., et al. (2010). Deprivation-specific psychological patterns: Effects of institutional deprivation. *Monographs of the Society for Research in Child Development, 75*(1, Serial No. 295).

Ryan, R. M., Fauth, R. C., & Brooks-Gunn, J. (2006). Childhood poverty: Implications for school readiness and early childhood education In B. Spodek & O. N. Saracho (Eds.), *Handbook of research on the education of young children* (2nd ed., pp. 323–346). Mahwah, NJ: Erlbaum.

Ryding, M., Konradsson, K., Kalm, O., & Prellner, K. (2002). Auditory consequences of recurrent acute purulent otitis media. *Annals of Otology, Rhinology, and Laryngology, 111*(3, Pt. 1), 261–266.

S

Saarni, C. (1999). *The development of emotional competence.* New York: Guilford.

Saarni, C. (2000). Emotional competence: A developmental perspective. In R. Bar-On & J. D. A. Parker (Eds.), *Handbook of emotional intelligence* (pp. 68–91). San Francisco: Jossey-Bass.

Saarni, C., Campos, J. J., Camras, L. A., & Witherington, D. (2006). Emotional development: Action, communication, and understanding. In N. Eisenberg (Ed.), *Handbook of child psychology: Vol. 3. Social, emotional, and personality development* (6th ed., pp. 226–299). Hoboken, NJ: Wiley.

Sabbagh, M. A., & Baldwin, D. A. (2001). Learning words from knowledgeable versus ignorant

speakers: Links between preschoolers' theory of mind and semantic development. *Child Development, 72,* 1054–1070.

Sabbagh, M. A., Xu, F., Carlson, S. M., Moses, L. J., & Lee, K. (2006). The development of executive functioning and theory of mind: A comparison of Chinese and U.S. preschoolers. *Psychological Science, 17,* 74–81.

Sacks, P. (2005). "No child left": What are schools for in a democratic society? In S. Olfman (Ed.), *Childhood lost: How American culture is failing our kids* (pp. 185–202). Westport, CT: Praeger.

Sadeh, A. (1997). Sleep and melatonin in infants: A preliminary study. *Sleep, 20,* 185–191.

Sadeh, A. (2007). Consequences of sleep loss or sleep disruption in children. *Sleep Medicine Reviews, 2,* 513–520.

Sadeh, A., Flint-Ofir, E., Tirosh, T., & Tikotzky, L. (2007). Infant sleep and parental sleep-related cognitions. *Journal of Family Psychology, 21,* 74–87.

Sadler, T. W. (2009). *Langman's medical embryology* (11th ed.). Baltimore: Lippincott Williams & Wilkins.

Saenger, P. (2003). Dose effects of growth hormone during puberty. *Hormone Research, 60*(Suppl. 1), 52–57.

Safe Kids USA. (2007*). Car seats, booster seats and seat belts.* Retrieved from usa.safekids.org

Safe Kids USA. (2008). *Report to the nation: Trends in unintentional childhood injury mortality and parental views on child safety.* Retrieved from usa.safekids.org

Saffran, J. R. (2009). What can statistical learning tell us about infant learning? In A. Woodward & A. Needham (Eds.), *Learning and the infant mind* (pp. 29–48). New York: Oxford University Press.

Saffran, J. R., Aslin, R. N., & Newport, E. L. (1996). Statistical learning by 8-month-old infants. *Science, 27,* 1926–1928.

Saffran, J. R., & Thiessen, E. D. (2003). Pattern induction by infant language learners. *Developmental Psychology, 39,* 484–494.

Saffran, J. R., Werker, J. F., & Werner, L. A. (2006). The infant's auditory world: Hearing, speech, and the beginnings of language. In D. Kuhn & R. Siegler (Eds.), *Handbook of child psychology: Vol. 2. Cognition, perception, and language* (6th ed., pp. 58–108). Hoboken, NJ: Wiley.

Sagi, A., van IJzendoorn, M. H., Aviezer, O., Donnell, F., Koren-Karie, N., Joels, T., & Harel, Y. (1995). Attachments in a multiple-caregiver and multiple-infant environment: The case of the Israeli kibbutzim. In E. Waters, B. E. Vaughn, G. Posada, & K. Kondo-Ikemura (Eds.), *Caregiving, cultural, and cognitive perspectives on secure-base behavior and working models: New growing points in attachment theory and research. Monographs of the Society for Research in Child Development, 60*(1, Serial No. 244), 71–91.

Sahlberg, P. (2010). Educational change in Finland. In A. Hargreaves, M. Fullan, A. Lieberman, & D. Hopkins (Eds.), *Second International handbook of educational change.* New York: Springer.

Saigal, S., Stoskopf, B., Streiner, D., Boyle, M., Pinelli, J., & Paneth, N. (2006). Transition of extremely low-birthweight infants from adolescence to young adulthood. *Journal of the American Medical Association, 295,* 667–675.

Saitta, S. C., & Zackai, E. H. (2005). Specific chromosome disorders in newborns. In H. W. Taeusch, R. A. Ballard, & C. A. Gleason (Eds.), *Avery's diseases of the newborn* (8th ed., pp. 204–215). Philadelphia: Saunders.

Salbe, A. D., Weyer, C., Lindsay, R. S., Ravussin, E., & Tataranni, P. A. (2002). Assessing risk factors for obesity between childhood and adolescence: I. Birth weight, childhood adiposity, parental obesity, insulin, and leptin. *Pediatrics, 110,* 299–306.

Salerno, M., Micillo, M., Di Maio, S., Capalbo, D., Ferri, P., & Lettiero, T. (2001). Longitudinal growth, sexual maturation and final height in patients with congenital hypothyroidism detected by neonatal screening. *European Journal of Endocrinology, 145,* 377–383.

Salihu, H. M., Shumpert, M. N., Slay, M., Kirby, R. S., & Alexander, G. R. (2003). Childbearing beyond maternal age 50 and fetal outcomes in the United States. *Obstetrics and Gynecology, 102,* 1006–1014.

Salley, B. J., & Dixon, W. E., Jr. (2007). Temperamental and joint attentional predictors of language development. *Merrill-Palmer Quarterly, 53,* 131–154.

Salmela-Aro, K., Nurmi, J.-E., Saisto, T., & Halmesmaki, E. (2000). Women's and men's personal goals during the transition to parenthood. *Journal of Family Psychology, 14,* 171–186.

Salmivalli, C., & Voeten, M. (2004). Connections between attitudes, group norms, and behaviour in bullying situations. *International Journal of Behavioral Development, 28,* 246–258.

Salovey, P., & Pizzaro, D. A. (2003). The value of emotional intelligence. In R. J. Sternberg, J. Lautrey, & T. I. Lubart (Eds.), *Models of intelligence: International perspectives* (pp. 263–278). Washington, DC: American Psychological Association.

Salter, D., McMillan, D., Richards, M., Talbot, T., Hodges, J., Bentovim, A., & Hastings, R. (2003). Development of sexually abusive behavior in sexually victimized males: A longitudinal study. *Lancet, 361,* 471–476.

Sameroff, A. (2006). Identifying risk and protective factors for healthy child development. In A. Clarke-Stewart & J. Dunn (Eds.), *Families count: Effects on child and adolescent development* (pp. 53–76). New York: Cambridge University Press.

Samuels, M. (2003). Viruses and sudden infant death. *Peaediatric Respiratory Review, 4,* 178–183.

Sanchez, M. M., & Pollak, S. D. (2009). Socioemotional development following early abuse and neglect: Challenges and insight from translational research. In M. de Haan & M. R. Gunnar (Eds.), *Handbook of developmental social neuroscience* (pp. 497–520). New York: Guilford.

Sandberg, D. E., & Voss, L. D. (2002). The psychosocial consequences of short stature: A review of the evidence. *Best Practice and Research in Clinical Endocrinology and Metabolism, 16,* 449–463.

Sanders, O. (2006). Evaluating the Keeping Ourselves Safe Programme. Wellington, NZ: Youth Education Service, New Zealand Police. Retrieved from www.nzfvc.org.nz/accan/papers-presentations/abstract11v.shtml

Sanderson, J. A., & Siegal, M. (1988). Conceptions of moral and social rules in rejected and nonrejected preschoolers. *Journal of Clinical Child Psychology, 17,* 66–72.

Sandler, J. C. (2006). Alternative methods of child testimony: A review of law and research. In C. R. Bartol & A. M. Bartol (Eds.), *Current perspectives in forensic psychology and criminal justice* (pp. 203–212). Thousand Oaks, CA: Sage.

Sandnabba, N. K., & Ahlberg, C. (1999). Parents' attitudes and expectations about children's cross-gender behavior. *Sex Roles, 40,* 249–263.

Sandstrom, M. J., & Cillessen, A. H. N. (2003). Sociometric status and children's peer experiences: Use of the daily diary method. *Merrill-Palmer Quarterly, 49,* 427–452.

Sangrigoli, S., Pallier, C., Argenti, A. M., Ventureyra, V. A. G., & de Schonen, S. (2005). Reversibility of the other-race effect in face recognition during childhood. *Psychological Science, 16,* 440–444.

Sann, C., & Streri, A. (2007). Perception of object shape and texture in human newborns: Evidence from cross-modal transfer tasks. *Developmental Science, 10,* 399–410.

Sann, C., & Streri, A. (2008). The limits of newborn's grasping to detect texture in a cross-modal transfer task. *Infant Behavior and Development, 31,* 523–531.

Sansavini, A., Bertoncini, J., & Giovanelli, G. (1997). Newborns discriminate the rhythm of multisyllabic stressed words. *Developmental Psychology, 33,* 3–11.

Sapp, F., Lee, K., & Muir, D. (2000). Three-year-olds' difficulty with the appearance–reality distinction: Is it real or is it apparent? *Developmental Psychology, 36,* 547–560.

Sarnecka, B. W., & Gelman, S. A. (2004). Six does not just mean a lot: Preschoolers see number words as specific. *Cognition, 92,* 329–352.

Sato, T., Matsumoto, T., Kawano, H., Watanabe, T., Uematsu, Y., & Semine, K. (2004). Brain masculinization requires androgen receptor function. *Proceedings of the National Academy of Sciences, 101,* 1673–1678.

Saucier, J. F., Sylvestre, R., Doucet, H., Lambert, J., Frappier, J. Y., Charbonneau, L., & Malus, M. (2002). Cultural identity and adaptation to adolescence in Montreal. In F. J. C. Azima & N. Grizenko (Eds.), *Immigrant and refugee children and their families: Clinical, research, and training issues* (pp. 133–154). Madison, WI: International Universities Press.

Saudino, K. J. (2003). Parent ratings of infant temperament: Lessons from twin studies. *Infant Behavior and Development, 26,* 100–107.

Saudino, K. J., & Cherny, S. S. (2001). Sources of continuity and change in observed temperament. In R. N. Emde & J. K. Hewitt (Eds.), *Infancy to early childhood: Genetic and environmental influences on developmental change* (pp. 89–110). New York: Oxford University Press.

Saudino, K. J., & Plomin, R. (1997). Cognitive and temperamental mediators of genetic contributions to the home environment during infancy. *Merrill-Palmer Quarterly, 43,* 1–23.

Saw, S. M., Carkeet, A., Chia, K. S., Stone, R. A., & Tan, D. T. (2002). Component dependent risk factors for ocular parameters in Singapore Chinese children. *Ophthalmology, 109,* 2065–2071.

Saxe, G. B. (1988, August–September). Candy selling and math learning. *Educational Researcher, 17*(6), 14–21.

Saxe, R. R., Whitfield-Gabrieli, S., Scholz, J., & Pelphrey, K. A. (2009). Brain regions for perceiving and reasoning about other people in school-aged children. *Child Development, 80,* 1197–1209.

Saxton, M., Backley, P., & Gallaway, C. (2005). Negative input for grammatical errors: Effects after a lag of 12 weeks. *Journal of Child Language, 32,* 643–672.

Saygin, A. P., Wilson, S. M., Dronkers, N. F., & Bates, E. (2004). Action comprehension in aphasia: Linguistic and non-linguistic deficits and their lesion correlates. *Neuropsychologia, 42,* 1788–1804.

Saylor, M. M. (2004). Twelve- and 16-month-old infants recognize properties of mentioned absent things. *Developmental Science, 7,* 599–611.

Saylor, M. M., Baldwin, D. A., & Sabbagh, M. A. (2005). Word learning: A complex product. In G. Hall & S. Waxman (Eds.), *Weaving a lexicon.* Cambridge, MA: MIT Press.

Saylor, M. M., Sabbagh, M. A., & Baldwin, D. A. (2002). Children use whole–part juxtaposition as a pragmatic cue to word meaning. *Developmental Psychology, 38,* 993–1003.

Saylor, M. M., & Troseth, G. L. (2006). Preschoolers use information about speakers' desires to learn new words. *Cognitive Development, 21,* 214–231.

Saywitz, K. J., Goodman, G. S., & Lyon, T. D. (2002). Interviewing children in and out of court: Current research and practice implications. In J. E. B. Myers & L. Berliner (Eds.), *The APSAC handbook on child maltreatment* (2nd ed., pp. 349–377). Thousand Oaks, CA: Sage.

Scarr, S., & McCartney, K. (1983). How people make their own environments: A theory of genotype–environment effects. *Child Development, 54,* 424–435.

Scarr, S., & Weinberg, R. A. (1983). The Minnesota adoption studies: Genetic differences and malleability. *Child Development, 54,* 260–267.

Schaal, B., Marlier, L., & Soussignan, R. (2000). Human fetuses learn odours from their pregnant mother's diet. *Chemical Senses, 25,* 729–737.

Schacht, P. M., Cummings, E. M., & Davies, P. T. (2009). Fathering in family context and child adjustment: A longitudinal analysis. *Journal of Family Psychology, 23,* 790–797.

Scharrer, E., & Comstock, G. (2003). Entertainment televisual media: Content patterns and themes. In E. L. Palmer & B. M. Young (Eds.), *The faces of televisual media: Teaching violence, selling to children* (pp. 161–193). Mahwah, NJ: Erlbaum.

Schauwers, K., Gillis, S., Daemers, K., De Beukelaer, C., De Ceulaer, G., Yperman, M., & Govaerts, P. J. (2004). Normal hearing and language development in a deaf-born child. *Otology and Neurotology, 25,* 924–929.

Schellenberg, E. G. (2004). Music lessons enhance IQ. *Psychological Science, 15,* 511–514.

Schellenberg, E. G., Nakata, T., Hunter, P. G., & Tamoto, S. (2007). Exposure to music and cognitive performance: Tests of children and adults. *Psychology of Music, 35,* 5–19.

Scher, A., Epstein, R., & Tirosh, E. (2004). Stability and changes in sleep regulation: A longitudinal study from 3 months to 3 years. *International Journal of Behavioral Development, 28,* 268–274.

Scher, A., Tirosh, E., Jaffe, M., Rubin, L., Sadeh, A., & Lavie, P. (1995). Sleep patterns of infants and young children in Israel. *International Journal of Behavioral Development, 18,* 701–711.

Schlaggar, B. L., & McCandliss, B. D. (2007). Development of neural systems for reading. *Annual Review of Neuroscience, 30,* 475–503.

Schlagmüller, M., & Schneider, W. (2002). The development of organizational strategies in children: Evidence from a microgenetic longitudinal study. *Journal of Experimental Child Psychology, 81,* 298–319.

Schmid, R. G., Tirsch, W. S., & Scherb, H. (2002). Correlation between spectral EEG parameters and intelligence test variables in school-age children. *Clinical Neurophysiology, 113,* 1647–1656.

Schmidt, L. A., Fox, N. A., Rubin, K. H., Sternberg, E. M., Gold, P. W., & Smith, C. C. (1997). Behavioral and neuroendocrine responses in shy children. *Developmental Psychobiology, 35,* 119–135.

Schmidt, L. A., Fox, N. A., Schulkin, J., & Gold, P. W. (1999). Behavioral and psychophysiological correlates of self-presentation in temperamentally shy children. *Developmental Psychobiology, 30,* 127–140.

Schmidt, L. A., Santesso, D. L., Schulkin, J., & Segalowitz, S. J. (2007). Shyness is a necessary but not sufficient condition for high salivary cortisol in typically developing 10-year-old children. *Personality and Individual Differences, 43,* 1541–1551.

Schmidt, M. E., Crawley-Davis, A. M., & Anderson, D. R. (2007). Two-year-olds' object retrieval based on television: Testing a perceptual account. *Media Psychology, 9,* 389–409.

Schmitz, S., Fulker, D. W., Plomin, R., Zahn-Waxler, C., Emde, R. N., & DeFries, J. C. (1999). Temperament and problem behaviour during early childhood. *International Journal of Behavioral Development, 23,* 333–355.

Schneider, B. H., Atkinson, L., & Tardif, C. (2001). Child–parent attachment and children's peer relations: A quantitative review. *Developmental Psychology, 37,* 86–100.

Schneider, W. (1986). The role of conceptual knowledge and metamemory in the development of organizational processes in memory. *Journal of Experimental Child Psychology, 42,* 218–236.

Schneider, W. (2002). Memory development in childhood. In U. Goswami (Ed.), *Blackwell handbook of childhood cognitive development* (pp. 236–256). Malden, MA: Blackwell.

Schneider, W., & Bjorklund, D. F. (1992). Expertise, aptitude, and strategic remembering. *Child Development, 63,* 461–473.

Schneider, W., & Bjorklund, D. F. (1998). Memory. In D. Kuhn & R. S. Siegler (Eds.), *Handbook of child psychology: Vol. 2. Cognition, perception, and language* (5th ed., pp. 467–521). New York: Wiley.

Schneider, W., & Bjorklund, D. F. (2003). Memory and knowledge development. In J. Valsiner & K. Connolly (Eds.), *Handbook of developmental psychology.* London: Sage.

Schneider, W., & Pressley, M. (1997). *Memory development between two and twenty* (2nd ed.). Mahwah, NJ: Erlbaum.

Scholl, B. J., & Leslie, A. M. (2000). Minds, modules, and meta-analysis. *Child Development, 72,* 696–701.

Scholl, T. O., Hediger, M. L., & Belsky, D. (1996). Prenatal care and maternal health during adolescent pregnancy: A review and meta-analysis. *Journal of Adolescent Health, 15,* 444–456.

Schonberg, R. L., & Tifft, C. J. (2007). Birth defects and prenatal diagnosis. In M. L. Batshaw, L. Pellegrino, & N. J. Roizen (Eds.), *Children with disabilities* (6th ed., pp. 83–96). Baltimore: Paul H. Brookes.

Schoppe-Sullivan, S. J., Brown, G. L., Cannon, E. A., Mangelsdorf, S. C., & Sokolowski, M. S. (2008). Maternal gatekeeping, coparenting quality, and fathering behavior in families with infants. *Journal of Family Psychology, 22,* 389–398.

Schoppe-Sullivan, S. J., Mangelsdorf, S. C., Brown, G. L., & Sokolowski, M. S. (2007). Goodness-of-fit in family context: Infant temperament, marital quality, and early coparenting behavior. *Infant Behavior and Development, 30,* 82–96.

Schor, J. B. (2002). Time crunch among American parents. In S. A. Hewlett, N. Rankin, & C. West (Eds.), *Taking parenting public* (pp. 83–102). Boston: Rowman & Littlefield.

Schott, J. M., & Rossor, M. N. (2003). The grasp and other primitive reflexes. *Journal of Neurological and Neurosurgical Psychiatry, 74,* 558–560.

Schuetze, P., & Eiden, R. D. (2006). The association between maternal cocaine use during pregnancy and physiological regulation in 4- to 8-week-old infants: An examination of possible mediators and moderators. *Journal of Pediatric Psychology, 31,* 15–26.

Schull, W. J. (2003). The children of atomic bomb survivors: A synopsis. *Journal of Radiological Protection, 23,* 369–394.

Schulte-Ruther, M., Markowitsch, H. J., Fink, G. R., & Piefke, M. (2007). Mirror neuron and theory of mind mechanisms involved in face-to-face interactions: A functional magnetic resonance imaging approach to empathy. *Journal of Cognitive Neuroscience, 19,* 1354–1372.

Schultz, D., Izar, C. E., Ackerman, B. P., & Youngstrom, E. A. (2001). Emotion knowledge in economically disadvantaged children: Self-regulatory antecedents and relations to social difficulties and withdrawal. *Development and Psychopathology, 13,* 53–67.

Schulz, M. S., Cowan, C. P., & Cowan, P. A. (2006). Promoting healthy beginnings: A randomized controlled trial of a preventive intervention to preserve marital quality during the transition to parenthood. *Journal of Consulting and Clinical Psychology, 74,* 20–31.

Schumann, C. M., & Amaral, D. G. (2010). The human amygdala in autism. In P. J. Whalen & E. A. Phelps (Eds.), *The human amygdala* (pp. 362–381). New York: Guilford.

Schumann, C. M., Barnes, C. C., Lord, C., & Courchesne, E. (2009). Amygdala enlargement in toddlers with autism related to severity of social and communication impairments. *Biological Psychiatry, 66,* 942–949.

Schunk, D. H., & Pajares, F. (2005). Competence perceptions and academic functioning. In A. J. Andrew & C. S. Dweck (Eds.), *Handbook of competence and motivation* (pp. 85–104). New York: Guilford.

Schwanenflugel, P. J., Henderson, R. L., & Fabricius, W. V. (1998). Developing organization of mental verbs and theory of mind in middle childhood: Evidence from extensions. *Developmental Psychology, 34,* 512–524.

Schwarte, A. R. (2008). Fragile X syndrome. *School Psychology Quarterly, 23,* 290–300.

Schwartz, C. E., Wright, C. I., Shin, L. M., Kagan, J., & Rauch, S. L. (2003). Inhibited and uninhibited infants "grown up": Adult amygdalar response to novelty. *Science, 300,* 1952–1953.

Schwartz, D., Proctor, L. J., & Chien, D. H. (2001). The aggressive victim of bullying: Emotional and behavioral dysregulation as a pathway to victimization by peers. In J. Juonen & S. Graham (Eds.), *Peer harassment in school: The plight of the vulnerable and victimized* (pp. 147–174). New York: Guilford.

Schwarz, N. (1999). Self-reports : How the questions shape the answers. *American Psychologist, 54,* 93–105.

Schwebel, D. C., & Bounds, M. L. (2003). The role of parents and temperament on children's estimation of physical ability: Links to unintentional injury prevention. *Journal of Pediatric Psychology, 28,* 505–516.

Schwebel, D. C., & Brezausek, C. M. (2007). Father transitions in the household and young children's injury risk. *Psychology of Men and Masculinity, 8,* 173–184.

Schwebel, D. C., & Gaines, J. (2007). Pediatric unintentional injury: Behavioral risk factors and implications for prevention. *Journal of Developmental and Behavioral Pediatrics, 28,* 245–254.

Schwebel, D. C., Brezausek, C. M., Ramey, S. L., & Ramey, C. T. (2004). Interactions between child behavior patterns and parenting: Implications for children's unintentional injury risk. *Journal of Pediatric Psychology, 29,* 93–104.

Schwebel, D. C., Hodgens, J. B., & Sterling, S. (2006). How mothers parent their children with behavior disorders: Implications for unintentional injury risk. *Journal of Safety Research, 37,* 167–173.

Schweiger, W. K., & O'Brien, M. (2005). Special needs adoption: An ecological systems approach. *Family Relations, 54,* 512–522.

Schweinhart, L. J., Montie, J., Xiang, Z., Barnett, W. S., Belfield, C. R., & Nores, M. (2005). *Lifetime effects: The High/Scope Perry Preschool Study through age 40.* Ypsilanti, MI: High/Scope Press.

Schweizer, K., Moosbrugger, H., & Goldhammer, F. (2006). The structure of the relationship between attention and intelligence. *Intelligence, 33,* 589–611.

Schwier, C., van Maanen, C., Carpenter, M., & Tomasello, M. (2006). Rational imitation in 12-month-old infants. *Infancy, 10,* 303–311.

Schwimmer, J. B., Burwinkle, T. M., & Varni, J. W. (2003). Health-related quality of life of severely obese children and adolescents. *Journal of the American Medical Association, 289,* 1813–1819.

Scott, K. D., Berkowitz, G., & Klaus, M. (1999). A comparison of intermittent and continuous support during labor: A meta-analysis. *American Journal of Obstetrics and Gynecology, 180,* 1054–1059.

Scott, L. S. (2009). *Two is enough.* Berkeley, CA: Seal Press.

Scrutton, D. (2005). Influence of supine sleeping positioning on early motor milestone acquisition. *Developmental Medicine and Child Neurology, 47,* 364.

Seibert, A. C., & Kerns, K. A. (2009). Attachment figures in middle childhood. *International Journal of Behavioral Development, 33,* 347–355.

Seifer, R., & Schiller, M. (1995). The role of parenting sensitivity, infant temperament, and dyadic interaction in attachment theory and assessment. In E. Waters, B. E. Vaughn, G. Posada, & K. Kondo-Ikemura (Eds.), *Caregiving, cultural, and cognitive perspectives on secure-base behavior and working models: New growing points of attachment theory and research. Monographs of the Society for Research in Child Development, 60*(2–3, Serial No. 244).

Sekido, R., & Lovell-Badge, R. (2009). Sex determination and SRY: Down to a wink and a nudge? *Trends in Genetics, 25,* 19–29.

Selman, R. L. (1976). Social-cognitive understanding: A guide to educational and clinical practice. In T. Lickona (Ed.), *Moral development and behavior: Theory, research, and social issues* (pp. 299–316). New York: Holt, Rinehart, & Winston.

Selman, R. L., & Byrne, D. F. (1974). A structural-developmental analysis of levels of role taking in middle childhood. *Child Development, 45,* 803–806.

Sen, M. G., Yonas, A., & Knill, D. C. (2001). Development of infants' sensitivity to surface contour information for spatial layout. *Perception, 30,* 167–176.

Senechal, M., & LeFevre, J. (2002). Parental involvement in the development of children's reading skill: A five-year longitudinal study. *Child Development, 73,* 445–460.

Senju, A., Csibra, G., & Johnson, M. H. (2008). Understanding the referential nature of looking: Infants' preference for object-directed gaze. *Cognition, 108,* 303–319.

Serbin, L. A., Powlishta, K. K., & Gulko, J. (1993). The development of sex typing in middle childhood. *Monographs of the Society for Research in Child Development, 58*(2, Serial No. 232).

Sermon, K., Van Steirteghem, A., & Liebaers, I. (2004). Preimplantation genetic diagnosis. *Lancet, 363,* 1633–1641.

Sesame Workshop. (2008). *Sesame Street season 37 press kit.* Retrieved from www.sesameworkshop.org/aboutus/pressroom/presskits/season37/sesame_street.php

Sevigny, P. R., & Loutzenhiser, L. (2010). Predictors of parenting self-efficacy in mothers and fathers of toddlers. *Child Care, Health and Development, 36,* 179–189.

Seymour, S. C. (1999). *Women, family, and child care in India.* Cambridge, UK: Cambridge University Press.

Shafer, V. L., & Garrido-Nag, K. (2007). The neurodevelopmental bases of language. In E. Hoff & M. Shatz (Eds.), *Blackwell handbook of language development* (pp. 21–45). Malden, MA: Blackwell.

Shah, T., Sullivan, K., & Carter, J. (2006). Sudden infant death syndrome and reported maternal smoking during pregnancy. *American Journal of Public Health, 96,* 1757–1759.

Shahar, S. (1990). *Childhood in the Middle Ages.* London: Routledge & Kegan Paul.

Shankaran, S., Laptook, A. R., Ehrenkranz, R. A., Tyson, J. E., McDonald, S. A., & Donovan, E. F. (2005). Whole-body hypothermia for neonates with hypoxic–ischemic encephalopathy. *New England Journal of Medicine, 353,* 1574–1584.

Shapiro, A. E., Gottman, J. M., & Carrere, S. (2000). The baby and the marriage: Identifying factors that buffer against decline in marital satisfaction after the first baby arrives. *Journal of Family Psychology, 14,* 59–70.

Shapka, J. D., & Keating, D. P. (2005). Structure and change in self-concept during adolescence. *Canadian Journal of Behavioural Science, 37,* 83–96.

Shatz, M. (2007). On the development of the field. In E. Hoff & M. Shatz (Eds.), *Blackwell handbook of language development* (pp. 1–20). Malden, MA: Blackwell.

Shaw, D. S., Lacourse, E., & Nagin, D. S. (2005). Developmental trajectories of conduct problems and hyperactivity from ages 2 to 10. *Journal of Child Psychology and Psychiatry, 46,* 931–942.

Shaw, D. S., Winslow, E. B., & Flanagan, C. (1999). A prospective study of the effects of marital status and family relations on young children's adjustment among African-American and European-American families. *Child Development, 70,* 742–755.

Shaw, P., Brierley, B., & David, A. S. (2005). A critical period for the impact of amygdala damage on the emotional enhancement of memory? *Neurology, 65,* 326–328.

Shaw, P., Eckstrand, K., Sharp, W., Blumenthal, J., Lerch, J. P., & Greenstein, D. (2007, November 16). Attention-deficit/hyperactivity disorder is characterized by a delay in cortical maturation. *Proceedings of the National Academy of Sciences Online.* Retrieved from www.pnas.org/cgi/content/abstract/0707741104v1

Sheehan, G., Darlington, Y., Noller, P., & Feeney, J. (2004). Children's perceptions of their sibling relationships during parental separation and divorce. *Journal of Divorce and Remarriage, 41,* 69–94.

Sheldon, J. P. (2004). Gender stereotypes in educational software for young children. *Sex Roles, 51,* 433–444.

Shenkin, J. D., Broffitt, B., Levy, S. M., & Warren, J. J. (2004). The association between environmental tobacco smoke and primary tooth caries. *Journal of Public Health Dentistry, 64,* 184–186.

Sherman, S. L., Allen, E. G., Bean, L. H., & Freeman, S. B. (2007). Epidemiology of Down syndrome. *Mental Retardation and Developmental Disabilities Research Reviews, 13,* 221–227.

Sherman, S. L., Freeman, S. B., Allen, E. G., & Lamb, N. E. (2005). Risk factors for nondisjunction of trisomy 21. *Cytogenetic Genome Research, 111,* 273–280.

Sherrod, L. R., & Spiewak, G. S. (2008). Possible interrelationships between civic engagement, positive youth development, and spirituality/religiosity. In R. M. Lerner, R. W. Roeser, & E. Phelps (Eds.), *Positive youth development and spirituality: From theory to research* (pp. 322–338). West Conshohocken, PA: Templeton Foundation Press.

Sherry, B., McDivitt, J., Brich, L. L., Cook, F. H., Sanders, S., Prish, J. L., Francis, L. A., & Scanlon, K. S. (2004). Attitudes, practices, and concerns about child feeding and child weight status among socioeconomically diverse white, Hispanic, and African-American mothers. *Journal of the American Dietetic Association, 104,* 215–221.

Shimada, S., & Hiraki, K. (2006). Infant's brain responses to live and televised action. *NeuroImage, 32,* 930–939.

Shinn, M., Schteingart, J. S., Williams, N. C., Carlin-Mathis, J., Bialo-Karagis, N., Becker-Klein, R., & Weitzman, B. C. (2008). Long-term associations of homelessness with children's well-being. *American Behavioral Scientist, 51,* 789–809.

Shipman, K. L., Zeman, J., Nesin, A. E., & Fitzgerald, M. (2003). Children's strategies for displaying anger and sadness: What works with whom? *Merrill-Palmer Quarterly, 49,* 100–122.

Shonkoff, J., & Phillips, D. (Eds.). (2001). *Neurons to neighborhoods: The science of early childhood development.* Washington, DC: National Academy Press.

Shwalb, D. W., Nakawaza, J., Yamamoto, T., & Hyun, J. H. (2004). Fathering in Japanese, Chinese, and Korean cultures: A review of the research literature. In M. E. Lamb (Ed.), *The role of the father in child development* (4th ed., pp. 146–181). Hoboken, NJ: Wiley.

Shweder, R. A., Goodnow, J. J., Hatano, G., LeVine, R. A., Markus, H. R., & Miller, P. J. (2006). The cultural psychology of development: One mind, many mentalities. In R. M. Lerner (Ed.), *Handbook of child psychology: Vol. 1. Theoretical models of human development* (6th ed., pp. 716–792). Hoboken, NJ: Wiley.

Sidappa, A., Georgieff, M. K., Wewerka, S., Worwa, C., Nelson, C. A., & deRegnier, R. (2004). Iron deficiency alters auditory recognition memory in newborn infants of diabetic mothers. *Pediatric Research, 55,* 1034–1041.

Sidebotham, P., Heron, J., & the ALSPAC Study Team. (2003). Child maltreatment in the "children of the nineties": The role of the child. *Child Abuse and Neglect, 27,* 337–352.

Siebert, A. C., & Kerns, K. A. (2009). Attachment figures in middle childhood. *International Journal of Behavioral Development, 33,* 347–355.

Siegal, M., Iozzi, L., & Surian, L. (2009). Bilingualism and conversational understanding in young children. *Cognition, 110,* 115–122.

Siegler, R. S. (1996). *Emerging minds: The process of change in children's thinking.* New York: Oxford University Press.

Siegler, R. S. (2002). Microgenetic studies of self-explanation. In N. Granott & J. Parziale (Eds.), *Microdevelopment: Transition processes in development and learning* (pp. 31–58). New York: Cambridge University Press.

Siegler, R. S. (2006). Microgenetic analyses of learning. In D. Kuhn & R. Siegler (Eds.), *Handbook of child psychology: Vol. 2. Cognition, perception, and language* (6th ed., pp. 464–510). Hoboken, NJ: Wiley.

Siegler, R. S. (2007). Cognitive variability. *Developmental Science, 10,* 104–109.

Siegler, R. S. (2009). Improving preschoolers' number sense using information-processing theory. In O. A. Barbarinb & B. H. Wasik (Eds.), *Handbook of child development and early education: Research to practice* (pp. 429–454). New York: Guilford.

Siegler, R. S., & Alibali, M. W. (2005). *Children's thinking* (4th ed.). Upper Saddle River, NJ: Prentice-Hall.

Siegler, R. S., & Booth, J. L. (2004). Development of numerical estimation in young children. *Child Development, 75,* 428–444.

Siegler, R. S., & Crowley, K. (1991). The microgenetic method: A direct means for studying cognitive development. *American Psychologist, 46,* 606–620.

Siegler, R. S., & Jenkins, E. A. (1989). *How children discover new strategies.* Hillsdale, NJ: Erlbaum.

Siegler, R. S., & Mu, Y. (2008). Chinese children excel on novel mathematics problems even before elementary school. *Psychological Science, 19,* 759–763.

Siegler, R. S., & Svetina, M. (2006). What leads children to adopt new strategies? A microgenetic/cross-sectional study of class inclusion. *Child Development, 77,* 997–1015.

Siervogel, R. M., Maynard, L. M., Wisemandle, W. A., Roche, A. F., Guo, S. S., Chumlea, W. C., & Towne, B. (2000). Annual changes in total body fat and fat-free mass in children from 8 to 18 years in relation to changes in body mass index: The Fels Longitudinal Study. *Annals of the New York Academy of Sciences, 904,* 420–423.

Sigman, M. (1995). Nutrition and child development: More food for thought. *Current Directions in Psychological Science, 4,* 52–55.

Signorielli, N. (2001). Television's gender-role images and contribution to stereotyping. In D. G. Singer & J. L. Singer (Eds.), *Handbook of children and the media* (pp. 341–358). Thousand Oaks, CA: Sage.

Silk, J. S., Morris, A. S., Kanaya, T., & Steinberg, L. D. (2003). Psychological control and autonomy granting: Opposite ends of a continuum or distinct constructs? *Journal of Research on Adolescence, 13,* 113–128.

Silk, J. S., Sessa, F. M., Morris, A. S., Steinberg, L., & Avenevoli, S. (2004). Neighborhood cohesion as a buffer against hostile maternal parenting. *Journal of Family Psychology, 18,* 135–146.

Silvén, M. (2001). Attention in very young infants predicts learning of first words. *Infant Behavior and Development, 24,* 229–237.

Silverman, W. K., & Pina, A. A. (2008). Psychosocial treatments for phobic and anxiety disorders in youth. In R. G. Steele, T. D. Elkin, & M. Roberts (Eds.), *Handbook of evidence-based therapies for children and adolescents: Bridging science and practice* (pp. 65–82). New York: Springer.

Simcock, G., & DeLoache, J. (2006). Get the picture? The effects of iconicity on toddlers' reenactment from picture books. *Developmental Psychology, 42,* 1352–1357.

Simcock, G., & Hayne, H. (2002). Breaking the barrier? Children fail to translate their preverbal memories into language. *Psychological Science, 13,* 225–231.

Simcock, G., & Hayne, H. (2003). Age-related changes in verbal and nonverbal memory during early childhood. *Developmental Psychology, 39,* 805–814.

Simion, F., Cassia, V. M., Turati, C., & Valenza, E. (2001). The origins of face perception: Specific versus non-specific mechanisms. *Infant and Child Development, 10,* 59–65.

Simons, L. G., Chen, Y. F., Simons, R. L., Brody, G., & Cutrona, C. (2006). Parenting practices and child adjustment in different types of households: A study of African-American families. *Journal of Family Issues, 27,* 803–825.

Simons, R. L., Whitbeck, L. B., Conger, R. D., & Chyi-In, W. (1991). Intergenerational transmission of harsh parenting. *Developmental Psychology, 27,* 159–171.

Simonton, D. K. (2009). Giftedness: The gift that keeps on giving. In T. Balchin, B. Hymer, & D. J. Matthews (Eds.), *The Routledge international companion to gifted education* (pp. 26–31). New York: Routledge.

Simpson, J. A., Rholes, W. S., Campbell, L., Tran, S., & Wilson, C. L. (2003). Adult attachment, the transition to parenthood, and depressive symptoms. *Journal of Personality and Social Psychology, 84,* 1172–1187.

Simpson, J. L., de la Cruz, F., Swerdloff, R. S., Samango-Sprouse, C., Skakkebaek, N. E., & Graham, J. M., Jr. (2003). Klinefelter syndrome: Expanding the phenotype and identifying new research directions. *Genetic Medicine, 5,* 460–468.

Singer, D. G., & Singer, J. L. (2005). *Imagination and play in the electronic age.* Cambridge, MA: Harvard University Press.

Singer, L. T., Minnes, S., Short, E., Arendt, R., Farkas, K., Lewis, B., & Klein, N. (2004). Cognitive outcomes of preschool children with prenatal cocaine exposure. *Journal of the American Medical Association, 291,* 2448–2456.

Singleton, J. L., & Newport, E. L. (2004). When learners surpass their models: The acquisition of American Sign Language from inconsistent input. *Cognitive Psychology, 49,* 370–407.

Sirios, S., & Jackson, I. (2007). Social cognition in infancy: A critical review of research on higher-order abilities. *European Journal of Developmental Psychology, 4,* 46–64.

Skinner, B. F. (1957). *Verbal behavior.* New York: Appleton-Century-Crofts.

Skinner, E. A., Zimmer-Gembeck, M. J., & Connell, J. P. (1998). Individual differences and the development of perceived control. *Monographs of the Society for Research in Child Development, 63*(2–3, Serial No. 254).

Slack, K. S., & Yoo, J. (2005). Food hardship and child behavior problems among low-income children. *Social Service Review, 79,* 511–536.

Slade, A., Belsky, J., Aber, J. L., & Phelps, J. L. (1999). Mothers' representations of their relationships with their toddlers: Links to adult attachment and observed mothering. *Developmental Psychology, 35,* 611–619.

Slater, A. (2001). Visual perception. In G. Bremner & A. Fogel (Eds.), *Blackwell handbook of infant development* (pp. 5–34). Malden, MA: Blackwell.

Slater, A., Bremner, G., Johnson, S. P., Sherwood, P., Hayes, R., & Brown, E. (2000). Newborn infants' preference for attractive faces: The role of internal and external facial features. *Infancy, 1,* 265–274.

Slater, A., Brown, E., Mattock, A., & Bornstein, M. H. (1996). Continuity and change in habituation in the first 4 months from birth. *Journal of Reproductive and Infant Psychology, 14,* 187–194.

Slater, A., & Johnson, S. P. (1999). Visual sensory and perceptual abilities of the newborn: Beyond the blooming, buzzing confusion. In A. Slater & S. P. Johnson (Eds.), *The development of sensory, motor and cognitive capacities in early infancy* (pp. 121–141). Hove, U.K.: Sussex Press.

Slater, A., & Quinn, P. C. (2001). Face recognition in the newborn infant. *Infant and Child Development, 10,* 21–24.

Sleet, D. A., & Mercy, J. A. (2003). Promotion of safety, security, and well-being. In M. H. Bornstein, L. Davidson, C. M. M. Keyes, K. A. Moore, & the Center for Child Well-Being (Eds.), *Well-being: Positive development across the life course* (pp. 81–97). Mahwah, NJ: Erlbaum.

Sloan, S., Gildea, A., Stewart, M., Sneddon, H., & Iwaniec, D. (2008). Early weaning is related to weight and rate of weight gain in infancy. *Child: Care, Health and Development, 34,* 59–64.

Slobin, D. I. (1985). Cross-linguistic evidence for language-making capacity. In D. I. Slobin (Ed.), *The cross-linguistic study of language acquisition: Vol. 2. Theoretical issues* (pp. 1157–1256). Hillsdale, NJ: Erlbaum.

Slobin, D. I. (1997). On the origin of grammaticalizable notions: Beyond the individual mind. In D. I. Slobin (Ed.), *The cross-linguistic study of language acquisition: Vol. 5* (pp. 265–324). Hillsdale, NJ: Erlbaum.

Slonims, V., & McConachie, H. (2006). Analysis of mother–infant interaction in infants with Down syndrome and typically developing infants. *American Journal of Mental Retardation, 111,* 273–289.

Sluzenski, J., Newcombe, N. S., & Kovacs, S. L. (2006). Binding, relational memory, and recall of naturalistic events: A developmental perspective. *Journal of Experimental Psychology: Learning, Memory, and Cognition, 32,* 89–100.

Small, M. (1998). *Our babies, ourselves.* New York: Anchor.

Smart, J., & Hiscock, H. (2007). Early infant crying and sleeping problems: A pilot study of impact on parental well-being and parent-endorsed strategies for management. *Journal of Paediatrics and Child Health, 43,* 284–290.

Smetana, J. G. (2006). Social-cognitive domain theory: Consistencies and variations in children's moral and social judgments. In M. Killen & J. G. Smetana (Eds.), *Handbook of moral development* (pp. 119–154). Mahwah, NJ: Erlbaum.

Smith, B. H., Barkley, R. A., & Shapiro, C. J. (2006). Attention-deficit/hyperactivity disorder. In E. J. Mash & R. A. Barkley (Eds.), *Treatment of childhood disorders* (3rd ed., pp. 65–136). New York: Guilford.

Smith, C. L., Calkins, S. D., Keane, S. P., Anastopoulos, A. D., & Shelton, T. L. (2004). Predicting stability and change in toddler behavior problems: Contributions of maternal behavior and child gender. *Developmental Psychology, 40*, 29–42.

Smith, J. R., Brooks-Gunn, J., Kohen, D., & McCarton, C. (2001). Transitions on and off AFDC: Implications for parenting and children's cognitive development. *Child Development, 72*, 1512–1533.

Smith, J., & Ross, H. (2007). Training parents to mediate sibling disputes affects children's negotiation and conflict understanding. *Child Development, 78*, 790–805.

Smith, L. B., Jones, S. S., Landau, B., Gershkoff-Stowe, L., & Samuelson, L. (2002). Object name learning provides on-the-job training for attention. *Psychological Science, 13*, 13–19.

Smith, P. K. (2003). Play and peer relations. In A. Slater & G. Bremner (Eds.), *An introduction to developmental psychology* (pp. 311–333). Malden, MA: Blackwell.

Smith, P., Perrin, S., Yule, W., & Rabe-Hesketh, S. (2001). War exposure and maternal reactions in the psychological adjustment of children from Bosnia-Hercegovina. *Journal of Child Psychology and Psychiatry and Allied Disciplines, 42*, 395–404.

Smith, R. (2007). Parturition. *New England Journal of Medicine, 356*, 271–283.

Smith, R., Smith, J. I., Shen, X., Engel, P. J., Bowman, M. E., McGrath, S. A., et al. (2009). Patterns of plasma corticotrophin-releasing hormone, progesterone, estradiol and estriol change and the onset of human labor. *Journal of Clinical Endocrinology and Metabolism, 94*, 2066–2074.

Snell, E. K., Adam, E. K., & Duncan, G. J. (2007). Sleep and the body mass index and overweight status of children and adolescents. *Child Development, 78*, 309–323.

Snidman, N., Kagan, J., Riordan, L., & Shannon, D. C. (1995). Cardiac function and behavioral reactivity. *Psychophysiology, 32*, 199–207.

Snow, C. E., & Beals, D. E. (2006). Mealtime talk that supports literacy development. In R. W. Larson, A. R. Wiley, & K. R. Branscomb (Eds.), *Family mealtime as a context of development and socialization* (pp. 51–66). San Francisco: Jossey-Bass.

Snow, C. E., & Kang, J. Y. (2006). Becoming bilingual, biliterate, and bicultural. In K. A. Renninger & I. E. Sigel (Eds.), *Handbook of child psychology: Vol. 4. Child psychology in practice* (6th ed., pp. 75–102). Hoboken, NJ: Wiley.

Snow, C. E., Pan, B. A., Imbens-Bailey, A., & Herman, J. (1996). Learning how to say what one means: A longitudinal study of children's speech act use. *Social Development, 5*, 56–84.

Snyder, J., Brooker, M., Patrick, M. R., Snyder, A., Schrepferman, L., & Stoolmiller, M. (2003). Observed peer victimization during early elementary school: Continuity, growth, and relation to risk for child antisocial and depressive behavior. *Child Development, 74*, 1881–1898.

Sobel, D. M. (2006). How fantasy benefits young children's understanding of pretense. *Developmental Science, 9*, 63–75.

Society for Research in Child Development. (2007). *SRCD ethical standards for research with children.* Retrieved from www.srcd.org/index.php?option=com_content&task=view&id&Itemid=110

Society of Obstetricians and Gynaecologists. (2008). *Record high caesarean rate raising concerns among Canada's obstetricians.* Retrieved from www.sogcorg/media/pdf/articles/artcaesareanrate080625.pdf

Soderstrom, M., Seidl, A., Nelson, D. G. K., & Jusczyk, P. W. (2003). The prosodic bootstrapping of phrases: Evidence from prelinguistic infants. *Journal of Memory and Language, 49*, 249–267.

Solomon, G. B., & Bredemeier, B. J. L. (1999). Children's moral conceptions of gender stratification in sport. *International Journal of Sport Psychology, 30*, 350–368.

Solomon, G. E. A., & Johnson, S. C. (2000). Conceptual change in the classroom: Teaching young children to understand biological inheritance. *British Journal of Development Psychology, 18*, 81–96.

Sondergaard, C., Henriksen, T. B., Obel, C., & Wisborg, K. (2002). Smoking during pregnancy and infantile colic. *Journal of the American Academy of Child and Adolescent Psychiatry, 41*, 147.

Sonuga-Barke, E. J, Schlotz, W., & Kreppner, J. (2010). Differentiating developmental trajectories for conduct, emotion, and peer problems following early deprivation. *Monographs of the Society for Research in Child Development, 75*(1, Serial No. 295), 102–124.

Sophian, C. (1995). Representation and reasoning in early numerical development: Counting, conservation, and comparisons between sets. *Child Development, 66*, 559–577.

Sosa, R., Kennell, J., Klaus, M., Robertson, S., & Urrutia, J. (1980). The effect of a supportive companion on perinatal problems, length of labor, and mother–infant interaction. *New England Journal of Medicine, 303*, 597–600.

South African Department of Health. (2009). *2008 National Antenatal Sentinel HIV and Syphilis Prevalence Survey.* Retrieved from www.doh.gov.za/docs/nassps-f.html

Sowell, E. R., Thompson, P. M., Welcome, S. E., Henkenius, A. L., Toga, A. W., & Peterson, B. S. (2003). Cortical abnormalities in children and adolescents with attention-deficit hyperactivity disorder. *Lancet, 362*, 1699–1707.

Sowell, E. R., Trauner, D. A., Camst, A., & Jernigan, T. (2002). Development of cortical and subcortical brain structures in childhood and adolescence: A structural MRI study. *Developmental Medicine and Child Neurology, 44*, 4–16.

Spadoni, A. D., McGee, C. L., Fryer, S. L., & Riley, E. P. (2007). Neuroimaging and fetal alcohol spectrum disorders. *Neuroscience and Biobehavioral Reviews, 31*, 239–245.

Spangler, G., Fremmer-Bomik, E., & Grossmann, K. (1996). Social and individual determinants of attachment security and disorganization during the first year. *Infant Mental Health Journal, 17*, 127–139.

Spector, A. Z. (2006). Fatherhood and depression: A review of risks, effects, and clinical application. *Issues in Mental Health Nursing, 27*, 867–883.

Speece, D. L., Ritchey, K. D., Cooper, D. H., Roth, F. P., & Schatschneider, C. (2004). Growth in early reading skills from kindergarten to third grade. *Contemporary Educational Psychology, 29*, 312–332.

Spelke, E. (2000). Core knowledge. *American Psychologist, 55*, 1233–1242.

Spelke, E. S. (2004). Core knowledge. In N. Kanwisher & J. Duncan (Eds.), *Attention and Performance* (Vol. 20, pp. 29–56). Oxford, UK: Oxford University Press.

Spelke, E. S., & Hermer, L. (1996). Early cognitive development: Objects and space. In R. Gelman & T. K. Au (Eds.), *Perceptual and cognitive development* (pp. 71–114). San Diego: Academic Press.

Spelke, E. S., & Kinzler, K. D. (2007). Core knowledge. *Developmental Science, 10*, 89–96.

Spelke, E. S., Phillips, A., & Woodward, A. L. (1995). Infants' knowledge of object motion and human action. In D. Sperber, D. Premack, & A. J. Premack (Eds.), *Causal cognition: A multidisciplinary debate* (pp. 44–78). New York: Oxford University Press.

Spence, M. J., & DeCasper, A. J. (1987). Prenatal experience with low-frequency maternal voice sounds influences neonatal perception of maternal voice samples. *Infant Behavior and Development, 10*, 133–142.

Spencer, J. P., & Perone, S. (2008). Defending qualitative change: The view from dynamical systems theory. *Child Development, 79*, 1639–1647.

Spencer, J. P., & Schöner, G. (2003). Bridging the representational gap in the dynamic systems approach to development. *Developmental Science, 6*, 392–412.

Spencer, J. P., Verejiken, B., Diedrich, F. J., & Thelen, E. (2000). Posture and the emergence of manual skills. *Developmental Science, 3*, 216–233.

Spencer, P. E. (2000). Looking without listening: Is audition a prerequisite for normal development of visual attention in infancy? *Journal of Deaf Studies and Education, 5*, 291–302.

Spencer, P. E., & Lederberg, A. (1997). Different modes, different models: Communication and language of young deaf children and their mothers. In L. B. Adamson & M. Romski (Eds.), *Communication and language acquisition: Discoveries from atypical development* (pp. 203–230). Baltimore: Paul H. Brookes.

Spencer, P. E., & Meadow-Orlans, K. P. (1996). Play, language, and maternal responsiveness: A longitudinal study of deaf and hearing infants. *Child Development, 67*, 3176–3191.

Spere, K. A., Schmidt, L. A., Theall-Honey, L. A., & Martin-Chang, S. (2004). Expressive and receptive language skills of temperamentally shy preschoolers. *Infant and Child Development, 13*, 123–133.

Spitz, R. A. (1946). Anaclitic depression. *Psychoanalytic Study of the Child, 2*, 313–342.

Spock, B., & Needlman, R. (2004). *Dr. Spock's baby and child care* (8th ed.). New York: Pocket.

Sporer, N., Brunstein, J. C., & Kieschke, U. (2009). Improving students' reading comprehension skills: Effects of strategy instruction and reciprocal teaching. *Learning and Instruction, 19*, 272–286.

Spruijt-Metz, D., Lindquist, C. H., Birch, L. L., Fisher, J. O., & Goran, M. I. (2002). Relation between mothers' child-feeding practices and children's adiposity. *American Journal of Clinical Nutrition, 75*, 581–586.

Sridhar, D., & Vaughn, S. (2001). Social functioning of students with learning disabilities. In D. P. Hallahan & B. K. Keogh (Eds.), *Research and global perspectives in learning disabilities* (pp. 65–91). Mahwah, NJ: Erlbaum.

Sroufe, L. A. (2002). From infant attachment to promotion of adolescent autonomy: Prospective, longitudinal data on the role of parents in development. In J. G. Borkowski & S. L. Ramey (Eds.), *Parenting and the child's world* (pp. 187–202). Mahwah, NJ: Erlbaum.

Sroufe, L. A. (2005). Attachment and development: A prospective, longitudinal study from birth to adulthood. *Attachment and Human Development, 7*, 349–367.

Sroufe, L. A., Egeland, B., Carlson, E., & Collins, W. (2005). *Minnesota Study of Risk and Adaptation from birth to maturity: The development of the person.* New York: Guilford.

Sroufe, L. A., & Waters, E. (1976). The ontogenesis of smiling and laughter: A perspective on the organization of development in infancy. *Psychological Review, 83*, 173–189.

Sroufe, L. A., & Wunsch, J. P. (1972). The development of laughter in the first year of life. *Child Development, 43*, 1324–1344.

St James-Roberts, I. (2007). Infant crying and sleeping: Helping parents to prevent and manage problems. *Sleep Medicine Clinics, 2*, 363–375.

St James-Roberts, I., Alvarez, M., Csipke, E., Abramsky, T., Goodwin, J., & Sorgenfrei, E. (2006). Infant crying and sleeping in London, Copenhagen and when parents adopt a "proximal" form of care. *Pediatrics, 117*, e1146–e1155.

Stacey, J., & Biblarz, T. (2001). (How) Does the sexual orientation of parents matter? *American Sociological Review, 66*, 159–183.

Stahl, S. A., & Miller, P. D. (2006). Whole language and language experience approaches for beginning reading: A quantitative research synthesis. In K. A. Dougherty Stahl & M. C. McKenna (Eds.), *Reading research at work: Foundations of effective practice* (pp. 9–35). New York: Guilford.

Stams, G. J. M., Juffer, F., & van IJzendoorn, M. H. (2002). Maternal sensitivity, infant attachment, and temperament in early childhood predict adjustment in middle childhood: The case of adopted children and their biologically unrelated parents. *Developmental Psychology, 38*, 806–821.

Standley, J. M. (1998). The effect of music and multimodal stimulation on responses of premature infants in neonatal intensive care. *Pediatric Nursing, 24*, 532–538.

Stanley, C., Murray, L., & Stein, A. (2004). The effect of postnatal depression on mother–infant interaction, infant response to the still-face perturbation, and performance on an instrumental learning task. *Development and Psychopathology, 16*, 1–18.

Stanovich, K. E. (2007). *How to think straight about psychology* (8th ed.). Boston: Allyn and Bacon.

Staub, F. C., & Stern, E. (2002). The nature of teachers' pedagogical content beliefs matters for students' achievement gains: Quasi-experimental evidence from elementary mathematics. *Journal of Educational Psychology, 94,* 344–355.

Steele, C. M. (1997). A threat in the air: How stereotypes shape intellectual identity and performance. *American Psychologist, 52,* 613–629.

Steele, J. (2003). Children's gender stereotypes about math: The role of stereotype stratification. *Journal of Applied Social Psychology, 33,* 2587–2606.

Steele, S., Joseph, R. M., & Tager-Flusberg, H. (2003). Developmental change in theory of mind abilities in children with autism. *Journal of Austism and Developmental Disorders, 33,* 461–467.

Steenhuis, I. H., & Vermeer, W. M. (2009). Portion size: Review and framework for interventions. *International Journal of Behavioral Nutrition and Physical Activity, 6,* 58.

Stehr-Green, P., Tull, P., Stellfeld, M., Mortenson, P. B., & Simpson, D. (2003). Autism and thimerosal-containing vaccines: Lack of consistent evidence for an association. *American Journal of Preventive Medicine, 25,* 101–106.

Stein, N., & Levine, L. J. (1999). The early emergence of emotional understanding and appraisal: Implications for theories of development. In T. Dalgleish & M. J. Power (Eds.), *Handbook of cognition and emotion* (pp. 383–408). Chichester, U.K.: Wiley.

Stein, Z., Susser, M., Saenger, G., & Marolla, F. (1975). *Famine and human development: The Dutch hunger winter of 1944–1945.* New York: Oxford.

Steinberg, L., Blatt-Eisengart, I., & Cauffman, E. (2006). Patterns of competence and adjustment among adolescents from authoritative, authoritarian, indulgent, and neglectful homes: A replication in a sample of serious juvenile offenders. *Journal of Research on Adolescence, 16,* 47–58.

Steinberg, L., Darling, N. E., & Fletcher, A. C. (1995). Authoritative parenting and adolescent development: An ecological journey. In P. Moen, G. H. Elder, Jr., & K. Luscher (Eds.), *Examining lives in context* (pp. 423–466). Washington, DC: American Psychological Association.

Steinberg, L., & Silk, J. S. (2002). Parenting adolescents. In M. H. Bornstein (Ed.), *Handbook of parenting: Vol. 1. Children and parenting* (pp. 103–134). Mahwah, NJ: Erlbaum.

Steiner, J. E. (1979). Human facial expression in response to taste and smell stimulation. In H. W. Reese & L. P. Lipsitt (Eds.), *Advances in child development and behavior* (Vol. 13, pp. 257–295). New York: Academic Press.

Steiner, J. E., Glaser, D., Hawilo, M. E., & Berridge, D. C. (2001). Comparative expression of hedonic impact: Affective reactions to taste by human infants and other primates. *Neuroscience and Biobehavioral Reviews, 25,* 53–74.

Stenberg, C. R., & Campos, J. J. (1990). The development of anger expressions in infancy. In N. Stein, B. Leventhal, & T. Trabasso (Eds.), *Psychological and biological approaches to emotion* (pp. 247–282). Hillsdale, NJ: Erlbaum.

Stenberg, G. (2003). Effects of maternal inattentiveness on infant social referencing. *Infant and Child Development, 12,* 399–419.

Stephens, B. E., & Vohr, B. R. (2009). Neurodevelopmental outcome of the premature infant. *Pediatric Clinics of North America, 56,* 631–646.

Stern, D. (1985). *The interpersonal world of the infant.* New York: Basic Books.

Stern, M., & Karraker, K. H. (1989). Sex stereotyping of infants: A review of gender labeling studies. *Sex Roles, 20,* 501–522.

Sternberg, R. J. (2001). Beyond g: The theory of successful intelligence. In R. J. Sternberg & E. L. Grigorenko (Eds.), *The general factor of intelligence: How general is it?* (pp. 447–479). Mahwah, NJ: Erlbaum.

Sternberg, R. J. (2003). The development of creativity as a decision-making process. In R. K. Sawyer, V. John-Steiner, S. Moran, R. J. Sternberg, D. H. Feldman, J. Nakamura, & M. Csikszentmihalyi

(Eds.), *Creativity and development* (pp. 91–138). New York: Oxford University Press.

Sternberg, R. J. (2005). The triarchic theory of successful intelligence. In D. P. Flanagan & P. L. Harrison (Eds.), *Contemporary intellectual assessment: Theories, tests, and issues* (pp. 103–119). New York: Guilford.

Sternberg, R. J. (2008). The triarchic theory of successful intelligence. In N. Salkind (Ed.), *Encyclopedia of educational psychology* (Vol. 2, pp. 988–994). Thousand Oaks, CA: Sage.

Sternberg, R. J., Forsythe, G. B., Hedlund, J., Horvath, J. A., Wagner, R. K., Williams, W. M., Snook, S. A., & Grigorenko, E. L. (2000). *Practical intelligence in everyday life.* Cambridge, U.K.: Cambridge University Press.

Sternberg, R. J., & Grigorenko, E. L. (2002). *Dynamic testing.* New York: Cambridge University Press.

Sternberg, R. J., & Jarvin, L. (2003). Alfred Binet's contributions as a paradigm for impact in psychology. In R. J. Sternberg (Ed.), *The anatomy of impact: What makes the great works of psychology great* (pp. 89–107). Washington, DC: American Psychological Association.

Stetsenko, A., Little, T. D., Gordeeva, T., Grasshof, M., & Oettingen, G. (2000). Gender effects in children's beliefs about school performance. *Child Development, 21,* 517–527.

Stevenson, H. W., Lee, S., & Mu, X. (2000). Successful achievement in mathematics: China and the United States. In C. F. M. van Lieshout & P. G. Heymans (Eds.), *Developing talent across the lifespan* (pp. 167–183). Philadelphia: Psychology Press.

Stevenson, R., & Pollitt, C. (1987). The acquisition of temporal terms. *Journal of Child Language, 14,* 533–545.

Stewart, P. W., Lonky, E., Reihman, J., Pagano, J., Gump, B. B., & Darvill, T. (2008). The relationship between prenatal PCB exposure and intelligence (IQ). *Environmental Health Perspectives, 116,* 1416–1422.

Stewart, R. B., Jr. (1990). *The second child: Family transition and adjustment.* Newbury Park, CA: Sage.

Stewart-Brown, S., & Edmunds, L. (2007). Assessing emotional intelligence in children: A review of existing measures of emotional and social competence. In R. Bar-On, M. J. Elias, & J. G. Maree (Eds.), *Educating people to be emotionally intelligent* (pp. 241–257). Westport, CT: Praeger.

Stiles, J. (2001a). Neural plasticity in cognitive development. *Developmental Neuropsychology, 18,* 237–272.

Stiles, J. (2001b). Spatial cognitive development. In C. A. Nelson & M. Luciana (Eds.), *Handbook of developmental cognitive neuroscience* (pp. 399–414). Cambridge, MA: MIT Press.

Stiles, J. (2008). *Fundamentals of brain development.* Cambridge, MA: Harvard University Press.

Stiles, J., Bates, E. A., Thal, D., Trauner, D. A., & Reilly, J. (2002). Linguistic and spatial cognitive development in children with pre- and perinatal focal brain injury: A ten-year overview from the San Diego longitudinal project. In M. H. Johnson & Y. Munakata (Eds.), *Brain development and cognition: A reader* (2nd ed., pp. 272–291). Malden, MA: Blackwell.

Stiles, J., Moses, P., Roe, K., Akshoomoff, N. A., Trauner, D., & Hesselink, J. (2003). Alternative brain organization after prenatal cerebral injury: Convergent fMRI and cognitive data. *Journal of the International Neuropsychological Society, 9,* 604–622.

Stiles, J., Reilly, J., Paul, B., & Moses, P. (2005). Cognitive development following early brain injury: Evidence for neural adaptation. *Trends in Cognitive Sciences, 9,* 136–143.

Stiles, J., Stern, C., Appelbaum, M., & Nass, R. (2008). Effects of early focal brain injury on memory for visuospatial patterns: Selective deficits of global–local processing. *Neuropsychology, 22,* 61–73.

Stilson, S. R., & Harding, C. G. (1997). Early social context as it relates to symbolic play: A longitudinal investigation. *Merrill-Palmer Quarterly, 43,* 682–693.

Stipek, D. (2002). At what age should children enter kindergarten? A question for policy makers and parents. *Social Policy Report of the Society for Research in Child Development, 16*(3).

Stipek, D. (2004). Teaching practices in kindergarten and first grade: Different strokes for different folks. *Early Childhood Research Quarterly, 19,* 548–568.

Stipek, D. J., & Byler, P. (1997). Early childhood education teachers: Do they practice what they preach? *Early Childhood Research Quarterly, 12,* 305–326.

Stipek, D. J., & Byler, P. (2001). Academic achievement and social behaviors associated with age of entry into kindergarten. *Journal of Applied Developmental Psychology, 22,* 175–189.

Stipek, D. J., Feiler, R., Daniels, D., & Milburn, S. (1995). Effects of different instructional approaches on young children's achievement and motivation. *Child Development, 66,* 209–223.

Stipek, D. J., Gralinski, J. H., & Kopp, C. B. (1990). Self-concept development in the toddler years. *Developmental Psychology, 26,* 972–977.

Stoch, M. B., Smythe, P. M., Moodie, A. D., & Bradshaw, D. (1982). Psychosocial outcome and CT findings after growth undernourishment during infancy: A 20-year developmental study. *Developmental Medicine and Child Neurology, 24,* 419–436.

Stocker, C. J., Arch, J. R., & Cawthorne, M. A. (2005). Fetal origins of insulin resistance and obesity. *Proceedings of the Nutrition Society, 64,* 143–151.

Stone, R. (2005). *Best classroom management practices for reaching all learners: What award-winning classroom teachers do.* Thousand Oaks, CA: Corwin Press.

Storch, S. A., & Whitehurst, G. J. (2001). The role of family and home in the literacy development of children from low-income backgrounds. In P. R. Britto & J. Brooks-Gunn (Eds.), *The role of family literacy environments in promoting young children's emerging literacy skills (New directions for child and adolescent development,* No. 92, pp. 53–71). San Francisco: Jossey-Bass.

Storey, A. E., Walsh, C. J., Quinton, R. L., & Wynn-Edwards, K. E. (2000). Hormonal correlates of paternal responsiveness in new and expectant fathers. *Evolution and Human Behavior, 21,* 79–95.

Stormshak, E. A., Bierman, K. L., McMahon, R. J., Lengua, L. J., & the Conduct Problems Prevention Research Group. (2000). Parenting practices and child disruptive behavior problems in early elementary school. *Journal of Clinical Child Psychology, 29,* 17–29.

Story, R. (2007). Asthma and obesity in children. *Current Opinion in Pediatrics, 19,* 680–684.

Strapp, C. M., & Federico, A. (2000). Imitations and repetitions: What do children say following recasts? *First Language, 20,* 273–290.

Straus, M. A., & Stewart, J. H. (1999). Corporal punishment by American parents: National data on prevalence, chronicity, severity, and duration, in relation to child and family characteristics. *Clinical Child and Family Psychology Review, 2,* 55–70.

Strayer, L., & Roberts, W. (2004). Children's anger, emotional expressiveness, and empathy: Relations with parents' empathy, emotional expressiveness, and parenting practices. *Social Development, 13,* 229–254.

Strazdins, L., Clements, M. S., Korda, R. J., Broom, D. H., & D'Souza, R. M. (2006). Unsociable work? Nonstandard work schedules, family relationships, and children's well-being. *Journal of Marriage and the Family, 68,* 394–410.

Streissguth, A. P., Bookstein, F. L., Barr, H. M., Sampson, P. D., O'Malley, K., & Young, J. K. (2004). Risk factors for adverse life outcomes in fetal alcohol syndrome and fetal alcohol effects. *Journal of Developmental and Behavioral Pediatrics, 25,* 228–238.

Streissguth, A. P., Treder, R., Barr, H. M., Shepard, T., Bleyer, W. A., Sampson, P. D., & Martin, D. (1987). Aspirin and acetaminophen use by pregnant women and subsequent child IQ and attention decrements. *Teratology, 35,* 211–219.

Streri, A. (2005). Touching for knowing in infancy: The development of manual abilities in very young infants. *European Journal of Developmental Psychology, 2,* 325–343.

Streri, A., Lhote, M., & Dutilleul, S. (2000). Haptic perception in newborns. *Developmental Science, 3,* 319–327.

Stretesky, P. B., & Lynch, M. J. (2001). The relationship between lead exposure and homicide. *Archives of Pediatrics and Adolescent Medicine, 155,* 579–582.

Striano, T., & Rochat, P. (2000). Emergence of selective social referencing in infancy. *Infancy, 1,* 253–264.

Striano, T., Tomasello, M., & Rochat, P. (2001). Social and object support for early symbolic play. *Developmental Science, 4,* 442–455.

Stright, A. D., Neitzel, C., Sears, K. G., & Hoke-Sinex, L. (2002). Instruction begins in the home: Relations between parental instruction and children's self-regulation in the classroom. *Journal of Educational Psychology, 93,* 456–466.

Strohschein, L. (2005). Parental divorce and child mental health trajectories. *Journal of Marriage and Family, 67,* 1286–1300.

Strohschein, L., Gauthier, A. H., Campbell, R., & Kleparchuk, C. (2008). Parenting as a dynamic process: A test of the resource dilution hypothesis. *Journal of Marriage and Family, 70,* 670–683.

Stromquist, N. P. (2007). Gender equity education globally. In S. S. Klein, B. Richardson, D. A. Grayson, L. H. Fox, & C. Kramarae (Eds.), *Handbook for achieving gender equity through education* (2nd ed., pp. 33–42). Mahwah, NJ: Erlbaum.

Stromswold, K. (2000). The cognitive neuroscience of language acquisition. In M. S. Gazzaniga (Ed.), *The new cognitive neurosciences* (pp. 909–932). Boston: MIT Press.

Stryer, B. K., Tofler, I. R., & Lapchick, R. (1998). A developmental overview of child and youth sports in society. *Child and Adolescent Psychiatric Clinics of North America, 7,* 697–719.

Sturge-Apple, M. L., Davies, P. T., Winter, M. A., Cummings, E. M., & Schermerhorn, A. (2008). Interparental conflict and children's school adjustment: The explanatory role of children's internal representations of interparental and parent–child relationships. *Developmental Psychology, 44,* 1678–1690.

Suárez-Orozco, C., Todorova, I., & Qin, D. B. (2006). The well-being of immigrant adolescents: A longitudinal perspective on risk and protective factors. In F. A. Villarruel & T. Luster (Eds.), *The crisis in youth mental health: Critical issues and effective programs: Vol. 2. Disorders in adolescence* (pp. 53–83). Westport, CT: Praeger.

Subbotsky, E. (2004). Magical thinking in judgments of causation: Can anomalous phenomena affect ontological causal beliefs in children and adults? *British Journal of Developmental Psychology, 22,* 123–152.

Subrahmanyam, K., Gelman, R., & Lafosse, A. (2002). Animate and other separably moveable things. In G. Humphreys (Ed.), *Category-specificity in brain and mind* (pp. 341–371). London: Psychology Press.

Suddendorf, T., Simcock, G., & Nielsen, M. (2007). Visual self-recognition in mirrors and live videos: Evidence for a developmental asynchrony. *Cognitive Development, 22,* 185–196.

Sullivan, M. C., McGrath, M. M. Hawes, K., & Lester, B. M. (2008). Growth trajectories of preterm infants: Birth to 12 years. *Journal of Pediatric Health Care, 22,* 83–93.

Sullivan, M. W., & Lewis, M. (2003). Contextual determinants of anger and other negative expressions in young infants. *Developmental Psychology, 39,* 693–705.

Sullivan, S., & Glanz, J. (2006). *Building effective learning communities: Strategies for leadership, learning, and collaboration.* Thousand Oaks, CA: Corwin Press.

Sullivan, S. A., & Birch, L. L. (1990). Pass the sugar, pass the salt: Experience dictates preference. *Developmental Psychology, 26,* 546–551.

Super, C. M. (1981). Behavioral development in infancy. In R. H. Monroe, R. L. Monroe, & B. B. Whiting (Eds.), *Handbook of cross-cultural human development* (pp. 181–270). New York: Garland.

Supple, A. J., & Small, S. A. (2006). The influence of parental support, knowledge, and authoritative parenting on Hmong and European American adolescent development. *Journal of Family Issues, 27,* 1214–1232.

Survey USA. (2005). *Disciplining a child.* Retrieved from www.surveyusa.com/50StateDisciplineChild0805SortedbyTeacher.htm

Svensson, A. (2000). Computers in school: Socially isolating or a tool to promote collaboration? *Journal of Educational Computing Research, 22,* 437–453.

Svirsky, M. A., Teoh, S. W., & Neuburger, H. (2004). Development of language and speech perception in congenitally profoundly deaf children as a function of age at cochlear implantation. *Audiology and Neuro-Otology, 9,* 224–233.

Sweet, M. A., & Appelbaum, M. L. (2004). Is home visiting an effective strategy? A meta-analytic review of home visiting programs for families with young children. *Child Development, 75,* 1435–1456.

Swingley, D. (2005). Statistical clustering and the contents of the infant vocabulary. *Cognitive Psychology, 50,* 86–132.

Symons, D. K. (2001). A dyad-oriented approach to distress and mother–child relationship outcomes in the first 24 months. *Parenting: Science and Practice, 1,* 101–122.

Szepkouski, G. M., Gauvain, M., & Carberry, M. (1994). The development of planning skills in children with and without mental retardation. *Journal of Applied Developmental Psychology, 15,* 187–206.

Szkrybalo, J., & Ruble, D. N. (1999). "God made me a girl": Sex-category constancy judgments and explanations revisited. *Developmental Psychology, 35,* 392–402.

Szlemko, W. J., Wood, J. W., & Thurman, P. J. (2006). Native Americans and alcohol: Past, present, and future. *Journal of General Psychology, 133,* 435–451.

T

Tabibi, Z., & Pfeffer, K. (2007). Finding a safe place to cross the road: The effect of distractors and the role of attention in children's identification of safe and dangerous road-crossing sites. *Infant and Child Development, 16,* 193–206.

Tacon, A., & Caldera, Y. (2001). Attachment and parental correlates in late adolescent Mexican American women. *Hispanic Journal of Behavioral Sciences, 23,* 71–88.

Tager-Flusberg, H., & Zukowski, A. (2009). Putting words together: Morphology and syntax in the preschool years. In J. B. Gleason & B. Ratner (Ed.), *The development of language* (7th ed., pp. 139–191). Boston: Allyn and Bacon.

Takahashi, K. (1990). Are the key assumptions of the "Strange Situation" procedure universal? A view from Japanese research. *Human Development, 33,* 23–30.

Takala, M. (2006). The effects of reciprocal teaching on reading comprehension in mainstream and special (SLI) education. *Scandinavian Journal of Educational Research, 50,* 559–576.

Tamis-LeMonda, C. S., & Bornstein, M. H. (1989). Habituation and maternal encouragement of attention in infancy as predictors of toddler language, play, and representational competence. *Child Development, 60,* 738–751.

Tamis-LeMonda, C. S., Shannon, J. D., Cabrera, N. J., & Lamb, M. E. (2004). Fathers and mothers at play with their 2- and 3-year-olds : Contributions to language and cognitive development. *Child Development, 75,* 1806–1820.

Tamis-LeMonda, C. S., Way, N., Hughes, D., Yoshikawa, H., Kalman, R. K., & Niwa, E. Y. (2008). Parents' goals for children: The dynamic coexistence of individualism and collectivism in cultures and individuals. *Social Development, 17,* 183–209.

Tammelin, T., Näyhä, S., Hills, A. P., & Järvelin, M. (2003). Adolescent participation in sports and adult physical activity. *American Journal of Preventive Medicine, 24,* 22–28.

Tamminen, K. (1991). *Religious development in childhood and youth.* Helsinki, Finland: Gummerus Kirjapaino Oy.

Tamrouti-Makkink, I. D., Dubas, J. S., Gerris, J. R. M., & van Aken, A. G. (2004). The relation between the absolute level of parenting and differential parental treatment with adolescent siblings' adjustment. *Journal of Child Psychology and Psychiatry, 45,* 1397–1406.

Tangney, J. P., Stuewig, J., & Mashek, D. J. (2007). Moral emotions and moral behavior. *Annual Review of Psychology, 58,* 345–372.

Tanimura, M., Takahashi, K., Kataoka, N., Tomita, K., Tanabe, I., Yasuda, M., et al. (2004). Proposal: Heavy television and video viewing poses a risk for infants and young children. *Nippon Shonika Gakkai Zasshi, 108,* 709–712 (in Japanese).

Tanner, J. M., Healy, M., & Cameron, N. (2001*).* *Assessment of skeletal maturity and prediction of adult height* (3rd ed.). Philadelphia: Saunders.

Tardif, T. (2006). But are they really verbs? Chinese words for action. In K. Hirsh-Pasek & R. M. Golinkoff (Eds.), *Action meets word: How children learn verbs* (pp. 477–498). New York: Oxford University Press.

Tardif, T., Fletcher, P., Liang, W., Zhang, Z., Kaciroti, N., & Marchman, V. A. (2008). Baby's first 10 words. *Developmental Psychology, 44,* 929–938.

Tardif, T., Gelman, S. A., & Xu, F. (1999). Putting the "noun bias" in context: A comparison of English and Mandarin. *Child Development, 70,* 620–635.

Tardif, T., Wellman, H. M., & Cheung, K. M. (2004). False belief understanding in Cantonese-speaking children. *Journal of Child Language, 31,* 779–800.

Tarren-Sweeney, M. (2006). Patterns of aberrant eating among preadolescent children in foster care. *Journal of Abnormal Child Psychology, 34,* 623–634.

Tarullo, A. R., & Gunnar, M. R. (2006). Child maltreatment and the developing HPA axis. *Hormones and Behavior, 50,* 632–639.

Tasker, F. (2005). Lesbian mothers, gay fathers, and their children: A review. *Developmental and Behavioral Pediatrics, 26,* 224–240.

Taumoepeau, M., & Ruffman, T. (2006). Mother and infant talk about mental states relates to desire language and emotion understanding. *Child Development, 77,* 465–481.

Taylor, C. A., Manganello, J. A., Lee, S. J., & Rice, J. C. (2010). Mothers' spanking of 3-year-old children and subsequent risk of children's aggressive behavior. *Pediatrics, 125,* e1057–e1065.

Taylor, E. (2004). ADHD is best understood as a cultural construct. *British Journal of Psychiatry, 184,* 8–9.

Taylor, J. S. (2002*).* Caregiver support for women during childbirth: Does the presence of a labor-support person affect maternal–child outcomes? *American Family Physician, 66,* 1205–1206.

Taylor, M., & Carlson, S. M. (1997). The relation between individual differences in fantasy and theory of mind. *Child Development, 68,* 436–455.

Taylor, M., & Carlson, S. M. (2000). The influence of religious beliefs on parental attitudes about children's fantasy behavior. In K. S. Rosengren, C. N. Johnson, & P. L. Harris (Eds.), *Imagining the impossible* (pp. 247–268). New York: Cambridge University Press.

Taylor, M., Carlson, S. M., Maring, B. L., Gerow, L., & Charley, C. M. (2004). The characteristics and correlates of fantasy in school-age children: Imaginary companions, impersonation, and social understanding. *Developmental Psychology, 40,* 1173–1187.

Taylor, M., Esbensen, B. M., & Bennett, R. T. (1994). Children's understanding of knowledge acquisition: The tendency for children to report that they have always known what they have just learned. *Child Development, 65,* 1581–1604.

Taylor, M. C., & Hall, J. A. (1982). Psychological androgyny: Theories, methods, and conclusions. *Psychological Bulletin, 92,* 347–366.

Taylor, M. G. (1996). The development of children's beliefs about the social and biological aspects of gender differences. *Child Development, 67,* 1555–1571.

Taylor, R. L. (2000). Diversity within African-American families. In D. H. Demo & K. R. Allen (Eds.), *Handbook of family diversity* (pp. 232–251). New York: Oxford University Press.

Teicher, M. H., Dumont, N. L., Ito, Y., Vaituzis, C., Giedd, J., & Andersen, S. L. (2004). Childhood neglect is associated with reduced corpus callosum area. *Biological Psychiatry, 56,* 80–85.

Tellings, A. (1999). Psychoanalytical and genetic-structuralistic approaches of moral development: Incompatible views? *Psychoanalytic Review, 86,* 903–914.

Temple, J. A., & Reynolds, A. J. (2006). Economic returns of investments in preschool education. In E. Zigler & S. Jones (Eds.), *A vision for universal prekindergarten* (pp. 37–68). New York: Cambridge University Press.

Temple, J. L., Giacomelli, A. M., Roemmich, J. N., & Epstein, L. H. (2007). Overweight children habituate slower than nonoverweight children to food. *Physiology and Behavior, 9,* 250–254.

ten Tusscher, G. W., & Koppe, J. G. (2004). Perinatal dioxin exposure and later effects—A review. *Chemosphere, 54,* 1329–1336.

Tenenbaum, H. R., & Leaper, C. (2002). Are parents' gender schemas related to their children's gender-related cognitions? A meta-analysis. *Developmental Psychology, 38,* 615–630.

Tenenbaum, H. R., & Leaper, C. (2003). Parent–child conversations about science: The socialization of gender inequities? *Developmental Psychology, 39,* 34–57.

Tenenbaum, H. R., Snow, C. E., Roach, K. A., & Kurland, B. (2005). Talking and reading science: Longitudinal data on sex differences in mother–child conversations in low-income families. *Journal of Applied Developmental Psychology, 26,* 1–19.

Terwel, J., Gillies, R. M., van den Eeden, P., & Hoek, D. (2001). Cooperative learning processes of students: A longitudinal multilevel perspective. *British Journal of Educational Psychology, 71,* 619–645.

Tessier, R., Cristo, M., Velez, S., Giron, M., Nadeau, L., & Figueroa, Z. (2003). Kangaroo mother care: A method of protecting high-risk premature infants against developmental delay. *Infant Behavior and Development, 26,* 384–397.

Teti, D. M., Gelfand, D. M., Messinger, D. S., & Isabella, R. (1995). Maternal depression and the quality of early attachment: An examination of infants, preschoolers, and their mothers. *Developmental Psychology, 31,* 364–376.

Teyber, E. (2001). *Helping children cope with divorce* (rev. ed.). San Francisco: Jossey-Bass.

Thacker, S. B., & Stroup, D. F. (2003). Revisiting the use of the electronic fetal monitor. *Lancet, 361,* 445–446.

Tharpe, A. M., & Ashmead, D. H. (2001). A longitudinal investigation of infant auditory sensitivity. *American Journal of Audiology, 10,* 104–112.

Thatcher, R. W., Walker, R. A., & Giudice, S. (1987). Human cerebral hemispheres develop at different rates and ages. *Science, 236,* 1110–1113.

Theil, S. (2006, September 4). Beyond babies. *Newsweek: International Edition.* Retrieved from www.msnbc.msn.com/id/14535863/site/newsweek

Thelen, E. (1989). The (re)discovery of motor development: Learning new things from an old field. *Developmental Psychology, 25,* 946–949.

Thelen, E., & Adolph, K. E. (1992). Arnold Gesell: The paradox of nature and nurture. *Developmental Psychology, 28,* 368–380.

Thelen, E., & Corbetta, D. (2002). Microdevelopment and dynamic systems: Applications to infant motor development. In N. Granott & J. Parziale (Eds.), *Microdevelopment: Transition processes in development and learning* (pp. 59–79). New York: Cambridge University Press.

Thelen, E., Fisher, D. M., & Ridley-Johnson, R. (1984). The relationship between physical growth and a newborn reflex. *Infant Behavior and Development, 7,* 479–493.

Thelen, E., Schöner, G., Scheier, C., & Smith, L. B. (2001). The dynamics of embodiment: A field theory of infant perseverative reaching. *Behavioral and Brain Sciences, 24,* 1–34.

Thelen, E., & Smith, L. B. (1994). *A dynamic systems approach to the development of cognition and action.* Cambridge, MA: Cambridge University Press.

Thelen, E., & Smith, L. B. (2006). Dynamic systems theories. In R. M. Lerner (Ed.), *Handbook of child psychology: Vol. 1. Theoretical models of human development* (6th ed., pp. 258–312). Hoboken, NJ: Wiley.

Théoret, H., Halligan, E., Kobayashi, M., Fregni, F., Tager-Flusberg, H., & Pascual-Leone, A. (2005). Impaired motor facilitation during action observation in individuals with autism spectrum disorder, *Current Biology, 15,* R84–R85.

Thiedke, C. C. (2001). Sleep disorders and sleep problems in childhood. *American Family Physician, 63,* 277–284.

Thiedke, C. C. (2003). Nocturnal enuresis. *American Family Physician, 67,* 1499–1506.

Thiessen, E.D., & Saffran, J. R. (2007). Learning to learn: Infants' acquisition of stress-based strategies for word segmentation. *Language Learning and Development, 3,* 75–102.

Thomaes, S., Stegge, H., & Olthof, T. (2007). Externalizing shame responses in children: The role of fragile-positive self-esteem. *British Journal of Developmental Psychology, 25,* 559–577.

Thoman, E., & Ingersoll, E. W. (1993). Learning in premature infants. *Developmental Psychology, 29,* 692–700.

Thomas, A., & Chess, S. (1977). *Temperament and development.* New York: Brunner/Mazel.

Thomas, A., Chess, S., & Birch, H. G. (1968). *Temperament and behavior disorders in children.* New York: New York University Press.

Thomas, K. A., & Tessler, R. C. (2007). Bicultural socialization among adoptive families: Where there is a will, there is a way. *Journal of Family Issues, 28,* 1189–1219.

Thomas, R. M. (2005). *Comparing theories of child development* (6th ed.). New York: New York University Press.

Thompson, A., Hollis, C., & Richards, D. (2003). Authoritarian parenting attitudes as a risk for conduct problems: Results of a British national cohort study. *European Child and Adolescent Psychiatry, 12,* 84–91.

Thompson, L. A., Goodman, D. C., & Little, G. A. (2002). Is more neonatal intensive care always better? Insights from a cross-national comparison of reproductive care. *Pediatrics, 109,* 1036–1043.

Thompson, P. M., Giedd, J. N., Woods, R. P., MacDonald, D., Evans, A. C., & Toga, A. W. (2000). Growth patterns in the developing brain detected by using continuum mechanical tensor maps. *Nature, 404,* 190–192.

Thompson, R. A. (1990). Vulnerability in research: A developmental perspective on research risk. *Child Development, 61,* 1–16.

Thompson, R. A. (2000). The legacy of early attachments. *Child Development, 71,* 145–152.

Thompson, R. A. (2006). The development of the person: Social understanding, relationships, conscience, self. In N. Eisenberg (Ed.), *Handbook of child psychology: Vol. 3. Social, emotional, and personality development* (6th ed., pp. 24–98). Hoboken, NJ: Wiley.

Thompson, R. A. (2009). Early foundations: Conscience and the development of moral character. In D. Narvaez & D. K. Lapsley (Eds.), *Personality, identity, and character: Explorations in moral psychology* (pp. 159–184). New York: Cambridge University Press.

Thompson, R. A., Easterbrooks, M. A., & Padilla-Walker, L. M. (2003). Social and emotional development in infancy. In R. M. Lerner & M. A. Easterbrooks (Eds.), *Social and emotional development in infancy* (pp. 91–112). New York: Wiley.

Thompson, R. A., & Goodvin, R. (2007). Taming the tempest in the teapot. In C. A. Brownell & C. B. Kopp (Eds.), *Socioemotional development in the toddler years: Transitions and transformations* (pp. 320–341). New York: Guilford.

Thompson, R. A., & Meyer, S. (2007). Socialization of emotion regulation in the family. In J. J. Gross (Ed.), *Handbook of emotion regulation* (pp. 249–268). New York: Guilford.

Thompson, R. A., Meyer, S., & McGinley, M. (2006). Understanding values in relationships: The development of conscience. In M. Killen & J. G. Smetana (Eds.), *Handbook of moral development* (pp. 267–298). Mahwah, NJ: Erlbaum.

Thompson, R. A., & Nelson, C. A. (2001). Developmental science and the media. *American Psychologist, 56,* 5–15.

Thompson, R. A., & Raikes, H. A. (2007). The social and emotional foundations of school readiness. In D. F. Perry, R. K. Kaufmann, & J. Knitzer (Eds.), *Social and emotional health in early childhood: Building bridges between services and systems* (pp. 13–35). Baltimore, MD: Paul H. Brookes.

Thompson, W. W., Price, C., Goodson, B., Shay, D. K., Benson, P., Hinrichsen, V. L., et al. (2007). Early thimerosal exposure and neuropsychological outcomes at 7 to 10 years. *New England Journal of Medicine, 357,* 1281–1292.

Thornton, S. (1999). Creating conditions for cognitive change: The interaction between task structures and specific strategies. *Child Development, 70,* 588–603.

Thorpy, M. J., & Yager, J. (2001). *Encyclopedia of sleep and sleep disorders.* New York: Facts on File.

Tienari, P., Wahlberg, K. E., & Wynne, L. C. (2006). Finnish adoption study of schizophrenia: Implications for family interventions. *Families, Systems, and Health, 24,* 442–451.

Tienari, P., Wynne, L. C., Laksy, K., Moring, J., Nieminen, P., Sorri, A., et al. (2003). Genetic boundaries of the schizophrenia spectrum: Evidence from the Finnish adoptive family study of schizophrenia. *The American Journal of Psychiatry, 160,* 1587–1594.

Tiggemann, M., & Anesbury, T. (2000). Negative stereotyping of obesity in children: The role of controllability beliefs. *Journal of Applied Social Psychology, 30,* 1977–1993.

Tincoff, R., & Jusczyk, P. W. (1999). Some beginnings of word comprehension in 6-month-olds. *Psychological Science, 10,* 172–175.

Tinsley, B. J. (2003). *How children learn to be healthy.* Cambridge, U.K.: Cambridge University Press.

Tizard, B., & Rees, J. (1975). The effect of early institutional rearing on the behaviour problems and affectional relationships of four-year-old children. *Journal of Child Psychology and Psychiatry, 16,* 61–73.

Tofler, I. R., Knapp, P. K., & Drell, M. J. (1998). The achievement by proxy spectrum in youth sports: Historical perspective and clinical approach to pressured and high-achieving children and adolescents. *Child and Adolescent Psychiatric Clinics of North America, 7,* 803–820.

Tokunaga, R. S. (2010). Following you home from school: A critical review and synthesis of research on cyberbullying victimization. *Computers in Human Behavior, 26,* 277–287.

Tomasello, M. (1992). *First verbs: A case study of early grammatical development.* New York: Cambridge University Press.

Tomasello, M. (1999). Having intentions, understanding intentions, and understanding communicative intentions. In P. D. Zelazo, J. W. Astington, & J. Wilde (Eds.), *Developing theories of intention: Social understanding and self-control* (pp. 63–75). Mahwah, NJ: Erlbaum.

Tomasello, M. (2000). Do young children have adult syntactic competence? *Cognition, 74,* 209–253.

Tomasello, M. (2003). *Constructing a language: A usage-based theory of language acquisition.* Cambridge, MA: Harvard University Press.

Tomasello, M. (2005). Beyond formalities: The case of language acquisition. *Linguistic Review, 22,* 183–197.

Tomasello, M. (2006). Acquiring linguistic constructions. In D. Kuhn & R. Siegler (Eds.), *Handbook of child psychology: Vol. 2: Cognition, perception, and language* (6th ed., pp. 255–298). Hoboken, NJ: Wiley.

Tomasello, M., & Akhtar, N. (1995). Two-year-olds use pragmatic cues to differentiate reference to objects and actions. *Cognitive Development, 10,* 201–224.

Tomasello, M., Akhtar, N., Dodson, K., & Rekau, L. (1997). Differential productivity in young children's use of nouns and verbs. *Journal of Child Language, 24,* 373–387.

Tomasello, M., & Brandt, S. (2009). Flexibility in the semantics and syntax of children's early verb use.

Monographs of the Society for Research in Child Development, 74(2, Serial No. 293), 113–126.

Tomasello, M., Call, J., & Hare, B. (2003). Chimpanzees understand psychological states—the question is which ones and to what extent. *Trends in Cognitive Sciences, 7,* 153–156.

Tomasello, M., Carpenter, M., & Liszkowski, U. (2007). A new look at infant pointing. *Child Development, 78,* 705–722.

Tong, S., Baghurst, P., Vimpani, G., & McMichael, A. (2007). Socioeconomic position, maternal IQ, home environment, and cognitive development. *Journal of Pediatrics, 151,* 284–288.

Tong, S., McMichael, A. J., & Baghurst, P. A. (2000). Interactions between environmental lead exposure and sociodemographic factors on cognitive development. *Archives of Environmental Health, 55,* 330–335.

Tong, V. T., Jones, J. R., Dietz, P. M., D'Angelo, D., & Bombard, J. M. (2009, May 29). Trends in smoking before, during, and after pregnancy—Pregnancy Risk Assessment Monitoring System (PRAMS), United States, 31 Sites, 2000–2005. *Morbidity and Mortality Weekly Report, 58* (No. SS-4).

Toomela, A. (1999). Drawing development: Stages in the representation of a cube and a cylinder. *Child Development, 70,* 1141–1150.

Toomela, A. (2002). Drawing as a verbally mediated activity: A study of relationships between verbal, motor, visuospatial skills and drawing in children. *International Journal of Behavioral Development, 26,* 234–247.

Torrance, E. P. (1988). The nature of creativity as manifest in its testing. In R. J. Sternberg (Ed.), *The nature of creativity: Contemporary psychological perspectives* (pp. 43–75). New York: Cambridge University Press.

Tottenham, N., Hare, T. A., & Casey, B. J. (2009). A developmental perspective on human amygdala function. In P. J. Whalen & E. A. Phelps (Eds.), *The human amygdala* (pp. 107–117). New York: Guilford Press.

Tough, S., Tofflemire, K., Benzies, K., Fraser-Lee, N., & Newburn-Cook, C. (2007). Factors influencing childbearing decisions and knowledge of preinatal risks among Canadian men and women. *Maternal and Child Health Journal, 11,* 189–198.

Townsend, D. A., & Rovee-Collier, C. (2007). *The transitivity of 6-month-olds' preconditioned memories in deferred imitation.* Paper presented at the annual meeting of the Eastern Psychological Association, Philadelphia.

Toyamo, N. (2000). "What are food and air like inside our bodies?" Children's thinking about digestion and respiration. *International Journal of Behavioral Development, 24,* 222–230.

Tracy, J. L., Robins, R. W., & Lagattuta, K. H. (2005). Can children recognize pride? *Emotion, 5,* 251–257.

Traurig, M., Mack, J., Hanson, R. L., Ghoussaini, M., Meyre, D., Knowler, W., et al. (2009). Common variation in SIM1 is reproducibly associated with BMI in Pima Indians. *Diabetes, 58,* 1682–1689.

Trautner, H. M., Gervai, J., & Nemeth, R. (2003). Appearance–reality distinction and development of gender constancy understanding in children. *International Journal of Behavioral Development, 27,* 275–283.

Trautner, H. M., Ruble, D. N., Cyphers, L., Kirsten, B., Behrendt, R., & Hartman, P. (2005). Rigidity and flexibility of gender stereotypes in childhood: Developmental or differential? *Infant and Child Development, 14,* 365–381.

Trautwein, U., Ludtke, O., Marsh, H. W., Koller, O., & Baumert, J. (2006). Tracking, grading, and student motivation: Using group composition and status to predict self-concept and interest in ninth-grade mathematics. *Journal of Educational Psychology, 98,* 788–806.

Trehub, S. E. (2001). Musical predispositions in infancy. *Annals of the New York Academy of Sciences, 930,* 1–16.

Tremblay, R. E. (2000). The development of aggressive behavior during childhood: What have we learned in

the past century? *International Journal of Behavioral Development, 24,* 129–141.

Tremblay, R. E. (2004). Decade of Behavior Distinguished Lecture: Development of physical aggression during infancy. *Infant Mental Health Journal, 25,* 399–407.

Tremblay, R. E., Japel, C., Perusse, D., Voivin, M., Zoccolillo, M., Montplaisir, J., & McDuff, P. (1999). The search for the age of "onset" of physical aggression: Rousseau and Bandura revisited. *Criminal Behavior and Mental Health, 9,* 8–23.

Trent, K., & Harlan, S. L. (1994). Teenage mothers in nuclear and extended households. *Journal of Family Issues, 15,* 309–337.

Trentacosta, C. J., & Shaw, D. S. (2009). Emotional self-regulation, peer rejection, and antisocial behavior: Developmental associations from early childhood to early adolescence. *Journal of Applied Developmental Psychology, 30,* 356–365.

Trevarthen, C. (2003). Infant psychology is an evolving culture. *Human Development, 46,* 233–246.

Triandis, H. C. (1995). *Individualism and collectivism.* Boulder, CO: Westview Press.

Triandis, H. C. (2005). Issues in individualism and collectivism research. In R. M. Sorrentino, D. Cohen, J. M. Olson, & M. P. Zanna (Eds.), *Culture and social behavior: The Ontario Symposium* (Vol. 10, pp. 207–225). Mahwah, NJ: Erlbaum.

Triandis, H. C. (2007). Culture and psychology: A history of their relationship. In S. Kitahama (Ed.), *Handbook of cultural psychology* (pp. 59–76). New York: Guilford Press.

Trickett, P. K., & Putnam, F. W. (1998). Developmental consequences of child sexual abuse. In P. K. Trickett & C. J. Schellenbach (Eds.), *Violence against children in the family and community* (pp. 39–56). Washington, DC: American Psychological Association.

Trocmé, N., & Wolfe, D. (2002). *Child maltreatment in Canada: The Canadian Incidence Study of Reported Child Abuse and Neglect.* Retrieved from http://www.hcsc.gc.ca/pphb-dgspsp/cm-vee

Troiano, R. P., Berrigan, D., Dodd, K. W., Mâsse, L. C., Tillert, T., & McDowell, M. (2007). Physical activity in the United States measured by accelerometer. *Medicine and Science in Sports and Exercise, 40,* 181–188.

Tronick, E. Z., Morelli, G., & Ivey, P. (1992). The Efe forager infant and toddler's pattern of social relationships: Multiple and simultaneous. *Developmental Psychology, 28,* 568–577.

Tronick, E. Z., Thomas, R. B., & Daltabuit, M. (1994). The Quechua manta pouch: A caretaking practice for buffering the Peruvian infant against the multiple stressors of high altitude. *Child Development, 65,* 1005–1013.

Troop-Gordon, W., & Asher, S. R. (2005). Modifications in children's goals when encountering obstacles to conflict resolution. *Child Development, 76,* 568–582.

Tropp, L. R., & Pettigrew, T. F. (2005). Relationships between intergroup contact and prejudice among minority and majority status groups. *Psychological Science, 16,* 951–957.

Troseth, G. L. (2003). Getting a clear picture: Young children's understanding of a televised image. *Developmental Science, 6,* 247–253.

Troseth, G. L., & DeLoache, J. S. (1998). The medium can obscure the message: Young children's understanding of video. *Child Development, 69,* 950–965.

Troseth, G. L., Saylor, M. M., & Archer, A. H. (2006). Young children's use of video as a source of socially relevant information. *Child Development, 77,* 786–799.

True, M. M., Pisani, L., & Oumar, F. (2001). Infant–mother attachment among the Dogon of Mali. *Child Development, 72,* 1451–1466.

Trzesniewski, K. H., Donnellan, M. B., & Robins, R. W. (2003). Stability of self-esteem across the life span. *Journal of Personality and Social Psychology, 84,* 205–220.

Tsujimoto, S. (2008). The prefrontal cortex: Functional neural development during early childhood. *Neuroscientist, 14,* 345–358.

Tuchfarber, B. S., Zins, J. E., & Jason, L. A. (1997). Prevention and control of injuries. In R. Weissberg, T. P. Gullotta, R. L. Hampton, B. A. Ryan, & G. R. Adams (Eds.), *Enhancing children's wellness* (pp. 250–277). Thousand Oaks, CA: Sage.

Tucker, C. J., McHale, S. M., & Crouter, A. C. (2001). Conditions of sibling support in adolescence. *Journal of Family Psychology, 15,* 254–271.

Tudge, J. R. H. (1992). Processes and consequences of peer collaboration: A Vygotskian analysis. *Child Development, 63,* 1364–1397.

Tudge, J. R. H., Hogan, D. M., Snezhkova, I. A., Kulakova, N. N., & Etz, K. E. (2000). Parents' child-rearing values and beliefs in the United States and Russia: The impact of culture and social class. *Infant and Child Development, 9,* 105–121.

Turati, C., Cassia, V. M., Simion, F., & Leo, I. (2006). Newborns' face recognition: Role of inner and outer facial features. *Child Development, 77,* 297–311.

Turiel, E. (2006). The development of morality. In N. Eisenberg (Ed.), *Handbook of child psychology: Vol. 3. Social, emotional, and personality development* (6th ed., pp. 789–857). Hoboken, NJ: Wiley.

Turiel, E., & Killen, M. (2010). Taking emotions seriously: The role of emotions in moral development. In W. F. Arsenio & E. A. Lemerise (Eds.), *Emotions, aggression, and morality in children: Bridging development and psychopathology* (pp. 33–52). Washington, DC: American Psychological Association.

Turkheimer, E., Haley, A., Waldron, M., D'Onofrio, B., & Gottesman, I. I. (2003). Socioeconomic status modifies heritability of IQ in young children. *Psychological Science, 14,* 623–628.

Turnbull, K. P., Anthony, A. B., Justice, L., & Bowles, R. (2009). Preschoolers' exposure to language stimulation in classrooms serving at-risk children: The contribution of group size and activity context. *Early Education and Development, 20,* 53–79.

Turnbull, M., Hart, D., & Lapkin, S. (2003). Grade 6 French immersion students' performance on large-scale reading, writing, and mathematics tests: Building explanations. *Alberta Journal of Educational Research, 49,* 6–23.

Turner, P. J., & Gervai, J. (1995). A multidimensional study of gender typing in preschool children and their parents: Personality, attitudes, preferences, behavior, and cultural differences. *Developmental Psychology, 31,* 759–772.

Turner, R. N., Hewstone, M., & Voci, A. (2007). Reducing explicit and implicit outgroup prejudice via direct and extended contact: The mediating role of self-disclosure and intergroup anxiety. *Journal of Personality and Social Psychology, 93,* 369–388.

Tuyen, J. M., & Bisgard, K. (2003). *Community setting: Pertussis outbreak.* Atlanta, GA: U.S. Centers for Disease Control and Prevention. Retrieved from www.cdc.gov/nip/publications/pertussis/chapter10.pdf

Twenge, J. M., & Campbell, W. K. (2001). Age and birth cohort differences in self-esteem : A cross-temporal meta-analysis. *Personality and Social Psychology Review, 5,* 321–344.

Twenge, J. M., & Crocker, J. (2002). Race and self-esteem: Meta-analyses comparing whites, blacks, Hispanics, Asians, and American Indians and comment on Gray-Little and Hafdahl (2000*). Psychological Bulletin, 128,* 371–408.

Twyman, K., Saylor, C., Taylor, L. A., & Comeaux, C. (2010). Comparing children and adolescents engaged in cyberbullying to matched peers. *Cyberpsychology, Behavior, and Social Networking, 13,* 195–199.

Tzuriel, D. (2001). *Dynamic assessment of young children.* New York: Kluwer Academic.

Tzuriel, D., & Kaufman, R. (1999). Mediated learning and cognitive modifiability: Dynamic assessment of young Ethiopian immigrant children to Israel. *Journal of Cross-Cultural Psychology, 30,* 359–380.

U

Uauy, R., Kain, J., Mericq, V., Rojas, J., & Corvalán, C. (2008). Nutrition, child growth, and chronic disease prevention. *Annals of Medicine, 40,* 11–20.

Ukrainetz, T. A., Justice, L. M., Kaderavek, J. N., Eisenberg, S. L., Gillam, R., & Harm, H. M. (2005). The development of expressive elaboration in fictional narratives. *Journal of Speech, Language, and Hearing Research, 48,* 1363–1377.

Ullrich-French, S., & Smith, A. L. (2006). Perceptions of relationships with parents and peers in youth sport: Independent and combined prediction of motivational outcomes. *Psychology of Sport and Exercise, 7,* 193–214.

Underwood, M. K. (2003). *Social aggression in girls.* New York: Guilford.

UNICEF (United Nations Children's Fund). (2006). *Immunization summary 2006.* Geneva, Switzerland: World Health Organization.

UNICEF (United Nations Children's Fund). (2007). *An overview of child well-being in rich countries, Innocenti Report Card 7.* Florence, Italy: UNICEF Innocenti Research Centre.

UNICEF (United Nations Children's Fund). (2008). *Immunization summary: A statistical reference containing data through 2006.* Geneva, Switzerland: World Health Organization.

UNICEF (United Nations Children's Fund). (2009a). *All children everywhere: A strategy for basic education and gender equality.* New York: Author.

UNICEF (United Nations Children's Fund). (2009b). *Children and AIDS: Fourth stocktaking report, 2009.* New York: United Nations.

UNICEF (United Nations Children's Fund). (2010). *Young champions for education: A progress review.* Retrieved from www.ungei.org/resources/1612_2341.html

United Nations. (2006). *World population prospects: The 2006 revision. Population database.* Retrieved from esa.un.org/unpp/index.asp?panel=2

U.S. Census Bureau. (2010a). *International data base.* Retrieved from www.census.gov/ipc/www/idb

U.S. Census Bureau. (2010b). *Statistical abstract of the United States* (129th ed.). Washington, DC: U.S. Government Printing Office.

U.S. Centers for Disease Control. (2009). Breastfeeding Report Card, United States: Outcome indicators. Retrieved from www.cdc .gov/breastfeeding/data/report_card2.htm

U.S. Department of Agriculture. (2009). Frequently asked questions about WIC. Retrieved from www .fns.usda.gov/wic/FAQs/faq.htm#3

U.S. Department of Education. (2006). *Calories in, calories, out: Food and exercise in public elementary schools, 2005.* Retrieved from nces.ed.gov /Pubs2006/nutrition

U.S. Department of Education. (2008). *The condition of education.* Retrieved from nces.ed.gov/programs /coe/list/i4.asp

U.S. Department of Education. (2009). *Digest of education statistics, 2008.* Washington, DC. U.S. Government Printing Office.

U.S. Department of Education. (2010). *Digest of education statistics, 2009.* Washington, DC: U.S. Government Printing Office.

U.S. Department of Health and Human Services. (2007a). *Prenatal care.* Retrieved from wwww.cdc .gov/nchs/fastats/prenatal.htm

U.S. Department of Health and Human Services. (2007b). *The Surgeon General's call to action to prevent and decrease overweight and obesity: Overweight children and adolescents.* Retrieved from www.surgeongeneral.gov/topics/obesity/calltoaction/fact_adolescents.htm

U.S. Department of Health and Human Services. (2007c, April). Trends in oral health status: United States, 1988–1994 and 1999–2004. *Vital and Health Statistics, 11*(No. 248).

U.S. Department of Health and Human Services. (2008a). CDC childhood injury report: Patterns of unintentional injuries among 0–19 year olds in the United States, 2000–2006. Atlanta, GA: National Center for Injury Control and Prevention.

U.S. Department of Health and Human Services. (2008b). *Child maltreatment 2006.* Retrieved from www.acf.hhs.gov/programs/cb/pubs/cm06/index .htm

U.S. Department of Health and Human Services. (2009a). *Benefits of breastfeeding.* Retrieved from www.womenshealth.gov/breastfeeding/benefits

U.S. Department of Health and Human Services. (2009b, January 7). Births: Final data for 2006. *National Vital Statistics Report, 57*(7).

U.S. Department of Health and Human Services. (2009c). *Child maltreatment 2007: Summary of key findings.* Retrieved from www.childwelfare.gov/pubs/factsheets/canstats.pdf

U.S. Department of Health and Human Services. (2009d). *Down syndrome.* Retrieved from www.cdc .gov/ncbddd/birthdefects/DownSyndrome.htm

U.S. Department of Health and Human Services. (2009e). *Key statistics from the National Survey of Family Growth.* Retrieved from www.cdc.gov/nchs/nsfg/abc_list_i.htm#impaired

U.S. Department of Health and Human Services. (2009f). National, state, and local vaccination coverage among children aged 19–35 months—United States, 2008. *Morbidity and Mortality Weekly Report, 58,* 921–926.

U.S. Department of Health and Human Services. (2009g). U.S. obesity trends 1985–2007. Retrieved from www.cdc.gov/obesity/data.trends.html

U.S. Department of Health and Human Services. (2010a). *Child maltreatment 2010.* Retrieved from www.acf.hhs.gov/programs/cb/stats_research/index .htm#can

U.S. Department of Health and Human Services. (2010b). *Head Start Impact Study: Final report.* Washington, DC: U.S Government Printing Office.

U.S. Department of Health and Human Services. (2010c). *Vital statistics—mortality.* Retrieved from www.cdc.gov/nchs/data_access/vitalstats /VitalStats_Mortality.htm

Ursano, R. J., & Shaw, J. A. (2007). Children of war and opportunities for peace. *Journal of the American Medical Association, 298,* 567.

Usta, I. M., & Nassar, A. H. (2008). Advanced maternal age. Part I: Obstetric complications. *American Journal of Perinatology, 25,* 521–534.

V

Vaillancourt, T., Hymel, S., & McDougall, P. (2003). Bullying is power: Implications for school-based intervention strategies. *Journal of Applied Social Psychology, 19,* 157–176.

Vaish, A., & Striano, T. (2004). Is visual reference necessary? Contributions of facial versus vocal cues in 12-month-olds' social referencing behavior. *Developmental Science, 7,* 261–269.

Vakil, E., Blachstein, H., Sheinman, M., & Greenstein, Y. (2009). Developmental changes in attention tests norms: Implications for the structure of attention. *Child Neuropsychology, 15,* 21–39.

Valdés, G. (1998). The world outside and inside schools: Language and immigrant children. *Educational Researcher, 27*(6), 4–18.

Valentine, J. C., DuBois, D. L., & Cooper, H. (2004). The relation between self-beliefs and academic achievement: A meta-analytic review. *Educational Psychologist, 39,* 111–133.

Valian, V. (1999). Input and language acquisition. In W. C. Ritchie & T. K. Bhatia (Eds.), *Handbook of child language acquisition* (pp. 497–530). San Diego: Academic Press.

Valiente, C., Eisenberg, N., Fabes, R. A., Shepard, S. A., Cumberland, A., & Losoya, S. H. (2004). Prediction of children's empathy-related responding from their effortful control and parents' expressivity. *Developmental Psychology, 40,* 911–926.

Valiente, C., Lemery-Chalfant, K., Swanson, J., & Reiser, M. (2008). Prediction of children's academic competence from their effortful control, relationships, and classroom participation. *Journal of Educational Psychology, 100,* 67–77.

van Aken, C., Junger, M., Verhoeven, M., van Aken, M. A. G., & Deković, M. (2007). The interactive effects of temperament and maternal parenting on toddlers' externalizing behaviours. *Infant and Child Development, 16,* 553–572.

Van Cleave, J., Gortmaker, S. L., & Perrin, J. M. (2010). Dynamics of obesity and chronic health conditions among children and youth. *Journal of the American Medical Association, 303,* 623–630.

Van de Vijver, P. J. R., Hofer, J., & Chasiotis, A. (2010). Methodology. In M. H. Bornstein (Ed.), *Handbook of cultural developmental science* (pp. 21–37). New York: Psychology Press.

Van den Bergh, B. R. H. (2004). High antenatal maternal anxiety is related to ADHD symptoms, externalizing problems, and anxiety in 8- and 9-year-olds. *Child Development, 75,* 1085–1097.

Van den Bergh, B. R. H., & De Rycke, L. (2003). Measuring the multidimensional self-concept and global self-worth of 6- to 8-year-olds. *Journal of Genetic Psychology, 164,* 201–225.

van den Boom, D. C., & Hoeksma, J. B. (1994). The effect of infant irritability on mother–infant interaction: A growth-curve analysis. *Developmental Psychology, 30,* 581–590.

van den Dries, L., Juffer, F., van IJzendoorn, M. H., & Bakermans-Kranenburg, M. J. (2009). Fostering security? A meta-analysis of attachment in adopted children. *Children and Youth Services Review, 31,* 410–421.

van der Meer, A. L. (1997). Keeping the arm in the limelight: Advanced visual control of arm movements in neonates. *European Journal of Paediatric Neurology, 4,* 103–108.

van der Wal, M. F., van Eijsden, M., & Bonsel, G. J. (2007). Stress and emotional problems during pregnancy and excessive infant crying. *Developmental and Behavioral Pediatrics, 28,* 431–437.

Van Eyk, J., & Dunn, M. J. (Eds.). (2008). *Clinical proteomics.* Weinheim, Germany: Wiley-VCH.

van IJzendoorn, M. H. (1995). Adult attachment representations, parental responsiveness, and infant attachment: A meta-analysis on the predictive validity of the Adult Attachment Interview. *Psychological Bulletin, 117,* 387–403.

van IJzendoorn, M. H., & Bakermans-Kranenburg, M. J. (2006). DRD4 7-repeat polymorphism moderates the association between maternal unresolved loss or trauma and infant disorganization. *Attachment and Human Development, 8,* 291–307.

van IJzendoorn, M. H., & Kroonenberg, P. M. (1988). Cross-cultural patterns of attachment: A meta-analysis of the Strange Situation. *Child Development, 59,* 147–156.

van IJzendoorn, M. H., & Sagi, A. (1999). Cross-cultural patterns of attachment. In J. Cassidy & P. R. Shaver (Eds.), *Handbook of attachment: Theory, research, and clinical applications* (pp. 713–734). New York: Guilford.

van IJzendoorn, M. H., Juffer, F., & Poelhuis, C. W. K. (2005). Adoption and cognitive development: A meta-analytic comparison of adopted and nonadopted children's IQ and school performance. *Psychological Bulletin, 131,* 301–316.

van IJzendoorn, M. H., Schuengel, C., & Bakermans-Kranenburg, M. J. (1999). Disorganized attachment in early childhood: Meta-analysis of precursors, concomitants, and sequelae. *Development and Psychopathology, 11,* 225–249.

van IJzendoorn, M. H., Vereijken, C. M. J. L., Bakermans-Kranenburg, M. J., & Riksen-Walraven, J. M. (2004). Assessing attachment security with the Attachment Q Sort: Meta-analytic evidence for the validity of the Observer AQS. *Child Development, 75,* 1188–1213.

Van Keer, H. (2004). Fostering reading comprehension in fifth grade by explicit instruction in reading strategies and peer tutoring. *British Journal of Educational Psychology, 74,* 37–70.

Vandell, D. L., & Mueller, E. C. (1995). Peer play and friendships during the first two years. In H. C. Foot, A. J. Chapman, & J. R. Smith (Eds.), *Friendship and social relations in children* (pp. 181–208). New Brunswick, NJ: Transaction.

Vandell, D. L., & Posner, J. K. (1999). Conceptualization and measurement of children's after-school environments. In S. L. Friedman & T. D. Wachs (Eds.), *Measuring environment across the life span* (pp. 167–196). Washington, DC: American Psychological Association.

Vandell, D. L., & Shumow, L. (1999). After-school child care programs. *Future of Children, 9*(2), 64–80.

Vandell, D. L., Reisner, E. R., & Pierce, K. M. (2007). *Outcomes linked to high-quality after-school programs: Longitudinal findings from the Study of Promising After-School Programs.* Retrieved from www.gse .uci.edu/childcare/pdf/afterschool/ PP%20Longitudinal%20Findings%20Final% 20Report.pdf

Vandell, D. L., Reisner, E. R., Pierce, K. M., Brown, B. B., Lee, D., Bolt, D., & Pechman, E. M. (2006). *The study of promising after-school programs: Examination of longer term outcomes after two years of program experiences.* Madison, WI: University of Wisconsin. Retrieved from www .wcer.wisc.edu/childcare/ statements.html

Vanderbilt-Adriance, E., & Shaw, D. S. (2008). Protective factors and the development of resilience in the context of neighborhood disadvantage. *Journal of Abnormal Child Psychology, 36,* 887–901.

Vandewater, E. A., & Bickham, D. S. (2004). The impact of educational television on young children's reading in the context of family stress. *Applied Developmental Psychology, 25,* 717–728.

Vandewater, E. A., Bickham, D. S., Lee, J. H., Cummings, H. M., Wartella, E. A., & Rideout, V. J. (2005). When the television is always on: Heavy television exposure and young children's development. *American Behavioral Scientist, 48,* 562–577.

Varela-Silva, M. I., Frisancho, A. R., Bogin, B., Chatkoff, D., Smith, P. K., Dickinson, F., & Winham, D. (2007). Behavioral, environmental, metabolic, and intergenerational components of early life undernutrition leading to later obesity in developing nations and in minority groups in the U.S.A. *Collegium Antropologicum, 31,* 39–46.

Varendi, H., & Porter, R. H. (2001). Breast odour as the only maternal stimulus elicits crawling toward the odour source. *Acta Paediatrica, 90,* 372–375.

Varnhagen, C. (2007). Children and the Internet. In J. Gackenbach (Ed.), *Psychology and the Internet* (2nd ed., pp. 37–54). Amsterdam: Elsevier.

Vaughn, B. E., & Bost, K. K. (1999). Attachment and temperament: Redundant, independent, or interacting influences on interpersonal adaptation and personality development? In J. Cassidy & P. Shaver (Eds.), *Handbook of attachment: Theory, research, and clinical applications* (pp. 265–286). New York: Guilford.

Vaughn, B. E., Colvin, T. N., Azria, M. R., Caya, L., & Krzysik, L. (2001). Dyadic analyses of friendship in a sample of preschool-age children attending Head Start: Correspondence between measures and implications for social competence. *Child Development, 72,* 862–878.

Vaughn, B. E., Kopp, C. B., & Krakow, J. B. (1984). The emergence and consolidation of self-control from eighteen to thirty months of age: Normative trends and individual differences. *Child Development, 55,* 990–1004.

Vaughn, B. E., Vollenweider, M., Bost, K. K., Azria-Evans, M. R., & Snider, J. B. (2003). Negative interactions and social competence for preschool children in two samples: Reconsidering the interpretation of aggressive behavior for young children. *Merrill-Palmer Quarterly, 49,* 245–278.

Velderman, M. K., Bakermans-Kranenburg, M. J., Juffer, F., & van IJzendoorn, M. H. (2006). Effects of attachment-based interventions on maternal sensitivity and infant attachment: Differential susceptibility of highly reactive infants. *Journal of Family Psychology, 20,* 266–274.

Venezia, M., Messinger, D. S., Thorp, D., & Mundy, P. (2004). The development of anticipatory smiling. *Infancy, 6,* 397–406.

Veneziano, R. A. (2003). The importance of paternal warmth. *Cross-Cultural Research, 37,* 265–281.

Vereijken, B., & Adolph, K. E. (1999). Transitions in the development of locomotion. In G. J. P. Savelsbergh, H. L. J. van der Maas, & P. C. L. van Geert (Eds.), *Non-linear analyses of developmental processes* (pp. 137–149). Amsterdam: Elsevier.

Verhulst, F. C. (2008). International adoption and mental health: Long-term behavioral outcome. In M. E. Garralda & J.-P. Raynaud (Eds.), *Culture and conflict in adolescent mental health* (pp. 83–105). Lanham, MD: Jason Aronson.

Verissimo, M., & Salvaterra, F. (2006). Maternal secure-base scripts and children's attachment security in an adopted sample. *Attachment and Human Development, 8,* 261–273.

Vernon-Feagans, L., Hurley, M., & Yont, K. (2002). The effect of otitis media and daycare quality on mother/child bookreading and language use at 48 months of age. *Journal of Applied Developmental Psychology, 23,* 113–133.

Vernon-Feagans, L., Pancsofar, N., Willoughby, M., Odom, E., Quade, A., & Cox, M. (2008). Predictors of maternal language to infants during a picture book task in the home: Family SES, child characteristics and the parenting environment. *Journal of Applied Developmental Psychology, 29,* 213–226.

Vidaeff, A. C., Carroll, M. A., & Ramin, S. M. (2005). Acute hypertensive emergencies in pregnancy. *Critical Care Medicine, 33,* S307–S312.

Vinden, P. G. (1996). Jun'n Quechua children's understanding of mind. *Child Development, 67,* 1707–1716.

Vinden, P. G. (2002). Understanding minds and evidence for belief: A study of Mofu children in Cameroon. *International Journal of Behavioral Development, 26,* 445–452.

Visher, E. B., Visher, J. S., & Pasley, K. (2003). Remarriage families and stepparenting. In F. Walsh (Ed.), *Normal family processes: Growing diversity and complexity* (pp. 153–175). New York: Guilford.

Vivanti, G., Nadig, A., Ozonoff, S., & Rogers, S. J. (2008). What do children with autism attend to during imitation tasks? *Journal of Experimental Psychology, 101,* 186–205.

Vogel, D. A., Lake, M. A., Evans, S., & Karraker, H. (1991). Children's and adults' sex-stereotyped perceptions of infants. *Sex Roles, 24,* 605–616.

Vohr, B., Jodoin-Krauzyk, J., Tucker, R., Johnson, M. J., Topol, D., & Ahlgren, M. (2008). Early language outcomes of early-identified infants with permanent hearing loss at 12 to 16 months of age. *Pediatrics, 122,* 535–544.

Volling, B. L. (2001). Early attachment relationships as predictors of preschool children's emotion regulation with a distressed sibling. *Early Education and Development, 12,* 185–207.

Volling, B. L., & Belsky, J. (1992). Contribution of mother–child and father–child relationships to the quality of sibling interaction: A longitudinal study. *Child Development, 63,* 1209–1222.

Volling, B. L., Mahoney, A., & Rauer, A. J. (2009). Sanctification of parenting, moral socialization, and young children's conscience development. *Psychology of Religion and Spirituality, 1,* 53–68.

Volling, B. L., McElwain, N. L., & Miller, A. L. (2002). Emotion regulation in context: The jealousy complex between young siblings and its relations with child and family characteristics. *Child Development, 73,* 581–600.

von Hofsten, C. (1993). Prospective control: A basic aspect of action development. *Human Development, 36,* 253–270.

von Hofsten, C. (2004). An action perspective on motor development. *Trends in Cognitive Sciences, 8,* 266–272.

von Hofsten, C., & Rosander, K. (1998). The establishment of gaze control in early infancy. In S. Simion & G. Butterworth (Eds.), *The development of sensory, motor and cognitive capacities in early infancy* (pp. 49–66). Hove, U.K.: Psychology Press.

Vondra, J. I., Hommerding, K. D., & Shaw, D. S. (1999). Stability and change in infant attachment in a low-income sample. In J. I Vondra & D. Barnett (Eds.), Atypical attachment in infancy and early childhood among children at developmental risk. *Monographs of the Society for Research in Child Development, 64*(3, Serial No. 258), pp. 119–144.

Vondra, J. I., Shaw, D. S., Searingen, L., Cohen, M., & Owens, E. B. (2001). Attachment stability and

emotional and behavioral regulation from infancy to preschool age. *Development and Psychopathology, 13,* 13–33.

Vouloumanos, A., & Werker, J. F. (2004). Tuned to the signal: The privileged status of speech for young infants. *Developmental Science, 7,* 270–276.

Vuoksimaa, E., Koskenvuo, M., Rose, R. J., & Kaprio, J. (2009). Origins of handedness: A nationwide study of 30,1671 adults. *Neuropsychologia, 47,* 1294–1301.

Vurpillot, E. (1968). The development of scanning strategies and their relation to visual differentiation. *Journal of Experimental Psychology, 6,* 632–650.

Vygotsky, L. S. (1978). *Mind in society: The development of higher psychological processes.* Cambridge, MA: Harvard University Press. (Original works published 1930, 1933, and 1935)

Vygotsky, L. S. (1987). Thinking and speech. In R. W. Rieber, A. S. Carton (Eds.), & N. Minick (Trans.), *The collected works of L. S. Vygotsky: Vol. 1. Problems of general psychology* (pp. 37–285). New York: Plenum. (Original work published 1934)

W

Wachs, T. D., & Bates, J. E. (2001). Temperament. In G. Bremner & A. Fogel (Eds.), *Blackwell handbook of infant development* (pp. 465–501). Oxford, U.K.: Blackwell.

Waddington, C. H. (1957). *The strategy of the genes.* London: Allen & Unwin.

Wadsworth, M. E., & Santiago, C. D. (2008). Risk and resiliency processes in ethnically diverse families in poverty. *Journal of Family Psychology, 22,* 399–410.

Wagenaar, K., Huisman, J., Cohen-Kettenis, P. T., & Delemarre-van de Waal, H. A. (2008). An overview of studies on early development, cognition, and psychosocial well-being in children born after in vitro fertilization. *Journal of Developmental and Behavioral Pediatrics, 29,* 219–230.

Wahlsten, D. (1994). The intelligence of heritability. *Canadian Psychology, 35,* 244–259.

Wainryb, C., & Ford, S. (1998). Young children's evaluations of acts based on beliefs different from their own. *Merrill-Palmer Quarterly, 44,* 484–503.

Wakeley, A., Rivera, S., & Langer, J. (2000). Can young infants add and subtract? *Child Development, 71,* 1477–1720.

Walberg, H. J. (1986). Synthesis of research on teaching. In M. C. Wittrock (Ed.), *Handbook of research on teaching* (3rd ed., pp. 214–229). New York: Macmilan.

Waldenström, U. (1999). Experience of labor and birth in 1111 women. *Journal of Psychosomatic Research, 47,* 471–482.

Waldfogel, J. (2001). International policies toward parental leave and child care. *Future of Children 11,* 52–61.

Waldman, I. D., Rowe, D. C., Abramowitz, A., Kozel, S. T., Mohr, J. H., & Sherman, S. L. (1998). Association and linkage of the dopamine transporter gene and attention-deficit hyperactivity disorder in children: Heterogeneity owing to diagnostic subtype and severity. *American Journal of Human Genetics, 63,* 1767–1776.

Walenski, M., Tager-Flusberg, H., & Ullman, M. T. (2006). Language in autism. In S. O. Moldin & J. L. R. Rubenstein (Eds.), *Understanding autism: From basic neuroscience to treatment* (pp. 175–203). Boca Raton, FL: CRC Press.

Walker, L. J., & Taylor, J. H. (1991). Family interactions and the development of moral reasoning. *Child Development, 62,* 264–283.

Walker-Andrews, A. S. (1997). Infants' perception of expressive behaviors: Differentiation of multimodal information. *Psychological Bulletin, 121,* 437–456.

Wall, M., & Côté, J. (2007). Developmental activities that lead to dropout and investment in sport. *Physical Education and Sport Pedagogy, 12,* 77–87.

Walton, G. E., Armstrong, E. S., & Bower, T. G. R. (1998). Newborns learn to identify a face in eight-tenths of a second? *Developmental Science, 1,* 79–84.

Wang, Q. (2004). The emergence of cultural self-constructs : Autobiographical memory and self-description in European American and Chinese children. *Developmental Psychology, 40*, 3–15.

Wang, Q. (2006a). Earliest recollections of self and others in European American and Taiwanese young adults. *Psychological Science, 17*, 708–714.

Wang, Q. (2006b). Relations of maternal style and child self-concept to autobiographical memories in Chinese, Chinese immigrant, and European American 3-year-olds. *Child Development, 77*, 1794–1809.

Wang, Q., Pomerantz, E. M., & Chen, H. (2007). The role of parents' control in early adolescents' psychological functioning: A longitudinal investigation in the United States and China. *Child Development, 78*, 1592–1610.

Wang, S., Baillargeon, R., & Paterson, S. (2005). Detecting continuity violations in infancy: A new account and new evidence from covering and tube effects. *Cognition, 95*, 129–173.

Warnock, F., & Sandrin, D. (2004). Comprehensive description of newborn distress behavior in response to acute pain (newborn male circumcision). *Pain, 107*, 242–255.

Warren, A. R., & Tate, C. S. (1992). Egocentrism in children's telephone conversations. In R. M. Diaz & L. E. Berk (Eds.), *Private speech: From social interaction to self-regulation* (pp. 245–264). Hillsdale, NJ: Erlbaum.

Warren, D. H. (1994). *Blindness and children: An individual difference approach.* New York: Cambridge University Press.

Warren, S. L., & Simmens, S. J. (2005). Predicting toddler anxiety/depressive symptoms: Effects of caregiver sensitivity on temperamentally vulnerable children. *Infant Mental Health Journal, 26*, 40–55.

Wasik, B. A., & Bond, M. A. (2001). Beyond the pages of a book: Interactive book reading and language development in preschool classrooms. *Journal of Educational Psychology, 93*, 243–250.

Wasserman, E. A., & Rovee-Collier, C. (2001). Pick the flowers and mind your As and 2s! Categorization by pigeons and infants. In M. E. Carroll & J. B. Overmier (Eds.), *Animal research and human health: Advancing human welfare through behavioral science* (pp. 263–279). Washington, DC: American Psychological Association.

Watamura, S. E., Donzella, B., Alwin, J., & Gunnar, M. R. (2003). Morning-to-afternoon increases in cortisol concentrations for infants and toddlers at child care: Age differences and behavioral correlates. *Child Development, 74*, 1006–1020.

Waters, E., & Cummings, E. M. (2000). A secure base from which to explore close relationships. *Child Development, 71*, 164–172.

Waters, E., Merrick, S., Treboux, D., Crowell, J., & Albersheim, L. (2000). Attachment security in infancy and early adulthood: A twenty-year longitudinal study. *Child Development, 71*, 684–689.

Waters, E., Vaughn, B. E., Posada, G., & Kondo-Ikemura, K. (Eds.). (1995). Caregiving, cultural, and cognitive perspectives on secure-base behavior and working models: New growing points of attachment theory and research. *Monographs of the Society for Research in Child Development, 60*(2–3, Serial No. 244).

Watkins, W. E., & Pollitt, E. (1998). Iron deficiency and cognition among school-age children. In S. G. McGregor (Ed.), *Recent advances in research on the effects of health and nutrition on children's development and school achievement in the Third World.* Washington, DC: Pan American Health Organization.

Watson, A. C., Nixon, C. L., Wilson, A., & Capage, L. (1999). Social interaction skills and theory of mind in young children. *Developmental Psychology, 35*, 386–391.

Watson, D. J. (1989). Defining and describing whole language. *Elementary School Journal, 90*, 129–141.

Watson, J. B., & Raynor, R. (1920). Conditioned emotional reactions. *Journal of Experimental Psychology, 3*, 1–14.

Watson, M. (1990). Aspects of self development as reflected in children's role playing. In D. Cicchetti & M. Beeghly (Eds.), *The self in transition: Infancy to*

childhood (pp. 281–307). Chicago: University of Chicago Press.

Watts-English, T., Fortson, B. L., Gibler, N., Hooper, S. R., & De Bellis, M. D. (2006). The psychobiology of maltreatment in childhood. *Journal of Social Issues, 62*, 717–736.

Waxman, S. R. (2003). Links between object categorization and naming: Origins and emergence in human infants. In D. H. Rakison & L. M. Oakes (Eds.), *Early category and concept development: Making sense of the blooming, buzzing confusion* (pp. 193–209). New York: Oxford University Press.

Waxman, S. R., & Lidz, J. L. (2006). Early word learning. In D. Kuhn & R. Siegler (Eds.), *Handbook of child psychology: Vol. 2. Cognition, perception, and language* (6th ed., pp. 464–510). Hoboken, NJ: Wiley.

Waxman, S. R., & Senghas, A. (1992). Relations among word meanings in early lexical development. *Developmental Psychology, 28*, 862–873.

Weaver, A., & Dobson, P. (2007). Nocturnal enuresis in children. *Journal of Family Health Care, 17*, 159–161.

Webb, N. M., Franke, M. L., Ing, M., Chan, A., De, T., Freund, D., & Battey, D. (2008). The role of teacher instructional practices in student collaboration. *Contemporary Educational Psychology, 33*, 360–381.

Webb, N. M., Nemer, K. M., & Chizhik, A. W. (1998). Equity issues in collaborative group assessment: Group composition and performance. *American Educational Research Journal, 35*, 607–651.

Webb, S. J., Monk, C. S., & Nelson, C. A. (2001). Mechanisms of postnatal neurobiological development: Implications for human development. *Developmental Neuropsychology, 19*, 147–171.

Weber, C., Hahne, A., Friedrich, M., & Friederici, A. (2004). Discrimination of word stress in early infant perception: Electrophysiological evidence. *Cognitive Brain Research, 18*, 149–161.

Wechsler, D. (2002). *WPPSI-III: Wechsler Preschool and Primary Scale of Intelligence* (3rd ed.). San Antonio, TX: Psychological Corporation.

Wechsler, D. (2003). *WISC-IV: Wechsler Intelligence Scale for Children* (4th ed.). San Antonio, TX: Psychological Corporation.

Weems, C. F., & Costa, N. M. (2005). Developmental differences in the expression of childhood anxiety symptoms and fears. *Journal of the American Academy of Child and Adolescent Psychiatry, 44*, 656–663.

Wehren, A., DeLisi, R., & Arnold, M. (1981). The development of noun definition. *Journal of Child Language, 8*, 165–175.

Weikart, D. P. (1998). Changing early childhood development through educational intervention. *Preventive Medicine, 27*, 233–237.

Weinberg, M. K., & Tronick, E. Z. (1994). Beyond the face: An empirical study of infant affective configurations of facial, vocal, gestural, and regulatory behaviors. *Child Development, 65*, 1503–1515.

Weiner, J., & Tardif, C. (2004). Social and emotional functioning of children with learning disabilities: Does special education placement make a difference? *Learning Disabilities Research and Practice, 19*, 20–32.

Weinert, F. E., & Hany, E. A. (2003). The stability of individual differences in intellectual development: Empirical evidence, theoretical problems, and new research questions. In R. J. Sternberg & J. Lautrey (Eds.), *Models of intelligence: International perspectives* (pp. 169–181). Washington, DC: American Psychological Association.

Weinert, F. E., & Schneider, W. (Eds.). (1999). *Individual development from 3 to 12: Findings from the Munich Longitudinal Study.* Cambridge, U.K.: Cambridge University Press.

Weinfield, N. S., Sroufe, L. A., & Egeland, B. (2000). Attachment from infancy to early adulthood in a high-risk sample: Continuity, discontinuity, and their correlates. *Child Development, 71*, 695–702.

Weinfield, N. S., Whaley, G. J. L., & Egeland, B. (2004). Continuity, discontinuity, and coherence in attachment from infancy to late adolescence: Sequelae of organization and disorganization. *Attachment and Human Development, 6*, 73–97.

Weinstein, R. S. (2002). *Reaching higher: the power of expectations in schooling.* Cambridge, MA: Harvard University Press.

Weinstock, M. (2008). The long-term behavioural consequences of prenatal stress. *Neuroscience and Biobehavioral Reviews, 32*, 1073–1086.

Weisner, T. S., & Wilson-Mitchell, J. E. (1990). Nonconventional family life-styles and sex typing in six-year-olds. *Child Development, 61*, 1915–1933.

Weiss, K. M. (2005). Cryptic causation of human disease: Reading between the germ lines. *Trends in Genetics, 21*, 82–88.

Weizman, Z. O., & Snow, C. E. (2001). Lexical output as related to children's vocabulary acquisition: Effects of sophisticated exposure and support for meaning. *Developmental Psychology, 37*, 265–279.

Wekerle, C., Wall, A.-M., Leung, E., & Trocmé, N. (2007). Cumulative stress and substantiated maltreatment: The importance of caregiver vulnerability and adult partner violence. *Child Abuse and Neglect, 31*, 427–443.

Wekerle, C., & Wolfe, D. A. (2003). Child maltreatment. In E. J. Mash & R. A. Barkley (Eds.), *Child psychopathology* (2nd ed., pp. 632–684). New York: Guilford.

Weller, E. B., Kloos, A. L., & Weller, R. A. (2006). Mood disorders. M. K. Dulcan & J. M. Wiener (Eds.), *Essentials of child and adolescent psychiatry* (pp. 267–320). Washington, DC: American Psychiatric Association.

Wellman, H. M. (1990). *The child's theory of mind.* Cambridge, MA: MIT Press.

Wellman, H. M. (2002). Understanding the psychological world: Developing a theory of mind. In U. Goswami (Ed.), *Blackwell handbook of child cognitive development* (pp. 167–187). Malden, MA: Blackwell.

Wellman, H. M., & Hickling, A. K. (1994). The mind's "I": Children's conception of the mind as an active agent. *Child Development, 65*, 1564–1580.

Wellman, H. M., Lopez-Duran, S., LaBounty, J., & Hamilton, B. (2008). Infant attention to intentional action predicts preschool theory of mind. *Developmental Psychology, 44*, 618–623.

Weng, X., Odouli, R., & Li, D.-K. (2008). Maternal caffeine consumption during pregnancy and the risk of miscarriage: A prospective cohort study. *American Journal of Obstetrics and Gynecology, 198*, 279e1–279e8.

Wentworth, N., Benson, J. B., & Haith, M. M. (2000). The development of infants' reaches for stationary and moving targets. *Child Development, 71*, 576–601.

Wentworth, N., & Haith, M. M. (1998). Infants' acquisition of spatiotemporal expectations. *Developmental Psychology, 24*, 247–257.

Werner, E. E. (1989, April). Children of the garden island. *Scientific American, 260*(4), 106–111.

Werner, E. E. (2001). *Journeys from childhood to midlife: Risk, resilience, and recovery.* Ithaca, NY: Cornell University Press.

Werner, E. E., & Smith, R. S. (1982). *Vulnerable but invincible: A study of resilient children.* New York: McGraw-Hill.

Werner, E. E., & Smith, R. S. (1992). *Overcoming the odds: High risk children from birth to adulthood.* Ithaca, NY: Cornell University Press.

Werner, E. E., & Smith, R. S. (2001). *Journeys from childhood to midlife: Risk, resilience, and recovery.* Ithaca, NY: Cornell University Press.

Werner, N. E., & Crick, N. R. (2004). Maladaptive peer relationships and the development of relational and physical aggression during middle childhood. *Social Development, 13*, 495–514.

Wesson, D. E., Stephens, D., Lam, K., Parsons, D., Spence, L., & Parkin, P. C. (2008). Trends in pediatric and adult bicycling deaths before and after passage of a bicycle helmet law. *Pediatrics, 122*, 605–610.

Westermann, G., Mareschal, D., Johnson, M. H., Sirois, S., Spratling, M. W., & Michael, S. C. (2007). Neuroconstructivism. *Developmental Science, 10*, 75–83.

Wexler, I. D., Branski, D., & Kerem, E. (2006). War and children. *Journal of the American Medical Association, 296*, 579–581.

Weyermann, M., Rothenbacher, D., & Brenner, H. (2006). Duration of breast-feeding and risk of overweight in childhood: A prospective birth cohort study from Germany. *International Journal of Obesity, 30,* 1281–1287.

Whalen, P. J., Davis, F. C., Oler, J. A., Kim, H., Kim, M. J., & Neta, M., (2009). Human amygdala responses to facial expressions of emotion. In P. J. Whalen & E. A. Phelps (Eds.), *The human amygdala* (pp. 265–288). New York: Guilford.

Whincup, P. H., Kaye, S. G., Owen, C. G., Huxley, R., Cook, D. G., Anazawa, S., et al. (2008). Birth weight and risk of type 2 diabetes: A systematic review. *Journal of the American Medical Association, 24,* 2886–2897.

Whipple, E. E. (2006). Child abuse and neglect: Consequences of physical, sexual, and emotional abuse of children. In H. E. Fitzgerald, B. M. Lester, & B. Zuckerman (Eds.), *The crisis in youth mental health: Vol 1. Childhood disorders* (pp. 205–229). Westport, CT: Praeger.

White, B., & Held, R. (1966). Plasticity of sensorimotor development in the human infant. In J. F. Rosenblith & W. Allinsmith (Eds.), *The causes of behavior* (pp. 60–70). Boston: Allyn and Bacon.

White, M. A., Wilson, M. E., Elander, G., & Persson, B. (1999). The Swedish family: Transition to parenthood. *Scandinavian Journal of Caring Sciences, 13,* 171–176.

Whitehurst, G. J., & Lonigan, C. J. (1998). Child development and emergent literacy. *Child Development, 69,* 848–872.

Whiteman, S. D., & Loken, E. (2006). Comparing analytic techniques to classify dyadic relationships: An example using siblings. *Journal of Marriage and Family, 68,* 1370–1382.

Whiteside-Mansell, L., Bradley, R. H., Owen, M. T., Randolph, S. M., & Cauce, A. M. (2003). Parenting and children's behavior at 36 months: Equivalence between African-American and European-American mother–child dyads. *Parenting: Science and Practice, 3,* 197–234.

Whiting, B., & Edwards, C. P. (1988). *Children in different worlds.* Cambridge, MA: Harvard University Press.

Whitington, V., & Ward, C. (1999). Intersubjectivity in caregiver–child communication. In L. E. Berk (Ed.), *Landscapes of development* (pp. 109–120). Belmont, CA: Wadsworth.

Wichmann, C., Coplan, R. J., & Daniels, T. (2004). The social cognitions of socially withdrawn children. *Social Development, 13,* 377–392.

Wigfield, A., Eccles, J. S., Schiefele, U., Roeser, R. W., & Davis-Kean, P. (2006). Development of achievement motivation. In N. Eisenberg (Ed.), *Handbook of child psychology: Vol. 3. Social, emotional, and personality development* (6th ed., pp. 933–1002). Hoboken, NJ: Wiley.

Wigfield, A., Eccles, J. S., Yoon, K. S., Harold, R. D., Arbreton, A. J., Freedman-Doan, C., & Blumenfeld, P. C. (1997). Changes in children's competence beliefs and subjective task values across the elementary school years: A three-year study. *Journal of Educational Psychology, 89,* 451–469.

Wilcox, A. J., Weinberg, C. R., & Baird, D. D. (1995). Timing of sexual intercourse in relation to ovulation: Effects on the probability of conception, survival of the pregnancy, and sex of the baby. *New England Journal of Medicine, 333,* 1517–1519.

Wilcox, T., & Woods, R. (2009). Experience primes infants to individuate objects. In A. Woodward & A. Needham (Eds.), *Learning and the infant mind* (pp. 117–143). New York: Oxford University Press.

Wilkinson, K., Ross, E., & Diamond, A. (2003). Fast mapping of multiple words: Insights into when "the information provided" does and does not equal "the information perceived." *Applied Developmental Psychology, 24,* 739–762.

Wilkinson, R. B. (2004). The role of parental and peer attachment in the psychological health and self-esteem of adolescents. *Journal of Youth and Adolescence, 33,* 479–493.

Willatts, P. (1999). Development of means–end behavior in young infants: Pulling a support to retrieve a distant object. *Developmental Psychology, 35,* 651–667.

Williams, C. (2006). Dilemmas in fetal medicine: Premature application of technology or responding to women's choice? *Sociology of Health and Illness, 28,* 1–20.

Williams, G. R. (2008). Neurodevelopmental and neurophysiological actions of thyroid hormone. *Journal of Neuroendocrinology, 20,* 784–794.

Williams, K., & Dunne-Bryant, A. (2006). Divorce and adult psychological well-being: Clarifying the role of gender and age. *Journal of Marriage and Family, 68,* 1178–1196.

Williams, K., Haywood, K. I., & Painter, M. (1996). Environmental versus biological influences on gender differences in the overarm throw for force: Dominant and nondominant arm throws. *Women in Sport and Physical Activity Journal, 5,* 29–48.

Williams, P. E., Weiss, L. G., & Rolfhus, E. (2003). *WISC-IV: Theoretical model and test blueprint.* San Antonio, TX: Psychological Corporation.

Williamson, J., Softas-Nall, B., & Miller, J. (2003). Grandmothers raising grandchildren: An exploration of their experiences and emotions. *Counseling and Therapy for Couples with Families, 11,* 23–32.

Willinger, M., Ko, C. W., Hoffman, H. J., Kessler, R. C., & Corwin, M. J. (2003). Trends in infant bed sharing in the United States, 1993–2000: The National Infant Sleep Position Study. *Archives of Pediatric and Adolescent Medicine, 157,* 43–49.

Winkler, I., Háden, G. P., Ladinig, O., Sziller, I., & Honing, H. (2009). Newborn infants detect the beat in music. *Proceedings of the National Academy of Sciences, 106,* 2468–2471.

Winner, E. (1986, August). Where pelicans kiss seals. *Psychology Today, 20*(8), 25–35.

Winner, E. (1988). *The point of words: Children's understanding of metaphor and irony.* Cambridge, MA: Harvard University Press.

Winner, E. (1996). *Gifted children: Myths and realities.* New York: Basic Books.

Winner, E. (1997). Exceptionally high intelligence and schooling. *American Psychologist, 52,* 1070–1081.

Winner, E. (2000). The origins and ends of giftedness. *American Psychologist, 55,* 159–169.

Winner, E. (2003). Creativity and talent. In M. H. Bornstein, L. Davidson, C. L. M. Keyes, K. A. Moore, & the Center for Child Well-Being, (Eds.), *Well-being: Positive development across the life course* (pp. 371–380). Mahwah, NJ: Erlbaum.

Winsler, A. (2009). Still talking to ourselves after all these years: A review of current research on private speech. In A. Winsler, C. Fernyhough, & I. Montero (Eds.), *Private speech, executive functioning, and the development of self-regulation.* New York: Cambridge University Press.

Winsler, A., Abar, B., Feder, M. A., Rubio, D. A., & Schunn, C. D. (2007). Private speech and executive functioning among high functioning children with autism spectrum disorders. *Journal of Autism and Developmental Disorders, Online First™.*

Winsler, A., Fernyhough, C., & Montero, I. (2009). *Private speech, executive functioning, and the development of verbal self-regulation.* New York: Cambridge University Press.

Winsler, A., Naglieri, J., & Manfra, L. (2006). Children's search strategies and accompanying verbal and motor strategic behavior: Developmental trends and relations with task performance among children age 5 to 17. *Cognitive Development, 21,* 232–248.

Wiseman, F. K., Alford, K. A., Tybulewicz, V. L. J., & Fisher, E. M. C. (2009). Down syndrome—recent progress and future prospects. *Human Molecular Genetics, 18,* R75–R83.

Witherington, D. C. (2005). The development of prospective grasping control between 5 and 7 months: A longitudinal study. *Infancy, 7,* 143–161.

Witherington, D. C., Campos, J. J., & Hertenstein, M. J. (2001). Principles of emotion and its development in infancy. In G. Bremner & A. Fogel (Eds.), *Blackwell handbook of infant development* (pp. 427–464). Malden, MA: Blackwell.

Wolak, J., Finkelhor, D., Mitchell, K. J., & Ybarra, M. L. (2008). Online "predators" and their victims: Myths, realities, and implications for prevention and treatment. *American Psychologist, 63,* 111–128.

Wolchik, S. A., Sandler, I. N., Millsap, R. E., Plummer, B. A., Greene, S. M., Anderson, E. R., et al. (2002). Six-year follow-up of preventive interventions for children of divorce: A randomized controlled trial. *Journal of the American Medical Association, 288,* 1874–1881.

Wolchik, S. A., Wilcox, K. L., Tein, J.-Y., & Sandler, I. N. (2000). Maternal acceptance and consistency of discipline as buffers of divorce stressors on children's psychological adjustment problems. *Journal of Abnormal Child Psychology, 28,* 87–102.

Wolf, A. W., Jimenez, E., & Lozoff, B. (2003). Effects of iron therapy on infant blood lead levels. *Journal of Pediatrics, 143,* 789–795.

Wolfe, D. A. (2005). *Child abuse* (2nd ed.) Thousand Oaks, CA: Sage.

Wolfe, D. A., Scott, K., Wekerle, C., & Pittman, A. (2001). Child maltreatment: Risk of adjustment problems and dating violence in adolescence. *Journal of the American Academy of Child and Adolescent Psychiatry, 40,* 282–289.

Wolfe, V. V. (2006). Child sexual abuse. In E. J. Mash & R. A. Barkley (Eds.), *Treatment of childhood disorders* (3rd ed., pp. 647–727). New York: Guilford.

Wolff, P. H. (1966). The causes, controls and organization of behavior in the neonate. *Psychological Issues, 5*(1, Serial No. 17).

Wolff, P. H., & Fesseha, G. (1999). The orphans of Eritrea: A five-year follow-up study. *Journal of Child Psychology and Psychiatry and Allied Disciplines, 40,* 1231–1237.

Wolfinger, N. H. (2000). Beyond the intergenerational transmission of divorce: Do people replicate the patterns of marital instability they grew up with? *Journal of Family Issues, 21,* 1061–1086.

Wong, M. M., Nigg, J. T., Zucker, R. A., Puttler, L. I., Fitzgerald, H. E., Jester, J. M., Glass, J. M., & Adams, K. (2006). Behavioral control and resiliency in the onset of alcohol and illicit drug use: A prospective study from preschool to adolescence. *Child Development, 77,* 1016–1033.

Wood, E., Desmarais, S., & Gugula, S. (2002). The impact of parenting experience on gender stereotyped toy play of children. *Sex Roles, 47,* 39–49.

Wood, J. J., Emmerson, N. A., & Cowan, P. A. (2004). Is early attachment security carried forward into relationships with preschool peers? *British Journal of Developmental Psychology, 22,* 245–253.

Woodward, A. (2009). Infants' grasp of others' intentions. *Current Directions in Psychological Science, 18,* 53–57.

Woodward, A. L., & Markman, E. M. (1998). Early word learning. In D. Kuhn & R. S. Siegler (Eds.), *Handbook of child psychology: Vol. 2. Cognition, perception, and language* (5th ed., pp. 371–420). New York: Wiley.

Woodward, J., & Ono, Y. (2004). Mathematics and academic diversity in Japan. *Journal of Learning Disabilities, 37,* 74–82.

Woody-Dorning, J., & Miller, P. H. (2001). Children's individual differences in capacity: Effects on strategy production and utilization. *British Journal of Developmental Psychology, 19,* 543–557.

Woolley, J. D. (1997). Thinking about fantasy: Are children fundamentally different thinkers and believers from adults? *Child Development, 68,* 991–1011.

Woolley, J. D. (2000). The development of beliefs about direct mental–physical causality in imagination, magic, and religion. In K. S. Rosengren, C. N. Johnson, & P. L. Harris (Eds.), *Imagining the impossible* (pp. 99–129). New York: Cambridge University Press.

Woolley, J. D., Browne, C. A., & Boerger, E. A. (2006). Constraints on children's judgments of magical causality. *Journal of Cognition and Development, 7,* 253–277.

Woolley, J. D., & Cox, V. (2007). Development of beliefs about storybook reality. *Developmental Science, 10,* 681–693.

World Cancer Research Fund/American Institute for Cancer Research. (2007). *Food, nutrition, physical activity, and the prevention of cancer: A global perspective.* Washington, DC: American Institute for Cancer Research.

World Health Organization. (2008a). *The global burden of disease: 2004.* Geneva, Switzerland: Author.

World Health Organization. (2008b). *World report on child injury prevention.* Geneva, Switzerland: Author.

World Health Organization. (2009a). *Obesity and overweight.* Retrieved from www.who.int /dietphysicalactivity/publications/facts/obesity/en/

World Health Organization. (2009b). *World health statistics, 2009.* Retrieved from www.who.int/whosis/ whostat/2009/en/index.html

World Health Organization. (2010a). *Population-based prevention strategies for childhood obesity.* Geneva, Switzerland: Author.

World Health Organization. (2010b). *The World Health Organization's infant feeding recommendation.* Retrieved from www.who.int/nutrition/topics/ infantfeeding_recommendation/en/index.html

Wright, B. C. (2006). On the emergence of the discriminative mode for transitive inference. *European Journal of Cognitive Psychology, 18,* 776–800.

Wright, J. C., Huston, A. C., Murphy, K. C., St. Peters, M., Pinon, M., Scantlin, R., & Kotler, J. (2001). The relations of early television viewing to school readiness and vocabulary of children from low-income families: The Early Window Project. *Child Development, 72,* 1347–1366.

Wright, M. J., Gillespie, N. A., Luciano, M., Zhu, G., & Martin, N. G. (2008). Genetics of personality and cognition in adolescents. In J. J. Hudziak (Eds.), *Developmental psychology and wellness: Genetic and environmental influences* (pp. 85–107). Washington, DC: American Psychiatric Publishing.

Wright, M. O., & Masten, A. S. (2005). Resilience processes in development. In S. Goldstein & R. B. Brooks (Eds.), *Handbook of resilience in children* (pp. 17–37). New York: Springer.

Wright, R. O., Tsaih, S. W., Schwartz, J., Wright, R. J., & Hu, H. (2003). Associations between iron deficiency and blood lead level in a longitudinal analysis of children followed in an urban primary care clinic. *Journal of Pediatrics, 142,* 9–14.

Wrotniak, B. H., Epstein, L. H., Raluch, R. A., & Roemmich, J. N. (2004). Parent weight change as a predictor of child weight change in family-based behavioral obesity treatment. *Archives of Pediatric and Adolescent Medicine, 158,* 342–347.

Wu, G., Bazer, F. W., Cudd, T. A., Meininger, C. J., & Spencer, T. E. (2004). Maternal nutrition and fetal development. *Journal of Nutrition, 134,* 2169–2172.

Wu, L. L., Bumpass, L. L., & Musick, K. (2001). Historical and life course trajectories of nonmarital childbearing. In L. L. Wu & B. Wolfe (Eds.), *Out of wedlock: Causes and consequences of nonmarital fertility* (pp. 3–48). New York: Russell Sage Foundation.

Wu, P., Robinson, C. C., Yang, C., Hart, C. H., Olsen, S. F., Porter, C. L., Jin, S., Wo, J., & Wu, X. (2002). Similarities and differences in mothers' parenting of preschoolers in China and the United States. *International Journal of Behavioral Development, 26,* 481–491.

Wulczyn, F. (2009). Epidemiological perspectives on maltreatment prevention. *Future of Children, 19,* 39–66.

Wust, S., Entringer, S., Federenko, I. S., Schlotz, W., Helhammer, D. H. (2005). Birth weight is associated with salivary cortisol responses to psychosocial stress in adult life. *Psychoneuroendocrinology, 30,* 591–598.

Wynn, K. (1992). Addition and subtraction by human infants. *Nature, 358,* 749–750.

Wynn, K., Bloom, P., & Chiang, W.-C. (2002). Enumeration of collective entities by 5-month-old infants. *Cognition, 83,* B55–B62.

Wynne-Edwards, K. E. (2001). Hormonal changes in mammalian fathers. *Hormones and Behavior, 40,* 139–145.

X

Xu, F., Spelke, E., & Goddard, S. (2005). Number sense in human infants. *Developmental Science, 8,* 88–101.

Xue, Y., & Meisels, S. J. (2004). Early literacy instruction and learning in kindergarten: Evidence from the Early Childhood Longitudinal Study—kindergarten classes of 1998–1999. *American Educational Research Journal, 41,* 191–229.

Y

Yale, M. E., Messinger, D. S., Cobo-Lewis, A. B., Oller, D. K., & Eilers, R. E. (1999). An event-based analysis of the coordination of early infant vocalizations and facial actions. *Developmental Psychology, 35,* 505–513.

Yan, Z. (2006). What influences children's and adolescents' understanding of the complexity of the Internet? *Developmental Psychology, 42,* 418–428.

Yang, B., Ollendick, T. H., Dong, Q., Xia, Y., & Lin, L. (1995). Only children and children with siblings in the People's Republic of China: Levels of fear, anxiety, and depression. *Child Development, 66,* 1301–1311.

Yang, C. (2008, April). *The influence of one-child policy on child rearing, family, and society in post-Mao China.* Invited address, Illinois State University.

Yang, C., Hart, C. H., Nelson, D. A., Porter, C. L., Olsen, S. F., Robinson, C. C., & Jin, S. (2003). Fathering in a Beijing Chinese sample: Associations with boys' and girls' negative emotionality and aggression. In R. D. Day & M. E. Lamb (Eds.), *Conceptualizing and measuring father involvement* (pp. 185–215). Mahwah, NJ: Erlbaum.

Yang, C.-K., & Hahn, H.-M. (2002). Cosleeping in young Korean children. *Developmental and Behavioral Pediatrics, 23,* 151–157.

Yarrow, M. R., Scott, P. M., & Waxler, C. Z. (1973). Learning concern for others. *Developmental Psychology, 8,* 240–260.

Yeates, K. O., Schultz, L. H., & Selman, R. L. (1991). The development of interpersonal negotiation strategies in thought and action: A social-cognitive link to behavioral adjustment and social status. *Merrill-Palmer Quarterly, 37,* 369–405.

Yeh, C. J., Kim, A. B., Pituc, S. T., & Atkins, M. (2008). Poverty, loss, and resilience: The story of Chinese immigrant youth. *Journal of Counseling Psychology, 55,* 34–48.

Yehuda, R., Engel, S. M., Brand, S. R., Seckl, J., Marcus, S. M., & Berkowitz, G. S. (2005). Transgenerational effects of posttraumatic stress disorder in babies of mothers exposed to the World Trade Center attacks during pregnancy. *Journal of Clinical Endocrinology and Metabolism, 90,* 4115–4118.

Yip, R., Scanlon, K., & Trowbridge, F. (1993). Trends and patterns in height and weight status of low-income U.S. children. *Critical Reviews in Food Science and Nutrition, 33,* 409–421.

Yirmiya, N., Erel, O., Shaked, M., & Solomonica-Levi, D. (1998). Meta-analyses comparing theory of mind abilities of individuals with autism, individuals with mental retardation, and normally developing individuals. *Psychological Bulletin, 124,* 283–307.

Yonas, A., Elieff, C., & Aterberry, M. E. (2002). Emergence of sensitivity to pictorial depth cues: Charting development in individual infants. *Infant Behavior and Development, 25,* 295–514.

Yonas, A., & Granrud, C. E. (2006). Infants' perception of depth from cast shadows. *Perception and Psychophysics, 68,* 154–160.

Yoshida, H., & Smith, L. B. (2003). Known and novel noun extensions: Attention at two levels of abstraction. *Child Development, 74,* 564–577.

Yoshinaga-Itano, C. (2003). Early intervention after universal neonatal hearing screening: Impact on outcomes. *Mental Retardation and Developmental Disabilities Research and Reviews, 9,* 252–266.

Young, J. F., & Mroczek, D. K. (2003). Predicting intraindividual self-concept trajectories during adolescence. *Journal of Adolescence, 26,* 589–603.

Youngblade, L. M., & Dunn, J. (1995). Individual differences in young children's pretend play with mother and sibling: Links to relationships and understanding of other people's feelings and beliefs. *Child Development, 66,* 1472–1492.

Young-Hyman, D., Tanofsky-Kraff, M., Yanovski, S. Z., Keil, M., Cohen, M. L., & Peyrot, M. (2006). Psychological status and weight-related distress in overweight or at-risk-for-overweight children. *Obesity, 14,* 2249–2258.

Youngstrom, E., Wolpaw, J. M., Kogos, J. L., Schoff, K., Ackerman, B., & Izard, C. (2000). Interpersonal problem solving in preschool and first grade: Developmental change and ecological validity. *Journal of Clinical Child Psychology, 29,* 589–602.

Yu, R. (2002). On the reform of elementary school education in China. *Educational Exploration, 129,* 56–57.

Yuan, A. S. V., & Hamilton, H. A. (2006). Stepfather involvement and adolescent well-being : Do mothers and nonresidential fathers matter? *Journal of Family Issues, 27,* 1191–1213.

Yuill, N., & Pearson, A. (1998). The developmental bases for trait attribution: Children's understanding of traits as causal mechanisms based on desire. *Developmental Psychology, 34,* 574–586.

Yumoto, C., Jacobson, S. W., & Jacobson, J. L. (2008). Fetal substance exposure and cumulative environmental risk in an African-American cohort. *Child Development, 79,* 1761–1776.

Yunger, J. L., Carver, P. R., & Perry, D. G. (2004). Does gender identity influence children's psychological well-being? *Developmental Psychology, 40,* 572–582.

Z

Zafeiriou, D. I. (2000). Plantar grasp reflex in high-risk infants during the first year of life. *Pediatric Neurology, 22,* 75–76.

Zahn-Waxler, C., Kochanska, G., Krupnick, J., & McKnew, D. (1990). Patterns of guilt in children of depressed and well mothers. *Developmental Psychology, 26,* 51–59.

Zahn-Waxler, C., Radke-Yarrow, M., & King, R. M. (1979). Child-rearing and children's prosocial initiations toward victims of distress. *Child Development, 50,* 319–330.

Zahn-Waxler, C., & Robinson, J. (1995). Empathy and guilt: Early origins of feelings of responsibility. In J. P. Tangney & K. W. Fischer (Eds.), *Self-conscious emotions* (pp. 143–173). New York: Guilford.

Zahn-Waxler, C., Schiro, K., Robinson, J. L., Emde, R. N., & Schmitz, S. (2001). Empathy and prosocial patterns in young MZ and DZ twins: Development and genetic and environmental influences. In R. N. Emde & J. K. Hewitt (Eds.), *Infancy to early childhood: Genetic and environmental influences on developmental change* (pp. 141–162). New York: Oxford University Press.

Zanetti-Daellenbach, R. A., Tschudin, S., Zhong, X. Y., Holzgreve, W., Lapaire, O., & Hösli, I. (2007). Maternal and neonatal infections and obstetrical outcome in water birth. *European Journal of Obstetrics and Gynecology and Reproductive Biology, 134,* 37–43.

Zaslow, M. J., Weinfield, N. S., Gallagher, M., Hair, E. C., Ogawa, J. R., Egeland, B., Tabors, P. O., & De Temple, J. M. (2006). Longitudinal prediction of child outcomes from differing measures of parenting in a low-income sample. *Developmental Psychology, 42,* 27–37.

Zeanah, C. H. (2000). Disturbances of attachment in young children adopted from institutions. *Journal of Developmental and Behavioral Pediatrics, 21,* 230–236.

Zelazo, N. A., Zelazo, P. R., Cohen, K. M., & Zelazo, P. D. (1993). Specificity of practice effects on elementary neuromotor patterns. *Developmental Psychology, 29,* 686–691.

Zelazo, P. D., Frye, D., & Rapus, T. (1996). An age-related dissociation between knowing rules and using them. *Cognitive Development, 11,* 37–63.

Zelazo, P. D., Muller, U., Frye, D., & Marcovitch, S. (2003). The development of executive function: Cognitive complexity and control—revised. *Monographs of the Society for Research in Child Development, 68(3),* 93–119.

Zeller, M. H., & Modi, A. C. (2006). Predictors of health-related quality of life in obese youth. *Obesity Research, 14,* 122–130.

Zeman, J., Shipman, K., & Suveg, C. (2002). Anger and sadness regulation: Predictions to internalizing and externalizing symptoms in children. *Journal of Clinical Child and Adolescent Psychology, 31,* 393–398.

Zeskind, P. S., & Barr, R. G. (1997). Acoustic characteristics of naturally occurring cries of infants with "colic." *Child Development, 68,* 394–403.

Zeskind, P. S., & Lester, B. M. (2001). Analysis of infant crying. In L. T. Singer & P. S. Zeskind (Eds.), *Biobehavioral assessment of the infant* (pp. 149–166). New York: Guilford.

Zhang, T.-Y., & Meaney, M. J. (2010). Epigenetics and the environmental regulation of the genome and its function. *Annual Review of Psychology, 61,* 439–466.

Zhou, M., & Bankston, C. L. (1998). *Growing up American: How Vietnamese children adapt to life in the United States.* New York: Russell Sage Foundation.

Zhou, M., & Xiong, S. (2005). The multifaceted American experiences of the children of Asian immigrants: Lessons for segmented assimilation. *Ethnic and Racial Studies, 28,* 1119–1152.

Zhou, Q., Lengua, L. J., & Wang, Y. (2009). The relations of temperament reactivity and effortful control to children's adjustment problems in China and the United States. *Developmental Psychology, 45,* 724–739.

Zhou, X., Huang, J., Wang, Z., Wang, B., Zhao, Z., Yang, L., & Zheng-zheng, Y. (2006). Parent–

child interaction and children's number learning. *Early Child Development and Care, 176,* 763–775.

Zhu, L., & Liu, G. (2007). Preschool children's understanding of illness. *Acta Psychologica Sinica, 39,* 96–103.

Zielinski, D. S., & Bradshaw, C. P. (2006). Ecological influences on the sequelae of child maltreatment: A review of the literature. *Child Maltreatment, 11,* 49–62.

Zimmerman, B. J., & Cleary, T. J. (2009). Motives to self-regulate learning: A social cognitive account. In K. R. Wenzel & A. Wigfield (Eds.), *Handbook of motivation at school* (pp. 247–264). New York: Routledge.

Zimmerman, F. J., & Christakis, D. A. (2005). Children's television viewing and cognitive outcomes. *Archives of Pediatrics and Adolescent Medicine, 159,* 619–625.

Zimmerman, F. J., Christakis, D. A., & Meltzoff, A. N. (2007). Television and DVD/video viewing in children younger than 2 years. *Archives of Pediatrics and Adolescent Medicine, 161,* 473–479.

Zimmerman, L. K., & Stansbury, K. (2004). The influence of emotion regulation, level of shyness, and habituation on the neuroendocrine response of three-year-old children. *Psychoneuroendocrinology, 29,* 973–982.

Zins, J. E., Garcia, V. F., Tuchfarber, B. S., Clark, K. M., & Laurence, S. C. (1994). Preventing injury in children and adolescents. In R. J. Simeonsson (Ed.), *Risk, resilience, and prevention: Promoting the well-being of all children* (pp. 183–202). Baltimore: Paul H. Brookes.

Zosuls, K. M., Ruble, D. N., Tamis-LeMonda, C. S., Shrout, P. E., Bornstein, M. H., & Greulich, F. K. (2009). The acquisition of gender labels in infancy: Implications for gender-typed play. *Developmental Psychology, 45,* 688–701.

Zucker, K. J. (2006). "I'm half-boy, half-girl": Play psychotherapy and parent counseling for gender identity disorder. In R. L. Spitzer, M. B. First, J. B. W. Williams, & M. Gibbon (Eds.), *DSM-IVTR Casebook: Vol. 2. Experts tell how they treated their own patients* (pp. 322–334). Washington, DC: American Psychiatric Publishing.

Zukow-Goldring, P. (2002). Sibling caregiving. In M. H. Bornstein (Ed.), *Handbook of parenting: Vol. 3* (2nd ed., pp. 253–286). Hillsdale, NJ: Erlbaum.

Zur, O., & Gelman, R. (2004). Young children can add and subtract by predicting and checking. *Early Childhood Research Quarterly, 19,* 121–137.

Zwart, M. (2007). The Dutch system of perinatal care. *Midwifery Today with International Midwife, 81*(Spring), 46.

Italic "n" following page number indicates caption or note accompanying figure, illustration, or table.

A

Aarnoudse-Moens, C. S., 137
Abbeduto, L. J., 385
Abecassis, M., 499
Aber, J. L., 27, 75, 77, 78, 523
Abikoff, H. B., 444, 445
Aboud, F. E., 494, 496
Achenbach, T. M., 139
Acker, M. M., 382
Ackerman, B. P., 251
Adachi-Mejia, A. M., 419
Adam, E. K., 418
Adams, A.-M., 336
Adams, R. J., 152
Adamson, D., 67
Adolph, K. E., 14, 145, 184, 185, 188, 193, 199
Afifi, T. O., 381
Afterschool Alliance, 517
Agatston, P. W., 502
Aggarwal, R., 302
Aguiar, A., 208
Ahadi, S. A., 257, 258
Ahlberg, C., 393
Ahlgren, M., 105
Ahmed, M. L., 413
Ahnert, L., 79, 230, 351
Aikens, N. L., 231, 350
Ainscow, M., 473
Ainsworth, M. D. S., 266, 267n, 270
Akhtar, N., 210, 354, 355
Akimoto, S. A., 254
Akinbami, L. J., 423
Aksan, N., 251, 258, 283, 380, 381
Akshoomoff, N. A., 170, 342
Alberman, E., 61
Albers, C. A., 228
Aldridge, M. A., 151
Alexander, J. M., 448, 449
Alexandre-Bidon, D., 12
Algarin, C., 146
Alhusen, J. L., 121
Ali, U. A., 134
Alibali, M. W., 21, 338
Aligne, C. A., 291
Alink, L. R. A., 386
Allen, M., 509
Allen, S. E. M., 463
Allhusen, V., 273
Allik, J., 508
Allison, J., 470
Allred, E. N., 414
Al-Namlah, A. S., 330
Alter, J., 73
Althaus, J., 133
Alwan, S., 106
Amaral, D. G., 342
Amato, M., 496
Amato, P. R., 94, 398, 507, 510, 512, 513, 515
Ambert, A.-M., 156, 508

American Academy of Pediatrics, 114, 173, 175n, 213, 445
American Academy of Pediatrics, Subcommittee on Attention-Deficit Hyperactivity Disorder, 445
American Diabetes Association, 118
American Psychiatric Association, 444
American Psychological Association, 43, 45, 45n, 221, 473n
Ames, E. W., 193
Amso, D., 191, 197
Amsterlaw, J., 340, 449
Anand, S. S., 417
Ananth, C. V., 135
Anderman, E. M., 487
Anders, T. F., 145
Andersen, E., 358
Anderson, C. A., 388
Anderson, D. M., 352
Anderson, D. R., 213
Anderson, K. G., 514
Anderson, K. J., 240, 503
Anderson, L. L., 190
Anderson, M. E., 147
Anderson, P. J., 56
Anderson, V. A., 170
Anderson, V. N., 92, 93n
Andersson, B.-E., 230
Andrews, D. W., 500
Andrews, G., 21, 327, 328, 343, 438, 441, 442
Andrews, M., 178
Andrews, S., 325, 325n
Anesbury, T., 419
Angelillo, C., 333
Ani, C., 177
Anisfeld, M., 182
Annahatak, B., 460
Annett, M., 293
Antle, B. J., 46
Aoki, M. F., 139
Apgar, V., 128, 129n
Appelbaum, M. L., 231
Aquan-Assee, J., 277
Aram, D., 312
Arauz, R. M., 225
Arbeau, K. A., 373
Arch, J. R., 105
Archer, A. H., 213
Arcus, D., 66
Ardila-Rey, A., 494
Arija, V., 416
Armer, M., 373
Armstrong, E. S., 152
Armstrong, L. M., 255
Arnett, J. J., 6

Arnold, D. H., 386
Arnold, M., 463
Arnold, M. L., 398
Arnold, P., 243
Arnold, R., 76, 77
Arnon, S., 138
Aronson, A. A., 304
Arriaga, R. I., 215
Arsenio, W. F., 387
Arslanian, S. A., 417
Artman, L., 440
Asakawa, K., 36
Asbjornsen, A. E., 304
Asher, S. R., 499, 501, 502
Ashmead, D. H., 151, 187, 194
Aslin, R. N., 190, 236, 241
Astington, J. W., 340, 448, 448n
Atance, C. M., 365
Aterberry, M. E., 192
Atkins, R., 75
Atkinson, L., 278
Atkinson, R. C., 22
Atlas, R., 33
Attewell, P., 472
Au, T. K., 324
Augustin, A., 413
Aumann, K., 273, 274, 275n, 516
Aunola, K., 398, 400
Autti-Raemoe, I., 109
Averhart, C. J., 495
Avis, J., 482
AWC Oslo, 303
Axelin, A., 150
Ayotte, V., 484, 485
Azar, S. T., 404
Azurmendi, A., 415

B

Bacallao, M. L., 36
Backley, P., 359
Baddeley, A., 218
Bader, A. P., 142, 143
Badzinski, D. M., 368
Baer, J., 42
Baghurst, P. A., 296
Bagwell, C. L., 32, 445, 498, 500
Bahrick, L. E., 181, 198, 214, 220
Bai, D. L., 193
Bailey, R. C., 290
Baillargeon, R., 208, 214, 339
Baillargeon, R. H., 386
Baird, D. D., 96
Baker, J. A., 470
Baker, J. M., 463
Bakermans-Kranenburg, M. J., 270, 271

Baker-Sennett, J., 445
Baker-Ward, L., 221
Balaban, M. T., 238
Baldi, A., 175n
Baldwin, D. A., 342, 355, 356
Baldwin, G., 356
Ball, H., 173
Balledux, M., 303
Baltes, P. B., 9, 83
Banaji, M. R., 496
Band, G. P. H., 428
Bandura, A., 18, 380, 381
Banish, M. T., 168
Banks, M. S., 152, 193
Bankston, C. L., 36
Barber, B. K., 399, 400
Bard, K. A., 280
Barenbaum, J., 518
Bar-Haim, Y., 196
Barker, D. J. P., 104, 105
Barkley, R. A., 444, 445
Barnea-Goraly, N., 414
Barnes, G. M., 76
Barnes-Josiah, D., 413
Barnett, D., 266
Barnett, W. S., 349
Baron, A. S., 496
Baron-Cohen, S., 342
Barr, H. M., 106, 109
Barr, R., 180, 210, 213, 219, 220n, 226, 277
Barr, R. G., 148, 149, 186
Barratt, M. S., 138
Barrett, J. L., 495
Barrett, K. C., 254
Barrett, M., 493
Barrett, T. M., 188
Barros, R. M., 433
Barsade, S. G., 457
Bartgis, J., 335, 443
Bartocci, M., 150
Barton, M. E., 358
Bartrip, J., 152, 196
Bartsch, K., 339
Bass, J. L., 136
Bassett, N. S., 128
Bassett, P., 467
Bastien, C. H., 110
Batal, H. A., 147
Batchelor, J., 178
Bates, E. A., 170, 234, 236, 240, 357
Bates, J. E., 83, 255, 256, 257, 258, 260, 261, 293, 369
Bathurst, K., 515
Battin, D., 521
Batty, G. D., 176
Bauer, C. R., 106
Bauer, P. J., 210, 220, 221, 336
Bauermeister, J. A., 426
Baughman, F. D., 335
Baumeister, R. F., 380, 496
Baumrind, D., 398, 400

Baumwell, L., 242
Bauserman, R., 513
Bavelier, D., 169
Baydar, N., 276
Bayless, S., 137
Bayley, N., 184n, 187n, 227
Baynes, K., 236
Beals, D. E., 464
Bean, R. A., 121
Beauchamp, G. K., 150
Becker, B. E., 72, 74
Becker, B. J., 270
Becker, G., 78
Becker, K., 87
Beckett, C., 169, 171n
Bedford, O. A., 371
Behnke, M., 106, 107
Beilin, H., 321
Beintema, D., 144n
Beitel, A. H., 275
Belay, S., 298, 299
Bell, C., 471
Bell, M. A., 193, 209
Bell, S. M., 472
Bellagamba, F., 211
Bellamy, C., 73
Bellinger, D. C., 111, 296
Bellmore, A. D., 500
Belmonte, M. K., 342
Belsky, D., 114
Belsky, J., 230, 268, 270, 272, 273, 277, 279, 351
Belyea, M., 147
Bem, D. J., 40
Bemmels, H. R., 85
Benarroch, F., 59
Bender, H. L., 381
Benenson, J., 499
Bengtson, H., 371
Bennett, K. E., 304
Bennett, M., 494
Bennett, R. T., 341
Benson, J. B., 187
Benson, P. L., 11
Bentler, P. M., 80
Berenbaum, S. A., 261, 282, 390, 392, 394, 397
Bergen, D., 319
Berger, A., 214
Berger, L. M., 347
Berger, S. E., 145, 185
Bergman, K., 115
Berk, L. E., 25, 226, 314, 319, 320n, 330, 331, 332, 350, 384n, 486, 495
Berkowitz, G., 131
Berkowitz, R. L., 63
Berlin, L. J., 270, 381, 382
Berman, P. W., 128
Berman, R. A., 463
Berndt, T. J., 499
Bernier, J. C., 445
Bernieri, F., 262

Berninger, V. W., 473
Bertenthal, B. I., 183, 193, 195, 209
Berthier, N. E., 187
Bertoncini, J., 151, 180
Besançon, M., 474
Best, D. L., 503
Betrán, A. P., 134
Betts, N. M., 300
Beyers, J. M., 400
Bhagavath, B., 55
Bhagwat, J., 223
Bhana, D., 426
Bhat, A., 187
Bhatt, R. S., 219, 222, 222n
Bialystok, E., 235, 327, 343, 465
Bianco, A., 115
Bibace, R., 426
Biblarz, T., 509
Bickham, D. S., 352
Bidell, T. R., 21, 28, 28n, 440, 442
Biederman, J., 444
Bielawska-Batorowicz, E., 155
Bierman, K. L., 377, 503
Bifulco, R., 471
Bigelow, A. E., 194, 270
Bigi, L., 448
Bigler, R. S., 22, 390, 396, 398, 494, 495, 496, 505, 506
Bimmel, N., 66
Bindrich, I., 116
Binet, A., 14
Bioethics Consultative Committee, 67
Birch, E. E., 192, 193
Birch, H. G., 257
Birch, L. L., 299, 300, 301, 420
Birch, S. A. J., 340
Birch, S. H., 375
Bird, A., 337
Bird, G. M., 337
Biringen, Z., 183
Birken, C. S., 424
Birney, D. P., 23
Bisanz, J., 345
Bisgard, K., 302
Bissaker, K., 398, 507
Bjork, E. L., 239
Bjorklund, D. F., 24, 216, 444, 446, 447
Black, B., 503
Black, J. E., 169, 172
Black, M. M., 178
Black, R. E., 300
Blackwell, L. S., 487
Blaga, O. M., 218
Blair, C., 334
Blakemore, J. E. O., 391, 504
Blasi, C. H., 24
Blass, E. M., 180
Blatchford, P., 467
Blatt, L., 253
Blatt-Eisengart, I., 399, 400
Bleeker, M. M., 487, 504
Bloom, L., 239, 354
Bloom, P., 214, 340, 357, 358, 378

Blumberg, M. S., 146
Blumenfeld, P. C., 23
Boardman, J. D., 75
Boat, B. W., 520
Bock, K., 357, 358
Bodrova, E., 25, 224, 335, 468
Boerger, E. A., 324
Bogartz, R. S., 208
Bogin, B., 162, 297, 413
Bohannon, J. N., III, 236, 359
Boldizar, J. P., 395
Bolen, R. M., 519
Bolisetty, S., 137, 137n
Bolzani, L. H., 251
Bond, J. T., 273, 274, 275n, 516
Bond, M. A., 343
Boniface, J., 219
Bonilla, S., 423
Bono, M. A., 219, 229, 335
Bonsel, G. J., 114
Bonvillian, J. D., 236
Boomsma, D. I., 455
Booth, J. L., 338
Booth-LaForce, C., 270
Borke, H., 323
Bornstein, M. H., 23, 196, 222, 225, 226, 242, 243, 274, 312
Boroughs, D. S., 519
Borst, C. G., 130
Bos, H. M. W., 509
Bosacki, S. L., 390
Bosquet, M., 168
Boss, B. J., 150
Bost, K. K., 271, 337
Botton, J., 176
Bouchard, C., 309n, 428
Bouchard, T. J., 85, 260
Boucher, O., 110
Boudreau, J. P., 192
Boukydis, C. F. Z., 149
Bouldin, P., 320
Boulton, M. J., 432, 502
Bounds, M. L., 424
Bower, T. G. R., 151, 152
Bower-Russa, M. E., 381
Bowlby, J., 9, 24, 265, 266, 274
Boyatzis, C. J., 311
Boyd, J. S., 345
Boyd-Franklin, N., 79
Boyd-Zaharias, J., 467
Boyer, K., 221
Boyle, M. H., 390
Boysson-Bardies, B. de, 237
Bracci, R., 135
Brackbill, Y., 133
Bracken, B. A., 347
Brackett, M. A., 457
Bradford, K., 387, 401
Bradley, P. J., 141
Bradley, R. H., 72, 139, 229, 229n, 231, 347, 347n
Bradshaw, C. P., 403
Braet, C., 418
Braine, L. G., 429
Braine, M. D. S., 357
Brainerd, C. J., 329

Branca, F., 418
Brand, S. R., 115
Brandt, S., 239
Branje, S. J. T., 41
Branski, D., 518
Branstetter, W. H., 31
Braswell, G. S., 310, 311
Bratt, R. G., 75
Braungart-Rieker, J. M., 242
Braver, S. L., 513
Bray, G. A., 420
Bray, J. H., 514
Bray, K. H., 141
Brazelton, T. B., 152, 153, 188
Bredekamp, S., 230n, 352n, 467n
Bredemeier, B. J. L., 430
Bremner, A. J., 208
Brennan, W. M., 193
Brenneman, K., 327
Brenner, E., 491
Brenner, H., 175n
Brenner, R. A., 306
Brent, M. R., 239
Breslau, N., 107
Bretherton, I., 266, 368
Brewaeys, A., 509
Brezausek, C. M., 305
Bridgett, D. J., 260, 262
Briefel, R. R., 176
Brierley, B., 295
Briggs, F., 495
Bright, G. M., 297
Broberg, A. G., 230
Brody, G. H., 75, 277, 401, 507, 508
Brody, L., 393
Brody, N., 453
Broberg, A. G., 230
Bronfenbrenner, U., 25, 26, 70, 84
Bronfman, E., 271, 279
Bronson, G. W., 195
Bronstein, P., 395
Brooker, I., 339
Brooks, K., 415
Brooks, P. J., 443, 463
Brooks, R., 237, 238
Brooks-Gunn, J., 75, 76, 79, 80, 139, 139n, 229, 230, 231, 276, 280, 350, 404, 458, 516
Brophy, J., 503
Brosseau-Lapré, F., 465
Brown, A. L., 469
Brown, A. M., 192
Brown, A. S., 112
Brown, C. S., 398, 494, 496, 497
Brown, G. L., 275, 365
Brown, J. L., 523
Brown, J. R., 369
Brown, P., 467
Brown, R. W., 357
Brown, S. R., 281
Brown, T. E., 444
Browne, C. A., 324
Browne, J. V., 153
Brownell, C. A., 278, 281, 367, 370
Bruce, D., 337

Bruck, M., 521
Bruer, J. T., 172, 235
Brunstein, J. C., 469
Brunt, J., 223
Bruschi, C. J., 491
Bruschweiler-Stern, N., 153
Bruzzese, J., 46
Bryan, A. E., 261
Bryant, P., 344
Buchanan, A., 402
Buchanan, C. M., 515
Buchanan-Barrow, E., 493
Buckhalt, J. A., 298
Budd, K. S., 178
Buescher, E. S., 175n
Bugental, D. B., 403, 404, 495
Buhrmester, D., 41, 507
Buhs, E. S., 375, 498, 501
Buist, K. L., 69
Buitelaar, J. K., 114, 115
Bukowski, W. M., 277, 373, 498, 500, 501
Bulk-Bunschoten, A. M., 303
Bullock, M., 280
Bumpass, L. L., 509
Bumpus, M. F., 516
Bunge, S. A., 292
Buonocore, G., 135
Burchinal, M. R., 33, 347
Burden, M. J., 109
Burgess, K. B., 259, 373, 400, 501
Burghard, B. H., 452
Burhans, K. K., 367
Buriel, R., 69
Burkam, D. T., 240, 344
Burke, A. S., 223
Burnham, M. M., 145
Burns, C. E., 290
Burns, E., 131
Burns, N. R., 442
Burns, T., 355
Burrell, N., 509
Burton, L. M., 231, 350
Burton, R., 457
Burts, D. C., 348, 401
Burwinkle, T. M., 419
Bus, A. G., 312
Bush, K. R., 72
Bushman, B. J., 388
Bushnell, E. W., 192
Bussey, K., 384, 493
Buswell, S. D., 173
Butcher, S., 238
Butler, M., 59
Butler, R., 483
Butler, R. J., 423
Butler, S., 393
Buttelmann, D., 339
Buur, H., 258
Bybee, J., 380
Byler, P., 348, 468
Byrne, D. F., 492n

C

Cabrera, N. J., 242, 274, 275, 401
Cahan, S., 440
Cahill, A. G., 134
Cain, K. M., 367, 487

Cairns, B. D., 13, 19
Cairns, R. B., 13, 19, 498
Calarco, K. E., 109
Caldera, Y. M., 26, 70, 276
Caldwell, B. M., 229, 347
Calkins, S. D., 254
Call, J., 234
Callaghan, T. C., 310, 340
Callanan, M. A., 310, 326, 355, 368
Callen, J., 176
Caltran, G., 148
Calvert, S. L., 353, 472
Camaioni, L., 211
Camann, W. R., 133
Cameron, C. A., 358
Cameron, N., 164
Cameron, P. A., 280
Cameron-Faulkner, T., 242
Cammu, H., 134
Campbell, A., 394
Campbell, D. A., 131
Campbell, F. A., 232, 232n
Campbell, S. B., 252, 270, 367, 370, 386
Campbell, T., 211
Campbell, W. K., 485, 486
Campos, J. J., 28, 192, 193, 214, 249, 251, 253
Campos, R. G., 148n
Camras, L. A., 28, 249, 250, 251, 255
Canada Campaign 2000, 80n
Candy, J., 394
Canobi, K. H., 452
Capaldi, D., 275
Capirci, O., 238
Capozzoli, M. C., 219, 319, 335
Carberry, M., 444
Card, N. A., 386
Carels, R., 485
CARE Study Group, 106
Carey, S., 206, 214, 321, 426, 442
Carlson, A., 92
Carlson, C., 486
Carlson, J. J., 283
Carlson, M., 171
Carlson, S., 178
Carlson, S. M., 35, 320, 340
Carlson, V. J., 270
Carmichael, S. L., 114
Carpenter, M., 210, 238, 239, 339
Carpenter, T. P., 199
Carper, R., 342
Carr, D., 419
Carr, J., 61
Carrere, S., 154
Carriger, M. S., 228
Carroll, J. B., 453
Carroll, M. A., 117
Carter, A. S., 255
Carter, J., 147
Caruso, D. R., 457
Carver, P. R., 506
Casalis, S., 451
Casas, J. F., 501
Casasola, M., 222, 223

Casby, M. W., 304
Case, R., 21, 218, 328, 429, 441, 442
Casey, B. J., 169, 292, 295
Casey, B. M., 312
Casey, R. J., 378
Cashon, C. H., 197, 208, 209, 214, 215, 222
Casper, L. M., 516
Caspi, A., 40, 41, 83, 86, 258, 260, 305
Cassia, V. M., 195, 196n
Cassidy, J., 270
Cassidy, S. B., 59
Catalano, R. A., 59
Caton, D., 133
Cauffman, E., 399, 400
Caughey, R. W., 105
Cavell, T. A., 486
Cawthorne, M. A., 105
Ceci, S. J., 440, 458, 459, 460, 521
Cecil, J. E., 300
Celano, D., 344
Center for Communication and Social Policy, 388
Center for Effective Discipline, 403
Cernoch, J. M., 151
Cervantes, C. A., 368
Chadwick, A., 374
Chall, J. S., 451n
Chalmers, J. B., 492
Chambers, P., 66
Champion, T. B., 460, 464
Chan, L. K. S., 487
Chan, R. W., 509
Chance, G., 198
Chandler, M. J., 340
Chandra, R. K., 113
Chang, F., 357, 358
Chang, L., 369
Chang, S., 416
Chao, R. K., 401
Chapman, R. S., 236
Charchut, S. W., 414
Charlesworth, R., 348
Charman, T., 225
Charpak, N., 139
Chase-Lansdale, P. L., 79, 229
Chasiotis, A., 34
Chater, N., 235
Chauhan, G. S., 395
Chavajay, P., 225, 447, 460
Chawarska, K., 342
Chazan-Cohen, R., 232
Cheah, C. S. L., 401
Cheatham, C. L., 171
Checkley, W., 302
Chen, D. W., 374, 376
Chen, F. S., 266, 266n
Chen, H., 401
Chen, L.-C., 185
Chen, M., 67
Chen, V., 401
Chen, X., 263, 263n, 374
Chen, Y.-C., 110
Chen, Y.-J., 110
Chen, Z., 211, 338
Cheng, T. O., 417

Cherny, S. S., 260
Chess, S., 256, 257, 262
Cheung, K. M., 340
Chiang, W.-C., 214
Chiarello, E., 222
Chien, D. H., 502
Children's Defense Fund, 27, 230, 305, 511
Childs, C. P., 25
Child Trends, 117
Chisholm, K., 269
Chitty, L. S., 64n
Chizhik, A. W., 471
Choby, B. A., 188
Choi, S., 223, 241
Chomsky, C., 463
Chomsky, N., 233
Chomtho, S., 176
Chorzempa, B. F., 470
Chouinard, M. M., 326, 359
Chow, V., 339
Christ, S. E., 56
Christakis, D. A., 213, 352, 353
Christenson, S. L., 77
Christensson, K., 306
Christiansen, M. H., 235
Christie, T., 320
Christophe, A., 180
Christophersen, E. R., 189
Chudley, A. E., 109
Chung, H. H., 465
Cibelli, C., 278
Cicchetti, D., 403, 404, 485, 519
Cillessen, A. H. N., 376, 497, 500, 501, 502
Clapp, J. F., 113
Clark, C. A., 137
Clark, E. V., 354, 359
Clark, K. E., 377
Clark, R., 155, 276
Clark, S. L., 134
Clark, S. M., 135
Clarke-Stewart, K. A., 12, 273, 377, 512
Clarkson, T. W., 110
Claxton, L. J., 188
Claxton, S. J., 340
Clearfield, M. W., 183, 393
Cleary, T. J., 449
Cleland, J. W., 148
Clements, D. H., 346, 353, 472
Cleveland, E. S., 337
Cleveland, H. H., 93n
Clifford, R. M., 348
Clifton, R. K., 187
Cluett, E. R., 131
Cnattingius, S., 105
Cobb, C. D., 471
Cohen, L. B., 197, 208, 209, 214, 215, 216, 222, 223
Cohen, R., 508
Cohen, S., 297
Cohen-Bendahan, C. C. C., 392
Cohn, J. E., 252
Coie, J. D., 32, 500
Colapinto, J., 392

Cole, D. A., 485, 487
Cole, J. D., 376, 385, 387, 501
Cole, M., 9
Cole, P., 451
Cole, P. M., 255, 491
Cole, R., 231
Cole, S. A., 271
Cole, T. J., 413
Coleman, M., 509
Coleman, S. M., 381
Coles, C. D., 106, 107
Coley, R. L., 510, 516
Collier, V. P., 465
Collins, W. A., 26, 84, 507
Colman, A. D., 121, 157
Colman, L. L., 121, 157
Colman, R. A., 369
Colombo, J., 218, 228
Colombo, M., 181
Colonnesi, C., 211
Coltrane, S., 516
Colwell, M. J., 319
Commission on Children at Risk, 522n
Committee on Injury, Violence, Poison Prevention, 306
Comstock, G., 352, 388
Conboy, B. T., 234, 465
Condron, D. J., 470
Conger, K. J., 11
Conger, R. D., 11, 72, 75
Conlon, E., 343
Connell, J. P., 487
Connell, M. W., 457
Conner, D. B., 332
Connolly, J. A., 319
Connolly, K. J., 92, 311, 311n
Connor, J. M., 434
Conrad, K., 23
Conti-Ramsden, G., 194
Conway, L., 506
Conyers, C., 18
Cook, A., 79
Cookston, J. T., 513
Cooper, H., 485
Cooper, R., 461
Cooper, R. P., 138, 151, 335
Coplan, R., 400
Coplan, R. J., 259, 373, 431, 503
Coppage, D. J., 222
Copple, C., 230n, 352n, 467n
Coppotelli, H., 500
Corapci, F., 177
Corbett, D., 170
Corbett, S. S., 178
Corbetta, D., 28
Corenblum, B., 495
Corkill, A. J., 443
Cornish, A. M., 155
Cornwell, A. C., 147
Correa-Chavez, M., 225
Cortes, R. C., 377
Corwyn, R. F., 72
Cosden, M., 106
Costa, N. M., 517
Côté, J. E., 431

Côté, S. M., 386, 387, 497
Coulton, C. J., 27, 403
Courage, M. L., 152, 181, 216, 224
Courchesne, E., 342
Covington, C. Y., 107
Cowan, C. P., 92, 93n, 120, 121, 154, 157, 500
Cowan, P. A., 92, 93n, 120, 121, 154, 157, 377, 500
Cox, M., 310
Cox, M. J., 275
Cox, S. M., 271
Cox, V., 324
Coyl, D. D., 274
Coyle, T. R., 446
Coyne, S. M., 276
Crago, M. B., 460, 463
Craig, C. M., 143
Craig, W. M., 33
Craighero, L., 182
Craik, F. I. M., 22
Crain, W., 17
Crair, M. C., 169
Craton, L. G., 192
Craven, R. G., 366, 485
Crawford, N., 506
Crawley-Davis, A. M., 213
Creasey, G. L., 319
Crick, N. R., 22, 376, 376n, 386, 387, 388, 498, 499, 500, 501, 508
Critser, G., 420
Crockenberg, S. C., 26, 255
Crocker, J., 485
Crocker, N. A., 107, 109
Croft, C. M., 271
Cronk, C., 238
Crosby, B., 298
Crosby, L., 500
Crosno, R., 470
Cross, D. R., 332
Crouch, J. L., 403
Crouter, A. C., 504, 507, 508, 516
Crowley, K., 43
Crowson, M., 342
Cruess, L., 334
Cruttenden, L., 209
Crystal, D., 498
Csibra, G., 209, 237
Csikszentmihalyi, M., 468
Csinady, A., 24
Cuevas, K., 220, 221
Culnane, M., 112
Cummings, E. M., 38, 38n, 70, 71, 265
Cunningham, A. E., 463
Curby, T. W., 375
Curran, M., 121
Currie, J., 349
Cutler, A., 190
Cutter, W. J., 62
Cyr, C., 278

D

Dabrowska, E., 357
Dack, L. A., 340
Dahl, R. E., 107

Dales, L., 302
Dal Santo, J. A., 305
Daltabuit, M., 148
Daly, M., 496, 496n
Damashek, A., 306, 307
Damhuis, I., 489
Damon, W., 374, 483, 484, 486, 499
Daniels, E., 431
Daniels, P., 119
Daniels, T., 503
Dannemiller, J. L., 196
Danziger, S. K., 80
Dapretto, M., 239
Darling, N. E., 77, 398
Darling-Hammond, L., 468, 471, 476
Darlington, R., 349
Darwin, C., 13
Das, D. A., 18
Davalos, M., 371
David, A. S., 295
Davidov, M., 491
Davidson, R. J., 168
Davies, P. T., 26, 70, 71
Davis, K. F., 145, 172
Davis, O. S. P., 82
Davison, K. K., 300
Daviss, B.-A., 132
Dawley, K., 116
Dawson, J. D., 434
Deafness Research Foundation, 243
Deák, G. O., 327, 355, 356
Dean, M., 521
Dearing, E., 75, 76, 517
Deary, I. J., 176, 453, 454
Deater-Deckard, K., 83, 262, 274, 381
DeBerry, K. M., 459
Deblinger, E., 519
DeBoer, T., 166
Debus, R., 485
DeCasper, A. J., 101, 102, 118, 151
De Corte, E., 452
de Haan, M., 99, 164, 165, 166, 168, 170, 191, 215, 220, 253, 292, 294, 414, 415, 443
Dekovic, M., 69, 385
Delahunty, K. M., 143
de la Ossa, J. L., 335
De Leon, J. M., 275
Delgado-Gaitan, C., 460
De Lisi, R., 396, 463
Dell, G. S., 357, 358
DeLoache, J. S., 211, 212, 213, 281, 320, 321, 336
Delobel-Ayoub, M., 137
Deltondo, J., 297
DelVecchio, W. F., 258
de Mare, J., 303
DeMarie, D., 446
Demetriou, A., 21, 442
Dempster, F. N., 443
DeNavas-Walt, C., 74, 79
Denham, S. A., 367, 368, 369, 457
Denissen, J. J. A., 485

Dennis, T., 107
Dennis, W., 186
Denton, N. A., 36
Deocampo, J. A., 213
de Pree, I. M., 303
de Pree-Geerlings, B., 303
Der, G., 176
deRegnier, R. A., 118, 166
de Ribaupierre, A., 455
de Rivera, J., 370, 490
DeRoche, K., 56
Derom, C., 293
DeRosier, M. E., 501, 502
de Rosnay, M., 341
De Rycke, L., 484
De Schipper, J. C., 351
de Schonen, S., 152, 196
Desmarais, S., 393
DeSouza, A. T., 263
De Souza, E., 61
Desrochers, S., 21
Dessel, A., 523
deUngria, M., 118
Deutsch, F. M., 120, 121
Deutsch, W., 464
Devi, N. P. G., 112
de Villiers, J. G., 340, 357
de Villiers, P. A., 340, 357
Devise, I., 243
DeVos, J., 208
DeVries, R., 468
de Waal, F. B. M., 391
de Weerd, A. W., 146, 147
de Weerth, C., 115, 176
de Winter, M., 303
De Wolff, M. S., 270
Deynoot-Schaub, M. J. G., 278
Diamond, A., 86, 209, 221, 294, 334, 334n, 335, 354
Diamond, M., 392
Diaz, V., 117
Dick, F., 234
Dickinson, D. K., 343, 344
Dick-Read, G., 130
Dickson, K. L., 251
Diehr, S., 423
Diener, M. L., 507
Dietrich, K. N., 111, 296
DiLalla, L. F., 347
Dildy, G. A., 115
DiMatteo, M. R., 131
Ding, Z. Y., 417
Dingel, A., 222
DiPietro, J. A., 101, 102
Dirix, C. E. H., 101, 181
Dirks, J., 460
Dishion, T. J., 39, 500
Dix, T., 261, 282
Dixon, W. E., Jr., 240
Dmitrieva, J., 273
Dobson, P., 422
Dodd, V. L., 139
Dodge, K. A., 22, 376, 376n, 383, 385, 387, 500, 501
Dodman, N., 132
D'Odorico, L., 241
Doherty, N. N., 181
Doherty, W. J., 154

Dohnt, H., 485
Dolan, A., 337
Dolenszky, E., 499
Dombrowski, K. J., 303
Dombrowski, S. C., 137
Domellof, E., 293
Dominy, N. J., 290
Domitrovich, C. E., 334, 377, 486
Dondi, M., 148
Donelan-McCall, N., 369
Dong, W., 487
Donnellan, M. B., 72, 75, 485, 486
Donnerstein, E., 388
D'Onofrio, B. M., 511
Dorius, C., 510, 512
Dornbusch, S. M., 515
Dorris, M., 108
Dorsey, S., 510
Doss, B. D., 154
dos Santos Silva, I., 105, 105n
Douglas, A. J., 143
Douglas, E. M., 513
Douglas, R. N., 447
Dowker, A., 345
Downe, S., 119
Downs, D. S., 113
Downs, R. M., 438
Doyle, A. B., 319, 494
Dozier, M., 271
Drabman, R. S., 418
Drell, M. J., 431
Drewett, R. F., 178
Driesenga, A., 495
Driscoll, M. C., 57
Drotar, D., 424
DuBois, D. L., 485
Dubois-Comtois, K., 278
Duckworth, A. L., 461
Dueker, G. L., 197
Duggan, A., 404
Duncan, G. J., 72, 334, 345, 418, 458
Duncan, S. R., 147
Dundek, L. H., 131
Dunger, D. B., 413
Dunham, Y., 496
Dunifon, R., 80
Dunn, J., 276, 277, 282, 369, 378, 507, 512, 515
Dunn, J. R., 75
Dunn, M. J., 65
Dunne-Bryant, A., 511
Dunphy-Lelii, S., 238
Dunsmore, J. C., 367
Durham, M., 347
Durkin, K., 342
Durkin, M. S., 424
Durlach, J., 114
Durlak, J. A., 516
Durston, S., 23, 292
Duszak, S., 112
Dutilleul, S., 149
Duxbury, L., 420
Dweck, C. S., 266, 266n, 367, 486, 487, 496
Dynarski, M., 76
Dzurova, D., 61

E
Earls, F., 171
Easterbrooks, M. A., 278, 279, 281
Eaton, M. M., 486
Ebeling, K. S., 323
Eberhard, J., 131
Eccles, J. S., 430, 470, 485, 503
Eckerman, C. O., 278
Economic Policy Institute, 477
Edelman, M. W., 81, 81n
Eder, R. A., 365
Edleson, J. L., 403
Edmondson, P., 243
Edmunds, L., 457
Edwards, A., 253, 387
Edwards, C. P., 391
Edwards, L. J., 147
Edwards, O. W., 458, 459
Edwards, S. M., 472
Egeland, B., 268, 272, 404, 520
Eggum, N. D., 387
Ehri, L. C., 312, 343
Ehrman, L., 293
Eichstedt, J. A., 390
Eidelman, A. I., 56, 139
Eiden, R. D., 106
Einspieler, C., 100
Eisbach, A. O., 341, 448
Eisen, M., 483
Eisenberg, N., 254, 258, 261, 369, 371, 379, 387
Eisenberg-Berg, N., 381
Eisenbud, L., 396
Ekeus, C., 306
Ekman, P., 250
Elder, G. H., Jr., 40, 470
Eliakim, A., 421
Elias, C. L., 319
Elias, M. J., 522
Elicker, J., 278
Elieff, C., 192
Elliott, J. G., 517
Elliott, K., 106
Ellis, A. E., 223
Ellis, L. A., 366
Ellis, W. E., 499
Elman, J. L., 236
Else-Quest, N. M., 255, 261, 283, 348, 390
El-Sheikh, M., 38, 38n
Eltzschig, H. K., 133
Eluvathingal, T. J., 171
Ely, R., 451, 464
Emde, R. N., 257
Emery, R. E., 513
Emmerson, N. A., 377
Emory, E. K., 133
Endestad, T., 521
Englund, M., 278
Ennemoser, M., 351, 352
Epstein, L. H., 421
Epstein, R., 174
Erath, S. A., 381
Erden, F., 394
Erickson, J. D., 106, 423
Erickson, M. F., 520

Erikson, E. H., 15, 248, 249, 364, 482
Erkulwater, J., 445
Ernst, M., 87
Eron, L. D., 388
Esbensen, B. M., 341
Espnes, G. A., 484
Espy, K. A., 347
Esser, G., 142
Estep, K., 369
Estourgie-van Burk, G. F., 174
Evanoo, G., 148n
Evans, A. M., 414
Evans, C. B., 79
Evans, D. E., 257, 258
Evans, G. W., 75, 77, 229
Evans, M. E., 401
Evenson, K. R., 113
Everman, D. B., 59

F
Fabes, R. A., 368, 369, 371, 379, 391, 394
Fabricius, W. V., 448
Fagan, J. F., III, 220, 228, 460
Fagard, J., 187
Fagot, B. I., 386, 393, 394, 395
Fahrmeier, E. D., 440
Falbo, T., 485, 508
Falk, D., 168
Fantuzzo, J. W., 470
Fantz, R. L., 193
Faraone, S. V., 83, 444
Farmer, T. W., 498
Farr, R. H., 509
Farrant, K., 337, 365
Farrar, M. J., 340
Farroni, T., 195, 196
Farver, J. M., 31, 374
Fasolo, M., 241
Fattibene, P., 110
Fauth, R. C., 75
Fearnow, M. D., 491
Fearon, R. M. P., 272, 278, 279
Federal Interagency Forum on Child and Family Statistics, 348, 510
Federico, A., 359
Federico, M. J., 423
Feeney, J. A., 120, 121, 154
Feigenbaum, P., 147
Fein, G. G., 373, 373n, 374
Feiring, C., 519
Feldkämper, M., 422
Feldman, D. H., 34
Feldman, J. F., 218, 228
Feldman, R., 37, 56, 138, 139, 141, 147, 255, 262, 274
Feng, Q., 107
Fenson, L., 240
Fenwick, K. D., 198
Ferguson, T. J., 489
Fergusson, D. M., 10, 176
Fernald, A., 240, 241, 354
Fernald, L. C., 177, 416
Fernandes, K. J., 190
Fernyhough, C., 25, 330
Ferrari, M., 418

Ferrell, J., 490
Fesseha, G., 518
Fiano, K., 133
Ficca, G., 172
Field, T. M., 114, 138, 139, 155, 371
Fiese, B. H., 271, 416
Fifer, W. P., 151
Figueroa, Z., 139
Fincham, F. D., 487
Findlay, L. C., 431
Fine, M. A., 400
Finger, B., 272
Finkelstein, E. A., 421
Finn, J. D., 467
Finnilä, K., 521
Fireman, G., 490
Fisch, H., 95
Fischer, A. D., 338
Fischer, K. W., 21, 28, 28n, 251, 255, 370, 440, 442, 489
Fischman, M. G., 313
Fish, M., 268
Fisher, C. B., 45, 46
Fisher, D. M., 144n, 145
Fisher, J. A., 299
Fisher, J. O., 300, 301, 420
Fisher, L., 269
Fisher, P. A., 240, 389
Fisher, S. E., 87
Fite, P. J., 387
FitzGerald, D. P., 492
Fivush, R., 221, 336, 337, 368, 393
Flanagan, C., 512
Flannery, K. A., 294
Flavell, E. R., 327, 339, 341, 490
Flavell, J. H., 327, 339, 341, 368, 443, 490
Flegal, K. M., 420, 421
Fletcher, A. C., 398, 431
Flett, G. L., 485
Flick, L., 113
Floccia, C., 180
Flom, R., 198, 214, 238
Flor, D. L., 401
Flynn, E., 43, 340
Flynn, J. R., 458, 459
Foehr, U. G., 351, 353, 389, 472
Fogel, A., 29, 251, 255
Fomon, S. J., 162
Ford, S., 493
Fordham, K., 259
Forgatch, M., 518
Forman, D. R., 155, 381
Forssell, S. L., 509
Foster, J. A., 421
Foster, M. A., 343, 347
Foster, W. A., 343, 451
Fowler, F., 398, 507
Fox, C. L., 502
Fox, N. A., 168, 193, 250, 254, 259, 271, 281
Foy, J. G., 343
Fradley, E., 330
Fraiberg, S., 250
Fraley, C., 260

Franco, P., 104
Frank, D. A., 107
Frank, J. B., 431
Franke, T. M., 80
Frankel, C. B., 28, 249
Frankenburg, E., 471
Franz, C., 371
Frederiksen-Goldsen, K. I., 516
Fredricks, J. A., 430, 485
Freed, G. L., 303
Freedman, J., 138
Freeman, H., 274
Freitag, C. M., 444
Fremmer-Bomik, E., 271
French, D. C., 374
French, L. A., 438
Freud, S., 15, 248, 249, 264
Frick, P. J., 387
Fried, P. A., 107, 108
Friederici, A. D., 236, 253
Friedman, C. K., 393
Friedman, J. M., 106
Friedman, M. A., 419
Friedman, S. L., 335
Friedrich, M., 236
Fries, A. B. W., 171, 269
Friesen, W., 250
Frith, L., 67
Frith, U., 342
Frost, L. A., 463
Frye, D., 443
Fryer, S. L., 107, 109
Fryns, J. P., 62n
Fu, G., 493
Fuchs, D., 474
Fuchs, L. S., 474
Fukumoto, A., 378
Fuligni, A. J., 36
Fuligni, A. S., 229
Fuller, C., 300
Fuller-Thomson, E., 275
Fullerton, J. T., 132
Fung, H., 366
Furman, W., 41, 507
Furusawa, T., 419
Fuson, K. C., 451, 452
Fussell, E., 157

G

Gaines, J., 305
Gaither, S. M., 488
Galambos, S. J., 516
Galinsky, E., 273, 274, 275n, 516
Gallagher, A. M., 396
Gallagher, L., 56, 353
Gallaway, C., 359
Galler, J. R., 177
Galloway, J. C., 185, 187
Gallup, G. G., 280
Ganchrow, J. R., 180
Gandy, J., 495
Ganea, P. A., 211, 212
Ganger, J., 239
Ganji, V., 300
Ganong, L. H., 509
Garber, J., 155
Garces, E., 349
Garcia, A., 213

Garcia, M. M., 387
Garcia-Bournissen, F., 106
García-Coll, C., 274, 401
Gardner, H., 34, 310n, 456, 456n, 457, 474, 475
Garner, P. W., 32, 254, 369, 491
Garrido-Nag, K., 234
Garrison, M. M., 353
Gartstein, M. A., 258, 261, 262
Garvey, A., 29
Gasden, V., 509
Gaskins, S., 333, 374
Gathercole, S. E., 336
Gathercole, V., 356
Gauthier, A. H., 157
Gauvain, M., 335, 439, 444
Gawlitzek-Maiwald, I., 465
Gaylor, E. E., 298
Gazelle, H., 498
Gazzaniga, M. S., 236
Geary, D. C., 24, 344, 345, 391
Geerts, M., 62n
Geesey, M. E., 117
Geissbuehler, V., 131
Gelman, R., 323, 324, 345
Gelman, S. A., 223, 241, 323, 324, 325, 326, 344, 365, 393, 393n, 426, 504
Gendler, M. N., 253
Genesee, F., 465
Gennetian, L. A., 80
Gentile, D. A., 388
Gentner, D., 354
George, S., 188
Georgsdottir, A., 474
Gerardi-Caulton, G., 260
Gerber, S. B., 467
Gerdes, A. C., 503
Gergely, G., 250, 253
Gershoff, E. T., 27, 77, 381, 382
Gershoff-Stowe, L., 354
Gerson, K., 92
Gerson, S., 211
Gervai, J., 393, 396
Gesell, A., 13
Gest, S. D., 486
Getchell, N., 308, 309n, 313, 428, 428n, 430
Geuze, R. H., 195
Gewirtz, A. H., 10, 403, 518
Ghim, H. R., 195, 195n
Ghulmiyyah, L. M., 135
Gibbons, A., 53
Gibbons, R., 53
Gibbs, J. C., 379, 384
Gibson, E. J., 192, 199
Gibson, J. J., 199
Gibson, K. A., 66
Giedd, J. N., 415
Gilbride, K., 224
Giles, J. W., 390
Giles-Sims, J., 381
Gill, M., 87
Gillespie, D. C., 169
Gillet, J.-P., 65
Gillette, P., 215
Gillies, R. M., 471

Gilliom, M., 369
Gilstrap, L. L., 521
Ginsburg, A. P., 193
Ginsburg, H. P., 345
Ginsburg-Block, M. D., 470
Giorgi, C., 294
Giovanelli, G., 151
Gissler, M., 107
Giudice, S., 292
Giuliani, A., 134
Glade, A. C., 121
Gladstone, I. M., 137
Gladwell, M., 419
Glanz, J., 469
Gleason, J. B., 233
Gleason, T. R., 319, 320
Gleitman, H., 356
Gleitman, L. R., 234, 355, 356
Glover, V., 115
Gluckman, P. D., 128
Gnepp, J., 368
Goddard, S., 215
Godfrey, K. M., 104
Goedereis, E. A., 276
Goeke-Morey, M. C., 71
Goering, J., 76
Goetz, T., 457
Gogate, L. J., 198, 220
Goh, Y. I., 114
Goldberg, A. E., 154
Golden, A., 419
Goldenberg, C., 36
Goldfield, B. A., 241
Goldhammer, F., 455
Golding, J., 423
Goldin-Meadow, S., 238, 327, 356
Goldschmidt, L., 107
Goldsmith, T., 423
Goldstein, A. S., 72
Goldstein, M. H., 237
Goldstein, S. E., 387
Goldwyn, R., 272
Goleman, D., 457
Golfier, F., 134
Golinkoff, R. M., 172, 239, 356
Golomb, C., 310
Golombok, S., 67, 393, 505, 509
Gomez-Perez, E., 443
Gomez-Smith, Z., 275
Göncü, A., 364, 373
Gonzales, N. A., 76
Gonzalez, A.-L., 398
Gonzalez-Rivera, M., 426
Good, T. L., 503
Goodlin-Jones, B. L., 145
Goodman, D. C., 140
Goodman, G. S., 521
Goodman, R., 425
Goodman, S. H., 376
Goodnow, J. J., 24, 381
Goodvin, R., 254, 365, 369
Goodwin, M. H., 394
Goossens, F., 273
Gopnik, A., 223, 241, 253, 324
Gordon, R. A., 79
Gore, S. A., 421

Gormally, S., 150
Gortmaker, S. L., 423
Goswami, U., 324
Gottesman, I. I., 84
Gottfried, A. E., 515
Gottfried, A. W., 515
Gottlieb, G., 9, 82, 84, 86, 86n
Gottman, J. M., 154
Goubet, N., 188
Gould, J. L., 54
Govaerts, P. J., 237
Graber, J. A., 388
Graham, J. A., 487
Graham, S., 470
Graham, S. A., 355
Gralinski, J. H., 282, 283
Granger, R. C., 516
Granic, I., 29
Granier-Deferre, C., 101, 102
Granrud, C. E., 192
Grant, K. B., 77
Grant, K. E., 276
Grantham-McGregor, S. M., 114, 177, 416
Grattan, M. P., 168
Gravitt, G. W., Jr., 376
Gray, K. A., 107
Gray, M. R., 398
Gray-Little, B., 485, 486
Greek, A., 276
Green, F. L., 327, 339, 341, 490
Green, G. E., 149
Green, J. A., 148
Greenbaum, C. W., 262
Greenberg, D., 304
Greenberg, M. T., 334, 377
Greenberger, E., 72
Greendorfer, S. L., 313
Greene, S. M., 512
Greenfield, P. M., 25, 78, 186, 440, 460
Greenhill, L. L., 445
Greenough, W. T., 169, 172
Greenwald, M., 419
Greer, T., 312, 312n
Gregory, A. M., 299
Gregory, R., 509
Grela, B., 213
Grieve, A. J., 228
Grigorenko, E. L., 458, 461
Groome, L. J., 101
Grossman, J. B., 341
Grossman, P. B., 486
Grossmann, K., 268, 271, 274, 276
Grossmann, T., 253
Grotuss, J., 24
Grover, T., 513
Grow-Maienza, J., 477
Gruendel, J., 78
Grusec, J. E., 379, 380, 381, 384n, 403, 486, 491
Grych, J. H., 276
Gugula, S., 393
Guignard, J.-H., 475
Guilford, J. P., 474
Guilleminault, C., 299
Guise, J. M., 134
Gulko, J., 503, 505

Gullone, E., 517
Gulotta, T. P., 11
Gunnar, M. R., 171
Gunnarsdottir, I., 176
Gunnoe, M. L., 383
Gunstad, J., 294
Guo, G., 94
Guo, J., 395
Guralnick, M. J., 503
Gurucharri, C., 492
Gust, D. A., 302
Gustafson, G. E., 148, 149
Gutman, L. M., 231
Gutteling, B. M., 115
Guttentag, R., 490
Gwiazda, J., 193

H

Hack, M., 140
Haddock, G., 419
Haden, C. A., 368
Hafdahl, A. R., 486
Hagan, R. I., 393
Hagerman, R. J., 59
Hagoort, P., 190
Hahn, D.-D., 477
Hahn, E. R., 354
Hahn, H. M., 173
Hahn, S., 64n
Haight, W. L., 226, 333
Hainline, L., 152
Haith, M. M., 187, 218
Hakuta, K., 235
Haladyna, T. M., 470
Halberstadt, A. G., 367
Hale, C. M., 340
Hales, V. N., 104
Halfon, N., 78
Halford, G. S., 21, 22, 217, 327, 328, 438, 441, 442
Halford, W. K., 121, 157
Hall, D. G., 355
Hall, G. S., 13
Hall, J. A., 395
Hall, J. G., 55, 55n
Halle, T. G., 249
Haller, J., 177, 416
Halperin, J. M., 445
Halverson, C. F., 396
Hamel, E., 352, 389, 472
Hamilton, H. A., 79, 514
Hamlin, J. K., 378
Hammer, S. J., 302
Hammes, B., 106
Hampl, J. S., 300
Hamre, B. K., 470
Han, W.-J., 229, 516
Hanawalt, B. A., 12
Hane, A. A., 259
Hanish, L. D., 391
Hanke, W., 108
Hankins, G. D., 135
Hannon, E. E., 189, 191
Hannon, T. S., 417
Hans, S. L., 106, 271
Hansen, M. B., 355
Hany, E. A., 228
Happaney, K., 403
Happé, F., 342
Harari, M. D., 423

Hardin, C. A., 341, 448
Harding, C. G., 230
Hare, B., 234
Hare, T. A., 295
Harlan, E. T., 260, 282
Harlan, S. L., 79
Harley, B., 465
Harley, K., 221
Harlow, H. F., 264
Harmon, R. J., 281
Harold, R. D., 503
Harris, C. J., 23
Harris, G., 150, 501
Harris, M. J., 262
Harris, P. A., 212
Harris, P. L., 324, 482
Harris, R. C., 258
Harris, S., 25, 330, 350
Harris, Y. R., 487
Harrison, A. O., 401
Harrison, Y., 172
Harrist, A. W., 501
Harsh, J., 298
Hart, B., 229, 239, 359
Hart, C., 417
Hart, C. H., 348, 386, 398,
    399, 400, 501, 508
Hart, D., 75, 465, 483, 484
Harter, S., 365, 366, 396, 425,
    483, 485, 489, 490
Harton, H. C., 499
Hartshorn, K., 219
Hartup, W. W., 319, 374, 375,
    499
Harvey-Arnold, E., 386
Harwood, M. D., 340
Harwood, R. L., 78, 270
Haryu, E., 355
Hasebe, Y., 494
Hasegawa, T., 214
Hastings, P. D., 259, 373
Hatton, D. D., 194
Hau, K.-T., 475
Hauck, F. R., 147
Hausenblas, H. A., 113
Hauser-Cram, P., 77
Hausfather, A., 230
Hawke, S., 94n
Hawkins, J. N., 485
Haws, R. A., 132
Hay, D. F., 155, 374
Hayne, H., 181, 182, 213, 219,
    220, 221, 221n, 222n,
    226, 277, 336
Hayslip, B., 275
Hayward, C., 512
Haywood, H. C., 461
Haywood, K. I., 313
Haywood, K. M., 308, 309n,
    313, 428, 428n, 430
Hazen, N. L., 274
He, Z., 339
Head Start Bureau, 349
Healy, M., 164
Heath, S. B., 74, 459
Heathcock, J., 187
Hebert, M., 520
Heckman, J. J., 80, 350
Hedges, L. V., 467
Hediger, M. L., 114, 137

Helburn, S. W. ., 230
Held, R., 188
Heller, L., 510
Heller, T. L., 377
Heller, W., 168
Helwig, C. C., 384, 385, 493,
    494
Henderson, H. A., 259
Henderson, R. L., 448
Henderson, S. O., 304
Hengst, J. A., 35
Henricsson, L., 470
Henriksen, T. B., 106
Hepper, P. G., 181, 293
Heraghty, J. L., 145
Herald, S. L., 375, 498
Herbert, J., 213, 220
Herbert, T. B., 297
Hermer, L., 196
Hernandez, D., 516
Hernandez, D. J., 36
Hernandez-Reif, M., 138,
    139, 181, 198, 220
Heron, J., 423
Herrenkohl, L. R., 468
Herrera, E., 155
Herrnstein, R. J., 458
Hertenstein, M. J., 249, 253
Hesketh, K., 352
Hespos, S. J., 143, 167, 168,
    214, 280
Hesse, E., 268
Hetherington, E. M., 510,
    511, 512, 513, 514, 515
Hewlett, B. S., 274, 276
Hewlett, S., 141
Hewstone, M., 497
Heyes, C., 182
Heyman, G. D., 325, 365, 367,
    390, 486, 503
Hickling, A. K., 323, 463
Hicks, J. H., 276
Higginbottom, G. M. A., 35
Higgins, A. C., 420
High, P. C., 344
Hilden, D., 218
Hildreth, K., 219
Hilgers, K. K., 290
Hill, A. L., 369
Hill, C. R., 469
Hill, E. J., 516
Hill, J. L., 139, 139n
Hilt, L. M., 488, 489n
Hind, H., 300
Hinojosa, T., 293
Hiraki, K., 182, 214
Hirsh-Pasek, K., 33, 172, 239,
    319, 356
Hiscock, H., 146
Hitch, G., 336
Hjälmäs, K., 423
Hjern, A., 306
Ho, E., 345
Hoch-Espada, A., 519
Hock, H. S., 446
Hodgens, J. B., 425
Hodges, J., 269
Hodges, R. M., 438
Hodnett, E. D., 131
Hoehn, T., 136

Hoeksma, J. B., 262
Hoekstra, R. A., 55n
Hofer, J., 34
Hoff, E., 37, 72, 240
Hoff, E. V., 320
Hofferth, S. L., 514
Hoffman, L. W., 282, 379,
    490, 515
Hoffman, M. K., 134
Hoffman, M. L., 282
Hoffmann, W., 110
Hoglund, W., 502
Hohmann, L. M., 320
Hohne, E. A., 190
Hokoda, A., 487
Holden, G. W., 381
Holditch-Davis, D., 147
Holland, A. L., 170
Holland, C. R., 228, 460
Hollich, G. J., 356
Hollis, C., 399
Holmes, R. M., 433
Holobow, N., 465
Holowka, S., 465
Homer, B., 448, 448n
Hommerding, K. D., 268
Honein, M. A., 106
Hong, M., 477
Hood, B. M., 208
Hood, M., 343
Hopkins, B., 168, 186
Hopkins, J., 271
Hopkins-Golightly, T., 136
Horgan, D., 357
Horn, J. M., 85, 459
Horne, R. S. C., 147
Horner, S. L., 488
Horner, T. M., 252
Horst, J. S., 220
Horwood, J., 10
Houck, G. M., 255
Houlihan, J., 110
Houts, A. C., 423
Hoven, C. W., 41
Howard, B. J., 298
Howard, K. S., 404
Howe, M. L., 181, 216, 224
Howe, N., 277
Howell, C. T., 139
Howell, K. K., 106, 107, 109
Howes, C., 278
Hoza, B., 501, 503
Hsu, C.-C., 110
Huang, C.-C., 510
Hubbs-Tait, L., 110
Huberty, P. D., 433
Hudson, J. A., 336, 337
Hudziak, J. J., 87
Huesmann, L. R., 388
Hueston, W. J., 117, 117n
Hughes, C., 340, 341, 369
Hughes, D. C., 303
Hughes, J. N., 469, 486
Huh, K., 461
Huizink, A. C., 107, 114
Human Genome Program,
    52
Humphrey, T., 149
Hunnius, S., 195

Hunt, C. E., 147
Huotilainen, M., 101
Hurewitz, F., 464
Hurley, M., 304
Hursti, U.-K., 299
Hurt, H., 107
Hurtado-Ortiz, M. T., 335
Huston, A. C., 352
Hutinger, P. L., 353
Huttenlocher, J., 208, 323
Huttenlocher, P. R., 164, 170,
    172, 214, 292
Huyck, M. H., 395
Hwang, C. P., 154
Hyde, J. S., 141, 155
Hymel, S., 500, 502
Hynd, G. W., 473
Hyppönen, E., 105

I
Ickovics, J., 119
Iglowstein, I., 172
Imai, M., 354, 355
Im-Bolter, N., 334
Indus, K., 508
Ingersoll, E. W., 180
Ingram, C. D., 143
Intraub, H., 195
Iocaboni, M., 182
Iozzi, L., 465
Irwin, J. R., 149
Isabella, R., 270
Isasi, R. M., 67
Ishihara, K., 111
Israel, M., 463
Israelashvili, R., 275
Itti, E., 62
Ivey, P., 252
Izard, C. E., 251, 389

J
Jaakkola, J. J., 107
Jackson, A. P., 80
Jackson, I., 339
Jackson, L. A., 472
Jackson, R. A., 66
Jacobs, J. A., 92
Jacobs, J. E., 485, 487, 503,
    504
Jacobs, J. N., 515
Jacobson, J. L., 104, 109, 110
Jacobson, S. W., 104, 109, 110
Jacobvitz, D., 404
Jacquet, P., 60
Jaffe, J., 270
Jaffee, S. R., 510
Jambor, T. W., 373
Jambunathan, S., 401
Jamieson, J. R., 243
Jankowski, J. J., 195, 195n,
    218
Jansen, A., 418
Jansen, J., 176
Janssens, J. M. A. M., 385
Janz, K. F., 434
Jason, L. A., 424, 425
Jaudes, P. K., 402

Jayakody, R., 509
Jean, G., 465
Jeffrey, J., 420
Jelalian, E., 417
Jenkins, E. A., 338
Jenkins, J. M., 340, 341, 507
Jenkins, R., 420
Jenni, O. G., 298, 299
Jennings, R. W., 63
Jensen, A. R., 83, 458, 459
Jeremy, R. J., 106
Jerome, E. M., 470
Jeynes, W. H., 77, 513
Ji, C. Y., 417
Ji, G., 508
Jiao, S., 508
Jimenez, E., 296
Jing, Q., 508
Jipson, J. L., 323
Jodl, K. M., 515
Joh, A. S., 193, 199
Johnson, C., 463
Johnson, D. C., 147
Johnson, D. E., 9
Johnson, E. K., 190
Johnson, J., 334
Johnson, J. G., 388, 388n
Johnson, K. C., 132
Johnson, M. H., 23, 164, 165,
    167, 195, 196n, 209, 215,
    237
Johnson, M. L., 162
Johnson, S. C., 266, 266n, 426
Johnson, S. P., 189, 190, 191,
    196, 197, 197n
Johnston, J., 401
Johnston, M. V., 166
Jones, E. F., 384
Jones, H. E., 107
Jones, I., 433
Jones, J., 111n, 112
Jones, N. A., 371
Jones, R. L., 296
Jones, S. M., 75, 523
Jones, S. S., 182
Jongbloet, P. H., 59
Joo, C.-A., 477
Jordan, B., 129, 132
Joseph, R. M., 342
Joshi, P. T., 518
Joy, M. E., 380
Juby, H., 515
Judge, S., 472
Juffer, F., 65, 67, 278, 458
Juhl, T., 155
Jumpstart Evaluation Team,
    350
Jürgensen, M., 392
Jusczyk, P. W., 151, 189, 190,
    196, 238, 241
Jussim, L., 470
Justice, E. M., 449
Juvonen, J., 497

K
Kable, J. A., 106, 107
Kagan, J., 8, 208, 214, 259,
    261, 271
Kahn, K. L., 131
Kahn, R. S., 87

Kaijser, M., 104
Kail, R. V., 218, 336, 428, 442, 443, 450
Kaiser Commission on Medicaid and the Uninsured, 303
Kaitz, M., 143
Kalil, A., 80, 509
Kalinka, J., 108
Kalish, C. W., 223, 325, 326
Kaller, C. P., 335
Kalra, L., 170
Kane, C. M., 79
Kane, P., 155
Kang, J. Y., 465
Kang, N. H., 477
Karafantis, D. M., 497
Karasik, L. B., 184, 188
Karraker, K. H., 261
Karrass, J., 242
Kaslow, N. J., 376
Kastens, K. A., 438, 439
Kato, I., 147
Katz, L. F., 369
Katz, V. L., 137
Katzmarzyk, P. T., 413
Kaufman, J., 209
Kaufman, R., 461, 462n
Kavanaugh, R. D., 319, 340
Kavoura, A., 502
Kavsek, M., 228
Kawakami, K., 261
Kaye, K., 206
Kazdin, A. E., 389, 390
Keating, D. P., 484
Keating-Lefler, R., 157
Keefe, M. R., 149
Keen, R., 188, 211
Keeton, W. T., 54
Keil, F. C., 324, 356
Keller, H., 281, 281n
Keller, S. S., 234
Kelley, M. L., 515
Kelley, S. A., 367, 370
Kellman, P. J., 151, 152n, 190
Kelly, D. J., 196
Kelly, J., 511, 512, 513
Kelly, N., 474
Kemeny, M. E., 297
Kempe, C. H., 402
Kendall, G., 136
Kendrick, D., 306
Kennedy, A. M., 302
Kennedy, J. M., 310
Kennell, J. H., 130, 131, 142
Kenney, G. M., 79
Kenny, S., 209
Kerem, E., 518
Keren, M., 226
Kern, S., 354
Kernis, M. H., 486
Kerns, K. A., 277, 508
Kerr, D. C. R., 379
Kesler, S. R., 62, 62n
Kessen, W., 144
Kessler, R. C., 445
Kettunen, S., 109
Kieffer, M. J., 466
Kieras, J. E., 254, 369
Kieschke, U., 469

Killen, M., 384, 385, 494, 496, 498, 504, 505n
Kilpatrick, S. W., 419
Kim, H., 275
Kim, J., 41, 485
Kim, J. M., 494
Kim, M., 354
Kim, Y. K., 374
Kimbro, R. T., 176
King, E. M., 73
King, N. J., 517
King, R. M., 379
King, V., 515
Kinney, H. C., 147
Kinnunen, M.-L., 174
Kinsht, I. A., 262
Kinzler, K. D., 214
Kirchner, G., 430
Kiriakidis, S. P., 502
Kiriakou, S., 305
Kirkham, N. Z., 334
Kirkpatrick, M., 470
Kisilevsky, B. S., 101, 252
Kisly, A., 115
Kistner, J., 371
Kitzmann, K. M., 403, 508
Kjønniksen, L., 434
Klahr, D., 21
Klaus, M. H., 131, 142
Klebanov, P. K., 229
Klein, M. C., 133
Klein, N., 140
Klein, P. J., 210, 220
Klein, P. S., 37
Klenberg, L., 443
Klesges, L. M., 107
Klibanoff, R. S., 345
Kliegman, R. M., 58n, 111n
Kliewer, W., 491
Klimes-Dougan, B., 371
Klingman, A., 518
Klingner, J. K., 473
Klitzing, K. von, 121
Klomsten, A. T., 484
Kloos, A. L., 415
Klute, M. M., 282
Knaack, A., 258, 260, 283, 380
Knafo, A., 379, 381
Knapp, P. K., 431
Knickmeyer, R. C., 165
Knight, N., 495
Knill, D. C., 192
Knobloch, H., 144, 144n
Knopf, M., 220
Knoppers, B. M., 67
Knox, D., 94n
Knutson, J. F., 381
Kobayashi, T., 214
Kobayashi, Y., 332
Kochanoff, A. T., 368
Kochanska, G., 251, 258, 260, 282, 283, 378, 379, 380, 381, 383
Kochel, K. P., 375
Kochenderfer-Ladd, B., 502
Koelsch, S., 236
Koenig, M. A., 325
Koestner, R., 371
Kohen, D. E., 76, 80
Kohlberg, L., 395

Kolomer, S. R., 275
Komsi, N., 258
Konner, M. J., 188
Konold, T. R., 375
Konstantopoulos, S., 467
Kontic-Vucinic, O., 114
Kooijman, V., 190
Kopp, C. B., 254, 278, 282, 283
Koppe, J. G., 111
Koren, G., 114
Korkman, M., 109, 443
Kornhaber, M. L., 476
Koslowski, B., 152, 153
Kossakowska-Petrycka, K., 155
Kotchick, B. A., 510
Kouba, E., 364, 373
Kovacs, S. L., 336
Koven, M., 366
Kowalski, K., 496
Kowalski, R. M., 502
Kozer, E., 106
Kozol, J., 471
Kozulin, A., 25
Krafft, K., 332
Krakow, J. B., 283
Krascum, R. M., 325, 325n
Kraus, U., 220
Krawinkel, M., 177
Krcmar, M., 213
Kreppner, J., 171
Kressley-Mba, R. A., 220
Krevans, J., 379
Krieg, D. B., 156
Krishnamoorthy, J. S., 417
Krogh, H. R., 505
Kroonenberg, P. M., 268n
Krumhansl, C. L., 189
Kuchner, J., 255
Kuczynski, L., 381, 398, 400, 507
Kuebli, J., 336, 393
Kugelmass, J., 473
Kuhl, P. K., 181, 191
Kuhn, D., 20, 43, 447
Kuklinski, M. R., 470
Kumar, S., 64n
Kumpf, M., 458
Kunisaki, S. M., 63
Kunzinger, E. L., III, 446
Kuppens, S., 399
Kurdek, L. A., 400
Kurtz-Costes, B., 485
Kwok, O., 469
Ky, K. N., 44
Kyratzis, A., 395

L
Lacourse, E., 381
Ladd, G. W., 375, 377, 498, 501
La Ferle, C., 472
Lafosse, A., 323
Lagattuta, K. H., 368, 490
Lagnado, L., 518
La Greca, A., 501
Lahti-Nuuttila, P., 443
Laible, D., 368, 377
Laird, R. D., 377, 500

Laitman, C. J., 106
Lalonde, C. E., 340
Lam, S., 488, 488n
Lamarche, V., 508
Lamaze, F., 130
Lamb, M. E., 79, 143, 230, 273, 275, 278, 351, 507
Lambert, S. M., 95
Lambert, W., 465
Lamphear, B. P., 296
Lampl, M., 162
Lancy, D. F., 333
Landry, S. H., 335
Lang, A. R., 109
Langdridge, D., 92
Lange, G., 449
Langer, J., 208, 215
Langman, L., 209
Lansford, J. E., 381, 382, 383, 500, 511, 512, 513
Lantieri, L., 522
Lantz, P. M., 303
Lanzi, R. G., 231, 350
Lapchick, R., 431
Lapkin, S., 465
Largo, R. H., 428
Larroque, B., 140
Larsen, J. A., 463
Larsen, J. T., 490
Larzelere, R. E., 382
Lashley, F. R., 53, 55, 55n, 58n
Latendresse, S. J., 72, 74, 74n
Latner, J. D., 419
Latz, S., 173
Laucht, M., 142
Lauderdale, D. S., 147
Lauer, J. A., 175
Lauer, P. A., 517
Laurent, H., 275
Laursen, B., 72, 502
Lavelli, M., 251
Lavigne, J. V., 298
Law, C., 420
Law, K. L., 107
Lawrence, K., 62
Lawson, K. R., 254
Layman, L. C., 55
Lazar, I., 349
Lazarus, B. N., 491
Lazarus, R. S., 491
Lazinski, M. J., 114, 115
Leadbeater, B., 502
Leaper, C., 240, 393, 394, 431, 503
Leavitt, L. A., 138
Lebeaux, D. S., 463
LeBlanc, L. A., 423
LeBourgeois, M. K., 298
Lecanuet, J.-P., 101, 102
Lecerf, T., 455
Lecuyer, E., 255
Lederberg, A., 243
Lederer, A., 461
LeFevre, J., 343
Legare, C. H., 503
Legerstee, M., 253
Le Grand, R., 169
Lehr, V. T., 150
Lehtonen, L., 150
Leiferman, J. A., 113
Leinbach, M. D., 386
Lemche, E., 332

Lee, V. E., 240, 344
Lee, W. N., 472
Lee, Y., 374
Leerkes, E. M., 26, 255
Leet, T., 113
LeFevre, J., 343
Legare, C. H., 503
Lemerise, E. A., 387
Lempert, H., 357, 463
Lengua, L. J., 258, 511
Lenhart, A., 472
Leon, K., 512
Leonard, W. R., 413
Leong, D. J., 25, 224, 335, 468
Lepage, J.-F., 183
Lerner, R. M., 4, 9, 31, 43, 70, 82
LeSieur, K., 377
Leslie, A. M., 214, 342
Lester, B. M., 9, 107, 148n, 149, 152, 153
Lett, D., 12
Leung, M.-C., 498
Leventhal, T., 75, 76
Levi, J., 422
Levin, I., 312
Levine, L. J., 368
LeVine, R. A., 73, 270
LeVine, S. E., 73
Leviton, A., 296
Levtzion-Korach, O., 194
Levy, G. D., 504
Levy, S. R., 496, 497
Levy-Shiff, R., 275
Lewis, C., 275, 341, 507
Lewis, M., 251, 254, 261, 280, 370, 489, 519
Lewis, M. D., 29, 250
Lewis, O., 472
Lewis, T. L., 169
Lewko, J. H., 313
Lhote, M., 149
Li, D.-K., 106, 147
Li, S.-C., 454
Li, Z., 263
Liben, L. S., 22, 321, 390, 396, 397, 438, 439, 505
Licklider, R., 9, 82, 84, 138, 198, 214
Lidz, C. S., 461
Lidz, J. L., 236, 355, 356, 358
Liebaers, I., 64n
Liebergott, J. W., 240
Lieberman, E. S., 133
Liebert, R. M., 381
Liederman, J., 294
Lieven, E., 242, 356
Li-Grining, C. P., 260
Lillard, A. S., 226, 319, 348
Lilly, A. R., 335, 443
Limber, S. P., 502
Lin, Z. L., 136
Linares, T. J., 107

Lincove, J. A., 468
Lindenberger, U., 9, 83
Lindsay, L. L., 26, 71
Lindsay-Hartz, J., 370, 490
Lindsey, E. W., 26, 70, 319, 377
Linebarger, D. L., 351
Linn, K., 213
Linn, R. L., 471
Lino, M., 92
Linscheid, T. R., 178
Linver, M. R., 229
Lipman, E. L., 390
Lipsitt, L. P., 147
Lipton, J. S., 215
Liszkowski, U., 238, 239
Litovsky, R. Y., 151, 194
Little, C., 255
Little, G. A., 140
Little, T. D., 385, 387
Littlejohn, A., 305, 306
Littlejohn, K., 310
Liu, A. H., 423
Liu, D., 340
Liu, G., 426
Liu, H.-M., 191
Liu, J., 177, 301, 416
Lloyd, L., 470
Lo, Y., 496
Loch, J., 116
Lochman, J. E., 387
Locke, J., 12
Lockhart, K. L., 324
Lockhart, R. S., 22
Lockman, J. J., 312, 312n
Lockwood, R. L., 508
Loeb, S., 351
Loehlin, J. C., 85, 260, 262, 459
Logan, A., 503
Loganovskaja, T. K., 110
Loganovsky, K. N., 110
Lohman, D. F., 455
Loken, E., 41
Lollis, S., 398, 507
London, K., 519
Longo, M. R., 183, 209
Longstaffe, S., 423
Lonigan, C. J., 242
Loock, C., 109n
Looker, D., 472
Loots, G., 243
Lopez, A., 111n, 112
Lorenz, K. Z., 23
Lorenz, R. P., 115
Lothian, J. A., 131
LoTurco, J. J., 165
Louie, V., 36
Louis, J., 146
Lourenco, O., 385
Loutzenhiser, L., 276
Love, J. M., 232, 273, 349
Lovell-Badge, R., 55
Low, J., 44
Low, J. A., 101
Lozoff, B., 173, 177, 296
Lubart, T. I., 474, 475
Luby, J., 371
Lucas, D. E., 146
Lucas-Thompson, R., 377

Luce, P. A., 151
Luciana, M., 23
Ludemann, P. M., 196
Luk, G., 465
Luna, B., 169, 335, 442, 443
Lund, N., 106
Lundy, B. L., 274, 276
Luo, Y., 147, 214
Lupyan, G., 223
Lussier, G., 513
Luthar, S. S., 72, 74, 74n
Lutkenhaus, P., 280
Lynam, D., 376, 385, 387, 501
Lynch, M. J., 296
Lynch, S. K., 381
Lynch, V., 79
Lyon, T. D., 341, 521
Lyons-Ruth, K., 271, 278, 279
Lytton, H., 56

M
Ma, L., 226
Ma, W., 354
Maas, F. K., 385
Macartney, S. E., 36
Maccoby, E. E., 391, 394, 507, 515
MacDorman, M. F., 140, 147
Machin, G. A., 55, 67
Mackey, K., 398
Mackey-Bilaver, L., 402
Mackie, S., 444
Macones, G. A., 134
Macpherson, A., 424
MacWhinney, B., 21, 239, 357
Madigan, S., 271
Madole, K. L., 220, 222
Madom, S., 470
Madrona, M. M., 132
Madsen, S. A., 155
Madsen, S. D., 507
Maggs, J. L., 516
Magnuson, K. A., 72
Magnussen, S., 521
Magos, L., 110
Maguire, M., 369
Mahoney, A., 379
Mahoney, L. T., 434
Main, M., 266, 268, 272
Majdandžić, M., 258
Majnemer, A., 186
Major, B., 461
Majorano, M., 241
Makin, J. E., 108
Makris, N., 495
Malatesta, C. Z., 255
Malina, R. M., 309n, 428
Malkin, C., 224
Mandara, J., 72
Mandler, J. M., 214, 222, 223
Manfra, L., 330
Mangelsdorf, S. C., 258, 365
Mann, T., 226, 319, 320n, 332
Mann, V., 343
Mao, A., 173
Maratsos, M., 357
Marchman, V. A., 170, 240, 354, 358
Marcon, R. A., 348, 350
Marcus, G. F., 190, 357

Marcus, J., 206
Mardh, P. A., 111n
Marentette, P. F., 237
Mareschal, D., 208
Margie, N. G., 384
Marian, V., 213
Mariano, K. A., 499
Mariner, C. L., 383
Markell, M., 494, 496
Markman, E. M., 206, 214, 355, 356
Markova, G., 253
Markovits, H., 499
Marks, K. S., 208
Marlier, L., 150, 150n, 151
Marrott, H., 210
Marschik, P. B., 100
Marsee, M. A., 387
Marsh, H. W., 366, 431, 475, 484, 485, 486
Marshall-Baker, A., 138
Marsland, K. W., 79
Martin, A., 229
Martin, C. L., 261, 282, 390, 391, 394, 396, 397
Martin, G. L., 18
Martin, M. M., 343, 465
Martin, N. G., 262
Martin, R., 61
Martin, R. P., 137
Martinez, I., 59
Martinez-Frias, M. L., 109
Martlew, M., 311, 311n
Martyn, C. N., 104
Marx, R. W., 23
Marzolf, D. P., 321
Masataka, N., 241
Masciadrelli, B. P., 516
Mascolo, M. F., 251, 255, 370, 489, 490
Mash, C., 222
Mashburn, A. J., 349, 375
Mashek, D. J., 371
Mason, A. D., 73
Massey, Z., 119
Masson, P., 95
Masten, A. S., 9, 10, 11, 520, 522n, 523
Masterov, D. V., 80, 350
Mastropieri, D., 151
Masur, E. F., 241, 443
Matheson, A., 253
Matheson, C. C., 278
Mathews, F., 114
Mathews, T. J., 140, 147
Mathiesen, K. S., 11
Matsuba, M. K., 75
Mattson, S. N., 107, 109
Matusov, E., 445
Mauer, D., 319
Maughan, B., 425
Maupin, R., 117
Maurer, D., 169
Mauro, J. A., 257
Mavroveli, S., 457
Mayberry, R. I., 119, 235
Maybery, M., 342
Mayeiux, L., 376, 497
Mayer, J. D., 457
Mayes, L. C., 107, 183

Mayes, R., 445
Mayeux, L., 501
Maynard, A. E., 25, 226, 440, 460
McAlister, A., 341
McBee, M. T., 476
McBride-Chang, C., 450, 465
McCabe, A., 343, 464
McCall, R. B., 228
McCandliss, B. D., 23
McCartney, G. R., 293
McCartney, K., 85, 230, 262, 273, 278, 469
McCarton, C., 80, 139
McCarty, M. E., 187, 188, 211
McClelland, M. M., 375
McColgan, K. L., 335
McConachie, H., 61
McCormack, T., 335
McCormack, V. A., 105
McCormick, M. C., 139
McCoy, J. K., 277, 507
McCune, L., 319
McDade, T., 173
McDonagh, M. S., 134
McDonough, L., 210, 222, 223
McDougall, P., 502
McDowell, D. J., 491
McElwain, N. L., 270, 277
McEwen, B., 9
McGee, C. L., 109
McGee, G., 67
McGee, L. M., 343, 343n, 345
McGillicuddy-De Lisi, A. V., 496, 496n
McGinley, M., 370
McGlothlin, H., 496
McGrath, S. K., 131
McGregor, K. K., 354
McHale, J. P., 70, 121, 154, 431
McHale, S. M., 394, 508, 516
McIntyre, C. W., 443
McKelvie, P., 44
McKenna, J. J., 173
McKie, P., 455
McKown, C., 460, 461, 461n, 470
McKusick, V. A., 56n, 58n, 59
McLanahan, S., 512
McLearn, K. T., 78
McLoyd, V. C., 231, 350, 381, 383
McMahon, C. A., 155
McManus, I. C., 293
McManus, K., 133
McMichael, A. J., 296
MCR Vitamin Study Research Group, 114
McWilliams, L., 386
Mead, G. H., 483
Mead, M., 129
Meadow-Orlans, K. P., 243
Meaney, J., 59
Meaney, M. J., 87
Mebert, C. J., 382, 382n
Mechelli, A., 465
Meek, J., 167
Mehlmadrona, L., 132

Meins, E., 330, 340
Meisels, S. J., 450
Meister, C., 469
Melby, J. N., 72
Melinder, A., 521
Melton, G. B., 81
Meltzoff, A. N., 181, 182, 182n, 209, 210, 211, 213, 220, 237, 238, 253, 352, 365
Melzi, G., 451, 464
Mendoza, J. R., 297
Mennella, J. A., 150
Ment, L. R., 138
Menyuk, P., 240
Mercy, J. A., 305
Meredith, N. V., 413
Merisca, R., 380
Merrilees, C. E., 70
Mervis, C. B., 325
Messinger, D., 251
Meyer, J. R., 521
Meyer, P. A., 296
Meyer, R., 174
Meyer, S., 369, 370
Mezulis, A. H., 155
Miccio, A. W., 304
Miceli, P. J., 263
Michael, G. F., 293
Michalik, N. M., 371
Michels, K. B., 105, 175n
Michiels, D., 276
Mick, E., 444
Midgett, C., 306
Midlin, M., 420
Milan, S., 298, 299
Milevsky, A., 398
Milgrom, J., 139
Miller, A. L., 277
Miller, C. F., 504
Miller, C. J., 473
Miller, J., 275
Miller, L. T., 455
Miller, M., 343, 451
Miller, M. A., 302
Miller, P. A., 491
Miller, P. D., 450
Miller, P. H., 154, 217, 334, 443, 444, 448
Miller, P. J., 35, 226, 366
Miller, S. A., 341, 448
Milligan, K., 340
Mills, D., 169, 234
Mills, R. S. L., 370, 380, 490
Mills, T. L., 275
Mindell, J. A., 298
Minkler, M., 275
Minkoff, H., 63
Mintz, J., 366
Miracle, J. A., 192
Misailidi, P., 490
Mischel, W., 381
Mishna, F., 46
Mistry, R. S., 72, 347
Mitchell, A., 150
Miura, I. T., 452
Mize, J., 377, 398, 507
Mocarelli, P., 111
Modi, A. C., 197, 419
Moens, E., 418

Moerk, E. L., 233
Moffatt, M. E., 423
Moffitt, T. E., 305
Mohite, P., 395
Molfese, V. J., 347
Moll, H., 323
Moll, I., 334
Moller, K., 154
Moller, L. C., 394
Möller, O., 177
Mondloch, C. J., 195, 196n
Monk, C., 115
Monk, C. S., 165, 342
Montague, D. P. F., 253
Montague, L., 354
Montemayor, R., 483
Montero, I., 25
Montessori, M., 348
Montgomery, D. E., 341, 448
Montgomery, G. L., 145, 172
Moolchan, E. T., 87
Moon, C., 151
Moon, R. Y., 147
Moonie, D. A., 423
Moore, C., 281, 390
Moore, E. G. J., 459
Moore, G. A., 252
Moore, J. B., 313
Moore, K. L., 54, 64n, 65n,
    96, 97n, 98, 98n, 99, 100,
    103n, 105, 163, 164
Moore, M. K., 181, 182, 182n,
    209, 210
Moore, P. J., 487
Moore, R. W., 193
Moore, S. G., 152
Moosbrugger, H., 455
Moran, G., 270, 271
Moran, G. F., 12
Moran, S., 34, 474, 475
Morelli, G. A., 173, 252, 333
Moreno, A. J., 282
Morgan, B., 342
Morgan, J. L., 190
Morgan, P. L., 75
Morgane, P. J., 113
Mori, L., 425
Morikawa, H., 241
Morris, G., 221
Morris, J. E., 516
Morris, J. K., 61
Morris, P. A., 26, 80, 84
Morrongiello, B. A., 198, 305,
    306, 425
Morse, S. B., 137
Morton, J., 152, 196
Mortweet, S. L., 189
Mosby, L., 383
Mosely-Howard, G. S., 79
Moses, L. J., 253, 340
Moss, E., 270, 272, 278
Mosteller, F., 466
Mota, J., 433
Mottus, R., 508
Moulden, A., 423
Mounts, N. S., 41
Mroczek, D. K., 485
Mrug, S., 503
Mu, X., 477
Mu, Y., 453

Muckle, G., 110
Mueller, C. M., 487
Mueller, E. C., 277
Muenchow, S., 79
Muentener, P., 213
Muir, D., 327
Mulder, E. J. H., 107, 114
Mullen, M., 183
Muller, F., 111n
Mullett-Hume, E., 41
Mulvaney, M. K., 332, 382,
    382n
Mumme, D. L., 253
Munakata, Y., 21, 22, 208,
    209, 236
Mundy, P., 281, 342
Munholland, K. A., 266
Munroe, R. L., 391
Muret-Wagstaff, S., 152
Muris, P., 517
Murphy, T. H., 170
Murray, A. D., 148
Murray, C., 458
Murray, K. T., 260, 282
Murray, L., 155
Murry, V. M., 508
Musick, K., 509
Mussen, P., 381
Mutti, D. O., 422
Myant, K. A., 426
Myers, G. J., 110
Myers, L. J., 438
Myowa-Yamakoshi, M., 181,
    182n

N
Nadel, J., 281
Nader, P. R., 417
Nafstad, P., 304
Nagel, K., 238
Nagel, S. K., 72
Nagin, D. S., 381
Naglieri, J., 330
Nagy, E., 181
Nagy, W. E., 463
Naigles, L. R., 355
Naito, M., 448
Namy, L. L., 354
Nánez, J., Sr., 192
Narr, K. L., 444
Nassar, A. H., 115
Nastasi, B. K., 353
Natale, R., 132
National Association for
    Sport and Physical
    Education, 313
National Center for
    Biotechnology
    Information, National
    Institutes of Health, 57
National Coalition for the
    Homeless, 75
National Council of Youth
    Sports, 430, 431
National Early Literacy Panel,
    344
National Institutes of Health,
    64
Navarrete, C., 59
Navarro, A. M., 132

Nawrocki, T., 371
Nazzi, T., 324
Neal, A., 496, 496n
Needham, A., 188, 197
Needleman, H. L., 296, 414
Needlman, R., 173
Neff, K. D., 494
Neiderman, D., 209
Neil, A., 114
Neisser, U., 213
Neitzel, C., 332
Nelson, C. A., 25, 99, 118,
    165, 165n, 166, 168, 170,
    191, 215, 220, 292, 294,
    387, 399, 414, 415, 443
Nelson, D. A., 276, 386, 399,
    401, 500, 501
Nelson, J., 384n
Nelson, K., 25, 195, 221, 239,
    365
Nelson, N. M., 393
Nelson, S. E., 162
Nemer, K. M., 471
Nemet, D., 421
Nemeth, R., 396
Nepomnyaschy, L., 141
Neri, Q., 67
Nesdale, D., 494, 496
Nettelbeck, T., 442
Netto, D., 198
Neuburger, H., 237
Neufeld, S. J., 254
Neuman, S. B., 240, 344, 345
Neumark-Sztainer, D., 416
Neville, H. J., 169, 235
Nevin, R., 296
Newachek, P., 303
Newcomb, A. F., 501
Newcombe, N. S., 208, 323,
    336
Newcombe, R., 337
Newell, L. D., 398, 399, 400,
    508
Newland, L. A., 274
Newman, A. J., 235
Newnham, C. A., 139
Newport, E. L., 190, 234, 235,
    236
Newson, E., 331
Newson, J., 331
Newton, N., 129
Ng, F. F., 488, 488n
Ng, S., 303
Nguyen, S. P., 393, 393n
Nguyen, T. M., 67
Ni, Y., 438
NICHD Early Child Care
    Research Network, 230,
    273, 351, 359
Nicholls, A. L., 310
Nichols, K. E., 281, 381
Nicholson, C., 167
Nicholson, J. M., 513, 515
Nickerson, P., 431
Nickman, S. L., 65, 68
Nicoladis, E., 465
Niehaus, M. D., 302
Nielsen, J., 420
Nielsen, M., 280, 320
Nielsen, S. J., 420

Nielsen Company, 472
Nievar, M. A., 270
Nigam, M., 21
Nigg, J. T., 107
Ningiuruvik, L., 460
Nippold, M. A., 463
Nisbett, R. E., 458, 459
Nishitani, S., 150
Nix, R. L., 399
Noe, G. F., 119
Noël, M.-P., 327
Noguera, P., 476
Noland, J. S., 107
Noller, P., 511
Noonan, C. W., 296
Noonan, K., 137
Nord, M., 178
Norwich, B., 474
Norwitz, E. R., 126, 134
Noterdaeme, M., 294
Nucci, L. P., 384, 385, 493,
    494
Nucci, M. S., 494
Nugent, J. K., 152, 153
Nunes, T., 344
Nurmi, J.-E., 398, 400
Nye, B., 467

O
Oakes, L. M., 220, 222, 223,
    326
Oakland, T. D., 458, 459
Oberecker, R., 236
Oberlander, T. F., 106
Obradović, J., 11, 75
O'Brien, A., 64n
O'Brien, J. G., 421
O'Brien, M., 65
O'Brien, M. A., 304
O'Callaghan, M. J., 294
O'Connor, A. R., 422
O'Connor, B. B., 299
O'Connor, E., 469
O'Connor, T. G., 115, 169,
    269, 271, 507
O'Dea, J. A., 416
Odouli, R., 106
OECD (Organisation for
    Economic Cooperation
    and Development), 80n,
    141
Ogan, A., 226, 319, 320n, 332
Ogbu, J. U., 487
Ogden, C. L., 417
Ohgi, S., 153
Ohlsson, G., 131
Okagaki, L., 456
Okami, P., 173
Okamoto, Y., 328, 429, 452
Okanda, M., 281
O'Keefe, M. J., 137
Olafson, E., 520
O'Laughlin, E. M., 92, 93n
Olds, D. L., 115, 116
O'Leary, S. G., 382
Olineck, K. M., 211
Ollendick, T. H., 517
Oller, D. K., 236
Olmstead, R., 173
Olsen, J. A., 400

Olsen, S. F., 398, 399, 400,
    508
Olson, D., 113
Olson, D. R., 464
Olson, S. L., 400
Olthof, T., 486
Ondejko, L., 305, 306
Ondrusek, N., 46
O'Neil, R., 72, 503
O'Neill, M., 241
Ong, K. K., 413
Ong, W., 470
Ono, Y., 477
Ontai, L. L., 340
Oosterwegel, A., 483
Openheimer, L., 483
Oppenheim, D., 275
O'Rahilly, R., 111n
Ordonana, J. R., 305
O'Reilly, A. W., 319
Orfield, G., 471
Orobio de Castro, B., 387
Osborn, C. N., 183
Oshima-Takane, Y., 358
Osmond, C., 104
Ostad, S. A., 330
Osterweil, P., 134
Ostrosky-Solis, F., 443
Ostrov, J. M., 386, 387, 388,
    508
Oude, L. H., 420
Ouko, L. A., 108
Oumar, F., 268
Ovando, C. J., 465
Ovelese, Y., 135
Overbaugh, J., 112
Overton, W. F., 9, 31, 43, 82
Owen, C. G., 175n
Owen-Kostelnik, J., 521
Owens, R. E., 233
Oyserman, D., 400
Ozanne, S. E., 104
Ozçaliskan, S., 356

P
Pacella, R., 422
Padilla-Walker, L. M., 279
Painter, G., 468
Painter, M., 313
Pajares, F., 449
Paladino, J., 330
Palermo, G. D., 67
Palincsar, A. S., 468
Palmer, J. R., 106
Palmers, E., 327
Pan, B. A., 358
Pan, H. W., 373
Pani, A. M., 325
Pani, J. R., 325
Papousek, M., 252
Papp, L. M., 71
Paquette, D., 274
Paradis, J., 465
Paradise, R., 333, 460
Parameswaran, G., 439n,
    440
Paris, A. G., 343, 451
Paris, S. G., 343, 451
Park, C. L., 446
Park, Y., 442

Parke, R. D., 69, 142, 274, 275, 377, 491
Parker, F. L., 350
Parker, J. G., 373, 498, 500
Parker, K. P., 145, 172
Parker, S., 522
Parker, S. W., 269
Parsons, E., 271, 279
Parsons, T., 521
Parten, M., 372
Pasamanick, B., 144, 144*n*
Pascalis, O., 191, 191*n*, 220
Pascual-Leone, J., 334
Pasley, K., 514
Pasterski, V. L., 392
Patel, D. R., 423
Paterson, D. S., 147
Paterson, S., 208
Patt, M. B., 364, 373
Pattee, L., 501
Pattenden, S., 108
Patterson, C. J., 508, 509
Patterson, G. R., 240, 389
Pattison, P. E., 452
Paul, J. J., 502
Pauli, S. A., 66
Paulozzi, L. J., 106
Paulussen-Hoogeboom, M. C., 262
Pawluski, J., 355
Paxson, C., 347
Payne, A., 374
PCA America, 404
Pear, J., 18
Pearl, P. L., 415
Pearlman, D. N., 423
Pearson, A., 483
Pechmann, T., 464
Pedersen, L. H., 106
Pedersen, S., 500, 501
Pederson, D. R., 270, 271
Peebles, D., 136
Peerson, S., 106
Peirano, P., 146
Pellegrini, A. D., 431, 432, 433
Pelletier, J., 340, 448, 448*n*
Pellicano, E., 342
Pemberton, C. K., 255
Peña, R., 73
Pennington, B. F., 23
Penny, H., 419
Pepler, D., 33
Peralta de Mendoza, O. A., 321
Perelle, I. B., 293
Pérez-Pereira, M., 194
Perfors, A., 240, 354
Perlman, M., 369
Perlmutter, M., 336
Perner, T., 339
Perone, S., 224
Perren, S., 121
Perrin, J. M., 423
Perris, E. E., 222*n*
Perrone, S., 135
Perry, D. G., 506
Perry, G. H., 290
Perry-Jenkins, M., 154

Persaud, T. V. N., 54, 64*n*, 65*n*, 96, 97*n*, 98, 98*n*, 99, 100, 103*n*, 105, 163, 164
Person, L., 73
Peshkin, A., 35, 77
Pesonen, A.-K., 262
Petch, J., 121, 157
Peterman, K., 278
Peters, R. D., 76, 77
Peterson, C., 521
Peterson, C. C., 341
Peterson, D. M., 340
Peterson, G. W., 72
Peterson, L., 306, 307, 425
Petinou, K. C., 304
Petitto, L. A., 237, 465
Petrides, K. V., 457
Petrill, S. A., 83
Petrovich, O., 495
Petrunka, K., 76, 77
Pettigrew, T. F., 496
Pettit, G. S., 377
Pettit, J., 355
Pezé, A., 187
Pfeffer, C. R., 41
Pfeffer, K., 443
Pfeifer, J. H., 496, 497
Philips, S. U., 225
Phillips, A., 222
Phillips, D., 172
Phillips, K. M. O., 338
Phillips, M., 469
Phillips, R. D., 143
Phillips, S., 441
Phillips-Grant, K., 337
Piaget, J., 19–21, 29, 33, 204–216, 224, 225, 226, 318–329, 330, 332, 334, 437–442, 467, 495
Pianta, R. C., 348, 375, 470, 520
Pick, A. D., 238
Pickard, M. B., 212
Pickens, J. N., 181, 220, 371
Pickett, K. E., 147
Pierce, K. M., 76
Pierce, S., 401
Pierce, S. H., 449
Pierroutsakos, S. L., 213
Pierson, L., 102
Pietilainen, K., 174
Pietz, J., 137
Piirto, J., 457
Pikhart, H., 61
Pina, A. A., 518
Pinderhughes, E. E., 72, 383, 520
Pine, J. M., 356, 357, 358
Pinelli, J., 176
Ping, R. M., 327
Pinker, S., 234, 358, 463
Pipp, S., 281
Pisani, L., 268
Pisoni, D. B., 241
Pitts, V. P., 495
Pizzaro, D. A., 457
Pleck, J. H., 516
Plomin, R., 82, 83, 85, 86, 229, 379, 381, 458
Pnevmatikos, D., 495

Poehlmann, J., 271, 275
Poelhuis, C. W. K., 65, 67, 458
Pohl, R., 78
Polka, L., 190, 304
Pollak, S. D., 269, 403
Pollatsek, A., 450
Pollitt, C., 354
Pollitt, E., 113, 301, 416
Polman, H., 387
Pomerantz, E. M., 401, 486, 487, 488, 488*n*, 503
Pong, S., 401
Pons, F., 490
Popkin, B. M., 420
Porter, R. H., 151
Portes, A., 36
Posada, G., 270
Posner, J. K., 76, 516
Posner, M. I., 214, 218, 254, 258
Poston, D. L., Jr., 508
Poulin-Dubois, D., 211, 339, 390
Povinelli, D. J., 365
Powell, C., 114
Powell, J. L., 10
Power, C., 105
Power, T. G., 432
Powers, C. J., 503
Powlishta, K. K., 394, 503, 505
Powls, A., 294
Pratt, M. W., 398
Prechtl, H. F. R., 100, 144, 144*n*
Preisler, G. M., 184, 194
Preissler, M. A., 321
Prencipe, A., 493
Prepin, K., 281
Pressley, M., 218, 446, 450
Previc, F. H., 293
Price, J. M., 375
Prinstein, M. J., 500, 501
Prior, M., 11
Proctor, B. D., 74, 79
Proctor, L. J., 502
Proctor, M. H., 419, 419*n*
Prodromidis, M., 273
Proffitt, D. R., 195
Profilet, S. M., 377
Programme for International Student Assessment, 476, 476*n*
Prosser, E., 486
Provins, K. A., 293
Pruden, S. M., 356
Prysak, M., 115
Puckett, K., 472
Puhl, R. M., 419
Pujol, J., 167
Punamaki, R. L., 67
Purcell-Gates, V., 343
Putallaz, M., 501
Putnam, F. W., 519
Putnam, S. P., 258

Q
Qin, D. B., 36
Quas, J. A., 521
Querido, J. G., 238

Quinn, P. C., 195, 196, 214, 222
Quinn, T. C., 112

R
Raboy, B., 509
Radan, A. E., 177
Radelet, M. A., 431
Radke-Yarrow, M., 379
Radunovic, N., 114
Radziszewska, B., 332
Raikes, H., 232
Raikes, H. A., 262, 272, 368, 369, 375
Rainie, L., 472
Rakison, D. H., 223
Rakoczy, H., 319
Raman, L., 426
Ramani, G. B., 281
Ramchandani, P. G., 155
Ramey, C. T., 231, 232, 350
Ramey, S. L., 231, 232, 350
Ramin, S. M., 117
Ramos, M. C., 257
Ramsay, D. S., 261, 280, 489
Ramsay, J. T., 75
Ramus, F., 151
Rankin, M. P., 310
Rao, G., 417
Rapus, T., 443
Rasbash, J., 507
Raskind, W. H., 473
Rasmussen, C., 345, 444
Rasnake, L. K., 178
Ratan, R., 170
Rathunde, K., 468
Rauber, M., 433
Rauer, A. J., 379
Rauscher, F. H., 44
Raver, C. C., 75, 516
Ravid, D., 462
Ravitch, D., 468, 476
Ray, J. A., 77
Ray, N., 509
Ray, S. D., 327
Rayner, K., 450
Raynor, H. A., 421
Raynor, R., 17
Raz, S., 136
Razza, R. P., 334
Reed, M. J., 11, 520
Reed, R. K., 129
Rees, J., 269
Reese, E., 221, 337, 365
Reeve, R. A., 452
Regehr, C., 46
Reilly, J. S., 170
Reis, S. M., 475
Reisman, J. E., 148*n*
Reisner, E. R., 76
Reiss, D., 85, 85*n*
Reissland, N., 155
Reiter, S., 38, 38*n*
Rennie, H., 425
Renninger, K. A., 470
Repacholi, B. M., 253
Reppucci, N. D., 521
Reschly, A. L., 77
Resnick, M., 353

Resnick, M. B., 142
Resta, R., 63
RESULTS, 73
Rettew, D. C., 87
Reynolds, A. J., 350
Rhoades, B. L., 334
Richards, D., 399
Richardson, H. L., 147
Richert, R. A., 495
Richgels, D. J., 343, 343*n*, 345
Richler, J., 302
Richmond, J., 181
Ridenour, T. A., 83
Rideout, R., 521
Rideout, V. J., 351, 352, 353, 389, 472
Ridley-Johnson, R., 144*n*, 145
Rigby, K., 502
Riggs, K. J., 340
Rijsdijk, F. V., 455
Riksen-Walraven, J. M., 176, 278
Riley, E. P., 109
Riordan, J., 133
Ripple, C. H., 80
Ris, M. D., 296
Rising, S. S., 119
Risley, T. R., 229, 359
Rissanen, A., 174
Riva, D., 294
Rivera, S. M., 208, 215
Rivkees, S. A., 101, 145
Rizzo, T. A., 118
Rizzolatti, G., 182
Roach, M. A., 138
Roazzi, A., 440
Robbins, M., 358
Roberts, B. W., 40, 258
Roberts, D. F., 351, 353, 389, 472
Roberts, J., 63
Roberts, J. E., 304, 347
Roberts, J. M., 523
Roberts, R. D., 457
Roberts, R. J., Jr., 23
Roberts, T., 312, 343
Roberts, W., 371
Robertson, J., 514
Robin, D. J., 187
Robins, R. W., 485, 490
Robinson, C. C., 373, 386
Robinson, J., 383
Robinson, J. L., 112, 282
Robinson, M. L., 87
Robinson, S., 342
Rochat, P., 143, 187*n*, 188, 213, 238, 253, 280, 280*n*, 281, 319
Rodemaker, J. E., 241
Rodgers, J. L., 93*n*, 94, 459
Rodkin, P. C., 500, 501
Rodriguez, A., 294
Roebers, C. M., 521
Roelfsema, N. M., 100
Roemmich, J. N., 421
Rogan, W. J., 296
Rogers, J. M., 107, 418
Rogge, M. M., 419

Roggman, L. A., 273
Rogoff, B., 25, 224, 225, 331, 332, 333, 439, 440, 444, 445, 447, 460, 482
Rohner, R. P., 276
Rohrbeck, C. A., 470
Roid, G., 346
Roisman, R., 260
Rolfhus, E., 454
Rollins, K. B., 324
Rolls, B. J., 301, 420
Romano, A. M., 131
Rome-Flanders, T., 238
Romney, A. K., 391
Rönnqvist, L., 168, 293
Roopnarine, J. L., 274, 374, 401
Rosander, K., 152, 187, 191, 197, 209
Rose, A. J., 499, 500, 502
Rose, H., 396
Rose, L., 142
Rose, S. A., 195, 195n, 218, 228
Rosen, A. B., 324
Rosenberger, L. R., 235
Rosenblatt, J. L., 522
Rosenbloom, A. L., 297
Rosenblum, T. B., 458
Rosenfeld, R. G., 297
Rosengren, K. S., 281, 313, 323
Rosenshine, B., 469
Roseth, C. J., 432
Rosetta, L., 175n
Ross, E., 354
Ross, H. S., 278, 369, 508
Rossor, M. N., 145
Rotenberg, N., 56
Rothbart, M. K., 83, 218, 254, 255, 256, 257, 258, 260, 261, 293, 369
Rothbaum, F., 261, 269
Rothenbacher, D., 175n
Rothstein-Fish, C., 460
Rotman, T., 154
Rouselle, L., 327
Rousseau, J. J., 13
Rovee-Collier, C. K., 180, 210, 219, 220, 220n, 221, 222, 222n
Rovers, M. M., 304
Rowe, D. C., 86, 93n
Rowe, M. L., 242
Rowe, R., 425
Rowland, C. F., 357
Rozin, P., 324
Rubin, C., 419
Rubin, K. H., 259, 263, 373, 373n, 377, 387, 400, 498, 500
Ruble, D. N., 261, 282, 390, 391, 394, 396, 397, 485, 496, 503
Ruchkin, V., 518
Rudolph, K. D., 377, 498
Rudy, D., 486
Ruff, C., 413
Ruff, H. A., 219, 254, 258, 319, 335
Ruffman, J., 339

Ruffman, T., 209, 255, 324, 340
Ruiz, I., 220
Ruiz-Peláez, J. G., 139
Rumbaut, R. G., 36
Runco, M. A., 474
Rushton, J. P., 83, 458
Russell, A., 398, 507
Russell, G., 507
Russell, J. A., 143, 368
Russell, R. B., 55
Rust, J., 394
Rutter, M., 9, 83, 86, 169, 269
Rvachew, S., 304
Ryan, E., 519
Ryan, R. M., 75
Rydell, A.-M., 470
Ryding, M., 422

S

Saarni, C., 249, 250, 252, 253, 254, 489, 490, 491
Sabbagh, M. A., 340, 355, 356
Sacks, P., 469
Sadeh, A., 146, 172, 298
Sadler, T. W., 98, 100
Saelens, B. E., 421
Saenger, P., 297
Safe Kids USA, 305, 306, 307
Saffran, J. R., 101, 151, 190, 236
Sagi, A., 268n, 269
Sahlberg, P., 477
Saigal, S., 139
St James-Roberts, I., 149
Saitta, S. C., 62n
Salamanca, F., 59
Salantera, S., 150
Salapatek, P., 193
Salbe, A. D., 417
Salerno, M., 297
Salihu, H. M., 115, 115n
Salley, B. J., 240
Salmela-Aro, K., 154
Salmivalli, C., 502
Salovey, P., 457, 491
Salsa, A. M., 321
Salter, D., 519
Salvaterra, F., 68
Sameroff, A. J., 10, 231
Samson, A. V., 258
Samuels, M., 147
Sanbinmatsu, D. M., 254
Sanchez, J., 473
Sanchez, M. M., 403
Sanchez, R. P., 211
Sandberg, D. E., 297
Sander, C. J., 136
Sanders, D. M., 419
Sanders, O., 520
Sanders, P., 240, 503
Sanderson, J. A., 385
Sandler, J. C., 521
Sandnabba, N. K., 393
Sandrin, D., 150
Sandstrom, M. J., 501
Sangrigoli, S., 196
Sann, C., 149, 198
Sansavini, A., 151
Santiago, C. D., 10
Sapp, F., 327

Sarama, J., 346, 353, 472
Sarnecka, B. W., 344
Sato, T., 391
Saucier, J. F., 36
Saudino, K. J., 229, 259, 260, 262, 262n
Saw, S. M., 422
Saxe, G. B., 25
Saxe, R. R., 448
Saxon, J. L., 487
Saxton, M., 359
Saygin, A. P., 236
Saylor, M. M., 211, 213, 355, 356
Saywitz, K. J., 521
Sbarra, D., 513
Scanlon, K., 300
Scarr, S., 85, 459
Schaal, B., 150, 150n, 151
Schacht, P. M., 70
Schaefer-McDaniel, N. J., 75
Schaeffel, F., 422
Scharrer, E., 352, 388
Schauwers, K., 237
Schellenberg, E. G., 44
Scher, A., 174
Scherb, H., 455
Schiller, M., 271
Schilling, T. H., 208
Schlackman, L. J., 133
Schlaggar, B. L., 23
Schlagmüller, M., 446, 449
Schlotz, W., 171
Schmid, R. G., 455
Schmidt, K. L., 381
Schmidt, L. A., 259
Schmidt, M. E., 213
Schmidt, M. H., 142
Schmitz, S., 257
Schneider, B. H., 278
Schneider, W., 351, 352, 444, 446, 447, 449, 521
Schnell, B., 73
Schofield, W., 114
Scholl, B. J., 342
Scholl, T. O., 114
Scholnick, E. K., 335
Schonberg, R. L., 61n, 63, 64
Schöner, G., 28
Schoppe, S. J., 258
Schoppe-Sullivan, S. J., 154, 262
Schor, J. B., 420
Schott, J. M., 145
Schuengel, C., 270
Schuetze, P., 106
Schull, W. J., 110
Schulte-Ruther, M., 182
Schultz, D., 490
Schultz, L. H., 376
Schultz, M. C., 240
Schulz, M. S., 157
Schumann, C. M., 342
Schunk, D. H., 449
Schwab-Stone, M., 518
Schwade, J. A., 237
Schwanenflugel, P. J., 448
Schwarte, A. R., 59
Schwartz, C. E., 259
Schwartz, D., 502

Schwartz, M., 416
Schwarz, N., 33
Schwebel, D. C., 305, 307, 424, 425
Schweiger, W. K., 65
Schweinhart, L. J., 349, 349n
Schweizer, K., 455
Schwier, C., 211
Schwimmer, J. B., 419
Scott, J. A., 463
Scott, K. D., 131
Scott, L. S., 92, 166
Scott, P. M., 380
Scott, R. M., 339
Scrutton, D., 186
Sebanc, A. M., 319
Sebastián, E., 356
Seibert, A. C., 277
Seid, M., 375
Seidl, A., 190
Seifer, R., 271
Seki, Y., 448
Sekido, R., 55
Seligman, M. E. P., 461
Selman, R. L., 376, 492, 492n
Sen, M. G., 192
Senechal, M., 343
Senghas, A., 355
Senior, G. J., 195, 195n
Senju, A., 237
Senman, L., 327
Sentz, J., 302
Serbin, L. A., 394, 503, 505
Sermon, K., 64n
Sesame Workshop, 351
Sevigny, P. R., 276
Sexton, C., 72
Seymour, S. C., 186
Shafer, V. L., 234
Shaffer, A., 11
Shaffer, T. G., 394
Shah, F., 136
Shah, T., 147
Shahar, S., 12
Shankaran, S., 136
Shannon, E. A., 293
Shannon, J. D., 242
Shapiro, A. E., 154
Shapiro, C. J., 445
Shapiro, L. R., 337
Shapka, J. D., 484
Sharlach, A. E., 516
Shastri, J., 395
Shatz, M., 236, 323
Shaw, D. S., 11, 268, 381, 500, 512
Shaw, G. L., 44
Shaw, G. M., 114
Shaw, J. A., 518
Shaw, P., 295, 444
Shea, A. K., 114, 115
Sheehan, G., 512
Sheeran, P., 92
Sheldon, J. P., 395
Shenkin, J. D., 291
Shepherd, J., 155
Sheridan, K., 457
Sherman, S. L., 61
Sherrod, L. R., 495
Sherry, B., 418

Sheu, C.-F., 293
Shic, F., 342
Shields, R., 306
Shiffrin, R. M., 22
Shimada, S., 182
Shiner, L., 83, 260
Shinn, M., 75
Shinskey, J. L., 208
Shipman, K. L., 491
Shirley, L., 394
Shonkoff, J., 172
Shrestha, S., 491
Shrout, P. E., 185
Shumow, L., 499
Shwalb, D. W., 274, 401
Shweder, R. A., 8, 35
Sidappa, A., 118
Sidebotham, P., 402
Sidle, A. L., 324
Siebert, A. C., 508
Siegal, M., 385, 465
Siegel, D. H., 445
Siegler, R. S., 21, 43, 327, 338, 338n, 345, 345n, 442, 446, 453
Siervogel, R. M., 413
Sigman, M., 416
Sigmundson, H. K., 392
Signorella, M. L., 397
Signorielli, N., 395
Silk, J. S., 71, 76, 399
Silvén, M., 238
Silver, E. J., 433
Silverman, B., 353
Silverman, W. K., 518
Simcock, G., 213, 221, 221n, 280, 321, 336
Simion, F., 148, 195, 196n
Simmens, S. J., 260
Simoni, H., 121
Simons, L. G., 79
Simons, R. L., 402
Simonton, D. K., 475
Simpson, J. A., 62, 62n, 155
Simpson, J. L., 62n
Singer, D. G., 352
Singer, J. L., 352
Singer, L. T., 107
Singleton, J. L., 235
Sinno, S., 384
Sirios, S., 339
Sizonenko, S. V., 128
Skaalvik, E. M., 484
Skinner, B. F., 17, 233
Skinner, E. A., 487
Skouteris, H., 139
Slaby, R. G., 388
Slack, K. S., 301
Slade, A., 272
Slater, A., 152, 191, 195, 196, 218
Sleet, D. A., 305
Slemmer, J. A., 191
Sloan, S., 176
Slobin, D. I., 358
Slobodskaya, H. R., 262
Sloman, J., 296
Slonims, V., 61
Sluzenski, J., 208, 336
Small, M., 149, 152

Small, S. A., 36
Smart, J., 146
Smetana, J. G., 384
Smith, A. L., 431
Smith, B. H., 445
Smith, C. L., 37
Smith, G. D., 105
Smith, J. [Julia], 381, 383
Smith, J. [Julie], 508
Smith, J. C., 74, 79
Smith, J. R., 80, 458
Smith, K. E., 516
Smith, L. B., 28, 185, 208, 224, 355
Smith, N. J., 302
Smith, P., 518
Smith, P. K., 374, 432
Smith, R. S., 10, 126, 142
Smokowski, P. R., 36
Smulian, J. C., 135
Snell, E. K., 418
Snidman, N., 259
Snow, C. E., 240, 358, 463, 464, 465
Snow, S., 298, 299
Snyder, J., 502
Snyder, K. A., 23
Sobala, W., 108
Sobel, D. M., 319
Sobolewski, J. M., 513
Society for Research in Child Development, 43, 45, 45n
Society of Obstetricians and Gynaecologists, 134
Soderstrom, M., 190
Soetens, B., 418
Softas-Nall, B., 275
Solomon, G. B., 430
Solomon, G. E. A., 426
Solomon, J., 266
Sondergaard, C., 107
Song, J., 368
Sonuga-Barke, E. J., 171
Sophian, C., 327
Sorensen, P. M., 330
Sosa, B. B., 337
Sosa, R., 130
Soto, P., 356
Soussignan, R., 150, 150n
South African Department of Health, 112
Sowell, E. R., 109, 168, 415, 444
Spadoni, A. D., 109
Spangler, G., 271
Sparrow, J. D., 188
Spatz, D. L., 173
Spector, A. Z., 155
Speece, D. L., 343
Spelke, E. S., 187, 196, 214, 215, 222
Spence, M. J., 101, 118, 151
Spencer, J. P., 28, 187, 224
Spencer, P. E., 243
Spere, K. A., 240
Spiewak, G. S., 495
Spinath, F. M., 83
Spinks, A., 424
Spinrad, T. L., 254, 371, 379
Spitz, R. A., 269

Spock, B., 173
Sporer, N., 469
Sprague, K. E., 344
Spruijt-Metz, D., 301
Spuhl, S. T., 332
Sridhar, D., 474
Sroufe, L. A., 9, 251, 268, 272, 278, 404
Stacey, J., 509
Stahl, S. A., 450
Stams, G. J. M., 67, 278
Standley, J. M., 138
Stangor, M., 498
Stanley, C., 155
Stanley-Hagan, M., 514
Stanovich, K. E., 34, 463
Stanowicz, L., 359
Stansbury, K., 259
Starr, M. S., 450
Stattin, H., 398, 400
Staub, F. C., 452
Staudinger, U. M., 9, 83
Stauffacher, K., 387, 508
Stedron, J. M., 209
Steele, C. M., 460
Steele, J., 504, 504n
Steele, K. H., 313
Steele, S., 342
Steenhuis, I. H., 420
Stegge, H., 486, 489
Stehr-Green, P., 302
Stein, A., 155
Stein, N., 368
Stein, R. E. K., 433
Stein, S., 131
Stein, Z., 113
Steinberg, L., 71, 77, 273, 398, 399, 400
Steiner, J. E., 150, 180
Steiner, M., 114, 115
Stella, J., 342
Stenberg, C. R., 251
Stenberg, G., 253
Stephens, B. E., 137
Stephens, B. R., 196
Sterling, S., 425
Stern, D., 252
Stern, E., 452
Stern, M., 261
Sternberg, K. J., 273
Sternberg, R. J., 14, 347, 453, 455, 456, 459, 461, 474
Stetsenko, A., 504
Stevenson, H. W., 477
Stevenson, J., 137
Stevenson, L. M., 439
Stevenson, R., 354
Stevenson-Hinde, J., 259
Stewart, J. H., 382, 382n, 383
Stewart, P. W., 110
Stewart, R. B., Jr., 156
Stewart, S. L., 259
Stewart-Brown, S., 457
Steyaert, J., 62n
Stifter, C. A., 219, 229, 335
Stiles, J., 164, 170
Stillman, R. D., 151
Stilson, S. R., 230
Stipek, D. J., 282, 348, 468
Stoch, M. B., 177

Stocker, C. J., 105
Stone, R., 469
Stoneman, Z., 277, 507
Storch, S. A., 343
Storey, A. E., 143
Stormshak, E. A., 70
Story, R., 423
Strambler, M. J., 460
Strapp, C. M., 359
Straus, M. A., 381, 382, 382n, 383
Strayer, L., 371
Strazdins, L., 516
Streri, A., 149, 198
Stretesky, P. B., 296
Striano, T., 238, 253, 280, 319
Stright, A. D., 332, 449
Strohschein, L., 94, 512
Stromquist, N. P., 73
Stromswold, K., 236
Strong, B. L., 353
Strosberg, R., 358
Stroup, D. F., 133
Stryer, B. K., 431
Stryker, M. P., 169
Stuewig, J., 371
Stuhlman, M., 470
Sturge-Apple, M. L., 155
Suárez-Orozco, C., 36
Subbotsky, E., 324
Subrahmanyam, K., 323, 460
Suddendorf, T., 280
Sugarman, D. B., 381
Sullivan, K., 147
Sullivan, M. C., 137
Sullivan, M. W., 251
Sullivan, S., 469
Sullivan, S. A., 300
Sulovic, N., 114
Super, C. M., 186
Supple, A. J., 36
Surian, L., 465
Survey USA, 382
Susman-Stillman, A., 507
Sussman, A. L., 141
Suveg, C., 491
Suzuki, L. K., 460
Svensson, A., 353
Svetina, M., 21, 327, 338, 442
Svirsky, M. A., 237
Sweeney, B., 219
Sweet, M. A., 231
Swenson, L. D., 355
Swenson, L. P., 500
Swingley, D., 190
Symons, D. K., 271
Szepkouski, G. M., 444
Szkrybalo, J., 396
Szlemko, W. J., 109

T
Tabibi, Z., 443
Tacon, A., 276
Tager-Flusberg, H., 236, 340, 342, 357
Takahashi, K., 173, 268
Takala, M., 469
Takeuchi, T., 67
Talmi, A., 153

Tam, H. P., 374
Tamang, B. L., 491
Tamis-LeMonda, C. S., 78, 184, 188, 225, 229, 242
Tammelin, T., 434
Tamminen, K., 495
Tamrouti-Makkink, I. D., 507
Tangney, J. P., 371
Tanimura, M., 213
Tanner, J. L., 6
Tanner, J. M., 164
Tardif, C., 278, 474
Tardif, T., 72, 239, 241, 340, 354
Tarren-Sweeney, M., 297
Tarullo, A. R., 171
Taska, L., 519
Tasker, F. L., 509
Tate, C. S., 358
Taumoepeau, M., 255, 340
Tavecchio, L. W. C., 351
Taylor, C. A., 382, 383
Taylor, C. L., 463
Taylor, E., 445
Taylor, J. H., 385
Taylor, J. S., 130
Taylor, M., 35, 319, 320, 341
Taylor, M. C., 395
Taylor, M. G., 393, 393n, 504
Taylor, R. L., 79
Teicher, M. H., 404
Tellings, A., 379
Temple, J. A., 350
Temple, J. L., 418
Tenenbaum, H. R., 393, 394, 503
Teoh, S. W., 237
Terwel, J., 471
Tessier, R., 139
Tessler, R. C., 68
Teti, D. M., 276
Teyber, E., 514n
Thacker, S. B., 133
Thal, D. J., 358, 465
Tharpe, A. M., 151
Thatcher, R. W., 292
Theil, S., 92
Thelen, E., 14, 28, 144n, 145, 185, 208, 209, 224
Théoret, H., 183, 342
Theuring, C., 185
Thiedke, C. C., 298, 422
Thiessen, E. D., 190
Thiessen, V., 472
Thomaes, S., 486
Thoman, E., 180
Thomas, A., 256, 257, 262
Thomas, D., 349
Thomas, D. G., 335, 443
Thomas, J. M., 501
Thomas, K. A., 68
Thomas, K. M., 99, 165, 166, 168, 170, 215, 220, 292, 294, 414, 415, 443
Thomas, R. B., 148
Thomas, R. M., 17
Thompson, A., 399
Thompson, C. K., 354
Thompson, L. A., 140
Thompson, N. R., 384

Thompson, P. M., 167, 292, 295
Thompson, R. A., 24, 45, 121, 165n, 254, 266, 268, 272, 278, 279, 340, 368, 369, 370, 375, 380
Thompson, W. W., 302
Thornton, S., 22, 22n
Thorpy, M. J., 299
Thurman, P. J., 109
Tienari, P., 83, 86
Tifft, C. J., 61n, 63, 64
Tiggemann, M., 419, 485
Tincoff, R., 238
Tinsley, B. J., 425
Tinsley, B. R., 142
Tirosh, E., 174
Tirsch, W. S., 455
Tisak, M. S., 387
Tizard, B., 269
To, Y. M., 490
Todd, C. M., 336
Todorova, I., 36
Tofler, I. R., 431
Tokunaga, R. S., 502
Tolchinsky, L., 462
Tomasello, M., 210, 234, 235, 236, 238, 239, 242, 253, 319, 323, 339, 355, 356, 357, 357n, 358, 463
Tong, S., 229, 296
Tong, V. T., 107
Toomela, A., 311, 311n
Torrance, E. P., 474
Torrance, N., 464
Torsheim, T., 434
Toth, S. L., 403
Tottenham, N., 295
Tough, S., 95
Tourigny, M., 520
Townsend, D. A., 210
Townsend, M. A. R., 492
Toyama, N., 426
Tracy, J. L., 490
Tracy, R., 465
Traupman, E., 188
Traurig, M., 419
Trautner, H. M., 391, 396, 504
Trautwein, U., 470
Trehub, S. E., 151, 189, 191
Tremblay, R. E., 385, 386, 497
Trent, K., 79
Trentacosta, C. J., 500
Trevarthen, C., 278
Triandis, H. C., 34, 78
Trickett, P. K., 519
Trocmé, N., 402, 405
Troiano, R. P., 433
Tronick, E. Z., 148, 152, 153, 250, 252
Troop-Gordon, W., 501
Tropp, L. R., 496
Troseth, G. L., 213, 356
Trowbridge, F., 300
True, M. M., 268
Trzesniewski, K. H., 485, 487
Tsao, F.-M., 191
Tseng, V., 36
Tsujimoto, S., 292

Tuchfarber, B. S., 424, 425
Tucker, C. J., 508
Tudge, J. R. H., 72, 332
Turati, C., 195, 196n
Turiel, E., 384, 385, 494
Turkewitz, G., 151
Turkheimer, E., 84
Turnbull, K. P., 343
Turnbull, M., 465
Turner, P. J., 393
Turner, R. N., 497
Tusscher, G. W., 111
Tuyen, J. M., 302
Twenge, J. M., 485, 486
Twyman, K., 502
Tzur, G., 214
Tzuriel, D., 461, 462n

U

Uauy, R., 146, 177
Ukrainetz, T. A., 464
Ullman, M. T., 342
Ullrich-French, S., 431
Umiltá, C., 195
Underwood, M. K., 386, 390
UNICEF, 73, 74, 78, 80n, 302
United Nations, 59, 302
Uppal, S., 486
Ursano, R. J., 518
U.S. Census Bureau, 67, 80n, 93, 95n, 140, 140n, 230, 275, 303, 348, 351, 464, 509, 510n, 515
U.S. Centers for Disease Control, 175
U.S. Department of Agriculture, 114
U.S. Department of Education, 80n, 348, 433, 477
U.S. Department of Health and Human Services, 60, 61, 95, 109, 116, 117n, 131, 133, 134, 137, 156, 176, 291, 302, 303, 349, 401, 402, 402n, 405, 414, 417, 421, 424, 433, 519
Usta, I. M., 115
Uttal, D., 281

V

Vaillancourt, T., 502
Vaish, A., 253
Vakil, E., 443
Valdés, G., 35
Valentine, J. C., 485
Valian, V., 359
Valiente, C., 371, 449
van Aken, C., 262
van Balen, F., 509
Van Cleave, J., 423
van de Beek, C., 392
Vandell, D. L., 76, 277, 499, 516, 517
Vandenberg, B., 373, 373n
Van den Bergh, B. R. H., 115, 484
van den Boom, D. C., 258, 262, 509

van den Bossche, A. S., 146, 147
van den Dries, L., 269
van den Oord, E., 93n
Vanderbilt-Adriance, E., 11
van der Meer, A. L., 187
van der Wal, M. F., 114
Van de Vijver, P. J. R., 34
Vandewater, E. A., 352, 353
van Eijsden, M., 114
Van Eyk, J., 65
van Goudoever, J. B., 137
van IJzendoorn, M. H., 65, 67, 267, 268n, 269, 270, 271, 272, 274, 278, 351, 458
Van Keer, H., 451
Van Orman, B., 495
Van Steirteghem, A., 64n
VanWey, L. K., 94
Varela-Silva, M. I., 413
Varendi, H., 151
Varnhagen, C., 389
Varni, J. W., 419
Vasquez, D. M., 171
Vaughn, B. E., 271, 283, 375, 386
Vaughn, S., 474
Velasco, R., 380
Velderman, M. K., 271
Veldhuis, J. D., 162
Venezia, M., 251
Veneziano, R. A., 276
Vereijken, B., 185
Verhulst, F. C., 65
Verissimo, M., 68
Vermeer, W. M., 420
Vernon, P. A., 455
Vernon-Feagans, L., 72, 304
Verschaffel, L., 452
Vidaeff, A. C., 117
Vihman, M. M., 237
Vinden, P. G., 340, 448
Vinovskis, M. A., 12
Vira, R., 121
Visher, E. B., 514
Visher, J. S., 514
Vivanti, G., 342
Voci, A., 497
Voeten, M., 502
Vogel, D. A., 261
Vohr, B. R., 137, 243
Volling, B. L., 255, 277, 379
Volpe, L. E., 173
Vondra, J. I., 266, 268
von Hofsten, C., 152, 187, 191, 197, 209
Voss, L. D., 297
Vouloumanos, A., 151
Vuoksimaa, E., 293
Vurpillot, E., 444
Vygotsky, L. S., 24, 330, 332

W

Wachs, T. D., 257, 258, 261
Waddell, K. J., 447
Waddington, C. H., 84
Wadsworth, M. E., 10
Wagenaar, K., 67
Wahlberg, K. E., 86

Wahlsten, D., 9, 82, 84, 84n
Wainryb, C., 493
Wakeley, A., 208, 215
Walberg, H. J., 468
Waldenström, U., 130, 294
Waldfogel, J., 139, 139n, 141, 347, 516
Waldman, I. D., 87
Walenski, M., 342
Walk, R. D., 192
Walker, A. M., 147
Walker, L. J., 385
Walker, R. A., 292
Walker, S. P., 416
Walker-Andrews, A. S., 198, 253
Wall, M., 431
Wall, S., 73
Wallace, I. F., 228
Waller, E. M., 500
Walsh, M. E., 426
Walton, G. E., 152
Wang, L., 263
Wang, Q., 337, 366, 401, 483, 488
Wang, S., 35, 208
Wang, Y., 258
Wänström, L., 459
Ward, C., 331
Warner, R. M., 457
Warnock, F., 150
Warren, A. R., 358
Warren, D. H., 194
Warren, S. L., 260
Wartella, E. A., 353
Wasik, B. A., 343
Wasserman, E. A., 222
Watamura, S. E., 273
Watanabe, H., 498
Waters, E., 251, 265, 267, 272
Watkins, W. E., 416
Watkinson, B., 108
Watson, A. C., 340
Watson, D. J., 450
Watson, J., 250, 253
Watson, J. B., 17
Watson, K. S., 373
Watson, M., 365
Watts-English, T., 404
Wax, J., 133
Waxler, C. Z., 380
Waxman, S. R., 223, 238, 355
Weaver, A., 422
Webb, N. M., 471
Webb, S. J., 165
Weber, C., 189
Wechsler, D., 346, 453, 454
Weems, C. F., 517
Wehren, A., 463
Weikart, D. P., 349
Weiling, E., 518
Weinberg, C. R., 96
Weinberg, M. K., 250
Weinberg, R. A., 459
Weinberger, J., 371
Weiner, J., 474
Weiner, S., 222n
Weinfield, N. S., 268, 272

Weinstein, R. S., 461, 461n, 470
Weinstock, M., 115
Weisglas-Kuperus, N., 137
Weisner, T. S., 173, 393
Weiss, K. M., 60
Weiss, L. G., 454
Weissberg, R. P., 516
Weisz, V., 503
Weizman, Z. O., 240, 463
Wekerle, C., 402, 403, 404
Weller, E. B., 415
Weller, R. A., 415
Wellman, H. M., 238, 323, 339, 340, 341, 368, 449, 463
Welner, K. G., 471
Welsh, J. A., 486
Welsh, M., 56
Weng, X., 106
Wentworth, N., 187, 218
Werker, J. F., 101, 151, 190
Werner, E. E., 10, 142
Werner, L. A., 101, 151, 190
Werner, N. E., 386, 498, 499
Wesson, D. E., 424
West, D. S., 421
Westermann, G., 23
Westra, T., 186
Wexler, I. D., 518
Weyermann, M., 175n
Whalen, J. C., 423
Whalen, P. J., 295
Whaley, G. J. L., 268
Wheeler, K., 228
Whincup, P. H., 104
Whipple, E. E., 402, 519
White, B., 188
White, K. J., 492
White, K. S., 190
White, M. A., 121
Whitehead, H., 278
Whitehurst, G. J., 242, 343
Whiteman, S. D., 41
Whitesell, N., 489
Whiteside-Mansell, L., 70
Whiting, B., 391
Whitington, V., 331
Whitley, M. E., 390
Wichmann, C., 503
Wickberg, B., 154
Wigfield, A., 485, 488, 489
Wilcox, A. J., 96
Wilcox, S. J., 197
Wiley, E., 235
Wilkinson, K., 354
Wilkinson, R. B., 486
Willatts, P., 211
Willerman, L., 85, 459
Williams, C., 63
Williams, G. R., 114
Williams, J. M., 426
Williams, K., 313, 511
Williams, P. E., 387, 454
Williams, W. M., 459
Williamson, J., 275
Willinger, M., 173
Wilson, M., 111n, 112, 384

Wilson, W. H., 441
Wilson-Mitchell, J. E., 393
Wimbarti, S., 374
Windecker-Nelson, B., 369
Winebarger, A., 381
Winkler, I., 151
Winner, E., 310, 310n, 356, 474, 475
Winsler, A., 25, 330
Winslow, E. B., 512
Wiseman, F. K., 61
Witherington, D. C., 188, 226, 249, 253
Wolak, J., 519
Wolchik, S. A., 512, 513
Wold, B., 434
Wolf, A. W., 173, 296
Wolfe, D. A., 402, 403, 404, 405
Wolfe, V. V., 519
Wolff, P. H., 146n, 518
Wolfgang, C. H., 394
Wolfinger, N. H., 512
Wolters, C. A., 398
Wong, J., 298
Wong, M. M., 11
Wood, E., 393
Wood, J. J., 377
Wood, J. W., 109
Wood, R. M., 148
Woods, R., 197
Woodward, A. L., 211, 222, 356
Woodward, J., 477
Woodward, L., 133
Woodward, L. J., 176
Woody-Dorning, J., 444
Woolley, J. D., 324, 495
World Cancer Research Fund/American Institute for Cancer Research, 417
World Health Organization, 175, 177, 301, 302, 305, 305n, 306, 417
Wright, B. C., 438
Wright, C. M., 178
Wright, J. C., 351, 352
Wright, K. L., 431
Wright, M. J., 66, 67, 83
Wright, M. O., 520, 522n
Wright, R. O., 296
Wright, S. B., 292
Wrotniak, B. H., 421
Wu, G., 105
Wu, L., 509
Wu, P., 34, 401
Wu, Y. W., 66
Wulczyn, F., 403
Wunsch, J. P., 251
Wust, S., 137
Wynn, K., 214, 215, 378
Wynne, L. C., 86
Wynne-Edwards, K. E., 143

X

Xie, H., 498
Xiong, S., 36
Xu, F., 215, 241
Xue, Y., 450

Y

Yager, J., 299
Yale, M. E., 250
Yan, Z., 473
Yang, B., 508
Yang, C., 173, 348, 387, 508
Yarrow, M. R., 380
Yeates, K. O., 376
Yeh, C. J., 36
Yehuda, R., 115
Yen, L., 355
Yip, R., 300
Yip, T., 36
Yirmiya, N., 262, 342

Yonas, A., 192
Yont, K., 304
Yoo, J., 301
Yoshida, H., 355
Yoshikawa, H., 36
Yoshinaga-Itano, C., 243
Young, J. F., 485
Young, S. H., 132
Youngblade, L. M., 369
Young-Hyman, D., 419
Youngstrom, E., 376
Yu, R., 263
Yuan, A. S. V., 514
Yudkin, P., 114
Yuill, N., 483

Yumoto, C., 104
Yunger, J. L., 506

Z

Zackai, E. H., 62n
Zafeiriou, D. I., 145
Zahn-Waxler, C., 379, 383
Zamsky, E. S., 79
Zanetti-Daellenbach, R. A., 131
Zarbatany, L., 499
Zarrett, N. R., 485
Zaslow, M. J., 347
Zeanah, C. H., 269

Zelazo, N. A., 145
Zelazo, P. D., 334, 384, 443
Zeller, M. H., 419
Zeman, J., 491
Zerwas, S., 281
Zeskind, P. S., 149
Zhang, D., 469
Zhang, T.-Y., 87
Zhou, M., 36
Zhou, Q., 258
Zhou, X., 453
Zhu, L., 426
Zielinski, D. S., 403
Zigler, E., 80, 141, 183

Zimmer-Gembeck, M. J., 487
Zimmerman, B. J., 449
Zimmerman, F. J., 213, 352
Zimmerman, L. K., 259
Zimmerman, R., 264
Zimmerman, S., 300
Zins, J. E., 424, 425
Zosuls, K. M., 282
Zucker, K. J., 506
Zukow-Goldring, P., 226
Zukowski, A., 236, 357
Zur, O., 345
Zwart, M., 141

Figures and tables are indicated by f and t following page numbers.

A

Ability grouping in schools, 470–471
Absence of father. *See* Father absence
Absenteeism. *See* School attendance
Abuse
  alcohol. *See* Alcohol use and abuse
  children. *See* Child maltreatment
  drugs. *See* Drug use and abuse
Abusive parenting. *See* Child maltreatment
Academic achievement
  ability grouping in schools and, 470–471
  Asian societies, 477
  authoritative parenting and, 398, 399t
  cognitive self-regulation and, 449
  cross-cultural research, 476–477
  cultural influences on, 476–477
  friendships and, 375
  immigrant youths, 36
  inclusive classrooms and, 473–474
  IQ scores and, 454
  learned helplessness and, 487
  memory and, 447
  peer relations and, 498
  self-esteem and, 485, 487
  teacher–student interaction and, 469–470
Academic learning. *See* Education; Schools
Academic preschools, 348, 352. *See also* Preschools
Academic self-efficacy, 449
Academic self-esteem, 485, 488–489
Academic subjects. *See also specific subjects (e.g., Mathematics and mathematical reasoning, Reading)*
  gender stereotyping of, 503–504, 504f
Accidents. *See also* Injuries
  bicycle accidents, 424–425
  motor vehicle. *See* Motor vehicle accidents
  pedestrian accidents, 424
Accommodation, in cognitive-developmental theory, 204, 321
Accreditation of child-care facilities, 231
Accutane, prenatal development and maternal use of, 106
Achievement-related attributions, 486–488, 488f
Acquired immune deficiency syndrome. *See* HIV/AIDS
Action words, in early vocabulary, 354
Active correlation, in genetic–environmental correlation, 85–86
Activity level, as temperament dimension, 257t
Adaptation. *See also* Coping strategies
  baby's adaptation to labor and delivery, 128
  cognitive-developmental theory, 204–205

Darwin's theory of survival of fittest, 13
  families and adaptation to change, 71
  immigrant youths, 36
Addiction. *See* Alcohol use and abuse; Drug use and abuse; Medications; Smoking
ADHD. *See* Attention-deficit hyperactivity disorder
Adjustment problems. *See also specific entries (e.g., Aggression, Depression)*
  ADHD and, 444
  child maltreatment, 403–404
  cognitive neuroscience and, 23
  gender identity development and, 395
  identity development and, 604–605
  left-handedness and, 294
  maternal depression and, 155
  neurotransmitters and, 415
  obesity and, 419
  paternal depression and, 155
  sexual abuse victims, 519–520
  sleep and, 299
  temperament and, 257, 262–263
Adolescence.
  adoptees in, 65, 67–68
  affluent families and, 74
  cognitive development in, 20
  defined, 6
  immigrant youths, adaptation in, 36
Adoption, 65–68
  attachment and, 269
  gay and lesbian families and, 508–509
  Romanian children, 169, 171
  single-parent families, 156
Adoption studies
  catch-up growth, 169–172
  intelligence and heritability estimates, 83–84
  IQ scores, 459
  twins reared apart, 83
Adrenal glands, 415
Adult-organized youth sports, 431
Adult work, children in village and tribal cultures participating in, 333
Advertising, teaching children to be critical of, 427
Advocacy for children's causes, 80–81
Affluent families, children from, 72, 74, 74f
Affordances, in differentiation theory, 199
African Americans
  asthma, 423
  child-rearing practices of, 401
  communication styles, 459
  cosleeping arrangements in infancy and childhood of, 173
  disciplinary practices, 383
  drug use, 560
  extended-family households, 79

food insecurity, 178
  gender typing, 394
  grandparents as primary caregivers, 275
  infant mortality among, 140
  IQ scores of, 458–461
  lead exposure risks, 296
  literacy skills and, 347, 575
  low birth weight among, 140
  narrative style and, 464
  obesity and, 417
  physical development, 164, 536–537
  poverty rate, 74
  prejudice against, 496, 496f
  school integration, 471
  self-esteem, 485
  self-fulfilling prophecies in teacher expectations, 470
  sickle cell anemia, 57
  single-parent families, 509
  skeletal development in infancy and toddlerhood, 165
  sleep routines for preschoolers, 298f, 298–299
African societies
  adult work, children in, 333
  breastfeeding, 175
  father–infant relationships, 276
  hand preference, 293
  industry in middle childhood, 482
  mother–infant relationship and attachment, 268
  motor development of infants, 188
  physical development
    early childhood, 290
    middle childhood, 413
  self-recognition of toddlers, 281, 281f
  sickle cell anemia, 57
  theory-of-mind tasks, performance of, 448
After-school programs, 516
Age. *See also* Milestones
  adapting to change, age of child and, 71
  children's response to divorce and, 511, 514
  corporal punishment and, 382, 382f
  eyewitness testimony by children, 521
  fetal viability, 100–102
  infertility and, 95
  maternal. *See* Maternal age
  paternal, 61, 95
  reproduction and, 54, 94–95, 95f
  skeletal age, 163, 164–165
  stages of development. *See* Stage concept of development
  stepfamilies, adjustment to and, 513
Aggression. *See also* Antisocial behavior; Violence
  child-rearing practices and, 386–387
  difficult child and. *See* Difficult child, as temperament type
  early childhood, 385–390
  family influences on, 386–387

friendships and, 499–500
  Internet and, 387–389
  intervention programs for, 389–390
  physical, 385
  popular-antisocial children, 500–501
  proactive, 385
  punishment and, 381
  reactive, 385
  rejected-aggressive children, 501, 503
  relational aggression, 386, 499, 500
  sex differences in, 386, 503
  television and, 387–389
  verbal, 385
  video and computer games and, 388–389
Agility, in middle childhood, 428. *See also* Motor development
AIDS. *See* HIV/AIDS
Aka of Central Africa, father–infant relationships among, 276
Alcohol use and abuse
  fetal alcohol syndrome (FAS), 108–109, 109t
  neurodevelopmental disorders and, 109, 109t
  prenatal development and, 108–109
Alleles, 56–57, 59
Allergies
  asthma, 423
  genomic imprinting and, 59
Altruistic behavior. *See* Prosocial behavior
Alzheimer's disease and Down syndrome, 61
Ambidextrous, 293
American Psychological Association, ethical guidelines for research, 43
American Sign Language, 234
Amnesia, infantile, 221
Amniocentesis, 63, 64t, 65f
Amnion, 98, 134
Amniotic fluid, 98
Amodal relations, perception of, 197
Amygdala, 294f, 295, 342
Analgesics, during childbirth, 133
Analogy, problem solving by, 211, 212t, 324
Anal stage of development (Freud), 15, 16t
Analytical intelligence (Sternberg), 455
Androgens, 143
  aggression and, 386
  gender typing and, 391–392
  middle childhood brain development and, 415
Androgynous traits, 395
Anemia
  Cooley's anemia, 58t
  iron-deficiency, 177
  sickle cell anemia, 423
Anencephaly and folic acid, 114
Anesthetics and newborns, 133, 149–150

Anger
  infancy and toddlerhood, 251, 283
  parents' anger, effect on children, 38, 38f
Animals. See also Ethology; Monkeys and chimps
  childhood injury prevention and, 307
  fears about, in early childhood, 370
  gender-typing experiments on, 391
  imprinting studies of geese, 265
  language acquisition among apes, 234
  smell responses in, 150
  stimulus deprivation of, 169
Animistic thinking, 321, 323–324
A-not-B search error, 207, 209
Anoxia, 135
Anthropomorphic view of God, 495
Antidepressant medications, effect on prenatal development, 106
Antisocial behavior. See also Aggression
  genetic–environmental correlation, 86
  peer acceptance and, 500–501
  popular-antisocial children, 500–501
  rejected-aggressive children, 501
Anxiety. See also Fear; Stress
  middle childhood, 517–519
  prenatal development and, 114–115
  separation. See Separation anxiety
  stranger anxiety, 252
Apes. See Monkeys and chimps
Apgar Scale, 128, 129t
  analgesics, effect on, 133
  SIDS and, 147
Aphasias, 234
Appearance, physical, 309, 485. See also Body image and physical attractiveness
Appearance vs. reality distinction, 327
Appetite. See Eating habits; Nutrition
Argentina, make-believe play with infants and toddlers, 226
Arithmetic. See Mathematics and mathematical reasoning
ARND (Alcohol-related neurodevelopmental disorder), 109, 109t
Arousal. See States of arousal
Arthritis, 423
Artistic expression, 310–311, 311f. See also Creativity; Drawing
Asian Americans, academic achievement, 36
Asian Pacific Islanders. See Pacific Islanders
Asians. See also specific countries or cultures
  academic achievement, 477
  achievement-related attributions, 488
  child-rearing practices, 261
  language development in early childhood, 241, 354
  mathematics and science achievement of students, 452–453
  myopia, 422
  physical development in middle childhood, 413
  self-concept, 483
  self-esteem, 485
  shame in, 371
Aspirin, prenatal development and maternal use of, 106

Assimilation, in cognitive-developmental theory, 204
Assisted discovery learning, 332
Associative play, 372
Asthma, 423
Athletics. See also Exercise; Extracurricular activities; Physical education
  adult-organized, 431
  developmentally appropriate organized sports, 432
  gender stereotyping in, 430
  middle childhood, 427–428
  self-esteem and, 485
  sex differences in performance and participation, 313
Attachment, 264–279
  adoption and, 269
  avoidant attachment, 267, 273
  behaviorist theories of, 264
  Bowlby's theory of, 265–266
  child care and, 273
  child maltreatment and, 271
  continuity of caregiving and, 269, 278
  cultural differences in, 268f, 268–269
  defined, 264
  disorganized/disoriented attachment, 267, 271, 278
  ecological systems theory and, 274
  ethological theory of, 265–266, 278
  factors affecting, 269–274
  family circumstances, 272
  fathers and, 274–275, 275f
  grandparents as primary caregivers, 275–276
  home environment and, 272
  infant characteristics and, 271
  institutionalized children, 171
  internal working model of, 266, 266f, 272
  later development and, 278–279
  measurement of attachment security, 266–267
  multiple attachments, 274–277
  newborns, bonding after birth, 143
  peer sociability and, 277–278
  phases of, 265
  psychoanalytic perspective on, 264
  quality of caregiving and, 270–271
  resistant attachment, 267, 270–271
  secure attachment, 266, 279
  siblings and, 276–277
  stability of, 268
  Strange Situation measurement technique, 266, 267t
"Attachment in the making" phase, 265
Attachment Q-Sort, 267
Attendance, school. See School attendance
Attention
  adaptability in, 443–444
  early childhood, 334–335
  habituation and, 219–220
  infancy and toddlerhood, 218–219
  information-processing theories, 218–219
  joint attention, 238, 241
  middle childhood, 443–445
  planning and, 444–445
  selectivity in, 443–444
  sustained, 218–219
Attention-deficit hyperactivity disorder (ADHD), 87, 444–445

Attention span, as temperament dimension, 257t
Attribution retraining, 488
Attributions. See also Personality traits
  achievement-related attributions, 486–488, 488f
  defined, 486
  learned-helplessness and, 487
  mastery-oriented attributions, 486–487
Atypical lateralization of brain, 293–294
Australia
  cesarean deliveries, 134
  child care, 230
  child health care, availability of, 303
  family size, 93
  gay and lesbian families, 509
  infant sleeping patterns, 174
  lead exposure risks, 296, 296f
  reproductive technology laws, 67
Authoritarian parenting, 399, 399t
Authoritative parenting, 398, 399t
  benefits of, 400
  defined, 398
  divorce and, 514
  maternal employment and, 515
  middle childhood, 507
  self-care children and, 516
  self-esteem and, 486
Autism, 342
  false belief and, 341
  fragile X syndrome and, 59
  immunization as possible cause of, 302
Auto accidents. See Motor vehicle accidents
Autobiographical memory, 221, 337, 365
Autonomic nervous system. See Brain development
Autonomy
  early childhood self-help skills and, 309
  independent self, 78
  infancy and toddlerhood, 282
  vs. shame and doubt, as psychosocial stage of development, 16t, 249
Autosomal diseases, 58t
Autosomes, 54
Avoidant attachment, 267, 273

B
Babbling, in language development, 236–237, 241
Babinski reflex of newborns, 144t
Baby Einstein products, 213
Baby fat, 163, 164f, 290
Baby teeth, loss of, 290, 414
"Back to basics" movement, 468
Bacterial diseases. See also Infectious diseases
  prenatal development and, 111t, 112
Baka hunters and gatherers of Cameroon, industry in middle childhood, 482
Balance
  cerebellum and, 294
  early childhood, 290, 308
  middle childhood, 428
  sex differences in, 313

Ball skills
  early childhood, 308, 308f, 313
  middle childhood, 428t
  sex differences in, 313
Bandura's social learning theory. See Social learning theory (Bandura)
Bases, of DNA, 52
Basic emotions, 250–252
Basic trust, vs. mistrust, as psychosocial stage of development, 16t, 248
Bayley Scales of Infant Development, 227
Bedsharing of infants with parents, 172–173
Bedwetting, 422–423
Behavioral assessment of newborns, 152–153
Behavioral genetics, 82
Behavior disorders. See Adjustment problems; Antisocial behavior; Delinquency
Behaviorism, 17–19, 30t. See also Classical conditioning; Operant conditioning
  attachment theory, 264
  language development theories, 233
  Locke as forerunner of, 12
Behavior modification, 18
Behavior, types of. See Antisocial behavior; Prosocial behavior
Beliefs. See also Bias; Spirituality and religiosity; Values
  false beliefs, children's understanding of, 339f, 339–340, 448, 448f
Bell-shaped distribution, in intelligence test scores, 228
Better Beginnings, Better Futures Project of Ontario, Canada, 77
Bhatto Bhatto (game in India), 374
Bias. See also Gender stereotyping
  against AIDS victims, 426
  against cancer victims, 426
  in cultural studies, 34
  "heightism," 297
  intelligence tests, bias in, 347, 454, 460–461
  against obesity, 419
  racial/ethnic, 494–497
  reducing racial/ethnic, methods for, 496–497
  stereotype threat, 460–461, 461f, 470
Biased samples in longitudinal research, 40
Bicycles and tricycles
  early childhood motor development, 308
  injuries caused by accidents, 424–425
Bidirectional influences
  ecological systems theory, 26, 70
  epigenesis, 86, 86f
  prenatal development and, 105
Bilingualism
  education and, 464–466
  language development and, 234, 235
Binet's intelligence test. See Stanford-Binet Intelligence Scales
Binocular depth cues, 192
Bioecological model of development (Bronfenbrenner), 26

Birth. *See* Childbirth; Conception; Newborns; Pregnancy; Prenatal development
  complications. *See* Birth complications
  defects. *See* Birth defects
Birth centers, 130
Birth complications, 135–153. *See also* Birth defects; Low birth weight; Preterm infants
  cesarean delivery, 134
  left-handedness and, 294
  long-term consequences of, 139–141
Birth control. *See* Contraceptive use
Birth defects
  Accutane, maternal use of and, 106
  chromosomal abnormalities, 60–62
  cleft palate, 114
  drug use during pregnancy and, 105–109
  environmental pollution and, 110–111
  fetal alcohol syndrome (FAS), 108–109
  fish consumption and mercury, 110
  infectious diseases during pregnancy and, 111–112
  lead exposure and, 111
  left-handedness and, 294
  nutrition during pregnancy and, 113–114
  radiation during pregnancy and, 110
  Rh factor incompatibility and, 115
  stress during pregnancy and, 114–115
  teratogens and, 102–112
  vitamin–mineral supplements to prevent, 113–114
Birth order, IQ scores and, 14
Birthrate, 93
Birth weight. *See also* Low birth weight
  average, 128
  health in later life and, 104–105
Blacks. *See* African Americans
Bladder control, 188–189
Blank slate (*tabula rasa*), 12
Blastocyst, 96f, 98
Blended families, 513–515
Blindness and infant development, 194, 250
Blood tests
  maternal blood analysis, 63, 64t
  for phenylketonuria, 56
Blood types, incompatible
  cesarean delivery and, 134
  prenatal development and, 115
Bloody show, at start of labor, 126
BMI (Body Mass Index), 416
Bodily-kinesthetic intelligence (Gardner), 456t
Body composition. *See also* Fat, body; Muscle development
  early childhood, 290
  hormones and, 532
  infancy and toddlerhood, 163, 164f
  middle childhood, 412f, 412–413
Body fat. *See* Fat, body
Body growth. *See* Growth spurt; Physical development; Prenatal development
Body image and physical attractiveness, self-esteem and, 485

Body Mass Index (BMI), 416
Body proportions
  early childhood, 290, 291f
  infancy and toddlerhood, 163
  middle childhood, 413
  newborns, 128
Body self-awareness, 281
Body size. *See* Body proportions; Height; Weight
Body weight. *See* Obesity; Weight
Bolivia, childbirth practices in, 129
Bonding. *See* Attachment
Bones. *See* Skeletal development
Botswana, !Kung of. *See* !Kung of Botswana
Bottle-feeding, 175
Boundary extension, 195
Bowel control, 188–189
Bowlby's theory of attachment, 265–266, 274
Brain activity. *See* Electroencephalograms (EEGs); Functional magnetic resonance imaging (fMRI); States of arousal
Brain damage
  child abuse victims, 404
  crying and, 149
  lateralization of brain and, 169
  newborns, oxygen-deprived, 136
  oxygen deprivation during childbirth, 136
  plasticity and, 169, 170
  reflexes of newborns and, 145
Brain development. *See also* Cerebral cortex; Prefrontal cortex
  bilingual development and, 465
  child abuse victims, 404
  cognitive neuroscience and, 23
  early childhood, 291–295
  experience-dependent brain growth, 172, 648
  experience-expectant brain growth, 172
  fetal alcohol syndrome (FAS) and, 109
  hearing-impaired individuals, 169
  hormones and, 415
  infancy and toddlerhood, 164–169
  information processing and, 442–443
  institutionalized orphans and, 169–171
  language areas, 234f, 234–235
  middle childhood, 414–415
  plasticity. *See* Brain plasticity
  prenatal development, 100–101
  prenatal malnutrition and, 113–114
  sensitive periods, 169–172
  states of arousal and, 172–174
  sudden infant death syndrome (SIDS) and, 147
Brain-imaging techniques. *See* Functional magnetic resonance imaging (fMRI)
Brain lateralization. *See* Lateralization of brain
Brain plasticity, 23, 168, 170, 292, 292f
Brain-wave patterns, 166
Brazil
  class-inclusion tasks, performance by children, 440
  diarrhea among children, 303
  mathematical learning among children, 25

Breast cancer and high birth weight, 105, 105f
Breast development, 531–532
Breastfeeding, 174–176
  advantages of, 179
  cosleeping arrangements and, 173
  obesity later in life and, 176
  rooting reflex and, 143
  smell responses in newborns and, 150
  sucking reflex and, 143, 144t
  weight gain and, 176
  Yurok Indians, 15–16
Breathing techniques during labor, 130
Breech position, 134
Broca's area of brain, 234, 234f
Bronfenbrenner's ecological systems theory. *See* Ecological systems theory (Bronfenbrenner)
Brown v. Board of Education (1954), 471
Buddhism and emotional self-regulation, 491
Bullying, 33, 502. *See also* Aggression; Antisocial behavior
Burns, 305

C
Caesarean (Cesarean) delivery, 134
Caffeine, effect on prenatal development, 106
Calcium in prenatal health care, 114
California, parental leave in, 141
Cameroon
  Baka hunters and gatherers, industry in middle childhood, 482
  Nso toddlers and self-recognition, 281, 281f
  theory-of-mind tasks, performance on, 448
Canada. *See also* Industrialized countries; Native Canadians
  aggression in early childhood, 388
  Better Beginnings, Better Futures Project (Ontario), 77
  bilingual families, 465, 466
  cesarean deliveries, 134
  child maltreatment, 404
  family size, 93–94
  health-care policy, 303
  immunization rate, 302
  language immersion programs, 466
  low birth weight, long-term effects of, 139–140
  moral reasoning, 492
  obesity incidence, 417
  parental leave policy, 141
  physical development in middle childhood, 413
  punishment to discipline children, 403
  reproductive technologies, 67
  television regulation, 388
Canalization, 84
Cancer
  children's understanding of, 426
  consequences of children having, 423
  diethylstilbestrol and, 105–106
  radiation and, 60, 110
  smoking during pregnancy and, 107
Car accidents. *See* Motor vehicle accidents
Cardinality, early childhood understanding of, 344

Cardiovascular system
  Apgar Scale, 129t
  heart disease and low birth weight, 104–105
Career. *See* Employment; Vocational development
Caribbean families' child-rearing styles, 401
Carolina Abecedarian Project, 231, 232f
Carriers, of inherited traits, 56–60
  autosomal diseases, 58t
  defined, 56
  detection, 63
  tests, 56–57
  X-linked diseases, 57, 59f
Car seats, 306, 307
Cartilage, 164, 164f
Case studies. *See* Clinical method of research
Cataracts, children born with, 169
Catching skills. *See* Ball skills
Catch-up growth, 169–172, 174
  growth faltering, 178
  hormone treatment and, 297
Categorization
  concrete operational stage of cognitive development, 438
  habituation and, 222, 222f
  infancy and toddlerhood, 218, 222f, 222–223
  information-processing theory, 218
  language development, relationship to, 224
  operant conditioning studies, 222f, 222–223
  preoperational stage of cognitive development, 324–326, 325f
  self-categorization, 282
Catholicism and understanding of God, 495
Cause-and-effect relationships, understanding of
  early childhood, 324, 328t
  infancy, 206
CDS (child-directed speech), 241–242
Cells, 52. *See also* Glial cells
  division (meiosis), 53–54, 54f
  duplication (mitosis), 52
Center of gravity, changes in, 308
Central conceptual structures, in information-processing theories, 441
Central executive, as part of working memory, 217f, 218, 342
Central nervous system. *See* Brain damage; Brain development
Centration, in preoperational stage, 322
Cephalocaudal trend, 162, 163
  prenatal development, 162, 163
Cerebellum, 294, 294f
Cerebral cortex, 167–169, 168f, 414. *See also* Brain damage; Brain development
  defined, 167
  dominance, 292
  early childhood, 292, 292f
  early temperament and prefrontal cortex, 260
  hemispheres, 168–169
  infancy, 168
  institutionalization and effects on, 171

Cerebral cortex (*cont.*)
　lateralization of. *See* Lateralization of brain
　measures of cortical functioning, 166–167, 166*t*
　middle childhood, 414
　mirror neurons, 182
　prenatal development, 100–101
　regions and functions of, 167–168
Cerebral palsy, 135
Certified nurse-midwives, 132
Cervix, 96, 126
Cesarean delivery, 134
Checkerboards, pattern perception of, 193, 193*f*
Chelation and lead exposure, 296
Chemical pollutants. *See* Environmental hazards
Chernobyl, Ukraine, and radiation exposure, 110
Chicken pox, 111*t*, 301
Child abuse. *See* Child maltreatment
Childbirth, 125–143. *See also* Birth complications; Newborns
　age at. *See* Maternal age
　approaches to, 129–132
　breech position, 134
　cesarean delivery, 134
　complications during. *See* Birth complications
　Down syndrome risk, 61
　fetal monitoring, 132–133
　home delivery, 131–132
　induced labor, 134
　instrument delivery, 133*f*, 133–134
　labor, commencement of, 126
　medical interventions, 132–134
　medications during, 133
　multiple births, 55*t*, 55–56. *See also* Twins
　natural (prepared) childbirth, 130–131
　positions for delivery, 131, 131*f*
　rooming in, 143
　stages of, 126–128, 127*f*
　vaginal birth after cesarean, 134
Child care, 350–352. *See also* Preschools
　attachment and, 273
　cognitive development and, 229–231, 348–351
　developmentally appropriate practice standards, 230, 231, 352
　ear infections and, 304
　early childhood, 350–351
　fear of, managing, 370
　illness spread and, 302–303
　infancy and toddlerhood, 230–231
　injury mortality rate and, 306
　otitis media and, 304
　quality of care studies, 229–231
Child-centered preschools, 348, 352. *See also* Preschools
Child custody, 508, 513
Child development. *See also specific periods (e.g., Early childhood, Infancy and toddlerhood)*
　basic issues, 7–11
　contexts for, 8, 23.*See also specific influences (e.g., Cultural differences, Environmental influences, Home environment)*

course of, 8–9, 30*t*. *See also* Continuous course of development; Discontinuous course of development
　Darwin's theory of, 13
　definition, 4
　determinants of, 9, 30*t*. *See also* Environmental influences; Genetics; Nature–nurture controversy
　domains of, 5.*See also specific domains (e.g., Cognitive development, Physical development)*
　field of study, 4–6
　historical foundations of, 11–13
　periods of, 6. *See also specific periods (e.g., Early childhood, Infancy and toddlerhood)*
　public policies, generally, 78–80. *See also* Public policies
　research on. *See* Research methods
　theories of. *See* Theories
　variations in. *See* Individual differences; *specific group differences (e.g., Ethnicity and race, Sex differences)*
Child-directed speech (CDS), 241–242
Child maltreatment, 401–405
　attachment and, 271
　community influences on, 402*t*, 403
　consequences of, 403–404
　cultural influences on, 402*t*, 403
　cycles of, repetition within families, 404
　ecological systems theory of, 402
　empathy in abused children, 371
　eyewitness testimony by children, 521
　family dynamics and, 402*t*, 402–403
　forms of, 401–402
　home visitation to prevent, 404, 405*f*
　incidence of, 401, 402
　intervention programs, 404–405
　newborns, crying and, 149
　origins of, 402*t*, 402–403
　partner abuse and, 402*t*, 403
　prevention of, 404–405
　punishment and, 381–382
　sexual abuse, 402, 519–520
　shaken baby syndrome and, 405
Child mortality. *See* Death; Infant mortality
Child neglect, 402. *See also* Child maltreatment
Child–parent relationship. *See* Attachment; Parent–child relationship
Child-rearing practices. *See also* Discipline; Families; Home environment
　adaptation to age changes, 71
　aggression and, 386–387
　Asian mothers, 261
　attachment and, 270–271
　authoritarian style. *See* Authoritarian parenting
　authoritative style. *See* Authoritative parenting
　child-rearing styles, 398–400. *See also specific styles (e.g., Authoritative parenting, Permissive parenting)*

cognitive development and, 229–231, 347
　cognitive self-regulation and, 449
　continuity of caregiving, 269, 278
　coregulation, 507
　cosleeping arrangements and, 298, 298*f*
　cultural differences, 400–401
　depression of child and, 155
　discipline, 382–384. *See also* Discipline
　divorce, adjustment of children to and, 512–514
　early childhood, 398–405
　eating habits and, 300–301
　emotional self-regulation and, 255, 370, 490–491
　empathy development and, 371
　extended-family households, 79
　family size and, 93–94
　fear management in children, 370
　gay and lesbian families, 508–509
　gender identity and, 504
　Gesell's approach to, 13–14
　goodness-of-fit model, 262–264, 380
　grandparents and, 275–276
　healthy lifestyles, fostering, 427
　injury prevention, 307
　Locke's philosophy of, 12
　marital relationship and, 70–71, 157
　maternal employment and, 515–517
　middle childhood, 506–507
　models of effective parenting, 121
　motor development and, 313–314
　newborns
　　adjustment to parenthood, 157
　　crying, 147–149
　　nutrition, 300–301
　permissive style. *See* Permissive parenting
　poverty and, 74–75
　preterm infants, 137–138
　Puritan doctrine of, 12
　responsive parenting, 270–271
　safety consciousness and, 306–307, 424–425
　self-care children and, 516
　self-conscious emotions and, 254
　self-control and, 283
　self-esteem and, 486
　sensitive caregiving, 270–271
　shy children, 259
　sibling relationship and, 277, 507–508
　single-parent families, 509–510
　social support for, 76
　socioeconomic influences on, 71–73
　sports and, 432
　stepfamilies, adjustment to, 513–515
　teenage parenthood, 559
　television and computers, regulating use of, 352–353, 387–389
　temperament and, 259
　uninvolved style. *See* Uninvolved parenting
Child-rearing styles, 398–400. *See also specific styles (e.g., Authoritative parenting, Permissive parenting)*
Children's Defense Fund, 81
Children's Health Insurance Program (CHIP), 303
Children's rights, 80–81
Child support, 509, 513
　divorce of parents and, 511

enforcement and public policy, 79–80
Chimpanzees. *See* Monkeys and chimps
China. *See also* Asians
　achievement-related attributions, 488, 488*f*
　child-rearing practices, 263, 400–401
　emotional self-regulation, 255, 257
　gender typing in, 394–395
　language and metacognition, 340
　language development, 241, 340
　mathematics instruction in, 452–453
　moral reasoning, 492
　obesity incidence, 417
　one-child family policy, 508
　parental leave, 141
　personal storytelling in early childhood, 367
　self-concept, 483
　self-conscious emotions, 255
　self-esteem, 485
　shame in, 401
　shyness valued in culture of, 263, 263*f*, 374
　temperament of infants, 260–261, 263
Chinese Americans. *See* Asian Americans
CHIP (Children's Health Insurance Program), 303
Chomsky's language acquisition device, 357
Chomsky's nativist theory of language development, 233–236
Chorion, 98
Chorionic villi, 98, 98*f*
Chorionic villus sampling, 63, 64*t*, 65*f*
Chromosomal abnormalities, 60–62
Chromosomes, 52, 52*f*
　autosomes, 54
　crossing over, 53
　dominant–recessive, 56*t*, 56–57
　sex chromosomes, 53–55
Chronic illnesses, 423–424, 426. *See also specific illnesses (e.g., Asthma)*
Chronosystem, in ecological systems theory, 26*f*, 27, 71
Cigarettes. *See* Smoking
Circular reactions, in sensorimotor stage of cognitive development, 205, 205*t*
Circumcision, 149–150
Classical conditioning, 179*f*, 179–180
Classification abilities. *See* Categorization abilities
Classification, hierarchical, 322, 325–328
Class-inclusion problems, 322, 438, 441
Classrooms. *See* Schools; Teachers and teaching techniques
"Clear-cut" attachment phase, 265
Cleft lip and palate, 114
Climate and physical development, 413
Clinical interviews, 20, 32*t*, 33
Clinical method of research, 16, 32*t*, 34
Coaching. *See* Athletics
Cocaine, effect on prenatal development, 106–107. *See also* Drug use and abuse
Cochlear implants, 237

Code switching and bilingual development, 465
Coercive parenting. *See* Authoritarian parenting
Cognition. *See* Cognitive development; Reasoning
abstract. *See* Abstract thinking
metacognition. *See* Metacognition
Cognitive development. *See also* Intelligence; Learning
bilingualism and, 465
brain damage and, 169–171
child care and, 229–231, 348–351
core knowledge perspective, 214–215
cultural influences on, 439–440
defined, 5f
early childhood, 317–361
early intervention programs, 232–233
emotional self-regulation and, 490–491
emotional understanding and, 368
environmental influences on, 229–230
environmental pollution and, 110–111
fetal alcohol syndrome and, 108–109
home environment and, 229–230, 347
individual differences in, 227–232, 453–462
infancy and toddlerhood, 203–245
information-processing perspective. *See* Information-processing perspective
innate knowledge and, 214
institutionalized orphans and, 169–171
language development and. *See* Language development
lead exposure risks, 296
linguistic knowledge and, 214
make-believe play and, 226
microgenetic research, 43
middle childhood, 437–479
milestones
early childhood, 408–409
infancy and toddlerhood, 290–291
middle childhood, 526–527
neurotransmitters and, 415
numerical knowledge and, 214, 215f
nutrition during pregnancy and, 113–114
perceptual development and, 208
phenylketonuria and, 56
physical knowledge and, 214
Piaget's theory of. *See* Cognitive-developmental theory (Piaget)
play and, 373–376
play materials and, 216
poverty and, 232–233
psychological knowledge and, 214
questions of children as catalyst for, 326
research on, 331–332
retardation and. *See* Mental retardation
self-concept and, 482–483
sex chromosomal disorders and, 61–62
social-cognitive theory of, 18
socially mediated process of, 25
sociocultural theory of. *See* Sociocultural theory of cognitive development (Vygotsky)
sociodramatic play and, 319

speed of thinking. *See* Speed of processing
symbolic understanding, 211–212
television and, 213
Cognitive-developmental theory (Piaget), 204–216
accommodation in, 204, 321
adaptation in, 204–205
assimilation in, 204
clinical interviews, 20, 33
disequilibrium in, 205
educational principles based on, 328–329, 467
equilibrium in, 205
evaluation of, 223–224
gender identity, 396
gender typing, 390
make-believe play and, 226
modifications to, 20–21, 216, 328, 441–442
moral development, 384–385
organization in, 205
repeating chance behaviors, 206
scaffolding in, 224
schemes in, 204–205
stages of, 329. *See also specific stages (e.g., Formal operational stage of cognitive development, Sensorimotor stage of cognitive development)*
Cognitive maps, 438–439, 439f
Cognitive neuroscience, developmental, 23
Cognitive psychology. *See* Information-processing perspective
Cognitive self-regulation, 449
Cohort effects, 41
Colic, 149
Collaborative style of communication, 460
Collectivist societies
cosleeping arrangements in infancy and childhood, 173
emotional self-regulation, 255
gender typing in, 395
individualistic societies vs., 78
make-believe play in infancy and toddlerhood, 226
play, 374
self-concept, 484
self-conscious emotions, 254
shame in, 371
shyness valued in Chinese culture, 263, 374
College education. *See* Higher education
Color vision in infancy, 190
Communication. *See* Language development; Speech
Communication styles
collaborative style, 460
cultural influences, 459–461
hierarchical style, 460
intelligence, 459–460
socioeconomic status, 459
topic-associating style, 464
topic-focused style, 464
Communities of learners, 469
Community influences, 75–77
childhood injuries, preventing, 306
child maltreatment, 402t, 403
immigrant youths and, 36
resilient children and, 11

Compassion. *See* Empathy; Prosocial behavior
Compliance. *See also* Conformity
defined, 282
toddlerhood, 282–283
Componential approach to intelligence, 455
Comprehension vs. production, in language development, 240
Computer-learning centers, 353
Computers
classroom learning centers, 353
classroom use, 472–473
metacognition and, 472
preschool children using, 353, 389
programming skills, 353
school-age children using, 471–472
sex differences in use, 472
Concealment, in research, 45t
Conception, 96. *See also* Fertility; Pregnancy; Prenatal development
breastfeeding's effect on, 175
donor insemination, 66
in vitro fertilization, 66–67
maternal age. *See* Maternal age
menarche and, 536
paternal age. *See* Paternal age
preconception steps for prospective parents, 68
zygote, 53–54, 54f
Concrete operational stage of cognitive development, 19t, 437–442
classification in, 438
conservation in, 438
defined, 438
evaluation of, 442
limitations of, 440
research on, 440–442
seriation in, 438, 440
spatial reasoning in, 438–440
Conditioned response (CR), 179f, 179–180
Conditioned stimulus (CS), 179f, 179–180
Conditioning. *See* Classical conditioning; Operant conditioning
Condoms. *See* Contraceptive use
Conflict. *See also* Aggression; Social problem solving; Violence
adult conflict, effect on children, 38, 38f
friendships in early childhood and, 375
marital. *See* Divorce
Resolving Conflict Creatively Program (RCCP), 522–523
sibling relationships, 508
Conformity, gender-role conformity and aggression, 386
Congo, Efe of. *See* Efe of Republic of Congo
Conscience. *See* Moral development; Superego
Consent to research, 45t, 45–46
Conservation
concrete operational stage of cognitive development, 438
defined, 321
preoperational stage of cognitive development, 321–322, 322f, 324
Constructive play, 373, 373t

Constructivist classrooms, 467–468
Context and intelligence (Sternberg), 456
Contexts for development, 8, 23. *See also specific influences (e.g., Environmental influences, Home environment)*
Continuous course of development, 7, 8f
cognitive development in early and middle childhood, 442
information-processing theories, 21–23
Locke's philosophy, 12
stance of major developmental theories, 30t
Continuum of acquisition, 440, 441
Contractions, in childbirth, 126–127
Contrast sensitivity, 193, 193f
Control deficiency, in attention and memory strategies, 443, 446
Control processes. *See* Mental strategies
Controversial children and peer acceptance, 500, 501
Convention on the Rights of the Child, 81
Convergent thinking, 474
Conversation. *See* Pragmatic development; Speech
Cooing, in language development, 236–237, 240–241
Cooley's anemia, 58t
Cooperation. *See* Compliance; Prosocial behavior
Cooperative learning, 468–469
ability grouping and, 470–471
defined, 471
inclusive classrooms and, 474
reciprocal teaching, 468–469
Cooperative play, 372
Coordination of secondary circular reactions, in sensorimotor stage of cognitive development, 205t
Coparenting, 70, 513
Coping strategies. *See* Emotional self-regulation
Coregulation, in supervision of children, 507
Core knowledge perspective, 214
Corporal punishment, 381–382, 382f, 403
Corpus callosum, 294f, 295, 414, 538
Corpus luteum, 96
Correlational research, 37, 39t, 229–230
Correlation coefficients, 37, 37f
Cortex. *See* Cerebral cortex; Prefrontal cortex
Corticotrophin-releasing hormone (CRH), 126
Cortisol
brain development and, 171
childbirth and, 126, 128
child maltreatment and, 404
stress response of mother, effect on prenatal development, 115
temperamental style and, 259
Cosleeping arrangements, 173, 298, 298f
Cost of raising a child, 92
Counseling
aggression, 389
bedwetting, 423

Counseling (cont.)
blended families, 515
chronic illnesses, 424
genetic counseling, 63, 68
postpartum depression, 155
sexual abuse victims, 520
Counting, in early childhood, 344
Course of development, 8–9. See also
Continuous course of
development; Discontinuous
course of development
comparison of major developmental
theories, 30t
Court proceedings. See Legal issues
and proceedings
CR (conditioned response), 179f,
179–180
Crawling, 185. See also Motor
development
depth perception and, 192–193
emotional self-regulation and, 255
Creatine, 534
Creative intelligence (Sternberg), 455
Creativity
defined, 474
gifted students, 474
Cretinism and prenatal nutrition, 114
Criminality. See Antisocial behavior;
Child maltreatment;
Delinquency; Violence
Critical period, 23. See also Sensitive
period
Critical thinking and constructivist
classrooms, 467
Cross-cultural research
academic achievement, 476–477
attachment patterns, 268f, 268–269
birth order and family size, 93
gay and lesbian family adoptions,
508
gender stereotyping
academic subject preferences, 504
personality traits, 503
infant mortality, 140f, 140–141
infant sleeping patterns, 174
language and verbal reasoning, 340
memory strategies, 447
motor development, 186
Neonatal Behavioral Assessment
Scale (NBAS), 152
parent–child relationship, 276
self-esteem, 486
separation anxiety, 269
sociocultural theory, 24–25
Crossing over, of chromosomes, 53
Cross-sectional research, 39t, 41–42
Crowning, in childbirth, 127
Crying
newborns, 147–149
soothing crying baby, 148–149
CS (conditioned stimulus), 179f,
179–180
Cultural bias
in intelligence tests, 347, 454,
461–462
in research, 34
Cultural differences. See also Cross-
cultural research; Ethnicity and
race; specific entries (e.g., African
societies, Native Americans)
academic achievement, 476–477
adult work, children in village
and tribal cultures participating
in, 333

extended-family households, 79
attachment, 268f, 268–269
body size, 413
childbirth practices, 129, 130, 131
child health care, availability of, 303
child maltreatment, 402t, 403
child-rearing styles, 400–401
cognitive development, 440
cosleeping arrangements of infants
with parents, 173
discipline, 383
drawing, development of, 311
emotional self-regulation and, 491
ethnographic research, 34–35
extended-family households, 79
food preferences, 300
gender typing, 394–395
God, children's understanding
of, 495
immigrant youths, adaptation by, 36
infant sleeping arrangements, 173
intelligence, 456, 459–461
language development, 240–241, 340
make-believe play, 226, 374
memory development, 447
moral development, 494
motor development, 186, 188
Neonatal Behavioral Assessment
Scale (NBAS), 152
newborn behavior and child-rearing
practices, 152–153
newborn health care, 140f, 140–141
paternal warmth, 276
peer relations, 374
physical discipline, 383
play, 226, 363, 374
prenatal health care, 117
psychosocial stages of development,
15–16
reaching, development of, 188
research methods, 35–39
self-concept, 367, 483–484
self-conscious emotions, expression
of, 254
self-development of toddlers, 281,
281f
self-esteem, 486
sociocultural theory. See
Sociocultural theory of cognitive
development (Vygotsky)
stranger anxiety among infants and
toddlers, 252
temperament, 260–261
tooth development, 290
war and violence, effect on children,
518
Custody of children, 508, 513
Cyberbullying, 502
Cystic fibrosis, 423
Cytoplasm, 53

D
Darwin's theory of evolution, 13
Day care. See Child care
Deafness. See Hearing and hearing
loss
Death. See also Infant mortality;
Suicide
diarrhea as cause of, 302
injuries as cause of, 305, 305f, 424f,
424–425
sex differences in child mortality, 59
suicide, 404
Debriefing in research, 46

Decentration, in concrete operational
stage, 438
Deception, 46
Decoding words, 450
Deferred imitation, 207, 210, 212t
Deformities. See Birth defects
Delay of gratification, 283
Delinquency
child abuse victims, 403
childhood aggression and, 387
peer rejection and, 500
sexual abuse victims, 519
Denmark
immunization rate, 302
in vitro fertilization, 67
poverty rate, 74
Dental development and care
breastfeeding and tooth
development, 175
bulimia damage to, 546
early childhood, 290
loss of primary (baby) teeth, 290, 414
malocclusion, 414
middle childhood, 414
tooth decay, 414
Deoxyribonucleic acid. See DNA
Dependent variables, in experimental
research design, 37
Depression. See also Suicide
maternal postpartum depression,
155
paternal, 155
preterm infants and maternal
depression, 271
Deprivation. See also Malnutrition;
Poverty; Sensitive period;
Socioeconomic influences
growth faltering, 178
sensory deprivation studies of
animals, 169
Depth perception, 192–193, 429, 429f
DES (diethylstilbestrol), effect on
prenatal development, 105–106
Despair, ego integrity vs.,16t. See also
Depression
Determinants of development, 9. See
also Environmental influences;
Genetics; Nature–nurture
controversy
stance of major developmental
theories, 30t
Developing countries
AIDS and prenatal development, 112
breastfeeding, 175
childbirth, 129
diarrhea among children, 302
education of girls in, 73
"kangaroo care" for preterm infants,
138
obesity trends, 417
prenatal malnutrition, 114
social interaction and learning in, 25
Development. See Child development;
specific entries (e.g., Cognitive
development, Physical
development)
Developmental cognitive
neuroscience, 23
Developmentally appropriate
practices
child-care and preschool programs,
230–231, 352, 375
sports, 432
Developmental quotients (DQs), 228

Developmental research designs,
40–43
Developmental science, defined, 4
Diabetes
as chronic illness, 423
genomic imprinting and, 59
insipidus, 58t
low birth weight and, 105
obesity and type 2, 417
in Pima Indians, 419
prenatal, 117
Diarrhea, 301–302, 304
Diet. See Eating habits; Malnutrition;
Nutrition
Diethylstilbestrol (DES), effect
on prenatal development,
105–106
Differentiation theory of perceptual
development, 198–199, 199f
Difficult child, as temperament type,
256, 351, 402
Digital divide, 472
Digit span, 336, 442–443
Dilation of cervix in childbirth, 126
Dioxins, effect on prenatal
development, 111
Disability. See specific disabilities
(e.g., Hearing loss)
Disadvantaged. See Deprivation;
Poverty; Socioeconomic
influences
Discipline. See also Child-rearing
practices; Punishment
(disciplinary)
aggression and, 387
cultural differences in, 383
effective discipline, principles of,
382–384
inductive, 379
moral development and, 378–379
positive discipline, 383
socioeconomic influences, 72
temperament and, 379
time out, 382, 383
Discontinuous course of
development, 8, 8f
cognitive development in early and
middle childhood, 442
stance of major developmental
theories, 30t
Discovery learning, 328–329, 332
Discrimination. See Bias; Ethnicity
and race; Racial/ethnic bias;
Socioeconomic influences
Diseases. See also Immune system;
Infectious diseases; specific
diseases (e.g., Cancer, Diabetes)
breastfeeding and, 175
children's understanding of, 426
chronic, 423–424
dominant–recessive inheritance,
56–60
early childhood development and,
301–304
middle childhood, 423–424
prenatal development and, 111t,
111–112
prenatal diagnosis, 58t, 63–65, 64t
X-linked inheritance, 57, 59f
Disequilibrium, in cognitive-
developmental theory, 205
Disorganized/disoriented attachment,
267, 271, 278–279
Displaced reference, 211, 212t

Disposition. *See* Personality traits; Temperament

Distractibility, as temperament dimension, 257

Distress. *See* Anxiety; Fear; Stress

Divergent thinking, 474, 475*f*

Diversity. *See* Cultural differences; Ethnicity and race; Racial/ethnic bias

Divorce, 510–513. *See also* Single-parent families
  age of child and response to, 511, 514
  child-rearing practices and, 512–514
  coparenting after, 513
  custody arrangements. *See* Custody of children
  family size and, 93
  gender of child and response to, 511
  immediate consequences of, 511–512
  incidence of, 510, 510*f*
  long-term consequences of, 512–513
  mediation, 513
  sex differences in response to, 511–512
  temperament of child and response to, 511–512

Dizygotic twins, 55. *See also* Twins; Twin studies

DNA (deoxyribonucleic acid), 52–53, 53*f*
  duplication (mitosis), 53
  mutation, 60
  radiation and, 60

Dogon of Mali, mother–infant relationship and attachment, 268

Domains of development, 5. *See also specific domains (e.g., Cognitive development, Physical development)*

Domestic violence. *See* Child maltreatment

Dominance hierarchy, 432

Dominant cerebral hemisphere, 293

Dominant–recessive inheritance, 56*t*, 56–57

Donor insemination, 66

Donor ova, 67

Doubt, autonomy vs. shame and, 249. *See also* Anxiety

Doula, role in childbirth, 130–131

Down syndrome, 61, 61*f*

DQs (developmental quotients), 228

Drama classes and intelligence, 44, 44*f*

Drawing
  cultural variations in development, 311, 311*f*
  early childhood, 309–311, 310–311*f*, 328
  middle childhood, 429, 429*f*
  realistic drawings, 310–311, 311*f*
  representational shapes and forms, 310
  scribbles, 310
  three-dimensional objects, 429, 429*f*

Dreams and REM sleep, 146

Dressing skills, 309, 309*t*

Dribbling skills. *See* Ball skills

Drill-oriented instruction in mathematics, 451–452

Drinking. *See* Alcohol use and abuse

Drowning, 305

Drug use and abuse. *See also* Medications
  prenatal development and maternal drug use, 105–109

Dual-earner households, 515–517. *See also* Maternal employment

Dual representation, 320–321, 327

Duchenne muscular dystrophy, 58*t*

Dutch. *See* Netherlands

Dwarfism, psychosocial, 297

Dynamic assessment of intelligence, 461–462, 462*f*

Dynamic systems perspective of development, 28*f*, 28–29, 30*t*
  emotional development and, 249–250
  information processing and, 217–224
  motor development and, 184–185, 308

Dyslexia. *See* Learning disabilities

E

Ear infections, 304, 422

Early childhood, 289–407
  academic training in, 349–350
  aggression in, 385–390
  artistic expression in, 310–311, 311*f*
  attention in, 334–335
  balance in, 290
  body composition in, 290
  body proportions in, 290, 291*f*
  bone density and milk drinking in, 300
  brain development in, 291–295
  child care in, 350–351
  child-rearing styles and practices in, 398–405
  cognitive development in, 317–361. *See also* Preoperational stage of cognitive development
  computer games in, 388–389
  computer use in, 353
  defined, 6
  diseases in, 301–304
  drawing in, 309–311, 310–311*f*, 328
  eating habits in, 299–301
  emergent literacy in, 343–344, 345
  emotional and social development in, 363–407
  emotional self-regulation in, 369–370
  emotions in, 367–372
  empathy in, 367, 371
  episodic memory in, 336
  fears in, 370
  fine-motor development in, 309*t*, 309–312
  friendships in, 374–375
  gender identity in, 395–397
  gender-stereotyped beliefs in, 390–391
  gender stereotyping in, 363, 396
  gender typing in, 390–398
  grammar in, 356–358
  gross-motor development in, 308–309, 309*t*
  guilt in, 380
  height in, 290
  information processing in, 334–346
  inhibition in, 334*f*, 334–335
  injuries in, 304–307
  intelligence tests in, 346–347
  intervention programs, 349–350

language development in, 318, 354–359
  literacy in, 341–344, 343*f*
  make-believe play in, 318–320, 323–324, 332, 374
  mathematical reasoning in, 344–346
  memory in, 335–337
  mental representation in, 318, 321
  metacognition in, 338–339
  milestones in, 408–409
  moral development in, 363, 378–390
  motor development in, 308*f*, 308–314
  nutrition in, 299–301
  parental relationships in. *See* Father–child relationship; Mother–child relationship; Parent–child relationship
  peer relations in, 372–377
  personal storytelling in, 366
  phobias in, 370
  phonological awareness in, 343
  physical development in, 289–315
  play in, 373, 373*t*
  pragmatics in, 358–359
  preschools, 348–351, 375, 394
  recall memory in, 336
  recognition memory in, 336
  self-concept in, 365–366
  self-conscious emotions in, 370–371
  self-esteem in, 266–267
  self-help skills in, 309
  shame in, 370, 371
  skeletal age in, 290
  skeletal development in, 290–291, 291*f*
  sleep habits and problems in, 298–299
  sociocultural theory, 330–334
  spelling in, 341–346
  taste in, 300
  television viewing in, 351–353, 387–389
  tooth development in, 290
  vocabulary in, 354–356
  walking in, 308, 309*t*
  weight in, 290
  writing in, 312, 341–346

Early Head Start, 232

Early intervention programs
  early childhood, 349–350
  infancy and toddlerhood, 231–232
  low-income, preterm babies, 139, 139*f*
  preschool, 349–350

Early learning centers, 172

Ears. *See also* Hearing and hearing loss
  infections in, 304, 422
  middle childhood, 422

Eastern Europe, gender-stereotyped beliefs, 504

Easy child, as temperament type, 256

Eating habits. *See also* Feeding practices; Nutrition
  early childhood, 299–301, 300*f*
  infancy and toddlerhood, 176
  middle childhood, 417–421
  obesity and, 417–422, 418*t*

Eclectic position on theories of child development, 29

Ecological systems theory (Bronfenbrenner), 25–27, 30*t*, 69
  attachment and, 274
  bidirectional influences, 26, 70

child maltreatment and, 402
  chronosystem, 26*f*, 27, 71
  definition, 25–26
  exosystem, 26*f*, 27, 75
  macrosystem, 26*f*, 27, 69
  mesosystem, 26*f*, 26–27, 75
  microsystem, 26, 26*f*, 69
  third-party influences, 26, 70

Economic development of countries and education of girls, 73

Economic influences. *See* Poverty; Socioeconomic influences

Ectoderm, 99

Education. *See also* Academic achievement; Learning; Schools; Teachers and teaching techniques; *specific subjects (e.g., Mathematics and mathematical reasoning, Reading)*
  bilingual, 464–466
  cognitive-developmental principles of, 329–330
  computer-learning centers in classrooms, 353
  developmentally appropriate practices for early childhood programs, 352
  early learning centers, 172
  expenditures on, 80*t*
  of girls in developing countries, 73
  health education in middle childhood, 425–427
  healthy lifestyles, fostering, 427
  high-quality education in elementary school, 467
  Home Observation for Measurement of the Environment (HOME), 229–230, 347
  infant caregiving skills, training parents in, 139
  information-processing principles of, 450–453
  Montessori, 348
  parenthood, preparation for, 120–121
  physical. *See* Physical education
  public education programs. *See* Public education programs
  safety education, 424
  sociocultural principles of, 332
  socioeconomic influences, 73
  television viewing, 387–389
  Tools of the Mind preschool curriculum, 335

Educational attainment
  poverty and, 80
  preschool intervention programs and, 349–350

Educational philosophies
  cognitive-developmental principles, 329–330, 467
  communities of learners, 469
  constructivist classroom, 467–468
  multiple intelligences theory, 475
  social-constructivist classroom, 468–469
  sociocultural principles, 332, 468
  traditional classroom, 467–468

Educational self-fulfilling prophecies, 470

Educational television, 351–353

EEG (electroencephalogram), 166*t*, 167*f*

Efe of Republic of Congo
  adult work, children in, 333
  physical development in early
    childhood, 290
  stranger anxiety among infants and
    toddlers, 252
Effacement of cervix in childbirth,
  126
Effective strategy use, in attention and
  memory strategies, 443
Effortful control, 254, 257–258, 257t,
  260, 261, 262, 282, 369, 379
  psychosexual theory of, 15
  psychosocial theory of, 17
Egocentric speech, 330
Egocentrism. See also Perspective
  taking
  defined, 321
  preoperational stage of cognitive
    development, 321, 323–324
Egypt
  education of girls, 73
  malnutrition, 416
Elaboration, as memory strategy, 337,
  446
Elaborative style, in conversing about
  past with children, 337
Electra conflict, 364
Electrical activity in cerebral cortex,
  166
Electroencephalogram (EEG), 166t,
  167f
Elementary schools. See Schools
Embarrassment, infancy and
  toddlerhood, 254
Embryonic disk, 98
Embryo, period of prenatal
  development, 97t, 99, 103f
Emergent literacy, 343–344, 345
Emotional abuse of children, 402
Emotional and social development.
  See also Emotions; Moral
  development; Personality traits;
  Temperament
  attachment and. See Attachment
  breastfeeding and, 175
  child maltreatment and, 404
  child-rearing practices and, 398–405
  cognitive development and, 368
  defined, 5f
  dynamic systems theory, 249–250
  early childhood, 363–407
  ethological theory and, 23
  games and, 430
  home environment and, 368
  infancy and toddlerhood, 247–285
  learning disabilities and, 473
  make-believe play and, 370
  middle childhood, 482–525
  milestones
    early childhood, 408–409
    infancy and toddlerhood, 290–291
    middle childhood, 526–527
  neighborhood environment and,
    75–76
  neurotransmitters and, 415
  obesity and, 419
  parental depression and, 155
  peer relations. See Peer relations
  play and, 363
  postpartum depression, 155
  psychosexual theory of. See
    Psychosexual theory of
    development (Freud)

psychosocial theory of. See
  Psychosocial theory of
  development (Erikson)
responding to others' emotions,
  252–253, 369
self-conscious emotions. See Guilt;
  Shame
self-regulation of emotions. See
  Emotional self-regulation
social learning theory of. See
  Social learning theory
  (Bandura)
sociodramatic play and, 374
understanding of emotions,
  252–253, 367–372, 490
visual impairment and, 194
Emotional competence, 367
Emotional contagion, 252
Emotional expression
  friendships in early childhood and,
    375
  sex differences in, 255
Emotional intelligence, 457
Emotional neglect of children. See
  Child maltreatment
Emotional self-efficacy, 491
Emotional self-regulation. See also
  Coping strategies
  early childhood, 369–370
  empathy and, 371
  infancy and toddlerhood, 254–255
  middle childhood, 490–491
Emotional stress. See Stress
Emotion-centered coping, 490–491
Emotions. See also Emotional and
  social development; specific
  entries (e.g., Anger, Fear)
  basic emotions, 250–252
  early childhood, 367–372
  individual differences in. See
    Temperament
  infancy and toddlerhood, 249–256
  lateralization of brain and, 168
  middle childhood, 489–491
  self-conscious. See Envy; Guilt;
    Pride; Self-conscious emotions;
    Shame
  self-regulation of. See Emotional
    self-regulation
Empathy. See also Prosocial behavior
  defined, 282
  early childhood, 367, 371
  guilt and, 380
  middle childhood, 490
  moral development and, 380
  perspective taking and, 491–492
  self-awareness and, 282
  toddlerhood, 282
Employment
  maternal employment. See Maternal
    employment
  work–life balance, 273
Endocrine system. See Hormones
Endoderm, 99
Endorphins, 150
England and Great Britain
  adopted children, mental test scores
    of, 171f
  childbirth practices, 131
  family size, 93
  immunization rate, 302
  infant sleeping patterns, 174
  parental depression, 155
  reproductive technology laws, 67

Enlightenment philosophies of
  childhood, 12
Enrichment programs. See Early
  intervention programs; Gifted
  children
Environmental hazards. See also
  Radiation
  asthma and, 423
  lead poisoning, 111
  prenatal development and, 110–111
Environmental influences, 69–81. See
  also Genetics; Nature–nurture
  controversy; specific influences
  (e.g., Cultural differences, Home
  environment)
  ADHD, 444–445
  behavioral genetics, 82
  cognitive development, 229–230
  community influences. See
    Community influences
  cultural influences. See Cultural
    differences
  families. See Families
  gene expression, 86–88
  gender typing, 393–395
  home environment. See Home
    environment
  intelligence, 83–84
  motor development, 314
  neighborhood influences, 75–77
  obesity, 417
  physical development, 178, 413
  prenatal development, 102–119
  prenatal environment and health in
    later life, 104–105
  relationship between heredity and
    environment, 82–88
  sudden infant death syndrome
    (SIDS), 147
  temperament, 261–262
Environmental pollutants. See
  Environmental hazards
Envy, 254. See also Jealousy
Epidural analgesia, 133
Epigenesis, 86, 86f, 87
Epilepsy and neurotransmitters, 415
Epiphyses, 164, 164f, 290
Episiotomy, in childbirth, 131
Episodic memory, 336
Equality and diversity, children's
  understanding of, 494–497
Equilibrium, in cognitive-
  developmental theory, 205
Erikson's psychosocial theory. See
  Psychosocial theory of
  development (Erikson)
Estimation, in basic arithmetic, 345
Estrogens, 143
Ethics
  reproductive technologies and, 67
  research, 43–46
Ethiopian children and dynamic
  assessment, effect on IQ scores,
  461–462, 462f
Ethnicity and race. See also African
  Americans; Cultural differences;
  Hispanics; Native Americans;
  Racial/ethnic bias
  child-rearing practices, 70
  face perception, own-race
    preference, 196
  fraternal twinning and, 55t
  friendships and, 499
  intelligence, definition of, and, 456

IQ scores and, 459–461
  middle childhood understanding of,
    494–497
  physical development and, 162, 290,
    413
  poverty and, 74
  prejudice based on. See Bias;
    Racial/ethnic bias
  school integration and magnet
    schools, 471
  self-esteem and, 488
  skeletal development, 163
  sleep routines for preschoolers, 298f,
    298–299
  sudden infant death syndrome
    (SIDS) and, 147
  temperament and, 260–261
Ethnography, as research method, 32t,
  34–35
Ethology, 23, 30t, 265, 278
Europe. See also specific countries or
  regions (e.g., Sweden, Western
  Europe)
  childbirth practices, 131
  child care in, 230
  child health care, availability of, 303
  cohabiting relationships, 157
  immunization rates, 302
  injury mortality rates, 306
  newborn care, 141
  physical development in middle
    childhood, 413
  reproductive technology laws, 67
Eustachian tube, 304, 422
Event-related potentials (ERPs), 166,
  166t
Evocative correlation, in
  genetic–environmental
  correlation, 85
Evolutionary developmental
  psychology, 24, 30t
Evolution, theories of
  Darwin and, 13
  ethology, 23
  on gender typing, 391
Exclusion, in peer groups, 498
Executive processing, 217f, 218, 342.
  See also Central executive, as part
  of working memory
Exercise. See also Athletics; Physical
  education
  middle childhood, 427, 433–434
  obesity and, 418t, 418–419,
    420–421
  prenatal development and, 113
  preschoolers, 313
  recess periods at school, 433
Exosystem, in ecological systems
  theory, 26f, 27, 75
Expansions, in language
  development, 359
Experience-dependent brain
  growth, 172, 648
Experience-expectant brain
  growth, 172
Experimental research design, 37–38,
  39t
Expressive style of language learning,
  240–241
Extended-family households, 79
  make-believe play and, 226
  never-married single parents and,
    509
Externalizing difficulties, 71

Extinction, in classical conditioning, 180
Extracurricular activities. *See also* Athletics
  after-school programs, 516
Eye blink reflex of newborns, 144*t*
Eyes. *See also* Vision
  postnatal development of, 151–152
  pupil dilation and temperamental style, 259
  REM sleep and, 146
  visual information processing by brain hemispheres, 168*f*
Eyewitness testimony by children, 521

F

Face perception, 195–196, 196*f*
Factor analysis of intelligence test scores, 453
Fairness. *See* Prosocial behavior
Faith. *See* Spirituality and religiosity
Fallopian tubes, 96, 96*f. See also* Reproductive system
Falls, 306
False beliefs, children's understanding of, 339*f,* 339–340, 448, 448*f*
False labor, 126
Familiarity preference, in habituation research, 181, 181*f*
Families, 69–71. *See also* Child-rearing practices; Grandparents; Home environment; Parent–child relationship; Sibling relationships
  adaptation to change, 71
  adoptive. *See* Adoption
  aggression in children and family dynamics, 386–387
  attachment and circumstances of, 272
  blended, 513–515
  child maltreatment and family dynamics, 402*t,* 402–403
  direct influences on children, 70
  divorce. *See* Divorce
  dual-earner, 515–517
  extended families. *See* Extended-family households
  gay and lesbian families, 508–509
  gender typing, influences on, 393*f,* 393–394
  health of, in developing countries, 73
  indirect influences on children, 70–71
  kinship studies. *See* Kinship studies
  maternal employment. *See* Maternal employment
  middle childhood and, 506–517
  never-married single-parent families, 509–510
  newborns, adjustment to, 154, 156
  one-child families, 508
  parent–child relationships, 506–507
  reconstituted, 513–515
  siblings. *See* Sibling relationships
  single-parent. *See* Single-parent families
  size of. *See* Family size
  skipped-generation families, 275
  socioeconomic influences on, 71–73
  stepfamilies, 513–515
Family planning, 92–95.
Family size, 93–94, 508
Family therapy. *See* Counseling

Family violence. *See* Child maltreatment
Fantasy play. *See* Make-believe play
FAS (Fetal alcohol syndrome), 108, 109*t*
FASD (Fetal alcohol spectrum disorder), 108, 109*t*
Fast mapping, in vocabulary development, 354
Fat, body. *See also* Obesity
  baby fat, 163, 164*f,* 290
  early childhood, 290
  middle childhood, 413
Father absence
  academic achievement and, 510
  antisocial behavior and, 510
  and divorce, 511
  in never-married single-parent families, 510
Father–adolescent relationship. *See* Parent–adolescent relationship
Father–child relationship. *See also* Father–infant relationship; Parent–child relationship; Father absence
  child-rearing styles of ethnic groups, 401
  divorce and, 512, 515
  favoritism in, 507
  gay and lesbian families, 508–509
  gender stereotyping and, 393, 503, 505, 507
  maternal employment and, 516
  never-married single-parent families, 510
  remarriage and, 515
  sibling relationships and, 507
Father–infant relationship. *See also* Parent–infant relationship
  attachment and, 274–275
  paternal warmth and development, 276
  newborns, 143, 156, 157
Father–stepmother families, 515
Fear
  conditioning of, 180
  early childhood, helping children manage in, 370
  infancy and toddlerhood, 252
  middle childhood, 517–519
  secure base and, 252
  stranger anxiety and, 252
Fearful distress, as temperament dimension, 257*t*
Feeding practices. *See also* Eating habits; Nutrition
  bottle-feeding, 175
  breastfeeding. *See* Breastfeeding
  early childhood motor development and, 309
  obesity and, 418
Feet first, reaching, 185*f,* 186
Female vs. male development. *See* Sex differences
Fertility. *See also* Conception; Infertility
  age of female and, 95
Fertility drugs and multiple births, 55, 55*t*
Fertilization, 96, 96*f. See also* In vitro fertilization
Fetal alcohol spectrum disorder (FASD), 108, 109*t*
Fetal alcohol syndrome (FAS), 108, 109*t*

Fetal medicine, 63–65
Fetal monitoring, 132–133
Fetoscopy, 64*t*
Fetus, period of prenatal development, 97*t,* 100–102
  habituation in, 181
  teratogens in, 103*f*
Field experiments, 38–39
Fijians, moral development among, 379
Fine-motor development
  defined, 183
  early childhood, 309*t,* 309–312
  enhancing, 313–314
  infancy and toddlerhood, 183–184, 184*t*
  middle childhood, 429
  milestones, 309*t*
  printing and, 312
  sex differences in, 313, 430
Finland
  academic achievement, 477
  adoption studies, 86
  cesarean deliveries, 134
  poverty rate, 74
Firearms, childhood injuries and death from, 307
First Amendment free-speech right, and TV regulation, 388
First-language learning, 234
First trimester of prenatal development, 97*t. See also* Embryo, period of prenatal development; Zygote
First words, 237, 238–239
Fitness. *See* Exercise; Health; Nutrition
Flexibility, physical, in middle childhood, 414, 428
fMRI (Functional magnetic resonance imaging), 166*t,* 166–167, 167*f*
Folic acid and prenatal health care, 114
Fontanels, 165, 165*f*
Food. *See* Eating habits; Feeding practices; Malnutrition; Nutrition
Food insecurity, 178. *See also* Malnutrition
Food supplement programs, prenatal, 114
Forceps use in childbirth, 133, 133*f*
Formula (bottle-feeding), 175
Fragile X syndrome, 59
France
  newborn smell response, 150
  reproductive technology laws, 67
Fraternal twins, 55, 55*t. See also* Twins; Twin studies
Freestanding birth centers, 130
Freud's psychosexual theory. *See* Psychosexual theory of development (Freud)
Friendships. *See also* Peer relations
  early childhood, 374–375
  middle childhood, 499–500
  sex differences in, 499–500
Frontal lobes, 168. *See also* Cerebral cortex; Prefrontal cortex.
  Broca's area, 234, 234*f*
Full inclusion of students with learning disabilities, 473
Functional magnetic resonance imaging (fMRI), 166*t,* 166–167, 167*f*

Functional play, 373, 373*t*
Fundamentalist views on make-believe, 35

G

Games. *See also* Athletics; Play; Toys
  language development and, 237*t,* 238
  middle childhood, 430
  organized games with rules, 430
  video games, 353
Gametes, 53–54. *See also* Ova; Sperm
Gardner's multiple intelligences theory, 456*t,* 456–458, 475
Gay and lesbian families, 508–509
Gays and lesbians. *See* Sexual orientation
Gender consistency, 396
Gender constancy, 395–396
Gender contentedness, 505
Gender differences. *See* Sex differences
Gender gap. *See* Sex differences
Gender identity
  cognitive-developmental theory of, 396
  defined, 395
  early childhood, 395–397
  gender schema theory of, 390, 396–397, 397*f*
  middle childhood, 505–506
  sex differences in development, 505
  social learning theory of, 396
  theories of, 396
Gender labeling, 395
Gender reassignment, 392
Gender-role adoption. *See* Gender stereotyping
Gender-role conformity and aggression, 386
Gender schema theory, 390, 396–397, 397*f*
Gender stability, 396
Gender stereotyping. *See also* Gender typing
  academic subjects and, 503–504, 504*f*
  categorizing self and, 282
  early childhood, 363, 390–391, 396
  infancy and toddlerhood, 261, 275
  middle childhood, 503–504
  motor development and, 313
  personality traits, 503
  reducing, 397–398
  sports and, 430
  temperament and, 261
  toys and, 261, 282
Gender typicality, 505–506
Gender typing. *See also* Gender identity; Gender stereotyping; Sex differences
  aggression and, 386
  biological influences on, 391–392
  child-rearing practices and, 393*f,* 393–394
  cognitive-developmental theory of, 390
  cultural influences, 394–395
  defined, 390
  early childhood, 390–398
  environmental influences on, 393–395
  family influences on, 393*f,* 393–394
  peer relations and, 394–395, 504, 505*f*

Gender typing (*cont.*)
 sibling relationships and, 393–394
 social learning theory of, 390
 teachers influencing, 394
Generativity, as psychosocial stage of development, 16*t*
Genes, 52–53. *See also* Genetics
 alleles, 56–57
 crossing over of, 53
 dominant–recessive inheritance, 56*t*, 56–57
 heterozygous pairing, 56
 homozygous pairing, 56
 Human Genome Project, 64
 modifier genes, 57
 mutation, 60
Gene therapy, 64
Genetic counseling, 63, 68
Genetic diagnosis, preimplantation, 64*t*
Genetic disorders, 60–62
Genetic engineering, 64
Genetic–environmental correlation, 85
 home environment influence and, 229
 temperament and, 261
Genetics, 52–62. *See also*
 Chromosomes; Genes;
 Inheritance; Nature–nurture controversy
 ADHD and, 444
 autism and, 59, 342
 behavioral genetics, 82
 canalization, 84
 chromosomal abnormalities, 60–62
 family studies of. *See* Kinship studies; Twin studies
 fraternal twinning and, 55*t*
 gender typing and, 391–392
 genetic disorders, 58*t*, 60–62
 hand preference and, 294
 heritability estimates. *See* Heritability estimates
 nocturnal enuresis and, 422
 obesity and, 417, 418*t*
 patterns of genetic inheritance, 56–62
 physical development and, 174, 297, 413
 relationship between heredity and environment, 82–88
 shyness versus sociability, 259
 sleep disorders and, 299
 temperament and, 260–261
Genital stage of development (Freud), 16*t*
Genome, 64
Genomic imprinting, 59–60
Genotype, 51, 86, 87, 87*f*
German measles, effect on prenatal development, 111
Germany
 attachment patterns of infants, 268, 268*f*, 276
 family size, 93
 parental leave, 141
 self-development of toddlers, 281
Germline mutation, 60
Gesell's timetable of child development, 13–14
Gestures, preverbal, 238, 242
GH (growth hormone), 297
Gibsons' differentiation theory, 198–199

Gifted children, 474–476
 clinical method research study of, 34
 defined, 474
 education of, 475–476, 476*f*
Glial cells, 100, 165
Goal-directed behavior, in sensorimotor stage of cognitive development, 206, 211
God, children's understanding of, 495
Goodness-of-fit model of child rearing, 262–264, 380
Government policies. *See* Public policies
Grammatical development. *See also* Language development
 early childhood, 356–358
 infancy and toddlerhood, 233–234, 236
 middle childhood, 463
Grandparents
 child-rearing practices and, 275–276
 extended-family households, 79
 influence of, 71
Grasping, development of, 186–188
Grasp reflex of newborns, 187
Gravity, infants' understanding of, 214
Gray matter in brain development, 414
Great Britain. *See* England and Great Britain
Greece
 false-belief understanding in early childhood, 341
 self-development of toddlers, 281, 281*f*
Gross-motor development
 defined, 183
 early childhood, 308–309, 309*t*
 enhancing, 313–314
 infancy and toddlerhood, 183–184, 184*t*
 middle childhood, 427–428, 428*t*
 milestones, 309*t*
 sex differences in, 313, 430
Group prenatal care, 119
Groups. *See* Peer groups
"Growing pains," 414
Growth. *See* Physical development
Growth faltering, 178
Growth hormone (GH), treating short children with, 297
Growth norms, 163, 413
Growth spurt
 adolescence, 532–534, 533*f*
 infancy and toddlerhood, 163
Growth stunting and prenatal health care, 105
Guatemala
 doula, role in childbirth, 130
 Mayan culture. *See* Mayans
Guidance Study (Berkeley), 40
Guided participation, 331
Guilt
 early childhood, 370–371, 380
 empathy-based, 380
 middle childhood, 489–490
 moral development and, 379, 380
 perspective taking and, 492
 psychosocial stage of development, 364
 toddlerhood, 254
Guns. *See* Firearms
Gusii of Kenya
 mother–infant relationship and attachment, 270
 motor development in infancy, 186

H
Habituation, 180–181, 181*f*
 attention and memory studies, 219–220
 categorization studies and, 222, 222*f*
 defined, 180–181
 familiarity preference and, 220
 fetus and, 101
 infant learning and, 180–181, 181*f*, 197
 intelligence predictions based on, 229
 novelty preference and, 220
 object perception studies, 196–197
 object permanence studies, 208–209
 prenatal evidence of, 181
 recovery and, 181
 to speech, faces, and music, 191, 191*f*
 time required for infants, 218
Hair, dominant–recessive inheritance, 56*t*, 56–57
Hall's theory of child and adolescent development, 13, 530
Handguns. *See* Firearms
Hand preference, 293–294
Happiness, 250–251
Harlem Hospital Injury Prevention Program, 424
Harsh punishment. *See* Child maltreatment; Punishment (disciplinary)
Hausa of Nigeria, conservation task performance, 440
Hawaii
 Kauai study of birth complications, 142
 obesity, 419
Head Start, 349–350
Head Start Impact Study, 349–350
Health. *See also* Diseases; Nutrition
 adolescence, 544–562
 children's understanding of, 426
 early childhood, 295–307
 immunization, 301–304
 middle childhood, 415–425
 prenatal environment and health in later life, 104–105
Health care and insurance. *See also* Diseases; Medications; *specific procedures (e.g., Blood tests)*
 childbirth. *See* Childbirth
 child health care, 303
 Children's Health Insurance Program (CHIP), 303
 diarrhea, 302
 growth hormone treatments, 297
 hearing screenings, 243
 prenatal. *See* Prenatal diagnosis; Prenatal health care
 preterm infants, 140–141
 public expenditures on, 80*t*
 public health programs, 303
 uninsured children, 303
 universal, 79, 117
Health concepts, development of, 426
Health education. *See also* Sex education
 chronic illnesses, 423
 middle childhood, 425–427
Healthy Families America, 404
Hearing and hearing loss. *See also* Ears
 brain development and, 169
 deaf parents of deaf and hearing babies, 237

ear infections and, 304, 422
 fetal response to sound, 101
 infancy and toddlerhood, 189–190
 intermodal perception, 197–198
 language development and, 169, 237, 241, 243
 middle childhood, 422
 newborn capacities, 151
 otitis media and, 422
 sign language, use of. *See* Sign language
Heart. *See* Cardiovascular system
Heart disease, low birth weight and, 104–105
Heart rate
 fetal monitoring, 132–133
 temperamental style and, 259
Height. *See also* Growth spurt
 diarrhea's effect on, 302
 early childhood, 290
 growth hormone treatments, 297
 infancy and toddlerhood, 163–164
 middle childhood, 413
 psychosocial dwarfism and, 297
"Heightism," 297
Helmets, protective, 424
Helplessness, learned. *See* Learned helplessness
Hemispheres of brain. *See* Lateralization of brain
Hemophilia, 58*t*, 65
Heredity. *See* Genetics; Inheritance; Nature–nurture controversy
Heritability estimates, 82–83
 attachment, 271
 IQ scores, 84, 458
 limitations of, 83–84
 temperament and personality, 259, 260, 261
Heroin. *See also* Drug use and abuse
 prenatal development and, 106–107
Herpes virus
 cesarean delivery due to, 134
 prenatal development and, 111*t*, 112
Heterozygous genes, 56
Hierarchical classification, in preoperational stage of cognitive development, 322, 325–328
Hierarchically structured self-esteem, 484, 484*f*
Hierarchical style of communication, 460
High birth weight and breast cancer, 105, 105*f*
Higher education. *See* Educational attainment
High-income households. *See* Affluent families; Socioeconomic influences
High schools. *See* Schools
High/Scope Perry Preschool Project, 349, 349*f*
High-stakes testing, 468, 476
Hinduism and emotional self-regulation, 491
Hippocampus, 118, 294, 294*f*
Hispanics
 bilingualism and academic achievement, 465–466
 breastfeeding, 175
 child-rearing practices, 274, 401
 father–infant relationship, 274
 food insecurity, 178
 gender typing, 394

grandparents as primary caregivers, 275
IQ scores, 458
obesity and, 417
poverty rate, 74
school integration, 471
self-fulfilling prophecies in teacher expectations, 470
sleep routines for preschoolers, 298f, 298–299
Historical events, cohort effects of, 41
Historical foundations of development theories, 11–13
HIV/AIDS
children's understanding of, 426
children with, 423
prenatal development and, 111t, 112
Home births, 131–132
Home environment. See also Families
ADHD and, 444–445
aggression in children and, 386–387
attachment and, 272
birth complications, long-term consequences of and, 141–142
cognitive development and, 229–230, 347
divorce's effect on, 511
eating habits and, 299–301
emotional and social development and, 368
injuries in childhood and, 307
Homelessness, 75. See also Poverty
Home Observation for Measurement of the Environment (HOME), 229–230, 347, 558
Home visiting
Nurse–Family Partnership, during pregnancy and infancy, 116
to prevent child maltreatment, 404, 405f
Homosexuality. See Sexual orientation
Homozygous genes, 56
Hopping
early childhood, 309t
middle childhood, 428t
Hormones
androgens. See Androgens
bedwetting and, 422
childbirth and, 126
estrogens. See Estrogens
gender typing and, 391–392
middle childhood, 415
newborn's production of, 128
oxytocin, 143
prolactin, 143
sex hormones, 143, 386
Hostile aggression, 385. See also Aggression; Anger; Antisocial behavior; Reactive aggression
Human Genome Project, 64
Human immunodeficiency virus. See HIV/AIDS
Humor, in vocabulary development, 463
Huntington disease, 57, 58t
Hyaline membrane disease, 136
Hyperactivity
ADHD, 87, 444–445
maternal smoking during pregnancy and, 87, 87f
Hypothesis, in research, 30

Identical twins, 54, 55, 82. See also Twins; Twin studies
Identification with same-sex parent, 364, 377
Identity. See also Gender identity; Self-concept
psychosocial stage of development, 16t
Id, psychosexual theory of, 15
Illegal drugs. See Drug use and abuse
Illnesses. See Diseases
Imaginary companions, 319
Imitation, 18. See also Modeling
cognitive-developmental theory, 207
deferred imitation, 207, 210, 212t
defined, 181
drawing and, 309
food preferences, 300
infant and toddler learning and, 181–183, 278
inferred imitation, 210–211, 212t
language development and, 233
mirror neurons, 182–183
in newborns, 182–183, 182f
Immigrant youths. See also specific cultural groups (e.g., Hispanics)
adaptation by, 36
bilingualism of, 465–466
Immune system
gene therapy, 65
middle childhood, 423
Immunization, 301–304
Implantation of blastocyst, 98
Imprinting, in ethological theory, 23, 265
Imprinting, genomic, 59–60
Impulsivity and ADHD, 87, 87f, 444
Incest. See Sexual abuse of children
Inclusive classrooms, 473
Incomplete dominance, 57
Independence. See Autonomy
Independent variables, in experimental research design, 37
India
play in early childhood, 374
spatial reasoning, 439f, 439–440
Individualistic societies
collectivist societies vs., 78
cosleeping arrangements in infancy and childhood, 173
emotional self-regulation and, 491
self-conscious emotions and, 254
Individual rights, 493–494
Indonesia, make-believe play with infants and toddlers in, 226
Induced labor, 134
Inductive discipline, 379
Indulgent parenting. See Permissive parenting
Industrialized countries. See also specific countries or regions (e.g., Western Europe)
AIDS and prenatal development, 112
breastfeeding, 175–176
childbirth, 129, 131–132
child health care, availability of, 303
choice to have children, 93
computers in schools, 472
diversity among families, 506
divorce rate, 510, 510f
early childhood literacy, 341
health and well-being of children, 80t

home delivery, 131
immunizations, 302
infant mortality rates, 140f, 140–141
infectious disease, 301
injuries during childhood, 306
male birth decline, 59
multiple births, 55
newborn baby care, 140–141
obesity trends, 416, 417f
physical development in middle childhood, 413
preschoolers' theory of mind, 341
social interaction and learning in, 25
socioeconomic status and family functioning, 71
transition to middle childhood, 482
Industry vs. inferiority, as psychosocial stage of development, 16t, 482
Infancy and toddlerhood, 162–202. See also Newborns
anger in, 251
attachment in. See Attachment
attention in, 218–219
autonomy in, 249
bladder control in, 188–189
body proportions in, 162
bowel control in, 188–189
brain development in, 164–169
brain plasticity in, 170
categorization in, 222f, 222–223
child care in, 230–231
cognitive attainments in, 212t, 212–216
cognitive development in, 203–245. See also Sensorimotor stage of cognitive development
compliance in, 283–284
cosleeping arrangements with parents, 173
death in. See Infant mortality
defined, 6
depth perception in, 192f, 192–193
early intervention programs in, 231–232
embarrassment in, 254
emotional and social development in, 247–285
emotional self-regulation in, 254–255
emotions in, 249–256
envy in, 254
fears in, 252
fine-motor development in, 183–184, 184t
gender stereotyping in, 261
gross-motor development in, 183–184, 184t
growth spurts in, 163
guilt in, 254
happiness in, 250–251
hearing in, 189–190
height in, 163–164
information processing in, 217–224
intelligence tests in, 227–228
language development in, 169, 233–236
laughter in, 250–251
low birth weight. See Low birth weight
make-believe play in, 226
malnutrition in, 176–178
memory in, 118, 217–218, 219–221

milestones in, 290–291
motor development in, 183–189, 184t
muscle development in, 163
musical perception in, 189, 191
nutrition in, 174–176
parental relationships in. See Father–infant relationship; Mother–infant relationship; Parent–infant relationship
peer relationships in, 277–278
perceptual development in, 189–199
physical development in, 162–202
preterm. See Preterm infants
pride in, 254
psychoanalytic theories of, 248
recall memory in, 220
recognition memory in, 220
sadness in, 251–252
self-awareness in, 280f, 280–282
self-categorization, 282
self-conscious emotions in, 253–254
self-control in, 282–284
self-development in, 279–284
self-recognition in, 280–281, 281f
shame in, 254
skeletal development in, 163–164
skull development in, 164
sleep in, 172–174
smiling in, 250–251
sociocultural theory of, 225
states of arousal in, 172, 174
television and video, learning from, 213
temperament in, 256–264
toilet training in, 188–189
toys in, 216
vision in, 190–197
visual acuity in, 190–191
vocabulary in, 234, 238–239
weight in, 163, 176
Infant–caregiver attachment. See Attachment
Infant Health and Development Project, 139
Infantile amnesia, 221
Infant mortality
cross-national perspective, 140, 140f
drug use during pregnancy and, 105–109
fetal monitoring and, 132–133
home delivery and, 132
Rh factor incompatibility and, 115
sex differences in, 59
SIDS as cause of. See Sudden infant death syndrome (SIDS)
small-for-date infants, 137
smoking during pregnancy and, 107–108
United States, rate in, 80t
Infant–parent relationship. See Attachment; Father–infant relationship; Mother–infant relationship; Parent–infant relationship
Infant-rearing practices. See Child-rearing practices
Infectious diseases. See also Diseases; specific diseases (e.g., HIV/AIDS)
early childhood, 301–304
immunization, 302–304
prenatal development and, 111t, 111–112

Inference, mental
  children's understanding of, 341, 448
  transitive, 438, 441
Inferred imitation, 210–211, 212t
Infertility, 66–67, 95
Information-processing perspective,
    21–23, 30t. See also Attention;
    Memory; Metacognition
  attention, 218–219
  categorization, 218
  cognitive self-regulation, 449
  compared to Piaget's theory, 22
  continuum of acquisition, 441
  early childhood, 334–346
  educational principles based on,
    450–453
  evaluation of, 223–224
  flowchart of steps, 22, 22f
  gender schema theory, 390, 396–397,
    397f
  infancy and toddlerhood, 217–224
  intelligence, 454–458
  mental strategies. See Mental
    strategies
  middle childhood, 442–453
  motor development and, 428
  social problem-solving model, 376
  social processing deficits, 387
  structure of system, 217–218
Informed consent of research
    participants, 45, 45t
In-group favoritism, 494–496
Inheritance. See also Genetics
  dominant–recessive, 56–57, 57f
  genomic imprinting, 59–60
  heritability estimates. See
    Heritability estimates
  mutation of genes, 60
  patterns of genetic inheritance,
    56–62
  polygenic, 60
  X-linked. See X-linked inheritance
Inhibited (shy) child, as temperament
    type, 258, 283. See also Shyness
Inhibition, 334f, 334–335, 443
Initiative vs. guilt, as psychosocial
    stage of development, 16t, 364
Injuries
  death, as cause of, 305, 305f
  early childhood, 304–307
  middle childhood, 424f, 424–425
  prevention, 306–307, 424–425
  sports-related, 431
Inner-city schools, 471
Inner speech, 330
Insomnia. See Sleep and sleep
    disorders
Institutionalization
  brain development, effect on,
    169–171
  infant attachment and, 269
  motor development and, 186, 188
Institutional review boards (IRBs), 45
Instruction. See Education; Learning;
    Schools; Teachers and teaching
    techniques; specific subjects (e.g.,
    Mathematics and mathematical
    reasoning, Reading)
Instrumental aggression, 385
Instrument delivery, 133f, 133–134
Insulin-like growth factor 1 (IGF-1),
    297
Insurance. See Health care and
    insurance

Integration of schools, 471
Integrity, as psychosocial stage of
    development, 16t
Intellectual development. See
    Cognitive development
Intelligence. See also Cognitive
    development
  alcohol use during pregnancy and,
    109
  canalization, 84
  cultural influences on, 459–461
  definitions of, 456
  emotional intelligence, 457
  environmental influences on,
    459–461
  genetic influences on, 458
  habituation as predictor of, 229
  information-processing approach to,
    454–455
  kinship studies, 82
  language customs and, 459–460
  measurement of. See Intelligence
    tests; IQ (Intelligence quotient)
  multiple intelligences theory
    (Gardner), 456t, 456–458, 475
  music lessons and, 44, 44f
  object permanence tasks as predictor
    of, 229
  reaction range and, 84, 84f
  sex chromosome disorders and,
    61–62
  theories of, 454–458
  triarchic theory of (Sternberg), 455f,
    455–456
Intelligence quotient. See IQ
Intelligence tests
  Binet, Alfred, 227
  computing scores, 227–228
  convergent thinking and, 474
  cultural bias in, 347, 454–455,
    461–462
  divergent thinking and, 474, 475f
  dynamic assessment approach,
    461–462, 462f
  early childhood, 346–347, 454–455
  factor analysis of components,
    453–454, 454f
  individually vs. group-administered,
    453
  infant intelligence tests, 227–228
  middle childhood, 453–454
  sample items, 454
  scores on. See IQ (Intelligence
    quotient)
  standardization sample, 227–228
  Stanford-Binet Intelligence Scales,
    454
  subtests in, 454
  Wechsler Intelligence Scales, 454
Intentional behavior, in sensorimotor
    stage of cognitive development,
    206–207
Intentions, understanding of, 493
Interactional synchrony, in
    attachment, 270
Interactionist theories of language
    development, 236
Interdependent self, 78
Interdisciplinary nature of child
    development studies, 4
Intermodal perception, 197–198, 280
Internalizing difficulties, 71
Internal working model, in
    attachment theory, 266, 266f, 272

International comparisons. See
    Cross-cultural research
Internet
  child sexual abuse and, 519
  educational use of, 472, 473f
  parental limits on use of, 389, 472
  violence portrayed via, 387–389
Internships for emerging adults, 652
Interpersonal behavior. See Families;
    Friendships; Marital relationship;
    Peer relations; Sibling
    relationships
Interpersonal intelligence
    (Gardner), 456t
Intersubjectivity, in sociocultural
    theory of cognitive
    development, 331
Intervention programs. See also Early
    intervention programs; Public
    education programs
  ADHD, 445
  aggression, 389–390
  attribution retraining, 488
  bully–victim problems, 502
  child maltreatment, 404–405
  chronic illnesses, 424
  Early Head Start, 232
  eyewitness testimony by children,
    521
  Head Start, 349–350
  healthy lifestyles, 427
  immunization, 302–303
  injury prevention, 424
  newborns
    adjustment to parenthood, 157
    NBAS-based interventions,
      152–153
    preterm infants, 138–139, 139f
  obesity, 420–422
  peer acceptance, 502–503
  postpartum depression, 155
  prenatal malnutrition, 114
  preterm infants, 138–139, 139f
  sexual abuse victims, 520
  social problem solving, 376
  supplementary preschool programs,
    350
  trauma curriculum after September
    11, 2001 attacks, 518
  violence by children and adolescents,
    522–523
  visual impairment in infancy and
    toddlerhood, 194
  war, effect on children, 518
Interview research methods, 32t, 33,
    258
Intimacy, psychosocial stage of
    development, 16t
Intrapersonal intelligence (Gardner),
    456t
Inuits
  communication styles, 460
  cosleeping arrangements in infancy
    and childhood, 173
  language of, 463
Invariant features, in differentiation
    theory, 198
Invisible displacement in object
    permanence, 207
In vitro fertilization, 66–67
  preimplantation genetic diagnosis,
    64t
  twin births and, 55, 55t
Iodine and prenatal health care, 114

Ionizing radiation. See Radiation
IQ (Intelligence quotient), 228–229,
    453–454
  componential analyses of, 455
  computation and distribution of,
    227–228
  early intervention programs and,
    232, 232 f,349
  ethnic differences in, 458–461
  gifted students, 474–476
  HOME scores and, 229–230
  lead exposure risks and, 296
  predicting later performance from,
    228
  socioeconomic differences in, 458
  stereotyping and, 460–461
Iran, motor development in infancy
    in, 186
Irish Americans, personal storytelling
    in early childhood, 366
Iron, prenatal health care and, 114,
    118
Iron-deficiency anemia, 177
Irreversibility in thinking, 322
Irritable distress, as temperament
    dimension, 257t
Isolettes, for preterm infants, 138
Isotretinoin, prenatal development
    and maternal use of, 106
Israel
  dynamic assessment, effect on IQ,
    461–462, 462f
  infant sleeping patterns, 174
Israeli kibbutzim
  attachment patterns of infants, 268f,
    269
  mother–infant relationship and
    attachment, 268f, 269
  stranger anxiety among infants and
    toddlers, 252
Italy, family size, 93

J
Jamaican West Indians, motor
    development in infancy of, 186
Japan. See also Asians
  academic achievement, 477
  attachment patterns of infants, 268,
    268f
  child-rearing practices, 261
  cosleeping arrangements in infancy
    and childhood, 173
  emotional self-regulation, 255
  family size, 93
  fathers' play with infants, 274
  gender-stereotyped beliefs, 504
  infant care, 149
  language development, 241
  make-believe play with toddlers, 226
  motor development in infancy, 186
  self-conscious emotions, 254, 255,
    260–261
  self-esteem, 485
  temperament of infants, 260–261
Jarara of South America, childbirth
    practices of, 129
Jealousy in sibling relationships, 277,
    507
Jobs. See Employment
Joint attention and language
    development, 238, 241
Joint custody of children, 513
Judaism, understanding of God
    and, 495

Jumping
early childhood, 309t
middle childhood, 313, 428t
sex differences in, 313
Jumpstart for Young Children, 350
Justice, understanding of, 493

K
"Kangaroo care," for preterm infants, 138, 176
Karma, in Hindu beliefs, 35
Karyotype of chromosomes, 52f
Kauai study on long-term consequences of birth complications, 142
Keeping Ourselves Safe (New Zealand), 520
Kenya
education of girls in, 73
Gusii, mother–infant relationship and attachment, 270
malnutrition and, 416
Kibbutzim. See Israeli kibbutzim
Kindergarten. See Preschools
Kinship studies, 82. See also Adoption studies; Twin studies
IQ scores, 458
Kipsigis of Kenya, motor development in infancy, 186
Klinefelter syndrome, 62, 62t
Korean Americans, play and peer relations in early childhood, 374
Korea
academic achievement, 477
cosleeping arrangements in infancy and childhood, 173
cultural differences in categorization development, 223
language development, 241
moral reasoning, 494
!Kung of Botswana
cosleeping arrangements in infancy and childhood, 173
grasping and reaching in infancy, 188
infant care, 149
Kwashiorkor, 177

L
Labor. See Employment
Laboratory experiments, 38
Labor, birthing. See Childbirth
Labor coaches, 130
Landmarks on maps, 438–439
Language acquisition device (LAD), 234, 357
universal grammar and, 234, 236
Language customs and intelligence, 459–460
Language development, 190. See also Reading; Speech; specific components (e.g., Grammatical development, Semantic development)
behaviorist theories of, 234
bilingualism and, 464–466
brain areas for, 234, 234f
brain damage, 169
categorization, relationship to, 223
child-directed speech and, 241–242
cognitive development and, 214
comprehension vs. production, 240
cooing and babbling, 236–237
cultural influences, 240–241

of deaf children, 243
delay in, 241, 243
early childhood, 318, 354–359
emotional self-regulation and, 255
expressive style of learning, 240–241
first-language learning, 234
first words, 237, 238–239
grammatical knowledge, innate, 233–234
hearing loss and, 236–237
imitation and, 233
individual differences in, 240–241
infancy and toddlerhood, 169, 214, 233–242
interactionist theories of, 236
lateralization of brain and, 169, 234, 235, 292, 292f
metalinguistic awareness, 462, 465
metaphors, 356, 463
middle childhood, 462–466
milestones
early childhood, 408–409
infancy and toddlerhood, 237t, 290–291
middle childhood, 526–527
nativist theory of, 233–236
operant conditioning and, 233
overextension in, 239
overregularization in, 357
parental interactions with infants and toddlers, 241–242
prelinguistic development, 237–238
referential style of learning, 240–241
second-language learning, 235, 464–466
self-control and, 281
sensitive periods, 235, 465
sex differences in, 240
supporting language learning, 241–242, 359
telegraphic speech in, 239
theories of, 233–236
theory of mind and, 340
two-word utterance phase, 239
underextension in, 239
Language immersion programs, 465–466
Language-making capacity, in grammatical development, 358
Lanugo, 100
Latency stage of development (Freud), 16t
Lateralization of brain, 168–169
atypical, 293–294
defined, 168
early childhood, 293
language development and, 169, 234, 235, 292, 292f
Latin Americans. See Hispanics
Laughter in infancy and toddlerhood, 250–251
Lead exposure risks, 111, 296, 296f
Learned helplessness, 449, 487
attribution retraining and, 488
peer acceptance and, 503
Learning. See also Cognitive development; specific forms (e.g., Imitation, Operant conditioning)
academic. See Education; Schools; specific subjects (e.g., Mathematics and mathematical reasoning, Reading)
achievement in. See Academic achievement

assisted discovery, 332
cultural influences on, 333
defined, 178
discovery learning, 328–329
guided participation, 331
individual differences in, 329
infancy and toddlerhood, capacities in, 178–183
observational. See Modeling
peer collaboration and, 332
readiness to learn, 329
scaffolding and, 224, 331, 332, 368, 469
social learning theory. See Social learning theory (Bandura)
verbal communication and, 332–333
Learning disabilities
attention-deficit hyperactivity disorder (ADHD), 87, 444–445
cognitive neuroscience and, 23
defined, 473
full inclusion of students, 473
inclusive classrooms and, 473
private speech and, 330
Learning goals, achievement-related attributions and, 487
Left-handedness, 168, 293–294
Legal issues and proceedings. See also Ethics; Public policies
child maltreatment, 405
child support, 513
divorce mediation, 513
eyewitness testimony by children, 521
reproductive technologies, 67
Lens of eye, development of, 151
Lesbian families, 508–509
Lesbian women. See Sexual orientation
Let's Move campaign, 422
Letter-sound correspondences, 343, 345
Lifespan. See Death; Infant mortality; Psychosocial period of development (Erikson)
Lightening, prior to childbirth, 126
Light, fetal response to, 100
Limbs. See Skeletal development
Linguistic development. See Language development
Linguistic intelligence (Gardner), 456t
Liquor. See Alcohol use and abuse
Literacy. See also Language development; Reading; Writing
development, supporting, 345
early childhood, 312, 341–346, 343f
emergent, 343–344, 345
interactive reading and, 343
letter-sound correspondences, 345
phonological awareness and, 343
socioeconomic influences on, 343–344, 344f
Locke's philosophy of child development, 12
Locomotion. See Crawling; Motor development; Running; Walking
Logical reasoning and problem solving
early childhood, 324
middle childhood, 438 441–442
Logico-mathematical intelligence (Gardner), 456t
Longitudinal research, 40–41
aggression, 388

attachment and later development, 268, 273
authoritative parenting, 400, 507
biased samples in, 40
birth complications, long-term consequences of, 142
birth order and parenting, 94
child care, 230
cohort effects, 41
corporal punishment, effects of, 382, 383
cosleeping arrangements in infancy and childhood, 173
disciplinary practices, 383
gender-stereotyping, 504
gender-typical and gender-contented children, 506
IQ fluctuations, 228
lead exposure risks, 296
literacy experiences and reading achievement, 343
memory strategies, 446
New York Longitudinal Study on temperament, 256
obesity trends, 417
peer sociability, 374
school readiness, 375
shyness and sociability, 259
television and aggression, 388
theory of mind development, 339, 340
visual impairment, 194
Longitudinal-sequential design, 39t, 41–42
Long-term memory, 217f, 218. See also Memory
Lorenz's study of imprinting, 265
Low birth weight, 136–137. See also Preterm infants
aspirin, maternal use of and, 106
caffeine, maternal use of and, 106
diabetes and, 105
drug use during pregnancy and, 106–107
environmental pollution and, 110–111
heart disease and, 104–105
lead exposure during pregnancy and, 111
neonatal mortality and, 140
prenatal malnutrition and, 113–114
small-for-date infants, 137
smoking during pregnancy and, 107–108
stress during pregnancy and, 114–115
stroke and, 104–105
Low-income households. See Poverty; Socioeconomic influences
Lungs. See Respiratory system
Lutheran understanding of God, 495

M
Macrosystem, in ecological systems theory, 26f, 27, 69
Magical thinking, 323–324
Magic Shrinking Machine, 221, 221f
Magnesium and prenatal health care, 114
Magnet schools, 471
Magnitude, in correlational coefficients, 37

Make-believe play
advantages of, 319–320, 332
cultural influences on, 35, 226
defined, 207
early childhood, 318–320, 323–324, 332, 373, 373*t*
emotional and social development and, 364, 370
infancy and toddlerhood, 208, 226, 241
literacy fostered by, 345
metacognition and, 340
preoperational stage of cognitive development, 318–320, 323–324
Malaria, 57, 111*t*
Malawi, Ngoni of, industry in middle childhood, 482
Male vs. female development. *See* Sex differences
Malnutrition. *See also* Nutrition
breastfeeding and, 175
diseases and, 301–302
early childhood, 301–302
infancy and toddlerhood, 176–178
middle childhood, 416
obesity and, 418, 418*t*
prenatal malnutrition, 113–114
small-for-date infants, 137
Malocclusion, 414
Maltreatment. *See* Child maltreatment
Maps, in concrete operational stage of cognitive development, 438–439, 439*f*
Marasmus, 177
Marfan syndrome, 58*t*
Marijuana. *See also* Drug use and abuse
prenatal development and, 107
Marital relationship. *See also* Divorce
child-rearing practices and, 26, 70–71, 154, 156
newborns, adjustments to, 154, 156
parenthood's effect on, 121
parent–infant relationship and, 275–276, 277
postpartum depression and, 155
remarriage, 514–515
Masculinity. *See* Sex differences
Mastery-oriented attributions, 486–489
Matching, in experimental research design, 38
Maternal age
Down syndrome and, 61, 61*f*
fertility problems, 95
fraternal twinning and, 55, 55*t*
prenatal and birth complications and, 115*f*, 115–116
Maternal blood analysis, 63
Maternal employment, 515–517
attachment and, 275–276
breastfeeding and, 176
child care and. *See* Child care
child development and, 515–516
delay in pregnancy due to, 95
father's increased involvement in child care, 516
incidence of, 230, 515
preschool-age children with employed mothers, statistics on, 348
support for employed mothers, 516
Maternal postpartum depression, 155

Maternal relationship. *See* Mother–child relationship; Mother–infant relationship
Maternity leave, 141
Mathematics and mathematical reasoning
cardinality principle, 344
drill-oriented instruction, 451–452
early childhood, 344–346
estimation, in basic arithmetic, 345
gender stereotyping of academic subjects, 504
gifted students, 476*f*
infancy, 214
information-processing research on, 451–453
logico-mathematical intelligence, 456*t*
middle childhood, 451–453
ordinality principle, 344
number board games, 345, 345*f*
"number sense" basis for instruction, 451
socioeconomic influences on, 345
Maturation
brain. *See* Brain development
concept of development, 13
Mayans
adult work by children, 333
attention in infancy and childhood, 225
childbirth practices, 129
communication styles, 460
cosleeping arrangements in infancy and childhood, 173
daily life of preschoolers, 374
memory skills, 447
physical development in middle childhood, 413
Means–end action sequences, in sensorimotor stage of cognitive development, 207
Measles. *See* Rubella
Media. *See* Computers; Internet; Public education programs; Television
Media multitasking and attention, 585
Mediation of divorce, 513
Medical insurance. *See* Health care and insurance
Medications. *See also* Drug use and abuse
ADHD, 445
anesthetics, 133, 149–150
for bedwetting, 423
childbirth use of, 133
childhood injury prevention, 307
postpartum depression, 155
prenatal development and maternal drug use, 105–109
suicide prevention and treatment, 632–633
Medicine, practice of. *See* Health care and insurance
Medieval philosophy of childhood, 11
Meiosis (cell division), 53–54, 54*f*, 60–62
Melatonin, 172
Memory
autobiographical, 221, 337, 365
context-dependent, 219
cultural influences on, 447
early childhood, 335–337

episodic memory, 336
everyday events and, 336–337
eyewitness testimony by children, 521
habituation and, 219–220
hippocampus and, 294
infancy and toddlerhood, 219–221
infantile amnesia, 221
knowledge acquisition and, 447
long-term memory, 220
mathematics learning and, 451–453
middle childhood, 446–447
operant conditioning studies, 219, 220*f*
prenatal iron deficiency, effect on infants' memory, 118
recall. *See* Recall memory
recognition. *See* Recognition memory
scripts in, 336–337
short-term. *See* Working (short-term) memory
strategies. *See* Memory strategies
verbal and non-verbal, 221, 221*f*
working memory. *See* Working (short-term) memory
Memory strategies
control deficiency, 443, 446
cultural influences on, 447
early childhood, 336
elaboration, 446
middle childhood, 446
organization, 446
production deficiency, 443
rehearsal, 446
utilization deficiency, 443, 446
Mennonite understanding of God, 495
Mental development. *See* Cognitive development; Intelligence
Mental health. *See* Adjustment problems; Counseling; *specific conditions (e.g., Anxiety, Depression, Stress)*
Mental inference. *See* Inference, mental
Mental representation
concepts in, 207
defined, 207
images in, 207
infantile amnesia and, 221
invisible displacement, 207
preoperational stage of cognitive development, 318, 321
sensorimotor stage of cognitive development, 205*t*, 207, 209–212
Mental retardation
Down syndrome and, 60–61
environmental pollution and, 110
fragile X syndrome and, 59
inclusive classrooms and, 473
infectious diseases during pregnancy, 111*t*
iodine deficiency and prenatal development, 114
left-handedness and, 294
phenylketonuria and, 56
Praeder-Willi syndrome, 59
Rh factor incompatibility and, 115
rubella during pregnancy and, 111
sex differences, 59
Mental testing movement, 14. *See also* Intelligence tests
Mercury, effect on prenatal development, 110

Mesoderm, 99
Mesosystem, in ecological systems theory, 26*f*, 26–27, 75
Metacognition
defined, 338
early childhood, 338–339
middle childhood, 447
scientific reasoning and, 571
Metalinguistic awareness, 462, 465
Metaphors, in language development, 356, 463
Methadone, effect on prenatal development, 106–107
Methods of research. *See* Research methods
Mexican Americans. *See* Hispanics
Mexico. *See also* Mayans
dietary preferences of preschoolers, 300
lead exposure risks, 296
make-believe play with infants and toddlers, 226
malnutrition and, 416
Pima Indians of Arizona, diet and obesity, 419
Zinacanteco Indians. *See* Zinacanteco Indians
Microgenetic research, 39*t*, 43, 338
Microsystem, in ecological systems theory, 26, 26*f*, 69
Middle childhood, 411–525
achievement-related attributions, 486–488
agility in, 428
anxiety in, 517–519
athletics in, 427–428, 431–434
attention in, 443–445
balance in, 428
bedwetting in, 422–423
blended families, 513–515
body composition in, 412*f*, 412–413
body growth in, 412*f*, 412–415
body proportions in, 412*f*, 412–415
brain development in, 414–415
bullies, 502
child care in, 516–517
child-rearing practices in, 506–507
cognitive development in, 437–479. *See also* Concrete operational stage of cognitive development
cognitive influences on self-concept in, 483–484
cognitive self-regulation in, 449
common development problems in, 517–523
coregulation in, 507
court appearance, preparation for, 521
defined, 6
diseases in, 423–424
divorce in, 510–513
dominance hierarchy in, 432
drawing in, 429, 429*f*
dual-earner families, 515–517
eating habits in, 417–421
emotional self-regulation in, 490–491
empathy in, 490
ethnic and political violence, effect on, 518
exercise in, 429, 433–434
eyewitness testimony in, 521
family influences in, 506–517
fears in, 517–519

fine-motor development in, 429
flexibility, physical in, 428
friendships in, 499–500
games in, 430
gay and lesbian families and, 508–509
gender identity in, 505–506
gender stereotyping in, 503–504
God, understanding of, 495
grammar in, 463
gross-motor development in, 427–428, 428t
guilt in, 489–490
health education in, 425–427
hearing in, 422
height in, 413
hormones in, 415
illnesses in, 423–424
immune system in, 423
information processing in, 442–453
injuries in, 424f, 424–425
intelligence tests in, 453–454
language development in, 462–466
malnutrition in, 416
memory in, 446–447
metacognition in, 447
milestones in, 526–527
moral development in, 492–497
motor development in, 427–434
muscle development in, 413
never-married single-parent families and, 509–510
nutrition in, 416
obesity in, 416–422
one-child families and, 508
parental relationships in. See Father–child relationship; Mother–child relationship; Parent–child relationship
peer acceptance in, 500–503
peer groups in, 498–499
peer relations in, 431, 497–503
perspective taking in, 491–492
phobias in, 517
physical development in, 411–435
physical education in, 432–434
play in, 427–434
pragmatic development in, 463–464
pride in, 489–490
propositional thought in, 568
prosocial behavior in, 490
reaction time in, 428
resilience, fostering in, 520–523
rough-and-tumble play in, 431–432
second-order false beliefs and, 448, 448f
secular trends in, 413
self-concept in, 482–483
self-conscious emotions in, 489–490
self-development in, 482–489
self-esteem in, 484–489
sexual abuse in, 519–520
shame in, 489–490
sibling relationships in, 507–508
skeletal development in, 414
spirituality and religiosity in, 495
teeth in, 414
violence, effect on, 518
vision in, 422
vocabulary in, 462–463
war, effect of, 518
weight in, 413
working (short-term) memory in, 446
writing in, 429

Middle East. See also specific countries
breastfeeding, 175
Middle-income households. See Socioeconomic influences
Middle schools. See Schools
Mid-twentieth-century theories of development, 14–21
Midwives, 132
Mild mental retardation, 473. See also Mental retardation
Milestones
brain development, 165
cognitive development of early childhood, 328t
early childhood, 408–409
fine-motor skills, 309t
gross-motor skills, 309t
infancy and toddlerhood, 290–291
language development during first two years, 237t
middle childhood, 526–527
prenatal development, 97t
reaching and grasping, 187f
"Mindblindness," 342
Minerals, dietary, 114, 300–301
Minorities. See Ethnicity and race; Racial/ethnic bias; specific minority groups (e.g., African Americans, Hispanics)
Min strategy, in math problem solving, 338, 344
Mirror neurons, 182–183
Miscarriage
diethylstilbestrol and, 106
fetal medicine and, 63
infectious diseases during pregnancy and, 111t
prenatal malnutrition and, 113–114
radiation during pregnancy and, 110
smoking during pregnancy and, 107
stress during pregnancy and, 114–115
Mitosis (cell duplication), 53
Modeling, 18. See also Imitation
gender identity, 396
literacy activities, 345
moral development and, 380
social support and, 76
Modified experimental research designs, 38–39
Modifier genes, 57
Monkeys and chimps
attachment experiment with, 264
cosleeping with babies, 173
discrimination of human and monkey faces by infants, 191, 191f
newborn imitation by, 182, 182f
sign language acquisition by, 234
Monozygotic twins, 55–56. See also Identical twins
Montessori education, 348
Moral development. See also Aggression; Moral reasoning; Prosocial behavior
child-rearing practices and, 385
cognitive-developmental perspective on, 384–385, 492–494
cultural influences on, 494
early childhood, 364, 378–390, 384–385
God, children's understanding of, 495
individual rights, understanding of, 483–484

middle childhood, 492–497
modeling and, 380
moral imperatives and social conventions, 384–385, 493
parenting and, 385
peer relations and, 385, 497–503
psychoanalytic perspective on, 379–380
religion, role in, 495
self-conscious emotions and, 370–371
social learning theory of, 380–384
temperament and, 379–380
theories of, 378–380
Moral imperatives, 384, 493
Moral reasoning. See also Moral development
early childhood, 384–385
Mormons, understanding of God and, 495
Moro reflex of newborns, 144, 144t
Mortality. See Death; Infant mortality
Mosaic pattern, of chromosomes, 61
Mother–adolescent relationship. See Parent–adolescent relationship
Mother–child relationship. See also Mother–infant relationship; Parent–child relationship
attachment and, 274–275
divorce and, 510–513
gay and lesbian families, 508–509
remarriage and, 514
Mother-headed households. See Single-parent families
Mother–infant relationship. See also Parent–infant relationship
attachment and, 274–275. See also Attachment
newborns, 143, 154–157
postpartum depression and, 155
sibling relationships and, 277
Mother–stepfather families, 514
Motor development. See also Sensorimotor stage of cognitive development; specific activities (e.g., Crawling, Drawing, Walking)
brain development and, 294
canalization, 84
cultural variations in, 186
depth perception and, 192f, 192–193
dynamic systems theory, 184–185, 308
early childhood, 308f, 308–314, 309t
environmental influences, 313–314
fine. See Fine-motor development
gross. See Gross-motor development
individual differences in, 312–313, 430
infancy and toddlerhood, 183–189, 184t
microgenetic research studies, 43
middle childhood, 427–434
rate of, 183–184
reaching and grasping in, 186–188
reflexes of newborns and, 144t, 144–145
sequence of, 183–184
sex differences in, 313
visual impairment and, 194
Motor vehicle accidents
early childhood, cause of injuries in, 305
middle childhood, cause of injuries in, 424–425
preventive safety measures, 307

Mouthing, 182
Movement. See Motor development
Mozart effect, 44
Multigrade classrooms, 470
Multiple births, 55–56, 67. See also Twins
Multiple intelligences theory (Gardner), 456t, 456–458
Mumps, effect on prenatal development, 111t
Muscle development
Apgar Scale, 129t
bladder control, 188–189
bowel control, 188–189
infancy and toddlerhood, 163
middle childhood, 413
Muscular dystrophy, Duchenne, 58t
Musical intelligence (Gardner), 456t
Musical perception, in infancy and toddlerhood, 189
Music lessons and intelligence, 44, 44f
Mutation of genes, 60
Mutual exclusivity bias, in vocabulary development, 355, 356
Myelin, 165
Myelination, 165, 166f, 168
adolescence, 537–538
early childhood, 292, 294–295
infancy and toddlerhood, 165, 165t
information-processing speed and capacity, 442
middle childhood, 414
Myopia, 422

N
NAEYC (National Association for the Education of Young Children), 231
Naps, 172, 298. See also Sleep and sleep disorders
Narratives and language development, 464
National Academy of Early Childhood Programs, 231 t,352t
National Assessment of Educational Progress, 477
National Association for Family Child Care, 231 t,352t
National Association for the Education of Young Children (NAEYC), 231
National Institute of Child Health and Development (NICHD), 273
Native Americans. See also specific peoples
alcohol abuse, 109
communication styles, 460
grandparents as primary caregivers, 275
infant mortality rate, 140
newborn behavior and child-rearing practices, 152
obesity and, 417
poverty rate, 74
Nativist theory of language development (Chomsky), 233–236
Natural childbirth, 130–131
Natural experiments, 38–39
Naturalistic observation research method, 32
Naturalist intelligence (Gardner), 456t
Natural selection, Darwin's theory of, 13

Nature–nurture controversy, 9, 82–88. *See also* Environmental influences; Genetics
  behavioral genetics, 82
  behaviorist theories, 17
  canalization and, 84
  comparison of child development theories and, 30t
  defined, 9
  epigenesis, 86, 86f
  genetic–environmental correlation, 229
  heritability estimates. *See* Heritability estimates
  intelligence and, 458
  Locke's philosophy on, 12
  reaction range, 84, 84f
  resilient children, 10
  stance of major developmental theorists, 9
  twins and, 84
NBAS (Neonatal Behavioral Assessment Scale), 152
Near-infrared spectroscopy (NIRS), 166t, 166–167, 167f
Near-sightedness, 422
Neglected children and peer acceptance, 500, 501
Neglectful parenting. *See* Uninvolved parenting
Neglect of children, 402. *See also* Child maltreatment
Neighborhood influences, 75–77. *See also* Community influences
  injuries in early childhood, 306
Neo-Freudians. *See* Psychoanalytic theories; Psychosocial theory of development (Erikson)
Neonatal Behavioral Assessment Scale (NBAS), 152
Neonatal Intensive Care Unit Network Neurobehavioral Scale (NNNS), 152
Neonatal mortality, 140. *See also* Infant mortality
Neonates. *See* Newborns
Neo-Piagetian theorists, 328, 441
Nepalese and emotional self-regulation, 491
Nervous system. *See* Brain damage; Brain development
Netherlands
  adoption research, 67
  childbirth practices, 131
  child health care, availability of, 303
  immunization rate, 302
  suicide rate of adolescents, 631
Neural tube, 99, 114
Neuroimaging techniques, 166t, 166–167, 167f
Neurons, 164–165, 165f. *See also* Brain damage; Brain development
  early childhood, 292
  infancy and toddlerhood, 164–166
  middle childhood, 414
  prenatal development of, 99
Neuroscience, developmental cognitive, 23
Neurotransmitters, 164, 415, 416
Never-married single-parent families, 509–510. *See also* Single-parent families

Newborns, 135–153. *See also* Infancy and toddlerhood
  adaptation to labor and delivery, 128
  appearance of, 128
  behavioral assessment of, 152–153
  bonding with, 143
  brain lateralization, 168
  breastfeeding. *See* Breastfeeding
  capacities of, 145–153
  caregiving behaviors after birth, 143
  cross-national policies on health care for, 140f, 140–141
  death of. *See* Infant mortality
  emotions in, 250–252
  family's adjustment to, 154–157
  imitation by, 181–183
  low birth weight. *See* Low birth weight
  oxygen-deprived, treatments for, 136
  physical assessment, 128, 129t
  preterm. *See* Preterm infants
  reflexes of, 143–145, 144t
  sensory capacities of, 149–152
  "small-for-date," 137
  states of arousal in, 145–146, 146t
  touch, sense of, 149–150
  training parents in caregiving skills for, 139
New Guinea, Jimi Valley children, development of drawing among, 311, 311f
New York Longitudinal Study, 256
New Zealand
  cesarean deliveries, 134
  child care, 230
  child health care, availability of, 303
  make-believe play with infants and toddlers, 226
  reproductive technology laws, 67
  sexual abuse education programs, 520
  suicide rate of adolescents, 631
Ngoni of Malawi, industry in middle childhood, 482
Niche-picking, 85
Nicotine. *See* Smoking
Nigeria, Hausa of, accomplishment of conservation tasks, 440
Nightmares in early childhood, 299
NIRS. *See* Near-infrared spectroscopy
NLSY. *See* U.S. National Longitudinal Survey of Youth
NNNS (Neonatal Intensive Care Unit Network Neurobehavioral Scale), 152
"Noble savages" of Rousseau, 13
No Child Left Behind Act (2001), 468, 476
Nocturnal enuresis, 422–423
Nonprescription drugs. *See* Medications
Non-rapid-eye-movement (NREM) sleep, in newborns, 146
Nonsocial activity, 372
Normal distribution, in intelligence test scores, 228, 228f
Normative approach to child study, 14
Norway
  child health care, availability of, 303
  immunization rate, 302
  poverty rate, 74
Nose, newborns' response to smell, 150–151

Novelty preference, in habituation research, 181, 181f, 220
NREM sleep, in newborns, 146
Nso toddlers (Cameroon) and self-recognition, 281, 281f
Nuclear radiation and birth defects, 110
Nucleus, of cells, 52
Numbers. *See* Mathematics and mathematical reasoning
Numerical knowledge, 214, 215f
Nurse–Family Partnership, 116
Nurse–midwives, 132
Nurture vs. nature. *See* Nature–nurture controversy
Nutrition. *See also* Eating habits; Malnutrition
  breastfeeding and, 174–176
  early childhood, 299–301
  infancy and toddlerhood, 174–176
  lead exposure risks and, 296
  maternal nutrition and fraternal twinning, 55t
  middle childhood, 416
  obesity and, 176
  physical development and, 413
  prenatal development and, 113–114
  vitamins. *See* Vitamins and minerals

O

Obama, Michelle, 422
Obesity, 416–422
  causes of, 417–419, 418t
  defined, 416
  epidemic of, 420–422, 421f
  health consequences of, 417
  incidence of, 416–417, 417f
  infant's weight correlated with, 176
  menarche and, 536–537
  middle childhood, 416–422
  Praeder-Willi syndrome, 59
  skeletal growth and, 290
  treatment of, 419–422
Object categorization. *See* Categorization
Object conservation. *See* Conservation
Object-hiding tasks, in sensorimotor stage of cognitive development, 208–209, 212t
Object labeling, in vocabulary development, 354–355
Object perception, 196–197, 197f
Object permanence, 207–209
  defined, 207
  intelligence prediction based on tasks of, 229
  sensorimotor stage, 207, 212t, 214, 229
Object solidity, 214
Object sorting, and categorization, 222–223
Object unity, perception of, 197, 197f
Observational learning, 18. *See also* Imitation; Modeling
Observation research methods, 32–33, 258
Occupations. *See* Employment
Oedipus conflict, 364
One-child families, 508
Only children, 508
Operant conditioning, 180
  categorization research, 222f, 222–223

Novelty preference, in habituation research, 181, 181f, 220
language development and, 233
memory research, 219, 220f
moral development and, 380
Operations, in preoperational stage of cognitive development, 321, 327
Oral rehydration therapy (ORT), 302
Oral sex, 555
Oral stage of development (Freud), 15, 16t
Ordinality, toddlerhood understanding of, 344
Organization
  cognitive-developmental theory, 205
  information-processing theories, 216
  memory strategy, 446
Organized games with rules, 430
Organs. *See also specific anatomic systems (e.g., Cardiovascular system, Respiratory system)*
  prenatal development of, 100
Orphanages. *See* Institutionalization
ORT (oral rehydration therapy), 302
Otitis media, 304, 422
Out-group prejudice, 494–496
Out-of-wedlock births. *See* Never-married single-parent families; Teenage pregnancy and parenthood
Ova, 53, 54, 67, 96
Overactivity. *See* Hyperactivity
Overextension, in language development, 239
Overlapping-waves theory, 338, 338f, 446
Overregularization, in grammatical development, 357
Over-the-counter drugs. *See* Medications
Overweight. *See* Obesity; Weight
Ovum. *See* Ova
Oxygen deprivation during childbirth, 135
Oxytocin, 134, 143, 171

P

Pacific Islanders
  child-rearing styles, 401
  obesity, 419
  physical development in middle childhood, 413
  Pukapukan childbirth practices, 129
Pacifier use, 304
Pain
  fetal response to, 101
  newborns' response to, 149–150
Pain-relievers, during childbirth, 133
Pakistani child-rearing practices and academic achievement, 582
Palate, cleft, 114
Palmar grasp reflex of newborns, 144
Papua New Guinea, Jimi Valley children, development of drawing among, 311, 311f
Parallel play, 372
Parasitic diseases, effect on prenatal development, 111t, 112. *See also* Infectious diseases
Parental consent, for research participation, 45, 45 t
Parental leave, 141, 516

Parent–child relationship. *See also* Child-rearing practices; Families; Father–child relationship; Home environment; Mother–child relationship
academic achievement and, 477
adapting to change, 71
autonomy, development of, 249
cultural influences on, 276
deaf parents' vs. hearing parents' relationship with deaf child, 243
divorce and, 512–514
emotional self-regulation and, 370
empathy development and, 371
growth faltering and, 178
intersubjectivity and, 331
language development and, 242
learned helplessness and, 487
make-believe play and, 226
middle childhood, 506–507
only children, 508
peer relations and, 377
resilient children, 11
scaffolding and, 331
Parenthood. *See also* Child-rearing practices; Families
ages of women at first births, 94–95, 95f
motivations for, 92–95
parents' relationship and, 121
pre-conception steps for prospective parents, 68
preparation for, 120–121
single parenting. *See* Single-parent families
transition to, 154, 156
Parent–infant relationship. *See also* Child-rearing practices; Families; Father–infant relationship; Home environment; Mother–infant relationship
attachment, 264–279, 275f. *See also* Attachment
balance of care, 248
cosleeping arrangements, 172–173
interactional synchrony in, 270
marital relationship and, 275–276, 277
operant conditioning and, 180
postpartum depression and, 155
preparation for parenthood, 120–121
sadness and, 251–252
sensitive caregiving, 270–271
single-parent families, 156–157
trust, development of, 248
visual impairment and, 194
Parents Anonymous, 404
Parent–school involvement, 477
Parent–teacher interaction. *See* Teacher–parent interaction
Parietal lobes, 414, 448
Partial fetal alcohol syndrome (p-FAS), 108, 109t
Participant observation, in ethnography, 35
Partner abuse and child maltreatment, 402t
Part-time work, maternal employment, 516
Passive correlation, in genetic–environmental correlation, 85

Passive smoking, effect on prenatal development, 108
Passive voice, in language development, 463
Paternal age
Down syndrome and, 61
fertility problems and, 95
Paternal depression, 155
Paternal relationship. *See* Father–child relationship; Father–infant relationship
Patient Protection and Affordable Care Act of 2010, 303
Pattern perception, 193f, 193–195, 195f
Pavlov's theory of classical conditioning, 17
PCBs effect on prenatal development, 110
Pedestrian accidents in middle childhood, 424
Pedigree, in genetic counseling, 63
Peer acceptance, 500–503
chronically ill children, 426
defined, 500
determinants of, 500–501
inclusive classrooms and, 473
intervention programs, 502–503
obesity and, 419
social preferences, 500
social prominence, 500
Peer collaboration and learning, 332, 472
Peer culture, 498, 583
Peer groups, 498–499
defined, 498
gender-segregated, 394, 504, 505f
middle childhood, 498–499
Peer relations. *See also* Friendships; Peer groups; Play; Sociability
ADHD and, 444
antisocial groups, 498
attachment security and, 277–278
cultural influences on, 374
dominance hierarchy, 432
early childhood, 322, 372–377
emotional understanding and, 369
exclusion, 498
gender typing and, 394–395
inclusive classrooms and, 473
infancy and toddlerhood, 277–278
middle childhood, 431, 497–503
moral development and, 385, 497–503
parental influences on, 377
play and, 374
preschools and school readiness, 375
self-concept and, 483
self-disclosure in friendships, 499
self-esteem and, 484
Peer tutoring, 474
Peer victimization, 502
Pencil grip, 312, 312f
Penis, 96
People's Republic of China. *See* China
Perceptual development. *See also* specific senses (e.g., Hearing, Touch, Vision)
cognitive development and, 208
culture-specific learning, 191
differentiation theory of, 198–199, 199f
habituation and, 180–181, 181f
infancy and toddlerhood, 189–199
intermodal perception, 197–198

newborns, 149–152
writing and, 312
Performance goals, achievement-related attributions and, 487
Periods of development. *See specific periods (e.g., Early childhood, Infancy and toddlerhood)*
Permissive parenting, 399t, 399–400, 486
Persistence
over time, in self-understanding, 365
temperament dimension, 257
Personal choice and moral development, 384, 493–494
Personality development. *See* Emotional and social development
Personality traits. *See also* Temperament; *specific traits (e.g., Aggression, Shyness)*
extreme personality styles, longitudinal study of, 40
gender stereotyping of, 390, 503
racial/ethnic bias and, 496
resilient children, 10–11
socioeconomic status and valuing of, 72
Personal storytelling, 366. *See also* Narratives; Autobiographical memory
Perspective taking, 323, 491–492, 492t
defined, 491
middle childhood, 491–492
self-concept and, 483
Selman's stages of, 492
Peru
diarrhea among children, 303
Quechua of
language and metacognition, 340
swaddling of infants, 148
PET (positron emission tomography), 166, 166t
p-FAS (Partial fetal alcohol syndrome), 108, 109t
Phallic stage of development (Freud), 16t
Pharmaceuticals. *See* Medications
Phenotype, 51
Phenylalanine, 56, 57
Phenylketonuria (PKU), 56, 58t
Phobias, 370, 517. *See also* Fear
Phonics, 450–451
Phonological awareness, 343, 345, 450–451, 465
Physical abuse of children, 381–382, 401. *See also* Child maltreatment
Physical activity. *See* Athletics; Exercise; Games; Motor development; Play
Physical aggression, 385. *See also* Aggression
Physical attractiveness. *See* Body image and physical attractiveness
Physical deformities. *See* Birth defects
Physical development. *See also* Motor development; Perceptual development; Skeletal development; *specific topics (e.g., Brain development, Height, Weight)*
defined, 5f
Down syndrome and, 60–61
early childhood, 289–315
emotional well-being and, 178

environmental influences on, 178
ethnic and race differences in, 165
fetal alcohol syndrome (FAS), 108–109
genetic influences on, 297
individual differences in, 413
infancy and toddlerhood, 162–202
malnutrition and, 176–178
middle childhood, 411–435
milestones
early childhood, 408–409
infancy and toddlerhood, 290–291
middle childhood, 526–527
nutrition and, 175, 175t, 300, 416
prenatal. *See* Prenatal development
recess periods at school and, 433
secular trends, 413
sex differences in, 163, 290, 412
sleep and, 298–299
Physical education. *See also* Athletics; Exercise
early childhood motor development and, 313–314
middle childhood, 432–434
Physical knowledge, in infancy, 222
Physical neglect of children. *See* Child maltreatment
Physical self-esteem, 485
Physical well-being. *See* Health
Piaget's cognitive-developmental theory. *See* Cognitive-developmental theory (Piaget)
Pictorial depth cues, 192
Pima Indians of Arizona, diet and obesity, 419
Pincer grasp, 188
Pituitary gland, 297
PKU (Phenylketonuria), 56, 58t
Placenta, 98, 98f
Placenta abruptio, 135
Placenta previa, 135
Planning
cultural tools, 336
defined, 336
early childhood, 335
middle childhood, 444–445
Plasticity of brain, 23, 168, 170, 292, 292f
Plasticity of development, 9, 12
Play. *See also* Games; Make-believe play; Peer relations; Toys
associative play, 372
child-care facilities, 231
cognitive development and, 216
constructive play, 373t
cooperative play, 372
cultural influences on, 364, 374
developmental sequence, 374t
early childhood, 314, 364, 373, 373t
emotional and social development and, 364
evolutionary influences, 432
functional play, 373, 373t
gender stereotyping of, 390–391, 394
motor development and, 313
parallel play, 372
rough-and-tumble play, 431–432
sociodramatic play, 319, 332, 374
Playgrounds
childhood injury prevention, 306, 307
motor development in early childhood and, 313
"Play years," 289

Poisoning prevention, 306
Pollution. See Environmental hazards
Polychlorinated biphenyls (PCBs), effect on prenatal development, 110
Polygenic inheritance, 60
Popular-antisocial children, 500–501
Popular children and peer acceptance, 500–501
Popular-prosocial children, 500
Positive affect, as temperament dimension, 257t
Positive discipline, 383
Positron emission tomography (PET), 166, 166t
Postpartum depression, 155
Poverty, 74–75. See also Socioeconomic influences
  birth complications, long-term consequences of and, 141
  child care and, 230
  child-rearing practices and, 74–75
  cognitive development and, 232–233
  educational attainment and, 80
  education of girls in developing countries and, 73
  emergent literacy and, 344
  health problems and, 415
  immunizations and, 302
  infant mortality and, 140–141
  injury mortality and, 306
  low birth weight and, 137
  neighborhood influences, 75–77
  obesity and, 418
  physical development and, 413
  prenatal health care and, 116
  prenatal malnutrition and, 114
  preterm infants and, 139, 139f
  United States rate, 74, 80t
  welfare-to-work program, 80
Practical intelligence (Sternberg), 455–456
Practice effects, in longitudinal research, 40
Praeder-Willi syndrome, 59
Pragmatics, in language development
  early childhood, 358
  middle childhood, 463–464
Preattachment phase, 265
Preeclampsia, 117
Prefrontal cortex, 168, 414
Pregnancy. See also Childbirth; Conception; Contraceptive use; Prenatal development
  adolescence. See Teenage pregnancy and parenthood
  age of. See Maternal age
  alcohol use and, 108–109
  drug use and, 106–107
  feeling fetal movements, 120
  health care during, 117, 119, 140–141
  healthy pregnancy do's and don'ts, 119
  infectious diseases and, 111t, 111–112
  miscarriage. See Miscarriage
  nutrition and, 113–114
  preparing for parenthood, 120–121
  radiation and, 110
  smoking and, 87, 87f, 107–108
  stress and, 114–115
Preimplantation genetic diagnosis, 64t
Prejudice. See Bias

Prelabor, 126
Premature infants. See Preterm infants
Prenatal abnormalities, elimination of, 98
Prenatal development, 91–123. See also Conception; Pregnancy
  age of viability, 100–102
  alcohol use of mother and, 108–109
  defined, 6
  dioxin exposure and, 111
  drug use by mother and, 105–109
  emotional attachment of parents, 121
  environmental influences on, 102–119
  habituation and, 181
  HIV/AIDS and, 111t, 112
  infectious diseases and, 111t, 111–112
  lead exposure and, 111
  malnutrition and, 113–114
  maternal smoking and, 87, 87f, 107–108
  maternal stress and, 114–115, 116
  mercury exposure and, 110
  milestones in, 97t
  nutrition and, 113–114
  PCB exposure and, 110
  phases of, 96–102
  pollutant exposure and, 110–111
  radiation exposure and, 110
  temperament of fetus, 101
  trimesters, 97t, 100–102
Prenatal diagnosis, 58t, 63–65, 64t
Prenatal health care, 116–119, 117f
  cultural differences in, 117, 140–141
  group prenatal care, 119
  infant mortality and, 140–141
  malnutrition, 113–114, 137
  teenage pregnancy, 557
Preoperational stage of cognitive development, 19t, 318–329
  accommodation in, 321
  animistic thinking in, 323–324
  appearance vs. reality, confusion in, 327
  categorization in, 324–326
  centration in, 322
  conservation in, 321–322, 322f, 324
  defined, 318
  egocentrism in, 321, 323–324
  evaluation of, 327–328, 328t
  hierarchical classification in, 322, 325–328
  irreversible thinking in, 322
  language in, 318
  limitations of, 321–322
  magical thinking in, 323–324
  make-believe play in, 318–320, 323–324
  mental representation in, 318, 321
  operations in, 321, 327
  research on, 323–327
  states-versus-transformations thinking in, 322
  symbol–real-world relations in, 320–321
Prepared childbirth, 130–131
Prereaching in infants, 187
Preschoolers. See Early childhood
Preschools, 348–351
  defined, 348
  developmentally appropriate practices, 375

intervention programs for at-risk preschoolers, 349–350
  sex differences in activities, 394
  types of, 348
Prescription drugs. See Medications
Pretending. See Make-believe play
Preterm infants, 136–141. See also Low birth weight
  breastfeeding, 176
  caregiving for, 137–139
  child maltreatment and, 138
  defined, 136
  drug use during pregnancy and, 105–109
  environmental pollution and, 110–111
  interventions for, 138–139, 139f
  lead exposure during pregnancy and, 111
  maternal depression and, 271
  medical interventions, 136
  "small for date" vs. preterm, 137
  smoking during pregnancy and, 107–108
  stress during pregnancy and, 114–115
  twins, 137
Prevention programs. See Intervention programs
Preverbal gestures, 238
Pride
  early childhood, 370
  toddlerhood, 254
  middle childhood, 489–490
Primary circular reactions, in sensorimotor stage of cognitive development, 205t, 206
Privacy rights of research participants, 45t
Private speech, 329–330, 330f
Privileges, withdrawal as disciplinary technique, 382
Proactive aggression, 385
Problems, emotional. See Adjustment problems; Stress
Problem solving. See also Reasoning
  by analogy, 211, 212 t, 324
  class inclusion problems, 322, 438, 441
  early childhood, 337–338, 338f
  emotional self-regulation and, 490–491
  infants
    IQ, as predictor of, 228
    reaching and grasping skills and, 188
  mathematical, 344–345, 451–452
  microgenetic research studies, 338
  overlapping-waves theory, 338, 338f, 446
  self-generated explanations and, 439
  social, 375–377
  three-mountains problem, 321, 321f
Processing capacity. See also Speed of processing
  infancy and toddlerhood, 218
  memory strategies and, 446
  middle childhood, 442
  synaptic pruning and, 442
Prodigies. See Gifted children
Production deficiency, in attention and memory strategies, 443
Production vs. comprehension of language, 240

Programme for International Student Assessment, 476f
Programming skills, computer, 353
Project Head Start, 349–350
Prolactin, 143
Promoting Alternative Thinking Strategies (PATHS) curriculum for preschool children, 376–377
Pronunciation, 241. See also Language development
Proprioception and reaching, 187
Prosocial behavior. See also Empathy
  defined, 371
  empathy and, 371
  friendships and, 500
  middle childhood, 490
  popular-prosocial children, 500
Prostate. See Reproductive system
Proteomics, 65
Proximal development, zone of. See Zone of proximal development
Proximodistal trend, 163
Psychoanalytic perspective, 15–17
Psychoanalytic theories. See also specific theories (e.g., Psychosocial theory of development (Erikson))
  attachment and, 264
  moral development and, 379–380
Psychological abuse of children. See Child maltreatment
Psychological control and authoritarian parenting, 399
Psychological disturbances. See Adjustment problems
Psychological knowledge, in core knowledge perspective, 214
Psychological stress. See Stress
Psychosexual theory of development (Freud). See also specific stages (e.g., Anal stage of development, Oral stage of development)
  Erikson's expansion of. See Psychosocial theory of development (Erikson)
  moral development and, 378
  overview of stages of, 15, 16t
Psychosocial dwarfism, 297
Psychosocial theory of development (Erikson)
  autonomy vs. shame and doubt, 249
  basic trust vs. mistrust, 248
  industry vs. inferiority, 482
  initiative vs. guilt, 364
  overview of stages of, 15–16, 16t
Psychotherapy. See Counseling
Public education programs
  child maltreatment, 404
  protective helmets and injuries, 424
  sexual abuse of children, 520
Public health programs, 303
Public policies. See also Intervention programs
  bilingual education, 465–466
  child development, generally, 78–80
  child care, 230, 273, 351
  child health care, availability of, 303
  childhood injuries, preventing, 306–307
  cognitive development, early intervention programs for, 231–232, 349–350
  defined, 78–79
  Head Start programs, 349–350
  immunization, 303

No Child Left Behind Act, 468
prenatal health care, 117, 140–141
preschool intervention programs, 349–350
reproductive technologies, 67
television programming, regulation of, 387–389
welfare reform, 80
Public television and children's programming, 351–353
Puerto Ricans
  attachment security, 270
  self-concept, 484
Pukapukans of Pacific Islands, childbirth practices, 129
Punishment (disciplinary)
  aggression and, 387
  child maltreatment and, 403
  corporal punishment, 381–382, 382f, 404–405
  empathy development and, 371
  moral development and, 379
  principles of effective punishment, 382–384
Punishment, in operant conditioning, 180
Puns, in vocabulary development, 463
Pupil dilation and temperamental style, 259
Puritan philosophy of childhood, 12
Pyloric stenosis, 114

Q

Quechua of Peru
  language and metacognition, 340
  swaddling of infants, 148
Questionnaires, as research method, 32t, 33, 258
Questions of children as catalyst for cognitive development, 326

R

Racial/ethnic bias
  development of, in middle childhood, 494–497
  intelligence tests, 347, 454–455, 461–462
Race. See Ethnicity and race; Racial/ethnic bias
Radiation
  genetic damage and, 60
  mutation of genes and, 60
  prenatal development and, 110
Random assignment, in experimental research design, 38–39
Range of reaction, 84, 84f
Rapid-eye-movement (REM) sleep
  infancy and toddlerhood, 172
  newborns, 146
Reaching and grasping, 186–188
Reaction range, 84, 84f
Reaction time, in middle childhood, 428
Reactive aggression, 385, 386, 387
Reactivity, as temperamental trait, 256, 257, 257t
Reading
  early childhood, 326, 341–346
  information-processing skills in, 450–451
  interactive, 343, 345
  language development and, 241
  letter-sound correspondences, 343, 345

phonics approach, 450–451
phonological awareness and, 343, 450–451
sequence of development, 451, 451t
socioeconomic influences on, 344, 344f
to toddlers, 241, 242
whole-language approach, 450
Reasoning
  abstract. See Abstract thinking
  by analogy, 211, 324
  mathematical reasoning in early childhood, 344–346
  measuring. See Intelligence tests
  moral. See Moral reasoning
  spatial. See Spatial reasoning and perception
Recall memory
  early childhood, 336
  infancy and toddlerhood, 220, 240
Recasts, in language development, 359
Recess periods at school, 433
Reciprocal relationship, formation of, in ethological theory of attachment, 265
Reciprocal teaching, 468–469
Recognition memory
  early childhood, 336
  infancy and toddlerhood, 220
Reconstituted families, 513–515
Recovery and habituation, 181. See also Habituation
Recreational drugs. See Drug use and abuse
Referential style of learning, in language development, 240–241
Reflexes
  Apgar Scale, 129t
  defined, 143
  Neonatal Behavioral Assessment Scale (NBAS), 152
  newborn, 143–145, 144t
    assessment of, 145, 152–153
    survival value of, 143
Reflexive schemes, in sensorimotor stage of cognitive development, 205t
Reformation philosophy of childhood, 12
Rehearsal, as memory strategy, 336, 446
Reinforcement
  defined, 17
  friendships in early childhood and, 374
  gender identity, 396
  moral development and, 380
Rejected-aggressive children, 501, 503
Rejected children and peer acceptance, 500–503
Rejected-withdrawn children, 501
Relational aggression, 386, 499, 500
Relationships. See specific types of relationships (e.g., Marital relationship, Parent–child relationship, Peer relations)
Religion. See Spirituality and religiosity
Remarriage, 513–515
Remote memory, 181
REM sleep
  infancy and toddlerhood, 172
  newborns, 146

Repetitive style, in conversing about past with children, 337
Representation, mental. See Mental representation
Reproduction. See Conception; Fertility; Pregnancy
Reproductive choices, 63–65. See also In vitro fertilization; Prenatal diagnosis
Reproductive system, 96, 96f
  DES and reproductive abnormalities, 106
Reproductive technologies, 66–67. See also In vitro fertilization
Republic of Congo, Efe of. See Efe of Republic of Congo
Research designs, 35–43. See also specific designs (e.g., Correlational research, Experimental research design, Longitudinal research)
  combining experimental and developmental designs, 43
  comparison of strengths and weaknesses, 39t
  correlational research, 37, 39t
  defined, 31
  developmental research designs, 40–43
  experimental research design, 37–38, 39t
  general research designs, 35–39, 39t
  sequential designs, 39t, 42, 42t
  strengths and limitations of, 39t
Research methods, 30t, 31–35. See also specific methods (e.g., Clinical method of research; Systematic observation research methods); topics or types of studies (e.g., Kinship studies, Twin studies)
  defined, 31
  ethics in, 43–46
Research rights of participants, 43, 45t, 45–46
Resilience
  birth complications, long-term consequences of, and, 141–142
  defined, 11
  infancy and toddlerhood, 279
  middle childhood, 520–523
Resistance to temptation. See Self-regulation
Resistant attachment, 267, 270–271
Resolving Conflict Creatively Program (RCCP), 522–523
Respiratory distress syndrome, 136
Respiratory system
  Apgar Scale, 129t
  asthma, 423
Responsive parenting. See also Authoritative parenting
  attachment and, 266, 266f, 270–271, 274
  basic trust and, 248
  compliance in toddlers and, 283
Retardation. See Mental retardation
Reticular formation, 294, 294f
Retina, 151
Retrieval of information. See Memory
Reversibility in thinking, 438
Rh factor and incompatible blood types, 115, 134
Riddles, in vocabulary development, 463
Right-handedness, 168, 293–294

Rights of children, 80–81
Romanian children, adoption of, 169, 171, 171f
Rooming in, after childbirth, 143
Rooting reflex of newborns, 144t
Rough-and-tumble play, 431–432
Rousseau's philosophy of child development, 13
Rubella
  effect on prenatal development, 111, 111t
  immunization and, 302
Rules, organized games with, 430
Running
  early childhood, 308, 309t
  middle childhood, 428t
  sex differences, 313
Russians
  gender-stereotyped beliefs, 504
  temperament of infants, 262

S

Sadness. See also Crying; Depression
  infancy and toddlerhood, 251–252
  still-face reaction, 251–252
Safety. See also Accidents; Injuries
  athletic activities, 547
  car seats, 306, 307
  child-rearing practices and, 306–307, 307t
  driving, 547
  protective helmets, 424
Safety education, 424
Samoans, obesity, 419
Sarcasm and language development, 579
Scaffolding, 331, 332, 368, 469
Scale errors, 281
Scanning, 191
Schemes
  in cognitive-developmental theory, 204–205
  defined, 204
  make-believe play and, 319
Schizophrenia, 83
Scholastic achievement. See Academic achievement
School absences, 423
School achievement. See Academic achievement
School-age children. See Middle childhood
School attendance, illness and absences, 423
School phobia, 517
Schools, 466–477. See also Education; Teachers and teaching techniques; specific subjects (e.g., Mathematics and mathematical reasoning, Reading)
  ability grouping in, 470–471
  absenteeism. See School attendance
  achievement in. See Academic achievement
  after-school programs, 516
  "back to basics" movement, 468
  bilingual education, 465–466
  class size and learning, 466–467
  computers in classrooms, 472–473
  constructivist classrooms, 467–468
  educational philosophies, 77, 467–469
  educational self-fulfilling prophecies, 470

Schools (*cont.*)
gifted children. *See* Gifted children
grouping practices in, 470–471
heterogeneous classes, 470–471
high-quality education in
elementary school, 467*t*, 471
high-stakes testing, 468
homogeneous classes, 470–471
inclusive classrooms in, 473
integration of, 471
Internet access, 472–473, 473*f*
magnet schools, 471
multigrade classrooms, 470
obesity reduction and, 422
peer tutoring, 470, 473
parent involvement in, 77
physical education programs. *See*
Physical education
preschools. *See* Preschools
recess, 433
safety education, 424
self-esteem and, 485
social-constructivist classrooms, 468
special-needs students, 473–476
suicide prevention programs, 632
traditional classrooms, 467
truancy. *See* School attendance
School years. *See* Middle childhood
Scientific studies. *See* Research
designs; Research methods
Scribbles, in early drawings, 310
Scripts and memory development,
336–337
Scrotum, 96
Seat belts, 307
Secondary circular reactions, in
sensorimotor stage of cognitive
development, 205*t*, 206, 212*t*
Secondary schools. *See* Schools
Second-language learning, 234, 235.
See also Bilingualism
Second-order false beliefs, 448, 448*f*,
492
Second trimester of prenatal
development, 97*t*, 100. *See also*
Fetus, period of prenatal
development
Secular trends
mental test performance, 459
physical development, 413
Secure attachment, 266, 279
Secure base, 252, 266
Self-awareness, 280*f*, 280–282
Self-blame. *See* Guilt
Self-care children, 516–517
Self-categorization, 282
Self-concept. *See also* Gender identity;
Identity; Self-esteem
cognitive influences on, 483–484
cultural influences on, 483–484
defined, 365
early childhood, 365–366
ideal self, 483
middle childhood, 482–483
personal storytelling and, 366
social comparisons, 483
Self-conscious emotions, 367. *See also*
Guilt; Shame
defined, 253
early childhood, 370–371
infancy and toddlerhood, 253–254
middle childhood, 489–490
Self-control. *See* Emotional self-
regulation; Self-regulation

Self-definition. *See* Self-concept
Self-development. *See also* Identity
early childhood, 365–367
infancy and toddlerhood, 249,
279–284
middle childhood, 482–489
Self-efficacy
academic, 449
emotional, 491
in social-cognitive theory, 18
Self-esteem, 484–489
academic. *See* Academic self-esteem
achievement-related attributions
and, 486–487
athletics and, 485
changes in level of, 485
child maltreatment and, 404
child-rearing practices and, 486
chronic illness and, 423
cultural influences on, 485–486
defined, 366
divorce of parents and, 512
early childhood, 266–267
gender identity and, 505
goal-setting, 487
hierarchically structured, 484, 484*f*
incremental view of ability, 486, 488
influences on, 485–489
maternal employment and, 515
middle childhood, 484–485
obesity and, 419
only children, 508
peer acceptance and, 500
peer victimization and, 502
racial/ethnic bias and, 496
resilience and, 522*t*
self-care children, 516
sex differences in, 485
sexual abuse victims, 519
shame and, 489–490
social support for, 76
Self-fulfilling prophecies, educational,
470
Self-help skills, in early childhood,
309
Self-image. *See* Self-concept
Self-recognition, 280–281, 281*f*
Self-reflective perspective taking, 492*t*
Self-regulation
cognitive self-regulation, 449
effortful control and, 254, 282
emotional. *See* Emotional self-
regulation
infancy and toddlerhood, 282–284
temperament and, 256, 257*t*
Self-report research methods, 32*t*,
33–34
Self-soothing of infants, 255
Self-understanding. *See* Self-
awareness; Self-concept
Self-world differentiation, in
infancy, 280
Self-worth. *See* Self-concept;
Self-esteem
Selman's stages of perspective taking,
492
Semantic bootstrapping, in
grammatical development,
357–358
Semantic development. *See* Language
development; Vocabulary
Semen, 95. *See also* Sperm
Sense of self. *See* Self-concept;
Self-esteem

Sensitive caregiving, and attachment,
270–271
Sensitive period
brain development and, 169–172
for culture-specific learning, 191
defined, 23–24
language development, 235, 465
prenatal development, 103, 103*f*, 112
Sensorimotor stage of cognitive
development, 19*t*, 205*t*, 205–207
attainments in infancy and
toddlerhood, 212*t*, 212–216
circular reactions in, 205, 205*t*
defined, 204
evaluation of, 212–216
language development and, 233–242
research on, 208–212
substages, 205, 205*t*
Sensory capacities of newborns,
149–152
Sensory register, in information
processing, 217, 217*f*
Separation
adolescent autonomy and, 619
marital. *See* Divorce
Separation anxiety
attachment and, 266, 267*t*
defined, 266
early childhood, 370
middle childhood, 517
September 11 terrorist attack and
children's stress reactions, 518
Sequential research designs, 39*t*,
42, 42*f*
Seriation, in concrete operational
stage of cognitive development,
438, 440
Serotonin and sudden infant death
syndrome (SIDS), 147
SES (socioeconomic status). *See*
Socioeconomic influences
Sesame Street, 351–352
Sex
chromosomes. *See* Sex chromosomes
differences. *See* Sex differences
hormones. *See* Sex hormones
Sex chromosomes, 53–55
abnormalities of, 61–62, 62*t*
dioxins, effect of, 111
genomic imprinting and, 59–60
Sex differences. *See also* Gender
stereotyping; Gender typing
achievement-related attributions,
487
ADHD diagnosis, 444
aggression, 386, 498, 503
asthma, 423
athletic performance and
participation, 430
blended families, adjustment to,
513–515
communication styles, 394
computer use, 472,
divorce of parents, response to,
511–512
education in developing countries, 73
emotional expression, 255
exclusion, 498
extreme personality styles,
longitudinal study of, 40
friendships, 499–500
gender identity development, 505
gender-role conformity, 393–394
health and mortality, 59

injuries, 305, 425
language development, 240
loss of primary (baby) teeth, 290
motor development, 313, 430
parent–child relationship, 393
physical development, 163, 290, 413
preschool activities, 394
rough-and-tumble play, 431–432
self-esteem, 485, 487
skeletal age, 165
spatial reasoning, 576–577
stepfamilies, adjustment to, 513
temperament, 261
Sex hormones, 386, 415. *See also*
Hormones; *specific hormones
(e.g., Androgens, Estrogens)*
"Sex sorter" reproductive technology,
66–67
Sex stereotyping. *See* Gender
stereotyping
Sex typing. *See* Gender typing
Sexual abuse of children, 402, 519–520.
See also Child maltreatment
Sexually transmitted diseases (STDs),
111*t*
Sexual orientation, gay and lesbian
families, 508–509
Shaken baby syndrome, 405
Shame
early childhood, 370
infancy and toddlerhood, 254
middle childhood, 489–490
Shape constancy, in object perception,
196
Sharing. *See* Prosocial behavior
Shoe-tying and motor development,
309, 309*t*
Short-term memory. *See* Memory;
Working (short-term) memory
Shyness
cultural differences in response to,
263, 263*f*, 374
development of, 259
infancy and toddlerhood, 259
Sibling relationships
aggression and, 387
attachment and, 276–277
cross-sectional study of, 41
and false-belief understanding, 341
firstborn's adjustment to newborn
sibling, 156
gender typing and, 393–394
make-believe play and, 226
middle childhood, 507–508
parental comparisons and, 507
social and emotional development
and, 369
Sibling rivalry, 507
Sickle cell anemia, 423
SIDS (Sudden infant death
syndrome), 147, 173, 186
Sign language
apes, language acquisition among,
234
deaf adults and, 169, 235, 243
in infancy and toddlerhood,
236–237, 243
Single-parent families. *See also*
Divorce
extended families and, 79
never-married, 509–510
transition to parenthood for,
156–157
welfare-to-work program, 80

Siriono childbirth practices, 129
Size constancy, in object perception, 196
Size of body. *See* Body proportions; Height; Weight
Size of family. *See* Family size
Skeletal age
  defined, 164
  early childhood, 290
  infancy and toddlerhood, 164–165
  psychosocial dwarfism and, 297
Skeletal development
  early childhood, 290–291, 291*f*
  infancy and toddlerhood, 163–164
  middle childhood, 414
  skull development, 164, 164*f*
Skinner's operant conditioning theory. *See* Operant conditioning
Skin, prenatal development of, 100
Skipped-generation families, 275
Skipping, 309
Skull development, 164, 164*f*
Sleep and sleep disorders
  bedwetting, 422–423
  cosleeping arrangements, 172–173, 298, 298*f*
  early childhood, 298–299
  fetal activity, 100–101
  genetic influences, 299
  infancy and toddlerhood, 172–174
  naps, 298
  newborns, 145–147
  obesity and, 418
  sudden infant death syndrome (SIDS) and, 147
Sleep terrors, 299
Sleepwalking in early childhood, 299
Slow-to-warm-up child, as temperament type, 257
Small-for-date infants, 137
Smell, 143
Smiling in infancy and toddlerhood, 250–251
Smoking
  early childhood development and, 290–291
  passive smokers, 108
  prenatal development and, 87, 87*f*, 107–108
Snacks, preferences of preschoolers, 300, 300*f*
Sociability. *See also* Peer relations
  attachment security and, 277–278
  development of, 259
  early childhood, 365, 373–374
  infancy and toddlerhood, 259
Social acceptance. *See* Peer acceptance
Social class. *See* Socioeconomic influences
Social-cognitive theory (Bandura), 18. *See also* Social learning theory (Bandura)
Social comparisons, 483
  defined, 483
  self-esteem and, 485–486
Social conflict. *See* Social problem solving.
Social-constructivist classrooms, 468
Social contract orientation in moral development, 61
Social conventions and moral development, 384, 492–493
Social development. *See* Emotional and social development

Social groups. *See* Peer groups
Social-informational perspective taking, 492*t*
Social interactions. *See* Social support; *specific types of relationships (e.g., Friendships, Peer relations)*
Social learning theory (Bandura), 17–18, 30*t*
  gender typing and, 390, 396
  moral development and, 380–384
Social phobia, 259
Social policy. *See* Public policies
Social preferences, and peer acceptance, 500
Social problem solving
  defined, 375
  early childhood, 375–377
Social prominence, and peer acceptance, 500
Social referencing, 253
Social self-esteem, 485–486
Social services. *See* Intervention programs
Social smile, 251
Social support
  benefits of, 76
  childbirth, during, 131–132
  child maltreatment and, 403, 404
  chronic illness in childhood, 424
  extended family households and, 78, 79
  resilient children and, 11, 522*t*
Societal perspective taking, 492*t*
Society for Research in Child Development, ethical guidelines for research, 43
Sociocultural theory of cognitive development (Vygotsky), 24–25, 30*t*
  early childhood, 329–334
  educational principles based on, 332
  evaluation of, 332–334
  guided participation, 331
  infancy and toddlerhood, 224–225
  intersubjectivity in, 331
  language development and, 359
  make-believe play and, 226
  private speech, 329–330, 330*f*
  scaffolding in, 331
  zone of proximal development. *See* Zone of proximal development
Sociodramatic play, 332, 374
Socioeconomic influences, 71–72. *See also* Poverty
  attachment security, 268
  child-care quality, 351, 517
  child-rearing styles, 401
  communications styles, 459
  computer use, 472
  dietary deficiencies, 300–301
  disciplinary practices, 383
  friendships, 499
  health care, availability of, 303
  hearing loss, 422
  immunization rate and, 302
  intelligence tests, 347
  IQ scores, 458
  lead exposure risks and, 296, 296*f*
  literacy and, 343–344, 344*f*
  mathematical reasoning and, 345
  motor development, 430
  myopia, 422
  neighborhood environment, 75–76
  obesity and, 417, 418*t*

physical development, 413
prenatal health care, 117
school integration and magnet schools, 471
school phobia, 517
self-care children and, 516
sexual abuse, 520
single-parent families, 509
television viewing, 352
tooth decay, 291
tooth development and, 414
Socioeconomic status (SES), 71–72. *See also* Socioeconomic influences
Somatic mutation, 60
Soothing crying baby, 148–149, 148*t*
Sound. *See also* Hearing and hearing loss
  fetal response to, 101
South Africa, HIV infection of pregnant women, 112
South America. *See also specific countries*
  Jarara childbirth practices, 129
  physical development in middle childhood, 413
Spanking. *See* Corporal punishment
Spatial intelligence (Gardner), 456*t*
Spatial reasoning and perception
  brain plasticity and, 168–169, 170
  brain damage and, 170
  concrete operational stage of cognitive development, 438–440
  lateralization of brain and, 168–169, 293
  visually impaired infants' development and, 194
Special-needs students, 473–476
Special Supplemental Food Program for Women, Infants, and Children (WIC), 114
Speech. *See also* Language development
  child-directed, 241–242
  early childhood conversations, 358–359
  egocentric, 330
  infants' perception of, 189–190, 197–198
  newborns' response to, 151
  private, 329–330, 330*f*
  statistical learning capacity and, 190
  telegraphic, 239
Speed of processing
  early childhood, 338
  IQ scores and, 454–455
  middle childhood, 442–443
Spelling in early childhood, 341–346
Sperm, 53, 95, 96
  donor banks, 67
  donor insemination, 66
Spina bifida, 64*t*, 114
Spinal block, during childbirth, 133
Spirituality and religiosity. *See also specific faiths (e.g., Catholicism, Judaism, Mormons)*
  God, children's understanding of, 495
  middle childhood, 495
  moral development and, 617
Sports. *See* Athletics; Extracurricular activities; Physical education
Sports-related injuries, 431

Stability
  attachment patterns, 268
  IQ scores, 228
  plasticity vs., in theories of development, 9
  temperament, 258–260
Stage concept of development, 8
  cognitive-developmental theory, 19*t*, 19–20. *See also specific stages (e.g., Formal operational stage of cognitive development, Sensorimotor stage of cognitive development)*
  psychosexual theory, 16t. *See also specific stages (e.g., Anal stage of development, Oral stage of development)*
  psychosocial theory, 16t. *See also specific stages (e.g., Autonomy, Trust)*
Rousseau's philosophy, 13
Standardization, of intelligence tests, 227–228
Stanford-Binet Intelligence Scales, 454
States of arousal. *See also* Sleep and sleep disorders
  infancy and toddlerhood, 172, 174
  newborns, 145–146, 146*t*
Statistics. *See also* Research methods
  correlation coefficients, 37, 37*f*
  factor analysis, 453
STDs (Sexually transmitted diseases), 111*t*
Stepfamilies, 513–515
Stepping reflex of newborns, 144*t*, 144–145
Stereotype threat, 460–461, 461*f*, 470
Stereotyping. *See* Bias; Gender stereotyping
Sternberg's triarchic theory of intelligence, 455*f*, 455–456
Steroids, anabolic, 534
Stigma. *See also* Bias
  gay and lesbian families, 509
  homosexuality, 553
Still-face reaction in infants and toddlers, 251–252
Stimulation
  brain development and, 165, 171–172
  emotional self-regulation and, 254
  motor development and, 188
  preterm infants, 138–139
  reaching and, 188
Stimulus
  conditioned, 179*f*, 179–180
  habituation to. *See* Habituation
  neutral, 179
  unconditioned, 179, 179*f*
Stop Bullying Now program, 502
Storytelling, personal, and early self-concept, 366
Stranger anxiety, 252
Strange Situation procedure to measure attachment, 266, 267*t*
Strategies
  coping. *See* Coping strategies
  memory. *See* Memory strategies
  mental strategies. *See* Mental strategies
  prevention. *See* Intervention programs

Stress
  aggression in children and family
    stress, 390
  attachment and family stressors, 272
  brain development and, 171
  child maltreatment and parental
    stress, 404
  cortisol and, 115, 171
  dual-earner families, 516
  ethnic and political violence, impact
    on children, 518
  extended family households and, 79
  institutionalized orphans and, 171
  poverty and, 75
  prenatal development and, 114–115
  resilient children and, 10–11, 520
  socioeconomic status and, 72
  World Trade Center collapse
    (September 11, 2001), 115
Stress hormones
  childbirth, and release by placenta
    of, 126
  newborn's production of, 128
  prenatal development and, 115
  in small-for-date infants, 137
Stress management. See Coping
  strategies
Stroke and low birth weight, 104–105
Structured interviews, 32t
Structured observation research
  method, 31–32
Students. See Academic achievement;
  Schools
Subcultures, 78
Substance abuse. See Alcohol use and
  abuse; Drug use and abuse
Sucking reflex of newborns, 144, 144t
Sudden infant death syndrome
  (SIDS), 147, 173, 186
Suggestibility, in eyewitness
  testimony, 521
Suicide, child maltreatment victims,
  404
Summer camps for chronically ill
  children, 424
Superego. See also Moral development
  psychosexual theory of, 15, 16t, 364,
    379
  psychosocial theory of, 364
Supersizing food portions, 420
Support groups. See Intervention
  programs
Surgery
  cesarean delivery, 134
  prenatal surgery, 64–64
Surrogate motherhood, 67, 264
Survival of fittest, Darwin's theory of,
  13
Sutures, in skull development, 164
Sweden
  childbirth practices, 131
  child care in, 230
  cohabitation, 652
  family size, 93
  immunization rate, 302
  poverty rate, 74
  prenatal attachment of parents to
    child, 121
  reproductive technology laws, 67
Swimming
  injury prevention, 307
  reflex of newborns, 143
Switzerland, reproductive technology
  laws, 67

Symbolic understanding of infants
  and toddlers, 211–212
Symbol–real-world relations, in
  preoperational stage of cognitive
  development, 320–321
Sympathy, 371. See also Empathy
Synapses, 164–166, 292, 292f, 414
Synaptic pruning, 165, 168, 292, 292f,
  343, 414–415, 442
Syntactic bootstrapping, in
  vocabulary development, 355,
  356
Syphilis, 111t
Systematic observation research
  methods, 31–33
Systems theory
  dynamic, 184–185
  ecological. See Ecological systems
    theory (Bronfenbrenner)

T
Tabula rasa, 12
Taiwan, academic achievement, 477
Talent, in gifted students, 474. See also
  Gifted children
Tanzanians, hand preference among,
  293
Taste
  early childhood, 300
  fetal acquisition of, 101
  newborns' response to, 150–151
Tay-Sachs disease, 58t, 68
Teacher–parent interaction, 77, 467
  academic achievement and, 77
  high-quality education in
    elementary school, 467
Teachers and teaching techniques. See
  also Education Learning;
  Schools; specific subjects (e.g.,
  Mathematics and mathematical
  reasoning; Reading)
  academic achievement and, 477
  achievement-related attributions
    and, 487, 488
  cognitive self-regulation and, 449
  communities of learners, 469
  constructivist classrooms, 468
  cooperative learning, 468–469
  gender typing, influence on, 394
  parent interaction. See
    Teacher–parent interaction
  philosophies of education. See
    Educational philosophies
  reciprocal teaching, 468–469
  self-fulfilling prophecies, 470
  social-constructivist classrooms, 468
  student interaction. See
    Teacher–student interaction
  traditional classrooms, 467
Teacher–student interaction, 469–470
  achievement-related attributions
    and, 487
  constructivist classrooms, 467–468
  high-quality education in
    elementary school, 467 t
  reciprocal teaching, 468–469
  self-fulfilling prophecies in, 470
  social-constructivist classrooms, 468
  traditional classrooms, 467
Teenage pregnancy and parenthood
  incidence of, 80t
  injury mortality rate and, 306
  prenatal development and, 116
  United States, rate of, 80t

Teeth. See Dental development and
  care
Telegraphic speech, 239
Television
  aggression and, 387–389, 388f
  children's programming, regulation
    of, 387–389
  early childhood, 351–353
  educational television, 351–353
  infant learning from, 213
  influence on children, 387–389
  obesity and television viewing, 176,
    418t, 418–419, 419f
  regulation of child's exposure to,
    389–390
  V-chip, 388–389
Temperament. See also Personality
  traits; specific traits (e.g., Anxiety,
  Shyness)
  attachment and, 271
  child maltreatment and, 404
  child-rearing practices and, 262–263
  child's unique experiences and,
    261–262
  corporal punishment and, 382, 382f
  defined, 256
  dimensions of, 257–258
  divorce of parents, response to, and,
    511–512
  effortful control of, 254, 257t,
    257–258, 260, 261, 262, 282
  emotional self-regulation and, 371
  empathy and, 371
  environmental influences on,
    261–262
  ethnic differences in, 261
  fetal responsiveness and, 101
  genetic influences on, 260–261
  goodness-of-fit model of child
    rearing and, 262–263, 380
  infancy and toddlerhood, 256–264
  injury proneness and, 305
  measurement of, 258
  models of, 256–258
  moral development and, 379–380
  New York Longitudinal Study of
    (Thomas & Chess), 256
  resilient children, 17, 520
  Rothbart's model of, 257, 257t
  safety issues and, 307
  sex differences in, 261, 390
  stability of, 258–260
  structure of, 256–258
  twin studies, 261–262, 262f
  types, 256–258, 257t, 259
Temperature and baby fat, 162
Teratogens, 102–112. See also specific
  agents (e.g., Alcohol abuse, PCBs,
  Rubella, Smoking)
Terrorism, effect on children, 518
Tertiary circular reactions, in
  sensorimotor stage of cognitive
  development, 205t, 207
Testes, 96
Testimony by children, 521
Tests. See specific tests (e.g., Blood tests,
  Intelligence tests)
"Test tube" babies, 66
Thalidomide, 105
Theories, 7–11. See also specific
  theories (e.g., Behaviorism,
  Psychoanalytic theories)
  attachment, 264
  comparison of, 29

  course of development, 8–9
  definition of theory, 7
  determinants of development, 9
  eclectic position on, 29
  gender identity, 395–397
  gender typing, 390
  historical foundations of, 11–14
  intelligence, 454–458
  language development, 233–236
  mid-twentieth century theories,
    14–29
  moral development, 379–380
  recent perspectives, 21–29
  scientific verification of, 7. See also
    Research methods
Theory of mind. See also False beliefs;
  Metacognition
  early childhood, 338–340
  factors contributing to, 340–341
  infancy and toddlerhood, 339
  limitations of young child's, 341
  middle childhood, 447–449
Therapy. See Counseling
Thinking. See Cognitive development
Third-party influences, in ecological
  systems theory, 26
Third-party perspective taking, 492t
Third trimester of prenatal
  development, 97t, 100–102. See
  also Fetus, period of prenatal
  development
Three-mountains problem, 321, 321f
Throwing skills. See Ball skills
Thumb sucking and malocclusion,
  414
Thyroid-stimulating hormone (TSH),
  297
Thyroxine, 297, 531, 532f
Time out, as disciplinary technique,
  382, 383
Timidity. See Anxiety
Tinbergen's study of imprinting, 23
Tobacco use. See Smoking
Toddlerhood. See Infancy and
  toddlerhood
Toilet training, 188–189
Tools of the Mind preschool
  curriculum, 335
Tonic neck reflex of newborns, 144,
  144t
Topic-associating narrative style, 464
Topic-focused narrative style, 464
Touch
  intermodal perception, 197–198
  newborns' response to, 149–150
  preterm infants and, 138–139
Toxemia, 117
Toxins. See Environmental hazards
Toxoplasmosis, effect on prenatal
  development, 111t, 112
Toys. See also Games; Play
  in child-care programs, 231t
  gender stereotyping of, 261, 282, 391
  infancy and toddlerhood, 216t
  make-believe play and, 320
Traditional classrooms, 467
Training. See Education; Intervention
  programs; Schools
Traits. See also specific traits (e.g.,
  Aggression, Shyness)
  androgynous. See Androgynous
    traits
  carriers of. See Carriers, of inherited
    traits

dominant–recessive, 56t, 56–60
personality. See Personality traits
polygenic inheritance, 60
Transition phase, in childbirth, 126–127
Transitions. See also Adjustment problems
  to middle childhood, 482
  to parenthood, 154
Transitive inference, in concrete operational stage of cognitive development, 438
Transitive inference, 441
Translocation pattern of chromosomes, in Down syndrome, 61
Treatment programs. See Counseling
Trial-and-error behavior, 211
Trials, legal. See Legal issues and proceedings
Triarchic theory of intelligence (Sternberg), 455f, 455–456
Tribal and village societies. See also specific societies
  accomplishment of conservation tasks, 440–441
  adult work, children in, 333
  childbirth practices among, 129, 132
  contexts of development and, 8
  infant caregiving, 148–149
Tricycles. See Bicycles and tricycles
Trimesters, in prenatal development, 97t
Triple X syndrome, 62
Trisomy 21 (Down syndrome), 61
Trophoblast, 98
Trust
  friendships and, 499
  parent–infant relationship and, 248
  vs. mistrust, psychosocial stage of development, 16t, 248
TSH (thyroid-stimulating hormone), 297
Tuberculosis, effect on prenatal development, 111t
Turner syndrome, 62
Tutoring in schools
  peer tutoring, 474
  students with learning difficulties, 474
TV. See Television
Twentieth century (mid-) theories of development, 14–29
Twins, 55–56
  ADHD among, 444
  maternal factors related to, 55, 55t
  myopia and, 422
  obesity among, 417
  preterm infants, 137
  sexual orientation,
  temperament and personality, 260, 261–262, 262f
Twin studies. See also Kinship studies
  adoption, 83
  aggression and, 86
  empathy, 379
  genetic–environmental correlation and, 85–86, 458
  hand preference, 293
  heritability estimates, 82–83
  IQ scores, 458
  niche-picking, 85–86
  physical development, 174

temperament and personality, 260, 261–262, 262f
Two-word utterance phase, 239

U
UCR (unconditioned response), 179, 179f
UCS (unconditioned stimulus), 179, 179f
Uganda, education of girls in, 73
Ulnar grasp, 187
Ultrasound, 64t, 100
Umbilical cord, 98, 135
U.N. See United Nations
Unconditioned response (UCR), 179, 179f
Unconditioned stimulus (UCS), 179, 179f
Underextension, in language development, 239
Underweight babies. See Low birth weight
Undifferentiated perspective taking, 492t
Uninhibited (sociable) child, as temperament type, 258. See also Sociability
Uninvolved parenting, 399t, 400
Unitarianism and understanding of God, 495
United Nations
  Convention on the Rights of the Child, 81
  on education of girls in developing countries, 73
Universal health care, 79, 117
U.S. National Longitudinal Survey of Youth (NLSY) on relationship of birth order and family size, 93f, 93–94
Uterus, 97, 98f. See also Reproductive system
Utilization deficiency, in attention and memory strategies, 443, 446
Utku Indians, moral development among, 378

V
Vaccination, 302, 304
Vacuum extraction, in childbirth, 133f, 133–134
Vagina, 96f
Vaginal birth after cesarean, 134
Values. See also Bias; Cultural differences; Moral development
  child maltreatment and cultural values, 403, 405
  immigrant youths, 36
  individualistic vs. collectivist, 78
  parenting practices and American values, 78–79
  shyness, valuing of, 236, 263f
Variables, in experimental research design, 37–38
Variations in development. See specific group differences (e.g., Ethnicity and race, Sex differences)
V-Chip (Violence-Chip), 388–389
Verbal abilities. See Language development; Speech
Verbal aggression, 385. See also Aggression
Vernix, 100
Victimization by bullies, 502

Video deficit effect, 213
Video and computer games, 353. See also Internet
Vietnamese Americans. See Asian Americans
Village societies. See Tribal and village societies
Violation-of-expectation method of research, 208, 208f, 209, 211, 212t, 214, 215, 215f, 339
Violence. See also Aggression
  childhood anxieties and, 518
  child maltreatment. See Child maltreatment
  children committing, 520–523
  cultural values and child maltreatment, 403, 405
  Internet access and, 472, 519
  partner abuse, 402t, 403
  television programming and, 387–389
  video and computer games and, 388–389, 472
  war, effect on children, 518
Viral diseases, 111t. See also Infectious diseases
Vision. See also Eyes
  color, in infancy, 152, 190
  depth perception, 192–193
  face perception. See Face perception
  impairment and delays in development, 194
  infancy, 190–197
  intermodal perception, 197–198
  middle childhood, 422
  myopia, 422
  newborn capacities, 151–152
  object perception, 196–197
  pattern perception, 193–195
  processing visual information by brain hemispheres, 168n
Visual acuity
  infancy, 190–191
  newborn, 151–152
Visual cliff studies (Gibson & Walk), 192, 192f, 250
Vitamins and minerals. See also Nutrition; specific entries (e.g., Calcium)
  childbearing-age women, 114
  early childhood, 300–301
  prenatal development and, 114
Vocabulary
  early childhood, 325, 354–356
  infancy and toddlerhood, 234
  metacognition and, 339
  middle childhood, 462–463
  spurt in, 239
Volunteering, reduction of prejudice through, 497
Vygotsky's sociocultural theory. See Sociocultural theory of cognitive development (Vygotsky)

W
Wales. See England and Great Britain
Walking. See also Motor development
  cultural variations in, 186
  depth perception and, 193, 199, 199f
  early childhood, 309t
  effect on social relationships, 183
  emotional self-regulation and, 255
  learning to walk, 184t, 185

stepping reflex of newborns, 144t, 144–145
War, effect on children, 518
Water birth, 131
Water safety, 307
Watson's theory. See Behaviorism
Weapons. See Firearms
Website-based learning activities, 472
Wechsler Intelligence Scales, 454
Weight. See also Obesity
  birth weight, 104–105, 128. See also Low birth weight
  breast cancer and high birth weight, 105, 105f
  early childhood, 290
  infancy and toddlerhood, 163, 176, 412
  middle childhood, 413
Welfare programs. See Intervention programs; Public policies
Welfare-to-work program, 80
Wernicke's area of brain, 234, 234f
Western countries, childbirth, 129
Western Europe. See also Industrialized countries
  gender-stereotyped beliefs, 504
  parental leave, 141
  prenatal health care, 141–142
White matter in brain development, 414
Whole-language approach to reading, 450
Whooping cough, 303
WIC (Special Supplemental Food Program for Women, Infants, and Children), 114
WISC–IV (Wechsler Intelligence Scale for Children–IV), 454
Withdrawal of privileges, as disciplinary technique, 382
Wives. See Marital relationship
Women. See Sex differences
Work. See Employment
Working (short-term) memory, 217, 217f, 441, 446–447. See also Memory
Working mothers. See Maternal employment
Worldviews. See Values
Writing. See also Literacy
  early childhood, 312
  letter-sound correspondences, 345
  middle childhood, 429
  phonological awareness and, 345
  socioeconomic influences on, 343

X
X chromosome, 54–55
X-linked inheritance of diseases, 57, 59f
XO (Turner) syndrome, 62
X-rays. See Radiation
XXX syndrome, 62
XXY (Klinefelter) syndrome, 62
XYY syndrome, 62

Y
Y chromosome, 54–55
Yolk sac, 98
Youths. See Adolescence
Yugoslavia and lead exposure risks, 296
Yurok Indians, breastfeeding customs of, 15–16

Z

Zambia, newborn behavior and child-rearing practices, 152

Zidovudine (ZDV) and prenatal AIDS transmission reduction, 112

Zinacanteco Indians
concrete operational thought, 440
make-believe play among siblings, 226
motor development in infancy, 186
social interaction and learning among, 25

Zinc
and prenatal health care, 114
dietary deficiency and lead exposure, 302

Zone of proximal development, in sociocultural theory of cognitive development
assisted discovery learning and, 332
cognitive development and, 330
defined, 224
dynamic testing and, 461
language development and, 242
private speech and, 330
scaffolding and, 331
teaching techniques and, 468

Zygote, 53–54

Zygote, period of prenatal development, 96–99, 103*f*